A Dictionary of

Business and Management

 SEE WEB LINKS

For recommended web links for this title,
visit http://oxfordreference.com/page/busman
when you see this sign.

GENR
Oxf
Std

The most authoritative and up-to-date reference books for both students and the general reader.

Many of these titles are also available online at www.oxfordreference.com

A Dictionary of

Business and Management

Management

SIXTH EDITION

OXFORD
UNIVERSITY PRESS

Great Clarendon Street, Oxford, OX2 6DP,
United Kingdom

Oxford University Press is a department of the University of Oxford.
It furthers the University's objective of excellence in research, scholarship,
and education by publishing worldwide. Oxford is a registered trade mark of
Oxford University Press in the UK and in certain other countries

First edition 1990 as *A Concise Dictionary of Business*
Second edition 1996
Third edition 2002
Fourth edition 2006
Fifth edition 2009
Sixth edition 2016

Impression: 2

Published in the United States of America by Oxford University Press
198 Madison Avenue, New York, NY 10016, United States of America

British Library Cataloguing in Publication Data

Data available

Library of Congress Control Number: 2015945929

ISBN 978-0-19-968498-4

Printed in Great Britain by
Clays Ltd, St Ives plc

Contents

Preface

A Dictionary of Business and Management is the sixth edition of *A Concise Dictionary of Business*, first published in 1990. The original edition was prepared on the assumption that it would be of use to students of all kinds of business courses, ranging from GCSE Business Studies to degree and postgraduate business subjects, as well as to business people and their professional advisers (lawyers, bankers, accountants, managers, insurers, etc.).

Although both sales and feedback suggest that the book succeeded admirably in this remit, subsequent editions were enlarged to reflect changes in business practice and culture. Most notably, perhaps, the fourth and fifth editions saw greatly increased coverage of management terms and theory to reflect the growing emphasis on human resources and organizational behaviour found in MBAs and business courses at all levels. Several hundred new entries were added to explain the concepts, vocabulary, and jargon associated with current theories of leadership, motivation, and team building. This trend has been continued in this new sixth edition, which has also been extensively revised in the light of the financial crisis of 2008, the ensuing global recession, and the sovereign debt crisis in Europe. The dictionary has also been fully updated to include the latest changes from such fast-moving fields as law, taxation, finance, and information technology (including mobile technology and social media). In particular, there is full coverage of the recent comprehensive reforms to UK accounting practice, which came into force in 2015.

J.L. 2015

Note: An asterisk (*) placed before a term in a definition indicates that this term can be found as an entry in the dictionary and will provide further information. Synonyms and abbreviations are usually found within brackets immediately following a headword.

Credits

Editor of the fourth, fifth, and sixth editions

Jonathan Law (Market House Books Ltd)

Editors of the earlier editions

John Pallister MA, PhD (Cardiff Business School)
Alan Isaacs BSc, PhD (Market House Books Ltd)

Market House Books Ltd staff

Amanda Garner-Hay
Anne Stibbs Kerr

Contributors to the sixth edition

Terry Stiastny
G. A. Williams

Contributors to earlier editions

Graham Betts
Barry Brindley BA
Peter Chadwick BA, MSc (University of Gloucestershire)
Leslie de Chernatony PhD (City University Business School)
Farooq Chudry MA (Bristol Business School)
Joan Gallagher MA (Personnel Consultant)
Nicholas Hand MSc, BComm (University of Greenwich)
Ian Holden BSc, MBA
Peter Lafferty MSc
Catherine Law MA, ACA
Clive Longhurst ACII
Gary Owen MSc, FFIS (University of Greenwich)
Edward Philips LLB, BCL (University of Buckingham)
John Smullen BSc, MA, MSc, MBA (University of Greenwich)
Stefan Szymanski BA, MSc, PhD (London Business School)
R. M. Walters MA, FCA
S. L. Williams MA (University of Buckingham)
Matthew Wright MA, MPhil

A1 A description of property or a person that is in the best condition. In marine insurance, before a vessel can be insured, it has to be inspected to check its condition. If it is 'maintained in good and efficient condition' it will be shown in *Lloyd's Register as 'A' and if the anchor moorings are in the same condition the number '1' is added. This description is also used in life assurance, in which premiums are largely based on the person's health. After a medical examination a person in perfect health is described as 'an A1 life'.

AA Abbreviation for *Advertising Association.

AAP Abbreviation for *affirmative action programme.

abandonment The act of giving up the ownership of something covered by an insurance policy and treating it as if it has been completely lost or destroyed. If the insurers agree to abandonment, they will pay a total-loss claim (*see* ACTUAL TOTAL LOSS; CONSTRUCTIVE TOTAL LOSS). This often occurs in marine insurance if a vessel has run aground in hazardous waters and the cost of recovering it would be higher than its total value and the value of its cargo. It also occurs during wartime when a vessel is captured by the enemy. If the owner wishes to declare a vessel and its cargo a total loss, **notice of abandonment** is given to the insurer; if, subsequently, the vessel or its cargo are recovered, they become the property of the insurer.

ABB Abbreviation for *activity-based budgeting.

abbreviated accounts A shorter form of *annual accounts that may be filed by a company qualifying as a small or medium-sized company under the UK Companies Acts. The use of abbreviated accounts can cut costs and save time. It can also minimize the information made available to others, especially business rivals. *See also* SUMMARY FINANCIAL STATEMENT.

ABC 1. Abbreviation for *Audit Bureau of Circulation. **2.** Abbreviation for *activity-based costing.

ABC classification (ABC ranking) A method of ranking items held in *inventory enabling particular attention to be given to those that, if incorrectly managed, will be most damaging to the effectiveness or the efficiency of an operation. Items are categorized according to their value of usage, i.e. their individual value multiplied by their usage rate. In most cases *Pareto's Rule then applies, so that approximately 20% of the items accounts for approximately 80% of the value of the stock held; these items are classified as Class A items. Class B covers the 30% of items that represent the next 10% of value. Class C covers the remaining 50%, which accounts for the remaining 10% of value. In *material requirements planning (MRP), ranking is used to categorize inventory by its impact value, i.e. whether or not production will stop if this item is out of stock.

ABCP Abbreviation for asset-backed *commercial paper.

ABI Abbreviation for *Association of British Insurers.

ability to pay The principle that taxes should be levied on the basis of taxpayers' ability to pay. This normally leads to the view that as income or wealth increases, its marginal utility (its value to its owner) decreases so that higher rates of tax can be levied on the higher slices. A typical *progressive tax of this sort is UK *income tax. *Compare* BENEFIT TAXATION; FLAT TAX; REGRESSIVE TAX.

ABMTN Abbreviation for asset-backed *medium-term note.

abnormal loss *See* NORMAL LOSS.

abnormal return A rate of return for taking a particular risk that is greater than that required by the market. The excess return is usually measured as being relative to that which the *capital asset pricing model or the *arbitrage pricing theory requires. *See also* ACTIVE MANAGEMENT; ANOMALY; EFFICIENT MARKETS HYPOTHESIS.

above par *See* PAR VALUE.

above-the-fold Originally denoting an advertisement displayed above the fold in printed media; in computer terms it indicates that a *banner advertisement or other content on a web page is displayed without the need to scroll. This is likely to give higher *clickthrough, but note that the location of the 'fold' within the *web browser is dependent on the screen resolution of a user's own computer.

above-the-line 1. Denoting those entries printed above the horizontal line on a company's *profit and loss account that separates the entries that establish the profit (or loss) from the entries showing how the profit is distributed. Prior to the introduction of Financial Reporting Standard (FRS) 3, Reporting Financial Performance, in 1992, it was understood that any exceptional items that were within the ordinary activities of the business were shown above the line, while any extraordinary items that were outside the ordinary activities of the business were shown below it. There was, however, criticism that the definitions of extraordinary and exceptional items could be manipulated to improve the *earnings per share figure. For example, if a building was sold for a large profit it could be interpreted as being

exceptional and included in the earnings per share, whereas if it was sold at a loss it could be interpreted as being extraordinary and not included in the earnings per share. Both exceptional and extraordinary items are now shown above the line and are included in the earnings per share. **2.** Denoting advertising expenditure on mass media advertising, including press, television, radio, and posters. It is traditionally defined as all advertising expenditure on which an *advertising agency would charge commission (as opposed to a flat fee). **3.** Denoting transactions concerned with revenue, as opposed to capital, in national accounts. *Compare* BELOW-THE-LINE.

ABP Abbreviation for *Associated British Ports.

absence culture An *organizational culture in which a certain degree of *absenteeism has come to be accepted as the norm. In companies with such a culture it may become routine for managers and workers to take occasional days off 'sick' when there is no justification for this.

absenteeism Absence from work for which there is no legitimate reason; it is often self-certified sick leave lasting for one day at a time. Most prevalent in large organizations, it can be a major problem. In order to combat it some organizations have introduced flexible working hours, increased annual leave, introduced personal days leave in addition to normal holiday entitlement, and devised incentive schemes for full attendance. High rates of absenteeism can be linked to low levels of *job satisfaction and an *absence culture in the workplace.

absolute cost advantage The cost advantage enjoyed by a country in producing certain goods, compared to costs in other countries. The costs of producing similar products vary between different countries because certain resources, such as labour, raw materials, and energy, will be cheaper in some countries than in others. Multinational enterprises are able to take advantage of these cost differences by buying components or products from countries that have these advantages. *Compare* COMPETITIVE ADVANTAGE.

absolute performance standard A standard set at the theoretical limit of performance. For example, in manufacturing, the theoretical quality standard of 'zero defects', which it is impossible to improve on, might be set as the absolute performance standard. Such standards may be achievable in practice or may form an ideal against which an organization may judge its progress.

absorption (cost absorption; overhead absorption) An accounting process, used in *absorption costing, in which the *overhead of an organization is charged to the production of that organization by the use of *absorption rates.

absorption costing (full absorption costing; total absorption costing) The *cost accounting system in which the *overheads of an organization are charged to the production by means of the process of *absorption. Costs are first apportioned to *cost centres, where they are absorbed using *absorption rates. Although this method has the advantage of simplicity, it involves an essentially *arbitrary allocation of costs; for this reason the system of *activity-based costing is now widely preferred. *Compare* MARGINAL COSTING.

absorption rate (overhead absorption rate; recovery rate) The rate or rates calculated in an *absorption costing system in advance of an accounting period for the purpose of charging the *overheads to the *production of that period. Absorption

rates are calculated for the accounting period in question using the following formula:

$$\text{budgeted overhead/budgeted production.}$$

In absorption costing production may be expressed in a number of different ways; the way chosen to express production will determine the absorption rate to be used. The seven major methods of measuring production, together with their associated absorption rate, are given in the table. The rate is used during the accounting period to obtain the absorbed overhead by multiplying the actual production achieved by the absorption rate.

These rates have been used by accountants for over a century and they are still widely applied. Many, however, would argue that they cannot provide the accurate *cause-and-effect allocations of costs that modern managers require; for this a system of *activity-based costing must be used. *See also* TRADITIONAL COSTING SYSTEM.

abstract of title A document used in conveyancing land to show how the vendor derived good title. For registered land, the abstract of title consists of official copies of the entries in the register. For unregistered land, the abstract generally comprises duplicate copies of those documents required to trace ownership back to a document that is at least 15 years old and that is held to show good title.

abuse of a dominant position Anti-competitive business practices by large enterprises, i.e. those having (usually) a market share of at least 40% in at least one

PRODUCTION MEASURE	ABSORPTION RATE
units, weight, or volume	rate per unit, weight, or volume
direct labour hours	rate per direct labour hour
machine hours	rate per machine hour
direct labour cost	% on direct labour cost
direct material cost	% on direct material cost
prime cost	% on prime cost
standard hours	rate per standard hour

Absorption rate.

EU state. Examples of such activities, which are contrary to Article 102 of the Treaty on the Functioning of the European Union and the UK Competition Act 1998, include refusing to supply an existing customer and engaging in *predatory pricing. The European Commission and the Competition and Markets Authority can fine businesses up to 10% of annual worldwide group turnover for breach of Article 102. High fines include €899 million against Microsoft in 2008.

ACA Abbreviation for Associate of the *Institute of Chartered Accountants.

ACAS Abbreviation for *Advisory Conciliation and Arbitration Service.

ACCA Abbreviation for *Association of Chartered Certified Accountants.

accelerated depreciation A rate of *depreciation of assets that is faster than the useful-life basis normally used to calculate depreciation. For example, a computer may be expected to have a useful life of four years when it is purchased; however, as a result of new product innovation, it is replaced after two years. If the useful-life basis had been used, the full cost would not have been charged to the accounts until the end of the fourth year; by accelerating the depreciation the full charge would be made earlier, reflecting the short life cycle of high-technology products. In the USA, the accelerated depreciation may be used to gain tax advantages.

acceptable use policy (AUP) The rules of permitted behaviour on a particular computer system, network, or website. Businesses and other organizations often require new users to sign an AUP document before providing access to their information systems. The main types of misuse proscribed typically include transmission of offensive or illegal material, breach of copyright or confidentiality, and any behaviour likely to lead to the corruption of data. The main aim of such documents is usually to avoid legal liability on the part of the organization. *See* CYBERLIABILITIES

acceptance 1. The signature on a *bill of exchange indicating that the person on whom it is drawn accepts the conditions of the bill. **2.** A bill of exchange that has been so accepted. Acceptances are divided into two categories: *banker's acceptances and trade acceptances. **3.** Agreement to accept the terms of an offer; for example, the agreement of an insurance company to provide a specified insurance cover or of a trader to accept a specified parcel of goods at the offer price.

acceptance credit A means of financing the sale of goods, particularly in international trade. It involves a commercial bank or merchant bank extending credit to a foreign importer, whom it deems creditworthy. An acceptance credit is opened against which the exporter can draw a *bill of exchange. Once accepted by the bank, the bill can be discounted on the *money market or allowed to run to maturity. In return for this service the exporter pays the bank a fee known as an **acceptance commission**.

acceptance number The number of sample units specified in a sampling plan that must conform to the specifications if the batch is to be accepted. *See* ACCEPTANCE SAMPLING.

acceptance sampling (lot acceptance sampling) A *statistical process-control technique that uses inspection of a *sample from a batch to decide whether to accept or reject the whole batch. In deciding the level of sampling, a balance has to be struck between achieving the desired quality levels and the cost of undertaking the sampling.

acceptance supra protest (acceptance for honour) The acceptance or payment of a *bill of exchange, after it has been dishonoured, by a person wishing to save the honour of the drawer or an endorser of the bill.

accepting house An institution specializing in accepting or guaranteeing *bills of exchange. A service fee is charged for guaranteeing payment, enabling the bill to be discounted at preferential rates on the *money market. The decline in the use of bills of exchange has forced the accepting houses to widen their financial activities, many of whom have returned to their original role as *merchant banks.

Accepting Houses Committee A committee representing the main *accepting houses in the City of London. Members of the committee are eligible for finer discounts on bills bought by the Bank of England, although this privilege has been extended to other banks.

acceptor The drawee of a *bill of exchange after acceptance of the bill, i.e. the acceptor has accepted liability by signing the face of the bill.

accessibility The degree to which a market segment can be reached and served.

access point (wireless access point) A device that acts as the core of a wireless computer network. It communicates with wireless nodes within its range and provides the necessary facilities for them to network successfully. Access points commonly also manage a link to a wired network, allowing their nodes to link with corporate networks, the Internet, etc.

access provider A company providing services to enable an organization or individual to access the Internet. Access providers are divided into *Internet service providers and online service providers.

accident analysis The use of analytical techniques drawn from *ergonomics to identify the causes of accidents, to recognize potential hazards in the workplace, and to create action plans for reducing the risks of injury and system damage. *See* ACCIDENT PRONENESS.

accident insurance An insurance policy that pays a specified amount of money to the policyholder in the event of the loss of one or more eyes or limbs in any type of accident. It also pays a sum to the dependants of the policyholder in the event

of his or her death. These policies first appeared in the early days of railway travel, when passengers felt a train journey was hazardous and they needed some protection for their dependants if they were to be killed or injured.

accident proneness The apparent propensity of some individuals to suffer (or cause) more than an average number of accidents. This is of particular interest in *industrial and organizational psychology, which is anxious to analyse the causes of accidents in the workplace in order to reduce their occurrence and their inevitable costs. There is, however, some doubt as to whether such a condition does in fact exist, or whether some people are simply the unlucky statistics that go to make up a *normal distribution of accident frequency.

On the other hand, it is not hard to imagine that accidents are more likely to occur at work (or anywhere else) if concentration is distracted by such extraneous factors as fatigue, illness, emotional preoccupation, or stress. Machine operators, for example, have certain skills at processing the information perceived by their senses so that an appropriate response is initiated. In addition to this skill, the personal qualities of the operator must also be involved in the smooth operation of the machine. If the operator is aware that his or her skill with the machine is less than it should be, this is not necessarily a recipe for accidents to occur; the intelligent operator will, under these circumstances, work more slowly, more cautiously, and with greater concentration. It is often, in fact, the more highly skilled operator, many of whose responses are automatic, who is more easily distracted by extraneous factors and thus more accident prone. Although organizational psychologists have been unable to provide a rigorous treatment of accident proneness, much valuable work has been done in analysing those activities that have high inherent risks and those environmental conditions (e.g. poor lighting, inappropriate room temperature) that increase the chances of accidents happening. Human error can be greatly reduced by improved design of equipment and work systems and through training programmes and other administrative interventions.

accommodating response A management strategy in which a company responds to criticism of its social or environmental record by accepting responsibility and seeking to improve its practices. *Compare* OBSTRUCTIVE RESPONSE; DEFENSIVE RESPONSE; PROACTIVE RESPONSE.

accommodation bill A *bill of exchange signed by a person (the accommodation party) who acts as a guarantor. The accommodation party is liable for the bill should the *acceptor fail to pay at maturity. Accommodation bills are sometimes known as **windbills** or **windmills**. *See also* KITE. .

accommodation endorser A person or a bank that endorses a loan to another party; for example, a parent company may endorse a bank loan to a subsidiary. The endorser becomes a guarantor and is secondarily liable in case of default. Banks may endorse other banks' acceptance notes, which can then be traded on the secondary market.

accord and satisfaction A device enabling one party to a *contract to avoid an obligation that arises under the contract, provided that the other party agrees. The accord is the agreement by which the contractual obligation is discharged and the satisfaction is the *consideration making the agreement legally operative. Such an agreement only discharges the contractual obligation if it is accompanied by consideration. For example, under a contract of sale the seller of goods may discharge the contractual obligation by delivering goods of different quality to that specified in the contract, provided there is agreement with the buyer (the accord) and the seller offers a reduction in the contract price (the satisfaction). The seller has therefore 'purchased' the release from the obligation. Accord and satisfaction refer to the discharge of an obligation arising under the law of tort.

account 1. A statement of indebtedness from one person to another. A provider of goods or services may render an account to a client or customer (*see* SALES INVOICE). **2.** A named segment of a *ledger recording transactions relevant to the person or the matter named. *See* BOOKS OF ACCOUNT. **3.** An account maintained by a *bank or a *building society in which a depositor's money is kept. *See* CHEQUE ACCOUNT; CURRENT ACCOUNT; DEPOSIT ACCOUNT; SAVINGS ACCOUNT. **4.** In an advertising, marketing, or public-relations agency, a client of the agency from whom a commission or fee is derived, in return for the services. **5.** *See* ANNUAL ACCOUNTS.

accountability An obligation to give an account. For limited companies, it is assumed that the directors of the company are accountable to the shareholders and that this responsibility is discharged, in part, by the directors providing an annual report and accounts (*see* ANNUAL ACCOUNTS). In an accountability relationship there will be at least one principal and at least one agent (*see* AGENCY RELATIONSHIP).

accountant A person who has passed the accountancy examinations of one of the recognized accountancy bodies and completed the required work experience. The bodies differ from each other in the way they train their students and the type of work expected to be undertaken. For example, accountants who are members of the Chartered Institute of Public Finance and Accountancy generally work in local authorities, the National Health Service, or other similar public bodies, while members of the Chartered Institute of Management Accountants work in industry (*see* MANAGEMENT ACCOUNTING). Wherever accountants work, their responsibilities centre on the collating, recording, and communicating of financial information and the preparation of analyses for decision-making purposes. *See also* CHARTERED

ACCOUNTANT; CHARTERED CERTIFIED ACCOUNTANT.

Accounting Council A body established in 2012 to take over certain functions of the former *Accounting Standards Board. Its main role is to advise its parent body, the *Financial Reporting Council (FRC), on matters of accounting and financial reporting policy. Responsibility for issuing *Financial Reporting Standards now belongs to the FRC, although the Accounting Council plays a role in their development.

account executive The person in an advertising, marketing, or public-relations agency responsible for implementing a client's business. This involves carrying out the programme agreed between the agency and client, coordinating the activities, and liaising with the client.

accounting code (cost code; expenditure code; income code) In modern accounting systems, a numerical reference given to each account to facilitate the recording of voluminous accounting transactions by computer.

accounting concepts (accounting principles; fundamental accounting concepts) The basic theoretical ideas devised to support the activity of accounting. As accounting developed largely from a practical base, it has been argued that it lacks a theoretical framework. Accountants have therefore tried to develop such a framework; although various concepts have been suggested, few have found universal agreement. In the UK, four have traditionally been seen as fundamental:

- the *going-concern concept assumes that the business is a going concern until there is evidence to the contrary, so that assets are not stated at their break-up value;
- the *accruals concept involves recording income and expenses as they accrue, as distinct from when they are received or paid;
- the *consistency concept demands that accounts be prepared on a basis that

clearly allows comparability from one period to another;
- the *prudence concept calls for accounts to be prepared on a conservative basis, not taking credit for profits or income before they are realized but making provision for losses when they are foreseen.

These four principles were laid down in *Statement of Standard Accounting Practice (SSAP) 2, Disclosure of Accounting Policies; they were also recognized in the EU's *Fourth Company Law Directive and the UK Companies Acts together with a fifth principle, the *accounting entity concept. From 2000 SSAP 2 was superseded by *Financial Reporting Standard (FRS) 18, which stated that the consistency concept and the prudence concept should no longer be regarded as fundamental. FRS 18 also identified four key objectives of financial information that can be regarded as fundamental principles: *comparability, *relevance, *reliability, and *understandability. The Financial Reporting Standard Applicable in the UK and Republic of Ireland issued in 2013 likewise emphasizes these qualities, together with those of timeliness, materiality, and completeness. The same qualities are recognized in the *International Accounting Standards Board's Conceptual Framework for Financial Reporting.

accounting entity (entity; business entity; reporting entity) The unit for which accounting records are maintained and for which *financial statements are prepared. The **accounting entity concept** (or **entity concept** or **separate entity concept**) is the principle that financial records are prepared for a distinct unit or entity regarded as separate from the individuals that own it. This will often be an incorporated *company, whose treatment as a separate accounting entity is required by law. For sole traders and partnerships accounts are also prepared to reflect the transactions of the business as an accounting entity, not those of the owner(s) of the business. Changing the boundaries of the accounting entity can have a significant impact on the accounts themselves, as these will reflect the purpose of the accounts and for whom they are prepared.

accounting event A transaction or change (internal or external) recognized by the accounting recording system. Events are recorded as debit and credit entries. For example, when a sale is made for cash the double entry for the sales transaction would be debit bank, credit sales (*see* DOUBLE-ENTRY BOOK-KEEPING).

accounting package *See* BUSINESS SOFTWARE PACKAGE.

accounting period 1. (financial period; period of account; reporting period) The period for which a business prepares its accounts. Internally, management accounts are usually produced monthly or quarterly. Externally, *financial statements are produced for a period of 12 months, although this may vary when a business is set up or ceases or if it changes its accounting year end. *See* ACCOUNTING REFERENCE DATE. **2. (chargeable account period)** A period in respect of which a *corporation tax assessment is raised. It cannot be more than 12 months in length. An accounting period starts when a company begins to trade or immediately after a previous accounting period ends. An accounting period ends at the earliest of:

- 12 months after the start date,
- at the end of the company's period of account,
- the start of a winding-up,
- on ceasing to be UK resident.

accounting policies The specific accounting bases adopted and consistently followed by an organization in the preparation of its *financial statements. These bases will have been determined by the organization to be the most appropriate for presenting its financial results and operations fairly; they will concentrate on such specific topics as pension schemes, *goodwill, research and development costs, and *foreign exchange. Companies are required to disclose their accounting policies in their *annual accounts.

accounting principles *See* ACCOUNTING CONCEPTS.

accounting rate of return (ARR) An *accounting ratio that expresses the profit of an organization before interest and taxation, usually for a year, as a percentage of the capital employed at the end of the period. Variants of the measure include using profit after interest and taxation, equity capital employed, and the average of opening and closing capital employed for the period. Although ARR can be used to forecast return on an investment project, *discounted cash flow measures are acknowledged to be superior for this purpose.

accounting ratio (financial ratio) A ratio calculated from two or more figures taken from the *financial statements of a company in order to provide an indication of the financial performance and position of that company. Ratios may be expressed as a percentage (e.g. *return on capital employed), in days (e.g. *debtor collection period), or as a multiple (e.g. *rate of turnover). *See* FINANCIAL-STATEMENT ANALYSIS; RATIO ANALYSIS.

accounting records The records kept by a company to comply with the Companies Act, which requires companies to keep accounting records sufficient to show and explain their transactions and to prepare accounts that give a true and fair view of their activities. Accounting records take the form of manual or computerized ledgers, journals, and the supporting documentation.

accounting reference date (ARD; reporting date) The date at the end of an **accounting reference period**, i.e. the financial year for a company, as notified to the *Registrar of Companies. For companies incorporated after 1 April 1990, it is normally taken as the last day of the month in which the anniversary of incorporation falls. Companies wishing to change their ARD must notify Companies House in advance.

Accounting Standards Board (ASB)
Formerly, the recognized body for setting
accounting standards in the UK. It was
established in 1990 to replace the
Accounting Standards Committee
(**ASC**). As well as issuing *Financial
Reporting Standards (FRS), the ASB issued
reports known as Abstracts through its off-
shoot, the Urgent Issues Task Force. In
2012 the ASB was abolished and responsibility for setting standards was transferred
to its parent body, the *Financial Reporting
Council. The ASB's other functions were
taken over by a new body, the *Accounting
Council

accounting technician A person qualified by membership of an appropriate body
(such as the *Association of Accounting
Technicians) to undertake tasks in the
accountancy field without being a fully
qualified *accountant.

account management group 1. A
group within an advertising, marketing, or
public-relations agency responsible for
planning, supervising, and coordinating all
the work done on behalf of a client. In large
agencies handling large accounts the group
might consist of an account director,
account manager, account or media plan-
ner, and *account executive. **2.** A group in
the sales department of an organization
that is responsible for managing the relationship with existing clients.

account of profits A legal remedy
available as an alternative to *damages in
certain circumstances, especially in breach
of *copyright cases. The person whose
copyright has been breached sues the person who breached it for a sum of money
equal to the gain made as a result of the
breach.

account payee only Words printed
between two vertical lines in the centre of a
UK cheque that, in accordance with the
Cheque Act 1992, make the cheque non-
transferable. This is to avoid cheques being
endorsed and paid into an account other
than that of the payee, although it should
be noted that banks may argue in some
circumstances that they acted in good faith

and without negligence if an endorsed
cheque is honoured by the bank. Most
cheques are now overprinted 'account
payee only' or 'A/C payee', and the words
'not negotiable' are sometimes added.

account reconciliation 1. A procedure
for confirming that the balance in a
chequebook matches the corresponding
*bank statement. This is normally done
by preparing a *bank reconciliation
statement. **2.** A procedure for confirming
the reliability of a company's *accounting
records by regularly comparing balances
of transactions. An account reconciliation
may be prepared on a daily, monthly, or
annual basis.

account rendered An unpaid balance
appearing in a *statement of account,
details of which have been given in a previous statement.

accounts 1. *See* ANNUAL ACCOUNTS.
2. *See* ACCOUNT; BOOKS OF ACCOUNT.

account sale A statement giving details of
a sale made on behalf of another person or
firm, often as an *agent. The account sale
shows the proceeds of the sale less any
agreed expenses, commission, etc.

Accounts Modernization Directive
An EU directive (2003) that requires companies to publish information that provides
a 'balanced and comprehensive' analysis of
their development and performance during
the financial year. This should include not
only key financial performance indicators
but also, where appropriate, non-financial
indicators, including information relating
to environmental and employee matters.
The directive, which is binding on medium
and large companies, has necessitated
changes to the UK regulations on the
*directors' report.

accounts payable (trade creditors;
trade payables) The amounts owed by a
business to suppliers (e.g. for raw materials). Accounts payable are classed as *current liabilities on the balance sheet, but
distinguished from *accruals and other

non-trade creditors (such as HM Revenue and Customs).

accounts receivable (trade debtors; trade receivables) The amounts owing to a business from customers for invoiced amounts. Accounts receivable are classed as *current assets on the balance sheet, but distinguished from prepayments and other non-trade debtors. A *provision for bad debts is often shown against the accounts receivable balance in line with the *prudence concept. This provision is based on the company's past history of bad debts and its current expectations. A general provision is often based on a percentage of the total credit sales, for example 2% of credit sales made during the period.

accrual (accrued charge; accrued expense; accrued liability) An estimate in the accounts of a business of a liability that is not supported by an invoice or a request for payment at the time the accounts are prepared. An accrual is a *current liability on the *balance sheet and will be charged under expenses in the *profit and loss account. An example would be telephone expenses, which are billed in arrears. At the end of the accounting period, if no bill has been received, an estimate (based on past bills) would be made and credited to an accruals account; the corresponding debit would be made to the telephone expense account. The telephone expense account is then cleared to the profit and loss account. *See* ACCRUALS CONCEPT.

accrual accounting A system of accounting in which *revenue is recognized when it is earned and expenses are recognized as they are incurred. Accrual accounting is a basic *accounting concept used in the preparation of the *profit and loss account and *balance sheet of a business. It differs from *cash accounting, which recognizes transactions when cash has been received or paid. In preparing *financial statements for an *accounting period using accrual accounting, there will inevitably be some estimation and uncertainty in respect of transactions.

accruals concept A fundamental *accounting concept recognized in the Financial Reporting Standard Applicable in the UK and Republic of Ireland. It requires that revenue and costs are recognized as they are earned or incurred, not as money is received or paid. Income and expenses should be matched with one another, as far as their relationship can be established or justifiably assumed, and dealt with in the *profit and loss account of the period to which they relate. *Accruals and *prepayments are examples of the application of the accruals concept in practice. For example, if a rates bill for both a current and future period is paid, that part relating to the future period is carried forward as a current asset (a prepayment) until it can be matched to the future periods.

The relevant international standard is *International Accounting Standard 18.

accrued benefits Benefits due under a *defined-benefit pension scheme in respect of service up to a given time. Accrued benefits may be calculated in relation to current earnings or protected final earnings. Section 28 of the Financial Reporting Standard Applicable in the UK and Republic of Ireland contains regulations on accounting for pension costs in financial accounts. UK listed companies have to comply with *International Accounting Standard 19, Employee Benefits.

accrued benefits method An actuarial method used in accounting for pension costs in which the actuarial value of liabilities relates at a given date to:

• the benefits, including future increases promised by the rules, for the current and deferred pensioners and their dependants;
• the benefits that the members assumed to be in service on the given date will receive for service up to that date only.

Allowance may be made for expected increases in earnings after the given date, and for additional pension increases not promised by the rules. The given date may be a current or future date. The further into the future the adopted date lies, the closer the results will be to those obtained by a prospective benefits valuation method.

accrued charge See ACCRUAL.

accrued income scheme An arrangement that applies in the UK when the owner of interest-bearing securities disposes of them. The interest accrued between the date of the last interest payment and the date of disposal is regarded, for tax purposes, as the income of the transferor. The transferee is able to deduct this sum from taxable income. The scheme does not apply to non-residents or if the transfer is part of a trade. Exemption also applies to individuals (husband and wife being regarded as one) if the total nominal value of the securities held does not exceed a certain amount.

accumulated depreciation (aggregate depreciation) The total amount of the *depreciation written off the cost price or valuation of a *fixed asset since it was brought into the balance sheet of an organization.

accumulated dividend A *dividend that has not been paid to a holder of *cumulative preference shares and is carried forward (i.e. accumulated) to the next accounting period. It represents a liability to the company. The Companies Act requires that where any fixed cumulative dividends on a company's shares are in arrears, both the amount of the arrears and the period(s) in arrears must be disclosed for each class of shares.

accumulated profits The amount showing in the *appropriation of profits account that can be carried forward to the next year's accounts, i.e. after paying dividends, taxes, and putting some to reserve.

accumulating shares Additional *ordinary shares issued to holders of ordinary shares in a company, instead of a dividend. Accumulating shares are a way of replacing annual income with capital growth; they avoid income tax but not capital gains tax. Usually tax is deducted by the company from the declared dividend,

in the usual way, and the net dividend is then used to buy additional ordinary shares for the shareholder.

accumulation and maintenance trust See DISCRETIONARY TRUST.

accumulation unit A unit in a *unit trust or an *investment trust in which dividends are ploughed back into the trust, after deducting income tax, enabling the value of the unit to increase. It is usually linked to a life-assurance policy.

achievement motivation theory A theory that establishes a relationship between personal characteristics, social background, and achievement. A person with a strong need for achievement tends to exhibit such characteristics as:

- regarding the task as more important than any relationship;
- having a preference for tasks over which they have control and responsibility;
- needing to identify closely, and be identified closely, with the successful outcomes of their actions;
- seeking tasks that are sufficiently difficult to be challenging, to be capable of demonstrating expertise, and to gain recognition from others, while also being sufficiently easy to be capable of achievement;
- avoiding the likelihood and consequences of failure;
- requiring feedback on achievements to ensure that success is recognized;
- needing opportunities for promotion.

The need for achievement is based on a combination of *intrinsic motivation (drives from within the individual) and *extrinsic motivation (pressures and expectations exerted by an organization, peers, and society). Achievement is also clearly influenced by education, social awareness, cultural background, and values. See MOTIVATION.

acid-test ratio See LIQUID RATIO.

ACII Abbreviation for Associate of the *Chartered Insurance Institute.

ACIS Abbreviation for Associate of the *Institute of Chartered Secretaries and Administrators.

ACMA Abbreviation for Associate of the Chartered Institute of Management Accountants. *See* ACCOUNTANT; MANAGEMENT ACCOUNTING.

ACORN Acronym for A Classification of Residential Neighbourhoods. This directory classifies 62 different types of neighbourhoods in the UK, assuming that people living in a particular postcode will have similar behaviour patterns, disposable incomes, etc. ACORN also identifies five main types of household: Wealthy Achievers, Urban Prosperous, Comfortably Off, Moderate Means, and Hard Pressed. It is used by companies to provide target areas for selling particular products or services (e.g. swimming pools, double glazing, etc.) or alternatively to exclude areas (particularly finance- and insurance-related) from a sales drive. It is also used extensively for selecting representative samples for questionnaire surveys. *See also* GEOGRAPHIC INFORMATION SYSTEM.

acquisition accounting The accounting procedures followed when one company is taken over by another. The *fair value of the purchase consideration should, for the purpose of consolidated financial statements, be allocated between the underlying net tangible and intangible assets, other than *goodwill, on the basis of the fair value to the acquiring company. Any difference between the fair value of the consideration and the aggregate of the fair values of the separable net assets (including identifiable intangibles, such as patents, licences, and trademarks) will represent goodwill. The results of the acquired company should be brought into the *consolidated profit and loss account from the date of acquisition only.

Acquisition accounting is now covered by Section 19 of the *Financial Reporting Standard Applicable in the UK and Republic of Ireland. UK listed companies are now required to follow *International Financial Reporting Standard 3, Business Combinations. *See* MERGER ACCOUNTING.

acquisition cost The average cost of acquiring a prospect or a customer. This is often calculated for setting marketing budgets in direct marketing. *See* ALLOWABLE MARKETING COST.

acquisition-development-retention (ADR framework) A measurement of a firm's activities derived from its website and based on its impact on the *a*cquisition, *d*evelopment, and *r*etention of customers.

Acrobat (Adobe Acrobat) A software application produced by Adobe Inc., used for producing and viewing electronic documents. The file format, known as **PDF** (portable document format), allows an exact reproduction of printed text, including fonts. It is widely used for Internet publication of official documents (e.g. annual accounts).

across the network Denoting a TV advertisement or programme series that is broadcast across all ITV regions simultaneously.

ACT 1. Abbreviation for *advance corporation tax. **2.** Abbreviation for *Association of Corporate Treasurers.

active management 1. A management style characterized by high levels of involvement in both task-related activities, such as initiating structures and setting goals, and interpersonal activities, such as listening, motivating, and providing feedback. *See* RELATIONSHIP-MOTIVATED; TASK-MOTIVATED. *See also* BLAKE–MOUTON MANAGERIAL GRID. **2.** A method of *portfolio management in which individual investments are selected with an eye to earning *abnormal returns. The general academic view is that this approach runs counter to the *efficient markets hypothesis and is therefore unlikely to be successful. The strategies of *diversification and following a market index are thought more likely to provide greater returns. *Compare* PASSIVE MANAGEMENT.

active partner A partner who has contributed to the business capital of a *partnership and who participates in its management. All partners are deemed to be active partners unless otherwise agreed. *Compare* SLEEPING PARTNER.

Active Server Page (ASP) A type of HTML page (denoted by an .asp file name) that includes *scripts (small programs) that are processed on a *web server before the web page is served to the user's *web browser. The main use of such programs is to process information supplied by the user in an online form. A query may then be run to provide specific information to the customer, such as delivery status of an order or a personalized web page. ASP is a Microsoft technology.

active stocks The stocks and shares that have been actively traded on a particular market on a given day.

ActiveX A programming language standard developed by Microsoft that enables complex customer applications to be written. ActiveX components are standard controls that can be incorporated into websites and automatically downloaded for users. Examples include graphics and animation, a calculator form for calculating interest on a loan, and a control for drawing graphs of stock exchange prices.

activist shareholders Investors who acquire an equity stake in a publicly traded company as a means of attempting to influence the company's practices or policies. Shareholders can be ethically motivated, such as wanting an improvement in the environmental or social impact of a business, or interested mainly in changing its business strategy or management.

activity In *activity-based costing systems, any operation performed within an organization that causes *costs to be incurred. Examples of activities therefore include processing an order, writing a letter, designing a product, and visiting a customer. The number of activities identified as such will vary from organization to organization. Activity-based costing is

founded on the recognition that resources generate costs, activities consume resources, and *cost objects (products, services, or customers) consume activities.

For purposes of *cost allocation, activities may be divided into several different categories:

- **Batch-level activities**, i.e. those activities that are performed each time a batch of goods is handled or processed. The cost incurred depends on the number of batches run rather than on the number of units in the batch. The cost is not therefore dependent on the volume of units. *See* BATCH COSTING.
- **Product-sustaining-level activities**, i.e. activities relating to specific products that must be carried out regardless of how many units are produced and sold.
- **Unit-level activities**, i.e. activities that must be performed for each unit of production.
- **Customer-level activities**, i.e. activities that are carried out for a customer but are not related to a specific product. *See also* FACILITY-SUSTAINING ACTIVITY.

activity analysis In *activity-based costing, the identification and description of *activities in an organization. Each department will determine the key activities, how many people work on the activities, and what resources are required to perform the activities. Some activities may be performed in a number of different departments.

activity-based budgeting (ABB) Establishing the activities that incur costs in each function of an organization, defining the relationships between activities, and using the information to decide how much resource should be allowed for each activity in the *budget. ABB also attempts to determine how well a particular section of the budget is being managed and to explain any variances from budgeted expenditure.

activity-based costing (ABC; activity costing) A system of costing proposed by Professors Johnson and Kaplan in their book *Relevance Lost: The Rise and Fall of Management Accounting* (1987), in which they questioned accounting techniques based on *absorption costing. Their method recognizes that costs are incurred by each activity that takes place within an organization and that products (or customers) should bear costs according to the activities they use. *Cost drivers are identified, together with the appropriate *activity cost pools, which are used to charge costs to products. Adherents of activity-based costing maintain that it provides accurate *cause-and-effect allocations of costs that cannot be obtained from *traditional costing systems.

activity-based management The use made by the management of an organization of *activity-based costing. The identification of activities and *cost drivers encourages the management to review how projected cost levels compare with the activity levels achieved.

activity cost pool (cost pool) In *activity-based costing, a collection of *indirect costs grouped according to the activity involved. To identify the costs of each activity, cost pool managers will have to ask questions such as:

• What staff are involved with the activity?
• What machinery, equipment, vehicles, and computers are used by staff?
• What materials are used for the activity?

Each activity cost pool has one or more relevant *activity measures (or *cost drivers) that are used in allocating costs: for some common examples, see the table.

The size of a particular cost pool will vary widely from one organization to another. For example, a cost pool for order processing may include hundreds of staff in a large organization, whereas a smaller organization may not have a separate cost pool for this activity as it involves only one or two staff. Note that some costs may not be included in any activity cost pool, usually because they are too minor or too difficult to allocate in this way.

activity measure In *activity-based costing systems, a measure of the volume or rate of *activity in an *activity cost pool used as a basis for allocating costs. Ideally, the activity measure chosen will be such that any rise or fall in the measure correlates closely with a rise or fall in the total cost of the activity. The terms activity measure and *cost driver are therefore often used synonymously (see also ALLOCATION BASE). Examples of activity measures include *direct labour hours, *machine hours, number of deliveries, units of output, and number of production run set-ups. In a large international organization there may be thousands of activity measures, whereas a smaller organization may identify only 20–30 such measures. It is important to state that there is no optimal number of activity measures for an organization. Note also that managers often identify more than one activity measure for each activity.

Some activity measures, such as labour hours, are very closely related to the volume of production, whereas others, such as the number of orders, are not.

activity-on-arrow (AOA) One of two alternative conventions for the visual representation of network diagrams (see NETWORK MODELLING). In AOA the activities, which make up the network, are depicted as arrows, with durations attached. The direction of the arrow indicates the direction of time. Compare ACTIVITY-ON-NODE.

ACTIVITY COST POOL	ACTIVITY MEASURE
Order processing	Number of orders
Product design	Number of product designs
Deliveries	Number of deliveries
Other costs not included	Not applicable

Activity cost pool. Some common cost pools with relevant activity measures.

activity-on-node (AON) One of two alternative conventions for the visual representation of network diagrams (*see* NETWORK MODELLING). In AON the activities, which make up the network, are located on nodes, with the lines in between simply indicating the logical sequence. *Compare* ACTIVITY-ON-ARROW.

activity ratio A ratio used in *management accounting consisting of the *production achieved for an accounting period divided by the production level regarded as achievable for that period.

activity sampling (work sampling) A technique in which a large number of observations are made over a period of a group of machines, processes, or workers. Each observation records what is happening at that instant; the percentage of observations recorded for a particular activity enables the total time during which that activity is occurring to be predicted. Traditionally carried out by industrial engineers using manual recording systems, this technique used to be dependent on the correct calculation of the number of observations required to give statistically valid data. Increasing use of online computerized data now enables managers to account for every second of their staff's time. The technique is particularly suitable for such processes as phone selling, customer services, etc. It can, however, also be applied in manufacturing systems and to groups, e.g. by requiring teams to bar-code themselves into a work area.

act of God A natural event that is not caused by any human action and cannot be predicted. It is untrue (as is sometimes thought) that insurance policies covering homes and businesses exclude acts of God. In fact, both cover such natural events as storms, lightning, and floods. However, some contracts exclude liability for damage arising from acts of God (see *FORCE MAJEURE*.)

act of war Anything that causes loss or damage as a result of hostilities or conflict. Such risks are excluded from all insurance policies (except life assurances). In marine and aviation insurance only, an extra premium may be paid to include war risks.

actual product A product's design, parts, quality level, features, brand name, packaging, and other attributes that combine to deliver a product with specified benefits.

actuals 1. (physicals) Commodities that can be purchased and used, as opposed to goods traded on a *futures contract. **2.** In futures contracts or forward dealing, the commodity underlying a contract. **3.** Expenses or receipts that have actually occurred, as opposed to targets, budgets, or other projections.

actual total loss The complete destruction or loss of an insured item or one that has suffered an amount of damage that makes it cease to be the thing it originally was. For example, a motor car would be an actual total loss if it was destroyed, stolen and not recovered, or damaged so badly that the repair cost exceeded its insured value. *See also* CONSTRUCTIVE TOTAL LOSS.

actuarial method A method used in *lease accounting to apportion rentals on the basis of compound *interest; it is also used in accounting for pensions to determine the charge to the *profit and loss account.

actuary A person trained in the application of statistics and probability theory to questions of commercial risk. Some are employed by insurance companies to calculate probable lengths of life, and advise insurers on the amounts that should be put aside to pay claims and the amount of premium to be charged for each type of risk. Actuaries also advise on the administration of pension funds; the *government actuary is responsible for advising the government on state pension schemes. *See also* INSTITUTE AND FACULTY OF ACTUARIES.

adapted marketing mix An international *marketing strategy for adjusting the elements of the *marketing mix of a product for each international target market. This strategy will add to the costs but is undertaken in the hope of attracting a larger market share and return.

adaptive customization The provision of the same basic product to all customers, who have the capability to filter out or alter various attributes of the item. Adaptive customization is often used with Internet software.

adaptive expectations In macro-economic theory, the hypothesis that economic agents form forecasts or expectations of the future values of certain economic variables by adjusting past values of the variable. This may lead agents to make systematic forecasting errors. In modern economic thought the theory of adaptive expectations has been largely superseded by that of *rational expectations.

adaptive exponential smoothing A *quantitative forecasting technique in which averages derived from historical data are smoothed by a coefficient, which is allowed to fluctuate with time in relation to changes in the demand pattern. The larger the coefficient, the greater the smoothing effect.

ad click See CLICKTHROUGH.

ad concept testing Obtaining the reactions of target customers to preliminary versions of a number of alternative approaches to an advertisement. See CONCEPT TEST.

added value See VALUE ADDED.

additional rate See HIGHER RATE OF INCOME TAX.

additional voluntary contribution (AVC) Additional pension-scheme contributions that employees can make, at their discretion, in order to increase the benefits available from their pension fund on retirement. Additional voluntary contributions can be paid into an employers' scheme or to a scheme of the employee's choice (a free-standing AVC).

add-on A supplementary accessory, replacement part, or a premium version of a product or service sold to a customer. See also CROSS-SELLING.

ad hoc mail survey A questionnaire sent to selected individuals with no prior contact or warning by a marketing research organization.

adhocracy An organization characterized by an absence of bureaucratic structures and rigid rule-based procedures. An adhocracy will develop new structures and working methods to meet each new goal or challenge. See also UNORGANIZATION.

adjudication The judgment or decision of a court, especially in *bankruptcy proceedings.

adjustable-rate mortgage (ARM) A *mortgage in which the interest rate is adjusted at periodic intervals, usually to reflect the prevailing rate of interest in the *money markets. Borrowers are sometimes protected by a *cap, or ceiling, above which the interest rate is not allowed to rise.

adjustable-rate preferred stock (ARP) Stock or cumulative preference shares in the USA whose dividends are linked to Treasury Bill interest rates. Minimum and maximum rates are specified by the application of a *collar. **Convertible adjusted-rate preferred stock** can be converted to common stock at a fixed price at specified dates.

adjusted present value A calculation of the *all-equity net present value of an investment or project that is then adjusted to allow for any other impacts, for example any tax concessions on financing. See also NET PRESENT VALUE; PRESENT VALUE.

adjuster See LOSS ADJUSTER.

adjusting entries Entries made at a *balance-sheet date under an *accrual accounting system to ensure that the income and expenditure of the business concerned are included in the correct period. Examples of adjustments include those made for *depreciation, *payments in advance, *accruals, and closing stock (items that will not be sold until future periods).

adjusting events Events that occur between a balance-sheet date and the date on which *financial statements are approved, providing additional evidence of conditions existing at the balance-sheet date. For example, a valuation of an asset held at the balance-sheet date that provides evidence of a permanent diminution in value would need to be adjusted in the financial statements. Such events include those that, because of statutory or conventional requirements, are reflected in financial statements. Current practice is set out in Section 32 of the Financial Reporting Standard Applicable in the UK and Republic of Ireland. *Compare* NON-ADJUSTING EVENTS.

adjustment bond A *bond issued in exchange for existing bonds when a business in financial difficulties is being restructured.

administered VMS (AVMS; administered strategic alliance) A *vertical marketing system in which a powerful *channel captain (quite often a major retailing chain) coordinates marketing activities at all levels in the channel, including planning and management, even though it does not directly own the other channel members. *Compare* CONTRACTUAL VMS; CORPORATE VMS.

administration order 1. An order made in a county court for the administration of the estate of a judgment debtor (*see* JUDGMENT CREDITOR). The order normally requires the debtor to pay the debts by instalments; so long as this is done, the creditors referred to in the order cannot enforce their individual claims by other methods without the leave of the court. Administration orders are issued when the debtor has multiple debts but it is thought that *bankruptcy can be avoided. **2.** An order of the court under the Insolvency Act 1986 made in relation to a company in financial difficulties with a view to securing its survival as a going concern or, failing

that, to achieving a more favourable realization of its assets than would be possible on a *liquidation. While the order is in force, the affairs of the company are managed by an *administrator and the firm is protected from legal action by the creditors to wind up the business. Since 2003 a form of **out-of-court administration** has also been possible. Under this procedure a company, its directors, or the holder of a floating *charge can appoint an administrator with a view to achieving the same purposes as an administrator appointed by a court.

administrative management A traditional view of *management that focuses on how a business should be organized and the practices an effective manager should follow. The two major contributors to this school of thought were Henri Fayol (1930) and Max Weber (1922). Fayol's 14 principles of management are still relevant, while Weber's bureaucracy model still has some relevance in medium and large organizations. *See also* CLASSICAL SCHOOL OF MANAGEMENT; SCIENTIFIC MANAGEMENT.

administrative receiver A *receiver appointed by the holder of a floating *charge covering the whole, or substantially all, of a company's assets. The administrative receiver has the power to sell the assets that are secured by the charge or to carry on the company's business. Subject to certain exceptions, an administrative receiver cannot be appointed by the holder of a floating charge created after 15 September 2003; it is now possible, however, for the holder of such a charge to appoint an *administrator without obtaining a court order.

administrator 1. Any person appointed by the courts, or by private arrangement, to manage the property of another. **2.** Any person appointed by the courts to take charge of the affairs of a deceased person, who died without making a will. This includes collection of assets, payment of debts, and distribution of the surplus to those persons entitled to inherit, according to the laws of intestacy (*see* INTESTATE). The administrator must be in possession of *letters of administration as proof of the authority vested by the courts. **3.** Any person appointed by the courts to implement an *administration order or undertake the duty of an *administrative receiver, or appointed to carry out an out-of-court administration of the affairs of a person or a company. Debt administration is now recognized as an *ancillary credit business.

adoption of innovations It has been suggested that those consumers who eventually accept an innovation can fall into the five groups shown in the diagram. Understanding each of these groups should help a company in devising effective marketing strategies.

- **Innovators**—the first to buy and use new products, i.e. they put the innovation on show to create the image of being venturesome. They are likely to communicate with and persuade others to try the product. This group is defined as the first 2½% to adopt the new product.
- **Early adopters**—tend to be opinion leaders and to adopt new ideas early but carefully. This group is defined as the next 13½% of the adopting consumers.
- **Early majority**—people regarded as being deliberate in their decisions, who are rarely leaders. These form the next 34% of the adopting consumers.

- **Late majority**—sceptics who only adopt an innovation after most other people have tried it. These form the next 34% of the adopting consumers.
- **Laggards**—the most tradition-bound, who are suspicious of changes and innovations. They tend only to adopt the innovation when it has become widely accepted (i.e. no longer an innovation).

The innovators are clearly critical to the process of adoption. Without their support an innovation is unlikely to be successful. *See also* PRODUCT LIFE CYCLE.

adoption process The mental and behavioural stages through which an individual passes before making a purchase or placing an order. The stages are: awareness→interest→evaluation→trial, and finally adoption of the product or service.

ADR 1. Abbreviation for *acquisition-development-retention (framework). **2.** Abbreviation for *American depositary receipt.

ad referendum (Latin: to be further considered) Denoting a contract that has been signed although minor points remain to be decided.

ADSL Abbreviation for asymmetric digital subscriber line; a method of high-speed digital transmission using existing copper telephone lines, employed especially in *broadband Internet connections. It

Adoption of innovations.

permits simultaneous use of the line for normal telephone calls. A special ADSL transceiver and configuration of the connection is required.

ADST Abbreviation for approved deferred share trust.

ad tracking research Marketing research that takes periodic measurements of the impact of an advertising campaign. While the goal of most advertising is to increase sales (and activity), there are many factors that can affect sales. Moreover, some advertisers judge the effectiveness of advertising by other criteria. The variables tracked are: unaided brand awareness, aided brand awareness, advertising awareness, playback, and proven recall.

ad valorem (Latin: according to value) Denoting a tax, duty, or commission that is calculated as a percentage of the total invoice value of goods or services. *VAT is an *ad valorem* tax.

advance A payment on account or a loan.

advance corporation tax (ACT) Formerly, an advance payment of *corporation tax, payable when a company made a *qualifying distribution. ACT was abolished in 1999. Larger companies must now pay corporation tax in instalments.

advance postcard (APC) A postcard sent in advance of a mail shot advising the recipient that the main mailing is coming.

adventure A commercial undertaking of a speculative nature, often associated with overseas trading.

adverse balance A deficit on an account, especially a *balance of payments account.

adverse opinion An opinion expressed in an *auditors' report to the effect that the financial statements do not give a *true and fair view of the organization's activities. This situation usually arises when there is a disagreement between the auditor and the directors, and the auditor considers the effect of the disagreement so material or pervasive that the financial statements are

seriously misleading. *See* AUDIT OPINION; QUALIFIED AUDIT REPORT.

adverse selection In the market for insurance products and loans, the tendency for the most risky customers to be the most likely to demand products that exempt them from disclosing their status. To reduce their exposure to large claims on this basis, sellers often raise premiums generally or exclude high-risk customers from such products. *See* UTMOST GOOD FAITH. *See also* ASYMMETRIC INFORMATION; MORAL HAZARD.

adverse variance *See* VARIANCE.

advertising A communication that is paid for by an identified sponsor with the object of promoting ideas, goods, or services. It is intended to persuade and sometimes to inform. The two basic aspects of advertising are the message and the medium. The media that carry advertising range from the press, television, cinema, radio, and posters to company logos on apparel. Advertising creates awareness of a product, extensive advertising creates confidence in the product, and good advertising creates a desire to buy the product. Advertising is a part of an organization's total marketing communications programme (i.e. its promotion mix). *See* ABOVE-THE-LINE; BELOW-THE-LINE; CONSUMER ADVERTISING; TRADE ADVERTISING.

advertising agency A business organization specializing in planning and handling *advertising on behalf of clients. A full-service agency provides a range of services to clients, including booking advertising space, designing and producing advertisements, devising media schedules, commissioning research, providing sales promotion advice, and acting as a marketing consultant. The departments within an agency include research, planning, creative design, media bookings, production, and accounts. Most advertising agents work on the basis of a commission on the total sums spent by the client.

advertising allowance A price concession given by a manufacturer of a product to a retailer to allow him to pay for local advertising. It is an effective way of advertising both the product and the retail outlet.

advertising appeal The central theme or idea behind an advertising message. Essentially its purpose is to tell potential buyers what the product offers and why the product is or should be appealing to them. To be meaningful, the appeal must be distinctive and credible.

Advertising Association (AA) An organization representing the interests of advertisers, *advertising agencies, and the media. Founded in 1926, it collects and assesses statistics on advertising expenditure as well as running an annual programme of seminars and training courses for people working in advertising, marketing, and sales promotion.

((()) SEE WEB LINKS

• Website of the Advertising Association: includes research and reports

advertising awareness A part of *ad tracking research in which consumers are asked whether they have seen or heard of any advertising for brands in a product category (e.g. coffee or mortgages) in the recent past (7 days, 14 days, 30 days, etc.).

advertising brief An agreement between an *advertising agency and a client on the objectives of an advertising campaign. It is important that the client knows exactly what the objectives are, helps to plan the overall strategy, and sets the budgets. Once the brief has been agreed the agency can prepare and evaluate the advertisements themselves and develop the media plan.

advertising evaluation An attempt to measure the effectiveness of an advertising campaign. Generally this involves an assessment of the communications and sales effects of the advertisement as well as copy testing. This testing can be done before or after an advertisement is broadcast or published. Testing before would

include direct rating, portfolio tests, and laboratory tests. Testing after would include recall tests (aided and unaided) as well as recognition tests. With communication and sales effectiveness, clearly the intention is to make consumers aware of and interested in the product, leading to the act of buying and producing satisfaction. It is recognized, however, that some potential buyers are unlikely to follow this course, particularly if the advertising is ineffective and the product does not meet the buyers' needs.

advertising network 1. A network that offers advertisers the ability to target specific audiences over the *Internet and to monitor results through DART (Dynamic Advertising Reporting and Targeting) technology. **2.** A collection of independent websites of different companies and media networks, each of which has an arrangement with a single advertising broker to place *banner advertisements.

advertising objective (communication goal) A specific communications (advertising) task to be achieved, with a specific target audience, during a specific period. In the context of marketing, the objectives will be to gain attention, to be understood, to be believed, and to be remembered (i.e. to inform, persuade, compare, and remind).

advertising rates The basic charges made by the advertising media for use of their services or facilities.

advertising schedule A list of planned or booked advertisements showing details of the media involved, sizes, timing, and costs.

Advertising Standards Authority (ASA) An independent body set up and paid for by the advertising industry to ensure that its system of self-regulation works in the public interest. The ASA must have an independent chairman, who appoints individuals to serve on the council, two-thirds of which must be unconnected with the advertising industry. The ASA maintains close links with central and local government, consumer organizations, and trade associations. All advertising must conform to the **UK Advertising Codes**, which are administered by the ASA; there are separate codes for broadcast media (television and radio commercials) and non-broadcast media (including electronic media and direct marketing). The Codes' requirement that adverts be legal, decent, honest, and truthful applies not only to what is said in an advertisement, but also what is shown. If it is claimed that one bar of chocolate contains one pint of milk, then the chocolate bar must contain that amount of milk. If the advertisement makes no claim, but shows a pint carton of milk, then the chocolate must still contain this amount of milk. The ASA controls the contents of advertisements by continuous monitoring of publications and by dealing with complaints from members of the public (now mainly via its website).

(((⊕))) SEE WEB LINKS
• Website of the ASA: includes text of the CAP code

advertising theme An *advertising appeal used in several different advertisements to give continuity to an advertising campaign. For example, Visa credit cards are advertised as the "most widely accepted card", while the theme of American Express card advertising is "the card has no spending limits".

advice note A note sent to a customer by a supplier of goods to advise him that an order has been fulfilled. The advice note may either accompany the goods or be sent separately, thus preceding the *sales invoice and any *delivery note. The advice note refers to a particular batch of goods, denoting them by their marks and numbers (if more than one package); it also details the date and method of dispatch.

advise fate A request by a collecting bank wishing to know, as soon as possible, whether a cheque will be paid on its receipt by the paying bank. The cheque is sent direct and not through the clearing system so that its *fate can be advised immediately.

Advisory Conciliation and Arbitration Service (ACAS) A UK government body set up in 1975 to mediate in industrial disputes in both the public and private sectors. Its findings are not binding on either side, but carry considerable weight. In some cases, especially those involving a dispute over the recognition of a trade union, it will refer a matter to the *Central Arbitration Committee. Its members include employers and trade unionists as well as academics and other independent persons. Since 1998 ACAS has also appointed arbitrators to give binding decisions in cases of alleged unfair dismissal. Under the Enterprise and Regulatory Reform Act 2013, anyone intending to bring a claim to an employment tribunal must first approach ACAS, with a view to achieving a pre-hearing settlement.

(((⊕))) SEE WEB LINKS
• Website of ACAS

advocacy promotion A firm's attempt to build customer goodwill and develop a better public image by promoting causes that are not naturally tied in to its products. A breakfast cereal producer supporting the WWF might be an example.

adware 1. Software that is free of charge to the user but makes money for its creator by displaying advertisements. Many Web sites are adware. **2.** Software that displays unwanted advertisements on the user's computer screen. Often concealed in downloaded web pages, it installs itself surreptitiously, either by exploiting security weaknesses or by tricking the user into giving consent, and is often difficult to remove. Adware is regarded as *malware and may include an element of *spyware.

affective commitment See ORGANIZATIONAL COMMITMENT.

affective component One of three main components of the *attitudes a person (potential customer) can have regarding an object or phenomenon. The affective component is concerned with the customer's emotional reactions and involves such questions as: Is this brand good or bad? Is it desirable? Is it likeable? It also involves such judgments as: 'I love BMWs'; 'The Japanese are not competent to make luxury cars'. While the former emotional response may be based upon 10 years' experience of BMWs, the latter may be based upon little cognitive information. The affective component of an attitude need not be based on experience.

affective engineering See KAIZEN.

affidavit A sworn written statement by a person, who signs it in the presence of a commissioner for oaths. In some circumstances evidence to be used in court proceedings may be taken by affidavit rather than by the witness appearing in person.

affiliate model (syndicated selling) An Internet marketing model in which a merchant uses a network of so-called 'affiliate' websites, often belonging to businesses with a similar customer base, to generate traffic to its own site via links, advertisements, special offers, etc. An affiliate earns commission on any sales made to customers who arrive at the merchant's site via the affiliate site. *Compare* AGGREGATOR MODEL.

affinity card A *credit card issued to members of a particular group (such as a club, college, etc.) or to supporters of a particular charity; the credit-card company pledges to make a donation to the charity or organization for each card issued and may also donate a small proportion of the money spent by card users. In the UK, affinity cards are sometimes called **charity cards**.

affirmation of contract Treating a *contract as being valid, rather than exercising a right to rescind it for a good reason. Affirmation can only occur if it takes place with full knowledge of the facts. It may take the form of a declaration of intention, or be inferred from such conduct as selling goods purchased under the contract, or allowing time to pass without seeking a remedy.

affirmative action programme (AAP) A programme adopted by an organization to correct former policies that discriminated against women and ethnic, or other, minorities, particularly in respect of employment. In the USA such programmes are required of all organizations with federal contracts. *See* DISCRIMINATION.

affordable method The method of setting a company's communications budget (including advertising) at a level the management thinks it can afford, rather than on the level of sales, profits, or the amount spent by competitors.

afghani (AFN) The standard monetary unit of Afghanistan, divided into 100 puli.

afloat Denoting goods, especially commodities, that are on a ship from their port of *origin to a specified port of destination; for example, 'afloat Rotterdam' means the goods are on their way to Rotterdam. The price of such goods will usually be between the price of spot goods and goods for immediate shipment from origin.

African, Caribbean, Pacific Group (ACP Group) The 79 countries in the developing world that are signatories to the **Cotonou Agreement** of June 2000, which establishes a partnership with the European Union. The main objectives of the Agreement are the reduction of poverty in ACP countries and the integration of these states with the rest of the global economy. Most ACP countries were former colonies of EU member states.

African Development Bank A regional bank, based on the model of the *International Bank for Reconstruction and Development (World Bank), created by independent African nations in 1964 to provide long-term development loans. Membership was originally restricted to African countries but was widened in 1989.

African Union (AU) An organization of African States created in 2001 as the successor to the **Organization of African Unity** (**OAU**) (formed in 1963). It aims to extend the OAU's policy of seeking cooperative solutions to the continent's political and economic problems, with the longer-term goal of establishing an economic union and a Pan-African parliament. Morocco is now the only African state not to be a member (although the memberships of Madagascar and Guinea-Bissau are currently in suspension).

after date The words used in a *bill of exchange to indicate that the period of the bill should commence from the date inserted on the bill, e.g. '…30 days after date, we promise to pay…'. *Compare* AFTER SIGHT; AT SIGHT.

after-hours deals Transactions made on a financial market after its official close at the end of its mandatory quote period. These deals are recorded as part of the next day's trading and referred to as **early bargains**.

after market *See* SECONDARY MARKET.

after-sales service Maintenance of products by the manufacturers or their agents after purchase. This often takes the form of a guarantee (*see* WARRANTY), which is effective for a stated period during which the service is free in respect of both parts and labour, followed by a maintenance contract for which the buyer of the product has to pay. Efficient and effective after-sales service is an essential component of good marketing policy, especially for such consumer durables as cars and computers; in the case of exported goods it is of overriding importance.

after sight The words used in a *bill of exchange to indicate that the period of the bill should commence from the date on which the drawee is presented with it for acceptance, i.e. has sight of it. *Compare* AFTER DATE; AT SIGHT.

AG Abbreviation for **Aktiengesellschaft*. It appears after the name of a German, Austrian, or Swiss company, being equivalent to the British abbreviation plc (i.e. denoting a public limited company). *Compare* GMBH.

age allowance *See* PERSONAL ALLOWANCE.

age analysis A listing of debtors' accounts (i.e. the amounts owing to a business),

usually produced monthly, which analyses the age of the debts by splitting them into such categories as those up to one month old, two months old, and more than two months old. As a basic part of the credit control system, the analysis should be regularly examined so that any appropriate follow-up action may be taken.

age and life-cycle segmentation The process of dividing the consumer market into different age and life-cycle groups, e.g. 30–39 years old, married, two children under 10 years old, etc. *See* MARKET SEGMENTATION.

age discrimination *See* DISCRIMINATION.

ageing schedule A breakdown of *accounts receivable by time period.

agency agreement 1. An agreement between a customer and a bank allowing the customer to bank cheques at one of its branches even though he or she does not have an account with that bank. It is usually entered into for logistical reasons. A charge is made by the bank for this service. **2.** Any agreement between an agent and a principal. *See* AGENCY RELATIONSHIP.

agency fee 1. In advertising, a sum of money paid for services provided based on a negotiated fee, as opposed to a commission. **2.** (**facility fee**) An annual fee paid to an agent for the work and responsibility involved in managing a loan after it has been signed.

agency loan A loan available for local-government authorities, public organizations, etc., from the *European Investment Bank.

agency relationship A relationship in which a principal engages an agent to perform some service on his or her behalf; this involves delegating authority by the principal. As it has to be assumed that the agent may not always act in the best interests of the principal, the principal incurs costs in monitoring and controlling the behaviour of the agent. In turn, the agent will incur bonding costs in convincing the principal that the interests of the principal will not be harmed. Even when carefully monitored, the agent may still take decisions that do not always maximize the welfare of the principal; these decisions can result in what is called a residual loss. The sum of the monitoring and bonding costs together with the residual loss form the **agency costs**. Even in an unregulated economy managers may choose to provide financial statements, examined by independent auditors, to shareholders and creditors in order to reduce agency costs. By supplying informative financial statements to external parties on the basis of information held by them, managers may avoid costly disputes and more expensive mechanisms for controlling their actions. These aspects of an agency relationship are sometimes referred to as **agency theory**. The so-called **agency problem** that arises when shareholders and managers have different interests and *asymmetric information was brought into sharp focus by the collapse of the US companies Enron and WorldCom in 2002. *See also* GOAL DIVERGENCE; SIGNALLING HYPOTHESIS.

agency worker A *worker who is supplied to an employer by an agency, usually on a temporary or contingent basis. Such workers are sometimes said to have a 'triangular' working relationship, in that they do their work for the client but are paid by the agency: they may have a contract with either, both, or neither. Because they have often found it difficult to prove that they are *employees of either the agency or the client, agency workers have tended to lack *employment protection. In order to decide whether such a worker is an employee the courts have looked for a regular pattern of mutual obligations between the parties. Regulations passed in 2003 and 2010 aim to ensure that agency workers are protected against exploitation; such workers now have a right to the same working and employment conditions as employees where they have undertaken the same role with the same hirer for 12 or more continuous weeks. They do not, however, have a right to claim *unfair dismissal. *See also*

CONTINGENT WORKER; TEMPORARY EMPLOYEE.

agenda The list of items to be discussed at a business meeting. For the *annual general meeting or an *extraordinary general meeting of a company, the agenda is usually sent to shareholders in advance. *See also* ORDER OF BUSINESS.

agent 1. Any person appointed by another (the *principal) to act on his or her behalf. *See* AGENCY RELATIONSHIP. **2.** In *contract law, a person appointed by a principal to negotiate a contract between the principal and a third party. If an agent discloses the principal's name (or at least the existence of a principal) to the third party in the transaction, the agent is not normally liable on the contract. An **undisclosed principal**, whose existence is not revealed by the agent to a third party, may still be liable on the contract, but in such cases the agent is also liable. However, an undisclosed principal may not be entitled to the benefit of a contract if the agency is inconsistent with the terms of the contract or if the third party has expressed a wish to contract with the agent personally.

In law, agents are either **general agents** or **special agents**. A general agent is one who has authority to act for the principal in all business of a particular kind, or who acts for the principal in the course of the agent's usual business or profession. A special agent is authorized to act only for a special purpose that is not in the ordinary course of the agent's business or profession. The principal of a general agent is bound by acts of the agent that are incidental to the ordinary conduct of the agent's business or the effective performance of the agent's duties, even if the principal has imposed limitations on the agent's authority. But in the case of a special agent, the principal is not bound by acts that are not within the authority conferred. In either case, the principal may ratify an unauthorized contract. A commercial (or mercantile) agent selling goods on behalf of the principal sometimes agrees to protect the principal against the risk of the buyer's insolvency. Such an agent is called a *del credere agent. **3.** A software program that can assist computer users to perform such tasks as finding particular types of information, for example, the best price for a product.

agent de change A stockbroker or securities house on the Paris Bourse (*see* BOURSE).

age of consent The age at which a person can enter into a legally binding *contract. It is set at 18 years by the Family Law Reform Act 1969. A contract entered into by someone below this age is not always capable of being enforced.

aggregate demand The sum of demands for all the goods and services in an economy at any particular time. Made a central concept in *macroeconomics by J. M. Keynes (1883–1946), it is usually defined as the sum of consumers' expenditure (*see* CONSUMPTION), *investment, government expenditure, and imports less exports. Keynesian theory proposes that the free market will not always maintain a sufficient level of aggregate demand to ensure *full employment and that at such times the government should seek to stimulate aggregate demand. However, many macroeconomists have questioned the feasibility of such policies and this remains a critical issue in macroeconomics. *See also* AGGREGATE SUPPLY.

aggregate planning An approach to planning that enables overall output levels and the appropriate resource input mix to be set for related groups of products over the near to medium term. Thus the aggregate plan for a car factory would consider the total number of units produced per month, but would not be concerned with the scheduling of individual models, colours, standards of finish, engine sizes, etc. It would be concerned with the labour and machine hours available in a given period but not with what each machine would be doing at a particular time. Aggregate planning assumes that the product/service mix remains stable over the period of the plan and that the capacity remains fixed, i.e. that problems cannot be solved by bringing new plant on stream within the timescale of the

plan. Aggregate planning may also seek to influence demand through such variables as price, advertising, and the product mix.

aggregate supply The total supply of all the goods and services in an economy. J. M. Keynes made *aggregate demand the focus of macroeconomics; however, since the 1970s many economists have questioned the importance of aggregate demand in determining the health of an economy, suggesting instead that governments should concentrate on establishing conditions to encourage the supply of goods and services. This could entail *deregulation, encouraging *competition, and removing restrictive practices in the labour market.

aggregator A firm that collates and presents information about an individual's bank accounts, investments, insurance policies, etc. so that the person concerned can manage all his or her financial affairs via a single website.

aggregator model An Internet business model in which a website is used to aggregate and display information about products or services from a variety of suppliers. The aggregator can earn revenue through advertising and from referral fees for transactions made through the site. This model is widely used in price comparison sites, as for insurance products etc. Success depends chiefly on being able to attract a large volume of traffic to the site.

AGM Abbreviation for *annual general meeting.

agora (*plural* **agorot**) A monetary unit of Israel, worth one hundredth of a *sheqel.

agreed bid A *takeover bid that is supported by a majority of the shareholders of the target company, whereas a **hostile bid** is not welcomed by the majority of the shareholders of the target company.

Agricultural Mortgage Corporation Ltd (AMC) A corporation established to grant loans to farmers against mortgages on their land by the Agricultural Credits Act 1928. The AMC offers loans for periods of

5 to 30 years. The capital of the corporation is supplied by the Bank of England, the commercial banks, and by the issue of state-guaranteed debentures. The corporation's loans are irrevocable except in cases of default and are usually made through the local branches of the commercial banking system.

agricultural property relief An *inheritance tax relief available on the transfer of agricultural property when certain conditions are met. Since March 1992 the relief has been at a rate of 100% or 50%. The 100% rate applies if the transferor has vacant possession of the property or the right to vacant possession within the following 12 months; it may also apply if the property was let after 31 August 1995. Otherwise the 50% rate applies.

AGV Abbreviation for *automated guided vehicle.

AIA Abbreviation for *Annual Investment Allowance.

AIDA In marketing and communications theory, an acronym for *a*ttention, *i*nterest, *d*esire, and *a*ction. AIDA presents a hierarchy of communication effects often regarded as a useful guideline in creating an advertisement or making a sale. The potential customer should be led from his or her initial awareness, through stages of heightened interest and desire, to the point of action (i.e. making a purchase). A fifth stage, satisfaction, is sometimes added creating the acronym **AIDAS**.

aided brand awareness One of the variables used in *ad tracking research; usually a researcher will ask respondents to indicate whether they are aware of various brands not mentioned in an unaided brand awareness question. Aided awareness is not regarded as a powerful indicator of future sales.

aided recall test See RECALL TEST.

aids to trade The formal study of commerce recognizes four aids to trade: advertising, banking, insurance, and transport.

AIFA Abbreviation for *Association of Independent Financial Advisers.

AIFM Directive See ALTERNATIVE INVESTMENT FUND MANAGERS DIRECTIVE.

AIM Abbreviation for *Alternative Investment Market.

AIO dimensions See LIFESTYLE.

air consignment note See AIR WAYBILL.

air date The date of first transmission of a commercial or an advertising campaign on television.

air freight 1. The transport of goods by aircraft, either in a scheduled airliner or chartered airliner carrying passengers (an all-traffic service) or in a freight plane (an all-freight service). Air cargo usually consists of goods that have a high value compared to their weight. **2.** The cost of transporting goods by aircraft. It is usually quoted on the basis of a price per kilogram.

airspace 1. The space that lies above a state's land and sea territory and is subject to its exclusive jurisdiction. **2.** The space above a piece of land. The owner of the land is entitled to the ownership and possession of the airspace above the land. This is not exclusive, however, and is limited by the reasonable and necessary use of that airspace by any neighbours as well as for the flight of aircraft.

airtime 1. The amount of time allocated to an advertisement on radio or television. **2.** The time of transmission of an advertisement on radio or television.

air waybill (air consignment note) A document made out by a consignor of goods by *air freight to facilitate swift delivery of the goods to the consignee. It gives the name of the consignor and the loading airport, the consignee and the airport of destination, a description of the goods, the value of the goods, and the marks, number, and dimensions of the packages.

Aktb Abbreviation for *Aktiebolaget*. It appears after the name of a Swedish joint-stock company.

Aktiengesellschaft A German, Austrian, or Swiss public limited company. *See* AG.

ALADI Abbreviation for *Latin American Integration Association.

ALCO Abbreviation for *asset and liability management committee.

algorithm A set of well-defined rules for solving a problem in a finite number of steps. Algorithms are extensively used in computer science. The steps in the algorithm are translated into a series of instructions that the computer can understand. These instructions form the computer program.

alienation A feeling of detachment that causes employees to believe that their work is neither a relevant nor an important part of their life. Because conflicts and disputes, leading to underperformance, can be caused by alienation, managers need to be aware of its existence and its causes if they are to improve relationships within a workforce. Some of the principal causes of alienation are:

- **powerlessness**—the inability to influence work conditions, quality, volume, etc.;
- **meaninglessness**—an absence of recognition of the contribution made by the individual to the output of work;
- **isolation**—the absence of human interaction during working hours; this may result from the nature of the location or a psychological gap between individuals and their supervisors and managers;
- **low self-esteem**—a reflection of the lack of value placed on individuals by an organization and its managers;
- **loss of identity with the organization**—the absence of pride in working for the organization, reinforced by the feeling that the individual's personal commitment is not recognized either financially or psychologically;

- **lack of prospects**—a feeling of frustration at being trapped in a situation that offers little prospect of advancement;
- **lack of equality**—a result of strict differentiation between the grades and levels in a hierarchical organization.

Only by addressing these causes can managers achieve groups of people who feel pride in their work, supported in solving their problems, and rewarded for their skills and effort. *See* MOTIVATION; ORGANIZATIONAL COMMITMENT.

alienation of assets The sale by a borrower of some or all of the assets that form the actual or implied security for a loan. It is therefore common practice to include a clause in the document setting up a loan, which restricts the disposal of the borrower's assets to specific circumstances.

alienative contract *See* PSYCHOLOGICAL CONTRACT.

all-equity net present value A calculation of *net present value made as if the firm, project, or investment were funded entirely by equity. In such cases, the *discount rate is the discount rate for equity. *See also* ADJUSTED PRESENT VALUE; PRESENT VALUE.

Allfinanz *See* BANCASSURANCE.

alliance *See* STRATEGIC ALLIANCE.

all-inclusive income concept A concept used in drawing up a *profit and loss account, in which all items of profit and loss are included in the statement to arrive at a figure of earnings; this is the approach adopted in the UK and the USA. Although it is claimed that this basis gives the fullest picture of the operation of an enterprise, it does lead to a volatility in earnings figures, as one-off costs, such as redundancies and sale of assets, will be included.

allocated quantity A quantity of an item held in stock that has already been allocated to an end use and is not therefore available to meet other requirements.

allocation base In *management accounting, the basis that is used to allocate costs to *cost objects. In a *traditional costing system there may be a single allocation base for each cost object, whereas in an *activity-based costing system there may be many such bases. In practice the term allocation base is often used synonymously with *activity measure or *cost driver. *See* COST ALLOCATION.

allonge An attachment to a *bill of exchange to provide space for further endorsements when the back of the bill itself has been fully used. With the decline in the use of bills of exchange it is now rarely needed.

all-or-nothing option *See* BINARY OPTION.

allotment A method of distributing previously unissued shares in a limited company in exchange for a contribution of capital. An application for such shares will often be made on the *flotation of a public company or on the privatization of a state-owned industry. The company accepts the application by dispatching a **letter of allotment** to the applicant stating how many shares have been allotted; the applicant then has an unconditional right to be entered in the *register of members in respect of those shares. If the number of shares applied for exceeds the number available (oversubscription), allotment is made by a random draw or by a proportional allocation. An applicant allotted fewer shares than applied for, is sent a cheque for the unallotted balance (an application must be accompanied by a cheque for the full value of the shares applied for). *See also* MULTIPLE APPLICATION.

allotted shares Shares distributed by *allotment to new shareholders (allottees).

allowable capital loss *See* CAPITAL LOSS.

allowable marketing cost The amount that can be spent on marketing while preserving the required profit margin. It is often calculated by deducting the cost of goods, the cost of fulfilment, and the desired profit from the total expected sales revenue. For example, if a company's sales revenue is £300,000, cost of producing goods is £130,000, cost of distribution, etc. is £30,000, and the required profit is £75,000, then the allowable marketing cost would be £65,000. Companies engaged in direct marketing activity often maintain cost control in this fashion.

allowance 1. Money paid to an employee for expenses incurred in the course of business. **2.** A deduction from an invoice for a specified purpose, such as substandard quality of goods, late delivery, etc. **3.** A price reduction or rebate given to a customer or intermediary on a large order or for some other specific reason. **4.** An agreed time used in *work measurement; it is added to the basic time in calculating the standard time (*see* STANDARD PERFORMANCE) for a particular job. These allowances provide time for rest, relaxation, and the workers' personal needs (e.g. toilet breaks). **5.** Promotional money paid by manufacturers to retailers in return for an agreement to feature the manufacturer's product in some way. **6.** An allowance against tax. *See* CAPITAL ALLOWANCES; INCOME TAX ALLOWANCES.

all-risks policy An insurance policy covering personal possessions against many risks but not, of course, all risks. A policy of this kind does not list the risks covered; instead it lists only the exclusions. Such wide cover often merits very high *premiums and items covered on this basis often include jewellery, photographic or electronic equipment, and other valuables.

alpha coefficient A measure of the expected return on a particular share compared to the expected return on shares with a similar *beta coefficient. It identifies the *specific risk associated with a share as opposed to the *systematic risk associated with securities of the same class.

alpha-release stage The first stage of testing a product or service in which *lead users, often company employees and loyal customers, test a new version. *See* BETA VERSION.

alteration of share capital An increase, reduction, or any other change in the *share capital of a company. If permitted by the *articles of association, a limited company can increase its capital as appropriate. It can also rearrange its existing capital and cancel unissued shares. The requirement for a company to specify its maximum *authorized share capital was removed under the Companies Act 2006. *See also* REDUCTION OF CAPITAL.

alternate director A person who can act temporarily in place of a named director of a company in his or her absence. An alternate director can only be present at a meeting of the board of directors if the *articles of association provide for this eventuality and if the other directors agree that the person chosen is acceptable to undertake this role.

alternative evaluation The stage in the process of *decision making in which the buyer uses information to evaluate the alternative brands available.

alternative finance arrangements A term applied in the UK Finance Acts to certain lending arrangements that comply with Islamic law (*see* ISLAMIC FINANCE). The Finance Act 2005 introduced a tax code under which tax is levied on the lender and relief is granted to the borrower as if (broadly) a proportion of each payment were interest.

Alternative Investment Fund Managers Directive (AIFM Directive) An EU directive (2011) that for the first time brought *hedge funds and *private equity firms under the supervision of a regulatory body. The directive, which has proved highly controversial within the industry, became binding on member states in July 2013.

Alternative Investment Market (AIM) A market of the *London Stock Exchange that opened in June 1995 to replace the Unlisted Securities Market, with the object of allowing small growing companies to raise capital and have their shares traded in a market, without the expense of a full market listing. Since its formation nearly 3000 smaller companies have traded their shares on this market and the number of institutions investing in the market is increasing.

(((●))) **SEE WEB LINKS**
• Information for companies, traders, and investors from the website of the London Stock Exchange

alternative trading system (ATS) In the USA, a financial trading platform that is not a recognized public exchange but is nevertheless approved and regulated by the *Securities and Exchange Commission. In many cases ATSs are fully electronic and buyers and sellers are matched to each other anonymously, so that a transaction only becomes public after it has been completed. There have been concerns that ATS trading provides too little information about trades and positions, thereby increasing the risk of market abuse. However, similar trading systems are now found in most of the world's main financial markets; the European equivalent to the ATS is the *multilateral trading facility.

Altman's Z score *See* Z SCORE.

amalgamation The combination of two or more companies. The combination may be effected by one company acquiring others, by the merging of two or more companies, or by existing companies being dissolved and a new company formed to take over the combined business. The relevant rules are set out in the *Financial Reporting Standard Applicable in the UK and Republic of Ireland and *International Financial Reporting Standard 3, Business Combinations. *See also* ACQUISITION ACCOUNTING; MERGER ACCOUNTING.

ambient computing *See* UBIQUITOUS COMPUTING.

ambulance stocks High performance stocks recommended by a broker to a client whose portfolio has not fulfilled expectations. They either refresh the portfolio— and the relationship between broker and client—or they confirm the client's worst fears.

AMC Abbreviation for *Agricultural Mortgage Corporation Ltd.

American depositary receipt (ADR) A receipt issued by a US bank to a member of the US public who has bought shares in a foreign country. The certificates are denominated in US dollars and can be traded as a security in US markets. The advantages of ADRs are the reduction in administration costs and the avoidance of stamp duty on each transaction.

American option *See* OPTION.

American terms A quotation of an exchange rate in terms of how many US dollars can be exchanged for one unit of another currency. *Compare* EUROPEAN TERMS.

amongst matter The position of an advertisement within a newspaper or magazine so that it is amongst editorial material.

amortization 1. The process of treating as an expense the annual amount deemed to waste away from a fixed asset. The concept is particularly applied to leases, which are acquired for a given sum for a specified term at the end of which the lease will have no value. It is customary to divide the cost of the lease by the number of years of its term and treat the result as an annual charge against profit. While this method does not necessarily reflect the value of the lease at any given time, it is an equitable way of allocating the original cost between periods. *Compare* DEPRECIATION.
*Goodwill may also be amortized. The Financial Reporting Standard Applicable in the UK and Republic of Ireland (Sections 18-19) requires the writing-off of goodwill to the *profit and loss account in regular instalments over the period of its economic life. **2.** The repayment of debt by a borrower in a series of instalments over a period. Each payment includes interest and part repayment of the capital. **3.** The spreading of the *front-end fee charged on

taking out a loan over the life of a loan, for accounting purposes. **4.** In the USA, another word for *depreciation.

amortization schedule A schedule that summarizes the dates on which specified amounts must be paid in the repayment of a loan.

amortized cost That part of the value of an asset that has been written off; it represents the *accumulated depreciation to date.

amortizing loan A loan in which the repayment is made in more than one instalment.

amortizing mortgage A *mortgage in which all the principal and all the interest has been repaid by the end of the mortgage agreement period. Although equal payments may be made during the term of the mortgage, the sums are divided, on a sliding scale, between interest payments and repayments of the principal. In the early years most of the payments go towards the interest charges, while in later years more repays the sum borrowed, until this sum is reduced to zero with the last payment. *Compare* BALLOON MORTGAGE.

amounts differ The words stamped or written on a cheque or bill of exchange by a banker who returns it unpaid because the amount in words differs from that in figures. Banks usually make a charge for returning unpaid cheques.

AMPS Abbreviation for *auction market preferred stock.

analysis of variance (ANOVA; variance analysis) 1. A commonly used method for examining the statistically significant differences between the means of two or more *populations. In its simplest form (**one-way analysis of variance**), it involves only one dependent variable (metric measurement level) and one or more independent variables (non-metric). For example, a researcher may be interested in establishing if there is a statistically significant difference in the average amount spent on alcohol per week between two samples of population (say, male and female). Here, the dependent variable is the amount spent and the independent variable is the gender of the participants. **2.** In *standard costing and *budgetary control, the analysis of *variances in order to seek their causes. The total *profit variance or *production cost variance is analysed into sub-variances, based on such factors as *direct labour, *direct materials, fixed and variable *overheads, and sales, in order to indicate the major reasons for the difference between budgeted figures and actual figures.

analytical estimating A *work measurement technique enabling an estimate of the time required to carry out the elements of a job to be produced at a defined level of performance. This level is based on previous knowledge, e.g. *standard performance and *synthetic standard times, and experience of the elements concerned.

anchor services *Internet service providers that form the basis of e-commerce websites by attracting traffic or providing credibility.

ancillary credit business A business involved in credit brokerage, debt adjusting, debt counselling, debt collecting, debt administration, or the operation of a credit-reference agency (*see* CREDIT RATING).

- **Credit brokerage** includes the effecting of introductions of individuals wishing to obtain credit to persons carrying on a consumer-credit business.
- **Debt adjusting** is the process by which a third party negotiates terms for the discharge of a debt due under consumer-credit agreements or consumer-hire agreements with the creditor or owner on behalf of the debtor or hirer. The latter may also pay a third party to take over an obligation to discharge a debt or to undertake any similar activity concerned with its liquidation.
- **Debt counselling** is the giving of advice (other than by the original creditor and certain others) to debtors or hirers about the liquidation of debts due under

consumer-credit agreements or consumer-hire agreements.
- A **credit-reference agency** collects information concerning the financial standing of individuals and supplies this information to those seeking it.
- **Debt administration**, which was legally recognized as a form of ancillary credit business in 2006, is the process in which an *administrator is appointed to manage the property of a debtor, including his or her salary or wages. The debt administrator may be appointed by court order (*see* ADMINISTRATION ORDER) or by a voluntary decision of the debtor.

The Consumer Credit Act 1974 provides for the licensing of ancillary credit businesses and regulates their activities.

Andean Community (CAN) An association of South American nations set up in 1969 to enhance economic cooperation. The original members were Bolivia, Chile, Colombia, Ecuador, Peru, and Venezuela; Chile withdrew in 1976 and Venezuela in 2006. The CAN signed a cooperation agreement with *Mercosur in 2004.

andon *See* VISIBLE CONTROL.

anergy *See* SYNERGY.

angel An investor in a high-risk enterprise. Traditionally, the term was applied to the financial backers of stage productions but it is now used increasingly for investors in e-business.

Annual Abstract of Statistics An annual publication of the *Office for National Statistics giving UK industrial, vital, legal, and social statistics. It is now available in an online version only. *Compare* MONTHLY DIGEST OF STATISTICS.

annual accounts (annual report; report and accounts) The *financial statements of an organization, generally published annually. In the UK, incorporated bodies have a legal obligation to publish annual accounts and file them at Companies House. Annual accounts consist of a *profit and loss account, *balance sheet, *cash-flow statement, *statement of total recognized gains and losses, and *reconciliation of movements in shareholders' funds, together with supporting notes and the *directors' report and *auditors' report. Companies falling into the legally defined *small companies and *medium-sized companies categories may file *abbreviated accounts and may also enjoy *audit exemption. Some bodies are regulated by other statutes; for example, many financial institutions and their accounts will have to comply with their own regulations. Non-incorporated bodies, such as partnerships, are not legally obliged to produce accounts but may do so for their own information, for their banks if funding is being sought, and for HM Revenue and Customs for taxation purposes. *See also* ANNUAL RETURN; PUBLISHED ACCOUNTS.

annual general meeting (AGM) An annual meeting of the shareholders of a company, which must be held every year; the meetings may not be more than 15 months apart. Shareholders must be given 14 days' notice of the meeting. The usual business transacted at an AGM is the presentation of the audited accounts, the appointment of directors and auditors and the fixing of their remuneration, and recommendations for the payment of dividends. Other business may be transacted if notice of it has been given to the shareholders. *See also* AGENDA; ORDER OF BUSINESS.

annual hours work plan A contractual arrangement in which staff agree to work a certain number of hours per year, rather than per week or month. This is particularly useful when there is a significant fluctuation in the demand for a product or service; it avoids the costs of overtime, part-time, or casual working, etc., to cover the peaks.

Annual Investment Allowance (AIA) A *capital allowance available from April 2008. It enables a business to offset 100% of its capital expenditure in any one year against corporation tax, to a limit of £500,000 (2015; £200,000 from 1 January 2016). The allowance is available to businesses of any size or legal form. It cannot be

claimed on non-commercial motor vehicles. *See also* FIRST-YEAR ALLOWANCE.

annually compounding yield (annual percentage yield) The annual *rate of return on an investment calculated on the assumption that interest payments are reinvested at the yield rate.

annual percentage rate (APR) The annual equivalent *rate of return on a loan or investment in which the rate of interest specified is chargeable or payable more frequently than annually. Most investment institutions are now required by law to specify the APR when the interest intervals are more frequent than annual. Similarly those charge cards that advertise monthly rates of interest (say, 2%) must state the equivalent APR; in this case it would be $[(1.02)^{12}-1] = 26.8\%$.

annual plan A short-term plan that describes a company's current situation, its objectives, strategy, action programme, and budgets for the year ahead, together with the controls included in the plan.

annual report *See* ANNUAL ACCOUNTS.

annual return A document that must be filed with the *Registrar of Companies within seven months of the end of the relevant accounting period (ten months for private companies). Information required on the annual return includes the address of the registered office of the company and the names, addresses, nationality, and occupations of its directors and secretary; details of the share capital and shareholders must also be included. The *directors' report must be annexed to the return, as must the *annual accounts (or *abbreviated accounts) and the *auditors' report (unless exempt from statutory audit).

annuitant A person who receives an *annuity.

annuity 1. A contract in which a person pays a premium to an insurance company, usually in one lump sum, and in return receives periodic payments for an agreed period or for the rest of his or her life. An annuity has been described as the opposite of a life assurance as the policyholder pays the lump sum and the insurer makes the regular payments. Annuities form the basis for private pensions in most developed countries. *See also* ANNUITY CERTAIN; DEFERRED ANNUITY. **2.** A payment made on such a contract.

annuity certain An *annuity in which payments continue for a specified period irrespective of the life or death of the person covered. In general, annuities cease on the death of the policyholder unless they are annuities certain.

anomaly An opportunity for *abnormal returns in financial markets. If markets are efficient there should be no anomalies (*see* EFFICIENT MARKETS HYPOTHESIS), and the assumption that this will indeed be the case dictates the pricing of many financial obligations, notably derivatives (*see* ARBITRAGE-FREE CONDITION).

anonymous FTP *See* FTP.

ANOVA Acronym for *analysis of variance.

ANSI Abbreviation for American National Standards Institute. This organization is the US equivalent of the *British Standards Institution or the Deutsches Institut für Normung (DIN).

Ansoff matrix *See* PRODUCT–MARKET STRATEGY.

ante-date To date a document before the date on which it is drawn up. This is not necessarily illegal or improper. For instance, an ante-dated cheque is not in law invalid. *Compare* POST-DATE.

anticipatory inventory *See* INVENTORY.

antidilution clause A term in a *warrant designed to protect the share price (and dividends per share) against such actions as *scrip issues. *See* DILUTION OF EQUITY.

anti-trust laws Laws passed in the USA, from 1890 onwards, making it illegal to do anything in *restraint of trade, set up monopolies, or otherwise interfere with free trade and competition.

Anton Piller order *See* SEARCH ORDER.

AOA Abbreviation for *activity-on-arrow.

AON Abbreviation for *activity-on-node.

APACS Acronym for *Association for Payment Clearing Services.

APC Abbreviation for *advance postcard.

APCIMS Abbreviation for Association of Private Client Investment Managers and Stockbrokers. *see* WEALTH MANAGEMENT ASSOCIATION.

APEX Acronym for Advance-Purchase Excursion: a form of return airline ticket offered at a discount to the standard fare, provided that bookings both ways are made a specified number of days in advance, with no facilities for stopovers or cancellations.

appellant A person or organization that appeals against the decision of a court. The party resisting the appeal is called the **respondent**.

applet A small program in the *Java programming language that can be incorporated in a web page to add additional features, such as sound or graphics.

application for listing The process by which a company applies to a stock exchange for its securities to be traded on that exchange. In obtaining the listing a company will be required to abide by the rules of the exchange. The advantage for a company in obtaining a listing is that it will be able to raise funds by issuing shares on the stock exchange and the marketability of the shares it issues will attract investors. *See also* FLOTATION; LISTING REQUIREMENTS.

application form A form, issued by a newly floated company with its *prospectus, on which members of the public apply for shares in the company. *See also* ALLOTMENT; MULTIPLE APPLICATION; PINK FORM.

application service provider (ASP) A supplier that brings together all the hardware and software needed to operate an e-commerce supply chain, provides the software on a central server, and permits customers access to the systems through browser software and an Internet link.

application services market A market in which expensive and complex software is located on a remote computer server and users, instead of installing the software themselves, access the server and pay a usage fee when running these programs.

applications software Computer programs that are designed for a particular purpose or application. For example, accounts programs, games programs, and educational programs are all applications software. Applications that can be downloaded to mobile devices such as smartphones are known as **mobile apps** or **apps**. *Compare* SYSTEMS SOFTWARE. *See* BUSINESS SOFTWARE PACKAGE.

applied research In *marketing research, research aimed at solving a specific business problem, such as obtaining a better understanding of the market, determining why a particular strategy or tactic failed, or reducing the uncertainty in making management decisions.

appraisal *See* PERFORMANCE APPRAISAL. *See also* ECONOMIC APPRAISAL; FINANCIAL APPRAISAL.

appraisal costs *See* COST OF QUALITY. *See also* ENVIRONMENTAL COSTS.

appreciation 1. An increase in the value of an asset, through inflation, a rise in market price, or interest earned. The directors of a company have an obligation to adjust the nominal value of land and buildings and other assets in balance sheets to take account of appreciation. *See* ASSET STRIPPING. **2.** An increase in the value of a currency with a *floating exchange rate relative to another currency. *Compare* DEPRECIATION; DEVALUATION.

apprentice A young employee who signs a contract (an **indenture** or **articles of apprenticeship**) agreeing to be trained in a particular skill for a set amount of time by a specific employer. During this time the wages will be relatively low but on completion of the apprenticeship they increase to reflect the increased status of the employee and to recognize the skills acquired.

appropriation 1. An allocation of the net profit of organizations in their accounts. Some payments may be treated as expenses and deducted before arriving at net profit; other payments are deemed to be appropriations of profit, once that profit has been ascertained. Examples of the former are such normal trade expenses as wages and salaries of employees, motor running expenses, light and heat, and most interest payments on external finance. Appropriations of the net profit include dividends or scrip dividends to shareholders, transfers to reserves, and amounts for taxation. In the case of partnerships, appropriations include salaries, interest on capital, and profit. *See also* ACCUMULATED PROFITS. **2.** The allocation of payments to a particular debt out of several owed by a debtor to one creditor. The right to make the appropriation belongs first to the debtor but if the debtor fails to do so, the creditor is entitled to. **3.** A document identifying a particular batch of goods to be supplied in fulfilment of a forward contract for a commodity. In some cases, for example, a forward contract may call for goods to be shipped in six months' time. At the time the contract is made the goods may not be identifiable. As the period for shipment approaches the supplier will notify the customer exactly which parcel of goods he is going to ship against the contract by identifying them (e.g. by the marks and numbers on the packages) in an appropriation.

apps *See* APPLICATIONS SOFTWARE.

APR Abbreviation for *annual percentage rate.

a priori segmentation The process of dividing markets on the basis of hunches, assumptions, or custom by the management of an organization, rather than on the basis of marketing research. *See* MARKET SEGMEN-TATION.

APT Abbreviation for *arbitrage pricing theory.

aptitude test A type of selection test intended to assess a candidate's promise, trainability, and potential rather than testing previously acquired competence. An intelligence test is often used as a measure of aptitude.

arbitrage The entering into a set of financial obligations to obtain profits with no risk, usually by taking advantage of differences in interest rates, exchange rates, or commodity prices between one market and another. Arbitrage is non-speculative because an arbitrageur will only switch from one market to another if the rates or prices in both markets are known and if the profit to be gained outweighs the costs of the operation. Thus, a large stock of a commodity in a user country may force its price below that in a producing country; if the difference is greater than the cost of shipping the goods back to the producing country, this could provide a profitable opportunity for arbitrage. Similar opportunities arise with *bills of exchange and with foreign currencies. A person or firm that engages in arbitrage is known as an **arbitrageur**.

arbitrage-free condition (no-arbitrage condition) The assumption, important in financial modelling, that there are no opportunities for risk-free excess returns in financial markets and no market *anomalies. These premises inform many aspects of finance, notably option pricing.

arbitrage pricing theory (APT) A model proposed by Stephen Ross in 1976 for calculating security returns in terms of the *arbitrage-free condition. It is an alternative to the *capital asset pricing model (CAPM). APT assumes a number of different *systematic risk factors without, however, definitively identifying the various types of risk. In setting *discount rates for decisions or valuations, companies therefore generally prefer to base their calculations on the CAPM.

arbitrary allocation A *cost allocation in which the *allocation base used is not likely to give accurate costs. For example, the cost of a lecture is not significantly dependent on the number of students: a class of 10 students requires one lecturer for (say) one hour as does a class of 200 students. Therefore using the number of students as an allocation base would result in an arbitrary allocation. The system of *activity-based costing is based on the idea that arbitrary allocations should be avoided and replaced with *cause-and-effect allocations.

arbitration The determination of a dispute by an arbitrator or arbitrators rather than by a court of law. Any civil (i.e. non-criminal) matter may be settled in this way; commercial contracts often contain **arbitration clauses** providing for this to be done in a specified way. Various industries and chambers of commerce have set up tribunals for dealing with disputes in their particular trades or business. The judgment of the arbitrator may be either binding or indicative. The current legal framework for arbitration is provided by the Arbitration Act 1996 *See also* ADVISORY CONCILIATION AND ARBITRATION SERVICE.

arbs Abbreviation for arbitrageurs, i.e. dealers specializing in *arbitrage.

architectural innovation An innovation that creates an improvement in the ways in which components, at least some of which may not in themselves be innovative, are put together. Examples include flexible manufacturing systems and networked computer systems. *Compare* COMPONENT INNOVATION.

archive A store for documents and magnetic disks or tapes containing records that are seldom used. Most computer users maintain an archive holding copies of disks or tapes containing vital information. If the original disk or tape becomes damaged, the archive copy is used to reinstate the information.

ARD Abbreviation for *accounting reference date.

ariary (MGA) The standard monetary unit of Madagascar, divided into five iraimbilanja.

arithmetic mean (arithmetic average) An average obtained by adding together the individual numbers concerned and dividing the total by their number. For example, the arithmetic mean of 7, 20, 107, and 350 is 484/4 = 121. This value, however, gives no idea of the spread of numbers and may prove misleading where there are a small number of extreme values. *Compare* GEOMETRIC MEAN; MEDIAN; WEIGHTED AVERAGE. *See also* NORMAL DISTRIBUTION.

ARM Abbreviation for *adjustable-rate mortgage.

arm's length 1. Denoting a transaction in which the parties to the transaction are or behave as if they are unrelated parties. For example, a transaction between two subsidiaries of the same parent organization could only be said to be at arm's length if it could be shown that the deal had been carried out at current market prices with no preference of any kind being shown in the trading terms. **2.** Denoting an investment portfolio in which the owner is not aware of the asset composition or the transactions entered into. *See* BLIND TRUST.

ARP Abbreviation for *adjustable-rate preferred stock.

ARR Abbreviation for *accounting rate of return.

arrangement 1. *See* DEED OF ARRANGEMENT; SCHEME OF ARRANGEMENT; VOLUNTARY ARRANGEMENT. **2.** A transaction or sale arranged by an intermediary, as in the case of an estate agent selling a mortgage as an agent for a bank.

arrears A liability that has not been settled by the due date. For example, *cumulative preference shares entitle the shareholders to receive an annual fixed dividend. If this is not paid, the dividend is said to be in arrears and this fact must be disclosed in the notes to the financial statements.

articled clerk 1. A trainee solicitor. In the UK all trainees are now graduates and will have taken professional examinations. They are then required to be articled to (i.e. to sign an agreement to learn from) a qualified solicitor for two years before being admitted as solicitors themselves. **2.** In certain Commonwealth countries, and formerly in the UK, a trainee accountant attached to a practising chartered accountant.

article of incorporation In the USA, an official document that details a company's existence. It is similar to the UK *memorandum of association.

articles of apprenticeship *See* APPRENTICE.

articles of association The document that governs the running of a company. It sets out voting rights of shareholders, conduct of shareholders' and directors' meetings, powers of the management, etc. Either the articles are submitted with the founding documents when application is made for incorporation or the relevant model articles contained in the Companies Regulations are adopted. In 2009 new model articles for private and public companies limited by shares were provided under the Companies Act 2006. The articles constitute a contract between the company and its members but this applies only to the rights of shareholders in their capacity as members. Therefore directors or company solicitors (for example) cannot use the articles to enforce their rights. The articles of a public company may be altered by a *special resolution of the members in a general meeting or by *written resolution.

articles of partnership *See* PARTNERSHIP AGREEMENT.

articulated accounts Accounts prepared under the *double-entry bookkeeping system, in which the retained earnings figure on the *profit and loss account equals the increase in net worth of the business on the *balance sheet, subject to any other increases, such as an injection of new capital.

artificial person An entity that is recognized by the law as a **legal person**, i.e. one having legal rights and duties distinct from the individuals who comprise it. For example, a company is a person in the sense that it can sue and be sued, hold property, etc., in its own name. It is not, however, an individual or natural person. *See* CORPORATION.

ASA Abbreviation for *Advertising Standards Authority.

ASA model Abbreviation for *attraction-selection-attrition model.

ASB 1. Abbreviation for *asset-backed security. **2.** Abbreviation for *Accounting Standards Board.

ascending tops A series of market peaks, each of which represents a higher level of prices than its predecessor. In *chartist analysis such a series is seen as a sign of a *bull market. *Compare* RISING BOTTOMS. *See also* DOUBLE TOP.

ASCII Acronym for American Standard Code for Information Interchange, a standard code adopted by many computer manufacturers to simplify the transfer of information between computers. The code represents the numbers, letters, and symbols used in computing by a standard set of numbers. It is based on coding with 7 bits and provides 2^7 (i.e. 128) distinct numbered characters. Other characters with values from 129 to 256 (based on 8 bits) form an extended character set (known as **extended ASCII**). In recent years ASCII has been largely superseded by *Unicode.

ASEAN Abbreviation for *Association of South East Asian Nations.

A shares In the USA, the most important class of *ordinary shares. A shares usually have greater voting power than *B shares and may carry various other privileges.

ASP 1. Abbreviation for *application service provider. **2.** Abbreviation for *Active Server Page.

as per advice Words written on a *bill of exchange to indicate that the drawee has been informed that the bill is being drawn on him.

aspirational groups *See* CONSUMER GROUPS.

assay A chemical test to determine the purity of a sample of metal or to determine the content of an alloy. In the UK assays are carried out by official Assay Offices, the marks of which appear in the *hallmarks of silver and gold articles.

assented stock A security, usually an ordinary share, the owner of which has agreed to the terms of a *takeover bid. During the takeover negotiations, different prices may be quoted for assented and **non-assented stock**.

assertiveness training Training courses designed to help employees to develop their abilities, exercise initiative, present themselves convincingly, translate ideas into action, and generally maximize their potential. Assertiveness training aims to raise trainees' self-esteem to enable them to accept that as individuals they have a right to express themselves, to be listened to, and to be taken seriously.

assessment The method by which a tax authority raises a bill for a particular tax and sends it to the taxpayer or his or her agent. The assessment may be based on figures already agreed between the authority and the taxpayer or it may be an estimate by the tax authorities. The taxpayer normally has a right of appeal against an assessment within a specified time limit. *See also* SELF-ASSESSMENT; DEFERRED ASSET.

assessment centre A part of the personnel department of an organization that uses a range of tests in selecting new employees and considering current employees for promotion. The tests include questionnaires, interviews, and practical exercises that attempt to identify the skills and qualities required for a particular job as well as the character traits of the individual.

The overall purpose of the assessment centre is to provide an organization with a process of assessment that is consistent, free of prejudice, and fair.

assessor *See* LOSS ASSESSOR.

asset Any object, tangible or intangible, that is of value to its possessor. In most cases it either is cash or can be turned into cash; exceptions include prepayments, which may represent payments made for rent, rates, or motor licences, in cases in which the time paid for has not yet expired. *Tangible assets include land and buildings, plant and machinery, fixtures and fittings, trading stock, investments, debtors, and cash; *intangible assets include *goodwill, patents, copyrights, and trademarks.

asset and liability management committee (ALCO) A senior management committee of a bank or financial institution that has overall responsibility for setting and overseeing risk-control policies in relation to the balance sheet (*see* ASSET–LIABILITY MANAGEMENT; GAP ANALYSIS). In some cases it will also be responsible for general management policy.

asset-backed commercial paper (ABCP) *See* COMMERCIAL PAPER.

asset-backed fund A fund in which the money is invested in tangible or corporate assets, such as property or shares, rather than being treated as savings loaned to a bank or other institution. Asset-backed funds can be expected to grow with inflation in a way that bank savings cannot. *See also* EQUITY-LINKED POLICY; UNIT-LINKED POLICY.

asset-backed medium-term note (ABMTN) *See* MEDIUM-TERM NOTE.

asset-backed security (ASB) A bond or note whose *collateral is the cash flows from a pool of financial obligations such as mortgages, car loans, or credit-card receivables. *See* SECURITIZATION. *See also* STRUCTURED FINANCE.

asset cover A ratio that provides a measure of the solvency of a company; it consists of its *net assets divided by its *debt. Those companies with high asset cover are considered the more solvent.

asset deficiency The condition of a company when its *liabilities exceed its *assets. Although each particular circumstance must be interpreted in its own context, the financial viability of an organization with an asset deficiency must be in question.

asset financing Funding arranged by using assets as collateral. Examples of asset financing are *factoring and *hire purchase agreements.

asset–liability gap *See* GAP.

asset–liability management The management of assets and liabilities in order to influence the *credit risk, *interest-rate risk, and *liquidity risk of a bank. *See* ASSET AND LIABILITY MANAGEMENT COMMITTEE; GAP ANALYSIS.

asset management 1. The management of the financial assets of a company in order to maximize the return on the investments. **2.** An investment service offered by banks and some other financial institutions. In the UK some private banks offer an asset management service for wealthy customers. *See also* PORTFOLIO.

asset stripping The acquisition or takeover of a company whose shares are valued below their *asset value, and the subsequent sale of the company's assets. Having identified a suitable company, an entrepreneur or investment company acquires a controlling interest in it by buying its shares; after revaluation, properties or other assets held can be sold for cash, which is distributed to shareholders (now including the entrepreneur). Subsequently, the entrepreneur can either revitalize the management of the company and later sell off the acquired shareholding at a profit or, in some cases, close the business down. Because the asset stripper is heedless of the welfare of the other shareholders, the employees, the suppliers, or creditors of the stripped company, the practice is

generally deprecated. *See also* PRIVATE
EQUITY FIRM.

asset turnover *See* CAPITAL TURNOVER.

asset valuation 1. The assessment of the
value of assets, most usually by a *present
value calculation. **2.** An assessment of the
value at which the *assets of an organization, usually the *fixed assets, should be
entered into its balance sheet. The valuation may be arrived at in a number of
ways; for example, a revaluation of land
and buildings would often involve taking
professional advice.

**asset value (per share) (break-up
value)** The total value of the assets of a
company less its liabilities, divided by the
number of ordinary shares in issue. This
represents in theory, although probably not
in practice, the amount attributable to each
share if the company was wound up. The
true value of the assets may well not be the
total of the values shown by a company's
balance sheet, since it is not the function of
balance sheets to value assets. It may,
therefore, be necessary to substitute the
best estimate that can be made of the
market values of the assets (including
goodwill) for the values shown in the balance sheet. If there is more than one class
of share, it may be necessary to deduct
amounts due to shareholders with a priority on winding up before arriving at the
amounts attributable to shareholders with
a lower priority. If a company goes into
liquidation or receivership, the break-up
value of the assets may well be below their
book value, especially if the assets include
obsolete technology saleable only for its
scrap value. The asset value per share is
also known as the **net asset value** (**NAV**).
See also BALANCE-SHEET ASSET VALUE;
BOOK VALUE.

assignment The act of transferring, or a
document (a **deed of assignment**) transferring, property to some other person.
Examples of assignment include the transfer of rights under a contract or benefits
under a trust to another person. *See also*
ASSIGNMENT OF LEASE.

assignment of copyright *See* COPY-
RIGHT.

assignment of insurable interest
Assigning to another party the rights and
obligations of the *insurable interest in an
item of property, life, or a legal liability to
be insured. This enables the person to
whom the interest is assigned to arrange
insurance cover, which would not otherwise be legally permitted.

assignment of lease The transfer of a
*lease by the tenant (assignor) to some
other person (assignee). Leases are freely
transferable at common law although it is
common practice to restrict assignment by
conditions (*covenants) in the lease. An
assignment that takes place in breach of
such a covenant is valid but it may entitle
the landlord to put an end to the lease and
re-enter the premises. An assignment
transfers the assignor's whole estate to the
assignee, unlike a sub-lease (*see* HEAD
LEASE). *See also* BUSINESS TENANCY.

assignment of life policies Transfer of
the legal right under a *life-assurance
policy to collect the proceeds. Assignment
is only valid if the life insurer is advised and
agrees; life assurance is the only form of
insurance in which the assignee need not
possess an *insurable interest. In recent
years policy auctions have become a
popular alternative to surrendering
*endowment assurances. In these auctions,
a policy is sold to the highest bidder and
then assigned to him or her by the original
policyholder.

assisted stock replenishment A system making use of *electronic-point-of-sale
data to generate stock replenishment
orders. Using the previous week's sales for
each item, new stock can be delivered in
advance and reviews of current sales
enable extra items to be supplied at short
notice.

Associated British Ports (ABP) A
statutory corporation set up by the Transport Act 1981 to administer the 19 ports
previously controlled by the British Transport Docks Board. ABP now administers 21

a

ports and is controlled by Associated British Ports Holding plc.

Association for Payment Clearing Services (APACS) An association set up by the UK banks in 1985 to manage payment clearing and overseas money transmission in the UK. It had four main Interest Groups: the Card Payments Group, the Cash Services Group, the Electronic Commerce Group, and the Liquidity Managers Group. APACS was succeeded by the *UK Payments Administration (UKPA) in 2009.

Association of Accounting Technicians An association set up in 1980 by the *Consultative Committee of Accountancy Bodies (CCAB) to provide a second-tier accounting qualification. This qualification can enable an individual to obtain subsequently a full CCAB qualification.

Association of British Insurers (ABI) A trade association representing some 380 insurance companies offering any class of insurance business, whose members transact over 90% of the business of the British insurance market. It was formed in 1985 by a merger of the British Insurance Association, the Accident Offices Association, the Fire Offices Committee, the Life Offices Association, and the Industrial Life Offices Association.

(((∙))) **SEE WEB LINKS**
• Website of the ABI: includes general insurance advice for businesses and private consumers

Association of Chartered Certified Accountants (ACCA) The professional association for *chartered certified accountants. It was formed in 1938 as the Association of Certified and Corporate Accountants and known as the **Chartered Association of Certified Accountants** from 1984 until 1996 when it adopted its present name. With over 140,000 members in 170 countries, it is one of the largest professional accountancy bodies in the world.

(((∙))) **SEE WEB LINKS**
• ACCA website: includes information on training and careers as well as advice on finding an accountant

Association of Corporate Treasurers (ACT) An organization set up to encourage and promote the study and practice of treasury management in companies. A small organization in relation to the professional accounting bodies, it has become influential in the field of corporate treasurership. Fellows of the Association are designated FCT and members as MCT.

Association of Independent Financial Advisers (AIFA) The trade body for *independent financial advisers in the UK, established in 1994. It represents the views of the profession to the *Financial Services Authority, parliament, and other policy makers, and promotes the benefits of financial advice to the public.

Association of Private Client Investment Managers and Stockbrokers (APCIMS) *See* WEALTH MANAGEMENT ASSOCIATION.

Association of South East Asian Nations (ASEAN) A political and economic grouping of certain nations of South East Asia, formed in 1967 and currently comprising: Thailand, Malaysia, Singapore, Philippines, Indonesia, Brunei, Laos, Burma, Vietnam, and Cambodia. The countries are very diverse—for example, the per capita income of Singapore is over 60 times that of Vietnam—and interests often diverge accordingly. Although ASEAN is committed to strengthening economic ties, progress has been limited. There has also been political, technological, and cultural cooperation. There are regular consultations between ASEAN and the major industrialized countries.

assurance *Insurance against an eventuality (especially death) that must occur. *See* LIFE ASSURANCE.

assured The person named in a life-assurance policy to receive the proceeds in the event of maturity or the death of the *life assured. As a result of the policy, the person's financial future is 'assured'.

AST Abbreviation for *automated screen trading.

asymmetric information The situation in which one party to an agreement or transaction has superior information to the other. Any serious or systematic imbalance of this kind can compromise the efficiency of markets and lead to *market failure. The problem of asymmetric information is often discussed in the context of *agency relationships, notably those between managers and shareholders: in most cases managers will have superior information to shareholders regarding the state of the latter's investment. Information asymmetry also occurs in insurance, where the purchaser of an insurance contract is likely to know more about the nature of the risks than the seller of the contract (*see* ADVERSE SELECTION; UTMOST GOOD FAITH). *See also* SIGNALLING HYPOTHESIS.

at A monetary unit of Laos, worth one hundredth of a *kip.

at and from Denoting a marine hull insurance cover that begins when the vessel is in dock before a voyage, continues during the voyage, and ends 24 hours after it has reached its port of destination.

at best (market order) An instruction to a broker to buy or sell shares, stocks, commodities, currencies, etc., as specified, at the best possible price at the time of transaction. It must be executed immediately irrespective of market movements. *Compare* AT LIMIT.

at call Denoting money that has been lent on a short-term basis and must be repaid on demand. *Discount houses are the main borrowers of money at call.

at limit (limit order) An instruction to a broker to buy or sell shares, stocks, commodities, currencies, etc., as specified, at a stated limiting price (i.e. not above a stated price if buying or not below a stated price if selling). When issuing such an instruction the principal should also state for how long

the instruction stands, e.g. for a day, a week, etc. *Compare* AT BEST.

ATM Abbreviation for *automated teller machine.

atmosphere An aspect of the environment designed to create or reinforce a buyer's inclination to buy a particular product. In large supermarkets, for example, the smell of freshly baked bread is extracted from the bakery and directed into the store to increase bread sales.

at par *See* PAR VALUE.

ATS Abbreviation for *alternative trading system.

at sight The words used on a *bill of exchange to indicate that payment is due on presentation. *Compare* AFTER DATE; AFTER SIGHT.

ATT Abbreviation for Associate of the Association of Tax Technicians, a qualification undertaken by employees working in taxation at a level below that of members of the *Chartered Institute of Taxation. The Association was set up in 1989 under the sponsorship of the Institute.

attachment 1. A procedure enabling a creditor, who has obtained judgment in the courts (the *judgment creditor), to secure payment of the amount due from the debtor. The judgment creditor obtains a further court order to the effect that money or property due from a third party to the debtor must be frozen and paid instead to the judgment creditor to satisfy the amount due. For instance, a judgment creditor may, through a *third-party debt order, attach the salary due to the debtor from the debtor's employer. **2.** A data file that is embedded in an *e-mail message. To users, the file appears as a distinct object attached to the message.

attest To bear witness to an act or event. The law requires that some documents are only valid and binding if the signatures on them have been attested to by a third party. This also requires the third party's signature on the document.

at the money Describing a call or put *option in which the exercise price is the same (or very nearly the same) as the current market price of the *underlying. Such an option has no *intrinsic value but will have some *time value. *See also* IN THE MONEY.

attitude The way in which a person views and evaluates something or someone. Attitudes determine whether people like or dislike things—and therefore how they behave towards them.

Attitude is traditionally divided into cognitive, behavioural, and *affective components, although the main emphasis now tends to fall on defining attitude in terms of affect—the person's feelings towards the object, brand, etc. Is the brand good or bad? Is it likeable? The importance of the cognitive and behavioural components is still accepted, but they are no longer regarded as critical components.

attitude research An investigation into the *attitudes of people towards an organization or its products. Attitude research is important to advertising specialists in planning campaigns. For example, it might reveal a 'Buy British' attitude among respondents, which would present a marketing and advertising problem to a US manufacturer.

attraction-selection-attrition model (ASA model) A theory holding that: (1) individuals are attracted to organizations whose members are similar to themselves in terms of personality, values, interests, and other attributes; (2) organizations are more likely to select those who possess knowledge, skills, and abilities similar to the ones their existing members possess; and (3) over time, those who do not fit in well are more likely to leave. Owing to these three factors, the personal characteristics of those who work for an organization are likely to become more similar over time, leading to the consolidation of *organizational culture.

attribute A characteristic of a product or service that can be measured by a rating having only two possible states, e.g. good or bad, acceptable or not acceptable, etc. *Compare* VARIABLE.

AU Abbreviation for *African Union.

auction A method of sale in which goods, securities, rights, etc. are sold in public to the highest bidder. Auctions are used for any property for which there are likely to be a number of competing buyers, such as houses, second-hand and antique furniture, works of art, etc., as well as for certain commodities, such as tea, bristles, wool, furs, etc., which must be sold as individual lots, rather than on the basis of a standard sample or grading procedure. In most auctions the goods to be sold are available for viewing before the sale and it is usual for the seller to put a *reserve price on the articles offered, i.e. the articles are withdrawn from sale unless more than a specified price is bid. The auctioneer acts as agent for the seller in most cases and receives a commission on the sale price. He

Attitude. The components of attitude.

must have the authority of the seller to sell, and must know of no defect in the seller's title to the goods, without promising that a buyer will receive good title for a specific object. An advertisement that an auction will be held does not bind the auctioneer to hold it. It is illegal for a dealer (a person who buys at auction for subsequent resale) to offer a person a reward not to bid at an auction. *See also* DOUBLE AUCTION; DUTCH AUCTION; VIRTUAL AUCTION.

auction enabler An online service that helps an auction house run an effective physical auction.

auction market preferred stock (AMPS) A US floating rate preferred stock whose dividend is set by *Dutch auction.

audience data syndicated services Research companies that collect, package, and sell data on media audiences to a variety of firms.

audience research Research to establish readership, audience, and circulation data, which is vital information in advertising. In the UK research into television audiences is undertaken by *BARB (Broadcasters' Audience Research Board), into radio audiences by RAJAR (*Radio Joint Audience Research), and into readership of newspapers and magazines by the *National Readership Survey and the *Audit Bureau of Circulation.

audimeter An electromechanical device used to record the channel that a television set is tuned to (if any). The information collected enables the marketing research company to say how many sets were tuned to a particular programme and for how long the television was on; it does not show how many persons were viewing or the length of time for which they were viewing.

audioconferencing A facility enabling several users in different places to conduct a business meeting over the telephone or by *VoIP. *See also* TELECONFERENCING; VIDEOCONFERENCING.

audio response device A output device, connected to a computer, that produces human speech. These devices are used, for example, in computerized telephone enquiry systems. They work by storing words, syllables, or phrases in the computer and linking them together to form more-or-less recognizable speech.

audit An independent examination of, and the subsequent expression of opinion on, the financial statements of an organization. This involves the auditor in collecting evidence by means of compliance tests (tests of control) and substantive tests (tests of detail). *External audits (i.e. audits performed by an auditor external to the organization) are required under statute for limited companies by the Companies Act and for various other undertakings, such as housing associations and building societies, by other Acts of Parliament. *Internal audits are performed by auditors within an organization, usually an independent department, such as an internal-audit department. Internal auditors examine various areas, including financial and non-financial concerns, with emphasis on ensuring that internal controls are working effectively. Internal auditors may assist the external auditor of an organization. Non-statutory audits can be performed at the request of the owners, members, or trustees of an undertaking, for example. Financial statements other than the annual accounts may also be audited; for example, summaries of sales made by an organization in a specified period. *See also* AUDIT OPINION; AUDITOR; AUDITORS' REPORT; STATUTORY AUDIT.

Audit Bureau of Circulation (ABC) An organization to which most advertising agencies, publishers of newspapers, magazines, and periodicals, and digital service providers belong. Its function is to collect and audit sales figures from publishers regularly and to publish monthly circulation figures; since 1996 it has also taken a leading role in measuring the reach of digital media. This data is of great value to advertisers and institutional investors. A newspaper, magazine, or periodical must have been publishing for a minimum of six months before it is registered with the ABC.

SEE WEB LINKS
• ABC website

audit committee In public companies, a committee of *non-executive directors that is responsible for oversight of financial reporting, internal and external audit, compliance with regulatory codes, and *risk management. The UK's *Corporate Governance Code recommends that all public companies establish audit committees to enhance accountability and public confidence. In the USA the role of such committees was strengthened by the *Sarbanes–Oxley Act 2002, passed in the wake of the Enron scandal. *See also* REMUNERATION COMMITTEE.

audit evidence The evidence required by an auditor on which to base an *audit opinion on the *financial statements of the company whose accounts are being audited. Sources of information include the accounting systems and the underlying documentation of the enterprise, its tangible assets, management and employees, its customers, suppliers, and any other third parties who have dealings with, or knowledge of, the enterprise or its business. The evidence will be obtained by means of **compliance tests** (tests to determine the effectiveness of a company's control procedures) and **substantive tests** (tests of the accuracy and completeness of accounting records and financial statements). Techniques involved in gathering the evidence include inspection, observation, enquiry, analysis, and *computer-assisted audit techniques.

audit exemption The exemption from *statutory audit by a registered auditor that can now be claimed by almost every *small company. Until October 2012 small companies with a turnover of more than £1 million (and a balance-sheet total of more than £2.8 million) could claim exemption from audit but still needed an **audit exemption report**. This was a document, drawn up by a **reporting accountant** and submitted

with the annual accounts, to the effect that (i) the accounts were consistent with the records kept by the company and the provisions of the Companies Acts and (ii) the company was entitled to the exemption on the basis of size. Such a report is no longer required.

audit fee (auditors' remuneration) The amount payable to an auditor for an audit; this has to be approved at the *annual general meeting of a company. In the *financial statements, audit fees must be distinguished from fees payable to the auditor for non-audit work.

audit opinion An opinion contained in an *auditors' report. It expresses a view as to whether or not the *financial statements audited have been prepared consistently using appropriate accounting policies, in accordance with relevant legislation, regulations, or applicable accounting standards. The opinion also has to state that there is adequate disclosure of information relevant to the proper understanding of the financial statements. If the auditors are satisfied on these points, and if any departure from legislation, regulations, or applicable accounting standards has been justified and adequately explained in the financial statements, an unqualified opinion will be given. If the scope of the auditors' examination has been limited, or the auditors disagree materially with the treatment or disclosure of a matter in the financial statements, or they do not comply with relevant accounting or other requirements, a *qualified audit report or *adverse opinion will be issued.

auditor A person or firm appointed to carry out an *audit of an organization. In the UK an external auditor must be a registered auditor or a member of a *Recognized Supervisory Body and be eligible for appointment under the rules of that body. The supervisory bodies are required to have rules designed to ensure that persons eligible for appointment as company auditors are either individuals who hold the appropriate qualification or firms controlled by properly qualified persons. These bodies must also ensure that eligible persons continue to maintain the appropriate level of competence and must monitor and enforce compliance with their rules. These rules do not apply to internal auditors.

auditors' remuneration *See* AUDIT FEE.

auditors' report (audit report) A report by the auditors appointed to *audit the accounts of a company or other organization. Auditors' reports may take many forms depending on who has appointed the auditors and for what purposes. Some auditors are engaged in an internal audit while others are appointed for various statutory purposes. The auditors of a limited company are required to form an opinion as to whether the annual accounts of the company give a *true and fair view of its profit or loss for the period under review and of its state of affairs at the end of the period; they are also required to certify that the accounts are prepared in accordance with the requirements of the Companies Act. The auditors' report is technically a report to the members of the company and it must be filed together with the accounts with the Registrar of Companies. The report must also include an audit of the directors' report with respect to consistency. The Companies Act 2006 creates a new criminal offence of knowingly or recklessly supplying false or deceptive information in an auditors' report.

audit software Computer programs used by an auditor to examine an enterprise's computer files. Utility programs may be used, for example, for sorting and printing data files. Package or tailor-made programs may be used to interrogate the computer-based accounting system of a client. More sophisticated *computer-assisted audit techniques (CAATs) include the use of embedded audit facilities, in which program codes and additional data are incorporated into the client's computerized accounting system to facilitate a continuous review of the system.

audit trail (paper trail) The sequence of documents, computer files, and other records examined during an *audit, showing how a transaction has been dealt with by an organization from start to finish. Documents will require cross-referencing so the trail is not broken. For example, a sales transaction can be traced from the item of stock sold, to the invoice, through the sales day book, to the sales account, and finally to the bank account. In securities dealing the audit trail should enable supervisory bodies to follow transactions and ensure that fair prices have been paid. *See also* COMPUTER-ASSISTED AUDIT TECHNIQUES.

augmented product Additional consumer services and benefits sold with a core product. The augmented product can be critical to the success of the core product. For example, a camcorder (the core product) may be marketed with a warranty, quick repair service, freephone number for problems, and possibly free lessons on how to use the device.

AUP Abbreviation for *acceptable use policy.

Australian Securities Exchange (ASX) An exchange based in Sydney, formed in 2006 from a merger of the **Australian Stock Exchange** and the Sydney Futures Exchange. The Australian Stock Exchange had itself been formed in 1987, when the Sydney exchange superseded the exchanges in Brisbane, Adelaide, Hobart, Melbourne, and Perth. It adopted fully automated trading in October 1997. The most important market index is now the S&P ASX200, covering the top 200 shares on the exchange, although the All-Ordinaries share index, covering some 500 shares, is still quoted.

authentication In e-commerce, *see* SECURITY.

authoritarian leader A leader who makes all major decisions himself or herself and takes a highly dominant role in interactions with subordinates. Experimental studies of *leadership style have found that work groups with authoritarian leaders tend to be more discontented than those with *democratic leaders or *laissez-faire

a

leaders and to be less productive than such groups when the leader is absent.

authorized auditor An individual granted special authorization to act as the auditor of a company under the Companies Act 1967. Authorizations were granted to individuals not otherwise eligible to act as auditors on the basis of their experience. The power to grant authorizations ended in 1978; since 1989 an authorized auditor is not eligible for appointment as an auditor of a listed company.

authorized minimum share capital In the UK, the statutory minimum of £50,000 for the share capital of a public company. There is no minimum share capital for private companies.

authorized share capital (nominal share capital; nominal capital; registered capital) The maximum amount of *share capital that may be issued by a company, as detailed in the company's *memorandum of association. There was formerly a statutory requirement for a company to specify its maximum authorized share capital; this was removed from late 2009 as part of the implementation of the Companies Act 2006. *See also* ISSUED SHARE CAPITAL.

automated answer *See* AUTOMATIC RESPONSE SYSTEM; AUTORESPONDER.

automated guided vehicle (AGV) A self-propelled vehicle guided by cables set in the floor, by radio or microwave transmitters, by onboard computer, or by optical guidance systems. AGVs are used to transport materials or components without human intervention. They are most often used in manufacturing plants, especially if these involve hazardous chemicals or structures, where AGVs can form an integrated part of the process design, replacing conveyor belts, etc.

automated screen trading (AST) Electronic dealing in securities or other financial instruments using visual-display units to display prices and the associated computer equipment to enter, match, and execute deals. The system does away with the need for face-to-face trading on a formal stock-exchange floor. It also reduces or eliminates paperwork. Many leading exchanges now operate entirely through automated screen trading, as do most *alternative trading systems. Automated trading has been taken to another level in modern high-speed trading, in which trades are executed entirely by algorithm.

automated teller machine (ATM) A computerized machine usually attached to the outside wall of a high-street bank or building society that enables customers to withdraw cash from their *current accounts at any hour of the day. The machines may also be used to effect transfers and obtain statements. They are operated by *cash cards or *multifunctional cards in conjunction with a *PIN. ATMs are often known colloquially as **cash dispensers**.

automatic debit transfer *See* GIRO.

automatic identification A means of identifying a product mechanically and entering the data obtained automatically into a computer. The most widely used method involves *bar codes. Other methods include *optical character recognition (OCR), magnetic ink character recognition (MICR), magnetic stripes, and voice systems.

automatic response system A software program designed to answer frequently asked questions (*see* FAQ) without human intervention.

automatic stabilizers Adjustments to fiscal policy that occur automatically during *business cycles and smooth the path of economic growth. For example, in a *recession the government will pump money into the economy by paying more in unemployment benefit without a change in policy. Automatic stabilizers counterbalance the feedback effect of changes in economic activity, although in practice their effectiveness is limited.

automatic vending Selling products by means of vending machines.

autonomous work groups (AWGs)
Small work units within an organization that are given considerable responsibility for organizing their activities and achieving results without guidance from management. Advocates of AWGs argue that improvements in performance can be attained if employees are highly motivated and fully involved in the direction and control of their work.

autoresponder A system enabling an answer to a query sent by e-mail to be automatically retrieved from a stored database and sent to the enquirer without human intervention. *See* FAQ.

available market The consumers who have interest in, sufficient income to buy, and access to a particular product or service. *See also* QUALIFIED AVAILABLE MARKET.

aval 1. A third-party guarantee of payment on a *bill of exchange or promissory note; it is often given by a bank. **2.** A signature on a bill of exchange that endorses or guarantees the bill.

AVC Abbreviation for *additional voluntary contribution.

average 1. A single number used to represent a set of numbers; mean. *See* ARITHMETIC MEAN; GEOMETRIC MEAN; MEDIAN; WEIGHTED AVERAGE. **2.** A partial loss in *marine insurance (from French: *avarie*, damage). In **general average** (**GA**), a loss resulting from a deliberate act of the master of the ship (such as throwing overboard all or part of the cargo to save the ship) is shared by all the parties involved, i.e. by the shipowners and all the cargo owners. *See* AVERAGE ADJUSTER; AVERAGE BOND. In a **particular average** (**PA**), an accidental loss is borne by the owners of the particular thing lost or damaged, e.g. the ship, an individual cargo, etc. Cargo can be insured either **free of particular average** (**FPA**) or **with average** (**WA**). An FPA policy covers the cargo against loss by perils of the sea, fire, or collision and includes cover for any contribution payable in the event of a general

average. A WA policy gives better cover as it also includes damage by heavy seas and sea-water damage. In addition, marine cargo can be covered by an *all-risks policy. *See also* FREE OF ALL AVERAGES; INSTITUTE CARGO CLAUSES. **3.** A method of sharing losses in property insurance to combat underinsurance. This is usually applied in an **average clause** in a fire insurance policy, in which it is stated that the sum payable in the event of a claim shall not be more than the proportion that the insured value of an item bears to its actual value.

average adjuster A person who handles marine insurance claims on behalf of the insurers. If there is a claim that involves general *average and contributions have to be made by all the parties involved it is the average adjuster who is responsible for apportioning payment.

average bond A promise to pay general *average contributions, if required. If a general-average loss occurs during a marine voyage the carrier has a right to take part of the cargo as payment of the cargo owners' contribution to the loss. As an alternative to the possibility of losing part of the cargo, the cargo owner may take out an average bond with insurers, who agree to pay any losses arising in this way.

average clause *See* AVERAGE.

average cost 1. The average cost per unit of output calculated by dividing the total costs, both *fixed costs and *variable costs, by the total units of output. **2.** (**AVCO; weighted-average cost**) A method of valuing units of *raw material or *finished goods issued from stock; it involves recalculating the unit value to be used for pricing the issues after each new consignment of raw materials or finished goods has been added to the stock. The average cost is obtained by dividing the total stock value by the number of units in stock. Because the issues are at an average cost, it follows that the valuation of the closing stock should be made on the same average cost basis. The method may also be used in *process costing to value the work in process at the end of an accounting period.

average life A somewhat artificial measure sometimes used to compare bonds of different duration and different repayment schedules. It is calculated as the average of the periods for which funds are available, weighted by the amounts available in each of these periods.

average order cost In *direct-mail selling, the total cost of orders, divided by the total number of orders.

average order value In *direct-mail selling, the total value of orders received, divided by the total number of orders.

average stock A method of accounting for stock movements that assumes goods are taken out of stock at the average cost of the goods in stock. *See* BASE STOCK; FIFO COST; LIFO COST; STOCK.

average variable cost An average taken over a specified period of the variable cost of producing units of production (*see* AVERAGE COST). The variable costs (such as the cost of raw materials, direct labour, machine time, etc.) of producing a unit are those that vary directly with the number of units produced. As they are likely to change from time to time it may be convenient for budgeting purposes to take an average.

averaging Adding to a holding of particular securities or commodities when the price falls, in order to reduce the average cost of the whole holding. **Averaging in** consists of buying at various price levels in order to build up a substantial holding of securities or commodities over a period. **Averaging out** is the opposite process, of selling a large holding at various price levels over a long period.

aviation broker A broker who arranges chartering of aircraft, air-freight bookings, insurance of air cargo and aircraft, etc.

aviation insurance The insurance of aircraft, including accident or damage to aircraft, insurance of air cargo, loss of life or injury while flying, and loss or damage to baggage.

AVMS Abbreviation for administered vertical marketing system. *See* ADMINISTERED VMS.

avo A monetary unit of Macao, worth one hundredth of a *pataca.

avoidable costs Costs that will not be incurred if a particular course of action is not taken. For example, if a specific product is not produced, certain material and labour costs may be avoided. *Variable costs are often avoidable costs, whereas *fixed costs, such as business rates, are not avoidable in the short term. *See also* RELEVANT COST.

AWGs Abbreviation for *autonomous work groups.

aw-shucks defence A legal defence in which a senior executive claims to have been ignorant of fraudulent or otherwise unlawful practices within their company. The term was coined by the prosecutor in the 2005 trial of Bernie Ebbers, the founder of WorldCom, who was found guilty of an $11 billion fraud. The failure of his defence meant that similar claims became less likely in subsequent trials.

baby boom A major increase in the annual birth rate following World War II, which lasted until the early 1960s. The **baby boomers**, now at or approaching retirement age, are a prime target for marketers, particularly as their own offspring will now have ceased to be a financial drain on them. *See also* GREY MARKET.

backdate 1. To put an earlier date on a document than that on which it was compiled, in order to make it effective from that earlier date. **2.** To agree that salary increases, especially those settled in a pay award, should apply from a specified date in the recent past.

back door One of the methods by which the *Bank of England injects cash into the *money market. The bank purchases Treasury bills at the market rate rather than lending directly to the discount houses (the **front door** method) when it acts as *lender of last resort.

back-end load The final charge made by an *investment trust or *unit trust when an investor sells shares in the fund. *Compare* FRONT-END LOAD.

backer A person or organization that invests in a new company or project and may require a share in the equity of the company.

backflush accounting A method of costing a product based on a management philosophy that includes having the minimum levels of *inventory available; in these circumstances, the valuation of stocks becomes less important, making the complex use of *absorption costing techniques unnecessary. Backflush accounting works backwards; after the actual costs

have been determined they are allocated between inventory and *cost of sales to establish profitability. There is no separate accounting for *work in progress.

back freight The cost of shipping goods back to the port of destination after they have been overcarried. If the master overcarried the goods for reasons beyond his control, the shipowner may be responsible for paying the back freight. If delivery was not accepted in reasonable time at the port of destination and the master took the goods on or sent them back to the port of shipment, the back freight would be the responsibility of the cargo owner.

backlog An accumulation of unfulfilled orders held by a firm. This may result from an inability to cope with the demand for a product during a particular period or it may be a deliberate policy to even out an irregular demand, or to avoid having to hold excessive stocks or to increase short-term production capacity by paying overtime rates.

back office *See* FRONT OFFICE–BACK OFFICE.

back-to-back credit (countervailing credit) A method used to conceal the identity of the seller from the buyer in a credit arrangement. When the credit is arranged by a British finance house, the foreign seller provides the relevant documentation. The finance house, acting as an intermediary, issues its own documents to the buyer, omitting the seller's name and so concealing the seller's identity.

back-to-back loan One loan of a matching pair of loans in different currencies: A lends to B and B lends to A where the loans are of the same value. The back-to-back loan was a precursor of the *currency swap and can be used to avoid currency restrictions.

back-to-back swaps Two swap that have been combined, sometimes as a method of winding up a *swap position.

back-up credit An alternative source of funds arranged if an issue of *commercial paper is not fully taken up by the market. Back-up credit is provided by a bank for a fee or by the deposit of credit balances at the bank of the issuer. The back-up is often a stand-by facility provided by the bank, which may be drawn upon if the paper is not placed.

backwardation 1. The situation in which (or the extent to which) the spot price of a commodity, plus any *carrying costs, is higher than the forward price. *Compare* CONTANGO. **2.** A situation that occasionally occurs on a stock exchange when a market maker quotes a buying price for a share that is lower than the selling price quoted by another market maker. This can only occur in a *quote-driven system.

backward channel A channel of distribution for recycling, in which the customary flow from producer to ultimate user is reversed. For example, bottles, cans, and paper are now returned to the producer for recycling.

backward integration *See* INTEGRATION.

Bacs *See* UK PAYMENTS ADMINISTRATION.

bad debt An amount owed by a debtor that is unlikely to be paid; for example, due to a company going into liquidation. The full amount should be written off to the *profit and loss account of the period or to a *provision for bad debts as soon as it is foreseen, on the grounds of prudence. Bad debts subsequently recovered either in part or in full should be written back to the profit and loss account of the period (or to a provision for bad and doubtful debts).

badges of trade The criteria that distinguish trading from investment for taxation purposes. Whereas six badges of trade were set out by the Royal Commission on the Taxation of Profits and Income in 1954, a total of nine such badges was identified in the important case *Rosemoore Investments v Inspector of Taxes* (2002). Dealing on the *commodity markets is normally regarded as trading and profits are subject to income tax or corporation tax; dealing on security markets is often (but not always) treated as investment and profits are subject to capital gains tax. The manner in which a capital gain is calculated frequently, but not invariably, gives a lower tax charge.

baht (THB) The standard monetary unit of Thailand, divided into 100 satang.

bailment A delivery of goods from the **bailor** (the owner of the goods) to the **bailee** (the recipient of the goods), on the condition that the goods will ultimately be returned to the bailor. The goods may thus be hired, lent, pledged, or deposited for safe custody. A delivery of this nature is usually also the subject of a contract; for example, a contract with a bank for the deposit of valuables for safekeeping. Nonetheless, in English law a bailment retains its distinguishing characteristic of a business relationship that arises outside the law of contract and is therefore not governed by it.

bailout Financial aid given to an economy or a company that is approaching collapse.

baiza A monetary unit of Oman, worth one hundredth of a *rial.

balance concentration The practice of consolidating the bank accounts of a group of companies in order to minimize overdraft costs.

balanced scales Measurement scales in marketing research, with the same number of positive and negative (or favourable and unfavourable) categories, i.e. there is no mid-point. They are therefore made up of even number categories—4, 6, 8, 10, etc.

balanced scorecard (BSC) An approach to management that integrates both financial and non-financial *performance measurement in a framework proposed by Professors Kaplan and Norton. The BSC was first reported in the *Harvard Business Review* in 1992 and has since been adopted by a wide range of organizations. It is considered one of the most significant recent developments in management accounting. The approach looks at performance from four interrelated perspectives:

• The **financial perspective**—how do we measure financial performance? Possible performance measures include *operating profits, *return on capital employed, and *unit costs.
• The **customer perspective**—how do we measure customer satisfaction? Possible performance measures include customer profitability, customer satisfaction, and market share.
• The **internal business-process perspective**—what must we excel at? Possible measures include time to develop new products, defect rates, and product returns.
• The **learning and growth perspective**—how can we continue to improve and create value? Possible measures include employee satisfaction and employee productivity.

The balanced scorecard approach requires managers to identify both lagging and leading measures. **Lagging measures** are financial measures that show the impact of decisions made in the past, whereas **leading measures** are non-financial measures relating to the customer, internal business-process, and learning and growth perspectives. The latter are the drivers of future financial performance.

balance of payments The accounts setting out a country's transactions with the outside world. They are divided into various sub-accounts, notably the **current account** and the **capital account**. The former includes the trade account, which records the balance of imports and exports (*see* BALANCE OF TRADE). Overall, the accounts must always be in balance.

A deficit or surplus on the balance of payments refers to the level of purchases or sales of the currency by the national government, usually through its central bank. The conventions used for presenting balance-of-payments statistics are those recommended by the *International Monetary Fund.

balance of trade The accounts setting out the results of a country's trading position. It is a component of the *balance of payments, forming part of the *current account. It includes *visibles (i.e. imports and exports in physical merchandise) but not *invisible earnings and expenditure (receipts and expenditure on such services as insurance, finance, freight, and tourism).

balance sheet (statement of financial position) A statement of the total assets and liabilities of an organization at a particular date, usually the last day of the *accounting period. The first part of the statement lists the fixed and current assets and the liabilities, whereas the second part shows how they have been financed; the totals for each part must be equal. Under the UK Companies Act the balance sheet is one of the primary statements to be included in the *annual accounts of a company. The Companies Act requires that the balance sheet of a company must give a *true and fair view of its state of affairs at the end of its financial year, and must comply with statute as to its form and content. A balance sheet does not necessarily value a company, as some assets may be given an unrealistic value and important *intangible assets may be omitted altogether (*see* ASSET VALUE (PER SHARE); BOOK VALUE). It can be difficult to compare the balance sheets of companies from different countries as they may disclose different information.

balance-sheet asset value The value of an asset as represented on the *balance sheet. For tangible fixed assets this is the cost less accumulated depreciation (although freehold land is generally not subject to depreciation). *Intangible assets are shown at cost less *amortization.

Current assets are valued at the lower of cost and *net realizable value. Under the alternative accounting rules given in the Companies Act, the historical cost of certain assets (for example, buildings and stocks) may be replaced by current cost. *See also* BOOK VALUE; NET BOOK VALUE.

balancing charge The charge that may be assessable to *corporation tax on the disposal of an asset when the proceeds realized on the sale of the asset exceed the *written-down value, for tax purposes. The balancing charge amounts to the difference between the proceeds and the written-down value. For example, if the written-down value is £23,000 and the proceeds on disposal were £30,000, there would be a balancing charge of the difference of £7,000. The balancing charge is deducted from the other allowances for the period. If the charge exceeds the allowances available, the net amount is added to the profit for the period and assessed to tax.

balboa (PAB) The standard monetary unit of Panama, divided into 100 centésimos.

Baldridge Award (Malcolm Baldridge National Quality Award; MBNQA) An annual award, named after a US Secretary of State for Commerce, given to US organizations that have 'excelled in quality management and quality achievement'. There are now six categories of winners: manufacturing, service, small business, healthcare, education, and nonprofit, with up to three awards in each category. The award is based on performance against a set of criteria now used by a wide range of companies as a benchmark for their own *total quality management systems, regardless of whether they enter for the award. The first-level categories are: leadership; strategic planning; customer and market focus; measurement, analysis, and knowledge management; workforce focus; process management; and results.

balloon A large sum repaid as an irregular instalment of a loan repayment. **Balloon loans** are those in which repayments are not made in a regular manner, but are made, as funds become available, in balloons.

balloon mortgage A *mortgage in which one or more large payments may be made as part of the repayment profile; it is also called a **non-amortizing mortgage**. With a balloon mortgage a lump sum often has to be repaid at the end of the term to cover the remaining debt.

ballot A random selection of applications for an oversubscribed *new issue of securities (*see also* FLOTATION). The successful applicants may be granted the full number of securities for which they have applied or a specified proportion of their applications. Applicants not selected in the ballot have their applications and cheques returned.

Baltic Exchange A former commodity and freight-chartering exchange in the City of London. It took its name from the trade in grain with Baltic ports, which was the mainstay of the business in the 18th century. Its activities, including the **Baltic International Freight Futures Exchange (BIFFEX)**, are now undertaken by a department of the *LIFFE, which is itself part of *Euronext NV.

ban (*plural* **bani**) A monetary unit of Romania and Moldova, worth one hundredth of a *leu.

bancassurance (Allfinanz) The combination of traditional loan and savings bank products with such assurance products as *life assurance and pensions. It is now common for major UK banks to provide this combined service and the practice is spreading worldwide.

Bancogiro *See* GIRO.

band 1. A trading range, set by upper and lower limits, of a commodity or currency. For example, the ERM II (*see* EUROPEAN ECONOMIC AND MONETARY UNION) now sets a band against a central rate of conversion to the euro of ± 15%. **2.** Four ranges of maturities set by the Bank of England to influence short-term interest rates in the money market. They are set on *Treasury bills, *local authority bills, and eligible bank bills (*see* ELIGIBLE PAPER); band 1 is from 1 to 14 days, band 2 from 15 to 33 days, band 3 from 34 to 63 days, and band 4 from 64 to 91 days.

banded pack A special offer of goods in which two or more related (or sometimes unrelated) items are bound together to form a single pack. This pack is offered at a lower price than the combined price of the individual items. Banded packs are sometimes offered with the slogan 'buy one, get one free'. *See* PRICE-BUNDLING STRATEGY.

bandwagon effect The phenomenon by which success breeds success; in business terms, the higher the market share the easier it is to make additional sales.

bandwidth In computer systems, the limit on the amount of data that can be sent through a particular channel. As a result of the increase in computer processing power, most systems now offer the option of transmitting text, voice, still pictures, and full video. Transmission systems installed only a few years ago to deal with simple text applications do not now have the bandwidth to carry all the data that is available. *See* BROADBAND.

bangtail A type of envelope usually having an attached perforated 'tail', which can be used as a response note or order form. Known as a two-in-one type of letter, it is normally used as part of one-piece mailer or self-mailer in *direct marketing. This arrangement reduces the costs of *direct-mail selling.

bank A commercial institution that takes deposits and extends loans. Banks are concerned mainly with making and receiving payments on behalf of their customers, accepting deposits, and making short-term loans to private individuals, companies, and other organizations. However, they also provide money transmission services and in more recent decades have diversified into many areas of finance, including high-risk speculative activities. Since the financial crisis of 2007–08 there have been widespread calls for the separation of the riskier forms of corporate and *investment

banking from traditional 'retail banking'. In the UK, the banking system comprises the *Bank of England (the central bank), the *commercial banks, *merchant banks, branches of overseas banks, and the *National Savings Bank. The first (1990) *building society to become a bank in the UK was the Abbey National (now part of Santander), after its public *flotation; many other building societies have now followed this precedent.

bank account *See* ACCOUNT; CHEQUE ACCOUNT; CURRENT ACCOUNT; DEPOSIT ACCOUNT; LOAN ACCOUNT; POSTAL ACCOUNT; SAVINGS ACCOUNT.

bank advance *See* BANK LOAN.

bank-aggregator payments *See* ELECTRONIC BILLING.

bank bill A bill of exchange issued or guaranteed (accepted) by a bank. It is more acceptable than a trade bill as there is less risk of non-payment and hence it can be discounted at a more favourable rate, although to some extent this depends on the bank's credit rating.

bank certificate A certificate, signed by a bank manager, stating the balance held to a company's credit on a specified date. It may be asked for during the course of an audit.

bank charge The amount charged to a customer by a bank, usually for a specific transaction, such as paying in a sum of money by means of a cheque or withdrawing a sum by means of an automated teller machine. However, modern practice is to provide periods of commission-free banking by waiving most charges on personal current accounts. Business customers invariably pay tariffs in one form or another.

bank deposit A sum of money placed by a customer with a bank. The deposit may or may not attract interest and may be instantly accessible or accessible at a time agreed by the two parties. Banks may use a percentage of their customers' deposits to lend on to other customers; thus most deposits may only exist on paper in the bank's books. Money on deposit at a bank is usually held in a *savings account, a *deposit account, or a *current account.

bank draft (banker's cheque; banker's draft) A cheque drawn by a bank on itself or its agent. A person who owes money to another buys the draft from a bank for cash and hands it to the creditor who need have no fear that it might be dishonoured. A bank draft is used if the creditor is unwilling to accept an ordinary cheque.

banker's acceptance A *time draft that promises to pay a certain sum and has been accepted by a bank. It is a form of promissory note, widely used in international trade; once signed and dated it can be traded before its maturity. *See also* THIRD-COUNTRY ACCEPTANCE.

banker's order *See* STANDING ORDER.

banker's reference (status enquiry) A report on the creditworthiness of an individual supplied by a bank to a third party, such as another financial institution or a bank customer. References and status enquiries are often supplied by specialist credit-reference agencies, who keep lists of defaulters, bad payers, and people who have infringed credit agreements. References must be very general and recent legislation has given new rights to the subjects of such reports, which restrict their value even further.

Bank for International Settlements (BIS) An international bank that fosters cooperation among central banks and other agencies in pursuit of monetary and financial stability. The BIS was originally established in 1930 as a financial institution to coordinate the payment of war reparations between European central banks. It was hoped that the BIS, with headquarters in Basle, would develop into a European central bank but many of its functions were taken over by the *International Monetary Fund (IMF) after World War II. Since then the BIS has fulfilled several roles including acting as a trustee and agent for such

international groups as the OECD, the European Monetary System, and the IMF. The frequent meetings of the BIS directors have been a useful means of cooperation between central banks, especially in combating short-term speculative monetary movements. The BIS also sets *capital adequacy ratios for banks. The original members were France, Belgium, West Germany, Italy, and the UK. There are now 55 members worldwide, including most European central banks (notably the ECB), as well as the monetary authorities of the USA, Japan, Russia, and China. The London agent is the Bank of England, whose governor is a member of the board of directors of the BIS.

bank giro credit (BGC) A preprinted paper slip used to pay cash or cheques into a specified bank account (often the customer's own). It is commonly found at the back of cheque books and at the bottom of utility and credit card bills. A completed BGC is not itself a payment instrument; it has no value apart from the cash or cheques that accompany it. *See* CREDIT TRANSFER; GIRO.

bank guarantee An undertaking given by a bank to settle a debt should the debtor fail to do so. A bank guarantee can be used as a security for a loan but the banks themselves will require good cover in cash or counter-indemnity before they issue a guarantee. A guarantee has to be in writing to be legally binding. Such guarantees often contain indemnity clauses, which place a direct onus on the guarantor. This onus leaves the guarantor liable in law in all eventualities.

Bank Holidays Public holidays in the UK, when the banks are closed. They are New Year's Day, Easter Monday, May Day (the first Monday in May), Spring Bank Holiday (the last Monday in May), August Bank Holiday (last Monday in August), and Boxing Day. In Scotland, Easter Monday is replaced by 2 January and the August Bank Holiday is on the first Monday in August. In Northern Ireland St Patrick's Day (17 March) and the Battle of the Boyne (12 July) are added. In the Channel Islands Liberation Day (9 May) is included. Bank Holidays have a similar status to Sundays in that *bills of exchange falling due on a Bank Holiday are postponed until the following day and also they do not count in working out *days of grace. Good Friday and Christmas Day are also public holidays, but any payment falling due (including *bills of exchange) on these days are payable on the preceding day. When Bank Holidays fall on a Sunday, the following day becomes the Bank Holiday.

banking The activities undertaken by banks; this includes personal banking (non-business customers), commercial banking (small and medium-sized business customers), and corporate and investment banking (large international and multinational corporations, pension funds, hedge funds). In the UK most banking for both business and personal customers is undertaken through the high-street banks, known as **branch banking** (*see also* COMMERCIAL BANK.)

Banking Acts UK Acts of Parliament (1979; 1987) defining a bank as a taker of deposits and investing supervision of *deposit-taking institutions in the *Bank of England. The Acts created safeguards to ensure that only fit and proper persons should be allowed to be managers, directors, or controllers of banks. The Acts also stipulate that the paid-up capital reserves of such an institution should be not less than £1 million. The only exceptions to this limit are authorized *building societies, municipal and school banks, and some central or international development banks. The UK legislation was made necessary by the First Banking Directive of the European Community.

banking directives Directives on various aspects of banking practice issued by the EU parliament and Council of Ministers; they include directives on solvency ratios, large exposures, and money laundering. The most important is the *Second Banking Directive, which concerns the

licensing of banks in EU countries other than their domicile. The *Investment Services Directive and *Markets in Financial Instruments Directive applied the principles outlined in the Second Directive to investment products.

Banking Ombudsman *See* FINANCIAL OMBUDSMAN SERVICE.

bank loan (bank advance) A specified sum of money lent by a bank to a customer, usually for a specified time, at a specified rate of interest. In most cases banks require some form of security for loans, especially if the loan is to a commercial enterprise. *See also* LOAN ACCOUNT; OVERDRAFT; PERSONAL LOAN.

bank mandate A document given by a customer of a bank to the bank, requesting that the bank should open an account in the customer's name and honour cheques and other orders for payment drawn on the account. The mandate specifies the signatures that the bank should accept for transactions on the account and also contains specimens of the signatures.

banknote An item of paper currency issued by a central bank. Banknotes developed in England from the receipts issued by London goldsmiths in the 17th century for gold deposited with them for safekeeping. These receipts came to be used as money and their popularity as a *medium of exchange encouraged the goldsmiths to issue their own banknotes, largely to increase their involvement in banking and, particularly, moneylending. Now only the Bank of England and the Scottish and Irish banks in the UK have the right to issue notes. Originally all banknotes were fully backed by gold and could be exchanged on demand for gold; however, since 1931 the promise on a note to 'pay the bearer on demand' simply indicates that the note is legal tender. *See also* PROMISSORY NOTE.

Bank of England The central bank of the UK. It was established in 1694 as a private bank by London merchants in order to lend money to the state and to deal with the national debt. It came under public ownership in 1946 with the passing of the Bank of England Act. The Bank of England acts as the government's bank, providing loans through ways and means advances and arranging borrowing through the issue of *gilt-edged securities. The bank helps to implement the government's financial and monetary policy as directed by the Treasury. Since May 1997 its *Monetary Policy Committee has had sole authority for setting the *base rate, which was formerly a joint decision of the Chancellor of the Exchequer and the Governor of the Bank of England (although the Chancellor retains the right to overrule the Governor in exceptional circumstances). It formerly had wide statutory powers to supervise the banking system, including the commercial banks, but these supervisory powers have now passed to the *Financial Services Authority. The bank, however, retains its responsibility for systemic stability and as *lender of last resort.

The Bank Charter Act 1844 divided the bank into an issue department and a banking department. The issue department is responsible for the issue of banknotes and coins as supplied by the *Royal Mint. The banking department provides banking services (including accounts) to commercial banks, foreign banks, other central banks, and government departments. The bank manages the national debt, acting as registrar of government stocks. It also manages the *exchange equalization account. The bank is controlled by a governor, two deputy governors, and a court (board) of 16 directors.

(⊕) SEE WEB LINKS
- Bank of England website

Bank of England Stock Register The register of holders of government stocks (*see* GILT-EDGED SECURITY) maintained by the *Bank of England. Purchases and sales of government stocks made by stockbrokers and banks are recorded on this register. Income tax on interest paid on these stocks is deducted at source, unlike stocks on the *National Savings Stock Register.

Bank of Japan (BoJ) The Japanese central bank, which controls monetary policy but does not regulate Japanese banks. Its main offices are in Tokyo and Osaka.

bank rate *See* BASE RATE.

bank reconciliation statement A statement that reconciles the bank balance in the books of an organization with the *bank statement. Differences may be due to cheques drawn by the organization but not yet presented to the bank, bank charges deducted from the account not yet notified to the organization, and payments made to the bank but not yet recorded by the organization. Bank reconciliations are usually performed weekly or monthly and are a form of internal control check.

bankruptcy The state of an individual who is unable to pay his or her debts and against whom a **bankruptcy order** has been made by a court. Such orders deprive bankrupts of their property, which is then used to pay their debts.

Bankruptcy proceedings are started by a **bankruptcy petition**, which may be presented to the court by
(1) a creditor or creditors;
(2) a person affected by a *voluntary arrangement to pay debts set up by the debtor under the Insolvency Act 1986;
(3) the Director of Public Prosecutions;
(4) the debtor himself.

The grounds for a creditors' petition are that the debtor appears to be unable to pay a debt for which a statutory demand has been made or that a court has ordered him or her to pay. The debt must amount to at least £750. The grounds for a petition by a person bound by a voluntary arrangement are that the debtor has not complied with the terms of the arrangement or has withheld material information. The Director of Public Prosecutions may present a petition in the public interest under the Powers of Criminal Courts Act 1973. The debtor may also present a petition on the grounds of being unable to pay his debts.

Once a petition has been presented, the debtor may not dispose of any property. The court may halt any other legal proceedings against the debtor. An interim receiver may be appointed. This will usually be the *official receiver, who will take any necessary action to protect the debtor's estate. A special manager may be appointed if the nature of the debtor's business requires it.

The court may make a **bankruptcy order** at its discretion. Once this has happened, the debtor is an *undischarged bankrupt, who is deprived of the ownership of all property and must assist the official receiver in listing it, recovering it, protecting it, etc. The official receiver becomes manager and receiver of the estate until the appointment of a **trustee in bankruptcy**. The bankrupt must prepare a statement of affairs for the official receiver within 21 days of the bankruptcy order. A public examination of the bankrupt may be ordered on the application of the official receiver or the creditors, in which the bankrupt will be required to answer questions about his or her affairs in court.

Within 12 weeks the official receiver must decide whether to call a **meeting of creditors** to appoint a trustee in bankruptcy. The trustee's duties are to collect, realize, and distribute the bankrupt's estate. The trustee may be appointed by the creditors, the court, or the Secretary of State and must be a qualified *insolvency practitioner or the official receiver. All the property of the bankrupt is available to pay the creditors, except for the following:

- equipment necessary for him to continue in employment or business;
- necessary domestic equipment;
- income required for the reasonable domestic needs of the bankrupt and his family.

The court has discretion whether to order sale of a house in which a spouse or children are living.

All creditors must prove their claims to the trustee. Only unsecured claims can be proved in bankruptcy. When all expenses have been paid, the trustee will divide the estate. The Insolvency Act 1986 sets out the order in which creditors will be paid (*see* PREFERENTIAL DEBTS).

The bankruptcy may end automatically after one year, but in some cases a court order is required. The bankrupt is discharged and receives a certificate of discharge from the court.

Bankruptcy Reform Act 1978 A US law that brought about major changes to bankruptcy law after 40 years of the previous legislation. The reforms made it easier to file petitions, amended the previous absolute rule giving priority to secured creditors in all cases, and gave federal bankruptcy judges more powers to hear cases. The reforms also added a clause covering tests for ability to pay under chapter 13 of the Bankruptcy Act. Under *chapter 11 a firm can apply to the court for protection from its creditors while it undergoes a reorganization in an attempt to pay its debts.

bank statement A regular record, issued by a bank or building society, showing the credit and debit entries in a customer's cheque account, together with the current balance. The frequency of issue will vary with the customer's needs and the volume of transactions going through the account. Cash dispensers enable customers to ask for a statement whenever one is needed.

bank transfer *See* CREDIT TRANSFER.

banner advertisement (banner ad) Typically, a rectangular graphic displayed on a web page for purposes of brand building or driving traffic to a site. It is normally possible to perform a *click-through to access further information from another website. Banners may be static or animated.

banques d'affaires The French name for an *investment bank.

Banque de France The central bank of France. Established in 1800 and nationalized in January 1946, it was granted operational independence in 1993 as a preparation for European Monetary Union. It is now linked to the *European Central Bank through the European System of Central Banks.

BARB Acronym for Broadcasters' Audience Research Board: a joint system for researching BBC and commercial television audiences, established in 1981. The board is responsible for commissioning television audience research, both quantitative (how many watched a particular programme) and qualitative (whether or not they liked the programme). The data is collected by online *audimeters attached to the TV sets of more than 5000 representative households in the UK. Regional panels vary in size according to the size of the population in a television area. The data is downloaded daily. The meter records accurately when the TV is switched on, but does not indicate who is actually watching. Thus the research is supplemented by push button handsets for each member of the household aged over four years, to record when they started and finished watching. Data is made available to subscribers, who pay an annual registration fee.

(⊕) SEE WEB LINKS
- BARB website: the public area includes a summary of the latest viewing figures and trends with monthly news bulletins

barbell A *portfolio made up predominantly of short- and long-term obligations, notably in bonds. Its name derives from the idea of such a portfolio being 'weighted' at both ends like a barbell or dumb-bell.

bar chart (bar diagram) A chart that presents statistical data by means of rectangles (i.e. bars) of differing heights. For example, the sales figures for a range of products for an accounting period may be presented in this way, the different sizes of the bars enabling the users to see at a glance how each product has performed during the period.

bar code (universal product code; UPC) A code, consisting of an array of parallel rectangular bars and spaces, printed on a package for sale in a retail outlet. When an optical scanner (**bar-code reader**) reads the bar code at the checkout till (*see* ELECTRONIC POINT OF SALE), the price and description of the goods are displayed on the till screen and the computer-controlled stock record is simultaneously reduced. This also enables the retailer to compile sales volume information.

bareboat charter A form of *chartering a ship in which the expenses incurred during the period of the charter are paid by the hirer, including the hiring of the master and crew, the provision of fuel and stores, etc. All the hirer gets is the ship. A bareboat charter often ends with the hirer acquiring title in the vessel; in such cases it is known as a **demise charter**.

bargain 1. A transaction on the London Stock Exchange. The bargains made during the day are included in the Daily Official List. **2.** A sale made at a specially low price, either as a means of sale promotion or to clear old stock.

barometer stock A security whose performance and price is regarded as an indicator of the overall health of the market. It will be a widely held *blue chip with a stable price record. In the USA such a stock is often termed a **bellwether security**.

barratry Any act committed wilfully by the master or crew of a ship to the detriment of its owner or charterer. Examples include scuttling the ship and embezzling the cargo. Illegal activities (e.g. carrying prohibited persons) leading to the forfeiture of the ship also constitute barratry. Barratry is one of the risks covered by *marine insurance policies.

barrel 1. A unit of capacity used in the oil industry equal to 42 US gallons (35 Imperial gallons). **2.** A unit of capacity used in the brewing industry equal to 36 Imperial gallons.

barrier option *See* IN-BARRIER OPTION; OUT-BARRIER OPTION.

barriers to entry Factors that prevent competitors from entering a particular market. These factors may be innocent, e.g. an absolute cost advantage on the part of the firm that dominates the market, or deliberate, such as high spending on advertising to make it very expensive for new firms to enter the market and establish themselves. Other entry barriers may result from a firm's technological advantage, often protected by patents, or from a firm's existing access to end users as a result of its control of the distribution network. Barriers to entry reduce the level of competition in a market, i.e. they make it less contestable, thereby by enabling incumbents to charge higher-than-competitive prices. *See also* LIMIT PRICE.

If a particular market for a product is dominated by a large multinational corporation, barriers to entry for smaller firms may be formidable: the multinational may be able to produce the product more cheaply because of *economies of scale, the existing product may have built up a strong *brand loyalty, the multinational may control the supply of raw material, or own the patent rights to all or part of the production process. *See also* MOBILITY BARRIERS.

barriers to exit Factors that make it difficult for a company to leave a market that is no longer profitable or that has ceased to provide an acceptable return on capital. For example, the workforce producing the product may not be redeployable, the plant and machinery producing it may be unsaleable, the product may have a niche in the company's product range that would affect sales of the whole range if it was withdrawn, etc.

BARS Abbreviation for *behaviourally anchored rating scales.

barter A method of trading in which goods or services are exchanged without the use of *money. It is a cumbersome system, which severely limits the scope for trade. Money, used as a medium of exchange, enables individuals to trade with each other at much greater distance and through whole chains of intermediaries, which are inconceivable in a barter system. The modern equivalent of barter is known as *countertrading.

base currency The currency used as the basis for an exchange rate, i.e. a foreign currency rate of exchange is quoted per single unit of the base currency, usually US dollars.

base date *See* BASE YEAR.

base metals The metals copper, lead, zinc, and tin. *Compare* PRECIOUS METALS. *See also* LONDON METAL EXCHANGE.

base rate 1. The rate of interest used as a basis by banks for the rates they charge their customers. In practice most customers will pay a premium over base rate on loans and will receive below the base rate on deposits with banks. **2.** An informal name for the rate at which a country's *central bank lends to the banking system, which effectively controls the lending rate throughout the banking system. In the UK, suspension of the official *minimum lending rate in 1981 heralded a loosening of government control over the banking system, but the need to increase interest rates in the late 1980s (to control inflation and the *balance of payments deficit) led to the use of a base rate. In 1997 sole responsibility for setting the base rate was given to the Bank of England. The base rate is more formally known as the **bank rate**.

base stock A certain volume of stock, assumed to be constant in that stock levels are not allowed to fall below this level. When the stock is valued, this proportion of the stock is valued at its original cost. This method is not normally acceptable for financial accounting purposes.

base-weighted index *See* INDEX NUMBER.

base year (base date) The first of a series of years in an index. The value of the index in that year is often denoted by the number 100, enabling percentage rises (or falls) to be seen at a glance. For example, if a price index indicates that the current value is 195, this will only be meaningful if it is compared to an earlier figure. This may be written: 195 (base year 1987 = 100), making it clear that there has been a 95% increase in prices since 1987.

BASIC Acronym for Beginner's All-purpose Symbolic Instruction Code, a family of languages used especially to program small computers. It is easy to learn and became virtually ubiquitous in the teaching of programming during the 1980s. **Visual Basic** was developed by Microsoft and launched in 1991. This was widely used by smaller businesses into the 2000s but is no longer supported.

basic rate of income tax In the UK, a rate of income tax below the higher rate. It is currently 20%, which is applied to the first £31,785 of *taxable income (2015–16). *See also* HIGHER RATE OF INCOME TAX.

basing-point pricing A pricing strategy in which the seller designates a particular city as a basing point and charges all customers the freight cost from that city to the customer's location, regardless of the city from which the goods are actually shipped. This strategy tends to be the case in large countries, such as the USA and Australia.

basis of assessment The basis upon which personal income or business profits are assessed in the UK for each *fiscal year. The individual rules for each income-tax *schedule identify the profits or income to be assessed in that year. These rules are complex and the advice of a tax expert should be sought. The basis of assessment does not necessarily equate to the actual tax year. In the case of a partnership that has been trading for many years, the profits for the year to 30 April 2015, i.e. those arising during the period 1 May 2014–30 April 2015, will form the basis of the assessment for the tax year 2015–16. This is known as the *current-year basis of assessment. Other income received during the year, e.g. building society interest received, is assessed on an actual basis and so for 2015–16 the basis of assessment will be the tax year, i.e. the interest received during the year 6 April 2015–5 April 2016.

basis point (point) One hundredth of one per cent; this unit is often used in finance when prices involve fine margins. *See also* TICK.

basis swap A *swap in which the payments are based on two variable interest rates. The swap may be either in a single currency or across currencies. *See* CROSS-CURRENCY INTEREST-RATE SWAP; INTEREST-RATE SWAP.

basket of currencies A group of selected currencies used to establish a value for some other unit of currency.

Basle Accords A series of international agreements concerning *capital adequacy regulations for banks. The first Accord (**Basle I**) was reached by the Basle Committee on Banking Supervision, representing the governors of the central banks of the G10 nations, in 1988. It stated that banks should hold specific types of capital to cover a minimum of 8% of their *capital at risk. Capital at risk was defined in terms of a set of multipliers to be attached to a number of different asset classes and multiplied by their balance-sheet worth. In 2004 the Accord was superseded by Basle II, which established a new framework for defining *capital at risk, based to a greater extent than previously on credit ratings and internal models. It also put in place a supervisory process to ensure that banks had adequate internal systems to understand and establish their capital at risk. A third Accord, **Basle III**, was agreed in 2011, largely as a response to the global banking crisis of 2008. The new Accord imposes more stringent capital adequacy requirements in several areas and introduces a Liquidity Coverage Ratio (LCR), requiring a bank to hold liquid assets sufficient to cover its cash outflows over a 30-day crisis period. The new provisions are being phased in between 2013 and 2018. The EU's Fourth Capital Requirements Directive will make the Basle III rules legally binding in all member states.

batch costing A form of costing in which the unit costs are expressed on the basis of a batch produced. This is particularly appropriate where the cost per unit of production would result in an infinitesimal unit cost and where homogeneous units of production can conveniently be collected together to form discrete batches. *See* BATCH PRODUCTION.

batch-level activities *See* ACTIVITY.

batch processing A method of processing data, using a computer, in which the programs to be executed are collected together into groups, or batches, for processing. All the information needed to execute the programs is loaded into the computer at the start so that it can work without further intervention. This contrasts with interactive processing, in which information is fed into the computer during processing. Batch processing is used for such tasks as preparing payrolls, maintaining inventory records, and producing reports.

batch production A manufacturing process in which medium to high volumes of similar items are made in batches, rather than continuously, with the product moving from process to process in batches. The key to batch production is the careful scheduling of work to ensure good utilization of capacity and to minimize the capital locked up in work in progress. Examples in which batch production are used include small engineering works and book printers. *See also* BATCH COSTING. *Compare* CONTINUOUS PROCESSING.

bath-tub curve (failure-rate curve) A graph, having the outline shape of a bath tub, in which the failure rate of a piece of machinery is plotted against time (on the horizontal axis). The graph has three phases: a burn-in or start-up phase, during which faults related to installation and assembly are likely to show up quickly; a normal phase, during which the machine will be reliable as long as it is maintained and used within its design parameters; and a wear-out phase, during which the machinery reaches the end of its design life and parts begin to fail at a rate that makes it uneconomical to repair. The extent of each phase will vary, e.g. a piece of electronic equipment might function perfectly until the moment that it fails. In practical terms, it has no wear-out phase.

baud A unit that measures the rate at which information is transmitted along a communications link. In normal computer usage, it is equivalent to bits per second (*see* BINARY NOTATION). Thus, a 300-baud communications link sends 300 bits of information per second.

B2B Abbreviation for business-to-business; denoting direct trading between commercial organizations, especially via the Internet.

BBA Abbreviation for *British Bankers' Association.

BCC Abbreviation for *British Chambers of Commerce.

BCG matrix *See* BOSTON MATRIX.

BCM Abbreviation for *business continuity management.

bear A dealer on a stock exchange, currency market, or commodity market who expects prices to fall. A **bear market** is one in which a dealer is more likely to sell securities, currency, or goods than to buy them. A bear may even sell securities, currency, or goods without having them. This is known as selling short or establishing a **bear position**. The bear hopes to close (or cover) such a short position by buying in at a lower price the securities, currency, or goods already sold. The difference between the purchase price and the original sale price represents the successful bear's profit. A concerted attempt to force prices down by one or more bears by sustained selling is called a **bear raid**. In a **bear squeeze**, sellers force prices up against someone known to have a bear position that has to be covered. *Compare* BULL.

bear closing The purchase of securities, currency, or commodities to close an open *bear position. Bear closing can have the effect of firming up a weak market.

bearer A person who presents for payment a cheque or *bill of exchange marked 'pay bearer'. As a bearer cheque or bill does not require endorsement it is considered a high-risk form of transfer.

bearer security (bearer bond) A security for which proof of ownership is possession of the security certificate; this enables such bonds to be transferred from one person to another without registration. This is unusual as most securities are registered, so that proof of ownership is the presence of the owner's name on the security register. *Eurobonds are bearer securities, enabling their owners to preserve their anonymity, which can have taxation advantages. Bearer bonds are usually kept under lock and key, often deposited in a bank. Dividends are usually claimed by submitting coupons attached to the certificate.

bear hug An approach to the board of a company by another company indicating that an offer is about to be made for their shares. If the target company indicates that it is not against the merger, but wants a higher price, this is known as a **teddy bear hug**.

bear note See BULL NOTE.

bear spread A position in the bond market that is long in short-dated securities and short in longer dated securities; it is intended to take advantage of a fall in commodity or security prices. *Compare* BULL SPREAD.

bed and breakfasting Formerly, an operation in which a shareholder sold a holding one evening and made an agreement with the broker to buy the same holding back again when the market opened the next morning. The object was generally to establish a loss, which could be set against other profits for calculating capital gains tax. Tax changes have made this set of transactions obsolete, as the time elapsed between sale and repurchase must now be above 30 days for the shareholder to benefit in this way. However, other assets (e.g. works of art) are still sometimes bed-and-breakfasted in this way.

behavioural finance The study of the role played by psychological factors in financial decision making and hence their effect on overall market outcomes. In particular, behavioural finance studies the ways in which individual and group behaviour deviates from the rational pursuit of self-interest posited by classical economic theory (*see* BOUNDED RATIONALITY; TIME INCONSISTENCY). A range of cognitive and emotional biases affecting decision making in conditions of uncertainty have been identified: these include systematic errors of judgment in estimating probability, the tendency to underreact to new information and then to 'compensate' by overreacting, and the unwillingness to realize a nominal loss (e.g. by selling shares that have fallen in value). Behavioural finance holds that such biases may create significant market anomalies, especially when they become self-reinforcing within a social group (e.g. in cases of panic selling). *See also* PROSPECT THEORY.

behavioural indicators See PERFORMANCE MEASUREMENT.

behaviourally anchored rating scales (BARS) A measure used in evaluating the job performance of employees. It involves disaggregating a particular job into its key tasks, identifying a range of possible behaviours that can be displayed by an employee undertaking each task, placing these behaviours on a scale ranging from ineffective to excellent performance, and assessing the jobholder against these scales for each of the tasks. This allows a total profile of job performance to be created for each employee, covering the various dimensions of his or her work. Involving jobholders themselves in the creation of performance scales can afford the BARS method greater validity. *Compare* BEHAVIOURAL OBSERVATION SCALE; MIXED-STANDARD SCALE. *See also* CRITICAL INCIDENT TECHNIQUE.

behavioural observation scale (BOS) A measure used in evaluating the performance of employees, often as part of a formal *performance appraisal. BOS involves a process of identifying the key tasks of a particular job and evaluating how frequently employees exhibit the required behaviour for effective performance. The scores for each of these observed behaviours can then be totalled to produce an overall performance measure. *Compare* BEHAVIOURALLY ANCHORED RATING SCALES; MIXED-STANDARD SCALE. *See also* CRITICAL INCIDENT TECHNIQUE.

behavioural segmentation The process of dividing a market (*see also* MARKET SEGMENTATION) into groups based upon the consumer's knowledge of a product, attitude to it, use for it, or response to it.

behavioural targeting An *online marketing technique in which software is used to track a person's Internet use (websites visited, activities on social media) so that advertising can be tailored to their individual profile. In this way businesses are able to direct advertising to those consumers more likely to be interested in their products or services; a person who visits a website providing diet advice, for example, may subsequently receive advertisements for weight-loss products. Behavioural targeting can be controversial when it gathers information that could be considered private without the consumer's knowledge or consent. *See also* COOKIE.

behavioural theories of leadership *See* LEADERSHIP THEORIES.

Beige Book The report on the current economic climate prepared by the US Federal Reserve Board ahead of one of the meetings (held at least four times a year) of the *Federal Open Market Committee.

bellwether security *See* BAROMETER STOCK.

below par *See* PAR VALUE.

below-the-line 1. Denoting entries below the horizontal line on a company's *profit and loss account that separates the entries that establish the profit (or loss) from the entries that show how the profit is distributed or where the funds to finance the loss have come from. **2.** Denoting advertising expenditure in which no commission is payable to an advertising agency. For example, direct mail, exhibitions, point-of-sale material, and free samples are regarded as below-the-line advertising. **3.** Denoting transactions concerned with capital, as opposed to revenue, in national accounts. *Compare* ABOVE-THE-LINE.

benchmarking The process of identifying the best practice in relation to products and processes, both within an industry and outside it, with the object of using this as a guide and reference point for improving the practice of one's own organization. Benchmarking can take place within an organization, when it may form part of a *total quality management (TQM) exercise; in relation to direct competitors, although such organizations may be unwilling to divulge the details of their practices; or in relation to organizations in totally different fields, in which case the main value of the practice is that it forces people to look outside their established patterns of behaviour.

Most of the early work in benchmarking was carried out in manufacturing but the technique is now applied in a wide range of organizations. Typical areas in which benchmarking can be expected to bring benefits to an organization include:

- **Customer satisfaction**. An organization wishing to improve some aspect of its performance (e.g. its website) might ask customers how this compares with that of competitors. By identifying and making improvements the company can expect to improve sales in the long run.
- **Cost reduction**. The benchmarking exercise may identify an area in which the organization has higher costs than competitors. Potential savings may be identified, such as reducing the number of suppliers or making better use of technology. Benchmarking can be applied to all departments.
- **Increased efficiency and effectiveness**. Benchmarking can help to streamline processes and identify ways of delivering a better service.

Before introducing benchmarking an organization will have to identify the costs of the exercise and the potential benefits and cost savings. The most significant cost will be the management time.

benchmark job A job that is used as a guide or reference point in setting remuneration packages for other jobs. To be suitable for this purpose a job should be well known within the industry, have a level of pay that is generally considered fair, and occupy a key point on the *job evaluation scale that is being used. Benchmark jobs play a key role in the *classification method and *factor-comparison method of job evaluation.

beneficial interest The right to the use and enjoyment of property, rather than to its bare legal ownership. For example, if property is held in trust, the trustee has the legal title but the beneficiaries have the beneficial interest in equity. The beneficiaries, not the trustee, are entitled to any income from the property and will be taxed on this income and on any chargeable gain arising if the property is sold.

beneficiary 1. A person for whose benefit a *trust exists. **2.** A person who benefits under a will. **3.** A person who receives money from the proceeds of a *letter of credit. **4.** A person who receives payment at the conclusion of a transaction, e.g. a retailer who has been paid by a customer by means of a *credit card.

benefit segmentation The process of dividing a market (see MARKET SEGMENTATION) according to the specific benefits consumers seek from a product. For example, some car buyers want comfort and reliability from their car, while others look for style and speed. A car manufacturer, therefore, has to decide which benefits to offer.

benefits in kind Benefits other than cash arising from employment. The UK tax legislation seeks to assess all earnings to tax, whether they be in the form of cash or in kind. The treatment of benefits depends on the level of total earnings, including the value of any benefits, and whether the employee is a director of a company. The general rule is to value benefits at their cash equivalent although some specific benefits (e.g. company cars) are subject to specific valuation rules. For employees earning less

than £8500, the benefits are only assessable if they are living accommodation or if they are capable of being turned into cash, such as credit tokens. For all *directors or higher-paid employees (i.e. those with total earnings, including benefits, in excess of £8500) the benefits must be reported on form P11D by the employer at the end of the *fiscal year. This form will include details of company cars and associated fuel provided by the employer, beneficial loans, mobile telephones or laptop computers, medical insurance provided by the employer, subscriptions paid, and any costs paid on the employee's behalf. These benefits will be assessed to tax. This often takes the form of a restriction to the *income tax code. See also FRINGE BENEFITS.

benefit taxation A form of taxation in which taxpayers pay tax according to the amounts of benefit that they receive from the system. Such a system of taxation is, in practice, very difficult to apply unless specific charges are made for specific services, as with metered water charges. Compare ABILITY TO PAY.

Benelux An association of countries in western Europe, consisting of Belgium, the Netherlands, and Luxembourg. As well as geographical proximity these countries have particularly close economic interests, recognized in their 1947 *customs union. In 1958 the Benelux countries joined the *European Economic Community.

Berne Union An association of credit insurers from the main industrial countries; its chief function is to facilitate an exchange of information, especially over credit terms. The *Export Credits Guarantee Department of the UK government is a member.

beta coefficient A measure of the volatility of a share. A share with a high beta coefficient is likely to respond to stock market movements by rising or falling in value by more than the market average. It is thus a measure of the *systematic risk associated with a particular security. See also ALPHA COEFFICIENT; CAPITAL ASSET PRICING MODEL.

beta version A preliminary version of a product or service, often provided free. The purpose of releasing the beta version is to allow selected customers to preview the product and provide valuable feedback to the organization. *See also* ALPHA-RELEASE STAGE.

BExA Abbreviation for *British Exporters Association.

BHAG Acronym (pronounced 'Bee-hag') for *Big Hairy Audacious Goal.

BI Abbreviation for *business intelligence.

BIBA Abbreviation for *British Insurance Brokers' Association.

bid 1. The price at which a buyer is willing to close a deal. If the seller has made an *offer that the buyer considers too high, the buyer may make a bid at a lower price (or on more advantageous terms). Having received a bid, the seller may accept it, withdraw, or make a counteroffer. **2.** The price or yield at which a buyer indicates that he or she is willing to buy a financial obligation. *See* BID PRICE. **3.** An approach by one company to buy the share capital of another. *See* TAKEOVER BID.

bid–offer spread The difference between an *offer price and the *bid price.

bid price The price at which a *market maker will buy shares, which is always somewhat lower than the same dealer's *offer price.

bid rate Short for *London Inter Bank Bid Rate (LIBID).

BIFFEX Acronym for Baltic International Freight Futures Exchange. *See* BALTIC EXCHANGE.

bifurcation The divestment of part of a business to improve the strategic focus of the remaining part.

Big Bang The upheaval on the *London Stock Exchange (LSE) when major changes in operation were introduced on 27 October 1986. The major changes enacted on that date were: (a) the abolition of LSE rules enforcing a dual-capacity system; (b) the abolition of fixed commission rates charged by *stockbrokers to their clients. The measures were introduced by the LSE in return for an undertaking by the government (given in 1983) that they would not prosecute the LSE under the Restrictive Trade Practices Act. Since 1986 the Big Bang has also been associated with the *globalization and modernization of the London securities market.

big-box store A very large shop occupying a box-like industrial-style building, typically in an out-of-town retail park. Such stores tend to be either *hypermarkets offering a variety of general merchandise at discounted prices or *category killers in a particular product area.

Big Four 1. The major high-street or *commercial banks in the UK: Barclays (incorporating the Woolwich), Lloyds, HSBC (formerly Midland), and the Royal Bank of Scotland Group (incorporating NatWest). In terms of market capitalization the four were joined in the 1990s by Abbey National (now part of Santander) and the Halifax (now HBOS and a wholly owned subsidiary of Lloyds), which changed their status from *building societies to banks. **2.** The four largest firms of accountants in the world, i.e. Deloitte, Ernst and Young, KPMG, and PricewaterhouseCoopers. **3.** In Japan, the four largest securities houses: Daiwa, Nikko, Nomura, and Yamaichi.

Big Hairy Audacious Goal (BHAG) A very ambitious long-term objective that serves to galvanize effort and build team spirit within a company. The concept was introduced by Jim Collins and Jerry Porras of Stanford University in the mid 1990s. They argued that an effective BHAG should be (a) audacious enough to be inspiring; (b) clear and unambiguous, so that it is obvious when the goal has been reached; (c) consistent with the company's core values and purposes; and (d) realizable over 10 to 30 years.

Big Mac Index An informal index sometimes used to judge whether current exchange rates are justified. It is based on the theory of *purchasing power parity and uses the price of a Big Mac in a particular currency as its indicator—this being one product that is made to an identical specification worldwide. For example, in country A a Big Mac costs 2.50 units of currency Z whereas in country B it costs 5.40 units of currency Y. In theory, the result of price in Z/price in Y (in this case 2.50/5.40 = 0.46) should equate to the number of units of currency Z that can be exchanged for one unit of Y. If the current rate is (say) 0.7:1, then currency Y is significantly overvalued.

bilateral bank facility A *facility provided by a bank to a corporate customer. The agreement is restricted to the two parties, which enables a relationship to develop between the bank and the customer (*see* RELATIONSHIP BANKING). *Compare* SYNDICATED BANK FACILITY.

bilateral contract A contract that creates mutual obligations, i.e. both parties undertake to do, or refrain from doing, something in exchange for the other party's undertaking. The majority of contracts are bilateral in nature. *Compare* UNILATERAL CONTRACT.

bilateral monopoly A situation in which a *monopoly seller bargains with a monopoly buyer (*see* MONOPSONY). The classic application of bilateral monopoly is to the negotiation of wages between a union and a firm. The most famous solution (1950) is that stated by John Nash, which suggests that both sides will settle for the wage that maximizes the benefits from cooperation.

bilateral netting 1. An agreement between two counterparties that mutual obligations will be settled by a single payment. 2. A method of reducing bank charges in which two related companies offset their receipts and payments with each other, usually monthly. In this way a single payment and receipt is made for the period instead of a number, which saves on both transaction costs and paperwork. *See also* MULTILATERAL NETTING.

bilateral trade agreement An agreement on trade policy between two countries, usually concerning a reduction in tariffs or other protective barriers. Although bilateral deals tend to fragment world trade, governments are attracted by their relative simplicity. The USA, in particular, has used such deals in free-trade agreements with Mexico and Canada and to hasten the resolution of problems with particular trading partners, notably Japan and other Asian countries.

bill broker (**discount broker**) A broker who trades in *bills of exchange.

biller-direct payments *See* ELECTRONIC BILLING.

billion Formerly, one thousand million (10^9) in the USA and one million million (10^{12}) in the UK; now it is almost universally taken to be one thousand million.

bill-me-later A facility offered by some suppliers of goods or services, who agree to give their customers credit by sending an invoice after the goods have been delivered. This facility eases an organization's *cash flow.

bill of entry A detailed statement of the nature and value of a consignment of goods prepared by the shipper of the consignment for *customs entry.

bill of exchange An unconditional order in writing, addressed by one person (the drawer) to another (the drawee) and signed by the person giving it, requiring the drawee to pay on demand or at a fixed or determinable future time a specified sum of money to or to the order of a specified person (the payee) or to the bearer. If the bill is payable at a future time the drawee signifies *acceptance, which makes the drawee the party primarily liable upon the bill; the drawer and endorsers may also be liable upon a bill. The use of bills of exchange enables one person to transfer to another an enforceable right to a sum of money. A bill of exchange is not only transferable but also negotiable, since, if a person without an enforceable right to the money transfers a bill to a *holder in due course, the latter obtains a good title to it. If the drawee or acceptor of the bill is a bank, the bill is known as a *bank bill or in the USA as a *banker's acceptance. If it is a trader, it is called a **trade acceptance**. These bills have a standard 90 days to maturity and their attractiveness will depend on whether they are eligible for rediscounting at the central bank. *See* ACCOMMODATION BILL; BILLS IN A SET; DISHONOUR.

bill of lading A document acknowledging the shipment of a consignor's goods for carriage by sea. It is used primarily when the ship is carrying goods belonging to a number of consignors (a general ship). In this case, each consignor receives a bill issued (normally by the master of the ship) on behalf of either the shipowner or a charterer under a charterparty. The bill serves three functions: it is a receipt for the goods; it summarizes the terms of the contract of carriage; and it acts as a document of title to the goods. A bill of lading is also issued by a shipowner to a charterer who is using the ship for the carriage of his or her own goods. In this case, the terms of the contract of carriage are in the charterparty and the bill serves only as a receipt and a document of title. During transit, ownership of the goods may be transferred by delivering the bill to another if it is drawn to bearer or by endorsing it if it is drawn to order. It is not, however, a negotiable instrument. The bill gives details of the goods; if the packages are in good order a **clean bill** is issued; if they are not, the bill will say so (*see* DIRTY BILL OF LADING). *See also* CONTAINERIZATION.

bill of materials (BOM) 1. A document listing all the materials required to produce a range of products, including all the components and their relevant quantities, the order in which they are assembled, and the *work centres that perform the assembly. The BOM is one of the main inputs into the *material requirements planning (MRP) system; in fact, the success of MRP depends on accurate BOMs. Their reliability has been improved by the use of *computer-aided design systems linked to *inventory status records. **2.** *See* BILL OF QUANTITIES.

bill of quantities (bill of materials) A document drawn up by a quantity surveyor showing in detail the materials and parts required to build a structure (e.g. factory, house, office block), together with the price of each component and the labour costs. The bill of quantities is one of the tender documents that goes out to contractors who wish to quote for carrying out the work.

bill of sale 1. A document by which a person transfers the ownership of goods to another. Commonly the goods are transferred conditionally, as security for a debt, and a **conditional bill of sale** is thus a mortgage of goods. The mortgagor has a right to redeem the goods on repayment of the debt and usually remains in possession of them; the mortgagor may thus obtain false credit by appearing to own them. An **absolute bill of sale** transfers ownership of the goods absolutely. The Bills of Sale Acts (1878; 1882) regulate the registration and form of bills of sale. **2.** A document recording the change of ownership when a ship is sold; it is regarded internationally as legal proof of ownership.

bill of sight A document that an importer, who is unable fully to describe an imported cargo, gives to the Customs and Excise authorities to authorize them to inspect the goods on landing. After the goods have been landed and the importer supplies the missing information the entry is completed and the importer is said to have **perfected the sight**.

bill of sufferance A document issued by the Customs and Excise enabling goods to be landed in the absence of detailed documentation, subject to the Customs being able to examine the goods at any time.

bill rate (discount rate) The rate on the *discount market at which *bills of exchange are discounted (i.e. purchased for less than they are worth when they mature). The rate will depend on the quality of the bill and the risk the purchaser takes. First-class bills, i.e. those backed by banks or well-respected finance houses, will be discounted at a lower rate than bills involving greater risk.

bills in a set One of two, or more usually three, copies of a foreign bill of exchange. Payment is made on any one of the three, the others becoming invalid on the payment of any one of them. All are made out in the same way, except that each refers to the others. The first copy is called the **first of exchange**, the next is the **second of exchange**, and so on. The duplication or triplication is to reduce the risk of loss in transit.

bills payable 1. The amounts owed by a business to its *creditors, such as trade suppliers. **2.** An item that may appear in a firm's accounts under current liabilities, summarizing the *bills of exchange being held, which will have to be paid when they mature.

bills receivable 1. The amounts owed to a business by its *debtors, i.e. its customers. **2.** An item that may appear in a firm's accounts under current assets, summarizing the *bills of exchange being held until the funds become available when they mature.

bill stuffer Any type of promotional material inserted into an envelope with an invoice or statement in order to save on postage. *See also* FREE RIDE.

BIMBO Acronym for buy-in management buy-out: a form of *management buy-out in which management invests in the venture together with outsider venture capitalists (such as a *private equity firm), who have more managerial control than is usual with a management buy-out.

binary notation A way of writing numbers using two symbols only. The symbols are usually written as 0 and 1, and called **binary digits** or **bits**. These bits are usually grouped in eights, called *bytes. Numbers written in binary notation are generally much longer than their decimal equivalents. For example, the binary number 1111

is equivalent to the decimal number 15. In a binary number the columns from the right represent 'units', 'twos', 'fours', 'eights', and so on. Binary notation is used in computing because digital computers represent numbers in terms of the presence (1) or absence (0) of an electrical pulse.

binary option (all-or-nothing option; cash-or-nothing option; digital option) An *exotic option in which the payoff is either a given value or nothing.

bin card (store card) A card attached to each site or bin in which individual items of *stock are stored to record the receipts, issues, and balances of each item of stock in units. The bin card balance should indicate the physical stock available at any time; regular reconciliations with the physical quantities should be made to ensure accuracy.

bingo card (reader service card) A reply card bound into a publication, which readers can complete to request further information or samples from companies that have either advertised or been referred to in the publication.

binomial process A process consisting of several stages, at each one of which there are two possible outcomes with separate probabilities. In finance, models based on binomial processes are used to consider the value of financial obligations, most notably certain option-pricing models. They are also sometimes used in decision making.

biodata In *personnel selection, items of biographical information about the candidates for a job that can be objectively assessed, e.g. qualifications, years of experience, positions of responsibility, etc. Each candidate is scored on the answers given and those whose total scores fall below a certain level are eliminated. This can be an effective way of selecting a short list. *See* STANDARD APPLICATION BLANK.

biological assets *Assets that are living plants or animals, such as trees in a plantation or orchard, cultivated plants, sheep and cattle, etc. The term was introduced in *International Accounting Standard 41, Agriculture, which became operative for annual financial statements covering periods beginning on or after 1 January 2003.

birr (ETB) The standard monetary unit of Ethiopia, divided into 100 cents.

BIS 1. Abbreviation for *Department for Business, Innovation and Skills. **2.** Abbreviation for *Bank for International Settlements.

bit Abbreviation for binary digit. *See* BINARY NOTATION.

bitcoin A digital currency launched in 2009. The currency units, bitcoins, are used as a *medium of exchange and store of value despite not being backed by any bank. They can be bought and sold using most recognized currencies or created from nothing by solving certain mathematical problems using specialized software, a process known as 'bitcoin mining'. Although transactions using bitcoins are recorded in a public ledger, the identities of those exchanging the currency for goods or services are withheld. This has caused questions to be raised about the extent of its use in illegal activities.

BlackBerry *Trademark* A type of *PDA. First released in 1999, it became very popular with business people as one of the first handheld devices that could be used for wireless e-mail.

black box An element in a system that is effectively opaque to those observing it. Inputs enter one end of the box and emerge, transformed, at the other. In terms of controlling the system, this may be perfectly adequate, however complex the processes might be within the element. The black box may be used as a way of representing the unobservable psychological processes that underlie a consumer's decision making. Researchers must focus on the input to and the output from the black box, as they are unable to observe the processes within it.

black economy Economic activity that is undisclosed, as to disclose it would render the earnings involved liable to taxation or even cause those engaged to be imprisoned (if they are claiming state benefits and have lied about their earnings). The black economy is thought to be significant in many countries, largely due to the benefits of evading tax. Earnings made in the black economy do not appear in national statistics.

black knight A person or firm that makes an unwelcome *takeover bid for a company. *Compare* GREY KNIGHT; WHITE KNIGHT.

blackleg 1. An employee who refuses to join a trade union. **2.** An employee who refuses to strike when an official strike has been declared.

black market An illegal market for a particular good or service. It can occur when regulations control a particular trade (as in arms dealing) or a particular period (as in wartime). *Compare* GREY MARKET.

Black Monday 1. Either of two Mondays notorious for spectacular stock market crashes. The original Wall Street crash occurred on Monday, 28 October 1929, when the *Dow Jones Industrial Average fell by 13%. On Monday, 19 October 1987, the Dow Jones Average lost 23%. **2.** The day in September 2008 that is often regarded as marking the beginning of the global financial crisis and subsequent 'Great Recession'. On Monday 15 September the US financial services giant Lehman Brothers filed for bankruptcy and the investment bank Merrill Lynch was sold to the Bank of America.

black swan In *risk management, a high-impact event that should not be regarded as impossible just because it is highly improbable. An example would be a market crash.

Black Wednesday Wednesday, 16 September 1992, when sterling was forced out of the Exchange Rate Mechanism, leading to a 15% fall in its value against the

Deutschmark. Because of the improved economic performance of the UK following this event, it is also sometimes known as **White Wednesday**. *See* EUROPEAN ECONOMIC AND MONETARY UNION.

Blake–Mouton managerial grid A model in which the *leadership style of a manager is described on two dimensions: concern for production and concern for people. Leadership behaviour is measured on a 9-point scale along each dimension, so that there is a total of 81 possible styles. These range from laissez-faire (production 1, people 1) to authoritarian (production 9, people 1) and country club (production 1, people 9), with the optimum score (production 9, people 9) representing true team leadership. The Blake–Mouton grid has often been used as the basis for organizational interventions designed to improve the performance of managers on both dimensions (a **grid organizational development**). It was devised by the US psychologists Robert R. Blake and Jane S. Mouton. *See also* RELATIONSHIP-MOTIVATED; TASK-MOTIVATED.

blank bill A *bill of exchange in which the name of the payee is left blank.

blank cheque *See* CHEQUE.

blank endorsed *See* ENDORSEMENT.

blanket policy An insurance policy that covers a number of items but has only one total sum insured and no insured sums for individual items. The policy can be of any type, e.g. covering a fleet of vehicles or a group of buildings.

blank transfer A share transfer form in which the name of the transferee and the transfer date are left blank. The form is signed by the registered holder of the shares so that the holder of the blank transfer has only to fill in the missing details to become the registered owner of the shares. Blank transfers can be deposited with a bank, when shares are being used as a security for a loan. A blank transfer can also be used when shares are

held by *nominees, the beneficial owner holding the blank transfer.

blind testing A marketing-research technique in which unidentified products are tested by consumers in order to determine their preference. It is often used to test a new product against an established product, especially one with a strong market position.

blind trust A trust that administers the private financial affairs of a person in public office without informing him or her of the transactions entered into, so that there can be no conflict of interest. *See also* ARM'S LENGTH.

blocked account A bank account from which money cannot be withdrawn for any of a number of reasons, the most likely being that the affairs of the holder of the account are in the hands of a receiver owing to *bankruptcy, or *liquidation in the case of a company. A bank account held in another country may be blocked owing to *exchange controls (*see* BLOCKED CURRENCY).

blocked currency A currency that cannot be removed from a country as a result of *exchange controls. Trading usually takes place in such currencies at a discount through brokers specializing in blocked-currency trading, who convert it to other funds for importers and exporters with blocked currency accounts.

blog (web log) A publicly accessible journal maintained on the Web by an individual or group. The topics covered in a blog are dictated by the author and so vary widely: some have become respected sources of information or opinion, while others are vehicles for corporations or other bodies to disseminate information and obtain feedback. Many blogs include facilities for readers to post comments and to engage in debate; blogs can also contain links to other blogs, forming an extended online community. It is now very easy to create and maintain a blog, using freely available software and services. *See* USER-GENERATED CONTENT.

Bloomberg A US-based financial information service founded in 1981. The **Bloomberg Terminal** is a computer system that displays and analyses data in real time and enables users to make trades. The company also owns TV and radio stations.

blow-in card A loose card (usually providing reply facilities) inserted into a publication for advertising purposes.

blue chip Colloquial name for any of the ordinary shares in the most highly regarded companies traded on a stock market. Originating in the USA, the name comes from the colour of the highest value chip used in poker. Blue-chip companies have a well-known name, a good growth record, and large assets. The main part of an institution's equity portfolio will consist of blue chips.

blue-collar worker A manual worker, normally one working on the shop floor, as opposed to an office worker, who is known as a *white-collar worker. The blue collar refers to the blue overalls often worn in factories and the white collar to the normal office attire of a white shirt and a tie.

blueprinting The detailed modelling of the production process for a new product or service, using *flow charts, *computer-aided design, or trial plants.

blue-sky law In the USA, a law providing for state regulation and supervision for issuing investment securities in that state. It includes broker licensing and the registration of new issues.

Bluetooth A wireless technology designed to replace cables between telephones, laptop computers, and other devices. It operates within the 2.4 GHz band. *See also* WiFi.

board of directors *See* DIRECTOR.

body corporate A *corporation consisting of a body of persons legally authorized to act as one person, while being distinct from that person. For example, the shareholders of a company are separate from the company. *See* ARTIFICIAL PERSON.

BOGOF Acronym for buy one get one free.

boilerplate A copy intended for use in making other copies. It is sometimes used to describe a group of instructions that is incorporated in different places in a computer program or the detailed standard form of words used in a contract, guarantee, etc.

boiler room 1. A colloquial name for a *bucket shop that specializes in selling securities over the telephone. So-called **boiler-room scams** involve the selling of worthless shares to gullible investors, usually by cold calling. **2.** That part of a business or organization in which the real day-to-day work takes place, unseen by the public (and possibly by higher management).

BoJ Abbreviation for *Bank of Japan.

bolívar (VEF) The standard monetary unit of Venezuela, divided into 100 céntimos.

boliviano (BOB) The standard monetary unit of Bolivia, divided into 100 centavos.

Bolsa de Madrid *See* MADRID STOCK EXCHANGE.

Bolsa de Valores de São Paulo (Bovespa) *See* SÃO PAULO STOCK EXCHANGE.

BOM Abbreviation for *bill of materials.

Bombay Stock Exchange (BSE) India's leading stock exchange, listing over 5,000 companies. British influence brought share trading to Mumbai in the 1830s; exchanges now exist in many other cities and the Indian government has created a Securities and Exchange Board of India (SEBI) to regulate the market. The main index is the BSE Sensex of 30 representative stocks. Derivatives have been traded since 2000. The *National Stock Exchange of India is also in Mumbai.

bona fide In good faith, honestly, without collusion or fraud. A bona fide purchaser for value without notice is a person who has bought property in good faith, without being aware of prior claims to it (for example, that it is subject to a trust). The purchaser will not be bound by those claims, unless (if the property is land) they were registered.

bona vacantia Goods without an apparent owner. An example could be the possessions of a person with no living relatives who has died intestate. The Crown is entitled to any personal property without an apparent owner. The prerogative may also be extended to real estate by the doctrine of **escheat**, the return of ownerless land to the superior landowner.

bond An IOU issued by a borrower to a lender. Bonds usually take the form of *fixed-interest securities issued by governments, local authorities, or companies. However, bonds come in many forms: with fixed or variable rates of interest, redeemable or irredeemable, short- or long-term, secured or unsecured, and marketable or unmarketable. Fixed-interest payments are usually made twice a year but may alternatively be credited at the end of the agreement (typically 5 to 10 years). The borrower repays a specific sum of money plus the face value (par) of the bond. Most bonds are unsecured and do not grant shares in an organization (*see* DEBENTURE). Bonds are usually sold against loans, mortgages, credit-card income, etc., as marketable securities. A discount bond is one sold below its face value; a premium bond is one sold above par. *See also* EUROBOND; INCOME BOND; PREMIUM BONDS. *Compare* NOTE.

bond credit rating A graded assessment of the creditworthiness of a bond issue, which measures the perceived likelihood of the issuer, such as a company or government, defaulting on its debt. The higher the *credit rating, the lower the risk associated with the bond and the lower the return on the investment. Ratings, which are issued by private credit *rating agencies such as Moody's or Standard and Poor's, range from AAA (the most secure) to C or D. On this basis bonds can be divided into those that are 'investment-grade'—relatively

safe—and those that are more or less speculative ('junk' bonds).

bonded goods Imported goods on which neither customs duty nor excise have been paid although the goods are dutiable. They are stored in a *bonded warehouse until the duty has been paid or the goods re-exported.

bonded warehouse A warehouse, usually close to a sea port or airport, in which goods that attract customs duty or excise are stored after being imported, pending payment of the duty or the re-export of the goods. The owners of the warehouse are held responsible for ensuring that the goods remain in bond until the duty is paid; they may only be released in the presence of a customs officer.

bond note A document, signed by an officer of the Customs and Excise, that enables goods to be released from a bonded warehouse, usually for re-export.

bond risk The *risk associated with holding bonds, which falls into two categories. In *interest-rate risk, the value of a bond falls if the rate of interest rises; in *credit risk, the rating of the bond may deteriorate, payments may be delayed, or the bond may default.

bond washing *See* DIVIDEND STRIPPING.

bonus 1. An extra payment made to employees by management, usually as a reward for good work, to compensate for something (e.g. dangerous work) or to share out the profits of a good year's trading. **2.** An extra amount of money additional to the proceeds, which is distributed to a policyholder by an insurer who has made a profit on the investment of a life-assurance fund. Only holders of *with-profits policies are entitled to a share in these profits and the payment of this bonus is conditional on the life assurer having surplus funds after claims, costs, and expenses have been paid in a particular year. **3.** Any extra or unexpected payment. *See also* NO-CLAIM BONUS; REVERSIONARY BONUS; TERMINAL BONUS.

bonus dividend A *dividend issued to a shareholder in addition to those expected. Typically, two dividends are issued each year. If an additional dividend is paid to shareholders, perhaps because of a take-over, this is known as a bonus dividend.

bonus rate The total rate of return on a *with-profits policy, including the *terminal bonus or any other bonuses paid by the insurance company.

bonus shares (bonus issue) Shares issued to the existing shareholders of a company following a *scrip issue. The number of shares received depends on the level of the shareholding prior to the bonus issue. The number of bonus shares is usu-ally one share for a specified number of shares held before the issue. For example, if the specified number is four this would be denoted as a 1:4 bonus issue. It is also possible to have a 2:1 bonus, when two shares are issued for every one held.

book 1. The totality of the purchases and sales that make up the *position of a trader on financial markets. The terms **long book**, **short book**, and **open book** are used synonymously with *long position, *short position, and *open position. **2.** To record an item in the accounts, usually a sale. **3.** Short for *book value.

book-keeping The keeping of the *books of account of a business. The records kept enable a *profit and loss account and the *balance sheet to be compiled. Most firms now use *business software packages of programs to enable the books to be kept by computer.

book of prime entry A book or record in which certain types of transaction are recorded before becoming part of the *double-entry book-keeping system. The most common books of prime entry are the *day book, the *cash book, and the *journal.

books of account The *ledgers, *jour-nals, and other accounting records in which a business records its transactions. If the business is a limited company the accounting records must show in sufficient

detail the position of the company at any time. *See* STATUTORY BOOKS.

book value 1. *See* NET BOOK VALUE.
2. (net asset value) The value of a com-pany calculated as that of its total assets less *intangible assets and *liabilities. The information required to calculate the book value is all in the *balance sheet. However, it can be very misleading to measure value on this basis, as assets (stocks, buildings, land) are historical accounting figures. The book value of a company is often compared to its *market value, particularly as a means of valuing intangible assets (*see* INTELLECTUAL CAPITAL). Coca-Cola and Dell Computers are examples of companies whose book value is 10% or less of the market value. The **market-to-book ratio** is calculated by taking current market price per share and dividing by the book value per share. This ratio indicates manage-ment's success in creating value for its shareholders, with a high ratio being pre-ferred. The ratio can be compared over time and against other companies. *See also* NET ASSETS; NET WORTH.

boom The part of the *business cycle that follows a recovery, in which the economy is working at full capacity. Demand, prices, and wages rise, while unemployment falls. If government control of the economy is not sufficiently tight a boom can lead to a recession and ultimately to a slump.

bootstrap 1. A *leveraged buy-out of the kind now mainly associated with *private equity firms. **2.** A takeover strategy in which a *two-tier tender offer is made to shareholders of the target company. Mul-tiple price offers are not permitted in the UK, but they are in some other countries, notably Germany and the USA. **3.** A com-pany that is started up with very little cap-ital, the intention being that costs will be met out of operating revenues. **4.** A technique enabling a computer to load a program of instructions. Before computer hardware can function, a program must be loaded into it. However, as a program is needed in the computer to enable it to load a program, preliminary instructions are stored permanently in the computer making it possible for longer programs to be accepted.

borrowing costs Costs that are incurred when an organization borrows money. Interest payments are an example of borrowing costs. In accounting, borrowing costs may be recognized as an expense when incurred or capitalized as part of the cost of an asset. For listed companies in the EU, the treatment of borrowing costs is now governed by *International Accounting Standard 23, Capitalization of Borrowing Costs.

borsa An Italian stock exchange.

Borsa Italiana The principal stock exchange of Italy, based in Milan. It was established in 1998, with the privatization and deregulation of the Milan Stock Exchange. It was acquired by the London Stock Exchange in 2007.

Börse A German stock exchange.

BOS Abbreviation for *behavioural observation scale.

Boston matrix (BCG matrix) A means of analysing and categorizing the performance of business units in large diversified firms by reference to market share and growth rates. It was developed by the Boston Consultancy Group (BCG), a leading firm of strategic consultants. Four main categories are displayed in a two-dimensional matrix, which seeks to identify those business units that generate cash and those that use it, and then to relate the position of the business units to the formulation of an overall business strategy. The Boston matrix has also been applied to a

company's product range so that an overall product development strategy can be implemented.

- **Cash Cows**: mature businesses or products with a high market share but low growth rate. Typically, most fixed investment has already been made and a substantial cash flow is generated, the surplus being used to develop and support other businesses or products requiring higher levels of investment and marketing support.
- **Stars**: businesses or products with a high rate of growth, which are often able to generate sufficient cash to fund the high investment necessary to meet increasing demand. As the market matures, such businesses or products should be managed in order to become future cash cows.
- **Question Marks** (or **Problem Children**): although operating in a growth market, the low market share is likely to mean that these business units are unable to sustain the required level of investment needed in order to try and turn them into stars. Competitor pressures may result in such a business or product becoming a dog.
- **Dogs**: the combination of low growth rate and market share is typical of these businesses and products, which operate in mature markets. Firms frequently face strategic decisions whether to continue to support dogs or to implement a divestment strategy. *Barriers to exit would also need to be considered.

See also GE MATRIX.

bot A background program that operates unsupervised on the Internet. Bots often perform repetitive tasks—a *web crawler is the most common example of this—or provide automated responses. Bots can also be used for malicious purposes: a **botnet** is a collection of computers compromised by bots controlled by the same intruder.

bottleneck *See* CAPACITY.

bottom An old mercantile name for a ship, which still occurs in references to

		Market Share	
		High	Low
Market Growth Rate	High	STAR	QUESTION MARK
	Low	CASH COW	DOG

Boston matrix.

shipments of cargo being 'made in one bottom' (i.e. in the same ship) and in bottomry bonds (*see* HYPOTHECATION).

bottom fishing The practice of seeking out very low-priced shares to invest in, or of waiting until the market as a whole is low before investing, in the hope of making a profit when prices rise.

bottom line A colloquial expression for *net profit after tax. This is the earnings figure used in the *earnings-per-share calculation of a company. UK listed companies or other entities choosing to disclose an earnings-per-share figure must now follow the rules set out in *International Accounting Standard 33, Earnings Per Share. *See also* ABOVE-THE-LINE.

bottomry bond *See* HYPOTHECATION.

bottom-up design An approach to product design based on research into the specific requirements of users, rather than on general design principles or existing models. *Compare* TOP-DOWN DESIGN.

bottom-up planning An approach to planning based on an awareness of what is feasible at the shop-floor level. Ideally, planning an organizational strategy should be an iterative process involving both a strategic awareness of market requirements and an operational awareness of organizational capabilities. Just as operations must be able to respond to opportunities identified by marketing, so marketing and the strategic decision makers should be able to respond to improved capabilities generated by operations.

bought day book *See* PURCHASE DAY BOOK.

bought deal 1. A method of raising capital for acquisitions or other purposes, used by listed companies as an alternative to a *rights issue or *placing. The company invites *market makers or banks to bid for new shares, selling them to the highest bidder, who then sells them to the rest of the market in the expectation of making a profit. Bought deals originated in the USA and are becoming increasingly popular in the UK, although they remain controversial as they violate the principle of *pre-emption rights. *See also* VENDOR PLACING. **2.** A *management buy-out or one in which the finance is obtained from a single institution.

bought ledger *See* PURCHASE LEDGER.

bought note *See* CONTRACT NOTE.

bounce back A technique for increasing sales by 'bouncing back' a further promotional offer to customers when fulfilling an order given in response to an earlier promotion.

boundaryless organization An organization in which there has been a concerted attempt by managers to break down (1) the internal barriers that separate different levels in the hierarchy, different functions (e.g. manufacturing and marketing), and different departments; and (2) the external barriers between the organization and its suppliers, customers, and even its competitors. Becoming boundaryless normally involves the creation of cross-functional teams, *delayering, and *empowerment of employees.

bounded rationality The type of rationality that most people (or organizations) resort to when faced with complex decisions in fast-moving, real-life situations where perfect information is unavailable. Given these constraints, decision makers will be content to find an alternative that gives satisfactory profits rather than one that maximizes profits. The concept of bounded rationality is thus a corrective to the assumption of many economic theories that economic agents make ideally rational decisions to optimize their self-interest. Similarly, some theorists have introduced the concepts of **bounded willpower** and **bounded self-interest** to explain decision making that appears to deviate from this model. *See* SATISFICING BEHAVIOUR. *See also* BEHAVIOURAL FINANCE.

bourse The French name for a *stock exchange (from the French *bourse*, purse). 'The Bourse' usually refers to the stock exchange in Paris (*see* PARIS BOURSE), but some other stock markets are also known by this name, e.g. the Bourse de Luxembourg and the Bourse de Montréal. In Belgium, the term denotes foreign-exchange dealing.

boutique 1. An office, usually with a shop front and located in a shopping parade, that offers financial advice to investors, often on a walk-in basis. **2.** Specialist investment bankers, who cover a particular sector of the market, e.g. management buy-outs, acquisitions, etc.

Bovespa *See* SÃO PAULO STOCK EX-CHANGE.

box spread A combination of call and put *options held at the same *exercise price.

boycott To refuse to supply a customer or potential customer with one's products or to refuse to buy the products of a particular supplier, usually for commercial rather than political reasons. *Compare* EMBARGO.

BPM Abbreviation for *business performance management.

BPR 1. Abbreviation for *business process re-engineering. **2.** Abbreviation for *business property relief.

bracket indexation A change in the upper and lower limits of any particular *taxation bracket in line with an index of inflation. This is needed in times of inflation to avoid fiscal drag (the tax system collecting unduly large amounts of tax).

BRAD Insight An information service formerly known as British Rates and Data (BRAD), that lists cover price, circulation, frequency, advertising rates, and contact details for national and provincial newspapers and consumer, trade, technical, and professional publications; similar data is also listed for television and radio stations and digital media outlets. BRAD Insight now provides an online service for subscribers, rather than publishing directories. It also compiles the **Account List File** (**ALF**), a directory of the UK's top-spending

advertisers, their brands, and the agencies they employ (with relevant contacts).

brainstorming A group discussion in order to invoke ideas and solve business problems. No idea is rejected, no matter how irrelevant it appears, until it has been thoroughly discussed and evaluated. A major rule of brainstorming is that the discussion of ideas should not be inhibited. *Compare* DELPHI TECHNIQUE.

branch accounting An accounting system in which each department or branch of a business is established as a separate *cost centre or *budget centre. The net profit per branch may be added together to arrive at the profit for the whole business. **Branch accounts** may be prepared to show the performance of both a main trading centre (i.e. the head office) and subsidiary trading centres (i.e. branches) but with all the accounting records being maintained by head office. Alternatively, **separate entity branch accounts** are prepared in which branches maintain their own records, which are later combined with head-office records to prepare accounts for the whole business.

brand (brand name) A tradename used to identify a specific product, manufacturer, or distributor. The sale of most branded products began in the UK at the turn of the century; some, such as Bovril (Trademark) and Horlicks (Trademark), were mid-Victorian, introduced when manufacturers wanted to distinguish their goods from those of their competitors. As consumers became more sophisticated, manufacturers placed more emphasis upon promoting their brands directly to consumers (rather than to distributors), spending considerable sums on advertising the high quality of their products. Manufacturers believe that if they invest in the quality of their brands they will build up a **brand image**, to which consumers will respond by asking for their goods by their brand names and by being willing to pay a premium for them (*see* BRAND LOYALTY). Manufacturers also believe they will be less susceptible to demands from distributors for extra discounts to stock their brands. For some products (e.g. perfumes and alcoholic drinks), considerable effort has been devoted to promoting brands to reflect the personality of their likely purchasers; marketing research has indeed shown that for these products consumers can be persuaded to buy brands that enhance the image they have of themselves. *See* BRAND VALUE; GENERIC PRODUCT; OWN BRAND.

brand equity In marketing, the value of a *brand beyond its functional purpose, based on the extent to which it commands *brand loyalty (expressed as repeat buying), name awareness, perceived quality, and strong brand associations. Market share and profit margins can be greater as a result of the *goodwill associated with the brand equity.

brand extension Using a successful brand name to launch a new or modified product in a separate category. A successful brand helps a company enter new product categories more easily. For example, a car manufacturer may use a brand name to launch a lawn mower. Brand extensions do not always work, however, as one manufacturer of canned foods found with the unsuccessful launch of a pet food.

brand image *See* BRAND.

brand loyalty Support by consumers for a particular *brand or product. Brand loyalty is usually the result of continued satisfaction with a product or its price and is reinforced by effective and heavy advertising. Strong brand loyalty, which is often subjective or subconscious, reduces the impact of competitive brand promotions and **brand switching** unless it is for an improved product.

brand management A marketing function that is concerned with maintaining and increasing the value of a company's *brands. Successful brand management involves creating strong positive associations for the branded product or service, largely through design, advertising, and publicity; it also requires vigilant attention to the quality of the product and the customer experience provided. The aim is to create a popular, trusted brand with a distinct identity, thereby promoting both brand recognition and *brand loyalty.

brand manager (product manager) The executive responsible for the overall marketing and promotion of a particular branded product. Responsibilities range from setting objectives for the product to managing and coordinating its sale. Brand managers emerged in the 1930s at Proctor and Gamble but are now employed by most producers of consumer goods.

brand mark A unique symbol that is part of a brand. Most well-known brands are associated with a brand name and a symbol that uniquely conjures up the image of the product or service.

brand switching *See* BRAND LOYALTY.

brand value The value of a brand name to a company as a reflection of the *market penetration the brand has achieved and the *brand loyalty it has acquired. The brand values of a company's range of products may be of importance in a *takeover bid; they may be shown in a company's balance sheets as *intangible assets.

breach of contract A failure by a party to a *contract to perform the obligations in that contract or an indication of an intention not to do so. An indication that a contract will be breached in the future is called **repudiation** or an **anticipatory breach**; it may be either expressed in words or implied from conduct. Such an implication arises as the only reasonable inference from a person's acts in this respect. For example, an anticipatory breach occurs if a person contracts to sell a car to A but sells and delivers it to B before the delivery date agreed with A. The repudiation of a contract entitles the injured party to treat the contract as discharged and to sue immediately for *damages for the loss sustained. The same procedure only applies to an actual breach if it constitutes a **fundamental breach**, i.e. a breach of a major term (*see* CONDITION) of the contract. In either an anticipatory or an actual breach, the injured party may, however, decide to affirm the contract instead (*see* AFFIRMATION OF CONTRACT). When an actual breach relates only to a minor term of the contract (a warranty) the injured party may sue for damages but has no right to treat the contract as discharged. The process of treating a contract as discharged by reason of repudiation or actual breach is sometimes referred to as *rescission. Other remedies available under certain circumstances for breach of contract are an *injunction and *specific performance.

breach of trust The contravention by a *trustee of the duties imposed by a *trust. If one of several trustees agrees to a breach of trust by a co-trustee, this also constitutes a breach of trust.

breach of warranty *See* WARRANTY.

breakeven analysis (cost-volume-profit analysis; CVP analysis) The technique used in *management accounting in which costs are analysed according to *cost behaviour characteristics into *fixed costs and *variable costs and compared to sales revenue in order to determine the level of sales volume, sales value, or production at which the business makes neither a profit nor a loss (*see* BREAKEVEN POINT). The technique is also used in decision making to assist management to determine such questions as the profit or loss likely to arise from any given level of production or sales, the impact on profitability of changes in the fixed or variable costs, and the levels of activity required to generate a desired profit. Breakeven analysis may either be carried out by drawing a *breakeven chart or by calculation. For example, the formula for determining the level of activity required to generate a desired profit is:

(total fixed costs + desired level of profit)/ contribution per unit of production.

See also CONTRIBUTION.

breakeven chart (breakeven graph) A graph on which an organization's total costs, analysed into *fixed costs and

*variable costs, are drawn over a given range of activity, together with the sales revenue for the same range of activity. The point at which the sales-revenue curve crosses the total-cost curve is known as the *breakeven point (expressed either as sales revenue or production/sales volume). The breakeven chart, like *breakeven analysis, may also be used to determine the profit or loss likely to arise from any given level of production or sales, the impact on profitability of changes in the fixed or variable costs, and the levels of activity required to generate a required profit.

breakeven point The level of production, sales volume, percentage of capacity, or sales revenue at which an organization makes neither a profit nor a loss. The breakeven point may be determined either by the construction of a *breakeven chart or by calculation. The formulae are:

breakeven point (units) =
  total fixed costs/contribution per unit;
breakeven point (sales) = (total fixed cost × selling price per unit)/ contribution per unit.

See also CONTRIBUTION.

break-forward (Boston option) A contract on the money market that combines the features of a *forward-exchange contract and a currency option. The forward contract can be undone at a previously agreed rate of exchange, enabling the consumer to be free if the market moves favourably.

breaking a leg (lifting a leg) Closing out one part of an arbitrage or spread transaction, while leaving the other part open. *See also* LEG; STRADDLE.

breaking bulk The practice of *bulk buying products, commodities, etc., and selling smaller quantities to users or consumers. This operation is often performed by a *wholesaler although it may be done by a *retailer.

breakout In *chartist analysis, a movement in the market price of a security above or below the limits within which it has recently fluctuated. When a security's price moves to a level above the usual price ceiling or below the usual price floor, this is thought to herald a continuing move in the same direction. *See also* RESISTANCE LEVEL.

break-up value 1. The value of the assets of an organization on the assumption that it will not continue in business. On this assumption the assets are likely to be sold piecemeal and probably in haste. **2.** The *asset value per share of a company.

bribery Under the Bribery Act 2010, the offence committed by anyone who gives, offers, or promises 'financial or other advantage' to induce another individual to act 'improperly' in the performance of 'any function of a public nature' or 'any activity connected with a business, trade, or profession'. Such a function is performed 'improperly' when the performance breaches: (i) a reasonable expectation of good faith or impartiality; or (ii) a reasonable expectation of how a person in a position of trust should behave. The Act likewise makes it an offence to accept or solicit bribes and creates the specific offence of bribing foreign public officials. The maximum penalty is 10 years' imprisonment together with an unlimited fine.

Under the Act a commercial organization commits an offence wherever it fails to prevent bribery on its behalf by any 'associated person'. Even where there is no deliberate wrongdoing or direct knowledge on the part of the organization, it will be guilty of the offence unless it can show that it has 'adequate procedures' to prevent bribery by third parties.

Before the passage of the 2010 Act, the term 'bribery' referred specifically to the common-law offence of making improper payments to judges, magistrates, or other judicial officers. Offences relating more generally to the improper influencing of public servants and other persons in a position of trust were referred to as **corruption**.

BRIC Denoting the economies of Brazil, Russia, India, and China, which experienced fast growth in the 2000s and are predicted to overtake many Western

economies by 2050. The acronyms **BRICET** (including Eastern Europe and Turkey) and **BRIMC** (including Mexico) are also sometimes used. Funds investing in these countries are known as **BRIC funds**. *See also* CIVETS; NEXT 11.

bricks-and-clicks *See* CLICKS-AND-MORTAR.

bridging loan A loan taken on a short-term basis to bridge the gap between the purchase of one asset and the sale of another. It is particularly common in the property and housing market.

Britannia coins A range of four British *gold coins (£100, £50, £25, and £10 denominations). They were introduced in October 1987 for investment purposes, in competition with the *Krugerrand. Although all sales of gold coins attract VAT, Britannia coins are dealt in as bullion coins.

British Bankers' Association (BBA) A London-based organization that represents the views of all the banks recognized in the UK. Founded in 1919, it is regarded as the banks' trade association. It established model contracts for financial instruments and publishes daily market interest rates in major currencies. It collects and publishes *London Inter Bank Offered Rate quotes, which are the basis for many financial contracts expressed on BBA terms.

(⊕) SEE WEB LINKS
• Website of the BBA: includes consumer information and LIBOR data

British Chambers of Commerce (BCC) A non-political organization representing local *chambers of commerce throughout the UK. It operates an accreditation scheme under which local chambers are admitted to the national network and a *benchmarking survey to encourage best practice. It was formed in 1993 from a merger of the Association of British Chambers of Commerce and the National Chamber of Trade.

(⊕) SEE WEB LINKS
• BCC website

British Exporters Association (BExA)
An association, formerly the British Export Houses Association (BEHA), that brings together UK manufacturers, export houses, bankers, and insurers. It also provides an information and networking forum for those engaged in the export business.

British Insurance Brokers' Association (BIBA) A trade association for registered insurance brokers. Formed in 1977, it widened its membership to include investment advisers in 1988 but subsequently (1994) set up a separate organization for such practitioners, the *Association of Independent Financial Advisers' Association (AIFA). BIBA provides public relations, free advice, representation in parliament, and a conciliation service for consumers.

British Standard 5750 A quality assurance standard applied to processes and procedures, rather than to products. The standard specifies processes capable of producing outputs that will satisfy the requirements of customers for high and consistent quality; these are formalized, documented, and inspected. Subsequent periodic inspections are then made to ensure that the certified procedures are being adhered to. At its inception, a BS 5750 accreditation was an order-winning criterion providing a competitive advantage. Now, in many industries, it is impossible to trade without it. *Compare* ISO 9000.

British Standards Institution (BSI Group) An institution founded in 1901, which received a royal charter in 1929. Its function is to formulate technical standards for building, engineering, chemical, textile, and electrical products, etc., ensuring that they maintain a specified quality. Products certified by the BSI are entitled to use the **Kitemark** logo as a symbol of reliability. Manufacturers who use the Kitemark do so under licence on condition that products are subject to regular inspection. The BSI also operates the European Union's CE certification scheme in the UK for products that come under the relevant EU directives. Apart from maintaining quality and safety standards in this way, the BSI attempts to ensure that the design of goods is restricted to a sensible number of patterns and sizes for one purpose, to avoid unnecessary variety. In this work the BSI collaborates closely with the *International Standards Organization.

A subdivision of the group, **BSI Management Systems**, provides quality assessments of management systems worldwide and advises organizations on how to improve their efficiency, health and safety record, and environmental sustainability.

((( ))) SEE WEB LINKS
- Website of the BSI
- Direct link to BSI Management Systems certification service

British Telecom (BT) The British Telecommunications Corporation was formed in 1981 as a public corporation to control the UK telephone and telecommunications system, which had previously been the responsibility of the Post Office. In 1984 this became British Telecommunications plc, when 51% of the shares were sold to the public; the remaining government shares were sold in the early 1990s. British Telecom no longer has a monopoly to run telecommunications in the UK but continues to provide virtually all the lines and exchanges for the country's fixed-line telephones.

broadband Referring to communications in which a wide range of frequencies can be transmitted at the same time, enabling data to be transmitted at very high speed. Broadband *Internet access allows much greater transmission rates than are possible with a dial-up connection. The most popular method is to use *ADSL.

broadbanding Adoption of an organizational pay structure that consists of a small number of broad pay 'bands', usually four or five in total. This allows greater scope for rewarding individual employees on the basis of performance, skill level, and market value without moving them into a different pay band or changing their job titles. *See also* DELAYERING.

broad money An informal name for M3 (or any wide definition of the *money supply). *Compare* NARROW MONEY.

broker An agent who brings two parties together, enabling them to enter into a contract to which the broker is not a principal. The broker's remuneration consists of a **brokerage**, usually calculated as a percentage of the sum involved in the contract but sometimes fixed by a tariff. Brokers are used because they have specialized knowledge of certain markets or to conceal the identity of a principal, in addition to introducing buyers to sellers. *See* AVIATION BROKER; BILL BROKER; COMMODITY BROKER; INSURANCE BROKER; SHIPBROKER; STOCKBROKER.

brokerage The commission earned by a *broker.

broker/dealer 1. An agent for buyers and sellers who also trades on his or her own account. **2.** A member of the *London Stock Exchange who, since the *Big Bang, has functioned both as a stockbroker and a jobber, but only in a single capacity in any particular transaction. *See* MARKET MAKER.

brownfield development A housing or industrial development within an existing urban area. *Compare* GREENFIELD DEVELOPMENT.

brown goods Televisions, hi-fi equipment, etc., which were formerly often housed in wood or imitation wood cabinets. *Compare* WHITE GOODS.

browser *See* WEB BROWSER.

BSC Abbreviation for *balanced scorecard.

BSE Abbreviation for *Bombay Stock Exchange.

B shares In the USA, a category of less important *ordinary shares. B shares are usually distinguished from *A shares by their limited voting power.

BSI Group *See* BRITISH STANDARDS INSTITUTION.

BTEC *See* VOCATIONAL TRAINING.

BTM Abbreviation for *business technology management.

bubble A situation in which asset prices are seriously inflated. The unstable boom thus created may lead to a market crash. The most infamous example of this was the South Sea Bubble of 1720, which led to the collapse of the British share market and the bankruptcy of many investors. A more recent example was the so-called 'dot.com bubble' of 1999–2000, in which the share prices of Internet start-up companies rose to wildly inflated levels before collapsing amidst panic selling.

bucket shop 1. A derogatory term for a firm of brokers, dealers, agents, etc., of questionable standing and frail resources, that is unlikely to be a member of an established trade organization. *See* BOILER ROOM. **2.** A travel agent who provides a service for travellers who book late, require the lowest prices, and will accept a minimum standard of service.

budget 1. A financial or quantitative statement, prepared prior to a specified accounting period, containing the plans and policies to be pursued during that period. It is used as the basis for *budgetary control. Generally a *functional budget is drawn up for each functional area within an organization, but in addition it is also usual to produce a *capital budget, a *cash-flow budget, stock budgets, and a *master budget, which includes a budgeted profit and loss account and balance sheet. **2.** (**the Budget**) In the UK, the government's annual budget, which is presented to parliament by the Chancellor of the Exchequer (traditionally, but not always, on a Tuesday in March). It contains estimates for the government's income and expenditure, together with the tax rates and the fiscal policies designed to meet the government's financial goals for the succeeding fiscal year.

budgetary control The process by which *financial control is exercised within an organization. *Budgets for income and expenditure for each *function of the organization are prepared in advance of an accounting period and are then compared with actual performance to establish any *variances. Individual function managers are made responsible for the *controllable costs within their budgets, and are expected to take remedial action if the adverse *variances are regarded as excessive.

budget centre A section or area of an organization under the responsibility of a manager for which *budgets are prepared; these budgets are compared with actual performance as part of the *budgetary control process. A budget centre may be a *function, department, section, individual, *cost centre, or any combination of these that the management wishes to treat as a budget centre. It is usual to produce regular financial statements on the basis of each budget centre so that each budget-centre manager is aware of its budgeted and actual performance and any *variances that arise.

budget committee The committee responsible for the operation of the *budgetary control process within an organization. The membership and responsibilities of the committee vary between organizations, but a typical committee might comprise a chief executive as chairman, the functional managers as members, and a financial manager as committee secretary or budget director. The committee is responsible for ensuring the formulation of the budgets according to the directives and policies communicated by the board of *directors, scrutinizing the various budgets for coordination and acceptability, and ultimately submitting the budgets (or budget revisions) to the board of directors for approval.

budget cost allowance The amount of budgeted expenditure that a *cost centre or *budget centre is allowed to spend according to its budget, having regard to the level of activity (or other basis of cost incurrence) actually achieved during the *budget period. The budget cost allowance is usually based on the level of activity achieved and whether the cost item is classified as a *fixed cost or a *variable cost.

budget deficit An excess of government expenditure over government income, which must be financed either by borrowing or by printing money. Keynesians have advocated that governments should run budget deficits during *recessions in order to stimulate aggregate demand. Monetarists and new classical macroeconomists, however, argue that budget deficits simply stimulate *inflation and crowd out private investment. Most economists now agree that, at least on average, governments should seek a balanced budget and that persistent deficits should be eliminated, either by reducing expenditure or increasing taxation. In some cases a **budget surplus** can be used during a boom to collect more revenue than is being spent. In the UK the budget deficit is now officially known as the *Public Sector Net Cash Requirement.

budgeted capacity The productive *capacity available in an organization for a budget period as expressed in the *budget for that period. It may be expressed in terms of *direct labour hours, *machine hours, or *standard hours.

budgeted cost A cost included in a *budget representing the cost expected to be incurred by a *budget centre, *cost centre, *cost unit, product, process, or job.

budgeted revenue The income level included in a *budget representing the income that is expected to be achieved during that budget period.

budget manual A manual setting out the administrative procedures and operations that should be applied in the operation of the *budgetary control system. It covers guidelines for the operation of the *budget committee and the *budget centres and includes such information as levels of responsibility, budget timetable, budget preparation, and budget-revision procedures.

budget period A period for which a *budget is prepared and during which it is intended to apply. It is usual for the budget period to be a year, but it is often broken down into shorter control periods, such as a month or a quarter. The budget periods should coincide with the *accounting periods adopted by the organization.

budget slack The surplus that arises when managers preparing a budget over-estimate costs or underestimate revenues. Most organizations would want to elimin-ate budget slack but some managers may be motivated to create it to improve their performance evaluations. In certain cases, slack may be deliberately created by organizations to protect against uncertainty in the environment: for example, a com-pany may hold excess stocks of a product to make sure that customers can always order the quantities they need. However, man-agers who create excessive slack in this way can be seen as inefficient.

budget surplus *See* BUDGET DEFICIT.

buffering The practice of isolating the operations within an organization from the effects of environmental uncertainty. This can be achieved either by holding *inven-tory or by the design of the organization's systems. While a degree of stability may be appropriate in some situations, manage-ment theory now favours a close relation-ship between operations and the ultimate customers, to ensure that the process is both effective in meeting the customers' needs and commercially efficient. *See* JUST IN TIME.

buffer inventory *See* INVENTORY.

buffer stock A stock of a commodity owned by a government or trade organiza-tion and used to stabilize the price of the commodity. Usually the manager of the buffer stock is authorized to buy the com-modity in question if its price falls below a certain level, which is itself reviewed peri-odically, to enable producers to find a

ready market for their goods at a profitable level. If the price rises above another fixed level, the buffer stock manager is author-ized to sell the commodity on the open market. Thus, producers are encouraged to keep up a steady supply of the commodity and users are reassured that its price has a ceiling. This arrangement is often effective, but may collapse during a boom or slump. *See also* UNITED NATIONS CONFERENCE ON TRADE AND DEVELOPMENT.

bug An error in a computer program, or a malfunction in a computer system. To **debug** a program is to find and correct all bugs.

Building Societies Act 1986 A UK Act of Parliament regulating the activities of *building societies. It widened their powers to include making unsecured loans and offering a range of financial services, such as providing foreign exchange, buying and selling shares, managing unit-trust schemes and personal-equity plans, arran-ging and giving advice on insurance, etc. The Act subjected building societies to a new regulatory agency, the Building Societies Commission, and additionally allowed societies to issue shares and become public limited companies, subject to the agreement of their members.

building society Traditionally, a finan-cial institution that accepts deposits, upon which it pays interest, and makes loans for house purchase or house improvement secured by *mortgages. They developed from the *Friendly Society movement in the late 17th century and were non-profit-making with mutual status. These institu-tions can be found in the UK, Australia, South Africa, Ireland, and New Zealand. The US *savings and loan associations are broadly similar organizations.

In the UK, the *Building Societies Act 1986 greatly widened the range of services they are permitted to offer; this has enabled them to compete with the commercial banks in many areas. They offer cheque accounts which pay interest on all credit balances, cash cards, credit cards, loans, money transmission, foreign exchange, and valuation and conveyancing services. The distinction between banks and building societies is fast disappearing; indeed many building societies have obtained the sanction of their members to become *public limited companies. This means that they become profit-making banks, owned by their shareholders, instead of non-profit-making societies owned by subscribing members. These changes have led to the merger of many building societies to provide a national network that can compete with the *Big Four banks. Competition is well illustrated in the close relationship of interest rates between banks and building societies as they both compete for the market's funds. Moreover, the competition provided by the building societies has forced the banks into offering free banking services, paying interest on current accounts, and Saturday opening. Similar changes have taken place in all the other countries that have building societies. The UK building societies are now regulated by the *Financial Conduct Authority.

built-in obsolescence *See* OBSOLESCENCE.

built-in software Computer programs that are built into a computer and available automatically when the computer is switched on. Examples include the *word processors, *spreadsheets, and graphics programs that are built into most desktop terminals.

built-to-flip Describing a start-up company, typically in the IT field, that is designed to be sold to an acquirer at the earliest opportunity rather than built up into an enduring concern. Such a company is designed to sell itself, or the idea on which it is based, rather than a product or service.

bulk buying The buying of products or commodities in sufficiently large quantities to take advantage of bulk discounts or other quantity discounts. *See also* BREAKING BULK.

bulk carrier A ship in which the cargo is carried in bulk, rather than in bags,

containers, etc. Bulk cargoes are usually homogeneous and capable of being loaded by gravity; examples include ores, coal, wheat, etc.

bulk discount *See* DISCOUNT.

bull A dealer on a financial market who expects prices to rise. A **bull market** is one in which prices are rising or expected to rise, i.e. one in which a dealer is more likely to be a buyer than a seller, even to the extent of buying without having made a corresponding sale, thus establishing a **bull position** or a **long position**. A bull with a long position hopes to sell these purchases at a higher price after the market has risen. *Compare* BEAR.

bulldog bond A fixed-interest *bond issued in the UK by a foreign borrower.

bullet 1. A security offering a fixed interest and maturing on a fixed date. **2.** The final repayment of a loan, which consists of the whole of the sum borrowed. In a **bullet loan**, interim repayments are interest-only repayments, the principal sum being repaid in the final bullet. *Compare* AMORTIZING LOAN.

bullion Gold, silver, or some other precious metal used in bulk, i.e. in the form of bars or ingots rather than in coin. Central banks use gold bullion in the settlement of international debts. In the **London bullion market**, bullion brokers act as agents for both buyers and sellers and also trade as principals.

bull note A bond whose redemption value is linked to a market index or a commodity price (e.g. the price of gold). Thus, a holder of a bull note will receive on redemption an amount greater than the principal of the bond if the relevant index or price has risen (but less if it has fallen). With a **bear note** the reverse happens. Bull and bear notes are therefore akin to an ordinary bond plus an *option, providing opportunities for hedging and speculating.

bull spread The simultaneous buying and selling of *options on the same commodity or security to take advantage of an

business analysis

anticipated rise in the price of the *underlying. *Compare* BEAR SPREAD.

bundling The marketing ploy of giving away a relatively cheap product with a relatively expensive one to attract customers; for example, incorporating one or more CD-ROMs with the software package supplied with a computer. *See* PRICE-BUNDLING STRATEGY.

burden In the USA, another word for *overheads.

bureaucracy A hierarchical administrative system designed to deal with large quantities of work in a routine manner, largely by adhering to a set of strict and impersonal rules; it is characterized by its permanence and stability, its body of experience and precedent, and its absence of a reliance on individuals. Bureaucracies have sprung up all over the world in the public and private sectors of an economy, in government, and in the service industries. It is generally believed to be the only viable structure for large sophisticated organizations. However, the modern strategies of *downsizing, *business process re-engineering, and *total quality management have to some extent undermined the inevitability of its structures.

bureaucratic leader A leader who depends on his or her position in a clearly defined hierarchy to influence followers, who adheres to established rules and procedures, and who is generally inflexible and suspicious of change. *Compare* CHARISMATIC LEADER. *See also* LEADERSHIP STYLE.

Bureau of Customs and Border Protection (CBP) The US agency responsible for collecting and administering import duties and for preventing the import of prohibited goods. In 2003 it became part of the Department of Homeland Security and acquired additional responsibilities for preventing illegal immigration and for maintaining the security of US borders.

bureaupathology (red-tape syndrome) The manifestations of exaggerated bureaucratic behaviour (*see* BUREAUCRACY). They include resistance to change, an obsessive reliance on rules and regulations, and an individual incapability of responding to unpredictable events. The bureaupath tends to believe the policies and procedures of an organization constitute an end in themselves, rather than a means to an end.

bureausis A reaction against bureaucratic behaviour (*see* BUREAUCRACY; BUREAUPATHOLOGY) by an individual (usually a client). The individual demands personal attention and refuses to abide by the rules and procedures followed by an organization.

burnout A work-related condition of emotional exhaustion in which interest in work, personal achievement, and efficiency decline sharply and the sufferer is no longer capable of making decisions. The condition is brought on by the unrelenting stress of pressure at work and is frequently experienced by individuals in jobs involving considerable involvement with people, who derive a major part of their self-esteem from their work, and have few interests outside it.

burnout turnaround The process of restructuring a company that is in trouble by producing new finance to save it from liquidation, at the cost of diluting the shareholding of existing investors.

burn rate The rate at which a new company or project uses up its funding before cash begins to come in from its trading activities. It is frequently used to evaluate high-tech or venture capital investments.

business analysis A means by which the current performance of a firm is evaluated as part of the strategic planning process. It should include an analysis of its current market performance in terms of *market share by product or service category, a *SWOT analysis of the firm (including major competitors), and a *PESTLE analysis of the environmental factors most likely to affect the firm's performance over the future planning period.

business buyer behaviour (industrial buyer behaviour) The shaping of business decisions by the purchaser of raw materials, components, industrial equipment, and services for an organization. The amount of time devoted to the process will depend on a number of factors, including the importance of the decision, the cost to the organization of the decision, the alternative products or services available, and the purchasing officer's experience. Three situations are recognized:

- **straight rebuy**—a familiar product (e.g. stationery, electricity) is bought from a regular supplier;
- **modified rebuy**—looking around for a product with improved performance, perhaps reflecting dissatisfaction with current suppliers;
- **new-task buying**—the buyer, on behalf of the organization, is attempting to fulfil a need or solve a problem that has not been previously encountered.

The higher the risk factor involved in a purchase (e.g. new production equipment, an innovative robotic machine), the larger will be the team forming the *decision-making unit (DMU) involved.

straight rebuy	modified rebuy	new-task buying

routine negotiations by buying department   new negotiations, probably involving the DMU

Business buyer behaviour.

business combination The combining of two or more companies by means of acquisition or merger. *See* INTEGRATION. *See also* ACQUISITION ACCOUNTING; MERGER ACCOUNTING.

business continuity management (BCM) A *risk management process designed to ensure the continuity of a business's key activities in the case of a major disruptive event (e.g. an IT systems breakdown or an epidemic of illness among staff). It involves identifying the key activities of a company, the resources needed to deliver them (e.g. personnel, systems, plant and machinery), and the major risks affecting these resources; a strategy must then be developed to restore key activities as soon as possible after any disruption. Once in place, a business continuity plan should be reviewed frequently in the light of any changes. *Scenario analysis can be used to test a BCM plan but should not be used to drive its formulation, because of the near-infinite number of possible scenarios.

business cycle (trade cycle) The process by which investment, output, and employment in an economy tend to move through a recurrent cycle of upturn, prosperity, downturn, and *recession. The cycle does not describe a regular pattern in either length or amplitude. Cycles in the immediate postwar period were of historically low amplitude, while those of the late 1970s and 1980s had greater amplitude and involved much deeper recessions. The reasons for the business cycle remain little understood. *See also* KONDRATIEFF CYCLE.

business entity *See* ACCOUNTING ENTITY.

business games Exercises used in personnel training in which teams of employees compete against one another in attempting to solve typical business or management problems. The games, which often involve role play, encourage participants to develop their problem-solving and decision-making abilities, to modify their ideas and attitudes, and to bond with other team members. *See also* TEAM-BUILDING EXERCISES.

business intelligence (BI) Any software system that enables firms to collect and analyse large quantities of raw data and to use these findings to inform their business decisions. The term was first used in 1958 by an IBM computer scientist, Hans Peter Luhn. Modern BI systems are used principally to measure, analyse, and report detailed information about a company's own operations, thereby shedding light on its various activities and overall performance. They combine *data warehousing and *knowledge management functions.

business-interruption policy (consequential-loss policy; loss-of-profits policy) An insurance policy that pays claims for financial losses occurring if a business has to stop or reduce its activities as a result of a fire or any other insurable risk. Claims can be made for lost profit, rent, rates, and other unavoidable overhead costs that continue even when trading has temporarily ceased.

business judgment rule The rule that the courts will not generally interfere in the conduct of a business. For example, the courts will not substitute their judgment for that of the directors of a company unless the directors are acting improperly. The rule is often invoked when directors are accused of acting out of self-interest in *takeover bids.

business market All the organizations that buy goods and services to use in the production of other products and services or for the purpose of reselling or renting them to others at a profit.

business marketing research *See* INDUSTRIAL MARKETING RESEARCH.

business name *See* REGISTERED NAME.

business performance management (BPM) A system of metrics for analysing whether *key performance indicators are being achieved by a company. Software systems for BPM typically use dashboards that show particular indicators and help executives to take decisions based on the information shown. A *balanced scorecard approach is often adopted. BPM is also known as **corporate performance management** (CPM) or **enterprise performance management** (EPM).

business plan 1. A detailed plan setting out the objectives of a business over a stated period, often three, five, or ten years. A business plan is drawn up by many businesses, especially if the business has passed through a bad period or if it has had

a major change of policy. For new businesses it is an essential document for raising capital or loans. The plan should quantify as many of the objectives as possible, providing monthly *cash flows and production figures for at least the first two years, with diminishing detail in subsequent years; it must also outline its strategy and the tactics it intends to use in achieving its objectives. Anticipated *profit and loss accounts should form part of the business plan on a quarterly basis for at least two years, and an annual basis thereafter. For a group of companies the business plan is often called a **corporate plan**. *See* APPENDIX: CHECKLIST FOR A BUSINESS PLAN. **2.** A forecast of the activity volumes and cash flows relating to a specific project within an organization.

business portfolio The collection of businesses and products that make up a company.

business process re-engineering (BPR; process innovation) An approach to the restructuring of organizations that seeks to introduce a fundamental and radical reassessment of the organizational processes. Rather than adjusting or improving on existing methods, BPR asks what the organization is trying to achieve, what are its core processes, and what are its predominant competencies. Based on the answers to these questions, it attempts to plan the most efficient, effective, and direct ways of achieving these ends. It has been argued that BPR simply updates the aims and techniques of *method study; however, while the underlying principles may be the same, the potential of the BPR approach can be significantly enhanced by the use of *information technology. Multiple-access databases, *local area networks, etc., allow parallel and simultaneous processing of tasks that would have been performed sequentially in traditional systems. This, in turn, permits much closer links between those who use the outputs from processes and those who produce the outputs. Modern technology also enables information to be shared across functions as well as geographically, so that organizational learning takes place more rapidly and more uniformly. However, experience shows that radical process innovation of this kind can be difficult to implement in practice, not least because of employee resistance. Employees may be concerned about losing their jobs, which will affect morale.

business promotion A *sales promotion designed to generate business leads, stimulate purchase, reward business customers, and motivate the salesforce.

business property relief An *inheritance tax relief available on certain types of business property. For an interest in an unlisted business, including a partnership share, the relief is 100%. Land or buildings owned and used in a company under the control of the donor, or a partnership in which the donor was a partner, attract 50% relief. A majority controlling interest in a listed company also attracts 50% relief.

business rates The local tax paid in the UK by businesses. It is based on a local valuation of the property occupied by the business and the **Uniform Business Rate** (**UBR**) set by central government.

business recipe An approach to business that seeks to identify the 'ingredients' (factors and resources) that have enabled a particular company to succeed, and to apply these lessons to new or established firms operating in a similar environment. The business recipe approach is thus based on an assumption that success can be explained and replicated.

Business Reply See INTERNATIONAL BUSINESS REPLY.

business segments Separately identifiable parts of the business operations of a company or group whose activities, assets, and results can be clearly identified. Companies are obliged to disclose in their annual report and accounts certain financial information relating to business segments (see SEGMENTAL REPORTING). Although *International Financial Reporting Standard 8, Operating Segments, provides guidance as to what comprises a business segment, many inconsistencies appear in the information provided by companies. Standard setters have recognized that companies are not keen to improve segmental reporting because they fear they could suffer some competitive disadvantage.

business software package (office suite) One of a wide range of *software programs sold in packages to enable computers to be used for a variety of business uses. They range in complexity and expense from those suitable for an individual PC to large systems operated on a mainframe or a network. A typical package would include one or more of: book-keeping programs, which provide facilities for keeping sales, purchase, and nominal ledgers; accounting packages, enabling balance sheets, budgetary control, and sale and purchase analysis to be undertaken automatically (see SPREADSHEET); payroll packages, dealing with wages, salaries, PAYE, National Insurance, pensions, etc.; and *database management systems to maintain company records. Business software packages may also include more general software, such as a *spreadsheet program and a word-processing application. The programs comprising the package are designed to work together and use each other's data. See also AUDIT SOFTWARE.

business strategy An overall longer-term policy for a firm that coordinates the separate functional areas of a business. It defines the business objectives, analyses the internal and external environments, and determines the direction of the firm. Each firm operates in a competitive environment and seeks to formulate a strategy that will provide it with an advantage over its rivals: design, quality, innovation, and branding are examples of ways in which *competitive advantage may be established. Some firms may seek to diversify into new markets, either through *internal growth (i.e. by expanding their existing products or introducing new ones) or by *external growth through mergers, takeovers, joint ventures, or strategic partnerships (see DIVERSIFICATION). Each of these methods carries different levels of risk. *See also* CLASSICAL SCHOOL OF STRATEGY; GENERIC STRATEGIES; STRATEGIC MANAGEMENT.

business structure The formal structure of a business. At the simplest level is a *sole proprietor, a small business run by a single owner. A *partnership is a business owned and controlled by two or more persons through a *partnership agreement; it is widely used by professional practices, such as accountants and solicitors, including the largest firms. A *private limited company is one in which the liability of the owners is restricted to their shareholdings and the shares are not available to a wider public. A *public company (plc), on the other hand, offers its shares for sale to the public and often has a very diverse ownership. A *co-operative is a business in which the ownership and control is held equally by its worker members.

business system The distinctive system of a nation's business organizations. The interaction of economic factors and social institutions within different countries has evolved in different ways. Business systems acquired their distinctive characteristics at an early stage of the industrialization process and they have subsequently developed and adapted to their environment. This helps to explain why the business systems in, say, Britain, Germany, and Japan have developed in different ways, as a result of such institutional factors as the system of government, the financial system, education and training, and industrial relations.

business technology management (BTM) 1. A strategic management process that aims to maximize value by achieving a complete integration of a company's IT practices with its structures, processes, decision-making, and evolving strategic goals. **2.** A comprehensive service offered to smaller companies that do not have their own IT department; it typically involves database and network management, security policy, and general advice and support.

business tenancy A tenancy of premises that are occupied for the purposes of a trade, profession, or employment. Business tenants have special statutory protection. If the landlord serves a notice to quit, the tenant can usually apply to the courts for a new tenancy. The landlord's wishes can only oppose the grant of a new tenancy on statutory grounds, which may include breaches of the tenant's obligations under the tenancy agreement or the provision of suitable alternative accommodation by the landlord. Otherwise the court will grant a new tenancy on whatever terms the parties agree or, if they cannot agree, on whatever terms the court considers reasonable. When the tenancy ends, the tenant may claim compensation for any improvements made.

Under the Landlord and Tenant (Covenants) Act 1995 when business tenancies are assigned (*see* ASSIGNMENT OF LEASE) the new tenant generally takes over the covenants (or promises and warranties) of the first tenant in the lease except when otherwise agreed. Previously the old tenant was always liable if a subsequent tenant defaulted on the lease.

business-to-business marketing (B2B marketing) Marketing aimed at selling a product for any use other than personal consumption. The buyer may be a manufacturer, a reseller, a government body, a non-profit-making institution, or any organization other than an ultimate consumer.

busted bond (old bond) A bond issued by a government or corporation that has already defaulted on the loan on which the bonds are based. Busted bonds are now collectors' items, especially those from pre-revolutionary Russia and those issued by US railroad companies. Occasionally promises are made to honour Russian or Chinese bonds.

butterfly A strategy used by dealers in traded *options. It involves simultaneously purchasing and selling call or put options at different *exercise prices. A butterfly is most profitable when the price of the underlying security fluctuates within narrow limits but the losses from the strategy are limited. *Compare* STRADDLE.

butut A monetary unit of the Gambia, worth one hundredth of a *dalasi.

buy-back 1. The buying back by a company of its shares from an investor, who put venture capital up for the formation of the company. The shares are bought back at a price that satisfies the investor, which has to be the price the company is willing to pay for its independence. The buy-back may occur if the company is publicly floated or is taken over. **2.** The buying back by a corporation, especially in the USA, of its shares to reduce the number on the market, either to increase the return on those shares still available or to remove threatening shareholders. **3.** Action by a developing country's government to reduce some or all of its debt to overseas banks by buying back that debt at the market price or at a substantial discount. The attraction for the banks is the removal of a damaging and negative debt, which may already have been provided for in its balance sheet. The advantage to the country in debt is a return to creditworthiness and the possibility of acquiring new loans.

buy earnings To invest in a company that has a low *yield but whose earnings are increasing, so that a substantial capital gain can be expected.

buyer 1. A person who makes a purchase of a product or service. Quite often, this person will be different from both the 'influencer' of the buying decision and the 'user' of the product or service (*see* CONSUMER BUYING BEHAVIOUR). For example, a mother may—on the advice of a friend—make a purchase, which is consumed by her child. **2.** A person in an organization's *buying centre (or *decision-making unit) with formal authority to select the supplier and arrange the terms of purchase. *See* BUSINESS BUYER BEHAVIOUR.

buyers' market A market in which the supply exceeds the demand, so that buyers can force prices down. At some point, however, sellers will withdraw from the market if prices fall too low; when this happens the supply will fall off and prices will begin to rise again. *Compare* SELLERS' MARKET.

buyers over A market in securities, commodities, etc., in which the sellers have sold all they wish to sell but there are still buyers. This is clearly a strong market, with an inclination for prices to rise. *Compare* SELLERS OVER.

buygrid The three classes of industrial buying: rebuying, which usually entails reordering from existing suppliers; modified rebuying, which involves reassessing existing policy, often seeking improved quality; and new-task buying, in which an organization buys something it has not bought before. *See* BUSINESS BUYER BEHAVIOUR.

buy-in The purchase of a holding of more than 50% in a company by (or on behalf of) a group of executives from outside the company, who wish to run the company.

buying centre All the individuals and units that participate in the business buying process for an organization.

buying forward Buying commodities, securities, foreign exchange, etc., for delivery at a date in the future in order to establish a *bull position or to cover a forward *bear sale. *See* FORWARD DEALING.

buying in The buying of securities, commodities, etc., by a broker because the original seller has failed to deliver. This invariably happens after a rise in a market price (the seller would be able to buy in himself if the market had fallen). The broker buys at the best price available and the original seller is responsible for any difference between the buying-in price and the original buying price, plus the cost of buying in. *Compare* SELLING OUT.

buy-out 1. An option, open to a member of an *occupational pension scheme on leaving, of transferring the benefits already purchased to an insurance company of his or her own choice. **2.** *See* LEVERAGED BUY-OUT. **3.** *See* MANAGEMENT BUY-OUT.

buy-to-let The purchase of a residential or other property as an investment for the income it will produce on letting.

BV Abbreviation for *Besloten Vennootschap*. It appears after the name of a Dutch company, being equivalent to the British abbreviation Ltd (denoting a private limited company). *Compare* NV.

by-product A product from a process that has secondary economic significance compared to the *main product of the process. For example, while the primary reason for cracking oil is to produce petroleum, other products produced as a result of the process, such as lubricating oil, paraffin, and other distillates, are by-products. *See also* PROCESS COSTING.

by-product pricing Setting the price for a *by-products in order to make the price of the main product more competitive. For example, in producing processed meats, chemicals, or oil there are often by-products, which—if they had to be disposed of—would make the main product uncompetitive. The producer therefore attempts to sell these by-products at the best possible price in order to keep the main product competitive.

byte A unit of information in a computer, consisting of a group of binary digits, that represents a number or character. Most computers use a byte with 8 binary digits. Byte and character are often used synonymously. For example, a USB flash drive holding 1 gigabyte will in theory store 1,000,000,000 characters.

C A language used to program computers. It was developed in the mid-1970s by the Bell laboratories in the USA. An extension of C, called **C++**, is widely used.

CA 1. Abbreviation for *chartered accountant. **2.** Abbreviation for *Consumers' Association.

CAATs Abbreviation for *computer-assisted audit techniques.

cabbage letter A letter used in *direct-mail selling, which contains illustrations, making it a hybrid between a letter and a leaflet.

CAC Abbreviation for *Central Arbitration Committee.

CAD 1. Abbreviation for *cash against documents. **2.** Abbreviation for *computer-aided design.

Cadbury Report A report on the financial aspects of *corporate governance in the UK issued in 1992 by a committee under Sir Adrian Cadbury. The so-called **Cadbury Code** of best practice recommended that *non-executive directors should be appointed for specified terms and reappointment should not be automatic, that such directors should be selected through a formal process, and that both their selection and their appointment should be a matter for the board as a whole. Together with the recommendations of the *Greenbury Report and the *Hampel Report, the Cadbury Code laid the foundations of the *Corporate Governance Code, first issued in 1998.

cafeteria plan In the USA, an agreement that permits employees to select a fringe benefit from a variety of such benefits (including cash); under the tax code, the benefit is not included in the gross income of the participants solely because the participants are required to choose from a variety of benefits.

calculative contract *See* PSYCHO-LOGICAL CONTRACT.

call 1. A demand from a company to its shareholders to pay a specified sum on a specified date in respect of their *partly paid shares (*see also* CALLED-UP SHARE CAPITAL). **2.** A notification that redeemable shares or bonds should be presented for repayment.

callable bonds Fixed-rate bonds, usually *convertibles, in which the issuer has the right, but not the obligation, to redeem (call) the bond during the life of the bond. A grace period during which the borrower is unable to call the bond will usually be included in the terms of the agreement. *Compare* PUTTABLE BONDS.

call bird A low-priced article used in the retail trade to encourage members of the public to come into a shop, in the hope that purchases for higher-priced goods will follow.

call centre An office whose sole purpose is to handle large numbers of incoming or outgoing telephone calls. It may be used for telephone sales, to carry out marketing research (*see* CENTRAL LOCATION TELEPHONE INTERVIEWING), or by large organizations wishing to deal with all enquiries centrally rather than in local branches. A **blended call centre** is one in which the same agents deal with both incoming and outgoing calls. The early 2000s saw a trend for major UK organizations to site their call centres in other English-speaking countries where labour is cheaper (e.g. India).

called-up share capital When the *issued share capital of a company consists of *partly paid shares, that part of the share capital that has been paid in by subscribers. *Compare* PAID-UP SHARE CAPITAL; RESERVE CAPITAL.

call money 1. Money put into the money market that can be called at short notice (*see also* MONEY AT CALL AND SHORT NOTICE). **2.** *See* OPTION MONEY.

call-of-more option *See* OPTION TO DOUBLE.

call option *See* OPTION.

callover A meeting of commodity brokers and dealers any of several fixed times during the day in order to form a market in that commodity. The callover has traditionally been used for trading in futures, in fixed quantities on a standard contract, payments being settled by differences through a *clearing house. Because traders usually formed a ring around the person calling out the prices, this form of market is often called **ring trading**. It has been largely superseded by *automated screen trading systems. *See also* OPEN OUTCRY; PIT.

call record sheets Marketing research interviewers' logs, listing the number of contacts or interviews conducted and their results.

call report A salesperson's periodic report listing the number of sales calls made, the sales concluded, and any other relevant activities. The call reports will usually be examined by a sales manager.

CAM Abbreviation for *computer-aided manufacturing.

campaign An organized course of action, carefully planned to achieve set objectives, especially in advertising, sales, public relations, or marketing.

Campaign A weekly magazine that gives details of new advertising campaigns, job

vacancies, personnel moves in advertising agencies, and general advertising gossip. It is now possible for subscribers to read the entire magazine online.

🌐 **SEE WEB LINKS**

- Campaign website: includes news, research, agency rankings, and jobs

cancellation The right to cancel a commercial contract after it has been entered into. The right to cancel exists generally for contracts concluded at a distance (*see* DISTANCE SELLING), such as mail order and Internet sales when the contract is with a *consumer, and in particular in such sectors as time-share sales and consumer credit.

cancellation price The lowest price at which the manager of a *unit trust may offer to redeem units on a particular day. The cancellation price is calculated on the basis of a formula laid down by the *Financial Conduct Authority.

c & m Abbreviation for *care and maintenance.

candlestick chart A type of graph used by *chartists in which each trading period is represented by a separate histogram. The blocks of the diagram represent the opening and closing prices, while the high and low periods are represented by vertical lines from the opening and closing prices, which in the case of the highs resemble candlewicks.

cannibalization A market situation in which increased sales of one brand results in decreased sales of another brand within the same *product line, usually because there is little differentiation between them. For instance, two drinks marketed by the same manufacturer and packaged in almost the same colour could cause increased sales of one to be achieved at the expense of decreased sales of the other.

cap A ceiling on a charge; for example, an interest-rate cap would set a maximum interest rate to be charged on a loan, regardless of prevailing general interest-rate levels. A lender would charge a fee for including a cap at the outset to offset this risk. Caps may also limit annual increases to a certain level. *Compare* FLOOR. *See also* COLLAR.

CAP Abbreviation for *Common Agricultural Policy.

capacity (system capacity) The highest sustainable output from an operating system in units per given time. A system's overall capacity is determined by the capacity of its 'narrowest' part, i.e. the **bottleneck**. For example, if a car assembly line can produce 120 cars per hour but the paint shop can only handle 100 cars in an hour, the overall capacity of the plant is 100. Identifying capacity in terms of services can be particularly difficult. For example, students per year provides an insufficient measure of the capacity of a university, as it fails to take into account the quality or effectiveness of the teaching. *See also* BUDGETED CAPACITY; DESIGNED CAPACITY; EFFECTIVE CAPACITY.

capacity requirements plan (CRP) Part of the second phase of *material requirements planning, which produces daily or weekly estimates of the workload on key machines and processes in each department of a plant. This enables proactive adjustment of capacity to be made, if possible, or feedback into the *master production schedule, so that adjustments can be made.

cap and collar mortgage A *mortgage in which the variable interest rate paid by the borrower cannot rise above or fall below specified levels; such a mortgage may be granted for the first few years of a loan. *See also* CAPPED MORTGAGE.

CAPAR Abbreviation for *computer-assisted panel research.

CAPI Abbreviation for *computer-aided personal interview.

capital 1. The total value of the assets of a person, less liabilities. **2.** The amount of the proprietors' interests in the assets of an organization, less its liabilities. **3.** The money contributed by the proprietors to an organization to enable it to function; thus *share capital is the amount provided by way of shares and the *loan capital is the amount provided by way of loans. However, the capital of the proprietors of companies not only consists of the share and loan capital, it also includes retained profit, which accrues to the holders of the ordinary shares. *See also* RESERVE CAPITAL. **4.** In economic theory, the man-made factor of production, usually either machinery and plant (**physical capital**) or money (**financial capital**). However, the concept can be applied to a variety of other assets, such as *human capital or *intellectual capital. Capital is generally used to enhance the productivity of other factors of production (e.g. combine harvesters enhance the productivity of land; tools enhance the value of labour) and its return is the reward following from this enhancement. In general, the rate of return on capital is called *profit.

capital account 1. An account in the financial records of a limited company showing the total amounts for each class of share capital, for example the *preference share capital and the *ordinary share capital. **2.** An account or series of accounts showing the interests of each partner in the net assets of a partnership. This account records the partners' capital contributions, goodwill valuation, and revaluations. In sole tradership accounts, the capital account records the interest the sole trader holds in the net assets of the business. *See also* CURRENT ACCOUNT. **3.** An account recording *capital expenditure on such items as land and buildings, plant and machinery, etc. **4.** A budgeted amount that can only be spent on major items, especially in public-sector budgeting. *Compare* REVENUE ACCOUNT. **5.** That part of the *balance of payments account that shows flows of money between currencies for investment purposes.

capital adequacy ratio (solvency ratio) The proportion of a bank's total assets that is held in the form of *shareholders' equity and certain other defined classes of capital. It is a measure of the bank's ability to meet the needs of its depositors and other creditors. The minimum international requirement was 8% but this will rise to 10.5–13% under the current Basle III proposals (*see* BASLE ACCORDS).

capital allocation The allocation of investment capital to particular units within an organization on the basis of possible losses, which are calculated by *value-at-risk techniques. This is particularly common in financial institutions. Capital allocation may also be related to the funding structure of units and is often used as a basis for the calculation of *shareholder value or *Economic Value Added. *See also* RISK-ADJUSTED RETURN ON CAPITAL.

capital allowances Allowances against UK income tax or corporation tax available to a business, sole trader, partnership, or limited company that has spent capital on *plant and machinery used in the business. Capital allowances are also given on industrial buildings and some agricultural and commercial buildings. The level of allowance varies according to the different categories of asset. Plant and machinery qualifies for a standard 18% *writing-down allowance. Certain *first-year allowances are from time to time made previously available to smaller businesses that invest in specified assets, and an all-purpose *Annual Investment Allowance was introduced in April 2008. An allowance of 8% is also available for certain long-life assets expected to last for 25 years or more. The allowances are treated as an expense in the computation of taxable profit and the capital allowance period reflects the period during which the accounts are prepared. If a business's capital allowances exceed its profit, it may obtain relief for the loss this generates by applying the usual loss relief rules.

SEE WEB LINKS

• Details of capital allowances from the HMRC website

capital asset *See* FIXED ASSET.

capital asset pricing model (CAPM) A statistical model to explain the expected or average return on an investment. It assumes that this return will be composed of the *risk-free rate of return and a *risk premium. The risk premium is related to those *systematic risks that cannot be avoided. Formally, the CAPM is based on the equation:

$$E(R_i) = R_f + \beta_i[E(R_m) - R_f],$$

where $E(R_i)$ is the expected/average return on the assets in portfolio i, R_f is the risk-free rate of return, $E(R_m)$ is the expected/average return on all assets, and β_i is the *beta coefficient of the asset or the portfolio i. The beta is the percentage that the return in i will change with a 1% change in R_m. The CAPM is a measure of the risk in the asset or the portfolio. It is the basis for calculating the required return on an investment and is frequently used to calculate the discount rate for a *net present value calculation.

capital at risk A measure of worst-case losses in excess of the average that is used in banking to calculate both capital requirements and certain performance measures, such as *risk-adjusted return on capital (RAROC). It is usually based on the *value-at-risk methodology. *See also* BASLE ACCORDS.

capital budget The sums allocated by an organization for future *capital expenditure. The capital budget may well encompass a longer period than the next accounting period.

capital budgeting The process by which an organization appraises a range of different investment projects with a view to determining which is likely to give the highest financial return. The approaches adopted include *net present value, the *internal rate of return, the *profitability index, and the *payback period method.

capital commitments (commitments for capital expenditure) Firm plans, usually approved by the board of directors in the case of companies, to spend sums of money on *fixed assets. Capital commitments must by law be shown by way of a note in the company accounts.

capital consumption The total depreciation in the value of the capital goods in an economy during a specified period. It is difficult to calculate this figure, but it is needed as it has to be deducted from the *gross national product (GNP) and the *gross domestic product (GDP) to obtain the net figures.

capital-conversion plan An *annuity that converts capital into income. Capital-conversion policies are often used to provide an income later in life for a person who might be liable to capital gains tax if his or her capital is not reinvested in some way.

capital distribution See DISTRIBUTION.

capital employed Either the sum of the *shareholders' equity in a company and its long-term debt or the *fixed assets of a company plus its *net current assets. Although this term is neither legally defined nor required to be disclosed in a *balance sheet, it is an important element of *ratio analysis, particularly in the calculation of *return on capital employed.

capital expenditure (capital costs; capital investment; investment costs; investment expenditure) The expenditure by an organization of a significant amount for the purchase or improvement of a *fixed asset; the amount expended would warrant the item being depreciated over an estimated useful life of a reasonably extended period. Capital expenditure is not charged against the profits of the organization when it takes place, but is regarded as an investment to be capitalized in the *balance sheet as a fixed asset and subsequently charged against profits by depreciating the asset over its estimated useful life. Relief against taxation is available through *capital allowances.

capital formation See FIXED CAPITAL FORMATION.

capital gain The gain on the disposal of an asset calculated by deducting the cost of the asset from the proceeds received on its disposal. Under *capital gains tax legislation the *chargeable gain may be reduced by various exemptions and reliefs. Capital gains by companies are adjusted by *indexation and are chargeable to *corporation tax.

capital gains tax (CGT) A UK tax on *capital gains. Most countries have a form of income tax under which they tax the profits from trading and a different tax to tax substantial disposals of assets either by traders for whom the assets are not trading stock (e.g. a trader's factory) or by individuals who do not trade (e.g. sales of shares by an investor). The latter type of tax is a capital gains tax. In the UK, capital gains tax is charged on the net amount of *chargeable gains accruing to an individual in a fiscal year after deducting any allowable *capital losses. There is a personal allowance for CGT (£11,100 for 2015–16) and gains from various types of asset are exempt (see CHARGEABLE ASSETS). Since April 2010 the tax has been levied at a rate of either 18% or 28%, depending on the total amount of an individual's taxable income during the tax year. The use of *taper relief and *indexation to reduce a chargeable gain was also abolished from April 2008, when *entrepreneurs' relief was introduced.

((⊕)) SEE WEB LINKS
• A guide to capital gains tax from the Gov.uk website

capital gearing See GEARING.

capital goods Long-term man-made factors of production, such as factories and machinery.

capital growth An increase in the value of invested capital. Investment in *fixed-interest securities or bonds provides income but limited capital growth (which may be improved in index-linked *gilt-edged securities). To have a chance of making substantial capital growth it is necessary to invest in equities (see ORDINARY SHARE), the value of which should increase more rapidly than *inflation. Investing in equities is thus said to be a hedge against inflation. *See* GROWTH STOCKS.

capital-intensive Denoting a technique of production that requires a high ratio of capital to labour costs. *Compare* LABOUR-INTENSIVE.

capital investment *See* INVESTMENT.

capitalism An economic system in which the *factors of production are privately owned and individual owners of *capital are free to make use of it as they see fit; in particular, for their own profit. In this system the market and the profit mechanism will play a major role in deciding what is to be produced, how it is to be produced, and who owns what is produced. *See also* FREE COMPETITION; PRIVATE ENTERPRISE.

capitalization 1. The act of providing *capital for a company or other organization. **2.** The structure of the capital of a company or other organization, i.e. the extent to which its capital is divided into share or loan capital and the extent to which share capital is divided into ordinary and preference shares. *See also* THIN CAPITALIZATION. **3.** The conversion of the reserves of a company into capital by means of a *scrip issue. **4.** The accounting practice of treating *capital expenditure as a fixed asset on the balance sheet rather than charging it against profits when it occurs.

capitalization issue *See* SCRIP ISSUE.

capitalization of borrowing costs *See* BORROWING COSTS.

capitalized value 1. The value at which an asset has been recorded in the balance sheet of a company or other organization, usually before the deduction of *depreciation. **2.** The capital equivalent of an asset that yields a regular income, calculated at the prevailing rate of interest. For example, a piece of land bringing in an annual income of £1,000, when the prevailing interest rate is 10%, would have a notational capitalized value of £10,000 (i.e. £1,000/0.1). This may not reflect its true value.

capital lease In the USA, a lease that does not legally constitute a purchase, although the leased asset should be recorded as an asset on the lessee's books if any one of the following four criteria is met:

- the lease transfers ownership of the property to the lessee at the end of the lease term;
- a **bargain purchase option** exists; i.e. an option exists enabling the lessee to buy the leased property at the end of the lease for a minimal amount or to renew the lease for a nominal rental (a **bargain renewal option**);
- the lease term is 75% or more of the life of the property;
- the *present value of minimum lease payments equals or exceeds 90% of the fair value of the property. *See also* FINANCE LEASE.

capital loss (allowable capital loss) The excess of the cost of an asset over the proceeds received on its disposal. Both individuals and companies may set capital losses against *capital gains to establish tax liability. *Indexation is not permitted to create or increase a capital loss.

capital maintenance concept 1. The **financial capital maintenance concept** is that the capital of a company is only maintained if the financial or monetary amount of its *net assets at the end of a financial period is equal to or exceeds the financial or monetary amount of its net assets at the beginning of the period, excluding any distributions to, or contributions from, the owners. **2.** The **physical capital maintenance concept** is that the physical capital is only maintained if the physical productive or operating capacity, or the funds or resources required to achieve this capacity, is equal to or exceeds the physical productive capacity at the beginning of the period, after excluding any distributions to, or contributions from, owners during the financial period.

capital market A market in which long-term *capital is raised by industry and commerce, the government, and local authorities. The money comes from private investors, insurance companies, pension funds, and banks and is usually arranged by *issuing houses and *merchant banks. *Stock exchanges are also part of the capital market in that they provide a market for the shares and loan stocks that represent the capital once it has been raised. It is the sophistication of their capital markets that distinguishes the industrial countries from the *developing countries, in that this facility for raising industrial and commercial capital is either absent or undeveloped in the latter.

capital movement The transfer of capital between countries, either by companies or individuals. *Exchange controls and restrictions on capital transfers between countries have been greatly reduced in recent decades. Capital movements seeking long-term gains are usually those made by companies investing abroad, for example to set up a factory. Capital movements seeking short-term gains are often more speculative, such as those taking advantage of temporarily high interest rates in another country or an expected change in the exchange rate.

capital profit See CAPITAL GAIN.

capital rationing The situation that arises when managers have insufficient money to invest in all projects with a positive *net present value. The term **soft capital rationing** is used of situations in which a company sets its own limits on the amount of money available for investment in projects; if there are external constraints on money available for investments, the term **hard capital rationing** is used. Whenever capital rationing exists, managers need to rank potential investments so that net present value can be maximised (see PROFITABILITY INDEX).

capital redemption reserve A reserve created if a company purchases its own shares in circumstances that result in a reduction of share capital. It is a reserve that cannot be distributed to the shareholders and thus ensures the maintenance of the capital base of the company and protects the creditors' buffer (which gives

creditors confidence to invest in the company, e.g. as suppliers or debenture holders). *See also* PERMISSIBLE CAPITAL PAYMENT.

capital reserves See UNDISTRIBUTABLE RESERVES.

capital risk The risk, in a lending operation, that the capital amount of the investment may be less than its *par value, even at maturity.

capital share See INVESTMENT TRUST; SPLIT-CAPITAL INVESTMENT TRUST.

capital stock In the USA, the equity shares in a corporation. The two basic types of capital stock are *common stock and *preferred stock.

capital structure (financial structure) **1.** The balance between the assets and liabilities of a company, the nature of its assets, and the composition of its borrowings. The assets may be fixed (tangible or intangible) or current (stock, debtors, or creditors); the borrowings may be long- or short-term, fixed or floating, secured or unsecured. The term is used particularly of the *debt–equity ratio of a company. *See also* GEARING. **2.** The mix of differently rated classes of debt in a *structured finance instrument. *See* TRANCHE.

capital surplus In the USA, the difference between the *par value of a share and its *issue price. It is the equivalent of a *share premium in the UK.

capital turnover (asset turnover) The ratio of the sales of a company or other organization to its *capital employed (i.e. its assets less current liabilities). It is presumed that the higher this ratio, the better the use that is being made of the assets in generating sales. *See also* RATE OF TURNOVER.

CAPM Abbreviation for *capital asset pricing model.

capped mortgage A *mortgage in which the variable interest rate paid by the borrower cannot rise above a specified level, usually for the first few years of the loan. The interest rate can, however, be reduced if interest rates fall generally. *See also* CAP AND COLLAR MORTGAGE.

captive audience An audience that is unlikely to be able to escape being exposed to an advertising message in toto. Examples include cinema audiences and conference audiences.

captive finance company A finance company controlled by an industrial or commercial company.

captive insurance company An insurance company that is totally owned by another organization and insures only, or mostly, the parent company's risks. In this way the parent organization is able to obtain insurance cover (particularly those classes that are compulsory by law) without having to pay premiums to an organization outside its trading group.

captive market A group of purchasers who are obliged to buy a particular product as a result of some special circumstance, such as the absence of an alternative supplier or product.

captive-product pricing Setting a price for products that have to be used with a main product, such as blades for a razor.

CAR Abbreviation for *compound annual return.

carat 1. A measure of the purity (fineness) of gold. Pure gold is defined as 24 carat; 14-carat gold contains 14/24ths gold, the remainder usually being copper. **2.** A unit for measuring the weight of a diamond or other gemstone, equal to 0.2 gram.

care and maintenance (c & m) Denoting the status of a building, machinery, ship, etc., that is not currently in active use, usually as a result of a fall in demand, but which is being kept in a good state of repair so that it can be brought back into use quickly, if needed.

career anchor A pattern of skills, interests, and values developed in the early stages of a person's career, when that person begins to recognize his or her abilities and the aspects of work that he or she enjoys most. Career anchors help to guide subsequent decisions about jobs and careers. The term was introduced by US organizational theorist Edgar H. Schein.

cargo insurance An insurance covering cargoes carried by ships, aircraft, or other forms of transport. In a *Free On Board (FOB) contract the responsibility for insuring the goods for the voyage rests with the buyer. The seller's responsibility ends once the goods have been loaded. In a *Cost and Freight (CFR) contract the buyer is likewise responsible for insurance, even though the seller arranges the shipment and pays the freight: if it is specified that the seller pays for insurance, this is a Cost Insurance and Freight (CIF) contract. Under a *Delivered Ex Ship (DES) contract, insurance is the responsibility of the seller up to the port of destination. *See* INCOTERMS. *See also* AVERAGE; FLOATING POLICY; OPEN COVER.

Caribbean Community (CARICOM) An association of Caribbean states established in 1973 (as the Caribbean Community and Common Market) to further economic cooperation, coordinate foreign policy, and provide common services in health, education, and communications. The members are Antigua and Barbuda, the Bahamas, Barbados, Belize, Dominica, Grenada, Guyana, Haiti, Jamaica, Montserrat, St Kitts and Nevis, St Lucia, St Vincent and the Grenadines, Suriname, and Trinidad and Tobago. **The Caribbean Single Market and Economy (CSME)** was established in 2006.

carriage cost The cost of delivering goods within a particular area (usually a country or major subdivision of a country). **Carriage forward** means that the cost of delivery has to be paid by the buyer. **Carriage paid** or **carriage free** means that they are paid by the seller.

Carriage Paid To *See* COST AND FREIGHT.

carried down (c/d) In book-keeping, describing an amount that is to be transferred as the opening balance in the next period.

carried forward (c/f) In book-keeping, describing the total of a column of figures that is to be the first item in the corresponding column on the next page.

carrier A person or firm that carries goods or people from place to place, usually under a contract and for a fee. Under UK law a **common carrier** is one who undertakes to provide a public service; such a carrier must carry any persons or goods (within certain restrictions) on regular routes; must charge a reasonable rate; and is liable for all loss or damage to goods in transit. All other carriers are **private carriers**; they reserve the right to accept or reject employment and owe only a duty of reasonable care.

carrying amount The balance-sheet value of an asset or liability. For example, a *fixed asset, such as a building, will be shown at the historical cost less the accumulated *depreciation to date, using the *historical-cost convention. Under alternative accounting rules it can be shown at the revalued amount less the accumulated depreciation to date.

carrying costs (cost of carry; holding costs) 1. The costs of maintaining an inventory, including any *opportunity costs, protective measures, wastage, etc. **2.** The costs of holding a particular financial *position; these may include funding costs and opportunity costs (often calculated as the prevailing *risk-free rate of return).

carry-over The quantity of a *commodity that is carried over from one crop to the following one. The price of some commodities, such as grain, coffee, cocoa, and jute, which grow in annual or biannual crops, is determined by the supply and the demand. The supply consists of the quantity produced by the current crop added to the quantity in the hands of producers and traders that is carried over from the previous crop. Thus, in some circumstances the

carry-over can strongly influence the market price.

car tax An excise duty levied in the UK on motor cars at the wholesale stage. It applies to both home-produced and imported cars and is additional to VAT.

cartel An association of independent companies formed to regulate the price and sales conditions of the products or services they offer. A cartel may be national or international, although some countries, including the UK and the USA, have legislation forbidding cartels to be formed on the grounds that they are *monopolies that function against the public interest. The International Air Transport Association is an example of an international price-fixing cartel that is regarded as acceptable because of fears that price-cutting of fares between airlines would jeopardize safety.

carve-out (equity carve-out) A form of corporate restructuring in which a parent firm sells shares in a subsidiary by means of an *initial public offering (IPO). A minority stake is usually sold in the subsidiary, leaving the parent company with a degree of control. *Compare* SPIN-OFF; SPLIT-OFF.

cascade shareholdings A form of *pyramiding in which a holding company has a controlling interest in a company that in turn has a controlling interest in further companies, and so on.

CASE Abbreviation for *computer-assisted self-explication.

case of need An endorsement written on a *bill of exchange giving the name of someone to whom the holder may apply if the bill is not honoured at maturity.

cash *Legal tender in the form of bank-notes and coins that are readily acceptable for the settlement of debts.

cash accounting 1. An accounting scheme for *value added tax enabling a *taxable person to account for VAT on the basis of amounts paid and received during the period of the VAT return. Relief for bad debts is automatically available under this scheme. In order to qualify for the scheme, expected turnover should not exceed £1.35M in the next 12 months. A business already in the scheme is allowed a tolerance limit of £1.6M. **2. (cash-flow accounting)** A system of accounting that records only the cash payments and receipts relating to transactions made by a business, rather than when the money is earned or when expenses are incurred, as in *accrual accounting. UK legislation does not permit this system of accounting to be used for *published accounts.

cash against documents (CAD) 1. Payment terms for exported goods in which the shipping documents are sent to a bank, agent, etc., in the country to which the goods are being shipped, and the buyer then obtains the documents by paying the invoice amount in cash to the bank, agent, etc. Having the shipping documents enables the buyer to take possession of the goods when they arrive at their port of destination; this is known as **documents against presentation**. *Compare* DOCU-MENTS AGAINST ACCEPTANCE. **2.** More generally, a description of any transaction involving simultaneous exchange of assets and payment.

cash and carry 1. A wholesaler, especially of groceries, who sells to retailers and others with businesses at discounted prices on condition that they pay in cash, collect the goods themselves, and buy in bulk. **2.** An operation that is sometimes possible on the futures market (*see* FUTURES CONTRACT), especially the *London Metal Exchange. In some circumstances the spot price of a metal, including the cost of insurance, warehousing, and interest for three months, is less than the futures-market price for delivery in three months. Under these conditions it is possible to buy the spot metal, simultaneously sell the forward goods, and make a profit in excess of the yield the capital would have earned on the money market.

cashback *See* ELECTRONIC FUNDS TRANSFER AT POINT OF SALE.

cash book The *book of prime entry in which are recorded receipts into and payments out of the organization's bank account (*compare* PETTY CASH). The cash book, unlike most other books of prime entry, is also an *account, as its balance shows the amount due to or from the bank.

cash budget *See* CASH FLOW.

cash card A plastic card enabling customers of banks and building societies to obtain cash from *automated teller machines, in conjunction with a *personal identification number. Many cash cards also function as *cheque cards and *debit cards.

cash cow *See* BOSTON MATRIX.

cash crop A crop that is sold for money as opposed to one that is consumed by the producer. In tropical and subtropical areas, cocoa, coffee, sugar and bananas are common cash crops. In cooler areas cash crops include grain and some vegetables. *Compare* SUBSISTENCE CROP.

cash cycle In manufacturing industry, the interval between an outlay of cash to buy raw materials and the receipt of payment for the manufactured goods produced from them.

cash deal A transaction (either buying or selling) on the *London Stock Exchange in which settlement is made immediately, i.e. usually on the following day.

cash discount A *discount receivable or allowable for settling an invoice for cash, or within a specified period. In the *profit and loss account, discounts receivable are classed as revenue; discounts allowable as expenditure.

cash dispenser *See* AUTOMATED TELLER MACHINE.

cash dividend A *dividend paid in cash rather than shares. Cash dividends are paid net of income tax, credit being given to the shareholder for the tax deducted.

cash flow 1. The movement of cash in and out of a business. A **cash-flow**

statement shows the inflows and outflows of cash and cash equivalents for a business over an accounting period under various set headings (operating activities; investing activities; financing activities). The Financial Reporting Standard Applicable in the UK and the Republic of Ireland requires nearly all companies to publish a cash-flow statement in their annual accounts. A **cash-flow projection** (or **cash budget**) sets out all the expected payments and receipts in a given period. This is different from the projected profit and loss account and, in times of cash shortage, may be more important. It is on the basis of the cash-flow projection that managers may arrange appropriate financing facilities and may also arrange for employees and creditors to be paid at appropriate times. *See also* DISCOUNTED CASH FLOW; FREE CASH FLOW. **2.** The net income from a particular transaction after all cash expenses have been met (non-cash expenses such as depreciation being specifically excluded from the calculation).

cash flow at risk A measure of the risks to a firm's cash flows, calculated by applying the concept of *value-at-risk.

cash inflows The cash receipts of a business. Cash inflows arise from transactions such as sales of trading stock, receipts from debtors for credit sales, and disposals of *fixed assets.

cashless society A society in which modern electronic credit and debit cards can be substituted for cash in all or nearly all purchases. *See* ELECTRONIC FUNDS TRANSFER AT POINT OF SALE.

cash management The planning, monitoring, and execution of a firm's policy regarding *liquidity.

cash management account A bank account in which deposits are invested by the bank, usually on the *money market; it is, however, a cheque account and the client is able to obtain loans if required.

cash on delivery (COD) Terms of trade in which a supplier will post goods to a customer, provided the customer pays the postman or delivery man the full invoice amount when they are delivered. It was extensively used in mail order (*see* MAIL-ORDER HOUSE), but the use of telephone and Internet ordering using credit cards has reduced the amount of COD business.

cash-or-nothing option *See* BINARY OPTION.

cash outflows The cash payments made by a business. Cash outflows arise from transactions such as purchase of materials, *direct labour costs, *overheads, and payment of taxes and dividends.

cash price The price at which a seller is prepared to sell goods provided that payment is received immediately in cash, i.e. no credit or commission to a credit-card company has to be given.

cash ratio (liquidity ratio) The ratio of the cash reserve that a bank keeps in coin, banknotes, etc., to its total liabilities to its customers, i.e. the amount deposited with it in current accounts and deposit accounts. Because cash reserves earn no interest, bankers try to keep them to a minimum, consistent with legal reserve requirements.

cash refund offer An offer to refund all or part of the purchase price of a product to consumers who send 'proof of purchase' to the manufacturer.

CASI Abbreviation for *computer-aided self-interview.

casino banking A pejorative term for the more speculative trading activities of a bank, as opposed to the provision of 'retail' banking services to private individuals and small businesses. *See* INVESTMENT BANKING.

casting vote A second or deciding vote. It is common practice to give the chairman of a meeting a second vote to be used to resolve a deadlock. In the case of a company meeting, the chairman is generally given this right by the articles of association, but has no common-law right to a casting vote.

catalogue A book, brochure, computer disk, or website containing details of items for sale, as used in *catalogue marketing. *See also* ELECTRONIC CATALOGUE.

catalogue marketing *Direct marketing by means of print, DVD, or electronic catalogues mailed to selected customers, made available in stores, or presented online. *See also* CATALOGUE STORE.

catalogue store A retail operation that sells a wide selection of fast-moving goods at discount prices. The selling medium is a *catalogue, with very little stock on display. The stores are not designed for the comfort of the customer, but the simple premises enable prices to be kept competitive.

catastrophe risk A *risk in which the potential loss is of the greatest size, such as the explosion of a nuclear power station or a major earthquake.

catching bargain (unconscionable bargain) An unfair *contract, often one in which one party has been taken advantage of by the other. Such a contract may be set aside or modified by a court.

category killer (category discounter) An exceptionally aggressive off-price retailer that offers branded merchandise in clearly defined product categories at heavily discounted prices. Their predatory pricing strategy and ability to decimate much of the competition in their sector explains the name. *See also* BIG-BOX STORE.

CATI Abbreviation for *computer-assisted telephone interviewing.

causal quantitative models Techniques used to forecast such future trends as demand for a product, based on establishing a causal relationship between two or more variables. For example, average temperature, time of year, and a local demographic profile can be used to predict ice-cream sales in an area. The reliability of the techniques is dependent on the correct identification of significant variables. Mathematical techniques, using *regression analysis, are used to establish a functional relationship between variables.

cause-and-effect allocation A *cost allocation in which the *allocation base is a significant determinant of the cost. To ensure that *indirect costs are accurately assigned to *cost objects, managers need to use cause-and-effect allocations rather than the *arbitrary allocations sometimes used in *traditional costing systems. *See* ACTIVITY-BASED COSTING.

cause–effect diagram (fish-bone diagram; Ishikawa diagram) A diagram that, by working back from a given problem, is used to identify the main categories of possible causes of the problem and then to generate detailed lists of specific possible causes. Attributed to Kaoru Ishikawa, the technique is one of a set taught to members of quality circles or quality-improvement teams within the *total quality management process. The method involves four steps: (1) identifying the problem or effect to be analysed; (2) identifying the main classes of possible causes using categories appropriate to the process under review; (3) identifying possible detailed causes under each of these categories; (4) recording these possible causes on the diagram to enable them to be discussed and clarified.

cautious shift *See* CHOICE-SHIFT EFFECTS.

caveat A proviso or qualification that limits liability by putting another party on notice. For example, a retailer may sell goods subject to the caveat that no guarantee of their suitability for a particular purpose is given. The purchaser in these circumstances has no remedy against the retailer should the goods in fact turn out to be unsuitable for that particular purpose.

caveat emptor (Latin: let the buyer beware) A maxim implying that the purchaser of goods must take care to ensure that they are free from defects of quality, fitness, or title, i.e. that the risk is borne by the purchaser and not by the seller. If the goods turn out to be defective, the purchaser has no remedy against the seller. The rule does not apply if the purchaser is unable to examine the goods, if the defects are not evident from a reasonable

Possible Causes

Machinery

Excessive downtime

Equipment failure

Human Resource

Section manager failed to update CPA

Technicians cut corners

Effect

Project not completed on time

Not to specification

Unexpected interactions

Control system inadequate

Delays in releasing cash

Materials

Methods

Money

Cause–effect diagram.

examination, or if the seller has behaved fraudulently. Some measure of protection for the unwary purchaser is afforded by a number of statutes, including the Unfair Contract Terms Act 1977, the Sale of Goods Act 1979, and the Consumer Protection Act 1987.

CBI Abbreviation for *Confederation of British Industry.

CBO Abbreviation for collateralized bond obligation. *See* COLLATERALIZED DEBT OBLIGATION.

CBP Abbreviation for *Bureau of Customs and Border Protection.

CBT Abbreviation for *computer-based training.

CCA Abbreviation for *current-cost accounting.

c.c.c. Abbreviation for *cwmni cyfyngedig cyhoeddus: the Welsh equivalent of plc.

CD Abbreviation for *certificate of deposit.

CDC Group A body set up by the UK government in 1948 (as the **Commonwealth Development Corporation**) to provide investment capital for private-sector businesses in the developing world. CDC is owned by the government but operationally independent. It invests through third-party fund managers rather than directly in businesses.

CDO Abbreviation for *collateralized debt obligation.

cedi (GHS) The standard monetary unit of Ghana, divided into 100 pesewas.

cell-based manufacturing A process design that identifies the common manufacturing characteristics in batches of apparently different products and groups of machinery to enable their common features to be organized in a way that provides some of the benefits of line production.

cellular layout A process design in which equipment used to make similar parts is grouped together. It is often associated with *job-design programmes aiming to overcome the perceived demotivating influence of conventional line production by putting staff together in relatively autonomous teams.

cellular network Any of the radio networks enabling mobile telephones to connect to the main telephone system. Such networks consist of a number of adjacent cells, each containing a transmit/receive station connected to the main telephone network and reached by the subscriber using a portable handset. As subscribers move from one geographical cell to another (e.g. by car), they are automatically switched to receive signals from the new area.

census An official count of a population for demographic, social, or economic purposes. In the UK, population censuses have been held every ten years since 1801 and since 1966 supplementary censuses have been held halfway through the ten-year periods. A **census of distribution**, quantifying the wholesale and retail distribution, has been carried out approximately every five years since 1950. A **census of production**, recording the output of all manufacturing, mining, quarrying, and building industries, together with that of all public services, has been held every year since 1968.

census tract A small geographical area (about 1200 households) in which the population has many socio-economic characteristics in common. The term is of US origin.

cent 1. A monetary unit of American Samoa, Antigua and Barbuda, Australia, the Bahamas, Barbados, Belau, Belize, Bermuda, the British Virgin Islands, Brunei, Canada, the Cayman Islands, Dominica, East Timor, Ecuador, El Salvador, Fiji, Grenada, Guam, Guatemala, Guyana, Hong Kong, Jamaica, Kiribati, Liberia, Malaysia, the Marshall Islands, Micronesia, Namibia, Nauru, New Zealand, Puerto Rico, Saint Kitts and Nevis, Saint Lucia, Saint Vincent and the Grenadines, Singapore, the Solomon Islands, Suriname,

Taiwan, Trinidad and Tobago, Tuvalu, the USA, the Virgin Islands, and Zimbabwe, worth one hundredth of a *dollar. **2.** A monetary unit of Andorra, Austria, Belgium, Cyprus, Estonia, Finland, France, French Guiana, Germany, Greece, Guadeloupe, Ireland, Italy, Kosovo, Latvia, Lithuania, Luxembourg, Madeira, Malta, Martinique, Mayotte, Monaco, Montenegro, The Netherlands, Portugal, Réunion, San Marino, Slovakia, Slovenia, and Spain, worth one hundredth of a *euro. **3.** A monetary unit of Ethiopia, worth one hundredth of a *birr. **4.** A monetary unit of Kenya, Somalia, Tanzania, and Uganda, worth one hundredth of a *shilling. **5.** A monetary unit of South Africa, worth one hundredth of a *rand. **6.** A monetary unit of Mauritius, the Seychelles, and Sri Lanka, worth one hundredth of a *rupee. **7.** A monetary unit of Swaziland, worth one hundredth of a *lilangeni. **8.** A monetary unit of Curaçao and Sint Maarten, worth one hundredth of a *guilder. **9.** A monetary unit of Sierra Leone, worth one hundredth of a *leone. **10.** A monetary unit of Eritrea, worth one hundredth of a *nakfa. **11.** A former monetary unit of The Netherlands, worth one hundredth of a guilder.

centas A former monetary unit of Lithuania, worth one hundredth of a *litas.

centavo 1. A monetary unit of Bolivia, worth one hundredth of a *boliviano. **2.** A monetary unit of Brazil, worth one hundredth of a *real. **3.** A monetary unit of Argentina, Chile, Colombia, Cuba, the Dominican Republic, Mexico, and the Philippines, worth one hundredth of a *peso. **4.** A monetary unit of Guatemala, worth one hundredth of a *quetzal. **5.** A monetary unit of Honduras, worth one hundredth of a *lempira. **6.** A monetary unit of Nicaragua, worth one hundredth of a *córdoba. **7.** A monetary unit of Cape Verde, worth one hundredth of an *escudo. **8.** A monetary unit of Mozambique, worth one hundredth of a *metical. **9.** A former monetary unit of Portugal and Madeira, worth one hundredth of an escudo (until 2002).

centesimo A former monetary unit of Italy and San Marino, worth one hundredth of a lira.

centésimo 1. A monetary unit of Panama, worth one hundredth of a *balboa. **2.** A monetary unit of Uruguay, worth one hundredth of a *peso.

centime 1. A monetary unit of Benin, Burkina-Faso, Burundi, Cameroon, the Central African Republic, Chad, Comoros, Congo, Congo-Brazzaville, The Democratic Republic of Congo, Côte d'Ivoire, Djibouti, Equatorial Guinea, Gabon, Guinea, Guinea-Bissau, Liechtenstein, Mali, Niger, Rwanda, Senegal, Switzerland, and Togo, worth one hundredth of a *franc. **2.** A monetary unit of Algeria, worth one hundredth of a *dinar. **3.** A monetary unit of Haiti, worth one hundredth of a *gourde. **4.** A monetary unit of Morocco, worth one hundredth of a *dirham. **5.** A former monetary unit of Andorra, Belgium, France, Luxembourg, and Monaco, worth one hundredth of a franc.

céntimo 1. A monetary unit of Costa Rica, worth one hundredth of a *colón. **2.** A monetary unit of Paraguay, worth one hundredth of a *guaraní. **3.** A monetary unit of Venezuela, worth one hundredth of a *bolívar. **4.** A monetary unit of Peru, worth one hundredth of a *new sol. **5.** A former monetary unit of Spain and Andorra, worth one hundredth of a peseta.

Central Arbitration Committee (CAC) A committee set up by the Employment Protection Act 1975 to arbitrate on matters voluntarily submitted to it through the *Advisory Conciliation and Arbitration Service by the parties to a trade dispute. Its main function is now determining claims for statutory recognition of trade unions under the Employment Relations Act 1999. CAC also adjudicates on disputes relating to an employer's disclosure of information to trade unions and issues arising from the European Works Council Directive.

central bank A bank that provides financial and banking services for the government of a country and its commercial banking system as well as implementing the government's monetary policy. The main functions of a central bank are: to manage the government's accounts; to accept deposits and grant loans to the commercial banks; to control the issue of banknotes; to manage the public debt; to help manage the exchange rate when necessary; to influence the interest rate structure and control the money supply; to hold the country's reserves of gold and foreign currency; to manage dealings with other central banks; and to act as lender of last resort to the banking system. Examples of major central banks include the *Bank of England in the UK, the *Federal Reserve Bank of the USA, and the *European Central Bank established in 1998.

central bank discount rate The rate of interest charged by a *central bank for discounting *eligible paper.

centralization The process or situation in which decision making is confined to the top managers of an organization. *Compare* DECENTRALIZATION.

central location telephone interviewing A marketing-research technique in which interviewers make telephone calls from a *call centre to interview respondents. In recent decades this has been the fastest growth area in marketing research; it is seen as a quick and cheap way of reaching opinion leaders and other groups.

centre-of-gravity method A method of calculating the ideal location for warehousing facilities by calculating the transport costs to each of the outlets to be served by the facility. The centre of gravity is the location giving the lowest total transport costs.

CEO Abbreviation for *chief executive officer.

certain annuity (terminable annuity) A form of investment contract that pays fixed sums at scheduled intervals to an individual after he or she attains a specified age; it runs for a specified number of years.

certainty equivalent method In *capital budgeting, a method of risk analysis in which a particularly risky return is expressed in terms of the *risk-free rate of return that would be its equivalent.

certificate of damage A certificate issued by a dock or wharfage company when it takes in damaged goods. The certificate, signed for or on behalf of the dock surveyor, states the nature of the damage and the cause, if known.

certificate of deposit (CD) A negotiable certificate issued by a bank in return for a term deposit of up to five years. They originated in the USA in the 1960s. From 1968, a sterling CD was issued by UK banks. They were intended to enable the *merchant banks to attract funds away from the *clearing banks with the offer of competitive interest rates. However, in 1971 the clearing banks also began to issue CDs as their negotiability and higher average yield had made them increasingly popular with the larger investors.

A secondary market in CDs has developed, made up of the *discount houses and the banks in the interbank market. They are issued in various amounts between £10,000 and £50,000, although they may be subdivided into units of the lower figure to facilitate negotiation of part holdings. *See also* ROLL-OVER CD.

certificate of incorporation The certificate that brings a company into existence; it is issued to the shareholders of a company by the Registrar of Companies. Until the certificate is issued, the company has no legal existence. *Compare* CERTIFICATE TO COMMENCE BUSINESS. *See also* ARTICLES OF ASSOCIATION.

certificate of insurance A certificate giving abbreviated details of the cover provided by an insurance policy. In a *motor-insurance policy or an *employers' liability insurance policy, the information that must be shown on the certificate of insurance is laid down by law and in both cases the policy cover does not come into force until the certificate has been delivered to the policyholder.

certificate of origin A document that states the country from which a particular parcel of goods originated. In international trade it is one of the shipping documents and will often determine whether or not an import duty has to be paid on the goods and, if it has, on what tariff. Such certificates are usually issued by a chamber of commerce in the country of origin.

certificate of quality A certificate to provide proof that goods to be traded in a *commodity market comply with an agreed standard.

certificate of value A statement made in a document certifying that the transaction concerned is not part of a transaction (or series of transactions) for which the amount involved exceeds a certain value. The statement is made in relation to stamp duty, denoting that either it is not payable or it is payable at a reduced rate.

certificate to commence business A document issued by the *Registrar of Companies to a public company on incorporation; it certifies that the nominal value of the company's share capital is at least equal to the authorized minimum of £50,000. Until the certificate has been issued, the company cannot do business or exercise its borrowing powers.

certified accountant *See* CHARTERED CERTIFIED ACCOUNTANT.

certified check *See* MARKED CHEQUE.

certified public accountant (CPA) In the US, an accountant licensed by a state authority to give an *audit opinion on a company's financial statements.

certified stock (certificated stock) Stocks of a commodity that have been examined and passed as acceptable for delivery in fulfilment of contracts on a futures market (*see* FUTURES CONTRACT).

CESR Abbreviation for Committee of European Securities Regulators.

cesser clause A clause in a charterparty (*see* CHARTERING), inserted when the charterer intends to transfer to a shipper the right to have goods carried. It provides that the shipowner is to have a lien over the shipper's goods for the freight payable under the charterparty and that the charterer's liability for freight ceases on shipment of a full cargo.

CET Abbreviation for *Common External Tariff.

CFC Abbreviation for Common Fund for Commodities. *See* UNITED NATIONS CONFERENCE ON TRADE AND DEVELOPMENT.

CFD Abbreviation for *contract for differences.

CFR Abbreviation for *Cost and Freight.

CFTC Abbreviation for *Commodity Futures Trading Commission.

CGT Abbreviation for *capital gains tax.

chaebol A large, often family-owned, conglomerate in South Korea. The Hanbo Business Group, which collapsed in 1997 with debts of $US 6 billion, is an example of a *chaebol*.

chain stores *See* MULTIPLE SHOPS.

chairman (chairwoman; chairperson; chair) The most senior officer in a company, who presides at the *annual general meeting of the company and usually also at meetings of the board of directors. He or she may combine the roles of chairperson and *managing director, especially in a small company of which he or she is the majority shareholder; alternatively, he or she may be a figurehead, without executive participation in the day-to-day running of the company. He or she is often a retired managing director. In the USA the person who performs this function is often called the **president**.

chairman's report (chairperson's report; chairwoman's report) A report by the chair of a company in the annual report and accounts (*see* ANNUAL ACCOUNTS), addressed to the *members of the company, giving an overview of the company's

activities during the financial period. These statements are not prescribed by regulation and often present a favourable view of the activities and prospects of an organization. The report often also gives a survey of what can be expected in the coming year. It is signed by the chairperson, who usually reads it at the *annual general meeting.

chamber of commerce In the UK, a voluntary organization, existing in most towns, of commercial, industrial, and trading business people who represent their joint interests to local and central government. The *London Chamber of Commerce is the largest such organization in the UK. Most UK chambers of commerce are affiliated to *British Chambers of Commerce, which represents their interests to government. Formerly, a distinction was recognized between chambers of commerce and **chambers of trade**, which represented local retailers and had a more limited range of interests. This distinction is now obsolete, with many organizations having the official title 'chamber of trade and commerce'.

change agent A group or individual whose purpose is to bring about a change in existing practices of an organization that have become entrenched routines. In many instances this role is fulfilled by outside management consultants as they are regarded as more objective and therefore their advice is more acceptable to those affected by the changes.

change management A systematic approach to dealing with both planned and unplanned change in an organization. A major part of change management is dealing with fear of or *resistance to change in the workforce. The best strategy for dealing with such resistance is usually one of communication, participation, encouragement, and support.

channel captain (channel leader) The most powerful member in the *distribution channel of goods. The channel consists of the manufacturer, wholesaler, and retailer, the channel captain usually being the manufacturer. There are, however, exceptions, most notably when the retailer is a major department further store or chain, whose buying power enables it to become the channel captain. The channel captain controls the distribution channel and can insist that products should be made to their own specifications. *See also* CHANNEL CONFLICT.

channel conflict A disagreement between members of a *distribution channel. Horizontal channel conflict can occur among retailers, if one retailer feels another is competing too vigorously through pricing or is using advertising to invade unauthorized sales territory. Vertical conflict occurs between retailers and their suppliers when either side feels dominated by the other. Conflict can arise when a manufacturer creates a new channel, such as direct e-commerce.

channel cooperation Cooperation between members of a *distribution channel as a result of harmonious marketing objectives and strategies. Problems can emerge when specific channel members have too much power or act negatively. Restriction of lines, limits on the number of new products, or the demand for promotional bonuses (typically a powerful retailer demanding cash for a promotion) by retailers and wholesalers can limit competition.

chaos theory A set of mathematical models according to which simple equations and initial conditions give rise to complicated paths for variables. Some of these models have been applied to financial markets.

CHAPS Co *See* UK PAYMENTS ADMINISTRATION.

chapter 7 In the USA, the statute of the Bankruptcy Reform Act 1978 that refers to liquidation proceedings. It provides for a trustee appointed by the court to make a management charge, secure additional financing, and operate the business in order to prevent further loss. The intention of the statute, which is based on fairness and public policy, is to accept that honest debtors may not always be able to discharge their debts fully and to give them an opportunity to make a fresh start both in their business and personal lives. In an attempt to prevent opportunistic bankruptcies, the Bankruptcy Abuse Prevention and Consumer Protection Act 2005 has made it more difficult for debtors to file under Chapter 7. *Compare* CHAPTER 11; CHAPTER 13.

chapter 11 In the USA, the statute of the Bankruptcy Reform Act 1978 that refers to the reorganization of partnerships, corporations, and municipalities, as well as sole traders, who are in financial difficulties. Unless the court rules otherwise, the debtor remains in control of the business and its operations. By allowing activities to continue, debtors and creditors can enter into arrangements, such as the restructuring of debt, rescheduling of payments, and the granting of loans. *Compare* CHAPTER 7; CHAPTER 13.

chapter 13 In the USA, the statute of the Bankruptcy Reform Act 1978 that refers to debt restructuring and provides for individuals to repay creditors over time. *Compare* CHAPTER 7; CHAPTER 11.

characteristics of easy movement *See* PRINCIPLES OF MOTION ECONOMY.

characteristics of services operations *See* SERVICE.

charge 1. A legal or equitable interest in land, securing the payment of money. It gives the creditor in whose favour the charge is created (the **chargee**) the right to payment from the income or proceeds of sale of the land charged, in priority to claims against the debtor by unsecured creditors. **2.** An interest in company property created in favour of a creditor (e.g. as a *debenture holder) to secure the amount owing. Most charges must be registered by the *Registrar of Companies (*see also* REGISTER OF CHARGES). A **fixed charge** is attached to specific fixed assets (e.g. premises, plant and machinery) and while in force prevents the company from dealing freely in those assets without the consent of the lender. A **floating charge** is not immediately attached to any specific asset but 'floats' over all the company's assets, to which it will not attach until **crystallization**, i.e. until some event (typically winding-up) causes it to become fixed. Before crystallization, the company may deal freely with such assets; this type of charge is suitable for *current assets, whose values must necessarily fluctuate. If the company goes into liquidation, fixed-charge holders are paid before *preferential creditors, who are paid before floating-charge holders.

A charge can also be created upon shares. For example, the articles of association usually give the company a lien in respect of unpaid calls, and company members may, in order to secure a debt owed to a third party, charge their shares, either by a full transfer of shares coupled with an agreement to retransfer upon repayment of the debt or by a deposit of the share certificate.

chargeable assets All forms of property, wherever situated, that are not specifically designated as exempt from tax on *capital gains. **Exempt assets** include private motor cars, National Savings Certificates, foreign currency for private use, betting winnings, life-insurance policies for those who are the original beneficial owners, works of art of national importance given for national purposes, principal private residences, *gilt-edged securities, personal possessions sold for less than £6000, and investments under *Individual Savings Accounts.

chargeable event Any transaction or event that gives rise to a liability to income tax, capital gains tax, or corporation tax.

chargeable gain In the UK, that part of a *capital gain arising as a result of the disposal of an asset that is subject to taxation. Non-chargeable gains include:

- gains resulting from proceeds that are taxable under *income tax;
- gains from exempt assets (*see* CHARGEABLE ASSETS);

- gains covered by other exemptions and reliefs (e.g. personal exemption from capital gains tax of £11,100 for 2015–16);
- gains not charged in full or at all owing to the system of *entrepreneurs' relief.

chargeable transfer A lifetime gift that is not covered by any of the exemptions and is therefore liable to *inheritance tax. A *potentially exempt transfer becomes a chargeable transfer where the death of the donor occurs within seven years of the transfer being made. A **chargeable lifetime transfer** is one that is neither an *exempt transfer nor potentially exempt; in practice, this applies only to payment into a *discretionary trust. Such a transfer is liable to inheritance tax at the lifetime rate of 20%, payable at the time of the transfer.

charge account (credit account) An account held by a customer at a retail shop that allows him or her to pay for any goods purchased at the end of a stated period (usually one month).

charge card A plastic card entitling the holder to purchase goods or services either up to a prescribed limit or (in some cases) without limit, provided that payment in full is made at regular intervals (usually monthly). Some charge cards are issued by retailers and may only be used in that retailer's outlets (*see* STORE CARD). However, most charge cards are issued by financial services companies (e.g. American Express, Diners' Club) and these have a wide acceptability similar to *credit cards. The main difference between a charge card and a credit card is that the former does not allow the customer to roll over credit from month to month (although some cards now allow for large purchases to be paid off over a longer period). Charge card users therefore pay a fixed annual fee rather than interest. Because charge cards were formerly issued very selectively, they are more prestigious than other forms of credit card.

charges forward An instruction to the effect that all carriage charges on a consignment of goods will be paid by the consignee after receipt.

charges register 1. *See* LAND REGISTRA-
TION. **2.** *See* REGISTER OF CHARGES.

charismatic leader A leader who
inspires his or her followers through personal magnetism and highly developed
communication skills. Charismatic leaders
tend to be confident, visionary, and
change-oriented and may display eccentric
or unusual behaviour. *Compare*
BUREAUCRATIC LEADER. *See also*
LEADERSHIP STYLE; POWER STYLES;
TRANSFORMATIONAL LEADERSHIP.

charitable trust A trust set up for a
charitable purpose that is registered with
the *Charity Commission. Charitable trusts
do not have to pay income tax if they
comply with the regulations of the
Commission.

Charity Commission The government
department that acts as both an adviser to,
and an investigator of, charities. It is
responsible to the Home Secretary and is
governed by the Charities Act 2011.

chartered accountant (CA) A qualified
member of the *Institute of Chartered
Accountants in England and Wales, the
Institute of Chartered Accountants of
Scotland, or the Institute of Chartered
Accountants in Ireland. These were the
original bodies to be granted royal charters.
Other bodies of accountants now have
charters (the *Association of Chartered
Certified Accountants, the Chartered
Institute of Management Accountants,
and the Chartered Institute of Public
Finance and Accountancy) but their
members are not known as chartered
accountants. Most firms of chartered
accountants are engaged in public practice concerned with auditing, taxation,
and other financial advice; however,
many trained chartered accountants fulfil
management roles in industry.

**Chartered Association of Certified
Accountants** *See* ASSOCIATION OF
CHARTERED CERTIFIED ACCOUNTANTS.

chartered bank A bank in the USA that is
authorized to operate as a bank by a charter

granted either by its home state (**state-
chartered bank**) or by the federal government (**nationally chartered bank**). In
Canada, a similar charter is granted to
banks by the Comptroller of Currency. The
use of charters dates back to the use of
Royal Charters, which predated Acts of
Parliament.

chartered certified accountant (CCA)
A member of the *Association of Chartered
Certified Accountants. The Association's
members are trained in industry, in the
public sector, and in the offices of practising accountants. Membership is granted on
the basis of completion of the Association's
examinations and of sufficient relevant
work experience. Members are recognized
by the UK Department for Business,
Innovation and Skills as qualified to audit
the accounts of companies. They may be
associates (ACCA) or fellows (FCCA) of the
Association and, although they are not
*chartered accountants, they fulfil much
the same role. Chartered certified
accountants were known as **certified
accountants** until 1996. In the USA the
equivalent is a **certified public accountant (CPA)**.

chartered company *See* COMPANY.

**Chartered Institute of Management
Accountants** *See* ACCOUNTANT;
MANAGEMENT ACCOUNTING.

**Chartered Institute of Marketing
(CIM)** A professional organization founded
in 1911 as the Sales Managers' Association.
Its goals are to promote the principles and
practices of marketing throughout industry,
to provide services for members and registered students, and to uphold professional
standards in the field. The Institute
received a Royal Charter in 1989.

(())) SEE WEB LINKS
• CIM website: provides news, analysis, and a
  wide range of information services

**Chartered Institute of Personnel
and Development (CIPD)** A professional
organization for personnel managers in the
UK, founded in 1913. The Institute, an

independent and non-political body, aims to encourage and assist the development of personnel management by promoting investigation and research and establishing standards of qualification and perform-ance. Previously known as the **Institute of Personnel Management** (**IPM**), it received the Royal Charter in 2000.

(SEE WEB LINKS)

• CIPD website: includes a wealth of resources on HR subjects ranging from employment law to training and development

Chartered Institute of Public Finance and Accountancy *See* ACCOUNTANT.

Chartered Institute of Public Rela-tions (CIPR) The professional organiza-tion, established in 1948, for UK public relations consultancies. It is the largest such organization in Europe.

Chartered Institute of Taxation (CIOT) A professional institute for those working within the taxation field, in accountancy practices, legal firms, banks, and commerce, as well as in HM Revenue and Customs. Members are designated CTA (Chartered Trust Advisor) or, for those qualifying before 1994, ATII or FTII (Asso-ciate or Fellow of the Taxation Institute Incorporated).

Chartered Insurance Institute (CII) An association of insurers and brokers in the insurance industry. Its origins date back to 1873; its first Royal Charter was granted in 1912. It provides training by post and at its own college, examinations leading to its associateship diploma (ACII) and fellow-ship diploma (FCII), and sets high stand-ards of ethical behaviour in the industry.

Chartered Management Institute (CMI) The principal UK professional body for managers, formed in 1992 from a mer-ger of the British Institute of Management and the Institute of Industrial Managers. Its purpose is to promote high professional standards among managers and to provide information and other benefits for its members. It was awarded a Royal Charter in 2002.

chartered secretary *See* INSTITUTE OF CHARTERED SECRETARIES AND ADMINISTRATORS.

chartered surveyor *See* ROYAL INSTITUTION OF CHARTERED SURVEYORS.

chartering Hiring the whole of a ship or aircraft. The hirer is called the **charterer** and the document setting out the terms and conditions of the contract is called the **charterparty**. In a *time charter the ship or aircraft is hired for a specified period, usu-ally with the owner operating it and the charterer paying fuel and stores costs. However, in a *bareboat charter, which is a form of time charter, the charterer pays for all crew expenses. In a *voyage charter, the ship or aircraft is hired for a single voyage between stated ports to carry a stated cargo and the owner pays all the expenses of running the ship. In an **open charter** the charterer may use the ship or aircraft to carry any cargo to any port.

chartist An *investment analyst who uses charts of prices and volumes in an attempt to predict what will happen in financial markets. Most chartist analysis is based on the assumption that history repeats itself and that the movements of share prices conform to a small number of repetitive patterns.

chase demand strategy (variable output plan) An approach to aggregate planning that attempts to match supply and output with fluctuating demand. Depend-ing on the product or service involved, the approach can incur costs by the ineffective use of capacity at periods of low demand, by the need to recruit or lay off staff, by learning-curve effects, and by a possible loss of quality. The advantages include low storage costs and greater ability to respond to the needs of the customer. *Compare* LEVEL OUTPUT STRATEGY.

chattels All property of whatever kind, excluding freehold land and anything per-manently affixed to freehold land. Interests in land (e.g. leaseholds) are **chattels real**. **Chattels personal** are all movable and tangible articles of property. Chattels include timber growing on land (whether freehold or leasehold) and articles of personal use.

cheap money (easy money) A monetary policy of keeping *interest rates at a low level. This is normally done to encourage an expansion in the level of economic activity by reducing the costs of borrowing and investment. It was used in the 1930s to help recovery after the Depression, during World War II to reduce the cost of government borrowing, and again in the wake of the financial crisis of 2007–08. *Compare* DEAR MONEY.

check The US spelling of *cheque.

check digit A digit often appended at the end of a string of digits; it is used for carrying out a check to verify the accuracy of a sequence or a customer number.

cheque A preprinted form on which instructions are given to an account holder (a bank or building society) to pay a stated sum to a named recipient. It is the most common form of payment of debts of all kinds (*see also* CHEQUE ACCOUNT; CURRENT ACCOUNT).

In a **crossed cheque** two parallel lines across the face of the cheque indicate that it must be paid into a bank account and not cashed over the counter (a **general crossing**). A **special crossing** may be used in order to further restrict the negotiability of the cheque, for example by adding the name of the payee's bank. An **open cheque** is an uncrossed cheque that can be cashed at the bank of origin. An **order cheque** is one made payable to a named recipient 'or order', enabling the payee to either deposit it in an account or endorse it to a third party, i.e. transfer the rights to the cheque by signing it on the reverse. In a **blank cheque** the amount is not stated; it is often used if the exact debt is not known and the payee is left to complete it. However, the drawer may impose a maximum by writing 'under £ . . .' on the cheque.

With the rise of electronic payment systems the use of cheques has fallen dramatically since the 1990s and most UK and European retailers no longer accept this form of payment. Cheques are still widely used in the USA (where the word is spelled **check**). *See also* MARKED CHEQUE; RETURNED CHEQUE; STALE CHEQUE.

cheque account An account with a bank or building society on which cheques can be drawn. The US name for such an account is a **checking account**. *See* CURRENT ACCOUNT.

cheque card A plastic card issued by a retail bank to its customers to guarantee cheques drawn on the customer's current account up to a specified limit. The card carries the account number, the name of the customer, and has to be signed by the customer. In the UK cheque cards have been replaced by *multifunctional cards, which also function as *cash cards and *debit cards.

cheque truncation The conversion of a paper *cheque into a digital reproduction, so that it can be transmitted electronically to the drawee bank rather than being presented physically. This may also involve the creation of a **substitute cheque** or **image replacement document**: a paper reproduction that serves as a complete legal substitute for the original cheque, provided that it contains a legible image of both sides of the instrument and all the original *MICR information. Cheque truncation has been legally possible in the UK since 1996 and in the USA since 2004.

chetrum A monetary unit of Bhutan, worth one hundredth of a *ngultrum.

Chicago Board of Trade (CBOT) A US exchange for trading in futures and options. It started in 1848, trading in grain, and began to offer standardized futures contracts in 1864. A screen-based trading system was introduced in 2000, but the exchange continues to use its traditional *open outcry method. CBOT was purchased by the *Chicago Mercantile Exchange in 2007.

Chicago Mercantile Exchange (CME)
The prime US futures and options market.
It was started in 1919 as a commodity
futures market but in 1972 opened the
International Monetary Market, the
world's first market for *financial futures.
CME became a public listed company in
2002 and acquired the *Chicago Board of
Trade in 2007 and the *New York Mercan-
tile Exchange in 2008.

(🌐) SEE WEB LINKS
• Website of the CME

chief executive officer (CEO) The person with responsibility for ensuring that an
organization functions efficiently and
makes a profit acceptable to the shareholders if it is profit-making. Although the
term was formerly more common in North
America than the UK, it is now sometimes
used in place of *managing director in
the UK.

Chinese wall A notional information
barrier between the parts of a business,
especially between the market-making part
of a stockbroking firm and the broking part.
It would clearly not be in investors' interests for brokers to persuade their clients to
buy investments from them for no other
reason than that the market makers in the
firm, expecting a fall in price, were anxious
to sell them.

CHIPS Acronym for *Clearing House Inter-
Bank Payments System.

choice criteria The critical attributes
made use of by a consumer in evaluating
alternative products. Choice criteria can
include the colour of the packaging, the
perceived taste of the product, expectations
related to the brand (e.g. the reliability of a
make of car), etc.

choice-shift effect The finding that after
participating in a group discussion, individuals tend to advocate more extreme
positions and call for riskier courses of
action than they would have done had they
not taken part in the discussion. This phenomenon is also known as the **risky shift**.
More recently, certain experimental

conditions have been found that lead group
discussion to inhibit risk (a so-called
cautious shift); as a result, the term
'choice-shift effect' is now sometimes
applied to both effects.

chon A monetary unit of North Korea and
South Korea, worth one hundredth of a
*won.

chooser option An *option in which the
holder has the freedom to decide, up to a
specified point before expiry, whether it is a
put or a call option.

chose in action A right of proceeding in a
court of law to obtain a sum of money or to
recover damages. Examples include rights
under an insurance policy, a debt, and
rights under a contract. A chose in action is
a form of property and can be assigned,
sold, held in trust, etc. *See also* CHOSE IN
POSSESSION.

chose in possession Moveable chattels
that a person possesses. Examples include
goods, merchandise, etc. All assets are
either choses in possession or *choses
in action.

churning 1. The practice by a broker of
encouraging an investor to change investments frequently in order to earn excessive
commissions. **2.** The practice by a bank,
building society, insurance broker, etc., of
encouraging a householder with an
endowment *mortgage to surrender the
policy and to take out a new one when
seeking to increase a mortgage or to raise
extra funds, instead of topping up the
existing mortgage. The purpose is to
increase charges and commissions at the
expense of the policyholder. **3.** A government policy of paying a benefit to a wide
category of persons and taxing it so that
those paying little or no taxes receive it
while the well-off return it through the tax
system. There have been suggestions that a
higher child benefit is suitable for
churning.

CIF Abbreviation for Cost, Insurance and
Freight. *See* COST AND FREIGHT.

CIFCI Abbreviation for cost, insurance, and freight plus commission and interest. A price quoted CIFCI is a *Cost and Freight price that also includes cargo insurance, an agreed commission payable by the seller to the buyer, and the interest charged by the seller's bank for negotiating the documents. Although prices are often quoted in these terms, CIFCI is not a recognized *Incoterm.

CII Abbreviation for *Chartered Insurance Institute.

CIM Abbreviation for *Chartered Institute of Marketing.

CIMS Abbreviation for *computer-integrated manufacturing system.

CIOT Abbreviation for *Chartered Institute of Taxation.

CIP Abbreviation for Carriage and Insurance Paid To. *See* COST AND FREIGHT.

CIPD Abbreviation for *Chartered Institute of Personnel and Development.

CIPR Abbreviation for *Chartered Institute of Public Relations.

circuit breakers Measures put in place by the major stock and derivatives exchanges to prevent very large market movements; for example, suspending trading on a particular market when certain extreme price fluctuations take place. These provisions were first instituted after the major stock market crash on *Black Monday 1987.

circuity of action The return of a *bill of exchange, prior to maturity, to the person who first signed it. Under these circumstances it may be renegotiated, but the person forfeits any right of action against those who put their names to it in the intervening period.

circular A notice or advertisement in any form distributed by post or by hand to large numbers of individuals or households.

circular letter of credit See LETTER OF CREDIT.

circulating assets *See* CURRENT ASSETS.

circulation 1. The distribution of a publication. **2.** The number of copies sold per issue of a publication.

CIT Abbreviation for *critical incident technique.

City The district of London that contains the Stock Exchange, the Bank of England, Lloyds, and the head offices of many financial institutions. Occupying the so-called **Square Mile** on the north side of the River Thames between Waterloo Bridge and Tower Bridge, the City has been an international merchanting centre since medieval times. Although many institutions remain in the square mile, others have migrated eastwards, to the Docklands area or westwards to former newspaper offices in Fleet Street.

City Code on Takeovers and Mergers
A code first laid down in 1968, and since substantially modified, giving the practices to be observed in company takeovers (*see* TAKEOVER BID) and *mergers. It is administered by a panel (the **Takeover Panel**) including representatives from major financial and business institutions. Under the Companies Act 2006 the code was given the force of law; previously the panel could only admonish offenders and refer them to their own professional bodies for disciplinary action or request the *Financial Services Authority to enforce its decisions.
   The code attempts to ensure that all shareholders, including minority shareholders, are treated equally, are kept advised of the terms of all bids and counterbids, and are advised fairly by the directors of the company receiving the bid on the likely outcome if the bid succeeds. Its many other rules are aimed at preventing directors from acting in their own interests rather than those of their shareholders, ensuring that the negotiations are conducted openly and honestly, and preventing a spurious market arising in the shares of either side. One of its rules is that if the number of shares controlled exceeds 30%

of the total, a general offer should be made for all the shares in the business.

Under the Companies Act 2006 the City Code was revised to incorporate articles of the EU's Takeover Directive (2005).

CIVETS Acronym for Colombia, Indonesia, Vietnam, Egypt, Turkey, and South Africa: countries identified in 2009–10 as emerging markets with prospects for growth and investment because of their perceived dynamic economies, young and growing populations, and relative political stability. *See also* BRIC; NEXT 11.

civil law 1. The law applied by the civil courts in the UK, as opposed to ecclesiastical, criminal, or military law. It is, thus, the law that regulates dealings between private citizens that are not subject to interference by the state. Its chief divisions include the law of contract, torts, and trusts. **2.** The law generally in force on the Continent, which has its basis in Roman law.

class action A legal action in which a person sues as a representative of a class of persons who share a common claim.

classical school of management The earliest formal theories of management, which developed in the late 19th century and held sway until the 1950s. Classical approaches to management are usually divided into the schools of *administrative management and *scientific management.

classical school of strategy An approach to *business strategy that emphasizes the role of rational, long-term planning by senior executives with the goal of establishing *competitive advantage and thus maximizing profits. It draws on traditions of military strategy and assumes that markets are efficient, managers rational, and organizations hierarchical. The classical school emerged in the 1960s and is exemplified by the work of the US mathematician and management guru Igor Ansoff. *See also* STRATEGIC MANAGEMENT.

classical system of corporation tax A system of taxing companies in which the company is treated as a taxable entity separate from its shareholders. The profits of companies under this system are therefore taxed twice, first when made by the company and again when distributed to the shareholders as dividends. *Compare* IMPUTATION SYSTEM.

classification method A method of *job evaluation in which jobs are placed in certain predefined categories on the basis of job title, *job description, and comparison with *benchmark jobs. It is mainly associated with large hierarchical organizations such as the civil service and local government. *Compare* FACTOR-COMPARISON METHOD; JOB-COMPONENT METHOD; POINT METHOD; RANKING METHOD.

classified advertising The form of *advertising that consists of small typeset or semi-display advertisements grouped together in such categories as cars for sale, furniture for sale, flats to let, etc., usually in a paper or magazine. They are usually inserted by direct contact between the advertiser and the advertising department of the publication.

Classified Directories UK trade directories (known colloquially as **Yellow Pages** because they are printed on yellow paper) issued by British Telecom for each business area. Businesses are listed by trade.

claused bill of lading *See* DIRTY BILL OF LADING.

clawback 1. Money that a government takes back from members of the public by taxation, especially through the *higher rate of income tax, having given the money away in benefits, such as retirement pensions. Thus the money is clawed back from those who have no need of the benefit (because they are paying higher-rate taxes). **2.** An agreement requiring the sponsors of a project to repay past profits in the event of a shortfall in later periods. This may be a condition in *project financing.

Clayton Act A US *anti-trust law passed in 1914; it placed restrictions on mergers and acquisitions that limited competition and debarred individuals from holding directorships on the boards of competing companies.

clean bill of lading *See* BILL OF LADING.

clean floating A government policy allowing a country's currency to fluctuate without direct intervention in the foreign-exchange markets. In practice, clean floating is rare as governments are frequently tempted to manage exchange rates by direct intervention by means of the official reserves, a policy sometimes called **managed floating** (*see also* MANAGED CURRENCY). However, clean floating does not necessarily mean that there is no control of exchange rates, as they can still be influenced by the government's monetary policy.

clean price The price of a *bond excluding the accrued interest since the previous dividend payment. Interest on fixed-interest securities accrues continuously although dividends are paid at fixed intervals (usually six months). Prices quoted in newspapers and other media outlets are usually clean prices, as are those given on US bond markets. On UK and European markets it is customary to quote the **dirty price**, i.e. the price of the bond including any unpaid interest. This is the price actually paid by the buyer.

clearance An indication from a taxing authority that a certain provision does not apply to a particular transaction. The procedure is only available when specified by statute, as, for example, on the reorganization of a company's share capital and on the demerger of a company's trade. Exceptionally, the Revenue grants a clearance under the extra-statutory concessional treatment whereby a dividend paid on the liquidation of a company is subject to capital gains tax and not to income tax.

clear days The full days referred to in a contract, i.e. not including the days on which the contract period starts or finishes.

cleared balance A balance on a bank account, excluding any receipts that have not yet been *cleared for value.

cleared for fate Denoting the date on which the payer's bank has confirmed that funds are available to provide value for a transfer in accordance with the instructions given in a cheque, etc. This may be up to four working days after the cheque has *cleared for value. Once a cheque has cleared for fate the funds transferred to the payee cannot be reclaimed unless there is evidence of deliberate fraud. *See* CLEARING CYCLE.

cleared for value Denoting the time at which a credit to a customer's bank account is used for calculating interest and for establishing the undrawn balance of an agreed overdraft facility. *See* CLEARING CYCLE.

clearing bank 1. In the UK, a bank that is a member of the central clearing system, to enable passage and clearance of cheques. It is often used as an alternative description for the major high-street banks. **2.** In the USA, a bank that settles federal, agency, and corporate securities for its customers.

clearing cycle The process by which a payment made by cheque, etc., through the banking system is transferred from the payer's to the payee's account. In the UK the average time for a cheque to be *cleared for value is two working days. However, it may be another two working days before the cheque is **cleared for withdrawal** (i.e. before the payee can withdraw money against the funds transferred) and six working days in all before the cheque is *cleared for fate.

clearing house A centralized and computerized system for settling indebtedness between members. The best known in the UK is Bacs (*see* UK PAYMENTS ADMINISTRATION), which enables the member banks to offset claims against one another for direct debits and credits. Similar arrangements exist in financial exchanges, in which sales and purchases are registered with the clearing house for settlement at the end of the accounting period. *See also* CLEARSTREAM; EUROCLEAR; LONDON CLEARING HOUSE; RECOGNIZED CLEARING HOUSE.

Clearing House Inter-Bank Payments System (CHIPS) A US bank *clearing house for large-value dollar transactions. It is owned by financial institutions and operated by the **Clearing House Payments Company**. Any bank may participate providing that it has a regulated US presence. *See also* FEDWIRE.

Clearstream A pan-European facility for the clearing and settlement of *eurobonds, based in Luxembourg. It was founded (as Clearstream International) in 2000, when *Deutsche Börse Clearing merged with the clearing company Centrale de Livraison de Valeurs Mobilières (Cedel International). It is now a wholly owned subsidiary of Deutsche Börse.

clickable Denoting a company or organization that operates on the *Internet. *See* E-COMMERCE.

click and collect A retail facility whereby shoppers order products online ('click') and pick them up from a designated physical location ('collect'). This multi-channel approach can offer advantages both to consumers, who are able to collect products at their convenience rather than waiting in to have them delivered at home, and to retailers, who gain access to a broad network of outlets such as convenience stores. In the UK click and collect grew in popularity in the early 2000s.

clicks-and-mortar (bricks-and-clicks) Denoting a business that combines *e-commerce ('clicks') with the use of physical premises such as retail outlets or warehouses.

clickstream The path that a user takes in navigating through a website. Monitoring clickstreams is important to designers of large websites.

clickthrough (ad click) The act of clicking on a *banner advertisement on a

website, which directs the user to a page that provides further information.

clickthrough fee (prospect fee) A payment made to a company for traffic generated by a link on the company's website, typically by means of a *banner advertisement.

clickthrough rate The percentage of visitors to a website who click on a particular *banner advertisement. Clickthrough rates of 1% or 2% are common for standard nonpersonalized advertisements.

click-tracker Software that automatically counts the number of times that particular links on a website have been clicked by visitors. It is typically used to measure advertisement *clickthrough.

client account A bank or building society account operated by a professional person (e.g. a solicitor, stockbroker, agent, etc.) on behalf of a client. A client account is legally required for any company handling investments on a client's behalf; it protects the client's money in case the company becomes insolvent and makes dishonest appropriation of the client's funds more difficult. For this reason money in client accounts should be quite separate from the business transactions of the company or the professional person.

climate change levy A UK tax charged on the supply of electricity, gas, coal, and coke, as they are supplies that are regarded as leading to global warming. The levy is imposed by the Finance Act 2000 on any supply made on or after 1 April 2001.

close company A company resident in the UK that is under the control of five or fewer participators or any number of participators who are also directors. There is also an alternative asset-based test, which applies if five or fewer participators, or any number who are directors, would be entitled to more than 50% of the company's assets on a winding-up. The principal consequences of being a close company are that the provision of certain *benefits in kind to shareholders can be treated by HM

Revenue as a *distribution, as can loans or quasi-loans. There are a number of other consequences. In the USA close companies are known as **closed companies**. *See also* CLOSE INVESTMENT HOLDING COMPANY.

closed economy A theoretical model of an economy that neither imports nor exports and is therefore independent of economic factors in the outside world. No such economy exists, although the foreign sector of the US economy is relatively small and most economic decisions are taken by the US government independently of the rest of the world.

closed-ended questions Questions on a questionnaire that ask the respondent to choose from a list of answers, e.g. asking which of a list of brands they have recently bought. *Compare* OPEN-ENDED QUESTION.

closed indent *See* OPEN INDENT.

closed shop Any organization in which there is an agreement between the employers and a trade union that only members of that union will be taken on as employees. Under the Trade Union and Labour Relations (Consolidation) Act, all employees are free to join a trade union or not, as they wish. If an employer takes action, short of dismissal, against an employee to enforce membership of a union, the employee can complain to an *employment tribunal, which can order the employer to pay him compensation. Dismissal for failure to belong to a trade union is automatically unfair (*see* UNFAIR DISMISSAL). A union that attempts to enforce a closed shop by industrial action has no immunity from legal action.

closed system A system that is unaffected by influences from outside its boundaries. While a real system that is totally immune to outside influences is hard to imagine, the concept can be useful as a theoretical model.

close investment holding company A *close company that does not exist wholly or mainly as a trading company, a property company letting to third parties, or a

holding company of a trading company. Such a company is subject to *corporation tax at the full rate on its profits; it cannot benefit from the lower rates and reliefs available to other companies.

closely held corporation In the USA, a public corporation that has only a limited number of stockholders and consequently few of its shares are traded.

close price The price of a share or commodity when the margin between the bid and offer prices is narrow.

closing The step in the selling process in which the salesperson asks the customer for an order.

closing balance The debit or credit balance on a ledger at the end of an *accounting period, which will be carried forward to the next accounting period. A debit closing balance (such as an *accrual) will be carried forward to the credit side of a ledger and a credit closing balance (such as a prepayment) will be carried forward to the debit side of a ledger.

closing deal A transaction on a financial market that closes a long or short position or terminates the liability of an *option holder.

closing out The final (or closing) results of either a direct mailing or direct response advertisement. For example, a 5% response rate indicates that 5% of those approached have responded positively to a mailing or advertising campaign.

closing prices The buying and selling prices recorded on a financial market at the end of a day's trading. *See* AFTER-HOURS DEALS.

closing signal A sign given by a prospective buyer indicating that a decision has been arrived at to make a purchase.

closing stock The *stock remaining within an organization at the end of an *accounting period as *raw materials, *work in progress, or *finished goods. It is necessary to establish the level of closing stocks so that the cost of their creation is not charged against the profits of the period (*see* OPENING STOCK). Closing stocks are therefore valued and deducted from the costs of the period and appear as *current assets in the *balance sheet.

cloud computing An approach to computing in which the end user connects to a remote network of computers ('the cloud') in order to run programs, store data, etc. This enables business and other users to access large amounts of data storage and computing power from anywhere in the world without having to own and maintain these resources themselves. Cloud computing became increasingly popular in the early 2010s.

club deal *See* SYNDICATED BANK FACILITY.

cluster sampling A method of selecting a *sample in which the members of the sample are chosen from one or more groups (clusters), rather than from the *population as a whole. This technique is often used when random sampling from the whole population would be impractical or expensive. In auditing, for example, groups of, say, invoices are chosen at random by the auditor and then each item in each group is examined in detail. In marketing research, clusters of respondents are often chosen according to their geographical areas in order to reduce travelling costs. *See also* SYSTEMATIC SAMPLING.

cluster theory A marketing theory stating that customers with similar demographic or other characteristics are also likely to share buying preferences.

CMA *See* COMPETITION AND MARKETS AUTHORITY.

CMI Abbreviation for *Chartered Management Institute.

CMS Abbreviation for *critical management studies.

CNAR Abbreviation for compound net annual rate. *See* COMPOUND ANNUAL RETURN.

Coase theorem In economic theory, an idea often invoked in discussions of *transaction costs, *externalities, and government regulation. Simply stated, the theorem holds that in an ideal world with clearly defined property rights, *perfect competition, and minimal transaction costs, private bargaining could be relied upon to produce an efficient outcome (i.e. one that maximizes social wealth) in any situation. The implication is that social costs (such as pollution) could be minimized by reducing, rather than increasing, external regulation. The theorem, which derives from the work of the economist Ronald Coase (1911–2013), remains highly controversial.

coaster A small cargo ship that makes short trips around the coast from port to port.

COBOL Acronym for *C*ommon *B*usiness-*O*riented *L*anguage. This language is widely used to program computers for business applications, such as invoice and payroll production. It is an easy-to-learn *high-level language that uses a limited number of English words. Programs written in COBOL can be run on different computers, provided that the standard version has been used. Because it was designed to make program writing easy, COBOL occupies considerable amounts of computer memory, making it more popular on larger systems than on microcomputers. However, microcomputer versions of COBOL are available.

co-branding An arrangement between two or more companies in which they agree to display joint *content and perform joint promotions using brand logos or *banner advertisements. The aim is to strengthen the bands by making them appear complementary. This is a reciprocal arrangement, which can occur without payment.

COD Abbreviation for *cash on delivery.

code of conduct A statement setting out guidelines regarding the ethical principles and standards of behaviour expected of a professional person or company. For example, the Market Research Society has a professional code of conduct and utility companies have customer charters. Codes of conduct have no statutory effect but can have legal consequences: e.g. a code of conduct for the handling of personal data in a particular trade may be referred to by a court in determining whether there is a prima facie case of misuse of data under the Data Protection Act.

coding notice A document issued by HM Revenue and Customs as part of the PAYE system showing the amount of *income tax allowances to be set against an individual's taxable pay. The total of allowances is reduced to a code by dropping the last digit and adding a letter depending on the taxpayer's circumstances.

coemption The act of buying up the whole stock of a commodity. *See* CORNER.

coercive contract *See* PSYCHOLOGICAL CONTRACT.

cognitive dissonance A state of mental conflict caused by a difference between a consumer's expectations of a product and its actual performance. As expectations are largely formed by advertising, dissonance may be reduced by making only realistic and consistent claims about a product's performance. Cognitive dissonance can increase if the buyer feels anxious about the decision, particularly if new information has been received about the product or service. The more negative the new information, the greater the dissonance.

cognitive processes The broad range of mental activities, including perception, learning, memory, thinking, information processing, and reasoning, that involve the interpretation of stimuli and the organization of thoughts and ideas. These processes have relevance to the *attitudes of potential customers and their evaluation of the flow of information provided for them by advertising and other communications seeking to persuade them to make purchases. *See also* HUMAN INFORMATION PROCESSING.

cognitive theories of leadership *See* LEADERSHIP THEORIES.

COGS Abbreviation for cost of goods sold. *See* COST OF SALES.

Cog's ladder A model that has been widely used in business and other organizations to understand group development and the way in which individuals learn to function as a team. The theory, which was first defined by George O. Charrier at Procter & Gamble in 1972, sets out five stages of teamwork: (i) the 'polite' stage, in which the group members are introduced to one another; (ii) the 'why we're here' stage, which establishes initial goals and relationships; (iii) the 'power' stage, which is characterized by competition between group members; (iv) the 'cooperation' stage, where greater teamwork emerges; and finally (v) the 'esprit' stage, where the team is cohesive and successful.

cohort effect Any effect associated with being a member of a group born at roughly the same time and bonded by common life experiences (e.g. growing up in the 1980s). The effect is of great interest to advertisers and others involved in marketing. In large organizations, cohorts are often defined by entry date and can retain some common characteristics (size, cohesiveness, competition) that affect the organization.

coinsurance The sharing of an insurance risk between several insurers. An insurer may find a particular risk too large to accept because the potential losses may be out of proportion to their claims funds. Rather than turning the insurance away, the insurer can offer to split the risk with a number of other insurers, each of whom would be asked to cover a percentage of the risk in return for the same percentage of the premium. The policyholder deals only with the first or leading insurer, who issues all the documents, collects all the premiums, and distributes shares to the others involved. A coinsurance policy includes a schedule of all the insurers involved and shows the percentage of the risk each one is accepting.

A policyholder can also become involved in coinsurance. In this case, a reduction of the premium by an agreed percentage is given, in return for an acceptance by the policyholder that all payments of claims are reduced by the same proportion.

cold calling A method of selling a product or service in which a sales representative makes calls, door-to-door, by post, by e-mail, or by telephone, to people who have not previously shown any interest in that product or service. In view of the high cost of maintaining a salesforce, many companies direct their sales representatives to those potential customers who are favourably disposed to the supplier (either as an existing customer or by replying to a press advertisement). When companies wish to extend their market to new customers, the sales representative must be willing to call on a large number of people, many of whom will show no interest in the product. The primary objective in cold calling is to establish a favourable relationship quickly, enabling the representative to explain the benefits of their product or service before being dismissed.

collaborative customization The tailoring of a product to meet a customer's unique requirements, based on a dialogue between the seller and the customer. *See* CUSTOMIZATION.

collar An arrangement in which both the maximum (*cap) and minimum (*floor) rate of interest payable on a loan are fixed in advance.

collateral A form of *security, especially an impersonal form of security, such as life-assurance policies or shares, used to secure a bank loan. In some senses such impersonal securities are referred to as a secondary security, rather than a primary security, such as a guarantee.

collateralize In the USA, to pledge assets to secure a debt. If the borrower defaults on the terms and conditions of the agreement the assets will be forfeited.

collateralized debt obligation (CDO) A *structured finance instrument consisting of a bond or note backed by a pool of fixed-income assets. Rights to the cash flows from this pool, along with different levels of credit risk, are allocated to different classes (*tranches) of note. Some specific types of CDO include **collateralized bond obligations** (CBOs), **collateralized loan obligations** (CLOs), and **collateralized mortgage obligations** (CMOs). A *structured investment vehicle is a specialized form of CDO. The collapse in the value of CDOs backed by *subprime mortgage loans was a major factor in the financial crisis of 2007–08; such instruments effectively became toxic assets with no market.

collecting bank (remitting bank) The bank to which a person who requires payment of a cheque (or similar financial document) has presented it for payment.

collective bargaining Bargaining between employers and employees over wages, terms of employment, etc., when the employees are represented by a trade union or some other collective body.

collective effort model In psychology, a model proposing that working on tasks as part of a group tends to weaken individual *motivation by (1) lowering the individual's expectancy that his or her actions can lead to the attainment of goals and (2) reducing the subjective value of these goals to the individual. *See* SOCIAL LOAFING; SUCKER EFFECT. *See also* PATH-GOAL LEADERSHIP MODEL; VALENCE-INSTRUMENTALITY-EXPECTANCY THEORY.

collectivism An economic system in which much of the planning is carried out by a central government and the means of production is owned by the state. This system was formerly common in eastern Europe and the developing world but has now been generally replaced by free-market systems.

collusion 1. An agreement between two or more parties in order to prejudice a third party, or for any improper purpose. Collusion to carry out an illegal, not merely improper, purpose is punishable as a conspiracy. In a business context, collusion may consist of an agreement to suppress competition by price fixing, conditions of sale, etc. *See* RESTRICTIVE TRADE PRACTICES. **2.** In legal proceedings, a secret agreement between two parties as a result of which one of them agrees to bring an action against the other in order to obtain a judicial decision for an improper purpose. **3.** A secret agreement between the parties to a legal action to do or to refrain from doing something in order to influence the judicial decision. For instance, an agreement between the plaintiff and the defendant to suppress certain evidence would amount to collusion. Any judgment obtained by collusion is a nullity and may be set aside.

collusive duopoly A form of *duopoly in which producers collude with each other in a price-fixing agreement, thus forming a virtual *monopoly, and negotiate a profit-sharing arrangement.

colón (*plural* **colónes**) (CRC) The standard monetary unit of Costa Rica, divided into 100 céntimos.

colophon A publisher's identifying emblem on a book or other published material. It was formerly an inscription at the end of the book giving the title, date of publication, and the printer.

column inches (column centimetres) A measurement of area of typeset matter equal to the width of a column of type in a newspaper or magazine multiplied by its depth. In practice, column centimetres have now largely replaced column inches, especially when it comes to selling advertisement space; however, most *public relations consultancies still refer to column inches when measuring the coverage their activities have achieved.

COM Abbreviation for *computer output microfilm.

Combined Code on Corporate Governance *See* CORPORATE GOVERNANCE CODE.

combined-transport bill of lading *See* CONTAINERIZATION.

comedian *See* RELATIONSHIP ROLES.

COMEX Acronym for *Commodity Exchange Inc. of New York.

command economy (planned economy) An economy in which the activities of firms and the allocation of productive resources is determined by government direction rather than market forces.

commercial An advertisement on television or radio.

commercial agency (credit-reference agency) An organization that gives a credit reference on businesses or persons. They specialize in collating information regarding debtors, bankruptcies, and court judgments in order to provide a widely based service to their clients. *See also* ANCILLARY CREDIT BUSINESS; CREDIT RATING.

commercial bank A bank that provides a wide range of financial services, both to the general public and to firms. The principal activities are operating current accounts, receiving deposits, taking in and paying out notes and coin, and making loans. Additional services include trustee and executor facilities, the supply of foreign currency, the purchase and sale of securities, insurance, a credit-card system, and personal pensions. They also compete with the *merchant banks by providing venture capital and trading on the financial markets and with *building societies by providing mortgages.

The main banks with national networks of branches in the UK are the so-called *Big Four (the Royal Bank of Scotland group, including NatWest; Barclays, including Woolwich; Lloyds, including HBOS; and HSBC), together with the Spanish-owned Santander Group, which includes the former building societies Abbey and Alliance and Leicester. These are also known as **high-street banks**, or **retail banks**.

commercial bill Any *bill of exchange other than a *Treasury bill. *See* BANK BILL; TRADE BILL.

commercial code Any of a number of codes used to reduce the cost of sending cables. However, the international use of Telex and fax has reduced the need for cables and writing in commercial codes.

commercial credit company A US finance house that gives credit to businesses rather than individuals.

commercialization The stage in the development of a new product during which a decision is made to embark on its full-scale production and distribution. *See* NEW PRODUCT DEVELOPMENT.

commercial law *See* MERCANTILE LAW.

commercial loan selling A transaction involving two banks and one business customer. Bank A grants a loan to the customer and then sells that loan agreement to Bank B. Bank A makes a profit on the sale; Bank B has a loan book it would not otherwise achieve; and the customer borrows at a favourable rate. Commercial loan selling is common in the USA.

commercial online services Companies that offer online information, entertainment, shopping, and other services to subscribers who pay the company a monthly fee. They make use of their own dedicated networks and operate their own computers, which are connected to the Internet, thus offering somewhat better security than the Internet itself.

commercial paper (CP) A relatively low-risk short-term (maturing at 60 days or less in the US but longer in the UK) form of borrowing. Commercial paper is often regarded as a reasonable substitute for Treasury bills, certificates of deposit, etc. The main issuers have traditionally been large creditworthy institutions, such as insurance companies, bank trust departments, and pension funds. Although commercial paper was traditionally unsecured, recent years have seen a major growth in **asset-backed commercial paper** (**ABCP**), in which the CP is secured against assets held by a *structured investment vehicle (usually longer-term debt). In 2007 the

market in ABCP was severely affected by the *subprime lending crisis.

commission A payment made to an intermediary, such as an agent, salesman, broker (*see also* BROKERAGE), etc., usually calculated as a percentage of the value of the goods sold. Sometimes the whole of the commission is paid by the seller (e.g. an estate agent's commission in the UK) but in other cases (e.g. some commodity markets) it is shared equally between buyer and seller. In *advertising, the commission is the discount (usually between 10% and 15%) allowed to an *advertising agency by owners of the advertising medium for the space or time purchased on behalf of their clients. A **commission agent** is an agent specializing in buying or selling goods for a principal in another country for a commission.

commission broker In the USA, a stock-exchange dealer who executes orders to buy or sell securities on payment of a fee or a commission based on the value of the deal.

commission disclosure The disclosure of commissions on insurance and investment business. Until the mid 1990s this was covered by a 'maximum commissions agreement' in the UK, resulting in the practice of **soft disclosure**. This meant that there was no need to make customers explicitly aware of commissions and charges, provided they were within the maximum limits set and the customer did not specifically ask for detailed information. In 1991, the *Office of Fair Trading objected that this practice was uncompetitive and amounted to an illegal price-fixing cartel. It was recommended that the industry move to a practice of **hard disclosure**. Initially, this took the form of disclosing the percentage of the commission charge rather than a strict monetary disclosure. But since 1995 there has been a practice of hard disclosure of the monetary value of commissions, expenses, charges and early surrender value to customers at the point of purchase.

commitment *See* ORGANIZATIONAL COMMITMENT.

commitment fee An amount charged by a bank to keep open a line of credit or to continue to make unused loan facilities available to a potential borrower. *See* FIRM COMMITMENT.

commitments for capital expenditure *See* CAPITAL COMMITMENTS.

committed costs Costs, usually *fixed costs, that the management of an organization have a long-term responsibility to pay. Examples include rent on a long-term lease and depreciation on an asset with an extended life.

committed facility An agreement between a bank and a customer to provide funds up to a specified maximum at a specified *interest rate (in the UK this is usually based upon an agreed margin over the *London Inter Bank Offered Rate) for a certain period. The total cost will be the interest rate plus the *mandatory liquid asset cost. The agreement will include the conditions that must be adhered to by the borrower for the facility to remain in place. *Compare* UNCOMMITTED FACILITY. *See also* REVOLVING BANK FACILITY.

commodity 1. A *good regarded in economics as the basis of production and exchange. **2.** Any raw material or primary product. **3.** A raw material traded on a *commodity market, such as grain, coffee, cocoa, wool, cotton, jute, rubber, pork bellies, or orange juice (sometimes known as *soft commodities) or base metals and other solid raw materials (known as hard commodities). In some contexts soft commodities are referred to as **produce**.

commodity broker A *broker who deals in *commodities, especially one who trades on behalf of principals in a *commodity market (*see also* FUTURES CONTRACT). The rules governing the procedure adopted in each market vary from commodity to commodity and the function of brokers may also vary. In some markets brokers pass on the names of their principals, in others they do not, and in yet others they are permitted to act as principals. Commodity brokers, other than those dealing in metals, are often called **produce brokers**.

commodity exchange *See* COMMODITY MARKET.

Commodity Exchange Inc. of New York (COMEX) A commodity exchange in New York that specializes in trading in metal *futures contracts and *options. Founded in 1933, it became a division of the *New York Mercantile Exchange (NYMEX) in 1994.

Commodity Futures Trading Commission (CFTC) A US government body set up in 1975 in Washington to regulate trading in commodity futures (*see* FUTURES CONTRACT). Its remit was extended to cover other forms of *derivatives trading in the early 1990s.

commodity market A market in which *commodities are traded. Historically, the main *terminal markets in commodities were in London, New York, and Chicago, but in some commodities there were also markets in the country of origin. There are now major commodity markets in India, China, and Kenya. Some commodities are dealt with at auctions (e.g. tea), each lot being sold having been examined by dealers, but most dealers deal with goods that have been classified according to established quality standards (*see* CERTIFIED STOCK). In these commodities both *actuals and futures (*see* FUTURES CONTRACT) are traded on **commodity exchanges**, in which dealers are represented by *commodity brokers. Many commodity exchanges offer *option dealing in futures, and settlement of differences on futures through a *clearing house. As commodity prices fluctuate widely, commodity exchanges provide users and producers with *hedging facilities with outside speculators and investors helping to make an active market, although amateurs are advised not to gamble on commodity exchanges.

The fluctuations in commodity prices have caused considerable problems in developing countries, from which many commodities originate, as they are often important sources of foreign currency, upon which the economic welfare of the country depends. Various measures have been used to restrict price fluctuations but none have been completely successful. *See also* INTERCONTINENTALEXCHANGE; INTERNATIONAL PETROLEUM EXCHANGE; LIFFE; LONDON METAL EXCHANGE; NEW YORK MERCANTILE EXCHANGE.

Common Agricultural Policy (CAP) A policy set up by the *European Economic Community to support free trade within the Common Market and to protect farmers in the member states. The *European Commission fixes a **threshold price**, below which cereals may not be imported into the European Union (EU), and also buys surplus cereals at an agreed **intervention price** in order to help farmers achieve a reasonable average price, called the **target price**. Prices are also agreed for meats, poultry, eggs, fruit, and vegetables, with arrangements similar to those for cereals. The European Commission is also empowered by the CAP to subsidize the modernization of farms within the community. The common policy for exporting agricultural products to non-member countries is laid down by the CAP. In the UK, the Intervention Board for Agricultural Produce is responsible for the implementation of EU regulations regarding the CAP. Important reforms designed mainly to eliminate surpluses and to uphold environmental and production standards were agreed in 1984, 1988, 1999, 2003, and 2014.

Common Budget The fund, administered by the *European Commission, into which all levies and customs duties on goods entering the European Union are paid and from which all subsidies due under the *Common Agricultural Policy are taken.

common carrier *See* CARRIER.

Common External Tariff (CET) The tariff of import duties payable on certain goods entering any country in the European Union from non-member countries.

Income from these duties is paid into the *Common Budget.

Common Fisheries Policy A fishing policy agreed between members of the European Community (EC) in 1983. An earlier agreement of 1971 introduced the principle of free access to European Community waters and a single fishing market. The key elements resulting from the 1983 agreement were: the setting of a Total Annual Catch (TAC) for the Community, which aimed to ensure conservation of stocks; a national TAC allocation; schemes for fleet restructuring; and negotiation with 'third party' nations. A radical reform of the policy imposing severe cuts in fishing quotas was agreed in 2013.

common law 1. The law common to the whole of the UK, as opposed to local law. **2.** Case law as opposed to legislation, i.e. the law that has evolved by judicial precedent rather than by statute. For instance, the rules relating to the formation of contracts is a product of the common law, and is not contained in any Act of parliament. **3.** The law of the UK as opposed to foreign law. In this sense, the common law would include case law as well as legislation.

Common Market *See* EUROPEAN ECONOMIC COMMUNITY; EUROPEAN UNION.

common stock The US name for *ordinary shares.

Commonwealth Development Corporation *See* CDC GROUP.

communication The result of any action (physical, written, or verbal) that conveys meanings between two individuals. In the context of marketing, the marketer wants the communication, in the form of a promotional message, to gain attention and to be understood, believed, and remembered. *See* ADVERTISING OBJECTIVE.

communication adaptation A global communication strategy for adapting advertising messages for local markets.

communication goals *See* ADVERTISING OBJECTIVE.

communication ring A shared communication structure on the Internet. Individuals in a communication ring can send messages to all the members of the ring, a subgroup of the ring, or each other. Examples include e-mail lists and instant messaging 'buddy lists' (of friends and acquaintances).

communications management A systematic approach to defining, managing, and monitoring the official channels of communication within an organization. The aim is to ensure that information flows freely and efficiently between the different levels and sections of a company, thereby improving decision making, motivation, and overall performance. Various processes and incentives can be devised to ensure that information flows in a bottom-up as well as a top-down direction, so that e.g. the experience of shop-floor workers is considered by management. Effective communications management is central to such modern philosophies as *total quality management.

communication timing The manner in which an Internet communication is scheduled, determining whether it is real-time or stored.

community of users The group of people who visit and use a particular site on the Internet.

community of values A network of users or contributors to an Internet site, who share knowledge, expertise, or similar outlooks.

Community Patent (unitary patent) A proposed European Union *patent that is likely to become available by 2016; it will consist of a single, unitary, centrally enforceable patent to cover all the member states of the EU except Spain, Italy, and possibly Poland. The EU Community Patent is distinct from the current European Patent, which is granted under the

European Patent Convention and does not have unitary effect.

commutation The right to receive an immediate cash sum in return for accepting smaller annual payments at some time in the future. This is usually associated with a pension in which certain life-assurance policyholders can, on retirement, elect to take a cash sum from the pension fund immediately and a reduced annual pension.

Companies Acts Legislation governing the activities of companies. In the UK, the first Companies Act was passed in 1844. More recently, the Companies Act 1985 contained comprehensive legislation and the Companies Act 1989 incorporated various EC directives into UK law. A new Companies Act, which replaced almost all the previous legislation, received the Royal Assent in 2006 and was fully implemented by late 2009.

(⊕) SEE WEB LINKS
- FAQs relating to the 2006 Act provided by BERR
- Full text of the Companies Act 2006

Companies House (Companies Registration Office) The office of the *Registrar of Companies in Cardiff. It contains a register of all UK private and public companies, their directors, shareholders, and balance sheets. All this information has to be provided by companies by law and is available to any member of the public for a small charge.

(⊕) SEE WEB LINKS
- Companies House website: includes guidance on incorporating and winding up a company

company A corporate enterprise that has a legal identity separate from that of its members; it operates as one single unit, in the success of which all the members participate. An **incorporated company** is a legal person in its own right, able to own property and to sue and be sued in its own name. A company may have limited liability (a *limited company), so that the liability of the members for the company's debts is limited. An *unlimited company is one in which the liability of the members is not limited in any way.

A **registered company**, i.e. one registered under the Companies Acts, is much the most common type of company. A company may be registered either as a *public limited company or a private company. A public limited company must have a name ending with the initials 'plc' and share capital of at least £50,000, of which at least £12,500 must be paid up. A private company is any registered company that is not a public company. The shares of a private company may not be offered to the public for sale. Unregistered companies include *joint-stock companies, in which the members pool their stock, **chartered companies**, formed under Royal Charter, and **statutory companies**, formed by special Act of Parliament (e.g. the privatized utilities).

There are legal requirements placed on companies to make certain financial information regarding their activities public. Such information normally comprises a *profit and loss account and *balance sheet and is included with other financial and non-financial information in an annual report and accounts (see ANNUAL ACCOUNTS). The term company is often used more widely to refer to any association of persons, such as a *partnership, joined together for the purpose of conducting a business, although legally there are significant differences. See also ARTIFICIAL PERSON; CORPORATION.

company and individual brand strategy A branding approach that focuses on the company name and individual brand name.

company doctor 1. An executive or accountant with wide commercial experience, who specializes in analysing and rectifying the problems of ailing companies. He or she may either act as a consultant or may be given executive powers to implement the policies recommended. **2.** A medical doctor employed by a company, either full-time or part-time, to look after its staff, especially its senior executives, and to advise on medical and public-health matters.

company formation The procedure to be adopted for forming a company in the UK. The *subscribers to the company must send to the *Registrar of Companies a statement giving details of the registered address of the new company together with the names and addresses of the first directors and secretary, with their written consent to act in these capacities. They must also give a declaration (**declaration of compliance**) that the provisions of the Companies Acts have been complied with and provide the *memorandum of association and the *articles of association. Provided all these documents are in order the Registrar will issue a *certificate of incorporation and, in the case of a public company, a certificate enabling it to start business. In the case of a *public limited company additional information is required.

Measures designed to simplify the process of company formation were enacted in the Companies Act 2006 and came into force in late 2009.

company limited by guarantee An incorporated organization in which the liability of members is limited by the *memorandum of association to the amount they agree to pay in the event of a *liquidation. Such a company does not issue shares to its members. See LIMITED COMPANY.

company limited by shares An incorporated organization in which the liability of members is limited by the *memorandum of association to the amounts paid, or due to be paid, for shares. See LIMITED COMPANY.

company policy See CORPORATE POLICY.

Company Reporting Directive An EU directive (2006) designed to enhance public confidence in financial reporting within the EU, chiefly by increasing the transparency of financial statements and reports. Listed companies are also required to publish information regarding their *corporate governance. Together with the *Statutory Audit Directive (also 2006), this directive is often seen as the European equivalent to the US *Sarbanes–Oxley Act (Sox); as such, the two directives are often referred to jointly as **Eurosox**.

company seal A seal with the company's name engraved on it in legible characters, often used to authenticate share certificates and other important documents issued by the company or affixed to contracts. Until the 1980s, certain types of contract were not binding unless made under seal.

company secretary An *officer of a company. The appointment is usually made by the directors. The secretary's duties are mainly administrative, including preparation of the agenda for directors' meetings. However, the modern company secretary has an increasingly important role, which may include managing the office and entering into contracts on behalf of the company. Duties imposed by law include the submission of the annual return and the keeping of minutes. The secretary of a public company is required to have certain qualifications, as set out in the Companies Acts. Under the Companies Act 2006 a private company is no longer required to appoint a company secretary. *See* INSTITUTE OF CHARTERED SECRETARIES AND ADMINISTRATORS.

company voluntary arrangement
See VOLUNTARY ARRANGEMENT.

comparability The accounting principle that financial information for a company should be comparable with financial information for other similar companies. Comparability is one of the most important characteristics of useful financial information. The concept is defined in the Financial Reporting Standard Applicable in the UK and the Republic of Ireland It is also recognized in the International Accounting Standards Board's Conceptual Framework.

comparable worth The view that jobs should be paid equally when the work requires equal training, skills, and responsibilities, and that this principle should override differences in job titles, status, or accepted market rates. The doctrine is mainly associated with the feminist point that jobs traditionally considered 'male' tend to be better paid than those considered 'female', even where the behavioural demands of these jobs are very similar.

comparative credit analysis A method of company evaluation in which a firm is compared with other similar firms that have a desired credit rating in order to decide on appropriate *accounting ratio targets for the company being analysed. *See* RATIO ANALYSIS.

comparative parity method A method of setting a promotional budget in which the marketer tries to match the expenditure of competitors. *Compare* AFFORDABLE METHOD.

comparison advertising Advertising that compares one brand, either directly or indirectly, with other brands. This is quite often used in car advertising, by comparing the availability of a range of features on competitors' models in the same price bracket. *See also* KNOCKING COPY.

compensable job factor In *job evaluation, any of a range of factors that are held to determine the value of a job to the organization and hence the level of remuneration paid to the job holder. These factors usually include the skills, training, and experience required to perform the job adequately and its behavioural demands in terms of effort, responsibility, and decision making. *See* FACTOR-COMPARISON METHOD; POINT METHOD.

compensation for loss of office A payment made by a company to a director, senior executive, or consultant who is forced to retire before the expiry of a service contract, as a result of a merger, takeover, or any other reason. This form of **severance pay** (*see also* REDUNDANCY) may be additional to a retirement pension or in place of it; it must also be shown separately in the company's accounts. Because these payments can be very large, they are known as **golden handshakes**. *See also* GOLDEN PARACHUTE.

compensation fund A fund set up by the *London Stock Exchange, to which member firms contribute. It provides compensation to investors who suffer loss as a result of a member firm failing to meet its financial obligations.

competency 1. Any of the skills, talents, and traits required to be able to perform a particular task to a given standard. The assessment of competencies is central to various key aspects of human resources management: setting standards of performance that can be expected from employees and appraising them against such standards; assessing the training and development needs of individual employees; and identifying the skills, abilities, and characteristics needed when recruiting and selecting new employees. **2.** *See* CORE COMPETENCY.

competition Rivalry between suppliers providing goods or services for a market. The consensus of most economic theory is that competition is beneficial for the public, largely because it brings prices down. Governments usually pursue policies aimed at increasing competition in markets, although there may sometimes be a conflict between policies that increase competition and those that promote the national interest. *See* MONOPOLISTIC COMPETITION; PERFECT COMPETITION.

Competition and Markets Authority (CMA) A new body that combines the functions of the former **Competition Commission**, which handled competition law and its enforcement in the UK, and the former *Office of Fair Trading. It was established under the Enterprise and Regulatory Reform Act 2013 and began operating in April 2014.

(((()))) SEE WEB LINKS
• CMA area of the Gov.uk website

competitive advantage An advantage over competitors gained by offering consumers greater value, either by means of lower prices or by providing greater benefits and better servicing facilities that could justify higher prices. This advantage may be achieved in various ways, including increased product performance, superior distribution methods, or creative advertising. Most forms of competitive advantage cannot be sustained in the longer term because competitors will initiate or find substitutes for the innovations that created it. A firm is said to have **sustainable competitive advantage** (**SCA**) when it has resources that cannot readily be imitated or substituted (*see* CORE COMPETENCY; RESOURCE-BASED VIEW).

competitive devaluation The *devaluation of a country's currency to make its economy more competitive in international trade, rather than to correct an ongoing disequilibrium in the exchange rate.

competitive exclusion The diversion of online traffic away from competitors by companies holding exclusive partnership deals with popular websites on the Internet.

competitiveness 1. The ability of an economy to supply increasing *aggregate demand and maintain exports. A loss of competitiveness is usually signalled by increasing imports and falling exports. Competitiveness is often measured in a narrower sense by comparing relative inflation rates. For instance, if the sterling–dollar exchange rate remains constant, but prices rise faster in the UK than in the US, UK goods will become relatively more expensive, reflecting a loss in competitiveness; this in turn may lead to a falling demand for exports. **2.** The ability of an organization to compete successfully with its commercial rivals. *See* COMPETITIVE ADVANTAGE; COMPETITOR ANALYSIS.

competitive strategy A strategy that strongly positions a company against competitors and gives that company the strongest possible strategic advantage.

competitor analysis The gathering of data about a competitor's products and prices in order to identify actual or future sources of *competitive advantage. An understanding of a competitor's objectives, strategies, strengths, and weaknesses will help an organization to develop its own strategy. The analysis should reveal which competitors to attack and which to avoid. *See* BENCHMARKING; SWOT.

competitor-centred company A company mainly motivated by its competitors' actions and reactions. Its principal preoccupation is tracking its competitors' market shares and trying to find strategies to increase its own share compared to its competitors' shares.

competitor intelligence Information gathered by a company so that it is informed of what the competition is doing or is planning.

completion The conveyance of land in fulfilment of a contract of sale. The purchaser will have obtained an equitable interest in the land at the date of the *exchange of contracts but will not become the full legal owner until completion. If the seller refuses to complete, the court may grant a decree of *specific performance. The date on which completion must take place is stated in the contract of sale.

completion risk The inherent risk in *project financing schemes that a construction project will not be completed. *Compare* SUPPLY RISK; TECHNOLOGICAL RISK.

complex buying behaviour *Consumer buying behaviour in situations in which a considerable amount of technical information has to be assessed and significant differences exist between brands. For example, in buying a new personal computer the buyer has to consider the relative merits of 'Pentium 4 chip' and '1 gig of RAM'; to do so means evaluating a large amount of data.

compliance Mechanisms within a company whose purpose is to ensure that decision makers are kept aware of all legal and regulatory obligations applying to the company and that these are observed in full. In the UK some of the main factors to be considered will be the Companies Act 2006, the Equality Act 2010, the Data Protection Act 1998, recent EU directives, the *Corporate Governance Code, financial reporting standards, all relevant health and safety legislation, and any non-statutory codes of conduct applying to particular professions.

compliments slip (**comp slip**) A slip of paper with the words 'With the compliments of . . . ' printed on it, followed by the name and address of the firm sending it. It is enclosed with material sent to another person or firm to identify the sender, when a letter is not necessary.

component innovation An innovation that creates an improvement in the capabilities of the individual components in a system, e.g. more powerful processors in computers. *Compare* ARCHITECTURAL INNOVATION.

composition An agreement between a debtor and his or her creditors discharging the debts in exchange for a proportion of what is due. The agreement may be registered as a *deed of arrangement or form part of an individual *voluntary arrangement. *See also* SCHEME OF ARRANGEMENT.

compound annual return (CAR) The total return available from an investment or deposit in which the interest is used to augment the investment. The more frequently the interest is credited, the higher the CAR.

$$\text{CAR} = 1 + (\text{nominal rate}/\text{number of times interest paid per annum})$$

The CAR is usually quoted on a gross basis. The return, taking into account the deduction of tax at the basic rate on the interest, is known as the **compound net annual rate** (**CNAR**).

compound interest *See* INTEREST.

compound net annual rate (CNAR) *See* COMPOUND ANNUAL RETURN.

comprehensive income statement

See STATEMENT OF COMPREHENSIVE INCOME.

comprehensive income tax An

income tax for which the tax base consists not only of income but also of *capital gains as well as other accretions of wealth, such as legacies. Although this is not a tax currently levied in the UK, tax theorists find it attractive since clear distinctions between income, capital gains, etc., are sometimes difficult to sustain. *See also* SINGLE-TAX SYSTEM.

compressed working week A work

pattern that involves the reallocation of work time into fewer and longer blocks during the week. The total length of work time remains unchanged, but each shift or period of work is lengthened. Typically, this means that the same basic hours are worked in four and a half days a week or nine days out of ten in a fortnight.

compression The process of reducing

the size of a digital file to enable it to occupy less storage space or to transmit more rapidly.

comptroller The title of the financial

director in some companies or chief financial officer of a group of companies. The title is more widely used in the USA than in the UK. *See also* CONTROLLER.

Comptroller of the Currency A US

Treasury Department official, appointed by the president, who is responsible for the regulation of the national banking system.

compulsory liquidation (compulsory

winding-up) The *liquidation of a company by a court. A petition must be presented both at the court and the registered office of the company. Those by whom it may be presented include: the company, the directors, a creditor, an official receiver, and the Secretary of State for Business, Innovation and Skills. The grounds on which a company may be wound up by the court include: a special resolution of the company that it be wound up by the court;

that the company is unable to pay its debts; that the number of members is reduced below two; or that the court is of the opinion that it would be just and equitable for the company to be wound up. The court may appoint a *provisional liquidator after the winding-up petition has been presented; it may also appoint a *special manager to manage the company's property. On the grant of the order for winding-up, the official receiver becomes the *liquidator and continues in office until some other person is appointed, either by the creditors or the members. *Compare* CREDITORS' VOLUNTARY LIQUIDATION; MEMBERS' VOLUNTARY LIQUIDATION.

compulsory purchase The compulsory

acquisition of land by the state when it is required for some purpose under the Town and Country Planning legislation. Compensation is paid on the basis of market value. *Compare* REQUISITIONING.

compulsory purchase annuity An

annuity that must be purchased with the fund built up from certain types of pension arrangements. When retirement age is reached, a person who has been paying premiums into this type of pension fund is obliged to use the fund to purchase an annuity to provide an income for the rest of his or her life. The fund may not be used in any other way (except for a small portion, which may be taken in cash).

Compumailer A machine that turns

continuous stationery into personalized letters and envelopes, enclosing one inside the other. It also seals the envelopes ready for mailing. Compumailers are frequently used by direct mailing organizations.

computer An electronic tool that

manipulates information in accordance with a predefined sequence of instructions. Computers have a simple 'brain', called the **central processing unit (CPU)**, that can do arithmetic and take decisions based on the results, and a **memory**, which stores the instructions and information. Strictly speaking, all other parts of a computer system are peripheral devices, but in practice all computers have at least: an input device, such as a keyboard, by means of which the information is fed in; an output device, such as a screen or printer, which displays the results of their work; and extra memory in the form of backing store (e.g. CDs or USB flash drives). Inside a computer, both information and instructions are represented by binary numbers (*see* BINARY NOTATION) and all processing is done using these numbers. A computer needs to be given detailed instructions, called a program, before it can perform even the simplest task. The art of composing these instructions is **computer programming**. The general term for the programs that a computer needs in order to operate is *software, while the computer and devices attached to it are called *hardware.

Traditionally, computers have been classified into three types according to size. The largest is the *mainframe, used typically for large-scale corporate data processing; and the smallest is the *personal computer, designed for a single user. Between these extremes is the *minicomputer. These distinctions have become blurred, as minicomputers and personal computers become more powerful. Moreover, mainframe and minicomputers have been replaced in many situations by groups of personal computers linked to form *local area networks.

computer-aided design (CAD) The use of computers to produce designs and to manipulate them rapidly. In many cases it can replace the need to produce expensive prototypes. In conjunction with live data, CAD can also be used for testing complex projects; for example, nuclear tests in the Pacific provided data enabling computer simulations to test future weapons. In conjunction with *virtual reality, CAD can allow potential customers to view new products at an early stage, before significant amounts of capital have been expended on plant, etc. CAD is also linked to *material requirements planning systems permitting rapid costing of new models to be made, together with the appropriate *bills of materials.

computer-aided manufacturing (CAM) The use of computers to control industrial processes, such as brewing, chemical manufacture, oil refining, and steel making. They are also used to control automatic machines that can be programmed to carry out different tasks, especially in the car-manufacturing industry. CAM is often used with *computer-integrated manufacturing as well as *computer-aided design.

computer-aided personal interview (CAPI) A method of interviewing in which researchers use laptop computers to conduct personal interviews and transmit the resulting data over the Internet. This dramatically reduces the time of the research process. It also allows on-screen presentation of stimuli to the respondent, reduces respondent fatigue, helps generate good-quality data, and allows fast collation of data from different geographical locations.

computer-aided self-interview (CASI) A method of interviewing in which the respondent interacts directly with the computer instead of through the interviewer. In theory, it is similar to a self-completion questionnaire and offers the same advantages (privacy and reduced interviewer bias). It is also called a **computerized self-administered questionnaire** (**CSAQ**).

computer-assisted audit techniques (CAATs) Techniques developed by auditors for performing audit tests on computer systems and the data they hold. There are two main categories of technique. (1) The auditor creates a set of input data to be processed by the computer programs; the results are then checked against the expected results. (2) Computer *audit software is used by the auditor to select data from a number of files. Various operations are then performed on the data and the results are transferred to a special audit file to be printed out in a required format.

computer-assisted panel research (CAPAR) A method of conducting panel research remotely. Panel members transmit details of specific purchases using bar-code scanners over the telephone to a host computer in which the information is accumulated. Television audience measurement is also conducted by this method.

computer-assisted self-explication (CASE) An online Internet system that asks visitors structured questions about their preferences and uses this information to produce rankings and recommendations on products and services for both consumers and producers.

computer-assisted telephone interviewing (CATI) A system in which a telephone interviewer conducts a sales or marketing interview, using a computer and a computerized questionnaire. This system reduces the number of errors as the interviewer keys in the respondent's answers as they are given and the computer follows a complex questionnaire routing efficiently, enabling the required statistics to be extracted automatically.

computer-assisted trading (CAT) See AUTOMATED SCREEN TRADING; HIGH-FREQUENCY TRADING.

computer-based training (CBT) The use of computers in training. Exercises are shown on the screen and participants have to key in answers to questions, which are assessed by the computer.

computer-integrated manufacturing system (CIMS) A system bringing together *computer-aided design, *computer-aided manufacturing, *flexible manufacturing systems, and outputs from integrated information processing systems. These systems are dependent on the adoption of common operating systems and transparent communications networks. Their success often depends on cultural and political issues rather than technical capabilities, as they often cut across traditional roles and power structures.

computer output microfilm (COM) A system that produces computer output on microfilm or microfiche. The information is recorded on film either by a camera that

photographs a miniature screen displaying the computer output, or by a laser beam recorder, which writes directly onto the film. COM is used where there is a large volume of output, particularly where immediate reference is not required.

concealed unemployment See HIDDEN UNEMPLOYMENT.

concentrated segmentation (niche marketing) A comparatively small segment of a market that has been identified, usually by a small company, in which to concentrate their efforts. For example, a company might decide to offer a service converting old cine films to DVD; as long as this activity does not threaten the profitability of the manufacturers of DVDs or anyone still selling cine films, it can establish a profitable niche in the market.

concentration The degree to which an industry is dominated by a small group of firms and thus closed to competitive pressure. According to a standard *industry structure analysis, this will be the major factor determining the nature of the market and the strategies necessary for succeeding within it. See also FOUR-FIRM CONCENTRATION RATIO; HERFINDAHL INDEX; STRUCTURE–CONDUCT–PERFORMANCE MODEL.

concept test A technique used in *marketing research to assess the reactions of consumers to a new product or a proposed change to an existing product (see NEW PRODUCT DEVELOPMENT). Before an organization invests in production facilities for a new product it writes a **concept statement** describing the proposed product and commissions a market researcher to interview a small number of potential consumers either in *group discussion or *depth interview. Respondents are shown the concept statement and their reactions are explored in detail. The results of these interviews help the organization to understand what it should do with the proposed product if it is to be successful.

concert-party agreement An agreement between apparently unconnected people to act together to manipulate the share price of a company or to influence its decision making. Under the Companies Act the shares of the parties to such an agreement should be treated as if they were owned by one person, from the point of view of disclosing interests in a company's shareholding.

conciliation *See* ADVISORY CONCILIATION AND ARBITRATION SERVICE; MEDIATION.

concurrent control (real-time control) An approach to controlling the performance of an operating system that attempts to bring together the monitoring of performance, comparison with parameters, and taking action stages. Thus in *total quality management members of staff take responsibility for the quality of every stage of a process as they are performing it, in contrast to a *feedback control system, in which the quality would not be inspected until the process had been completed. In some specialist environments the use of electronic data-capture has enabled the feedback cycle to become very short. Processes can be adjusted within milliseconds, thus minimizing any cost penalties. *See also* FEEDFORWARD CONTROL.

concurrent engineering (interactive engineering; simultaneous engineering) An approach to the design and introduction of new products that aims to shorten lead times and reduce costs by running development stages in parallel. In traditional systems, each stage in development is discrete, i.e. production planning can only begin when the product design has been finalized. In concurrent engineering, production planning will start as soon as there is a reasonable level of confidence in the likely outcome of the preceding phase. In this way, not only is each stage able to start earlier but it is also able to provide feedback that helps to optimize the preceding stage. This approach has been facilitated by the development of *computer-integrated manufacturing systems. Full exploitation may require application of *business process re-engineering techniques.

condition 1. A major term of a contract that, if unfulfilled, constitutes a fundamental *breach of contract and may invalidate it. *Compare* WARRANTY. **2.** A provision that does not form part of a contract but either suspends the contract until a specified event has happened (**condition precedent**) or brings it to an end in specified circumstances (**condition subsequent**). An example of a condition precedent is an agreement to buy a particular car if it passes its MOT test; an example of a condition subsequent is an agreement that entitles the purchaser of goods to return them if they prove unsatisfactory.

conditional bid *See* TAKEOVER BID.

conditionality The terms under which the *International Monetary Fund (IMF) provides balance-of-payments support to member states. The principle is that support will only be given on the condition that it is accompanied by steps to solve the underlying problem. Programmes of economic reform are agreed with the member; these emphasize the attainment of a sustainable balance-of-payments position and boosting the supply side of the economy. Lending by commercial banks is frequently linked to IMF conditionality.

conditional sale agreement A contract of sale under which the price is payable by instalments and ownership does not pass to the buyer (who is in possession of the goods) until specified conditions relating to the payment have been fulfilled. The seller retains ownership of the goods as security until being paid in full.

Confederation of British Industry (CBI) An organization that lobbies for British business on matters of concern, chiefly to the UK government but also to the European Union and other international bodies. Its objective is to help create and sustain the conditions in which British business can compete and prosper. The CBI was formed from a merger of several other employers' organizations in 1965 and now represents some 240,000 UK companies. Its ruling body is the CBI Council, which meets on a quarterly basis in

London. There are also 12 regional councils.

conference lines *See* SHIPPING CONFERENCE.

conferencing *See* AUDIOCONFERENCING; VIDEOCONFERENCING.

confidence indicators *See* PERFORMANCE MEASUREMENT.

confidentiality clause A clause in a contract of employment that details certain types of information the employee will acquire on joining the firm that may not be passed on to anyone outside the firm.

confirmation note A document confirming the main facts and figures of a deal between two parties, usually a deal that has been agreed verbally or by telephone.

confirmed letter of credit *See* LETTER OF CREDIT.

confirming house An organization that purchases goods from local exporters on behalf of overseas buyers. It may act as a principal or an agent, invariably pays for the goods in the exporters' own currency, and purchases on a contract that is enforceable in the exporters' own country. The overseas buyer, who usually pays the confirming house a commission or its equivalent, regards the confirming house as a local buying agent, who will negotiate the best prices on its behalf, arrange for the shipment and insurance of the goods, and provide information regarding the goods being sold and the status of the various exporters.

conflict management The control of conflict within an organization. There are three main philosophies of conflict management:

• **traditionalists** hold that all conflict is bad and potentially destructive for an organization;

• **behaviourists** see conflict as inevitable in an organization and attempt to harness it in a positive way;

• **interactionists** see conflict as essential to the survival of an organization and as something that should be encouraged.

See also CHANGE MANAGEMENT; DIVERSITY MANAGEMENT.

conflict of interests A situation that can arise if a person (or firm) acts in two or more separate capacities and the objectives in these capacities are not identical. The conflict may be between self-interest and the interest of a company for which a person works or it could arise when a person is a director of two companies, which find themselves competing. The proper course of action in the case of a conflict of interests is for the person concerned to declare any interests, to make known the way in which they conflict, and to abstain from voting or sharing in the decision-making procedure involving these interests. *See also* GOAL DIVERGENCE

confused positioning A *positioning error that leaves consumers with a confused image of a company, its products, or brands.

conglomerate A diverse group of companies, usually managed by a *holding company. There is usually little integration and few transactions between each of the subsidiaries, often because their activities and products are unrelated. This form of business structure is generally disliked by investors because conglomerates may lack a clear strategic focus and the overall value of the group can undervalue the combined individual values of the operating subsidiaries.

conjoint analysis A statistical method that attempts to determine the relative importance consumers attach to salient *attributes and the utilities they attach to the levels of attributes. The technique is based on the premise that products and services are made up of features or attributes that vary according to the identified preferences of consumers. The more dominant the interest in a particular attribute of a product, the higher will be the utility value given to it by actual or potential purchasers. It is widely used in marketing for various purposes, including concept identification of new products, competitive analysis, market segmentation, pricing, advertising, and distribution. *See also* UTILITY THEORY.

connected person In the context of the Companies Act (disclosure requirements for directors and connected persons), a director's spouse, child, or stepchild (under 18 years of age), a body corporate with which a director is associated, a trustee for a trust that benefits a director or connected person, or a partner of a director.

consequential-loss policy *See* BUSINESS-INTERRUPTION POLICY.

conservatism A prudent and not over-optimistic view of the state of affairs of a company or other organization. Because it is regarded as imprudent to distribute to shareholders profits that may not materialize, it is a general principle of accounting not to anticipate profits before they are realized but to anticipate losses as soon as they become foreseeable. *See also* PRUDENCE CONCEPT.

consideration 1. A tangible benefit that is exchanged as part of a *contract. It is essential if a contract (other than a deed) is to be valid. It usually consists of a promise to do or not to do something or to pay a sum of money. **2.** The money value of a contract for the purchase or sale of securities on the *London Stock Exchange, before commissions, charges, stamp duty, and any other expenses have been deducted.

consignee 1. Any person or organization to whom goods are sent. **2.** An agent who sells goods, usually in a foreign country, on *consignment on behalf of a principal (consignor).

consignment 1. A shipment or delivery of goods sent at one time. **2.** Goods sent **on consignment** by a principal (consignor) to an agent (consignee), usually in a foreign

country, for sale either at an agreed price or at the best market price. The agent, who usually works for a commission, does not normally pay for the goods until they are sold and does not own them, although usually having possession of them. The final settlement, often called a **consignment account**, details the cost of the goods, the expenses incurred, the agent's commission, and the proceeds of the sale.

consignment note A document accompanying a consignment of goods in transit. It is signed by the *consignee on delivery and acts as evidence that the goods have been received. It gives the names and addresses of both consignor and consignee, details the goods, usually gives their gross weight, and states who has responsibility for insuring them while in transit. It is not a negotiable document (*compare* BILL OF LADING) and in some circumstances is called a **way bill**.

consignment stock Stock held by one party (the dealer) but legally owned by another; the dealer has the right to sell the stock or to return it unsold to its legal owner. Because it can be difficult to distinguish between the commercial realities of the transaction and the legal agreement, consignment stock has sometimes been used as a means of *creative accounting.

consignor 1. Any person or organization that sends goods to a *consignee. **2.** A principal who sells goods on *consignment through an agent (consignee), usually in a foreign country.

consistency concept One of four fundamental *accounting concepts identified in *Statement of Standard Accounting Practice (SSAP) 2, Disclosure of Accounting Policies; it was also recognized in the UK Companies Act 1985 and the EU's *Fourth Company Law Directive. The concept requires consistency of treatment of like items within each accounting period and from one period to the next; it also requires that *accounting policies are consistently applied. Under current guidance the consistency concept is no longer recognized as a fundamental principle. Rather, an entity is required to implement those policies that are judged most appropriate to its circumstances for the purpose of giving a *true and fair view. *Comparability is therefore held to be a more important characteristic of financial statements than consistency.

consolidated accounts *See* CONSOLI-DATED FINANCIAL STATEMENTS.

consolidated annuities *See* CONSOLS.

consolidated balance sheet The *balance sheet of a group providing the financial information contained in the individual financial statements of the parent company of the group and its subsidiary undertakings, combined subject to any necessary *consolidation adjustments. It must give a *true and fair view of the state of affairs of a group as at the end of the financial year, and its form and content should comply with the Companies Act. If the balance sheet formats require the disclosure of the balances attributable to group undertakings (creditors, debtors, investments), the information should be analysed to show the amounts attributable to parent and fellow subsidiary undertakings of the parent company, and amounts attributable to unconsolidated subsidiaries.

consolidated financial statements (consolidated accounts; group accounts; group financial statements) The financial statements of a group of companies obtained by *consolidation. These are required by the Companies Act and the Financial Reporting Standard Applicable in the UK and Republic of Ireland. The information contained in the individual financial statements of a group of undertakings is combined into consolidated financial statements, subject to any *consolidation adjustments. The consolidated accounts must give a *true and fair view of the profit or loss for the period and the state of affairs as at the last day of the period of the undertakings included in the consolidation. Subsidiary undertakings within the group may be excluded from consolidation and the parent company itself may be exempt from preparing consolidated accounts.

UK listed companies are required to follow *International Accounting Standard 27, Consolidated and Separate Financial Statements, and *International Financial Reporting Standard 3, Business Combinations.

Consolidated Fund The Exchequer account, held at the Bank of England and controlled by the Treasury, into which taxes are paid and from which government expenditure is made. It was formed in 1787 by the consolidation of several government funds.

consolidated goodwill The difference between the *fair value of the consideration given by an acquiring company when buying a business and the aggregate of the fair values of the separable net assets acquired. *Goodwill is generally a positive amount. According to the Financial Reporting Standard Applicable in the UK and Republic of Ireland (Section 19), goodwill should be capitalized on the *balance sheet and *amortized to the *profit and loss account over the period of its useful economic life; if this cannot be reliably estimated, it must be assumed to be no more than five years. The international accounting standards relevant to the treatment of consolidated goodwill are *International Financial Reporting Standard 3, Business Combinations, *International Accounting Standard (IAS) 36, Impairment of Assets, and IAS 38, Intangible Assets.

consolidated profit and loss account A combination of the individual *profit and loss accounts of the members of a *group of organizations, subject to any consolidation adjustments. The consolidated profit and loss account must give a *true and fair view of the profit and loss of the undertakings included in the consolidation. A parent company may be exempted, under the Companies Act, from publishing its own profit and loss account if it prepares group accounts. The individual profit and loss account must be approved by the directors, but may be omitted from the company's annual accounts. In such a case, the company must disclose its profit or loss for the financial year and also state in its notes that it has taken advantage of this exemption.

consolidation 1. An increase in the *nominal price of a company's shares, by combining a specified number of lower-price shares into one higher-priced share. In most cases this can be done by an ordinary resolution at a general meeting of the company. **2.** The inclusion of one or more subsidiary companies in a parent company's financial statements. *See* CONSOLIDATED FINANCIAL STATEMENTS.

Consols Government securities that pay interest but have no redemption date. The present bonds, called **consolidated annuities** or **consolidated stock**, are the result of merging several loans at various different times going back to the 18th century. Their original interest rate was 3% on the nominal price of £100; some now pay 2½% and therefore stand at a price that makes their annual *yield comparable to long-dated *gilt-edged securities, e.g. at £31 they yield about 8%.

consortium A combination of two or more businesses formed on a temporary basis, often to quote for and carry out a single large project. The purpose of forming a consortium may be to eliminate competition between the members or to pool skills, not all of which may be available to the individual companies. Consortia often involve the setting up of a *special purpose vehicle or a *joint venture. *See also* CONSORTIUM RELIEF.

consortium relief A modified form of *group relief applying to consortia. A consortium is held to exist if 20 or fewer companies each own at least 5% of the ordinary share capital of the consortium company and together the consortium members hold at least 75% of the ordinary shares of the consortium company. Losses can be surrendered between the consortium members and the consortium company. The loss that can be surrendered is restricted to the proportion of the claimant's profits that corresponds with the surrendering company's interest in the consortium. From 1 April 2000 members of a consortium no longer have to be resident in the UK to qualify for relief.

constant-dollar plan The US name for *pound cost averaging, i.e. the investment of a specified sum of money at regular intervals in the acquisition of assets. It is sometimes called **dollar-cost averaging**.

constant sum scales Scales used in marketing research asking the respondent to divide (usually) 100 points between two or more attributes based on their importance to the respondent. For example, the respondent may be asked to allocate points to the attributes speed, comfort, fuel consumption, and reliability by a car manufacturer. If the average scores of all respondents are: speed 10, comfort 10, fuel consumption 30, and reliability 50, the manufacturer will have useful information to assist the engineering and design departments.

constraint A circumstance that prevents an organization achieving higher levels of performance. A constraint results from the impact of a limiting factor (or principal budget factor), which must be eliminated or reduced before the constraint is removed. For example, at various times a shortage of skilled labour, materials, production capacity, or sales volume may constitute a limiting factor. Constraints are also brought into the statement of problems in *linear programming. *See* THEORY OF CONSTRAINTS.

constructive dismissal A situation that arises when an employer's behaviour towards an employee is so intolerable that the employee is left with no option but resignation. In these circumstances the employee can still claim compensation for *wrongful dismissal.

constructive total loss A loss in which the item insured is not totally destroyed but is so severely damaged that it is not financially worth repairing. The Marine Insurance Act 1906 defines a constructive total loss as one in which 'the subject matter insured is reasonably abandoned on account of its actual total loss appearing to be unavoidable, or because it could not be preserved from actual total loss without an expenditure which would exceed its value when the expenditure had been incurred.'

consular invoice An export invoice that has been certified in the exporting country by the consul of the importing country. This form of invoice is required by the customs of certain countries (especially South American countries) to enable them to charge the correct import duties. A *certificate of origin may also be required. The fee charged by the consul for this or any other commercial service is called the **consulage**.

Consultative Committee of Accountancy Bodies (CCAB) A committee set up in 1970 by the six main accountancy bodies in the UK and Ireland to foster closer cooperation. It plays an active part in many financial accounting and reporting issues. The Chartered Institute of Management Accountants withdrew from the CCAB in 2011.

consumable materials Materials that are used in a production process although, unlike *direct materials, they do not form part of the *direct cost of sales. Examples are cooling fluid for production machinery, lubricating oil, and sanding discs. In circumstances in which direct materials of small value are used, such as cotton or nylon thread or nails and screws, they are sometimes treated in the same way as consumable materials.

consumer A private individual acting otherwise than in the course of a business. Consumers are often given special legal protection when entering into contracts, for example by having a right to avoid certain unfair terms or to cancel the contract (*see* CONSUMER PROTECTION; DISTANCE SELLING).

consumer advertising The *advertising of goods or services specifically aimed at the potential end-user, rather than at an intermediary in the selling chain. *Compare* TRADE ADVERTISING.

consumer buying behaviour The buying behaviour of individuals and households who buy goods and services for personal consumption. A number of different people, playing different roles, have been identified in the decision to make a specific purchase:

- **initiator**, the person who first suggests or thinks of the idea of buying a particular product or service;
- **influencer**, a person whose views or advice influences the buying decision;
- **decider**, the person who ultimately makes the decision to buy (or any part of it); this decision includes whether to buy, what to buy, how to buy, and where to buy;
- **buyer**, the person who makes the actual purchase;
- **user**, the person who uses the product or service.

It is usual to regard a consumer's decision to make a specific purchase as having five stages:

problem recognition

↓

information search

↓

evaluation of alternatives

↓

choice

↓

post purchase experience

This model emphasizes that the decision process is sequential and combines both mental and physical activities. In broad terms, the first four of these stages constitute the decision phase. This is followed by the actual purchase, and the subsequent experience of using the newly acquired product. If this experience is positive it can act as a reinforcement to make further similar purchases. A negative experience will encourage a change to another product or supplier.

consumer credit Short-term loans to the public for the purchase of goods. The most common forms of consumer credit are credit accounts at retail outlets, personal loans from banks and finance houses, *hire purchase, and *credit cards. Since the *Consumer Credit Act 1974, the borrower has been given greater protection, particularly with regard to regulations establishing the true rate of interest being charged when loans are made (*see* ANNUAL PERCENTAGE RATE). The Act also made it necessary for anyone giving credit in a business (with minor exceptions) to obtain a licence. The Consumer Credit Act 2006 introduced further safeguards and extended the remit of the *Financial Ombudsman Service to include consumer credit agreements. *See* CONSUMER-CREDIT REGISTER.

Consumer Credit Act 1974 A UK Act of Parliament aimed at protecting the borrower in credit agreements, loans, and mortgages. The Act requires full written details of the true interest rate (i.e. *annual percentage rate) to be quoted; a *cooling-off period to be given, during which borrowers may change their minds and cancel agreements; and all agreements to be in writing. The Act does not cover overdrafts. The **Consumer Credit Act 2006** updates and extends the scope of the 1974 Act.

Consumer Credit Protection Act 1968 The US equivalent of the UK *Consumer Credit Act 1974. The Act is enforced by the Federal Reserve Bank.

consumer-credit register The register kept by the *Office of Fair Trading, as required by the Consumer Credit Acts 1974 and 2006, relating to the licensing or carrying on of consumer-credit businesses or consumer-hire businesses. The register contains particulars of undetermined applications, licences that are in force or have at any time been suspended or revoked, and decisions under the Act and any appeal from them. The public is entitled to inspect the register, which can now be viewed online.

consumer goods Goods that are purchased by members of the public. **Consumer durables** are consumer goods, such as cars, refrigerators, and television

sets, whose useful life extends over a relatively long period. The purchase of a consumer durable falls between *consumption and *investment. **Consumer non-durables** or **disposables** are goods that are used up within a short time after purchase. They include food, drink, newspapers, etc.

consumer groups The groups to which consumers belong and which influence their behaviour. These groups can be small primary groups, such as the family or a work group, or they can be larger secondary groups, such as professional associations or trade unions. **Reference groups** serve as direct (face-to-face) or indirect points of reference, providing comparisons that help to form a person's attitudes or behaviour. Within these groups are **aspirational groups**, to which people would like to belong; quite often, the aspiring person assumes the values, attitudes, and even the dress of the group. **Opinion leaders** are important within reference groups, because their special skills, knowledge, or personality enables them to influence others.

consumer instalment loan The US name for *hire purchase.

consumerism An organized movement of citizens and government agencies to improve the rights and power of buyers in relation to sellers.

consumer market The market for *consumer goods, as opposed to the industrial market, in which buyers of goods are not the end users.

consumer-oriented marketing A principle of enlightened marketing holding that a company should view and organize its marketing activities from the point of view of the consumers of its products and services.

consumer preference The way in which consumers in a free market choose to divide their total expenditure in purchasing goods and services. Using a limited number of assumptions, an individual's preferences can be built up into a utility function (*see* CONSUMER THEORY). Applying *price theory to the utility functions of individuals enables a model to be constructed of the behaviour of markets in an economy.

Consumer Price Index (CPI) 1. In the UK, the usual name for the **Harmonized Index of Consumer Prices** (**HICP**), a measure of price level introduced in 1997 to enable comparisons within the EU. In the UK government inflation targets are now based on the CPI rather than the *Retail Price Index. **2.** In the USA, the measure of price level calculated monthly by the Bureau of Labor Statistics. It is commonly known as the cost-of-living index and gives the cost of specific consumer items compared to the base year of 1967. Since 2000 the Federal Reserve Board has preferred to base its inflation forecasts on the Personal Consumption Expenditure Price Index (PCEPI), which is regarded as a more sophisticated measure.

(⊕) SEE WEB LINKS

• HICP data from the Office for National Statistics

consumer profile A profile of a typical consumer of a product, in terms of age, sex, social class, and other characteristics. *See also* CONSUMER GROUPS.

consumer promotion A sales promotion designed to stimulate consumer purchasing. It may offer samples, coupons, rebates, price reductions, premiums, patronage rewards, displays, contests, sweepstakes, etc.

consumer protection The protection, especially by legal means, of consumers. It is the policy of current UK legislation to protect consumers against unfair contract terms. In particular they are protected by the Unfair Contract Terms Act 1977 and the Sale of Goods Act 1979 against terms that attempt to restrict the seller's implied undertakings that he or she has a right to sell the goods, that the goods conform with either description or sample (*see* TRADE DESCRIPTION), and that they are of merchantable quality and fit for their particular purpose. Consumers are further protected

in these respects by the Unfair Terms in Consumer Contracts Regulations 1999. There is also provision for the banning of unfair consumer trade practices in the Fair Trading Act 1973, which established the *Office of Fair Trading. Consumers (including individual businesspeople) are protected when obtaining credit by the Consumer Credit Acts 1974 and 2006 (*see also* CONSUMER-CREDIT REGISTER). There is provision for the imposition of standards relating to the safety of goods under the Consumer Protection Act 1987, which makes the producer of a product liable for any damage it causes (*see* PRODUCT LIABILITY), and the General Product Safety Regulations 1994. The Consumer Protection from Unfair Trading Regulations (2008) and Business Protection from Misleading Marketing Regulations (2008) restrict unfair, aggressive, and misleading marketing practices (including *viral marketing).

consumer relationship-building promotion A sales promotion that promotes a product's *positioning and includes a selling message.

consumer research Any form of *marketing research undertaken among the final consumers of a product or service. For example, a manufacturer supplying man-made fibres to a shirt factory might undertake consumer research, interviewing purchasers of shirts, in order to establish the merits, or otherwise, of the fibres. *Compare* INDUSTRIAL MARKETING RESEARCH.

Consumers' Association (CA) A UK charitable organization formed in 1957 to provide independent and technically based guidance on the goods and services available to the public. The Consumers' Association tests and investigates products and services and publishes comparative reports on performance, quality, and value in its monthly magazine *Which?*. It also publishes various books, including *Working for Yourself* and *Save and Invest*. The US equivalent is the **Consumer Advisory Council**.

- *Which*? website: provides guidance on a wide range of consumer issues

consumers' expenditure *See* CONSUMPTION.

consumer theory The theory explaining the choices made by individuals and households in terms of the concept of utility. Consumers are assumed to be able to order their preferences (*see* CONSUMER PREFERENCE) in such a way that they can choose a basket of goods that maximize their utility, subject to the constraint that their income is limited. The application of *price theory and demand theory to this problem forms the basis of *microeconomics (together with the theory of the firm) and also of *macroeconomics.

consumption 1. The using up of *consumer goods and services for the satisfaction of the present needs of individuals, organizations, and governments. **2.** The amount of money spent by the whole of an economy on consumer goods and services. Economists contrast this amount of money (sometimes called **consumers' expenditure**) with the amount spent on *investment, which provides for future consumption. In most economies about 80% of national income is spent on consumption, the balance going to investment. However, the distinction between consumption and investment is not always clear as some goods, such as consumer durables, provide for both present and future consumption.

containerization The use of large rectangular containers for the shipment of goods. Goods are packed into the containers at the factory or loading depot and transported by road in these containers to the port of shipment, where they are loaded direct onto the ship without unpacking. At the port of destination they can again be transported by road to the final user. It is usual for such shipments to be covered by a **container bill of lading (combined-transport bill of lading)**.

contango 1. (forwardation) The situation in which (or the extent to which) the price for future delivery is greater than the spot price. *Compare* BACKWARDATION. **2.** The former practice of carrying the purchase of stocks and shares over from one *account day on the London Stock Exchange to the next.

contempt of court An act that hinders the course of justice or that constitutes disrespect to the lawful authority of the court. Contempt may be divided into acts committed in court (for instance, unseemly behaviour or refusing to answer a question as a witness) and acts committed out of court (such as intimidating a witness or refusing to obey a court order). Contempt of court is punishable by fine or imprisonment or both.

content In website design, the text, graphical information, and design features that constitute a web page. Good content is the key to attracting customers to a website and retaining their interest or achieving repeat visits.

content analysis A technique used to study written material (often advertising copy) to reduce it to meaningful units, using carefully applied rules. It provides an objective and systematic description of a communication's content.

contingencies Potential gains and losses known to exist at the balance-sheet date although the actual outcomes will only be known after one or more events have occurred (or not occurred). Depending on the nature of a particular contingency, it may be appropriate to include it in the financial statements or to show it as a *note to the accounts; Section 21 of the Financial Reporting Standard Applicable in the UK and Republic of Ireland provides guidance on the appropriate accounting treatment. Generally, accountants apply the *prudence concept and will disclose *contingent liabilities much more readily than *contingent assets.

contingency insurance An insurance policy covering financial losses occurring as a result of a specified event happening. The risks covered by policies of this kind are various and often unusual, such as a missing documents indemnity, the birth of twins, or *pluvial insurance.

contingency plan A plan that is formulated to cope with some event or circumstances that may occur in the future. For example, the contingency may be an increase in sales, in which case the plan would include means of increasing production very quickly.

contingency theories of leadership In *industrial and organizational psychology, various models stating that the performance of a leader will depend not only on his or her qualities or methods but also on certain key aspects of the work situation. The leader will be most effective when his or her *leadership style is best suited to the characteristics of the group (e.g. level of experience) and the nature of the group task (e.g. whether clearly structured or not). One of the earliest and most influential of such theories, that of Fred Fiedler, proposes that *task-motivated leaders will be most successful in very favourable or very unfavourable situations and that *relationship-motivated leaders will be most successful when the situation is not so extreme. Some other models suggest that it may be easier for the leader to alter the work situation to suit his or her style than vice versa. *See* LEADERSHIP THEORIES. *See also* SITUATIONAL LEADERSHIP THEORY; TANNENBAUM–SCHMIDT CONTINUUM; VROOM–YETTON–JAGO MODEL.

contingency theory of management accounting The theory that there is no single *management accounting system acceptable to all organizations or any system that is satisfactory in all circumstances in a single organization. Consequently, accounting systems are contingent upon the circumstances that prevail at any time; they must be capable of development in order to take into consideration such factors as changes in the environment, competition, organizational structures, and technology.

contingent agreement *See* EARN-OUT AGREEMENT.

contingent annuity (reversionary annuity) An annuity in which the payment is conditional on a specified event happening. The most common form is an annuity purchased jointly by a husband and wife that begins payment after the death of one of the parties (*see* JOINT-LIFE AND LAST-SURVIVOR ANNUITIES).

contingent asset (contingent gain) A possible asset that arises from past events and whose existence will be confirmed only by the occurrence of one or more uncertain future events, which are not wholly in the control of the accounting entity. For example, if a company is making a substantial legal claim against another organization, the company has a contingent asset (depending upon the successful outcome of the claim). Under the Financial Reporting Standard Applicable in the UK and Republic of Ireland, an entity should not recognize a contingent asset unless the appropriate economic events are virtually certain (in which case the asset is not really a contingent asset). *Compare* CONTINGENT LIABILITY.

contingent consideration A payment that is contingent on a particular factor or factors occurring. The concept often used in relation to *earn-out agreements.

contingent interest *See* VESTED INTEREST.

contingent liability (contingent loss) **1.** A possible obligation that arises from past events, whose existence will be confirmed only by the occurrence of one or more uncertain future events not wholly within an entity's control. For example, if there is a substantial legal claim for damages against a company, there is a contingent liability (depending on the outcome of the claim). **2.** A present obligation that arises from past events in which either the amount of the obligation cannot be measured reliably or it is not probable that a transfer of economic benefits will be required to settle the obligation. Generally, an entity should disclose a contingent liability but not recognize it as a liability. *Compare* CONTINGENT ASSET. *See also* CONTINGENT LOSS.

contingent reinforcement In management and leadership, the use of rewards and penalties to motivate followers and achieve compliance with organizational goals and norms. Reliance on contingent reinforcement is a hallmark of *transactional leadership. The term is associated with behaviouristic schools of psychology that emphasize the correlation of stimulus and response. *Compare* HUMAN RELATIONS THEORY.

contingent time off (job and finish) A *job-design practice in which staff are allowed to go home as soon as an agreed amount of work has been completed to an agreed standard.

contingent worker A *worker who has a conditional arrangement with an employer, such as a temporary, agency, or casual worker. Contingent workers tend to be employed by organizations when they have temporary need for a particular service, technology, or skill at a particular time and place. *See also* AGENCY WORKER; TEMPORARY EMPLOYEE.

continual access Twenty-four-hours-a-day, seven-days-a-week access; sometimes referred to as 24/7.

continuance commitment *See* ORGANIZATIONAL COMMITMENT.

continuation An arrangement between an investor and a stockbroker in which the broker reduces the *commission for a series of purchases by that investor of the same stock over a stated period.

continuity The commissioning and scheduling of advertisements to appear evenly within a given period.

continuity programs Special services and benefits extended to important customers to encourage them to make further purchases. Airline 'frequent flyer' programs are an example.

continuity series A marketing method in which a customer is offered a series of similar products over an extended period.

continuous improvement The ongoing process of improving an organization's goods or services, with the aim of increasing customer satisfaction. In a highly competitive environment, organizations need to search actively for ways of reducing costs, improving quality, and eliminating waste. *See also* ITERATIVE DESIGN; *KAIZEN*; *KANSEI* ENGINEERING; TOTAL QUALITY MANAGEMENT.

continuous-operation costing A system of costing applied to industries in which the method of production is *continuous processing; examples include electricity generation, and bottling. Because the product is homogeneous, this costing system is essentially a form of *average costing in which the unit cost is obtained by dividing the total production cost by the number of units produced. *Compare* PROCESS COSTING.

continuous processing A process in which very high volumes are produced on dedicated plant continuously, e.g. cement production or electricity generation. The plant usually involves very high capital expenditure. Unplanned shut-downs are very costly, typically involving a major refurbishment, for example to replace cracked furnace linings. Most continuous processes are largely self-controlling or are monitored by computer (*see* COMPUTER-AIDED MANUFACTURING) with only minor operator involvement. The product is often made to stock and is therefore vulnerable to market fluctuations. *Compare* BATCH PRODUCTION. *See* PROCESS CHOICE.

contra A book-keeping entry on the opposite side of an account to an earlier entry, with the object of cancelling the effect of the earlier entry. *See also* PER CONTRA.

contra accounts Accounts that can be offset, one against the other. For example, if Company A owes money to Company B and Company B also owes money to

Company A, the accounts can be offset against each other, enabling both debts to be settled by one payment.

contraband Illegally imported or exported goods, i.e. goods that have been smuggled into or out of a country.

contract A legally binding agreement. Agreement arises as a result of an *offer and *acceptance, but a number of other requirements must be satisfied for an agreement to be legally binding:

- there must be a *consideration (unless the contract is by deed);
- the parties must have an intention to create legal relations;
- the parties must have capacity to contract (i.e. they must be competent to enter a legal obligation, by not being a minor, mentally disordered, or drunk);
- the agreement must comply with any formal legal requirements;
- the agreement must be legal;
- the agreement must not be rendered void either by some common-law or statutory rule or by some inherent defect.

In general, no particular formality is required for the creation of a valid contract. It may be oral, written, partly oral and partly written, or even implied from conduct. However, certain contracts are valid only if made by deed (e.g. transfers of shares in statutory companies, transfers of shares in British ships, legal *mortgages, certain types of *lease) or in writing (e.g. *hire-purchase agreements, *bills of exchange, *promissory notes, contracts for the sale of land made after 21 September 1989), and certain others, though valid, can only be enforced if evidenced in writing (e.g. guarantees, contracts for the sale of land made before 21 September 1989). *See also* SERVICE CONTRACT.

Certain contracts, though valid, may be liable to be set aside by one of the parties on such grounds as misrepresentation or the exercise of undue influence. *See also* AFFIRMATION OF CONTRACT; BREACH OF CONTRACT.

contract costing A costing technique applied to *long-term contracts, such as

civil-engineering projects, in which the costs are collected by contract. A particular problem of long-term projects is the determination of annual profits to be taken to the profit and loss account when the contract is incomplete. This requires the valuation of *work in progress at the end of the financial year.

contract for differences (CFD) A *derivative contract in which one party (the issuer) agrees to pay another (the buyer) the difference between the current value of an *underlying (e.g. an equity, bond, or index) and the value at the time the contract was made: if the difference is negative, the buyer pays the issuer. Settlement is on a daily basis for as long as the contract remains open. CFDs enable investors to speculate on the price movements of an asset without buying it: the buyer pays only a small principal to the issuer but receives the full benefits of owning the asset (including dividends on shares) and is likewise fully responsible for any losses. Exchange-traded CFDs went on sale for the first time in August 2007, on the Australian Stock Exchange.

contract for services A contract undertaken by a self-employed individual. The distinction between a contract for services (self-employed) and a *contract of employment (employee) is fundamental, not least in establishing the tax position. In practice, however, the distinction may not always be clear (*see* WORKER). With a contract for services the person may hire and pay others to carry out the work, will be responsible for correcting unsatisfactory work at their own expense, and may make losses as well as profits.

contract guarantee insurance An insurance policy designed to guarantee the financial solvency of a contractor during the performance of a contract. If the contractor becomes financially insolvent and cannot complete the work the insurer makes a payment equivalent to the contract price, which enables another contractor to be paid to complete the work. *See also* CREDIT INSURANCE.

contract manufacturing A joint venture in which a company contracts with a manufacturer, generally in a foreign market, to produce a particular product for the company to sell or distribute.

contract note 1. A document containing details of a contract sent from one counterparty to the contract to the other. **2.** A document sent by a stockbroker or commodity broker to a client as evidence that the broker has bought (in which case it may be called a **bought note**) or sold (a **sold note**) securities or commodities in accordance with the client's instructions. It will state the quantity of securities or goods, the price, the date (and sometimes the time of day at which the bargain was struck), the rate of commission, the cost of the transfer stamp and VAT (if any), and the amount due and the settlement date.

contract of employment A contract by which an *employee agrees to undertake certain duties under the direction and control of the employer in return for a specified wage or salary. The contract need not be in writing, but under the Employment Rights Act 1996 the employee must be given a written statement of terms of employment (for details *see* STATEMENT OF TERMS OF EMPLOYMENT). Implied in every contract are the employer's duty to protect the employee from danger and risks to health, and the employee's duty to do the work to the best of his or her ability. Employees who have been continuously employed in the same business for certain minimum periods have statutory rights, relating for example to *unfair dismissal and *redundancy, that do not apply to the self-employed. A self-employed person is engaged under a *contract for services and owes his employer or customer no other duty than to complete the specified work in accordance with the terms of the individual contract. Termination of a contract of employment in breach of the terms of the contract is *wrongful dismissal and may be remedied at law.

contractual VMS A *vertical marketing system in which independent firms at different levels of production and distribution contract to join together to obtain more economies or greater sales impact than they could achieve alone. *Compare* ADMINISTERED VMS; CORPORATE VMS.

contra proferentem A rule of legal interpretation primarily applying to documents. If any doubt or ambiguity arises in the interpretation of a document, the rule requires that the doubt or ambiguity should be resolved against the party who drafted it. For instance, a defendant who claims that a clause in a contract that he drafted exempts him from liability can expect that any ambiguity in the terms of the clause will be resolved against him. The expression derives from the Latin: *verba chartarum fortuis accipiuntur contra proferentum*, the words of a contract are construed more strictly against the person proclaiming them.

contribution 1. In *marginal-costing systems, the amount that a given transaction produces to cover fixed overheads and to provide profit. The **unit contribution** is normally taken to be the selling price of a given unit of merchandise, less the variable costs of producing it. Once the total contributions exceed the fixed overheads, all further contribution represents pure profit. The **total contribution** is the product of the unit contribution and the number of units produced. This is based on the assumptions that the marginal cost and the sales value will be constant. **2.** The sharing of claim payments between two or more insurers who find themselves insuring the same item, against the same risks, for the same person. As that person is not entitled to claim more than the full value of the item once, each insurer pays a share. For example, if a coat was stolen from a car, it might be insured under both a personal-effects insurance and a motor policy. As the policyholder is only entitled to the value of the coat (and cannot profit from the theft), each insurer contributes half of the loss.

contribution income statement The presentation of an *income statement or *profit and loss account using the

	PRODUCT A	PRODUCT B	TOTAL
Sales revenue	2000	5000	7000
Variable costs	1400	2900	4300
Contribution	600	2100	2700
Total Fixed costs			1200
Total profit			1500

Contribution income statement. A simplified example.

*marginal costing layout. In such a treatment the *fixed costs are not charged to the individual products produced as in *absorption costing but are treated as a deduction from the total *contribution of all the products. A simplified contribution income statement is shown above.

contributory Any person who is liable to contribute towards the assets of a company on liquidation. The list of contributories will be settled by the liquidator or by the court. This list will include all shareholders, although those who hold fully paid-up shares will not be liable to pay any more.

contributory pension A *pension in which the employee as well as the employer contribute to the pension fund. *Compare* NON-CONTRIBUTORY PENSION.

control The ability to direct the financial and operating policies of another undertaking with a view to gaining economic benefits from its activities. One company is said to control another company if it holds more than 50% of that company's share capital, voting power, distributable income, or net assets in a winding-up. If one company has control in this sense over another, the two companies should produce *consolidated financial statements.

control accounts Accounts in which the balances are designed to equal the aggregate of the balances on a substantial number of subsidiary accounts. Examples are the sales ledger control account (or total debtors account), in which the balance equals the aggregate of all the individual debtors' accounts, the purchase ledger control account (or total creditors account), which performs the same function for creditors, and the stock control account,

whose balance should equal the aggregate of the balances on the stock accounts for each item of stock. This is achieved by entering in the control accounts the totals of all the individual entries made in the subsidiary accounts. The purpose is two-fold: to obtain total figures of debtors, creditors, stock, etc., at any given time, without adding up all the balances on the individual records, and to have a cross-check on the accuracy of the subsidiary records.

control chart A graphical representation of the statistically derived performance limits (normally ±2 *standard deviations), which is used in *statistical process control. By recording samples on a control chart, it is possible to identify the trends and to take remedial action before performance goes outside the limits. *See also* CONCURRENT CONTROL; FEEDFORWARD CONTROL.

controllability concept The principle that managers should only be held responsible for *controllable costs and *controllable investment. This concept is often difficult to apply in practice. Many costs are not easily classified as either controllable or uncontrollable and others are clearly only partially controllable. For example, the manager at a building society branch is not responsible for advertising costs, staff salaries, or interest rates on savings or loans. *See* CONTROLLABLE CONTRIBUTION.

controllable contribution The sales revenue of a division less those costs that are controllable by the divisional manager (*see* CONTROLLABLE COSTS). Controllable contribution is the most appropriate measure of a divisional manager's performance. In practice, however, it can be difficult to distinguish between controllable costs and *uncontrollable costs. Where a division is a *profit centre, *depreciation is not a controllable cost, as the manager is not responsible for investment decisions. However, the manager of an investment centre is responsible for investments and therefore depreciation is a controllable cost.

controllable costs Costs identified as being controllable and therefore able to be influenced by a particular level of management. Information about those costs is therefore directed to the correct management personnel in the appropriate *operating statements. In any system of responsibility accounting, managers can only be regarded as responsible for those costs over which they have some control.

controllable investment The *capital employed that is controllable by a divisional manager. When calculating *performance measures for a division it is important to ensure that only those assets and liabilities that a manager can influence are included. See CONTROLLABLE CONTRIBUTION.

controllable turnover See LABOUR TURNOVER RATE.

controllable variance In *standard costing or *budgetary control, a *variance that is regarded as controllable by the manager responsible for that area of an organization. The variance occurs as a result of the difference between the *budget cost allowance and the actual cost incurred for the period. See also CONTROLLABLE COSTS.

controlled foreign company A foreign company in which a UK resident company or individual has a *controlling interest. A UK resident company can be charged to UK tax in respect of profits from a controlled foreign company where these profits may be expected to have arisen in the UK if tax-planning arrangements had not been effected to move them out of UK tax charge. The tax rules applying to

controlled foreign companies are very complex and underwent major changes in the Finance Act 2012.

controller In the USA, the chief accounting executive of an organization. The controller will normally be concerned with financial reporting, taxation, and auditing but will leave the planning and control of finances to the *treasurer. See also COMPTROLLER.

controlling interest An interest in a company that gives a person or another company control of it. To have a controlling interest in a company, a shareholder would normally need to own or control more than half the voting shares. However, in practice, a shareholder might control the company with considerably less than half the shares, if the other shares were divided among a large number of different holders. For legal purposes, a director is said to have a controlling interest in a company if he or she alone, or together with his or her spouse or civil partner, minor children, and the trustees of any settlement in which he or she has an interest, owns more than 50% of the voting shares in a company or in a company that controls that company. See also MINORITY INTEREST; PARTICIPATING INTEREST.

control process A process that helps an organization to determine whether or not its objectives are being achieved and whether or not adjustments need to be made to meet them. A good control system should help managers to determine why goals and objectives are not being met; knowing the cause of failure will help to decide the corrective actions. Control activities should relate directly to tactical and operational plans; in turn, these will affect and influence the organization's long-term strategic plans.

convenience product A consumer product that customers usually buy frequently, immediately, and with a minimum of comparison and buying effort.

convenience store A store that trades primarily on the convenience it offers to

Long-term strategic goals and plans are set

Managers determine short-term tactical and operational objectives and plans

Control standards are established in line with objectives

Performance is measured

Comparisons are made between performance and standards

Corrective action is taken; the standard is changed or performance is continued

Control process. Steps in the control system of an organization.

customers. The products stocked may be influenced by local tastes or ethnic groups and the stores are often open long hours as well as being conveniently placed for customers in residential areas. They are often members of a multiple chain.

conventional distribution channel A channel consisting of one or more independent producers, wholesalers, and retailers, each a separate business seeking to maximize its own profits even at the expense of profits for the system as a whole.

convergence The general trend in which computers, telecommunications, and the broadcast media have become increasingly interdependent and have assumed similar functions for many business and other purposes. *See* INFORMATION TECHNOLOGY.

convergence criteria (Maastricht criteria) The economic tests used to

determine whether member states of the European Union are ready to adopt the euro, as set out in the 1991 *Maastricht Treaty. The four principal criteria concern (i) the inflation rate; (ii) ratios of government deficit and government debt to GDP; (iii) long-term interest rates; and (iv) membership of the *Exchange Rate Mechanism (ERM). *See* EUROPEAN ECONOMIC AND MONETARY UNION.

conversational systems *See* INTERACTIVE.

conversion The tort (civil wrong) equivalent to the crime of theft. It is possible to bring an action in respect of conversion to recover damages, but this is uncommon.

conversion cost The costs incurred in a production process as a result of which raw material is converted into finished goods. The conversion costs usually include *direct labour and *manufacturing overheads but exclude the costs of *direct material itself.

convertible 1. A *bond or preferred stock that can be changed into other securities, usually equity, on predetermined conditions. **2.** A government security in which the holder has the right to convert a holding into new stock instead of obtaining repayment.

convertible adjusted-rate preferred stock *See* ADJUSTABLE-RATE PREFERRED STOCK.

convertible revolving credit A *revolving credit that can be converted by mutual agreement into a fixed-term loan.

convertible term assurance A *term assurance that gives the policyholder the option to widen the policy to become a *whole life policy or an *endowment assurance policy, without having to provide any further evidence of good health. All that is required is the payment of the extra premium. The risks of AIDS has meant that policies of this kind are no longer available, as insurers are not now prepared to offer any widening of life cover without evidence of good health.

conveyancing The transfer of ownership of land from the person currently holding title to a new owner. *See also* ELECTRONIC CONVEYANCING.

cookie A small text file stored on an end-user's computer (quite often without the user's knowledge) to enable websites to identify the user. It enables a company to identify a previous visitor to a site and may be used to build up a profile of that visitor's behaviour. In general, cookies help the user and in some cases they are essential. For example, if the user is buying a number of items online, then a cookie is necessary for the server to keep track of items from different pages placed in a 'shopping cart'. However, their use has raised privacy concerns and the law now requires that websites provide clear information about what cookies are set and a simple method enabling users to block them if they so choose.

cooling-off period 1. The 14 days that begins when a life-assurance policy, credit agreement, etc., is effected, during which new policyholders, borrowers, etc., can change their minds. During this period any policies or agreements entered into can be cancelled with a full refund of any premiums, arrangement fees, etc. **2.** The time that must elapse after a failed *takeover bid before a new bid can be made.

co-operative 1. (**worker co-operative**) A type of business organization sometimes adopted in labour-intensive industries, such as agriculture, and often associated with socialist systems. Agricultural co-operatives have been encouraged in the developing countries, where individual farmers are too poor to take advantage of expensive machinery and large-scale production. In this case several farms pool resources to jointly purchase and use agricultural machinery. The principle has sometimes been extended to other industries, as when factory employees arrange a worker buy-out in order to secure threatened employment. The overall management of such co-operatives is usually vested in a committee of the employee-owners. **2.** (**consumer co-operative**) A movement launched in 1844 by 28 Rochdale weavers who combined to establish retail outlets where members enjoyed not only the benefits of good-quality products at fair prices but also a share of the profits (a dividend) based on the amount of each member's purchases.

copyright The exclusive right to reproduce or authorize others to reproduce artistic, dramatic, literary, or musical works. It is conferred by the Copyright Act 1988, which also extends to sound broadcasting, cinematograph films, television broadcasts, and computer programs. In EU countries copyright lasts for the author's lifetime plus 70 years from the end of the year of death (or from the end of the year of publication, if later); it can be assigned or transmitted on death. The principal remedies for breach of copyright (*see* PIRACY) are an action for *damages and account of profits or an *injunction. It is a criminal offence to make or deal in articles that infringe a copyright.

copy testing The process of measuring the communication effect of an advertisement, either before or after it is printed or broadcast. The advertising copy is usually tested on likely buyers of the product or service.

copywriter A person who writes the text for advertisements or other promotional material. Copywriters are usually employed by an *advertising agency, although in the case of highly technical advertising matter they are often employed by the company manufacturing or distributing the product.

córdoba (NIO) The standard monetary unit of Nicaragua, divided into 100 centavos.

core competency Any distinctive capability that endows a particular business with a *competitive advantage over its rivals. The degree to which the business can exploit this unique competence varies according to the extent to which it can be imitated by rival firms. Some skills, such as technologies or processes, may be protected by patents; others may have been built up by reputation or by marketing expertise. *See also* RESOURCE-BASED VIEW.

core inflation The rate of inflation calculated to exclude certain items that are subject to sudden and shortlived price movements, mainly food and energy. Core inflation is considered a better indicator of overall long-term trends than unadjusted headline inflation.

core job characteristics The five characteristics that have been identified by *job characteristics theory as inducing the critical psychological states required for *motivation at work:

- **skill variety**—the degree to which the job includes different activities drawing on several skills and abilities;
- **task identity**—the extent to which a person is able to complete a task from start to finish;
- **task significance**—the degree to which a person carrying out a task perceives it to be important to the organization and its clients;
- **autonomy**—the degree to which a person has discretion as to how and when the task will be done;
- **feedback**—the extent to which the person receives feedback on the quality of performance from the task itself.

These core job characteristics are important to the psychological well-being of the individual. If they are lacking, then *job satisfaction (and hence motivation) may well suffer unless a programme of *job enlargement or *job enrichment is instituted.

core product The problem-solving service or core benefit that a consumer is really buying when purchasing a product.

core strategy The identification of a group of customers for whom a firm has a differential advantage prior to *positioning itself in that market.

corner The situation in which an individual or organization succeeds in establishing a controlling influence over the supply of a particular good or service. It will then force the price up until further supplies or substitutes can be found. This objective has often been attempted, but rarely achieved, in international *commodity markets. Because it is undesirable and has antisocial effects, 'cornering the market' in this way is now generally prevented by government restrictions on monopolies and antitrust laws.

corporate anorexia A malaise that affects businesses after a severe cost-cutting phase. The firm's ability to expand production to maintain its competitive position in the market may, for example, be compromised by a misguided pressure to reduce costs by *downsizing, resulting in the elimination of personnel who made a long-term contribution to the company's viability.

corporate bond A *bond issued by a private corporation.

corporate brand licensing A form of licensing enabling a firm to rent a corporate trademark or logo made famous in one product or service category to use in a related category.

corporate brand strategy A brand strategy designed to make a company's name the dominant brand identity for all of its products.

corporate citizenship The idea that a business is part of civil society and thus has responsibilities beyond maximizing its profit while obeying the law. Good corporate citizenship requires that a company subject both its internal and its external practices to the test of *corporate social responsibility.

corporate culture *See* ORGANIZATIONAL CULTURE. *See also* CORPORATE IMAGE.

corporate finance 1. The branch of financial economics concerned with business funding, decision making, and mergers and acquisitions. **2.** An activity in investment and merchant banks in which advice and funding for mergers and acquisitions, etc., is provided to large corporations. **3.** Loans made to large companies by banks.

corporate governance The manner in which organizations, particularly limited companies, are managed and the nature of *accountability of the managers to the owners. This topic has been of increased importance since the publication of the *Cadbury Report in 1992, which set out a code of practice later incorporated into the *Corporate Governance Code.

Corporate Governance Code A code of best practice in the field of *corporate governance, first issued with the *Hampel Report of 1998. The Code, which incorporated the earlier recommendations of the *Cadbury Report and the *Greenbury Report, concerns such matters as the role of *non-executive directors, directors' remuneration, and general issues of audit, accountability, and relations with shareholders. UK listed companies are required to disclose whether or not they have complied with the Code, and to explain any departures from it. Earlier versions of the Code, which is reissued approximately every two years, were often referred to as the **Combined Code on Corporate Governance**. *See also* Higgs Report; Turnbull Report.

( ) SEE WEB LINKS
- Full text of the Code (2012) from the Financial Reporting Council website

corporate image The image that a company projects of itself. To gain a benevolent image for the way a company treats its employees or the environment, for example, can be as important to its sales as its individual brand images. In recent years there has been an increase in advertising to create an acceptable corporate image. For example, Shell has spent considerable sums advertising its concern for the unspoilt countryside.

corporate manslaughter An offence introduced by the Corporate Manslaughter and Corporate Homicide Act 2007. It occurs where: (i) the death of a person

(such as an employee or a customer) has been caused by a gross breach of a relevant duty of care owed to that person by the company; and (ii) the breach involved a serious failing by senior management in the way the company's activities were organized or managed. The offence can be committed only by companies and certain other organizations (including partnerships and trade unions). Individuals, such as directors of a company, can also be prosecuted under the common law for manslaughter.

corporate modelling The use of simulation models to assist the management of an organization in carrying out planning and decision making. A budget is an example of a corporate model.

corporate performance management *See* BUSINESS PERFORMANCE MANAGEMENT.

corporate plan *See* BUSINESS PLAN.

corporate policy (company policy) A set of written guidelines intended to govern the actions of a company's managers and its other employees in specified situations. Typically, corporate policy will be both internal and external. Internal policies cover issues such as the behaviour of employees at work and the procedures used to deal with human resources questions; external policies govern behaviour towards customers and the broader public.

corporate raider A person or company that buys a substantial proportion of the equity of another company (the target company) with the object of either taking it over or of forcing the management of the target company to take certain steps to improve the image of the company sufficiently for the share price to rise enough for the raider to sell the holding at a profit.

corporate restructuring A change in the *business strategy of a company by *diversification into new areas, which it considers more attractive. Alternatively, following poor performance, it may seek to withdraw from an area by *divestment or closure of parts of its business, which it no longer considers to be part of its future strategic focus. *See also* DOWNSIZING; RIGHTSIZING.

corporate social reporting *See* SOCIAL RESPONSIBILITY REPORTING.

corporate social responsibility (CSR) The notion that a company has responsibilities to society that go beyond its legal obligations and its duties to shareholders. Corporate social responsibility considerations include the company's impact on the environment, any ethical issues arising from its trading or investment practices, and the policies of the company internally, for instance with regard to transparency and the fair and equal treatment of employees. *See* TRIPLE BOTTOM-LINE ACCOUNTING.

corporate venturing The provision of *risk capital by one company, either directly or by means of a venture-capital fund, for another company. This may be undertaken as a means of obtaining information about the company requiring venture capital or its market, of taking a first step towards acquiring the company, or of moving into a new market cheaply and without needing to acquire the relevant expertise and personnel.

Corporate Venturing Scheme (CVS) A former UK scheme designed to encourage established companies to invest in the ordinary shares of companies of the same kind as those qualifying under the *Enterprise Investment Scheme. Companies investing through the CVS obtained *corporation tax relief (at 20%) on the amount invested provided that the shares were held for at least three years. The scheme was discontinued in 2010.

corporate VMS A *vertical marketing system that combines successive stages of production and distribution under single ownership in order to establish channel leadership. *Compare* ADMINISTERED VMS; CONTRACTUAL VMS.

corporate website A site set up by a company on the *World Wide Web, which carries information and other features designed to answer customer's questions, build customer relationships, and generate interest in the company, rather than to sell its products or services directly. The website handles interactive communications initiated by the consumer.

corporation A succession of persons or body of persons authorized by law to act as one person and having rights and liabilities distinct from the individuals forming the corporation. The *artificial person may be created by Royal Charter, statute, or common law. The most important type is the registered *company formed under the Companies Act. **Corporations sole** are those having only one individual forming them; for example, a bishop, the sovereign, the Treasury Solicitor. **Corporations aggregate** are composed of more than one individual, e.g. a limited company. They may be formed for special purposes by statute; the BBC is an example. Corporations can hold property, carry on business, bring legal actions, etc., in their own name. Their actions may, however, be limited by the doctrine of *ultra vires. *See also* PUBLIC CORPORATION.

corporation tax (CT) Tax charged on the total profits of a company *resident in the UK arising in each *accounting period. The rate of corporation tax depends on the level of profits of the company. The small companies rate of 20% currently (2015–16) applies to companies with total profits of £300,000 or less. Full-rate corporation tax of 21% currently applies to companies with total profits of over £1.5 million. There is a *marginal relief for those companies with total profits between £300,000 and £1.5 million. Large companies pay corporation tax in instalments: other companies pay CT nine months after the end of the company's chargeable accounting period. Certain *capital allowances are deductible for corporation tax purposes, as are losses carried forward from previous years. Any *chargeable gains from the disposal of fixed assets are included in the total profits for corporation tax purposes.

( ) SEE WEB LINKS
- A guide to corporation tax from the Gov.uk website

correspondent bank A bank in a foreign country that offers banking facilities to the customers of a bank in another country. These arrangements are usually the result of agreements, often reciprocal, between the two banks. The most frequent correspondent banking facilities used are those of money transmission.

corruption 1. The introduction of errors into computer data through mechanical accident or malfunction. All forms of electronic or magnetic data storage are vulnerable to corruption, which can occur for no discernible reason. Corruption can also occur when data is sent over telephone lines between communicating computers. **2.** *See* BRIBERY.

corset 1. A restriction of the movements of currency exchange values imposed by certain formal market mechanisms. **2.** A government restriction on the growth of bank deposits and thus indirectly on bank lending and the *money supply.

cosmetic customization The practice of presenting a standard product in different ways for different audiences without actually changing the product. *See* CUSTOMIZATION.

cost 1. An expenditure, usually of money, for the purchase of goods or services. **2.** An expenditure, usually of money, incurred in achieving a goal, e.g. producing certain goods, building a factory, or closing down a branch. *See also* CURRENT COST; ECONOMIC COSTS; FIXED COST; HISTORICAL COST; MARGINAL COST; OPPORTUNITY COST; REPLACEMENT COST.

cost accounting The techniques used in collecting, processing, and presenting financial and quantitative data within an organization to ascertain the cost of the *cost centres, the *cost units, and the various operations. Cost accounting is now regarded as a division of *management accounting, which also incorporates the techniques of planning, decision making, and control.

cost allocation The process of assigning costs to one or more *cost objects when it is not possible to trace a cost directly. *Indirect costs (overheads) always have to be assigned to cost objects using cost allocations. The basis on which costs are assigned to cost objects is called the *allocation base or *cost driver. The purposes of cost allocation can be briefly summarized as follows:
- to provide information for decisions: an example would be deciding whether or not to replace a machine;
- to set selling prices;
- to measure profits accurately (product profitability and customer profitability);
- to motivate management or employees.

Broadly, two types of systems can be used to assign indirect costs to cost objects: *traditional costing systems and *activity-based costing. Traditional costing systems focus on product costs and are often criticized for relying on *arbitrary allocations. Activity-based costing systems use *cause-and-effect allocations.

Cost and Freight (CFR) An *Incoterm denoting an export contract in which the seller pays the cost of shipping the goods to the port of destination; if the seller also pays costs of marine insurance it is known as a **Cost, Insurance and Freight (CIF)** contract. In either case, risk passes to the buyer once the goods have crossed the ship's rail at the port of shipment. A **Carriage Paid To (CPT)** or **Carriage and Insurance Paid To (CIP)** contract is made on exactly the same terms except that the seller's responsibilities end when the goods are handed over at a named destination (not necessarily a port); it can therefore be used with any mode of transport, or combination of modes. *Compare* DELIVERED EX SHIP.

cost assignment (cost attribution) The procedures by which direct or indirect costs are charged to or made the responsibility of particular *cost centres, and ultimately charged to the products manufactured or services provided by the organization. Procedures used to achieve cost attribution include *absorption costing, *activity-based costing, and *marginal costing. *See also* COST ALLOCATION; COST TRACING.

cost behaviour The changes that occur to total costs as a result of changes in activity levels within an organization. The total of the *fixed costs tends to remain unaltered by changes in activity levels in the short term, whereas the total of the *variable costs tends to increase or decrease in proportion to activity. There are also some costs that demonstrate *semi-variable cost behaviour, i.e. they have both fixed and variable elements. The study of cost behaviour is important for *breakeven analysis and also when considering decision-making techniques.

cost-benefit analysis A technique used in *capital budgeting that takes into account the estimated costs to be incurred by a proposed investment and the estimated benefits likely to arise from it. In a *financial appraisal the benefits may arise from an increase in the revenue from a product or service, from saved costs, or from other cash inflows, but in an *economic appraisal the economic benefits, such as the value of time saved or of fewer accidents resulting from a road improvement, often require to be valued.

cost centre The area of an organization for which costs are collected for the purposes of cost ascertainment, planning, decision making, and control. Cost centres are determined by individual organizations; they may be based on a function, department, section, individual, or any group of these. Cost centres are of two main types: **production cost centres** in an organization are those concerned with making a product, while **service cost centres** provide a service (such as stores, boilerhouse, or canteen) to other parts of the organization.

cost classification The process of grouping expenditure according to common characteristics. Costs are initially divided into *capital expenditure and *revenue expenditure. In a production organization the revenue expenditure is classified sequentially to enable a product cost to build up in the order in which these costs tend to be incurred. Revenue costs would normally include:

- direct material,
- direct labour,
- direct expenses,
- production overheads,
- administration overheads,
- selling overheads,
- distribution overheads,
- research overheads.

cost control The techniques used by various levels of management within an organization to ensure that the costs incurred fall within acceptable levels. Cost control is assisted by the provision of financial information to management by the accountant and by the use of such techniques as *budgetary control and *standard costing, which highlight and analyse any variances.

cost convention The custom used as a basis for recording the costs to be charged against the profit for an accounting period. The cost convention used may be based on *historical cost, *current cost, or *replacement cost.

cost driver In a system of *activity-based costing, any factor such as number of units, number of transactions, or duration of transactions that drives the costs arising from a particular *activity. When such factors can be clearly identified and measured, they will be used as a basis for allocating costs to cost objects. The term cost driver is therefore effectively synonymous with both *activity measure and *allocation base and the literature often uses them interchangeably. *See also* ACTIVITY COST POOL; COST ALLOCATION.

cost effectiveness 1. Achieving a goal with the minimum of expenditure. **2.** Achieving a goal with an expenditure that makes the achievement viable in commercial terms.

cost focus *See* FOCUS STRATEGY.

cost function A formula or equation that represents the way in which particular costs behave when plotted on a graph. For example, the most common cost function represents the total cost as the sum of the *fixed costs and the *variable costs in the equation $y = a + bx$, where y is the total cost, a is the total fixed cost, b is the variable cost per unit of production or sales, and x is the number of units produced or sold.

Cost, Insurance and Freight *See* COST AND FREIGHT.

cost leadership strategy *See* LOW-COST STRATEGY.

cost minimization The behavioural assumption that an individual or firm will seek to purchase a given amount of goods or inputs at the least cost, other things being equal. By making certain assumptions, there will exist a single cost-minimizing combination of inputs for any level of output. Thus, assuming that firms or *entrepreneurs choose to minimize costs, their behaviour can be predicted. It can be shown that the profit-maximizing level of output for a firm is also cost minimizing; however, it need not be assumed that firms actually maximize profits, which is a different behavioural assumption.

cost object Any item for which a separate measurement of *costs is desired. This may be a product, a service, a customer, or a specific operation associated with any of these (e.g., designing a new product, processing a mortgage application, making a telephone call to a customer). The number of cost objects identified and the frequency of measuring the costs will vary between organizations; a product cost will normally be calculated on a weekly or monthly basis, whereas the cost of processing a mortgage

application may only be calculated on an annual basis.

cost of capital The return, expressed in terms of an interest rate, that an organization is required to pay for the capital used in financing its activities. This will vary according to the type or types of capital employed (e.g., *equity capital, *loan capital, or some mixture of the two). One approach to establishing the cost of capital is therefore to compute a unique *weighted average cost of capital for each organization, based on its particular mix of capital sources. The cost of capital is often used as a *hurdle rate in *discounted cash flow calculations.

cost of carry *See* CARRYING COSTS.

cost of debt The effective overall rate of interest that a company pays on its loans, bonds, and other debts, as used in calculating the total *cost of capital for that firm. This is usually calculated as an after-tax figure. The more risky the company's debts, the higher its cost of debt will be.

cost of equity The rate of return that a company's shareholders expect for holding stock in that company, used as part of the calculation of the total *cost of capital for a firm. It represents the *opportunity cost to investors of holding shares. The cost can be calculated by a formula dividing dividends per share by current market value, and adding the dividend growth rate.

cost of funds The cost to banks of borrowing in the principal *money markets, which determines their rates of interest when lending to their customers.

cost of goods manufactured (manufacturing cost of finished goods) The total *production cost of the *finished goods transferred from the production facility of an organization during an accounting period. It is made up of the total expenditure for the period on *direct materials, *direct labour, *direct expenses, and *manufacturing overheads adjusted by the opening and closing stocks of raw materials and the *work in progress at the beginning and end of the period.

cost of quality The total costs of ensuring good quality or rectifying poor quality. Ultimately, by improving quality managers will reduce costs and improve profits. Four categories of costs are useful for this analysis:

- **prevention costs**. These are the costs incurred in preventing mistakes. Examples include training, quality planning, process controls, and market research. Expenditure in this area is seen as an investment.
- **appraisal costs**. These include the costs of inspecting parts from suppliers, inspecting and testing products in manufacture, and performing quality audits.
- **internal failure costs**. These are the costs incurred when a product does not conform to quality standards. Examples include the costs of scrap, repairs to defective products, and downtime. They are incurred before the customer receives the product.
- **external failure costs**. These are the costs incurred when the customer receives a poor quality product. Examples include the costs of investigating complaints, of replacing products returned by the customer, and warranty charges. If the customer is dissatisfied and finds a new supplier, the total cost will be much higher. *See also* ENVIRONMENTAL COSTS.

cost of sales (cost of goods sold; COGS) A figure representing the cost to an organization of supplying goods or services for sale, excluding administration and other general overheads. In a sales organization, it is the *opening stock at the beginning of an accounting period plus the purchases for the period, less the closing stock at the end of the period. In a manufacturing organization, the purchases for the period would be replaced by the *production cost of finished goods for the period. In a service providing organization, the cost of sales would be calculated as *direct costs adjusted by the opening and closing values

of *work in progress. The cost of sales figure is deducted from the sales revenue to obtain the *gross profit for the period.

cost per enquiry (CPE) A commonly used method of calculating costs in *direct marketing in which the total cost of the mailing is divided by the number of resultant enquiries received. For example, if 1,000 enquiries were generated by a mailing operation costing £5,000, the CPE would be £5 (i.e. 5,000/1,000).

cost per mille (CPM) The cost of an advertisement per thousand people who will see or hear it.

cost per order (CPO) The total cost of a mailing divided by the total number of orders received.

cost per product The cost needed to generate a visit to a website. For advertising on the web it is the cost per *banner advertisement divided by the *click-through rate.

cost per targeted mille (CPTM) The cost of an advertisement per targeted thousand people who will see or hear it.

cost-plus contract A contract entered into by a supplier in which the goods or services provided to the customer are charged at cost plus an agreed percentage markup. This method of pricing is very common if the cost of producing the commodity is unknown or if its production will involve significant research work. However, because simple cost-plus contracts do not encourage suppliers to minimize their costs, there has been a move away from this type of contract in UK government orders with private industry.

cost-plus pricing An approach to establishing the selling price of a product or service in a commercial organization, in which the total cost of the product or service is estimated and a percentage *mark-up is added in order to obtain a profitable selling price. A variation to this approach is to estimate the costs to a particular stage, say the costs of production only, and then to add a percentage mark-up to cover both the other overheads (including administration, selling, and distribution costs) and the profit margin. This approach to costing is very different from *target costing. *Compare* FULL COST PRICING; MARGINAL COST PRICING.

cost-plus transfer prices *Transfer prices set by *cost-plus pricing, which include a mark-up to provide a profit for the supplying division. When *variable costs rather than full costs are used in this calculation, the mark-up will need to be higher to cover both the *fixed costs and a profit margin. This method involves a problem for managers, as cost-plus transfer pricing does not identify the output levels that will maximize prices.

cost-push inflation An increase in the prices of goods or services caused by increases in the cost of inputs (especially wages and raw materials). As an explanation of *inflation, cost-push theories became popular in the 1970s when they appeared to explain the rapid inflation of that period, which followed on from very rapid rises in wages and the increases in oil prices. However, the theory is also widely criticized as: (a) it describes only changes in relative prices (e.g. oil) rather than rises in the general price level (which is how inflation is defined); and (b) most economists would now agree that price rises can only continue if there is an accompanying increase in the *money supply.

cost tracing The process of assigning *direct costs to the relevant *cost objects. *Compare* COST ALLOCATION.

cost unit A unit of production for which the management of an organization wishes to collect the costs incurred. In some cases the cost unit may be the final item produced, for example a chair or a light bulb, but in other more complex products the cost unit may be a sub-assembly, for example an aircraft wing or a gear box. Cost units may also be expressed as batches of items, particularly when the unit cost of the individual product would be very small; for example, the cost unit for a manufacturer of

pens might be the cost per thousand pens. *See also* COST OBJECT.

Cotonou Agreement *See* AFRICAN, CARIBBEAN, PACIFIC GROUP.

counterbid 1. A bid made in an auction that exceeds a bid already made (which then becomes the **underbid**). **2.** A second bid made in reply to a *counteroffer.

countercyclical stock A stock whose value tends to move in the opposite direction to prevailing economic trends, i.e. one that rises in a recession and falls during periods of economic growth. Such stocks could include those in firms that sell low-priced essential goods or inexpensive 'feel-good' items (*see* LIPSTICK EFFECT).

counteroffer A reply made to a *bid. If a seller makes an *offer of goods on specified terms at a specified price, the buyer may accept it or make a bid against the offer. Sellers who find the bid unacceptable may make a counteroffer, usually on terms or at a price that are a compromise between those in the offer and bid. If the buyers still find the counteroffer unacceptable they may make a *counterbid.

counterparty A person who is a party to a contract.

counterparty risk The *risk that either of the parties to a contract (counterparties) will fail to honour their obligations under the contract. In such organized markets as the *LIFFE (now Euronext.liffe) this risk is reduced by the *clearing house becoming counterparty to the contract, i.e. the buyer contracts to buy from LCH and the seller contracts to sell to LCH (*see* NOVATION). The risk is, however, greater in over-the-counter transactions.

countertrading The practice in international trading of paying for goods in a form other than by hard currency. For example, a South American country wishing to buy aircraft may countertrade (usually through a third party) by paying in coffee beans.

countervailing credit *See* BACK-TO-BACK CREDIT.

countervailing duty An extra import duty imposed by a country on certain imports. It is usually used to prevent *dumping or to counteract export subsidies given by foreign countries.

country risk The *risk of conducting transactions with, or holding assets of entities within, a particular country, arising from political or economic events within that country. *See* POLITICAL CREDIT RISK; TRANSFER CREDIT RISK.

coupon 1. One of several dated slips attached to a *bond, which must be presented to the agents of the issuer or the company to obtain an interest payment or dividend. They are usually used with *bearer securities; the **coupon yield** is the *yield provided by a bearer bond. 2. The rate of interest paid by a fixed-interest bond. The annual payment is a percentage of the bond's nominal value. 3. (**coupon security**) A bond or note on US Treasury Markets. 4. A fixed-rate payment on an interest or currency swap.

coupon stripping A financial process in which the *coupons are stripped off a *bearer bond and then sold separately as a source of cash, with no capital repayment; the bond, bereft of its coupons, becomes a *zero-coupon bond and is also sold separately.

coupon yield *See* COUPON.

covenant 1. A promise made in a *deed. Such a promise can be enforced by the parties to it as a contract, even if the promise is gratuitous: for example, if A covenants to pay B £100 per month, B can enforce this promise even without having done anything in return. Covenants were formerly used to minimize income tax, by transferring income from taxpayers to non-taxpayers (such as children or charities). However, since the Finance Act 1988 and the introduction of the *gift aid system, covenants can no longer be used for tax planning in this way.

Covenants may be entered into concerning the use of land, frequently to restrict the activities of a new owner or tenant (e.g. a covenant not to sell alcohol or run a fish-and-chip shop). Such covenants may be enforceable by persons deriving title from the original parties. This is an exception to the general rule that a contract cannot bind persons who are not parties to it. 2. An undertaking in a loan agreement the breaching of which will make the loan repayable immediately. *See also* EVENT OF DEFAULT; RATIO COVENANT.

cover 1. The security provided by *insurance or *assurance against a specified risk. 2. *See* DIVIDEND COVER. 3. Collateral given against a loan or credit, as in option dealing. 4. A *hedge purchased to safeguard an *open position. 5. Money set aside from income to meet potential bad debts or losses.

CPA 1. Abbreviation for certified public accountant. 2. Abbreviation for critical-path analysis. *See* NETWORK MODELLING. 3. Abbreviation for *customer profitability analysis.

CPE Abbreviation for *cost per enquiry.

CPM 1. Abbreviation for *cost per mille. 2. Abbreviation for corporate performance management. *See* BUSINESS PERFORMANCE MANAGEMENT.

CPO Abbreviation for *cost per order.

CPP accounting Abbreviation for *current purchasing power accounting.

C2 Principles A code of best practice, established by Thomas Dunfee and David Hess of the University of Pennsylvania, describing how a company and its employees should deal with any attempt to make or solicit improper payments.

CPT Abbreviation for Carriage Paid To. *See* COST AND FREIGHT.

CPTM Abbreviation for *cost per targeted mille.

CQ Abbreviation for *cultural intelligence.

craft union *See* TRADE UNION.

crash 1. A rapid and serious fall in the level of prices in a market. **2.** A breakdown of a computer system. A program is said to crash if it terminates abnormally.
A computer is said to crash either if it suffers a mechanical failure, or if one of the programs running on it misbehaves in a way that causes the computer to stop. Generally, the computer must then be switched off, any necessary repairs made, and restarted.

crawling peg (adjustable peg; sliding peg) A method of *exchange control that accepts the need for the stability given by fixed (or pegged) exchange rates, while recognizing that fixed rates can be prone to serious misalignments, which in turn can cause periods of financial and economic upheaval. Under crawling-peg arrangements, countries alter their pegs by small amounts at frequent intervals, rather than making large infrequent changes. This procedure provides flexibility and, in conjunction with the manipulation of interest rates, reduces the possibility of destabilizing speculative flows of capital. However, it is exposed to the criticism made against all fixed-rate regimes, that they are an inefficient alternative to the free play of market forces. At the same time, the crawling peg loses a major advantage of fixed rates, which is to inject certainty into the international trading system and more stable inflationary expectations. The rates may move as frequently as daily under a crawling-peg policy.

creative accounting Misleadingly optimistic, though not illegal, forms of accounting. This can occur because there are a number of accounting transactions that are not subject to regulations or the regulations are ambiguous. Companies sometimes make use of these ambiguities in order to present their financial results in the best light possible (so-called *window dressing). In particular, companies often wish to demonstrate increasing accounting profits and a strong balance sheet. Two examples of transactions that have

permitted creative accounting are those involving *consignment stocks and *repurchase agreements. In these contexts, creative accounting involves the separation of legal title from the risks and rewards of the activities, the linking of several transactions to make it difficult to determine the commercial effect of each transaction, or the inclusion in an agreement of *options, which are likely to be exercised. In the 1990s and 2000s a series of scandals raised the profile of issues such as *corporate governance and the responsibilities of auditors, leading governments and standard-setting bodies to address some of the worst abuses. However, the banking crisis of 2008 revealed the extent to which financial institutions had used *securitizations, *special purpose vehicles, and other complex *off-balance-sheet arrangements to present accounts that many would consider highly misleading.

creative destruction A phrase describing the dynamic, destabilizing effects of free-market capitalism, in which established businesses, industries, and ways of doing things are constantly overturned by new products, technologies, markets, and organizational structures. The phrase is chiefly associated with the Austrian economist Joseph Schumpeter (1883–1950). *See also* SCHUMPETERIAN GROWTH.

credit 1. The reputation and financial standing of a person or organization.
2. The sum of money that a trader or company allows a customer before requiring payment. **3.** The funding of members of the public to purchase goods and services with money borrowed from finance companies, banks, and other money lenders. **4.** An entry on the right-hand side of an *account in double-entry book-keeping, usually showing a sale or a liability.
5. A payment into an account.

credit account *See* CHARGE ACCOUNT.

credit balance A balancing amount of an account in which the total of credit entries exceeds the total of debit entries. Credit balances represent revenue, liabilities, or capital.

credit brokerage *See* ANCILLARY CREDIT BUSINESS.

credit call A national or international telephone call that is charged to the caller's credit card.

credit card A plastic card issued by a bank or finance organization to enable holders to obtain credit in shops, hotels, restaurants, petrol stations, etc. The retailer or trader receives monthly payments from the credit-card company equal to its total sales in the month by means of that credit card, less a service charge. Customers also receive monthly statements from the credit-card company, which may be paid in full within a certain number of days with no interest charged, or they may make a specified minimum payment and pay interest on the outstanding balance. Credit cards may be used to obtain cash either at a bank or its ATMs. *See also* CHARGE CARD; DEBIT CARD; GOLD CARD.

credit control Any system used by an organization to ensure that its outstanding debts are paid within a reasonable period. It involves establishing a **credit policy**, *credit rating of clients, and chasing accounts that become overdue. *See also* FACTORING.

credit crunch A period during which lenders are unwilling to extend credit to borrowers or the costs of borrowing rise. The term is particularly associated with the period beginning in late 2007, when the previous era of 'easy credit' came to a sudden end in the wake of the *subprime lending fiasco. *See also* CREDIT SQUEEZE.

credit enhancement The use of various techniques to raise the credit rating of *asset-backed securities. This is known as **internal enhancement** when it is carried out by the issuer of the security and **external enhancement** when it is done by a third party, such as a *monoline insurer.

credit guarantee 1. A type of insurance provided by credit guarantee associations, government institutions, or lenders to enable small firms to obtain credit from banks. **2.** An undertaking in which a holding company commits itself to paying any debts incurred by a subsidiary company. **3.** *See* CREDIT INSURANCE.

credit insurance 1. An insurance policy that continues the repayments of a particular debt in the event of the policyholder being financially unable to do so because of illness, death, redundancy, or any other specified cause. **2. (credit guarantee)** A form of insurance against losses arising from bad debts. This is not usually undertaken by normal insurance policies but by specialists known as factors (*see* FACTORING). *See also* EXPORT CREDITS GUARANTEE DEPARTMENT.

credit line 1. The extent of the credit available to a borrower or the user of a *credit card as set down in the initial credit agreement. **2.** The facility for borrowing money over a given period to a specified extent.

credit note A document expressing the indebtedness of the organization issuing it, usually to a customer. When goods are supplied to a customer an invoice is issued; if the customer returns all or part of the goods the invoice is wholly or partially cancelled by a credit note.

creditor One to whom an organization or person owes money. The *balance sheet of a company shows the total owed to creditors and a distinction has to be made between creditors who will be paid during the coming accounting period and those who will not be paid until later than this.

creditor–days ratio A ratio that gives an estimate of the average number of days' credit taken by an organization before the creditors are paid. It is calculated by the formula:

$$(\text{trade creditors} \times 365)/\text{annual purchases on credit}.$$

creditors' committee A committee of creditors of an insolvent company or a bankrupt individual, which represents all the creditors. They supervise the conduct of the administration of a company or the bankruptcy of an individual or receive reports from an administrative *receiver.

creditors' ledger See PURCHASE LEDGER.

creditors' voluntary liquidation (CVL) The winding-up of a company by special resolution of the members when it is insolvent. A **meeting of creditors** must be held within 14 days of such a resolution and the creditors must be given seven days' notice of the meeting. The creditors also have certain rights to information before the meeting. A *liquidator may be appointed by the members before the meeting of creditors or at the meeting by the creditors. If two different liquidators are appointed, the creditors' nominee is usually preferred. CVLs, also known as **creditors' voluntary winding-ups**, are the most common form of liquidation in use in the UK. *Compare* MEMBERS' VOLUNTARY LIQUIDATION.

credit rating An assessment of the creditworthiness of an individual or a firm, i.e. the extent to which they can safely be granted credit. Traditionally, banks have provided confidential trade references (*see* BANKER'S REFERENCE), but recently **credit-reference agencies** (also known as **rating agencies**) have grown up, which gather information from a wide range of sources, including the county courts, bankruptcy proceedings, hire-purchase companies, and professional debt collectors. This information is then provided as a **credit reference**, for a fee, to interested parties. The consumer was given some protection from such activities in the *Consumer Credit Act 1974, which allows an individual to obtain a copy of all the information held by such agencies relating to that individual, as well as the right to correct any discrepancies. There are also agencies that specialize in the corporate sector, giving details of a company's long-term and short-term debt. This can be extremely important to the price of the company's shares on the market, its ability to borrow, and its general standing in the business community. Credit ratings for the debt instruments of large corporations are provided by such

organizations as Moody's Investor Service and Standard and Poor's (*see* BOND CREDIT RATING). *See also* ANCILLARY CREDIT BUSINESS.

credit risk 1. The *risk taken when a loan is made on which the borrower will default, or delay repayment of the principal, or fail to keep up with scheduled payments of interest. *See also* POLITICAL CREDIT RISK; TRANSFER CREDIT RISK **2.** The risk that the value of a flow of payments from a credit derivative will decline due to an adverse movement in the *credit rating.

credit sale agreement See HIRE PURCHASE.

credit squeeze A government measure, or set of measures, to reduce economic activity by restricting the money supply. Measures used include increasing the interest rate (to restrain borrowing), controlling moneylending by banks and others, and increasing down payments or making other changes to hire-purchase regulations.

credit transfer A system of making payments by transferring money through a bank. The payer gives instructions naming the receiver and giving the receiver's address and account number. Several receivers may be listed and settled by a single transaction. The popularity of this system in the UK led the banks to introduce a credit-clearing system in 1961 and the Post Office to do so in 1968. The Bankers' Automated Clearing System (now Bacs) was introduced in 1969 (*see* UK PAYMENTS ADMINISTRATION). *See also* BANK GIRO CREDIT; GIRO.

creditworthiness An assessment of a person's or a business's ability to pay for goods purchased or services received. Creditworthiness may be presented in the form of a *credit rating.

creeping takeover The accumulation of a company's shares, by purchasing them openly over a period on a stock exchange, as a preliminary to a takeover (*see* TAKEOVER BID). There are regulations governing this process and stipulating the maximum number of shares that can be acquired before formal notification must be made and a bid undertaken.

CREST An electronic share settlement system created by the Bank of England for the securities industry that began operation in 1996. Using CREST, shares are registered electronically, purchases and sales are settled instantaneously on the due date, and the dividends can be paid electronically direct to the shareholder's bank. Paper certificates and associated paperwork have been abolished for those who join CREST. As with paper shares, the company register of shareholders provides proof of ownership. Those wishing to retain paper certificates are able to do so. Since September 2002 CREST has been wholly owned by *Euroclear.

critical event In critical-path analysis, an event—i.e. the start and/or completion of an activity—that lies on a critical path (*see* NETWORK MODELLING).

critical incident technique (CIT) An analytical technique used to identify those factors that are critical to the success or failure of individuals or systems in a given setting. People with first-hand experience (e.g. factory supervisors) are asked to describe incidents in which behavioural or other factors had a critical effect. These findings are then collated and analysed. The technique has mainly been used to devise rating scales for *employee evaluation (*see* BEHAVIOURALLY ANCHORED RATING SCALES; BEHAVIOURAL OBSERVATION SCALE) but is also used in *accident analysis, analysis of customer complaints, and various other applications.

critical management studies (CMS) A radical approach to management studies and organizational theory that emerged in the 1990s. It has its roots in post-structuralism, feminism, and environmentalism and is deeply critical of traditional managerialist assumptions.

critical mass A threshold number of users or customers needed for the sustainable growth of a product or service. Critical mass is required for the success of many online communities and for competing standards.

critical-path analysis (CPA) *See* NETWORK MODELLING.

critical success factors The strengths and weaknesses that most affect an organization's success. These are measured relative to those of its competitors.

CRM system *See* CUSTOMER RELATIONSHIP MANAGEMENT SYSTEM.

crore *See* LAKH.

cross-border listing The practice of listing shares in a company on the stock exchanges of different countries in order to create a larger market for the shares.

cross-currency interest-rate swap A *swap of two interest rates in two different currencies. This usually involves swapping a fixed rate for a floating rate (or vice versa); if both rates are floating it is known as a *basis swap. *See* CURRENCY SWAP; INTEREST-RATE SWAP.

crossed cheque *See* CHEQUE.

cross-holding A situation in which two or more companies hold shares in each other in order to cement business ties and forestall takeovers.

crossing the chasm A common problem in new-product marketing in which there is a gap between the use of a technology by *early adopters and its adoption by more pragmatic mainstream consumers.

cross-selling The practice of selling related products and services to existing customers. For example, a car dealer may also offer its customers servicing of the vehicle, valeting, re-upholstering, etc. An insurance broker may also offer motor-car insurance to its house-insurance customers. Businesses often cross-sell as part of their customer loyalty and retention strategy. Research evidence suggests that the greater the number of different products or services a customer buys from the same vendor, the lower the defection rate. *See also* UP-SELLING.

crowdfunding The financing of a new company or other project by selling shares or bonds directly to small private investors via the Internet. Despite its attractions, there have been fears that this growing practice offers scant legal protection to investors or to entrepreneurs, who may find their ideas are stolen and developed by others. In the UK and the USA crowdfunding platforms have increasingly been brought within the remit of the regulatory authorities. *See also* PEER-TO-PEER LENDING.

crown jewel option A form of *poison pill in which a company, defending itself against an unwanted *takeover bid, writes an *option that would allow a partner or other friendly company to acquire one or more of its best businesses at an advantageous price if control of the defending company is lost to the unwelcome predator. The granting of such an option may not always be in the best interests of the shareholders of the defending company.

CRP Abbreviation for *capacity requirement plan.

cruzeiro *See* REAL.

crystallization *See* CHARGE.

CSR Abbreviation for *corporate social responsibility.

CT Abbreviation for *corporation tax.

cultural environment Institutions and other forces that affect society's basic values, perceptions, preferences, and behaviours.

cultural intelligence (CQ) An individual's sensitivity to and ability to work positively with cultural differences. In today's globalized business environment this is an increasingly valued (and studied) attribute.

cum- *See* EX-.

cum-new Denoting a share that is offered for sale with the right to take up any *scrip issue or *rights issue. *Compare* EX-NEW.

cumulative preference share A type of *preference share that entitles the owner to receive any dividends not paid in previous years. Companies are not obliged to pay dividends on preference shares if there are insufficient earnings in any particular year. Cumulative preference shares guarantee the eventual payment of these dividends in arrears before the payment of dividends on ordinary shares, provided that the company returns to profit in subsequent years.

cumulative preferred stock In the USA, stock in which the dividends accumulate if not paid out in a particular financial period.

currency 1. Any kind of money that is in circulation in an economy. **2.** Anything that functions as a *medium of exchange, including coins, banknotes, cheques, *bills of exchange, promissory notes, etc. **3.** The money in use in a particular country. *See* FOREIGN EXCHANGE. **4.** The time that has to elapse before a bill of exchange matures.

currency future A *financial futures contract in which a currency for forward delivery is bought or sold at a particular exchange rate.

currency option A contract giving the right either to buy or to sell a specified currency at a fixed exchange rate within a given period. The price agreed is called the *exercise price or strike price. This is the price at which the buyer has the right to buy or sell the currency.

currency risk *See* EXCHANGE-RATE EXPOSURE.

currency swap A *swap in which specified amounts of one currency are exchanged for another currency at agreed principles over time. In an ordinary currency swap both currencies bear interest at a fixed rate: if both currencies bear interest at a floating rate the transaction is known as a *basis swap and if one rate is floating and the other fixed it is a *cross-currency interest-rate swap.

current account 1. An active account at a bank or building society into which deposits can be paid and from which withdrawals can be made by cheque (*see also* CHEQUE ACCOUNT). Building societies usually make no charges and pay interest on balances maintained in a current account. Banks, in order to remain competitive, have been obliged to follow the same practice for most non-business accounts. **2.** The part of the *balance of payments account that records non-capital transactions. It includes trade in visibles and invisibles. **3.** An account in which intercompany or interdepartmental balances are recorded. **4.** An account recording the transactions of a partner in a partnership that do not relate directly to his or her capital in the partnership (*see* CAPITAL ACCOUNT).

current assets (circulating assets; circulating capital; floating assets)
Those assets of an organization that form part of the *working capital and are constantly changing their form, circulating from cash to goods and back to cash again. Cash is used to purchase raw materials, which become work in progress when issued to a production department. The work in progress becomes finished goods, which once they are sold, become debtors or cash from an accounting point of view. Debtors are ultimately changed into cash when they pay, thus completing the cycle. *Compare* FIXED ASSET.

current cost 1. A cost calculated to take into consideration current circumstances of cost and performance levels. **2.** The sum that would be required at current prices to purchase or manufacture an asset. This may be the replacement cost or the historical cost adjusted for inflation by means of an appropriate price index. **3.** (**constant dollar**) In the USA, the method of converting historical cost to current cost and then adjusting to constant purchasing power by using the average *Consumer Price Index for the current year.

current-cost accounting (CCA) A form of accounting in which the approach to capital maintenance is based on maintaining the operating capability of a business. Assets are valued at their *value to the business, which is the loss that a business would suffer if it were to be deprived of the use of the asset. This may be the *replacement cost of the asset, its *net realizable value, or its *economic value to the business. Current-cost accounting ensures that a business maintains its operating capacity by separating holding gains from *operating profits, thereby preventing them from being distributed to shareholders. The current-cost accounting profit figure is derived by making a number of adjustments to the *historical-cost accounting profit and loss account: these are the cost of sales adjustment, *depreciation adjustment, monetary *working-capital adjustment, and the *gearing adjustment. The current-cost reserve in the balance sheet is used to 'collect' the current cost adjustments. This method of accounting was widely used in the UK in the late 1970s and early 1980s, when inflation was high; it was not popular, however, and as inflation has reduced it has been largely abandoned.

current liabilities Amounts owed by a business to other organizations and individuals that should be paid within one year from the balance-sheet date. These generally consist of trade creditors, *bills of exchange payable, amounts owed to group and related companies, taxation, social-security creditors, proposed dividends, accruals, deferred income, payments received on account, bank overdrafts, and short-term loans. Any long-term loans repayable within one year from the balance-sheet date should also be included. Current liabilities are distinguished from long-term liabilities on the balance sheet.

current marketing situation The section of a marketing plan that describes a target market and a company's position in it.

current purchasing power accounting (constant purchasing power accounting; CPP accounting) A form of accounting that measures profit after allowing for the maintenance of the purchasing power of the shareholders' capital. The *Retail Price Index is used to adjust for general price changes to ensure that the shareholders' capital maintains the same monetary purchasing power. There is no requirement to allow for the maintenance of the purchasing power of the loan creditors' capital. Current purchasing power accounting was covered by the provisional *Statement of Standard Accounting Practice 7, issued in 1974 but withdrawn in 1978.

current ratio (working-capital ratio) The ratio of the *current assets of a business to the *current liabilities, expressed as x:1 and used as a test of liquidity. For example, if the current assets are £250,000 and the current liabilities are £125,000 the current ratio is 2:1. There is no simple rule of thumb, but a low ratio, e.g. under 1:1, would usually raise concern over the liquidity of the company. Too high a ratio, e.g. in excess of 2:1, may indicate poor management of *working capital; this would be established by calculating the *stock turnover ratio and *debtor collection period ratio. Care must be taken when making comparisons between companies to ensure that any industry differences are recognized. The *liquid ratio is regarded as a more rigorous test of liquidity. See also SOLVENCY RATIO.

current-year basis The *basis of assessment for tax purposes in the UK in which tax is charged in a *fiscal year on profits arising in the accounts for the period ending in that tax year.

current yield See YIELD.

curriculum vitae (Latin: the course of one's life) An account of one's education, qualifications, and career prepared by a candidate for a job and given to a prospective employer. It should be typed and give full details. It is usual to add a section on outside interests. In the USA it is often called a **resumé**.

customer acquisition costs See ACQUISITION COST.

customer agent A software package or online shopping service that goes to different websites to compare prices and terms of sale on behalf of a customer.

customer capital See INTELLECTUAL CAPITAL.

customer-centred company A company that focuses on customer developments in designing its *marketing strategies and on delivering superior value to its target customers.

customer coalitions Groups of customers working together to obtain preferential prices for specific goods or services or to ensure high quality service by the provider.

customer database An organized collection of comprehensive information about individual customers or prospects, including geographic, demographic, and psychographic data as well as information about buying behaviour. See also LIVE-MARKETING DATABASE.

customer delivered value The difference between total customer value and the total customer cost of a marketing offer. It can be regarded as 'profit' to the customer.

customer-level activities See ACTIVITY.

customer lifetime value See LIFETIME VALUE.

customer perspective See BALANCED SCORECARD.

customer processing technology The technology that either provides the immediate interface between an organization and its customers (e.g. a bank *automated teller machine) or facilitates human interaction with customers. Direct interaction between the customer and the organization has traditionally been a low-technology activity. Increasingly, *information technology is being used to make that interaction more efficient; for example, by giving salespersons up-to-date product information and allowing them to transmit orders instantly. This both speeds the back-office operation and makes customers feel that they have received a more customized and responsive service.

customer profitability analysis (CPA)

The analysis of profits by customer. In the past, management accounting reports focused exclusively on product profitability, but in recent years it has become clear that managers need to understand both product and customer profitability. Typically, organizations that introduce CPA discover that a relatively small number of customers account for most of the profit; identifying profitable customers can therefore be very important. *See also* LIFETIME VALUE.

customer relationship management system (CRM system)

A computer application used to integrate a company's information about its customers with the knowledge of how best to use this information. It essentially combines a *sales-force automation system with a *marketing information system

customer service

The services an organization offers to its customers, especially of industrial goods and expensive consumer goods, such as computers or cars. Customer services cover a wide variety of forms, including after-sales servicing, such as a repair and replacement service, extended guarantees, regular mailings of information, and, more recently, freephone telephone calls in case of complaints. The appeal of a company's products is greatly influenced by the customer services it offers.

customer value

A consumer's assessment of the overall capacity of a product to satisfy his or her needs.

customer value analysis

An analysis undertaken to determine what benefits target customers value and how they rate the relative value of various competitors' offers.

customer value delivery system

The system made up of the value chains of a company and its suppliers, distributors, and ultimately its customers, who work together to deliver value to customers.

customization

The design and development of a product to meet the specific requirements of a single customer. Because of the high cost and time required to produce a unique product, most firms prefer to provide a product that consists of a set of standard features, some of which have been modified. Many cars, for example, are available in several different body styles, colours, and trim combinations. In addition, optional extras are specified to enable buyers to customize their purchases.

custom of the trade

A practice that has been used in a particular trade for a long time and is understood to apply by all engaged in that trade. Such customs or practices may influence the way in which a term in a contract is interpreted and courts will generally take into account established customs of a trade in settling a dispute over the interpretation of a contract.

Customs and Excise

See REVENUE AND CUSTOMS, HM.

customs entry

The record kept by the Customs of goods imported into or exported from a country. In the UK a *bill of entry is used for either imports (**entry in**) or exports (**entry out**). If no duty is involved with a consignment it is given **free entry**.

customs invoice

An invoice for goods imported or exported, which is prepared especially for the customs authorities.

customs tariff

A listing of the goods on which a country's government requires customs duty to be paid on being imported into that country, together with the rate of customs duty applicable. For the UK the Customs Tariff is published by the *Stationery Office.

customs union

A union of two or more states to form a region in which there are no import or export duties between members but goods imported into the region bear the same import duties. The *European Union is an example.

CVA Abbreviation for company *voluntary arrangement.

CVL Abbreviation for *creditors' voluntary liquidation.

CVS Abbreviation for *Corporate Venturing Scheme.

cwmni cyfyngedig cyhoeddus (c.c.c.) Welsh for *public limited company.

cwo Abbreviation for cash with order.

cybercafé (Internet café) A place with several computers that members of the public can use to access the Internet, usually for a fee on a walk-in basis.

cybercrime Crime committed on or using a computer or computer network. The main categories are computer fraud (e.g. *phishing scams), identity theft, breaking into confidential networks (*see* HACKER), and deliberately spreading computer viruses or *malware.

cyberliabilities The risks to an organization from misuse of the Internet and e-mail by its staff. These include the risks of virus infection, leakage of confidential information, and damage to a company's reputation resulting from unofficial e-mails or use of *social media (e.g. the forwarding of jokes that might be found offensive). The risks can be minimized by developing clear policies on appropriate and inappropriate use and the installation of software to check for viruses and content. If such measures are neglected, directors or senior managers may be liable in law for the actions of employees (e.g. in sending libellous or racist e-mails). *See* ACCEPTABLE USE POLICY.

cybermediaries Intermediaries who bring together buyers and sellers on the Internet or those who need and those who supply particular information or services.

cycle The medium-term wavelike rise and fall of the sales of a product, resulting from changes in general economic and competitive activity. *See also* BUSINESS CYCLE.

cycle inventory *See* INVENTORY.

cycle time The length of time required from the placing of an order by a customer to the delivery of the product or service. In companies using *just-in-time techniques, this should be equivalent to the time taken from start to finish of the manufacturing process. Reducing cycle times is very important for just-in-time companies; some ways in which this can be done include reducing set-up times, improving quality to reduce time spent on inspection and replacing faulty parts, and preventative maintenance to reduce machine downtime.

DA Abbreviation for *deposit account.

D/A Abbreviation for *documents against acceptance.

Daily Official List *See* OFFICIAL LIST.

daimyo bond A *bearer security issued on the Japanese markets and in the *euro-bond market by the *World Bank.

daisy chain The buying and selling of the same items several times over, for example stocks and shares. This may be done to 'inflate' trading activity (that is, the sale of the same items are being included in the sales figure more than once).

dalasi (GMD) The standard monetary unit of the Gambia, divided into 100 bututs.

damages Compensation, in monetary form, for a loss or injury, breach of contract, tort, or infringement of a right. Damages refers to the compensation awarded, as opposed to damage, which refers to the actual injury or loss suffered. The legal principle is that the award of damages is an attempt, as far as money can, to restore injured parties to the position they were in before the event in question took place; i.e. the object is to provide restitution rather than profit.

Damages are not assessed in an arbitrary fashion but are subject to various judicial guidelines. The general principle is that the claimant is entitled to full compensation for his or her losses. The purpose of damages in *tort is to put the claimant in the position that he or she would have been in had the tort not been committed. The purpose of damages in contract is to put the claimant in the position that he or she would have

been in had the *contract been performed. In either case the claimant must take all reasonable steps to mitigate his or her losses.

Damages can be further classified as liquidated or unliquidated, general or specific, and substantial, nominal, or exemplary.

Damages capable of being quantified in monetary terms are known as **liquidated damages**. In particular, liquidated damages include instances in which a genuine pre-estimate can be given of the loss that will be caused to one party if a contract is broken by the other party. If the anticipated breach of contract occurs this will be the amount, no more and no less, that is recoverable for the breach. Liquidated damages must be distinguished from any penalties specified in a contract as payable on its breach (which do not usually constitute a genuine estimate of the likely loss). Another form of liquidated damages is that expressly made recoverable under a statute. These may also be known as **statutory damages** if they involve a breach of statutory duty or are regulated or limited by statute. **Unliquidated damages** are those fixed by a court rather than those that have been estimated in advance.

General damages represent compensation for general damage, which is the kind of damage the law presumes to exist in any given situation. They are recoverable even without being specifically claimed and are awarded for the usual or probable consequences of the wrongful act complained of. For example, in an action for medical negligence, pain and suffering is presumed to exist, therefore if the action is successful, general damages would be awarded as compensation even though not specifically claimed or proved. Loss of earnings by the injured party, however, must be specifically claimed and proved, in which case they are known as **specific damages**.

Prospective damages are awarded to a plaintiff, not as compensation for any loss suffered at the time of a legal action but in respect of a loss it is reasonably anticipated will be suffered at some future time. Such an injury or loss may sometimes be considered to be too remote and therefore not recoverable.

Substantial damages are awarded to provide compensation when actual damage has been caused. By contrast, **nominal and contemptuous damages** are awarded for trifling amounts – usually when the court is of the opinion that although the plaintiff's rights have been infringed no real loss has been suffered, or, that although actual loss has resulted, the loss has been caused in part by the conduct of the plaintiff. The prospect of receiving only nominal or contemptuous damages prevents frivolous actions being brought. The award is usually accompanied by an order that each party bears their own legal costs.

Exemplary damages, on the other hand, are punitive damages awarded not merely as a means of compensation but also to punish the party responsible for the loss or injury. This usually occurs when the party causing the damage has done so wilfully or has received financial gain from the wrongful conduct. Exemplary damages will be greater than the amount that would have been payable purely as compensation.

danger money *See* OCCUPATIONAL HAZARD.

dark patterns Elements incorporated in the design of a website with the deliberate intention of benefiting the site's owner at the expense of the user. Dark patterns in the user interface of a site may cause consumers to opt in to services that they did not knowingly choose or, conversely, make it difficult to access an advertised benefit, such as a special offer. Users may be compelled to provide extra personal data, find themselves signed up by default to newsletters and e-mails, or in some cases incur additional hidden costs with their purchases. *See also* FORCED CONTINUITY.

data The information that is processed, stored, or produced by a computer. The distinction between program (instructions) and data is a fundamental one in computing.

database An organized collection of information held on a computer. A special computer program, called a **database management system** (**DBMS**), is used to organize the information held in the database according to a specified schema, to update the information, and to help users find the information they seek. There are two kinds of DBMS: simple DBMS, which is the electronic equivalent of a card index; and programmable DBMS, which provides a programming language that allows the user to analyse the data held in the database. On large computer systems, other programs can generally communicate with the DBMS and use its facilities. The term **data bank** is used for a collection of databases. *See also* DATA WAREHOUSING; MANAGEMENT INFORMATION SYSTEM.

databased marketing Marketing based on extensive use of computerized databases of customers. The databases usually contain customers' names, addresses, phone numbers, past purchases, and other data. These databases can be owned by the company doing the marketing (e.g. listing a bank's own customers) or they can be purchased from companies who supply consolidated lists.

data capture The insertion of information into a computerized system. For example, information about the sale of an item (the item sold, the sales price, and discount given, date and location of sale, etc.) is taken into the accounting system either at the point of sale in a retail organization by an electronic till or by keyboarding into the system when the invoice is prepared. This information is then readily available and up-to-date; it can also be used to adjust stock levels.

data file A *file on a computer system that contains *data, as opposed to one that contains a program. A data file is usually subdivided into records and fields.

data flow chart (data flow diagram) A chart that illustrates the way in which specified data is handled by a computer program. Its purpose is to specify the data, to show where it is used or changed, where it is stored, and which reports use it.

data integrity The accuracy, consistency, and completeness of the information held on a computer database. Data integrity can be compromised by human error (e.g. in inputting), software or mechanical faults, and system errors (e.g. inadequate procedures to make sure that changes made to local files are transferred to master files). Various checks, mechanisms, and standards have been developed to protect data integrity.

data mining The process of extracting useful knowledge from the huge volumes of data kept in modern computer databases. Sophisticated algorithms and statistical techniques are used to identify significant trends or patterns within complex data and to form predictive models. Major business applications include the mining of *electronic point of sale data to build customer profiles and identify regional or seasonal buying patterns. In finance, data mining is used to formulate the algorithms used in automated *high-frequency trading.

data processing (DP) Computing operations that manipulate large quantities of information. In business, these operations include book-keeping, printing invoices and mail shots, payroll calculations, and general record keeping. Data processing forms a major use of computers in business, and many firms have full-time data-processing departments.

data protection Safeguards relating to personal data, i.e. personal information about individuals that is stored on a computer or in 'relevant manual filing systems'. Legislation to prevent the potential misuse of such data has now been enacted in many countries.

In the UK the principles of data protection, the responsibilities of data controllers, and the rights of data subjects are now governed by the Data Protection Act 1998, which came into force on 1 March 2000. As compared to the Data Protection Act 1984, the 1998 Act extends the operation of protection beyond computer storage, replaces the system of registration with one of notification, and demands that the level of description by data controllers is more general than the detailed coding system previously required. Under the 1998 Act, the eight principles of data protection are:

(1) The information to be contained in personal data shall be obtained, and personal data shall be processed, fairly and lawfully.

(2) Personal data shall be held only for specified and lawful purposes and shall not be used or disclosed in any manner incompatible with those purposes.

(3) Personal data held for any purpose shall be relevant to that purpose and not excessive in relation to the purpose(s) for which it is used.

(4) Personal data shall be accurate and, where necessary, kept up to date.

(5) Personal data held for any purpose shall not be kept longer than necessary for that purpose.

(6) Personal data shall be processed in accordance with the rights of data subjects.

(7) Appropriate technical and organizational measures shall be taken against unauthorized and unlawful processing of personal data and against accidental loss or destruction of, or damage to, personal data.

(8) Personal data shall not be transferred to a country or territory outside the European Union unless that country or territory ensures an adequate level of protection for the rights and freedoms of data subjects in relation to the processing of personal data.

Data controllers must now notify their processing of data (unless they are exempt) with the **Information Commissioner** by completing and returning a notification form (this can now be done online). Notification is renewable annually; a data controller who fails to notify his or her processing of data, or any changes that have been made since notification, commits a criminal offence.

The Information Commissioner can seek information from and ultimately take enforcement action against data controllers for noncompliance with their full obligations under the 1998 Act. Appeals against decisions of the Commissioner may be made to the **Data Protection Tribunal**. Apart from non-notification, strict liability criminal offences under the 1998 Act include:

- obtaining, disclosing (or bringing about the disclosure), or selling (or advertising for sale) personal data, without consent of the data controller;
- obtaining unauthorized access to data;
- asking another person to obtain access to data;
- failing to respond to an information and/ or enforcement notice.

Data subjects have considerable rights conferred on them under the 1998 Act. They include:

- the right to find out what information is held about them;
- the right to seek a court order to rectify, block, erase, and destroy personal details if these are inaccurate, contain expressions of opinion, or are based on inaccurate data;
- the right to prevent processing where such processing would cause substantial unwarranted damage or substantial distress to themselves or anyone else;
- the right to prevent the processing of data for direct marketing;
- the right to compensation from a data controller for damage or damage and distress caused by any breach of the 1998 Act.

Datastream A UK financial information provider. It is now part of the Thomson Reuters Corporation.

data warehousing Computer technology enabling data from multiple operational processing systems to be brought together into a single source, which can then be accessed and interrogated. The data can be both current and historical. Warehousing differs from previous *management information systems in that designers do not need to think about what questions might be asked of the system. The data is held in detail, rather than prespecified categories; it is therefore possible to ask questions and to relate variables that may never have seemed relevant before, without having to interrupt ongoing operational processes. *See also* DECISION SUPPORT SYSTEM; EXPERT SYSTEM; ONLINE ANALYTICAL PROCESSING.

dated security A stock that has a fixed *redemption date.

date stamp A date stamped on the packaging of prepacked perishable food to indicate either the date by which it must be sold by a retailer (**sell-by date**) or the date by which it must be consumed by the consumer (**consume-by date**). This is a legal requirement for prepacked perishable food sold in the UK.

dawn raid An attempt by one company or investor to acquire a significant holding in the equity of another company by instructing brokers to buy all the shares available in that company as soon as the stock exchange opens, usually before the target company knows that it is, in fact, a target. The dawn raid may provide a significant stake from which to launch a *takeover bid. The conduct of dawn raids is now restricted by the *City Code on Takeovers and Mergers.

day book A specialized *book of prime entry recording specific transactions. For example, the *sales day book records invoices for sales, the *purchase day book records invoices received from suppliers. Day-book entries are transferred to memorandum *ledgers, such as the debtors' ledger and the creditors' ledger, while totals of entries are transferred to the *nominal ledger control accounts, such as the debtors' ledger control account and the creditors' ledger control account.

day order An order to a stockbroker, commodity broker, etc., to buy or sell a specified security or commodity. The order is valid for the day on which it is given and automatically becomes void at the close of trading on that day.

days of grace (grace period; period of grace) 1. The interval between the establishment of a loan and the first due date for repayment. **2.** Time given to defaulters to satisfy their obligations (*see* GRACE AND NOTICE PROVISION). **3.** The extra time allowed for payment of a *bill of exchange or insurance premium after the actual due date. With bills of exchange the usual custom is to allow 3 days of grace (not including Sundays and *Bank Holidays) and 14 days for insurance policies.

DBM Abbreviation for *disk-by-mail.

DBMS Abbreviation for database management system. *See* DATABASE.

DB scheme Abbreviation for *defined-benefit pension scheme.

DCF Abbreviation for *discounted cash flow.

DCI Abbreviation for *direct computer interviewing.

DC scheme Abbreviation for *defined-contribution pension scheme.

dead-cat bounce A temporary recovery on a stock exchange, after a substantial fall. It does not imply a reversal of the downward trend.

dead freight *Freight charges incurred by a shipper for space reserved but not used.

deads Mail that the postal service has been unable to deliver to the addressee on at least two occasions. Sometimes this is due to their death, but more often because they have moved away.

deadweight cargo Any cargo, such as minerals and coal, for which the *freight is charged on the basis of weight rather than volume.

deadweight debt A debt that is incurred to meet current needs without the security of an enduring asset. It is usually a debt incurred by a government; the national debt is a deadweight debt incurred by the UK government during the two World Wars.

deadweight tonnage *See* TONNAGE.

dealer 1. A trader of any kind. **2.** A person who deals as a principal on a financial market rather than as a broker or agent.

dealer brand Any product on which a middleman, usually a retailer, puts its own brand name. For example, St Michael is the dealer brand for Marks and Spencer's products.

dear money (tight money) A monetary policy in which loans are difficult to obtain and only available at high rates of interest. *Compare* CHEAP MONEY.

death-valley curve A curve on a graph showing how the venture capital invested in a new company falls as the company meets its start-up expenses before its income reaches predicted levels. This erosion of capital makes it difficult for the company to interest further investors in providing additional venture capital. *See also* MAXIMUM SLIPPAGE.

debenture 1. The most common form of long-term loan taken by a company. It is usually a loan repayable at a fixed date, although some debentures are *irredeemable securities; these are sometimes called *perpetual debentures. Most debentures also pay a fixed rate of interest, and this interest must be paid before a *dividend is paid to shareholders. Most debentures are also secured on the borrower's assets, although some, known as **naked debentures** or *unsecured loan stock, are not. In the USA debentures are usually unsecured, relying only on the reputation of the borrower. In a *secured debenture, the bond may have a fixed *charge (i.e. a charge over a particular asset) or a floating charge. If debentures are issued to a large number of people (for example in the form of **debenture stock** or **loan stock**) trustees may be appointed to act on behalf of the debenture holders. There may be a premium on redemption and some debentures are *convertible, i.e. they can be converted into ordinary shares on a specified date, usually at a specified price. The advantage of debentures to companies is that they carry lower interest rates than, say, overdrafts and are usually repayable a long time into the future. For an investor, they are usually saleable on a stock exchange and involve less risk than *equities. **2.** A *deed under seal setting out the main terms of such a loan. **3.** A form of bank security covering corporate debt, either fixed or floating; in either case the bank ranks as a preferred creditor in the event of liquidation.

debit An entry on the left-hand side of an *account in double-entry book-keeping, showing an amount owed by the organization keeping the book. In the case of a bank account, a debit shows an outflow of funds from the account.

debit balance The balance of an account whose total *debit entries exceed the total of the *credit entries. Debit balances represent expenditure and *assets.

debit card A plastic card issued by a bank or building society to enable its customers to pay for goods or services at certain retail outlets by using the telephone network to debit their accounts directly. It is also known as a **payment card**. The retail outlets need to have a computerized input device, into which the card is inserted; the customer is usually required to tap in a *personal identification number. Most debit cards also function as *cash cards and *cheque cards. In the USA these cards are sometimes called **asset cards**.

debit note A document sent by an organization to a person showing that the recipient is indebted to the organization for the amount shown in the debit note. Debit notes are rare as invoices are more

regularly used; however, a debit note might be used when an invoice would not be appropriate, e.g. for some form of inter-company transfer other than a sale of goods or services.

debt 1. A sum owed by one party to another. In commerce, it is usual for debts to be settled within one month of receiving an invoice, after which *interest may be incurred. **2.** Any funding instrument other than equity, such as a *bond, *bill of exchange, or *promissory note. *See also* DEBENTURE.

debt adjusting *See* ANCILLARY CREDIT BUSINESS.

debt administration *See* ADMINISTRATOR; ANCILLARY CREDIT BUSINESS.

debt collection agency An organization that specializes in collecting the outstanding debts of its clients, charging a commission for doing so. Because of the historical stigma attached to the phrase 'debt collection', these agencies prefer to be called **commercial collection agencies**. *See also* ANCILLARY CREDIT BUSINESS.

debt counselling *See* ANCILLARY CREDIT BUSINESS.

debt discounting The purchase of a *debt from a trader, especially an exporter at a discount. *See* DEBT COLLECTION AGENCY; FORFAITING.

debt–equity ratio A ratio used to examine the financial structure or *gearing of a business. The long-term debt, normally including *preference shares, of a business is expressed as a percentage of its equity. A business may have entered into an agreement with a bank that it will maintain a certain debt–equity ratio; if it breaches this agreement the loan may have to be repaid. The debt–equity ratio is now sometimes expressed as the ratio of the debt to the sum of the debt and the equity. *See* GEARING RATIOS. *See also* MODIGLIANI– MILLER THEOREM.

debt-for-equity swap A transaction in which debt is swapped for equity. It often accompanies the reorganization of companies in *financial distress. *See* DEBT RESTRUCTURING.

debt instrument A document used to raise non-equity finance consisting of a *promissory note, *bill of exchange, or any other legally binding *bond.

debtor One who owes money to another. In *balance sheets, debtors are those who owe money to the organization and a distinction has to be made between those who are expected to pay their debts during the next accounting period and those who will not pay until later.

debtor collection period (average collection period) The period, on average, that a business takes to collect the money owed to it by its trade debtors. If a company gives one month's credit then, on average, it should collect its debts within 45 days. The **debtor collection period ratio** is calculated by dividing the amount owed by trade debtors by the annual sales on credit and multiplying by 365. For example if debtors are £25,000 and sales are £200,000, the debtors collection period ratio will be:

$$(£25,000 \times 365)/£200,000 = 46 \text{ days}$$
approximately.

debtors' ledger *See* SALES LEDGER.

debt rescheduling Any change in the terms of an outstanding loan in which the debtor has repayment difficulties that involves deferring interest or principal repayments. When the new agreement also involves a lowering of interest rates or writing off part of the principal it is usually referred to as *debt restructuring.

debt restructuring The adjustment of a debt, either as a result of legal action or by agreement between the interested parties, to give the debtor a more feasible arrangement for meeting the creditors for meeting the financial obligations. This may take the form of a *debt-for-equity swap. The management of a company may also voluntarily restructure debt, for example by replacing long-term debt with short-term debt. Debt restructuring can also involve sovereign entities, as in March 2012 when Greece agreed to the biggest debt restructuring in history in order to secure an aid package from the European Union. *See* SOVEREIGN DEBT.

debt service ratio (DSR) The proportion of annual export earnings needed to service a country's external debts, including both interest payments and repayment of principal. The DSR is an important statistic, indicating the severity of a country's indebtedness. The effect of rescheduling programmes can be examined by comparing pre- and post-rescheduling DSRs.

debt swap The exchange of an outstanding loan to a third party between one bank and another. The loans are usually to governments of countries in the developing world and are often expressed in the local currency.

debug *See* BUG.

decentralization The delegation of decision-making responsibilities to the subunits of an organization. The advantages claimed for decentralization are that local managers are more aware of immediate problems, are better motivated, and have greater control over local circumstances. The disadvantages of decentralization are the possibility of wasteful competition between subunits, the duplication of certain services and functions, and the loss of central control and access to information. *See* DIVISIONALIZATION.

deceptive advertising *See* MISLEADING ADVERTISING.

decider *See* CONSUMER BUYING BEHAVIOUR; DECISION-MAKING UNIT.

decimal currency A currency system in which the standard unit is subdivided into 100 parts. Following the example of the USA in 1792, most countries have introduced a decimal system. However, it was not until 15 February 1971 that decimalization was introduced in the UK, following the recommendations of the Halesbury Committee of 1961.

decision making The act of deciding between two or more alternative courses of action. In the running of a business, accounting information and techniques are used to facilitate decision making, especially by the provision of decision models, such as *discounted cash flow, *network modelling, *marginal costing, and *breakeven analysis.

decision-making unit (DMU) The informal group of individuals within an organization that decides which items the organization should buy. Commercial buying is undertaken by a group of people, rather than by individuals; it is important for the seller to discover the composition of this group within each of his potential customers, and to recognize that membership changes periodically. The group's composition varies according to the cost and complexity of the item being bought, but might comprise: the company's purchasing manager, the proposed user of the item (the **internal user**), the **influencer** (one or more people, such as the production scheduler, indirectly associated with the use of the item), and the **decider** (one or more people, such as a director, who authorize the purchase).

decision model A model that simulates the elements or variables inherent in a business decision, together with their relationships to each other and the constraints under which they operate; the purpose of the model is to enable a solution to be arrived at in keeping with the objectives of the organization. For example, a *linear programming decision model may arrive at a particular production mix that, having regard to the constraints that exist, either minimizes costs or maximizes the *contribution. Other decision models include *decision trees and *discounted cash flow.

decision support system (DSS) A computer system specifically designed to assist managers in making unstructured or semistructured decisions, i.e. when the nature of the problem requiring a decision is not known in advance. A language subsystem has to be included in the DSS to allow users to communicate easily with the system and a problem processing subsystem, such as a *spreadsheet, is also required. Typically, a system of this type has a store of internal data and is able to access external data. A **group decision support system (GDSS)** is designed to facilitate group decision making, whereas an **executive information system (EIS)** is specially tailored for senior executives. *See also* DATA WAREHOUSING; EXPERT SYSTEM; MANAGEMENT INFORMATION SYSTEM.

decision table A table used to aid decision making. The table shows the problems requiring actions to be considered and estimated probabilities of outcomes. Where probabilities are difficult to estimate, the maximax and maximin criteria are often used, the former leading to the selection of the option with the greatest maximum outcome, the latter to the selection of the action with the greatest minimum outcome.

decision tree A diagram that illustrates the choices available to a decision maker and the estimated outcomes of each possible decision. Each possible decision is shown as a separate branch of the tree, together with each estimated outcome for each decision and the subjective *probabilities of these outcomes actually occurring. From this information the *expected values for each outcome can be determined, which can provide valuable information in decision making. For an example see the diagram.

deck cargo Cargo that is carried on the deck of a ship rather than in a hold. This may increase the insurance premium—depending on the nature of the cargo.

declaration of dividend A statement in which the directors of a company announce that a *dividend of a certain amount is recommended to be paid to the shareholders. The liability should be recognized as soon as the declaration has been made and the appropriate amount is included under *current liabilities on the *balance sheet.

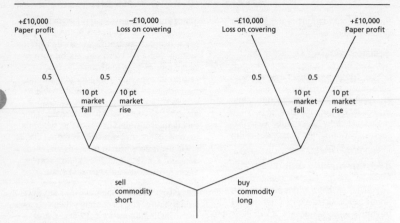

Decision tree. A decision tree showing the outcome of a speculative sale and purchase of a commodity, assuming that there is an equal probability of a 10 point market rise and a 10 point market fall. It is assumed that there is a stop loss order to cover after an adverse market movement of 10 points, but profits are allowed to run.

declaration of solvency A declaration made by the directors of a company seeking voluntary liquidation that it will be able to pay its debts within a specified period, not exceeding 12 months from the date of the declaration. It must contain a statement of the company's assets and liabilities, and a copy must be sent to the Registrar of Companies.
A director who participates in a declaration of solvency without reasonable grounds will be liable to a fine or imprisonment on conviction. *See* MEMBERS' VOLUNTARY LIQUIDATION.

decline stage The stage in a *product life cycle when the sales of the product begin to fall, because of such factors as reduced popularity, obsolescence, and market saturation.

decreasing term assurance A form of *term assurance in which the amount to be paid in the event of the death of the *life assured reduces with the passage of time. These policies are usually arranged in conjunction with a cash loan or mortgage and are designed to repay the loan if the *life assured dies. As the amount of the loan decreases with successive repayments the sum assured reduces at the same rate.

deductible The amount deducted from a claim in an *excess policy; whereas 'excess' is the usual word in motor-vehicle and householders' policies, 'deductible' is used in large commercial insurances. It is an amount that is deducted from every claim that is paid. If a claim is made for a figure below the deductible no payment is made. Deductibles are usually applied to policies in return for a premium reduction.

deductions at source A method of tax collection in which a person paying income to another deducts the tax on the income and is responsible for paying it to the authorities. Tax authorities have found that, in general, it is easier to collect tax from the payer rather than the recipient of income, especially if paying the tax is made a condition of the payer's obtaining tax relief for the payment. The payee receives a credit against any tax liability for the tax already suffered. Examples of this in the UK tax system are *PAYE, share dividends, interest on government securities, deeds of covenant, trust income, and subcontractors in the building industry.

deduplication The removal of names and addresses that appear in a customer or prospect list more than once. Duplicate records often occur because data is collated from a variety of sources. Furthermore, names and addresses are not always listed in exactly the same way and details are often incomplete. Good deduplication software, usually known as de-duping software, should be able to identify and flag these anomalies.

deed A written document that states clearly that it is intended to be a deed and that has been validly executed as a deed. These factors make a deed different from an ordinary written agreement. Until 1990 all deeds required a seal in order to be validly executed but it is now only necessary for a deed to be signed, witnessed, and delivered. Delivery may be actual or constructive, i.e. by carrying out some act to show that the deed is intended to be operative. Some transactions, such as conveyances of land, must be carried out by deed to be effective.

deed of arrangement A written agreement between a debtor and his or her creditors that has been registered as such with the Insolvency Service. The agreement may take the form of a *composition of debts or a *scheme of arrangement of the debtor's affairs. Unlike an individual *voluntary arrangement, a deed of arrangement can only be entered into when no bankruptcy order has been made.

deed of assignment *See* ASSIGNMENT.

deed of partnership A *partnership agreement drawn up in the form of a deed. It covers the respective *capital contributions of the partners, their entitlement to interest on their capital, their profit-sharing percentages, agreed salary, etc.

deed of variation A written *deed that identifies the specific provisions of a will to be varied. It must be signed by any person who would otherwise have benefited from the will as originally drawn. No payment or inducement must pass between the *beneficiaries in order to encourage them to enter into the variation. In order to apply, the deed must have been executed within two years of the testator's death and must have been filed within six months of the deed being executed.

deed poll A *deed used when only one party is involved in an action, e.g. when a person declares a wish to be known by a different name. Such a deed was formerly distinguished by having a straight edge at the top, as opposed to an *indenture. Deeds of all kinds now commonly have straight edges.

deep-line strategy *See* FULL-LINE STRATEGY.

deeply discounted security A loan stock or government security issued at a discount of more than 15% of the amount on redemption or, where it is held for more than 30 years, at a discount of more than 1/2% for each completed year between issue and redemption. The discount will normally be treated as income accruing over the life of the stock and charged to income tax on sale or redemption. For example, a **deep-discount bond** might be a four-year loan stock issued at £95 for every £100 nominal (the discount exceeds 1/2% per annum) or a 25-year loan stock issued at £75 for every £100 nominal (the discount exceeds 15% in total).

deep market A market for a security, commodity, currency, etc. in which there are currently a large number of transactions. In such a market the *spread between bid and offer prices will be narrow and sizable transactions can take place without moving the price of the security, etc. A deep market is highly liquid. *Compare* THIN MARKET.

de facto (Latin: in fact) Denoting that something exists as a matter of fact rather than by right. For example, a plaintiff may have de facto control of a property. This compares to **de jure** (Latin: in law), which denotes that something exists as a matter of legal right. For example, a planning authority may have acted de jure in refusing a planning application. In international law, one government may recognize another de facto, i.e. acknowledge that it is in control of the country even though it has no legal right to be. De jure recognition acknowledges that it has a legal right to govern. The basis of the distinction, however, is more political than legal.

de facto director A person who is not legally or formally appointed as a director of a company but may be regarded as such as a matter of fact, because he or she is allowed to occupy the position of director or assumes the responsibilities of a director. Such a person owes the same fiduciary duties to a company as a de jure director. *Compare* SHADOW DIRECTOR.

defalcation Embezzlement of property belonging to another party.

default 1. Failure to do something that is required by law, especially failure to comply with the rules of legal procedure. **2.** Failure to comply with the terms of a contract. A seller defaults by failing to supply the right quality goods at the time contracted. A buyer defaults by failing to take up documents or pay for goods according to contract. Before taking legal action against a defaulter a **default notice** must be served on him or her. **3.** Failure to make required payments, as on a mortgage or other loan.

defended takeover bid A *takeover bid for a company in which the directors of the target company oppose the bid.

defender strategy A competitive strategy in which a business concentrates on its existing products or services and attempts to protect (rather than expand) its market share by offering superior quality, low prices, and strong customer service. Such a policy requires firm cost control and is usually only successful in an established, stable market where there is little scope for innovation. *Compare* PROSPECTOR STRATEGY.

defensive interval ratio A ratio that demonstrates the ability of a business to satisfy its current debts by calculating the time for which it can operate on current liquid assets, without needing revenue from the next period's sales. Current assets less stock is divided by the projected daily operational expenditure less non-cash charges. Projected daily operational expenditure is calculated by dividing by 365 the total of the *cost of sales, operating expenses, and other cash expenses.

defensive response A management strategy in which a company responds to disquiet about its social or environmental practices by taking only the minimum steps necessary to avoid legal or regulatory action. *Compare* ACCOMMODATING RESPONSE; OBSTRUCTIVE RESPONSE; PROACTIVE RESPONSE.

defensive security A stable *security that is expected to have relatively good performance in periods of recession or downturn in financial markets.

deferred annuity An *annuity in which payments do not start at once but either at a specified later date or when the policyholder reaches a specified age.

deferred asset An *asset the realization of which is likely to be considerably delayed.

deferred credit (deferred liability) Income received or recorded before it is earned, under the *accruals concept. The income will not be included in the *profit and loss account of the period but will be carried forward on the *balance sheet until it is matched with the period in which it is earned. A common example of a deferred credit is a government grant. The grant is shown as a separate item or under *creditors in the balance sheet, and an annual amount is transferred to the profit and loss account until the deferred credit balance is brought to nil.

deferred debit (deferred asset; deferred expense) An item of expenditure incurred in an accounting period but, under the *accruals concept, not matched with the income it will generate. Instead of being treated as an operating cost for that period, it is treated as an *asset with the intention of treating it as an operating cost to be charged against the income it will generate in a future period. An example is rent paid for a period beyond the end of the accounting period.

deferred income *See* DEFERRED CREDIT.

deferred ordinary share 1. A type of *ordinary share, formerly often issued to founder members of a company, in which dividends are only paid after all other types of ordinary share have been paid. They often entitle their owners to a large share of the profit. **2.** A type of share on which little or no dividend is paid for a fixed number of years, after which it ranks with other ordinary shares for dividend.

deferred-payment agreement *See* HIRE PURCHASE.

deferred pricing A situation in which a transaction is agreed upon before the price of the transaction is settled.

deferred rebate A rebate offered by a supplier of goods or services to customers on the understanding that further goods and services are purchased from the same supplier. The rebate is usually paid periodically, after the supplier has seen that he has the customer's continued support. Some shipping companies offer a deferred rebate to shippers.

deferred taxation A sum set aside for tax in the accounts of an organization that will become payable in a period other than that under review. It arises because of timing differences between tax rules and accounting conventions. The principle of **deferred-tax accounting** is to reallocate a tax payment to the same period as that in which the relevant amount of income or expenditure is shown. Historically, the most common reason for this timing difference is because the percentages used for the calculation of *capital allowances have differed from those used for *depreciation.

deficit financing The creation of a government *budget deficit for the purpose of expanding economic activity by fiscal policy.

defined-benefit pension scheme (DB scheme) An occupational pension scheme in which the rules specify the benefits to be received on retirement and the scheme is funded accordingly. The benefits are normally calculated on a formula incorporating years of service and salary levels (*see* FINAL SALARY SCHEME). Accounting for pension costs poses a number of difficulties for accountants; the basic regulations are set out in *International Accounting Standard 19, Employee Benefits and Section 28 of the new Financial Reporting Standard Applicable in the UK and Republic of Ireland.

In recent years rising costs have led many companies to close their existing DB schemes to new employees, who are obliged to join *defined-contribution pension schemes.

defined-contribution pension scheme (DC scheme) A pension scheme in which the benefits are based on the value of the contributions paid in by each member. The rate of contribution is normally specified; the amount of pension an individual will receive will depend on the size of the fund accumulated and the annuity that can be obtained from it at the date of retirement. *Compare* DEFINED-BENEFIT PENSION SCHEME.

deflation The situation in which there is a general decrease in prices, especially when this is accompanied by falling levels of output, employment, and trade. Because of these associations, advocates of anti-inflationary policies usually now prefer the term *disinflation. *Compare* INFLATION.

defunct company A company that has been wound up and has therefore ceased to exist.

degearing The process in which some of the fixed-interest loan stock of a company is replaced by *ordinary share capital. *See* GEARING.

de-industrialization A substantial fall in the importance of the manufacturing sector in the economy of an industrialized nation as it becomes uncompetitive with its neighbours. This may result from bad industrial relations, poor management, inadequate investment in capital goods, or short-sighted government economic policies. In many cases each of these factors contributes to de-industrialization.

de jure *See* DE FACTO.

delayering The removal of layers of middle management (usually) from organizational structures, in order to bring an organization closer to the customer and generally to be more flexible and responsive. The process is facilitated by increased use of *information technology, which allows hierarchies of sequential decision making to be replaced by less bureaucratic procedures. *See also* BROADBANDING.

del credere agent A selling *agent who guarantees to pay for any goods sold on behalf of a principal if the customer fails to do so. An extra commission is charged for covering this risk.

delegatus non potest delegare
(Latin: a delegate cannot further delegate) The rule that a person to whom a power, trust, or authority is given to act on behalf, or for the benefit of, another, cannot delegate this obligation unless expressly authorized to do so. For instance, an auditor who has been appointed to audit the accounts of a company cannot delegate the task to another unless expressly allowed to do so. If express authorization has not been granted the auditor will have acted **ultra vires*.

deliberate strategy A business strategy in which decisions are made according to a preconceived plan and outcomes are realized as planned. In 1978 the business academic Henry Mintzberg contrasted such a strategy with an *emergent strategy, in which some or all decisions occur in response to events. According to Mintzberg (who defines a strategy as a 'pattern in a stream of decisions'), a pure deliberate strategy must satisfy three conditions: that intentions are precise and detailed; that these intentions are known to all within an organization; and that they are realized exactly as they were formulated. In practice this is very rare, with most real-world strategies occurring somewhere along a continuum from purely deliberate to purely emergent. *See also* PRESCRIPTIVE STRATEGY.

Delivered Ex Ship (DES) An *Incoterm denoting an export contract in which the seller pays all freight and insurance charges up to the port of destination. If the seller also agrees to pay for lighterage and unloading this is correctly styled a **Delivered Ex Quay** (**DEQ**) contract. In a DES or DEQ contract, unlike a Cost, Insurance and Freight Contract (*see* COST AND FREIGHT), risk passes to the buyer at the port of destination, not that of shipment.

delivered price (freight-allowed price) A quoted price that includes the cost of packing, insurance, and delivery to the destination given by the buyer (usually a port or airport).

delivery date 1. The day in the month that commodities on a futures contract have to be delivered. **2.** The maturity date for foreign exchange in a forward exchange contract. **3.** The date that a buyer of securities receives the relevant certificates.

delivery month The month in which the *underlying of a futures contract must be handed over to the buyer. Usually any day within the specified month will fulfil the contract obligations.

delivery note A document, usually made out in duplicate, that is given to the consignee of goods when they are delivered to him. The consignee, or his representative, signs one copy of the delivery note as evidence that the goods have been received. *See also* ADVICE NOTE.

delivery order A written document from the owner of goods to the holder of the goods (e.g. a warehouse company) instructing them to release the goods to the firm named on the delivery order or to the bearer (if made out to 'bearer'). A delivery order backed by a dock or warehouse *warrant may be accepted by a bank as security for a loan.

Delphi technique A *qualitative forecasting technique that seeks to eliminate the effects of personal relationships and domination by strong personalities. A coordinator sends a written question to each relevant expert, who then replies in writing. The replies are edited and summarized. On the basis of the summary, new questions are issued to the experts, who again reply in writing. The cycle is repeated until the coordinator is satisfied that the process has provided an objective assessment of the issue in question (e.g. the likely sales of a new product).

demand curve A curve on a graph relating the quantity of a good demanded to its price. Economists usually expect the demand curve to slope downwards, i.e. an increase in the price of a good brings a lower level of demand.

demand deposit An instant-access checking account (i.e. current account) in the USA.

demand-pull inflation A rise in prices caused by an excess of demand over supply in the economy as a whole. When the labour force and all resources are fully employed extra demand will only disappear as a result of rising prices. *Compare* COST-PUSH INFLATION.

demarcation dispute An industrial dispute between trade unions or between members of the same union regarding the allocation of work between different types of tradesmen or workers.

demarketing The process of discouraging consumers from either buying or consuming a particular product, such as cigarettes. It may also be used if a product is found to be faulty and the producers do not wish to risk their reputation by continuing to sell it.

demerger A business strategy in which a large company or group of companies

splits up so that its activities are carried on by two or more independent companies. Alternatively, subsidiaries of a group are sold off. Demerging was popular in the late 1980s when large *conglomerates became unfashionable. One of the main reasons for demerging is to improve the value of the company's shares, particularly if one part of a group's value can be better reflected by a separate share quotation.

Deming Prize A prize instituted in 1951 by the Union of Japanese Scientists and Engineers, in honour of W. Edwards Deming, one of the leading *total quality management (TQM) theorists, who introduced the idea that quality control should be a strategic activity led by senior management. The prize is given to organizations or divisions of organizations that can demonstrate successful 'company-wide quality control', using *statistical process control techniques. There is also a prize for individuals who have made an outstanding contribution to the study or development of TMQ.

demise charter *See* CHARTERING.

democratic leader A leader who maintains an egalitarian atmosphere within the group and who is prepared to delegate planning, decision making, and other responsibilities to followers. Experimental studies of *leadership style have found that work groups with democratic leaders tend to be more flexible, innovative, and highly motivated than those with *authoritarian leaders or *laissez-faire leaders.

demographic segmentation Dividing a market into groups based on such demographic variables as age, sex, family size, family life cycle, income, occupation, education, religion, race, or nationality (*see also* MARKET SEGMENTATION). While demographic segmentation has been popular in marketing, it is now used together with benefit, life-stage, and life-cycle segmentation to try to produce more predictable market information. *See also* GEODEMOGRAPHIC SEGMENTATION.

demography The study of human populations, including their size, composition (by age, sex, occupation, etc.), and sociological features (birth rate, death rate, etc.).

demurrage 1. Liquidated *damages payable under a charterparty (*see* CHARTERING), at a specified daily rate for any days (**demurrage days**) required for completing the loading or discharging of cargo after the *lay days have expired. **2.** Unliquidated damages to which a shipowner is entitled if, when no lay days are specified, the ship is detained for loading or unloading beyond a reasonable time. **3.** Liquidated damages included in any contract to compensate one party if the other is late in fulfilling his obligations. This occurs frequently in building contracts. Even if the loss caused by the delay is less than the demurrage, the demurrage must be paid in full.

demutualization The act by which a *mutual, such as a *building society, changes its status to that of a public limited company. In the 1980s and 1990s this was seen in the retail financial services industry worldwide.

denar (MKD) The standard monetary unit of Macedonia, divided into 100 deni.

denationalization *See* PRIVATIZATION.

deni A monetary unit of Macedonia, worth one hundredth of a *denar.

department A discrete section of an organization under the responsibility of a **department manager**; separate costs and, where appropriate, income are allocated or apportioned to the department for the purposes of costing, performance appraisal, and control.

Department for Business, Innovation and Skills (BIS) The UK government department responsible for consumer and competition policy, company legislation, employment law, science and research, higher education, and adult learning. It was formed in 2009 from a merger of the **Department for Business,**

Enterprise and Regulatory Reform (BERR) and the Department for Innovation, Universities and Skills (DIUS).

(((●))) SEE WEB LINKS
• BIS area of the Gov.uk website

Department for International Development The UK government department responsible for providing economic, technical, and other assistance to overseas countries with the goals of eradicating extreme poverty and promoting sustainable development.

Department for Work and Pensions A UK government department formed in 2001 from parts of the former Department of Education and Employment and the Department of Social Security. It is responsible for helping unemployed people back into work and for administering unemployment benefit and other *social security payments, including state pensions.

department store A retail organization that carries a wide variety of products—typically clothing, home furnishings, and household goods; each department is managed by specialist buyers or merchandisers. Historically, department stores have occupied large multistorey buildings in city centres.

dependent demand The situation arising when the demand for one product is derived from or depends on the demand for other items. If a car manufacturer, for example, knows how many vehicles to produce in a month, this will fix how many engines, wheels, doors, seats, etc., have to be ordered. *Compare* INDEPENDENT DEMAND.

depletion The using up of an *asset, especially a mineral asset. For example, a quarry is depleted by the extraction of stone. *See also* WASTING ASSET.

depolarization *See* POLARIZATION.

deposit 1. A sum of money paid by a buyer as part of the sale price of something in order to reserve it. Depending on the terms agreed, the deposit may or may not be returned if the sale is not completed. **2.** A sum of money left with an organization, such as a bank, for safekeeping or to earn interest or with a broker, dealer, etc., as a security to cover any trading losses incurred. **3.** A sum of money paid as the first instalment on a *hire-purchase agreement. It is usually paid when the buyer takes possession of the goods.

deposit account (DA) An *account with a bank or building society from which money cannot be withdrawn without notice and on which interest is paid. *See also* SAVINGS ACCOUNT.

deposit-taking institution An institution whose main function is to take deposits. This is the basis of the legal definition of a bank as laid down in the *Banking Acts. In the UK regulation of deposit-taking institutions was transferred from the Bank of England to the *Financial Services Authority in 2001. *See also* FINANCIAL INSTITUTION.

depreciation 1. A measure of the diminution in value of a *fixed asset due to *wear and tear or *obsolescence over an accounting period. A **provision for depreciation** can be computed by means of a number of generally accepted techniques, including the *straight-line method, the *diminishing-balance method, the *sum-of-the-digits method, the *production-unit method, and the *revaluation method. The depreciation reduces the book value of the asset and is charged against income of an organization in the income statement or *profit and loss account. Section 17 of the new Financial Reporting Standard Applicable in the UK and the Republic of Ireland deals with the subject of depreciation in the accounts. The relevant *International Accounting Standard is IAS 16, Property, Plant and Equipment. **2.** A fall in the value of a currency with a *floating exchange rate relative to other currencies. Depreciation can refer both to day-to-day movements and to long-term realignments in value. For currencies with a *fixed exchange rate a *devaluation

or *revaluation of currency is required to change the relative value. *Compare* APPRECIATION.

depreciation rate The percentage rate used in the *straight-line method and *diminishing-balance method of *depreciation in order to determine the amount of depreciation that should be written off a *fixed asset and charged against income or the profit and loss account.

depression (slump) An extended or severe period of *recession. Depressions occur infrequently. The most recent Great Depression occurred in the 1930s; prior to that they occurred in the periods 1873–96, 1844–51, and 1810–17. Depressions are usually associated with falling prices (*see* DEFLATION) and large-scale involuntary unemployment. They are often preceded by major financial crashes, e.g. the Wall Street crash of 1929. *See also* BUSINESS CYCLE.

depth interview An unstructured interview that explores a marketing issue for purposes of *marketing research. The interviewer, a specialist acting on behalf of a client, will have previously compiled a topic guide that identifies the points to be explored; the respondent is part of a *sample chosen to match certain criteria (e.g. if the problem concerned tea all respondents would be tea drinkers). The interview is conducted informally and the interviewer adopts a passive role; he encourages the respondent to talk and ask questions, while ensuring that all the points on the topic guide are covered. After a minimum of ten such interviews, the interviewer reports back to his client with his marketing recommendations. Depth interviews are a qualitative procedure (*see* QUALITATIVE MARKETING RESEARCH).

depth of product line The number of different items in a line of products. For example, a soap manufacturer may have eight brands of soap in the bar soap line.

DEQ Abbreviation for Delivered Ex Quay. *See* DELIVERED EX SHIP.

deregulation The removal of controls imposed by governments on the operation of markets. Many economists and politicians believe that during the mid-20th century governments imposed controls over markets that had little or no justification. Since the 1980s many governments have followed a deliberate policy of deregulation. However, most economists still argue that certain markets should be regulated, particularly where there is a natural monopoly or a state of *market failure. The extent to which deregulation of the US financial sector played a role in precipitating the financial crisis of 2007–08 is a matter of considerable dispute.

derivative A financial instrument, the price of which has a strong relationship with an *underlying commodity, currency, economic variable, or financial instrument. The main types of derivatives are *futures contracts, forwards (*see* FORWARD DEALING), *swaps, and *options. They are traded on **derivative markets** or *over the counter (OTC). The market-traded derivatives are standard, while the OTC trades are specific and customized. The 1990s and 2000s saw massive growth in the market for complex derivatives products and the lack of transparency associated with these instruments is seen as a major factor in the global financial collapse of 2008 (*see* COLLATERALIZED DEBT OBLIGATION). *See also* SECURITIZATION; STRUCTURED FINANCE.

derivative action A legal action brought by a shareholder on behalf of a company, when the company cannot itself decide to sue. A company will usually sue in its own name but if those against whom it has a cause of action are in control of the company (i.e. directors or majority shareholders) a shareholder may bring a derivative action. The company will appear as defendant so that it will be bound by, and able to benefit from, the decision. The need to bring such an action must be proved to the court before it can proceed.

descriptive research Marketing research aimed at providing good descriptions of marketing problems, situations, or markets. Descriptive research explores the market potential for a product, the demographics of a market, and the attitudes of consumers. Most marketing research in the UK is of this type.

descriptive statistics (univariate statistics) The branch of statistics that provides marketing researchers with a summary of the available data. Usually a single variable is analysed alone, such as the mean age of the consumers of a product or the consumption level of a type of food.

design & build A contract used in the construction industry to cover a situation in which one company takes the responsibility for both the design and building of a major building, such as a school or office block. It brings together the usually separated activities of architectural design and building construction in order to achieve greater integration to meet the client's needs.

Designated Professional Body (DPB) A professional body registered with the *Financial Services Authority as having statutory responsibility for regulating its profession. There are now 10 DPBs: the Association of Chartered Certified Accountants, the Council for Licensed Conveyancers, the Institute of Actuaries, the Institute of Chartered Accountants in England and Wales, the Institute of Chartered Accountants in Ireland, the Institute of Chartered Accountants of Scotland, the Law Society, the Law Society of Northern Ireland, the Law Society of Scotland, and the Royal Institute of Chartered Surveyors. The DPBs were formerly known as **Recognized Professional Bodies** (RPBs).

designed capacity The maximum theoretical output of an *operating system in units per time, taking no account of such operational limitations as staffing decisions, set-up times, unforeseeable failures, maintenance, etc. *Compare* EFFECTIVE CAPACITY.

desirable products Products that give both high immediate satisfaction and high long-run benefits.

deskilling The process of removing the requirement for individual skills as part of an operating system. Techniques to improve the efficiency of systems tend to simplify and standardize procedures, so that they can be repeated at minimum cost. Computers and information technology can also play a role in replacing human decision making. Deskilling can result in a loss of motivation on the part of employees.

desk research A *marketing research study using mainly external published data and material but also including some internal reports, company records, etc. *See also* OFF-THE-PEG RESEARCH.

desktop publishing (DTP) An application of computers that enables small companies and individuals to produce reports, advertising, magazines, etc., to near-typeset quality. Modern systems, which simulate many of the functions of professional typesetting systems, consist of a *personal computer, using DTP software, and a *laser printer. The software is designed to format text into pages using a wide range of different typefaces. A common feature is the ability to preview each page on the computer's screen before it is printed and to import pictures and diagrams into the page.

destination site Any website visited following a click on a *hyperlink, especially one visited following a *clickthrough on a *banner advertisement.

Deutsche Börse An international market place organizer for trading in securities, commodities, and derivatives, with its headquarters in Frankfurt, Germany. Established as a holding company in 1992, Deutsche Börse AG owns and operates the *Frankfurt Stock Exchange and (since 2000) the clearing and settlement facility *Clearstream. It is also joint owner of the electronic derivatives exchange *Eurex, which acquired the US-based *International Securities Exchange in 2007. Deutsche

Börse introduced the electronic trading platform Xetra in 1997 and became a public listed company in 2001.

(⊕) **SEE WEB LINKS**
• Deutsche Börse Group website

Deutschmark Formerly, the standard monetary unit of Germany, divided into 100 Pfennige. It was replaced by the euro in 2002.

devaluation A reduction in the value of a currency relative to gold or to other currencies. Governments engage in devaluation when they feel that their currency has become overvalued, for example through high rates of inflation making exports uncompetitive or because of a substantially adverse *balance of trade. The intention is that devaluation will make exports cheaper and imports dearer, although the loss of confidence in an economy forced to devalue invariably has an adverse effect. Devaluation is a measure that need only concern governments with a *fixed exchange rate for their currency. With a *floating exchange rate, devaluation or revaluation takes place continuously and automatically (*see* DEPRECIATION; REVALUATION OF CURRENCY).

developing countries Countries that often have abundant natural resources but lack the capital and entrepreneurial and technical skills required to develop them. The average income per head and the standard of living in these countries is therefore far below that of the industrial nations.

The developing countries, in which nearly 80% of the world's population lives, are characterized by mainly agricultural economies from which poverty, hunger, and disease have not been eliminated. Many depend on a single product for their exports and are therefore vulnerable in world markets. Some have developed small low-technology companies, but market mechanisms (particularly distribution) do not exist.

development costs *See* RESEARCH AND DEVELOPMENT COSTS.

development stage The stage in the development of a new product during which the concept is transformed into a prototype and the basic marketing strategy is developed. *See* NEW PRODUCT DEVELOPMENT.

diary method A procedure for collecting purchase data and the media habits of consumers; it requires respondents to complete a written report (in a diary) of their behaviour. This is either collected by or mailed to a marketing research company weekly or monthly.

diary panel A group of shops and shoppers who keep a regular record of all purchases or purchases of selected products, for the purpose of *marketing research.

dichotomous question A question that asks the respondent to choose between two answers, generally 'yes' or 'no'.

difference option An *option that pays the difference between the price of two assets. The buyer's profit will depend on how the price differential at the *exercise date compares with the price differential at the time of purchase.

differential analysis (incremental analysis) An assessment of the impact on costs and revenues of specific management decisions. Such an analysis will focus on identifying the **differential** (or **incremental) cash flows**, i.e. those costs or revenues that will change as a result of a specific decision. In decision making, the **differential costs** are the only *relevant costs. *See also* OUT-OF-POCKET COSTS.

differential pricing A method of pricing a product in which the same product is supplied to different customers, or different market segments, at different prices. This approach is based on the principle that to achieve maximum market penetration the price charged should be what a particular market will bear. *See* DISCRIMINATING MONOPOLY; REVENUE MANAGEMENT.

differentiated culture *See* ORGANIZATIONAL CULTURE.

differentiated marketing (multiple market segmentation) 1. Marketing in which provision is made to meet the special needs of certain consumers. For example, weight watchers require diet drinks and left-handed people require left-handed scissors. **2.** A marketing exercise in which the marketer selects more than one target market and then develops a separate marketing mix for each. The differentiation strategy for each of these target markets is a strategy in which the marketer offers a product that is unique in the industry, provides a distinct advantage, or is otherwise set apart from competitors' brands in some way other than price.

differentiation focus *See* FOCUS STRATEGY.

differentiation strategy A strategy that aims to gain *competitive advantage for a product or service across the whole of an industry by making it distinct from its competitors in terms of quality or *brand image. The strategy was described by Michael Porter in 1980, who distinguished it from the *low-cost strategy and the *focus strategy. Such an approach is most likely to succeed where the market is not highly price-sensitive and there is scope for effective branding. *See* GENERIC STRATEGIES.

diffusion of innovation *See* ADOPTION OF INNOVATIONS.

digital brand (online brand) A brand identity of a product or company online that differs from the traditional brand.

digital economy The sector of the economy that is based on the use of digital technologies to allocate resources and generate wealth; it thus comprises all transactions conducted over the *Internet and (in the widest definition) any other commerce that is enabled by modern *information technology. The phrase was first coined by Don Tapscott in his 1995 book of this name. In the early 21st century the digital economy was characterized by rapid change, constant technological development, and high rates of growth. At the same time governments faced challenges in responding to the competition and regulation issues raised by these changes.

digital option *See* BINARY OPTION.

digital signature *See* ELECTRONIC SIGNATURE.

digital whiteboard An area on a computer screen that can be written or drawn on by several users, enabling them to participate in audio- and video-conferencing as well as joint document creation.

digitizing The translation of text, illustrations, etc., into digital form.

dilapidations Disrepair of leasehold premises. The landlord may be liable to repair certain parts of domestic premises (e.g. the structure and exterior, and the sanitary appliances) under the Landlord and Tenant Act 1985 if the lease is for less than seven years. Otherwise, the lease will usually contain a covenant by either the landlord or the tenant obliging them to keep the premises in repair. Under the Landlord and Tenant Act 1985, a landlord cannot enforce a repairing covenant against a tenant by ending the lease prematurely unless a notice is first served specifying the disrepair and giving time for the repairs to be carried out. If there is no covenant in the lease, the tenant is under a common-law duty not to damage the premises and must keep them from falling down.

Dilbert principle The adage that large corporations knowingly promote their most incompetent staff to higher management, in the hope that this will prevent them from doing too much harm. The assumption is that all the real work of a company is done by those lower in the hierarchy. The principle was formulated by the US cartoonist Scott Adams (1957–), creator of the *Dilbert* comic strip. *See also* PARKINSON'S LAWS; PETER PRINCIPLE.

diluted earnings per share *See* FULLY DILUTED EARNINGS PER SHARE.

dilution of equity An increase in the number of ordinary shares in a company without a corresponding increase in its assets or profitability. The result is a fall in the value of the shares and lower dividends. The percentage of the equity held by each existing shareholder (and hence his or her voting power) will likewise be reduced. *See also* STOCK WATERING.

diminishing-balance method (reducing-balance method) A method of computing the *depreciation of a *fixed asset in an accounting period, in which the percentage to be charged against income is based on the depreciated value at the beginning of the period (*see* NET BOOK VALUE). This has the effect of reducing the annual depreciation charge against profits year by year. The annual percentage to be applied to the annual depreciated value is determined by the formula:

$$\text{rate of depreciation} = 1 - (S/C)^{1/N},$$

where N is the estimated life in years, S is the estimated scrap value at the end of its useful life, and C is the original cost.

dinar 1. (DZD) The standard monetary unit of Algeria, divided into 100 centimes. **2.** The standard monetary unit of Bahrain (BHD), Iraq (IQD), Jordan (JOD), and Kuwait (KWD), divided into 1,000 fils. **3.** (TND) The standard monetary unit of Tunisia, divided into 1,000 millimes. **4.** (RSD) The standard monetary unit of Serbia, divided into 100 paras. **5.** (LYD) The standard monetary unit of Libya, divided into 1,000 dirhams. **6.** A monetary unit of Iran, worth one hundredth of a *rial.

dinkie Denoting an affluent couple without children who may be expected to be extensive purchasers of consumer goods. The word is formed from *double-income no-kids.*

diram A monetary unit of Tajikistan, worth one hundredth of a *somoni.

direct-action advertising *See* DIRECT-RESPONSE TV ADVERTISING.

direct computer interviewing (DCI) A form of interviewing in which the respondent interacts directly with a computer programmed to ask questions and accept responses. This interactive process often encourages respondents to give information that they may be unwilling to disclose to an interviewer.

direct costs 1. Product costs that can be directly traced to a product or *cost unit. They are usually made up of *direct materials costs (which can be charged directly to the product by means of materials requisitions), *direct labour costs (charged by means of time sheets, time cards, or computer direct data entries), and *direct expenses (which are subcontract costs charged by means of an invoice from the subcontractor). The total of direct materials, direct labour, and direct expenses is known as the **prime cost** or **direct cost of sales. 2.** Departmental or *cost centre overhead costs that can be traced directly to the appropriate parts of an organization, without the necessity of *cost allocation. For example, the costs of a maintenance section that serves only one particular cost centre should be charged directly to that cost centre. *Compare* INDIRECT COSTS.

direct customer dialogue Two-way communication between a firm and its customers without the services of intermediaries.

direct debit A form of *standing order given to a bank by an account holder to pay regular amounts from his cheque account to a third party. Unlike a normal standing order, however, the amount to be paid is not specified; the account holder trusts the third party to claim from his bank an appropriate sum. In the USA this system is known as **reverse wire transfer**.

direct expense Expenditure that would not have been incurred had a particular product not been produced, excluding the costs of direct labour and materials. Direct expenses are included in the *direct cost of an item.

direct exporting A form of the export trade in which a domestic producer sells products directly to foreign buyers. Other

than transportation, there are no other intermediaries.

direct foreign investment Investment of capital by a government, company, or other organization in production (assembly or manufacturing facilities) and marketing operations that are located in a foreign country.

direct investment *See* FOREIGN INVESTMENT.

directive 1. A legislative decision by the European Union's Council of Ministers and Parliament, which is binding on member states but allows them to decide how to enact the required legislation. **2.** An instruction to carry out certain money-market operations, particularly instructions given by the US Federal Reserve Open Market Committee.

direct labour Workers directly concerned with the production of a product, service, or *cost unit, such as machine operators, assembly and finishing operators, etc. *Compare* INDIRECT LABOUR.

direct labour cost (direct wages) Expenditure on wages paid to those operators who are directly concerned with the production of a product, service, or *cost unit. It is one of the *cost classifications making up the *direct cost of a cost unit; it is quantified as the product of the time spent on each activity (collected by means of time sheets or job cards) and the rate of pay of each operator concerned. A percentage of the direct labour cost is sometimes used as a basis for absorbing production overheads to the cost unit in *absorption costing.

direct letter of credit *See* LETTER OF CREDIT.

direct-mail selling (direct-mail marketing) A form of *direct marketing in which sales literature or other promotional material is mailed directly to selected potential purchasers. The seller may be the producer of the products or a business that specializes in this form of marketing. The seller may build up his own list of potential customers or he may buy or rent a list (*see* LIST RENTING). *See also* MAIL-ORDER HOUSE.

direct marketing Selling by means of dealing directly with consumers rather than through retailers. Traditional methods include mail order (*see* MAIL-ORDER HOUSE), *direct-mail selling, *cold calling, *telephone selling, and door-to-door calling. More recently telemarketing, direct radio selling, magazine and TV advertising, and online computer shopping have been developed. *See also* DIRECT-RESPONSE TV ADVERTISING; HOME SHOPPING CHANNELS.

Direct Marketing Association UK (DMA) A trade association for marketers and suppliers in the *direct-marketing industry, formed in 1992 from a merger of several similar bodies. It publishes a code of conduct (the **DM Code**), issues best practice guidelines, and operates an awards system for the industry.

(((●))) SEE WEB LINKS
• DMA website: includes full text of the DM Code of Practice

direct materials Materials that are directly incorporated in the final product or *cost unit of an organization. For example, in the production of furniture, direct materials would include wood, glue, and paint. *Compare* INDIRECT MATERIALS.

direct materials cost Expenditure on *direct materials. It is one of the *cost classifications that make up the *direct cost of a *cost unit and is ascertained by collecting together the quantities of each material used on each product by means of materials requisitions and multiplying the quantities by the cost per unit of each material. A percentage on direct materials cost is sometimes used as a basis for absorbing production overheads to the cost unit in *absorption costing.

director A person appointed to carry out the day-to-day management of a company. A public company must have at least two directors, a private company at least one. The directors of a company, collectively known as the **board of directors**, usually act together, although power may be conferred (by the *articles of association) on one or more directors to exercise executive powers; in particular there is often a managing director with considerable executive power.

The first directors of a company are usually named in its articles of association or are appointed by the subscribers; they are required to give a signed undertaking to act in that capacity, which must be sent to the *Registrar of Companies. Subsequent directors are appointed by the company at a general meeting, although in practice they may be appointed by the other directors for ratification by the general meeting. Directors may be discharged from office by an *ordinary resolution with special notice at a general meeting, whether or not they have a *service contract in force. They may be disqualified for *fraudulent trading or *wrongful trading or for any conduct that makes them unfit to manage the company.

Directors owe duties of honesty and loyalty to the company (fiduciary duties) and a duty of care; their liability in *negligence depends upon their personal qualifications (e.g. a chartered accountant must exercise more skill than an unqualified person). The Companies Act 2006 sets out seven specified duties of directors:

• the duty to act within the powers of the company's constitution and to exercise the powers for the purposes for which they are conferred;
• the duty to act in good faith to promote the success of the company for the benefit of its members as a whole;
• the duty to exercise independent judgment;
• the duty to exercise reasonable care, skill, and diligence;
• the duty to avoid conflicts of interest;
• the duty not to accept benefits from third parties;
• the duty to declare an interest in any proposed transaction or arrangement with the company.

Directors' remuneration consists of a salary and in some cases directors' fees, paid to them for being a director, and an expense allowance to cover their expenses incurred in the service of the company. Directors' remuneration must be disclosed in the company's accounts and shown separately from any pension payments or *compensation for loss of office. *See also* EXECUTIVE DIRECTOR; NON-EXECUTIVE DIRECTOR; SHADOW DIRECTOR.

directors' authority to act In law, a director's power to act on behalf of a company may be based on actual or apparent authority. **Actual authority** is either express or implied. **Express authority** is an explicit conferring of authority on a director from, for example, the *articles of association or a contract of employment. **Implied authority** comprises usual authority (i.e. those powers that fall within the usual scope of the office to which the individual has been appointed) or authority based on the conduct of the parties. **Apparent** (or **ostensible**) **authority** is the authority of an agent as it appears to others—i.e. the particular agent has been held out by their principal as possessing the requisite authority.

directors' interests *See* REGISTER OF DIRECTORS' INTERESTS.

directors or higher-paid employees Under UK tax law, a 'higher-paid employee' is defined as one earning more than £8,500 per annum. This amount, which has remained unaltered since it was set in 1979 and is now below the *minimum wage, includes remuneration together with benefits and reimbursed expenses. An employer must account to HM Revenue and Customs, on form P11D, for all the benefits received by a higher-paid employee or director (for whom there is no earnings limit). These benefits are assessed at the cost to the employer, although special rules apply to certain benefits, e.g. company cars. *See* BENEFITS IN KIND.

directors' remuneration (directors' emoluments) The amounts received by directors from their office or employment, including all salaries, fees, wages, perquisites, and other profit as well as certain expenses and benefits paid or provided by the employer, which are deemed to be remuneration or emoluments.

directors' report An annual report by the directors of a company to its shareholders, which forms parts of the accounts required to be filed with the Registrar of Companies under the Companies Act. The information that must be given includes the principal activities of the company, a fair review of the performance and position of the business with likely future developments, details of research and development, significant issues regarding the sale, purchase, or valuation of assets, recommended dividends, transfers to reserves, names of the directors and their interests in the company during the period, employee statistics, and any political or charitable gifts made during the period. The UK government issued new regulations for the directors' report in 2005; these required a more comprehensive review of the company's performance and a description of the principal risks and uncertainties affecting its future. The scope of the directors' report was further expanded by the Companies Act 2006, which requires public companies to include information on employees, crucial supply chains, and the company's environmental record; in the case of larger companies, *key performance indicators must be cited. *See also* ACCOUNTS MODERNIZATION DIRECTIVE.

directory A web site that provides a structured listing of links to other sites in different categories. Yahoo! and the Open Directory Project are the best known examples of web directories. The distinction between a *search engine and a directory has to some extent become blurred, since many sites now include both facilities as part of a portal service.

direct placing A *placing of shares in a company direct to investors, without recourse to underwriters to back the deal or to public subscription.

direct quote (reciprocal exchange rate) An exchange rate expressed in terms of the number of units of domestic currency corresponding to one unit of the foreign currency. In eurozone countries, for example, a direct quote for the US dollar might be €0.75. *Compare* INDIRECT QUOTE.

direct-response TV advertising (DRTV advertising; direct-action advertising) A television advertisement designed to stimulate immediate purchase or encourage some other direct response. Television spots, typically 60 to 120 seconds long, attempt to describe a product or service, persuade viewers of its merits, and provide a free phone number for ordering or for further information. *See also* HOME SHOPPING CHANNELS.

direct taxation Taxation, the effect of which is intended to be borne by the person or organization that pays it. Economists distinguish between direct taxation and *indirect taxation. The former is best illustrated by *income tax, in which the person who receives the income pays the tax and his or her income is thereby reduced. The latter is illustrated by *VAT, in which the tax is paid by traders but the effects are borne by the consumers who buy the trader's goods. In practice these distinctions are rarely clear-cut. For example, *corporation tax is a direct tax but there is evidence that its incidence can be shifted to consumers by higher prices or to employees by lower wages.

direct write-off method In the USA, the procedure of writing off bad debts as they occur instead of creating a provision for them. Although this practice is unacceptable for financial reporting purposes, it is the only method allowed for tax purposes.

dirham 1. (MAD) The standard monetary unit of Morocco, divided into 100 centimes. **2.** (AED) The standard monetary unit of the United Arab Emirates, divided into 100 fils. **3.** A Qatari monetary unit, worth one hundredth of a *riyal. **4.** A Libyan monetary unit, worth one thousandth of a *dinar.

dirty bill of lading (foul *or* claused bill of lading) A *bill of lading carrying a clause or endorsement by the master or mate of the ship on which goods are carried to the effect that the goods (or their packing) arrived for loading in a damaged condition.

dirty price *See* CLEAN PRICE.

disbursement 1. A payment by a bank under a facility or other agreement. **2.** A payment made by an agent, often a professional such as a solicitor, on behalf of a client.

discharge To release a person from a binding legal obligation by agreement, by the performance of an obligation, or by law. For example, the payment of a debt discharges the debt; similarly, a judicial decision that a contract is frustrated discharges the parties from performing it.

disclaimer A clause in a contract that reduces potential liability. For instance, a liquidator of a company may disclaim its lease to avoid liability for the rent.

disclosure 1. The obligation, in contract law, that each party has to the other to disclose all the facts relevant to the subject matter of the contract. *See* UTMOST GOOD FAITH. **2.** The obligation, in company law, that a company has to disclose all relevant information and results of trading to its shareholders and other interested parties. The information is normally given in the *directors' report and the *annual accounts. **3.** The declaration of all relevant information about a company or a security in the interests of market transparency. In order for a company to be publicly traded in the US, the *Securities and Exchange Commission (SEC) requires it to make public all relevant financial or other information so that potential investors can be aware of any material facts that might affect their decisions. Likewise the Disclosure and Transparency Regulations of the UK *Financial Conduct Authority require listed companies to disclose all relevant price-sensitive information. There are also detailed rules that oblige investors to disclose certain types of holding in listed companies (especially in relation to any takeover bid) and that require traders to disclose certain types of financial position (usually a *short position).

discontinuous innovation An entirely new product introduced to the market to perform a function that no previous product has performed. Such a product requires new consumption or usage patterns to be developed. The introduction of the home personal computer, for example, illustrates how new marketing systems had to be established. In addition to new retailers, consumers had to be encouraged to buy and use PCs. *Compare* DYNAMICALLY CONTINUOUS INNOVATION.

discount 1. A deduction from a *bill of exchange when it is purchased before its maturity date. The party that purchases (discounts) the bill pays less than its face value and therefore makes a profit when it matures. The amount of the discount consists of interest calculated at the *bill rate for the length of time that the bill has to run. *See* DISCOUNT MARKET. **2.** A reduction in the price of goods below list price, for buyers who pay cash (**cash discount**), for members of the trade (*see* TRADE DISCOUNT), for buying in bulk (**bulk** or **quantity discount**), for retailers who advertise a manufacturer's product (**promotional discount**), etc. **3.** The amount by which the market price of a security is below its *par value. A £100 par value loan stock with a market price of £95 is said to be at a 5% discount. **4.** To convert a *future value into a *present value, as by the *discounted cash flow method.

discount broker *See* BILL BROKER.

discounted cash flow (DCF) A method used in *capital budgeting, *capital expenditure appraisal, and decision appraisal that predicts the future stream of cash flows, both inflows and outflows, over time and discounts them, using a *cost of capital rate or *hurdle rate, to *present values in order to determine whether the project or decision is likely to be financially sensible. A number of appraisal approaches use the DCF principle, namely *net present value, *internal rate of return, and the *profitability index. Most computer spreadsheet programs now include a DCF appraisal routine.

discounted payback method A method of *capital budgeting in which managers calculate the time required before the forecast discounted cash inflows from an investment will equal the initial investment expenditure (*see* DISCOUNTED CASH FLOW). This method is similar to the *payback period method but makes some allowance for the *time value of money. Despite theoretical problems, it is widely used in practice.

discounted value *See* PRESENT VALUE.

discount factor (present-value factor) A factor that, when multiplied by a particular year's predicted cash flow, brings the cash flow to a *present value. The factor takes into consideration the number of years from the inception of the project and the *hurdle rate that the project is expected to earn before it can be regarded as feasible. The factor is computed using the formula:

$$\text{discount factor} = 1/(1+r)^t,$$

where r is the hurdle rate required and t is the number of years from project inception.

In practice there is little necessity to compute discount factors when carrying out appraisal calculations as they are readily available in discount tables. Most computer spreadsheet programs now include a *discounted cash flow routine, which also obviates the need for using discount factors.

discount house 1. A company or bank on the *discount market that specializes in discounting *bills of exchange, especially *Treasury bills. **2.** *See* DISCOUNT STORE.

discounting 1. The application of *discount factors to each year's cash flow projections in a *discounted cash flow appraisal calculation. **2.** The process of selling a *bill of exchange before its maturity at a price below its face value.

discount market In the UK, the part of the *money market consisting of banks, *discount houses, and *bill brokers. By borrowing money at short notice from commercial banks or discount houses, bill brokers are able to discount bills of exchange, especially Treasury bills, and make a profit.

discount rate 1. The *hurdle rate of interest or *cost of capital rate applied to the *discount factors used in a *discounted cash flow appraisal calculation. The discount rate may be based on the cost-of-capital rate adjusted by a risk factor based on the risk characteristics of the proposed investment in order to create a hurdle rate that the project must earn before being worthy of consideration. Alternatively, the discount rate may be the interest rate that the funds used for the project could earn elsewhere. **2.** *See* BILL RATE. **3.** The interest rate charged by the US Federal Reserve Banks when lending to other banks.

discount store A retail organization that regularly sells standard merchandise (national brands) at lower prices than supermarkets, etc., by accepting lower margins and selling a higher volume. In the UK, several major grocery retailers operate in this way.

discretionary account (DA) An account placed with a stockbroker, securities house, commodity broker or other authorized investment manager in which they are empowered to carry out transactions on this account without referring back for approval to the principal. Principals normally set parameters for their accounts, but with a discretionary account the broker has more discretion, only reporting back on purchases, sales, profits and losses, and the value of the portfolio.

discretionary costs (managed costs) Costs incurred as a result of a managerial decision; the extent of these costs is consequently subject to managerial discretion. A characteristic of such costs is that they are often for a specified amount or subject to a specific formula, such as a percentage of sales revenue. Examples include advertising and research expenditure.

discretionary order 1. An order given to a stockbroker, commodity broker, etc., to buy or sell a stated quantity of specified securities or commodities, leaving the broker discretion to deal at the best price. **2.** A similar order given to a stockbroker in which the sum of money is specified but the broker has discretion as to which security to buy for his client.

discretionary trust 1. A *trust in which the shares of each beneficiary are not fixed by the settlor in the trust deed but may be varied at the discretion of some person or persons (often the trustees). Such trusts may be particularly useful when the needs of the beneficiaries are likely to change, as in the case of children. Formerly, many discretionary trusts took the form of **accumulation and maintenance (A & M) trusts**, in which income could be carried forward from one year to the next with no distributions to the beneficiaries being required. Apart from their other advantages, such trusts were widely used to avoid liability to *inheritance tax, leading to a series of changes to the law. Most discretionary trusts are now *relevant property trusts for tax purposes; from April 2008 all existing A & M trusts were reclassified as either *18–25 trusts or relevant property trusts, thereby losing their remaining tax advantages. **2.** In the USA, an *investment trust in which the managers can decide what investments to make.

discriminating monopoly A *monopoly in which the supplier's products or services are sold to consumers at different prices; by dividing the market into segments and charging each market segment the price it will bear, the monopolist increases profits. An example is the different domestic and industrial tariffs operated by suppliers of electricity in many countries.

discriminating tariff A *tariff that is not imposed equally by a country or group of countries on all its trading partners. The abolition of discriminating tariffs is one of the purposes of the *World Trade Organization.

discrimination The practice of treating some people less favourably than others on grounds unrelated to merit, normally because they belong to a particular group or category. Under the Equality Act 2010 it is illegal to discriminate on grounds of sex, race, disability, religious or other belief, marriage or civil partnership, pregnancy or maternity, sexual orientation, gender reassignment, or age. **Indirect discrimination** is deemed to occur where a provision, criterion, or practice is applied to everyone but the result is to put one group at a particular disadvantage. In employment, the Act applies to decisions about who to employ, the terms and conditions of employment, and access to training and promotion. Discrimination may include *harassment of an individual or any sort of victimization of a person who brings or supports a complaint under the legislation. The Act also applies to the provision of goods and services. *See also* EQUAL PAY; REASONABLE ADJUSTMENTS.

disguised observation The research process of monitoring people, objects, or occurrences when the people do not know they are being watched. This can only take place in public, where people can reasonably expect to be observed.

dishonour 1. To fail to pay a cheque when the account of the drawer does not have sufficient funds to cover it. When a bank dishonours a cheque it marks it 'refer to drawer' and returns it to the payee through his or her bank. **2.** To fail to accept a *bill of exchange (**dishonour by non-acceptance**) or to fail to pay a bill of exchange (**dishonour by non-payment**). **3.** To fail to honour any other financial obligation.

disinflation A fall in the rate of *inflation, especially one that is not accompanied by falls in output and employment. *See* DEFLATION.

disintermediation 1. The elimination of such middlemen as brokers and bankers from financial transactions. Disintermediation has been a consequence of new technology, deregulation, and *globalization. Although it enables both parties to a transaction to save costs on commissions and fees, these savings have to be offset by the increase in the *credit risk. **2.** The elimination of a layer of intermediaries from a marketing channel or the displacement of traditional resellers by radically new types of intermediaries.

disinvestment The reducing of investment in an activity, asset, company, or location.

disk-by-mail (DBM) In marketing research, an interviewing method in which a respondent is sent a disk containing the questionnaire through the post. This has to be completed using a personal computer. The disk is then returned to the researcher for processing. Completed questionnaires can also be returned by e-mail. The dangers of importing computer viruses must be taken into account by researchers.

dismissal The termination of an employee's contract of employment by the employer. An employer usually dismisses the employee by giving him or her the required period of notice, but dismissal without notice may be justified in certain circumstances (e.g. for gross misconduct). An employer's failure to renew a fixed-term employment contract also counts as dismissal. An employee having the required length of service in the business can apply to an employment tribunal if he or she is unfairly dismissed (*see* UNFAIR DISMISSAL). An employee dismissed for *redundancy after two years' continuous employment in the business is entitled to a redundancy payment under the Employment Rights Act 1996. An employee dismissed without due notice or before a fixed-term contract expires can also claim damages in the courts for *wrongful dismissal.

dispatching rules Rules used to decide the priorities for fulfilling orders. Examples include:
- **first-come-first-served (FCFS)**;
- **first-in-first-out (FIFO)**—often seen as a fair rule, especially by the customer, but in practice it leads to overall inefficiency;
- **earliest-due-date (EDD) first**—the job due out first is processed first: this ignores arrival times and processing times;

- **shortest processing time (SPT) first**— an ideal method for getting small jobs out of the way and minimizing work in progress, but it can make large jobs late and it ignores due dates and arrival times;
- **longest processing time (LPT) first**— this tends to increase work in progress and to make short jobs late;
- **truncated shortest processing time (TSPT)**—jobs that have been waiting longer than a predetermined time are given priority (if no work has been waiting long, SPT rules apply);
- **critical ratio (CR)**—this is the ratio of the time until the due date to the processing time: jobs with the lowest CR are processed first.

display advertising Advertising, such as a full-page or quarter-page advertisement, often containing a logo or illustration, rather than simple *classified advertising.

disposable income 1. The income a person has available to spend after payment of taxes, National Insurance contributions, and other deductions, such as pension contributions. **2.** In national income accounts, the total value of income of individuals and households available for consumer expenditure and savings, after deducting income tax, National Insurance contributions, and remittances overseas.

disposables *See* CONSUMER GOODS.

disposals account An account used to record the disposal of a fixed *asset. The original cost (a debit entry), *accumulated depreciation (a credit entry), and the amount received (credit entry) are transferred to the account, the balancing figure being any profit (debit entry) or loss (credit entry) on disposal.

disproportionate stratified sampling A sampling method in which the size of the *sample drawn from a particular stratum is not proportional to the relative size of that stratum. For example, a stratum could be large supermarkets, which may only account for 20% of all grocery stores— although they account for 80% of grocery sales. In this case, a disproportionate

sample would be used to represent the large supermarkets to reflect their sales (i.e. 80%) rather than the number of stores. *Compare* PROPORTIONATE STRATIFIED SAMPLING. *See* STRATIFIED SAMPLING.

distance selling The sale of goods or services to a consumer in which the parties do not meet, such as sale by mail order, telephone, digital TV, e-mail, or the Internet. The EU distance selling directive implemented from October 2000 in the UK by the Consumer Protection (Distance Selling) Regulations 2000 contains the relevant law. In particular, consumers have rights to certain information about the contract to be entered into and, in many cases, the right to cancel the contract within a certain period, often seven working days from the day after receipt of the goods. The right applies whether the goods are defective or not, but it does not apply in certain important categories (such as auctions, betting, goods specifically made for a consumer, and food that will deteriorate).

distrain To seize goods as a security for the performance of an obligation, especially the seizure of goods by a landlord because a tenant is in arrears with his rent.

distributable profits (distributable reserves) The profits of a company that are legally available for distribution as *dividends. They consist of a company's accumulated *realized profits after deducting all realized losses, except for any part of these net realized profits that have been previously distributed or capitalized. *Public companies, however, may not distribute profits to such an extent that their net assets are reduced to less than the sum of their *called-up share capital and their *undistributable reserves.

distributed processing A system of processing data in which several computers are used at various locations within an organization instead of using one central computer. The computers may be linked to each other in a *local area network, allowing them to cooperate, or they may be linked to a larger central computer, although a significant amount of the processing is done without reference to the central computer.

distribution 1. A payment by a company from its *distributable profits, usually by means of a *dividend. **2. (capital distribution)** A final payment made on the winding up of a company, which may include the repayment of share capital. A capital distribution to an individual is usually subject to capital gains tax, rather than income tax. **3.** The division of a person's property and assets according to law, e.g. in cases of bankruptcy or after death. **4.** The allocation of goods to consumers by means of wholesalers and retailers.

distribution bond An *investment bond issued by an insurance policy, in which the investment is a mixture of *fixed-interest securities and ordinary shares.

distribution centre A large highly automated warehouse designed to receive goods from various suppliers, take orders, fulfil them efficiently, and deliver goods to customers as quickly as possible.

distribution channel The network of firms necessary to distribute goods or services from the manufacturers to the consumers; the channel therefore consists of manufacturers, distributors, wholesalers, and retailers.

distribution overhead (distribution cost; distribution expense) The *cost classification that includes the costs incurred in delivering a product to the customers. Examples include postage, transport, packaging, and insurance.

distribution to owners In the USA, a payment of a *dividend to shareholders (stockholders).

distributor An intermediary, or one of a chain of intermediaries (*see* DISTRIBUTION CHANNEL), that specializes in transferring a manufacturer's goods or services to the consumers.

distributor brand *See* OWN BRAND.

diversification 1. Movement by a manufacturer or trader into a wider field of products. This may be achieved by buying firms already serving the target markets or by expanding existing facilities. It is often undertaken to reduce reliance on one market, which may be diminishing (e.g. tobacco), to balance a seasonal market (e.g. ice cream), or to provide scope for general growth. **2.** The spreading of an investment *portfolio over a wide range of assets to avoid serious losses if a recession is localized to one sector of the market.

diversity management Management that embraces the challenges of managing a workforce that is heterogeneous in terms of culture, ethnicity, religious belief, and political affiliation. The growing diversity of the workforce in most countries today means that many former assumptions about shared attitudes, values, and cultural norms no longer apply. Successful diversity management requires that managers acknowledge cultural differences in the workforce, understand the ways in which these can translate into different work-related attitudes (e.g. in terms of attitudes toward authority or individual competitiveness), and accept this diversity as an asset rather than a liability to the organization.

divestment A *business strategy in which a part of a business is sold off. It may be motivated either by a firm's decision to focus on certain aspects of its operation by selling those parts that no longer fit, or by the need to reduce costs and improve the profitability of the business by selling unprofitable parts. Competitors may seek to increase their market position by buying a divested business, or other companies may purchase a divested business as part of a *diversification strategy.

dividend 1. The distribution of part of the earnings of a company to its shareholders. The dividend is normally expressed as an amount per share on the *par value of the share. Thus a 15% dividend on a £1 share will pay 15p. However, investors are usually more interested in the **dividend yield**, i.e.

the dividend expressed as a percentage of the share value; thus if the market value of these £1 shares is now £5, the dividend yield would be $1/5 \times 15\% = 3\%$. The size of the dividend payment is determined by the board of directors of a company, who must decide how much to pay out to shareholders and how much to retain in the business; these amounts may vary from year to year. In the UK it is usual for companies to pay a dividend every six months, the largest portion (the **final dividend**) being announced at the company's AGM together with the annual financial results. A smaller **interim dividend** usually accompanies the interim statement of the company's affairs, six months before the AGM. In the USA dividends are usually paid quarterly. *See also* DIVIDEND COVER; YIELD.

Interest payments on *gilt-edged securities are also sometimes called dividends although they are fixed. **2.** A payment made out of profits by a *co-operative society to its members. It is usually related to the amount the member spends and is expressed as a number of pence in the pound.

dividend cover The number of times a company's *dividends to ordinary shareholders could be paid out of its *net profits after tax in the same period. For example, a net dividend of £400,000 paid by a company showing a net profit of £1M is said to be covered 2½ times. Dividend cover is a measure of the probability that dividend payments will be sustained (low cover might make it difficult to pay the same level of dividends in a bad year's trading) and of a company's commitment to investment and growth (high cover implies that the company retains its earnings for investment in the business). Negative dividend cover is unusual, and may be a sign that a company is in difficulties. In the USA, the dividend cover is expressed as the **pay-out ratio**, the total dividends paid as a percentage of the net profit. *See also* PRICE–DIVIDEND RATIO.

dividend mandate A document in which a shareholder of a company notifies the company to whom dividends are to be paid.

dividend stripping (bond washing) The practice of buying *gilt-edged securities after they have gone ex-dividend (*see* EX-) and selling them cum-dividend just before the next dividend is due. This procedure enables the investor to avoid receiving dividends, which in the UK are taxable as income, and to make a tax-free *capital gain. Dividend stripping was once popular among higher-rate taxpayers but has now become of little interest since the rules regulating the taxation of accrued interest were changed.

dividend tax A UK tax on *dividends introduced from April 2016 as a replacement for the former *tax credit system. No tax is paid on the first £5,000 of income from dividends. Where dividend income exceeds this figure, *basic-rate taxpayers pay tax at a rate of 7.5%, *higher-rate taxpayers at 32.5%, and additional-rate taxpayers at 38.1%.

dividend waiver A decision by a major shareholder in a company not to take a dividend, usually because the company cannot afford to pay it.

dividend warrant Under the *tax credit system, the cheque issued by a company to its shareholders when paying *dividends. It states the tax deducted and the net amount paid.

dividend yield *See* DIVIDEND.

divisionalization 1. The splitting up of a large organization into separate divisions, based on the products or services provided or on the geographical location of a particular plant. Although some management functions are repeated separately in each division, and economies of scale are not maximized, many large organizations that encompass a diversity of activities are structured in this way. Because decision making is decentralized to the divisional managers, a swift response to a change in markets is possible. Coordination between divisions is achieved by a central management. *See* DECENTRALIZATION.

2. The process of transforming the subsidiary organizations in a group into divisions of a single integrated company.

DJIA Abbreviation for *Dow Jones Industrial Average.

DMA Abbreviation for *Direct Marketing Association UK.

DMAIC *See* SIX SIGMA.

DMU Abbreviation for *decision-making unit.

DNI framework The keywords *d*igital, *n*etworked, *i*ndividuals that represent the fundamental forces shaping Internet marketing.

DNS Abbreviation for *Domain Name System.

dobra (STD) The standard monetary unit of São Tomé e Príncipe, divided into 100 centavos.

dock receipt (wharfinger's receipt) A receipt for goods given by a dock warehouse or wharf, acknowledging that the goods are awaiting shipment. A more formal document is a **dock warrant** or wharfinger's warrant (*see* WARRANT), which gives the holder title to the goods.

documentary bill A *bill of exchange attached to the shipping documents of a consignment of goods. These documents include the *bill of lading, insurance policy, dock warrant, invoice, etc.

documentary credit *See* LETTER OF CREDIT.

document merge The process of combining two or more documents to produce a single document. This is a common operation in word processing. An example is the combining of data produced by a *spreadsheet program into a document produced by a word processing program.

documents against acceptance (D/A) A method of payment for goods that have been exported in which the exporter sends

the title and *shipping documents with a *bill of exchange to a bank or agent at the port of destination. The bank or agent releases the goods when the bill has been accepted by the consignee. Provided the documents are in order, there is an obligation to pay for them even if the goods have been lost in transit. In these circumstances, the buyer would hold the insurance policy to provide recompense for the lost goods. *Compare* CASH AGAINST DOCUMENTS.

documents against presentation (D/P) *See* CASH AGAINST DOCUMENTS.

Dodd-Frank Act 2010 US legislation that provided for comprehensive changes to the framework of financial regulation in the USA following the crisis of 2007–08. The Act was named after its sponsors, Senator Chris Dodd and Representative Barney Frank. Its main provisions include new capital requirements and risk limits for banks and the creation of new government agencies to oversee the protection of consumers and the regulation of financial institutions and credit-rating agencies.

dog *See* BOSTON MATRIX.

dollar The standard monetary unit of American Samoa (USD), Antigua and Barbuda (XCD), Australia (AUD), the Bahamas (BSD), Barbados (BBDS), Belau (USD), Belize (BZD), Bermuda (BMD), the British Virgin Islands (USD), Brunei (BND), Canada (CAD), the Cayman Islands (KYD), Dominica (XCD), East Timor (USD), Ecuador (USD), El Salvador (USD), Fiji (FJD), Grenada (XCD), Guam (USD), Guatemala (USD), Guyana (GYD), Hong Kong (HKD), Jamaica (JMD), Kiribati, Liberia (LRD), the Marshall Islands (USD), Micronesia (USD), Namibia (NAD), Nauru (AUD), New Zealand (NZD), Puerto Rico (USD), St Kitts and Nevis (XCD), St Lucia (XCD), St Vincent and the Grenadines (XCD), Singapore (SGD), the Solomon Islands (SBD), Taiwan (TWD), Trinidad and Tobago (TTD), Tuvalu, the USA (USD), the Virgin Islands (USD), and Zimbabwe (USD), in all cases divided into 100 cents.

dollarization The adoption by a country of the US dollar in place of its own currency, usually as a means of controlling inflation and interest-rate volatility. Partial dollarization is said to occur when a country gives the US dollar equal status to its own currency or pegs its currency one-to-one with the dollar.

dollar stocks US or Canadian securities.

domain name A registered address for an organization or an individual for use on the Internet. Domain names are hierarchical with the parts separated by full stops, known as dots. The highest hierarchical part is called the **top-level domain**; this identifies the nature of the site:

.gov a government department
.com a commercial company
.org a non-commercial organization
.edu an educational establishment
and so on.

The domain may also identify the country in which the organization is situated:

.uk the United Kingdom
.fr France
and so on.

The **subdomain** identifies the organization and sometimes department of an organization or an individual in it:

jsmith.ucsd.edu
            identifies John Smith at the University of California, San Diego campus.
jsmith.ford.co.uk
            identifies John Smith at the Ford Motor Company in the UK.

The **Domain Name System** (DNS) is the Internet system in which the domain name is given a unique numeric Internet Protocol (IP) address (e.g. 162.18.2.3). When the domain name is keyed into the Internet to access a website the name is automatically translated into its numeric equivalent to enable it to be used by the Internet routing software. The **Domain Name Service** is the Internet system that implements the Domain Name System and retains in its databases both the domain name and its IP address, which can be accessed by the user. *See also* UNIFORM RESOURCE LOCATOR.

domain strategy The branding and positioning of a firm to enable its website to be found easily, especially the *domain name and subdomains chosen.

domicile (domicil) 1. The country or place of a person's permanent home, which may differ from that person's nationality or place where they are a *resident. Domicile is determined by both the physical fact of residence and the continued intention of remaining there. For example, a citizen of a foreign country who is resident in the UK is not necessarily domiciled there unless there is a clear intention to make the UK a permanent home. In order to prove that the **domicile of origin** has been relinquished in favour of the **domicile of choice**, tangible changes have to be made. Links with the domicile of origin must be severed and active steps taken to become involved with the country that is the domicile of choice, e.g. by making a will under its laws. Under the common law, it is domicile and not residence or nationality that determines a person's civil status. Whether a person is domiciled in the UK may affect their liability to UK taxation (*see* NON-DOMICILED). A corporation may also have a domicile, which is determined by its place of registration. **2.** In banking, an account is said to be domiciled at a particular branch and the customer will usually treat that branch as his or her main banking contact. Computer technology, however, now allows customers to use other branches exactly as if their account was domiciled there.

dông (VND) The standard monetary unit of Vietnam, divided into 10 hào.

donor A person making a gift or transferring property to another person (the **donee**).

donor list A list of all those who have donated to a particular charity. Lists of this type are of great importance to direct-marketing agencies specializing in marketing for charities.

door-to-door retailing Selling door-to-door, office-to-office, or at home-sales parties. Originally started in the USA with the Fuller Brush Company, this is now a popular method of marketing. In the UK cosmetics and plastic containers are widely marketed at home-sale parties. The Japanese market is the largest direct-sales market, mainly because most Japanese cars have traditionally been sold door-to-door.

dormant company A company that has had no significant accounting transactions for the accounting period in question. Such a company need not appoint auditors.

DOS *See* MS-DOS.

dot.com bubble *See* BUBBLE.

double auction An *auction in which both bids and offers are competitive. An example is an *open outcry market, in which buyers and sellers shout out the prices at which they are willing to trade. *See* CALLOVER.

double bottom In *chartist analysis, the situation in which the prices of a security fall, then rise, then fall again to the same level, producing a 'W' pattern on a graph. This pattern is thought to indicate that the security has much support at the price at the bottom of the W. *Compare* DOUBLE TOP. *See* SUPPORT LEVEL.

double declining balance method A method of *depreciation in which the historical cost (or revalued amount) of an *asset less its estimated residual value (*see* NET RESIDUAL VALUE) is divided by the number of years of its estimated useful life and the resulting amount is multiplied by two to give the depreciation figure. For example, in the first year an asset costing £12,000 with an estimated residual value of £2,000 and an estimated useful life of 10 years would have a depreciation charge of £2,000, i.e. $2 \times [(£12,000 - £2,000)/10]$.

double-entry book-keeping A method of recording the transactions of a business in a set of *accounts, such that every transaction has a dual aspect and therefore needs to be recorded in at least two accounts. For example, when a person (debtor) pays cash to a business for goods

purchased, the cash held by the business is increased and the amount due from the debtor is decreased by the same amount; similarly, when a purchase is made on credit, the stock is decreased and the amount owing to creditors is increased by the same amount. This double aspect enables the business to be controlled because all the *books of accounts must balance.

double option A combination of a put *option and a call option. It is less flexible, since the put and call cannot be separated.

double taxation Taxation that falls on the same source of income in more than one country. Taxation is normally levied on a person's worldwide income in the country of residence but, in addition, most countries also levy a charge on income that arises within that country whether it is from interest or a business. As a result a large number of treaties (**double-taxation agreements**) have been concluded between countries to ensure that their own residents are not doubly taxed. The agreements also attempt to cover fiscal evasion.

As a result there are several different kinds of relief from double taxation available: (1) relief by agreement, providing for exemption, in whole or in part, of certain categories of income; (2) credit agreement, in which tax charged in one country is allowed as a credit in the other; (3) deduction agreement, in which the overseas income is reduced by the foreign tax paid on it; (4) if there is no agreement the UK tax authorities will allow the foreign tax paid as a credit up to the amount of the corresponding UK liability.

See UNILATERAL RELIEF.

double top In *chartist analysis, a pattern of fluctuation in the price of a security, in which a rise is followed by a fall, then a second rise to the same level. This pattern is thought to indicate that the security is meeting resistance to a move to a higher level. *Compare* DOUBLE BOTTOM. *See also* ASCENDING TOPS; RESISTANCE LEVEL.

doubtful debts Money owed to an organization, which it is unlikely to receive. A provision for doubtful debts may be created, which may be based on specific debts or on the general assumption that a certain percentage of debtors' amounts are doubtful. As the doubtful debt becomes a *bad debt, it may be written off to the provision for doubtful debts or alternatively charged to the *profit and loss account if there is no provision. *See* PROVISION FOR BAD DEBTS.

Dow Jones Industrial Average (DJIA) An index of security prices used on the *New York Stock Exchange; it is issued by Dow Jones & Co., a US firm providing financial information. The Dow is a narrowly based index, having 30 constituent companies. The index was founded in 1884, based then on 11 stocks (mostly in railways), but was reorganized in 1928 when it was given the value of 100. Its lowest point was on 2 July 1932, when it reached 41. In 2007 it exceeded 14,000. Dow Jones also publishes other indices, and the DJIA is now just one of a number of US stock price indices.

(∰) SEE WEB LINKS

• Dow Jones Indexes website

download To retrieve electronic information, such as a web page or e-mail, from another location, such as a *web server.

downsizing A reduction in the size of an organization, especially by cutting the number of direct employees. The main purpose of downsizing is to improve profitability by reducing costs, although there may also be gains in both focus and flexibility. Apart from the damage to staff morale, the main danger is that the loss of experienced employees will lead to loss of customers and 'business memory'. *Compare* RIGHTSIZING.

downstream 1. To borrow funds for use by a subsidiary company at the better rates appropriate to the parent company, which would not have been available to the subsidiary company. *Compare* UPSTREAM. **2.** Denoting the respondent bank (**downstream bank**) in an arrangement with a *correspondent bank. **3.** Denoting a later stage in the production process or *value chain.

down time The period during which a computer is out of action, usually because of a fault or for routine maintenance work.

DP Abbreviation for *data processing.

D/P Abbreviation for documents against presentation. *See* CASH AGAINST DOCUMENTS.

DPB Abbreviation for *Designated Professional Body.

drachma Formerly, the standard monetary unit of Greece, divided into 100 lepta. It was replaced by the *euro in 2002.

draft 1. *See* BANK DRAFT. **2.** Any order in writing to pay a specified sum, e.g. a *bill of exchange. **3.** A preliminary version of a document, before it has been finalized.

dragon bond A foreign *bond issued in the Asian bond markets.

dragon markets A colloquial name for those markets and economies in the Pacific basin that developed rapidly in the 1980s and early 1990s, notably Indonesia, Malaysia, the Philippines, and Thailand. They enjoyed dynamic growth and high savings ratios until 1997, when the region suffered a severe financial and economic crisis.

dram (AMD) The standard monetary unit of Armenia, divided into 100 louma.

drawback The refund of import duty by HM Revenue and Customs when imported goods are re-exported. Payment of the import duty and claiming the drawback can be avoided if the goods are stored in a *bonded warehouse immediately after unloading from the incoming ship or aircraft until re-export.

drawdown 1. The drawing of funds against a *credit line. *See also* FLEXIBLE DRAWDOWN. **2.** The movement of a customer's funds from one account to another account, which may be in another bank.

drawee 1. The person on whom a *bill of exchange is drawn (i.e. to whom it is addressed). The drawee will accept it (*see* ACCEPTANCE) and pay it on maturity. **2.** The bank on whom a cheque is drawn, i.e. the bank holding the account of the individual or company that wrote it. **3.** The bank named in a *bank draft. *Compare* DRAWER.

drawer 1. A person who signs a *bill of exchange ordering the *drawee to pay the specified sum at the specified time. **2.** A person who signs a cheque ordering the drawee bank to pay a specified sum of money on demand.

drawings *Assets (cash or goods) withdrawn from an unincorporated business by its owner. If a business is incorporated, drawings are usually in the form of *dividends or *scrip dividends. Drawings are shown in a **drawings account**, which is used, for example, by the partners in a *partnership.

drip-feed To fund a new company in stages rather than by making a large capital sum available at the start.

drop-date A specified date upon which direct-mailing envelopes will be delivered to the postal service for distribution.

drop-dead fee A fee paid by an individual or company that is bidding for another company to the organization lending the money required to finance the bid. The fee is only paid if the bid fails and the loan is not required. Thus, for the price of the drop-dead fee, the bidder ensures that the interest charges are only incurred if the money is required. It is sometimes called a **termination fee**.

drop lock A bond initially issued with a variable rate of interest which becomes a fixed-rate bond if the index or rate falls below a trigger at a coupon reset date.

drop ship A method of processing orders in *direct marketing in which the marketers pass orders to manufacturers to deliver the goods direct to the consumer.

DRTV advertising Abbreviation for *direct-response TV advertising.

dry test A test in which consumers are asked to order a particular product before it has been manufactured. The manufacturer will only proceed with production if the response rate is sufficiently high to ensure a specified profit. If the desired level of response is not reached, the product is not manufactured. In such cases compensation is often offered.

DSR Abbreviation for *debt service ratio.

DSS Abbreviation for *decision support system.

DTP Abbreviation for *desktop publishing.

dual-capacity system A system of trading on a stock exchange in which the functions of *stockjobber and *stockbroker are carried out by separate firms. In a **single-capacity system** the two functions can be combined by firms known as *market makers. Dual capacity existed on the *London Stock Exchange prior to October 1986 (*see* BIG BANG), when a single-capacity system was introduced.

dual distribution A method of using two separate distribution channels to market a product. For example, a manufacturer may sell a product over the Internet as well as by direct-response television.

dual-rate transfer prices *Transfer prices that are set at different levels for the supplying and receiving divisions of an organization. The dual prices method charges a low price, say a price based on the *marginal cost, to the buying division, while at the same time crediting a high price, say a price based on *full cost pricing, to the selling division. The idea is that this will encourage a buying division to buy within the organization without penalizing the selling division. However, this is only likely to be beneficial to the organization as a whole if the selling division has sufficient spare capacity to supply the buying division's needs. A compensating entry to eliminate unrealized profits is required in the books of the head office when the divisional results are consolidated. Managers rarely use this method in practice as it can lead to confusion.

due date The date on which a debt is due to be settled, such as the maturity date of a *bill of exchange.

due diligence The process of evaluating and scrutinizing the assets, liabilities, profitability, cash flow, policies, and *compliance of a company prior to a potential transaction, such as the purchase of the business. Due diligence is typically conducted by the prospective buyer in conjunction with legal, accountancy, and other relevant experts to ensure that all material facts are declared and understood. The term is sometimes used in an older legal sense to mean the care a reasonable person should take before entering into an agreement.

dummy name A method of tracking the usage of a proprietary mailing list in *list renting by inserting a unique name in the list. For example, if a list is rented for using once only the presence of this name would indicate if it has been used on more than one occasion.

dump 1. To transfer the contents of a computer's main memory onto a backing memory. This provides a back-up copy of the main memory for security reasons. **2.** A printout of the contents of computer memory, or of a *file, used to diagnose such problems as *crashes.

dumping The selling of goods abroad at prices below their marginal cost, which implies that the seller is making a loss. It has often been argued that developing countries wishing to establish an industry should use tariffs and quotas to ensure a monopoly for producers at home, while selling goods cheaply overseas. However, this practice inevitably leads to claims of dumping by other countries. The *World Trade Organization allows countries to prevent dumping by imposing tariffs on goods that are being dumped, although it is always difficult to establish conclusively that a particular price level constitutes dumping. Dumping is prohibited in the EU.

duopoly A market in which there are only two producers or sellers of a particular product or service and many buyers. The profits in such an imperfect form of competition are in practice usually less than could be achieved if the two suppliers

merged to form a *monopoly but more than if the two allowed competition to force them into *marginal costing. *See also* COLLUSIVE DUOPOLY.

durables *See* CONSUMER GOODS.

duration driver A measure of the amount of time required to perform an *activity when this is a significant *cost driver. Duration drivers provide a more accurate basis for allocating costs than the number of transactions when there is a significant variation in the time required to complete an activity. For example, if all deliveries are completed in 10 minutes then it is simple (and accurate) to use the number of deliveries as a cost driver. If one delivery requires 10 minutes and another two hours, then using time for deliveries as the cost driver will improve the accuracy of the costing system. However, duration drivers are often seen as more expensive to measure and record than transaction drivers.

dustbin checkers *See* GARBOLOGISTS.

Dutch auction An *auction sale in which the auctioneer starts by calling a very high price and reduces it until a bid is received.

Dutch disease The deindustrialization of an economy as a result of the discovery of a natural resource, so named because it occurred in Holland after the discovery of North Sea gas. The discovery of such a resource lifts the value of the country's currency, making manufactured goods less competitive; exports therefore decline and imports rise.

duty A government tax on certain goods or services. *See* EXCISE DUTY; IMPORT DUTY; STAMP DUTY; TARIFF.

duty of care *See* NEGLIGENCE.

dynamically continuous innovation The development of new products that are different from previously available products but that do not strikingly change buying or usage patterns. Thus the company remains in the same product and markets but continues to improve the products.

This needs to be done dynamically (to save time and increase effectiveness), as well as continuously, because of the effect of the *product life cycle. *Compare* DISCONTINUOUS INNOVATION.

dynamic capabilities A *strategic management framework that emphasizes a firm's ability to adapt quickly to fast-changing environments as the main source of *competitive advantage in the modern business world. Some key capabilities of this kind include: proactive *environmental scanning; a focus on market demand, consumer feedback, and *continuous improvement; successful *business technology management; and a readiness to reconfigure the company's structures, resources, and competencies in innovative ways. The dynamic capabilities approach is usually seen as a development of the *resource-based view.

E & OE Abbreviation for errors and omissions excepted. In the past, this was frequently printed on invoice forms to protect the sender from the consequences of any clerical or accounting errors in the preparation of the invoice.

EAP Abbreviation for *employee assistance programme.

ear The advertising space at the top left or right corner of a newspaper's front page.

early adopter *See* ADOPTION OF INNOVATIONS.

early bargains *See* AFTER-HOURS DEALS.

early majority *See* ADOPTION OF INNOVATIONS.

early payment A reduction offered as reward for payment of an invoice before a specified date.

EARN Acronym for *Euro Area Reference Note.

earned income For tax purposes, the following types of income are treated as earned income:

- income from employment;
- income from trades, professions, and vocations;
- foreign business profits;
- patent and copyright income received by the creator;
- a proportion of the annuity paid to a retired partner.

There is little difference in the tax treatment of earned and *unearned income under the present UK taxation system.

earnings before interest and tax *See* EBIT; EBITDA.

earnings per share (eps) The *profit in pence attributable to each *ordinary share in a company, based on the consolidated profit for the period, after deducting *minority interests and *preference share dividends. This profit figure is divided by the weighted average number of equity shares in issue during the period. The eps may be calculated on a **net basis** or a **nil basis**. Using the net basis, the tax charge includes any variable elements of tax, such as unrelieved overseas tax arising from the payment or proposed payment of dividends (*see* OVERSEAS-INCOME TAXATION). The nil basis excludes such items from the tax charge. The eps should be shown on the face of the *profit and loss account, both for the period under review and for the corresponding previous period. The basis of calculating the earnings per share should be disclosed on the face of the profit and loss account or in the notes to the accounts.

Earnings per share was seen as an important measure of performance in the 1950s and 1960s but its significance has since declined. UK listed companies or other entities choosing to disclose an earnings-per-share figure must now follow the rules set out in *International Accounting Standard 33. This requires the disclosure of both basic eps and *fully diluted earnings per share on the profit and loss account. *See also* BOTTOM LINE.

earnings retained *See* RETAINED EARNINGS.

earnings yield *See* YIELD.

earn-out agreement (contingent contract) An agreement to purchase a company in which the purchaser pays a lump sum at the time of the acquisition, with a promise to pay more (a *contingent consideration) if certain criteria, usually specified earnings levels, are met for a specified number of years. This method of acquisition has been popular in 'people' businesses, in particular advertising agencies. The agreement provides a means of retaining the previous owners in the business, with a motivation to maintain the company's profitability.

easement A right, such as a right of way, right of water, or right of support, that one owner of one piece of land (the dominant tenement) may have over the land of another (the servient tenement). The right must benefit the dominant tenement and the two pieces of land must be reasonably near each other. The right must not involve expenditure by the owner of the servient tenement and must be analogous to those rights accepted in the past as easements. An easement may be granted by *deed or it may be acquired by prescription (lapse of time, during which it is exercised without challenge); it may also be acquired of necessity (for example, if A sells B a piece of land that B cannot reach without crossing A's land) or when 'continuous and apparent' rights have been enjoyed with the part of the land sold before it was divided. Existing easements over the land of third parties pass with a conveyance of the dominant tenement.

easy money *See* CHEAP MONEY.

e-banking *See* HOME BANKING.

Ebay The largest online auction house on the Internet. *See* VIRTUAL AUCTION.

e-billing *See* ELECTRONIC BILLING.

EBIT Abbreviation for earnings before interest and tax, the *profit of a company as shown on the *profit and loss account, before deducting the variables of interest and tax. This figure, which is used in calculating many ratios, enables better comparisons to be made with other companies.

EBITDA Abbreviation for earnings before interest, taxation, depreciation, and amortization. This figure is frequently cited by

investment analysts since it represents a *cash-flow vision of shareholders' return.

ECB Abbreviation for *European Central Bank.

ECGD Abbreviation for *Export Credits Guarantee Department.

ECMAScript *See* JAVASCRIPT.

ecocentric management Management that treats environmental issues as a core business concern, rather than an *externality. Recognizing the relationship that the firm has with the natural environment, it regards taking full account of the environmental impact it produces as part of management's responsibility.

e-commerce (electronic commerce) The use of the *Internet to buy and sell goods and services. At the simplest level, a company will probably have a website that provides details of products and contacts. *See* DIGITAL ECONOMY; ELECTRONIC SHOPPING.

Economic and Labour Market Review A monthly publication of the UK *Office for National Statistics devoted to economic data and analyses; it is available in both online and print formats.

economic appraisal A method of *capital budgeting that makes use of *discounted cash flow techniques to determine a preferred investment. However, instead of using annual projected cash flows in the analysis, the technique discounts over the project's life the expected annual *economic costs and *economic benefits. It is mainly used in the assessment of governmental or quasi-governmental projects, such as road, railway, and port developments.

economic batch quantity A refinement of the *economic order quantity to take into account circumstances in which the goods are produced in batches. The formula is:

$$Q = [2cdr/h(r - d)]^{1/2}$$

where Q is the quantity to be purchased or manufactured, c is the cost of processing an order for delivery, d is the demand in the period for that stock item, h is the cost of holding a unit of stock, and r is the rate of production.

economic benefits The projected benefits revealed by an *economic appraisal. Economic benefits are usually gains that can be expressed in financial terms as the result of an improvement in facilities provided by a government, local authority, etc. For example, the economic benefits arising from the construction of a new or improved road might include lower vehicle operating costs, time savings for the road users, and lower accident costs as a result of fewer accidents. In each case the savings would be in economic terms, that is, excluding the effect of taxes and subsidies within the economy. See ECONOMIC COSTS.

economic costs The projected costs revealed by an *economic appraisal. Economic costs differ from financial costs in that they exclude the transfer payments within the economy, which arise when an investment is made. In the construction of a road, for example, the economic costs exclude taxes and import duties on the materials and plant used in its construction, while any subsidies made are added back to the costs. See ECONOMIC BENEFITS.

economic duress Historically, in *contract law, a claim that a contract was voidable for duress could only be successful if a threat to the person (i.e. physical duress) had induced the contract. Now, however, a contract may be voidable for economic duress. The essential elements are that an illegitimate threat has been made (e.g. to breach an existing contract or to commit a tort) and that the injured party has no practical alternative to agreeing to the terms set out by the person making the threat.

economic environment Factors that affect the buying power and spending patterns of consumers. These factors include income distribution, changes in purchasing power as a result of inflation, the state of the country's economy, etc. While the economic environment can be influenced extensively by government activity, companies need to monitor these changes in order to predict their sales estimates.

economic good See GOOD.

economic growth The expansion of the output of an economy, usually expressed in terms of the increase of national income. Nations experience different rates of economic growth mainly because of differences in population growth, investment, and technical progress.

economic order quantity (EOQ) A decision model, based on differential calculus, that determines the optimum order size for purchasing (sometimes called the **economic purchase quantity**) or manufacturing (**economic manufacturing quantity**) an item of stock. The optimum order quantity is that which equates the total ordering and total *carrying costs. The formula used is:

$$Q = \sqrt{(2cd/h)},$$

where Q is the quantity to be purchased or manufactured, c is the cost of processing an order for delivery, d is the demand in the period for that stock item, and h is the cost of holding a unit of stock. See also ECONOMIC BATCH QUANTITY.

economic sanctions Action taken by one country or group of countries to harm the economic interest of another country or group of countries, usually to bring about pressure for social or political change. Sanctions normally take the form of restrictions on imports or exports, or on financial transactions. They may be applied to specific items or they may be comprehensive trade bans. There is considerable disagreement over their effectiveness. Critics point out that they are easily evaded and often inflict more pain on those they are designed to help than on the governments they are meant to influence. They can also harm the country that imposes sanctions, through the loss of export markets or raw material supplies. In addition the target country may impose retaliatory sanctions. See also EMBARGO.

economic value The *present value of expected future *cash flows. For example, the economic value of a *fixed asset would be the present value of any future revenues it is expected to generate, less the present value of any future costs related to it.

Economic Value Added (EVA) A performance measure used to evaluate a company's **economic profit** (i.e., the value added to a company by its activities in a given time period). It is the calculation of a company's net *operating profit after taxes, minus a *cost of capital charge for the investment or capital employed in the business. The Stern Stewart consulting organization registered EVA as a tradename in the 1990s.

economies of scale (scale effect) Reductions in the average cost of production, and hence in the unit costs, when output is increased. If the average costs of production rise with output, this is known as **diseconomies of scale**. Economies of scale can enable a producer to offer his product at more competitive prices and thus to capture a larger share of the market. **Internal economies of scale** occur when better use is made of the factors of production and by using the increased output to pay for a higher proportion of the costs of marketing, financing, and development, etc. Internal diseconomies can occur when a plant exceeds its optimum size, requiring a disproportionate unwieldy administrative staff. **External economies** and diseconomies arise from the effects of a firm's expansion on market conditions and on technological advance.

economies of scope See SCOPE ECONOMIES.

economy, efficiency, and effectiveness The primary performance measures for an *operating system. In order for a system to be effectively managed, it is necessary to have feedback. **Economy** requires feedback on the cost of the inputs to a system. **Efficiency** measures how successfully the inputs have been transformed into outputs. **Effectiveness** measures how successfully the system achieves its desired outputs. Because effectiveness involves the subjective reaction of the customer, it is the most difficult to measure.

ECP Abbreviation for *euro-commercial paper.

ECU Abbreviation for *European Currency Unit.

EDI Abbreviation for *electronic data interchange.

editorial advertisement An advertisement in a newspaper or magazine written in the form of an editorial feature. Such advertisements must, however, be clearly labelled 'advertisement'.

EDSP Abbreviation for Exchange Delivery Settlement Price. *See* SETTLEMENT PRICE.

EEA Abbreviation for *European Economic Area.

effective annual rate The total interest paid or earned in a year expressed as a percentage of the principal amount at the beginning of the year.

effective capacity The capacity of a system in units per time, taking into account such factors as staffing decisions (e.g. whether to run 24 hours a day, 7 days a week, or to operate one 8-hour shift, 5 days a week), set-up times, maintenance, and an allowance for unforeseeable failures. *Compare* DESIGNED CAPACITY.

effective tax rate The average tax rate that is applicable in a given circumstance. In many cases the actual rate of tax applying to an amount of income or to a gift may not, for various reasons, be the published rate of the tax; these reasons include the necessity to gross up, the complex effects of some reliefs, and peculiarities in scales of rates. The effective rate is therefore found by dividing the additional tax payable as a result of the transaction by the amount of the income, gift, or whatever else is involved in the transaction.

effective yield *See* GROSS REDEMPTION YIELD.

efficiency 1. (**technical efficiency**)
A measure of the ability of an organization
to produce the maximum output of
acceptable quality with the minimum of
time, effort, and other inputs. One company is said to be more efficient than
another if it can produce the same output
as the other with less input, irrespective of
the price factor. *See* ECONOMY, EFFICIENCY,
AND EFFECTIVENESS. **2.** (**economic efficiency**) A measure of the ability of an
organization to produce and distribute its
product at the lowest possible cost. A firm
can have a high technical efficiency but a
low economic efficiency because its prices
are too high to meet competition.

efficiency ratio A ratio that measures
the efficiency of labour or an activity over a
period by dividing the *standard hours
allowed for the production by the actual
hours taken. It is usually expressed as a
percentage, using the formula:

$$(\text{standard hours allowed} \times 100)/\text{actual hours worked.}$$

efficient markets hypothesis A central theory of modern finance holding that
transactors in financial markets cannot
make *abnormal returns on the basis of
exploiting information, since market prices
incorporate all available information. The
US economist Eugene Fama has defined
three categories of market efficiency:
weak-form efficiency, in which only historical information is incorporated into the
market prices; **semi-strong-form efficiency**, in which all publicly available
information, past or present, is incorporated; and **strong-form efficiency**, in
which all public or private information is
incorporated. *See also* ACTIVE
MANAGEMENT; ANOMALY.

EFQM Award An award instituted in 1992
by the European Foundation for Quality
Management. It is given to companies that
can demonstrate success across all nine
areas of the **EFQM Excellence Model**:
leadership; strategy; people; partnerships
and resources; processes, products, and
services; customer results; people results;
society results; and key results. The Award

was formerly known as the **European
Quality Award**.

EFTA Acronym for *European Free Trade
Association.

EFTPOS Abbreviation for *electronic funds
transfer at point of sale.

EGM Abbreviation for *extraordinary general meeting.

EIB Abbreviation for *European Investment Bank.

18–25 trust A *trust established for the
benefit of a young person, who becomes
absolutely entitled to the trust property on or
before his or her 25th birthday. An 18–25 trust
can now only be created by the will of the young
person's parent or step-parent (until April 2008
it could also be created by converting an existing accumulation and maintenance trust; *see*
DISCRETIONARY TRUST). The trust is charged to
*inheritance tax (i) on settlement; (ii) when any
distribution is made to the beneficiary, he or
she being over 18 years old; and (iii) when the
beneficiary becomes absolutely entitled, he or
she being over 18 years old.

Eighth Company Law Directive An
EU directive (1984) concerning the role and
regulation of auditors. Its provisions were
incorporated into UK law in the Companies
Act 1989. In 2006 it was superseded by a
revised and expanded version, the *Statutory Audit Directive.

EIS 1. Abbreviation for *Enterprise Investment Scheme. **2.** Abbreviation for executive
information system. See DECISION SUPPORT
SYSTEM.

e-learning (**electronic learning**) Any
form of training or education that uses
computer technology as an essential part of
the teaching process. Typically, computerized data and programs substitute partly or
completely for the human teacher and
students engage with all or part of the
course remotely (e.g. over the Internet).

elective resolution Formerly, a *resolution by all the members of a private
*company to dispense with certain

requirements of the Companies Act 1985, such as the holding of an *annual general meeting. The need for such a resolution was removed by the Companies Act 2006.

electronic banking *See* HOME BANKING.

electronic billing (e-billing) The facility to send invoices and accept payments for goods and services over the Internet. The payment and presentment services can be divided into two types: **biller-direct payments**, in which the supplier sends the consumer a statement of account by electronic means and receives payment in the same way; and **bank-aggregator payments**, in which online banking enables a bank-account holder to pay bills to a variety of other users.

electronic catalogue 1. An online *catalogue of goods for purchase. **2.** An interactive *videotex system in which consumers see products on their home TV screens, using touch-tone phones to control the sequence and to place orders.

electronic commerce *See* E-COMMERCE.

electronic conveyancing (e-conveyancing) The transfer of land by electronic means instead of by paper documents. A legal framework for such conveyancing was set in place by the Electronic Communications Act 2000 and the Land Registration Act 2002. Although electronic conveyancing is not yet a reality, the land registers are already kept in electronic form and it is possible to discharge mortgages of registered land electronically. *See* LAND REGISTRATION.

electronic data interchange (EDI) The use of electronic data-transmission networks to move information from one computer system to another, in general without human intervention. For example, EDI can be used for orders, invoices, and payments to suppliers, customers, banks, etc., without recourse to hard copy. EDI is dependent on users having compatible technology and systems that are transparent to the other members of the network.

electronic funds transfer at point of sale (EFTPOS) The automatic debiting of a purchase price from the customer's bank or credit-card account by a computer link between the checkout till and the bank or credit-card company. The system can only work when the customer has a *debit card or *credit card recognized by the retailer. In the now dominant **chip and pin** system the transaction is ratified by use of the customer's *personal identification number (PIN), rather than by signature of a printed voucher. Many larger shops now permit customers buying goods by EFTPOS to withdraw cash as part of the same transaction. This **cashback** facility has advantages for shops, as it minimizes the amount of cash that needs to be counted, stored, and banked.

electronic learning *See* E-LEARNING.

electronic mail survey (EMS) A relatively easy, low cost, and fast method of conducting marketing surveys in which potential respondents are sent the questionnaire by group mail. Respondents e-mail the completed questionnaires back to the researchers. Evidence suggests that e-mail surveys produce a faster but lower response rate than mail (postal) surveys.

electronic mall *See* VIRTUAL MALL.

electronic marketspace *See* MARKETSPACE.

electronic point of sale (EPOS) A computerized method of recording sales in retail outlets, using a laser scanner at the checkout till to read *bar codes printed on the items' packages. Other advantages over conventional checkout points include a more efficient use of checkout staff time, the provision of a more detailed receipt to the customer, and real-time stock control, enabling rapid replenishment of stock and minimizing the stock that has to be held. In consumer goods sales, the data can also be used to produce consumer profiles for marketing purposes.

electronic shopping (e-shopping) The buying of goods or services over the

Internet. Payment is generally by credit card or *PayPal, although various types of electronic cash have been devised (*see* BITCOIN). Delivery may be by shipping to a designated address, downloading of digital products (e.g. music files or computer software), printing out of coupons etc., or customer pick-up (e.g. of theatre or concert tickets at the box office; *see also* CLICK AND COLLECT).

electronic signature An item of data incorporated into or associated with an electronically transmitted document or contract that fulfils the function of a written signature. Under the Electronic Communications Act 2000 electronic signatures are recognized in legal proceedings and as having legal effect. They can be purchased from such bodies as the Post Office and the London Chamber of Commerce on production of relevant identification documents. There is a distinction between an electronic signature in this legal sense and a **digital signature**, which may be simply an authentication code to verify the source of a document.

electronic transfer of funds (ETF) The transfer of money from one bank account to another by means of computers and communications links. Banks routinely transfer funds between accounts using computers; ETF is also used in *home banking services. *See also* ELECTRONIC FUNDS TRANSFER AT POINT OF SALE.

eligibility Criteria that determine which bills the Bank of England will discount, as *lender of last resort. Such bills are known as *eligible paper.

eligible list A listing of the names of banks entitled to discount acceptances at the Bank of England.

eligible paper 1. Treasury bills, short-dated gilts, and any first-class security, accepted by a British bank or an accepting house and thus acceptable by the *Bank of England for rediscounting, or as security for loans to discount houses. The Bank of England's classification of eligible paper influences portfolios because of the ability

to turn them into quick cash, and thus reinforces the Bank's role as *lender of last resort. **2.** Acceptances by US banks available for rediscounting by the *Federal Reserve System.

eligible reserves Cash held in a US bank plus the money held in its name at its local *Federal Reserve Bank.

e-mail (electronic mail) Software that enables messages (e.g. letters, memos, documents) between individuals or from individuals to groups to be exchanged by computer. Its operation can be restricted to a *local area network or it can be open to a wide area network, such as the *Internet. Many systems now support the delivery of **multimedia mail**, which can combine text, graphics, voice, and other forms of information in a single message.

embargo A ban on some or all of the trade with one or more countries. A trade embargo is a form of *economic sanction. Prominent examples include the continuing US embargo against Cuba and the former international ban on trade in arms with South Africa. Full embargos are rare and difficult to apply in practice.

embezzlement A form of theft in which an employee dishonestly appropriates money or property given to him or her on behalf of an employer. The special offence of embezzlement ceased to exist in 1969.

emergent strategy A business strategy in which decisions are made in response to events as they occur, rather than according to a preconceived plan. The term was introduced by the academic Henry Mintzberg in 1978. Mintzberg defines an emergent strategy as one in which either (i) no plan was formulated at the outset or (ii) the initial strategy was displaced along the way. *Compare* DELIBERATE STRATEGY; PRESCRIPTIVE STRATEGY.

EMIs Abbreviation for *Enterprise Management Investments.

emissions trading *See* POLLUTION PERMITS.

emoluments Amounts received from an office or employment including all salaries, fees, wages, perquisites, and other profits as well as certain expenses and benefits paid or provided by the employer, which are deemed to be emoluments. They are subject to *income tax. *See also* DIRECTORS' REMUNERATION.

emotional appeal The attempt by advertising to stir up negative or positive emotions to motivate a purchase. Much marketing and advertising is geared to creating fear, guilt, shame, love, pride, or joy in the potential customer rather than evoking dispassionate appraisal on the basis of objective criteria.

emotional selling proposition (ESP) The unique associations established by consumers with particular products. Many car marques evoke an emotional response that ensures their continual success, even though other makers offer superior performance at the same price.

employee A person who works under the direction and control of another (the employer) in return for a wage or salary. An employee works for the employer under a *contract of employment, whereas an independent contractor who is contracted to perform a specific task works under a *contract for services. The distinction is crucial since employees enjoy more protection under employment legislation. The question as to whether someone is or is not an employee is governed by a number of tests laid down by the courts over many years and can be far from clear. *Compare* WORKER.

employee assistance programme (EAP) A confidential personal counselling service funded by an employer. EAPs provide professional counsellors with whom employees can discuss their work and non-work-related problems, which may be emotional, financial, or legal or related to alcohol or drug misuse.

employee buy-out *See* MANAGEMENT BUY-OUT.

employee empowerment *See* EMPOWERMENT.

employee evaluation A formal assessment of an employee's performance in his or her job, as measured by certain objective indicators (e.g. sales figures, absenteeism) or by more subjective rating procedures. The employee may be evaluated in absolute terms or by comparison with others doing similar work, as in the *paired comparison method. The results are usually presented to the employee as part of his or her *performance appraisal.

employee participation 1. The encouragement of motivation in a workforce by giving shares in the company to employees. Employee shareholding (*see* EMPLOYEE SHARE OWNERSHIP PLAN) can be an important factor in improving industrial relations. **2.** The appointment to a board of directors of a representative of the employees of a company, to enable the employees to take part in the direction of the company. *See* PARTICIPATIVE DECISION MAKING.

employee report A simplified version of the statutory annual report and accounts of a company prepared for the employees of the company (*see* ANNUAL ACCOUNTS). Although this is a voluntary practice, such documents should comply with the provisions of the Companies Act relating to *non-statutory accounts. Employee reports were particularly popular in the 1930s and the 1970s.

employee share ownership plan (ESOP) A method of providing the employees of a company with shares in the company. The ESOP buys shares in its sponsoring company, usually with assistance from the company concerned. The shares are then allocated to employees who satisfy certain performance targets. The advantage claimed for ESOPs is that they do not require dilution of the sponsoring company's share capital by the creation of new shares. In the USA they are known as **employee stock option plans**. *See also* EMPLOYEE SHARE OWNERSHIP TRUST; SHARE INCENTIVE SCHEME; SHARE OPTION.

employee share ownership trust

(ESOT) A trust set up by a UK company, under the provisions introduced in 1989, to acquire shares in the company and distribute them to the employees. The company's payments to the trust are tax-deductible. The trust deed sets out the specified period of employment and all those employees who fulfil the requirements must be included in the class of beneficiaries of the trust. *See also* EMPLOYEE SHARE OWNERSHIP PLAN; SHARE INCENTIVE PLAN; SHARE INCENTIVE SCHEME.

employers' liability insurance An

insurance policy covering an employer's legal liability to pay compensation to any of his employees suffering or contracting injury or disease during the course of their work. This type of insurance is compulsory by law for anyone who employs another person (other than members of their own family) under a contract of service. A *certificate of insurance must be displayed at each place of work, confirming that employer's liability insurance is in force and giving details of the policy number and the insurer's name and address. *See also* PUBLIC-LIABILITY INSURANCE.

employment agency An organization

that introduces suitable potential employees to employers, charging the employer a fee, usually related to the initial salary, for the service. Employment agencies also provide temporary staff, in which they are the employers, the temporary staff member being charged out at an hourly rate. Employment agencies that specialize in finding suitable managers and executives for a firm, or finding suitable jobs for executives who want a change, are often known as **head hunters**. Such agencies will often provide a short list of candidates in order to save their client's time in personnel selection. Employment agencies run by the government are called *job centres.

employment costs The expenditure

incurred in employing personnel. It includes salaries, wages, bonuses, incentive payments, employer's National Insurance

contributions, and employer's pension scheme contributions.

employment protection The legal

safeguards applying to an *employee's position with regard to his or her employment. *See* CONTRACT OF EMPLOYMENT; REDUNDANCY; UNFAIR DISMISSAL. *See also* WRITTEN STATEMENT OF TERMS OF EMPLOYMENT.

(((●))) **SEE WEB LINKS**

• Guide to employment rights from the TUC's WorkSMART website

employment tribunal Any of the bod-

ies established under the UK employment protection legislation to hear disputes between employers and employees or trade unions relating to statutory terms and conditions of employment. For example, the tribunals hear complaints concerning *unfair dismissal, *redundancy, *equal pay, and *maternity rights. Tribunals may also hear complaints from members of trade unions concerning unjustifiable disciplining by their union. The tribunal often consists of a legally qualified chairperson and two independent lay members, but employment judges may also sit alone. Under the Enterprise and Regulatory Reform Act 2013 legal officers may decide certain claims, provided both parties agree. The tribunal differs from a civil court in that it cannot enforce its awards (this must be done by separate application to a court) and it can conduct its proceedings informally. Strict rules of evidence need not apply and the parties can present their own case or be represented by anyone they wish at their own expense. From 2013 fees must be paid by anyone bringing a claim. The tribunal has powers to declare a dismissal unfair and to award compensation; in some cases it may order the reinstatement or re-engagement of a dismissed employee.

empowerment In *human-resource

management, the giving of increased responsibility and a measure of control to employees in their working lives. The concept is based on the view that people need personal satisfaction and fulfilment in their work and that responsibility and control increase satisfaction. Employees like empowerment because an increase in responsibility usually leads to greater rewards and enhanced prospects. On the other hand, it has been criticized because staff are asked to become more account-able without being given more authority. Empowerment also has the added advan-tage that it enables potential talents to be identified and developed, either by the employing organization or the individual.

As well as being a motivational strategy, empowerment may occur as part of a process of re-engineering organizational structures to remove layers of management (*see* DELAYERING), so that the system can respond more rapidly to customers' requirements.

EMS 1. Abbreviation for *electronic mail survey. **2.** Abbreviation for European Monetary System. *See* EUROPEAN ECONOMIC AND MONETARY UNION.

EMU Abbreviation for EUROPEAN ECONOMIC AND MONETARY UNION.

EMV Abbreviation for *expected monetary value.

encourager *See* RELATIONSHIP ROLES.

encryption The encoding of electronic data so that it can be transmitted without interception. With the growing use of the *Internet for commercial purposes, there has been an ongoing need for secure encryption methods, notably in the transmission of credit card details. *See* SECURITY.

encumbrance (incumbrance) A charge or liability, such as a *mortgage or registered judgment, to which land is subject.

end-of-day sweep An automatic trans-fer of funds from one bank account held by a company to another of its bank accounts, usually one that pays interest on deposits. The sweep takes place at the end of every day, or at the end of the day when certain conditions are met.

endogenous growth *See* SCHUM-PETERIAN GROWTH.

endorsement (indorsement)
1. A signature on the back of a *bill of exchange or cheque, making it payable to the person who signed it. A bill can be endorsed any number of times, the pre-sumption being that the endorsements were made in the order in which they appear, the last named being the holder to receive payment. If the bill is **blank endorsed**, i.e. no endorsee is named, it is payable to the bearer. In the case of a **restrictive endorsement** of the form 'Pay X only', it ceases to be a *negotiable instrument. A **special endorsement**, when the endorsee is specified, becomes payable **to order**, which is short for 'in obedience to the order of'. **2.** A signature required on a document to make it valid in law. **3.** An amendment to an *insurance policy or cover note, recording a change in the con-ditions of the insurance. **4.** Another term for a guarantee.

endowment assurance An assurance policy that pays a specified amount of money on an agreed date or on the death of the *life assured, whichever is the earlier. As these policies guarantee to make a pay-ment (either to the policyholder or his or her dependants) they offer both life cover and a reasonable investment. A *with-profits policy will also provide bonuses in addition to the sum assured. These policies are often used in the repayment of an *endowment mortgage or as a form of saving.

endowment mortgage A *mortgage in which repayment of the principal is made principally by means of an *endowment assurance policy. In the 1980s and 1990s, many first-time home buyers in the UK were encouraged to take out this form of mortgage (which earns the mortgagor's agent an immediate commission from the life cover provider). However, with the subsequent poor performance of invest-ments on the stock exchange, many endowment mortgagees are facing a short-fall in the principal at the end of the mortgage's life; in some cases, the courts have ordered the mortgage provider to compensate the mortgagee, on the grounds that the policy was mis-sold. As a result of these problems endowment mortgages are now rarely sold.

Engel's law The law stating that the lower a family's income the greater is the proportion spent on food. As the income rises the family's spending is spread across a wider range of goods and services, such as housing, transport, consumer goods, leisure activities, etc. It was stated by the German statistician Ernst Engels (1821–96).

enlightened marketing A marketing philosophy holding that a company's marketing should support the best long-run performance of the marketing system; its five principles are consumer-oriented marketing, innovative marketing, value marketing, sense-of-mission marketing, and societal marketing.

enquiry (inquiry) An initial request from a potential purchaser for information regarding the quality, price, delivery date, etc., of a particular product. This may be the standard practice in some trades and commercial markets or it may be a consumer's response to an advertisement, sales promotion, or *direct marketing approach.

enquiry test (inquiry test) A method of testing the response to an advertisement or a particular medium by comparing the number of enquiries received as a result of it.

Enterprise Finance Guarantee A UK government scheme intended to facilitate bank lending to smaller companies by guaranteeing 75% of a company's overdraft in return for a 2% annual premium (borrowers are nevertheless responsible for repayment of 100% of the loan). The scheme is available to all UK companies with a turnover of no more than £41 million. It replaced the former **Small Firms Guarantee Scheme**, which had a more limited eligibility, from January 2009.

Enterprise Investment Scheme (EIS) An investment scheme in the UK that replaced the Business Expansion Scheme (BES) on 1 January 1994. Its purpose is to help certain types of small higher-risk unlisted trading companies to raise capital. Individuals who invest between £500 and £1M in eligible shares in any one year are entitled to a tax relief of 30% of the amount subscribed. Gains on the sale of shares issued under the scheme are exempt from capital gains tax. Investors may hold paid directorships of the companies concerned. Tax relief of 50% of an investment of up to £100,000 made between 6 April 2012 and 6 April 2017 is also available under the **Seed Enterprise Investment Scheme**. *See also* CORPORATE VENTURING SCHEME; VENTURE CAPITAL TRUST.

(⊕) **SEE WEB LINKS**
• A guide to the EIS from the Gov.uk website

Enterprise Management Incentives (EMIs) An approved *share option scheme designed to help small high-risk unlisted companies attract and retain key employees. Under the scheme, an employee of a qualifying company (broadly, an independent trading company with fewer than 250 full-time employees and gross assets of no more than £30M) may receive share options of a value up to £250,000 free of tax. On disposal of the shares, he or she is entitled to *entrepreneurs' relief on any capital gain.

enterprise performance management (EPM) *See* BUSINESS PERFORMANCE MANAGEMENT.

enterprise resource planning (ERP) A single computer-based information system that aims to integrate all key functions of an enterprise, including *material requirements planning, *customer relationship management, human resources, accounting and payroll, and a *decision support system for managers.

enterprise zone An area, designated as such by the UK government, in which its aim is to restore private-sector activity by removing certain tax burdens and by relaxing certain statutory controls. Benefits, which are available for a 10-year period, include: exemption from rates on industrial and commercial property; 100% allowances for corporation- and income-tax purposes for capital expenditure on industrial and commercial buildings; exemption from industrial training levies; and a simplified planning regime.

entity concept See ACCOUNTING ENTITY.

entrepôt trade Trade that passes through a port, district, airport, etc., before being shipped on to some other country. The entrepôt trade may make use of such a port because it is conveniently situated on shipping lanes and has the warehouses and customs facilities required for re-export or because that port is the centre of the particular trade concerned and facilities are available there for sampling, testing, auctioning, breaking bulk, etc. Much entrepôt trade used to pass through London, but since the decline of the London docks other European ports, such as Rotterdam, have taken its place. Singapore and Hong Kong are also centres of the entrepôt trade.

entrepreneur An individual who undertakes (from the French *entreprendre* to undertake) to supply a good or service to the market for profit. The entrepreneur will usually invest capital in the business and take on the risks associated with the investment. In most modern capitalist economies the initiative of entrepreneurs is regarded as an important element in creating a society's wealth; governments are therefore led to establish conditions in which they will thrive.

entrepreneurs' relief A *capital gains tax relief introduced from 6 April 2008, when it replaced *taper relief and *indexation allowance. Under the relief, gains arising from the disposal of all or part of a business are charged at an effective rate of 10%, rather than the normal rate of 18%: the relief can be claimed more than once, up to a lifetime total of £1M of gains qualifying for relief.

entry A record made in a book of account, register, or computer file of a financial transaction, event, proceeding, etc. *See also* DOUBLE-ENTRY BOOK-KEEPING.

entry-level criteria See ORDER-QUALIFYING CRITERIA.

enumeration district A geographical area of approximately 150 households corresponding to the census breakdown of Great Britain, used for the segmentation of consumer markets using data lists.

environmental accounting See GREEN REPORTING; SOCIAL RESPONSIBILITY REPORTING.

environmental audit (green audit) An *audit of the impact of the activities of an organization on the environment. Its purpose is usually to ensure that the organization has clear environmental policies, that its operations comply with the stated environmental policies, and that its policies are subject to regular review. Environmental audits may be conducted internally or externally by environmental consultants. Areas covered by a green audit include energy usage, wastage and recycling procedures, conservation of raw materials, and adopting cleaner technologies. *See also* GREEN REPORTING; SOCIAL AUDIT; SOCIAL RESPONSIBILITY REPORTING; TRIPLE BOTTOM-LINE ACCOUNTING.

environmental costs The *costs of making sure that a company's activities do not damage the environment or that any such damage is put right. There are many types of environmental costs and these are often difficult to identify as they are hidden in *overheads. Measuring environmental costs is now an important issue for many companies, as national regulations become more stringent and penalties or fines more severe. It is useful to classify environmental costs into four categories:

- **environmental appraisal costs**. These are the costs of activities performed to monitor environmental effects that a firm is responsible for. Examples include the costs arising from inspection of products and contamination testing.

- **environmental prevention costs**. These are the costs of activities performed to prevent the production of waste that could cause damage to the environment. Examples include the costs of recycling products, training staff, and carrying out environmental studies.
- **environmental internal failure costs**. These are the costs of activities that have to be performed when contaminants and waste have been produced by a company but not discharged into the environment. Examples include treating toxic waste and maintaining pollution equipment.
- **environmental external failure costs**. These are the costs incurred by a company if it discharges waste into the environment. Examples include the costs of cleaning up oil spills or cleaning a polluted river. A company may also incur fines or other penalties or lose sales if it acquires a poor environmental reputation. *See also* COST OF QUALITY.

environmental management perspective A management outlook in which a firm takes aggressive action to affect the people and forces controlling its marketing environment, rather than simply watching them and reacting to them.

environmental scanning An examination of the environment of a business in order to identify its marketing opportunities, competition, etc.

EONIA Acronym for Euro Overnight Index Average, the overnight *reference rate for the eurozone *interbank market, as computed by the European Central Bank. *Compare* EURONIA. *See also* EURO INTER BANK OFFERED RATE.

EOQ Abbreviation for *economic order quantity.

EPM Abbreviation for enterprise performance management. *See* BUSINESS PERFORMANCE MANAGEMENT.

EPOS Abbreviation for *electronic point of sale.

EPP Abbreviation for *executive pension plan.

eps Abbreviation for *earnings per share.

equal opportunities *See* DISCRIMINATION.

equal pay The requirement of the Equality Act 2010 (and before that of the Equal Pay Act 1970) that men and women in the same employment must be paid at the same rate for like work or work rated as equivalent. Work is rated as equivalent when the employer has undertaken a study to evaluate his employees' jobs in terms of the skill, effort, and responsibility demanded of them and the woman's job is given the same grade as the man's or when an independent expert appointed by an *employment tribunal evaluates the two jobs as of equal value.

equipment trust certificate (ETC) In the USA, a document setting out the details of a loan used to fund the purchase of a major item of equipment. The holder of the certificate has a secured interest in the asset in the event of a corporate default. The arrangement is therefore similar to a mortgage, and like house mortgages ETCs are often *securitized.

equitable apportionment The process of sharing common costs between *cost centres in a fair manner, using a basis of apportionment that reflects the way in which the costs are incurred by the cost centres.

equitable interest An interest in, or ownership of, property that is recognized by *equity but not by the *common law. A beneficiary under a trust has an equitable interest. Any disposal of an equitable interest (e.g. a sale) must be in writing. Some equitable interests in land must be registered or they will be lost if the legal title to the land is sold. Similarly, equitable interests in other property will be lost if the legal title is sold to a bona fide purchaser for value who has no notice of the equitable interest. In such circumstances the owner of the equitable interest may claim damages from the person who sold the legal title.

equity 1. A beneficial interest in an asset. For example, a person having a house worth £250,000 with a mortgage of £100,000 may be said to have an equity of £150,000 in the house. *See also* NEGATIVE EQUITY. **2.** The amount of money returned to a borrower in a mortgage or hire-purchase agreement, after the sale of the specified asset and the full repayment of the lender of the money. **3.** The net assets of a company after all creditors (including the holders of *preference shares) have been paid off. **4.** The ordinary share capital of a company (*see* EQUITY CAPITAL). **5.** The market value of a company's issued *ordinary shares. **6.** The system of law developed by the medieval chancellors and later by the Court of Chancery. It is distinguished from the *common law, which was developed by the king's courts, having originated from the residual jurisdiction delegated by the king to the chancellor. A citizen dissatisfied by the common law could petition the chancellor, who might grant relief on an ad-hoc basis. In time this developed into a complementary but separate system of law providing remedies unavailable at common law, such as specific performance of a contract rather than damages. Until 1873 equity was applied and administered by the Court of Chancery, and equitable remedies were not available in the common law courts (and vice versa). However, the Judicature Acts of 1873 and 1875 merged the two systems so that any court may now apply both common law and equity. If the two sets of rules contradict each other, the equitable rule prevails. Equity has been particularly important in the development of the law of trusts, land law, administration of estates, and alternative remedies for breach of contract. *See also* NEGATIVE EQUITY.

equity accounting The practice of showing in a company's accounts a share of the undistributed profits and a share of the net assets of another company in which it holds a share of the *equity (usually a share of between 20% and 50%). The share of profit shown by the equity-holding company is usually equal to its share of the equity in the other company. Although none of the profit may actually be paid over, the company has a right to this share of the undistributed profit.

equity capital (equity share capital) 1. Generally, the part of the share capital of a company owned by ordinary shareholders. For certain purposes, such as *pre-emption rights, other classes of shareholders may be deemed to share in the equity capital and therefore be entitled to share in the profits of the company or any surplus assets on winding up. *See also* A SHARES. **2.** The *market value of a company's issued *ordinary shares.

equity carve-out *See* CARVE-OUT.

equity dilution *See* DILUTION OF EQUITY.

equity dividend cover A ratio that shows how many times the *dividend to ordinary shareholders can be paid out of the profits of a company available for distribution. The higher the cover, the greater the certainty that dividends will be paid in the future.

equity finance Finance raised from shareholders in the form of *ordinary shares and reserves, as opposed to *non-equity shares and to borrowing.

equity gearing *See* GEARING.

equity-linked policy An insurance or assurance policy in which a proportion of the premiums paid are invested in equities. The surrender value of the policy is therefore the selling price of the equities purchased; as more premiums are paid the portfolio gets larger. Although investment returns may be considerably better on this type of policy than on a traditional endowment policy, the risk is greater, as the price of equities can fall, dramatically reducing the value of the policy. With *unit-linked policies, a much wider range of investments can be achieved and the risk is correspondingly reduced.

equity share capital *See* EQUITY CAPITAL.

ERG theory. The existence, relatedness, and growth theory of motivation.

equity theory A cognitive theory of *motivation, based on the work of J. Stacey Adams, which claims that employees will be motivated if they believe that they are fairly treated in the workplace. The theory proposes that employees form an estimate of how the total benefits they receive from a job (pay, status, interest) compare with their total input (effort, skill, experience); this ratio is then compared with that of other people doing similar work. If the latter comparison is unfavourable, motivation will suffer.

equivalent units (effective units) Unfinished units of production that remain in a process at the end of a period as *work in progress (or process). Degrees of completion are assigned to each cost classification, which, when applied to the number of units in work in progress, give an equivalent number of completed units. For example, if the number of units of work in progress is, say, 3,000 units to the following degrees of completion, the effective units are given in the table overleaf. The equivalent units have an impact on the valuation of opening and closing work in process.

ERDF Abbreviation for *European Regional Development Fund.

ergonomics (human factors) The discipline that draws on human physiology and psychology in order to design jobs, equipment, and work environments that are safe and efficient. For example, such human characteristics as size, reach, and flexibility must match the machines and tools that people have to use.

ERG theory (existence, relatedness, and growth theory) A theory of human *motivation that focuses on three groups of needs that form a hierarchy: **existence needs** (physical and material wants); **relatedness needs** (the desire for interpersonal relationships and for deeper relationships with the important people in one's life); and **growth needs** (desires to be creative and productive). The theory suggests that these needs change their position in the hierarchy as circumstances change (see diagram). A need does not have to be fully satisfied for upward movement to occur; a downward movement can occur when a need is not

COST CLASSIFICATION	WORK IN PROGRESS (UNITS)	DEGREES OF COMPLETION (%)	EQUIVALENT UNITS
direct materials	3000	100	3000
direct labour	3000	50	1500
overheads	3000	50	1500

Equivalent units. A simple example.

satisfied. In the deficiency cycle at the bottom of the hierarchy the individual can become obsessed with satisfying existence needs. The enrichment cycle leads a person to learn and grow, generally in multiple environments (i.e. work, home, etc.). The theory, which was developed from *Maslow's motivational hierarchy by the US organizational psychologist Clayton P. Alderfer (1940–), has been widely applied to issues of workplace motivation and consumer behaviour.

ERM Abbreviation for Exchange Rate Mechanism. *See* EUROPEAN ECONOMIC AND MONETARY UNION.

ERP Abbreviation for *enterprise resource planning.

errors and omissions excepted *See* E & OE.

escalation clause A clause in a contract authorizing the contractor to increase the price in specified conditions of all or part of the services or goods he has contracted to supply. Escalation clauses are common in contracts involving work over a long period in times of high inflation. The escalation may refer to either or both labour and materials and may or may not state the way in which the price is permitted to escalate. An escalation clause does not convert a contract into a *cost-plus contract, but it represents a move in that direction.

escalation of commitment Increasing the resources available to an unsuccessful venture in the hope of recovering past losses. This is sometimes called a **creeping commitment**. This policy is often adopted in *new product development when the company continues to pour in funds, irrespective of the likelihood of success, in an attempt to recover some of its investment. It is known colloquially as throwing good money after bad.

escape clause A clause in a contract releasing one party from all or part of the contractual obligations in certain specified circumstances.

escrow A *deed that has been validly executed but is delivered on the condition that it will not become operative until some stated event happens. It will become effective as soon as that event occurs and it cannot be revoked in the meantime. Banks often hold escrow accounts, in which funds accumulate to pay taxes, insurance on mortgaged property, etc.

escudo 1. The standard monetary unit of Cape Verde (CVE), divided into 100 centavos. **2.** The former monetary unit of Portugal, divided into 100 centavos. It was replaced by the *euro in 2002.

ESM Abbreviation for *European Stability Mechanism.

ESOP Abbreviation for *employee share ownership plan (or, in the USA, employee stock option plan).

ESOT Abbreviation for *employee share ownership trust.

ESP Abbreviation for *emotional selling proposition.

estate 1. The sum total of a person's assets less his or her liabilities (usually as measured on his or her death for the purposes of *inheritance tax.) **2.** A substantial piece of land, usually attached to a large house.

estate in land The length of time for which a piece of land will be held; for example, a life estate would last only for the life of the owner. *See* FEE SIMPLE.

estoppel 1. A rule of evidence by which a person is prevented from denying that a certain state of affairs exists, having previously asserted that it does. **2. (promissory estoppel)** The rule that if a person has declared that the strict legal rights under a contract will not be insisted upon, they cannot be insisted upon later if the other party has relied on that declaration. The strict legal rights may, however, be enforced on giving reasonable notice, if this would not be inequitable. **3. (proprietary estoppel)** The rule that if one person allows or encourages another person to act to his or her detriment in respect of land, he or she will not later be able to refuse to grant something that he or she allowed the other person to expect. For example, if A encourages B to build a garage, which can only be reached by driving over A's land, saying that a right of way will be granted, A will not later be able to refuse to do so.

ETC Abbreviation for *equipment trust certificate.

ETF Abbreviation for *electronic transfer of funds.

Ethernet A high-speed *local area network system. When first introduced in the 1980s, Ethernet worked at a standard 10 million *bits per second; Fast Ethernet and Gigabit Ethernet working at respectively 10 and 100 times this speed have since become available.

ethical behaviour Behaviour judged to be good, just, right, and honourable, based on principles or guides from a specific ethical theory. However, ethical theories may vary from person to person, country to country, or company to company. Ethical realism accepts that although morality does not apply internationally, the ethical values of a trading partner should be respected.

ethical dilemmas The moral quandaries that can occur in running a business. While not confronting the law, most of these dilemmas arise as a result of conflict between what the businessperson sees as necessary in the interests of the business and his or her personal ethical values. These dilemmas may be related to entrepreneurial activities (Does the product or service offered conflict with one's social responsibility?), to one's behaviour to competitors (Have the claims for the superiority of one's product or service overstepped the limits of fair competition?), to one's shareholders (Are they earning a fair return on their capital?), and most of all, perhaps, to one's customers (Does the product or service offer fair value for money?).

ethical indicators See PERFORMANCE MEASUREMENT.

ethical investment (socially responsible investment) An investment made in a company not engaged in an activity that the investor considers to be unethical, such as armaments or tobacco, or an investment in a company of which the investor approves on ethical grounds, e.g. one having a good environmental or employment record.

ethnic segmentation Recognizing the special strengths or needs of an ethnic community in offering it appropriate products and services using an appropriate marketing approach. See MARKET SEGMENTATION.

ethnocentrism Belief, often unconscious, in the superiority of one's own ethnic group or the universality of one's own culture-bound practices and preferences. In a global economy, such assumptions may be particularly dangerous in the fields of marketing and advertising.

EU Abbreviation for *European Union.

Euratom Abbreviation for *European Atomic Energy Community.

Eurex An electronic derivatives exchange formed by a merger of the Deutsche Terminbörse and the Swiss Options and Financial Futures Exchange in 1998. The electronic system on which trading occurs is accessible in some 700 locations worldwide. Eurex is now owned wholly by *Deutsche Börse. Plans to acquire the US-based *International Securities Exchange were announced in 2007 but have yet to be approved.

Euribor Acronym for *Euro Inter Bank Offered Rate.

euro The currency unit of the European Union's *eurozone, divided into 100 cents. In January 1999 it was adopted for all purposes except cash transactions by Austria, Belgium, Finland, France, Germany, Ireland, Italy, Luxembourg, The Netherlands, Portugal, and Spain; Greece followed suit in 2001. Euro-denominated notes and coins were issued in January 2002 and the national currencies were withdrawn after a short period of dual circulation. Slovenia adopted the euro in 2007, as did Cyprus and Malta in 2008, Slovakia in 2009, Estonia in 2011, Latvia in 2014, and Lithuania in 2015. Andorra, Monaco, San Marino, and Vatican City also use the euro through agreements with the EU; Kosovo and Montenegro likewise use the euro but without any such agreement. The euro is also used in the Azores, the Canary Islands, French Guiana, Guadeloupe, Madeira, Martinique, Mayotte, Réunion, Saint-Barthélemy, and Saint-Pierre-et-Miquelon. *See* EUROPEAN ECONOMIC AND MONETARY UNION.

Euro-ad An advertisement designed to be used in all countries of the European Union. Certain products, particularly those that have been in use for long enough for national traditions to build up, are not suitable for multinational advertisements. Food is an example: there would be no point in advertising tinned baked beans in France. On the other hand, advertisements for cars, a more recent product, can have an equal appeal in all European countries.

Euro Area Reference Note (EARN) A euro-denominated bond first issued by the *European Investment Bank in 1999 to establish a market in euro-denominated securities.

eurobanks Financial intermediaries that deal in the *eurocurrency market.

eurobond A *bond issued in a *eurocurrency. The eurobond market is now one of the largest markets for raising money (it is much larger than the UK stock exchange). The reason for this popularity is that *secondary market investors can remain anonymous, usually for the purpose of avoiding tax. For this reason it is difficult to ascertain the exact size and scope of operation of the market. Issues of new euro-bonds normally take place in London, largely through syndicates of US and Japanese investment banks; they are *bearer securities, unlike the shares registered in

most stock exchanges, and interest payments are free of any *withholding taxes. There are various kinds of eurobonds. An ordinary bond, called a **straight**, is a fixed-interest loan of 3 to 8 years duration; others include **floating-rate notes**, which carry a variable interest rate based on the *London Inter Bank Offered Rate; and **perpetuals**, which are never redeemed. Some carry *warrants and some are *convertible. Eurobonds in British pounds are referred to as **eurosterling bonds**.

euro certificate of deposit (Euro CD) A *certificate of deposit denominated in a *eurocurrency. London is the main issuing centre.

Euroclear A pan-European provider of clearing, settlement, and related services for bond, equity, and investment-fund transactions. Based in Brussels, it was set up in 1968 by the US bank J. P. Morgan. With *Clearstream, it is one of the two main clearing systems for *eurobonds. *See also* CREST.

euro-commercial paper (ECP) *Commercial paper issued in a *eurocurrency, the market for which is centred in London. It provides a quick way of obtaining same-day funds by the issue of unsecured notes, for example in Europe for use in New York.

eurocredit A loan in a *eurocurrency.

eurocurrency A currency deposit at a bank located outside the country where the currency is issued as a legal tender. For example, dollars deposited in a bank in Switzerland are *eurodollars, yen deposited at a US bank are euroyen, etc. The deposit need not be held at a European bank or in Europe. Eurocurrency is used for lending and borrowing; the **eurocurrency market** often provides a cheap and convenient form of liquidity for the financing of international trade and investment. The main borrowers and lenders are the commercial banks, large companies, and the central banks. By raising funds in eurocurrencies it is possible to secure more favourable terms and rates of interest, and sometimes to avoid domestic regulations and taxation.

The deposits and loans were initially on a short-term basis but increasing use is being made of medium-term loans, particularly through the raising of *eurobonds. This has to some extent replaced the syndicated loan market, in which banks lent money as a group in order to share the risk.

eurodeposit A deposit using the currency of another country, i.e. a transaction in the *eurocurrency market.

eurodollars Dollars deposited in financial institutions outside the USA. The eurodollar market evolved in London in the late 1950s when the growing demand for dollars to finance international trade and investment coincided with a greater supply of dollars. The prefix 'euro' indicates the origin of the practice but it now refers to all dollar deposits made anywhere outside the USA. *See also* EUROCURRENCY.

euroequity An *equity issue made on a stock exchange outside the country of the issuing company but denominated in the currency of that country.

Eurofirst 300 Index *See* FTSE INDEXES.

Euro Inter Bank Offered Rate (Euribor) The rate of interest charged on interbank loans within the eurozone. *See* INTERBANK MARKET. *See also* EONIA; EURONIA.

euromarket 1. A market that emerged in the 1950s for financing international trade. Its principal participants are *commercial banks, large companies, the European Central Bank, and the central banks of member states of the EU. Its main business is in *eurobonds, *euro-commercial paper, *euronotes, and *euroequities issued in *eurocurrencies. The largest euromarket is in London, but there are smaller ones in Paris, Brussels, and Frankfurt. **2.** The European Union, regarded as one large market for goods.

Euronext.liffe *See* LIFFE. *See also* EURONEXT NV.

Euronext NV A market and clearing system for equities and traded derivatives,

established in September 2000 with the merger of the Amsterdam, Brussels, and Paris stock exchanges. It acquired the London futures exchange *LIFFE (now Euronext.liffe) in 2001 and the Lisbon Stock Exchange (now Euronext Lisbon) in 2002. A merger with NYSE Group, the owner of the *New York Stock Exchange, was approved in December 2006, leading to the creation of **NYSE Euronext**—the world's first global stock market.

(⊕) SEE WEB LINKS
- Euronext website

EURONIA Acronym for Euro Overnight Index Average, a *reference rate computed as a weighted average of euro overnight funding rates in the London interbank market. *Compare* EONIA; SONIA. *See* OVERNIGHT RATE.

euronote A form of *euro-commercial paper consisting of short-term negotiable *bearer securities. They may be in any currency but are usually in dollars or euros. The **euronote facility** is a form of *note issuance facility set up by a syndicate of banks, which underwrites the notes.

European Atomic Energy Community (Euratom) The organization set up by the six members of the *European Coal and Steel Community in 1957; the *European Economic Community was established at the same time. Euratom was formed to create the technical and industrial conditions necessary to produce nuclear energy on an industrial scale. Its controlling bodies were absorbed into the *European Commission in 1967.

European Central Bank (ECB) The central bank of the *European Union, which was established in 1998 under the terms of the *Maastricht Treaty and became fully operational on 1 January 1999. From that date it superseded the *European Monetary Institute and the European Monetary Cooperation Fund. It is responsible for *eurozone monetary policy and in particular the setting of interest rates. It is independent of national governments but works with the central banks of the individual eurozone countries through the **Euro System**. It is based in Frankfurt am Main, Germany. Since 2010 the ECB has taken a leading role in attempting to resolve the *sovereign debt crisis affecting the eurozone (*see* EUROPEAN STABILITY MECHANISM). *See also* EUROPEAN ECONOMIC AND MONETARY UNION; EUROPEAN SYSTEM OF CENTRAL BANKS.

(((⊕))) SEE WEB LINKS
• Website of the ECB

European Coal and Steel Community (ECSC) The first of the European Communities (EC), founded in 1953. The ECSC created a common market in coal, steel, iron ore, and scrap between the original six members of the EC (Belgium, France, West Germany, Italy, Luxembourg, and the Netherlands). These six countries, in 1957, signed the Treaty of Rome setting up the *European Economic Community.

European Commission The single executive body formed in 1967 (as the Commission of the European Communities) from the three separate executive bodies of the *European Coal and Steel Community, the *European Atomic Energy Community, and the *European Economic Community. It now consists of 28 Commissioners, one from each member state (France, Germany, Italy, Spain, and the UK were formerly allotted two Commissioners each). The Commissioners accept joint responsibility for their decisions, which are taken on the basis of a majority vote. The Commission initiates and implements EU legislation and mediates between member governments. The Commissioners are backed by a staff of some 33,000 civil servants.

European Community *See* EUROPEAN ECONOMIC COMMUNITY; EUROPEAN UNION.

European Currency Unit (ECU) A former currency medium and unit of account created in 1979 to act as the reserve asset and accounting unit of the European Monetary System (EMS). ECU reserves were held in the European Monetary Cooperation Fund. With the introduction

of the *euro in January 1999 the ECU ceased to exist. *See* EUROPEAN ECONOMIC AND MONETARY UNION.

European Economic and Monetary Union (EMU) The EU policy that culminated in the creation of the *European Central Bank (1999) and a single European currency for participating states. Monetary cooperation between the member states of the European Union began in 1979, with the establishment of the **European Monetary System** (EMS), a system of exchange-rate stabilization.

The EMS consisted of two main elements: the Exchange Rate Mechanism (ERM), under which participating countries committed themselves to maintaining the values of their currencies within agreed limits, and a *balance of payments support mechanism, organized through the European Monetary Cooperation Fund. The ERM operated by giving each currency a value in *European Currency Units (ECUs) and drawing up a parity grid giving exchange values in ECUs for each pair of currencies. If market rates differed from the agreed parity by more than a permitted percentage (2.25% or 6% depending on the currency), the relevant governments were required to take action to correct the disparity.

The EMS suffered a major crisis in September 1992, when two currencies, the UK pound and the Italian lira, were effectively forced out of the ERM by speculative pressure (*see* BLACK WEDNESDAY). The lira subsequently rejoined but the pound did not. From 1993 the currencies in the system were allowed wider (plus or minus 15%) fluctuations.

Although some participants had seen the EMS as no more than a means of stabilizing exchange rates, the view that its ultimate goal should be **Economic and Monetary Union** (EMU), with a single currency and a single monetary policy directed by a European central bank, became official EU policy in 1989. The decision to create a common currency was enshrined in the *Maastricht Treaty of 1991, which created the *European Monetary Institute to coordinate the process of convergence.

In June 1998 11 EU countries – all the then member states except Denmark, Greece, Sweden, and the UK—committed themselves to monetary union. Their currencies were locked together irrevocably and the *European Central Bank (ECB) was established to direct the single monetary policy essential for EMU. A common currency, the *euro, was launched in January 1999 for all purposes except cash transactions. Euro bank notes and coins came into circulation from January 2002 and the national currencies were withdrawn after a short transitional period.

A new exchange-rate mechanism, known as **ERM II**, was established in January 1999 to enable those EU states remaining outside the *eurozone to link their currencies to the euro if they so wished (with fluctuation rates of plus or minus 15% as the basic rule). Its initial members were Denmark and Greece (the latter of which adopted the euro in 2001).

With the single currency established, all countries subsequently joining the EU are required to participate in ERM II as soon as this is judged economically practicable and to adopt the euro in due course. Countries must participate in ERM II for a minimum of two years before adopting the euro. Of the 13 states that have joined the EU since 2004, Slovenia joined the eurozone in 2007, Cyprus and Malta in 2008, Slovakia in 2009, Estonia in 2011, Latvia in 2014, and Lithuania in 2015. Of the established members, only Sweden and the UK remain outside the European Monetary System. *See also* CONVERGENCE CRITERIA.

European Economic Area (EEA) The organization formed in 1992 between the members of the *European Union and the members of the *European Free Trade Association (EFTA) except Switzerland. The EEA was intended to come into force in 1993, with the single market of the EU, but owing to Switzerland's rejection of the plan, this was delayed until 1994. The EEA is controlled by a committee of EU and EFTA members and meetings of ministers.

European Economic Community (EEC; Common Market) The European

common market set up by the six member states of the *European Coal and Steel Community (ECSC) in 1957. At the same time the *European Atomic Energy Community (Euratom) was set up. The European Parliament and the European Court of Justice were formed in accordance with the Treaty of Rome in 1957. The treaty aimed to forge a closer union between the countries of Europe by removing the economic effects of their frontiers. This included the elimination of customs duties and quotas between members, a common trade policy to outside countries, the abolition of restrictions on the movement of people and capital between member states, and a *Common Agricultural Policy. In addition to these trading policies, the treaty envisaged a harmonization of social and economic legislation to enable the Common Market to work. The **European Community (EC)** was created in 1967, when the controlling bodies of the EEC, ECSC, and Euratom were merged to form the Commission of the European Communities (*see* EUROPEAN COMMISSION) and the Council of the European Communities. The UK, Ireland, and Denmark joined the EC in 1973, Greece joined in 1981, and Portugal and Spain became members in 1986. In 1992, following the ratification of the *Maastricht Treaty, the European Community became the *European Union.

European Free Trade Association (EFTA) A trade association formed in 1960 between Austria, Denmark, Norway, Portugal, Sweden, Switzerland, and the UK. Finland, Iceland, and Liechtenstein joined later while the UK, Denmark, Portugal, Austria, Finland, and Sweden left on joining the *European Union (or its earlier forms). EFTA is a looser association than the EU, dealing only with trade barriers rather than generally coordinating economic policy. All tariffs between EFTA and EU countries were abolished finally in 1984. EFTA is governed by a council in which each member has one vote; decisions must normally be unanimous and are binding on all member countries. In 1992 the *European Economic Area (EEA) was formed to facilitate the movement of goods, services, capital, and labour between all EU and EFTA countries with the exception of Switzerland.

European Investment Bank (EIB) A bank set up under the Treaty of Rome in 1958 to finance capital-investment projects in the *European Economic Community (EEC). It grants long-term loans to private companies and public institutions for projects that further the aims of the Community. The members of the EIB are the member states of the *European Union, all of whom have subscribed to the Bank's capital; however, most of the funds lent by the bank are borrowed on the EU and international capital markets. The bank is non-profit-making and charges interest at a rate that reflects the rate at which it borrows. Its headquarters are in Luxembourg.

European Monetary System (EMS) The former system of exchange-rate stabilization involving the countries of the *European Union. See EUROPEAN ECONOMIC AND MONETARY UNION.

European option See OPTION.

European Patent Court (Unified Patent Court) A proposed court that will exercise specialized jurisdiction in patent disputes throughout the EU, thus avoiding the need for multiple litigation in up to 28 member states. An agreement to establish such a court was signed by 25 EU states (all the current members except Poland, Spain, and Croatia) in 2013. The court is expected to be based in London.

European Quality Award See EFQM AWARD.

European Regional Development Fund (ERDF) A fund set up in 1975 by the European Union to allocate money usually in regions of high unemployment or social deprivation. In its earlier years the fund concentrated on infrastructure projects but it now invests in such areas as tourism, culture, education, information technology, and the environment.

European Stability Mechanism (ESM) An intergovernmental body established in September 2012 to provide permanent financial stability for the *eurozone; as such it replaced both the **European Financial Stability Facility** and the **European Financial Stabilization Mechanism**, which were introduced as emergency measures in 2010. Unlike these bodies, the ESM was given a formal basis in EU treaty law. It is empowered to provide financial assistance to any member of the eurozone facing unusual economic difficulties, provided that recipients accept such measures of reform as are imposed by the ESM, the European Central Bank, and the International Monetary Fund. Assistance may take the form of stability support loans, a bank recapitalization programme, precautionary credit lines, or intervention in the primary or secondary markets for government debt. The ESM is based in Luxembourg.

European System of Central Banks The group of central banks comprising the *European Central Bank and the central banks of all 28 member states of the EU (i.e. including those countries that are not in the *eurozone). Its objectives are the maintenance of price stability throughout the EU and the facilitation of monetary cooperation between the eurozone countries and other members of the EU.

European terms The quotation of foreign-exchange rates in terms of how many units of a currency can be exchanged for one US dollar. *Compare* AMERICAN TERMS.

European Union (EU) The 28 nations that have joined together to form an economic community, with common monetary, political, and social aspirations. The EU was created in 1993 from the European Community (EC), which itself grew from the European Coal and Steel Community, the European Atomic Energy Community, and the *European Economic Community. The 12 nations of the EC (Belgium, Denmark, France, Germany, Greece, Ireland, Italy, Luxembourg, the Netherlands, Portugal, Spain, and the UK) were joined by Austria, Sweden, and Finland in 1995, by (Greek) Cyprus, the Czech Republic,

Estonia, Hungary, Latvia, Lithuania, Malta, Poland, Slovakia, and Slovenia in 2004, by Bulgaria and Romania in 2007, and by Croatia in 2013. Its executive body is the *European Commission, which was formed in 1967 with the Council of the European Communities. EU policy emerges from a dialogue between the Commission, which initiates and implements the policy, and the Council, which takes the major policy decisions. The European Parliament, formed in 1957, exercises democratic control over policy, and the European Court of Justice imposes the rule of law on the EU, as set out in its various treaties. A draft EU Constitution, providing for the creation of an EU president and foreign minister, was published in 2004 but rejected by the electorates of France and the Netherlands. Elements of the proposed constitution were retained in a treaty agreed in October 2007 (the Lisbon Treaty), but this was rejected by the Irish electorate in 2008. *See* EUROPEAN ECONOMIC AND MONETARY UNION.

Europort Any of the main European ports, especially Rotterdam.

eurosecurities Financial instruments traded on *euromarkets, notably *euro-commercial paper, *euronotes, *euro-bonds, and *euroequities.

Eurosox *See* COMPANY REPORTING DIRECTIVE.

Euro-Top 100 Index *See* FTSE INDEXES.

eurozone The 19 member countries of the European Union that have adopted the *euro as their currency, namely Austria, Belgium, Cyprus, Estonia, Finland, France, Germany, Greece, Ireland, Italy, Latvia, Lithuania, Luxembourg, Malta, The Netherlands, Portugal, Slovakia, Slovenia, and Spain. Monetary policy in these countries is now the responsibility of the *European Central Bank. In 2010 confidence in the eurozone was threatened by mounting *sovereign debt in several member states, most notably Greece. European finance ministers responded by creating the European Financial Stability Facility (bail-out fund) to provide emergency assistance; this

was replaced by the *European Stability Mechanism in 2012. *See* EUROPEAN ECONOMIC AND MONETARY UNION.

EV Abbreviation for *expected value.

EVA Abbreviation for *Economic Value Added.

evaluation of training An assessment of the effectiveness of personnel training programmes. Ideally, such a review should be carried out at four levels:

(1) **reaction**—What did the trainees themselves think of the programme? This involves collecting data directly from trainees about their reaction to the length, depth, pace, difficulty, and usefulness of the training.

(2) **learning**—How much new knowledge has been acquired by the trainees? This can be assessed by testing trainees on the information content of the course.

(3) **behaviour**—How has the programme affected the behaviour of trainees? To answer this, supervisors must find evidence of new skills or positive behavioural traits that can be attributed directly to the programme.

(4) **results**—How has the effectiveness of the group or organization as a whole benefitted from the training? This involves relating the answers received for questions (1), (2), and (3) to an agreed system of *performance measurement for the organization.

event of default In a loan agreement, a specified occurrence that will make the loan repayable immediately. The breaching of any *covenant clause will be an event of default. Events of default also include failure to pay, failure to perform other duties and obligations, false *representation and warranty, *material adverse change, bankruptcy, and *alienation of assets.

evergreen fund A fund that provides capital for new companies and supports their development for a period with regular injections of capital.

ex- (Latin: without) A prefix used to exclude specified benefits when a security is quoted. A share is described as **ex-dividend** (xd or ex-div) when a potential purchaser will no longer be entitled to receive the company's current dividend, the right to which remains with the vendor. Government stocks go ex-dividend 36 days before the interest payment. Similarly, **ex-rights**, **ex-scrip**, **ex-coupon**, **ex-capitalization** (**ex-cap**), and **ex-bonus** mean that each of these benefits belongs to the vendor rather than the buyer. **Ex-all** means that all benefits belong to the vendor. **Cum-** (Latin: with) has exactly the opposite sense, meaning that the dividend or other benefits belong to the buyer rather than the seller. The price of a share that has gone ex-dividend will usually fall by the amount of the dividend, while one that is **cum-dividend** will usually rise by this amount. However, in practice market forces usually mean that these falls and rises are often slightly less than expected.

ex-all *See* EX-.

ex ante (Latin) Before the event. The phrase is used, for example, of a budget that is prepared as an estimate and subsequently compared with actual figures. *Compare* EX POST.

ex-capitalization (ex-cap) *See* EX-.

Excel *Trademark* A widely used *spreadsheet program supplied by Microsoft.

excepted peril A *risk that is expressly excluded from an insurance policy. In the carriage of goods, excepted perils exclude *acts of God, *inherent vice, *negligence, and loss resulting from action of the Queen's enemies. *See also* INSURABLE RISK.

exceptional items Costs or income affecting a company's *profit and loss account that arise from the normal activities of the company but are of exceptional magnitude, either large or small. Under current UK rules they are included in the calculation of the normal trading profit or loss but disclosed separately. Neither exceptional nor *extraordinary items are recognized under *International Financial Reporting Standards.

excess 1. An initial sum which the holder of an insurance policy must bear before any claim is met by the insurer. It is most often used in car insurance, e.g. the first £50 of any claim has to be borne by the insured party. **2.** A bank or other financial institution's margin of assets over liabilities. *See also* EXCESS RESERVES. **3.** *See* EXCESS SHARES.

excess capacity The part of the output of a plant or process that is not currently being utilized but which, if it could be, would reduce the average cost of production. The excess capacity is thus the amount by which the present output must be increased to reduce the average cost per unit to a minimum.

excess policy An insurance policy in which the insured is responsible for paying a specified sum (the **excess**) of each claim and cannot make claims of a lower value than this excess. For example, a £100 excess on a motor-insurance policy means that the insured has to pay the first £100 of any claim and cannot make a claim on the policy for less than £100. This arrangement enables the insurer to offer the insurance at a lower premium than would otherwise be the case as he avoids the administrative cost of small claims and also makes a saving on claims paid out. *See also* DEDUCTIBLE; FRANCHISE.

excess reserves Higher reserves than required, held by banks. This usually undesirable state occurs as a result of poor demand for loans or high interest rates. Banks often sell excess reserves to one another.

excess shares Shares not taken up by other shareholders in a *rights issue, for which an invitation to purchase is sent to shareholders with their standard letters of *allotment.

exchange 1. The trading of goods, stocks, shares, commodities, paper currencies, or other financial instruments. **2.** The place in which such trading occurs, e.g. a stock exchange or commodities exchange. This may not necessarily have a physical location. **3.** An agreement to swap, as in *exchange of contracts.

exchange control Restrictions on the purchase and sale of foreign exchange. This has taken various forms in different countries, in particular those who experience shortages of *hard currencies; sometimes different regulations apply to transactions that would come under the capital account of the *balance of payments. Recent decades have seen a general movement toward dismantling exchange controls by developed countries. The UK abolished all forms of exchange control in 1979.

Exchange Delivery Settlement Price (EDSP) *See* SETTLEMENT PRICE.

exchange equalization account An account set up in 1932 and managed by the *Bank of England on behalf of the government. It contains the official gold and foreign-exchange reserves (including *Special Drawing Rights) of the UK and is used to manage the value of sterling. Although all *exchange controls were abolished in 1979, the Bank of England still makes use of this account to help to stabilize rates of exchange.

exchange of contracts A procedure adopted in the sale and purchase of land in which both parties sign their copies of the contract, having satisfied themselves as to the state of the property, etc., and agreed that they wish to be bound. There need be no physical exchange of documents; the parties or their advisers can exchange contracts by agreeing to do so orally (for example, by telephone). From that moment the contract is binding and can normally be enforced by specific performance. Contracts for the sale of land must be in writing.

exchange offer A proposal to debt or equity holders that they should exchange their existing securities for new securities, the terms of which are usually less favourable. It is a mechanism for capital restructuring in situations of *financial distress.

exchange rate *See* RATE OF EXCHANGE.

exchange-rate exposure (currency risk; exchange-rate risk; foreign-exchange rate risk) The risk associated with uncertain exchange rates.

Exchange Rate Mechanism (ERM) *See* EUROPEAN ECONOMIC AND MONETARY UNION.

exchange-traded option (exchange option; listed option) An option traded on one of the institutional markets, such as the *LIFFE, as opposed to one sold on the *over-the-counter market; such options have standard terms and conditions.

Exchequer The account held by the *Bank of England for all government funds.

Exchequer stocks *See* GILT-EDGED SECURITY.

excise duty A duty or tax levied on certain goods consumed within a country, such as alcoholic drinks and tobacco products, unlike customs duty, which is levied on imports. In the UK, both excise and customs duties are collected by HM Revenue and Customs.

exclusive distribution 1. The use by a manufacturer of a single retailer or wholesaler in a particular market for a particular product. **2.** A situation in which a distributor carries the products of one manufacturer and not those of competing manufacturers; this may give the distributor the exclusive right to distribute the company's products in other territories. *See* EXCLUSIVE TERRITORY.

exclusive economic zone *See* TERRITORIAL WATERS.

exclusive territory 1. An area, defined by geographical boundaries or population, assigned by a manufacturer to a retailer, wholesaler, or other dealer with the understanding that no other distributors will be allowed to sell the manufacturer's products in that area. **2.** A practice used by some manufacturers in which intermediaries may only sell their products within a designated geographical area.

executive director (working director)
A *director of a company who is also an employee (usually full-time) of that company. An executive director will often have a specified role in the management of the company, such as finance director, marketing director, production director, etc. By contrast a *non-executive director is involved in planning and policy-making, but not in the day-to-day management of the company.

executive information system (EIS)
See DECISION SUPPORT SYSTEM.

executive pension plan (EPP)
A pension for a senior executive or director of a company in which the company provides a tax-deductible contribution to the premium. An executive pension plan may be additional to any group pension scheme provided by the company, as long as the pension limit of two-thirds of the working salary is not exceeded.

executive share option scheme
An approved *share option scheme that entitles a specified class of directors or employees to purchase shares in the company in which they are employed. *See* SAVINGS RELATED SHARE OPTION SCHEME.

executor
A person named in a will of another person to gather in the assets of that estate, pay liabilities, and distribute any residue to the beneficiaries in accordance with the instructions contained in the will.

exempt gilts
In the UK, government *gilt-edged securities that pay interest gross, unlike ordinary gilts, on which tax is deducted from interest payments. These gilts are of particular interest to foreign buyers and others, such as institutions, who do not pay income tax.

exempt supplies
Supplies of goods or services in the categories of items that are identified as exempt from *value added tax, as given in the Value Added Tax Act 1994. The main categories are: land (including rent), insurance and financial services, postal services, betting, sport, charities (except on their business activities), education (non-profitmaking), health services, and burial and cremation.

exempt transfers
Transfers resulting in no liability to *inheritance tax. These are:
- the first £3,000 transferred in any tax year;
- gifts to a spouse or civil partner;
- normal expenditure out of income;
- small gifts, up to £250, to any number of individuals;
- marriage gifts, up to £5,000 for each parent and £2,500 for grandparents of the parties to the marriage, but limited to £1,000 for other gifts;
- gifts to charities;
- gifts for national purposes;
- gifts for public benefit;
- gifts to political parties;
- certain transfers to employee trusts.

See also POTENTIALLY EXEMPT TRANSFER.

exempt unit trust
A *unit trust in which only institutional investors who are not subject to taxation are allowed to invest, i.e. it is restricted to charities and pension funds.

exercise
To make use of the right to carry out a transaction on previously agreed terms, mainly in the *options market.

exercise date
The date on which the holder of an *option can exercise the right to implement the option contract. It is normally after three, six, or nine months.

exercise notice
Formal notification from the *taker of an *option to the *writer expressing an intention to exercise the option to buy (for a call option) or sell (for a put option) at the *exercise price on the *exercise date.

exercise price (strike price; striking price)
The price per share at which a traded *option entitles the owner to buy the *underlying in a call option or to sell it in a put option.

ex gratia
(Latin: as of grace) Denoting a payment made out of gratitude, moral

obligation, kindness, etc., rather than to fulfil a legal obligation. When an ex gratia payment is made, no legal liability is admitted by the payer.

ex gratia pension A pension paid by an employer although there is no legal, contractual, or implied commitment to provide it.

ex growth (of a share or a company) Having had substantial growth in the past but now not holding out prospects for immediate growth of earnings or value.

exhibition list A list of visitors to an exhibition. Such lists are often used as a data source for *direct marketing to business customers.

Eximbank *See* EXPORT-IMPORT BANK OF THE USA.

existence needs *See* ERG THEORY.

exit charge The charge to *inheritance tax made when an asset is taken out of a *discretionary trust.

exit interview An interview in which an employee who has handed in his or her resignation is questioned by personnel staff. Such interviews can be useful to the employer because they provide a means of finding out the reasons why the employee is leaving, which may be helpful in designing policies that can help to retain staff (e.g. by improving promotion opportunities or job satisfaction).

exit value The *net realizable value of an asset, i.e. its market price at the date of a balance sheet less the selling expenses. Exit values are effectively *break-up values and are not consistent with the *going-concern concept, which assumes that a business is continuing to trade.

ex-new Describing a share that is offered for sale without the right to take up any *scrip issue or *rights issue. *Compare* CUM-NEW.

exotic options (exotics) Options that have unusual features, particularly in relation to their *exercise price, payoff formula, or *underlying. Examples include *binary options and *exploding options.

expected monetary value (EMV) In decision making, the sum of the products of the outcomes in monetary terms and the probabilities of these outcomes arising. In *decision trees subjective probability estimates are assigned to each possible outcome. In the EMV, the outcomes are expressed in terms of money. In the example given in the table, the EMV is 3900. *Compare* EXPECTED VALUE.

expected value (EV) A statistical measure of central value often used in decision making. It is the sum of the possible outcomes in quantitative terms, such as units of output or sales, weights, or volumes, multiplied by the respective probabilities of these outcomes arising. *Compare* EXPECTED MONETARY VALUE.

expenditure The costs or expenses incurred by an organization. They may be *capital expenditure or *revenue expenditure. Although expenditure is usually incurred by an outlay of money, expenditure may also arise in accounting by the acknowledgement of a liability, for example rent accrued due, which is regarded as expenditure in the period accrued although it will not be paid until a later date.

POSSIBLE OUTCOMES (£)	SUBJECTIVE PROBABILITY (P)	PRODUCT (£ × P)
3000	0.5	1500
4000	0.3	1200
6000	0.2	1200
	1.0	EMV = 3900

Expected monetary value. In this simple example the EMV of a project is calculated as £3900.

expenditure tax (outlay tax) A tax on the expenditure of individuals or households. This form of taxation, of which VAT is an example, is often preferred by tax theorists to income taxes, as it does not distort the incentive to work. *See also* SALES TAX.

expense 1. A sum spent for goods or services, which therefore no longer represents an asset of the purchasing organization. Expenses are normally shown as charge against profit in the *profit and loss account. **2.** A sum of money spent by an employee during the course of his work. The employee records this expenditure in an **expense account**, for refund by the company and submission to HM Revenue and Customs on a P11D form for assessment of any taxable element.

expense account 1. An account, opened in either the cost ledger or the nominal ledger, for each *expenditure heading in which the costs of an organization are recorded before being totalled and transferred to the *profit and loss account at the end of an accounting period. **2.** The amount of money that certain staff members are allowed to spend on personal expenses in carrying out their activities for an organization.

experience curve A relationship between the costs of production and cumulative output, showing that efficiency increases with the repetition of the process. As experience increases, costs fall, adding to the competitive advantage of a firm. This may be a continuous process as improvements are regularly made to the manufacture of a product over its life cycle.

experiencing focus groups *Focus groups that enable a client to listen to consumers' thoughts and feelings regarding specific products and services.

experimental marketing research The gathering of primary data by selecting matched groups of subjects, giving them different treatments, controlling related factors, and checking for differences in group responses.

expert networks Firms that refer clients to outside consultants with expertise in their fields in return for a fee. Expert networks are often used by financial professionals to obtain specialized information relevant to investment decisions, for example whether or not to back a new product or company. However, such advice has the potential to cause conflicts of interest when confidential or proprietary information is involved and may give rise to allegations of *insider dealing.

expert system A computer application used to solve problems in a particular area of knowledge. The system uses the computer's ability to store, organize, and retrieve large amounts of information and is programmed to make decisions of the type that would be made by an expert in the field. Typically, an expert-system program asks questions of the user, who chooses one of several possible answers. This leads to other questions, and eventually to a conclusion. A common successful use is in basic medical diagnosis, but expert systems can also be designed for analysis of company results, review of loan applications, buying stocks and shares, and other financial purposes.

expiry date 1. The date on which a contract expires. **2.** The day on which an *option expires. In a European option the option must be taken up or allowed to lapse on this date. In an American option the decision can be taken at any time up to the expiry date.

exploding option An *exotic option in which exercise is automatic if the price of the *underlying reaches the *exercise price.

exploratory focus groups *Focus groups that aid in the precise definition of a problem, in pilot testing, in generating hypotheses for testing, or suggesting concepts for further *marketing research.

exploratory research Preliminary *marketing research to clarify the exact nature of a problem to be solved. Quite often sales managers recognize that there is a problem but do not understand the dimensions of the problem. In these circumstances preliminary research is conducted with small numbers of potential customers to define the nature of the problem.

exponential smoothing *See* ADAPTIVE EXPONENTIAL SMOOTHING.

Export Credits Guarantee Department (ECGD) A UK government department that now operates under the name UK Export Finance. It encourages exports from the UK by making export credit insurance available to exporters and guaranteeing repayment to UK banks that provide finance for exports on credit terms of two years or more. It also insures British private investment overseas against war risk, expropriation, and restrictions on the making of remittances. Some sections of the ECGD were privatized in 1991, including short-term credit insurance.

(()) SEE WEB LINKS
• UK Export Finance area of the Gov.uk website

Export-Import Bank of the USA (Eximbank) A US bank established by the US government to foster trade with the USA. It provides export credit guarantees and guarantees loans made by commercial banks to US exporters.

export incentive An incentive offered by a government to exporters. These can be subsidies, grants, tax concessions, credit facilities, etc.

export licence A licence required before goods can be exported from a country. Export licences are only required in the UK for certain works of art, antiques, etc., and certain types of arms and armaments.

exports Goods or services sold to foreign countries. Export selling may be achieved by using international marketing middlemen (**indirect exporting**) or by a company's own overseas branch or sales representatives or by a company's *agents abroad (**direct exporting**). In terms of the *balance of payments ECGD website, goods are classified as *visibles, while such

services as banking, insurance, and tourism are treated as invisibles. The UK has traditionally relied on its invisibles to achieve its trade balance as it tends to spend more on imports than it receives in exports. *See also* EXPORT CREDITS GUARANTEE DEPARTMENT.

ex post (Latin) Short for *ex post facto*: after the event. This abbreviation is used, for example, to refer to the collection of financial data for transactions after they have been effected. *Compare* EX ANTE.

exposure The degree of *risk involved in holding a particular *position on a financial market.

extended community An Internet community that is larger and more extensive than a *personal community.

extended guarantee A servicing and maintenance cover that a manufacturer offers to a customer for a specified additional amount of time beyond the original guarantee. Extended guarantees usually have to be paid for.

extended marketing mix An addition to the traditional *marketing mix of product, price, place, and promotion (the four Ps) to include three further Ps, when marketing services, i.e.:

• **physical evidence**—the tangible elements of a service that enable consumers to evaluate it;
• **people**—an evaluation of the personnel providing the service (e.g. knowledge, competence, politeness);
• **process**—an evaluation of the overall experience provided by the service to ensure that all the elements of which it consists operate effectively together.

extended trial balance A *trial balance that gives a vertical listing of all the *ledger account balances with three additional columns for adjustments, *accruals, and *payments in advance, and a final two columns (each containing a debit and a credit side) that show the entries in the *profit and loss account and the *balance sheet.

extendible bond issue A *bond, the maturity of which can be extended at the option of all the parties.

Extensible Business Reporting Language (XBRL) A computer language that has become a global standard for communicating business and financial data. XBRL is a type of extensible mark-up language (XML) that allows business facts to be identified and analysed by computer. It is the format mandated by the US *Securities and Exchange Commission for reporting since 2010.

extension risk The *risk associated with an agreement that permits one of the partners to extend its term, so that payments take place later than expected. It is the opposite of *prepayment risk.

extension service An alliance partner to an *anchor service on the Internet; if, for example, the anchor service is an airline, an extension service might be provided by a firm of travel agents.

external audit An *audit of an organization carried out by an auditor who is external to, and independent of, the organization. An example would be a *statutory audit carried out on behalf of the shareholders of a limited company. *Compare* INTERNAL AUDIT.

external environment The institutions and people outside a business organization that affect it; these include national and local government, trade unions, competitors, customers, suppliers, etc. The external environment is one of the contingency factors that has to be taken into account in designing an organization.

external failure costs *See* COST OF QUALITY. *See also* ENVIRONMENTAL COSTS.

external growth The means by which a business can grow by merger, takeover, or joint ventures, rather than by growing organically through its own internal development (*see* BUSINESS STRATEGY). External growth is widely used by companies as it can offer greater speed in achieving its corporate objectives than internal

development. Typically firms can increase their market share by merging with or taking over a competitor in the same field (horizontal diversification). In mature or declining markets, restructuring of combined operations can lead to cost savings. Alternatively, a company may seek to gain greater control of its supply chain by expanding through merging or taking over a supplier or distributor (vertical integration). Unrelated external expansion may take place when a firm buys into a market in which it has no existing expertise; often the time taken to develop a significant presence on its own account is considered to be too long and risky, compared to buying an established business. Although great benefits may accrue from external growth, it also carries high risks, since the expected gains may often be slow to appear as a result of the restructuring and organizational changes involved as well as the high costs of financing the merger or takeover. *Joint ventures, often between rival firms, sometimes between companies from different countries, are becoming a more common form of external growth. In such cases, the parties bring complementary strengths (technology, operations, marketing) and share the risks of the venture, although differences in company and country culture may cause difficulties.

externality A cost or benefit to an economic agent that is not matched by a compensating financial flow. For example, siting a railway station close to a housing estate represents an externality to householders on that estate. It is an external economy if the householders benefit from shorter journey times to work (and consequent rising house prices) and an external diseconomy if the noise of trains keeps them awake at night. In business, externalities can be defined as those economic effects of an entity that are not recorded in its accounts as they do not arise from individual transactions. For example, local overcrowding may arise because a large number of employees have been attracted to the neighbourhood, thus incurring extra costs for roads, schools, health care, etc. It is usually argued that governments should take steps to internalize external diseconomies, such as pollution, by means of taxation or other penalties. *See also* FREE RIDE; MARKET FAILURE.

external link A web link that takes the user to a different, usually independent, website.

extranet An *intranet extended beyond a company to its customers, suppliers, collaborators, or even competitors. Like an intranet, an extranet is password-protected to prevent access by general Internet users.

extraordinary general meeting (EGM) Any general meeting of a company other than the *annual general meeting. Most company's articles give the directors the right to call an EGM whenever they wish. Members have the right to requisition an EGM if they hold not less than 10% of the paid-up share capital; a resigning auditor may also requisition a meeting. Directors must call an EGM when there has been a serious loss of capital. The court may call an EGM if it is impracticable to call it in any other way. Those entitled to attend must be given 14 days' notice of the meeting (21 days if a special resolution is to be proposed). *See also* AGENDA; ORDER OF BUSINESS.

extraordinary items Costs or income affecting a company's *profit and loss account that do not derive from the normal activities of the company, are not expected to recur, and, if undisclosed, would distort the normal trend of profits. In traditional UK accounting practice, such items were disclosed after the normal trading profit or loss had been shown. However, under current rules virtually all previously extraordinary items are now treated as *exceptional items and included in the profit and loss. The concepts of extraordinary and exceptional standards are not recognized in *International Financial Reporting Standards.

extraordinary resolution Formerly, a type of *resolution submitted to a general meeting of a company; 14 days' notice of such a resolution was required and 75% of those voting had to approve the resolution for it to be passed. Under the Companies Act 1985 certain decisions (e.g. to wind up a company) could only be effected by extraordinary resolution; the Companies Act 2006 removed such a requirement, although it may still be present in the articles of a company.

extrapolation *See* INTERPOLATION.

extrinsic motivation An incentive to do something that arises from factors outside the individual, such as rewards or penalties. The promise of a bonus if one meets agreed performance targets is an obvious example of such *motivation. *Compare* INTRINSIC MOTIVATION. *See* EXTRINSIC REWARD.

extrinsic reward A positive outcome that is obtained by performing work but which is separate from and not inherent to the work task. The most obvious extrinsic rewards are the pay and benefits that workers receive in return for work, though others might include praise from superiors and a sense of career progression. *Compare* INTRINSIC REWARD. *See* EXTRINSIC MOTIVATION.

Ex Works (EXW) An *Incoterm denoting a delivery contract in which the buyer has to pay for transporting the goods away from the seller's factory, warehouse, etc. and bears all the risks of doing so. The seller is responsible for preparing the goods for transit and packing them (if necessary) but not for loading them.

eyrir (*plural* **aurar**) A monetary unit of Iceland, worth one hundredth of a *króna.

faa Abbreviation for *free of all averages.

Facebook A social networking website established in 2004. With about 1.4 billion (2015) active users each month, it is one of the most frequently accessed websites in the world and increasingly used for business marketing purposes. *See* SOCIAL MEDIA.

face value 1. The value printed on a banknote or coin. **2.** *See* PAR VALUE.

facility An agreement between a bank and a company that grants the company a line of credit with the bank. This can either be a *committed facility or an *uncommitted facility.

facility-sustaining activity In *activity-based costing, an *activity that is performed to sustain the organization as a whole. Examples include security, safety, maintenance, and plant management. It is not possible to identify these costs with particular products.

fact book A file containing information on the history of a product, including data on sales, distribution, competition, customers, and relevant marketing research undertaken, as well as a detailed record of the product's performance in relation to the marketing effort made on its behalf.

factor 1. A firm that engages in *factoring. **2.** An individual or firm that acts as an agent (often called a **mercantile agent**) in certain trades, usually receiving a **factorage** (commission or fee) based on the amount of sales achieved. Unlike some other forms of agent, a factor takes possession of the goods and sells them in his own name.

factor-comparison method A method of *job evaluation in which jobs are compared with each other in terms of *compensable job factors. These may include skill, effort, decision making, working conditions, and responsibility for people, finance, or equipment. Ideally, all factors should be present in all the jobs being evaluated to some degree, so that each job can be scored under each factor heading. The total scores across factors can then determine the sorting of jobs into a set of pay grades, usually by comparison with a number of *benchmark jobs. *Compare* CLASSIFICATION METHOD; HAY METHOD; JOB-COMPONENT METHOD; POINT METHOD; RANKING METHOD.

factoring The buying of the trade debts of a manufacturer, assuming the task of debt collection and accepting the credit risk, thus providing the manufacturer with working capital. **With service factoring** involves collecting the debts, assuming the credit risk, and passing on the funds as they are paid by the buyer. **With service plus finance factoring** involves paying the manufacturer up to 90% of the invoice value immediately after delivery of the goods, with the balance paid after the money has been collected. This form of factoring is clearly more expensive than with service factoring. In either case the factor, which may be a bank or finance house, has the right to select its debtors. *See also* UNDISCLOSED FACTORING.

factors of production The resources required to produce economic goods. They are land (including all natural resources), labour (including all human work and skill), *capital (including all money, assets, machinery, raw materials, etc.), and entrepreneurial ability (including organizational and management skills, inventiveness, and the willingness to take risks). For each of these factors there is a price, i.e. rent for land, wages for labour, interest for capital, and profit for the entrepreneur.

factory costs (factory expenses) The expenditure incurred by the manufacturing section of an organization. Factory costs include *direct materials, *direct labour, *direct costs, and *manufacturing overheads but not mark-up or profit.

factory overhead *See* MANUFACTURING OVERHEAD.

factory shop (factory outlet) A retailing operation owned and operated by a manufacturer to sell the manufacturer's surplus, discontinued, or irregular goods.

facultative reinsurance A form of *reinsurance in which the terms, conditions, and reinsurance premium is individually negotiated between the insurer and the reinsurer. There is no obligation on the reinsurer to accept the risk or on the insurer to reinsure it if it is not considered necessary. The main differences between facultative reinsurance and *coinsurance is that the policyholder has no indication that reinsurance has been arranged. In coinsurance, the coinsurers and the proportion of the risk they are covering are shown on the policy schedule. Also, coinsurance involves the splitting of the premium charged to the policyholder between the coinsurers, whereas the reinsurers charge entirely separate reinsurance premiums.

fad A fashion that enters the market quickly, is adopted with great enthusiasm, peaks early, and declines rapidly. Fashion clothing and many novelty products fall into this category.

failure mode and effect analysis (FMEA) A technique for analysing how systems might fail and what the consequences of that failure would be. Primarily used to calculate and predict risks for safety and insurance purposes, FMEA identifies all the ways in which it is possible for each

component to fail and then follows through the consequence of each type of failure. From this data it is possible to develop preventive maintenance and contingency plans.

failure-rate curve *See* BATH-TUB CURVE.

fair average quality *See* FAQ.

fair presentation The requirement that *financial statements should not be misleading. 'Fair presentation' is the US and *International Accounting Standards equivalent of the British requirement that financial statements give a *true and fair view.

fair trade The policy of benefiting producers in developing countries by buying such commodities as rice and coffee directly from them at a guaranteed price. In the UK, consumer demand for fairly traded products has grown rapidly in recent years.

fair value (fair market value) The amount of money for which it is assumed an asset or liability could be exchanged in an *arm's length transaction between informed and willing parties. The concept is essential in *acquisition accounting. It is also important, if controversial, in accounting for derivatives and other complex financial instruments. The *Financial Reporting Standard Applicable in the UK and the Republic of Ireland permits *fair value accounting in a much wider range of circumstances than was the case in previous UK accounting practice.

fair value accounting (FVA) A form of accounting in which assets are measured at their current market price (or an estimate of that price), with all changes in that value being recognized in the *profit and loss. FVA developed in the 1980s and 1990s with the growth in the derivatives trade and the practice of marking these products to their market value or to an accepted pricing model. This form of accounting differs from traditional *historical-cost accounting in that it allows for the recording of unrealized gains where the market price of assets has risen above their historical cost. Owing to the nature of the derivatives market, fair value accounting can therefore introduce a high degree of volatility to the profit and loss account (*see* HEDGE ACCOUNTING). Critics of FVA argue that it exacerbated the banking crisis of 2008, as mark-to-market rules helped to create a downward price spiral in which complex derivatives products held by the banks rapidly became 'toxic' assets for which there was no longer a functioning market. Nevertheless, it is now enshrined in *International Financial Reporting Standards and the Financial Reporting Standard Applicable in the UK and Republic of Ireland.

fallen angel A security in the US market that has dropped below its original value; it may be sold for its increased *yield.

falsification of accounts A dishonest entry in a firm's *books of account, made by an employee with the object of covering up the theft of goods or money from the firm.

FAME Film Audience Measurement and Evaluation: a UK audience-research survey that profiles film audiences by age, sex, and lifestyle and analyses their viewing in the cinema and on television, DVD, and the Internet. It replaced the earlier CAVIAR (Cinema and Video Industry Audience Research) survey in 2006.

family brand A group of brand names for the products of a company, all of which contain the same word to establish their relationship in the minds of the consumers. *See also* PRODUCT LINE.

family life cycle The six stages of family life based on demographic data: (1) young single people; (2) young couples with no children; (3) young couples with youngest child under six years; (4) couples with dependent children; (5) older couples with no children at home; (6) older single people. These groups have been useful in marketing and advertising for defining the markets for certain goods and services, as each group has its own specific and distinguishable needs and interests.

Fannie Mae Colloquial name for the US *Federal National Mortgage Association (FNMA).

FAO Abbreviation for *Food and Agriculture Organization.

faq 1. Abbreviation for frequently asked questions. Standard answers to such questions are often prepared and made available in e.g. information and instruction manuals or in the form of *automated answers. **2.** Abbreviation for fair average quality. This is a trade description of certain commodities that are offered for sale on the basis that the goods supplied will be equal to the average quality of the current crop or recent shipments rather than on the basis of a specification or quality sample.

FAS Abbreviation for *Free Alongside Ship.

FASB Abbreviation for *Financial Accounting Standards Board.

fast food Food served in restaurants or other outlets with limited and standardized menus. They are often takeaway or self-service establishments offering the same quality of product throughout the country or, in some cases, internationally.

fast-moving consumer goods (FMCG) Products that move off the shelves of retail shops quickly, which therefore require constant replenishing. Fast-moving consumer goods include standard groceries, etc., sold in supermarkets as well as bestselling CDs and DVDs.

fate Whether or not a cheque or bill has been paid or dishonoured. A bank requested by another bank to *advise fate of a cheque or bill is being asked if it has been paid or not. *See also* CLEARED FOR FATE.

FATF Abbreviation for *Financial Action Task Force on Money Laundering.

fault trees An analytical technique used to provide a model of the way components interact during the course of the failure of a system.

favourable variance *See* VARIANCE.

fax A method of communication between businesses, linked to the international telephone system. Use of a fax machine enables messages, copies of documents, diagrams, plans, etc., to be sent for the cost of a telephone call of equal duration (approximately 30–60 seconds per A4 page). The system operates worldwide. In recent years it has been increasingly replaced by *e-mail.

FCA **1.** Abbreviation for *Financial Conduct Authority. **2.** Abbreviation for *Free Carrier. **3.** Abbreviation for Fellow of the *Institute of Chartered Accountants.

FCPA Abbreviation for *Foreign Corrupt Practices Act 1977.

feasibility study An investigation to determine which of a range of decisions is likely to give a satisfactory return in a *financial appraisal or *economic appraisal of the alternatives.

FED Abbreviation for the *Federal Reserve System.

Federal funds (Fed funds) Non-interest-bearing deposits held at the US *Federal Reserve System that are traded between member banks.

Federal funds rate (Fed funds rate) The highly volatile and sensitive interest rate charged between member banks of the *Federal Reserve System. As the *overnight rate paid on Federal funds, it is a key indicator of money-market interest rates. Every transaction can alter the level at which the rate is fixed. In practice the *Federal Open Market Committee sets a target rate as part of its *monetary policy, which is then enforced through *open-market operations.

Federal Home Loan Banks Twelve regional organizations in the USA that supply credit for *savings and loans associations (the US equivalent of *building societies) and other organizations providing domestic mortgages. They are independent organizations but regulated by the **Federal Housing Finance Agency**. The same legislation made it a duty for district banks to provide cheap mortgage finance for borrowers on low incomes.

Federal Home Loan Mortgage Corporation (FHLMC) A corporation established in the USA in 1970 to buy mortgages from *savings and loan associations in order to resell them in the secondary market packaged as securities. The stock of the corporation is held by the *Federal Home Loan Banks. The FHLMC is often referred to as **Freddie Mac**. Following a collapse in its share value, it was taken into temporary public ownership in September 2008.

Federal National Mortgage Association (FNMA) A government sponsored publicly traded company formed in the USA to trade in *mortgages, guaranteed by the Federal Housing Finance Board (*see* FEDERAL HOME LOAN BANKS). It is the largest source of housing finance in the USA. FNMA is often referred to as **Fannie Mae**. Following a collapse in its share value, it was taken into temporary public ownership in September 2008.

Federal Open Market Committee (FOMC) The policy committee of the *Federal Reserve System, which sets the level of money and credit in the US banking system. Its members, the governors of the Federal Reserve Board and the presidents of the 12 *Federal Reserve Banks (seven of whom cannot vote on policy), meet at least four times a year and regulate the money supply by instructing the federal banks to buy or sell securities. *See* FEDERAL FUNDS RATE.

Federal Reserve Bank Any of the 12 banks that together form the *Federal Reserve System in the USA; they are situated in Boston, New York, Philadelphia, Cleveland, Richmond, Atlanta, Chicago, St Louis, Minneapolis, Kansas City, Dallas, and San Francisco. They provide *central bank services and are involved with the Federal Reserve Board of Governors in developing and enacting monetary policy, as well as regulating local commercial and savings banks. Each Federal Reserve Bank is owned by the local banks in its district.

Federal Reserve System (FED) The organization, consisting of the 12 *Federal Reserve Banks, that functions as the *central bank of the USA. Created by the Federal Reserve Act 1913, the system controls monetary policy, regulates the cost of money and the money supply to local banks, and supervises international banking by means of its agreement with the central banks of other countries. The system is administered centrally by the **Federal Reserve Board**, based in Washington DC.

(⊕) SEE WEB LINKS
• Website of the Board of Governors of the Federal Reserve System

Federal Trade Commission (FTC) The US government agency established in 1915 by the Federal Trade Commission Act 1914 to promote free and fair competition in interstate commerce and to prevent unfair methods of competition. Its wide brief covers takeovers, mergers, cartels, price fixing, and fraudulent advertising.

(⊕) SEE WEB LINKS
• Website of the FTC

Fed funds *See* FEDERAL FUNDS.

Fed funds rate *See* FEDERAL FUNDS RATE.

FEDMA Abbreviation for Federation of European Direct and Interactive Marketing (formerly the Federation of Direct Marketing Associations).

fedwire A high-speed electronic link in the USA between the 12 *Federal Reserve Banks and the Treasury, used to move large sums of money for themselves and their customers. The transactions are generally completed within minutes of being initiated. With the *Clearing House Inter-Bank Payments System (CHIPS) it constitutes the main US network for large-value payments.

feedback Information or opinions about the performance of a product, system, intervention (e.g. a *management development or training program), or employee. Important sources of feedback include

clients and customers, users of a product or system, and an employee's supervisors or fellow workers. Regular and reliable feedback is essential to *employee evaluation and *performance appraisal, and its absence may be detrimental to *job satisfaction (*see* CORE JOB CHARACTERISTICS). Feedback also plays a key role in modern management philosophies of *continuous improvement, such as *total quality management. *See* MULTISOURCE FEEDBACK.

feedback control A method for controlling the performance of an *operating system by monitoring outputs and comparing them with the system's design parameters. Because the approach is based on past activities it is essentially reactive. Although it may allow adjustments to be made to avoid problems in the future, it cannot avoid the cost of the original divergence from targets. *Compare* CONCURRENT CONTROL; FEEDFORWARD CONTROL.

feedforward control An approach to controlling the performance of an *operating system that attempts to forecast a future state and to take the necessary action before problems arise. For example, in a *statistical process control system the operation may remain in control, but knowledge of the system enables the operator to extrapolate trends in control data and to take the action necessary to avoid the system becoming out of control. The success of this approach is dependent on the ability to predict the consequences of a particular event. *Compare* CONCURRENT CONTROL; FEEDBACK CONTROL.

fee simple The most usual freehold *estate in land. Although all land in England is theoretically held by the Crown, the owner of a fee simple (or his or her heirs) will own the land forever and may dispose of it as they wish both during the lifetime of the owner and by will. The land will revert to the Crown only if the owner dies without leaving a will and with no surviving relatives. This is the only type of freehold estate that can now exist in common law, as opposed to in equity.

fen A monetary unit of China worth one hundredth of a *yuan.

feninga A monetary unit of Bosnia and Hercegovina, worth one hundredth of a marka.

FHLMC Abbreviation for *Federal Home Loan Mortgage Corporation.

fiat money Money that a government has declared to be legal tender, although it has no intrinsic value and is not backed by reserves. Most of the world's paper money is now fiat money.

fictitious asset An *asset shown in a balance sheet that does not exist. The asset may have been inadvertently left on the books despite having ceased to exist or no longer having any value (as with *goodwill); alternatively, it may be shown as part of a deliberate fraud.

fidelity guarantee An insurance policy covering employers for any financial losses they may sustain as a result of the dishonesty of employees. Policies can be arranged to cover all employees or specific named persons. Because of the nature of the cover, insurers require full details of the procedure adopted by the organization in recruiting and vetting new employees and they usually reserve the right to refuse to cover a particular person without giving a reason.

fiduciary A person who holds property in trust or as an executor. Persons acting in a fiduciary capacity do so not for their own profit but to safeguard the interests of some other person or persons.

fiduciary deposit Funds deposited in a bank and managed for the benefit of the depositor by the bank.

fiduciary issue Banknotes issued by a central bank without backing in gold, the value of the issues relying entirely on the reputation of the issuing bank.

fiduciary loan A loan that is made on trust, rather than against some security.

field experiments Marketing tests conducted outside the laboratory in a real market environment. See TEST MARKETING.

field sales manager A district or regional sales manager (so called because his or her main concern is the control of salespeople in the field). The primary task of the field sales manager is to motivate and supervise sales personnel. Depending on the organization, the field sales manager may also be involved in setting salesforce objectives, designing the strategy, and recruiting, selecting, training, and evaluating the field sales personnel.

field selling Non-retail selling that takes place outside the employer's place of business, usually on the prospective customer's premises. The sales personnel involved are the company's personal link with customers and can bring back to the company much needed information about the customers.

FIFO cost Abbreviation for *first-in-first-out cost.

file In computing, a collection of related information held on backing store that is treated as a unit. A file may contain data of any kind.

file server See SERVER; LOCAL AREA NETWORK.

file transfer protocol See FTP.

fillér A monetary unit of Hungary worth one hundredth of a *forint.

fils 1. A monetary unit of the United Arab Emirates, worth one hundredth of a *dirham. 2. A monetary unit of Bahrain, Iraq, and Kuwait, worth one thousandth of a *dinar. 3. A monetary unit of Yemen, worth one hundredth of a *riyal.

final accounts The *annual accounts produced at the end of a company's financial year as opposed to any interim accounts produced during the year.

final dividend See DIVIDEND.

final invoice An invoice that replaces a *proforma invoice for goods. The proforma invoice is sent before all the details of the goods are known. The final invoice contains any missing information and states the full amount still owing for the goods.

final salary scheme An occupational pension scheme in which payments are determined by the employee's final salary. *See* DEFINED-BENEFIT PENSION SCHEME.

finance 1. The practice of manipulating and managing money. **2.** The capital involved in a project, especially the capital that has to be raised to start a new business. **3.** A loan of money for a particular purpose, especially by a *finance house. **4.** An academic discipline within the general field of economics dealing with funding, financial markets, and the funding implications for managing businesses.

Finance Act The annual UK Act of Parliament that changes the law relating to taxation, giving the rates of income tax, corporation tax, etc., proposed in the preceding *Budget.

finance bill A *bill of exchange used for short-term credit. It cannot be sold on to another party in the same way as a *banker's acceptance.

finance company A company that provides finance, normally in the form of loans. As it tends to finance ventures with a high risk factor, the cost of borrowing is likely to be higher than that made by a clearing bank.

finance house Any organization, many of which are owned by *commercial banks, that provides finance for *hire-purchase or *leasing agreements. A consumer, who buys an expensive item (such as a car) from a trader and does not wish to pay cash, enters into a hire-purchase contract with the finance house, who collects the deposit and instalments. The finance house pays the trader the cash price in full, borrowing from the commercial banks in order to do so. The finance house's profit is the difference between the low rate of interest it pays to the commercial banks to borrow and the high rate it charges the consumer.

finance lease A lease in which the lessee acquires all the financial benefits and risks attaching to ownership of whatever is being leased. In accounting, it is as if the business owned the assets. Section 20 of the Financial Reporting Standard Applicable in the UK and Republic of Ireland provides detailed guidance on whether a lease should be classified as a finance lease. *Compare* OPERATING LEASE.

finance vehicle An entity set up by a company to obtain some financial benefit. The setting up of overseas companies so as to lower tax liabilities is a prime example of a finance vehicle.

financial accounting The branch of accounting concerned with classifying, measuring, and recording the transactions of a business. At the end of a period, usually a year but sometimes less, a *profit and loss account, a *balance sheet, a *statement of total recognized gains and losses, and a *cash-flow statement are prepared to show the performance and position of the business. Financial accounting is primarily concerned with providing a *true and fair view of the activities of a business to parties external to it. To ensure that this is done correctly considerable attention will be paid to *accounting concepts and to any requirements of legislation, accounting standards, and (where appropriate) the regulations of the *stock exchange. Financial accounting can be separated into a number of specific activities, such as conducting *audits, *taxation, book-keeping, and *insolvency. **Financial accountants** need not be qualified, in that they need not belong to an accountancy body, although the majority of those working in public practice will be. *Compare* MANAGEMENT ACCOUNTING.

Financial Accounting Standards Board (FASB) In the USA, a non-government body founded in 1973 with the responsibility of promulgating *generally accepted accounting principles. This is achieved by the issue of *Statements of

Financial Accounting Standards, which certified public accountants are expected to follow. Owing to the FASB's close relationship with the *Securities and Exchange Commission, US companies that desire a market listing have to comply with the standards it issues.

SEE WEB LINKS
• Website of the FASB

Financial Action Task Force on Money Laundering (FATF) An organization founded in 1989 by the *Organization for Economic Cooperation and Development to curtail the practice of *laundering money, chiefly by persuading individual governments to legislate against it. Its policies have been codified in the Forty Recommendations on money laundering and, more recently, in the Nine Special Recommendations on terrorist financing.

financial adviser 1. Anyone who offers financial advice to someone else, especially one who advises on *investments. *See also* INDEPENDENT FINANCIAL ADVISER. **2.** An organization, usually a merchant bank, who advises the board of a company during a takeover (*see* TAKEOVER BID).

financial analysis *See* FINANCIAL-STATEMENT ANALYSIS; RATIO ANALYSIS.

financial appraisal The use of financial evaluation techniques to determine which of a range of possible alternatives is preferred. Financial appraisal usually refers to the use of *discounted cash flow techniques but it may also be applied to any other approaches used to assess a business problem in financial terms, such as *ratio analysis, *profitability index, or risk analysis. *Compare* ECONOMIC APPRAISAL.

Financial Conduct Authority (FCA)
The new regulatory body for the UK financial services industry that was established in April 2013; it is one of two successor bodies to the *Financial Services Authority (FSA) created under the Financial Services Act 2012, the other being the *Prudential Regulation Authority. The FCA is responsible for regulating conduct in both retail and wholesale financial markets and the infrastructure that supports them. The new body is intended to be a more robust regulator than the FSA; it has said that it will intervene more quickly to ban risky financial products and enforce its rulings with tougher penalties.

SEE WEB LINKS
• Website of the FCA

financial control (financial management) The actions of the management of an organization taken to ensure that the costs incurred and revenue generated are at acceptable levels. Financial control is assisted by the provision of financial information to management by the accountant and by the use of such techniques as *budgetary control and *standard costing, which highlight and analyse any *variances.

financial crisis A collapse in the price of financial obligations, which may lead to a collapse in the economy. The major financial crisis in the history of world finance took place after the Wall Street Crash of 1929. This crisis led to a widespread failure in the US banking system and the interwar recession. The 1980s and 1990s saw a number of financial crises, notably in Russia, South-East Asia, and Latin America, but none of these had an impact spreading to the international economy. In the late 2000s reckless *subprime lending in the US mortgage industry, compounded by the *securitization of these loans in complex derivatives products, led to the crisis of September–October 2008, which saw the failure or bail-out of major institutions and a collapse in stock-market values. The result was a global economic recession.

financial distress The situation in which the activity of a business is influenced by the possibility of impending insolvency. The costs of distress can be divided into those related to bankruptcy and those incurred without bankruptcy. The costs of bankruptcy are those directly incurred in winding up or restructuring the business. The costs short of bankruptcy are those arising from a sudden change in suppliers' and customers' behaviour, prompted by their concerns over dealing with a potentially insolvent firm. They also include costs engendered by the diversion of managerial focus and conflicts between stakeholders, notably managers, debt holders, and shareholders. As a firm increases the level of its debt or *gearing, so the costs of financial distress will rise (and hence the cost of funding). The costs of financial distress are an important factor in determining the firm's level of gearing.

financial futures A *futures contract in currencies, interest rates (*see* INTEREST-RATE FUTURES), or other financial assets. The contract is a standard one, which is exchange-traded. Until about 1970 trading in financial futures did not exist, although futures and options were dealt in widely on *commodity markets. However, instantaneous trading across the world coupled with accelerated international capital flows combined to produce great volatility in interest rates, stock-market prices, and currency exchanges. The result has been an environment in which organizations and individuals responsible for managing large sums need a financial futures and options market both to manage risks effectively and as a source of additional profit. In the UK financial futures and options are traded on the *LIFFE (now Euronext.liffe). *See also* HEDGE; INDEX FUTURES; PORTFOLIO INSURANCE.

financial gearing *See* GEARING; DEBT–EQUITY RATIO.

financial institution An organization whose core activity is to provide financial services or advice in relation to financial products. Financial institutions include state bodies, such as central banks, and private companies, such as banks, savings and loan associations, and also financial markets. At one time there was a clear distinction and regulatory division between *deposit-taking institutions, such as banks, and non-deposit-taking institutions, such as brokers or life-insurance companies. This is no longer the case; brokers and

other companies now often invest funds for their clients with banks and in the money markets.

financial instrument A contract involving a financial obligation. Examples are stocks, bonds, loans, and derivatives.

financial intermediary 1. An institution, be it a bank, building society, finance house, insurance company, investment trust, etc., that holds funds borrowed from lenders in order to make loans to borrowers. **2.** In the *Financial Services Act 1986, a person or organization that sells insurance but is not directly employed by an insurance company (e.g. a broker, insurance agent, bank). *See also* INDEPENDENT INTERMEDIARY.

financial investment *See* INVESTMENT.

financial leverage *See* GEARING.

financial management *See* FINANCIAL CONTROL.

financial modelling The construction and use of planning and decision models based on financial data to simulate actual circumstances in order to facilitate decision making within an organization. The financial models used include *discounted cash flow, *economic order quantity, *decision trees, *learning curves, and *budgetary control.

Financial Ombudsman Service (FOS) A UK body set up to deal with complaints in relation to financial services and products. It was established by the *Financial Services and Markets Act 2000 to replace the separate complaint schemes for banks, building societies, insurance, investments and pensions.

⊕ SEE WEB LINKS
- Website of the Financial Ombudsman Service

financial perspective *See* BALANCED SCORECARD.

financial planning The formulation of short-term and long-term plans in financial terms for the purposes of establishing goals for an organization to achieve, against which its actual performance can be measured.

financial report The *financial statements of a company. *See also* ANNUAL ACCOUNTS.

Financial Reporting Council (FRC) A UK body set up in 1990 to promote high-quality *corporate governance and financial reporting. The structure of the FRC and its operating bodies was subject to reform in 2012. There are now two divisions: the Codes and Standards division, which is advised by the *Accounting Council, the Actuarial Council, and the Audit and Assurance Council; and the Conduct division, which exercises monitoring, oversight, and disciplinary functions in the accounting, actuarial, and audit professions. *See also* ACCOUNTING STANDARDS BOARD; FINANCIAL REPORTING REVIEW PANEL.

((()) SEE WEB LINKS
• Website of the FRC

Financial Reporting Review Panel (FRRP) An operating body of the *Financial Reporting Council, which acts as its sole director. The panel investigates departures from the accounting requirements of the Companies Acts and is empowered to take legal action to remedy any such departures. Its remit covers the financial reports of public companies and large private companies.

Financial Reporting Standard (FRS) Any of a series of standards issued by the *Accounting Standards Board and the *Financial Reporting Council (FRC). In 2013 the reorganized FRC issued FRS 102: **The Financial Reporting Standard Applicable in the UK and Republic of Ireland;** from 1 January 2015 this supersedes FRSs 1–30 in their entirety, largely in the interests of harmonizing UK practice with the standards published by the *International Accounting Standards Board. UK listed companies have been required to follow *International Financial Reporting Standards since January 2005.

((()) SEE WEB LINKS
• Full text of the Financial Reporting Standard Applicable in the UK and Republic of Ireland

financial risk The *risk that an organization will not be able to meet its monetary commitments, notably any debt-related payments.

financials A shorthand term for the *financial statements of an organization.

Financial Services Act 1986 A UK Act of Parliament that came into force in April 1988. Its objectives were to regulate investment business and to promote competition in industry by means of the Securities and Investment Board and its Self-Regulating Organizations. It provided legislation for many of the recommendations of the Gower Report. The Act was superseded by the *Financial Services and Markets Act 2000.

Financial Services Action Plan (FSAP) A communication published by the European Commission in 1999, consisting of 42 proposed measures designed to complete the integration of EU financial markets by 2005. The legislative phase of FSAP was largely completed by 2007, with the approval of such key measures as the *Markets in Financial Instruments Directive (MiFID), the Capital Requirements Directive, and the expanded *Eighth Company Law Directive.

Financial Services and Markets Act 2000 Legislation, implemented in November 2001, establishing a regulatory framework for UK banking, insurance, and investment. Under the terms of the Act, the *Financial Services Authority became the key regulator, taking over functions from the Bank of England, the Building Societies Commission, and the Treasury. However, the Bank of England retained a regulatory interest where systemic risk to the UK financial system was concerned. *See also* FINANCIAL OMBUDSMAN SERVICE.

Financial Services Authority (FSA) An independent, nongovernmental body set up in 1997 to regulate the financial services industry in the UK. It was given statutory

FINANCIAL REPORTING STANDARDS

1. Cash Flow Statements, issued 1991
2. Accounting for Subsidiary Undertakings, issued 1992
3. Reporting Financial Performance, issued 1992
4. Capital Instruments, issued 1993
5. Reporting the Substance of Transactions, issued 1994
6. Acquisitions and Mergers, issued 1994
7. Fair Values in Acquisition Accounting, issued 1994
8. Related Party Transactions, issued 1995
9. Associates and Joint Ventures, issued 1997
10. Goodwill and Intangible Assets, issued 1997
11. Impairment of Fixed Assets and Goodwill, issued 1998
12. Provisions, Contingent Liabilities and Contingent Assets, issued 1998
13. Derivatives and Other Financial Instruments: Disclosures, issued 1998
14. Earnings Per Share, issued 1998
15. Tangible Fixed Assets, issued 1999
16. Current Tax, issued 1999
17. Retirement Benefits, issued 2000
18. Accounting Policies, issued 2000
19. Deferred Tax, issued 2000
20. Share-based Payment, issued 2004
21. Events After the Balance Sheet Date, issued 2004
22. Earnings Per Share, issued 2004
23. The Effects of Change in Foreign Exchange Rates, issued 2004
24. Financial Reporting in Hyperinflationary Economies, issued 2004
25. Financial Instruments: Disclosures and Presentation, issued 2004
26. Financial Instruments: Measurement, issued 2004
27. Life Assurance, issued 2004
28. Corresponding Amounts, issued 2005
29. Financial Instruments: Disclosures, issued 2005
30. Heritage Assets, issued 2009
100. Application of Financial Reporting Requirements, issued 2012
101. Reduced Disclosure Framework, issued 2012
102. The Financial Reporting Standard Applicable in the UK and Republic of Ireland, issued 2013
103. Insurance Contracts, issued 2014

powers by the Financial Services and Markets Act 2000, which specified four statutory objectives for the FSA: to maintain market confidence; to promote public understanding of the financial system; to ensure a satisfactory degree of consumer protection; and to reduce the possibilities for financial crime. In 2013 the FSA was abolished and its responsibilities divided between two new bodies, the *Financial Conduct Authority and the *Prudential Regulation Authority.

Financial Services Compensation Scheme A scheme set up under the UK *Financial Services and Markets Act 2000 to provide compensation for private investors who stand to lose money as a result of the default or bankruptcy of an authorized investment firm. It is funded by a levy on the industry.

Financial Services Directive An EU directive (1996) on the regulation of financial services. It is based on the principle that a firm authorized to undertake business in one EU state under local regulations should be able to conduct business in any other member state. It also provides for the harmonization of minimum standards. *See also* INVESTMENT SERVICES DIRECTIVE; MARKETS IN FINANCIAL INSTRUMENTS DIRECTIVE.

Financial Services Modernization Act 1999 (Gramm–Leach–Bliley Act) Legislation enacted in the USA that removed the restrictions on banks undertaking securities business that had been imposed by the *Glass–Steagall Act 1933. It also empowered companies to set up financial holding companies to supply banking, insurance, and investment services. Critics of the Act have argued that these provisions contributed directly to the financial crisis of 2008.

financial-statement analysis Analysis of the *financial statements of a company to assess its position and performance. The standard analysis will consider the business from the perspectives of managerial performance, liquidity, and stock-exchange performance. *See* ACCOUNTING RATIO; RATIO ANALYSIS.

Financial Statement and Budget Report (FSBR) The document published by the Chancellor of the Exchequer on Budget Day. It summarizes the provisions of the *Budget as given in the Chancellor's speech to the House of Commons. It is sometimes known as the **Red Book**.

financial statements The annual statements summarizing a company's activities over the last year. They consist of the *profit and loss account, *balance sheet, *statement of total recognized gains and losses, and, if required, the *cash-flow statement, together with supporting notes.

Financial Times–Stock Exchange Share Indexes *See* FTSE INDEXES.

financial year 1. Any year connected with finance, such as a company's *accounting period or a year for which budgets are made up. **2.** In the UK, a specific period relating to *corporation tax, i.e. the 12 months beginning on 1 April in one year and ending on 31 March in the next year. Corporation-tax rates are fixed for specific financial years by the Chancellor in the Budget; if a company's accounting period falls into two financial years the profits have to be apportioned to the relevant financial years to find the rates of tax applicable. *Compare* FISCAL YEAR.

financier A person who finances a business deal or venture or who makes arrangements for such a deal or venture to be financed by a merchant bank or other *financial institution. The term often implies a hands-on approach, in addition to providing finance.

fine paper *See* FIRST-CLASS PAPER.

fine trade bill A *bill of exchange that is acceptable to the Bank of England as security, when acting as *lender of last resort. It will be backed by a first-class bank or finance house.

fine tuning The implementation of economic policy, in particular monetary and fiscal policy, by means of small, incremental policy changes. Doubt has been cast on any real possibility of fine-tuning economies, given their lack of short-term forecastability. Critics argue that, if an economy is impossible to forecast in detail, then it follows that it is also impossible to determine appropriate short-term incremental policies.

finished goods stock (finished goods inventory) The value of goods that have completed the manufacturing process and are available for distribution to customers. In any accounting period there will be *opening stock of finished goods at the beginning of the period and *closing stock of finished goods at the end of the period. Methods of valuing finished goods stock may include *first-in-first-out cost or *average cost methods.

finite capacity loading *Loading based on the assumption that capacity is finite, i.e. cannot be increased. This parameter aligns load to the available capacity, enabling realistic lead times to be calculated. *Compare* INFINITE CAPACITY LOADING.

fire insurance An insurance policy covering financial losses caused by damage to property by fires. Most fire insurance policies also include cover for damage caused by lightning and explosions of boilers or gas used for domestic purposes. On payment of an additional premium, fire insurers are usually prepared to widen the cover to include such special perils as those arising from various weather-related or man-made causes.

firewall 1. In a conglomerate, a barrier created between the organization, funding, and ownership of one business entity and those of other entities in the group, so that problems experienced by the one do not affect others. **2.** A system usually inserted between a *local area network and the *Internet to filter incoming traffic, to try to eliminate viral infection, and to restrict the access of *hackers to the system. It may create a bottleneck in the transmission of data to and from the system.

firm 1. Any business organization. **2.** A business partnership.

firm commitment 1. An undertaking by a bank to lend up to a maximum sum over a period at a specified rate; a *commitment fee usually has to be paid by the borrower, which is not returned if the loan is not taken up. **2.** In the USA, an agreement in which an underwriter of a flotation assumes the risk that not all the securities issued will be sold, by guaranteeing to buy all the excess securities at the offer price. **3.** Any binding commitment to enter into an agreement.

firm offer An offer to sell goods that remains in force for a stated period. For example, an "offer firm for 24 hours" binds the seller to sell if the buyer accepts the offer within 24 hours. If the buyer makes a lower *bid during the period that the offer is firm, the offer ceases to be valid. An offer that is not firm is usually called a *quotation.

firm order An order to a broker (for securities, commodities, currencies, etc.) that remains firm for a stated period or until cancelled. A broker who has a firm order from a principal does not have to refer back if the terms of the order can be executed in the stated period.

firmware Computer programs or data that are stored in a memory chip. These are often built into a computer to make it unnecessary to load the programs or data from disk or from the keyboard. Word-processing programs, for example, on read-only memory (ROM) chips are built into some business computer systems. Firmware is also used where absolute reliability is required, for example in air-traffic control.

first-class paper (fine paper) A *money-market instrument that is backed by a bank with a high credit rating.

first-in-first-out cost (FIFO cost) A method of valuing units of *raw material or *finished goods issued from stock based on using the earliest unit value for pricing the issues until all the stock received at that price has been used up. The next latest price is then used for pricing the issues, and so on. Because the issues are based on a FIFO cost, the valuation of closing stocks is described as being on the same FIFO basis. The method may also be used in *process costing to value the work in process at the end of an accounting period. *Compare* LAST-IN-FIRST-OUT COST; NEXT-IN-FIRST-OUT COST.

first-loss policy A property insurance policy in which the policyholder arranges cover for an amount below the full value of the items insured and the insurer agrees not to penalize him for under-insurance. The main use of these policies is in circumstances in which a total loss is virtually impossible. For example, a large warehouse may contain £2.5M worth of wines and spirits but the owner may feel that no more than £500,000 worth could be stolen at any one time. The solution is a first-loss policy that deals with all claims up to £500,000 but pays no more than this figure if more is stolen. First-loss policies differ from *coinsurance agreements with the policyholders because the insured is not involved in claims below the first-loss level and the premiums are not calculated proportionately. In the above example, the premium might be as much as 80–90% of the premium on the full value.

first mortgage debenture A *debenture with the first charge over property owned by a company. Such debentures are most commonly issued by property companies.

first notice day 1. The date on which a seller in a futures market contract gives notice of an intention to deliver according to the terms of a particular *futures contract. **2.** The date on which the buyer is notified of such an arrangement.

first of exchange *See* BILLS IN A SET.

first preferred stock In the USA, *preferred stock with prior rights where dividends are concerned or in the event of liquidation.

first-tier market The main market on which the equity of large companies is traded. There is customarily a high level of regulation and supervision in such markets. *Compare* SECOND-TIER MARKET.

first-year allowance In the UK, a special *capital allowance against *corporation tax that is granted in the year of purchase of an asset in place of the standard *writing-down allowance of 25%. Various first-year allowances, often targeted at smaller businesses wishing to invest in new technology, have been made available at various times. *See also* ANNUAL INVESTMENT ALLOWANCE.

fiscal agent 1. A third party who acts on behalf of a bond issuer to pay subscribers to the issue and generally assist the issuer. **2.** An agent for one of the national *financial institutions in the USA who acts as an adviser, for example, to the National Mortgage Association for its debt securities. **3.** In the USA, an agent empowered to collect taxes, revenues, and duties on behalf of the government. For example, the *Federal Reserve Banks perform this function for the US Treasury.

fiscal drag The deflationary impact on a country's economy of a steady increase in tax revenues. Because most developed countries have progressive rates of taxation, the proportion of national income paid in taxes rises as national income grows.

fiscal policy The use of government spending and taxation to influence macroeconomic conditions. Fiscal policy was actively pursued to sustain full employment in the post-war years; however, monetarists and others have argued that this set off the inflation of the 1970s. Fiscal policy has remained generally 'tight' in most Western countries since the 1980s. *Compare* MONETARY POLICY.

fiscal year In the UK, the 12-month period beginning on 6 April in one year and ending on 5 April in the next (the fiscal year 2015–16 runs from 6 April 2015 to 5 April 2016). Income tax, capital gains tax, and annual allowances for inheritance tax are all calculated for fiscal years, and the UK Budget estimates refer to the fiscal year. In the USA the fiscal year now runs from 1 October to the following 30 September. The fiscal year is sometimes called the **tax year** or the **year of assessment**. *Compare* FINANCIAL YEAR.

fish-bone diagram *See* CAUSE–EFFECT DIAGRAM.

fixed asset (capital asset) An asset of a business intended for continuing use, rather than a short-term *current asset (such as stock). Fixed assets must be classified in a company's *balance sheet as intangible, tangible, or investments. Examples of *intangible assets include *goodwill, *patents, and *trademarks. Examples of tangible fixed assets include land and buildings, plant and machinery, fixtures and fittings. Fixed assets must be written off to the *profit and loss account over their useful economic life; this is effected by the *amortization of intangible fixed assets and the *depreciation of tangible fixed assets. An investment included as a fixed asset is shown at its purchase price, market value, or directors' valuation, or using the equity method of accounting (*see* EQUITY ACCOUNTING).

fixed capital The amount of an organization's *capital that is tied up in its *fixed assets.

fixed capital formation An investment over a given period, as used in the national income accounts. It consists primarily of investment in manufacturing and housing. **Gross fixed capital formation** is the total amount of expenditure on investment, while **net fixed capital formation** includes a deduction for the *depreciation of existing capital.

fixed charge 1. *See* CHARGE. **2.** The part of an expense that remains unchanged, irrespective of the amount of the commodity or service used or consumed. For example, in the UK both the electricity and gas industries operate tariffs consisting of a fixed charge, which remains unchanged irrespective of the consumption of energy, and a variable charge, based on the energy consumed.

fixed cost (fixed expense) An item of expenditure that remains unchanged, in total, irrespective of changes in the levels of production or sales. Examples are business rates, rent, and some salaries. *Compare* SEMI-VARIABLE COST; VARIABLE COST.

fixed debenture A *debenture that has a *fixed charge as security. *Compare* FLOATING DEBENTURE.

fixed exchange rate A *rate of exchange between one currency and another that is fixed by government and maintained by that government's economic policy and its buying or selling its currency to support or depress it. *Compare* FLOATING EXCHANGE RATE.

fixed-for-fixed Denoting a *currency swap in which both parties pay a fixed rate of interest.

fixed-for-floating Denoting an *interest-rate swap or *cross-currency interest-rate swap in which one party pays a fixed rate, while the other pays a floating rate.

fixed-interest security A type of *security that gives a fixed stated interest payment. They include *gilt-edged securities, *bonds, *preference shares, and *debentures; as they entail less risk than *equities they offer less scope for capital appreciation. They do, however, often give a better *yield than equities.

The prices of fixed-interest securities tend to move inversely with the general level of interest rates, reflecting changes in the value of their fixed yield relative to the market. Fixed-interest securities tend to be particularly poor investments at times of high and increasing inflation as their value does not adjust to changes in the price level. To overcome this problem some gilts now give index-linked interest payments.

fixed overhead cost The elements of the *indirect costs of an organization's product that, in total, remain unchanged irrespective of changes in the levels of production or sales. Examples include administrative salaries, sales personnel salaries, and rent.

fixed-price tender A bid to undertake an activity for a given price. *See* TENDER.

fixed production overhead The elements of an organization's *manufacturing overheads that, in total, remain unchanged irrespective of changes in the level of production or sales. Examples include factory rent, depreciation of machinery using the *straight-line method, and the factory manager's salary.

fixed-rate loan A loan on which the interest rate is fixed at the start of the loan.

fixed-rate mortgage A *mortgage in which the rate of interest paid by the borrower is fixed, usually for the first few years of the loan.

fixed spot A television advertising spot for which a premium is paid (normally 15%) to ensure that it is transmitted in a preselected commercial break during a particular programme.

fixtures and fittings Items normally forming part of the setting in which an organization conducts its business, as distinct from the *plant and machinery it uses in conducting the business.

flag of convenience The national flag of a small country, such as Panama, Liberia, or the Bahamas, flown by a ship that is registered in one of these countries, although the ship is owned by a national of another country. The practice of registering ships in these countries, and sailing them under flags of convenience, grew up in the 1920s and still continues despite attempts to control it. The object for the shipowners is to avoid taxation, high labour costs, and the more stringent safety and humanitarian conditions imposed on ships and their crews by the larger sea-going nations.

flash report In the USA, a management report that highlights key data for corrective action.

flat tax (proportional tax) A tax with a single rate (as opposed to one in which the rate of tax increases with the size of the *tax base) and with no reliefs or exemptions apart from a standard personal allowance. In recent years a flat rate of income tax has been introduced in Russia and a number of Eastern European economies. The advantages claimed for such a system are that it is very simple to understand and operate, thereby reducing administrative costs for both government and business, that it eliminates many forms of tax avoidance, that the abolition of the higher-rate tax bands encourages enterprise and wealth creation, and that the raising of the threshold at which people begin to pay tax benefits the lowest earners (who also gain from the elimination of poverty traps). Opponents argue that it denies governments flexibility in setting tax policy and offends against the *ability to pay principle by shifting the burden of tax from the wealthiest to those on middle incomes. *Compare* PROGRESSIVE TAX; REGRESSIVE TAX. *See also* SINGLE-TAX SYSTEM.

flat yield *See* YIELD.

fleet rating A single special premium rate quoted by an insurer for covering the insurance on a number of ships or vehicles owned by one person or company, rather than considering each one individually. The fleet need not consist of identical vehicles or vessels but common ownership is essential. A common method of fleet rating is to examine the claims history of the fleet against the total premium. In this way one fleet member may have several claims (which would individually merit a premium adjustment) but if the rest of the fleet is claim-free no adjustment need be made. Insurers vary on the minimum number constituting a fleet.

flexibility The ability to adapt an *operating system to respond to changes in the environment. Increasingly seen as a source of competitive advantage in a rapidly changing market, it is an area of *operations management in which Japanese practices have had a major impact. Flexibility has two dimensions: how quickly and how far an organization can change. Changes may be called for in terms of the product or service, i.e. the flexibility to introduce new products; mix flexibility is the ability to provide a wide range or mix of products; volume flexibility is the ability to produce different volumes to suit demand; delivery flexibility is the ability to change (usually advance) the delivery date.

flexible budget A budget that takes into account the fact that values for income and expenditure on some items will change with changing circumstances. Consequently, in a flexible budget the *budget cost allowances for each variable cost item will change to allow for the actual levels of activity achieved. A budget that has been adjusted in this way is known as a **flexed budget**.

flexible drawdown The *drawdown in stages of funds available under a credit agreement.

flexible manufacturing system (FMS) An automated and computerized production line that can be reprogrammed to produce more than one product line. Use of a flexible manufacturing system enables companies to lower costs and vary production quickly in response to changes in consumer demand. The ability to reprogramme machines by means of software rather than the physical set-up makes FMS particularly applicable to handling batches of a fairly small range of products.

flexible mortgage A *mortgage on a property in which the lender (mortgagee) allows a measure of flexibility in the repayments made by the borrower (mortgagor). In some flexible mortgages the borrower may overpay on the nominal repayments in order to pay off the debt more quickly. Others permit underpayments or even a repayment holiday for one instalment. Some flexible mortgages offer loans including all these concessions.

flexible working Employees who have children aged under 17, a disabled child aged under 18, or who care for an adult dependent, have the legal right to request a change in their working hours and conditions, including the option of working from home. Although employers have no obligation to grant such a request, they are legally obliged to consider it seriously and to give a written explanation for any refusal. The government has announced plans to extend the right to request flexible working to all employees.

flexitime (flexihours) A system of working, especially in offices, in which employees are given a degree of flexibility in the hours they work. Provided they work an agreed number of hours per day, they may start or finish work at different times. The object is usually to reduce time spent in rush-hour travelling or to adjust work schedules to other demands, such as responsibility for children.

flier *See* FREE-STANDING STUFFER.

flight to quality A movement of investors into safer assets in times of uncertainty. Government securities, *blue-chip stocks, short-term government debt, gold, and US investments all typify the type of assets that are bought at such times.

flip-flop FRN A perpetual *floating-rate note (i.e. one without redemption), which can be converted into a short-term note of up to four years' maturity and back again into a perpetual FRN.

float 1. In the USA, the proportion of a corporation's stocks that are held by the public rather than the corporation or institutional investors. **2.** Money created as a result of a delay in processing cheques, e.g. when one account is credited before the paying bank's account has been debited. **3.** Money set aside as a contingency fund or an advance to be

reimbursed. **4.** *See* FLOTATION. **5.** *See* SLACK TIME.

floater A colloquial name for a *floating-rate note.

floating charge *See* CHARGE.

floating debenture A *debenture that has a floating *charge as security. *Compare* FIXED DEBENTURE.

floating debt 1. The part of the national debt that consists primarily of short-term *Treasury bills. *Compare* FUNDED DEBT. *See also* FUNDING OPERATIONS. **2.** Short-term borrowing (i.e. for less than one year). **3.** Debt with a floating rate of interest.

floating exchange rate A *rate of exchange between one currency and others that is permitted to float according to market forces. Most major currencies and countries now have floating exchange rates but governments and central banks intervene, buying or selling currencies when rates become too high or too low. *Compare* FIXED EXCHANGE RATE.

floating policy An insurance policy that has only one sum insured although it may cover many items. No division of the total is shown on the policy and the policyholder is often able to add or remove items from the cover without reference to the insurers, provided that the total sum insured is not exceeded. Cover for contractors' plant and machinery is often arranged on this basis, because it enables them to purchase specialist equipment for a particular contract, without having to contact the insurers on every occasion.

floating-rate certificate of deposit (FRCD) A certificate of deposit with a variable interest rate, normally for interbank lending purposes. Commonly bearing a one-year maturity, these certificates have interest rates that may be adjusted (e.g. every 90 days); they are usually expressed in eurodollars at a rate linked to LIBOR.

floating-rate interest An *interest rate on certain bonds, certificates of deposit, etc., that changes with the market rate in a predetermined manner, usually in relation to the *base rate.

floating-rate loan A loan that does not have a fixed interest rate throughout its life. Floating-rate loans can take various forms but they are all tied to a short-term market indicator; in the UK this is usually the *London Inter Bank Offered Rate.

floating-rate note (FRN) A *eurobond with a *floating-rate interest, usually based on the *London Inter Bank Offered Rate. They first appeared in the 1970s and have a maturity of between 7 and 15 years. They are usually issued as negotiable *bearer bonds. A **perpetual FRN** has no *redemption. *See also* FLIP-FLOP FRN.

floating warranty A guarantee given by one person to another that induces this other person to enter into a contract with a third party. For example, a car dealer may induce a customer to enter into a hire-purchase contract with a finance company. If the car does not comply with the dealer's guarantee, the customer may recover damages from the dealer, on the basis of the hire-purchase contract, even though the dealer is not a party to that contract.

floor 1. (trading floor) The area in a financial market set aside for face-to-face dealing between *floor traders. With the increased use of *automated screen trading, floor trading has become much less frequent. *See also* PIT. **2.** The minimum interest rate on a loan or other obligation, as set in advance by the lender. *Compare* CAP. *See also* COLLAR.

floor trader A member of a stock exchange, commodity market, etc., who is permitted to enter the dealing room of these institutions and deal with other traders, brokers, underwriters, etc. Each institution has its own rules of exclusivity, but in most computer dealing has largely or wholly replaced face-to-face floor trading.

florin (AWG) The standard monetary unit of Aruba, divided into 100 cents.

flotation The process of launching a public company for the first time by inviting the public to subscribe in its shares (also known as 'going public'). It applies both to private and to previously nationalized share issues, and can be carried out by means of an *introduction, *issue by tender, *offer for sale, *placing, or *public issue. After flotation the shares can be traded on a stock exchange. Flotation allows the owners of the business to raise new capital or to realize their investments.

flotation cost The total cost incurred by a company in offering its securities to the public.

flotsam 1. The collection of items from a cargo or ship that is itself floating on the sea after a shipwreck. In British waters, it can be claimed by the ship's owners for 366 days after the shipwreck; thereafter it belongs to the Crown. *Compare* JETSAM. **2.** In *marine insurance, items or rights that are lost as a result of breach of *warranty. In such cases the policyholder has no right to make an insurance claim.

flow chart A chart used to provide a model for the flow of material, information, or people through a system. The primary purpose of a flow chart is to identify the activities taking place within a system and to enable this information to be presented graphically. Flow charts can be used in the initial design layout of a process, to diagnose problems, or to optimize existing processes by, for example, identifying duplication of effort or elements in which no value is added. The principles of flow charting now form the basis for a range of computer packages enabling production and service environments to be simulated with 'what-if' scenarios. There are a number of conventional symbols used in flow charts. The important ones are the process box, which indicates a process taking place, and the decision lozenge, which indicates where a decision is needed.

flurry A burst of activity on a speculative market, especially on a financial market.

flyposting *See* POSTER.

FMCG Abbreviation for *fast-moving consumer goods.

FMEA Abbreviation for *failure mode and effect analysis.

FMS Abbreviation for *flexible manufacturing systems.

FNMA Abbreviation for *Federal National Mortgage Association.

FOB Abbreviation for *Free On Board.

FoC Abbreviation for father of chapel. This is the person in charge of a trade-union chapel, usually a unit of the union within a particular printing or publishing firm.

focused improvement An approach to improving a system's performance that concentrates on identifying the current *constraints on performance and taking steps to eliminate them one at a time. Advocates of focused improvement argue that it yields immediate measurable benefits more readily than more general approaches such as *continuous improvement and *total quality management. *See* THEORY OF CONSTRAINTS.

focused strategy A business strategy in which firms seek to divest themselves of all but their core activities, using the funds so raised to enhance their *core competencies. This strategy developed as a reaction to the trend towards *diversification and the development of *conglomerates.

focus group An exploratory research group of 8 to 12 participants, led by a moderator, who meet for an in-depth discussion on one particular topic or concept. The participants are generally chosen for their relevance to the particular topic or concept. By skilful use of probes and other interviewing devices, the group members are encouraged to respond in depth to the moderator. These group discussions largely depend for their success on the moderator, who must establish the right atmosphere in order to gain the maximum involvement and cooperation of all the group members. Focus groups are useful in the early stages of developing methods to understand the nature of business or organizational problems and for suggesting issues that should be covered in a questionnaire survey. Discussions are usually recorded and observed through see-through mirrors (with the full knowledge of the group members). Normally, these groups last for between one and three months.

focus-group facility A facility belonging to a marketing research agency consisting of a conference room with a separate observation room. The facility could have audiovisual recording equipment, enabling observers to see and hear what is happening in the conference room, and sometimes see-through mirrors. *See* FOCUS GROUP.

focus-group moderator A person appointed by a marketing research agency on behalf of a client to lead a *focus group. This person may need a background in psychology or sociology or, at least, in marketing.

focus strategy A strategy in which a business chooses to operate in a narrow area of the market and to specialize within these constraints. Such an approach was recognized as one of three *generic strategies by Michael Porter in 1980. He further defined two types of focus strategy: the first, **cost focus**, aims to give the business cost advantage in its target market; the second, **differentiation focus**, seeks to distinguish its product within the defined sector. *Compare* DIFFERENTIATION STRATEGY; LOW-COST STRATEGY.

follow-the-leader strategy A pricing strategy in which an organization sets prices at the level established by the market leader. This strategy is especially common in organizations in weak competitive positions. It applies to both price increases and reductions.

follow-up The last step in the *selling process, in which the salesperson follows up the customer after the sale to ensure satisfaction and in the hope of achieving repeat business.

FOMC Abbreviation for *Federal Open Market Committee.

Food and Agriculture Organization (FAO) A specialized agency of the United Nations with its headquarters in Rome. It is responsible for organizing world agriculture, especially in developing countries, to improve nutrition and avoid famine.

footprint The physical space occupied by a commercial organization. A retailer, for example, with many stores may wish to shrink its footprint if profits are falling, by selling off some of its premises.

FOOTSIE Colloquial name for the FTSE 100 Share Index. *See* FTSE INDEXES.

FOR Abbreviation for Free On Rail. *See* FREE ON BOARD.

forbearance The position taken by a lender who chooses not to exercise his or her legal right of *foreclosure when a borrower defaults. Instead, the lender may renegotiate the terms of the loan.

forced continuity 1. A marketing strategy in which a special introductory offer is used to persuade consumers to sign up to a longer-term obligation that entails regular payments. Those who join such schemes, which typically include subscription services, book clubs, and gym memberships, may find that rules about e.g. notice periods make it more difficult to withdraw than they had supposed. **2.** In Internet sales, a *dark pattern on a website that operates so that a consumer who enters his or her bank details (either to make a payment or to enjoy a 'free trial') is subsequently charged on a recurring basis, usually without having given explicit authorization. The charges may be small and irregular in the hope that the consumer will not notice them.

forced sale A sale that has to take place because it has been ordered by a court or because it is necessary to raise funds to avoid bankruptcy or liquidation.

forced saving A government measure imposed on an economy with a view to increasing savings and reducing expenditure on *consumer goods. It is usually implemented by raising taxes, increasing interest rates, or raising prices.

forced scale In marketing research, a rating scale that does not include a 'no opinion' or 'no knowledge' category; it therefore requires respondents to indicate their position on the attitude scale.

force-field analysis An analytical technique, usually presented graphically (see diagram); it is used to identify all the positive forces and all the negative forces acting on a problem.

Force-field analysis. A simple force-field diagram analysing whether or not to move house.

force majeure (French: superior force) An event outside the control of either party to a contract (such as a strike, riot, war, act of God) that may excuse either party from fulfilling his contractual obligations in certain circumstances, provided that the contract contains a force majeure clause. If one party invokes the *force majeure* clause the other may either accept that it is applicable or challenge the interpretation. In the latter case an *arbitration would be involved.

forecasting The art of estimating future demand for goods or services by anticipating how buyers are likely to react under given sets of conditions. *See* QUALITATIVE FORECASTING TECHNIQUES; QUANTITATIVE FORECASTING TECHNIQUES.

foreclosure The legal right of a lender of money if the borrower fails to repay the money or part of it on the due date. The lender must apply to a court to be permitted to sell the property that has been held as security for the debt. The court will order a new date for payment in an order called a foreclosure nisi. If the borrower again fails to pay, the lender may sell the property. This procedure can occur when a mortgagor fails to pay the mortgagee (bank, building society, etc.) the *mortgage instalments, in which the security is the house in which the mortgagor lives. The bank, etc., then forecloses the mortgage, dispossessing the mortgagor.

foreign bill *See* INLAND BILL.

foreign bond A bond held by a resident of one country that is denominated in the currency of another country and issued by a non-domestic creditor. *See* BULLDOG BOND; YANKEE BOND.

Foreign Corrupt Practices Act 1977 (FCPA) A US statute that prohibits a company from using bribes to obtain business in another country or to prevent the restriction of its business. In 1998 the **Foreign Corrupt Practices Amendment** extended the scope of the Act to include actions by foreign citizens and companies while on US territory.

foreign currency cross-rate A mechanism whereby an exchange rate can be calculated between two currencies for which no direct rate of exchange exists. The US dollar, which is customarily used as the vehicle currency in foreign-exchange trading, is the common denominator of such calculations. Thus, there may not be a direct rate between, say, the Barbados dollar and the Argentine peso. A cross-rate is calculated by divided the $US rate for the peso by the $US rate for the Barbados dollar, showing how many Barbados dollars are needed to purchase one peso.

foreign exchange (FX) The currencies of foreign countries, as bought and sold on a *foreign-exchange markets. Firms or organizations require foreign exchange to purchase goods from abroad or for purposes of investment or speculation.

foreign-exchange broker A *broker who specializes in arranging deals in foreign currencies on the *foreign-exchange markets. Most transactions are between commercial banks and governments. Foreign-exchange brokers do not normally deal direct with the public or with firms who require foreign currencies for buying goods abroad (who buy from commercial banks).

foreign-exchange dealer A person who buys and sells *foreign exchange on a *foreign-exchange market, usually as an employee of a *commercial bank. Banks charge fees or commissions for buying and selling foreign exchange on behalf of their customers; dealers may also be authorized to speculate in forward exchange rates.

foreign-exchange market An international market in which foreign currencies are traded. It consists primarily of foreign-exchange dealers employed by *commercial banks (acting as principals) and foreign-exchange brokers (acting as intermediaries). Although tight *exchange controls have been abandoned by many governments, including the UK government, the market is not entirely free in that it is to some extent manipulated by governments. Currency dealing has a *spot market for delivery of foreign exchange within two days and a forward-exchange market (*see* FORWARD-EXCHANGE CONTRACT) in which transactions are made for foreign currencies to be delivered at agreed dates in the future. This enables dealers, and their customers who require foreign exchange in the future, to hedge their purchases and sales. Options and futures on forward-exchange rates can also be traded on various world markets, both *over-the-counter (OTC) and on exchanges.

foreign investment Investment in the domestic economy by foreign individuals or companies. Foreign investment takes the form of either **direct investment** in productive enterprises or investment in financial instruments, such as a portfolio of shares. Countries receiving foreign investment tend to have a mixed attitude towards it. While the creation of jobs and wealth is welcome, there is sometimes antagonism on the grounds that the country is being 'bought by foreigners'. Similarly, there may be resentment in the country whose nationals invest overseas, especially if there is domestic unemployment. Nevertheless, foreign investment is increasingly important in the economy of the modern world.

foreign sector The part of a country's economy that is concerned with external trade (imports and exports) and capital flows (inward and outward).

foreign trade multiplier The mutually beneficial effect on national income that occurs when one country buys another's exports. The rise in employment and income levels in the exporting country will enable workers there to spend more on products from the other country.

foreign trade zone *See* FREE PORT.

forensic accounting 1. Accounting undertaken in relation to proceedings in a court of law. In such circumstances accountants may be called on to provide expert evidence. **2.** Accounting that sets out to determine the nature of past business activity, often on the basis of partial documentation.

FOREX *See* FOREIGN EXCHANGE.

forfaiting A form of *debt discounting for exporters in which a forfaiter accepts at a discount, and without recourse, a *promissory note, *bill of exchange, *letter of credit, etc., received from a foreign buyer by an exporter. Maturities are normally from one to three years. Thus the exporter receives payment without risk at the cost of the discount.

forfeited share A partly paid share in a company that the shareholder has to forfeit because of a failure to pay a subsequent part or final payment. Such shares must be sold or cancelled by a public company but a private company is not regulated in this respect.

forgery The legal offence of making a false instrument in order that it may be accepted as genuine, thereby causing harm to others. Under the Forgery and Counterfeiting Act 1981, an instrument may be a document or any device on which information is recorded. An instrument is considered false, for example, if it purports to have been made or altered by someone who did not do so, on a date or at a place when it was not, or by someone who does not exist. It is also an offence to copy or use a false instrument knowing it to be false or to make or possess any material meant to be used to produce such specified false instruments as money, cheques, share certificates, credit or debit cards, passports, or registration certificates.

for information only Denoting a quotation given to provide a client with a guide to current market prices. It cannot be treated as a firm offer either to buy or to sell at the quoted price.

forint (HUF) The standard monetary unit of Hungary, divided into 100 fillér.

formation expenses The expenses incurred on setting up a company. According to the Companies Act, these expenses must not be treated as an asset of the company.

Form 10-K An annual report supplied to the US *Securities and Exchange Commission (SEC) by companies listed on the national stock exchanges, detailing financial and other information on the operations of the business. In most cases, the form must be filed within 90 days of the end of a company's financial year (larger companies now have a shorter deadline of 60–75 days).

Form 10-Q A quarterly submission by publicly listed companies to the US *Securities and Exchange Commission (SEC). The information it required is less detailed than that on *Form 10-K and does not have to be audited.

Fortran Acronym for *fo*rmula *tran*slation, a computer programming language. The first *high-level language to gain widespread acceptance for mathematical and scientific work, Fortran has been dominant in this field since the 1950s. A vast amount of software has been written in it, forming an investment that ensures its continued popularity despite advances in programming language design.

forwardation *See* CONTANGO.

forward-dated *See* POST-DATE.

forward dealing Dealing in commodities, securities, currencies, freight, etc., for delivery at some future date at a price agreed at the time the contract (called a **forward contract**) is made. This form of trading enables dealers and manufacturers to cover their future requirements by hedging their more immediate purchases (*see* HEDGE). Strictly, a forward contract differs from a *futures contract in that the former cannot be closed out by a matching transaction, whereas a futures contract can be, and often is. However, this distinction is not always adhered to and the terms are sometimes used synonymously.

forward delivery Terms of a contract in which goods are purchased for delivery at some time in the future (*compare* SPOT GOODS). Commodities may be sold for forward delivery up to one year or more ahead, often involving shipment from their port of origin.

forward differential *See* FORWARD POINTS.

forward-exchange contract An agreement to purchase *foreign exchange at a specified date in the future at an agreed exchange rate. In international trade, with floating rates of exchange, the forward-exchange market provides an important way of eliminating risk on future transactions that will require foreign exchange. *See also* FINANCIAL FUTURES; FOREIGN-EXCHANGE MARKET.

forwarding agent *See* SHIPPING AND FORWARDING AGENT.

forward integration *See* INTEGRATION.

forward margin *See* FORWARD POINTS.

forward points (forward differential; forward margin) The amount to be added to or deducted from the spot foreign-exchange rate to calculate the forward-exchange rate.

forward price The fixed price at which a given amount of a commodity, currency, or a financial instrument is to be delivered on a fixed date in the future. A forward contract differs from a *futures contract in that each forward deal stands alone.

forward-rate agreement (FRA)
1. A contract between two parties that determines the rate of interest that will apply to a future loan or a deposit, which may or may not materialize. **2.** A specified amount of a specified currency to be exchanged on an agreed future date at a specified rate of exchange.

FOS Abbreviation for *Financial Ombudsman Service.

foul bill of lading *See* DIRTY BILL OF LADING.

founders' shares Shares issued to the founders of a company. They often have special rights to dividends. *See also* DEFERRED ORDINARY SHARE.

four-firm concentration ratio The combined *market share of the four largest firms in a particular industry expressed as a percentage. For example, the combined market share of the four largest UK supermarkets has been calculated at nearly 80%. The four-firm ratio is often held to indicate the form or structure of a market in respect of competition (i.e. whether it takes the form of *monopolistic competition, *oligopoly, or *monopoly). A concentration ratio of over 40%, for example, is usually held to indicate an oligopoly. *See also* HERFINDAHL INDEX.

four-plus cover An advertising campaign in which a particular advertisement is exposed to the public at least four times. It is based on the theory that four exposures is the most likely number to persuade a person to buy a particular product.

Fourth Company Law Directive An EU directive (1978) concerning the harmonization of company law and accounting practices in member states. It recognized five *accounting concepts as fundamental: the *accounting entity concept, the *accruals concept, the *consistency concept, the *going-concern concept, and the *prudence concept. In 2006 it was superseded by the *Company Reporting Directive and the *Statutory Audit Directive.

FPA Abbreviation for free of particular average. *See* AVERAGE.

FRA Abbreviation for *forward-rate agreement.

FRAC Abbreviation for frequency, recency, amount, and category. A method of scoring based on a customer's behavioural data. It is normally used in *databased marketing to provide easy access to that customer's transactional information.

Frequency refers to time elapsed between purchases. Recency is the date of the last purchase. Amount is the average value of that customer's purchases. Category refers to the category of the product in which the customer is interested. Each customer is given a score based on these parameters, which can be used to divide customers into groups. A company may use this information at both tactical and strategic levels in its direct marketing effort.

fractional banking A practice that some governments and central banks impose on their banks, requiring a fixed fraction between cash reserves and total liabilities. If the monetary authorities increase the ratio of reserves to deposits, this indicates a tighter credit policy. *See* MONETARY POLICY.

fragmentation culture *See* ORGANIZATIONAL CULTURE.

fragmented industry An industry characterized by having many opportunities to create competitive advantages although each advantage is small.

franc 1. The standard monetary unit of various former French colonies and some French dependencies: Benin (XOF), Burkina-Faso (XOF), Burundi (BIF), Cameroon (XAF), the Central African Republic (XAF), Chad (XAF), Comoros (KMF), Congo-Brazzaville (XAF), the Democratic Republic of Congo (CDF), Côte d'Ivoire, (XOF), Djibouti (DJF), Equatorial Guinea (XAF), Gabon (XAF), Guinea (GNF), Guinea-Bissau (XOF), Mali (XOF), Niger (XOF), Rwanda (RAF), Senegal (XOF), and Togo (XOF). In all countries it is divided into 100 centimes. **2.** (**Swiss franc**) the standard monetary unit of Switzerland and Liechtenstein, divided into 100 centimes. **3.** The former standard monetary unit of France, most French dependencies, Monaco, and (with the peseta) Andorra (**French franc**); of Belgium (**Belgian franc**); and of Luxembourg (**Luxembourg franc**). In each case it was replaced by the euro in 2002.

franchise 1. A licence given to a manufacturer, distributor, trader, etc., to enable them to manufacture or sell a named product or service in a particular area for a stated period. The holder of the licence (**franchisee**) usually pays the grantor of the licence (**franchisor**) a royalty on sales, often with a lump sum as an advance against royalties. The franchisor may also supply the franchisee with a brand identity as well as finance and technical expertise. Franchises are common in the fast-food business, petrol stations, travel agents, etc. **2.** A clause in an insurance policy, often a marine-insurance policy, that excludes the payment of claims up to a specified level but agrees to pay in full all claims above it. For example, a £50 franchise would mean that insurers would not deal with claims below £50 but a claim for £51 would be met in full. Franchise clauses are used by insurers to avoid administratively expensive small claims, while still providing the policyholder with full cover for larger claims. *See also* EXCESS POLICY.

franco (Spanish: free) Export delivery terms in which the seller of goods pays for all transport and insurance to the buyer's warehouse, even when this is in a foreign country. In some countries the term **rendu** is used.

franked investment income Formerly, dividends and other distributions from UK companies received by other companies. The principle of the *imputation system was that once one company had paid corporation tax, any dividends it paid could pass through any number of other companies without incurring a further tax charge.

Frankfurt Stock Exchange (Frankfurt Wertpapierbörse) The oldest and largest of eight regional stock exchanges in Germany, accounting for more than 75% of equity trading in Germany. It first recorded trading in 1820 and was subsequently recognized as a centre for dealing in bonds. Trading is now on four markets; the *Amtlicher Handel* for Government bonds and major companies, the *Geregelter Markt* for smaller companies, the *Freiverkehr*, or third market, and the *Neuer Markt*, launched in 1997 for companies involved in Internet trading. Prices are determined on an auction basis by the official brokers (*Kursmakler*) and free brokers (*Freimakler*), who base them on buying and selling orders from the banks. The main market indicator is the Deutsche Aktienindex (DAX index). The exchange is owned by *Deutsche Börse.

franking machine A machine supplied to businesses who wish to frank their own mail. Instead of taking mail to a post office and using gummed stamps, the business uses the machine to print the postage and the date. Some machines will automatically gauge the weight and size of an item and price it accordingly. The machine records the amount of money due, which has to be remitted to the Royal Mail.

fraud A false representation by means of a statement or conduct, in order to gain a material advantage. A contract obtained by fraud is voidable on the grounds of fraudulent *misrepresentation. If a person uses fraud to induce someone to part with money he or she would not otherwise have parted with, this may amount to theft. *See*

also FRAUDULENT CONVEYANCE; FRAUDULENT PREFERENCE; FRAUDULENT TRADING.

fraudulent conveyance The transfer of property to another person with the aim of putting it beyond the reach of creditors. For example, if a man transfers his house into the name of his wife because he realizes that his business is about to become insolvent, the transaction may be set aside by the court under the provisions of the Insolvency Act 1986.

fraudulent preference Putting a creditor of a company into a better position than he would have been in, at a time when the company was unable to pay its debts. If this occurs because of an act of the company within six months of winding-up (or two years if the preference is given to a person connected with the company), an application to the court may be made to cancel the transaction. The court may make any order that it thinks fit, but no order may prejudice the rights of a third party who has acquired property for value without notice of the preference.

fraudulent trading Carrying on business with intent to defraud creditors or for any other fraudulent purpose. This includes accepting money from customers when the company is unable to pay its debts and cannot meet its obligations under the contract. Such conduct is a criminal offence. The liquidator of a company may apply to the court for an order against any person who has been a party to fraudulent trading to make such contributions to the assets of the company as the court thinks fit. 'Fraudulent' in this context implies actual dishonesty or real moral blame. *Compare* WRONGFUL TRADING.

FRC Abbreviation for *Financial Reporting Council.

FRCD Abbreviation for *floating-rate certificate of deposit.

Freddie Mac Colloquial name for the US *Federal Home Loan Mortgage Corporation (FHLMC).

Free Alongside Ship (FAS) An *Incoterm denoting an export contract in which the seller pays for sending the goods to the port of shipment and bringing them alongside the ship but not for loading them. The seller must pay for any lighterage required. Once the goods are within reach of the ship's crane, all costs and risks pass to the buyer. The seller is responsible for arranging export documentation. *Compare* FREE ON BOARD. *See also* FREE CARRIER.

free asset ratio The ratio of the market value of an insurance company's assets to its liabilities.

free capital 1. Capital in the form of cash. *See also* LIQUID ASSETS. **2.** The shares in a public company that are available to the general public, i.e. those not held by controlling shareholders. In the USA it is known as the **free float**.

Free Carrier (FCA) An *Incoterm denoting an export contract in which the seller pays for sending the goods to a named destination, where they are handed over to the main carrier. At this point all costs and risks pass to the buyer. The seller is responsible for clearing the goods for export. The term is suitable for all modes of transport and is often used as the air-freight equivalent for *Free Alongside Ship.

free cash flow A measure of the cash that a company is generating or consuming. Free cash flow is often defined as after-tax *operating profit less net *capital expenditure:

free cash flow = revenues − operating expenses + depreciation − taxes − capital expenditure costs

However, there is no precise definition of free cash flow: another equation might include changes in *working capital. Making comparisons between companies on this basis is not very useful if they are using different definitions. Free cash flow is not determined in accordance with *generally accepted accounting principles (GAAP) and should be considered in addition to, not as a substitute for, financial measures determined in accordance with GAAP.

Free cash flow is important for managers as a positive cash flow can be used to pay dividends, acquire other companies, or invest in new opportunities. It is also an important measure of a company's ability to reduce debt. The value of a company can be calculated as the sum of the future discounted free cash flows (*see* DISCOUNTED CASH FLOW).

free competition An economy in which free interaction between economic agents is allowed to determine prices, incomes, etc., without government interference. *See* COMPETITION; FREE MARKET.

free depreciation A method of granting tax relief to organizations by allowing them to charge the cost of *fixed assets against taxable profits in whatever proportions and over whatever period they choose. This gives businesses considerable flexibility, enabling them to choose the best method of *depreciation depending on their anticipated cash flow, profit estimates, and taxation expectations.

free enterprise *See* PRIVATE ENTERPRISE.

free fall *See* FREE-STANDING STUFFER.

Freefone A telephone service provided to businesses by BT in which the business pays for incoming calls. A customer who dials a Freefone number (generally beginning with the prefix 0800 or 0808) from a land line will not have to pay for the call; however, mobile operators now usually charge for access to Freefone. This service is much used by *mail-order houses and lines dealing with customer complaints.

freehold An *estate in land that is now usually held in *fee simple. Land that is not freehold will be *leasehold land.

free in and out Denoting a selling price that includes all costs of loading goods (into a container, road vehicle, ship, etc.) and unloading them (out of the transport).

free issue *See* SCRIP ISSUE.

free-keeper A small gift given as a reward for placing an order by mail. Normally the gift can be kept even if the buyer returns the goods ordered.

free list A list, issued by the Customs and Excise, of the goods that can be imported into the UK without paying duty.

free lunch A non-existent benefit. The phrase derives from a 19th-century tavern that advertised free food, it being clearly understood that anyone attempting to exploit this offer without buying a drink would be thrown out. It is now used to convey the idea that wherever there appears to be a free benefit, someone, somewhere, always pays for it. *See also* FREE RIDE.

freely callable Describing a bond that the issuer may choose to redeem at any time from the issue date. *See* CALLABLE BONDS.

free market 1. A market that is free from government interference, prices rising and falling in accordance with supply and demand. **2.** A security that is widely traded on a stock exchange, there being sufficient stock on offer for the price to be uninfluenced by availability. **3.** A *foreign-exchange market that is free from influence on rates by governments, rates being free to rise and fall in accordance with supply and demand.

free of all averages (faa) Denoting a marine insurance that covers only a total loss, general *average and particular average losses being excluded.

free of capture Denoting a *marine insurance in which capture, seizure, and mutiny are excluded. This usually applies to policies taken out in wartime.

free of particular average (FPA) *See* AVERAGE.

Free On Board (FOB) An *Incoterm denoting an export contract in which the seller pays for sending the goods to the port of shipment and loading them on to the ship. Thereafter all costs and risks are assumed by the buyer. The seller is responsible for arranging export

documentation. If the goods are to travel by air or rail the terms **FOB Airport** or **Free On Rail** (**FOR**) are sometimes used, although these are not recognized Incoterms. *Compare* FREE ALONGSIDE SHIP. *See also* FREE CARRIER.

free port A port, such as Bremerhaven, Gdansk, Rotterdam, or Singapore, that is free of customs duties. The area around the port, known as a **foreign trade zone** or **free zone**, specializes in *entrepôt trade, as goods are landed and warehoused before re-export without the payment of customs duties.

Freepost A UK business reply service provided by the Royal Mail. Members of the public reply to advertisements and the advertiser pays the cost of postage after the reply is delivered.

free ride The situation in which an economic agent benefits from the expenditure of others without making a contribution. A free ride is a type of *externality and a source of market imperfection. An example of free riding in financial markets is when small investors benefit from the monitoring of firms carried out by institutional investors.

freesheets Local newspapers and magazines that are published and distributed without charge. As they are entirely dependent upon advertising revenue they must ensure high circulation and low costs to survive. For this reason, the advertising to editorial ratio is exceptionally high.

free-standing stuffer (free-fall; flier) A promotional item distributed by being inserted into a newspaper or a magazine.

free trade The flow of goods and services across national frontiers without the interference of laws, tariffs, quotas, or other restrictions. Since World War II, under the auspices of GATT and the World Trade Organization, trade barriers have continuously, if slowly, fallen.

free trade agreement An agreement to abolish tariffs between two or more countries. Notable examples are the agreement to set up the *European Free Trade Association (EFTA) in 1960 and the *North American Free Trade Agreement (NAFTA), concluded in 1994 between the USA, Canada, and Mexico.

freeze-out Pressure applied to minority shareholders of a company that has been taken over, to sell their stock to the new owners.

freezing injunction An order of the court preventing the defendant from dealing with specified assets. Such an order will be granted in cases in which the plaintiff can show that there will be a substantial risk that any judgment given against the defendant will be worthless, because the defendant will sell assets to avoid paying it. It is usually granted to prevent assets leaving the jurisdiction of the English courts, but may in exceptional circumstances extend to assets abroad. It was formerly called a **Mareva injunction** after the 1975 case *Mareva Compania Naviera SA v International Bulkcarriers SA.*

free zone *See* FREE PORT.

freight 1. The transport of goods by sea (**sea freight**) or air (**air freight**). **2.** The goods so transported. **3.** The cost of shipping goods for a particular voyage by sea or by air. Freight is charged on the basis of weight (*see* DEADWEIGHT CARGO) or the volume occupied, described as **weight or measurement**. Usually the rate is quoted per tonne or per cubic metre, the freight paid being whichever is the greater amount. Air freights are usually quoted on the basis of per kilo or per 7,000 cubic centimetres, whichever is the greater. Certain cargoes are charged on an *ad valorem* basis, expressed as a percentage of the *Free On Board (FOB) value. Freight is normally paid when the goods are delivered for shipment but in some cases it is paid at the destination (**freight forward**).

freight-absorption pricing A geographic pricing strategy in which a company absorbs all or part of the freight

charges in delivering the goods in order to capture the business.

freight-allowed price *See* DELIVERED PRICE.

freight insurance A form of marine or aviation insurance in which a consignor or a consignee covers loss of sums paid in *freight for the transport of goods.

freight note An invoice from a shipowner to a shipper showing the amount of *freight due on a shipment of goods.

freight release An endorsement on a *bill of lading made by a shipowner or his agent, stating that *freight has been paid and the goods may be released on arrival. Sometimes the freight release is a separate document providing the same authority.

frequency 1. The number of times the average person in a target market is exposed to an advertising message during a given period. **2.** The number of times an advertisement is repeated in a given medium (television, radio, etc.) within a given period, usually a month. **3.** In statistics, a measurement of the likelihood of a particular event occurring.

frequency marketing Special services and benefits extended to customers who make frequent purchases from the same seller.

frictional unemployment A minimal level of *unemployment that will occur in even the most efficient economy. Frictional unemployment exists because of lags between workers leaving one job and taking up another and because there are times of the year when many new workers (such as school and college leavers) enter the labour market; in these circumstances there is some delay in finding them all jobs.

friction-free capitalism A term coined by the US founder of Microsoft, Bill Gates (1955–), to refer to the enhanced efficiency of markets resulting from the widespread use of the Internet; this is held to have abolished such traditional market imperfections as physical distance, lack of information, lack of choice, and local regulation.

Friendly Society A UK non-profit-making association registered as such under the Friendly Society Acts (1896–1992). Mutual insurance societies of this kind date back to the 17th century and remained widespread until the introduction of National Insurance in 1946, after which many closed. Those that remain offer a range of personal assurance and insurance benefits relating to sickness, pensions, and unemployment. The 1992 Act created a new framework for Friendly Societies, enabling them to extend their services and to compete with other organizations. Their activities are now regulated by the *Financial Conduct Authority.

fringe benefits 1. Non-monetary benefits offered to the employees of a company in addition to their wages or salaries. They include company cars, expense accounts, the opportunity to buy company products at reduced prices, private health plans, canteens with subsidized meals, cheap loans, gym memberships, etc. Some of these benefits, such as company cars, do not escape the tax net. *See* BENEFITS IN KIND. **2.** Benefits, other than dividends, provided by a company for its shareholders. They may include reduced prices for the company's products or services, Christmas gifts, etc. *See* SHAREHOLDERS' PERKS.

FRN Abbreviation for *floating-rate note.

front door *See* BACK DOOR.

front-end fee A charge levied by a lender when a loan is set up or when the first payment of the loan is taken.

front-end load The initial charge made by a *unit trust, life-assurance company, or other investment fund to pay for administration and commission for any introducing agent. The investment made on behalf of the investor is, therefore, the total initial payment less the front-end load. *Compare* BACK-END LOAD.

front office–back office The division between those elements of an *operating system that are transparent to the customer and with which they can interact (**front office**), and those that are hidden (**back office**). In the service sector there is a trade-off between the benefits that accrue from close and open relationships with the customer and the greater ease with which operations can be controlled when they are out of sight. Application of information technology to many service operations has allowed the customer to experience what appears to be a customized service, while at the same time allowing standardization of procedures.

front running The generally illegal practice in which brokers or intermediaries make their own deals on advance information provided by their investment analysis department, before acting for their clients on the basis of the same information. *See also* CHINESE WALL.

frozen assets Assets that for one reason or another cannot be used or realized. This may happen when a government refuses to allow certain assets to be exported. *See* FREEZING INJUNCTION.

FRRP Abbreviation for *Financial Reporting Review Panel.

FRS Abbreviation for *Financial Reporting Standard.

frugging (fund raising under the guise of research) The unethical practice of deliberate deception by fund raisers masquerading as market researchers. Respondents are often invited to take part in a survey as a lead-in to a presentation, or as an attempt to obtain information that could be used for donor leads or mailing lists. *Compare* SUGGING.

frustration of contract The termination of a *contract as a result of an unforeseen event that makes its performance impossible or illegal. A contract to sell an aircraft could be frustrated if it crashed before the contract was due to be implemented. Similarly an export contract could be frustrated if the importer was in a country that declared war on the country of the exporter.

FSA Abbreviation for *Financial Services Authority.

FSAP Abbreviation for *Financial Services Action Plan.

FSBR Abbreviation for *Financial Statement and Budget Report.

FTC Abbreviation for *Federal Trade Commission.

FTP (file transfer protocol) The protocol used to transfer files across the *Internet from one computer to another. **Anonymous FTP** is the mechanism that enables Internet users to retrieve data from a network file server without having a named account with the server.

FTSE Indexes Share Indexes compiled by the FTSE Group, an independent company owned jointly by the *Financial Times* and the London Stock Exchange. They consist of weighted arithmetic averages for 10 broad sectors of the market (general industrial, cyclical consumer goods, etc.), which are further divided into 38 industry subsectors. They are widely used by investors and portfolio managers.

The widest measure of the market is provided by the **FTSE All-Share Index** of over 600 shares and fixed-interest stocks, which includes a selection from the financial sector. Calculated after the end of daily business, it covers over 98% of the market and some 90% of turnover by value.

For many years the **Financial Times Ordinary Share Index** (**FT 30**) was the main day-to-day market barometer. It records the movements of 30 leading industrial and commercial shares, chosen to be representative of British industry rather than of the Stock Exchange as a whole; it therefore excludes banks, insurance companies, and government stocks. The index, which started from a base of 100 in 1935, is an unweighted geometric average, calculated hourly during the day and closing at 4.30 pm.

The FT 30 has been superseded as the main indicator of market activity by the **FTSE 100 Index** (**Footsie**), a weighted index representing the price of 100 securities with a base of 1,000 on 3 January 1984. This is calculated minute-by-minute and its constituents—the 100 largest UK companies on the LSE—are reviewed quarterly.

In 1992 the UK index series was extended to create two further real-time indexes, the **FTSE 250**, comprising companies capitalized between £150 million and £1 billion, and the **FTSE 350**, which aggregates the FTSE 100 and the FTSE 250. They are calculated both inclusive and exclusive of investment companies. The FTSE 350 is the source for the **FTSE 350 Supersectors**, a series of 18 indexes based on industry baskets that provide an instant view of industry performance across the market.

There are also several indexes for smaller companies. **The FTSE SmallCap Index** covers 270 companies capitalized between £20 million and £150 million; it is calculated at the end of the day's business, both including and excluding investment trusts. The **FTSE Fledgling Index** covers all those companies that are too small to be included in the SmallCap Index but that meet the other criteria for inclusion in the UK Index series. The mainly smaller companies on the London Stock Exchange's *Alternative Investment Market are covered by the **FTSE AIM Index Series**.

The **Financial Times Government Securities Index** measures the movements of government stocks (gilts).

Several indexes now measure the performance of companies resident and incorporated in the European Union. These include the **Euro-Top 100 Index** of the 100 most highly capitalized EU companies, the **FTSE Euro 100 Index** of *eurozone companies, and the **FTSE New EU Index**, which covers the markets of the ten countries that joined the EU in May 2004. In 2003 FTSE Ltd launched the Euro.rst Index series in conjunction with the cross-border derivatives exchange Euronext NV; the most important of these is the **FTSE Eurofirst 300 Index** of blue-chip European companies.

The **FTSE All World Index Series** was launched in 1987 and now covers over 2,800 share prices from 49 countries. With sectors for the developed, emerging, and advanced emerging economies, it is calculated daily and published in sterling, euros, US dollars, and yen.

fulfilment The process of dealing with an order from its receipt to delivery of the goods.

fulfilment operations The operations that occur between a customer placing an order for a product or service and the successful delivery of that product. These include inventory, warehousing, and logistics operations and are of key importance in e-commerce involving physical products.

full consolidation The method of accounting in which the whole impact of subsidiaries is incorporated into group accounts (*see* CONSOLIDATED FINANCIAL STATEMENTS). If a subsidiary undertaking is less than 100% owned, the percentage pertaining to the *minority interest must be adjusted for. This method of consolidation is generally adopted in the UK.

full cost pricing An approach to setting selling prices that attempts to ensure that the price of a good or service is based on all the costs incurred in its supply, including *overheads. It usually involves an *absorption approach to the costing of units. *Compare* COST-PLUS PRICING; MARGINAL COST PRICING.

full-cost transfer prices *Transfer prices that are set by *full cost pricing but do not include a profit margin for the supplying division. This method is widely used in practice. However, there can be problems for managers if they do not have accurate cost information, which may lead to poor decision making.

full employment The state in which all the economic resources of a country (and more specifically, its labour force) are fully utilized.

full-line strategy (deep-line strategy) A strategy that involves a company in offering a large number of variations of its products. Companies employing a full-line strategy are seeking both a high market share and market growth. Leading detergent manufacturers offer up to 15 brands of their detergents.

full listing The status of a company whose shares appear on the *Official List of the *main market of the *London Stock Exchange. *See* LISTING REQUIREMENTS.

fully diluted earnings per share The *earnings per share (eps) for a company that takes into account not only the number of shares in issue but also those that may be issued as a result of such factors as convertible loans and options or warranties. *International Accounting Standard 33 requires that diluted earnings per share be disclosed on the face of the profit and loss account as well as basic earnings per share. The US equivalent is **primary earnings per share**.

fully paid share A *share on which the full nominal or *par value has been paid by the shareholder (plus any premium). *Compare* PARTLY PAID SHARE. *See also* PAID-UP SHARE CAPITAL.

function A section or department of an organization that carries out a discrete activity, under the control of a manager or director. It is the section of the business for which *functional budgets are produced. Examples of separate functions are production, sales, finance, and personnel.

functional budget A financial or quantitative statement prepared for a *function of an organization; it summarizes the policies and the level of performance expected to be achieved by that function for a *budget period.

functional discount A price reduction offered by the seller of goods to those trade channel members that perform certain functions, such as selling, storing, and record keeping. *See also* TRADE DISCOUNT.

functional leader In the social psychology of groups, any group member who performs the functions associated with the role of leader, whether he or she has a formal leadership role or not. These functions may be either goal-oriented (e.g. suggesting solutions to problems, inciting action) or relationship-oriented (e.g. reducing conflict, raising morale).

functional strategy The contribution to the overall organizational objectives made by individual functions. Functional strategy is particularly concerned with the management of functions to achieve the optimum outputs and to maximize systems synergy.

function costing The technique of collecting the costs of an organization by *function and presenting them to the functional management in operating statements on a regular basis.

functions of money In economics, money fulfils the functions of acting as a *medium of exchange, a *unit of account, and a store of value. None of the functions occur in an economy based on barter.

fund 1. A resource managed on behalf of a client by a *financial institution. **2.** A separate pool of monetary and other resources used to support designated activities.

fundamental term A term in a *contract that is of such importance to the contract that to omit it would make the contract useless. Fundamental terms cannot be exempted from a contract, whereas lesser terms, known as conditions and *warranties, can be exempted by mutual consent.

funded debt 1. The part of the national debt that the government is under no obligation to repay by a specified date. This consists mostly of *Consols. *Compare* FLOATING DEBT. *See also* FUNDING OPERATIONS. **2.** Borrowing with a maturity in excess of a year.

funded pension scheme A pension scheme that pays benefits to retired people from a pension fund invested in securities. The profits produced by such a fund are paid out as pensions to the members of the scheme. *Compare* PAY-AS-YOU-GO PENSION SYSTEM.

funding Paying short-term debt by arranging long-term borrowing. *See* FUNDING OPERATIONS.

funding operations 1. The replacement of short-term fixed-interest debt (*floating debt) by long-term fixed-interest debt (*funded debt). This is normally associated with the government's handling of the National Debt through the operations of the Bank of England. The bank buys Treasury bills and replaces them with an equal amount of longer-term government bonds, thus lengthening the average maturity of government debt. This has the effect of tightening the monetary system, as Treasury bills are regarded by the commercial banks as liquid assets while bonds are not. **2.** A change in the *gearing of a company, in which short-term debts, such as overdrafts, are replaced by longer-term debts, such as *debentures.

fund manager (**investment manager**) An employee of one of the larger institutions, such as an insurance company, *investment trust, or *pension fund, who manages its investment fund. The fund manager decides which investments the fund shall hold, in accordance with the specified aims of the fund, e.g. high income, maximum growth, etc.

fund of funds A *unit trust belonging to an institution in which most of its funds are invested in a selection of other unit trusts owned by that institution. It is designed to give maximum security to the small investor by spreading the investment across a wide range.

fund supermarket An Internet facility that provides private investors with a wide range of investment opportunities, generally for a lower charge than established fund *management companies. Under new rules introduced in 2013, fund supermarkets must now charge an upfront fee for their services, rather than taking commission.

fungible issue 1. A *bond issued on the same terms and conditions as a bond previously issued by the same company. It has the advantage of having paperwork consistent with the previous bond and of increasing the depth of the market of that particular bond (*see* DEEP MARKET; THIN MARKET). The *gross redemption yield on the fungible issue will probably be different from that of the original issue, which is achieved by issuing the bond at a discount or a premium. **2.** Any security that is interchangeable with another of the same class.

fungibles 1. Interchangeable goods, securities, etc., that allow one to be replaced by another without loss of value. *Bearer securities and banknotes are examples. **2.** Perishable goods the quantity of which can be estimated by number or weight.

futures contract An agreement to buy or sell a fixed quantity of a particular commodity, currency, or security for delivery at a fixed date in the future at a fixed price. Unlike an *option, a futures contract involves a definite purchase or sale and not an option to buy or sell; it therefore may entail a potentially unlimited loss. However, **futures** provide an opportunity for those who must purchase goods regularly to *hedge against changes in price and for speculators to make large profits. In London, futures are traded in a variety of markets. *Financial futures are traded on the *LIFFE (now Euronext.liffe), whose commodity department deals with shipping and with cocoa, coffee, and other foodstuffs; the *London Metal Exchange deals with metals; and the *International Petroleum Exchange (ICE Futures Europe) with oil. In many cases actual goods (*see* ACTUALS) do not pass between dealers in these **futures markets**, a bought contract being cancelled out by an equivalent sale contract, and vice versa; money differences arising as a result are usually settled through a *clearing house. In some futures markets only brokers are allowed to trade; in others, both dealers and brokers are permitted to do so. *See also* FORWARD DEALING.

future value The value that a sum of money (the *present value) invested at compound interest will have in the future. If the future value is F, and the present value is P, at an annual rate of interest r, compounded annually for n years, $F = P(1+r)^n$. Thus a sum with a present value of £1,000 will have a future value of £1,973.82 at 12% p.a., after six years.

FX Abbreviation for *foreign exchange.

G7; G8; G10; G11; G20 *Abbreviations for* *Group of Seven; *Group of Eight; *Group of Ten; *Group of Eleven; *Group of Twenty.

GA Abbreviation for general average. *See* AVERAGE.

GAAP Abbreviation for *generally accepted accounting principles or *generally accepted accounting practice.

GAAR Abbreviation for *General Anti-Abuse Rule.

GAAS Abbreviation for *generally accepted auditing standards.

GAB Abbreviation for *general arrangements to borrow.

gaiatsu Foreign pressure on Japan to bring its trade and financial policies more in line with those of the rest of the developed world.

gaijin A foreign investor on the Tokyo Stock Exchange.

gain sharing A form of output-based incentive that operates at company or workplace level. There are a variety of forms, including the Scanlon and Rucker plans and Improshare, but common to most is an attempt to link payment to a measure of *value added. Here, value added is calculated by removing labour costs and expenditure on raw materials, energy, and support services from the income derived from the sale of the finished product. If value added increases above a target level, then it is shared between workforce and company in accordance with a preset formula. The aim is to create a group incentive that reflects

the contribution of the work force to business performance more directly than *profit-sharing schemes or *profit-related pay.

game theory A mathematical theory, developed by J. von Neumann (1903–57) and O. Morgenstern (1902–77) in 1944, concerned with predicting the outcome of games of strategy (rather than games of chance) in which the participants have incomplete information about the others' intentions. Under *perfect competition there is no scope for game theory, as individual actions are assumed not to influence others significantly; under *oligopoly, however, this is not the case. Game theory has been increasingly applied to economics and the theory of industrial organizations. The theory was further elucidated by the economists John Nash, John Harsanyi, and Reinhard Selten, who received the Nobel Prize for Economics in 1994.

gaming contract A *contract involving the playing of a game of chance by any number of people for money. A **wagering contract** involves only two people. In general, both gaming contracts and wagering contracts are solid and no action can be brought to recover money paid or won under them.

Gantt chart A chart presenting a planned activity as a series of horizontal bands against a series of vertical lines representing dates (see illustration on p. 272). It can be used to measure progress on a project or to compare planned production in a period to actual production. It was invented by Henry L Gantt in 1917. *See also* SCHEDULE.

GAO Abbreviation for *Government Accountability Office.

JOB	Wk 1	Wk 2	Wk 3	Wk 4	Wk 5	Wk 6	Wk 7	Wk 8	Wk 9	Wk 10
Foundations	███	███								
Floorslab			██							
Walls			███	███	███	███				
Drains		███	███							
Roof							███	███		
Windows/Doors								███	███	
Second Fixing									███	███

Gantt chart. A Gantt chart showing the stages of building a house.

gap 1. Any disparity between goals, expectations, or requirements on the one hand and the actual situation on the other, as between the predicted and actual performance of a business or business unit or between consumer expectations and the quality of goods or services supplied. *See* SERVQUAL; STRATEGIC GAP ANALYSIS. **2.** (**asset–liability gap**) A measure of *interest-rate risk used in banking. It comprises the difference between rate-sensitive assets (i.e. loans) and rate-sensitive liabilities (i.e. deposits) within a particular range of repricing time periods. If short-term rate-sensitive assets are greater than short-term liabilities, the gap will lead to a situation in which an interest-rate fall will lower the profitability and value of a bank. *See also* MISMATCH.

gap analysis 1. A methodical tabulation of all the known requirements of consumers in a particular category of products, together with a cross-listing of all the features provided by existing products to satisfy these requirements. Such a chart shows up any gaps that exist and therefore provides a pointer to any new products that could supply an unfulfilled demand. **2.** (**gap management**) The management of a bank's *interest-rate risk by monitoring and controlling *gaps between rate-sensitive assets

and liabilities. *See also* ASSET–LIABILITY MANAGEMENT. **3.** *See* STRATEGIC GAP ANALYSIS.

garage To transfer assets and liabilities internationally in order to benefit from tax advantages.

garbage in garbage out (GIGO) An enunciation of the important computing principle that all input, however absurd, will be processed according to a program's algorithms and appropriate output generated. If the input is garbage, then the output will inevitably also be garbage.

garbologists (dustbin checkers) Marketing researchers who sort through people's dustbins to analyse household consumption patterns. This normally has to be done with the permission of the householder.

garden leave clause A clause in an employment contract that provides for a long period of notice, during which the employee will be remunerated in full but will not be required to attend at the workplace. Such clauses are used by employers wishing to safeguard trade secrets or prevent a highly skilled employee from leaving to work for a rival firm. An employee who has been head-hunted could be required to serve 'garden leave' for a period of up to one year in order to lawfully terminate his or her existing contract. Throughout this period the employee will be subject to all the normal contractual restraints. Management sees the use of such clauses as an expensive, but reliable and enforceable, alternative to traditional *restraint of trade clauses.

gatekeeper 1. A manager in a large company who controls the flow of information. It is the gatekeeper who decides what information shall be passed upwards to a parent company and downwards to a subsidiary. **2.** See RELATIONSHIP ROLES.

GATT Abbreviation for *General Agreement on Tariffs and Trade.

Gaussian distribution See NORMAL DISTRIBUTION.

gazump To raise the price of, or accept a higher offer for, land, buildings, etc., on which a sale price has been agreed but before the *exchange of contracts has taken place. The intending purchaser with whom the sale price had been agreed has no remedy, even though he or she may have incurred expenditure on legal fees, surveys, etc.

gazunder To reduce an offer on a house, flat, etc., immediately before exchanging contracts, having previously agreed a higher price. The buyer is assuming that the seller will be extremely anxious to sell, having incurred legal expenses and perhaps having bought another property.

GDP Abbreviation for *gross domestic product.

GDP deflator The factor by which the value of GDP (see GROSS DOMESTIC PRODUCT) at current prices must be reduced (deflated) to express GDP in terms of the prices of some base year (e.g. 2000). The GDP deflator is thus a measure of *inflation.

GDSS Abbreviation for group *decision support system.

gearing (capital gearing; equity gearing; financial gearing; leverage) The relative size of the funds provided to a company by its ordinary shareholders and the long-term funds with a fixed interest charge, such as *debentures and *preference shares. A company is said to be high geared when its fixed interest capital is dominant and low geared when its capital is predominantly in ordinary shares, especially in relation to other similar companies. A high-geared company is considered to be a speculative investment for the ordinary shareholder and will be expected to show good returns when the company is doing well. See also DEBT–EQUITY RATIO; FINANCIAL DISTRESS.

gearing adjustment In *current-cost accounting, an adjustment that reduces the charge to the owners for the effect of price changes on *depreciation, *stock, and *working capital. It is justified on the grounds that a proportion of the extra financing is supplied by the *loan capital of the business.

gearing ratios (leverage ratios) Ratios that express a company's capital *gearing. There are a number of different ratios that can be calculated from either the *balance sheet or the *profit and loss account. Ratios based on the balance sheet usually express *debt as a percentage of *equity, or as a percentage of debt plus equity (see DEBT–EQUITY RATIO). **Income gearing** is normally calculated by dividing the *profit before interest and tax by the gross interest payable to give the *interest cover.

geisha bond See SHOGUN BOND.

GE matrix (McKinsey Matrix) A tool for analysing the relative strengths of brands or business units within a large diversified corporation. A range of measures are used to score items on each of two dimensions: (i) the attractiveness of the industry or market; and (ii) the strength of the product or business. On this basis, each item is assigned to one of nine cells on a two-dimensional grid:

Business Strength

	High	Medium	Low
High			
Medium			
Low			

Industry Attractiveness

The corporation should invest in items that appear towards the top left-hand corner of the grid and consider disinvesting from those towards the bottom right-hand corner. Those that appear between these extremes require the most careful appraisal.

To add further dimensions, individual items are usually shown on the grid as pie charts of varying size; the diameter of the pie indicates the size of the relevant market and the size of the 'slice' indicates the market share.

The GE matrix is essentially a more sophisticated development of the *Boston matrix. It is so-called because it was first used by the management consultants McKinsey in their work for General Electric (GE).

gender segmentation Dividing a market on the basis of gender, i.e. into male and female. *See* MARKET SEGMENTATION.

General Agreement on Tariffs and Trade (GATT) A trade treaty that operated from 1948 until 1995, when it was replaced by the *World Trade Organization (WTO). GATT was supported by 95 nations and a further 28 nations applied its rules de facto. Its objectives were to expand world trade and to provide a permanent forum for international trade problems. GATT was especially interested in extending *free trade, which it achieved in eight 'rounds': Geneva (1947), Annecy (1948), Torquay (1950), Geneva (1956), Dillon (1960–61), Kennedy (1964–67), Tokyo (1973–79), and Uruguay (1986–94).

General Anti-Abuse Rule (GAAR) In the UK, a measure designed to counter *tax avoidance by outlawing any arrangement that creates a tax advantage through means that are judged 'artificial and abusive'. The test for the terms 'artificial and abusive' is based on a concept of reasonableness: would it be reasonable to enter into the arrangements in question for any purpose other than reducing liability to tax? If not, then these arrangements may be abusive. The measure, which applies to all the main forms of direct taxation (including inheritance tax), came into force on the royal assent to the Finance Act 2013. It will not be applied to any arrangements entered into before that time.

general arrangements to borrow (GAB) The special arrangements made by the *Group of Ten (G10) to enable the *International Monetary Fund to increase its lending to members of G10. They came into effect in 1962 and were augmented in 1983 when Switzerland, though not a member of the IMF, joined the GAB, enabling it to extend its loan facilities to non-members.

general average (GA) *See* AVERAGE.

General Commissioners In the UK, an unpaid local body of persons of good standing appointed to hear appeals against income tax, corporation tax, and capital gains tax assessments or matters of dispute arising from them. General Commissioners can appoint their own clerk, often a lawyer, who can advise them on procedure and legal matters. *Compare* SPECIAL COMMISSIONERS.

general crossing *See* CHEQUE.

general insurance Insurance cover against the occurrence of certain specified events. The most common examples of general insurance relate to the risks of fire, automobile damage or loss, and theft.

generally accepted accounting practice (GAAP) In the UK, the practices generally followed by accountants in preparing company accounts. These are defined chiefly by issued accounting standards but also by theoretical *accounting concepts and the requirements of company law and the stock exchange. Increasingly, UK tax law has taken accounting practice as the rule to determine the amount of profit on which tax is imposed. In the Finance Act 2000, statute, for the first time, used the concept of 'normal accounting practice' to enact anti-avoidance legislation (in this case, to prohibit a company from obtaining a tax advantage by triggering a capital gain on the sale of its future rents).

generally accepted accounting principles (GAAP) In the USA, the rules, accounting standards, and *accounting concepts followed by accountants in measuring, recording, and reporting transactions. There is a requirement to state whether *financial statements conform with GAAP.

generally accepted auditing standards (GAAS) In the USA, the broad rules and guidelines set down by the Auditing Standards Board of the American Institute of Certified Public Accountants (AICPA). In carrying out audit work for a client, a certified public accountant is also obliged to apply *generally accepted accounting principles.

general meeting A meeting that all the members of a company or association may attend. *See also* ANNUAL GENERAL MEETING; EXTRAORDINARY GENERAL MEETING.

general need description The stage in the business buying process in which a company describes the general characteristics and quantity required of an item it wishes to purchase. *See* BUSINESS BUYER BEHAVIOUR.

general obligation bond In the USA, a security in which the municipal department with the authority to levy taxes has unconditionally promised payment.

general offer An offer of sale made to the general public rather than to a restricted number of people. For example, an object displayed in a shop window with a price tag is a general offer; the shopowner must sell to anyone willing to pay the price.

general partner *See* PARTNERSHIP.

general power of investment A power, introduced by the Trustee Act 2000, that allows trustees to make any kind of investment that they could make if they were absolutely entitled to the assets of the trust fund. Previously, trustees were only permitted to make certain authorized investments. This much wider general power of investment may be expressly excluded in the trust instrument. There are still some restrictions on investments in land. In exercising the general power of investment, trustees are required by the Act to consider the suitability of the proposed investment to the trust and the need for diversification of investment. Trustees are also required to review the investments from time to time with the same criteria in mind.

general price level An index that gives a measure of the purchasing power of money. In the UK, the best-known measure is the *Retail Price Index; in the USA it is the *Consumer Price Index.

general union *See* TRADE UNION.

generic advertising Advertising a type of product or service rather than a branded product or service. Wool and fabric conditioners are both products that have benefitted from generic advertising.

generic brand *See* GENERIC PRODUCT.

generic demand (primary demand) Demand for a class of products (e.g. cars, television sets, etc.), without regard to brand.

genericide The process in which a trademarked brand name acquires such wide usage that it comes to be applied generically (i.e. to all similar products). Although many firms resist the unauthorized use of their trade names, some nevertheless enter the language, such as aspirin, hoover, and escalator.

generic name The name of a class or category of products, such as videos or pens. Sometimes the name of an extensively promoted and successful brand comes to be used as a generic name; examples include Biro, Hoover, and Walkman, which are then often written without an initial capital letter.

generic product (generic brand) A product that carries neither a manufacturer's name nor a distributor's *brand. The goods are plainly packaged with stark lettering that simply lists the contents. These no-name brands offer no guarantees of quality and are produced and sold inexpensively.

generic strategies A framework for helping businesses to find the best means of gaining *competitive advantage for their product, as set out by Michael Porter in 1980. The main strategies are the *focus strategy, the *low-cost strategy, and the *differentiation strategy. Deciding between these generic approaches entails choices as to whether a business looks at the whole industry or one niche, and whether it competes on price or by distinguishing its product offer.

Gensaki The market for the resale and repurchase of short- and medium-term government securities that provides a money market substitute in Japan.

geodemographic segmentation *Market segmentation in which consumers are grouped according to demographic variables, such as income and age, and identified by a geographic variable, such as post code or zip code. The base data is obtained from the census data. Two principles are involved: (1) people who live in the same neighbourhood, defined by a census enumeration district, are likely to share similar buying habits; (2) neighbourhoods can be categorized in terms of their populations: two or more neighbourhoods with similar populations can be placed in the same category. *See* GEOGRAPHIC INFORMATION SYSTEM.

geographic information system (GIS) A tool for interpreting data based on *geodemographic segmentation. It consists of a demographic database, digitized maps, and computer software; lifestyle data may also be included in the analysis. The two main systems currently available in the UK are *ACORN, which has 56 neighbourhood types classified into 17 groups, and **Mosaic**, which identifies 61 types of neighbourhood with a wide range of variables classified into 11 market groupings. Both systems now operate at the level of individual postcodes, thereby targeting potential customers more closely.

geography-based organization An organizational structure in which a market area is divided into territories; marketing efforts are specialized and carried out by geographic area.

geometric mean An average obtained by calculating the nth root of a set of n numbers. For example the geometric mean of 7, 100, and 107 is $\sqrt[3]{74{,}900} = 42.15$, which is considerably less than the *arithmetic mean of 71.3.

Gesellschaft The German name for a limited company. *See* AKTIENGESELLSCHAFT; GESELLSCHAFT MIT BESCHRÄNKTER HAFTUNG.

Gesellschaft mit beschränkter Haftung (GmbH) The German name for a private limited company. The letters GmbH after the name of a company is equivalent to Ltd in the UK. *Compare* AKTIENGESELLSCHAFT.

Giffen good A product that, contrary to normal theories of economic demand, tends to be bought in greater quantities as its price rises. It is typically an inferior good, such as a cheap staple food, for which there are limited substitutes. When the price of bread rises, for example, poorer families are less able to afford more expensive substitutes and will therefore consume more bread. The concept is named after the economist Sir Robert Giffen. *Compare* VEBLEN GOOD.

gift aid A system enabling individuals and companies to donate money to charities and for the charities to recover the tax paid on these donations. The taxpayer must make a **gift aid declaration** to the charity, stating that the payment is to be treated as gift aid. This system was first introduced in 1990, but tax relief was subject to the donation being of a minimum value. From April 2000 the system was extended to gifts of any value, including regular and one-off payments. It replaced the *deed of covenant in favour of charities from that date, although existing covenants remain valid. There are equivalent arrangements whereby tax relief can be obtained on gifts of land, stocks and shares, or plant and machinery.

gifts *inter vivos* Gifts made during an individual's lifetime. The treatment of such gifts, for *inheritance tax purposes, depends on the amount of the gift, the occasion of the gift, and the recipient of the gift. Small gifts can be covered by the small gifts exemption (if less than £250) or by the individual's annual exemption (if less than £3,000). Additional gifts are exempt if they are given on the occasion of marriage. Any gift from one individual to another individual is a *potentially exempt transfer and only becomes liable to tax if the donor dies within seven years of making the gift. Gifts to *relevant property trusts are chargeable to inheritance tax at the lifetime rate, which is half the death rate. The level of charge is dependent on the size of the transfer to the trust and the amount of previous *chargeable transfers within the preceding seven years. *See also* EXEMPT TRANSFERS.

gift tax A US federal tax on property given away, levied on the donor.

gift with reservation A gift in which the donor retains some benefit from the asset given away. Examples include:

- shares given away in which the donor continues to receive the dividends;
- property given by a parent to a child, although the parent continues to live in the property, rent-free. HM Revenue and Customs has detailed rules to cover gifts with reservation to ensure that such gifts are not used as a means of avoiding tax.

GIGO *See* GARBAGE IN GARBAGE OUT.

gilt-edged market makers (primary dealers) The *market makers approved and supervised by the Bank of England for dealing directly with the Bank of England in gilt-edged securities. They have to some extent taken over the role of the *government broker.

gilt-edged security (gilt) A *fixed-interest security or stock issued by the British government in the form of **Exchequer stocks** or **Treasury stocks**. Gilts are among the safest of all investments, as the government is unlikely to default on interest or on principal repayments. They may be irredeemable (*see* CONSOLS) or redeemable. **Redeemable gilts** are classified as: **long-dated gilts** or **longs** (not redeemable for 15 years or more), **medium-dated gilts** or **mediums** (redeemable in 5 to 15 years), or **short-dated gilts** or **shorts** (redeemable in less than 5 years).

Like most fixed-interest securities, gilts are sensitive not only to interest rates but also inflation rates. This led the government to introduce **index-linked gilts** in the 1970s, with interest payments moving in a specified way relative to inflation.

Most gilts are issued in units of £100. If they pay a high rate of interest (i.e. higher than the current rate) a £100 unit may be worth more than £100 for a period of its life, even though it will only pay £100 on *redemption.

gilt repo market A market in the sale and repurchase of *gilt-edged securities set up by the Bank of England in 1996. Its size relative to the money market has made it an attractive market for the implementation of monetary policy with regard to the liquidity of the banking system.

gilts primary dealers *See* GILT-EDGED MARKET MAKERS.

gilt strip A discount UK government stock that has been issued by the Bank of England since 1996. A bond can be divided into a set of payments, which are made by the state and sold at a discount.

gilt unit trust A *unit trust that invests in *gilt-edged securities only.

Ginnie Mae 1. Colloquial name for the US *Government National Mortgage Association (GNMA). **2.** Colloquial name for a mortgage-supported bond issued by the Government National Mortgage Association. A **Ginnie Mae pass-through** is a bond backed by mortgages guaranteed by the GNMA, entitling the buyer to part of a pool of residential mortgages. These securities are called 'pass-throughs' because the investor receives both the principal and interest from the bank or originating mortgage supplier, who retains no margin or profit.

giro 1. A banking arrangement for clearing and settling small payments that has been used in Europe for many years. In 1968 the Post Office set up the UK National Girobank (subsequently **Girobank plc**) as a system for settling debts between people who did not have bank accounts. It subsequently offered many of the services provided by *commercial banks, including services to businesses. In 1990 Girobank was acquired by Alliance and Leicester (now Santander UK).

Bank Giro is a giro system operated in the UK by the clearing banks. It has no central organization, being run by bank branches. The service enables customers to make payments from their accounts by *credit transfer to others who may or may not have bank accounts. **Bancogiro** is a giro system in operation in Europe, enabling customers of the same bank to make payments to each other by immediate book entry. **2.** A colloquial name for a *social security payment made by the UK Department for Work and Pensions to a person in need of financial support.

glass ceiling An invisible artificial barrier (sometimes generated by management) that can limit the career advancement of employees, particularly women and members of minority groups. The expectations and aspirations of all staff within an organization should be met equally. While standards of practice in this area are laid down by law in many countries, they are not always observed. *See* EQUAL EMPLOYMENT OPPORTUNITY LEGISLATION.

Glass–Steagall Act 1933 US legislation that separated commercial banking and securities operations by banks. It was introduced in the aftermath of the great stock-market crash of 1929 to lessen the likelihood of such panics occurring again. These provisions of the Act were largely repealed by the *Financial Services Modernization Act 1999, a move that some commentators now see as contributing to the financial crisis of 2007–08. Similar provisions were re-enacted in a weaker form as part of the *Dodd-Frank Act 2010.

global bond 1. A bond traded in a number of different markets. **2.** A single bond for the total amount of a new issue of bonds, issued on a temporary basis to the bank (normally the *paying agent) that has responsibility for distributing the actual bonds to investors. In due course the global bond, sometimes referred to as a **global bearer bond**, is exchanged for the actual bonds.

global custody Safekeeping, usually by banks, of securities held on behalf of clients. It can include full portfolio services, with valuation and reporting, settlement of trades, registration of ownership, use of specialized nominee companies, collection of domestic and foreign income, and tax accounting. These services span markets and securities in a number of countries.

global firm An organization that operates in more than one country. Global firms have research, production, marketing, and financial advantages in their costs and reputation that are not available to purely domestic competitors.

global information system An organized collection of telecommunications equipment, computer software, data, and personnel designed to capture, store, update, manipulate, analyse, and display on computer a broad range of information about worldwide business activity.

globalization 1. The process that has enabled investment in financial markets to be carried out on an international basis. It has come about as a result of improvements in technology and *deregulation; with globalization, for example, investors in London can buy shares or bonds directly from Japanese brokers in Tokyo rather than passing through intermediaries. *See also* DISINTERMEDIATION. **2.** The process by which the world economy has become dominated by powerful *multinational enterprises operating across national and geographical barriers. The emergence since the 1980s of a single world market in which companies can easily move their operations from one country to another to take advantage of factors such as lower labour costs has affected the ability of national governments to order their own economic affairs. The benefits and drawbacks of this process, and the extent to which it may be controlled or influenced, are the subject of much controversy. **3.** The internationalization of products and services by large firms (*see* GLOBALIZATION STRATEGY; GLOBAL PRODUCT.)

globalization strategy (standardization strategy) A *marketing strategy that is standardized for use throughout the world. The strategy assumes that the behaviour of many consumers throughout the world has become very similar. It assumes that members of market segments require the same features and buy for the same reasons. It also anticipates that the cost savings obtained from production and marketing on a global scale will more than offset the lower sales achieved because the product has not been adapted for local markets. Part of the globalization strategy is to make use of these *economies of scale to support the development of new products.

global offering A security issued in a number of different markets at the same time.

global organization A form of international organization in which top corporate management and staff plan worldwide manufacturing or operational facilities, marketing policies, financial flows, and logistical systems. The global operating unit reports directly to the chief executive, rather than an international divisional head.

global product A product that is marketed throughout the world with the same *brand name, such as Coca Cola, Guinness, Levi, and McDonalds. The advantage of a global product is that it usually enables an advertisement or image to be used worldwide. However, one drawback is that some advertising slogans do not travel well. For example, 'things come alive with Pepsi', when translated into Chinese, led the populace to believe that their ancestors would be brought back from the dead; the Vauxhall Nova encountered similar problems in Spain, where Nova means 'no go'.

Globex (CME Globex) A global round-the-clock electronic trading platform for futures and options, introduced in 1992 by the *Chicago Mercantile Exchange.

GmbH Abbreviation for *Gesellschaft mit beschränkter Haftung. Compare* AG.

GNMA Abbreviation for *Government National Mortgage Association, often referred to as *Ginnie Mae.

gnomes of Zürich An unflattering term applied to Swiss bankers and financiers, alluding to their secrecy and speculative activity. It was popularized by the Labour politician George Brown during the sterling crisis of 1964.

GNP Abbreviation for *gross national product.

goal divergence The situation in which there is a disparity or conflict between the goals of those who should ideally be working together to achieve mutually beneficial outcomes. In business, goal divergence may arise between shareholders and managers, managers and workers, or between a manufacturer or service provider and its marketing channels. The creation of **goal convergence**, rather than divergence, is a major concern of agency theory (*see* AGENCY RELATIONSHIP.)

goal setting The practice of setting individual performance targets for employees. To maximize performance and increase *motivation four general principles should be followed: (1) goals should be challenging but realistic; (2) goals should be specific, not vague; (3) employees should have involvement in setting these goals; and (4) goals should be measurable. *See also* PERFORMANCE MEASUREMENT.

godfather offer A *tender offer pitched so high that the management of the target company is unable to discourage shareholders from accepting it.

going-concern concept A fundamental *accounting concept recognized in the Financial Reporting Standard Applicable in the UK and Northern Ireland. It is the assumption that an enterprise will continue in operation for the foreseeable future, i.e. that there is no intention or necessity to liquidate or significantly curtail the scale of the enterprise's operation. The implication of this principle is that assets are shown at cost, or at cost less depreciation, and not at their *break-up values; it also assumes that liabilities applicable only on liquidation are not shown. The **going-concern value** of a business is higher than the value that would be achieved by disposing of its individual assets, since it is assumed that the business has a continuing potential to earn profits. This assumption will underlie the preparation of *financial statements. If an auditor thinks that a business may not be a going concern, the *auditors' report should be qualified.

Users of financial statements may assume that the going-concern concept has been applied unless there is clear warning to the contrary.

going-rate pricing Setting the price of products largely by following competitors' prices rather than by basing them on company costs or demand.

gold card A *credit card that entitles its holder to various benefits (e.g. an unsecured overdraft, some insurance cover, a higher limit, lower interest rates) in addition to those offered to standard card holders. The cards are available only to those on higher-than-average incomes.

gold clause A clause in a loan agreement between governments stipulating that repayments must be made in the gold equivalent of the currency involved at the time either the agreement or the loan was made. The purpose is to protect the lender against a fall in the borrower's currency, especially in countries suffering high rates of inflation.

gold coins Coins made of gold ceased to circulate after World War I. At one time it was illegal to hold more than four post-1837 gold coins and there have been various restrictions on dealing in and exporting gold coins at various times. Since 1979 (Exchange Control, Gold Coins Exemption, Order) gold coins may be imported and exported without restriction, except that gold coins more than 50 years old with a value in excess of £8,000 cannot be exported without authorization from the Department for Business, Innovation and Skills. *See also* BRITANNIA COINS; KRUGERRAND.

golden handcuffs Financial incentives offered to key staff to persuade them to remain with an organization.

golden handshake *See* COMPENSATION FOR LOSS OF OFFICE.

golden hello A payment made to induce an employee to take up employment. The tax treatment depends on the nature of the payment; in some cases the taxpayer has successfully argued that the payment should be tax-free.

golden parachute A clause in an employment contract, usually of a senior executive, that provides for financial and other benefits if this person is sacked or decides to leave as the result of a takeover or change of ownership.

golden share A share in a company that controls at least 51% of the voting rights. A golden share has been retained by the UK government in some *privatization issues to ensure that the company does not fall into foreign or other unacceptable hands.

Goldilocks economy A colloquial term for an economy that combines low inflation with steady economic growth. Such an economy is 'not too hot, not too cold, but just right'—like the porridge in the story of *Goldilocks and the Three Bears*.

gold market The market for buying and selling gold, which can be traded as *bullion, as coins, or in the futures and forward markets.

gold reserves Reserves held in the form of gold by a country for intervention on foreign-exchange markets.

gold standard A former monetary system in which a country's currency unit was fixed in terms of gold. In this system a currency was freely convertible into gold and free import and export of gold was permitted. It formed the basis for stable prices, since it linked the money supply to the quantity of gold reserves in a country. The UK was on the gold standard from the early 19th century until it finally withdrew in 1931. Most other countries withdrew soon after. *See also* INTERNATIONAL MONETARY FUND.

gold tranche *See* RESERVE TRANCHE.

good A *commodity or *service that is regarded by economists as satisfying a human need. An **economic good** is one that is both needed and sufficiently scarce to command a price. A **free good** is also needed but it is in abundant supply and therefore does not need to be purchased; air is an example. However, a commodity or service that is free but has required an effort to produce or obtain is not a free good in this sense. *See also* CONSUMER GOODS.

good delivery Delivery on the terms specified by the contract.

Goodhart's law Originally, an economic theory stating that if a particular definition of the *money supply were to be used as the basis for monetary policy, the stability of its statistical relationship with spending on the economy would break down and the policy would prove ineffective. The law is now used more widely to highlight the problems of focusing on the value of any specific variable as an indicator. In simple terms, when a measure becomes a target, it ceases to be a good measure. The applications to *performance measurement in management accounting and other aspects of business are obvious.

goods-in-transit insurance An insurance policy covering property against loss or damage while it is in transit from one place to another or being stored during a journey. Policies often specify the means of transport to be used, which may include the postal service. Goods shipped solely by sea are not covered by this type of policy, in which case a *marine insurance policy would be used.

goodwill An *intangible asset reflecting a business's customer connections, reputation, and similar factors. It can be valued as the difference between the value of the separable net assets of a business and the total value of the business. *Purchased goodwill is the difference between the fair value of the price paid for a business and the aggregate of the fair values of its separable net assets. It is generally recognized as an intangible asset in the balance sheet and written off by *amortization to the *profit and loss account over its useful economic life (which is assumed to be no more than five years if it cannot be realistically estimated). Internally generated goodwill should not be recognized in the financial statements of an organization. The treatment of goodwill is now governed by Section 19 of the Financial Reporting Standard Applicable in the UK and Republic of Ireland. The relevant *International Accounting Standards are

IAS22, Business Combinations; IAS36, Impairment of Assets; and IAS38, Intangible Assets.

gopik A monetary unit of Azerbaijan worth one hundredth of a *manat.

go private To take a listed company into private ownership, thus removing its shares from the stock exchange. *Compare* GO PUBLIC.

go public To apply to a stock exchange to become a *public limited company. *Compare* GO PRIVATE. *See* FLOTATION.

Gordon growth model A model used to value businesses or shares based on applying a *present-value formula to future dividends. It assumes that the value of shares is the present value of future dividends, which will grow at a fixed rate g, and is expressed in the formula:

$$P_t = D_i + 1/(r - g),$$

where P_t is the value of a share or business in time period t; D_i + 1 is the value of the dividend in time period t plus one time period; r is the appropriate present value discount rate; and g is the growth rate of dividends per time period. The formula will only work if r is greater than g, which will be the case for mature companies.

go slow A form of *industrial action in which employees work at a deliberately slow pace. *See also* WORK-TO-RULE.

gourde (HTG) The standard monetary unit of Haiti, divided into 100 centimes.

Government Accountability Office (GAO) The audit and investigation department of the US Congress, established in 1921 as the **General Accounting Office**. Its mission is to carry out financial and performance audits of government organizations and programmes.

government actuary A government officer who works with a small team of *actuaries to produce detailed population projections on the basis of observed trends and to assess their implications for national planning and public expenditure. He or she provides a consulting service to government departments and the public sector, giving advice on social security schemes, superannuation arrangements, and on government supervision of insurance companies.

government broker The senior broker appointed by the Bank of England to sell government securities on the London Stock Exchange. The government broker is also the broker to the National Debt Commissioners. Until October 1986 (*see* BIG BANG) the government broker was traditionally the senior partner of Mullins & Co. Since then, however, he or she has been appointed from the gilt-edged division of the Bank of England; many of the functions formerly carried out by the government broker are now undertaken by the *gilt-edged market makers.

government grant An amount paid to an organization to assist it to pursue activities considered socially or economically desirable. Grants may be revenue-based, i.e. made by reference to a specified category of revenue expenditure. Revenue-based grants should be credited to the *profit and loss account in the same period as the revenue expenditure to which they relate. Capital-based grants are made by reference to specified categories of capital expenditure and should be credited to the profit and loss account over the useful economic life of the asset to which they relate. Section 24 of the new Financial Reporting Standard Applicable in the UK and Republic of Ireland gives guidance with respect to the treatment of grants.

government market The market consisting of national and local government units that purchase or hire goods and services for carrying out their main functions. This includes defence procurement, education requirements (school buildings, books, teachers), medical services, road building, etc.

Government National Mortgage Association (GNMA) A US government-owned corporation that guarantees payment on securities backed by mortgages granted by such national organizations as the Federal Housing Association. *See also* GINNIE MAE.

government security (government stock) A security issued by a government, e.g. US Treasury bonds or UK Treasury or Exchequer stock (*see* GILT-EDGED SECURITY).

grace and notice provision The provision in a loan agreement that a borrower who fails on the due date to meet either an interest obligation or capital repayment obligation or who fails to comply with an undertaking is not initially in default. The grace and notice provision is inserted into a loan agreement to avoid problems arising because of administrative mistakes, such as payments not being made on the correct day.

Gramm–Leach–Bliley Act *See* FINANCIAL SERVICES MODERNIZATION ACT 1999.

grandfathered activity A transaction or practice that may be continued by those already engaged in it, but that is forbidden to new participants by changes in the legal or regulatory framework.

grant-in-aid Any grant from central government to a local authority for particular services, other than the rate-support grant.

grant of probate An order from the High Court in the UK authorizing the executors of a will to deal with and distribute the property of the deceased person. If the person died intestate or did not appoint executors, the administrator of the estate has to obtain *letters of administration.

graphical user interface (GUI) A system that enables the user of a computer or hand-held device to operate software without a keyboard or without needing to learn a command language. GUIs rely on graphically presented menus, button-bars, and icons, which are activated by using a mouse or touching the screen.

graphic rating scale A technique for evaluating the performance of an employee that can be used as part of the formal

appraisal process (*see* EMPLOYEE EVALUATION; PERFORMANCE APPRAISAL). It involves listing the desirable traits that the jobholder should possess (e.g. integrity, drive, reliability, etc.) and rating (on a 5–7 point scale) each employee for each of these traits. These trait scores can then be aggregated into overall performance scores.

graphics Any computer output except alphanumeric characters, especially the drawings, graphs, and symbols that can be produced on computers. Most *business software packages include a graphics program that can produce graphs, histograms, and piecharts. More powerful graphics programs are used for *computer-aided design and animation.

graphology The analysis of handwriting as a tool of *personnel selection. In theory, a person's handwriting is supposed to reveal aspects of their personality and character, so a company might use a graphologist to produce profiles of the candidates for a job based on handwriting samples. This method of profiling candidates has low validity but is nonetheless sometimes used by management.

greater-fool theory The theory that in rising markets it can be advisable for an investor to buy securities or other assets that he or she suspects to be overvalued, as it will always be possible to find a purchaser to buy them at an even higher price (the 'greater fool'). This way of thinking is held to be a factor in many speculative bubbles.

green audit *See* ENVIRONMENTAL AUDIT.

Greenbury Report A report on *corporate governance issued in 1995 by a committee under the chairmanship of Sir Richard Greenbury. Developing a number of recommendations of the *Cadbury Report, it stressed the importance of a *remuneration committee of *non-executive directors, the provision of information on remuneration policy in the annual report and accounts, and the restriction of notice and contract periods to less than one year. Many of its recommendations were incorporated in the *Corporate Governance Code. *See also* HAMPEL REPORT.

green currencies The currencies of members of the European Union using artificial rates of exchange for the purposes of the *Common Agricultural Policy (CAP). Their object was to protect farm prices in the member countries from wide variations caused by fluctuations in the real rates of exchange. The need for green currencies was greatly reduced by the European Monetary System and with the advent of the single European currency the term is now seldom used (*see* EUROPEAN ECONOMIC AND MONETARY UNION).

greenfield development A housing or industrial development on a virgin site in the country. *Compare* BROWNFIELD DEVELOPMENT.

greenmail (greymail) The purchase of a large block of shares in a company, which are then sold back to the company at a premium over the market price in return for a promise not to launch a bid for the company. This practice is not uncommon in the USA, where companies are much freer than in the UK to buy their own shares. Although the morality of greenmail is dubious, it can be extremely profitable.

green marketing Marketing products that benefit the environment. The ecological properties of products are important in order that companies produce ecologically safer products, including recyclable and biodegradable packing. Better pollution controls and more energy-efficient production processes and product performance also form a part of green marketing. *See* PRODUCT LIFE CYCLE.

green product A product that its manufacturers claim will not cause damage to the environment, especially a new product or formulation that is being launched to replace one that is said to cause environmental damage.

green reporting (environmental accounting) A report by the directors of a company that attempts to quantify the costs and benefits of that company's operations in relation to the environment. At present relatively few companies disclose such information in their *annual accounts and report. This is, however, a growing practice and reflects the concerns of many investors, consumers, and other stakeholders. New Zealand is one of several countries that have recently introduced legislation on green reporting. The European Union's *Accounts Modernization Directive, which is binding on publicly listed companies from 1 January 2005, states that company information should disclose the environmental impact of a business's activities 'where appropriate'. *See also* ENVIRONMENTAL AUDIT; ENVIRONMENTAL COSTS; SOCIAL RESPONSIBILITY REPORTING; TRIPLE BOTTOM-LINE ACCOUNTING.

greenshoe (greenshoe option) An option given by an issuer of securities to an *underwriter entitling the latter to buy and sell extra shares in an issue if there is high public demand. The term derives from the first company to provide such an arrangement, the Green Shoe Manufacturing Co.

grey-hair investment *See* GREY WAVE.

grey knight In a takeover battle, a counter bidder whose ultimate intentions are undeclared. The original unwelcome bidder is the *black knight, the welcome counter bidder for the target company is the *white knight. The grey knight is an ambiguous intervener whose appearance is unwelcome to all.

greymail *See* GREENMAIL.

grey market 1. Any market for goods that are in short supply. It differs from a *black market in being legal. **2.** A market in shares that have not been issued, although they are due to be issued in a short time. Market makers will often deal with investors or speculators who are willing to trade in anticipation of receiving an allotment of these shares or are willing to cover their deals after flotation. This type of grey market provides an indication of the market

price (and premium, if any) after flotation.
3. The market for goods or services created by older people with a comfortable disposable income and a willingness to spend.

grey wave (grey-hair investment) A company that is thought to be potentially profitable and ultimately a good investment, but that is unlikely to fulfil expectations in the near future. The fruits of an investment in the present should be available when the investor has grey hair.

grid organizational development *See* BLAKE–MOUTON MANAGERIAL GRID.

Groschen A former monetary unit of Austria, worth one hundredth of a *Schilling.

gross domestic product (GDP) The monetary value of all the goods and services produced by an economy over a specified period. It is measured in three ways:

(1) on the basis of expenditure, i.e. the value of all goods and services bought, including consumption, capital expenditure, increase in the value of stocks, government expenditure, and exports less imports;

(2) on the basis of income, i.e. income arising from employment, self-employment, rent, company profits (public and private), and stock appreciation;

(2) on the basis of the value added by industry, i.e. the value of sales less the costs of raw materials.

In the UK, statistics for GDP are published monthly by the government on all three bases, although there are large discrepancies between each measure. Economists are usually interested in the real rate of change of GDP to measure the performance of an economy, rather than the absolute level of GDP. *See also* GDP DEFLATOR; GROSS NATIONAL PRODUCT; NET NATIONAL PRODUCT.

gross income 1. The income of a person or an organization before the deduction of the expenses incurred in earning it.
2. Income that is liable to tax but from which the tax has not been deducted. For many types of income, tax may be deducted at source (*see* DEDUCTIONS AT SOURCE) leaving the taxpayer with a net amount.

grossing up Converting a net return into the equivalent gross amount. For example, if a net dividend (*d*) has been paid after deduction of *r*% tax, the gross equivalent (*g*) is given by:

$$g = 100d/(100 - r).$$

gross interest The amount of interest applicable to a particular loan or deposit before tax is deducted. Interest rates may be quoted gross (as they are on government securities) or net (as in most building society deposits or bank deposits). The gross interest less the tax deducted at the basic rate of income tax gives the net interest. Any tax suffered is usually, but not always, available as a credit against tax liabilities.

gross investment *See* NET INVESTMENT.

gross margin *See* GROSS PROFIT.

gross margin ratio *See* GROSS PROFIT PERCENTAGE.

gross national product (GNP) The *gross domestic product (GDP) with the addition of interest, profits, and dividends received from abroad by UK residents and with those payments made from the UK to overseas residents deducted. The GNP better reflects the welfare of the population in monetary terms, although it is not as accurate a guide as to the productive performance of the economy as the GDP. *See also* NET NATIONAL PRODUCT.

gross profit (gross margin; gross profit margin) The difference between the sales revenue of a business and the *cost of sales. It does not include the costs of finance, administration, or distribution. *Compare* NET PROFIT.

gross profit percentage (gross margin ratio) A ratio of financial performance calculated by expressing the *gross profit as a percentage of sales. With retailing companies in particular, it is regarded as a prime measure of their trading success. The only ways in which a company can improve its gross margin ratio are to increase selling prices and/or reduce its *cost of sales.

gross receipts The total amount of money received by a business in a specified period before any deductions for costs, raw materials, taxation, etc. *Compare* NET RECEIPTS.

gross redemption yield (effective yield; yield to maturity) The internal rate of return of a bond bought at a specified price and held until maturity; it therefore includes all the income and all the capital payments due on the bond. The tax payable on the interest and the capital repayments are ignored.

gross tonnage (gross register tonnage) *See* TONNAGE.

gross weight 1. The total weight of a package including its contents and the packing. The **net weight** is the weight of the contents only, i.e. after deducting the weight of the packing (often called the **tare**). **2.** The total weight of a vehicle (road or rail) and the goods it is carrying, as shown by a weighbridge. The **net weight** is obtained by deducting the tare of the vehicle.

grosz (*plural* **groszy**) A monetary unit of Poland worth one hundredth of a *zloty.

ground rent Rent payable under a lease that has been granted or assigned for a capital sum (premium). Normally, long leases on offices, flats, etc., are granted for such a premium, payable when the lease is first granted; in addition the leaseholder pays the landlord a relatively small annual ground rent. *See also* RENT.

group A parent undertaking and its subsidiary or subsidiaries. In UK tax law, two or more companies constitute a group where one company holds more than 50% of the shares in the other(s). This test is usually applied to the voting share capital only. Where there is a group of companies, the availability of the lower rates of corporation tax is restricted. Where the links between companies are made by share ownership of

75% or over, assets can be passed among the companies without a tax charge in respect of *capital gains. *See* CONSOLIDATED FINANCIAL STATEMENTS; GROUP RELIEF. *See also* MEDIUM-SIZED GROUP; SMALL GROUP.

group accounts (group financial statements) *See* CONSOLIDATED FINANCIAL STATEMENTS.

group decision support system (GDSS) *See* DECISION SUPPORT SYSTEM.

group discussion A *marketing research technique that brings between six and eight respondents together for at least an hour to discuss a marketing issue under the guidance of an interviewer. It has been found that, once such a group is relaxed, it will fully explore issues in a manner that shows what is important to it, using its own rather than marketers' terminology. The interviewer, who is a specialist acting on behalf of a client, first draws up a **topic guide** that identifies the points to be explored. A *sample of respondents—who must not know one another—is recruited to match certain criteria (e.g. if the problem concerned tea all respondents would be tea drinkers). The group meets in the interviewer's home or in a hotel; with the discussion being tape-recorded, the interviewer describes the problem and then adopts a passive role, allowing the group to discuss their views and interjecting further questions only if some aspect of the problem is not being explored adequately. After a minimum of four group discussions, the interviewer will have sufficient material to write a report and recommend a particular action. Group discussions are a qualitative procedure (*see* QUALITATIVE MARKETING RESEARCH) frequently used to determine attitudes to particular products or advertisements. *See also* FOCUS GROUP.

group income A *dividend paid by one company in a group to another. The dividends received are not subject to *corporation tax.

group life assurance A *life-assurance policy that covers a number of people, usually a group of employees or the members of a particular club or association. Often a single policy is issued and premiums are deducted from salaries or club membership fees. In return for an agreement that all employees or members join the scheme, insurers are prepared to ask only a few basic questions about the health of a person joining. However, with the advent of AIDS insurers are no longer prepared to waive all health enquiries, as they were some years ago.

Group of Eight (G8) The *Group of Seven plus Russia, which was admitted as a full member of this economic summit grouping in 1998. In 2014 Russia was suspended from the G8 in response to its annexation of Crimea. *see* GROUP OF TWENTY.

Group of Eleven (G11) A group of 11 lower-income countries established with the aim of narrowing the income gap with the world's rich nations, mainly through debt forgiveness and increased access to world markets. The members are Croatia, Ecuador, El Salvador, Georgia, Honduras, Indonesia, Jordan, Morocco, Pakistan, Paraguay, Sri Lanka, and Tunisia. It was formed in 2006 at the instigation of King Abdullah of Jordan.

Group of Seven (G7) The seven leading Western industrial nations: namely, the USA, Japan, Germany, France, UK, Italy, and Canada. This group evolved from the first economic summit held in 1976 and now holds an annual meeting attended by heads of state. The original aim was to discuss economic coordination but the agenda broadened to include political issues. From 1991 Russia attended G7 meetings, initially as an observer but from 1998 as a full participant (*see* GROUP OF EIGHT). With the subsequent rise of China, India, and other non-Western economies the continuing role of the G7 and/or G8 has become a matter of some uncertainty. *See* GROUP OF TWENTY.

Group of Ten (G10; the Paris Club) The ten prosperous industrial nations that agreed in 1962 to lend money to the

*International Monetary Fund (IMF), namely Belgium, Canada, France, (West) Germany, Italy, Japan, The Netherlands, Sweden, UK, and the USA. They inaugurated *Special Drawing Rights. Switzerland, although not a member of the IMF, is a party to the *general arrangements to borrow, which the G10 countries established to provide additional credit facilities. Luxembourg is also an associate member.

Group of Thirty A group of economic experts comprising individuals from central and commercial banks and finance ministries, as well as academic economists. The group was founded in 1978 by the Rockefeller Foundation to carry out research into international economic issues.

Group of Twenty (G20) A group of 19 leading economies plus the European Union. Meetings of G20 finance ministers and central bank governors have been held regularly since 1999. The first summit of G20 heads of state was held in November 2008 as a response to the global financial crisis and it was subsequently agreed that the G20 would take over from the *Group of Eight as the main forum for the world's wealthy nations. Summit meetings are now held annually.

group registration Registration for *value added tax for a group of companies under common control. The business carried on by any group member is treated as that of the representative member. VAT is not charged on supplies between group members.

group relief Relief available to companies within a 75% group as a result of which *qualifying losses can be transferred to other group companies. The losses transferred are available to set against the other group members' profits chargeable to corporation tax, thus reducing the overall tax liability for the group. A 75% group, for group relief, exists if one company holds 75% or more of:

- the ordinary share capital, and
- the distributable income rights, and
- the rights to the net assets in a winding-up. From 1 April 2000 members of a

group no longer have to be resident in the UK to qualify for relief. *See also* CONSORTIUM RELIEF.

group roles Certain identifiable roles (i.e. coherent sets of behaviours) that tend to be adopted by the different members of a group, partly as a matter of personal inclination but also as a response to the expectations of others. These will include *relationship roles, such as the group encourager or comedian, as well as *task roles, such as the initiator or summarizer.

groupthink In group decision making, the tendency to drift into ill-conceived policies or decisions without adequate debate. This can be a result of various pressures, including the illusion of ingroup superiority and the wish to achieve consensus and avoid painful disagreements.

groupware Computer software that enables collaborative working on a joint project. Using groupware, members of a team can work together despite being in different locations (e.g. by using shared documents). Groupware was a precursor of web-based collaborative working systems.

growth 1. An increase in the value of an asset. If growth is sought in an investment, it is an increase in its capital value that is required. *See also* GROWTH STOCKS. **2.** The expansion of an economy, usually expressed in terms of an increase of national income.

growth curve A curve on a graph in which a variable is plotted as a function of time. The curve thus illustrates the growth of the variable. This may be used to show the growth of a population, sales of a product, price of a security, etc.

growth fund A managed fund holding assets that are expected to grow in value and provide capital gains. In general, these funds are supposed to provide higher returns but with greater risks.

growth industry Any industry that is expected to grow faster than GDP.

growth needs *See* ERG THEORY.

growth rate The amount of change over a period in some of the financial characteristics of a company, such as sales revenue or profits. It is normally measured in percentage terms and can be compared to the *Retail Price Index, or some other measure of inflation, to assess the real performance of the company.

growth recession *See* RECESSION.

growth stage The stage in a *product life cycle during which a product's sales start climbing rapidly.

growth stocks Securities that are expected to offer the investor sustained *capital growth. Investors and investment managers often distinguish between growth stocks and income stocks. The former are expected to provide *capital gains; the latter, high income. The investor will usually expect a growth stock to be an ordinary share in a company whose products are selling well and whose sales are expected to expand, whose capital expenditure on new plant and equipment is high, whose earnings are growing, and whose management is strong, resourceful, and investing in product development and long-term research.

G-SIFIs *See* SIFIs.

guaraní (PYG) The standard monetary unit of Paraguay, divided into 100 céntimos.

guarantee 1. *See* WARRANTY. **2.** A promise made by a third party (**guarantor**), who is not a party to a contract between two others, to accept liability if one of the parties fails to fulfil the contractual obligations. For example, a bank may make a loan to a person, provided that a guarantor is prepared to repay the loan if the borrower fails to do so. The banker may require the guarantor to provide some *security to support his guarantee. *See also* BANK GUARANTEE.

guaranteed bond (guaranteed stock) A *bond in which payments of principal or interest are guaranteed by a party other than the issuer. In the USA this is often a state.

guaranteed-income bond A bond issued by a life-assurance company that guarantees the purchaser a fixed income as well as a guaranteed return of capital at the end of the term or on prior death. *See also* SINGLE-PREMIUM ASSURANCE.

guarantor *See* GUARANTEE.

GUI Abbreviation for *graphical user interface.

guide price *See* COMMON AGRICULTURAL POLICY.

guilder 1. The standard monetary unit of Curaçao (ANG) and Sint Maarten (ANG), divided into 100 cents. **2.** The former standard monetary unit of The Netherlands, divided into 100 cents. It was replaced by the euro in 2002.

guinea A former British coin, originally made from gold from Guinea. First issued in 1663, it had various values; during most of the 18th century it stood at 21 shillings. Although it was replaced in 1817 by the sovereign, it persisted, not as a coin but as a unit of 21 shillings for charging for some professional services, until decimalization (1971). Prices are still sometimes quoted in guineas in the sale of livestock or horses, especially when this is by auction.

g

habitual buying behaviour Consumer behaviour in the buying of cheap frequently purchased items, characterized by low consumer involvement and few significant *brand differences. Purchases are made out of habit, rather than a strong commitment to a brand. Generally, price and sales promotions are used to stimulate sales, as consumers tend to base their decisions on past behaviour and have no need for further information.

hacker An individual with a good understanding of the structure and operation of computer networks, who deliberately breaks into confidential systems. In many cases there are no malign intentions, although hackers can cause damage by inadvertently introducing viruses or commands that disrupt the proper working of the system. Those with more malign intentions are sometimes known as **crackers**. *See also* CYBERCRIME.

halal Acceptable under Islamic law. The term is applied to those forms of banking and finance that avoid the religious prohibition against taking interest payments. *Compare* HARAAM. *See* ISLAMIC FINANCE.

halala A monetary unit of Saudi Arabia, worth one hundredth of a *riyal.

haler (*plural* **haleru** or **halers**) A monetary unit of the Czech Republic (and former monetary unit of Slovakia) worth one hundredth of a *koruna.

half-commission man A person who is not a member of a stock exchange but works for a *stockbroker, introducing clients in return for half, or some other agreed share, of the commission.

hallmark In the UK, a series of marks (usually four) stamped on articles made of gold, silver, platinum, or (from 2010) palladium to indicate the maker, the hall or *assay office making the mark, the quality of the metal, and the date of assay. Each of the four halls (London, Birmingham, Sheffield, and Edinburgh) have distinguishing marks (e.g. a leopard for London, an anchor for Birmingham). The quality of gold was indicated by a *carat mark (22, 18, 14, and 9 carats) until 1975, after which it was expressed in parts of gold per 1000 (e.g. 22 carat = 916, 14 carat = 585, 9 carat = 375). The quality mark for sterling silver (925 parts per 1000) in England is a lion (passant) and in Scotland a thistle or lion (rampant). Britannia silver (958) is indicated by a full-length figure of Britannia. Platinum is indicated by an orb. The date is indicated by a letter in a specifically shaped shield. Hallmarks on precious metals are accepted internationally and there are heavy penalties for forging them or selling articles made in the UK of these metals (except those exempt) without them. The future of hallmarks is, however, uncertain, owing to current moves to make the marking of precious metals consistent throughout the EU. Since January 1999 all articles made in the EU of gold, silver, or platinum must carry a numeral indication of purity (in parts per 1000) in addition to any hallmarks.

hall test A marketing research test conducted in a room or hall close to a shopping centre. Consumers, selected at random, are invited to come to the hall to participate in the test, which involves answering questions about their buying habits, purchases, etc.

halo effect *See* HORNS AND HALO EFFECT.

hammering The removal of a member firm from the *London Stock Exchange because it is unable to meet its obligations. This was formerly (until 1970) announced by three blows of a hammer, followed by the broker's name.

Hampel Report A report issued in 1998 by a committee under the chairmanship of Sir Ronald Hampel. It reviewed the implementation of the Cadbury Code (*see* CADBURY REPORT) and the Greenbury recommendations (*see* GREENBURY REPORT) and combined these into a new *Corporate Governance Code.

handbill A form of printed advertisement delivered into the hands of likely customers; handbills may also be attached to their cars or put through their letter boxes.

Hang Seng Index An arithmetically weighted index based on the capital value of selected stocks on the *Hong Kong Stock Exchange. It was first quoted in 1964 and takes its name from the Hang Seng Bank. The number of stock was initially 33, because this is a lucky number in Chinese astrology. There are now 49 constituent stocks.

hào A monetary unit of Vietnam, worth one tenth of a *dồng.

haraam Forbidden by Islamic law. In financial contexts, this applies chiefly to lending or borrowing money at interest. Various schemes enable Muslims to take out loans, notably mortgages, without violating this principle of faith. *Compare* HALAL. *See* ISLAMIC FINANCE.

harassment A form of prohibited *discrimination on grounds of sex, race, age, gender reassignment, sexual orientation, religion or belief, or disability that occurs where someone is subjected to unwanted conduct that has the purpose or effect of violating their dignity or creating an intimidating, hostile, degrading, humiliating, or offensive environment. **Sexual harassment** occurs where the unwanted conduct is of a sexual nature.

hard commodity *See* COMMODITY.

hard currency A currency that is commonly accepted throughout the world; they are usually those of the Western industrialized countries although other currencies have achieved this status, especially within regional trading blocs. Holdings of hard currency are valued because of their universal purchasing power. Countries with *soft currencies go to great lengths to obtain and maintain stocks of hard currencies, often imposing strict restrictions on their use by the private citizen.

hard dollars A fee paid to a US stockbroker, investment adviser, etc., for research, analysis, or advice, as opposed to **soft dollars**, which refers to the commission earned on purchases made.

hard sell The use of selling methods that emphasize the supposed virtues of a product, repeat its name, and attempt to force it upon the consumer by forceful and unsubtle means. *Compare* SOFT SELL.

hard systems Systems that consist entirely of non-human elements, e.g. machines. The behaviour of all the elements in the system should be predictable and amenable to mathematical or other scientific modelling methods. *Compare* SOFT SYSTEMS METHODOLOGY.

hardware The electronic and mechanical parts of a computer system; for example, the central processing unit, disk drive, screen, and printer. *Compare* SOFTWARE.

Harmonized Index of Consumer Prices (HICP) *See* CONSUMER PRICE INDEX.

harmonizer *See* RELATIONSHIP ROLES.

harvesting strategy Making a short-term profit from a particular product shortly before withdrawing it from the market. This is often achieved by reducing the marketing support it enjoys, such as advertising, on the assumption that the effects of earlier advertising will still be felt and the product will continue to sell.

haulage The charge made by a **haulier** (**haulage contractor**) for transporting goods, especially by road. If the goods consist of a large number of packages (e.g. 100 tonnes of cattlefood packed in 2000 bags each weighing 50 kilograms) there will be a separate charge for loading and unloading the vehicle.

Hawthorne studies Research conducted in the 1920s and 1930s at the Western Electric Company's Hawthorne plant in Chicago. The programme set out to explore the effects of physical working conditions on employee productivity but became known more for its major finding of the importance of the social dimension of workplace relations. Although output increased significantly after changes were made in working conditions, it was subsequently concluded that this owed more to the workers' sense that they were receiving special treatment than to the changes themselves. The Hawthorne studies laid the basis for the *human relations theory of management.

Hay method A *job evaluation system based on three core factors: know-how, problem solving, and accountability. The system, which is named after the US management expert Edward N. Hay, is essentially a combination of the *point method and the *factor-comparison method.

hazardous waste Any waste substance that is considered harmful to human health or the environment because it possesses one or more of 15 properties listed in the EU's Revised Waste Framework Directive (2008). A list of such substances can be found in the European Waste Catalogue. There are stringent regulations governing the production, pretreatment, movement, and disposal of all such wastes and imposing a regime of monitoring and inspection. *See also* WASTE DISPOSAL.

head hunter *See* EMPLOYMENT AGENCY.

head lease The main or first *lease, out of which **sub-leases** may be created. For example, if A grants a 99-year lease to B and B then grants a 12-year lease of the same property to C, the 99-year lease is the head lease and the 12-year lease is a sub-lease.

headline inflation *See* CORE INFLATION.

Health and Safety Executive (HSE) A UK government body appointed to look after the health, safety, and welfare of people at work; to protect the public from risks arising from work activities; and to control the use and storage of explosives and other dangerous substances. It is composed of representatives from trade unions, employers, and local authorities, with a full-time chairman. The HSE enforces its policies through inspection of industrial and other premises.

(⊕) **SEE WEB LINKS**

• Website of the HSE: provides information and guidelines on a wide range of health and safety topics, including those applicable to particular industries

hedge A financial transaction or position designed to mitigate the risk of other transactions or positions. For example, a manufacturer may contract to sell a large quantity of a product for delivery over the next six months. If the product depends on a raw material that fluctuates in price, and if the manufacturer does not have sufficient raw material in stock, an open position will result. This open position can be hedged by buying the raw material required on a *futures contract; if it has to be paid for in a foreign currency the manufacturer's currency needs can be hedged by buying that foreign currency forward or on an *option. Operations of this type do not offer total protection because the prices of *spot goods and futures do not always move together, but it is possible to reduce the vulnerability of an open position substantially by hedging.

Buying futures or options as a hedge is only one kind of hedging; it is known as **long hedging**. In **short hedging**, something is sold to cover a risk. For example, a fund manager may have a large holding of long-term fixed income investments and is worried that an anticipated rise in interest rates will reduce the value of the *portfolio. This risk can be hedged by selling interest-rate futures on a *financial futures market. If interest rates rise the loss in the value of the portfolio will be offset by the profit made in covering the futures sale at a lower price.

hedge accounting Certain accounting treatments that may be followed when an entity uses financial *derivatives to hedge against risk. Their purpose is to offset the extreme movements that may appear in a company's profit and loss account when a volatile derivative is measured using *fair value accounting methods. The Financial Reporting Standard Applicable in the UK and Republic of Ireland (Section 12) limits the availability of such treatments; in general, hedge accounting may only be used with the less complex forms of derivative. UK listed companies should follow *International Accounting Standard 39, Financial Instruments: Recognition and Measurement.

hedge fund A *unit trust that is subject to minimum regulation, typically a partnership or mutual fund that attempts to achieve large gains by exploiting market anomalies. These funds are often high-return and are regarded as speculative. Typically, they accept only accredited investors, require a high minimum level of investment (£500,000 or more), and pay high performance-related fees to managers. Many are domiciled in offshore financial centres.

hedging against inflation Protecting one's cash flow, income, or capital against inflation by buying *equities or making other investments that are likely to rise with the general level of prices.

hereditament *Real property. Originally, it was property that would be inherited by the heir on intestacy. **Corporeal hereditaments** are physical real property, such as land, buildings, trees, and minerals. **Incorporeal hereditaments** are intangible rights, such as easements or profits *à prendre*, attached to land.

Herfindahl Index A measure of the degree of competition within a particular industry. It is calculated as the sum of the squares of the individual *market shares of all known players in that industry. The Index is considered a better measure than simple *concentration ratios (e.g. the *four-firm concentration ratio) because it reflects the distribution of market share throughout an industry while giving greatest weight to that of the largest firms. An index figure of 1,000 or more is usually held to indicate a fairly high level of concentration: although regulatory regimes differ, a merger that caused a further significant rise in the index (say by 50 points) would normally prompt the interest of competition watchdogs.

Herstatt risk *See* SETTLEMENT RISK.

Herzberg's two-factor theory *See* HYGIENE FACTORS; MOTIVATORS.

HFT Abbreviation for HIGH-FREQUENCY TRADING.

HICP Abbreviation for Harmonized Index of Consumer Prices. *See* CONSUMER PRICE INDEX.

hidden reserve Funds held in reserve but not disclosed on the balance sheet (they are also known as **off balance sheet reserves** or **secret reserves**). They arise when an asset is deliberately either undisclosed or undervalued. Such hidden reserves are permitted for some banking institutions but are not permitted for limited companies as they reduce profits and therefore the corporation tax liability of the company.

hidden tax *See* STEALTH TAX.

hidden unemployment (concealed unemployment) *Unemployment that does not appear in government statistics, which are usually based on figures for those drawing unemployment benefit (since 1996 known as jobseeker's allowance in the UK). In addition to these people there will be some who are doing very little productive work, although they are not registered as unemployed. These include workers on short time for whom their employers are expecting to be able to provide work shortly; workers who are not usefully employed, although their employers think they are; people who are not in full-time work but who do not qualify for the jobseeker's allowance for various reasons (including those drawing alternative benefits, such as income support or incapacity benefit); and others who choose not to claim benefit. *See also* RESIDUAL UNEMPLOYMENT.

hierarchy of effects The steps in the persuasion process that lead a consumer to purchase a particular product. They are awareness, knowledge, liking, preference, conviction, and finally a decision to purchase.

hierarchy of needs *See* MASLOW'S MOTIVATIONAL HIERARCHY.

Higgs Report A report on the role and effectiveness of *non-executive directors produced by a committee under Sir Derek Higgs; it was published with the **Smith Report** on the independence of auditors in 2003. The findings of both reports led to revisions in the *Corporate Governance Code.

higher rate of income tax A rate of *income tax that is higher than the *basic rate of income tax. For 2015–16 higher rate tax is payable on taxable income, after *personal allowances and other allowances, of over £31,785. The rate of tax is 40%. An **additional rate** of 45% is payable on taxable income over £150,000.

high-frequency trading (HFT) A computerized trading strategy in which complex algorithms are used to generate and execute orders at high speed, so that large volumes of shares may be held for very short periods of time before being automatically resold. The role of HFT in sudden market movements or 'flash crashes' has made the practice controversial. Although the US *Securities and Exchange Commission has sought to regulate such trading, it now accounts for a majority of all equities trades in the USA and Europe.

high-involvement management An approach to management that emphasizes the need to develop *organizational commitment amongst employees, on the grounds that this will lead to improved *motivation, better performance, and a lower *labour turnover rate. It argues that employee commitment can be enhanced through training, incentives, sharing of information, and participation in decision making.

high-involvement product A product that involves the consumer in taking time and trouble before deciding on a purchase. This will include looking in several catalogues, shops, etc., to compare prices and the products themselves. High-involvement products include such major purchases as cars and houses, as well as computers, home entertainment systems, and many other domestic products. *Compare* LOW-INVOLVEMENT PRODUCT.

high-level language A computer-programming language that is designed to reflect the needs of the programmer rather than the capabilities of the computer. Such languages use abstract data and control structures, and symbolic names for variables. There are a large number of high-level languages; *BASIC, *COBOL, *Fortran, and *C are examples.

high net-worth individuals (HNWIs) People in possession of either very high net incomes, very large net assets, or both. Under most regulatory regimes, certified HNWIs become eligible to be sold personalized financial products and services in which there is a substantially higher risk to their investment. The current UK net income threshold for HNWIs is £300,000 per year. In the USA an informal figure of $1 M in liquid assets is often cited.

high-street bank *See* COMMERCIAL BANK.

high yielder A stock or share that gives a high yield but is more speculative than most, i.e. its price may fluctuate.

HIP Abbreviation for *human information processing.

hire purchase (HP) A method of buying goods in which the purchaser takes possession of them as soon as an initial instalment of the price (a **deposit**) has been paid and obtains ownership of the goods when all the agreed number of subsequent instalments have been paid. A **hire-purchase agreement** differs from a **credit-sale agreement** and **sale by instalments** (or a **deferred payment agreement**) because in these transactions ownership passes when the contract is signed. It also differs from a contract of hire, because in this case ownership never passes. Hire-purchase agreements were formerly controlled by government regulations stipulating the minimum deposit and the length of the repayment period. These controls were removed in 1982. Hire-purchase agreements were also formerly controlled by the Hire Purchase Act 1965, but most are now regulated by the Consumer Credit Act 1974. In this Act a hire-purchase agreement is regarded as one in which goods are bailed in return for periodical payments by the bailee; ownership passes to the bailee if the terms of the agreement are complied with and the option to purchase is exercised.

A hire-purchase agreement often involves a *finance company as a third party. The seller of the goods sells them outright to the finance company, which enters into a hire-purchase agreement with the hirer.

histogram A graph of a frequency distribution constructed with rectangles, in which the areas of the rectangles are proportional to the frequencies.

historical cost The value of a unit of stock or other asset calculated on the basis of the original cost to the organization of purchasing or manufacturing it, rather than on the basis of its current value to the organization. *Compare* CURRENT COST.

historical-cost accounting A system of accounting based on the principle that assets should be valued at *historical cost. It is relaxed to some extent by such practices as the valuation of stock at the lower of cost and *net realizable value and, in the UK, revaluation of *fixed assets. The advantages of historical-cost accounting are that it is relatively objective, easy to

apply, difficult to falsely manipulate, and suitable for audit verification. In times of high inflation, however, the results of historical-cost accounting can be misleading as profit can be overstated, assets understated in terms of current values, and *capital maintenance is only concerned with the nominal amount of the capital invested rather than its purchasing power. Because of these defects it is argued that historical-cost accounting is of little use for decision making, but attempts to replace it with such other methods as *current-cost accounting have failed.

Company legislation sets out the rules for the application of historical-cost accounting to *financial statements. Companies may also choose to use alternative accounting rules based on the **modified historical-cost convention**, in which certain assets are included at revalued amounts.

historical summary A voluntary statement appearing in the *annual accounts and report of some companies in which the main financial results are given for the previous five to ten years.

HMRC Abbreviation for HM *Revenue and Customs.

HNWIs Abbreviation for *high net-worth individuals.

hockey-stick growth Very rapid exponential growth, in which a graph of, for example, revenue or visitors to a website against time is shaped like a hockey stick.

Hofstadter's law The adage that a task will always take longer than expected, even when Hofstadter's law is taken into account. The law is therefore endlessly recursive. Although often taken facetiously, the law makes the serious point that something unexpected is very likely to occur in the completion of any complex task, no matter how carefully one plans. It is therefore a good antidote to *planning fallacy and *optimism bias. The law is named after the US academic Douglas Hofstadter (1945–).

holder The purchaser of a financial obligation, i.e. a dealer who has a *long position in this obligation.

holding company (parent company) A company that holds shares in other companies in a *group (usually, but not necessarily, its subsidiaries).

holding costs See CARRYING COSTS.

holdout A situation in which creditors refuse to agree to a particular reorganization proposal for a firm in *financial distress.

holiday pay Wages or salary paid to a *worker during a period of vacation leave to which he or she is entitled. In the UK full-time workers are now legally entitled to a minimum of 28 days paid annual leave per year, including bank holidays; part-time workers have a pro-rata entitlement. The right to holiday pay was first enshrined in English law under the Holidays with Pay Act 1938. The USA has no statutory minimum-leave entitlement.

holistic evaluation An evaluation of an advertising or marketing campaign as a whole, as distinct from an analysis of the results of its constituent parts.

holon See SOFT SYSTEMS METHODOLOGY.

home audit Marketing research conducted in the home by means of panels of householders who keep a diary on a regular basis recording the products they buy and when they buy them.

home banking Carrying out banking transactions by means of a home computer linked to a bank's computer via the Internet (**e-banking** or **online banking**) or by means of a telephone link to a call centre or a computerized system (**telephone banking**). This enables the account-holder to carry out certain operations—most commonly checking the balance held or transferring sums between accounts—at any time of the day or night without leaving the home or office. Although regular transfers, such as direct debits, can be arranged, and payments to third parties can often be made, paying in cheques is not possible in home banking (although it is using a *postal account). In the UK these services are now offered by all the high-street banks but only a minority of account-holders make regular use of them. Home banking is, however, a growing trend among business customers. A number of Internet-only banks, with no branch offices, now exist.

home page A document, usually in graphical form, that acts as the entry point to a *World Wide Web server. Set out in a page format, it provides hypertext access to related menus and files.

home service assurance See INDUSTRIAL LIFE ASSURANCE.

home shopping channels A form of television direct marketing in which television programmes or entire channels are dedicated to selling goods and services. While relatively small in money terms in the UK and Europe, in the USA it is estimated that more than $10 billion is spent in this manner annually on goods and services. Compare DIRECT-RESPONSE TV ADVERTISING.

Hong Kong Stock Exchange (SEHK) The main market for listed securities in Hong Kong, first established in 1947. It is currently the second largest exchange in Asia by market capitalization, after the Tokyo Stock Exchange. The leading market indicator is the *Hang Seng Index.

(⊕) SEE WEB LINKS
• Website of Hong Kong Exchanges and Clearing Ltd

honour policy A marine insurance policy that covers the risk of a person who has an interest in a voyage in circumstances in which the interest may be difficult to establish.

horizontal integration See INTEGRATION.

horizontal job enlargement See JOB ENLARGEMENT.

horizontal marketing systems A channel arrangement in which two or more companies, at one level, join together to follow a new marketing opportunity. Such *joint ventures have become more commonplace as companies combine their capital, production facilities, and marketing resources to compete in global markets.

horizontal mobility *See* MOBILITY OF LABOUR.

horizontal spread A combination of *options with different expiry dates, such as a long put option combined with a short put option.

horns and halo effect An effect in which one person's judgment of another is unduly influenced by a first impression; it may be either unfavourable (horns) or favourable (halo). The effects can be misleading when interviewing job applicants. For example, a well-qualified candidate who arrives late for an interview, for a good reason, may be passed over as a bad time-keeper, while a poorly qualified but punctual and well-groomed candidate may be offered the job.

hostile bid A *takeover bid that is unwelcome either to the board of directors of the target company or to its shareholders.

hot list The most up-to-date names on a mail-order buyer or enquirer list. Hot lists are of great value in *direct marketing.

hot money **1.** Money that moves at short notice from one financial centre to another in search of the highest short-term interest rates, for the purposes of *arbitrage, or because its owners are apprehensive of some political intervention in the money market, such as a *devaluation. Hot money can influence a country's *balance of payments. **2.** Money that has been acquired dishonestly and must therefore be untraceable.

house brand *See* OWN BRAND.

household insurance 1. An insurance policy that covers the structure of a home (often called **buildings insurance**). **2.** An insurance policy covering the personal goods and effects kept inside a home (**contents policy**). A **comprehensive householder's policy** will cover both the buildings and the contents.

house journal A journal produced by a large organization for the benefit of its employees. It usually seeks to keep all levels of employees informed of the general policy of the company, to function as a forum for employees, and often to provide social news. It often helps to create a corporate identity, especially if employees are widely distributed geographically.

house list A direct-mail seller's own list of names of either current or lapsed customers, prospects, members, etc.

HP Abbreviation for *hire purchase.

HRM Abbreviation for *human-resource management.

hryvna (UAH) The standard monetary unit of Ukraine, divided into 100 kopiykas.

HSE Abbreviation for *Health and Safety Executive.

HTML (hypertext markup language) The computer language used to write *hypertext. A particular feature of HTML is the use of tags to display *hyperlinks.

HTTP (hypertext transfer protocol) A standard protocol for the transmission of information on the World Wide Web. *See* HYPERTEXT; INTERNET.

hull insurance *Marine insurance or aircraft insurance covering the structure of a ship, boat, hovercraft, or aeroplane and the equipment maintained permanently on board.

human capital The skills, general or specific, acquired by an individual in the course of training and work experience. The concept was introduced by Gary Becker (1930–2014) in the 1960s in order to point out that wages reflect in part a return on human capital. This theory has been used to explain large variations in wages for apparently similar jobs and why even in a recession a firm may retain its workers on relatively high wages, despite high levels of involuntary unemployment. *See also* INTELLECTUAL CAPITAL.

human factors *See* ERGONOMICS.

human information processing (HIP) The *cognitive processes involved in thinking, remembering, interpreting, and *decision making. The importance of HIP to business is that an understanding of the way in which people use information in the decision-making process should make it possible to determine the most appropriate information to be provided and the most suitable form.

human relations theory An approach to management based on the idea that employees are motivated not only by financial reward but also by a range of social factors (e.g. praise, a sense of belonging, feelings of achievement and pride in one's work). The theory, which developed from empirical studies carried out in the 1920s and 1930s (*see* HAWTHORNE STUDIES), holds that attitudes, relationships, and *leadership styles play a key role in the performance of an organization. *See* MOTIVATION; SELF-ACTUALIZATION.

human-resource accounting (human-asset accounting) An attempt to recognize the human resources of an organization, quantify them in monetary terms, and show them on the *balance sheet. A value is placed on such factors as the age and experience of employees as well as their future earning power for the company. Although this approach has aroused some interest, in practice considerable difficulty has been met in quantifying the value of human resources.

human-resource management (HRM) The management of people to achieve individual behaviour and performance that will enhance an organization's effectiveness. HRM encourages individuals to set personal goals and rewards, guiding them to shape their behaviour in accordance with the objectives of the organization that employs them.

HRM was traditionally called **personnel management** and involved such responsibilities as interviewing job applicants, providing training, and storing personal data on employees. However, current trends place a greater emphasis on the morale and *motivation of employees, which is increasingly seen as the key to competitiveness. Strategies for achieving enhanced *job satisfaction may include training employees to do more than one job and encouraging all the members of a workforce to accept responsibility (*see* EMPOWERMENT).

hundredweight 1. (Abbreviation: cwt) A former unit of weight used in the UK, equal to 112 lb; 20 cwt equal 1 long ton (2240 lb). It has been largely replaced by metric units; many bags that used to contain 1 cwt of material now contain 50 kilos. 1 cwt = 50.8 kilograms. Under the Weights and Measures Act 1985 and the EU directive on metric measures adopted into British law in January 2000 it is no longer legal to use the hundredweight in trade. **2.** A unit of weight used in the USA, equal to 100 lb; 20 hundredweights = 1 short ton (2000 lb).

hurdle rate The rate of interest in a *capital budgeting study that a proposed project must exceed before it can be regarded worthy of consideration. The hurdle rate is often based on the *cost of capital or the *weighted average cost of capital, adjusted by a factor to represent the risk characteristics of the projects under consideration.

hybrid A synthetic financial instrument formed by combining two or more individual financial instruments, such as a bond with a warrant attached.

hybrid marketing channels Two or more marketing channels set up by a single firm to reach one or more customer segments. In this form of multichannel distribution a variety of direct and indirect approaches are used to deliver the firm's goods to its customers.

hygiene factors In the two-factor theory of *motivation introduced by Frederick Herzberg, those aspects of the work situation that can cause dissatisfaction if they are lacking or inadequate but cannot by themselves create *job satisfaction. They include quality of supervision, job security, remuneration, and physical working conditions. *Compare* MOTIVATORS.

hypercompetition A market situation in which there is an unusually high degree of competition between companies. Hypercompetition tends to arise in sectors characterized by rapid technological and structural change and low *barriers to entry; as a result, no one firm can sustain its *competitive advantage over time. Such situations are typical of new and emerging industries.

hyperinflation A situation in which levels of *inflation are so high that money becomes virtually worthless and monetary exchange breaks down, to be replaced by a system of barter. The appropriate accounting treatment is set out in Section 31 of the Financial Reporting Standard Applicable in the UK and Republic of Ireland. UK listed companies must apply *International Accounting Standard 29.

hyperlink A word, phrase, or image on a web page that is clickable and enables navigation to another page on the site or another site on the World Wide Web. Hyperlinks are generally indicated to the user by text highlighted by underlining and/or a different colour. *See* HYPERTEXT; INTERNET.

hypermarket A very large shop, usually having a selling area of at least 50,000 square feet (4,645 square metres), that sells a wide range of products under one roof. Hypermarkets are often located adjacent to towns and base their attraction on low prices and the convenience to car-owning consumers, who can make many of their purchases in one place where parking facilities are provided. *See also* BIG-BOX STORE; SUPERMARKET; SUPERSTORE.

hypertext A document format used in multimedia and on the *Internet in which a page of text contains links, usually in the form of highlighted words or icons (*see* HTML). Selecting one of these *hyperlinks takes the user directly to related documents, enabling them to pursue a line of investigation without having to search for each item individually. Links could be to further documents directly relating to the initial search subject, to related subjects, or even to further specialist sources. The connections can therefore increase exponentially.

hypothecation 1. An authority given to a banker, usually as a **letter of hypothecation**, to enable the bank to sell goods that have been pledged (*see* PLEDGE) to them as security for a loan. It applies when the bank is unable to obtain the goods themselves. The goods have often been pledged as security in relation to a documentary bill, the banker being entitled to sell the goods if the bill is dishonoured by non-acceptance or non-payment. **2.** A mortgage granted by a ship's master to secure the repayment with interest, on the safe arrival of the ship at her destination, of money borrowed during a voyage as a matter of necessity (e.g. to pay for urgent repairs). The hypothecation of a ship itself, with or without cargo, is called **bottomry** and is effected by a **bottomry bond**; that of its cargo alone is **respondentia** and requires a **respondentia bond**. The bondholder is entitled to a maritime *lien. **3.** The practice of reserving the revenue from a tax or duty for spending on a particular stated purpose; for example dedicating revenues received from the tax on tobacco products to health spending.

IA Abbreviation for *information acceleration.

IAB Abbreviation for *Internet Advertising Bureau.

IAP Abbreviation for Internet access provider. *See* ACCESS PROVIDER.

IAS Abbreviation for *International Accounting Standard.

IASB Abbreviation for *International Accounting Standards Board.

IBF Abbreviation for *international banking facility.

IBNR claims reserve A reserve held by an insurance company for claims 'incurred but not yet reported'.

IBOR Abbreviation for Inter Bank Offered Rate. *See* INTERBANK MARKET.

IBRD Abbreviation for *International Bank for Reconstruction and Development.

ICC Abbreviation for *International Chamber of Commerce.

ICE Abbreviation for *IntercontinentalExchange.

ICE Futures Europe A London-based subsidiary of *Intercontinental Exchange (ICE) that trades futures and options in energy (especially crude and refined oil) and carbon emissions allowances. It was established following ICE's acquisition of the *International Petroleum Exchange in 2001. The exchange has been fully electronic since 2005.

(((⊕))) SEE WEB LINKS
• Information from the ICE website

ICE Futures US A New York-based subsidiary of *Intercontinental Exchange (ICE) that trades futures and options in *soft commodities, currencies, and equity indexes. It was established in 2007, when ICE acquired the *New York Board of Trade.

ICMA Abbreviation for *International Capital Market Association.

ICSA Abbreviation for *Institute of Chartered Secretaries and Administrators.

IDA Abbreviation for *International Development Association.

idea generation The systematic search for new product ideas. *See* NEW PRODUCT DEVELOPMENT.

idea screening Screening new-product ideas in order to identify and develop good ideas and drop poor ones as soon as possible.

identifiable assets and liabilities (separable assets and liabilities) Those *assets and *liabilities of a business that could be disposed of separately, i.e. without disposing of the business as a whole.

idle capacity The part of the *budgeted capacity within an organization that is unused. It is measured in hours using the same measure as production. Idle capacity can arise as a result of a number of causes in all of which the actual hours worked are less than the budgeted hours available. The reasons can include non-delivery of raw materials, shortage of skilled labour, or lack of sales demand.

idle time The time, usually measured in labour hours or machine hours, during which a production facility is unable to operate. *See also* IDLE CAPACITY; WAITING TIME.

IFA Abbreviation for *independent financial adviser.

IFAD Abbreviation for *International Fund for Agricultural Development.

IFC Abbreviation for *International Finance Corporation.

IFRS Abbreviation for *International Financial Reporting Standard.

IIB Abbreviation for *Institute of Insurance Brokers.

ijarah See ISLAMIC FINANCE.

ijarawa-iktina See ISLAMIC FINANCE.

illegal contract A *contract prohibited by statute (e.g. one between traders providing for minimum resale prices) or illegal at common law on the grounds of *public policy. An illegal contract is totally void, but neither party (unless innocent of the illegality) can recover any money paid or property transferred under it, according to the maxim *ex turpi causa non oritur actio* (a right of action does not arise out of an evil cause). Related transactions may also be affected. A related transaction between the same parties (e.g. if X gives Y a promissory note for money due from him under an illegal contract) is equally tainted with the illegality and is therefore void. The same is true of a related transaction with a third party (e.g. if Z lends X the money to pay Y) if the original illegality is known to that party.

illegal partnership A *partnership formed for an illegal purpose and therefore disallowed by law. A partnership of more than 20 partners is illegal, except in the case of certain professionals, e.g. accountants, solicitors, and stockbrokers.

ILO Abbreviation for *International Labour Organization.

IMA 1. Abbreviation for *Institute of Management Accountants. **2.** Abbreviation for *Investment Management Association.

image A composite mental picture formed by people about an organization or its products. *See* BRAND; CORPORATE IMAGE.

image replacement document *See* CHEQUE TRUNCATION.

IMF Abbreviation for *International Monetary Fund.

immediate annuity An *annuity contract that begins to make payments as soon as the contract has come into force.

immediate holding company A company that has a *controlling interest in another company, even though it is itself controlled by a third company, which is the *holding company of both companies.

immigrant remittances Money sent by immigrants from the country in which they work to their families in their native countries. These sums can be a valuable source of foreign exchange for the native countries.

impact day The first day on which a newly issued security may be traded by subscribers. Trading will reveal whether the market price of the security is above or below the *issue price.

Imperial units A system of units formerly widely used in the UK and the rest of the English-speaking world. It includes the pound (lb), quarter (qt), *hundredweight (cwt), and *ton (ton); the foot (ft), yard (yd), and mile (mi); and the gallon (gal), British thermal unit (btu), etc. These units have been largely replaced by metric units, although Imperial units persist in some contexts. In January 2000 an EU regulation outlawing the sale of goods in Imperial measures was adopted into British law; an exception was made for the sale of beer and milk in pints. *Compare* METRIC SYSTEM; US CUSTOMARY UNITS.

impersonal account A *ledger account that does not bear the name of a person or company, such as a *nominal account or *real account.

implied term A provision of a *contract not agreed to by the parties in words but either regarded by the courts as necessary to give effect to their presumed intentions or introduced into the contract by statute (as in the case of contracts for the sale of goods). An implied term may constitute either a *condition of the contract or a *warranty; if it is introduced by statute it often cannot be expressly excluded.

implied warranty In contract law, the unwritten contract between a seller and a buyer that goods or services traded are fit for their usual purpose. The buyer has the right to expect that their purchase conforms to certain standards, even where there is no written *warranty.

import deposit A method of restricting importation to a country, in which the importer is required to deposit a sum of money with the customs and excise authorities when goods are imported. It is sometimes used as an alternative to raising import duties.

import duty A tax or *tariff on import goods. Import duties can either be a fixed amount or a percentage of the value of the goods. They have been a major type of barrier used to protect domestic production against foreign competition and they have also been an important source of government revenue, especially in developing countries.

import entry form A form completed by a UK importer of goods and submitted to HM Revenue and Customs for assessment of the *import duty, if any. When passed by the Customs the form functions as a *warrant to permit the goods to be removed from the port of entry.

import licence A permit allowing an importer to bring a stated quantity of certain goods into a country. Import licences are needed when *import restrictions include *import quotas, currency restrictions, and prohibition. They also function

as a means of exchange control, the licence both permitting importation and allowing the importer to purchase the required foreign currency.

import quota An *import restriction imposed on imported goods, to reduce the quantity of certain goods allowed into a country from a particular exporting country, in a stated period. The purpose may be to conserve foreign currency, if there is an unfavourable *balance of payments, or to protect the home market against foreign competition (*see* PROTECTIVE DUTY). Quotas are usually enforced by means of *import licences.

import restrictions Restrictions imposed on goods and services imported into a country, which usually need to be paid for in the currency of the exporting country. This can cause a serious problem to the importing country's *balance of payments, hence the need for restrictions, which include *tariffs, *import quotas, currency restrictions, and prohibition. Prohibition will also apply to preventing the importation of illegal goods (e.g. drugs, arms). The restrictions may also be imposed to protect the home industry against foreign competition (*see* PROTECTIVE DUTY) or during the course of political bargaining.

imports Goods or services purchased from another country. *See* IMPORT DUTY; IMPORT QUOTA; IMPORT RESTRICTIONS.

import surcharge An extra tax applied by a government on certain imports in addition to the normal *tariff. It is usually applied as a temporary measure by a government that is in difficulty with its *balance of payments, but does not wish to violate its international tariff agreements.

impression management *See* POWER STYLES.

imprest account A means of controlling *petty-cash expenditure in which a person is given a certain sum of money (float or imprest). When some of it has been spent, that person provides appropriate vouchers for the amounts spent and is then reimbursed so that the float is restored. Thus at any given time the person should have either vouchers or cash to a total of the amount of his float.

impulse buying The buying of a product by a consumer without previous intention and almost always without evaluation of competing brands. Impulse buying is encouraged by such factors as prominent shelf position; manufacturers are therefore keen to persuade retailers to give these advantages to their products.

imputation system A *corporation tax system in which a company making a *qualifying distribution pays tax on the dividend paid. The shareholder receiving the dividend also receives a credit representing the tax paid by the company and this can be used to offset his or her tax liability. The UK operated an imputation system until 1999 (*see* ADVANCE CORPORATION TAX; FRANKED INVESTMENT INCOME).

imputed cost A cost that is not actually incurred by an organization but is introduced into the *management accounting records in order to ensure that the costs incurred by dissimilar operations are comparable. For example, if rent is not payable by an operation it will be introduced as an imputed cost so that the costs may be compared with an operation that does pay rent.

IMS Abbreviation for *Institute of Management Services.

inactive buyer A customer of a *direct marketing company, who has not made a purchase for a specified time.

in-barrier option An *option that is eliminated if the price of the *underlying fails to pass a certain level. In such cases the premium paid for the option is partly reimbursed. *Compare* OUT-BARRIER OPTION.

in-basket test *See* WORK-SAMPLE TESTS.

in bond Delivery terms for goods that are available for immediate delivery but are held in a *bonded warehouse. The buyer has to pay the cost of any Customs duty due, the cost of loading from the warehouse, and any further on-carriage costs.

incentive-compatible contract A contract designed to ensure mutually beneficial behaviour by the parties. So, for example, the employment contracts of a company's managers might incorporate a bonus system to make sure that their interests and those of the shareholders are congruent. *See* AGENCY RELATIONSHIP; GOAL DIVERGENCE.

incentive system A scheme in which rewards are offered to managers or other employees conditional on certain performance targets being met. Apart from cash bonuses, such rewards may include shares or share options (*see* SHARE INCENTIVE SCHEME), health insurance, gym membership, or corporate entertainment.

incestuous share dealing The buying and selling of shares in companies that belong to the same group, in order to obtain an advantage of some kind, usually a tax advantage. The legality of the transaction will depend on its nature.

inchoate instrument A *negotiable instrument in which not all the particulars are given. The drawer of an inchoate instrument can authorize a third party to fill in a specified missing particular.

incidence of taxation The impact of a tax on those who bear its burden, which may not be limited to those who are charged to pay it. For example, *value added tax (VAT) is paid by traders, but part of the ultimate *tax burden falls on the consumer of the trader's goods or services. Again, a company may pay corporation tax but if it then raises its prices or reduces its employees' wages to recoup some or all of the tax, it may be said to have shifted the incidence.

income 1. Any sum that a person or organization receives either as a reward for effort (e.g. salary or trading profit) or as a return on investments (e.g. rents or interest). From the point of view of taxation, income has to be distinguished from *capital. *See* EARNED INCOME; GROSS INCOME; TOTAL INCOME. **2.** In economics, the flow of economic value attributed to an individual or group of individuals over a particular period. The total of income throughout an individual's life, minus expenditure, is equal to that person's wealth. Note that both income and wealth are generally considered to include more than simply money; for example, benefits in kind, services rendered by governments, and *human capital should all be included.

income and expenditure account An account, similar to a *profit and loss account, prepared by an organization whose main purpose is not the generation of profit. It records the income and expenditure of the organization and results in either a surplus of income over expenditure or of expenditure over income. Such an organization's accounts do not use the *accruals concept.

income bond 1. (National Savings Income Bond) A type of bond introduced by the Department for *National Savings in 1982. They offer monthly interest payments on investments of between £500 and £1 million. Interest is taxable but not deducted at source. **2.** *See* GUARANTEED-INCOME BOND.

income distribution 1. The proportions of income paid to different sections of a community. *See* INCOME REDISTRIBUTION. **2.** The payment by a *unit trust of its half-yearly income to unit holders, in proportion to their holdings. The income distributed is the total income less the manager's service charge and income tax at the standard rate.

income in kind *See* BENEFITS IN KIND.

income redistribution The use of taxation to ensure that the incomes of the richer members of the community are reduced and those of the poorer members are increased. Tax theorists have tended to favour *progressive taxes for this purpose,

combined with various forms of income support for the poorer members of the community.

income segmentation Dividing a market into different income groups.

income share *See* INVESTMENT TRUST; SPLIT-CAPITAL INVESTMENT TRUST.

income smoothing The manipulation by companies of certain items in their *financial statements so that they eliminate large movements in profit and are able to report a smooth trend over a number of years. The practice is pursued because of the belief that investors have greater confidence in companies that are reporting a steady increase in profits year by year. It is doubtful if any regulations can totally prevent this form of *creative accounting.

incomes policy A government policy aimed at controlling inflation and maintaining full employment by holding down increases in wages and other forms of income and prices by means of statute or *moral suasion.

income statement In the USA, the equivalent of a UK *profit and loss account.

income stock A stock or share bought primarily for the steady and relatively high income it can be expected to produce. This may be a fixed-interest *gilt-edged security or an ordinary share with a good *yield record.

income tax (IT) A direct tax on an individual's income. In general, individuals can earn income without paying tax up to a threshold, with subsequent income giving rise to tax liabilities, usually at increasing rates as income increases (*progressive taxation).

In UK tax legislation income is not defined; rather, amounts received are classified under seven headings according to their source: (i) income from employment; (ii) income from trading; (iii) pensions income; (iv) savings and investment income; (v) income from social security payments; (vi) income from property; (vii) other miscellaneous income. In order to be potentially liable to income tax an amount received must fall under one of these headings. There are some specific occasions when the legislation requires capital receipts to be treated as income for taxation purposes, e.g. when a landlord receives a lump sum on the granting of a lease. In the UK the importance of the distinction between income and capital has diminished since income and capital gains are now charged at essentially the same rate. The tax is calculated on the taxpayer's taxable income, i.e. gross income less any *income tax allowances and deductions. If the allowances and deductions exceed the gross income in a *fiscal year, no income tax is payable. In the UK, there are currently three tax-rate bands for *earned income: a *basic rate of income tax of 20% on taxable earnings up to £31,785; a *higher rate of income tax of 40% on taxable earnings over £31,785; and an additional rate of 45% on taxable earnings over £150,000 (2015–16 figures). The starting rate of 10% was abolished from April 2008 for earned income. *See also* PAYE.

income tax allowances Allowances that may be deducted from a taxpayer's gross income before calculating the liability to *income tax. Every individual who is a UK resident is entitled to a *personal allowance, the level of which currently depends on his or her age. After 5 April 2000 the former married couple's allowance was discontinued for all couples in which the elder spouse was under 65 on that date; if one spouse was born before 6 April 1935, the allowance is a maximum of £8,355 (2015–16), relief for this amount being available at a rate of 10%. From April 2015 either spouse in such a marriage may choose to transfer up to 10% of their personal allowance to their partner (but not where one or both pays higher-rate tax). There is also a registered blind person's allowance of £2,290. For savings income, there is now an allowance of £1,000 (£500 for higher-rate tax payers). From April 2016 there will be an allowance of £5,000 for dividend income (*see* DIVIDEND TAX).

income tax code A code number issued by HM Revenue and Customs that takes account of the *personal allowance available to the taxpayer together with any other additional allowances to which he or she is entitled, e.g. age allowance. The code is used by the employer through the *PAYE scheme to calculate the taxable pay using tables supplied by the Revenue (now usually in the form of computer software). The income tax code can also be used to tax *benefits in kind, such as company cars, by reducing the code number and so collecting more tax each tax week or month. The code provides a means of ensuring that the tax due for the *fiscal year is deducted from the employee's earnings in equal weekly or monthly amounts.

income tax month *See* TAX MONTH.

income tax year *See* FISCAL YEAR.

income velocity of circulation *See* VELOCITY OF CIRCULATION.

incompatibility The inability of one computer to handle data and programs produced for a different type of computer.

inconvertible currency A currency that cannot be legally converted into other currencies. It is often the case that currencies are inconvertible for certain purposes, such as overseas investment. Currencies are most likely to be inconvertible where the underlying economy is weak or underdeveloped.

inconvertible paper money Paper money that cannot be converted into gold. Most paper money now falls into this category, although until 1931, in the UK, the Bank of England had an obligation to supply any holder of a bank note with the appropriate quantity of gold.

incorporated company *See* COMPANY.

Incorporated Society of British Advertisers Ltd (ISBA) A society founded in 1900 as the Advertisers Protection Society. It is open to any advertising company and is concerned with all matters relating to advertising, including *direct marketing, *public relations, and sponsorship.

Incoterms A glossary of terms used in international trade, published by the *International Chamber of Commerce (ICC) in Paris. It gives precise definitions of such terms as *Ex Works (EXW), *Free On Board (FOB), and *Cost and Freight (CFR) to eliminate misunderstandings between buyers and sellers in different countries. The latest version, Incoterms 2010, is available in 31 languages.

(((⊕))) SEE WEB LINKS

• A short guide to Incoterms from the ICC website

increasing capital An increase in the number or value of the shares in a company to augment its authorized *share capital. If the *articles of association of the company do not permit this to be done (with the agreement of the members), the articles will need to be changed. A company cannot increase its share capital unless authorized to do so by its articles of association.

incremental analysis See DIFFERENTIAL ANALYSIS.

incremental cost of capital The overall cost of raising extra finance. For example, if extra debt is incurred, this increases the risk to equity and debt funders, who will in turn demand a higher rate of return on their investment. The concept is also applied to funding raised to implement specific decisions, and should reflect the risks involved in the activity. See COST OF CAPITAL.

indemnity 1. An agreement by one party to make good the losses suffered by another, usually by payment of money, repair, replacement, or reinstatement. This is the function of *indemnity insurance. **2.** An undertaking by a bank's client, who has lost a document (such as a share certificate or bill of lading), that the bank will be held harmless against any consequences of the document's absence if it proceeds to service the documents that have not been mislaid. The bank usually requires a *letter of indemnity to make sure that it suffers no loss.

indemnity insurance Any insurance designed to compensate a policyholder for a loss suffered, by the payment of money, repair, replacement, or reinstatement. In every case the policyholder is entitled to be put back in the same financial position as he or she was immediately before the event insured against occurred. There must be no element of profit to the policyholder nor any element of loss. Most—but not all—insurance policies are *indemnity contracts. For example, personal accident and life-assurance policies are not contracts of indemnity as it is impossible to calculate the value of a lost life or limb (as the value of a car or other property can be calculated).

indenture 1. A *deed, especially one creating or transferring an estate in land. It derives its name from the former practice of writing the two parts of a two-part deed on one piece of parchment and separating the two parts by an irregular wavy line. The two parts of the indenture were known to belong together if the indented edges fitted together. A deed with a straight edge was known as a *deed poll. **2.** A document establishing the terms and conditions of a securities issue. **3.** See APPRENTICE.

Independent Commission on Banking A commission set up by the UK government in 2010 under the chairmanship of Sir John Vickers: its report (the **Vickers Report**) recommended the *ring-fencing of mass-market retail banking to insulate it from the risks involved in wholesale and *investment banking by the same institutions. Legislation has since been proposed to enforce the separation of retail from investment banking in the UK, with banks being given a deadline of 2019 to comply. The commission's other recommendations, which have been largely adopted by government, include higher capital ratios and measures to encourage greater competition.

independent demand The situation in which the demand for a product is independent of the production process, i.e. it is subject to market forces and therefore demand has to be forecast. When a car manufacturer produces a car, the number of wheels required is known before each unit can be sent out of the factory. However, the manufacturer does not know how many transmissions will fail, or whether individuals will buy their replacements from other suppliers. They cannot therefore predict accurately how many spares to produce. *Compare* DEPENDENT DEMAND.

independent financial adviser (IFA) A person or firm defined under the *Financial Services Act 1986 as an adviser on pensions, investments, or life assurance who is not committed to the products of any company or organization. Such a person or firm is now licensed to operate by the *Financial Conduct Authority. With no loyalties except to the customer, the IFA is bound legally to give 'best advice' on products from the whole of the market. This distinguishes the IFA from both a **tied adviser**, who advises on products from a single provider, and a **multi-tied adviser**, who is committed to a selection of providers. New rules introduced at the end of 2012 state that independent financial advisers selling investment products (including pensions, life policies, and unit trusts) must now charge an upfront fee for their advice rather than taking payment in the form of commission. This does not apply to mortgages or insurance products. *See also* POLARIZATION.

independent intermediary A person who acts as a representative of a prospective policyholder in the arrangement of an insurance or assurance policy. In *life assurance and *pensions it is a person who represents more than one insurer and is legally bound to offer advice to clients on the type of assurance or investment contracts best suited to their needs. In general insurance the independent intermediary can represent more than six insurers and is responsible for advising clients on policies that best suit their needs. They must,

themselves, have *professional indemnity insurance to cover any errors that they may make. Although, in both cases, intermediaries are the servants of the policyholder (and the insurer is therefore not responsible for their errors), they are paid by the insurer in the form of a commission, being an agreed percentage of the first or renewal premium paid by the policyholder.

independent retailer A small *retailer, generally owning between one and nine shops. They are now less important than *multiple shops in many areas of retailing.

indexation 1. The policy of connecting such economic variables as wages, taxes, social-security payments, annuities, or pensions to rises in the general price level. This policy is often advocated by economists in the belief that it mitigates the effects of *inflation. In practice, complete indexation is rarely possible, so that inflation usually leaves somebody worse off (e.g. lenders, savers) and somebody better off (borrowers). *See* RETAIL PRICE INDEX. **2.** The practice of adjusting the *chargeable gain from the sale of an asset to take account of inflation over the period of ownership of the asset. In the UK *corporation tax system an indexation factor derived from the rise in the *Retail Price Index during the period of ownership is applied to the cost, or 31 March 1982 value, of an asset. The indexed cost or value is then deducted from the proceeds of sale on disposal of the asset, in order to establish the chargeable gain. Until April 1998 indexation was also applied to gains chargeable to *capital gains tax. In the case of assets acquired before that date and disposed of before April 2008, the indexation allowance was calculated to 5 April 1998 and this figure was used to calculate the chargeable gain.

indexed security 1. A *security that has its coupon payment or redemption value adjusted for inflation. **2.** A security in which the coupon or the principal is related to the performance of a financial index.

index futures A *financial futures contract on a financial index. On the FTSE 100

Index (*see* FTSE INDEXES) the trading unit is £10 per index point; thus if a futures contract is purchased when the index stands at 2,400, say, the buyer is covering an equivalent purchase of equities of £24,000. If the index rises 100 points the purchaser can sell a matching futures contract at this level, making a profit of £1,000. *See also* PORTFOLIO INSURANCE.

index-linked gilts *See* GILT-EDGED SECURITY; INDEXATION.

index-linked savings certificates *See* INDEXATION; NATIONAL SAVINGS.

index number A number used to represent the changes in a set of values between a *base year and the present. If the index reflects fluctuations in a single variable, such as the price of a commodity, the index number can be calculated using the formula:

$$100(p_n/p_0),$$

where p_0 represents the price in the base year and p_n represents the price in the current year. In practice many indices reflect variations in a combination of variables, such as the raw materials required to manufacture a product. In this situation it is necessary to produce an index that weights the important variables, e.g. labour costs. These are known as **weighted aggregate indices**. If both costs and quantities have varied over a period, it is further necessary to find a way of using the same quantities for the numerator and denominator of the index. When the calculation uses base-year quantities as the fixed point, the resultant index is a **base-weighted** (or **Laspeyres'**) **index**, i.e.:

100(total cost of base year quantities at current prices/total cost of base year quantities at base year prices),

or

$$100(\Sigma\, p_n q_0/\Sigma\, p_0 q_0),$$

where p represents the price and q represents the quantity. When the calculation uses current year quantities, it is known as

a **current-weighted** (or **Paasche's**) **index**, i.e.:

100(total cost of current quantities at current prices/total cost of base year quantities at current prices),

or

$$100(\Sigma p_n q_n/\Sigma p_0 q_n).$$

Index of Production A UK index produced each month by the *Office for National Statistics to show changes in the volume of production of the main British industries and of the economy as a whole.

index tracking Setting up a *portfolio or investment product in such a way that it should provide the same returns as a particular market index. An **index fund** or **tracker fund** is one that has been weighted in the same proportions as a leading financial index.

indication of interest A mechanism whereby investors give indications of their possible reactions to the pricing of new share issues. This information is then used in establishing the *issue price.

indicative prices On a financial market, prices quoted as indicators of the likely prices at which market makers or dealers will trade. They are not explicit commitments to deal at those prices.

indicator A measurable variable that gives information regarding performance or prospects. Examples of macroeconomic indicators are price, money supply, income, imports, and exports. Most organizations will use a range of financial and other indicators to assess the performance of individuals, departments, or the company as a whole. *See* KEY PERFORMANCE INDICATORS; PERFORMANCE MEASUREMENT.

indirect costs (indirect expenses) Expenses that cannot be traced directly to a *product or *cost unit and are therefore *overheads (*compare* DIRECT COSTS). Some indirect product costs may, however, be regarded as *cost centre direct costs; the indirect cost centre costs are usually those costs requiring apportionment to cost centres in an *absorption costing system.

indirect discrimination *See* DISCRIMINATION.

indirect labour 1. Employees of a contractor who carry out work for another organization. This organization employs the contractor to supply the labour for a particular task. For example, some councils use a contractor, and indirect labour, to collect refuse. **2.** The part of a workforce in an organization that does not directly produce goods or provide the service that the organization sells. Indirect labour includes office staff, cleaners, canteen workers, etc. *Compare* DIRECT LABOUR.

indirect materials Those materials that do not feature in the final product but are necessary to carry out the production, such as machine oil, cleaning materials, and consumable materials. *Compare* DIRECT MATERIALS.

indirect method The method used for a *cash-flow statement in which the operating profit is adjusted for non-cash charges and credits to reconcile it with the net cash flow from operating activities.

indirect quote The expression of an exchange rate in terms of the number of units of a foreign currency corresponding to a single unit of the domestic currency. For example, in the UK an indirect quote for the dollar might be $1.8 = £1. *Compare* DIRECT QUOTE.

indirect shareholder *See* NOMINEE SHAREHOLDING.

indirect taxation Taxation that is intended to be borne by persons or organizations other than those who pay the tax (*compare* DIRECT TAXATION). The principal indirect tax in the UK is VAT, which is paid by traders as goods or services enter into the chain of production, but which is ultimately borne by the consumer of the goods or services. One of the advantages of indirect taxes is that they can be collected from comparatively few sources while their economic effects can be widespread.

individual marketing Tailoring products and marketing programmes to the needs and preferences of individual customers.

individual network value The value to a specific individual of belonging to and using a network.

individual retirement account (IRA) A US pension plan that allows annual sums to be set aside from earnings free of tax and accumulated in a fund, which pays interest. Basic-rate tax is payable once the saver starts to withdraw from the account, which must be done no later than the participant's 70th birthday. The concession is not available to employees in a company-pension scheme or profit-sharing scheme.

Individual Savings Account (ISA) A savings portfolio for small investors introduced in the UK in 1999, replacing personal equity plans (PEPs) and Tax Exempt Special Savings Accounts (TESSAs). Under current rules ISAs entitle individuals to save up to £15,240 per year free of tax in the form of cash, stocks and shares, or any combination of the two. The former restriction on the amount that could be saved in cash was abolished from July 2014. ISAs can be cashed in at any time without loss of the tax relief, which includes exemption from personal income tax and capital gains tax. In 2011 the government introduced **Junior ISAs**, which currently entitle individuals born on or after 3 January 2011 to invest up to £4,080 per year; money cannot normally be withdrawn until the holder is 18. **Help to Buy ISAs**, which were introduced in 2015, are for those saving for the deposit on a house; for each £200 saved, the government will add an extra £50 (to a maximum of £3,000 added). *See also* ISA MORTGAGE.

individual voluntary arrangement *See* VOLUNTARY ARRANGEMENT.

indorsement *See* ENDORSEMENT.

industrial action Any form of coordinated action in an **industrial dispute** by employees, with or without the support of a trade union, that seeks to force employers to agree to their demands relating to wages, terms of employment, working conditions, etc. It may take the form of a *go slow, *overtime ban, *work-to-rule, *sit-down strike, or *strike.

industrial and organizational psychology (industrial psychology; organizational psychology) The application of psychological concepts to the issues and problems that arise in business, industry, and other organizational settings. An understanding of individual and group psychology is particularly relevant to such areas as *motivation, decision making, leadership (*see* LEADERSHIP THEORIES), team work, *human-resource management, and *personnel selection.

industrial bank 1. A relatively small *finance house that specializes in *hire purchase, obtaining its own funds by accepting long-term deposits, largely from the general public. **2.** A US bank that specializes in industrial leasing.

industrial buyer behaviour *See* BUSINESS BUYER BEHAVIOUR.

industrial democracy Any system in which workers participate in the management of an organization or in sharing its profits. *Participative decision making can improve *industrial relations and add to workers' *job satisfaction and *motivation. Various schemes have been tried, including worker directors on the boards of some nationalized industries, workers' councils, and *profit-sharing schemes.

industrial disability benefit Benefits paid by the UK Department for Work and Pensions to compensate for disablement resulting from an industrial accident or from certain diseases arising from the nature of a person's employment. A weekly payment is made on a scale of disablement ranging from 14% to 100%. No benefit is paid for less than 14% disablement, except in the case of certain respiratory diseases. Claimants have to submit to a medical examination. The payment is made if the claimant is still suffering disability 15 weeks

or more after the accident or onset of the disease.

industrial dispute *See* INDUSTRIAL ACTION; TRADE DISPUTE.

industrial engineering The application of *work study techniques. It was traditionally regarded as a specialist function within organizations, with its own professional bodies. Increasingly, it is being taught as techniques to operations managers in organizations that take the more holistic approach associated with *total quality management.

industrial espionage Spying on a competitor to obtain *trade secrets by dishonest means. The information sought often refers to the development of new products, innovative manufacturing techniques, commissioned market surveys, forthcoming advertising campaigns, research plans, etc. The means used include a wide range of telephone- and computer-tapping devices, infiltration of the competitor's workforce, etc.

industrial estate *See* TRADING ESTATE.

industrial life assurance (home service assurance) A type of life-assurance policy, usually for a modest amount, the premiums for which were collected on a regular basis by an agent of the assurance company, who called at the policyholder's home. Records of the premium payments were kept in a book, which had to be produced to make a claim. This type of assurance began in industrial areas (hence its name), where small weekly policies were purchased to help pay the funeral expenses of the policyholder. The company agent was known in certain areas as a tally man. This type of insurance is now virtually obsolete, owing to its high costs and low revenues.

industrial marketing research (business marketing research) Any form of *marketing research undertaken among organizations that buy and add value to products and services but are not the final consumers. *Compare* CONSUMER RESEARCH.

industrial medicine The health care provided by employers for their employees. Apart from the provision of first aid and nursing care in larger organizations, its main aims are prophylactic: the prevention of accidents by providing adequate guards for machinery, the prevention of disease by controlling noxious fumes, dusts, etc., and the prevention of stress by providing the best possible working environment. In addition, regular check-ups are often provided to monitor the health of members of staff.

industrial organization economics An approach to *microeconomics that focuses on the *strategic behaviour of firms in a state of imperfect competition. In particular, it explores the ways in which different market forms (e.g. *monopolistic competition, *oligopoly, *monopoly) demand different competitive strategies in such areas as production, pricing, marketing and advertising, and investment. The role of government regulation is also analysed. Although highly theoretical in many respects, the field has direct applications in *strategic management and government competition policy. In recent decades it has been much influenced by *game theory and *behavioural finance. *See also* STRUCTURE–CONDUCT–PERFORMANCE MODEL.

industrial product A product bought by individuals and organizations for further processing or for use in conducting a business.

industrial psychology *See* INDUSTRIAL AND ORGANIZATIONAL PSYCHOLOGY.

industrial relations The relationship between the management of an organization and its workforce. If industrial relations are good, the whole workforce will be well motivated to work hard for the benefit of the organization and its customers. The job satisfaction in such an environment will itself provide some of the rewards for achieving good industrial relations. If the industrial relations are bad, both management and workers will find the workplace an uncongenial environment, causing discontent, poor motivation, and a marked tendency to take self-destructive *industrial action.

industrial tribunal *See* EMPLOYMENT TRIBUNAL.

industrial union *See* TRADE UNION.

industry 1. An organized activity in which *capital and labour are utilized to produce *goods. **2.** The sector of an economy that is concerned with manufacture. **3.** A group of firms that offer a product or class of products that are close substitutes for each other. The set of all sellers of a product or service, e.g. the car industry or the steel industry.

industry life cycle An analysis of business sectors that aims to characterize particular industries in terms of the stage they have reached in their natural rise and fall; the usual purpose is to clarify investment decisions. An industry life cycle is normally divided into four stages: the emergence of a new industry at a time of rapid change; its growth; its maturity, at which point the market is saturated; and finally its decline.

industry structure analysis The analysis of a particular industry in terms of the opportunities and threats presented to a firm by the prevailing *microenvironment. This can be used: (i) to appraise the attractiveness of the industry to investors or new entrants; and (ii) to devise competitive strategies appropriate to the industry in question. The standard tool for such an analysis is *Porter's Five Forces, which focuses on competition between existing firms, *barriers to entry, pressure from substitute products or services, the bargaining power of customers, and the bargaining power of suppliers.

inertia selling A form of selling in which unrequested goods are sent to a potential customer on a sale-or-return basis. This method is especially prevalent with book and CD clubs.

infant industry A new industry that may merit some protection against foreign competition in the short term. The argument in favour of providing protection, say in the form of a tariff on imported competitors' goods, is that it would provide a period during which the new industry could streamline its process and make the necessary economies in order for it to become truly competitive with all market producers.

infinite capacity loading *Loading based only on the due dates for deliveries, taking no notice of whether capacity is available. This parameter encourages a critical examination of the options available for expanding capacity, e.g. overtime, subcontracting. *Compare* FINITE CAPACITY LOADING.

inflation A general increase in prices in an economy and consequent fall in the purchasing value of money. *See also* CORE INFLATION; HYPERINFLATION; STAGFLATION.

inflation accounting Any method of accounting that, unlike *historical-cost accounting, attempts to take account of the fact that a monetary unit (e.g. the pound sterling) does not have a constant value; because of the effects of inflation, successive accounts expressed in that unit do not necessarily give a fair view of the trend of profits. The principal methods of dealing with inflation have been *current-cost accounting and *current purchasing power accounting.

inflationary bias The bias towards inflationary measures that is sometimes held to characterize any *monetary policy conducted according to the discretion of the policy-making body, as opposed to one governed by fixed pre-announced rules. Most obviously, where monetary policy is set by government a resolve to maintain price stability may be compromised by short-term electoral pressures, such as a desire to increase consumer spending or reduce unemployment. The wish to eliminate inflationary bias has been a major factor in the recent tendency for government to cede responsibility for monetary policy to independent central banks. However, some theorists maintain that the policies of the central bank will still have inflationary bias if they are not constrained by mechanical rules.

inflationary gap The difference between the total spending in an economy (both private and public) and the total spending that would be needed to maintain full employment in a given time period.

inflation targeting A policy in which the government or central bank announces a target rate for inflation in the medium term, as measured by a specified index, and then uses changes in interest rates or other tools of *monetary policy in an attempt to achieve this rate. The policy was pioneered in New Zealand from 1990 and has now been adopted by over 50 countries including the UK (where the target rate is currently 2%). In the USA the Federal Reserve operates a somewhat less strict regime in which a target range for inflation is announced.

influencer *See* CONSUMER BUYING BEHAVIOUR; DECISION-MAKING UNIT.

infomediary An *intermediary business whose main source of revenue is obtained from capturing consumer information and developing detailed profiles of individual customers for use by third parties.

infomercial A television commercial, usually 30 minutes long, that has the appearance of being a programme. The product advertised is repeatedly demonstrated, together with a telephone number to enable the viewer to order. Infomercials are widely used in the USA.

infopreneurial industry The manufacture and sale of electronic office and factory equipment for the distribution of information. *See* INFORMATION TECHNOLOGY.

information acceleration (IA) A *virtual reality system designed to place a consumer in a virtual buying environment similar to one in which he or she normally makes purchase decisions. It is used to measure the intentions, perceptions, and preferences of consumers.

Information and Consultation Regulations A set of UK government regulations, introduced in 2004, that require all businesses with more than 50 employees to notify and consult with their workforce about certain plans and decisions affecting the business. Issues that must be dealt with in this way include the possible sale of the business, significant redundancies, or changes to pension schemes.

information flow management *See* SUPPLY-CHAIN MANAGEMENT.

information goods Products with a high information content. Such products can be digitized and delivered online.

information practice statement A discrete statement that describes a particular use or practice regarding consumers' personal information and/or a choice offered to consumers about their personal information.

information search *See* CONSUMER BUYING BEHAVIOUR.

information technology (IT) The use of computers and other electronic means to process and distribute information. Information can be transferred between computers using cables, satellite links, or telephone lines and the cellular network (mobile phones). Networks of connected computers can be used to send *e-mail, to interrogate remote *databases using the *Internet, and to transmit sound, pictures, and moving images. These systems also enable *electronic transfer of funds between banks, as well as *home banking, automated screen trading in stocks and shares, and the buying of goods and services online. In doing so, they have played a major role in the *globalization of financial and other markets since the 1980s. The entertainment industry has seen a similar convergence of the broadcast media with computers and telecommunications.

informative advertising Advertising used to inform consumers about a new product or feature in order to build primary demand.

infrastructure The goods and services, usually requiring substantial investment, considered essential to the proper functioning of an economy. For example, roads, railways, sewerage, and electricity supply constitute essential elements of a community's infrastructure. Since the infrastructure benefits the whole of an economy, it is often argued that it should be funded, partly if not wholly, by the government by means of taxation.

inherent vice A defect or weakness of an item, especially of a cargo, that causes it to suffer some form of damage or destruction without the intervention of an outside cause. For example, certain substances, such as jute, when shipped in bales, can warm up spontaneously, causing damage to the fibre. Damage by this cause is excluded from most cargo insurance policies as an *excepted peril.

inheritance tax (IHT) A tax introduced in the Budget of 1986. Inheritance tax is chargeable on the death of an individual domiciled in the UK on all property, wherever it is situated. A non-UK domiciled individual is charged on death to inheritance tax on all UK property. In order to prevent too obvious avoidance, inheritance tax is also charged retrospectively on certain lifetime gifts. Some classes of gifts, such as those between husbands and wives, are totally exempt (*see* EXEMPT TRANSFERS). Others are liable to tax if the transferor should die within seven years of making the gift; these are known as *potentially exempt transfers. The threshold at which inheritance tax takes effect is currently (2015–16) £325,000. Since April 2008 it has been possible to transfer the allowance of the first spouse or civil partner to die to the surviving partner, effectively raising the current threshold to £650,000. From April 2017 there will be an additional allowance for a main family home, the intention being to raise the total threshold to £500,000 (for an individual) by 2020. No tax is payable if the cumulative total of all *chargeable transfers is less than the threshold. Above this amount, tax is payable on the excess at a single rate of 40%.

( ) SEE WEB LINKS

• A guide to inheritance tax from the Gov.uk website

initial charge The charge paid to the managers of a *unit trust by an investor when units are first purchased. For most trusts the initial charge ranges between 5% and 6%, as laid down in the trust deed. *Money-market unit trusts and *exempt unit trusts have lower initial charges and in some cases no initial charge.

initial public offering (IPO) The first sale of shares by a *private limited company to the public. It can be difficult to set an *issue price that will be low enough to attract sufficient investors to take up the whole issue and yet high enough to give the company the maximum capital. An IPO is underpriced if the issue price is less than the market price and overpriced if the issue price is greater than the market price. *See* FLOTATION; OFFER FOR SALE; PUBLIC ISSUE.

initial yield The gross initial annual income from an asset divided by the initial cost of that asset. *Compare* GROSS REDEMPTION YIELD.

initiator 1. *See* TASK ROLES. **2.** *See* CONSUMER BUYING BEHAVIOUR.

injunction An order by a court that a person shall do, or refrain from doing, a particular act. This is an equitable remedy that may be granted by the court wherever 'just and convenient'. An **interim injunction**, lasting only until the main action is heard, may be granted on the application of one party without the other being present if there is great urgency. **Prohibitory injunctions** forbid the doing of a particular act; **mandatory injunctions** order a person to do some act. Failure to obey an injunction is contempt of court and punishable by a fine or imprisonment.

inland bill A *bill of exchange that is both drawn and payable in the UK. Any other bill is classed as a **foreign bill**.

innominate terms (intermediate terms) Terms of a *contract that cannot be classified as a *condition or *warranty. The parties to a contract may label the terms of the contract as either conditions or warranties and those labels will usually be respected by the courts provided that the result is reasonable. Similarly, certain terms have traditionally been treated as conditions or warranties even though they have not been labelled as such (for example, time clauses in mercantile contracts are to be treated as conditions). Innominate terms are those that will not fit the above categories. The remedy for breach of an innominate term will depend on whether or not the breach is of a fundamental nature, i.e. that the injured party has been deprived of substantially the whole of the benefit of the contract. If the injured party has been so deprived, he or she will be entitled to treat the contract as repudiated and claim damages. If not, the injured party will be entitled to damages only. *See also* BREACH OF CONTRACT.

innovation Any new approach to designing, producing, or marketing goods or services that creates value and gives the innovating company an advantage over competitors. In business literature, innovation is often distinguished from invention: while the latter involves coming up with a new idea or insight, and is usually the product of individual ingenuity, innovation involves bringing a new idea into practical effect, and is more often achieved within the organization. The restructuring of an organization or its processes to achieve significant improvements can be an important form of innovation. In economic theory, innovation is seen as a driver of *Schumpeterian growth (*see also* CREATIVE DESTRUCTION) and is recognized as a key concept in the *knowledge triangle. *See* DISCONTINUOUS INNOVATION; DYNAMICALLY CONTINUOUS INNOVATION.

innovative marketing A principle of enlightened marketing that requires a company to seek real improvements in its products and its marketing.

innovators *See* ADOPTION OF INNOVATIONS.

input substitution The substitution of a cheaper raw material input for other inputs that have stayed the same price or become more expensive.

input tax *Value added tax paid by a *taxable person on purchasing goods or services from a VAT-registered trader. The input tax, excluding irrecoverable input VAT, is set against the *output tax in order to establish the amount of VAT to be paid to the tax authorities.

inquiry test *See* ENQUIRY TEST.

inscribed stock (registered stock) Shares in loan stock, for which the names of the holders are kept in a register rather than by the issue of a certificate of ownership. On a transfer, a new name has to be registered, which makes them cumbersome and unpopular in practice.

inside director In the USA, an employee of a company who has been appointed to the board of directors.

insider dealing (insider trading) Dealing in company securities with a view to making a profit or avoiding a loss while in possession of price-sensitive information that is not generally known (**insider information**). Under the UK Companies Securities (Insider Dealing) Act 1985 those who are or have been connected with a company (e.g. the directors, the company secretary, employees, and professional advisers) are prohibited from such dealing on or, in certain circumstances, off the stock exchange if they acquired the information by virtue of their connection and in confidence. The prohibition extends to certain unconnected persons to whom the information has been conveyed. Similar laws on insider dealing now operate in most developed countries.

insolvency The inability to pay one's debts when they fall due. In the case of individuals this may lead to *bankruptcy and in the case of companies to *liquidation. In both of these cases the normal procedure is for a specialist, a trustee in bankruptcy or a liquidator, to be appointed to gather and dispose of the assets of the insolvent and to pay the creditors. Insolvency does not always lead to bankruptcy and liquidation, although it often does. An insolvent person may have valuable assets that are not immediately realizable.

insolvency practitioner A person authorized to undertake insolvency administration as a *liquidator, provisional liquidator, *administrator, *administrative receiver, or nominee or supervisor under a *voluntary arrangement. Insolvency practitioners must be members of an approved professional body, such as the **Insolvency Practitioners Association** or the Institute of Chartered Accountants.

insolvency risk 1. The *risk that a borrower may be unable to repay a debt. **2.** The risk that a *counterparty may be unable to honour a contract owing to insolvency. *See* COUNTERPARTY RISK.

Insolvency Service An executive agency of the *Department for Business, Innovation and Skills that investigates the affairs of bankrupts and of firms that have been liquidated by the court (*see* COMPULSORY LIQUIDATION). It can also act as a *liquidator and supervise individual *voluntary arrangements as well as performing various other administrative functions. *See* BANKRUPTCY.

inspection and investigation of a company An inquiry into the running of a company made by inspectors appointed by the Department for Business, Innovation and Skills. Such an inquiry may be held to supply company members with information or to investigate fraud, unfair prejudice, nominee shareholdings, or *insider dealing. The inspectors' report is usually published.

inspector general In the USA, the head of one of the 73 federal offices that perform audit and investigative activities on federal agencies, making periodic reports to Congress.

Inspector of Taxes A civil servant responsible to HM *Revenue and Customs for issuing tax returns and assessments, the conduct of appeals, and agreeing tax liabilities with taxpayers.

instalment One of a series of payments, especially when buying goods on *hire purchase, settling a debt, or buying a new issue of shares.

instalment sale The USA equivalent of a UK retail sale by hire purchase.

instant Of the current month. In commercial English it used to be common to refer to a date as, for example, the 5th instant, or more usually 5th inst., meaning the 5th of the current month. **Ultimo** refers to the previous month; for example, the 5th ultimo, or more usually the 5th ult., means the 5th of last month. **Proximo** refers to the next month; the 5th proximo, or 5th prox., means the 5th of next month.

Institute and Faculty of Actuaries The professional body to which UK *actuaries belong. It was formed in 2010 by a merger of the **Institute of Actuaries**, based in London, and the Edinburgh-based **Faculty of Actuaries**. The roots of the profession go back to 1756, when a Fellow of the Royal Society, James Dodson, produced the first table of premiums for life assurance, having been turned down for an assurance policy on the grounds of his age.

Institute cargo clauses Clauses, originally issued by the Institute of London Underwriters in the early 1980s, that are added to standard *marine insurance policies for cargo to widen or restrict the cover given. Each clause has a wording agreed by a committee of insurance companies and *Lloyd's underwriters. By attaching particular clauses to the policy the insurers are able to create an individual policy to suit the clients' requirements.

Institute for Fiscal Studies An independent UK economic research institute that specializes in the microeconomic analysis of public finances and tax policy. The politically impartial think-tank produces regular analyses of the UK Budget and studies the impact of government policies in broader areas, such as welfare, productivity, and inequality.

Institute of Chartered Accountants Any of the three professional accountancy bodies in the UK, the **Institute of Chartered Accountants in England and Wales** (ICAEW), the **Institute of Chartered Accountants of Scotland** (ICAS), and the **Institute of Chartered Accountants in Ireland** (ICAI). The institutes are separate but recognize similar codes of practice. The largest is the England and Wales institute, with some 138,000 members, who are identified by the letters ACA or FCA (as are members of the Ireland institute; in Scotland members use the letters CA). The institutes ensure high standards of education and training in accountancy, provide qualification by examination, and supervise professional conduct in the service of clients and of the public. They are members of the Consultative Committee of Accountancy Bodies, whose Accounting Standards Committee is responsible for drafting accounting standards. *See also* CHARTERED ACCOUNTANT.

SEE WEB LINKS

- Website of the Institute of Chartered Accountants in England and Wales: provides technical information, advice on training and careers, and help in finding a chartered accountant

Institute of Chartered Secretaries and Administrators (ICSA) A professional body for company secretaries and administrators; although based in the UK, it now operates in some 70 countries worldwide. Founded in 1891 and granted a Royal Charter in 1902, the institute represents members' interests to government bodies on such matters as company law; publishes journals, reports, pamphlets, and papers;

promotes the professional standing of members; and conducts the education and examination of members.

Institute of Directors (IoD)
A non-political organization for directors of companies, founded in London in 1903. There are approximately 40,000 members in the UK and more than 65,000 worldwide. Membership has increased more than 50% since the 1990s and includes directors from many sectors of the economy. The Institute encourages members to improve their standards of performance and represents the views of business leaders to government and other organizations. Members receive a variety of benefits including information, advice, training, conferences, and publications.

SEE WEB LINKS
- Website of the Institute of Directors

Institute of Insurance Brokers (IIB)
The UK professional association for insurance broking firms, established in 1987. It represents the views of its members to the *Financial Conduct Authority, parliament, and other policy makers.

Institute of Management Accountants (IMA)
A US-based international accountancy body established in 1919 as the National Association of Cost Accountants. There are now more than 65,000 members worldwide.

Institute of Management Services (IMS)
An institution, founded in 1941, that is the professional and qualifying body for people in *management services. Its main aims are to create and maintain professional standards for the practice of management services; to provide a system of qualifying examinations; and to encourage research and development in management services.

SEE WEB LINKS
- Website of the IMS: explains many tools and techniques used in management services

Institute of Practitioners in Advertising (IPA)
The professional organization,

established in 1917, for UK advertising agencies. Its members handle some 95% of all UK advertising.

Institute of Sales Promotion (ISP)
The professional organization for UK sales-promotion agencies. Its aims are to raise awareness of the benefits of sales promotion, to encourage excellence within the industry, and to promote responsible self-regulation. The Institute was formed in 1978, following the reorganization of the Sales Promotion Executives Association, itself founded in 1969.

institutional advertisement
An advertisement designed to promote the image of an organization, to stimulate *generic demand for a product (e.g. coffee), or to build goodwill for an industry.

institutional broker
A securities firm or broker dealing with financial institutions.

institutional investor (institution)
A large organization, such as an insurance company, unit trust, bank, trade union, or a pension fund of a large company, that has substantial sums of money to invest on a stock exchange, usually in the UK, in both gilts and equities. Institutions usually employ their own investment analysts and advisors; they are usually able to influence stock exchange sentiment more profoundly than private investors and their policies can often affect share prices. Because institutions can build up significant holdings in companies, they can also influence company policy, usually by making their opinions known at shareholders' meetings, especially during *takeover-bid negotiations.

insurable interest
The legal right to enter into an insurance contract. A person is said to have an insurable interest if the event insured against could cause that person a financial loss. For example, anyone may insure their own property as they would incur a loss if an item was lost, destroyed, or damaged. If no financial loss would occur, no insurance can be arranged. For example, a person cannot insure a next-door neighbour's property.

The limit of an insurable interest is the value of the item concerned, although there is no limit on the amount of life assurance a person can take out on his or her own life, or that of a spouse, because the financial effects of death cannot be accurately measured.

Insurable interest was made a condition of all insurance by the Life Assurance Act 1774. Without an insurable interest, an insured person is unable to enforce an insurance contract (or life-assurance contract) as it is the insurable interest that distinguishes insurance from a bet or wager.

insurable risk (static risk) The possibility of suffering some form of loss or damage that can be described sufficiently accurately for a calculation to be made of the probability of its happening, on the basis of past records. Fire, theft, accident, etc., are all insurable *risks because underwriters can assess the probability of having to pay out a claim and can therefore calculate a reasonable *premium. If the risk is met so infrequently that no way of calculating the probability of the event exists, no underwriter will insure against it and it is therefore an **uninsurable risk**.

insurance A legal contract in which an insurer promises to pay a specified amount to another party, the *insured, if a particular event (known as the peril), happens and the insured suffers a financial loss as a result. The insured's part of the contract is to promise to pay an amount of money, known as the *premium, either once or at regular intervals. In order for an insurance contract to be valid, the insured must have an *insurable interest. It is usual to use the word 'insurance' to cover events (such as a fire) that may or may not happen, whereas *assurance refers to an event (such as death) that must occur at some time (*see also* LIFE ASSURANCE). The main branches of insurance are: *accident insurance, *fire insurance, holiday and travel insurance, *household insurance, *liability insurance, *livestock and bloodstock insurance, loss-of-profit insurance (*see* BUSINESS-INTERRUPTION POLICY), *marine insurance, *motor insurance, *pluvial insurance, *private health insurance, and *property insurance. *See also* REINSURANCE.

insurance broker A person who offers advice on all insurance matters and arranges cover, on behalf of the client, with an *insurer. Insurance brokers act as intermediaries and their income comes from commission paid to them by insurers, usually in the form of an agreed percentage of the first premium or on subsequent premiums. Insurance brokers are regulated by the *Financial Services Authority. *See also* LLOYD's.

insurance policy A document that sets out the terms and conditions of an *insurance contract, stating the benefits payable and the *premium required. *See also* LIFE ASSURANCE.

insurance premium *See* INSURANCE; PREMIUM.

insured A person or company covered by an *insurance policy. In some policies that cover death, the alternative word *assured may be used for the person who receives the payment in the event of the *life assured's death.

insurer A person, company, syndicate, or other organization that underwrites an insurance risk.

intangible asset (invisible asset) An asset that can neither be seen nor touched. The most common of these are competencies, *goodwill, and *intellectual properties such as *patents, *trademarks, and copyrights. Goodwill is probably the most intangible and invisible of all assets as no document provides evidence of its existence and its commercial value is difficult to determine. However, it frequently does have very substantial value as the capitalized value of future profits, not attributable purely to the return on *tangible assets. While goodwill is called either an intangible asset or an invisible asset, such items as insurance policies and less tangible overseas investments are usually called invisible assets. Intangible assets are increasingly seen as the key to competitive advantage and the *market value of a firm (*see also* BOOK VALUE; INTELLECTUAL CAPITAL).

The accounting treatment for intangible assets has been a controversial topic. Under the Companies Act intangible assets is a main heading that should appear on the face of the balance sheet. The following subheadings are required but may be shown either on the face of the balance sheet or in the notes: *research and development costs; concessions, patents, licences, trademarks, and similar rights and assets; goodwill; payments on account. Accounting for intangible assets is now covered by Sections 18 and 19 of the Financial Reporting Standard Applicable in the UK and Republic of Ireland. The relevant *International Accounting Standards are IAS 22, Business Combinations; IAS 36, Impairment of Assets; and IAS 38, Intangible Assets.

integrated accounts A single set of accounting records containing both the financial accounts and the cost accounts of an organization in an integrated form (*see* FINANCIAL ACCOUNTING; MANAGEMENT ACCOUNTING). This avoids the necessity of reconciling separate financial and cost books and at the same time ensures that both records are based on the same data.

integrated logistics management A physical distribution concept that recognizes the need for a firm to integrate its logistics system with those of its suppliers and customers. The aim is to maximize the performance of the entire distribution system.

integrated marketing communications Marketing communications in which all the elements of *promotional mix are coordinated and systematically planned to be in harmony with each other.

integrated office system (IOS) A program for use on a personal computer or small multiuser business computer that combines some of the functions otherwise performed by a series of single-purpose programs. A typical mix of functions in an integrated office system might be *spreadsheet, word processor, *database management system, and graphics. The outputs of the various sections can usually be merged to form a final document containing pictorial, tabular, and textual material.

integration The combination of two or more companies under the same control for their mutual benefit, by reducing competition, saving costs by reducing overheads, capturing a larger market share, pooling resources, cooperating on research and development, enhancing competitive advantage, etc. In **horizontal** (or **lateral**) **integration** the businesses carry out the same stage in the *value chain or produce similar products or services; they are therefore competitors. In a monopoly, horizontal integration is complete, while in an oligopoly there is considerable horizontal integration. In **vertical integration** a company obtains control of its suppliers (sometimes called **backward integration**) or of the concerns that buy its products or services (**forward integration**). Conglomerate integration takes place between firms in different value chains.

integrative culture *See* ORGANIZATIONAL CULTURE.

intellectual capital A complex concept that includes human knowledge, information systems, brand names, and reputation. One popular definition is given by the equation:

intellectual capital = *human capital + structural capital + relationship capital.

Here **human capital** includes knowledge, competences, and the experience and expertise of staff, **structural capital** includes information systems and databases, and **relationship** (or **customer**) **capital** includes customer relationships, *brands, and trademarks.

In accounting, intellectual capital is often treated as being synonymous with *intangible assets and valued in the same way, that is, by calculating the difference between the *market value of a company and its *book value. Measuring the intellectual capital is important if one is buying or selling a company or comparing the performance of one company with another. In some companies the book value is only a small percentage of the market value. For example, in 2012 Apple had a market capitalization of over $500 billion with tangible assets valued at less than $50 billion. The intellectual capital of Apple was therefore valued at over $450 billion. Clearly, the balance sheet for Apple is not reporting the all-important intellectual capital of the company, which includes technology, patents, brands, and human knowledge.

intellectual property An *intangible asset, such as a copyright, *patent, *trademark, or design right. Intellectual property is an asset, and as such it can be bought, sold, licensed, or exchanged. Further, the intellectual property owner has the right to prevent the unauthorized use or sale of the property.

Examples of intellectual properties include inventions, literary and artistic works, names, images, designs used in commerce, and computer programs. *See also* ROYALTY.

Intellectual Property Office (IPO) The UK government agency that administers the Patent Acts, the Registered Designs Act, and the Trade Marks Act. It also deals with questions relating to the Copyright Acts and provides an information service about *patent specifications. The IPO was known as the **Patent Office** until 2007.

(((•))) SEE WEB LINKS
• Information on copyright, patents, trademarks, and registration of designs from the IPO area of the Gov.uk website

intelligent terminal A computer terminal that is able to process data without the help of the computer to which it is connected. An example is a point-of-sale terminal that adds up the cost of the items purchased and also informs the main stock computer that they are no longer in stock.

intensive distribution A distribution strategy aimed at obtaining the maximum number of outlets to stock a product at the wholesale or retail level. Such products as

sweets, chewing gum, disposable razors, soft drinks, and camera film are sold in numerous outlets (including supermarkets, newsagents, and petrol stations) to provide maximum brand exposure and consumer convenience.

interactive Denoting a computer system or application in which there is continuous two-way communication between the computer and its operator. The computer program prompts the operator when it needs information and stops running until the information is supplied. Interactive computer systems are also called **conversational systems**. *Compare* BATCH PROCESSING.

interactive banner advertisement A *banner advertisement that enables the user to enter information.

interactive design strategies *See* CONCURRENT ENGINEERING.

interactive engineering *See* CONCURRENT ENGINEERING.

interactive marketing Marketing by a service firm recognizing that perceived service quality depends heavily on the quality of buyer–seller interaction.

interbank market The wholesale *money market in which banks lend to and borrow from one another. The importance of the market is that it allows individual banks to adjust their liquidity positions quickly, covering shortages by borrowing from banks with surpluses. This reduces the need for each bank to hold large quantities of liquid assets, thus releasing funds for more profitable lending transactions. The **Inter Bank Offered Rate** (IBOR) is the rate of interest charged on interbank loans in a particular financial centre. *See* LONDON INTER BANK OFFERED RATE.

intercompany transactions (intragroup transactions) Transactions between the companies in a *group. These may be in the form of charges or the transfer of goods or services. It is important in the preparation of *consolidated financial statements that such transactions are eliminated or suitable adjustments made as they do not reflect transactions between the group and external parties. *See also* CONSOLIDATION.

Intercontinental Exchange (ICE) The world's leading electronic market for energy and soft commodities contracts. It was established in 2000 as a platform for over-the-counter energy trading and expanded into futures in 2001, when it acquired London's *International Petroleum Exchange (now *ICE Futures Europe). The ICE became a publicly traded company in 2005 and acquired the *New York Board of Trade (now *ICE Futures US) in 2007 and *NYSE Euronext in 2012. Its headquarters are in Atlanta, Georgia.

🌐 **SEE WEB LINKS**
• Website of the ICE

inter-dealer broker 1. A broker who acts as an intermediary between buyers and sellers in the *interbank market or bond market; he or she typically uses *voice broking to maintain constant contact with potential customers and to establish deals and prices. **2.** A specialized brokerage firm that acts in the same capacity. The leading such firm is the London-based ICAP.

interdict An *injunction in Scottish law.

interest 1. The charge made for borrowing a sum of money. The *interest rate is the charge made, expressed as a percentage of the total sum loaned, for a stated period of time (usually one year). Thus, a rate of interest of 15% per annum means that for every £100 borrowed for one year, the borrower has to pay a charge of £15, or a charge in proportion for longer or shorter periods. In **simple interest**, the charge is calculated on the sum loaned only, thus $I = Prt$, where I is the interest, P is the principal sum, r is the rate of interest, and t is the period. In **compound interest**, the charge is calculated on the sum loaned plus any interest that has accrued in previous periods. In this case $I = P\left[(1 + r)^n - 1\right]$, where n is the number of periods for which interest is separately calculated. Thus, if £500 is loaned for two years at a rate of 12%

per annum, compounded quarterly, the value of n will be $4 \times 2 = 8$ and the value of r will be $12/4 = 3\%$. Thus, $I = 500\left[(1.03)^8 - 1\right] =$ £133.38, whereas on a simple-interest basis it would be only £120. These calculations of interest apply equally to deposits that attract income in the form of interest.

In general, rates of interest depend on the money supply, the demand for loans, government policy, the risk of nonrepayment as assessed by the lender, the period of the loan, and relative levels of foreign-exchange rates into other currencies. **2.** A share of ownership. *See* CONTROLLING INTEREST; MINORITY INTEREST; PARTICIPATING INTEREST.

interest arbitrage Transactions between financial centres in foreign currencies that take advantage of differentials in interest rates between the two centres and the difference between the forward and spot exchange rates. In some circumstances it is possible to make a profit by borrowing money on domestic markets at fixed rates, buying a foreign currency, lending the foreign currency at fixed rates, and entering into a forward contract to buy domestic currency.

interest cover (fixed-charge–coverage ratio) A ratio showing the number of times interest charges are covered by earnings before interest and tax (*see* EBIT). For example, a company with interest charges of £12 million and earnings before interest and tax of £36 million would have its interest covered three times. The ratio is one way of analysing *gearing and reflects the vulnerability of a company to changes in interest rates or profit fluctuations. A highly geared company, which has a low interest cover, may find that an increase in the interest rate will mean that it has no earnings after interest charges with which to provide a dividend to shareholders.

interest factors An individual's personal interests and likes or dislikes, as revealed in answers to a standardized questionnaire or derived from his or her hobbies, leisure activities, etc. In *personnel selection and vocational guidance, interest factors are seen as revealing stable personality traits and therefore as predictors of successful performance in a particular job or type of job. **Interest tests**, such as the Strong Interest Inventory and the Kuder Occupational Interest Survey, require participants to express their preferences among a range of activities, characteristics, and values; their answers can then be compared with the patterns of answers obtained from individuals who have proved successful in a particular occupation.

interest-in-possession trust A type of fixed-interest *trust in which there is an entitlement to the income generated by the trust assets. The *beneficiaries of an interest-in-possession trust, the life tenants, are entitled to the income arising for a fixed period or until their death. The capital in the trust then passes absolutely to a recipient known as the remainderman.

Formerly, any lifetime transfer into an interest-in-possession trust was a *potentially exempt transfer for purposes of *inheritance tax; from March 2006, however, such transfers are no longer possible unless the trust is for the benefit of a disabled person. *Compare* DISCRETIONARY TRUST.

interest-only yield *See* YIELD.

interest rate The amount charged for a loan, usually expressed as a percentage of the sum borrowed. Conversely, the amount paid by a bank, building society, etc., to a depositor on funds deposited, again expressed as a percentage of the sum deposited. *See* ANNUAL PERCENTAGE RATE; BASE RATE; LONDON INTER BANK BID RATE; LONDON INTER BANK OFFERED RATE.

interest-rate cycle The notion that the movement of interest rates is cyclical and related to the *business cycle. Historically, the variable path of inflation has modified any cyclical pattern in rates.

interest-rate exposure *See* INTEREST-RATE RISK.

interest-rate futures A form of *financial futures that enables investors, portfolio

managers, borrowers, etc., to obtain protection against future movements in interest rates. Interest-rate futures also enable dealers to speculate on these movements. In the UK, interest-rate futures are dealt in on London's *LIFFE exchange (now Euronext.liffe), using contracts for three-month sterling, eurodollars, euros, etc., in the short term and long gilts, US Treasury bonds, euro bonds, etc., in the long term. For long gilts, for example, the standard contract is for £50,000 of nominal value and the *tick size is 0.01% of the nominal value. *See* HEDGE.

interest-rate guarantee An indemnity sold by a bank, or similar financial institution, that protects the purchaser against the effect of future movements in interest rates. It is similar to a *forward-rate agreement, but the terms are specified by the customer.

interest-rate margin 1. The difference between the interest rate at which banks lend and the rate they pay on deposits. It is likely to be a major indicator of a bank's profitability. **2.** The amount charged to borrowers over and above the *base rate. This margin is the bank's profit on the transaction but has to take account of risk of loss or default by the borrower.

interest-rate option A form of *option enabling traders and speculators to *hedge themselves against future changes in interest rates. It is an option to purchase a specific debt instrument.

interest-rate policy A policy in which governments or central banks set *interest rates in an attempt to influence the *money supply. Higher rates of interest will reduce the demand for money, giving a downward impetus to output, employment and prices. Lower interest rates will have the opposite effect. Responsibility for interest-rate policy was restored to the Bank of England by the UK government in 1997. *See* MONETARY POLICY.

interest-rate risk (interest-rate exposure) The *risk arising from changes in interest rates. In recent decades the different forms of interest-rate risk have been the subject of much analysis, monitoring, and scrutiny. In the 1980s, for example, the *savings and loan associations (S & L) in the USA faced a major crisis as a result of continuing to offer fixed-rate loans despite a steadily climbing interest rate; this meant that their interest revenues remained at a constant level while their interest costs rose. The main forms of interest-rate risk are: the risk that interest-rate changes will impact on the value of fixed-interest assets and liabilities; the risk of mismatches in terms of the repricing of interest on assets and liabilities (as illustrated by the S & L example); *prepayment risk, in which a borrower repays an obligation, such as a mortgage, early; the risk that reinvestment may take place at lower rates; and the risk that, as rates rise, repayments will take longer than expected. *See* GAP.

interest-rate swap A form of dealing between banks, security houses, and companies in which institutions exchange interest-rate payments on a notional capital value. *Swaps can be in the same currency or cross-currency (*see* CROSS-CURRENCY INTEREST-RATE SWAP). If a swap is in the same currency it will usually involve a fixed interest payment in exchange for a floating interest payment; a swap involving two different floating rates is called a *basis swap. *See also* RATE ANTICIPATION SWAP.

interest-sensitive Denoting an activity that is sensitive to changes in the general level of interest rates. For example, the demand for consumer goods usually bought on some form of *hire-purchase basis is interest-sensitive because they cost more as interest rates rise.

interim accounts *See* INTERIM FINANCIAL STATEMENTS.

interim dividend A *dividend paid during a *financial year.

interim financial statements (**interim accounts; interim report**) *Financial statements issued for a period of less than a financial year. Although there are provisions under the Companies Acts that refer to interim accounts in certain circumstances relating to the distribution of *dividends, there are no legal requirements obliging companies to produce interim accounts on a regular basis. However, *listed companies on the *London Stock Exchange are required to prepare a half-yearly report on their activities and *profit and loss during the first six months of each financial year. The interim financial statement must be either sent to the holders of the company's listed *securities or advertised in at least one national newspaper not later than four months after the end of the period to which it relates. A copy of the interim financial statements must also be sent to the Company Announcements Office and to the competent authority of each other state in which the company's shares are listed. The vast majority of companies choose to send the interim statement to shareholders with a brief announcement of the headline figures reported in the press. There is no requirement for the interim statements to be audited. Although the stock-exchange regulations require mainly profit information, there is a trend for the larger companies to also provide *balance sheet and *cash-flow statements. In the UK, the requirements only call for six-monthly financial statements, but some larger companies with interests in the USA follow the US practice of issuing reports quarterly.

intermarket spread swap Swapping securities in the hope of improving the spread between the yields of the securities.

intermediaries Firms in a distribution channel that help a company to find customers or make sales to them. Intermediaries include brokers, agents, dealers, wholesalers, and retailers that buy and resell goods.

intermediate-term *See* MEDIUM-TERM.

intermediate terms *See* INNOMINATE TERMS.

intermediation The activity of a bank, similar financial institution, broker, etc., in acting as an intermediary between the two parties to a transaction; the intermediary can accept all or part of the credit risk or the other commercial risks. *Compare* DISINTERMEDIATION.

intermodalism A method of using more than one form of transport in the delivery of goods. In the USA, for example, an increasing number of manufacturers and *shipping and forwarding agents are delivering goods by combining low-cost long-haul rail transport with the flexibility of road transport to the final destination.

internal audit An *audit that an organization carries out on its own behalf, normally to ensure that its own internal controls are operating satisfactorily. Whereas an external audit is almost always concerned with financial matters, this may not necessarily be the case with an internal audit; internal auditors may also concern themselves with such matters as the observation of the safety and health at work regulations or of the equal opportunities legislation. It may also be used to detect any theft or fraud (*see also* INTERNAL CONTROL).

internal business-process perspective *See* BALANCED SCORECARD.

internal control The measures an organization employs to ensure that opportunities for fraud or misfeasance are minimized. Examples range from requiring more than one signature on certain documents, security arrangements for stock-handling, division of tasks, keeping of *control accounts, use of special passwords, handling of computer files, etc. It is one of the principal concerns of an *internal audit to ensure that internal controls are working properly so that the external auditors can have faith in the accounts produced by the organization. Internal control should also reassure management of the integrity of its operations.

internal control system A system of controls, both financial and non-financial, set up by the management of a company to carry out the business of the company in an orderly and efficient manner. The system

should ensure that management policies are adhered to, assets are safeguarded, and the records of the company's activities are both complete and accurate. The individual components of an internal control system are the individual internal controls.

internal customer A unit, division, or individual employee who is the recipient of materials, products, information, or services from another unit in the same organization (the **internal supplier**). The concept encourages employees to treat their co-workers as though they were external customers or suppliers, thereby raising quality consciousness within the organization.

internal failure costs *See* COST OF QUALITY. *See also* ENVIRONMENTAL COSTS.

internal growth (organic growth) The means by which a business can grow using its own resources (*see* BUSINESS STRATEGY). A business will grow by increased *market penetration at the expense of its competitors, by *new product development, and by market development through seeking new applications and markets for existing products or services. All these means utilize a firm's *core competencies and while some may have a relatively short lead time (e.g. market penetration) others, notably product development, can involve significant lead times and development costs. Firms that have a successful record of innovation are usually more successful at internal growth, whereas others favour greater reliance on *external growth.

internal marketing Marketing in which a service firm trains and effectively motivates its customer-contact employees and the supporting service team to work together to provide customer satisfaction.

internal rate of return (IRR) An interest rate that gives a *net present value of zero when applied to the projected cash flow from an asset, liability, or financial decision. This interest rate, where the *present values of the cash inflows and outflows are equal, is the internal rate of return for a project under consideration, and the decision to adopt the project will depend on its size compared with the *cost of capital. The approximate IRR can be computed manually by interpolation but most computer *spreadsheet programs now include a routine enabling the IRR to be computed quickly and accurately. The IRR technique suffers from the possibility of multiple solution rates in some circumstances. If it suggests a different decision to that obtained from *net present value it should be disregarded, because net present value is a superior decision tool.

Internal Revenue Code (IRC) The federal tax law of the USA, which comprises the regulations applied to taxpayers.

Internal Revenue Service (IRS) In the USA, the branch of federal government responsible for collecting most types of taxes. The IRS administers the *Internal Revenue Code, investigates tax abuses, and makes criminal prosecution for tax fraud through the US tax court.

internal supplier *See* INTERNAL CUSTOMER.

internal user *See* DECISION-MAKING UNIT.

International Accounting Standard (IAS) Any of the accounting standards issued by the board of the International Accounting Standards Committee (IASC) between 1973 and 2001. In 2001 the IASC

INTERNATIONAL ACCOUNTING STANDARDS

1. Presentation of Financial Statements (revised 2007)
2. Inventories (revised 2005)
7. Cash Flow Statements
8. Accounting Policies, Changes in Accounting Estimates, and Errors (revised 2003)
10. Events After the Balance Sheet Date (revised 2003)
11. Construction Contracts
12. Income Taxes
14. Segment Reporting (revised 2003)
16. Property, Plant and Equipment (revised 2003)
17. Leases (revised 2003)
19. Employee Benefits (revised 2011)
20. Accounting for Government Grants and Disclosure of Government Assistance
21. The Effects of Changes in Foreign Exchange Rates (revised 2003)
23. Capitalization of Borrowing Costs
24. Related Party Disclosures (revised 2009)
26. Accounting and Reporting by Retirement Benefit Plans
27. Consolidated and Separate Financial Statements (revised 2003)
28. Investments in Associates (revised 2011)
29. Financial Reporting in Hyperinflationary Economies
30. Disclosures in the Financial Statements of Banks and Similar Financial Institutions
31. Interests In Joint Ventures (revised 2003)
32. Financial Instruments: Presentation (revised 2003)
33. Earnings Per Share (revised 2003)
34. Interim Financial Reporting
36. Impairment of Assets (revised 2004)
37. Provisions, Contingent Liabilities and Contingent Assets
38. Intangible Assets (revised 2004)
39. Financial Instruments: Recognition and Measurement (revised 2005)
40. Investment Property (revised 2003)
41. Agriculture

As indicated, many IASs have been issued in revised form under the International Accounting Standards Board's Improvements Project.

was replaced by the *International Accounting Standards Board (IASB), which announced that its accounting standards would be designated *International Financial Reporting Standards (IFRS). The IASB stated that all of the International Accounting Standards issued by the IASC would continue to be applicable unless and until they were amended or withdrawn by the new body. For years starting on or after 1 January 2005, listed companies in the EU are required to use adopted IASs in their financial statements.

International Accounting Standards Board (IASB) An independent, privately funded body responsible for establishing and improving international accounting standards. It superseded the **International Accounting Standards Committee** (IASC) in 2001. According to the mission statement of the IASB, its objectives are:

• to develop, in the public interest, a single set of high-quality, understandable, and enforceable global accounting standards that require high-quality, transparent, and comparable information in financial statements and other financial reporting, thereby helping participants in the world's capital markets and other users make economic decisions;

• to promote the use and rigorous application of those standards;

• to bring about convergence of national accounting standards with *International Accounting Standards and *International Financial Reporting Standards.

The IASB has no authority to require compliance with its accounting standards. However, many countries (including the USA and member states of the EU) now require that statements of publicly traded companies are prepared in accordance with IASB standards. The process of bringing UK *Financial Reporting Standards into harmony with IASB standards was essentially completed by January 2015. The organization is based in London.

(⊕) SEE WEB LINKS

• Website of the IASB and the IFRS Foundation: includes summaries of standards in issue

International Bank for Reconstruction and Development (IBRD) A specialized agency established by the Bretton Woods Conference of 1944 to help finance post-war reconstruction and to help raise standards of living in developing countries, by making loans to governments or guaranteeing outside loans. It lends on broadly commercial terms, either for specific projects or for more general social purposes; funds are raised on the international capital markets. The Bank and its affiliates, the *International Development Association and the *International Finance Corporation, are often known as the **World Bank**; it is owned by the governments of 185 (2007) countries. Members must also be members of the Bank's sister organization, the *International Monetary Fund. The headquarters of the Bank are in Washington, with a European office in Paris and a Tokyo office.

(⊕) SEE WEB LINKS

• Website of the World Bank Group

international banking facility (IBF) A banking facility in the USA that is authorized by the *Federal Reserve System to participate in *eurocurrency lending. Such facilities are exempt from reserve requirement and may have many other advantages usually associated with offshore banking.

International Business Reply Service (IBRS) A service offered by the Royal Mail enabling a company to supply its customers in 200 countries worldwide with a prepaid business reply card, envelope, or label so that they can reply to direct-mail shots, ask for follow-up literature, pay bills promptly, etc., free of postal charges.

International Capital Market Association (ICMA) A trade association and self-regulatory organization for European participants in the international debt capital market, including banks, exchanges, dealers and brokers, asset managers, and investors. It was formed in 2005 by a merger of the **International Securities Market Association** (ISMA) and the International Primary

Market Association. ICMA is based in Zurich.

International Chamber of Commerce (ICC) An international business organization that represents business interests by promoting open markets and the free movement of capital. It also conducts arbitrations and promotes business self-regulation. Its office is in Paris. *See also* INCOTERMS.

international commodity agreements Agreements between governments that aim to stabilize the price of commodities. This is often important for producing nations, for whom the revenue from commodity sales may make a major contribution to the national income. Methods tried include government-financed buffer stocks and the imposition of price limits between which the price of the commodity is allowed to fluctuate. Among the commodities for which agreements have been made are coffee, sugar, wheat, cocoa, and tin.

International Development Association (IDA) An affiliate of the *International Bank for Reconstruction and Development (IBRD) established in 1960 to provide assistance for poorer developing countries. It is funded by subscription and

transfers from the net earnings of IBRD. The headquarters of the IDA are in Washington, with offices in Paris and Tokyo.

international division A division of an international marketing organization that handles all a firm's international activities. Marketing, manufacturing, research, planning, and specialist staff are organized into operating units according to geography or product groups, or organized as an international subsidiary responsible for its own sales and profitability.

International Finance Corporation (IFC) An affiliate of the *International Bank for Reconstruction and Development (IBRD) established in 1956 to provide assistance for private investment projects. Although the IFC and IBRD are separate entities, both legally and financially, the IFC is able to borrow from the IBRD and reloan to private investors. The headquarters of the IFC are in Washington. Its importance increased in the 1980s, when it began to issue its own bonds.

International Financial Reporting Standard (IFRS) Any of the accounting standards issued by the *International Accounting Standards Board (IASB) since its institution in 2001. For financial years

---

INTERNATIONAL FINANCIAL REPORTING STANDARDS

There are currently 13 IRFRs:
1. First-time Adoption of International Financial Reporting Standards
2. Share-based Payment
3. Business Combinations
4. Insurance Contracts
5. Non-current Assets Held for Sale and Discontinued Operations
6. Exploration for and Evaluation of Mineral Assets
7. Financial Instruments: Disclosures
8. Operating Segments
9. Financial Instruments
10. Consolidated Financial Statements
11. Joint Arrangements
12. Disclosure of Interests in Other Entities
13. Fair Value Measurement

starting on or after 1 January 2005 listed companies in the EU are required to follow IFRSs in their published accounts. *See also* INTERNATIONAL ACCOUNTING STANDARD.

International Fund for Agricultural Development (IFAD)

A fund, proposed by the 1974 World Food Conference, that began operations in 1977 with the purpose of providing additional funds for agricultural and rural development in developing countries. It currently has 168 member states. The headquarters of the IFAD are in Rome.

International Labour Organization (ILO)

A special agency of the United Nations, established under the Treaty of Versailles in 1919, with the aim of promoting lasting peace through social justice. The ILO establishes international labour standards, runs a programme of technical assistance to developing countries, and attacks unemployment through its World Employment Programme. The ILO is financed by contributions from its member states. Its headquarters, The International Labour Office, is in Geneva.

International Monetary Fund (IMF)

An international organization established in 1947 to enhance stability and convertibility in the international monetary system. The Fund assists any member experiencing short-term balance of payments difficulties by supplying the amount of foreign currency it wishes to purchase in exchange for the equivalent amount of its own currency. The member repays this amount by buying back its own currency in a currency acceptable to the Fund, usually within three to five years. High levels of borrowing are conditional on the implementation of IMF suggested policies for a country. The Fund is financed by subscriptions from its members, the amount determined by an estimate of their means. The organization has a weighted voting system in which the larger countries have more votes. The day-to-day working of the IMF is carried on by an executive board representing its 188 members; this is based in Washington. *See also* CONDITIONALITY.

SEE WEB LINKS
• Website of the IMF

International Monetary Market *See* CHICAGO MERCANTILE EXCHANGE.

International Organization for Standardization (ISO)

An organization founded in 1946 to standardize measurements and other standards for industrial, commercial, and scientific purposes. The *British Standards Institution is a member. *See also* ISO 9000.

International paper sizes

International paper sizes are based upon a rectangle of paper with an area of one square metre, the sides of which are in the proportion $1:\sqrt{2}$. This geometrical relationship is used so that any lengthways halving of the original rectangle of paper produces another rectangle of paper with the same geometric relationship. For example, the A series is shown here.

There are three series of international paper size; A, B, and C. A is the most common series, with A4 being the favoured size for business correspondence. The B series is often used for posters, wall charts, other large items and where circumstances dictate a size of paper intermediate between any two adjacent sizes of the A series. The C series is used mainly when it is necessary to fit an envelope inside another envelope. The range and sizes of the three series are as follows:

A series (mm)

A0	841 × 1189	A4	210 × 297	A8	52 × 74
A1	594 × 841	A5	148 × 210	A9	37 × 52
A2	420 × 594	A6	105 × 148	A10	26 × 37
A3	297 × 420	A7	74 × 105		

B series (mm)

B0	1000 × 1414	B4	250 × 353	B8	62 × 88
B1	707 × 1000	B5	176 × 250	B9	44 × 62
B2	500 × 707	B6	125 × 176	B10	31 × 44
B3	353 × 500	B7	88 × 125		

C series (mm)

C4	324 × 229	C5	229 × 162	C6	162 × 114

International Petroleum Exchange (IPE)

An exchange, founded in London in 1980, that dealt in *futures contracts and *options in oil (gas oil, Brent crude oil, and heavy fuel oil) with facilities for making an exchange of futures for physicals (*see* ACTUALS). The IPE was acquired by the US-based *Intercontinental Exchange in 2001 and is now known as **ICE Futures Europe**.

International Securities Exchange (ISE)

A fully electronic exchange for securities and security options launched in the USA in 2000. It currently consists of a stock exchange, an options exchange, and the Alternative Markets platform for trading derivatives and other sophisticated instruments. ISE was acquired by *Eurex in 2007 and operates as an independent subsidiary.

International Securities Market Association

See INTERNATIONAL CAPITAL MARKET ASSOCIATION.

international security identification number (ISIN)

An identification system for all securities issues on the international market.

International Standard on Auditing (ISA)

Any of the statements on basic principles and essential procedures in auditing issued by the International Auditing and Assurance Standards Board. In the UK, auditors are required to comply with ISAs (UK and Ireland) for any audit of *financial statements for periods commencing on or after 15 December 2004.

international strategy

An approach to operating a *multinational enterprise in which a significant degree of autonomy is given to the units of the business in different countries. Such a strategy allows each unit to adapt to local market conditions, which may not be possible where a high degree of control and homogenization is imposed from the centre.

International Telecommunication Union (ITU)

A special agency of the United Nations founded in Paris in 1865 as the International Telegraph Union. It sets up international regulations for telecommunication and radio services; promotes international cooperation for the improvement of telecommunications; and is concerned with the development of technical facilities. It is responsible for the allocation and registration of radio frequencies for communications. Its headquarters are in Geneva.

International Union of Credit and Investment Insurers

See BERNE UNION.

Internet (the Net)

A global communications system consisting of millions of computer networks interconnected by modems, telephone cables, wireless networks, and satellite links, with associated software controlling the movement of data. It offers facilities for accessing remote databases, transfer of data between computers, and *e-mail. In addition, there are high-level services. **MBONE** (multicast backbone service), for example, allows transmission to more than one destination and is used for *videoconferencing. The **World Wide Web** is a multimedia facility allowing pictures, sound, and video to be displayed. A particular feature of the Web is the availability of *hyperlinks between pages and documents.

Originally, the Internet was mainly used by the academic community, but the wider availability of personal computers led to an enormous growth in the number of individual users during the 1990s and 2000s: in 2003 it was estimated that some 77% of people in the developed world were Internet users. This has resulted in ever increasing commercial exploitation in such areas as electronic shopping, *B2B trading, *supply-chain management, *home banking, financial services, advertising, marketing research, and customer contact (*see* DIGITAL ECONOMY). Recent developments include the growth of *cloud computing, *social media, and access to the Internet via mobile devices (smartphones and tablet computers). *See also* INFORMATION TECHNOLOGY.

Internet access provider (IAP) *See* ACCESS PROVIDER.

Internet Advertising Bureau (IAB) The UK trade association for online advertising, representing brands, digital media, and agencies. Established in 1997, the body carries out research, issues guidance to its members, and represents their interests to government in response to current and proposed regulation.

Internet café *See* CYBERCAFÉ.

Internet marketing The application of the Internet and related digital technologies to achieve marketing objectives.

It can be divided into web marketing (through a company website, affiliate networks, or on search engines), e-mail marketing, and marketing on *social media (including *viral marketing).

Internet relay chat (IRC) A communications tool that enables a text-based 'chat' to take place between different Internet users, who are logged on at the same time.

Internet service provider (ISP) A company that provides home or business users with a connection to access the Internet. Internet service providers can also host websites or provide a link from web servers to enable other companies and consumers access to a corporate website.

Internet tool Software that is used on the Internet. An example is a *web browser.

internship A period of temporary work, typically undertaken by a student or recent graduate, that allows a person to gain experience and insight into a particular industry or profession by working at a junior level. Internships usually last for a few months only and do not guarantee future employment; the intern may be paid or unpaid. The practice of offering unpaid internships has been criticized as exploitative and for allowing wealthier young people greater employment opportunities.

interpolation Estimation of the value of an unknown quantity that lies between two of a series of known values. For example, one can estimate by interpolation the population of a country at any time between known 10-year census figures. This would normally be done on a graph, the shape of the curve between known points enabling a good estimate to be made of the interpolated value. **Extrapolation** involves estimating an unknown quantity that lies outside a series of known values. Thus one could obtain a figure for the population of a country five years after its last census, by extending the population curve after the last known value.

intervention price *See* COMMON AGRICULTURAL POLICY.

interviewer error An error in marketing research that results from conscious or unconscious bias on the part of the interviewer. For example, the interviewer may guess incorrectly the age of the respondent or may assume that because someone is driving a car they own the car.

inter vivos **gifts** *See* GIFTS INTER VIVOS.

intestate A person who dies without having made a will. The estate, in these circumstances, is divided according to the rules of **intestacy**. The division depends on the personal circumstances of the deceased. If there is a spouse or civil partner then there is a fixed statutory legacy, with the remainder being split between an *interest-in-possession trust for the surviving partner and the children's absolute entitlement to the other half, if they are over 18. Where there is no surviving spouse the estate is divided between the children or their issue. Where there are no children then the split is rather more complicated and can include parents, brothers and sisters, grandparents, uncles, and aunts.

in the money Describing an *option that would generate a gain if currently exercised. An option that would not generate a gain is described as being **out of the money**, whereas one that would generate neither a gain nor a loss is *at the money. *See* INTRINSIC VALUE.

intraday limit 1. The maximum price movement in a single day's trading that is permitted by the rules of a particular financial market. **2.** The limit placed on a given trader's *exposure in a single day.

intranet A network within a single company or other organization that provides access to private information using the familiar tools of the Internet, such as *web browsers and e-mail. Only staff within the company or organization can access the intranet, which is usually protected by a password.

intrapreneur An executive or senior manager of a large firm who uses the entrepreneurial approach to management. In order to encourage entrepreneurship, it has become common for firms to encourage risk-taking and profit-orientated behaviour among its managers by organizing a business into a number of separate profit centres. Each centre is responsible for making a profit by intra-group trading and, where appropriate, by building up its external sales and clients. This approach has been used in the service departments of large companies, giving subsidiary companies the choice of using the internal services or of going outside to independent suppliers. This process of developing an internal market for services has also been applied by the public sector; for example, the UK National Health Service was encouraged to use this intrapreneurial approach in the 1990s. Critics, however, suggest that in these circumstances decisions will often be taken too narrowly, rather than for the benefit of the whole organization; the internal market in the NHS was discontinued largely for this reason in 1999.

intrinsic motivation An incentive to do something that arises from factors within the individual, such as a need to feel useful or to seek *self-actualization. *Compare* EXTRINSIC MOTIVATION. *See* INTRINSIC REWARD; MOTIVATION.

intrinsic reward A positive outcome of performing work that is integral to the work task itself, such as love of or pride in one's work, a sense of challenge or achievement, etc.

intrinsic value When a traded *option is *in the money, the difference between the *exercise price of the option and the market value of the underlying. If the option is not in the money, the intrinsic value is zero. *Compare* TIME VALUE.

introduction A method of issuing new securities in which a broker or issuing house takes small quantities of the company's shares and issues them to clients at opportune moments. It is also used by existing public companies that wish to issue additional shares. *Compare* OFFER FOR SALE; PLACING.

introduction stage *See* PRODUCT LIFE CYCLE.

inventoriable costs Costs that can be included in the valuation of *inventory (raw materials, *work in progress, or finished goods). *See* INVENTORY VALUATION.

inventory 1. (stock; stock-in-trade) The products or supplies of an organization on hand or in transit at any time. For a manufacturing company the types of inventory are raw materials, work in progress, and finished goods. An inventory count usually takes place at the end of the *financial year to confirm that the actual quantities support the figures given in the *books of account. The differences between the inventories at the beginning and the end of a period are used in the calculation of *cost of sales for the *profit and loss account and the end inventory is shown on the *balance sheet as a *current asset. **2.** More broadly, the total accumulation of material resources within an *operating system (not only what is held deliberately in stock). It includes all the transformed resources that are locked up in the system, such as work in progress, scrap, rejects, etc. All operations have some inventory, which represents locked-up capital. The task of *operations is to ensure that levels are kept to the minimum without affecting the efficiency and effectiveness of the transformation process.

Inventory, in this sense, falls into a number of different categories:

- **Anticipatory inventory** is produced in periods of relatively low demand in anticipation of a later increase in demand. This is only possible if the goods are non-perishable and is only economically viable if the costs of storage are less than the costs of changing production levels to match demand.

- **Uncoupling inventory** is the amount of material held to decouple elements of the *transformation system, such as the raw-material supplier from the manufacturer, one machine from another, or the manufacturer from the customer. This provides an element of operational flexibility.

- Similar to uncoupling inventory is the **buffer inventory**, which protects against variations in supply, demand,

and lead times. It represents a safety margin and is therefore directly related to the reliability of demand forecasting, etc.

- **Pipeline inventory** is that part of the inventory that is locked up in the system. Because all processes take time, the pipeline is a function of a *transformation system rather than performing a function within it. If organizations have to sub-contract part of their products or if elements of the system are widely separated geographically, the amount of resource locked up in the pipeline can increase dramatically. Modern process-monitoring systems based on *information technology are designed to ensure that the pipeline inventory in particular is kept to a minimum.

- **Cycle inventory** is a function of the *economic order quantity (EOQ) calculation and represents a trade-off between minimizing the inventory and the costs of setting up and changing processes. *Just-in-time techniques are designed to rely on a minimum EOQ. Clearly there is some overlap between these different types of inventory.

inventory control *See* STOCK CONTROL.

inventory effect The fact that the relationship between price and demand for a product is much more sensitive in the short term than the long term for non-perishable products. This is largely because consumers know that they can stock and safely store non-perishables during a sale.

inventory status record A data file containing up-to-date information on the status of every item, component, etc., controlled by the *material requirements planning system. This file contains the identification number, quantity in hand, safety stock level, quantity allocated, and procurement lead time of every item.

inventory valuation (stock valuation) The valuation of stocks of raw material, work in progress, and finished goods. For accounting purposes, inventories should be valued at the lower of cost or *net realizable value. This effectively means that finished goods and work in progress should include both fixed and variable production costs but exclude the selling and distribution costs. In the UK valuing stocks at cost, the *first-in-first-out cost, or the *average cost may be used, but not the *last-in-first-out cost or the *next-in-first-out cost. *Marginal cost may be used as a basis of stock valuation for *management accounting purposes but is unacceptable for *financial accounting.

investment 1. The purchase of capital goods, such as plant and machinery in a factory in order to produce goods for future consumption. This is known as **capital investment**; the higher the level of capital investment in an economy, the faster it will grow. **2.** The purchase of assets, such as securities, works of art, bank and building-society deposits, etc., with a primary view to their financial return, either as income or capital gain. This form of **financial investment** represents a means of saving. The level of financial investment in an economy, will be related to such factors as the rate of interest, the extent to which investments are likely to prove profitable, and the general climate of business confidence.

investment analyst A person employed by stockbrokers, banks, insurance companies, unit trusts, pension funds, etc., to give advice on the making of investments, especially investments in securities, commodities, etc. Many pay special attention to the study of *equities in the hope of being able to advise their employers to make profitable purchases of ordinary shares. To do this they use a variety of techniques, including a comparison of a company's present profits with its future trading prospects; this enables the analyst to single out the companies likely to outperform the general level of the market. This form of **technical analysis** is often contrasted with **fundamental analysis**, in which predicted future market movements are related to the underlying state of an economy and its expected trends. Analysts who rely on past movements to predict the future are called *chartists.

investment bank A US bank that fulfils many of the functions of a UK *merchant bank. It is usually one that advises on mergers and acquisitions and provides finance for industrial corporations by buying shares in a company and selling them in relatively small lots to investors. Capital provided to companies is usually long-term and based on fixed assets. In the USA, commercial banks were excluded from selling securities for many years but the law was relaxed in the late 1980s and most of the remaining restrictions were removed in 1999 (*see* FINANCIAL SERVICES MODERNIZATION ACT 1999). The financial crisis of 2008 saw the demise of several leading investment banks, notably Lehman Brothers, Bear Sterns, and Merrill Lynch.

investment banking Those activities of a bank that do not involve taking deposits from or providing financial services to the general public or *SMEs; typically these include arranging finance for large corporations and public bodies, assisting in mergers and acquisitions, trading on financial markets, and managing assets on behalf of investors through e.g. *unit trusts or *hedge funds. When these activities are short-term and high-risk in character they are often referred to disparagingly as *casino banking.

investment bond A single-premium life-assurance policy in which an investment of a fixed amount is made (usually over £1,000) in an *asset-backed fund. Interest is paid at an agreed rate and at the end of the period the investment is returned with any growth. Investment bonds confer attractive tax benefits in some circumstances. *See also* SINGLE-PREMIUM ASSURANCE; TOP SLICING.

investment club A group of investors who, by pooling their resources, are able to make more frequent and larger investments on a stock exchange, often being able to reduce brokerage and to spread the risk of serious loss. The popularity of investment clubs has waxed and waned with the developments of investment vehicles and the value of stocks.

investment company *See* INVESTMENT TRUST.

investment-grade Describing a bond that has been given a relatively high credit rating by a major *rating agency, namely Baa and above by Moody's or BBB and above by Standard & Poor's or Fitch's. Lower-rated bonds may promise a higher yield but are inherently more speculative.

investment grant (investment incentive) A grant made to a company by a government to encourage investment in plant, machinery, buildings, etc. The incentives may take various forms, some being treated as a deduction for tax purposes, others being paid whether or not the company makes a profit.

investment income 1. A person's income derived from investments. **2.** The income of a business derived from its outside investments rather than from its trading activities.

Investment Management Association (IMA) The UK trade association for unit trust and investment fund managers.

investment manager *See* FUND MANAGER.

investment portfolio *See* PORTFOLIO.

investment properties Properties owned by a company that holds investments as part of its business, such as an *investment trust or a property-investment company. Investment properties may also include properties owned by a company whose main business is not the holding of investments. An investment property is defined by Section 16 of the Financial Reporting Standard Applicable in the UK and Republic of Ireland as being an interest in land and/or buildings that is held for its investment potential or rental income or both. A property owned and occupied by a company for its own purposes is not an investment property, but a property let to and occupied by another company in the same group is an investment property for the purposes of its own accounts or the *consolidated financial statements. Investment properties should be included in the *balance sheet at their open-market value, movements being taken to the *profit and loss account; if the market value of the property cannot be measured reliably without undue cost and effort, it should be depreciated in the same way as plant and machinery. The relevant *International Accounting Standard is IAS 40: Investment Property.

Investment Services Directive (ISD) An EU directive (1993) providing a regulatory framework for securities dealing. It enshrined the principle that securities firms admitted by their domestic regulator should be allowed to operate at a European level. From 2007 the ISD was superseded by the *Markets in Financial Instruments Directive (MiFID), which greatly strengthens the single market for financial services.

investment tax credit In the USA, an incentive to investment in which part of the cost of an asset subject to depreciation is used to offset income tax falling due in the year of purchase.

investment trust (investment company) A company that invests the funds provided by shareholders in a wide variety of securities. It makes its profits from the income and capital gains provided by these securities. The investments made are usually restricted to securities quoted on a stock exchange, but some will invest in unlisted companies. The advantages for shareholders are much the same as those with *unit trusts, i.e. spreading the risk of investment and making use of professional managers. Investment trusts, which are not generally *trusts in the usual sense, but private or public limited companies, differ from unit trusts in that in the latter the investors buy units in the fund but are not shareholders. Some investment trusts aim for high capital growth (**capital shares**), others for high income (**income shares**).

The profits of an investment trust are subject to *corporation tax at the full rate; the lower rates of tax applied to trading companies are not available. They are also subject to special provisions in relation to dividends. *See also* SPLIT-CAPITAL INVESTMENT TRUST; VENTURE CAPITAL TRUST.

invisible assets *See* INTANGIBLE ASSET.

invisible earnings (invisibles) The earnings from abroad that contribute to the *balance of payments as a result of transactions involving services, such as insurance, banking, shipping, and tourism (often known as **invisibles**), rather than the sale and purchase of goods. Invisibles can play an important part in a nation's current account, although they are often difficult to quantify. The UK relies on a substantial invisible balance in its balance of payments.

invitation to treat *See* OFFER.

invoice *See* SALES INVOICE.

invoice discounting A form of debt discounting in which a business sells its invoices to a *factoring house at a discount for immediate cash. The service does not usually include sales accounting and debt collecting.

IOS Abbreviation for *integrated office system.

IoD Abbreviation for *Institute of Directors.

IOU A written document providing evidence of a debt, usually in the form 'I owe you . . .'. It is not a *negotiable instrument or a *promissory note and requires no stamp (unless it does include a promise to pay). It can, however, be used as legal evidence of a debt.

IPA Abbreviation for *Institute of Practitioners in Advertising.

IPE Abbreviation for *International Petroleum Exchange.

IPO 1. Abbreviation for *initial public offering. **2.** Abbreviation for *Intellectual Property Office.

Ipsos MORI A marketing research organization engaged in a wide variety of research activities. Formed from a merger

of Ipsos and MORI (Market and Opinion Research International) in 2005, it is best known for its research on social and political attitudes and its opinion polls.

IR35 A rule introduced in the Finance Act 2000 that requires an individual who provides services to an employer through an intermediary (such as a limited company) to be taxed on the basis that he is an employee rather than self-employed. This requires deduction of tax at source under the *PAYE rules, imposes Class 1 National Insurance contributions, and gives less favourable treatments for the deduction of expenses than formerly.

IRA Abbreviation for *individual retirement account.

iraimbilanja A monetary unit of Madagascar, worth one fifth of an *ariary.

IRC Abbreviation for *Internet relay chat.

Irish Stock Exchange (ISE) An independent exchange that opened in Dublin in 1995; the Dublin exchange had previously been part of the London Stock Exchange (then known as the International Stock Exchange of Great Britain and the Republic of Ireland). Fully automated trading was introduced in 2000.

IRR Abbreviation for *internal rate of return.

irredeemable securities (irredeemables) Securities, such as some government loan stock (*see* CONSOLS) and some *debentures, on which there is no date given for the redemption of the capital sum. The price of fixed-interest irredeemables on the open market varies inversely with the level of interest rates.

irrevocable documentary acceptance credit A form of irrevocable confirmed *letter of credit in which a foreign importer of UK goods opens a credit with a UK bank or the UK office of a local bank. The bank then issues an irrevocable letter of credit to the exporter, guaranteeing to accept *bills of exchange drawn on it on presentation of the shipping documents.

Once the letter of credit has been drawn up, the importer has to 'accept' that he or she will pay, by signing the acceptance.

irrevocable letter of credit *See* LETTER OF CREDIT.

IRS Abbreviation for *Internal Revenue Service.

ISA Abbreviation for *Individual Savings Account.

ISA mortgage A *mortgage in which the borrower repays only the interest on the loan to the lender, but at the same time puts regular sums into an *Individual Savings Account (ISA). When the ISA matures it is used to repay the capital. An ISA mortgage is similar to an *endowment mortgage, except that it does not provide any life-assurance cover and that ISA funds are untaxed.

ISBA Abbreviation for *Incorporated Society of British Advertisers Ltd.

Ishikawa diagram *See* CAUSE–EFFECT DIAGRAM.

ISIN Abbreviation for *international security identification number.

Islamic finance A system of finance that is bound by religious laws that prevent the taking of interest payments (*see* HALAL; HARAAM). Joint ventures in which the funder and the borrower share profits and risks are, however, acceptable. There are a number of different techniques by which this takes place. **Murabaha** is a good vehicle for temporary idle funds, which are used to purchase goods from a supplier for immediate sale and delivery to the buyer, who pays a predetermined margin over cost on a deferred payment date. The term can be as short as seven days. **Musharaka transactions** involve participation with other parties in trade financing, leasing, real estate, and industrial projects. Net profits are shared in proportions agreed at the outset. **Shirkah** is a partnership between a bank and a customer to share the risks and gains of a project. **Muqarada** is a joint venture by finance providers.

Ijarah involves profit from rental income on real estate. **Ijarawa-iktina** is leasing of large capital items, such as property or plant and machinery. Leasing is achieved by the equivalent of monthly rental payments, and at the expiry the lessee purchases the equipment. *See also* ALTERNATIVE FINANCE ARRANGEMENTS.

ISO Abbreviation for *International Organization for Standardization.

ISO 9000 An international process quality standard, issued by the *International Organization for Standardization and based largely on *British Standard 5750. A revised version of the standard, **ISO 9001**, was published in 2000; this places an enhanced emphasis on process management, *continuous improvement, and focus on customer satisfaction.

ISP 1. Abbreviation for *Institute of Sales Promotion. **2.** Abbreviation for *Internet service provider.

issue 1. The number of shares or the amount of stock on offer to the public at a particular time. *See also* NEW ISSUE; RIGHTS ISSUE; SCRIP ISSUE. **2.** The number of banknotes distributed by the Bank of England at a particular time.

issue by tender (sale by tender; tender offer) A type of *offer for sale in which an issuing house asks investors to tender for a new issue of shares or other securities, which are then allocated to the highest bidders. It is usual for the tender documents to state the lowest price acceptable. This method is not frequently employed. *Compare* PUBLIC ISSUE.

issued share capital (subscribed share capital) The amount of the *authorized share capital of a company for which shareholders have subscribed. *See also* CALLED-UP SHARE CAPITAL; PAID-UP SHARE CAPITAL; SHARES OUTSTANDING.

issue price (offering price) The price at which a new issue of shares is sold to the public. Once the issue has been made the securities will have a market price, which may be above (at a premium on) or below (at a discount on) the issue price (*see also* STAG). In an *introduction or *public issue, the issue price is fixed by the company on the advice of its stockbrokers and bankers; in an *issue by tender the issue price is fixed by the highest price that can be obtained for the whole issue; in a *placing the issue price is negotiated by the issuing house or broker involved. *See also* INITIAL PUBLIC OFFERING; OFFER FOR SALE.

issuing house A financial institution, usually a *merchant bank or *investment bank, that specializes in the *flotation of private companies on a *stock exchange. In some cases the issuing house will itself purchase the whole issue (*see* UNDERWRITER), thus ensuring that there is no uncertainty in the amount of money the company will raise by flotation. It will then sell the shares to the public, usually by an *offer for sale, *introduction, *issue by tender, or *placing.

IT 1. Abbreviation for *income tax.
2. Abbreviation for *information technology.

iterative design The practice of making *continuous improvements in the design of a product on the basis of testing, expert evaluation, and consumer feedback. *See also* KAIZEN; KANSEI ENGINEERING.

ITU Abbreviation for *International Telecommunication Union.

IVA Abbreviation for individual *voluntary arrangement.

jailbreaking Modifying the operating system of a digital device, such as an iPhone or iPod, in order to run applications that are not authorized by the manufacturer. In 2010 the US copyright office determined that jailbreaking was permitted as an exemption to the Digital Millennium Copyright Act.

Japan Bank for International Cooperation (JBIC) A Japanese bank that provides finance for Japanese overseas investment, promotes exports and imports, and provides low-interest loans to projects in the developing world. It was created in 1999, through a merger of the Export-Import Bank of Japan and the Overseas Economic Cooperation Fund.

Java A programming language and associated software platform that enable complex and graphical customer applications to be written and then accessed from a *web browser. An example might be a form for calculating interest on a loan.

JavaScript A scripting language originally designed to add features to web pages but now used in many other applications. It is loosely based on Java. The standardized form of the language is officially named **ECMA Script**.

jerque note A certificate issued by a UK customs officer to the master of a ship, stating that he is satisfied that the cargo on his ship has been correctly entered on the *manifest and that no unentered cargo has been found after searching the ship.

jetsam Items of a ship's cargo that have been thrown overboard and sink below the surface of the water. *Compare* FLOTSAM.

jettisons Items of a ship's cargo that have been thrown overboard to lighten the ship in dangerous circumstances. If the items are insured they constitute a general average loss (*see* AVERAGE).

jiao A monetary unit of China, worth one tenth of a *yuan.

JICWEBS Acronym for the Joint Industry Committee for Web Standards in the UK and Ireland, the media industry trade body established to develop standards and guidelines for online advertising. The body sets standards for measuring web traffic so that meaningful comparisons can be made across the industry.

JIT Abbreviation for *just in time.

job An identifiable discrete piece of work carried out by an organization. For costing purposes a job is usually given a *job number.

job analysis A detailed study of a particular job, the tools and equipment needed to do it, and its relation to other jobs in an organization. The analysis should also provide the information needed to say how the job should best be done and the qualifications, experience, or aptitudes of the person best suited to doing it. Data is usually collected by questioning those already doing or supervising the job and is subjected to various forms of interpretation by a **job analyst**. Accurate job analysis is crucial to effective *job evaluation, *employee evaluation, and *personnel selection. *See also* JOB DESCRIPTION; JOB DIMENSIONS.

job and finish *See* CONTINGENT TIME OFF.

jobber 1. *See* STOCKJOBBER. **2.** A dealer who buys and sells commodities, etc., for his or her own account.

jobbing A type of process in which small numbers of products are made to order. It involves high levels of skill and the movement of resources to the product. Examples of jobbing include prototype engineering, cabinet making, etc.

jobbing backwards Looking back on a transaction or event and thinking about how one might have acted differently, had one known then what one knows now.

Jobcentre Plus A UK government agency that seeks work for those out of a job, assists employers to find suitable employees, and offers occupational advice on retraining. The agency operates **Universal Jobmatch**, an online service that aims to match jobseekers to vacancies on the basis of their skills and experience. It also administers claims for and payments of *social security benefits.

job characteristics theory A theory that describes how *job design can affect motivation, performance, and job satisfaction. A number of specific *core job characteristics are held to induce high levels of motivation and performance.

job-component method A method of *job evaluation in which jobs are ranked according to a statistical analysis of the behavioural demands they impose. The data is usually obtained from employees' answers to a standardized questionnaire. *Compare* CLASSIFICATION METHOD; FACTOR-COMPARISON METHOD; POINT METHOD; RANKING METHOD.

job costing (job order costing; specific order costing) A costing process to assess the individual costs of performing each *job. It is important in organizations in which the production of different products is carried out, and also in service organizations, in which the cost is required of each service provided.

job description An official document that states the purpose of a specific job,

together with tasks or duties involved, performance objectives, and the reporting relationships. It also provides information on the remuneration and working hours. In large organizations, a job description is usually arrived at through a formal process of *job analysis; it can then be used to compile a *personnel specification defining the skills and other attributes necessary to successful performance of the job. *See also* JOB DIMENSIONS; PERSONNEL SELECTION.

job design The process of putting together the various elements of work that constitute an *operating system, to form jobs that individuals will perform (*see* WORK STUDY). The process involves a balance between the needs of the individual to be healthy, safe, and motivated and the needs of the organization to be economic, efficient, and effective. There is no single solution: each compromise will reflect the strategy and management philosophy favoured by a particular organization.

job dimensions The general scope of a particular job in terms of the tasks or duties that are typically required, e.g. secretarial duties or responsibility for financial decisions. Most *job descriptions now cite the key dimensions of a job rather than attempting a comprehensive list of all the tasks that may be involved. The notion of job dimensions is sometimes extended to include the key *competencies, including personality traits, that are held to be essential to performance of a job.

job enlargement An approach to *job design that seeks to enhance staff motivation by increasing either (a) the number and variety of related tasks given to an individual (**horizontal job enlargement**) or (b) the complexity of the tasks and the autonomy and responsibility of the worker performing them (**vertical job enlargement**).

job enrichment An approach to *job design that aims to increase motivation and job satisfaction by giving workers a greater level of autonomous decision making and personal control. For example, production line workers might be given responsibility for preventive maintenance of their work station and for running their own *statistical process control.

job evaluation An assessment of the work involved in a particular job, the responsibilities borne by the person who does it, and the skills, experience, or qualifications required, all with a view to evaluating the appropriate remuneration for the job and the differentials between it and other work in the same organization. Job evaluation enables different jobs to be compared with agreed common standards. These standards may be specific to an organization or an industry or they may be universal. Several procedures for job evaluation are in common use; *see* BENCHMARK JOB; CLASSIFICATION METHOD; FACTOR-COMPARISON METHOD; JOB-COMPONENT METHOD; POINT METHOD; RANKING METHOD.

job interview *See* SELECTION INTERVIEW.

job number A number assigned to each job where *job costing is in operation; it enables the costs to be charged to this number so that all the individual costs for a job can be collected.

job rotation An approach to *job design that reduces boredom, and thus increases motivation, by rotating staff through a range of jobs. This process can also increase the flexibility of a system by introducing an element of multiskilling. The key is to make use of rotation with a minimum of disruption and learning-curve effects, and to retain the element of freshness.

job satisfaction The sense of fulfilment and pride felt by people who enjoy their work and do it well. This feeling is enhanced if the significance of the work done and its value are recognized by those in authority (*see* EMPOWERMENT; MOTIVATION; SELF-ACTUALIZATION).

The factors that determine job satisfaction are investigated by *industrial and organizational psychology because it is widely accepted that a satisfied workforce is more productive and compliant than a

dissatisfied force. The general conclusion is that to motivate and reassure employees, managers should encourage the sense of community felt by everyone in a successful organization, in addition to broadening their jobs (*see* JOB ENLARGEMENT; JOB ENRICHMENT) and praising their work.

An absence of job satisfaction has been blamed for *absenteeism, *accident proneness, high *labour turnover rates, poor *industrial relations, and a demotivated workforce that produces shoddy work (*see* ALIENATION).

Organizational psychologists have shown that apart from the human needs fulfilled by working, satisfaction is also related to the expectations aroused by the job: both the needs and the expectations require fulfilment if the job is to provide satisfaction. *See also* HYGIENE FACTORS; MOTIVATORS.

job sharing Dividing the work of one full-time employee between two or more part-time employees.

job specification *See* PERSONNEL SPECIFICATION.

Johannesburg Securities Exchange *See* JSE.

joint account A bank or building-society account held in the names or two or more people, often husband and wife. On the death of one party the balance in the account goes to the survivor(s), except in the case of partnerships, executors' accounts, or trustees' accounts. Normally, any of the holders of a joint account is entitled to operate it alone.

joint and several liability A liability that is entered into as a group, on the understanding that if any of the group fail in their undertaking the liability must be shared by the remainder. Thus if two people enter into a joint and several guarantee for a bank loan, if one becomes bankrupt the other is liable for repayment of the whole loan.

Joint Industry Committee for Web Standards *See* JICWEBS.

joint investment A security purchased by more than one person. The certificate will bear the names of all the parties, but only the first named will receive notices. To dispose of the holding all the parties must consent.

joint-life and last-survivor annuities Annuities that involve two people (usually husband and wife). A joint-life annuity begins payment on a specified date and continues until both persons have died. A last-survivor annuity only begins payment on the death of one of the two people and pays until the death of the other. *Compare* SINGLE-LIFE PENSION.

jointness of supply The situation in which the cost of supplying a good to the first user is the same, or nearly the same, as supplying it to many users. This is true of most digital goods.

joint-stock bank A UK bank that is a *public limited company rather than a partnership. During the 19th century many private banks failed; the joint-stock banks became stronger, however, largely as a result of amalgamations and careful investment. In the 20th century, they evolved into the *commercial banks or high-street banks.

joint-stock company A *company in which the members pool their stock and trade on the basis of their joint stock. This differs from the earliest type of company, the merchant corporations or regulated companies of the 14th century, in which members traded with their own stock, subject to the rules of the company. Joint-stock companies originated in the 17th century; they are now rare.

joint supply (complementary supply) The supply of two or more separate commodities that are produced by the same process; examples include milk and butter, wool and mutton, and petrol and heavy oil. If the demand for one increases, the supply of the other will also increase, but its price will fall unless its demand also increases.

joint tenants Two or more persons who jointly own an interest in land. When one dies, the other(s) takes his share by right of survivorship. No one tenant has rights to any particular part of the property and no tenant may exclude another.

joint venture A commercial undertaking entered into jointly by two or more entities. Joint ventures are generally governed by the Partnership Act 1890 but they differ from *partnerships in that they are limited by time or by activity. Separate books are not usually kept and the joint venturers will have a profit- or loss-sharing ratio for the purpose of the joint venture only. Joint venturers often carry on their principal businesses independently of, and at the same time as, the joint venture. Joint ventures have become increasingly common as companies cooperate with each other in international markets, in order to share costs, exploit new technologies, or gain access to new markets. According to the Financial Reporting Standard Applicable in the UK and Republic of Ireland (Section 15), a joint venture only exists where strategic decisions require the unanimous consent of all the parties to the venture.

journal 1. A *book of prime entry in which transfers from one *account to another are recorded. It is used for transfers not recorded in any other of the books of prime entry, such as the *sales day book or the *cash book. **2.** Any *day book.

JSE The principal stock exchange of South Africa, established in 1887 as the **Johannesburg Stock Exchange**. It changed its name following its move to the suburb of Sandton in 2000. The JSE is the largest exchange in the African continent.

judgment creditor A creditor who has obtained a court judgment against a debtor (the **judgment debtor**), ordering him or her to pay the sum owed. If the judgment debtor fails to pay, the judgment creditor must return to the court asking for the judgment to be enforced. *See also* THIRD-PARTY DEBT ORDER.

judgment sampling A form of *non-probability sampling in which a researcher selects a *sample from a population on the basis of his or her judgment, rather than by using statistical sampling techniques. For example, in marketing research an interviewer might interview a woman with a child because the questions relate to children's clothing. Although such an approach can be valuable in *qualitative marketing research, its drawback is that it does not permit an inference from the sample to a larger population.

junk bond A *bond that offers a high rate of interest because it carries a higher than usual probability of default. **High-yield** or **speculative-grade bonds**, as they are also known, are defined as those with a rating of Ba or lower from Fitch or BB or lower from Moody's or Standard & Poor's. The practice of issuing junk bonds to finance the takeover of large companies developed in the USA during the 1980s and has since spread elsewhere (*see* LEVERAGED BUY-OUT). *Compare* INVESTMENT-GRADE.

just in time (JIT) An approach to manufacturing that aims to reduce stocks of raw materials and finished goods, queues and bottlenecks, excess transport, and levels of scrap and defective units. Whereas traditional systems isolate operations from the environment, for example by uncoupling *inventory, JIT recognizes that without

protection processes can go wrong but, if they do, the reasons should be found and the process put right. It seeks to improve all performance variables, such as cost, quality, speed, dependability, and flexibility. The key elements of JIT are:

- respect for the contribution that employees can make;
- encouragement of personal responsibility and process ownership from a multi-skilled workforce that is proactive in problem solving;
- a demand-pull system in which material only flows when needed;
- *kanban*;
- standardized product design;
- accelerated learning-curve effects;
- preventive rather than reactive maintenance;
- level scheduling;
- reduction of set-up times;
- efficient plant layout, eliminating places in which inventory can get lost;
- JIT purchasing involving close liaison with suppliers;
- *total quality management committed to *continuous improvement.

JIT has been facilitated by the advent of cheap computing power and *computer-aided manufacturing systems. It is easier to install JIT techniques from the outset, rather than attempting to introduce them piecemeal when a process is running. *See also* LEAN PRODUCTION.

kaizen The Japanese concept of *continuous improvement that underlies both *total quality management and *just-in-time techniques. Its prime consideration is to ensure that problems are continuously sought out and rectified and that opportunities for improvement, in any aspect of the system, are exploited. Rather than concealing problems, staff are encouraged to bring them to the surface and to suggest solutions; a degree of employee *empowerment is therefore required. The aim of this approach is to prevent the large-scale change that may be required if a system is allowed to stagnate and then has to be brought back into line.

Kaldor–Hicks efficiency In economic theory, an alteration in the allocation of resources is said to be Kaldor-Hicks efficient when it produces more benefits than costs. A *Pareto efficiency arises when at least one person is made better off and no one is made worse off. In practice, however, it is extremely difficult to make any change without making at least one person worse off. Under the Kaldor–Hicks efficiency test, an outcome is efficient if those who are made better off could *in theory* compensate those who are made worse off and so produce a Pareto efficient outcome. Although all Kaldor–Hicks efficient situations are Pareto optimal, in that no further Pareto improvements can be made, the reverse is not true. Conversely, although every Pareto improvement is a Kaldor–Hicks improvement, most Kaldor–Hicks improvements are not Pareto improvements.

kamikaze pricing The practice of offering goods and services at exceptionally low rates, usually as part of a *market penetration strategy or in an attempt to force competitors out of the market (*see* PREDATORY PRICING STRATEGY). It is named after the Japanese suicide pilots of World War II.

kanban A Japanese method of controlling the movement of materials through a *just-in-time system. Literally meaning 'visual record', *kanban* cards provide authority for a work station to produce or to transfer materials.

kangaroos An informal name for Australian shares, especially in mining, land, and tobacco companies, on the London Stock Exchange.

Kansei engineering (affective engineering) An approach to product design and development in which a company seeks out users' emotional and aesthetic reactions to the product and attempts to incorporate these into subsequent models. *Kansei* is a Japanese word meaning 'psychological feeling'. *See* ITERATIVE DESIGN.

Kassenobligation A German term for a medium-term financial obligation, most notably in the form of three- to five-year federal government securities.

keelage A fee paid by the owners of a ship for being permitted to dock in certain ports and harbours.

keepwell A guarantee by a *holding company that it will maintain financial backing for a subsidiary for a stated period.

The usual purpose is to enhance the creditworthiness of the subsidiary.

Keidanren The Japanese name for the **Japan Business Federation** (formerly the Japan Federation of Economic Organizations), which is the most powerful of the Japanese business organizations. It functions as the main voice of the business community; its members are the major trade associations and the prominent companies.

keiretsu In Japan, a group of companies that have interlocking *cross-holdings. These are usually minor shareholdings to cement relationships and typically involve at least one financial institution. The *keiretsu* is now the main form of business organization in Japan. *Compare* ZAIBATSU.

Keogh plan A US savings scheme to create a pension plan for self-employed people, in which tax is deferred until withdrawals are made. It can be held at the same time as a corporate pension or *individual retirement account. Keogh plans originated with the Self-Employment Individuals Retirement Act 1982.

kerb market Any informal financial market, such as one for dealing in securities not listed on a stock exchange. The term derives from the former practice of trading on the street after the formal close of business of the London Stock Exchange.

keyed advertisement An advertisement designed to enable the advertiser to know where a respondent saw it, for instance by including a code number of a particular department in the return address.

key performance indicators (KPIs) Specific measures of the performance of an individual, team, or department in defined **key performance areas** (KPAs). In the case of an individual employee, these will be based on that person's *job description and may be specified in his or her contract of employment. *See* EMPLOYEE EVALUATION; PERFORMANCE MEASUREMENT.

key-person assurance An assurance policy on the life of a key employee, especially a senior executive in a small company, whose death would be a serious loss to the organization. In the event of the key person dying, the benefit is paid to the company. Where a policy also provides cover for critical illness it is known as **key-person protection**.

khoum A monetary unit of Mauritania, worth one fifth of an *ouguiya.

kickback A colloquial term for an illegal payment made to secure favourable treatment in the award of a contract.

killer bee An investment banker who helps a business to resist a predatory *takeover bid by devising strategies to make the target company appear a less attractive proposition. *See* POISON PILL; PORCUPINE PROVISIONS.

kina (PGK) The standard monetary unit of Papua New Guinea, divided into 100 toea.

kip (LAK) The standard monetary unit of Laos, divided into 100 at.

kite An informal name for an *accommodation bill. **Kite-flying** or **kiting** is the discounting of a kite (accommodation bill) at a bank, knowing that the person on whom it is drawn will dishonour it.

Kitemark *See* BRITISH STANDARDS INSTITUTION.

kiting 1. *See* KITE. **2.** An informal US name for the dishonest practice of improving the apparent cash position in a company's accounts by paying a large cheque on the last day of the accounting period from one of its current accounts into a second current account. Because the first account will not have been debited, but the second account will have been credited, the overall cash position is temporarily overstated. **3.** The act of changing a cheque illegally by altering the amount to be drawn. **4.** The practice of artificially driving up the market price of a share.

knock-for-knock agreement An agreement between motor insurers that they will pay for their own policyholders' accident damage without seeking any contribution from the other insurers, irrespective of blame but provided that the relevant policies cover the risk involved. The agreement works on the principle that, having paid for their own policyholder's damage, insurer A refrains from claiming the payment back from insurer B, even though it may be clear that A's client was to blame for the accident. On another occasion the roles might be reversed; insurer B then refrains from claiming from A even though A's client was responsible.

Before the knock-for-knock agreement, insurers found they were exchanging roughly similar amounts in payment of these claims. The agreement has cut down the expensive administration of claim and counterclaim, which has helped to reduce the cost of premiums.

knocking copy Advertising copy that attacks a rival product.

knowledge management The creation and sharing of knowledge in an organization. Knowledge management is a relatively new concept and there are many different definitions. Successful knowledge management initiatives will typically lead to improved employee involvement, improved individual and organizational creativity, and enhanced intrapreneurship and innovation.

knowledge triangle The interaction of research (which produces knowledge), education (which diffuses knowledge), and *innovation (which applies knowledge). The knowledge triangle is seen as a key driver of success in modern knowledge-based economies, as recognized in the EU's Lisbon Strategy and its plans for a European Institute of Innovation and Technology.

knowledge worker An individual who is employed to analyse and communicate ideas and information.

kobo A monetary unit of Nigeria, worth one hundredth of a *naira.

Kondratieff cycle A hypothesis, first suggested by the economist Nikolai Kondratieff, that the international economy is characterized by 50-year price cycles. The term has also been used more generally to support the notion that there are 50-year cycles in economic activity. *See* BUSINESS CYCLE.

kopeck A monetary unit of Russia and Belarus, worth one hundredth of a *rouble.

kopiyka A monetary unit of Ukraine, worth one hundredth of a *hryvna.

Korea Exchange A financial market in Seoul that is now one of Asia's largest and most modern. It was formed from a merger of the Korea Stock Exchange, which dates back to 1911, with the Korea Futures Exchange and KOSDAQ, an electronic exchange.

koruna 1. (CZK) The standard monetary unit of the Czech Republic, divided into 100 haleru. **2.** The former standard monetary unit of Slovakia, divided into 100 haleru. It was replaced by the euro in 2009.

KPAs Abbreviation for key performance areas. *See* KEY PERFORMANCE INDICATORS.

KPIs Abbreviation for *key performance indicators.

krona (SEK) The standard monetary unit of Sweden, divided into 100 öre.

króna (*plural* **krónor**) **(ISK)** The standard monetary unit of Iceland, divided into 100 aurar.

krone (*plural* **kroner**) The standard monetary unit of Denmark (DKK), the Faeroe Islands, Greenland, and Norway (NOK), divided into 100 øre.

kroon The former standard monetary unit of Estonia, divided into 100 senti. It was replaced by the euro in 2011.

Krugerrand A South African coin containing 1 troy ounce of gold, minted since 1967 for investment purposes.

KRX Abbreviation for *Korea Exchange.

KSAOs Abbreviation for *k*nowledge, *s*kills, *a*bilities, and *o*ther characteristics: attributes of an employee or job applicant that are assessed for such purposes as *personnel selection, *performance appraisal, and career development. In larger organizations, the KSAOs required for a particular job will be identified by a formal process of *job analysis and itemized in a *personnel specification.

kuna (*plural* **kune**) **(HRK)** The standard monetary unit of Croatia, divided into 100 lipas.

kuru (*plural* **kuruş**) A monetary unit of Turkey, worth one hundredth of a *lira.

kwacha 1. (MWK) The standard monetary unit of Malawi, divided into 100 tambala. **2.** (ZMW) The standard monetary unit of Zambia, divided into 100 ngwee.

kwanza (AOA) The standard monetary unit of Angola, divided into 100 lwei.

kyat (MMK) The standard monetary unit of Burma, divided into 100 pyas.

k

laari A monetary unit of the Maldives, worth one hundredth of a *rufiyaa.

labor union US name for a *trade union.

labour costs (wages costs) Expenditure on wages paid to those operators who are both directly and indirectly concerned with the production of the product, service, or *cost unit. *See also* DIRECT LABOUR COST; INDIRECT COSTS.

labour-intensive Denoting an industry, company, production process, or project in which the remuneration paid to employees represents a high proportion of the total costs. *Compare* CAPITAL-INTENSIVE.

labour turnover rate The ratio, usually expressed as a percentage, of the number of employees leaving an organization or industry in a stated period to the average number of employees working in that organization or industry during the period. An important distinction is made between **uncontrollable turnover**, as by death, superannuation, or unavoidable redundancy, and **controllable turnover**. A high rate of controllable voluntary turnover (i.e. by resignation) can be a sign of low *job satisfaction in an organization; a high rate of controllable involuntary turnover (e.g. by dismissal for misconduct or poor performance or by retirement owing to work-related illness) is usually a sign that the organization has graver problems.

laches (Norman French *lasches*: negligence) Neglect and unreasonable delay in enforcing an equitable right. If a plaintiff with full knowledge of the facts takes an unnecessarily long time to bring an action (e.g. to set aside a contract obtained by fraud) the court will be of no assistance;

hence the maxim 'the law will not help those who sleep on their rights'. No set period is given but if the action is covered by limitation-of-actions legislation, the period given will not be shortened. Otherwise the time allowed depends on the circumstances.

laddered portfolio A *portfolio holding a range of fixed-interest bonds or other securities with fixed values in different maturities. *See also* BARBELL.

Lady Macbeth strategy A strategy used in takeover battles in which a third party makes a bid that the target company would favour, i.e. it appears to act as a *white knight, but subsequently changes allegiance and joins the original bidder.

laesio enormis (Latin: extraordinary injury) A doctrine of Roman law that is included in some European legal systems but not in English law. It states that the price given in a contract by way of *consideration must be fair and reasonable or the contract may be rescinded.

laggards *See* ADOPTION OF INNOVATIONS.

lagging measures *See* BALANCED SCORECARD.

LAIA Abbreviation for *Latin American Integration Association.

laissez-faire economy An economy in which government intervention is kept to a minimum and *market forces are allowed to rule. The term, attributed to the French merchant J. Gourlay (1712–59), is best translated as 'let people do as they think best'. *See* FREE COMPETITION.

laissez-faire leader A leader who effectively abdicates from the leadership role by allowing members of the group freedom of action and providing little guidance or structure. Experimental studies of *leadership style have found that work groups with laissez-faire leaders tend to be more apathetic and less productive than those with *authoritarian leaders or *democratic leaders.

lakh In the Indian subcontinent, a unit of 10^5 (100,000), often used in citing sums of money. For example, twenty lakh Indian rupees = IRS 2 million. A hundred lakh make one **crore** (10^7 or 10,000,000). Separators are often used to indicate the number of lakh rather than the number of millions, so that e.g. 4.5 million (45 lakh) is written 45,00,000.

lame duck A company that has national prestige and is a large employer of labour (especially in an area of high unemployment) or is a leader in a particular technology but, being unable to meet foreign competition, is unable to survive without government support.

LAN Abbreviation for *local area network.

land In law, the part of the earth's surface that can be owned, including all buildings, trees, minerals, etc., attached to or forming part of it. It also includes the airspace above the land necessary for its reasonable enjoyment. In law, a first-floor flat can constitute a separate piece of land, although it has no contact with the soil, just as a cellar may be a separate *estate in land.

land bank The amount of land a developer owns that is awaiting development.

land certificate A document that takes the place of a *title deed for registered land. It is granted to the registered proprietor of the land and indicates ownership. It will usually be kept in the *Land Registry if the land is subject to a mortgage.

land charges Encumbrances, such as contracts, payments, or other matters, to which *land is subject; if they are not dealt with before the land is sold, they will usually bind the purchaser. Formerly, they bound a purchaser who had notice of them. Now most of them must be registered if they are to remain effective, either under the Land Charges Act 1972 (applicable to unregistered land) or under the Land Registration Act 1925 (applicable to registered land).

Land Charges Register 1. The register of *land charges on unregistered land, kept at the *Land Registry. Charges are registered against the name of the estate owner. The kinds of charges that must be registered are set out in the Land Charges Act 1972 and include estate contracts, equitable easements, restrictive covenants, and HM Revenue charges. Registration constitues actual notice to any person of the existence of the charge. If a charge is not registered it will not bind a purchaser for money or money's worth of a legal estate in the land, even if he had notice of the charge. Some charges, if not registered, will not bind the purchaser for value of any interest (whether legal or equitable) in the land. **2. (Local Land Charges Register)** A register kept by each London borough, the City of London, and each unitary authority or district council. Public authorities may register statutory restrictions on land, e.g. under town and country planning legislation. These are registered against the land itself, not the estate owner. If restrictions are not registered, the purchaser is still bound by them, but will be entitled to compensation.

landed Denoting an export price in which the exporter pays all the charges to the port of destination and also pays the *landing charges but not any dock dues or onward carriage charges to the importer's factory or warehouse. The corresponding *Incoterm is Delivered Ex Quay (DEQ); *see* DELIVERED EX SHIP. *Compare* FRANCO.

landfill tax A tax charge, introduced in the Finance Act 1996, on the commercial disposal of waste by way of landfill. *See* WASTE DISPOSAL.

landing account An account prepared by a public warehousing company to the owner of goods that have recently been landed from a ship and taken into the warehouse. The account, which is usually accompanied by a *weight note, states the date on which the warehouse rent begins and also the quantity of goods and their condition (from the external appearance of the packages).

landing charges The charges incurred in disembarking a cargo, or part of it, from a ship at the port of destination.

landing order A permit enabling an importer to remove goods from a ship or quay to a *bonded warehouse, pending payment of duty or their re-export.

landlord and tenant The parties to a *lease. The landlord grants the lease to the tenant. The landlord may be the freehold owner of the land or may be a tenant of a superior landlord (*see* HEAD LEASE). The law of landlord and tenant is that governing the creation, termination, and regulation of leases. Many leases, both business and residential, are subject to statutory control. This means that the right of the landlord to end a lease and evict tenants may be restricted and the rent may be controlled. It is therefore essential to consider statutory rights when considering the relation between landlord and tenant, as well as those given by the lease.

land registration The system of registration of title introduced by the Land Registration Act 1925 and overhauled by the Land Registration Act 2002. Land is registered by reference to a map rather than against the name of any estate owner. Three registers are kept:

- the **property register**, which records the land and estate; it refers to a map and mentions any interests benefiting the land, e.g. *easements and restrictive *covenants;
- the **proprietorship register**, which sets out the name of the owner, the nature of the title (e.g. freehold or leasehold), and any restrictions on the way the land may be dealt with (e.g. if the land is subject to a trust);

- the **charges register**, which contains notice of rights adverse to the land, such as mortgages and *land charges as defined in the Land Charges Act 1972.

The owner's title is guaranteed by registration in most circumstances. Rights in registered land may be a registered interest, which amounts to ownership of the freehold or leasehold estate; an overriding interest, which binds a purchaser without needing to be registered; or a minor interest, which needs to be protected by an entry on the register (e.g. interest under a trust or restrictive covenant). The purpose of the system is to simplify conveyancing, so that instead of checking title deeds, a search of the register will reveal all relevant matters. Eventually, all land in England and Wales will be registered, enabling unregistered conveyancing to disappear; this process is now over 80% complete. *See also* ELECTRONIC CONVEYANCING; RECTIFICATION OF REGISTER.

Land Registry The official body that keeps the various land registers (*see* LAND REGISTRATION) and is responsible for implementing the policy of registering title to all land in England and Wales. The main registry is in Lincoln's Inn Fields in London, but there are also regional registries and information is now held electronically. Title information and a location plan for any registered land can be downloaded by the general public for a small fee. There is also a service for registered business users. *See also* RECTIFICATION OF REGISTER.

(⊕) SEE WEB LINKS

- Land Registry area of the Gov.uk website

language laboratory A room equipped with audiovisual apparatus for the study of foreign languages. The object is to acquire a proficiency in the spoken language as quickly as possible and to this end extensive use is made of recording equipment, pre-recorded CDs, and interactive computer software. A supervisor can plug into recordings made by students, to monitor their progress and correct errors, especially of pronunciation.

Lanham Trademark Act 1947 A US law prohibiting brand names and trademarks from being confusingly similar to registered trademarks.

lapping In the USA, the fraudulent practice of concealing a shortage of cash by delaying the recording of cash receipts. In the UK it is referred to as **teeming and lading**. There are a number of variations, but essentially the cashier conceals the theft of cash received from the first customer by recording the cash received from the second customer as attributable to the first, and so on with subsequent customers. The cashier hopes to be in a position to replace the cash before the dishonesty is discovered. As such hopes are frequently based on attempts at gambling, the deception is often discovered.

laptop computer A small portable personal computer that can be operated from its own rechargeable batteries, has a flat display screen that folds over the keyboard when not in use, and is generally suitable for use while travelling. Laptops usually have all the features of an equivalent desktop model. Small versions of laptops are sometimes called **notebook computers**. *See also* PDA; TABLET COMPUTER.

lari (GEL) The standard monetary unit of Georgia, divided into 100 tetri.

laser printer A type of high-speed, high-quality printer used with computers and *desktop publishing equipment. The characters to be printed are formed by a low-power laser, which alters the electrical charge on appropriate areas of the surface of a photoconductive rotating drum, as in *xerography.

LASH Acronym for *l*ighter *a*board *sh*ip. This is a method of cargo handling in which cargo-carrying barges (lighters) are lifted on and off ocean-going ships by the ship's own crane, thus reducing to a minimum the need for port facilities.

Laspeyres' index *See* INDEX NUMBER.

last-in-first-out cost (LIFO cost) A method of valuing units of raw material or finished goods issued from stock by using the latest unit value for pricing the issues until all the quantity of stock received at that price is used up. The next earliest price is then used for pricing the issues, and so on. Because the issues are based on a LIFO cost, the valuation of closing stocks is described as being on the same LIFO basis. The method may also be used in *process costing to value the work in process at the end of an accounting period. This method of costing is not normally acceptable for stock valuation in the UK. *Compare* FIRST-IN-FIRST-OUT COST; NEXT-IN-FIRST-OUT COST.

last-survivor policy 1. An *assurance policy on the lives of two people, the sum assured being paid on the death of the last to die. *See also* JOINT-LIFE AND LAST-SURVIVOR ANNUITIES. **2.** A contract (formerly called a **tontine**) in which assurance is arranged by a group of people, who all pay premiums into a fund while they are alive. No payment is made until only one person from the group is left alive. At that point the survivor receives all the policy proceeds. Contracts of this kind are not available in the UK because of the temptation they provide to members to murder their fellows, in order to be the last survivor.

last trading day The last day on which commodity trading for a particular delivery period can be transacted.

late majority *See* ADOPTION OF INNOVATIONS.

lateral integration *See* INTEGRATION.

Latin American Integration Association (LAIA; ALADI) An economic grouping of South American countries with headquarters in Montevideo. It superseded the **Latin American Free Trade Area (LAFTA)** in 1981. Its members are Argentina, Bolivia, Brazil, Chile, Colombia, Cuba, Ecuador, Mexico, Panama, Paraguay, Peru, Uruguay, and Venezuela. Nicaragua is currently (2015) in the process of joining. *See also* MERCOSUR.

lats Formerly, the standard monetary unit of Latvia, divided into 100 santimes. It was replaced by the *euro in 2014.

laundering money Processing money acquired illegally (as by theft, drug dealing, etc.) so that it appears to have come from a legitimate source. This may be achieved by paying the illegal cash into a foreign bank and transferring its equivalent to a bank with a good name in a hard-currency area. There are now stringent controls on this activity.

lay days The number of days allowed to a ship to load or unload without incurring *demurrage. **Reversible lay days** permit the shipper to add to the days allowed for unloading any days he has saved while loading. Lay days may be calculated as *running days (all consecutive days), *working days (excluding Sundays and public holidays), or *weather working days (working days on which the weather allows work to be carried out).

laying off Suspending or terminating the employment of workers because there is no work for them to do. If the laying off involves a permanent termination of employment, *redundancy payments will be involved.

lay-off pay US for *redundancy payment.

LBO Abbreviation for *leveraged buy-out.

LCH Abbreviation for *London Clearing House.

LCM Abbreviation for *lower of cost or market.

lead The first named underwriting syndicate on a Lloyd's insurance policy. When a broker seeks to cover a risk he will first try to get a large syndicate to act as lead, which encourages smaller syndicates to cover a share of the risk. The premium rate is calculated by the lead; if others wish to join in the risk they have to insure at that rate. On a collective policy the lead insurer is the first insurer on the schedule of insurers; he issues the policy, collects the premiums, and distributes the proportions to the coinsurers.

lead bank *See* LEAD MANAGER.

leadership continuum theory *See* TANNENBAUM–SCHMIDT CONTINUUM.

leadership style The traits, behavioural tendencies, and characteristic methods of a person in a leadership position. An important dimension of leadership style is the extent to which the leader is willing to delegate responsibility and encourage input from followers; some key styles here are those of the *authoritarian leader, *democratic leader, and *laissez-faire leader. Another basic dimension is the extent to which a leader is *task-motivated (concerned with defining goals and the means to achieve them) or *relationship-motivated (concerned with supporting and encouraging subordinates). A distinction can also be drawn between the *charis-matic leader, who relies on his or her per-sonal qualities to inspire followers, and the *bureaucratic leader, who depends on his or her position in the hierarchy and an established set of rules and procedures. *See* TRANSACTIONAL LEADERSHIP; TRANSFORMATIONAL LEADERSHIP. *See also* POWER STYLES.

leadership theories In *industrial and organizational psychology, various theories that have been put forward to explain the successful or unsuccessful performance of leaders. Such theories tend to fall into three main categories:

- **Trait theories of leadership** focus on the role played by certain key personality traits in the leader. These usually include decisiveness, organizational ability, con-fidence, and communication skills.
- **Behavioural theories of leadership** focus on issues of *leadership style, notably the extent to which the leader can be described as *task-motivated or *relationship-motivated. *Contingency theories of leadership attempt to define the different leadership behaviours demanded by different situations.
- **Cognitive theories of leadership** focus on the ways in which followers' ideas and

perceptions can affect the performance of their leaders.

See also PATH-GOAL LEADERSHIP MODEL; SITUATIONAL LEADERSHIP THEORY; TANNENBAUM–SCHMIDT CONTINUUM; VROOM–YETTON–JAGO MODEL.

leading and lagging 1. Techniques often used at the end of a financial year to enhance a cash position and reduce borrowing. This is achieved by arranging for the settlement of outstanding obligations to be accelerated (leading) or delayed (lagging). **2.** The use of similar techniques to benefit from the expected change in a currency value.

leading indicators Key variables in a *time-series analysis that change in the same direction but in advance of company sales.

leading measures *See* BALANCED SCORECARD.

lead manager (lead bank) A bank or other financial institution chosen to underwrite a new issue of bonds or to head a *syndicated bank facility. It is usually chosen either because it has a close relationship with the borrower or because it has been successful in a competitive *bought deal contest. The lead manager is the main organizer of the transactions and takes a larger fee than the other institutions involved.

lead users The first users of a new product or service, who are asked to assess its advantages and disadvantages in relation to those of its competitors. They are often company employees, loyal customers, or people who have the relevant expertise.

leakage 1. The loss of a liquid from a faulty container. **2.** An allowance for loss of a liquid in transit, due to evaporation or other causes.

lean back A period of cautious inaction by a government agency before intervening in a market. For example, a central bank might allow a lean-back period to elapse to allow exchange rates to stabilize, before intervening in the foreign exchange market.

lean production An approach to manufacturing that focuses on eliminating waste and improving work flow. It is particularly associated with the production system established at Toyota in the 1950s and 1960s, with its twin pillars of *just-in-time inventory management and automated quality control. In recent decades the principles of 'lean thinking' have been increasingly applied within the service industries. *See also* KAIZEN; KANBAN; SHINGO'S SEVEN WASTES.

learning and growth perspective *See* BALANCED SCORECARD.

learning curve A technique that takes into account the reduction in time taken to carry out production as the cumulative output rises. The concept is based on a doubling of output, so that a 70% learning curve means that the cumulative average time taken per unit falls to 70% of the previous cumulative average time as the output doubles. The cumulative average time per unit is measured from the very first unit produced. The formula for the learning curve is:

$$y = ax^{-b},$$

where y is the cumulative average time per unit of production, a is the time taken to produce the first unit, x is the cumulative number of units manufactured to date, and b is the learning coefficient.

learning organization An organization that is dedicated to the idea of continuous learning and improvement. Such an organization will see the training and development of its work force as a major priority, will constantly seek out and evaluate new ideas and approaches, and will establish structures and processes that maximize the opportunities for learning presented by each work task.

lease A contract between the owner of a specific asset, the **lessor**, and another party, the **lessee**, allowing the latter to hire the asset. The lessor retains the right of ownership but the lessee acquires the right to use the asset for a specific period of time in return for the payment of specific rentals or payments. The Financial Reporting Standard Applicable in the UK and Republic of Ireland classifies leases into *operating leases and *finance leases with differing accounting treatments (Section 20). The relevant *International Accounting Standard is IAS 17, Leases.

leaseback (renting back) An arrangement in which the owner of an *asset (such as land or buildings) sells it to another party but immediately enters into a *lease agreement with the purchaser to obtain the right to use the asset. Such a transaction is a method for raising funds and can affect the *financial statements of a company, depending on whether a *finance lease or an *operating lease is entered into.

leased department retailer An independent retailer who owns the merchandise stocked and displayed but who leases floor space from another (usually larger) retailer, often using their own retailing name. This arrangement is sometimes called a shop within a shop.

leasehold land Land held under a *lease. The land will eventually revert to the freehold owner, although there has been some statutory modification of this right to repossession (e.g. in the Rent Acts). This is the most common way for blocks of offices to be owned. The landlord maintains possession of the common parts and creates separate leases for each office. The ownership of each office may subsequently change as leases are assigned.

lease-purchase agreement A lease in which the payments go towards the purchase of the asset. *See also* HIRE PURCHASE.

leasing Hiring equipment, such as a car or a piece of machinery, to avoid the capital cost involved in owning it. In some companies it is advantageous to use capital for other purposes and to lease some equipment, paying for the hire out of income. The equipment is then an asset of the leasing company rather than the lessor.

Sometimes a case can be made for leasing rather than purchasing, on the grounds that some equipment quickly becomes obsolete.

Least Preferred Co-worker Scale (LPC Scale) A measure used to identify the extent to which a leader is predominantly *task-motivated or *relationship-motivated. The participant is asked to think of the co-worker with whom he or she has had the most problems in the past and to rate this person on a series of dimensions, such as intelligent–unintelligent, honest–dishonest, and so on. A total score is then derived from these ratings. Leaders who score their least preferred co-worker relatively highly are assumed to be *relationship-motivated; those who are more critical are assumed to be *task-motivated. *See also* CONTINGENCY THEORIES OF LEADERSHIP; LEADERSHIP STYLE.

ledger A collection of *accounts of a similar type. Traditionally, a ledger was a large book with separate pages for each account; in modern systems they will usually consist of computer records. The most common ledgers are the *nominal ledger containing the *impersonal accounts, the *sales ledger containing the accounts of an organization's customers, and the *purchase ledger containing the accounts of an organization's suppliers.

leg One element in a complex set of financial transactions. *See* BREAKING A LEG; STRADDLE.

legal capital In the USA, the amount of stockholders' equity which cannot be reduced by the payment of dividends. This is the value of a company's shares in the balance sheet.

legal person *See* ARTIFICIAL PERSON.

legal reserve The minimum amount of money that building societies, insurance companies, etc., are bound by law to hold as security for the benefit of their customers.

legal tender Money that must be accepted in discharge of a debt. It may be

limited legal tender, i.e. it must be accepted but only up to specified limits of payment; or **unlimited legal tender**, i.e. acceptable in settlement of debts of any amount. Bank of England notes and the £2 and £1 coins are unlimited legal tender in the UK. Other Royal Mint coins are limited legal tender; i.e. debts up to £10 can be paid in 50p and 20p coins; up to £5 by 10p and 5p coins; and up to 20p by bronze coins.

lek (ALL) The standard monetary unit of Albania, divided into 100 qindars.

lempira (HNL) The standard monetary unit of Honduras, divided into 100 centavos.

lender of last resort A country's *central bank with responsibility for controlling its banking system. In the UK, the Bank of England fulfils this role, lending to *discount houses, either by repurchasing *Treasury bills, lending on other paper assets, or granting direct loans, charging the *base rate of interest. *Commercial banks do not go directly to the Bank of England; they borrow from the discount houses.

lending multiple 1. The ratio of a bank's deposits to its highly liquid assets. **2.** In the UK housing market, a multiple of the borrower's income used to calculate the maximum amount that will be lent on a mortgage.

leone (SLL) The standard monetary unit of Sierra Leone, divided into 100 cents.

lepton (*plural* **lepta**) A former monetary unit of Greece, worth one hundredth of a *drachma.

lessee The party to a *lease contract who uses the asset and makes the lease payments.

lessor The party to a *lease contract who provides the asset and receives the lease payments.

letter of allotment *See* ALLOTMENT.

letter of comfort 1. A letter to a bank from the parent company of a subsidiary that is trying to borrow money from the bank. The letter gives no guarantee for the repayment of the projected loan but offers the bank the comfort of knowing that the subsidiary has made the parent company aware of its intention to borrow; the parent also usually supports the application, giving, at least, an assurance that it intends that the subsidiary should remain in business and that it will give notice of any relevant change of ownership. **2.** A letter by one party to a bank indicating a relationship that will make a second party more likely to repay a bank loan.

letter of credit (documentary credit) A letter from one banker to another authorizing the payment of a specified sum to the person named in the letter on certain specified conditions (*see* LETTER OF INDICATION). Commercially, letters of credit are widely used in the international import and export trade as a means of payment. In an export contract, the exporter may require the foreign importer to open a letter of credit at the importer's local bank (the issuing bank) for the amount of the goods. This will state that it is to be negotiable at a bank (the negotiating bank) in the exporter's country in favour of the exporter; often, the exporter (who is called the beneficiary of the credit) will give the name of the negotiating bank. On presentation of the shipping documents (which are listed in the letter of credit) the beneficiary will receive payment from the negotiating bank.

An **irrevocable letter of credit** cannot be cancelled by the person who opens it or by the issuing bank without the beneficiary's consent, whereas a **revocable letter of credit** can. In a **confirmed letter of credit** the negotiating bank guarantees to pay the beneficiary, even if the issuing bank fails to honour its commitments (in an **unconfirmed letter of credit** this guarantee is not given). A confirmed irrevocable letter of credit therefore provides the most reliable means of being paid for exported goods. However, all letters of credit have an expiry date, after which they can only be negotiated by the consent of all the parties.

A **circular letter of credit** is an instruction from a bank to its correspondent banks to pay the beneficiary a stated sum on presentation of a means of identification. It has now been replaced by *traveller's cheques.

Although the term 'letter of credit' is still widely used, in 1983 the International Chamber of Commerce recommended **documentary credit** as the preferred term for these instruments.

letter of hypothecation *See* HYPOTHECA-TION.

letter of indemnity 1. A letter stating that the organization issuing it will compensate the person to whom it is addressed for a specified loss. *See also* INDEMNITY. **2.** A letter written to a company registrar asking for a replacement for a lost share certificate and indemnifying the company against any loss that it might incur in so doing. It may be required to be counter-signed by a bank. **3.** A letter written by an exporter accepting responsibility for any losses arising from faulty packing, short weight, etc., at the time of shipment. If this letter accompanies the *shipping documents, the shipping company will issue a clean *bill of lading, even if the packages are damaged, enabling the exporter to negotiate the documents and receive payment without trouble.

letter of indication (letter of identification) A letter issued by a bank to a customer to whom a *letter of credit has been supplied. The letter has to be produced with the letter of credit at the negotiating bank; it provides evidence of the bearer's identity and a specimen of his or her signature. It is used particularly with a circular letter of credit carried by travellers, although *traveller's cheques are now more widely used.

letter of intent A letter in which a person formally sets out his or her intentions to do something, such as signing a contract in certain circumstances, which are often specified in detail in the letter. The letter does not constitute either a contract or a promise to do anything, but it does indicate the writer's serious wish to pursue the course set out.

letter of licence A letter from a creditor to a debtor, who is having trouble raising the money to settle the debt. The letter states that the creditor will allow the debtor a stated time to pay and will not initiate proceedings against the debtor before that time. *See also* ARRANGEMENT.

letter of regret A letter from a company, or its bankers, stating that an application for an allotment from a *new issue of shares has been unsuccessful.

letter of renunciation 1. A form, often attached to an *allotment letter, on which a person who has been allotted shares in a *new issue renounces any rights to them, either absolutely or in favour of someone else (during the **renunciation period**). **2.** A form on the reverse of some *unit-trust certificates, which the holder completes to dispose of the holding. The holder sends the completed certificate to the trust managers.

letter of set-off *See* SET-OFF.

letters of administration An order authorizing the person named (the *administrator) to distribute the property of a deceased person, who has not appointed anyone else to do so. The distribution must be in accordance with the deceased's will, or the rules of intestacy if he or she died *intestate.

leu (*plural* **lei**) The standard monetary unit of Romania (RON) and Moldova (MDL), divided into 100 bani.

lev (*plural* **leva**) **(BGN)** The standard monetary unit of Bulgaria, divided into 100 stotinki.

level output strategy An approach to *aggregate planning that aims to regulate production at a constant level, regardless of fluctuation in demand. It involves storing the product in times of low demand and is not therefore an option available to the providers of services. The benefits include maintaining a stable workforce and the optimum use of capacity. The disadvantages include the costs of storage and the difficulty of responding to major changes in demand. *Compare* CHASE DEMAND STRATEGY.

level scheduling *See* UNIFORM LOAD SCHEDULING.

leverage 1. A US word, now increasingly used in the UK, for *gearing. **2.** The use by a company of its limited assets to guarantee substantial loans to finance its business.

leveraged buy-out (LBO) The acquisition of one company by another through the use of borrowed funds. The intention is that the loans will be repaid from the cash flow of the acquired company. In the 1980s many takeovers in the USA were financed by the issue of *junk bonds in highly leveraged buyouts. More recently, LBOs have become associated with the activities of *private equity firms.

leveraged lease A *lease in which the lessor borrows as part of the finance of the asset to be leased.

leverage ratios *See* GEARING RATIOS.

liability 1. The funding of a business debt. *See* CURRENT LIABILITIES; DEFERRED CREDIT; LONG-TERM LIABILITY; SECURED LIABILITY. **2.** An obligation to make a financial payment. *See* CONTINGENT LIABILITY. **3.** The acceptance of an insurance risk.

liability insurance A form of insurance policy that promises to pay any compensation and court costs the policyholder becomes legally liable to pay because of claims for injury to other people or damage to their property as a result of the policyholder's negligence. Policies often define the areas in which they will deal with liability, e.g. personal liability or employers' liability (*see* EMPLOYERS' LIABILITY INSURANCE).

LIBID Abbreviation for *London Inter Bank Bid Rate.

LIBOR Abbreviation for *London Inter Bank Offered Rate.

licence 1. Official permission to do something that is forbidden without a licence (e.g. sell alcohol or own a TV or a firearm). Licences may be required for social reasons or simply to enable revenue to be collected. Since the Consumer Credit Act 1974 all businesses involved with giving credit to purchasers of goods must be licensed by the Office of Fair Trading. **2.** Formal permission to enter or occupy land. Such licenses are of three kinds. (a) The simplest gives the licensee the permission of the landowner to be on land (e.g. the right of a visitor to enter a house). It may be revoked at any time. (b) **Contractual licences** are permissions to be on land in the furtherance of some contractual right (e.g. the right of the holder of a cinema ticket to be in the cinema). (c) Licences coupled with an interest are those that go with a recognizable interest in the land of another. Such licences are irrevocable and assignable. **3.** *See* FRANCHISE. **4.** A *carrier's licence.

licensed brand A product or service using a registered brand name offered by the brand owner to a licensee for an agreed fee or royalty.

licensed dealer A dealer licensed under the *Financial Services Act 1986 to provide investment advice and deal in securities, either as an agent or principal. Licensed dealers are not members of the *London Stock Exchange and are not covered by its compensation fund.

licensing In international marketing, an agreement by which a company (the licensor) permits a foreign company (the licensee) to set up a business in the foreign market using the licensor's manufacturing processes, patents, trademarks, trade secrets, etc., in exchange for payment of a fee or royalty.

lien The right of one person to retain possession of goods owned by another until the possessor's claims against the owner have been satisfied. In a **general lien**, the goods are held as security for all the outstanding debts of the owner, whereas in a **particular lien** only the claims of the possessor in respect of the goods held must be satisfied. Thus an unpaid seller may in some contracts be entitled to retain the goods until receiving the price, a carrier may have a lien over goods being transported, and a repairer over goods being repaired. Whether a lien arises or not depends on the terms of the contract and usual trade practice. This type of lien is a **possessory lien**, but sometimes actual possession of the goods is not necessary. In an **equitable lien**, for example, the claim exists independently of possession. If a purchaser of the property involved is given notice of the lien it binds him; otherwise he will not be bound. Similarly a **maritime lien**, which binds a ship or cargo in connection with some maritime liability, does not depend on possession and can be enforced by arrest and sale (unless security is given). Examples of maritime liens are the lien of a salvor, those of seamen for their wages and of masters for their wages and outgoings, that of a bottomry or respondentia bondholder (*see* HYPOTHECATION), and that over a ship at fault in a collision in which property has been damaged.

life annuity An *annuity that ceases to be paid on the death of a specified person, which may or may not be the *annuitant.

life assurance An *insurance policy that pays a specified amount of money on the death of the *life assured or, in the case of an *endowment assurance policy, on the death of the life assured or at the end of an agreed period, whichever is the earlier. Life assurance grew from a humble means of providing funeral expenses to a means of saving for oneself or one's dependants, with certain tax advantages. *With-profits policies provide sums of money in excess of the sum assured by the addition of *bonuses. *Unit-linked policies invest the premiums in funds of assets, by means of buying units in the funds. See also WHOLE LIFE POLICY.

life assured The person upon whose death a life-assurance policy makes an agreed payment. The life assured need not be the owner of the policy.

lifeboat 1. A fund set up to rescue dealers on an exchange in the event of a market collapse and the ensuing insolvencies. **2.** The rescue of a company that is in financial difficulty by new or restructured loans from its group of bankers.

life-cycle costing An approach to determining the total costs of a *fixed asset that takes into account all the costs likely to be incurred both in acquiring it and in operating it over its effective life. For example, the initial cost to an airline of an aircraft is only part of the costs relevant to the decision to purchase it. The operating costs over its effective life are also relevant and would therefore be part of the decision-making data. This is an aspect of *terotechnology.

life-cycle segmentation An approach to marketing that recognizes that consumers' needs change at different stages of their lives.

life office A company that provides *life assurance.

lifestyle The activities, interests, opinions, and values of individuals as they affect their mode of living. Lifestyle reflects more than social class or personality; it provides a profile of a person's whole pattern of behaviour and interaction with the world. Lifestyles are important in marketing because they influence the way in which people elect to make purchases. The technique for measuring lifestyle is part of *psychographic segmentation. It involves measuring primary characteristics, known as **AIO dimensions** (activities, interests, and opinions). Lifestyle classifications have been developed out of this, particularly the **Values and Lifestyles Typology** (**VALS**), which classifies consumers into lifestyle groups. The current VALS system uses a questionnaire to classify people into eight segments according to their demographic characteristics and 'primary motivations'.

lifestyle business A small business run by owners with a personal interest in the product. The business reflects their lifestyles and provides them with a comfortable income, but is not a growth venture. Compilers of reference books could fall into this category.

lifestyle format An advertising format that reflects a target market's *lifestyle.

lifestyle segmentation Segmentation of a market based on *lifestyles. More companies are segmenting their markets by lifestyles, as these are increasingly seen as good predictors of consumer behaviour. Most companies use off-the-shelf research-agency classifications, because of the high cost and complexity of developing their own. *See* MARKET SEGMENTATION.

lifetime transfers *See* POTENTIALLY EXEMPT TRANSFER.

lifetime value (customer lifetime value; customer equity) The future long-term profitability of a particular customer, i.e. the amount by which the revenue received from this customer will exceed the cost of attracting, selling to, and servicing him or her. There is no clear agreement on how lifetime value can be measured. One technique is to forecast future cash flows for the customer, identify an appropriate *discount rate or *cost of capital, and then calculate the *net present value of the cash flows. This is a relatively simple calculation but it does involve managers making difficult assumptions. One key assumption is customer retention. Managers may not agree on how loyal a customer will be in the future and whether sales will increase or decrease. A company will always be looking at strategies for maximizing the lifetime value of customers. *See also* CUSTOMER PROFITABILITY ANALYSIS.

LIFFE The London International Financial Futures and Options Exchange. A *financial futures market opened in 1982, in London's Royal Exchange, to provide facilities within the European time zone for dealing in options and futures contracts, including those in government bonds, share indexes, foreign currencies, and interest rates. In 1991 LIFFE moved into its own premises in the City of London. The London Traded Options Market merged with LIFFE in 1992, when the words 'and Options' was added to its full name, although the familiar acronym (pronounced 'lifey') remained unchanged. Electronic trading via the LIFFE CONNECT system was introduced in 1989 but did not replace live *pit trading until 1998. In 1996 LIFFE merged with the London Commodity Exchange, making it the first exchange to provide futures and options contracts on financial, equity, and commodity products and equity indices. Since 2002 it has been part of the pan-European exchange *Euronext NV, with markets in Amsterdam, Brussels, Lisbon, and Paris. The London exchange is now known as **Euronext.liffe**.

LIFO cost Abbreviation for *last-in-first-out cost.

lifting a leg *See* BREAKING A LEG.

light dues A levy on shipowners for maintaining lighthouses, beacons, buoys, etc., collected in the UK by HM Revenue and Customs on behalf of *Trinity House.

lighter A flat-bottomed cargo barge, usually without its own means of propulsion, that is towed by a tug for short distances, as between a ship and a quay or along a river from a port to a warehouse. The charge for transporting goods by lighter is the **lighterage**. *See also* LASH.

lilangeni (*plural* **emalangeni**) **(SZL)** The standard monetary unit of Swaziland, divided into 100 cents.

LIMEAN Abbreviation for *London Inter Bank Mean Rate.

limit 1. The *maximum fluctuations (up or down) allowed in certain markets over a stated period (usually one day's trading; *see* INTRADAY LIMIT). In some volatile circumstances the market moves the limit up (or down). The movement of prices on the Tokyo Stock Exchange is limited in this way as it is on certain US commodity markets. In some markets, if the limit is reached trading is stopped for the day or for a cooling-off period. **2.** A restriction on a derivatives or commodity exchange on the number of contracts or positions one party can hold.

limitation of actions Statutory rules limiting the time within which civil actions can be brought. Actions in simple contract and tort must be brought within six years of the cause of action. There are several special rules, including that for strict liability actions for defective products, in which case the period is three years from the accrual of the cause of action or (if later) the date on which the plaintiff knew, or should have known, the material facts, but not later than ten years from the date on which the product was first put into circulation. The present UK law is contained in the Limitations Act 1980, the Latent Damage Act 1986, and the Consumer Protection Act 1987.

limited by guarantee *See* COMPANY LIMITED BY GUARANTEE; LIMITED COMPANY.

limited company A *company in which the liability of the members in respect of the company's debts is limited. It may be **limited by shares**, in which case the liability of the members on a winding-up is limited to the amount (if any) unpaid on their shares. This is by far the most common type of registered company. The liability of the members may alternatively be **limited by guarantee**; in this case the liability of members is limited by the memorandum to a certain amount, which the members undertake to contribute on winding-up. These are usually societies, clubs, or trade associations. Since 1980 it has not been possible for such a company to be formed with a share capital, or converted to a company limited by guarantee with a share capital. *See also* PUBLIC LIMITED COMPANY.

limited-function wholesaler *See* LIMITED-SERVICE MERCHANT WHOLESALER.

limited liability *See* LIMITED COMPANY; LIMITED LIABILITY PARTNERSHIP.

limited liability partnership (LLP) A legally recognized entity under the Limited Liability Partnership Act 2000. This type of business organization is intended to combine the flexibility of a traditional *partnership with the corporate notion of limited liability. Persons intending to set up a limited liability partnership must register it with *Companies House. There are also several disclosure requirements that are similar in nature to those required by companies. Much of the pressure for this change in the law was led by accountancy and audit partnerships, wishing to limit the liability of partners against claims for *negligence.

limited market A market for a particular security in which buying and selling is difficult, usually because a large part of the issue is held by very few people or institutions.

limited partner *See* PARTNERSHIP. *See also* LIMITED LIABILITY PARTNERSHIP.

limited recourse financing *See* PROJECT FINANCING.

limited-service merchant wholesaler (limited-function wholesaler) A wholesaler that offers less than full service for customers but charges lower prices than a full-service merchant wholesaler.

limited-service retailer A retailer that provides only a limited number of services to shoppers, but usually sells goods at a discount.

limit order *See* AT LIMIT.

limit price The highest price that established sellers in a market can charge for a product, without inducing a new seller to enter the market. The limit price is usually lower than the monopoly price but higher than the competitive price. Limit pricing enables established sellers to make higher profits than they would if they sold at the competitive price and it also ensures that new firms will not enter the market and drive the prices down to competitive levels.

line and staff management A system of management used in large organizations in which there are two separate hierarchies; the **line management** side consists of **line managers** with responsibility for deciding the policy of and running the organization's main activities (such as manufacturing, sales, etc.), while the **staff management**, and its separate **staff managers**, are responsible for providing such supporting services as warehousing, accounting, transport, personnel management, and plant maintenance.

linear cost function *Cost behaviour that, when plotted on a graph against activity levels, results in a straight line. For example, total fixed cost levels and variable costs per unit of activity will both result in a straight line horizontal to the x-axis when activity, production, or sales is plotted on the x-axis. Total variable costs will also result in a straight line and is thus a linear cost function.

linear depreciation *Depreciation charges that, when plotted on a graph against time on the x-axis, result in a straight line, as a constant amount per annum is written off the assets concerned. Both the *straight-line method of depreciation and the *rate per unit of production method, when the depreciation charge is plotted against production levels, result in linear depreciation.

linear programming A modelling technique that determines an optimal solution for attaining an objective by taking into consideration a number of *constraints. The objective function, often to optimize profits or minimize costs, is expressed as an equation and the constraints are also expressed in mathematical terms. Where only two products and few constraints are involved a solution may be obtained graphically. More than two products requires a computer program.

line extending Increasing a line of products by adding variations of an existing brand. For example, Coca Cola extended its line with Diet Coke. Line extending runs

the risk of weakening the brand name. *Compare* LINE FILLING.

line filling Adding products to an existing line of products in order to leave no opportunities for competitors. Line filling can be horizontal or vertical. In horizontal line filling, a video manufacturer may produce machines with a variety of features, such as half-speed copying, multi-recording memory, etc., at the top end of the price range, and relatively cheap cost-effective machines at the opposite end; a competitor can therefore only compete on price. In vertical line-filling a manufacturer may produce a wide variety of brand names within a single product line; some detergent manufacturers do this. *Compare* LINE EXTENDING.

line management *See* LINE AND STAFF MANAGEMENT.

line production (mass production) A type of process in which high volumes of identical, or very similar, products are made in a set sequence of operations. It involves high capital expenditure and depends on efficient plant layouts and procedures, as well as good product design to minimize unit costs. The levels of skill required are not usually high. In recent years a number of organizations have experimented with systems that trade off the benefits of full line production in exchange for the increased levels of motivation following from giving staff more ownership of the product, e.g. through *cellular layout. The introduction of computerized control systems has enabled some manufacturers to produce apparently unique products without losing the benefits of the line process. For example, some Japanese car manufacturers have put together a relatively small range of standard components, trims, finishes, etc., to the customer's specification, which enables them to claim that no two of their cars are identical.

LinkedIn A *social media platform that is chiefly used for professional networking. The site, which was launched in 2003 and became a public company in 2011, is increasingly important as a place to make business contacts and to find jobs or candidates for jobs.

lipa A monetary unit of Croatia, worth one hundredth of a *kuna.

lipstick effect (lipstick indicator) The tendency for sales of lipstick and similar items to rise sharply during or immediately before a recession. In times of low consumer confidence, it is said, women will increase their spending on small indulgences, such as lipstick, as a substitute for major purchases, such as designer dresses or handbags.

liquid assets (liquid capital; quick assets; realizable assets) Assets held in cash or in something that can be readily turned into cash with minimal capital loss (e.g. deposits in a bank current account, trade debts, marketable investments). The ratio of these assets to current liabilities provides an assessment of an organization's *liquidity or solvency. *See also* LIQUID RATIO; MANDATORY LIQUID ASSETS.

liquidation (winding-up) The distribution of a company's assets among its creditors and members prior to its dissolution. This brings the life of the company to an end. The liquidation may be voluntary (*see* CREDITORS' VOLUNTARY LIQUIDATION; MEMBERS' VOLUNTARY LIQUIDATION) or by the court (*see* COMPULSORY LIQUIDATION).

liquidation committee A committee set up by creditors of a company being wound up in order to consent to the *liquidator exercising certain of his powers. When the company is unable to pay its debts, the committee is usually composed of creditors only; otherwise it consists of creditors and *contributories.

liquidator A person appointed by a court, or by the members of a company or its creditors, to regularize the company's affairs on a *liquidation (winding-up). In the case of a *members' voluntary liquidation, it is the members of the company who appoint the liquidator. In a *creditors' voluntary liquidation, the liquidator may

be appointed by company members before the **meeting of creditors** or by the creditors themselves at the meeting; in the former case the liquidator can only exercise his or her powers with the consent of the court. If two liquidators are appointed, the court resolves which one is to act. In a *compulsory liquidation, the court appoints a *provisional liquidator after the winding-up petition has been presented; after the order has been granted, the court appoints the *official receiver as liquidator, until or unless another officer is appointed.

The liquidator is in a relationship of trust with the company and the creditors as a body; a liquidator appointed in a compulsory liquidation is an officer of the court, is under statutory obligations, and may not profit from the position. A liquidator must be a qualified *insolvency practitioner, according to the Insolvency Act 1986. On appointment, the liquidator assumes control of the company, collects the assets, pays the debts, and distributes any surplus to company members according to their rights. In the case of a compulsory liquidation, the liquidator is supervised by the court, the *liquidation committee, and the Department for Business, Innovation and Skills. The liquidator receives a *statement of affairs from the company officers and must report on these to the court.

liquid capital *See* LIQUID ASSETS.

liquid instrument A *negotiable instrument that the purchaser is able to sell before maturity.

liquidity The extent to which an organization's assets are liquid (*see* LIQUID ASSETS), enabling it to pay its debts when they fall due and also to move into new investment opportunities.

liquidity index A measure of a company's liquidity assessed by calculating the number of days it would take for current assets to be converted into cash.

liquidity premium The relative advantage of holding assets in liquid form. Investors are prepared to receive lower returns on *liquid assets, because they can easily be transferred into cash with little capital loss. Liquid assets are thus to some extent a hedge against uncertainty.

liquidity risk The risk, in lending operations, that an investment cannot be liquidated during its life without significant costs.

liquidity trap A situation in which investors hold on to cash because they are worried about the likelihood of a fall in the price of financial assets. J. M. Keynes argued that in these circumstances monetary policy becomes ineffective, because monetary expansion will not lower interest rates.

liquid market A financial market in which *spreads are narrow, there are many buyers and sellers, and large transactions do not have a marked impact on the market price.

liquid ratio (quick ratio) A ratio used for assessing the *liquidity of a company; it is the ratio of the *liquid assets (i.e. the *current assets less the *stock) to the *current liabilities. For example, a company has current assets of £250,000, including stock of £150,000, and liabilities of £120,000. This gives a liquid ratio of:

$$(£250,000 - £150,000)/£120,000 = 0.83,$$

i.e. 83% or 0.83:1. This may be interpreted as the company having 83 pence of liquid assets for every £1 of current liabilities. If, for some reason, the company was obliged to repay the current liabilities immediately there would be insufficient liquid assets to allow it to do so. The company might therefore be forced into a hurried sale of stock at a discount to raise finance. Although there is no rule of thumb, and there are industry differences, a liquid ratio significantly below 1:1 will give rise to concern. The liquid ratio is regarded as an acid test of a company's solvency and is therefore sometimes called the **acid-test ratio**.

lira 1. (TRY) The standard monetary unit of Turkey, divided into 100 kuruş. **2.** Formerly, the standard monetary unit of Italy and San Marino, divided into 100 centesimi. It was replaced by the *euro in 2002. **3.** Formerly, the standard monetary unit of Malta, divided into 100 cents. Malta adopted the euro in 2008.

lisente A monetary unit of Lesotho, worth one hundredth of a *loti.

listed company A company that has a listing agreement (*see* LISTING REQUIRE- MENTS) with a major stock exchange and whose shares have a quotation on that exchange. In the UK such companies were formerly called **quoted companies**.

listed option *See* EXCHANGE-TRADED OPTION.

listed security 1. In general, a security that has a *quotation on a recognized *stock exchange. **2.** On the *London Stock Exchange, a security that has a quotation in the Official List of Securities of the *main market. *See also* FLOTATION; LISTING REQUIREMENTS; YELLOW BOOK.

listing requirements The conditions that must be satisfied before a security can be traded on a stock exchange. To achieve a quotation in the Official List of Securities of the *main market of the *London Stock Exchange, the requirements contained in a **listing agreement** must be signed by the company seeking quotation. The two main requirements of such a listing are usually:

- that the value of the company's assets should exceed a certain value;
- that the company publish specific financial and operating information, both at the time of *flotation and regularly thereafter.

Listing requirements are generally more stringent the larger the market. For example, the main market in London demands considerably more information from companies than the *Alternative Investment Market. The listing requirements are set out in the *Yellow Book.

list price 1. The retail price of a consumer good as recommended by the manufacturer and shown on his price list. If no price-maintenance agreements apply, a discount on the list price may be offered by the retailer to attract trade. **2.** A supplier's price as shown on an invoice to a retailer or wholesaler, before deduction of any discounts.

list renting The practice of renting a list of potential customers to an organization involved in *direct-mail selling or to a charity raising funds. When the terms of hiring restrict the use of the list to one mail shot, it is usual for the owner of the list to carry out the mailing, so that the hirer cannot copy it for subsequent use.

lists closed The closing of the application lists for a *new issue on the London Stock Exchange, after a specified time or after the issue has been fully subscribed.

litas Formerly, the standard monetary unit of Lithuania, divided into 100 centai. It was replaced by the *euro in 2015.

litigation 1. The taking of legal action. The person who takes it is called a **litigant. 2.** The activity of a solicitor when dealing with proceedings in a court of law.

live-marketing database An abbreviated version of a full *customer database. A live-marketing database sacrifices some degree of customer information to enable marketing decisions to be made more quickly.

livery company One of some 80 chartered companies in the City of London that are descended from medieval craft guilds. Now largely social and charitable institutions, livery companies owe their name to the elaborate ceremonial dress (livery) worn by their officers. Several support independent schools (e.g. Merchant Taylors, Haberdashers, Mercers) and although none are now trading companies, some still have some involvement in their trades (e.g. Fishmongers). In 1878 they joined together to form the City and Guilds of London Institute, which founded the City and Guilds College of the Imperial College of Science and Technology and has been involved in other forms of technical education.

livestock and bloodstock insurance An insurance policy covering the owners against financial losses caused by the death of an animal. Policies may be widened to include cover for treatment fees for certain specified diseases or lost profits for stud animals. Insurances can be arranged to cover single animals or for whole herds.

living company A company that is managed for long-term success rather than for short-term profit. Such companies tend to be sensitive to changes in the business environment but wary of fashionable ideas and cautious with finance; they usually have a cohesive *organizational culture and a commitment to developing the talents of their employees over the mid-to-long term.

Lloyd's A corporation of underwriters (**Lloyd's underwriters**) and insurance brokers (**Lloyd's brokers**) that developed from a coffee shop in Tavern Street in the City of London in 1689. It takes its name from the proprietor of the coffee shop, Edward Lloyd. By 1774 it was established in the Royal Exchange and in 1871 was incorporated by act of parliament. It now occupies a building in Lime Street (built in 1986 by Richard Rogers). As a corporation, Lloyd's itself does not underwrite insurance business; all its business comes to it from some 176 Lloyd's brokers, who are in touch with the public, and is underwritten by some 75 *syndicates of Lloyd's underwriters, who are approached by the brokers and who do not, themselves, contact the public.

The 20,000 or so Lloyd's underwriters must each deposit a substantial sum of money with the corporation and accept unlimited liability before they can become members. They are grouped into syndicates, run by a syndicate manager or agent, but most of the members of syndicates are **names**, underwriting members of Lloyd's who take no part in organizing the underwriting business, but who share in the profits or losses of the syndicate and provide the risk capital. Lloyd's has long specialized in marine insurance but now covers almost all insurance risks. In the period 1988 to 1994 Lloyd's lost some

£8 billion. This brought severe hardship to many names and a number of changes to the way in which the organization is run, including allowing limited liability companies to become underwriters.

Lloyd's agent A person situated in a port to manage the business of Lloyd's members, keeping the corporation informed of shipping movements and accidents, arranging surveys, helping in the settlement of marine insurance claims, and assisting masters of ships. A Lloyd's agent will be found in every significant port in the world.

Lloyd's broker *See* LLOYD'S.

Lloyd's List A daily newspaper founded in Lloyd's coffee shop, London, in 1734. It gives details of the movements of ships and aircraft, accidents, etc. **Lloyd's Loading List**, published weekly, lists ships loading in British and continental ports, with their closing dates for accepting cargo. It also gives general news on the insurance market.

Lloyd's Register A society formed (as **Lloyd's Register of Shipping**) in Lloyd's coffee house, London, in 1760 to inspect and classify all ocean-going vessels in excess of 100 tons. Ships are still periodically surveyed by **Lloyd's surveyors** and classified according to the condition of their hulls, engines, and trappings. The society also provides technical advice. In addition to its annual publication, *Lloyd's Register of Ships*, it now supplies a range of electronic information services. The Register enables underwriters to have instant access to the information they need to underwrite marine risks, even when the vessels may be thousands of miles away. In recent decades it has diversified into other areas of risk management, notably offshore energy.

Lloyd's underwriter *See* LLOYD'S.

LLP Abbreviation for *limited liability partnership.

LME Abbreviation for *London Metal Exchange.

load 1. The cumulative amount of work assigned at any time to a work centre for processing in the future. **2.** *See* BACK-END LOAD; FRONT-END LOAD.

loading 1. The process of allocating jobs or orders to work centres within a production facility. If there is a range of jobs there could be a range of possible routes through the various work centres. Building up a profile of the load on each location enables approximate completion dates for each job to be estimated and bottlenecks in the system to be identified. Loading is based on average times and does not take into account job interference, etc. **Forward loading** begins with the present date and loads jobs forwards. **Backward loading** begins with the completion date and works backwards. *See* FINITE CAPACITY LOADING; INFINITE CAPACITY LOADING. **2.** The addition of a charge to cover incidental expenses, administrative costs, profit, etc., on an insurance policy, bank account, or purchases of unit trusts. *See* BACK-END LOAD; FRONT-END LOAD.

load line One of a series of lines marked on the hull of a ship to show the extent to which the hull may be immersed in the water. Originally introduced by Samuel Plimsoll MP in 1874 and running right round the hull, the **Plimsoll Line** made a great contribution to safety at sea. The modern markings consist of a series of lines, usually painted on the hull amidships, applying to different conditions. The line marked TF applies to tropical fresh water, F fresh water, T tropical sea water, S summer sea water, W winter sea water and WNA winter in the North Atlantic. Shipowners and masters who allow vessels to be overloaded face heavy penalties.

loan Money lent on condition that it is repaid, either in instalments or all at once, on agreed dates and usually that the borrower pays the lender an agreed rate of interest (unless it is an **interest-free loan**). *See also* BALLOON; BANK LOAN; BRIDGING

LOAN; BULLET; LOCAL LOAN; PERSONAL LOAN.

loan account An account opened by a bank in the name of a customer to whom it has granted a loan, rather than an *overdraft facility. The amount of the loan is debited to this account and any repayments are credited; interest is charged on the full amount of the loan less any repayments. The customer's current account is credited with the amount of the loan. With an overdraft facility, interest is only charged on the amount of the overdraft, which may be less than the full amount of the loan.

loanback An arrangement in which an individual can borrow from the accumulated funds of his pension scheme. Usually a commercial rate of interest has to be credited to the fund for the use of the capital. Some life assurance companies offer loan facilities on this basis of up to fifteen times the annual pension premium.

loan-backed Describing an *asset-backed security in which the assets are portfolios of loans. For example, credit-card portfolios or portfolios of unsecured personal loans are loan-backed securities.

loan capital (borrowed capital; debt capital) Capital used to finance an organization that is subject to payment of interest over the life of the loan, at the end of which the loan is normally repaid. There are different categories of loan capital: *mortgage debentures are secured on specific assets of the organization, while convertible debentures may be converted into equity according to the terms of the issue.

loan creditor A person or institution that has lent money to a business. For example, when a bank loan is obtained the bank becomes a loan creditor.

loan note A form of loan stock (*see* DEBENTURE) in which an investor takes a note rather than cash as the result of a share offer to defer tax liability. The yield is often variable and may be linked to the *London Inter Bank Offered Rate. Loan notes are not usually marketable but are usually repayable on demand.

loan-price ratio The ratio of the value of a loan to the value of any *collateral. This formula is often used to judge the risk exposure for mortgages.

loan selling The sale of bank loans by one bank to another. For example, the debt of a developing country may be sold at a discount to the market value in order to reduce the burden of the debt on a particular bank. Loans to individuals may also be sold in this way, from one financial institution to another, often without the borrower knowing that the lender has changed. *See also* EUROBOND.

loan stock *See* DEBENTURE.

local A person who has a seat on a financial market and who deals for his or her own account.

local area network (LAN) A network of microcomputers, printers, and other devices connected together in a localized area, such as an office building. Individual microcomputers (**workstations**) are able to use data on their own local hard disk. In addition, they can access data and software held on a central shared unit (the **file server**), which also controls the operation of the network.

local authority bill A *bill of exchange drawn on a UK local government authority.

localization Altering the content of a product such as a website, computer program, etc., so that it is appropriate to users in a particular country or language group.

local loan A loan issued by a UK local government authority for financing capital expenditure.

location strategy The process of choosing where to locate a unit producing goods or services. This must take account of a range of variables to achieve the minimum cost that optimizes the overall strategy of the particular organization. There are three basic strategies. In a **product-**

based strategy, independent facilities are used to produce each product in a company's range. This permits dedicated design and organization of facilities, which may vary from product to product.

A **market-based** strategy gives priority to locating as close to customers as possible. This is clearly important in the case of services and for organizations offering a quick response to customer requirements, e.g. in fast-moving consumer goods. A **vertically differentiated** strategy locates different elements of the process at different sites, according to the economic characteristics of each element. These considerations are particularly important for transnational and global operations.

lockbox In the USA, a Postal Service box used for the collection of customer payments. The recipient's bank will arrange collection from these boxes throughout the day, deposit the funds, and provide a computer listing of the payments with the daily total. This method is effective for small number of payments with a high value as the bank's charges per item are relatively high.

lock-out A form of industrial action in which the employer refuses to allow employees access to their place of work unless they accept the employer's terms of employment.

lock-up An investment in assets that are not readily realizable, or one that is specifically intended to be held for a long period—say, over ten years.

loco Denoting a price for goods that does not include any loading or transport charges; i.e. the goods are located in a specified place, usually the seller's warehouse or factory, and the buyer has to pay all the charges involved in loading, transporting, or shipping them to their destination. A **loco price** might be quoted in the form: £500 per tonne, loco Islington factory. The equivalent *Incoterm is *Ex Works (EXW).

locus poenitentiae (Latin: an opportunity to repent) An opportunity for the parties to an illegal contract to reconsider their positions, decide not to carry out the illegal act, and so save the contract from being void. Once the illegal purpose has been carried out, no action in law is possible.

log file A file stored on a *web server that records every item *downloaded by users. **Log file analysers** are used to build a picture of the amount of usage of different parts of a website, based on the information contained in the log file.

logical incrementalism An approach to business planning that emphasizes small, incremental changes to strategy as the best means of adapting to changing circumstances. The concept was introduced in 1980 by James Quinn, who characterized it as an evolutionary, fragmented, and intuitive method of approaching change, in which past experience is used as a basis for future plans. Logical incrementalism thus contrasts with models that see planning and strategy in terms of big, overarching decisions.

logistics 1. *See* SUPPLY-CHAIN MANAGEMENT. **2.** The detailed planning of any complex operation.

logo (logtype) A brand name or company name written in a distinctive way.

Lombard rate 1. The rate of interest at which the German central bank, the Bundesbank, lends to German commercial banks, usually ½% above the *discount rate. **2.** The interest rate charged by a European commercial bank lending against security.

Lombard Street The street in the City of London that is the traditional centre of the *money market. Many commercial banks have offices in or near Lombard Street, as do many bill brokers and discount houses. The Bank of England is round the corner.

London acceptance credit A method of providing immediate cash for a UK exporter of goods. On shipment of the goods the exporter draws a *bill of exchange on the foreign buyer. The accepted bill is then pledged to a *merchant bank in London, which accepts an *accommodation bill drawn by the exporter. The acceptance can be discounted on the bank's reputation, to provide the exporter with immediate finance, whereas the foreign buyer's acceptance would be difficult, or impossible, to discount in London.

London approach The approach adopted by London banks to customers facing a cash-flow crisis. The key feature is that the banks remain supportive for as long as possible, decisions are made collectively, and all information and any money paid is shared between the lending banks on an equitable basis.

London Bankers' Clearing House Formerly, the organization that daily set off all cheques drawn for and against the *clearing banks in the UK. It was established in Lombard Street, in the City of London, in the 1770s. In 1985 it was superseded by the Association for Payment Clearing Services (now the *UK Payments Administration).

London Bullion Market The world's largest market for gold and silver trading. Market makers mainly quote prices in US dollars per troy ounce for spot and forward delivery. It is operated by the London Bullion Market Association (LBMA), whose primary task is to ensure that refiners of gold and silver meet the required standards of quality. The Association maintains close links with the Bank of England, which is responsible for the supervision of the market and for publishing its code of conduct.

SEE WEB LINKS
• Website of the LBMA

London Chamber of Commerce The largest *chamber of commerce in the UK. It provides the normal services of a chamber of commerce and in addition runs courses and examinations in business subjects.

London Clearing House (LCH) A *clearing house established in 1888 (known before 1991 as the International

Commodities Clearing House). It provides futures and options markets with netting and settlement services as well as becoming a counterparty (*see* COUNTERPARTY RISK) to every transaction between its members. In this capacity LCH takes the risk of its members defaulting, which it covers by collecting *margins from members; it also provides an independent guarantee from its shareholders and from the insurance market. Exchanges making use of LCH facilities include the *London Stock Exchange, the *London Metal Exchange, and the *International Petroleum Exchange (*ICE Futures Europe). In 2003 LCH merged with the Continental clearing house Clearnet to form **LCH.Clearnet**; the group serves markets across Europe and is the sole clearer for *Euronext NV.

London code of conduct *See* NIPS CODE.

London Inter Bank Bid Rate (LIBID) The rate of interest at which banks bid for funds to borrow from one another on the London *interbank market. *See* LONDON INTER BANK OFFERED RATE.

London Inter Bank Mean Rate (LIMEAN) The average of the *London Inter Bank Offered Rate (LIBOR) and the *London Inter Bank Bid Rate (LIBID).

London Inter Bank Offered Rate (LIBOR) The rate of interest at which banks offer to lend to each other on the London *interbank market. The loans are for a minimum of £250,000 for periods from overnight up to five years. LIBOR is the most significant interest rate for international banks. It is also used as a benchmark for lending to bank customers and as a reference rate for many derivatives. In 2012 evidence emerged of a major scandal in which leading banks had manipulated LIBOR for their own profit; oversight of LIBOR has now been passed from the British Bankers' Association to the *Intercontinental Exchange group. *See also* LONDON INTER BANK BID RATE.

London International Financial Futures and Options Exchange *See* LIFFE.

London Metal Exchange (LME) The world's largest non-ferrous metals exchange, the total value of contracts each year being around $15,000 billion. Established in 1877, it is now regulated by the UK *Financial Conduct Authority. The LME trades in *futures and *options contracts in copper, aluminium, nickel, zinc, and lead. An electronic trading platform was introduced in 2001, but *open outcry trading remains important.

(⊕) SEE WEB LINKS
• Website of the LME

London rules A set of guidelines, approved by the Bank of England, relating to the treatment of distressed borrowers.

London Stock Exchange The market in London that deals in securities. Dealings in securities began in London in the 17th century. The name Stock Exchange was first used for New Jonathan's Coffee House in 1773, although it was not formally constituted until 1802. The development of the industrial revolution encouraged many other share markets to flourish throughout the UK, all the remnants of which amalgamated in 1973 to form The Stock Exchange of Great Britain and Ireland. After the *Big Bang in 1986 this organization became the International Stock Exchange of the UK and Republic of Ireland Ltd (ISE) in an attempt to stress the international nature of the main UK securities market; it is now the London Stock Exchange plc. The reforms of 1986 included:

• allowing banks, insurance companies, and overseas securities houses to become members and to buy existing member firms;
• abolishing scales of commissions, allowing commissions to be negotiated;
• abolishing the division of members into jobbers and brokers, enabling a member firm to deal with the public, to buy and sell shares for their own account, and to act as *market makers;
• the introduction of the *Stock Exchange Automated Quotations System, a computerized dealing system that has virtually abolished face-to-face dealing on the floor of exchange.

The London Stock Exchange now has four core business areas:

• **equity markets**—the *main market for listed companies and the *Alternative Investment Market for unlisted securities;
• **trading services**—trading platforms that are used by broking firms around the world to buy and sell securities;
• **market information**—the provision of prices and news;
• **derivatives**—a recent diversification beyond the core equity markets. In collaboration with the Nordic exchange group *OMX, the London Stock Exchange created the derivatives platform EDX London (now absorbed by *Turquoise) in 2003

(⊕) SEE WEB LINKS
• Website of the LSE: includes information for companies and traders and much educational material for private investors

long-dated gilt *See* GILT-EDGED SECURITY.

long hedging *See* HEDGE.

longitudinal design A marketing research design in which the views of a fixed population sample are measured over a period to show trends and changes in audiences. Many of the consumer panels, TV audience panels, and readership panels are of this type.

long lease A lease that has more than 50 years to run, as defined by the Companies Act. *Compare* SHORT LEASE.

long position A *position held in securities, commodities, currencies, derivatives, etc., such that a rise in the market increases the value of the position. *Compare* SHORT POSITION.

long-range plan A plan that describes the principal factors and forces affecting an organization during the coming years, including long-term objectives, the chief marketing strategies used to attain them, and the resources required.

longs 1. *See* GILT-EDGED SECURITY.
2. Securities, commodities, currencies, etc., held in a *long position.

long tail The situation in which a wide range of items sell in modest quantities individually but make up a considerable volume of sales collectively. The term alludes to a distribution curve in which a peak at the far left of the graph (representing the top-scoring 20% or so of items) falls away sharply to form a long thin 'tail' to the right (the remaining 80% of items: *see* PARETO'S RULE). Traditionally, the long tail has provided opportunities for small-scale niche selling, in which specialist companies have made modest profits by targeting a small segment of the market (*see* CONCENTRATED SEGMENTATION). However, the advent of e-commerce – with its low inventory, marketing, and distribution costs – has focused attention on the gains to be made from 'selling less of more'. The classic example of a company that makes serious profits from selling small quantities of a very large number of items is Amazon.

long-term bond A bond that does not mature in less than one year.

long-term contract A contract that falls into two or more accounting periods before being completed. Such a contract may be for the design, manufacture, or construction of a single substantial asset, for example in the construction or civil engineering industries. From an accounting point of view, there is a problem in determining how much profit can be reasonably allocated to each accounting period, although the contract is not complete. Generally, contracts should be assessed on an individual basis and shown in the *profit and loss account by recording turnover and related activity as the contract progresses. Where the outcome of the contract can be assessed with reasonable certainty, even

though it is not complete, the part of the profit that can be attributed to the work performed by an accounting date may be recognized in the profit and loss account. Attributable profit is that part of the total profit currently estimated to arise over the duration of the contract, after allowing for estimated remedial costs, maintenance costs, and increases in costs not recoverable under the contract agreement. Construction contracts are dealt with in Section 23 of the Financial Reporting Standard Applicable in the UK and Republic of Ireland. The relevant International Accounting Standards are IAS 18, Revenue, and IAS 11, Construction Contracts.

long-term debt Loans and debentures that are not due for repayment for at least ten years.

long-term liability A sum owed that does not have to be repaid within the next accounting period of a business. In some contexts a long-term liability may be regarded as one not due for repayment within the next three, or possibly ten, years.

long ton *See* TON.

loose insert An advertising leaflet distributed with another publication and usually inserted loosely within its pages.

loss adjuster A person appointed by an insurer to negotiate an insurance claim. The loss adjuster, who is independent of the insurer, discusses the claim with both the insurer and the policyholder, producing a report recommending the basis on which the claim should be settled. The insurer pays a fee for this service based on the amount of work involved for the loss adjuster, not on the size of the settlement. *Compare* LOSS ASSESSOR.

loss assessor A person who acts on behalf of the policyholder in handling a claim. A fee is charged for this service, which is usually a percentage of the amount received by the policyholder. *Compare* LOSS ADJUSTER.

loss leader A product or service offered for sale by an organization at a loss in order to attract customers. This practice was curbed in the UK by the Resale Prices Act 1976, although it still continues, especially in supermarkets.

loss-of-profits policy *See* BUSINESS-INTERRUPTION POLICY.

loss ratio The total of the claims paid out by an insurance company, underwriting *syndicate, etc., expressed as a percentage of the amount of premiums coming in in the same period. For example, if claims total £2M and premiums total £4M, the result is a 50% loss ratio. Insurers use this figure as a guide to the profitability of their business when they are reconsidering premium rates for a particular risk.

loss reliefs Relief available to sole traders, partnerships, and companies making losses, as adjusted for tax purposes. *Capital allowances can create a trading loss or can enhance it. Trading losses can be carried forward to set against future trading profits.

For sole traders and partnerships, trading losses can be set against other income for the year of the loss and for the previous year. Partners can decide individually how to use their share of the losses. Special rules apply to trading losses in the early years of a trade. These losses can be carried back three years to a period before the trade commenced. It is possible to set trading losses against capital gains if the loss cannot be used first by setting against other income during the year.

For companies, a trading loss can be set off against the profits of the previous 12-month period provided the company was carrying on the same trade during that period. *Capital losses can be set against capital gains in the same period. Any surplus capital loss that cannot be utilized during the current year must be carried forward to set against future capital gains. Capital losses cannot be set against other income, unlike trading losses. *See also* TERMINAL-LOSS RELIEF.

loti (plural maloti; LSL) The standard monetary unit of Lesotho, divided into 100 lisente.

low-cost strategy (cost leadership strategy) A *generic strategy in which a company aims to gain *competitive advantage across the whole of an industry by focusing on price as the key feature distinguishing its product or service from those of its competitors. The strategy was described in 1980 by Michael Porter, who distinguished it from the *differentiation strategy and the *focus strategy. In order to succeed, the business must drive down its own costs so that it can lower costs to consumers.

lower of cost or market (LCM) A method of valuing a *current asset of an organization in which the value taken is either its purchase (or production) price or the cost of replacing it (by purchase or manufacture), whichever is the lower. The Companies Act requires that a current asset be valued at either its purchase (or production) price or its *net realizable value, whichever is the lower.

low-involvement product A product that involves the consumer in little or no trouble or deliberation when making a purchase. Such products are invariably cheap; manufacturers try to make them more interesting and appealing by means of advertising with the intention of developing a brand loyalty. *Compare* HIGH-INVOLVEMENT PRODUCT.

loyalty techniques Incentive schemes in which customers receive points for repeat purchases. These points can be converted into discounts, free products, or cash. Most supermarkets now operate schemes in which customers' points are recorded by means of plastic **loyalty cards**, which are swiped through the checkout till at the time of purchase. In **online incentive schemes** customers may receive points for visiting certain websites.

LPC Scale Abbreviation for *Least Preferred Co-worker Scale.

Ltd The usual abbreviation for limited. This (or the Welsh equivalent) must appear in the name of a private *limited company. *Compare* PLC.

luma A monetary unit of Armenia, worth one hundredth of a *dram.

lump sum 1. A sum of money paid all at once, rather than in instalments. **2.** A sum of money paid for freight, irrespective of the size of the cargo. **3.** An insurance benefit, such as a sum of money paid on retirement or redundancy or to the beneficiaries on the death of an insured person. Retirement *pensions can consist of a lump sum plus a reduced pension. **4.** A form of *damages; a **lump-sum award** is given in tort cases.

Lutine Bell A bell that hangs in the underwriting room at *Lloyd's and is rung for ceremonial occasions, and rarely to draw the attention of underwriters to an important announcement. It was formerly rung once if a ship sank and twice for good news. It was recovered from the *Lutine*, a ship that was insured by Lloyd's and sank in the North Sea in 1799, with a cargo of bullion (£1.4M value).

lwei A monetary unit of Angola, worth one hundredth of a *kwanza.

M0; M1; M2; M3; M4; M5 *See* MONEY SUPPLY.

Maastricht Treaty Legislation, signed in 1992, creating the *European Union (EU) from the existing 12 member countries of the European Community (EC). In the main financial provisions of the treaty, the states agreed to a process of Economic and Monetary Union (EMU), with the creation of a single European currency as its ultimate goal. Monetary union was designed to be achieved in three stages, starting with participation in the Exchange Rate Mechanism (ERM). The second stage created the European Monetary Institute (EMI) to set qualifying conditions for the move towards the single currency (*see* CONVERGENCE CRITERIA). The third stage, achieved by January 1999, locked member states into a fixed exchange rate and activated the *European Central Bank as the governor of economic and monetary policy throughout the currency union. The euro was fully adopted in 12 EU countries in January 2002. *See* EUROPEAN ECONOMIC AND MONETARY UNION.

machine-down time The period during which a machine cannot be used, usually because of breakdown. If a machine is 'down', clearly production is not taking place, but it is customary in costing to attribute costs to the down time.

machine hour A measurement of production in terms of the time taken for a machine operation to complete a given amount of production.

machine hour rate An *absorption rate used in *absorption costing, obtained by the formula:

budgeted *cost centre overheads/ budgeted machine hours.

machine-idle time The period during which a machine is not being used. This is similar in effect to *machine-down time though it may be caused by lack of work rather than by a fault in the machine.

machine-readable Denoting any form of data that can be input directly into a computer. It includes data that has been stored on a magnetic or optical disk or a USB flash drive and data that has been prepared for *OCR.

macroeconomics The branch of economics that studies economies as a whole rather than the behaviour of particular economic agents. Modern macroeconomics is largely concerned with the relationships between such factors as money supply, employment, interest rates, government spending, investment, and consumption, and with the role that government should play in a national economy. In recent economic thinking the distinction between macroeconomics and *microeconomics has become less clear cut than previously.

macroenvironment The wider environment that creates the forces that shape every business and non-profit enterprise. The physical environment, social and cultural forces, demographic make-up, economic climate, prevailing political beliefs, and current legal infrastructure are components of the macroenvironment. Generally, most companies have no control over these factors. *Compare* MICROENVIRONMENT.

macroprudential regulation An approach to financial regulation that involves using a set of targeted rules to reduce levels of instability and systemic risk across the financial system as a whole. Such an approach has been adopted in many countries as a response to the financial crisis of 2007–08. In the UK the Bank of England's Financial Policy Committee, set up in 2013, is the authority charged with this type of regulation. *Compare* MICROPRUDENTIAL REGULATION.

MAD Abbreviation for *mean absolute deviation.

mad dog An informal name for a company with the potential to grow quickly, providing it can obtain substantial capital; risks are likely to be high. The information technology industry is an example of a sector that has included a number of mad dogs.

Madrid Protocol A treaty concerning the international registration of trademarks, agreed in Madrid in 1996. It has now been ratified by most of the world's major trading nations, including the USA, Japan, the EU, and India.

Madrid Stock Exchange (Bolsa de Madrid) The largest of four stock exchanges in Spain, the others being in Barcelona, Bilboa, and Valencia. They all now use a centralized settlement system, with the markets modelled on the London system. The markets are overseen by a national securities commission, the Comisión del Mercado de Valores (CNMV).

Magnuson–Moss Warranty Act 1975 A US federal law requiring that guarantees provided by sellers should be made available to buyers before a purchase is made and that they specify who the warrantor is, what products (or parts of products) are covered, what the warrantor must do if the product is defective, how long the warranty applies, and the obligations of the buyer.

mailing list A list of names and addresses used in *direct-mail selling, advertising, fund raising, etc. *See also* LIST RENTING.

mail-order house A firm that specializes in selling goods direct to customers by post. Orders are obtained from an illustrated catalogue supplied by the firm or by agents, who introduce the catalogue. The low costs of selling, especially the absence of retail premises, enable the mail-order houses to offer goods at competitive prices. *See also* DIRECT-MAIL SELLING.

mail shot Selling, advertising, or fund-raising material sent to all the names on a mailing list.

mail survey Marketing research conducted by mail. As respondents have time to consider their answers, this form of research has advantages over both telephone surveys and face-to-face surveys. However, it does suffer from low returns.

mainframe The largest type of *computer, requiring an air-conditioned room and special staff. They are used by large organizations, such as banks, as they can handle vast amounts of information with ease and calculate at high speed. They can also handle many users simultaneously (*see* TIME SHARING). *Compare* LOCAL AREA NETWORK; PERSONAL COMPUTER; MINICOMPUTER.

main market The premier market for the trading of *equities on the *London Stock Exchange. The *listing requirements are more stringent, and the liquidity of the market is greater, than on the *Alternative Investment Market. A company wishing to enter this market must have audited trading figures covering at least five years and must place 25% of its shares in public hands. The main market currently deals in over 1300 securities.

main product The product of a process that has the greatest economic significance. Other products of secondary economic importance are regarded as *by-products; however, if all products have equal economic significance they are regarded as joint products. *See also* PROCESS COSTING.

maintenance margin The minimum *margin required in a brokerage account by a particular exchange or brokerage firm.

making a price On the *London Stock Exchange, the quoting by a *market maker of a selling price and a buying price for a particular security, usually without knowing whether the broker or other person asking for a price wishes to buy or sell. Having made a price, the market maker is bound to buy or sell at the prices quoted, though the quantity may be limited if the broker stipulates the quantity at the time of making the price.

Malcolm Baldridge National Quality Award (MBNQA) See BALDRIDGE AWARD.

mall intercept interviewing A form of interviewing in which shoppers are intercepted in the public areas of shopping centres and malls to be interviewed face-to-face. The population samples so selected are usually *judgment samples or convenience samples.

malpractice insurance See PROFESSIONAL INDEMNITY INSURANCE.

malware An inclusive term for any computer software with a subversive purpose. Malware includes viruses, *adware, and *spyware.

managed costs See DISCRETIONARY COSTS.

managed currency (managed floating) A currency in which the government influences the exchange rate. This control is exerted by the central bank buying and selling in the foreign-exchange market and by its overall economic policy. See also CLEAN FLOATING.

managed fund A fund, made up of investments in a wide range of financial obligations, that is actively managed by a life-assurance company to provide low risk investments for the smaller investor, usually in the form of *investment bonds, *unit trusts, or unit-linked saving plans (see UNIT-LINKED POLICY). The *fund managers will have a stated investment policy favouring a specific category of investments.

management 1. The running of an organization or part of it. Management has perhaps three main components: an organizational skill, an entrepreneurial sense, and an ability to get the best out of followers. The organizational skill, involving many traditional principles and techniques of management, is taught at colleges and business schools (see ADMINISTRATIVE MANAGEMENT; SCIENTIFIC MANAGEMENT); the entrepreneurial sense, recognizing and making use of opportunities, predicting market needs and trends, and achieving one's goals by sustained drive, skilful negotiation, and articulate advocacy, is not so easily taught, although contact with the market place in association with a successful entrepreneur will encourage an inherent ability to develop. The third component, the ability to motivate subordinates, has become an increasingly prominent part of management theory and training (see LEADERSHIP STYLE; LEADERSHIP THEORIES; MOTIVATION), although the extent to which such leadership skills can be taught in the abstract remains disputable. See also ACTIVE MANAGEMENT; CHANGE MANAGEMENT; CONFLICT MANAGEMENT; DIVERSITY MANAGEMENT; HIGH-INVOLVEMENT MANAGEMENT; HUMAN-RESOURCE MANAGEMENT; SALESFORCE MANAGEMENT; SUPPLY-CHAIN MANAGEMENT; TOTAL QUALITY MANAGEMENT. **2.** The people involved in the running of an organization. **Top management** includes the *chief executive officer (see also MANAGING DIRECTOR) of an organization, his or her deputy or deputies, the board of *directors, and the managers in charge of the divisions or departments of the organization. **Middle management** consists largely of the managers to whom top management delegates the day-to-day running of the organization.

Management is traditionally broken down into the categories formalized in *line and staff management: the line managers organize the production of the goods or oversee the services provided by the organization, while the staff management provides such support as personnel management, transport management, service management, etc.

management accounting The techniques used to collect, process, and present financial and quantitative data within an organization to help effective performance measurement, cost control, planning, pricing, and decision making to take place. The major professional body of **management accountants** in the UK is the Chartered Institute of Management Accountants (CIMA).

management audit An independent review of the management of an organization, carried out by a firm of *management consultants specializing in this type of review. The review will cover all aspects of running the organization, including the control of production, marketing, sales, finance, personnel, warehousing, etc.

management buy-in The acquisition of a company by an outside team of managers, usually specially formed for the purpose, often backed by a venture-capital organization. In the past a typical target might have been a small family-owned company, which the owners wished to sell, or an unwanted subsidiary of a public company. In recent years, however, *private equity firms have successfully targeted leading public companies.

management buy-out (MBO) The acquisition of a company or a subsidiary by the existing management, often as an alternative to closure. This generally occurs after the acquisition of the parent company by new owners who wish to divest themselves of a particular subsidiary but occasionally as a result of owners wishing to dispose of the whole business through a trade sale. The new owner-managers of the buy-out frequently improve its performance as they usually are well aware of any remedial action required and have a serious incentive in the form of their equity stake. Additional capital is provided by financial institutions and venture capitalists and also in many cases by allowing other employees to buy shares. In a few

instances, all employees have participated in a buy-out; these are sometimes called **employee buy-outs**. In a highly leveraged buy-out, funding will usually consist of a small amount of equity (allowing the management team to retain control), considerable straight debt, and a certain amount of *mezzanine finance. *See also* BIMBO.

management by exception 1. A principle of management in which a management decision that cannot be made at one level is passed up to the next level for a decision; i.e. exceptional decisions are passed up the management tree. **2.** The principle used in *budgetary control in which items of income or expenditure that show no *variances or small variances require no action, whereas exceptional items showing adverse variances to an unacceptable degree require action to be taken.

management by objectives (MBO) A management technique in which all levels of management are encouraged to specify and agree quantitative and/or qualitative objectives to be achieved within a set period and to answer to higher levels of management for the actual performance achieved against these objectives.

management by walking around (MBWA) The practice by managers of spending a significant part of their time listening to staff problems and ideas while walking around an office or plant. The opportunity to communicate with managers can be seen as providing an important contribution to staff motivation.

management company A company that manages *unit trusts. Its fees, known as **management charges**, are usually stated in the agreement setting up the trust; they are paid by the unit holders.

Management Consultancies Association (MCA) An association founded in 1956 to establish and maintain the professional standards of the management consultancy profession in the UK.

management consultant A professional adviser who specializes in giving advice to organizations on ways for improving their efficiency and hence their profitability. They come into an organization as total outsiders, uninfluenced by either internal politics or personal relationships, and analyse the way the business is run. At the end of a period, during which two or more members of the consultant firm have spent a considerable time in the organization, they provide a detailed report, giving their suggestions for improving efficiency. Their advice usually spans board-level policy-making and planning, the use of available resources (department by department), the best use of manpower, and a critical assessment of industrial relations, production, marketing, and sales.

management contracting The practice in which a domestic firm supplies the management know-how to a foreign company that provides the capital, in order to create a *joint venture; the domestic firm exports management services rather than products.

management development The process of ensuring that an organization has the appropriate management skills and competencies to meet its developing needs. Existing skills and abilities are assessed and actual or potential shortfalls are identified with the aim of ameliorating them. Various programmes and interventions may be used for this purpose, including training, *mentoring, or role-play and *team-building exercises.

management discussion and analysis (MD&A) In the USA, the section in the annual report to stockholders (*see* ANNUAL ACCOUNTS) and in *Form 10-K that is required by the *Securities and Exchange Commission. The purpose of the MD&A is to assist investors to understand the impact of changes in accounting and business activity that have affected comparisons with the results of previous years. Management should summarize and discuss, among other matters, the reasons for changes in the results of operations, capital resources, and liquidity.

management information system (MIS) An information system designed to provide financial and quantitative information to all the levels of management in an organization. Modern management information systems provide the data from an integrated computer *database, which is constantly updated from all areas of the organization in a structured way. Access to the data is usually restricted to the areas regarded as useful to particular managers, and access to confidential information is limited to top management. An MIS should run parallel to the configuration of the physical and organizational structures. The systematic application of *information technology has enabled MIS to drive these structures (*see* BUSINESS TECHNOLOGY MANAGEMENT). *See also* DECISION SUPPORT SYSTEM.

management letter A letter written by an auditor to the management of a client company at the end of the annual *audit to suggest any possible improvements that could be made to the company's accounting and internal control system or to communicate any other such information that the auditor believes would be of benefit to the client.

management services The department of an organization that is concerned with systematic attempts to improve its productivity and quality of output through such methods as *industrial engineering, *work studies, *systems analysis, and *business process re-engineering. Professionals in these fields qualify through the *Institute of Management Services.

management system A computer application that enables the owner of a *franchise network to access and coordinate information about the business activities of the franchisees. Such systems provide data about marketing, salesforce activity, customer relationships, and royalties across the network and thereby allow analysis of the operations of the business as a whole and comparison of individual units.

managerial capitalism The prevailing form of capitalism for most of the 20th century, in which markets were dominated by large bureaucratic organizations led by teams of salaried executives. This differed from earlier forms of capitalism, in which decision making and most day-to-day management functions were carried out directly by the owners. In the view of many commentators, the managerial model began to wane in the late 20th century, owing to a range of factors that includes the advent of *information technology, the growing importance of *intellectual capital, and the emergence of new patterns of organizational structure and career development.

managing director (MD) The company director responsible for the day-to-day running of a company. Second in the hierarchy only to the *chairman, if there is one, the managing director is the company's *chief executive officer, a title that is becoming increasingly popular in both the USA and the UK. In the USA the *president is often the equivalent of the MD. If a company has more than one MD, they are known as **joint managing directors**.

manat 1. (AZN) The standard monetary unit of Azerbaijan, divided into 100 gopik. **2.** (TMM) The standard monetary unit of Turkmenistan, divided into 100 tenesi.

mandate 1. A written authority given by one person (the **mandator**) to another (the **mandatory**) giving the mandatory the power to act on behalf of the mandator. It is usually revocable until acted upon and comes to an end on the death, mental illness, or bankruptcy of the mandator. A cheque is a mandate from a customer to his or her bank. **2.** A document instructing a bank to open an account in the name of the mandator (customer), giving details of the way it is to be run, and providing specimen signatures of those authorized to sign cheques, etc.

mandatory liquid assets Certain *liquid assets, the structure and nature of which is defined by regulatory requirement, that a bank is required to maintain on its balance sheet. Such a policy may be implemented as an instrument of monetary control or as a protection against 'runs' on particular banks. The regulatory trend is away from this type of control, since it often gives a market advantage to short-term government debt, which is a major part of the specified assets.

man-hour (person-hour) The amount of work done by one person in one hour. It is sometimes convenient in costing a job to estimate the number of man-hours it will take.

manifest A list of all the cargo carried by a ship or aircraft. It has to be signed by the captain (or first officer) before being handed to the customs on leaving or arriving at a port or airport.

manufacturer brand A *brand name used by a manufacturer, as opposed to one used by a distributor or retailer. *Compare* OWN BRAND.

manufacturer's agent A commission agent who usually has a *franchise to sell a particular manufacturer's products in a particular country or region for a given period.

manufacturers' recommended price (MRP) *See* RECOMMENDED RETAIL PRICE.

manufacturing account (manufacturing statement) An accounting statement forming part of the internal final accounts of a manufacturing organization; for a particular period, it is constructed to show, inter alia, *direct cost of sales, *manufacturing overhead, total *production cost, and *cost of goods manufactured. In some cases a *manufacturing profit is also computed.

manufacturing cost of finished goods *See* COST OF GOODS MANUFACTURED.

manufacturing costs (manufacturing expenses) Items of expenditure incurred to carry out the manufacturing process in an organization. They include *direct materials, *direct labour, *direct expenses (such as subcontract costs), and *manufacturing overhead. *See* COST OF GOODS MANUFACTURED; COST OF SALES.

manufacturing overhead (factory overhead; production overhead) The costs of production that cannot be traced directly to the product or *cost unit. Apart from the *direct costs, all other costs incurred in the manufacturing process are the manufacturing overhead; examples include depreciation of machinery, factory rent and business rates, cleaning materials, and maintenance expenses.

manufacturing profit/loss (production profit/loss) The difference between the value of the goods transferred from a *manufacturing account to a *trading account at a price other than the *cost of goods manufactured, and the cost of goods manufactured. This difference is measured in organizations wishing to submit the production department to market prices; it involves crediting production according to some formula, such as a price per unit.

maquiladora (Spanish: twin-plant) In Mexico, a factory or plant built near the US border to enable US companies to take advantage of lower Mexican labour costs.

margin 1. The *profit margin on sales of goods or services. It is often expressed as a percentage of revenue. *See* GROSS PROFIT; GROSS PROFIT PERCENTAGE; NET PROFIT; NET PROFIT PERCENTAGE. *See also* CONTRIBUTION; MARK-UP. **2.** The difference between the prices at which a *market maker or commodity dealer will buy and sell. This is also known as the *bid–offer spread and colloquially as a **haircut**. **3.** In banking, the difference between the rate of interest on funds lent and funds borrowed by a bank. **4.** Money or securities advanced by a client to a stockbroker or dealer to cover any possible losses the client may make. *See* MARGIN CALL.

marginal cost The additional cost incurred as a result of the production of one additional unit of production. In accounting, it usually equates to the variable costs per unit of production. The variable costs are usually regarded as the direct costs plus the variable overheads.

marginal costing (direct costing; variable costing) A costing and decision-making technique that charges only the *marginal costs to the *cost units and treats the *fixed costs as a lump sum to be deducted from the total *contribution, in obtaining the profit or loss for the period. In some cases, *inventory valuation is also at marginal cost, although this approach is used for internal reporting purposes only. *Compare* ABSORPTION COSTING.

marginal cost pricing The setting of product selling prices based on the charging of *marginal costs only to the product. The approach is only likely to be used in exceptional circumstances, such as when competition is intensive, as its application to the complete range of products is likely to cause the business to make losses by its failure to cover its *fixed costs. *Compare* COST-PLUS PRICING; FULL COST PRICING.

marginal-cost transfer prices *Transfer prices set by *marginal cost pricing. When there is no market for the goods and services that are bought and sold between the divisions of an organization, the transfer price should be the marginal cost, which is normally assumed to be short-term *variable cost. Setting transfer prices equal to marginal costs helps managers to identify the output levels that will maximize profits. There can be problems if managers do not have accurate cost information.

marginal rate of tax The amount of extra tax that is incurred if a taxpayer earns £1 more than his or her current income. Under a *progressive tax regime, the marginal rate of tax rises as incomes rise. *See also* ABILITY TO PAY.

marginal relief (small companies relief) In the UK, relief available when the profits chargeable to *corporation tax of a company fall between the upper and lower limits for the *financial year (currently between £300,000 and £1,500,000).

marginal revenue The additional revenue that a producer will achieve by selling one additional unit of production.

margin call A call to a client from his commodity broker or stockbroker to increase his *margin, i.e. the amount of money or securities deposited with the broker as a safeguard. This usually happens if the client has an *open position in a market that is moving adversely for this position.

margin of safety The difference between the level of activity at which an organization breaks even and a given level of activity greater than the *breakeven point. The margin of safety may be expressed in the same terms as the breakeven point, i.e. sales value, number of units, or percentage of capacity.

margin of safety ratio The *margin of safety expressed as a percentage of a given level of activity. For example, if the sales level achieved is £500,000 and the sales level breakeven point is £400,000, the margin of safety is £100,000 and the margin of safety ratio will be:

$$(£100,000 \times 100)/£500,000 = 20\%.$$

marine insurance The insurance of ships or their cargo against specified causes of loss or damage that might be encountered at sea. The definition has widened over the years to include the transit of cargo over land at each end of the voyage and the term 'vessel' now extends to include ships under construction or repair and drilling rigs.

marka (BAM) The standard monetary unit of Bosnia and Hercegovina, divided into 100 feninga.

marked cheque A cheque that the bank on which it is drawn has marked 'good for payment', so that it is effectively a cash equivalent. This practice has been replaced in the UK by *bank drafts, although it is still used in the USA, where such cheques are called **certified checks**.

marker barrel A standard oil price based on one barrel of Saudi Arabian oil. It sets standard prices for oil in the rest of the world.

market 1. An arena in which buyers and sellers exchange goods and services, usually for money. It does not have to have a physical location. **2.** An organized gathering for trading in financial obligations, such as a stock exchange, commodity market, etc. **3.** The demand for a particular product or service, often measured by sales during a specified period.

marketable security A *security (stock, share, bond, etc.) that can be bought or sold on a *stock exchange. *Compare* NON-MARKETABLE SECURITIES.

market assessment The identification and evaluation of a market for a particular good or service to ascertain its size and to estimate the price that the product or service would command. *See also* MARKETING RESEARCH.

market-based transfer prices *Transfer prices that are based on market prices. When there is a perfectly competitive market for the goods and services that are bought and sold between divisions of an organization, the transfer price should be the market price. The transfer price may be slightly lower than the market price if the selling expenses are lower for interdivisional transfers, e.g. because there is no advertising cost for transfers between divisions. There is a problem for managers in that market prices may fluctuate.

market capitalization *See* MARKET VALUE.

market-centred company A company that pays balanced attention to both customers and competitors in designing its marketing strategies.

market challenger A firm that is fighting to increase its market share. Generally, such a company is second in market share and aggressively challenging the *market leader.

market development A strategy by which an organization attempts to sell an existing product to new customers, usually by introducing the product in a new geographical area. *See* PRODUCT–MARKET STRATEGY.

market failure A situation in which a market does not operate efficiently. Factors that may cause market failure include the possession of *market power by transactors, *externalities, or information problems (*see* ASYMMETRIC INFORMATION). *See also* EFFICIENT MARKETS HYPOTHESIS.

market follower A firm that is usually second to the *market leader in an industry and wants to hold its share without upsetting the status quo. Market followers do not want to challenge the leader, but can maintain their market share with much lower investment costs than the leader.

market forces The forces of supply and demand that in a *free market determine the quantity available of a particular product or service and the price at which it is offered. In general, a rise in demand will cause both supply and price to increase, while a rise in supply will cause both a fall in price and a drop in demand, although many markets have individual features that modify this simple analysis.

marketing The process of planning and executing the conception, pricing, promotion, and distribution of ideas, products, and services to create exchanges that will satisfy the needs of individuals and organizations. Marketing a product involves such tasks as anticipating changes in demand (usually on the basis of *marketing research), promotion of the product (*see* SALES PROMOTION), ensuring that its quality, availability, and price meet the needs of the market, and providing after-sales service. *See also* DIRECT MARKETING.

marketing audit A review of an organization's marketing capabilities based on a structured appraisal of a marketing department's internal strengths and weaknesses, which helps the company decide how best to respond to external opportunities and threats. Sales are analysed, the effectiveness of the *marketing mix is assessed, and, externally, the *marketing environment is monitored. When the marketing audit has been completed, a *marketing plan is drawn up based on its results.

marketing control The process of measuring and evaluating the results of *marketing strategies to ensure that corrective action can be taken to enable *marketing objectives to be attained. This is usually achieved by means of the *marketing plan.

marketing costs The costs incurred by an organization in carrying out its marketing activities. These would include sales promotion costs, salesmen's salaries, advertising, and point-of-sale promotional material, such as display stands.

marketing database An organized set of data about individual customers or prospective customers that can be used to generate and qualify customer leads, sell products and services, and maintain customer relationships.

marketing environment The combined influence of all the factors external to a company that could affect its sales. These factors include: cultural traditions, technological developments, competitors' activity, government policies, and changes in distribution channels. The marketing environment cannot be controlled by the company and, because it may change frequently, requires constant monitoring.

marketing implementation The process that converts *marketing strategies and plans into action in order to accomplish *marketing objectives.

marketing information system (MkIS) An organized set of procedures and methods by which pertinent, timely, and accurate information is continually gathered, analysed, and evaluated for use by marketing decision makers. Modern systems are computerized and usually consist of a data-collection system and a *decision support system.

marketing intelligence Data about the *marketing environment gathered from a variety of disparate sources and subjected to a structured analysis. The data should include information from customers, sales personnel, suppliers, retailers, agencies, monitoring of competitors, and government bodies.

marketing intermediaries Firms that help a company to promote, sell, and distribute its products to final buyers. They include middlemen, wholesalers, retailers, distribution firms, marketing-service agencies, and financial intermediaries.

marketing logistics *See* LOGISTICS; PHYSICAL DISTRIBUTION.

marketing management The planning and implementation of programmes designed to create, build, and maintain sales of a product. This is achieved by the *marketing mix.

marketing mix The factors controlled by a company that can influence consumers' buying of its products. The four components of a marketing mix (often called the **four Ps**) are:

- the product—quality, branding, packaging, and other features;
- pricing—recommended retail price, discounts for large orders, and credit terms;
- promotion—*see* SALES PROMOTION;
- place—where to sell the product, which distributors and transport services to use, and desirable stock levels.

The potential profitability of a particular marketing mix and its acceptability to its market are assessed by *marketing research. *See also* EXTENDED MARKETING MIX.

marketing myopia A failure to define an organization's purpose in terms of its function from the consumers' point of view. For example, railway companies that define their markets in terms of trains,

rather than transportation, fail to recognize the challenge of competition from cars, airlines, and buses. It is therefore necessary to define the needs of the consumer in more general terms rather than product-specific terms.

marketing objective A statement about the level of performance an organization, business unit, or operating unit intends to achieve. Objectives must be defined in measurable terms.

marketing plan A detailed statement (usually prepared annually) of how a company's *marketing mix will be used to achieve its *market objectives. A marketing plan is usually prepared following a *marketing audit.

marketing research The systematic collection and analysis of data to resolve problems concerning *marketing, undertaken to reduce the risk of inappropriate marketing activity. Data is almost always collected from a *sample of the target market, by such methods as observation, interviews, and audit of shop sales. Interviews (*see* OPEN-ENDED QUESTION; STRUCTURED INTERVIEW) are the most common technique, and can be carried out face-to-face, by telephone, over the Internet, or by post. When the results have been analysed (usually by computer), recommendations regarding the original problem can be made. *See also* QUALITATIVE MARKETING RESEARCH; QUANTITATIVE MARKETING RESEARCH.

  Market research, which is often used synonymously with the preferred term 'marketing research', is more correctly used to refer to research with the restricted objective of discovering the size of the market for a particular brand or product.

marketing-service agency A marketing research firm, advertising agency, marketing consultancy firm, or other service provider that helps a company to promote its products in the market.

marketing strategy A plan identifying what marketing goals and objectives will be pursued to sell a particular product or product line and how these objectives will be achieved in the time available.

marketing warfare strategy An aggressive marketing plan based on principles or metaphors taken from military strategy. The 1980s saw a vogue for such analogies, in which lessons were drawn from the thinking of Napoleon, Clausewitz, Sun Tzu, and others. Marketing strategies were identified as either defensive or offensive; direct confrontation could be avoided through flanking movements (e.g. concentrating on an overlooked market segment) or a 'guerrilla'-style campaign. The assumption behind all such strategies is that business is a zero-sum game, in which success depends on overpowering or outwitting the 'enemy'. Contemporary theorists tend to be more cautious, arguing that a competitor-oriented (as opposed to customer-oriented) approach of this kind is suitable only to established markets with little scope for growth.

marketing website A site on the World Wide Web created by a company to interact with consumers for the purpose of moving them closer to a purchase or other marketing outcome. The site is designed to handle interactive communication initiated by the company.

market leader The firm in a particular industry with the largest market share. The market leader usually dominates other firms in price changes, the introduction of new products, distribution coverage, and promotion spending. This firm may or may not be admired by other companies, but generally these companies accept the dominance.

market maker 1. Any intermediary who creates a market for a financial obligation. 2. A dealer in securities on the *London Stock Exchange who undertakes to buy and sell securities as a principal and is therefore obliged to announce buying and selling prices for a particular security at a particular time. Before October 1986 (*see* BIG BANG) this function was performed by a *stockjobber, who was then obliged to deal with the public through a *stockbroker.

Since that date market makers have combined dealing in securities as principals with acting as agents, working for a commission. While this dual role may create a conflict of interest for market makers (*see* CHINESE WALL; FRONT RUNNING), it avoids the restrictive trade practice of the former system and reduces the cost of dealing in the market.

market manager An individual responsible for administering all the marketing activities of a company that relate to a particular market, including forecasting, product planning, and pricing.

market objectives The objectives to be fulfilled by a *marketing plan. Marketing objectives are determined by interpreting the relevant parts of a corporate plan (*see* BUSINESS PLAN) in the light of a *marketing audit.

market order *See* AT BEST.

market orientation *See* PRODUCT ORIENTATION.

market overhang The situation in which sellers, worried by falling prices, prefer to postpone their sales until there is greater market demand. By reducing transactions, this behaviour can itself delay the hoped for recovery.

market penetration (penetration)
1. The process of entering a market to establish a new brand or product. Market penetration may be achieved by offering the brand or product at a low initial price to familiarize the public with its name. This is known as **market-penetration pricing**. 2. The extent to which a product or an advertisement has been accepted by, or has registered with, the total number of possible users. It is usually expressed as a percentage. *Compare* MARKET SHARE. 3. A marketing strategy based on low prices and extensive advertising to increase a product's market share. For penetration strategy to be effective the market will have to be large enough to be able to sustain low profit margins. *See* PRODUCT–MARKET STRATEGY.

market portfolio *See* MARKOWITZ MODEL.

market positioning *See* POSITIONING.

market power The ability of a transactor to influence market prices, owing to the very large share of the demand or supply in a particular market that this transactor controls. The major UK supermarkets are often said to possess market power of this kind.

market price The price of a raw material, product, service, security, etc., in an open market. In formal markets, such as a stock exchange, commodity market, foreign-exchange market, etc., there is often a *margin between the buying and selling price; there are, therefore, two market prices. In these circumstances the market prices often quoted are the average of the buying and selling price (*see* MIDDLE PRICE). *See also* MARKET VALUE.

market price to book ratio *See* BOOK VALUE.

market–product strategy *See* PRODUCT–MARKET STRATEGY.

market rate of discount *See* BILL RATE.

market research *See* MARKETING RESEARCH.

Market Research Society (MRS) A UK-based professional association for those who use survey techniques for marketing, social, and economic research. The MRS aims to maintain professional standards, to provide its members with training programmes and information about new techniques, and to represent the interests of its members to government and commerce.

(((🌐))) SEE WEB LINKS
• MRS website

market risk The *risk inherent in dealing on a market where prices may change. The obvious market risks are buying on a market that subsequently falls and selling on a market that rises; these risks can be reduced by hedging (*see* HEDGE), especially by means of *futures contracts or *options, but they can never be eliminated. These forms of market risk are the obverse of the market opportunities that provide speculators with the chance of making a profit.

market segmentation The division of a *market into homogeneous groups of consumers, each of which can be expected to respond to a different *marketing mix. There are numerous ways of segmenting markets, the more traditional being by age, sex, family size, income, occupation, and social class; more recently *geodemographic segmentation, which identifies housing areas in which people share a common lifestyle and will be more likely to buy certain types of products, has become more popular. Another frequently used method is *benefit segmentation. Once a segment has been identified, the marketer can then develop a unique marketing mix to reach it, for example by advertising only in the newspapers read by that market segment. Therefore, to be of practical value a market segment must be large enough to warrant the development costs.

market share The share of the total sales of all brands or products competing in the same market that is captured by one particular brand or product, usually expressed as a percentage. For example, if brands A, B, and C are the competing brands of a product and in a particular month they achieved sales of £480,000, £620,000, and £900,000, respectively, brand A's market share would be

$$(480,000/(480,000 + 620,000 + 900,000)) \times 100 = 24\%.$$

Markets in Financial Instruments Directive (MiFID) An EU directive (2004) providing a comprehensive regulatory regime for financial services and markets throughout the *European Economic Area. It superseded the *Investment Services Directive in November 2007. The main aims are to increase competition and enhance investor protection.

market-skimming pricing Setting a high price for a new product in order to skim the maximum revenues, layer by layer, from the market segments willing to pay the high price. Using this high-price strategy, the company makes fewer but more profitable sales.

marketspace (electronic marketspace) A virtual marketplace in which no direct contact occurs between buyers and sellers.

market targeting The process of evaluating each market segment and selecting the most attractive segments to enter with a particular product or product line.

market testing *See* TEST MARKETING.

market timing An investment strategy based on the forecasting of changes in the direction of market prices. However, there is little evidence to suggest that investors can apply such a strategy systematically and even if it were possible, it would violate the *efficient markets hypothesis.

market-to-book ratio *See* BOOK VALUE.

market value 1. (market capitalization) The value of a company obtained by multiplying the number of its issued ordinary shares by their *market price. This may differ widely from the *book value of the company. **2. (open market value; OMV)** The value of an asset if it were to be sold on the open market at its current *market price. When land is involved it may be necessary to distinguish between the market value in its present use and that in some alternative use; for example, a factory site may have a market value as a factory site, and be so valued in the company's accounts, which may be less than its market value as building land. *See* FAIR VALUE.

markings The official number of bargains that have taken place during a working day on the *London Stock Exchange.

marking to market The valuation of financial obligations according to current *market prices (or an estimate of such prices).

marking to model The valuation of financial obligations according to pricing models. This occurs when there is not a current market price for the obligation, for example in relation to derivatives sold on the *over-the-counter market.

markka The former standard monetary unit of Finland, divided into 100 penniä. It was replaced by the euro in 2002.

Markowitz model A method of selecting the optimum investment *portfolio devised by H. M. Markowitz (1927–), who received the Nobel prize in Economics for this work in 1990. It assumes that investors are *risk-averse —i.e. they are attracted by high average returns on an investment but dislike high standard deviations of returns. It concludes that investors should diversify as widely as possible and opt for the level of risk and return they find most acceptable by varying the proportions they borrow, lend, and invest in risky assets.

mark-up The amount by which the cost of a service or product has been increased to arrive at the selling price. It is calculated by expressing the *profit as a percentage of the cost of the good or service. For example, if a product cost £8 and is sold for £12, the mark-up would be:

$$£4/£8 \times 100 = 50\%.$$

Note that the *margin is calculated by expressing the profit as a percentage of the selling price; in this case it would be:

$$£4/£12 \times 100 = 33.3\%.$$

The mark-up is widely used in retailing, both for setting prices and as a ratio for control and decision making. *See* GROSS PROFIT PERCENTAGE; NET PROFIT PERCENTAGE.

Maslow's motivational hierarchy (Maslow's hierarchy of needs) A model of human *motivation developed by the US psychologist Abraham Maslow (1908–70). It posits a hierarchy of human needs (or motives) with five levels: physiological needs, such as food and sleep; safety needs; love needs; esteem needs, such as competence and recognition; and meta needs, such as the needs for beauty, knowledge, and *self-actualization. Essentially, the higher levels of motivation come into play after the lower needs have been satisfied. Maslow developed this model largely as a reaction against behaviouristic theories of motivation, which focus on the role of physical and material rewards. It has proved widely influential in *human relations theory and other aspects of industrial and organizational psychology. *See also* ERG THEORY.

mass customization The ability to create tailored marketing messages or products for individual customers, or a group of similar customers (a bespoke service), while retaining the *economies of scale and the capacity of mass marketing or production.

mass marketing Marketing in which the same product, price, promotion, and distribution is used for all consumers in a particular market.

mass media *See* MEDIA.

mass production *See* LINE PRODUCTION.

mass service technology The type of technology used in labour-intensive service industries, with low customer contact, e.g. university teaching. *Compare* PROFESSIONAL SERVICE TECHNOLOGY.

master The captain of a merchant ship.

master production schedule (MPS) A schedule developed from firm orders or from forecasts of demand. The MPS is a key input into a *material requirements planning (MRP) system. The MPS identifies how many of each end product need to be produced and when they need to be produced by within each planning period. This data forms one of three key inputs enabling an MRP system to produce detailed timings for component manufacture and material purchases. It summarizes what the business plans to make and drives the operation in terms of what is assembled, what is made, and what is bought in. In addition it forms the basis for planning the utilization of labour and equipment and determines the requirements for materials and cash.

matched bargain A transaction in which a sale of a particular quantity of stock is matched with a purchase of the same quantity of the same stock. On the *London Stock Exchange transactions of this kind are now carried out electronically by *SETS. A matched-bargain system is an *order-driven system.

matched sale–purchase agreement (MSP) A device used by the US Federal Reserve in which it sells money-market instruments for immediate effect and couples the sale with the forward purchase of the same instrument, to facilitate the distribution of reserves of the banking system.

material adverse change A clause in a loan agreement or bank facility stating that the loan will become repayable if there should be a material change in the borrower's credit standing. The clause can be contentious because it is not always clear what constitutes a material change.

material fact **1.** Any important piece of information that a person seeking insurance must disclose to the insurer to enable the insurer to decide whether or not to accept the insurance and to calculate the premium. What is and what is not material may have to be decided by a court of law, but very often it is obvious. While a person cannot be penalized for not revealing facts that are not known or cannot reasonably be expected to be known, an insurance contract can become void if the facts have been deliberately concealed from the insurer if they could have influenced the acceptance of the risk, the premium charged, or the exceptions made. **2.** Relevant information about a company that must be made public in its *prospectus, if it is seeking a flotation on a stock exchange. **3.** Any information that could be provided by a witness in court proceedings and could influence the decision of the court.

materiality The extent to which an item of accounting information is material. Information is considered material if its omission or misstatement could influence the decision making of its users. Materiality is therefore not an absolute concept but is dependent on the size and nature of an item and the particular circumstances in which it arises. It is recognized as an important principle in the Financial Reporting Standard Applicable in the UK and Republic of Ireland.

material requirements planning (MRP) A computer-based information system that uses known orders and forecast orders to produce a commitment to manufacture a given number of products in a given period. MRP is often divided into two phases: MRPI produces the commitment to manufacture, while MRPII develops the concept to assess the financial implications of the material requirements.

materials cost The expenditure incurred by an organization on *direct materials or *indirect materials. The expenditure on direct materials is part of *direct cost of sales and that on indirect materials is a *manufacturing overhead.

materials management See SUPPLY-CHAIN MANAGEMENT.

maternity rights The rights of a woman when she is absent from work because of her pregnancy or confinement. The current law is contained in the Employment Rights Act 1996 as amended by the Work and Families Act 2006 and supplemented by the Maternity and Parental Leave Regulations 1999, 2002, and 2006. The statutory rights are:

- All pregnant employees are entitled to reasonable time off work, with pay, for antenatal care.
- An employee is entitled not to be dismissed because of pregnancy or any reason connected with it.
- A pregnant employee who meets certain qualifying conditions is entitled to receive **statutory maternity pay** from her employer for up to 39 weeks. Employers can recover 92% of such payments by setting the amount against their National Insurance payments.
- An employee who continues to be employed by her employer until the beginning of the 11th week before the

expected week of confinement is entitled to **maternity leave** of 52 weeks, consisting of 26 weeks of ordinary leave and up to 26 weeks of additional leave.
- An employee entitled to maternity leave is also entitled to return to work with her employer. An employee who returns at the end of her ordinary maternity leave is entitled to return to the same job on the same terms and conditions. An employee who returns at the end of her additional maternity leave has the same entitlement unless the employer can show that this is not practicable, in which case she must be offered a similar job on terms and conditions no less favourable.
- Throughout the maternity leave period the employee is entitled to continue to benefit from all contractual terms of her employment with the exception of remuneration (money payment).
- During her maternity leave an employee is entitled to do up to ten days' paid work in order to 'keep in touch': however, the employer may not demand this.
- Pregnant women, and women who have recently given birth or who are breastfeeding, have the right to be offered any suitable alternative work, rather than being suspended on maternity-related health and safety grounds.

In the UK men enjoyed no statutory **paternity rights** until 1999, when an EU directive was adopted into British law entitling a parent of either sex to take a total of 13 weeks unpaid leave in the first five years of a child's life (but only four weeks in any one year). New fathers became entitled to two weeks' statutory paternity pay in April 2003. It is also now possible for a new father to claim additional paternity leave and pay if his partner returns to work before the end of her statutory maternity leave or pay. A growing number of companies now operate contractual schemes providing for a period of paid and/or unpaid paternity leave.

mate's receipt A document signed by the mate of a ship as proof that the goods specified in the document have been loaded onto his ship, especially if they have been delivered direct to the ship, rather than from a quayside warehouse. The mate's receipt functions as a document of title, which may be required as proof of loading in a *Free On Board (FOB) contract, pending the issue of the *bill of lading.

matrix organization A management structure in which some employees report to two (or more) managers in different departments. It is often used if two separate areas of the external environment demand management attention. For example, if a wholesaler of an organization's product requires extra credit, the distribution management and the finance management would both need to be consulted. In effect, this would involve the employees concerned in a multiple-authority structure rather than a simple chain of command (see diagram).

maturity date The date on which a document, such as a *bond, *bill of exchange, or insurance policy, becomes due for payment. In some cases, especially for redeemable government stocks, the maturity date is known as the **redemption date**. *See also* REDEMPTION.

maturity stage *See* PRODUCT LIFE CYCLE.

maximum allowable cycle time The maximum time that can elapse between consecutive items leaving a production

process, if the designated *capacity of the process is to be achieved.

maximum fluctuation The maximum daily price fluctuation that is permitted on a financial market. *See* LIMIT.

maximum investment plan (MIP) A unit-linked endowment policy marketed by a life-assurance company that is designed to produce maximum profit rather than life-assurance protection. It calls for regular premiums, usually over ten years, with options to continue. These policies normally enable a tax-free fund to be built up over ten years and, because of the regular premiums, *pound cost averaging can be used, linked to a number of markets. Such investment products are now largely obsolete, since there is now a general preference for separating the life assurance and investment elements of products.

maximum slippage The period between the date on which a new company expects to start earning income and the date up to which it can survive on its venture capital. After this date has passed, the company would be unable to raise further funds and would sink into insolvency. *See also* DEATH-VALLEY CURVE.

MB Abbreviation for megabyte.

MBA Abbreviation for Master of Business Administration.

Matrix organization.

MBNQA Abbreviation for Malcolm Baldridge National Quality Award. *See* BALDRIDGE AWARD.

MBO 1. Abbreviation for *management buy-out. **2.** Abbreviation for *management by objectives.

MBS Abbreviation for *mortgage-backed security.

MBWA Abbreviation for *management by walking around.

MCA Abbreviation for *Management Consultancies Association.

m-commerce *See* MOBILE COMMERCE.

MD Abbreviation for *managing director.

MDS Abbreviation for *multi-dimensional scaling.

mean *See* ARITHMETIC MEAN; GEOMETRIC MEAN. *Compare* MEDIAN.

mean absolute deviation (MAD) In statistics, the *arithmetic mean of the deviations (all taken as positive numbers) of all the numbers in a set of numbers from their arithmetic mean. For example, the arithmetic mean of 5, 8, 9, and 10 is 8, and therefore the deviations from this mean are 3, 0, 1, and 2, giving a mean deviation of 1.5. *Compare* STANDARD DEVIATION.

mean price *See* MIDDLE PRICE.

means test Any assessment of the income and capital of a person or family to determine their eligibility for benefits provided by the state or a charity.

measurability The degree to which the size, purchasing power, and profitability of a market segment can be measured.

measured daywork A method of assessing wages in which a daily production target is set and a daily wage agreed on this basis. If the target is reached the worker receives the agreed daily wage; if it is not reached (or is exceeded) the worker is paid pro rata.

measurement tonnage *See* TONNAGE.

mechanical observation Observation techniques involving mechanical observers either in conjunction with, or in place of, human observers. Examples include the motion-picture or video camera, the *audimeter, the psychogalvanometer, the eye-camera, and the pupilometer. None of these would be used without the knowledge and permission of the respondent.

mechanistic organization An organization characterized by clearly specified roles and clear definitions of the rights and obligations of individuals within the hierarchical structure. Interaction and communication are largely vertical. This type of structure is appropriate if the environment is certain. *Compare* ORGANIC ORGANIZATION.

media (mass media) The means, such as television, radio, newspapers, and magazines, by which advertisers, politicians, etc., communicate with large numbers of members of the general public.

media analysis (media research; media planning; media selection) An investigation into the relative effectiveness and the relative costs of using the various advertising *media in an advertising campaign. Before committing an advertising budget it is necessary to carry out marketing research on potential customers, their

| MECHANISTIC ORGANIZATION | | ORGANIC ORGANIZATION |

CERTAINTY ◄─────────────────────► UNCERTAINTY

EXTERNAL ENVIRONMENT

Mechanistic and organic organizations.

reading habits, television-watching habits, how many times the advertisers wish the potential customers to see an advertisement, how great a percentage of the market they wish to reach, etc. These elements all need to be considered and balanced to plan a campaign that will effectively reach its target audience at a reasonable cost.

media equation The equation 'media = real life', indicating that users of communications technology tend to interact with the media much as they do with other people in the real world.

media impact The qualitative value of exposure through a given medium. For example, messages on TV are likely to create more impact than messages on the radio.

median A typical value that is identified by arranging a set of numbers in an ascending or descending scale and selecting the middle number (if there is an odd number in the set) or the arithmetic mean of the middle two numbers (if there is an even number). This can give a more representative average in some circumstances than an *arithmetic mean or a *geometric mean.

media schedule A schedule identifying the media to be used for an advertising programme and the dates on which advertisements are to appear. Decisions have to be made on:

- reach (the percentage of market that would be expected to see the ad);
- frequency (how often the target market would see the ad);
- impact (qualitative value of the ad);
- major media to be used (TV, Internet, newspapers and magazines, etc.);
- media vehicles (specific media to be used, e.g. *The Times* newspaper);
- media timing (the schedule of the appearance of the ads in the chosen media).

mediation The intervention of a neutral third party in an industrial dispute. The object is to enable the two sides to reach a compromise solution to their differences, which the mediator usually does by seeing representatives of each side separately and then together. If the mediator has power to make binding awards the process is known as *arbitration; if the mediator can only suggest means of settling the dispute it is known as **conciliation**. *See* ADVISORY CONCILIATION AND ARBITRATION SERVICE.

media vehicle A specific channel, such as a particular magazine, television show, or radio programme, within each general media type.

medical insurance *See* PRIVATE HEALTH INSURANCE.

medium-dated gilt *See* GILT-EDGED SECURITY.

medium of exchange A substance or article of little intrinsic value that is used to pay for goods or services. In primitive economies various articles, such as sea shells, have been used for this purpose but *money is now used universally.

mediums *See* GILT-EDGED SECURITY.

medium-sized company A company that is entitled to certain filing exemptions because it meets two out of three of the following criteria for the current and preceding year, or the two preceding financial years:

- the company's *net worth should not exceed £12.9 million;
- the *turnover should not exceed £25.9 million
- the average number of employees should not exceed 250.

In a company's first *financial year it need only meet the conditions for that year; in its second financial year it may claim the filing exemptions of a medium-sized company if it met the conditions in its first financial year. A *public limited company, a banking or insurance company, an authorized person under the Financial Services Act 1986, or a member of an ineligible group may not claim medium-sized company filing exemptions.

A medium-sized company must prepare full audited *financial statements for distribution to its shareholders but it may file *abbreviated accounts instead of full accounts with the *Registrar of Companies. *See also* SMALL COMPANY; SME.

medium-sized group A *group that meets two out of three of the following criteria for the current and preceding year, or the two preceding financial years:

• the group's *net worth should not exceed £12.9 million net or £15.5 million gross;
• its *turnover should not exceed £25.9 million net or £31.1 million gross;
• the average number of employees should not exceed 250.

Formerly, a parent company was not required to prepare *group accounts for a financial year in which the group headed by that parent qualified as a medium-sized group. However, for accounting periods beginning on or after 6 April 2008 medium-sized groups are no longer eligible for this exemption other than in certain specified circumstances. *See also* SMALL GROUP.

medium-term (intermediate-term) Denoting a time period of medium duration, the extent of which will differ according to context. For example, in accounting 'medium-term' describes liabilities of between one and ten years, in money markets it means maturities of greater than a year, in bond markets a period of five to ten years, and in *eurobond markets one of two to seven years.

medium-term note (MTN) A *note issued in a eurocurrency with a maturity of about three to six years. Although MTNs were traditionally unsecured, recent years have seen a growth in **asset-backed medium-term notes (ABMTN)**, in which the MTN is secured against assets held by a *structured investment vehicle.

meeting of creditors *See* BANKRUPTCY; CREDITORS' VOLUNTARY LIQUIDATION; LIQUIDATOR.

meltdown A disastrous and uncontrolled fall in share prices. The expression is derived from the disaster that results when the core of a nuclear reactor melts uncontrollably.

member bank A bank that belongs to a central banking or clearing system. In the UK a member bank is a *commercial bank that is a member of the *Association for Payment Clearing Services. In the USA it is a commercial bank that is a member of the *Federal Reserve System.

member firm A firm of brokers or *market makers that is a member of the *London Stock Exchange. Banks, insurance companies, and overseas securities houses can now become corporate members.

member of a company A shareholder of a company whose name is entered in the *register of members. Founder members (*see* FOUNDERS' SHARES) are those who sign the *memorandum of association; anyone subsequently coming into possession of the company's shares becomes a member.

member profile The accumulated information on a member of a *community of users. This information will include details of their lifestyle, buying habits, membership of clubs, etc.

membership group A social group to which a person feels that he or she belongs and that has a direct influence on that person's behaviour. Such groups may include clubs and societies, political parties, religious organizations, etc.

membership rules Qualifications or characteristics required for an individual to become part of a *community of users.

members' voluntary liquidation (members' voluntary winding-up) The winding-up of a company by a special resolution of the members in circumstances in which the company is solvent. Before making the winding-up resolution, the directors must make a *declaration of solvency. It is a criminal offence to make such a declaration without reasonable grounds for believing that it is true. When the resolution has been passed, a *liquidator is appointed; if, during the course of the winding-up, the liquidator believes that the company will not be able to pay its debts, a meeting of creditors must be called and the winding-up is treated as a members' *compulsory liquidation.

memorandum of association An official document that must be submitted to the Registrar of Companies when a new company is formed.

Until 1 October 2010, when the Companies Act 2006 came into force, the memorandum formed part of the company's constitution and included such information as the objects of the company, the type of company (e.g. public limited company), and the *authorized share capital. The memorandum is now a much shorter document stating simply that the members wish to form a company. *See also* ARTICLES OF ASSOCIATION.

memorandum of satisfaction A document stating that a mortgage or charge on property has been repaid. It has to be signed by all the parties concerned and a copy sent to the *Registrar of Companies, if the mortgage or charge was made by a company.

mentoring The process in which a senior employee takes an active role in a junior colleague's development. The mentor usually provides support and encouragement as well as advice on how the mentee can develop his or her competencies to progress along a successful career path. In larger organizations, mentors are often formally assigned to those at an earlier stage of their career.

menu A list of choices displayed by a computer. When many options are available the user may be presented first with a main menu, from which more detailed menus can be selected. A well-designed menu system can make a complicated program simple to use.

menu costs The costs incurred by a firm when it changes its prices. The term alludes to the case of a restaurant, which is obliged

to reprint its menus every time it changes a price; this means that it will only make such changes when the costs of not doing so clearly outweigh the cost and inconvenience of reprinting. Menu costs are frequently cited as one explanation for the *stickiness of prices, i.e. their failure to respond immediately to shifts in supply and demand. Some analysts have argued that e-commerce will eradicate most traditional forms of menu costs.

mercantile agent *See* FACTOR.

mercantile law The commercial law, which includes those aspects of a country's legal code that apply to banking, companies, contracts, copyrights, insolvency, insurance, patents, the sale of goods, shipping, trademarks, transport, and warehousing.

merchandising The promotion by a retailer of selected products. Commonly used techniques include displays to encourage *impulse buying, free samples and gifts, and temporary price reductions. Merchandising policy is usually designed to influence the retailer's sales pattern and is influenced by such factors as the firm's *market, the speed at which different products sell, *margins, and service considerations. Sometimes merchandising is used to attract customers into the shop rather than to promote the product itself.

merchant A trader who buys goods for resale, acting as a principal and usually holding stocks. Typically a merchant sells goods in smaller lots than he buys and often exports goods or is involved in *entrepôt trade.

merchantable quality An implied condition respecting the state of goods sold in the course of business. Such goods should be as fit for their ordinary purpose as it is reasonable to expect, taking into account any description applied to them, the price (if relevant), and all the other relevant circumstances. The condition does not apply with regard to defects specifically drawn to the buyer's attention or defects that should have been noticed in an examination of the goods before the contract was made.

merchant bank A bank that formerly specialized in financing foreign trade, an activity that often grew out of its own merchanting business. This led them into accepting *bills of exchange and functioning as accepting houses. More recently they have tended to diversify into the field of *hire-purchase finance, the granting of long-term loans (especially to companies), providing venture capital, advising companies on flotations and *takeover bids, underwriting new issues, and managing investment portfolios and unit trusts. Many of them are old-established and some offer a limited banking service. Their knowledge of international trade makes them specialists in dealing with the large multinational companies. They are most common in Europe, but some merchant banks have begun to operate in the USA; the US equivalent in terms of current activity is known as an **investment bank**. Several UK merchant banks were taken over in the 1990s either by the commercial banks or by large overseas banks.

merchant wholesaler An independently owned business that functions as a wholesaler and takes title to the merchandise it handles, i.e. it takes goods into stock and supplies its customers from stock, rather than acting as an agent or distributor for a manufacturer.

MERCOSUR (Southern Common Market) An association of South American nations formed in 1991 with the aim of establishing a common market between member states and harmonizing their economic and social policies. The current members are Argentina, Brazil, Paraguay, Uruguay, and Venezuela; Bolivia, Chile, Colombia, Ecuador, and Peru are associated members. Paraguay's membership was suspended in 2012. In 2004 Mercosur signed a cooperation agreement with the **Andean Community (CAN)**, which comprises Bolivia, Colombia, Ecuador, Peru, and Venezuela. The ultimate goal is now the complete integration of the two blocs to form a continent-wide association on the model of the *European Union. *See also* LATIN AMERICAN INTEGRATION ASSOCIATION.

merger A combination of two or more businesses on a relatively equal footing that results in the creation of a new reporting entity. The shareholders of the combining entities mutually share the risks and rewards of the new entity and no one party to the merger obtains control over another. Financial Reporting Standard 6, Acquisitions and Mergers, which is now discontinued, laid down four criteria by which a merger may be identified:

- no party is the acquirer or acquired;
- all parties to the combination participate in establishing the management structure of the new entity;
- the combining entities are relatively equal in terms of size;
- the consideration received by the equity shareholders of each party consists primarily of equity shares in the combined entity, any other consideration received being relatively immaterial.

However, true mergers (as opposed to disguised takeovers) are very rare in the contemporary business environment. Owing to its widespread abuse, *merger accounting has been effectively limited to cases of reconstruction within an existing group.

merger accounting A method of accounting that treats two or more businesses as combining on an equal footing. It is usually applied without any restatement of *net assets to fair value and includes the results of each of the combined entities for the whole of the *accounting period, as if they had always been combined. It does not reflect the issue of shares as an application of resources at fair value. The difference that arises on *consolidation does not represent *goodwill but is deducted from, or added to, *reserves. In the past merger accounting was often used to avoid recognizing goodwill in combinations that were essentially takeovers rather than true mergers. The recent Financial Reporting Standard Applicable in the UK and Republic of Ireland permits merger accounting only in cases of group reconstruction. *International Financial Reporting Standard 3, Business Combinations, prohibits merger accounting for all business combinations falling within its scope. *Compare* ACQUISITION ACCOUNTING.

merger relief Relief from adding to, or setting up, a *share premium account when issuing shares at a premium if an issuing company has secured at least a 90% equity holding in another company. This relief applies if the issuing company is providing for the allotment of equity shares in the issuing company in exchange for the equity shares (or non-equity shares) in the other company or by the cancellation of any such shares not held by the issuing company. *See* MERGER RESERVE.

merger reserve (merger capital reserve) A *reserve credited in place of a *share premium account when *merger relief is made use of. *Goodwill on consolidation may be written off against a merger reserve (unlike the share premium account).

merit bonus A *bonus granted to an employee as a reward for good work.

message board A website showing messages and information to visitors about a specific company or area of interest.

message source The source from which an advertising message proceeds. This can be a company, its brand name, the salesperson, or the actor in the advertisement who endorses a product.

meta search engine A *search engine that submits keywords typed by users to a range of other search engines in order to increase the number of relevant pages, since different search engines may have indexed different sites.

meta tags In an HTML file (*see* HYPERTEXT), tags containing text that is not displayed by the browser. This **meta text** may summarize the content of the site (**content meta tag**) and relevant keywords (**keyword meta tag**), which are matched against the keywords typed into *search engines.

Metcalfe's law The law that the value of a network of people using the same Internet site(s) increases with the square of the number of participants. This is strictly true only if all users belong to a *community of values.

methodological log A journal of detailed and time-sequenced notes on the investigative techniques used during a market-research enquiry, with special attention to biases or distortions each technique may have introduced.

method study A critical examination of existing and proposed ways of carrying out work, with the object of seeking methods that are more effective, more efficient, or cheaper. Normally a method study is carried out before *work measurement as there is no point in measuring an inappropriate method. *See also* WORK STUDY.

METI The Japanese Ministry for Economy, Trade and Industry, formerly known as MITI (Ministry for International Trade and Industry). This government body played a vital role in Japan's postwar economic boom.

metical (*plural* **meticais**) (MZN) The standard monetary unit of Mozambique, divided into 100 centavos.

metrics for Internet marketing Measures that indicate the effectiveness of *Internet marketing activities in meeting customer, business, and marketing objectives.

metric system A system of measurement based on the decimal system. It was first formalized in France at the end of the 18th century and by the 1830s was being widely adopted in Europe. In the UK *Imperial units remained supreme until 1963, when the yard was redefined as 0.9144 metre and the pound as 0.453 592 37 kilogram. The Metrication Board set up in 1969 failed to achieve its target of the **metrication** of British industry by 1975. However, the Weights and Measures Act 1985, the 1994

Amendment Order, and the 1994 Regulations took into account directives issued by the European Union. As a result certain traditional units such as the hundredweight, ton, pound, ounce, yard, foot, inch, gallon, bushel, square mile, cubic yard, and cubic foot were outlawed for purposes of trade. Finally, in January 2001, the UK adopted into law an EU directive making it illegal (with a few specified exceptions) to sell goods in any measures other than the gram, kilogram, millimetre, and metre. The pint (for milk and draught beer), the mile (for road traffic signs), and the acre (for land registration) are authorized without time limit. For all scientific purposes and many trade and industrial purposes the form of the metric system known as *SI units is now in use. In the USA metrication has been even slower than in the UK.

metric ton *See* TON.

metrology The scientific study of weights and measures. The subject has long been closely associated with trade and commerce, which is based on the exchange of measured quantities of goods or services for money or measured quantities of other goods or services. *See* IMPERIAL UNITS; METRIC SYSTEM; SI UNITS.

metropolitan statistical area (MSA) A unit of the US Census Bureau consisting of either: (1) a city with 50,000 or more inhabitants or (2) an urban centre with at least 50,000 inhabitants together with adjacent territory that is socially and economically integrated with this centre.

mezzanine finance 1. Finance, usually provided by specialist financial institutions, that is neither pure equity nor pure debt. It can take many different forms and can be secured or unsecured; it usually earns a higher rate of return than pure debt but less than equity. Conversely, it carries a higher risk than pure debt, although less than equity. It is often used in *management buy-outs. **2.** A form of finance used by venture capitalists after *seed capital has been provided.

M-form Describing a type of organizational structure consisting of a relatively large number of relatively small semiautonomous units, which are controlled mainly by the setting of financial targets from the centre. 'M' stands for 'multidivisional'. Recent years have seen a trend towards M-form and *N-form structures.

MICEX Abbreviation for Moscow Interbank Currency Exchange; *see* MOSCOW EXCHANGE.

MICR Magnetic ink character recognition: a process in which ferromagnetic ink is used on cheques and other documents to enable them to be automatically sorted and the characters to be read and fed into a computer.

microcomputer *See* PERSONAL COMPUTER.

microcredit The lending of small sums of money on very low security, especially to small businesses or to small producers in the developing world.

microeconomics The analysis of economic behaviour at the level of individual market participants, chiefly individual businesses or consumers. For an individual or household microeconomics is concerned with the optimal allocation of a given budget, the labour supply choice, and the effects of taxation. For a business it is largely concerned with the production process, costs, and the marketing of output, dependent on the type of competition faced. *Compare* MACROECONOMICS.

micro-entity A very *small company with an annual turnover of not more than £632,000, a balance-sheet total of not more than £316,000, and (on average) no more than 10 employees. Under EU regulations adopted into UK law in November 2013, such an entity is exempt from the requirements of the *Company Reporting Directive and may present annual accounts with a simplified balance sheet and profit-and-loss format; only the former need be filed at *Companies House. A company that opts to be treated as a micro-entity is not permitted to apply *fair value accounting methods.

An entity that is not eligible for the small companies accounting regime (e.g. because it is a member of a group containing a public company) cannot qualify as a micro-entity whatever its size; nor can a parent company that prepares *consolidated financial statements or a subsidiary included in group accounts by the method of *full consolidation.

microenvironment The environment close to a company, which affects its ability to serve its customers. This includes the company itself, firms in its market channel, customer markets, and competitors. *Compare* MACROENVIRONMENT.

micromanagement A management style characterized by excessive attention to small details and constant interference in the work of subordinates. Apart from being inefficient, micromanagement can have a severely demotivating effect on workers, who may feel that their abilities and experience are not respected.

micromarketing A form of target marketing in which companies tailor their marketing programmes to the needs of a narrowly defined geographic, demographic, psychographic, or behavioural market segment.

microprocessor In computer technology, an integrated circuit that contains on one chip the arithmetic, logical, and control functions of the central processing unit. Microprocessors are used as control systems in many devices, including car electronics and cameras, as well as in *personal computers.

microprudential regulation An approach to the regulation of the financial system that is based on scrutinizing operations at the level of the individual and the firm. Such an approach emphasizes e.g. levels of *capital adequacy in banks, the outlawing of unfair or anticompetitive practices, and measures to protect investors and consumers of financial services. Since the financial crisis of 2007–08

microprudential regulation has been increasingly supplemented by *macroprudential regulation.

middleman A person or organization that makes a profit by trading in goods as an intermediary between the producer and the consumer. Middlemen include agents, brokers, dealers, merchants, factors, wholesalers, distributors, and retailers. They earn their profit by providing a variety of different services, including finance, bulk buying, holding stocks, breaking bulk, risk sharing, making a market and stabilizing prices, providing information about products (to consumers) and about markets (to producers), providing a distribution network, and introducing buyers to sellers.

middle management *See* MANAGEMENT.

middle price (mean price) The average of the *offer price of a security, commodity, currency, etc., and the *bid price. It is the middle price that is often quoted in the financial press.

MiFID Abbreviation for *Markets in Financial Instruments Directive.

MIGA Abbreviation for *Multilateral Investment Guarantee Agency.

migrant worker A worker who has come from another country or region to work. Attracted by better wages in the country or region to which they have migrated, such workers may or may not bring their family with them. In many cases they will not have done so and will therefore be sending a substantial proportion of their earnings back to their native country. This can have an adverse effect on the *balance of payments of countries that attract substantial numbers of migrant workers and conversely can be advantageous to countries from which many workers migrate.

mil A monetary unit of Malta, worth one thousandth of a *lira.

Milan Stock Exchange *See* BORSA ITALIANA.

milk round An annual visit to universities by the personnel managers of large companies seeking graduates to join their organizations.

millime A Tunisian monetary unit, worth one thousandth of a *dinar.

minicomputer A *computer that is less powerful than a *mainframe but more powerful than a *personal computer. It is unable to handle as many people or programs at the same time as a mainframe, but it is adequate for a wide range of business and scientific applications.

minimum lending rate (MLR) Between 1971 and 1981, the minimum rate at which the Bank of England would lend to the *discount houses. This was a published figure; the present more informal *base rate does not have the same status.

minimum subscription 1. The minimum sum of money, stated in the *prospectus of a new company, that the directors consider must be raised if the company is to be viable. **2.** The smallest bid required in terms of the number of new securities at issue.

minimum wage The minimum wage that an employer may legally pay an employee. In some countries there are statutory national minimum wages and in other countries there may be agreed minimum wages within certain industries. The UK introduced its first statutory minimum wage in 1999; the current (2014–15) rates are £6.50 per hour for those aged 21 or over, £5.13 for those aged 18–20, and £3.79 for those under 18. Special rules apply to apprentices. From April 2016 employers will be required to pay workers over the age of 25 a **National Living Wage**, initially set at £7.25 per hour.

minority interest The interest of individual shareholders in a company more than 50% of which is owned by a *holding company. For example, if 60% of the ordinary shares in a company are owned by a holding company, the remaining 40% will represent a minority interest. These

minority shareholders will receive their full share of profits in the form of dividends although they will be unable to determine company policy as they will always be outvoted by the majority interest held by the holding company. *See* CONTROLLING INTEREST; PARTICIPATING INTEREST.

minority protection Remedies evolved to safeguard a minority of company members from the abuse of majority rule. They include just and equitable winding-up, applying for relief on the basis of *unfair prejudice, bringing a *derivative or representative action, and seeking an *inspection and investigation of the company.

mint A factory, owned by a government or a bank, in which coins and banknotes are manufactured. *See* ROYAL MINT.

mint par of exchange The rate of exchange between two currencies that were on the *gold standard. The rate was then determined by the gold content of the basic coin.

MIP 1. Abbreviation for monthly investment plan. **2.** Abbreviation for *maximum investment plan.

MIPS Abbreviation for millions of instructions per second, used as a measure of computer power.

mirror swap *See* OFFSETTING SWAP.

MIS Abbreviation for *management information system.

misdeclaration penalty A penalty of up to 15% of the *value added tax lost in understating the VAT liability or overstating the VAT refund due on the VAT return, when the amounts involved are material. The penalty will apply if the inaccuracy equals the lesser of £1 million and 30% of the total amount of tax due for the period of the VAT return. The penalty can be avoided if the *taxable person can show that there was reasonable excuse, that there had been a voluntary disclosure, or that the taxable person had reason to believe that their VAT affairs were under investigation by HM

Revenue and Customs. *See also* PERSISTENT MISDECLARATION PENALTY.

misery index A measure of economic distress calculated by adding the unemployment rate to the inflation rate at any time. Some versions include additional measures, such as the base rate, annual GDP, and the number of bankruptcies.

misfeasance 1. The negligent or otherwise improper performance of a lawful act. **2.** An act by an officer of a company in the nature of a breach of trust or breach of duty, particularly if it relates to the company's assets.

misfeasance summons An application to the court by a creditor, contributory, liquidator, or the official receiver during the course of winding up a company. The court is asked to examine the conduct of a company officer and order restitution to be made if the officer is found guilty of breach of trust or duty.

misleading advertising (deceptive advertising) Advertising that, although not strictly untrue, leads consumers to less-than-accurate conclusions. Intentionally misleading consumers is an extreme form of misleading advertising and is against the advertising standards code of conduct (*see* ADVERTISING STANDARDS AUTHORITY).

mismatch 1. Any financial *position that is not perfectly *offset. **2.** A *floating-rate note in which the coupon is paid monthly but the interest rate paid is that applicable to a note of longer maturity. **3.** The situation in which the assets (loans made) and liabilities (deposits taken) of a bank are not matched, typically because the bank borrows short-term and lends long-term. This is usually acceptable as long as deposits keep coming in. *See* ASSET–LIABILITY MANAGEMENT; GAP.

misrepresentation An untrue statement of fact, made by one party to the other in the course of negotiating a contract, that induces the other party to enter into the contract. The person making the misrepresentation is called the **representor**, and

the person to whom it is made is the **representee**. A false statement of law, opinion, or intention does not constitute a misrepresentation; nor does a statement of fact known by the representee to be untrue. Moreover, unless the representee relies on the statement so that it becomes an inducement (though not necessarily the only inducement) to enter into the contract, it is not a misrepresentation. The remedies for misrepresentation vary according to the degree of culpability of the representor. If guilty of **fraudulent misrepresentation** (i.e. if the truth of a statement is not honestly believed, which is not the same as saying that it is known to be false) the representee may, subject to certain limitations, set the contract aside and may also sue for *damages. If guilty of **negligent misrepresentation** (i.e. if the statement is believed without reasonable grounds for doing so) the representee may also rescind (*see* RESCISSION) the contract and sue for damages. If the representor has committed merely an **innocent misrepresentation** (one reasonably believed to be true) the representee is restricted to rescinding the contract.

missionary sales personnel Salespersons who visit prospective customers, distribute information to them, and handle their questions and complaints but do not usually take orders from them. Sales personnel who perform these functions tend to be employed by an agency and are hired out to the selling company.

mission statement (vision statement) A statement that encapsulates the overriding purpose and objectives of an organization. It is used to communicate this purpose to all stakeholder groups, both internal and external, and to guide employees in their contribution towards achieving it. *See also* STRATEGIC INTENT; VALUE STATEMENT.

mistake In law, a misunderstanding or erroneous belief about a matter of fact (**mistake of fact**) or a matter of law (**mistake of law**). In civil cases, mistake is particularly important in the law of *contract. Mistakes of law have no effect on the validity of agreements, and neither do many mistakes of fact. When a mistake of fact does do so, it may render the agreement void under common-law rules (in which case it is referred to as an **operative mistake**) or it may make it voidable, i.e. liable, subject to certain limitations, to be set aside under the more lenient rules of equity.

When both parties to an agreement are under a misunderstanding, the mistake may be classified as either a **common mistake** (i.e. a single mistake shared by both) or a **mutual mistake** (i.e. each misunderstanding the other). In the case of common mistake, the mistake renders the contract void only if it robs it of all substance. The principal (and almost the only) example is when the subject matter of the contract has, unknown to both parties, ceased to exist. A common mistake about some particular attribute of the subject matter (e.g. that a document is an original, not a copy) is not an operative mistake. However, a common mistake relating to any really fundamental matter will render a contract voidable. In the case of mutual mistake, the contract is valid if only one interpretation of what was agreed can be deduced from the parties' words and conduct. Otherwise, the mistake is operative and the contract void. When only one party to a contract is under a misunderstanding, the mistake may be called a **unilateral mistake** and it makes the contract void if it relates to the fundamental nature of the offer and the other party knew or ought to have known of it. Otherwise, the contract is valid so far as the law of mistake is concerned, though the circumstances may be such as to make it voidable for *misrepresentation.

A deed or other signed document (whether or not constituting a contract) that does not correctly record what both parties intended may be rectified by the courts. When one signatory to a document was fundamentally (but not carelessly) mistaken as to the character or effect of the transaction it embodies, the signatory may plead the mistake as a defence to any action based on the document.

mitigation of damage Minimizing the loss incurred by the person who suffered the loss and is claiming *damages as a result of it. The injured party has a duty to take all reasonable steps to mitigate any loss and the courts will not, therefore, award damages to compensate for a loss that could have been avoided by reasonable action.

mixed economy An economy in which some goods and services are produced by the government and some by private enterprise. A mixed economy lies between a *command economy and a complete *laissez-faire economy. In practice, however, most economies are mixed; the significant feature is whether an economy is moving towards or away from a more laissez-faire situation.

mixed-standard scale A measure used in evaluating the job performance of employees. An example of good, average, and poor behaviour is identified for each of the key elements of a job; supervisors are then asked to rate the performance of the employee in terms of whether it is better than, equal to, or worse than each of the identified behaviours. A total score is derived from these responses. *Compare* BEHAVIOURALLY ANCHORED RATING SCALES; BEHAVIOURAL OBSERVATION SCALE.

MMDA Abbreviation for *money-market deposit account.

MNE Abbreviation for *multinational enterprise.

mobile advertising Advertising in which products are promoted on mobile devices such as smartphones and tablet computers, and through applications and messaging for such devices. The benefits for advertisers can include the very immediate and targeted nature of such messages; mobile advertising allows businesses to interact directly with prospective customers and can be both time- and location-sensitive.

mobile commerce (m-commerce) Selling goods or services to customers over the

Internet via their smartphones and tablet computers. Transactions are carried out using websites, particularly those tailored for handheld devices, or through applications (apps) that enable purchases from particular firms. Increasingly, mobile devices can also be used as a direct means of payment. For instance, transport or event tickets can be bought in this way without using a bank card.

mobility barriers Those factors that restrict the ability of a firm to move from one *strategic group within an industry to another (in effect, to adopt a radically different and more competitive strategy). As described by Michael Porter in 1980, these may include investment costs, the nature of the market, and the firm's internal capacities. Mobility barriers are thus analogous to the *barriers to entry or exit that apply to an industry as a whole.

mobility of labour The extent to which workers are willing to move from one region or country to another (**geographical mobility**) or to change from one occupation to another (**occupational mobility**). In **horizontal mobility** there is no change of status, whereas in **vertical mobility** there is. An upward change in status will increase a worker's mobility, whereas a downward change will reduce it. The more highly skilled a worker, the less his occupational mobility will be, but he will often be highly geographically mobile. An unskilled worker will often be both occupationally and geographically mobile. In the UK, many government retraining schemes aim to increase occupational mobility; at the same time considerable effort goes into encouraging new industries into areas of high unemployment to reduce the need for geographical mobility.

mock auction An *auction during which a lot is sold to someone at a price lower than his highest bid, part of the price is repaid or credited to the bidder, the right to bid is restricted to those who have bought or agreed to buy one or more articles, or articles are given away or offered as gifts. Under the Mock Auction Act 1961 it is an

offence to promote or conduct a mock auction.

mode *See* NORMAL DISTRIBUTION.

modem Abbreviation for *mo*dulator-*dem*odulator, a device that enables a computer to transmit and receive data by means of a communications link, such as a telephone line. The process of converting computer signals into a form suitable for transmission is called modulation. The reverse process, making the transmitted signals intelligible to the computer, is called demodulation. Modems provide access to the telephone network for *e-mail and for the *Internet.

moderator 1. An individual who supervises activities in Internet marketing research or in Internet chat rooms or discussions in order to maintain relevance and quality. **2.** *See* FOCUS-GROUP MODERATOR.

modified accounts The original name for what are now called *abbreviated accounts.

modified rebuy A situation in which a buyer is unhappy with current suppliers or products and is looking at competitors' products and prices rather than automatically rebuying the same product as before. *See* BUSINESS BUYER BEHAVIOUR.

Modigliani–Miller theorem (MM hypothesis) A theory of corporate finance, first advanced by Franco Modigliani and Merton Miller in 1958, which holds that the *capital structure of a firm has, under certain assumptions, no effect on the firm's value. The theorem states that, in a perfect market with no taxation or costs of *financial distress, neither the relative levels of debt and equity in a firm, nor its dividend policy, would affect the market value. In real-world markets, this is by no means the case.

modular design A design technique that aims to provide a variety of products using combinations of a small range of components. The end result is that customer

m

choice is maximized while operational complexity is minimized.

monadic testing A technique used in marketing research in which consumers are presented with a product to test on its own, rather than being asked to compare it with a competing product (*see* PAIRED COMPARISONS).

monetary assets *Assets, such as *cash and *debtors, that have a fixed monetary exchange value and are not affected by a change in the price level. If there are no regulations requiring companies to account for changing price levels, monetary assets remain in the *financial statements at their original amounts. If the principle of accounting for changes in price levels is applied, the monetary assets will be indexed.

monetary control The deliberate management of the *money supply by a central bank or other authority, usually as a means of maintaining price stability.

monetary policy The procedures by which governments or central banks try to affect macroeconomic conditions by influencing the supply of money. Apart from simply printing more money, which is now rarely used in practice (but *see* QUANTITATIVE EASING), there are four main options:

- using *open-market operations (i.e., the sale or purchase of government debt) to expand or contract the *money supply;
- raising or lowering reserve requirements (i.e. the percentage of their assets that banks must hold in cash) to affect liquidity;
- controlling the amount of money supplied to the banking system through short-term funds;
- changing the interest rate as a means of indirectly influencing the money supply.

The traditional Keynesian view has been that monetary policy is at best a blunt instrument, while monetarism holds the opposite view. In practice, most Western governments have come to accept the case for 'tight' monetary policies as a means of restraining inflation, except where there is a serious risk of deflation. This has led many governments to cede control of monetary policy to an independent central bank. *See also* INFLATION TARGETING. *Compare* FISCAL POLICY.

Monetary Policy Committee (MPC) The committee of *Bank of England officials and outside economic experts that has been responsible for setting interest rates in the UK since 1997. Prior to this date, interest rates were set by the Treasury.

monetary reform The revision of a country's currency by the introduction of a new currency unit or a substantial change to an existing system. Examples include decimalization of the UK currency (1971), the change from the austral to the peso in Argentina (1992), and the introduction of the *euro (2002).

monetary system 1. The system used by a country to provide the economy with money for internal use and to control the exchange of its own currency with those of foreign countries. It also includes the system used by a country for implementing its **monetary policy**, i.e. its policy regarding the *money supply. **2.** A system used to control the exchange rate of a group of countries, such as the Exchange Rate Mechanism of the *European Monetary System and its successor, ERM II.

monetary union A group of countries using a single currency. *See* EUROPEAN ECONOMIC AND MONETARY UNION.

monetary unit The standard unit of currency in a country. The monetary unit of each country is related to those of other countries by a *foreign exchange rate.

money A *medium of exchange that functions as a *unit of account, a store of value, and a means for deferred payment. Originally money enhanced economic development by enabling goods to be bought and sold without the need for barter. However, throughout history money has been beset by the problem of its debasement as a store of value as a result of *inflation. Now that the supply of money is a monopoly of the state, most governments are committed in principle to stable prices. The word 'money' is derived from the Latin *moneta*, which was one of the names of Juno, the Roman goddess whose temple was used as a mint.

money at call and short notice One of the assets that appears in the balance sheet of a bank. It includes funds lent to discount houses, money brokers, the stock exchange, bullion brokers, corporate customers, and increasingly to other banks. **At call money** is repayable on demand, whereas **short notice money** implies that notice of repayment of up to 14 days will be given. After cash, money at call and short notice are the banks' most liquid assets. They are usually interest-earning secured loans but their importance lies in providing the banks with an opportunity to use their surplus funds and to adjust their cash and liquidity requirements.

money broker In the UK, a *broker who arranges short-term loans in the *money market, i.e. between banks, discount houses, and dealers in government securities. Money brokers do not themselves lend or borrow money; they work for a commission arranging loans on a day-to-day and overnight basis. Money brokers also operate in the *eurobond markets.

money laundering *See* LAUNDERING MONEY.

moneylender A person whose business it is to lend money, other than pawnbrokers, friendly or building societies, corporate bodies with special powers to lend money, banks, or insurance companies. The Consumer Credit Act 1974 replaced the earlier Moneylenders Acts and requires all moneylenders to be registered, to obtain an annual licence to lend money, and to state the true *annual percentage rate (APR) of interest at which a loan is made.

money market 1. The wholesale market for short-term loans and debt instruments. In the UK, *money brokers arrange for loans between the banks, the government,

the *discount houses, and the *accepting houses, with the Bank of England acting as *lender of last resort. The main items of exchange are *bills of exchange, *Treasury bills, and trade bills. The market has traditionally taken place in and around *Lombard Street in the City of London. Private investors, through their banks, can place deposits in the money market at a higher rate of interest than bank deposit accounts. These are considered to be safe investments. *See also* INTERBANK MARKET. **2.** The *foreign-exchange market and the bullion market in addition to the short-term loan market.

money-market deposit account (MMDA) A type of high-yielding savings account introduced in the USA in 1982 to allow *deposit-taking institutions to compete with the money markets for savers' funds. Typically, such accounts require a minimum balance of between $1,000 and $2,500 and restrict withdrawals to six a month, of which only three may be transfers for bill payment.

money-market line An agreement between a bank and a company that entitles the company to borrow up to a certain limit each day in the *money markets, on a short-term basis (often overnight or in some cases up to one month). *See* UNCOMMITTED FACILITY.

money-market unit trust (cash unit trust) A *unit trust that invests in money-market instruments in order to provide investors with a risk-free income.

money-purchase pension scheme A *defined-contribution pension scheme as opposed to a *defined-benefit pension scheme.

money supply The quantity of money issued by a country's monetary authorities (usually the central bank). If the demand for money is stable, the widely accepted quantity theory of money implies that increases in the money supply will lead directly to an increase in the price level, i.e. to inflation. Since the 1970s most Western governments have attempted to reduce inflation by controlling the money supply. This raises two issues:

(i) how to measure the money supply;
(ii) how to control the money supply (*see* MONETARY POLICY).

In the UK various measures of the money supply have been used, from the very narrow M0 to the very broad M5. They are usually defined as:

M0—notes and coins in circulation plus the banks' till money and the banks' balances with the Bank of England;
M1—notes and coins in circulation plus private-sector current accounts and deposit accounts that can be transferred by cheque;
M2—notes and coins in circulation plus non-interest-bearing bank deposits plus building society deposits plus National Savings accounts;
M3—M1 plus all other private-sector bank deposits plus certificates of deposit;
M3c—M3 plus foreign currency bank deposits;
M4—M1 plus most private-sector bank deposits plus holdings of money-market instruments (e.g. Treasury bills);
M5—M4 plus building society deposits.

In some contexts the amount of money existing in an economy is called the **monetary stock**. To obtain the money supply the monetary stock has to be multiplied by the *velocity of circulation. See also* MONETARY POLICY.

monoline insurer A company that provides guarantees to bond issuers as a form of *credit enhancement. In recent years monoline insurers have been very active in the markets for *collateralized debt obligations and other complex *structured finance instruments. The *subprime lending disaster of 2007 led to major losses for some monoline insurers.

monopolistic competition A market for a particular product or service in which there are many competing sellers offering similar but non-identical goods. Such a market resembles *perfect competition in that there are a multiplicity of buyers and sellers and few *barriers to entry. However,

because each specific good can only be obtained from one seller, the producer acquires a power to influence market prices that would not exist under perfect competition: it has, in effect, a *monopoly in its own product. In such a market *product differentiation becomes essential, and branding, advertising, and marketing will be crucial to a firm's success.

monopoly A market in which there are multiple buyers but only one seller, who is thus largely able to control the terms of trade (e.g. price). Governments usually try to eliminate monopolies as being against the public interest. In recent decades some of the services formerly regarded as natural monopolies, such as electricity and water supply, have been privatized to encourage competition and eliminate the monopolistic element. *See also* CARTEL; CORNER; OLIGOPOLY.

monopsony A market in which there are many sellers but only a single buyer, who therefore has a decisive influence on the market price. An example of a monopsony would be the labour market in a town or industry where there is only one significant employer.

Monte Carlo simulation A *simulation in which random data are generated from specified distributions and used as an input into predictive or other models. In finance, such simulations are used to price complicated derivatives and portfolios and provide the basis for many *risk-management systems. Firms also employ them in their decision-making and capital-appraisal models.

Monthly Digest of Statistics A monthly publication of the UK *Office for National Statistics providing statistical information on business and industry, national income, and the UK population. It is available in both print and online form.

moonlighting Having two jobs, one a full-time daytime job, the other a part-time evening job. Often the second job is undertaken on a self-employed basis and income is not returned for tax purposes.

moral appeal An appeal in an advertisement or sales literature that is directed to the audience's sense of what is right and proper.

moral hazard The situation in which a person or organization has no incentive to act honestly or with due prudence. The term is mainly used in the insurance world, where a typical example of a person exposed to moral hazard would be the owner of an insured car, who has little or no incentive to guard against theft. Moral hazard is closely associated with the concept of *adverse selection, as when a person purchasing health insurance declines to reveal his or her greater likelihood to need health treatment than the average. Most recently, the phrase has been widely used in relation to the financial crisis of 2007–08, it being held that the lack of transparency associated with complex *structured finance products constituted a moral hazard that encouraged irresponsible risk taking. Similarly, the *too big to fail principle associated with the banks and other major financial institutions has been seen as a form of moral hazard.

moral suasion A regulatory body's use of argument and persuasion, rather than coercion or legislation, to influence the activities of those within its purview. The term is often applied to the efforts of the Federal Reserve Board (*see* FEDERAL RESERVE SYSTEM) to persuade its members to comply with its policies.

moratorium 1. An agreement between a creditor and a debtor to allow additional time for the settlement of a debt. **2.** A period during which one government permits a government of a foreign country to suspend repayments of a debt. **3.** A period during which all the trading debts in a particular market are suspended as a result of some exceptional crisis in the market. In these circumstances, not to call a moratorium would probably lead to more insolvencies than the market could stand. The intention of such a moratorium is, first, that firms should be given a breathing space to find out exactly what their liabilities are

and, secondly, that they should be given time to make the necessary financial arrangements to settle their liabilities.

MORI *See* IPSOS MORI.

mortality rate (death rate) The crude death rate, i.e. the number of deaths per 1,000 of the average population in a given year. It can be subdivided into different rates for different age groups of the population and for different regions.

mortality table (life table) An actuarial table prepared on the basis of mortality rates for people in different occupations in different regions of a country. It provides life-assurance companies with the information they require to quote for life-assurance policies, annuities, etc.

mortgage An interest in property created as a security for a loan or payment of a debt and terminated on payment of the loan or debt. The borrower, who offers the security, is the **mortgagor**; the lender, who provides the money, is the **mortgagee**. *Building societies and banks are the usual mortgagees for house purchasers. In either case the mortgage is repaid by instalments over a fixed period (often 25 years), either of capital and interest (**repayment mortgage**) or of interest only, with other arrangements being made to repay the capital, for example by means of an *endowment assurance policy (this is known as an **endowment mortgage**). Business uses of the mortgage include using property to secure a loan to start a business. Virtually any property may be mortgaged (though land is the most common).

  Under the Law of Property Act (1925), which governs mortgage regulations in the UK, there are two types of mortgage, legal and equitable. A **legal mortgage** confers a legal estate on the mortgagee (lender). Under the 1925 Act, the only valid mortgages are:

(a) a lease granted for a stated number of years, which terminates on repayment of the loan at or before the end of that period; and

(b) a deed expressed to be a *charge by way of legal mortgage.

All other mortgages are equitable mortgages, in which the mortgagee obtains an equitable interest in the property only. Such a mortgage may arise in two ways:

(1) If the mortgagor (borrower) has only an equitable, as opposed to a legal, interest in the property (e.g. because he or she is a beneficiary under a trust of the property) he or she can only grant an equitable mortgage. Provided that the mortgage is created by deed, the rights of the parties are very similar to those under a legal mortgage.

(2) An equitable mortgage can also be created of a legal or equitable interest by an informal written agreement, e.g. the mortgagor hands the title deeds to the mortgagee as security for a loan. The great majority of mortgages are now of this kind. Such a mortgagee has the remedies of repossession and foreclosure only.

A second or subsequent mortgage may be taken out on the same property, provided that the value of the property is greater than the amount of the previous mortgage(s). All mortgages of registered land are noted in the *register of charges on application by the mortgagee, and a charge certificate is issued. When mortgaged land is unregistered, a first legal mortgagee keeps the title deeds. A subsequent legal mortgagee and any equitable mortgagee who does not have the title deeds should protect their interests by registration.

Under the so-called equity of redemption, the mortgagor is allowed to redeem the property at any time on payment of the loan together with interest and costs, which may include a penalty for early redemption; any provisions in a mortgage deed to prevent redemption (known as clogs) are void.

In theory, the mortgagee always has the right to take possession of mortgaged property even if there has been no default. However, this right is usually excluded by building-society mortgages until default, and its exclusion may be implied in any instalment mortgage. Where residential property is concerned, the court has power to delay the recovery of possession if there is a realistic possibility that the default will be remedied in a reasonable time. In case of default, the mortgagee has a statutory right to sell the property, but this will normally be exercised after obtaining possession first. Any surplus left after the debt and the mortgagee's expenses have been met must be paid to the mortgagor. The mortgagee also has a statutory right to appoint a *receiver to manage mortgaged property in the event of default; this power is useful where business property is concerned. As a final resort, a mortgage may be brought to an end by *foreclosure, in which the court orders the transfer of the property to the mortgagee. This is not common in times of rising property prices, as the mortgagor would lose more than the value of the debt, so the court will not order foreclosure where a sale would be more appropriate.

mortgage-backed security (MBS) A *security in which cash flows derive from an underlying pool of mortgages. They are very widely used in the USA. *See also* SECURITIZATION; SUBPRIME LENDING.

mortgage bond In the USA, a bond in which a debt is secured by a real asset (land or property). **Senior mortgage bonds** have first claim on assets and **junior mortgage bonds** are subordinate. A mortgage bond may have a closed-end provision, which prevents an organization issuing further bonds of a similar nature on the same asset or open-end provision, which permits further issues with the same status.

mortgage debenture A loan made to a company by an investor, secured on the real property of the company. *See* DEBENTURE.

mortgagee *See* MORTGAGE.

mortgagor *See* MORTGAGE.

Mosaic *See* GEOGRAPHIC INFORMATION SYSTEM.

Moscow Exchange The principal stock exchange in Russia, formed in 2011 through a merger of the Moscow Interbank Currency Exchange (MICEX) and the Russian Trading System.

most-favoured-nation clause A clause in a trade agreement between two countries stating that each will accord to the other the same treatment as regards tariffs and quotas as they extend to the most favoured nation with which each trades. Both the World Trade Organization and the EU have used this concept.

motion A proposal put before a meeting for discussion. Usually members of a company who attend a meeting of the company receive a **notice of motion** to enable them to consider the motion before the meeting. If the motion is passed by a majority of the members of the company it becomes a *resolution. If the meeting decides to amend the motion, the amended motion, known as the **substantive motion**, is then discussed and voted upon.

motivation The mental processes that arouse, sustain, and direct human behaviour. Motivation may stem from processes taking place within an individual (*intrinsic motivation) or from the impact of factors acting on the individual from outside (*extrinsic motivation); in most cases these two influences are continually interacting.

The vocabulary associated with motivation is large; such terms as purpose, desire, need, goal, preference, perception, attitude, recognition, achievement, and incentive are commonly used. Many of these drives can act on an individual simultaneously, causing varying degrees of conflict. A consumer deciding between buying chocolate and buying ice cream is in conflict. An employee who wants to disagree with the boss but also wants to keep his or her job is in conflict.

In a business context, an understanding of human motivation is crucial to understanding *consumer buying behaviour. It is also vital to the design of organizational norms and structures, including reward structures, that encourage effort and

achievement on the part of employees. In the realm of theory considerable importance has been given to the hierarchy of needs investigated by Abraham Maslow (1908–70; *see* MASLOW'S MOTIVATIONAL HIERARCHY), which places the basic needs of human survival at the bottom of the scale of human motivation and *self-actualization at the top. The more flexible *ERG theory focuses on three groups of needs that form a hierarchy: existence needs (physical and material wants); relatedness needs (the desire for interpersonal relationships); and growth needs (desires to be creative and productive).

Although most psychologists now believe that human needs and motives are too variable to be confined to a fixed hierarchy, these theories have the merit of emphasizing that, besides goals, ambitions, and rewards, there is a need for success to be recognized by others and a need to develop and progress. A person in an organization never works in a vacuum; there can be a real conflict between different motivations that relate to the organization: Would I be worse paid working elsewhere? But would I be more secure/ better trained/more appreciated elsewhere? *See* ACHIEVEMENT MOTIVATION THEORY; ALIENATION; THEORY X AND THEORY Y; THEORY Z; VALENCE-INSTRUMENTALITY-EXPECTANCY THEORY.

motivational research A form of *marketing research in which the motivations for consumers preferring one product rather than another are studied. It may form the basis of a plan to launch a competitive product or of a campaign to boost sales of an existing product.

motivators In the two-factor theory of *motivation proposed by Frederick Herzberg (1923–2000), those aspects of the work situation that can motivate employees by providing positive *job satisfaction (as opposed to a mere absence of dissatisfaction). They include responsibility, autonomy, variety, and the *intrinsic rewards arising from the work itself. *Compare* HYGIENE FACTORS.

motor insurance A form of insurance covering loss or damage to motor vehicles and any legal liabilities for bodily injury or damage to other people's property. Drivers have a legal obligation to be covered against third-party claims (*see* THIRD-PARTY INSURANCE), but most drivers or owners of vehicles have a **comprehensive insurance**, providing wide coverage of all the risks involved in owning a motor vehicle. An intermediate cover is known as third-party, fire, and theft. *See also* NO-CLAIM BONUS.

moving average A series of *arithmetic means calculated from data in a time series, which reduces the effects of temporary seasonal variations. For example, a moving average of the monthly sales figures for an organization might be calculated by averaging the 12 months from January to December for the December figure, the 12 months from February to January for the January figure, and so on.

MPC *See* MONETARY POLICY COMMITTEE.

MPS Abbreviation for *master production schedule.

MRP 1. Abbreviation for manufacturers' recommended price. *See* RECOMMENDED RETAIL PRICE. **2.** Abbreviation for *material requirements planning.

MRS Abbreviation for *Market Research Society.

MSA Abbreviation for *metropolitan statistical area.

MS-DOS *Trademark* Abbreviation for Microsoft Disk Operating System. Designed originally for the IBM Personal Computer, it became the standard operating system for larger *personal computers. Earlier versions of *Windows ran on MS-DOS.

MSF Abbreviation for *multisource feedback.

MSP Abbreviation for *matched sale–purchase agreement.

MTF Abbreviation for *multilateral trading facility.

MTN Abbreviation for *medium-term note.

multibrand strategy A strategy in which a seller develops two or more brands in the same product category.

multichannel marketing Marketing one's products or services using two or more marketing channels, often to reach more than one market segment (*see* MARKET SEGMENTATION). Retail chains, for example, besides using the shops to distribute their products, quite often also use catalogue selling.

multi-component euronote facility A *euronote issued in a variety of currencies.

multi-dimensional scaling (MDS) A technique used to assist understanding of a consumer's perception of competing brands or products. A 'perceptual map' is often drawn showing how consumers perceive competitive products along certain dimensions or attributes. For example, respondents may be asked to rank pairs of brands in terms of their perceived similarities, so that some understanding can be gained of their choice criteria.

multifunctional card A plastic card issued by a bank or building society to its customers to function as a debit card, *cash card, and *cheque card. Multifunctional cards operate in conjunction with a *personal identification number.

Multilateral Investment Guarantee Agency (MIGA) An affiliate of the *International Bank for Reconstruction and Development (IBRD) established in 1988 to encourage foreign investment in developing countries by providing investors with guarantees, and developing countries with an advisory service.

multilateral netting 1. The centralizing of international payments of a group of companies so that payments and receipts in different currencies can be offset, thus reducing transaction and hedging costs. **2.** A method of reducing bank charges in which the subsidiaries of a group offset their receipts and payments with each other, usually monthly, resulting in a single net intercompany payment or receipt made by each subsidiary to cover the period concerned. This saves both on transaction costs and paperwork. *See also* BILATERAL NETTING; NETTING.

multilateral trade agreement A trading arrangement between a number of nations in which there is agreement to abolish quotas and tariffs or to accept that there will be a surplus or deficit on the balance of payments.

multilateral trading facility (MTF) In the EU, any platform for financial trading that is not a regulated exchange run by a recognized market operator. MTFs were first defined and regulated by the *Markets in Financial Instruments Directive, which became effective in late 2007. In most cases these platforms are fully electronic and buyers and sellers are often matched to each other anonymously. An MTF is thus the European equivalent of a US *alternative trading system (ATS). The largest and best known example is Chi-X Europe.

multimedia The integration of text, graphics, sound, and still or moving pictures in the storing and presentation of information by computers. Personal computers are now able to present information in a wide variety of forms from a wide variety of sources. Networked systems are able to transfer live TV pictures together with text and graphics. However, the ability of organizations to exploit this technology, e.g. for conferencing, may be restricted by the *bandwidth of their systems.

multimedia mail *See* E-MAIL.

multinational enterprise (MNE) A corporation that has production operations in more than one country for various reasons, including securing supplies of raw materials, utilizing cheap labour sources, servicing local markets, taking advantage of tax differences, and bypassing protectionist barriers. Multinationals may be seen as an efficient form of organization, making effective use of the world's resources and transferring technology between countries.

On the other hand, some have excessive power, are beyond the control of governments (especially weak governments), and are able to exploit host countries, especially in the developing world, where they are able to operate with low safety levels and inadequate control of pollution. *See* GLOBALIZATION.

multiple *See* PRICE–EARNINGS RATIO.

multiple application The submission of more than one application form for a new issue of shares that is likely to be oversubscribed. In many countries it is illegal to do so either if the applications are made in the same name or if false names are used.

multiple-choice question A question requiring a respondent to select an answer from a list of answers provided with the question. For example, the respondent may be asked to name the brand of cigarettes purchased in the last week from a list of major brands. *Compare* OPEN-ENDED QUESTION.

multiple exchange rate An exchange rate quoted by a country that has more than one value, depending on the use to which the currency is put. For example, some countries have quoted a specially favourable rate for tourists or for importers of desirable goods.

multiple market segmentation *See* DIFFERENTIATED MARKETING.

multiple niching A marketing strategy in which several independent offers of a product are made, which are intended to appeal to several different types of customer.

multiple shops (chain stores) A large chain of shops (usually ten or more) owned by the same *retailer. Compared with *independent retailers, they benefit from *economies of scale and so can charge lower prices to consumers. Multiple shops have therefore become dominant in many areas of retailing, such as packaged groceries.

multiple taxation Taxation of the same income by more than two countries. *Compare* DOUBLE TAXATION.

multiple-unit pricing Selling more than one unit of a product at a lower price than twice the unit price. 'Buy two, get one free' is an example.

multisource feedback (MSF) A system of *employee evaluation that involves collecting performance *feedback from multiple sources, including manager, subordinates, colleagues, and possibly clients and customers. This is sometimes extended to a system of *360° feedback.

multitasking Describing a computer system that can run more than one program at the same time.

multi-tied adviser *See* INDEPENDENT FINANCIAL ADVISER.

multivariate analysis A statistical procedure that simultaneously analyses multiple measurements on each individual or object under study in a marketing-research enquiry. Examples of the procedures used include multiple regression, factor analysis, cluster analysis (*see* CLUSTER THEORY), and *conjoint analysis.

municipal bond A bond issued by a local government authority, especially one in the USA.

muqarada *See* ISLAMIC FINANCE.

murabaha *See* ISLAMIC FINANCE.

musharaka *See* ISLAMIC FINANCE.

mutual A company that is owned by its members or depositors. In the UK *building societies used to have this structure, but most have now demutualized, becoming *public limited companies. **Mutual life-assurance** companies developed out of the *Friendly Societies. There are no shareholders, and apart from benefits and running expenses there are no other withdrawals from the fund; thus any profits are distributed to policyholders.

mutual fund A mostly US name for a *unit trust, especially an *open-end trust.

mutually exclusive projects A number of alternative projects being considered for appraisal, no one of which can be pursued in conjunction with any of the others. For example, a parcel of land may be used to build a factory, an office block, or a mixture of the two. Each alternative is mutually exclusive because the choice of one alternative automatically excludes the others. Mutually exclusive projects arise when there is a scarce resource, in this case land.

mutual mistake *See* MISTAKE.

mystery shoppers People employed by retailers to pose as customers at their own or their competitors' stores to compare prices, offers, displays, staff attitude, etc.

NAFTA Abbreviation for *North American Free Trade Agreement.

naira (NGN) The standard monetary unit of Nigeria, divided into 100 kobo.

naive quantitative methods A simple approach to forecasting future trends (e.g. the demand for a product) in which an average value is obtained from historical data and it is assumed that the same average will obtain for values in the future. No attempt is made to establish a causal relationship between variables, or to use such techniques as e.g. *adaptive exponential smoothing to reduce the effect of seasonal or cyclic variations within time series data. *Compare* CAUSAL QUANTITATIVE MODELS.

Nakasone bond A bond issued by the Japanese government in a foreign currency. It is named after the prime minister in office when it was introduced (1982).

naked call writing Selling (writing) a call *option on assets that one does not own. A person may do this if he or she expects the price of a particular asset to fall or remain unchanged. It is, however, a dangerous strategy because if the price rises the assets will have to be purchased at the market price in order to deliver them, thus involving an unlimited risk.

naked debenture An unsecured *debenture.

naked position *See* OPEN POSITION.

nakfa (ERN) The standard monetary unit of Eritrea, divided into 100 cents.

name *See* LLOYD's; SYNDICATE.

narrow money An informal name for M0, or sometimes M1: the part of the *money supply that can directly perform the function of a *medium of exchange. *Compare* BROAD MONEY.

NAS Abbreviation for network-attached storage, a specialized device for storing data on a computer network. It fulfils a similar role to a *server, but more efficiently because it is dedicated to and optimized solely for storing data efficiently and securely. *Compare* SAN.

NASDAQ A US electronic market for securities that began operations in 1971, as the National Association of Securities Dealers Automated Quotations System. The first screen-based trading system to have no market floor, it is now the largest stock market in the USA, listing more than 3,000 companies. The system was owned and operated by the National Association of Securities Dealers, Inc. until 2002. In 2008 NASDAQ acquired the Swedish exchange group OMX.

(((•))) SEE WEB LINKS
• NASDAQ website

national banks US commercial banks established by federal charter (approved by the *Comptroller of the Currency), which requires them to be members of the *Federal Reserve System. They were created by the National Bank Act 1863 and formerly issued their own banknotes.

National Consumer Council *See* NEW NATIONAL CONSUMER COUNCIL.

National Insurance contributions (NICs) Payments made by those with earned income that contribute to the

National Insurance Fund, from which benefits are paid. These benefits include retirement pensions, unemployment pay, widow's benefits, invalidity benefit, and certain sickness and maternity benefits. There are six different classes of National Insurance contributions; the class applicable to a person depends on the type of earned income received by that person.

Class 1 is paid by those with earnings from employment. There are two parts to class 1, primary contributions paid by the employee and secondary contributions paid by the employer. The rates of contributions depend on the level of earnings and also whether or not the employee is a member of a contracted-out occupational, personal, or stakeholder pension scheme; for employees the standard rate is 12% on weekly earnings between £155 and £815 and 2% on weekly earnings thereafter (2015–16 figures). Employers also pay Class 1 contributions at a standard rate of 13.8%; there is currently (2015–16) an allowance of £2,000.

Class 2 is a flat-rate contribution paid by the self-employed; it is £2.80 per week for 2015–16.

Class 3 is voluntary, and is also at a flat rate – £14.10 per week for 2015–16. It is paid by those wishing to maintain their contribution record even though they may be unemployed or their level of earnings is below that for mandatory contributions.

Class 4 is paid by the self-employed at a rate of 9% on income between a lower limit of £8,060 per year and an upper limit of £42,385 per year and 2% on yearly income thereafter.

Class 1A was introduced in 1991 and is payable by employers who provide their employees with benefits in kind (typically cars for private as well as business use). The current rate is 13.8% of the cash equivalent figure.

Class 1B is payable by employers in value of any items included in a PAYE settlement with HM Revenue and Customs.

(((⊕))) SEE WEB LINKS
• Guide to NICs from the Gov.uk website

nationalization The process of bringing the assets of a business into the ownership of the state. Examples of industries nationalized in the past in the UK include the National Coal Board and British Rail. Historically, nationalization has been achieved through compulsory purchase, although this need not necessarily be the case. Nationalization has often been pursued as much for political as economic ends and the economic justifications themselves are varied. One argument for nationalization is that if a company possesses a natural monopoly, then it should not be run for private profit; another is that certain industries are strategically important for the nation. In the 1980s and 1990s Conservative governments reversed the nationalizations of the post-war Labour governments with a series of *privatization measures, on the grounds that competition would increase efficiency and reduce prices. Labour administrations after 1997 proved reluctant to renationalize until the financial crisis of 2008, when several leading banks (notably the Royal Bank of Scotland) were partly nationalized to prevent their collapse.

National Readership Survey (NRS) A non-profit organization that provides publishers, advertisers, and others with estimated readership figures for over 250 newspapers and magazines in the UK. Readership is also analysed in terms of sex, age, region, social class, and a range of other demographic and lifestyle characteristics. The data is derived from a stratified random sample involving some 36,000 computer-assisted interviews in a continuous survey lasting 12 months. Updated data is published online four times a year. Since 2012 NRS has also provided figures for the reach of non-print platforms, such as the online versions of daily newspapers.

(((⊕))) SEE WEB LINKS
• Website of the NRS: includes estimates of average readership for all publications on the survey

National Savings A wide range of schemes for personal savers, administered by National Savings and Investments (NSI), a government agency established in 1969 as the Post Office Savings Department. They include *premium bonds, income bonds, and Children's Bonds. The Department also offers *Individual Savings Accounts (ISAs) and (since January 2004) Easy Access Savings Accounts. The **National Savings Bank (NSB;** formerly the Post Office Savings Bank) was founded in 1861.

National Savings Stock Register A facility that enables members of the public to buy certain Treasury stocks and other *gilt-edged securities without going through a stockbroker; it is now administered by the Bank of England and provides an alternative to the main *Bank of England Stock Register. Purchases and sales are made by post and the interest paid is taxable, but is paid before deduction of tax. The lower rates of commission make this the cheapest way of buying gilts. However, because transactions are carried out by post, it does not provide the maximum flexibility in a moving market.

National Stock Exchange of India (NSE) A stock exchange in Mumbai, established by a group of leading financial institutions in 1993. It now trades in equities, debt, futures, and options. The main index is the S&P CNX Nifty.

National Vocational Qualification (NVQ) See VOCATIONAL TRAINING.

natural justice The minimum standard of fairness to be applied by a court when resolving a dispute. The main rules of natural justice include: (1) the right to be heard – each party to the dispute should be given an opportunity to answer any allegations made by the other party; (2) the rule against bias – the person involved in settling the dispute should act impartially, in particular by disclosing any interest in the outcome of the dispute. The rules of natural justice apply equally in judicial as well as in administrative proceedings. Alleging a breach of natural justice is the method commonly used to challenge an administrative decision before the courts.

natural rate of interest See INTEREST.

natural wastage The method by which an organization can contract without making people redundant, relying on resignations, retirements, or deaths. If the time is available, this method of reducing a workforce causes the least tension. See also REDUNDANCY.

NAV Abbreviation for net asset value. See ASSET VALUE (PER SHARE); BOOK VALUE.

navigation On the Internet, the process of finding and moving between different information and pages on a website. It is governed by menu arrangements, site structure, the layout of individual pages, and, sometimes, searching facilities.

NBV Abbreviation for *net book value.

NCI Abbreviation for *New Community Instrument.

NDP Abbreviation for *net domestic product.

near money (quasi money) An asset that is immediately transferable and may be used to settle some but not all debts, although it is not as liquid as banknotes and coins. *Bills of exchange are examples of near money. Near money is not included in the *money supply definitions.

need recognition The first stage of *consumer buying behaviour, in which the consumer recognizes a problem or need.

negative cash flow A *cash flow in which the outflows exceed the inflows.

negative equity 1. The difference between the value of a property (usually residential) and the outstanding amount borrowed against it where the latter is the greater. For example, if a property's current market value is £250,000 and the borrowing against it is £260,000, there is a negative *equity to the extent of £10,000. Negative equities were common in the mid-1990s when the economic recession had an adverse effect on property prices. House owners who paid more for their houses than their current market value were

unable to sell without realizing the loss.
2. More generally, any asset that has a
market value below the sum of money
borrowed to purchase it.

negative income tax (NIT) A means of
targeting social security benefits to those
most in need using the income-tax system.
After submitting an income-tax return
showing an income level below a set minimum, an individual would receive a direct
subsidy from the tax authorities bringing
income up to that level.

negative interest A charge made by a
bank or other deposit taker for looking after
a sum of money for a given period.

negative net worth The value of a
company whose liabilities exceed its assets.

negative pledge A *covenant in a loan
agreement in which a borrower promises
that no secured borrowings will be made
during the life of the loan, or will ensure
that the loan is secured equally and ratably
with any new borrowings as specifically
defined.

negligence In law, a tort in which a
breach of a **duty of care** results in damage
to the person to whom the duty is owed.
Such a duty is owed by manufacturers to
the consumers who buy their products, by
accountants, solicitors, doctors, and other
professional persons to their clients, by a
director of a company to its shareholders,
etc. A person who has suffered loss or
injury as a result of a breach of the duty of
care can claim *damages in tort. The risk of
being sued for negligence makes it essential for partners in firms that are not
*limited liability partnerships to obtain
*professional indemnity insurance.

negotiability The ability of a document
that entitles its owner to some benefit to
change hands, so that legal ownership of
the benefit passes by delivery or endorsement of the document. For a document to
be negotiable it must also entitle the holder
to bring an action in law if necessary. *See*
NEGOTIABLE INSTRUMENT.

negotiable instrument A document
of title that can be freely negotiated (*see*
NEGOTIABILITY). Such documents are
*cheques and *bills of exchange, in which
the stated payee of the instrument can
negotiate the instrument by either inserting
the name of a different payee or by making
the document 'open' by endorsing it (signing one's name), usually on the reverse.
Holders of negotiable instruments cannot
pass on a better title than they possess. Bills
of exchange, including cheques, in which
the payee is named or that bear a restrictive
endorsement, such as 'not negotiable', are
non-negotiable instruments.

**negotiable order of withdrawal
(NOW)** A type of cheque used in US savings
accounts that are interest-bearing and from
which sums can be withdrawn. If no interest is paid the account is called a **NINOW**.

negotiate 1. To confer with a view to
arriving at mutually acceptable terms for a
contract or agreement. **2.** To transfer a *bill
of exchange or cheque to another for consideration (*see* NEGOTIABILITY; NEGOTIABLE
INSTRUMENT).

negotiated transfer prices *Transfer
prices set by negotiation between the supplying and receiving divisions of an organization. Negotiated transfer prices are
appropriate when there is an imperfect
market for the goods and services that are
bought and sold between divisions. Negotiation may be seen as a way of reducing
conflicts between managers. The relative
bargaining power of the divisions is
important; a mediator may be used to help
the negotiations.

nem con (abbreviation of Latin *nemine
contradicente*: no-one disagreeing) These
words are often used in the minutes of a
meeting when no-one has voted against a
proposition.

nested-ad content Advertising material
on the same website to which a person is
directed by clicking on a banner (as
opposed to being redirected to a corporate
or brand site).

net Denoting an amount remaining after specific deductions have been made. For example, **net profit before taxation** is the profit made by an organization after the deduction of all business expenditure but before the deduction of the *taxation charge.

net assets The assets of an organization less its *current liabilities. The resultant figure is equal to the *capital of the organization. Opinion varies as to whether long-term liabilities should be treated as part of the capital and are therefore not deductible in arriving at net assets, or whether they are part of the liabilities and therefore deductible. The latter view is probably technically preferable and is more common. A further practice is to split long-term liabilities and to treat those described as the 'finance element' as part of the capital. *Compare* NET CURRENT ASSETS. *See also* BOOK VALUE; NET TANGIBLE ASSETS; NET WORTH.

net asset value (NAV) *See* ASSET VALUE (PER SHARE); BOOK VALUE.

net basis The basis upon which the *earnings per share of a company is calculated, taking into account both constant and variable elements in the company's tax charge. According to *International Accounting Standard 33, Earnings per Share, a *listed company must show the earnings per share on the net basis on the face of the *profit and loss account. *Compare* NIL BASIS.

net book value (NBV; book value) The value at which an asset appears in the books of an organization (usually as at the date of the last balance sheet). This is the purchase cost or latest revaluation less any depreciation applied since purchase or revaluation. The net book value is also known as the **depreciated value** or **depreciated cost**. *See* BALANCE-SHEET ASSET VALUE.

net current assets *Current assets less *current liabilities. The resultant figure is also known as *working capital, as it represents the amount of the organization's capital that is constantly being turned over

in the course of its trade. *See also* NET ASSETS.

net dividend The *dividend paid by a company to its shareholders, after excluding the *tax credit received by the shareholders.

net domestic product (NDP) The *gross domestic product of a country less *capital consumption (i.e. depreciation).

net income 1. The income of a person or organization after the deduction of the appropriate expenses incurred in earning it. **2.** *Gross income from which tax has been deducted.

net interest Interest paid into a savings or current account at a UK bank or building society after the deduction of tax at source. Interest on bank and building society accounts is currently taxed at 20%.

net investment The addition to the stock of capital goods in an economy during a particular period (the **gross investment**) less *capital consumption (i.e. depreciation).

net margin *See* NET PROFIT.

net margin ratio *See* NET PROFIT PERCENTAGE.

net national product (NNP) The *gross national product less *capital consumption (i.e. depreciation) during the period. NNP is therefore equal to the national income, i.e. the amount of money available in the economy for expenditure on goods and services. However, NNP cannot be considered a very accurate measure, as it is difficult to calculate depreciation reliably.

net position The difference between a dealer's long and short *positions in the same security or market.

net present value (NPV) A method of *capital budgeting in which the value of an investment is calculated as the total *present value of all *cash inflows and *cash outflows minus the cost of the initial investment. If the net present value is positive, the return will be greater than that required by the capital markets and the investment should be considered. A negative net present value indicates that the investment should be rejected. Many spreadsheet programs now include a calculator for NPV. *See also* DISCOUNTED CASH FLOW.

net price The price a buyer pays for goods or services after all discounts have been deducted.

net profit (net margin; net profit margin) The *gross profit less all the other costs of an organization in addition to those included in the *cost of sales. It is shown before and after taxation in the *profit and loss account.

net profit percentage (net margin ratio) A ratio of financial performance calculated by expressing the *net profit as a percentage of sales revenue. *Compare* GROSS PROFIT PERCENTAGE. *See also* MARGIN; MARK-UP.

net realizable value (NRV) **1.** The sales value of the stock of an organization less the additional costs likely to be incurred in getting the stocks into the hands of the customer. It is the value placed on the closing stock when the NRV is lower than cost. **2.** The amount at which any asset could be disposed of, less any direct selling costs.

net receipts The total amount of money received by a business in a specified period after deducting costs, raw materials, taxation, etc. *Compare* GROSS RECEIPTS.

net relevant earnings A person's non-pensionable earned income before *personal allowances have been deducted but after deduction of expenses, capital allowances, losses, or any stock relief agreed with HM Revenue and Customs. It forms income from which any tax relief on pension contributions can be calculated.

net reproduction rate The number of female children in a population divided by the number of female adults in the previous generation. This figure gives a good guide to population trends; if it exceeds unity the population is expanding.

net residual value (disposal value) The expected proceeds from the sale of an asset, net of the costs of sale, at the end of its estimated useful life. It is used for computing the *straight-line method and *diminishing-balance method of depreciation, and also for inclusion in the final year's cash inflow in a *discounted cash flow appraisal.

net return The profit made on an investment after the deduction of all expenses, either before or after deduction of *capital gains tax.

net tangible assets The *tangible assets of an organization less its *current liabilities. In analysing the affairs of an organization the net tangible assets indicate its financial strength in terms of being solvent, without having to resort to such nebulous (and less easy to value) assets as *goodwill.

netting The process of setting off matching sales and purchases against each other, especially sales and purchases of futures, options, and forward foreign exchange. This service is usually provided for an exchange or market by a *clearing house. It also provides a means by which a firm can deal with its risks, notably *exchange-rate exposure. *See* BILATERAL NETTING; MULTILATERAL NETTING. *See also* NOVATION.

net tonnage (net register tonnage) *See* TONNAGE.

net weight *See* GROSS WEIGHT.

network *See* LOCAL AREA NETWORK.

network-attached storage *See* NAS.

network computer A simple access device designed for use on a computer network; it depends on a powerful central server for programs and storage.

network modelling Techniques that enable complex projects to be scheduled, taking into account the precedence of each activity.

Critical-path analysis (**CPA**) involves identifying all the activities that constitute the project to be modelled, determining their sequence or order of precedence, and estimating the time required for each activity. This information is used to build a graphical representation of the whole project and to establish the chain of activities that defines its overall length, i.e. the critical path. As well as being a powerful analytical tool, the visual qualities of CPA charts make them extremely useful aids to communications. With computer-based CPA programmes, managers can produce rapid updates when unexpected changes occur (e.g. the failure to complete an activity on time). These programmes also enable the appropriate resources to be allocated to the activities and detailed costings to be produced. The key to their successful use is that they should be updated continuously. Considerable resources are required to produce a CPA; if changes, postponements, etc., are not noted the chart quickly becomes irrelevant.

Programme evaluation and review technique (**PERT**) was developed in 1958 by the US Navy to assist in the construction of the first Polaris submarines. It is based on the same principles as CPA but uses statistical techniques to project optimistic, most probable, and pessimistic times for each activity.

net worth The value of an organization when its liabilities have been deducted from the value of its assets. Often taken to be synonymous with *net assets, net worth so defined can be misleading in that balance sheets rarely show the real value of assets. *See* BOOK VALUE.

neuroeconomics An interdisciplinary field of study that applies insights from neuroscience and psychology to explain the economic decisions of individuals, which are assumed to have a biological basis. In particular, neuroeconomics seeks to explain decisions that conventional economics cannot account for, such as those that appear irrational or that result in suboptimal outcomes. The field, which has a strong emphasis on experimental observation, has emerged since 2000. *See* BEHAVIOURAL FINANCE.

New Community Instrument (NCI) Loans organized on the international money market by the *European Investment Bank.

new entrants 1. Those looking for work for the first time. The main group comprises school leavers but housewives are also important, especially with the recent opportunities for job sharing. **2.** Firms entering an industry for the first time. They may be new organizations or established organizations entering a new field.

new for old The basis for household insurance policies in which payments of claims are not subject to a deduction for wear and tear. As a result, a claim for an old and worn-out table would be met by the payment of the price of a new table of a similar type.

new issue Any new security, but especially a share being offered on a *stock exchange for the first time. *See* FLOTATION.

New National Consumer Council A UK statutory organization established in 2007 through a merger of the **National Consumer Council** and the consumer bodies for the energy and postal services; its remit is to watch over consumer interests and to speak for the consumer to the government, industry, and commerce. The council, which now operates under the name **Consumer Futures**, deals only with issues of policy (i.e. it does not issue consumer advice or deal with complaints). Since April 2014 it has been part of the Citizens Advice Service.

new product development (**NPD**) A marketing procedure in which new ideas are developed into viable new products or extensions to existing products or product ranges. New ideas, which are generated either internally (e.g. by scientific research) or by feedback from consumers, are first screened for prima facie viability; the few that remain are further reduced by

| Stage 1 Idea Generation | Stage 2 Screening | Stage 3 Business Analysis |

Strategic

| Generation of new service or product from modification of existing products or from new | Assessing the compatability with the organization's aims, objectives, and resource capabilities | Project costed, sales forecast, and profits estimated |

| Stage 4 Development | Stage 5 Test Marketing | Stage 6 Commercialization |

Tactical Implementation

| The commercial and technical development of the brand personality and other aspects of marketing | Test launch to evaluate NPD and business objectives | Launch regionally or nationally against objectives |

New product development.

*concept tests and detailed analysis of their potential profitability. Any ideas that survive these obstacles are subjected to extensive product development. Prototypes are made and tested within the company and among consumers, and improvements made. This cycle is repeated until satisfactory marketing research results are obtained, when the new product will be launched (possibly at first in a restricted area; *see* TEST MARKETING). *See also* NEW-PRODUCTS COMMITTEE.

new-products committee A group within an organization assigned to creating new-product policies, evaluating options, and deciding whether to commercialize new products. Membership usually includes the heads of the organization's functional departments and the new-products director (if there is one).

new sol (PEN) The standard monetary unit of Peru, divided into 100 céntimos.

news release A brief written statement sent to the press describing a company's new product, product improvement, price change, or some other development of interest. The release will only be published if it is sufficiently newsworthy.

New York Board of Trade (NYBOT) The parent company established in 1998 with the amalgamation of the New York Cotton Exchange and the Coffee, Sugar and Cocoa Exchange Inc. of New York. It became a subsidiary of *Intercontinental Exchange in January 2007 and is now known as *ICE Futures US. Following the destruction of its headquarters and trading facility in the World Trade Centre, NYBOT moved into the *New York Mercantile Exchange; it finally closed its trading pit in 2007.

New York Mercantile Exchange (NYMEX) A futures exchange in New York dealing chiefly in oil products and metals. In 1994 it acquired the *Commodity Exchange Inc. of New York (COMEX), becoming the world's largest market in commodity futures. NYMEX became a publicly traded company in 2006 and a designated contracts market of the Chicago-based CME group in 2008.

(( )) SEE WEB LINKS
• Information from the CME Group website

New York Stock Exchange (NYSE) The main US stock exchange. It was founded in 1792 under the Buttonwood Agreement (the name of the tree under which 24 merchants agreed to give each other preference in their dealings); it moved to Wall Street in 1793. The New York Stock & Exchange Board was formally established in 1817; it was renamed the New York Stock Exchange in 1983. In 2006 the NYSE combined with the pan-European exchange *Euronext NV to create *NYSE Euronext, the world's first global exchange. It acquired the electronic exchange Archipelago Holdings in 2006 and the American Stock Exchange in 2008. The main indexes are the *Dow Jones Industrial Average and the NYSE Composite Index, which covers all common stock listed on the exchange.

(( )) SEE WEB LINKS
• Information for traders, companies, and private investors from the NYSE Euronext website

Next 11 (N-11) Eleven countries identified in the mid 2000s as emerging markets with large populations and considerable economic potential: namely, Bangladesh, Egypt, Indonesia, Iran, Mexico, Nigeria, Pakistan, Philippines, Turkey, South Korea, and Vietnam. The term was coined by Jim O'Neill of Goldman Sachs to complement his earlier coinage of the term *BRIC. *See also* CIVETS.

next-in-first-out cost (NIFO cost) A method of valuing units of raw material or finished goods issued from stock by using the next unit price at which a consignment will be received for pricing the issues. It is effectively using *replacement cost as a stock valuation method, which is not normally acceptable as a stock valuation system in the UK when computing profits for taxation purposes. *Compare* FIRST-IN-FIRST-OUT COST; LAST-IN-FIRST-OUT COST.

N-form Describing a type of organizational structure in which several smaller companies representing different stages in the production process establish informal links with one another rather than joining together in vertical *integration. The 'N' stands for 'network'. Recent years have seen a trend towards N-form and *M-form structures.

NGT Abbreviation for *nominal group technique.

ngultrum (BTN) The standard monetary unit of Bhutan, divided into 100 chetrum.

ngwee A monetary unit of Zambia, worth one hundredth of a *kwacha.

NICs Abbreviation for *National Insurance contributions.

niche marketing See CONCENTRATED SEGMENTATION.

NIF Abbreviation for *note issuance facility.

NIFO cost Abbreviation for *next-in-first-out cost.

night safe A service provided by commercial banks, enabling customers to deposit cash with the bank after banking hours. By using this service shopkeepers, etc., can avoid keeping large sums overnight. A special wallet provided by the bank is inserted into a safe in the outside wall of the bank to which customers are given the key. The following day the wallet is opened, either by the customer or by a bank clerk, and the customer's account is credited accordingly.

Nikkei Stock Average (Nikkei Index) An index of prices on the *Tokyo Stock Exchange. It was originally known as the **Nikkei Dow Jones Index** and first calculated on 16 May 1949, based at 176.21. The Nikkei Stock Average is a price-weighted index of 225 Japanese companies representing 19% of first section issues, and accounting for about 51% of market value. It was restructured for the first time in its history in late 1991 by its administrator, the Nikon Keizai Shimbun financial newspaper group, to try to reduce the impact of futures-related trading on the index (Nikkei is a shortening of the full name of the newspaper group). Membership of the index is now reviewed annually, when up to six members can be replaced if their shares become illiquid or unrepresentative. Previously changes only occurred when companies were taken over or liquidated.

nil basis The basis upon which the *earnings per share of a company is calculated taking into account only the constant elements in the company's tax charge. *Compare* NET BASIS.

NIPS Code A code of best practice, issued by the Bank of England, for traders and brokers in the wholesale markets in Non-Investment Products (NIPs), specifically the sterling, foreign exchange, and bullion markets. It replaced the former London Code of Conduct in 2001.

NIT Abbreviation for *negative income tax.

NL Abbreviation for no liability. It appears after the name of an Australian company, being equivalent to the British abbreviation *plc (denoting a public limited company).

NMS Abbreviation for *Normal Market Size.

NNP Abbreviation for *net national product.

no-arbitrage condition See ARBITRAGE-FREE CONDITION.

no-claim bonus A reward, in the form of a premium discount, given to policyholders if they complete a year or more without making a claim. The system is mostly used in motor insurance. In every case, the bonus is allowed for remaining claim-free and is not dependent on blame for a particular accident.

node See LOCAL AREA NETWORK.

noise 1. In communication theory, any interference or distraction that disrupts the communication process. **2.** In statistics, random fluctuations in data.

nominal account A ledger *account that is not a *personal account in that it bears the name of a concept, e.g. light and heat, bad debts, investments, etc., rather than the name of a person. These accounts are normally grouped in the *nominal ledger. *See also* REAL ACCOUNT.

nominal capital (authorized capital) *See* SHARE CAPITAL.

nominal group technique (NGT) A group problem-solving technique in which each member of the group is asked to write down a list of ideas without talking to their colleagues. The ideas elicited in this way are then discussed and criticized by the group, who are not told which members contributed which ideas. Similar ideas are grouped or merged; when the discussion has finished the panel ranks the remaining ideas, again without discussion. The individual rankings are then combined mathematically to find the favoured solution, which is adopted. The NGT is intended to eliminate such problems of group decision making as *groupthink, deference to authority, political manoeuvring, and personal likes or dislikes.

nominal interest rate 1. An interest rate not adjusted for inflation. **2.** The interest rate on a fixed-interest security calculated as a percentage of its par value rather than its market price.

nominal ledger The *ledger containing the *nominal accounts and *real accounts necessary to prepare the accounts of an organization. This ledger is distinguished from the personal ledgers, such as the *sales and *purchase ledgers, which contain the accounts of customers and suppliers respectively.

nominal partner See PARTNERSHIP.

nominal price 1. A minimal price fixed for the sake of having some *consideration for a transaction. It need bear no relation to the market value of the item. **2.** The price given to a security when it is issued. This is the maximum amount the holder can be required to contribute to the company. See PAR VALUE.

nominal value See PAR VALUE.

nominal yield See YIELD.

nomination The person to whom the proceeds of a life-assurance policy should be paid, as specified by the policyholder. See ASSIGNMENT OF LIFE POLICIES.

nominee A person named by another (the **nominator**) to act on his or her behalf, often to conceal the identity of the nominator. See NOMINEE SHAREHOLDING.

nominee shareholding A shareholding held in the name of a bank, stockbroker, company, individual, etc., that is not the name of the beneficial owner of the shares (the **indirect shareholder**). A shareholding may be in the name of nominees to facilitate dealing or to conceal the identity of the true owner. Although this cover was formerly used in the early stages of a takeover, to enable the bidder clandestinely to build up a substantial holding in the target company, this practice was prevented by the Companies Act 1985, which made it mandatory for anyone holding 5% or more of the shares in a public company to declare that interest to the company. The earlier Companies Act 1967 made it mandatory for directors to openly declare their holdings, and those of their families, in the companies of which they are directors. The Companies Act 2006 extends information and voting rights to indirect shareholders.

non-acceptance The failure by the person on whom a *bill of exchange is drawn to accept it on presentation.

non-adjusting events Any events occurring between the balance-sheet date and the date on which the *financial statements of an organization are approved that relate to conditions that did not exist at the balance-sheet date. If they are sufficiently material for their non-disclosure to affect a user's understanding of the financial statements, non-adjusting events should be disclosed in the notes to the accounts. If a non-adjusting event suggests that the *going-concern concept is no longer applicable to the whole, or a material part, of the company, changes in the amounts to be included in the financial statements should be made. For example, if serious industrial action has occurred, which if it continues could threaten the continued existence of the business, an appropriate provision should be made in the accounts. *Compare* ADJUSTING EVENTS.

non-adopter A member of the group of consumers who never buys a particular new product or adopts a certain new style. *See* ADOPTION OF INNOVATIONS.

non-assented stock *See* ASSENTED STOCK.

non-business days *See* BANK HOLIDAYS.

non-contributory pension A *pension in which the full premium is paid by an employer or the state and the pensioner makes no contribution. *Compare* CONTRIBUTORY PENSION.

non-cumulative preference share A *preference share that does not have the right to *dividends unpaid in previous years. *Compare* CUMULATIVE PREFERENCE SHARE.

non-cumulative quantity discount A price discount determined by the size of an individual purchase order. The larger the order, the larger the discount.

non-domiciled Denoting a person whose country of *domicile is not the same as his or her country of residence for tax purposes. Before April 2008 a person resident but not domiciled in the UK paid no UK tax on foreign investment income unless this was remitted to the UK. From that date so-called **non-doms** who have been resident in the UK for seven of the last ten years pay a flat annual charge of £30,000 if they wish to avoid paying UK tax on foreign income and gains.

non-durables Consumer non-durables. *See* CONSUMER GOODS.

non-equity share Under former UK accounting rules, a *share in a company having any of the following characteristics:

• any of the rights of the share to receive payments are for a limited amount that is not calculated by reference to the company's assets or profits or the dividends on any class of equity share;

• any of the rights of the share to participate in a surplus on *liquidation are limited to a specific amount that is not calculated by reference to the company's assets or profits;

• the share is redeemable either according to its terms or because the holder, or any party other than the issuer, can require its redemption.

Until 2005 so-called *preference shares were classed as non-equity share capital (*see* PREFERENCE SHARE CAPITAL); these are now considered liabilities rather than *shareholders' equity. The concept of non-equity shares is not recognized under *International Financial Reporting Standards.

non-executive director A director of a company who is not involved in the day-to-day management of the business but who is appointed to bring independent judgment on issues of strategy, performance, resources, and standards of conduct. In the UK the *Corporate Governance Code requires public listed companies to appoint non-executive directors or to explain why they have not done so. Apart from their watchdog role, such directors are often employed for their prestige, experience, contacts, or specialist knowledge.

non-marketable securities Securities that are not sold on financial markets, notably (in the UK) savings bonds and National Savings Certificates.

non-monetary advantages and disadvantages Those aspects of an employment that are not connected with its financial remuneration. They include the employees' subjective opinion of their working environment, the stimulation or boredom of the work itself, the companionship or isolation experienced in their place of work, the distance travelled to reach work, etc. These aspects of an employment, together with the salary, bonuses, commission, and fringe benefits, make employees decide either to stay in their present jobs or seek another. *See* INTRINSIC REWARD; JOB SATISFACTION.

non-negotiable instruments *See*
NEGOTIABLE INSTRUMENT.

non-participating preference share
A *preference share that does not carry a
right to participate in the profits of a company beyond a fixed rate of *dividend. This
is the most common type of preference
share.

non-personal communication channel A channel of communication that carries messages without personal contact
or feedback, including the media, radio,
TV, etc.

non-price competition A form of competition in which two or more producers
sell goods or services at the same price but
compete to increase their share of the
market by such measures as advertising,
sales promotion campaigns, improving the
quality of the product or service, delivery
time, and (for goods) improving the packaging, offering free servicing and installation, or giving free gifts of unrelated
products or services.

non-probability sampling A sampling
procedure in which the sample is chosen
on the basis of convenience, personal
judgment (*see* JUDGMENTAL SAMPLING),
quota controls (*see* QUOTA SAMPLING), or
some other principle, rather than on the
basis of random selection from a population. *Compare* PROBABILITY SAMPLING.

non-production overhead costs The
*indirect costs of an organization that are
not classified as *manufacturing overhead.
They include administration overheads,
*selling overhead, *distribution overhead,
and (in some cases) *research and development costs.

nonprofit marketing (social marketing) Organized marketing used by nonprofit organizations, including those
involved in education, culture, health care,
charity, social causes, politics, and religion.

nonprofit organization A body, typically working in the charitable or social
enterprise sector, that does not seek to
make a profit for itself but rather distributes

any surplus accrued to further its objectives, whether internally or externally. In the
US such organizations are eligible for
exemption from federal income tax. *See
also* SOCIAL ENTREPRENEURSHIP.

non-qualifying policy A UK life-assurance policy that does not satisfy the qualification rules contained in Schedule 15 of
the Income and Corporation Taxes Act
1988.

non-resident The status of an individual
who has never lived in a particular country
for fiscal purposes or who has moved to
another country, either for employment or
permanently. This person's liability to tax
in the first country is restricted to income
from sources within that country. Interest
on all British government stocks is exempt
from UK tax for non-residents. *See also*
DOUBLE TAXATION; RESIDENT. *Compare*
NON-DOMICILED.

non-revolving bank facility A loan
from a bank to a company in which the
company has a period (often several years)
in which to make its *drawdowns, as well as
flexibility with regard to the amount and
timing of the drawdowns, but once drawn
an amount takes on the characteristics of a
*term loan. *Compare* REVOLVING BANK
FACILITY.

non-sampling errors All the errors that
can occur in *marketing research other
than the *sampling error. These can
include a badly phrased questionnaire, an
error made by the interviewer, an error
made by the respondent, etc.

non-statutory accounts Any financial
statement issued by a company that does
not form part of the statutory *annual
accounts. Under the Companies Act a
company has to make a statement on any
non-statutory accounts it issues to the
effect that they are not the statutory
accounts. Such accounts are often reported
in the media.

non-systematic risk *See* SPECIFIC RISK.

non-tariff office *See* TARIFF OFFICE.

non-tariff trade barrier A non-monetary barrier to a foreign product or service, such as a bias against a foreign company's product standards or a rejection of a foreign country's political record.

non-taxable income Income that is specifically exempt from tax. Examples of such income include:

- shares allotted by an employer under an approved share option scheme;
- bonuses paid as part of a *savings related share option scheme;
- statutory redundancy pay;
- income received under a maintenance agreement or court order in cases of divorce or separation;
- income from *Individual Savings Accounts (ISAs);
- up to £4,250 annually from a 'rent-a-room' scheme;

- income from scholarships;
- winnings from betting (including the National Lottery) and competition prizes.

no par value capital stock In the USA and Canada, stock (shares) that have no *par value printed on the stock certificate. An advantage of such stock is that it avoids a *contingent liability to stockholders in the event of a stock discount. For accounting purposes, on the issue of no par value capital stock, cash is debited and a capital stock account credited with the total proceeds received. No premium account is required. No par value shares are not permitted under UK law.

normal distribution (Gaussian distribution) The symmetrical bell-shaped frequency curve formed when the frequency of a range of values is plotted on the vertical

Normal distribution curve. Figure 1: the bell-shaped normal distribution curve.

Figure 2: normal distribution curves having the same mean but different standard deviations.

axis against the value of a random variable on the horizontal axis. The bell shape indicates that extreme values (both large and small) occur infrequently, while the more frequent occurrences are clustered around the *arithmetic mean value, which in a normal distribution is also equal to the *median and the **mode** (the value that occurs most frequently in a set of data).

A wide variety of natural, social, and economic phenomena fall approximately into a normal distribution, which is therefore an important concept in statistical analysis. From Figure 1 it can be seen that if a population is investigated, the **range** of values is six times the *standard deviation (SD), i.e. almost all the values from the population lie within three SDs either side of the mean. For a normal distribution, one SD either side of the mean can be seen to cover 68% (34% + 34%) of observed values (or the area under the curve); for two SDs it covers 95%; and for three SDs it covers 99%.

The SD is important in marketing research as it provides the researcher with some idea of the range of answers to a question. In Figure 2 two sample populations, A and B, have the same mean, but population B has a greater SD than population A (indicated by the spread of the curve). While the researcher may have asked both populations the same

questions, with both populations on average agreeing (i.e. the same mean), there is a greater dispersion in population B, indicating a greater variation of opinion than in A.

normal loss The loss arising from a manufacturing or chemical process through waste, seepage, shrinkage, or spoilage that can be expected, on the basis of historical studies, to be part of that process. It may be expressed as a weight or volume or in other units appropriate to the process. It is usually not valued but if it is, a notional scrap value is used. It is axiomatic in costing that normal losses are part of the normal *manufacturing cost, whereas the cost of abnormal losses should not be borne by the good output. *See also* WASTE.

Normal Market Size (NMS) A classification system for trading in securities, which in January 1991 replaced the alpha, beta, gamma, and delta classification used on the *London Stock Exchange. The old system had developed in a way that, contrary to the original intention, had made it a measure of corporate virility. NMS is the minimum size of the package of shares in a company traded in normal-sized market transactions; there are 12 categories. The main purpose of the system is to fix the size of transactions in which *market makers are obliged to deal, and to set a basis on which the bargains should be published.

normal retirement age The age at which an individual is expected to retire. Until 2010 this was normally 65 for a man and 60 for a woman in the UK; this is now gradually adjusting to 65 for both in 2018 and 67 for both in 2028. It is at these ages that state pensions begin. However, other policies can nominate other pre-agreed dates, which HM Revenue will accept in certain cases.

normative contract *See* PSYCHOLOGICAL CONTRACT.

North American Free Trade Agreement (NAFTA) A trade agreement between the USA, Canada, and Mexico that provided for the elimination of all trade *tariffs between these countries within a 10-year period. It was originally concluded between the USA and Canada in 1988, with Mexico joining in 1992.

nostro account A bank account conducted by a UK bank with a bank in another country, usually in the currency of that country. *Compare* VOSTRO ACCOUNT.

notary public A legal practitioner, usually a solicitor, who is empowered to attest deeds and other documents, and notes (*see* NOTING) dishonoured *bills of exchange.

note 1. A *promissory note. **2.** A negotiable record of an unsecured loan (*see* COMMERCIAL PAPER). The word 'note' is now used in preference to *bond when the principal sum is repayable in less than five years. **3.** A *banknote. **4.** An inscription on an unpaid *bill of exchange (*see* NOTING) made by a *notary public.

notebook computer *See* LAPTOP COMPUTER.

note issuance facility (NIF; note purchase facility) A means of enabling short-term borrowers in the *eurocurrency markets to issue euronotes, with maturities of less than one year, when the need arises rather than having to arrange a separate issue of euronotes each time they need to borrow. A **revolving underwriting facility (RUF)** achieves the same objective.

notes to the accounts (notes to financial statements) Information supporting that given on the face of a company's *financial statements. Many notes are required to be given by law, including those detailing *fixed assets, investments, *share capital, *debentures, and *reserves. Other information may be required by accounting standards or be given to facilitate the users' understanding of the company and its current and future performance.

notice day The day on which notice must be given that goods will be supplied to fulfil a commodity-market contract, rather than

having it cancelled out by a matching contract.

notice in lieu of distringas *See* STOP NOTICE.

notice of abandonment *See* ABANDONMENT.

notice of motion *See* MOTION.

noting 1. The procedure adopted if a *bill of exchange has been dishonoured by non-acceptance or by non-payment. Not later than the next business day after the day on which it was dishonoured, the holder has to hand it to a *notary public to be noted. The notary re-presents the bill; if it is still unaccepted or unpaid, the circumstances are noted in a register and also on a **notarial ticket**, which is attached to the bill. The noting can then, if necessary, be extended to a *protest. **2.** In advertising research, noticing a particular advertisement when first looking through a newspaper or magazine in which it appears. *See* NOTING SCORE.

noting score The average number of readers *noting a particular advertisement or editorial item in a newspaper or magazine, expressed as a percentage of the total readership.

not negotiable Words marked on a *bill of exchange indicating that it ceases to be a *negotiable instrument, i.e. although it can still be negotiated, the holder cannot obtain a better title to it than the person from whom it was obtained, thus providing a safeguard if it is stolen. A cheque is the only form of bill that can be crossed 'not negotiable'; other forms must have it inscribed on their faces.

novation The replacement of one legal agreement by a new obligation, with the agreement of all the parties. For example, on financial exchanges using a *clearing house, transactions between members are novated so that matching contracts are created between the buyer and the clearing house and between the clearing house and the seller (*see* COUNTERPARTY RISK).

NOW Abbreviation for *negotiable order of withdrawal.

NPD Abbreviation for *new product development.

NPV Abbreviation for *net present value.

NRS Abbreviation for *National Readership Survey.

NRV Abbreviation for *net realizable value.

NSE Abbreviation for *National Stock Exchange of India.

nudum pactum (Latin: nude contract) An agreement that is unenforceable in British law because no *consideration is mentioned. *See* CONTRACT.

numbered account A bank account identified only by a number. This service, offered by some Swiss banks at one time, encouraged funds that had been obtained illegally to find their way to Switzerland. A numbered account is now more frequently used to ensure legitimate privacy.

numerically controlled machine tools Computer-controlled machine tools that store within their built-in memories the parameters of the components they are producing. This enables them to produce work to consistent standards using relatively unskilled labour.

NV Abbreviation for *Naamloze Vennootschap*. It appears after the name of a Dutch company, being equivalent to the British abbreviation Ltd (i.e. denoting a limited liability company). *Compare* BV.

NVQ Abbreviation for National Vocational Qualification. *See* VOCATIONAL TRAINING.

NYBOT Abbreviation for *New York Board of Trade.

NYMEX Abbreviation for *New York Mercantile Exchange.

NYSE Abbreviation for *New York Stock Exchange.

NYSE Arca An electronic platform for trading in shares and options, with its headquarters in Chicago. It originated as Archipelago, later ArcaEx, in 1996, and took over the former Pacific Exchange in 2005. A year later it was itself acquired by the *New York Stock Exchange (subsequently *NYSE Euronext). After *NASDAQ, it is the largest electronic trading system in the world by volume of shares traded.

NYSE Euronext The global corporation formed in 2006 by the merger of the *New York Stock Exchange (NYSE) and the pan-European equities and derivatives market *Euronext NV. NYSE had acquired the electronic trading system ArcaEx (*see* NYSE ARCA) earlier that same year. In December 2012 it was announced that NYSE Euronext had itself been acquired by the electronic commodities market *Intercontinental Exchange.

O & M *See* ORGANIZATION AND METHODS.

objective and task method A method of setting a promotional budget in which the marketer decides the objective to be accomplished and the tasks necessary to achieve the objective. The budget is decided by estimating the costs of carrying out the tasks.

objectivity An *accounting concept attempting to ensure that any subjective actions taken by the preparer of accounts are minimized. The aim of the rules and regulations required to achieve objectivity is that users should be able to compare *financial statements for different companies over a period with some confidence that the statements have been prepared on the same basis (*see* COMPARABILITY). One of the major advantages claimed for *historical-cost accounting is that it is objective, but necessarily some subjective decisions will have been made.

objects clause Formerly, a clause contained in the *memorandum of association of a company setting out the objects for which the company was formed. If the company undertook any activities not included in the objects clause, it would have been acting beyond its powers, i.e. *ultra vires*. The Companies Act 2006 removed the requirement for a company to state its objects in such a clause and effectively abolished the concept of *ultra vires*.

obligation 1. The duty of a borrower to repay a loan, and that of the lender to ensure that repayment is made. **2.** A bond or other promise to pay a sum of money.

obligatory expenditure The spending of the European Union, governed by such treaties as the *Common Agricultural Policy and the *European Regional Development Fund. The European Parliament can add to the amount spent but if it wishes to reduce it, it must obtain the agreement of the Council of Ministers, or reject the whole of the Union Budget in that year.

observation research Marketing research in which a respondent's actions are monitored without direct interaction, without using an interviewer.

OBS Abbreviation for *off-balance-sheet.

obsolescence A fall in the value of an asset as a result of its age. For example, plant and equipment may not have actually worn out but may have become out of date because technology has advanced and more efficient plant has become available. It also applies to consumer durables (*see* CONSUMER GOODS), in which a change of style may render a serviceable piece of equipment, such as a car or washing machine, out of date. In accounting, obsolescence is an important factor both for *depreciation of fixed assets and for valuation of stock.

  Built-in obsolescence or **planned obsolescence** is a deliberate policy adopted by a manufacturer to limit the durability of a product in order to encourage the consumer to buy a replacement more quickly than he or she otherwise might have to. The morality of this policy has been frequently questioned but is usually defended on two grounds. Firstly, in the modern world, the pace of technological improvement is such that many consumers will choose to buy new computers, cameras, mobile phones, etc., before their existing models have worn out. In these circumstances, it makes sense for manufacturers to produce cheap products that will function well for a fairly short period rather than more expensive ones that will function long after they have become technically obsolete. Secondly, Western economies depend on strong consumer demand; if such consumer durables as cars and washing machines were built to last for their purchaser's lifetime, demand would be reduced to a level that would create enormous unemployment.

obstructive response A management strategy in which a company responds to criticism of its social or environmental practices by denial of the problem or concealment of evidence. This contrasts with an *accommodating response, *defensive response, or *proactive response, which to varying degrees seek to engage with the issues raised.

occasion segmentation Dividing a market into groups according to the occasions on which buyers get the idea to buy, actually make their purchase, or use the purchased item.

occupational hazard A risk of accident or illness at one's place of work. Dangerous jobs usually command higher salaries than those involving no risks, the increase being known as **danger money**. *See also* HEALTH AND SAFETY EXECUTIVE.

occupational pension scheme (superannuation; workplace pension) A pension scheme open to employees within a certain trade or profession or working for a particular firm. An occupational pension scheme can either be insured or self-administered. If it is insured, an insurance company pays the benefits under the scheme in return for having the premiums to invest. In a self-administered scheme, the pension-fund trustees are responsible for investing the contributions themselves. In the UK, work-related pensions are regulated by the *Pensions Regulator. From 2017 UK employers will be legally obliged to enrol all employees who meet certain

criteria in a workplace pension scheme and to make contributions; staff who do not wish to be enrolled will have to opt out. *See also* DEFINED-BENEFIT PENSION SCHEME; DEFINED-CONTRIBUTION PENSION SCHEME.

(⊕) **SEE WEB LINKS**
- Website of the Pensions Regulator: includes Codes of Practice and guidance for employers, trustees, and their advisers
- An introduction to automatic enrolment

OCR Abbreviation for *optical character recognition.

OD Abbreviation for *organizational development.

odd-even pricing The pricing of a product so that the price ends in an odd number of pence, which is not far below the next number of pounds. For example, £4.99 might be used in preference to £5.00 in order to make the product appear cheaper.

odd lot *See* ROUND LOT.

OECD Abbreviation for *Organization for Economic Cooperation and Development.

OEIC Acronym (pronounced 'oik') for *open-ended investment company.

Ofcom *See* OFFICE OF COMMUNICATIONS.

off-balance-sheet (OBS) Denoting assets or liabilities that do not appear on the *balance sheet of a company. Various off-balance-sheet arrangements have been used by companies wishing to avoid full disclosure of their assets or liabilities; these include complex legal agreements, the use of *joint ventures or specifically created subsidiaries, and *securitizations and other *structured finance arrangements. In **off-balance-sheet finance** a company removes some or all of its finance from the balance sheet, usually to enhance its *accounting ratios, such as the *gearing ratio and *return on capital employed, or to avoid breaking any agreements it has made with the banks in respect of the total amount it may borrow. Similarly, banks have used a variety of off-balance-sheet methods, typically involving securitizations and *special purpose vehicles, to avoid their obligations under the *capital adequacy rules. The accounting profession has attempted to counter these practices by emphasizing that accounting should reflect the commercial reality of transactions and not simply their legal form. In the USA, the *Sarbanes–Oxley Act of 2002 introduced new regulations concerning the disclosure of off-balance-sheet arrangements in the wake of the scandal surrounding the collapse of the energy-trading giant Enron. In the banking and financial sector, the lack of transparency arising from complex off-balance-sheet practices has been identified as a factor in the financial crisis of 2008. *See* CREATIVE ACCOUNTING; HIDDEN RESERVE.

off-balance-sheet reserve *See* HIDDEN RESERVE.

off-card rate An advertising charging rate that is different from that shown on the *rate card, having been separately negotiated.

offer The price at which a seller makes it known that he or she is willing to sell something. If there is an *acceptance of the offer a legally binding *contract has been entered into. In law, an offer is distinguished from an **invitation to treat**, which is an invitation by one person or firm to others to make an offer. An example of an invitation to treat is to display goods in a shop window. *See also* FIRM OFFER; OFFER PRICE; QUOTATION.

offer by prospectus An offer to the public of a new issue of shares or debentures made directly by means of a *prospectus, a document giving a detailed account of the aims, objects, and capital structure of the company, as well as its past history. The prospectus must conform to the provisions of the Companies Acts. *Compare* OFFER FOR SALE.

offer document A document sent to the shareholders of a company that is the subject of a *takeover bid. It gives details of the offer being made and usually provides shareholders with reasons for accepting the terms of the offer.

offer for sale An invitation to the general public to purchase the stock of a company through an intermediary, such as an issuing house or *merchant bank (*compare* OFFER BY PROSPECTUS); it is one of the most frequently used means of *flotation. An offer for sale can be in one of two forms: a *public issue (the more usual), in which stock is offered at a fixed price and some form of balloting or rationing is required if the demand for the shares exceeds supply; or an *issue by tender, in which individuals offer to purchase a fixed quantity of stock at or above some minimum price and the stock is allocated to the highest bidders. *Compare* INTRODUCTION; PLACING.

offer price 1. The price at which a security is offered for sale by a *market maker. *Compare* BID PRICE. **2.** The price at which an institution will sell units in a *unit trust.

offer to purchase *See* TAKEOVER BID.

Office for Budget Responsibility The independent economic forecasting watchdog established by HM Treasury in May 2010 to provide economic data and analysis for the UK government. Its main duties include producing twice-yearly economic forecasts; judging progress towards fiscal targets set by the government; analysing the long-term sustainability of public finances; and scrutiny of Treasury costings of Budget proposals.

((⊕)) SEE WEB LINKS
• Website of the Office for Budget Responsibility: includes public finance data and medium-term forecasts for the UK economy

Office for National Statistics (ONS) The UK government's statistical unit, formed by a merger of the **Central Statistical Office** and the Office of Population Censuses and Surveys in 1996. It is an independent body responsible for collecting economic statistics for the government. Among its publications are *Financial Statistics* (monthly), *Economic and Labour Market Review* (monthly), *UK National Accounts* (the *Blue Book*; annually), *UK*

Balance of Payments (the *Pink Book*; annually), and the *Annual Abstract of Statistics.*

(⊕)) SEE WEB LINKS
* Free access to data produced by the Office for National Statistics

Office of Communications (Ofcom) A UK government body set up in 2003 to supervise the communications industries. It was formed from a merger of the Office for Telecommunications (Oftel) and the various regulatory bodies for radio and television broadcasting. It is responsible for issuing licences, regulating competition, and protecting the interests of the consumer. Since 2011 it has also been responsible for regulating the UK's postal services.

office of exit In the EU, the customs office though which exported goods pass on the point of leaving EU territory. This may or may not be in the goods' country of origin.

Office of Fair Trading (OFT) A former government department, established in 1973, to enforce competition law and consumer protection regulations. It was abolished in 2014, when many of its functions were transferred to a new *Competition and Markets Authority.

Office of Government Commerce (OGC) An office of HM Treasury established to help government departments and other public sector organizations deliver best value for money. It issues standards on best practice in procurement, project management, and service management and measures performance against these standards.

officer of a company A person who acts in an official capacity in a company. Company officers include the directors, managers, the company secretary, and in some circumstances the company's auditors and solicitors. The Companies Act empowers a court dealing with a *liquidation to investigate the conduct of the company's officers with a view to recovering any money they may have obtained illegally or incorrectly.

office suite *See* BUSINESS SOFTWARE PACKAGE.

Official List 1. A list of all the securities traded on the *main market of the *London Stock Exchange. *See* LISTED SECURITY; LISTING REQUIREMENTS. **2. (Daily Official List)** A list prepared daily by the London Stock Exchange, recording all the bargains that have been transacted in listed securities during the day. It also gives dividend dates, rights issues, prices, and other information.

(⊕)) SEE WEB LINKS
* Official List of securities on the LSE from the Financial Conduct Authority website

official rate The rate of exchange given to a currency by a government. If the official rate differs from the market rate, the government has to be prepared to support its official rate by buying or selling in the open market to make the two rates coincide.

official receiver (OR) A person appointed by the Secretary of State for Business, Innovation and Skills to act as a *receiver in *bankruptcy and winding-up cases. The High Court and each county court that has jurisdiction over insolvency matters has an official receiver, who is an officer of the court. Deputy official receivers may also be appointed. The official receiver commonly acts as the *liquidator of a company being wound up by the court.

official strike *See* STRIKE.

offline 1. Not connected to a computer or the Internet. **2.** Denoting computer equipment that is not usable, either because it is not connected to a computer or because the system has been forbidden to use it. *Compare* ONLINE.

offprint A reprint or photocopy of an article from a periodical or paper.

offset 1. The right that enables a bank to seize any bank-account balances of a guarantor or debtor if a loan has been defaulted upon. **2.** A code on the magnetic strip of a plastic card that, together with the

*personal identification number (PIN), verifies that the user of the card is entitled to use it. **3.** To cancel a futures contract or options contract by entering into a reverse agreement.

offsetting swap (mirror swap) A *swap in which cash flows exactly offset those of an existing swap.

offshore banking *See* OFFSHORE FINAN-CIAL CENTRES.

offshore company 1. A company not registered in the same country as that in which the persons investing in the company are resident. **2.** A company set up in a foreign country or *tax haven by a financial institution with the object of benefiting from tax laws or exchange control regulations in that country.

offshore financial centres Centres that provide advantageous deposit and lending rates to non-residents because of low taxation, liberal exchange controls, and low reserve requirements for banks. Some countries have made a lucrative business out of **offshore banking**; the Cayman Islands is currently one of the world's largest offshore centres. In Europe, Switzerland, the Channel Islands, and the Isle of Man are very popular. Such locations are often described as *tax havens because they can reduce customers' tax liabilities in entirely legal ways. The USA and Japan have both established domestic offshore facilities enabling non-residents to conduct their business under more liberal regulations than domestic transactions. Their objective is to stop funds moving outside the country.

offshore fund 1. A fund that is based in an *offshore financial centre to avoid UK taxation. Offshore funds operate in the same way as *unit trusts but are not supervised by the UK's regulatory authorities. **2.** Any fund held outside the country of residence of the holder.

offshoring The transfer of some operations or processes of a business to another country, typically in order to take advantage of lower costs there. Costs reduced in this way may include the costs of labour, costs of goods, or taxation. Offshoring may also take advantage of lower levels of regulation in another jurisdiction.

off-the-peg research Marketing research that uses existing data, rather than a fresh investigation of a market. *See also* DESK RESEARCH.

off-the-shelf company A company that is registered with the *Registrar of Companies although it does not trade and has no directors. It can, however, be sold and reformed into a new company with the minimum of formality and expense. Such companies are easily purchased from specialist brokers.

OFT Abbreviation for *Office of Fair Trading.

OGC Abbreviation for *Office of Government Commerce.

OIS Abbreviation for *overnight index swap.

OLAP Abbreviation for *online analytical processing.

Old Lady of Threadneedle Street An affectionate name for the *Bank of England, coined by the English politician and dramatist R B Sheridan (1751–1816). The street in which the Bank stands (since 1734 in a Renaissance building by George Sampson) probably takes its name from the thread and needle used by the Merchant Taylors, a guild whose hall is in the same street.

oligopoly A market in which relatively few sellers supply many buyers. Each seller recognizes that prices can be controlled to a certain extent and that competitors' actions will influence profits. There is therefore a risk of *collusion. An oligopoly is often defined as a market in which the four largest players have a combined market share of over 40% (*see* FOUR-FIRM CONCENTRATION RATIO). *See also* MONOPOLY.

oligopsony A market in which there are numerous potential sellers but a small number of buyers. Under oligopsony, buyers are in a strong position to dictate terms and can pass many costs and risks on to the supplier. Markets in soft commodities are often oligopsonistic, especially where large Western companies buy from numerous small producers in the developing world.

omnibus research *Marketing research surveys based on multipart questionnaires sent out regularly to a panel of respondents. Space on the questionnaire is available to companies that have specific marketing research needs, especially those having a limited number of questions to ask, which would not alone justify setting up a separate research study.

OMV Abbreviation for open market value. *See* MARKET VALUE.

OMX A company that owns and operates stock exchanges in Scandinavia and the Baltic States; it also markets advanced electronic trading systems for derivatives products that are used in many other exchanges worldwide. It originated in 1985 as an options exchange in Stockholm; this later moved to London (1990–2003) to circumvent changes in Sweden's tax regime. OMX acquired the Stockholm Stock Exchange in 1998, the Helsinki Exchange in 2003, and the Copenhagen Exchange in 2005. In 2008 it became a wholly owned subsidiary of *NASDAQ.

on approval (on appro) The practice of allowing potential buyers to take possession of goods in order to decide whether or not they wish to buy them. The potential buyer is a bailee (*see* BAILMENT) and is obliged to return the goods in perfect condition after deciding not to purchase them. Many department stores and mail-order firms allow their customers to take goods on appro.

on consignment *See* CONSIGNMENT.

oncost 1. The additional costs incurred as a consequence of employing personnel, i.e.

wages oncost, or the additional costs incurred by storing and handling direct materials, i.e. **materials oncost** or **stores oncost. 2.** A rarely used alternative name for *overheads.

on demand Denoting any liability that may be subject to immediate repayment.

one-month money Money placed on the *money market for one month, i.e. it cannot be withdrawn without penalty during this period.

one-to-one marketing A form of marketing in which dialogue occurs directly between a company and individual customers (or, less strictly, with groups of customers with similar needs). The dialogue involves a company listening to the needs of a customer and responding with services to meet these needs.

one-year money Money placed on the *money market for one year, i.e. it cannot be withdrawn without penalty for one year.

online 1. Of, relating to, or connected to the Internet. **2.** Denoting computer equipment that is connected to a computer system and is usable by it. *Compare* OFFLINE.

online advertising Advertising on the Internet, whether in the form of display advertising on web pages (typically *banner advertisements or pop-up ads, which appear when a user opens a particular page) or via e-mail, social media, or mobile phones (*see* MOBILE ADVERTISING). In 2013 it was estimated that 20% of all money spent on advertising was spent on Internet and mobile content. A recent development is the growth of highly targeted advertising, in which offers and promotions are directed at individual users on the basis of their browsing history (*see* BEHAVIOURAL TARGETING).

online analytical processing (OLAP) A software application that enables users to extract very specific types of data from a large, multidimensional database and to analyse that information in several ways at once. OLAP systems can therefore provide swift answers to very detailed and complex inquiries from managers about e.g. products, sales, and marketing costs. *See* DATA WAREHOUSING.

online banking *See* HOME BANKING.

online brand *See* DIGITAL BRAND.

online focus groups A form of Internet research in which participants attend a virtual *focus group meeting held at a website. It is particularly useful if collecting all the group participants in one location is difficult.

online incentive schemes *See* LOYALTY TECHNIQUES.

online marketing Direct marketing conducted through interactive online computer services that provide two-way systems, electronically linking consumers with sellers.

ONS Abbreviation for *Office for National Statistics.

on stream Denoting that a specified investment or asset is providing the expected revenues.

OPEC Abbreviation for *Organization of the Petroleum Exporting Countries.

open auction An *auction in which each participant is aware of the value of the others' bids.

open charter *See* CHARTERING.

open cheque *See* CHEQUE.

open cover (open policy) A marine cargo insurance policy in which the insurer agrees to cover any voyage undertaken by the policyholder's vessel(s) or any cargo shipped by a particular shipper. A policy condition requires a declaration to be completed on a weekly, monthly, or quarterly basis indicating the vessels involved, the commodities carried, and the voyages undertaken. Insurers use the declaration to calculate the premium. The main advantage of a policy of this kind is that the insurer can be confident that all cargos have insurance cover without the need to notify insurers of the details before the voyage. In some cases there may be a policy limit above which the insurance ceases. On such policies it is necessary to keep a running total of the sums insured to make sure that the policy limit is not exceeded.

open credit Unlimited credit offered by a supplier to a trusted client.

open-door policy An import policy of a country in which all goods from all sources are imported on the same terms, usually free of import duties.

open economy An economy in which a significant percentage of its goods and services are traded internationally and a significant percentage of total domestic spending is on imports from abroad. The degree of openness of an economy depends on the amount of overseas trade in which the country is involved or the policies of its government. Thus the UK economy is relatively open, as the economy is significantly dependent on foreign trade, while the US economy is relatively closed, as imports are not important to its economy.

open-ended investment company (OEIC) An investment business that operates an *open-end trust. The size of its fund depends on the number of units sold.

open-ended question A question that requires respondents to provide answers in their own words, rather than 'yes', 'no', or 'don't know'. Such questions as Why . . . ? What . . . ? When . . . ? are asked without providing answers from which to choose. Open-ended questions are often used in *exploratory research. *Compare* MULTIPLE-CHOICE QUESTION; STRUCTURED INTERVIEW.

open-end trust (open-end fund) A form of *unit trust in which the managers of the trust may vary the investments held without notifying the unit holders. Open-end trusts are common in the USA.

open general licence An import licence for goods on which there are no import restrictions.

open indent An order to an overseas purchasing agent to buy certain goods, without specifying the manufacturer. If the manufacturer is specified this is a **closed indent**.

opening prices The *bid prices and *offer prices made at the opening of a day's trading on any security or commodity market. The opening prices may not always be identical to the previous evening's *closing prices, especially if any significant events have taken place during the intervening period.

opening stock The inventory held by an organization at the beginning of an accounting period as *raw materials, *work in progress, or *finished goods. The *closing stocks of one period become the opening stocks of the succeeding period and it is necessary to establish the level of closing stocks so that the cost of their creation is not charged against the profits of that period but brought forward as opening stocks to be charged against the profits of the succeeding period.

open-market operations The purchase or sale by a central bank of government bonds in exchange for money, with the aim of influencing *monetary policy. Buying debt provides liquidity and selling debt reduces liquidity in the private banking sector.

open market value (OMV) See MARKET VALUE.

open outcry Quoting prices, making offers, bids, and acceptances, and concluding transactions by word of mouth in a financial market, usually in a trading *pit. See also CALLOVER; DOUBLE AUCTION.

open policy See OPEN COVER.

open position (naked position) A trading position in which a dealer has commodities, *securities, or currencies bought but unsold or unhedged (see HEDGE), or sales that are neither covered nor hedged. In either case the dealer is vulnerable to market fluctuations until the position is closed or hedged.

open-pricing agreement An agreement between firms operating in an oligopolistic market in which prices and intended price changes are circulated to those taking part in the agreement in order to avoid a *price war.

open shop See CLOSED SHOP.

open-source Denoting computer software that is freely available with its source code, to be used or altered by anybody as they wish. Commonly the only restriction is that it cannot be charged for, that its free distribution should not be hindered, and that the work of others should be properly respected. This cooperative approach reflects a belief that the best way to create high quality software is through widespread inspection, modification, and correction of the source code by any interested party. It is contrasted especially with the traditional proprietary model, where source code is a closely guarded commercial secret.

open standards Software protocols and operations on the Internet that are readily available, widely documented, and not controlled by a private company.

open system A system that is affected by influences from outside its system boundary and that is able to affect other systems. *Compare* CLOSED SYSTEM.

operating budget A forecast of the financial requirements for the future trading of an organization, including its planned sales, production, cash flow, etc. An operating budget is normally designed for a fixed period, usually one year, and forms the plan for that period's trading activities. Any divergences from it are usually monitored and, if appropriate, changes can then be made to it as the period progresses. See BUDGETARY CONTROL.

operating costs See OVERHEAD.

operating doctrine Stock-control policies that specify when and how much stock should be reordered.

operating lease A lease that is not a *finance lease, i.e. one in which the risks and rewards of owning the asset remain substantially with the lessor. In practice this is generally a lease under which an asset is hired out to a lessee for a period that is substantially shorter than its useful economic life. Section 30 of the Financial Reporting Standard Applicable in the UK and Republic of Ireland provides detailed guidance.

operating profit/loss The profit or loss made by a company as a result of its principal trading activity. This is arrived at by deducting its **operating expenses** from its *trading profit, or adding its operating expenses to its trading loss; in either case this is before taking into account any *extraordinary items.

operating statement A financial and quantitative statement provided for the management of an organization to record the performance achieved by that area of the operation for which the management is responsible, for a selected budget period. An operating statement may include production levels, costs incurred, and (where appropriate) revenue generated, all compared with budgeted amounts and the performance in previous periods.

operating system 1. The collection of programs that controls the basic operation of a *computer. Usually purchased with the computer, it controls such tasks as start-up routines, input and output, and memory allocation. It is also responsible for loading and executing programs. In small systems, the operating system loads a program and then gives it control of the machine. In larger *multitasking systems, the operating system always retains control of the machine, ensuring that the separate programs do not interfere with each other and controlling the amount of processing time each receives. **2.** The configuration of the activities concerned with transforming resources within an organization. The way in which a particular organization arranges the components of its operating system will be a product of its *operations strategy.

While there may be areas of similarity between successful organizations, there is no single right way to set up an operating system. Each system is an attempt to achieve the optimum match between organizational capabilities and perceived environmental conditions.

operational flexibility See FLEXIBILITY.

operational gearing (operational leverage) The ratio of a company's *fixed costs to its total costs. The higher the level of operational gearing, the greater the risk, since fixed costs have to be covered before a profit can be recorded.

operational indicators See PERFORMANCE MEASUREMENT.

operational research (operations research) A scientific method of approaching industrial and commercial problems in order to arrive at the most efficient and economic method of achieving the desired objective. It basically consists of making a clear statement of the problem, designing a model to represent the possible solutions using different strategies, and applying the solutions obtained from the analysis of the model to the real problem. It makes use of *game theory, critical-path analysis, *simulation techniques, etc.

operational risk The risk of direct or indirect loss resulting from inadequate or failed internal processes and systems, or from a wide variety of external events. The control of operational risk has been the object of much attention in recent years, for example in the *Basle Accords concerning the *capital adequacy of banks and in the *Turnbull Report in the UK. It has also led to changes in the regulation of financial institutions and the requirements for the listing of public companies. Some major categories of operational risk include fraud and theft, legal action (e.g. by employees or customers), natural disaster, vandalism (including cybervandalism), and computer system failure.

operation job card A card or form on which an employee writes up the details of a particular task and the length of time it took to complete. It is used in *work studies.

operations A set of activities concerned with transforming resource inputs into desired outputs, i.e. goods or services. Every purposeful organization has desired outputs and, as every output requires inputs of some sort, all purposeful organizations are involved in operations. Traditionally, the word has been used to refer exclusively to manufacturing processes, but it applies equally to the service sector and to non-profit-making organizations. In some organizations it is possible to identify a single coherent sub-system as performing the operations function. In others, responsibility for various elements may be split between different linked departments.

operations management The management of an *operating system to achieve the desired organizational outputs within an optimum balance of economy, efficiency, and effectiveness.

operations manager A manager with responsibility for running the resource inputs that constitute an *operating system. Most managers have an operational function within their overall job description, e.g. a human resource manager (*see* HUMAN-RESOURCE MANAGEMENT) has to make use of inputs consisting of cash, skilled personnel, documentation, etc., to produce an output consisting of an appropriately skilled workforce.

operations strategy A plan to transform an organization's overall strategic objectives into operational deliverables. It involves the design of the product or service and the processes by which the product or service is produced; the way in which production is managed and controlled; and the design of processes for the constant improvement of the operation. If, at the strategic level, the organization decides to compete in the market on the basis of superior quality, the operations strategy has to plan to produce a package

incorporating the specified quality within stated financial constraints. If the strategy is to compete on cost, the plan must produce the product cheaply within the limits of acceptable quality.

opinion giver *See* RELATIONSHIP ROLES.

opinion leaders *See* CONSUMER GROUPS.

opinion poll A poll using marketing research techniques that is specifically concerned with political opinion. Public opinion polls are usually commissioned by the media (especially television and newspapers) in order to keep their readers or viewers informed. Private opinion polls are usually commissioned by the political parties in order to help develop campaign strategies.

opinion seeker *See* RELATIONSHIP ROLES.

opportunities to see The number of times a member of the public (or an audience) may, on average, be expected to see a particular advertisement.

opportunity cost The economic cost of an action measured in terms of the benefit foregone by not pursuing the best alternative course of action. The cost of funds, for example, must be measured in terms of the returns they could earn in the capital markets for taking the same degree of risk. Opportunity cost is an important factor in decision making (*see* COST-BENEFIT ANALYSIS), although it represents costs that are not recorded in the accounts of the relevant organization.

OPT Abbreviation for *optimized production technology.

optical character recognition (OCR) The recognition of printed characters by a light-sensitive optical scanner. The scanner recognizes the shape of a letter by scanning it with a very fine point of light. It then uses a computer to compare the pattern of reflected light with the patterns of the letters of the alphabet stored in its memory. OCR is often used to read responses on questionnaires, thus reducing human error and increasing the speed of analysis.

optical scanner A light-sensitive optical device used to capture photographs, diagrams, printed characters, etc. in a digitized form so that they can be stored electronically.

optimism bias The tendency for people to be optimistic about future events, especially those seen as following from their own plans and actions. Studies have suggested that this is a universal cognitive bias, possibly with a biological origin. Although optimism may be a stimulus to enterprise, it has obvious dangers: these include increased risk taking (including neglect of basic precautions), failure to estimate probabilities accurately, and inadequate contingency planning. In drawing up plans, schedules, and budgets there is a demonstrated tendency for managers to underestimate costs and duration and to overestimate benefits (*see* PLANNING FALLACY). This being so, there is now an explicit requirement for those managing government projects in the UK to include an adjustment for optimism bias. *See also* STRATEGIC MISREPRESENTATION.

optimized production technology (OPT) A computer-based system for planning production and the allocation of resources. In contrast to other methods that aim to use machines to their full capacity, for OPT the management of bottlenecks is the key to efficient and effective plant utilization. Maximization of throughput in areas that are not bottlenecks only increases the build-up of work in these areas, and thus locks up capital in work in progress. While an appropriate quantity of work is necessary, too much is counterproductive. *See* FOCUSED IMPROVEMENT; THEORY OF CONSTRAINTS.

opt-in A customer or potential customer who chooses to give permission for use of personalized information or to receive solicitation, particularly via *direct marketing and the Internet. *Compare* OPT-OUT.

opt-in e-mail An e-mail sent to a customer only when he or she has explicitly asked for information to be sent (usually when filling in an on-screen form).

option The right to buy or sell a fixed quantity of a commodity, currency, *security, etc., at a particular date at a particular price (the *exercise price). Unlike the buyer of a *futures contract, the purchaser of an option is not obliged to buy or sell at the exercise price and will only do so if it is profitable; the purchaser may allow the option to lapse, in which case only the initial purchase price of the option (the option money or premium) is lost.

An option to buy is known as a **call option** and is usually purchased in the expectation of a rising price; an option to sell is called a **put option** and is bought in the expectation of a falling price or to protect a profit on an investment. Options, like futures, allow individuals and firms to *hedge against the risk of wide fluctuations in prices; they also allow dealers and speculators to gamble for large profits with limited initial payments.

Professional traders in options make use of a large range of potential strategies, often purchasing combinations of options that reflect particular expectations or cover several contingencies. A **traded option** is one that can be bought or sold on an exchange at any time, as opposed to a **traditional option**, which once bought cannot be resold. There is a further distinction between **European options**, in which the buyer can only exercise the right to take up the option or let it lapse on the expiry date, and **American options**, in which this right can be exercised at any time up to the expiry date. American options are generally worth more than European options because the option holder has more chance of buying or selling at a favourable price. American options are also more difficult to value. *See also* REAL OPTION.

option money The price paid for an *option. The cost of a call option is often known as the **call money** and that for a put option as the **put money**.

option period The time during which an option remains open, i.e. before the buyer has to make a final choice whether or not to exercise the option.

option to double 1. An *option by a seller to sell double the quantity of securities for which he or she has sold an option, if it is so desired. In some markets this is called a **put-of-more option**. **2.** An option by a buyer to buy double the quantity of securities for which he or she has bought an option, if desired. In some markets this is called a **call-of-more option**.

option to purchase 1. A right given to shareholders to buy shares in certain companies in certain circumstances at a reduced price. **2.** A right purchased or given to a person to buy something at a specified price on or before a specified date. Until the specified date has passed, the seller undertakes not to sell the property to anyone else and not to withdraw it from sale.

opt-out A customer who chooses to receive no solicitation, particularly via *direct marketing or the Internet. *Compare* OPT-IN.

opt-out e-mail An e-mail sent to a customer who will not be contacted again if he or she expresses a wish not to be contacted in future. Opt-out or *unsubscribe options are usually available within the e-mail itself.

OR Abbreviation for *official receiver.

order cheque *See* CHEQUE.

order driven Denoting a market in which prices are determined by the publication of orders to buy or sell shares, with the objective of attracting a counterparty. *Compare* QUOTE DRIVEN.

order of business The sequence of the items on the *agenda of a business meeting. It is usual to adopt the following order: apologies for absence; reading and signing of the minutes of the last meeting; matters arising from these minutes; new correspondence received; reading and adoption of reports, accounts, etc.; election of officers and auditors; any special motions; any other business; date of next meeting. *See also* ANNUAL GENERAL MEETING; EXTRAORDINARY GENERAL MEETING.

order-qualifying criteria (entry-level criteria) The characteristics that a product or service has to have before customers will consider buying it, i.e. before it can gain entry to the market.

order-routine specification The stage of the business buying process in which the buyer writes the final order with the chosen supplier(s), listing the technical specifications, quantity needed, expected time of delivery, and warranties.

order-winning criteria The characteristics of a product or service that are most important in deciding whether or not a customer will make a purchase. These are the characteristics that positively differentiate a particular product from similar products in the market. Clearly order-winning criteria vary from customer to customer. *Compare* ORDER-QUALIFYING CRITERIA.

ordinary activities Any activities undertaken by an organization as part of its business and any related activities in which it engages in furtherance of, incidental to, or arising from, these activities. Ordinary activities include the effects on the reporting entity of any event in the various environments in which it operates, including the political, regulatory, economic, and geographical environments, irrespective of the frequency or unusual nature of the events. *See also* EXTRAORDINARY ITEMS.

ordinary resolution A *resolution that is valid if passed by a majority of the votes cast by the members of a company, whether in person or by proxy. No notice that the resolution is to be proposed at a meeting is required. It is appropriate where no other type of resolution is expressly required by the Companies Act 2006 or the *articles of association. *Compare* EXTRAORDINARY RESOLUTION; SPECIAL RESOLUTION.

ordinary share A fixed unit of the *share capital of a company. Shares in publicly owned quoted companies (*see* PLC; QUOTATION) are usually traded on *stock exchanges and represent one of the most important types of security for investors. Shares yield dividends, representing a proportion of the profits of a company (*compare* FIXED-INTEREST SECURITY; PREFERENCE SHARE). In the long term, ordinary shares, by means of *capital growth, yield higher rewards, on average, than most alternative forms of securities, which compensates for the greater element of risk they entail. *See also* CONVERTIBLE; GROWTH STOCKS.

ordinary share capital The total *share capital of a company consisting of *ordinary shares.

öre A monetary unit of Sweden, worth one hundredth of a *krona.

øre A monetary unit of Denmark, the Faeroe Islands, Greenland, and Norway, worth one hundredth of a *krone.

organic growth *See* INTERNAL GROWTH.

organic organization An organization characterized by roles that are not well defined, tasks being redefined as individuals interact; there is little reliance on authority, with control and decision making decentralized, and communication is both lateral and vertical. This type of organization, which is a feature of the computer software industry, is appropriate if the external environment is uncertain. *Compare* MECHANISTIC ORGANIZATION.

organizational behaviour The ways in which people behave, individually and collectively, when working together in organizations. The study of organizational behaviour involves attention to such issues as *organizational commitment, *organizational culture, and group decision making. *See* INDUSTRIAL AND ORGANIZATIONAL PSYCHOLOGY.

organizational buying The way in which an organization (as opposed to an individual consumer) identifies, evaluates, and chooses the products it buys. *See* DECISION-MAKING UNIT.

organizational commitment An individual's psychological attachment to an organization and desire to remain part of it. It is normally measured by attitudinal dimensions, e.g. identification with the goals and values of the organization; desire to belong to the organization; and willingness to display effort on behalf of the organization. A distinction is sometimes made between **affective commitment**, which involves a sense of loyalty and shared values, and mere **continuance commitment**, which arises from inertia or the problems of finding alternative employment. *Compare* ALIENATION.

organizational culture (**corporate culture**) The values, customs, rituals, attitudes, and norms shared by members of an organization, which have to be learnt and accepted by new members of the organization. It is argued that there are at least three different types of organizational culture:

- In an **integrative culture** the objective is to obtain a consensus regarding the values and basic assumptions of the organization and to produce consistent actions. This integration brings unity, predictability, and clarity to work experiences.
- In a **differentiated culture**, subcultures develop that have internal consensus about values and basic assumptions but differ greatly between each subculture; this produces inconsistencies throughout the organization.
- In a **fragmentation culture** there are multiple interpretations of values and assumptions, which produce great ambiguity. This can arise from fast changes within the organization, the growing diversity of the workforce, and the increasingly global environment with which organizations are faced.

organizational design The way in which managers structure their organization in order to achieve the organization's goals. The formal design of an organization is laid out in an *organization chart, which indicates the duties, tasks, and responsibilities of both individuals and departments. Reporting relationships and the number of levels in the organization's hierarchy are other elements in the design. Organizational design has two basic functions:

- to ensure that information reaches the appropriate person to enable effective decisions to be made;
- to assist in the coordination of the interdependent parts of the organization.

organizational development (OD) A long-term, systematic, and prescriptive approach to planned organizational change. It applies the concepts of the social and behavioural sciences to the problem of changing an organization; in doing so it treats the organization as a complex social and technical system, which should have enough flexibility to change its design according to the nature of its tasks and external environment.

Its purpose is to derive strategies and initiatives for improving the effectiveness of an organization, largely by making the best use of the qualities and capabilities of its human resources. To be effective, organizational development should pervade the whole organization, forming part of the strategy that informs all the activities within it. It requires a total corporate commitment, requiring full understanding and acceptance by everyone in the organization. Inherent in organizational development is an overall purpose to address issues and solve problems in a way that is consistent with the *organizational culture. *See also* ORGANIZATIONAL BEHAVIOUR; ORGANIZATIONAL DESIGN; ORGANIZATIONAL THEORY.

organizational psychology *See* INDUSTRIAL AND ORGANIZATIONAL PSYCHOLOGY.

organizational theory The study of the design, structure, and process of decision making in organizations (*see* ORGANIZATIONAL DESIGN). The sociology of organizational systems, and the structure of relationships within them, are central to organizational theory.

Considerable work has been carried out on the way in which decisions are made, both by individuals and groups (committees) within organizations. The extent to which managers are influenced by

organizational politics, rather than being guided by reason and economics, in making their decisions is an aspect of considerable importance.

organization and methods (O & M) A form of *work study involving the organization of procedures and controls in a business and the methods of implementing them in management terms. It is usually applied to office procedures rather than factory production.

organization chart (organogram) A chart illustrating the structure of an organization; in particular it will show for which function of the business each manager is responsible and the chain of responsibility throughout the organization. Some organization charts include managers by name; others show the management positions in the structure.

Organization for Economic Cooperation and Development (OECD) An organization formed in 1961, replacing the Organization for European Economic Cooperation (OEEC), to promote cooperation among industrialized member countries on economic and social policies. Its objectives are to assist member countries in formulating policies designed to achieve high economic growth while maintaining financial stability, contributing to world trade on a multilateral basis, and stimulating members' aid to developing countries. Members are Australia, Austria, Belgium, Canada, Chile, the Czech Republic, Denmark, Estonia, Finland, France, Germany, Greece, Hungary, Iceland, Ireland, Israel, Italy, Japan, South Korea, Luxembourg, Mexico, The Netherlands, New Zealand, Norway, Poland, Portugal, Slovakia, Slovenia, Spain, Sweden, Switzerland, Turkey, UK, and the USA. Its headquarters are in Paris.

(⊕) SEE WEB LINKS
- Website of the OECD: links to detailed economic statistics for all member countries

Organization of the Petroleum Exporting Countries (OPEC) An organization created in 1960 to unify and coordinate the petroleum policies of

Organization chart. A chart of the top management of a typical company.

member countries and to protect their interests, individually and collectively. Present members are Algeria, Angola, Ecuador, Iran, Iraq, Kuwait, Libya, Nigeria, Qatar, Saudi Arabia, UAE, and Venezuela.

organized market A formal market in a specific place in which buyers and sellers meet to trade according to agreed rules and procedures. Stock exchanges, financial futures exchanges, and commodity markets are examples of organized markets.

organogram See ORGANIZATION CHART.

origin 1. The country from which a commodity originates. **Shipment from origin** denotes goods that are shipped directly from their country of origin, rather than from stocks in some other place. See also CERTIFICATE OF ORIGIN. **2.** The country from which a person comes. A person's country of origin is not necessarily his country of *domicile or residence (see RESIDENT).

original cost The cost of an item at the time of purchase or creation. This applies particularly to *fixed assets in which depreciation by the *straight-line method uses the original cost as a basis for the calculation. See also HISTORICAL COST.

original-entry book See BOOK OF PRIME ENTRY.

original goods Natural products that have no economic value until factors of production are applied to them. They include virgin land, wild fruit, natural waterways, etc.

OTC Bulletin Board (OTCBB) A regulated quotation service for equities sold on the US *over-the-counter market. It provides real-time quotes and last-sale prices for stocks that are not listed on one of the major US exchanges. The OTCBB was created by the National Association of Securities Dealers Inc. (NASD) in 1990.

⊕ SEE WEB LINKS
• OTCBB information

OTE Abbreviation for on-target earnings, which represents the salary and commission a salesman should be able to earn.

ouguiya (MRO) The standard monetary unit of Mauritania, divided into 5 khoums.

out-barrier option An *option that is eliminated when the value of the *underlying reaches a certain level, at which point the initial premium is partly refunded. *Compare* IN-BARRIER OPTION.

outdoor training programme An intervention in which employees are taken to a remote location, often in a National Park or similar area, and presented with a series of challenging physical exercises, which typically involve an element of group problem solving. The aim is usually to develop leadership potential, boost confidence, and build a sense of belonging to a team (*see* TEAM-BUILDING EXERCISES).

outlay cost The expenditure incurred as the initial cost of a project or activity. The outlay cost may include both *capital expenditure and expenditure on working capital, such as stocks of raw material.

outlay tax *See* SALES TAX.

out-of-control process *See* STATISTICAL PROCESS CONTROL.

out-of-pocket costs The additional costs that will be incurred as the result of a particular decision. In some circumstances, these costs will be more relevant to decision making than the total differential cash flows. For example, an organization with limited cash resources may decide to pursue an investment alternative that would not have been the first choice had it not offered the lowest level of out-of-pocket costs. *See also* RELEVANT COST.

out of the money *See* IN THE MONEY.

outplacement counselling Helping employees who are made redundant to come to terms with the situation and find jobs elsewhere. When faced with making workers redundant, progressive employers will often arrange for their employees to receive psychological support as well as career advice and assistance in seeking alternative work.

output tax The VAT that a trader adds to the price of the goods or services he supplies. He or she must account for this output tax to HM Revenue and Customs, having first deducted the *input tax.

outside broker A stockbroker who is not a member of a stock exchange but acts as an intermediary between the public and a stockbroker who is a member.

outside director A US term for a *non-executive director.

outsourcing The buying in of components, sub-assemblies, finished products, and services from outside suppliers rather than by supplying them internally. A firm may decide to buy in rather than supply internally because it lacks the expertise, investment capital, or physical space required to do so. It may also be able to buy in more cheaply or more quickly than manufacturing in-house. More recently this decision may be taken in the process of *business process re-engineering or *downsizing, when specific activities have been redefined as noncore activities. In certain instances, computer, legal, and personnel services have been outsourced as well as the more traditional manufactured components.

outstanding shares *See* SHARES OUTSTANDING.

outwork Work carried out in a person's own home or workshop rather than on a company's premises. The term is mainly applied to poorly paid manual work, as opposed to white-collar *teleworking. In Western countries, the use of outworkers declined in the earlier part of the 20th century but the practice is still common in developing economies (e.g. in the garment industry).

overbought 1. Having purchased more of a good than one needs or has orders for. **2.** Having purchased more securities or commodities than are covered by margins deposited with a broker or dealer. In a falling market, for example, a bull speculator can become overbought without having made a fresh purchase. **3.** Denoting a market that has risen too rapidly as a result of excessive buying. An overbought market is unstable and likely to fall if unsupported. *Compare* OVERSOLD.

overcapacity The situation that arises when a firm or industry has greater capacity than the market demand. It may be caused by a temporary downturn in the economy or *business cycle, overinvestment in capacity by existing or new entrants, or a permanent decline in demand for a product or service. In the last case, it is likely to be followed by restructuring throughout the industry, resulting in capacity being reduced through merger and closure in order to bring it into line with demand.

overcapitalization A condition in which an organization has too much *capital for the needs of its business. If a business has more capital than it needs it is likely to be overburdened by interest charges or by the need to spread profits too thinly by way of dividends to shareholders. Businesses can now reduce overcapitalization by repaying long-term debts or by buying their own shares. *Compare* UNDERCAPITALIZATION.

overdraft A loan made to a customer with a cheque account at a bank or building society, in which the account is allowed to go into debit, usually up to a specified limit (the **overdraft limit**). Interest is charged on the daily debit balance. This is a less costly way of borrowing than taking a *bank loan (providing the interest rates are the same) as, with an overdraft, credits are taken into account.

over-entry certificate A document issued by HM Revenue and Customs stating that imported goods have paid excessive duty on entry into the country, which may be reclaimed. If too little duty has been paid, **post-entry** duty is claimed.

overhead (overhead cost) An *indirect cost of an organization. Overheads are usually classified as *manufacturing overheads, administration overheads, *selling overheads, *distribution overheads, and *research and development costs.

overheating The state of an economy during a boom, with increasing *aggregate demand leading to rising prices rather than higher output. Overheating reflects the inability of some firms to increase output to keep up with demand; they therefore choose to profit from the excess demand by raising prices.

overinsurance The practice of insuring an item for a greater amount than its value. This is pointless as insurers are only obliged to pay the full value (usually the replacement value) of an insured item and no more, even if the sum insured exceeds this value. If insurers find a policyholder has overinsured an item, the premium for the cover above the true value is returned.

overinvestment Excessive investment of capital, especially in the manufacturing industry towards the end of a boom as a result of over-optimistic expectations of future demand. When the boom begins to fade, the manufacturer is left with surplus capacity and can therefore make no further capital investments, which itself creates unemployment and fuels the imminent recession. It is often seen with new technology investment booms.

overnight index swap A *fixed-for-floating *interest-rate swap in which a fixed rate is swapped with a floating rate derived from an overnight index, such as *SONIA or *EONIA. *See* OVERNIGHT RATE.

overnight loan A loan made by a bank to a *bill broker to enable the broker to take up *bills of exchange. Initially the loan will be repayable the following day but it is usually renewable. If it is not, the broker must turn to the *lender of last resort, i.e. the Bank of England in the UK.

overnight position An *open position held overnight.

overnight rate The interest rate at which major banks lend to one another on the overnight market (i.e. for repayment the next day). Indexes of the average overnight rate, such as *SONIA and *EONIA, provide an important *reference rate.

overpositioning A *positioning error in which too narrow a picture of a company, its product, or a brand is communicated to target customers.

overseas company A company incorporated outside the UK that has a branch or a subsidiary company in the UK. Overseas companies are subject to the provisions of the Companies Act 2006 relating to registration, accounts, constitution, directors, etc.

overseas-income taxation Taxation of income that has been subject to taxation outside the jurisdiction of the UK tax authorities. When the same income is subject to taxation in more than one country, relief for the double tax is given either under the provisions of the *double taxation agreement with the country concerned or unilaterally.

overseas investment Investment by the government, industry, or members of the public of a country in the industry of another country. For members of the public this is often most easily achieved by investing through foreign stock exchanges.

overseas joint ownership A *joint venture in which a company joins investors in a foreign market to create a local business in which the company shares ownership and control.

overshooting On financial markets, the tendency for a security, commodity, currency etc. to jump (or fall) suddenly in value and then to drop (or rise) slowly until it finds a new equilibrium. Overshooting has been used as an explanation of exchange-rate movements arising from adjustment problems in economies.

overside delivery The unloading of a cargo over the side of a ship into *lighters.

oversold 1. Having sold more of a product or service than one can produce or purchase. **2.** Denoting a market that has fallen too fast as a result of excessive selling. It may therefore be expected to have an upward reaction.

oversubscription The situation that arises when there are more applications for a *new issue of securities than there are securities available. In these circumstances, applications have to be scaled down

according to a set of rules devised by the company issuing the shares or their advisors. Alternatively some companies prefer to allocate the shares by ballot (*see* ALLOTMENT). Oversubscription usually occurs because of the difficulty in arriving at an issue price that will be low enough to attract sufficient investors to take up the whole issue and yet will give the company the maximum capital. Speculative purchases by *stags also make it difficult to price a new issue so that it is neither oversubscribed nor undersubscribed. In the case of **undersubscription**, which is rare, the *underwriter has to take up that part of the issue that has not been bought by the public. Undersubscription can occur if some unexpected event occurs after the announcement of the issue price but before the issue date.

over-the-counter market (OTC market) A market in which financial obligations are bought and sold outside the jurisdiction of a recognized financial market; it was originally so named in the 1870s, from the practice of buying shares over bank counters in the USA. OTC markets are used for trading in specific tailor-made *derivative products. The world's largest OTC market is *NASDAQ.

overtime Hours worked in excess of an agreed number per week or per day. The payment made for overtime work is usually higher than the basic rate of pay. Unions therefore have an interest in making the basic working week as short as possible, so that those working longer hours earn as much as possible. Employers, on the other hand, want to make the working week as long as possible.

overtime ban A form of *industrial action in which employees refuse to work *overtime, thus causing considerable dislocation to normal working but clearly less than would occur in a total *strike. Overtime bans are usually supported and often organized by unions. *See also* WORK-TO-RULE.

overtrading Trading by an organization beyond the resources provided by its existing capital. Overtrading tends to lead to *liquidity problems as too much stock is bought on credit and too much credit is extended to customers, so that ultimately there is not sufficient cash available to pay the debts as they arise. The solution is either to cut back on trading or to raise further permanent capital.

own brand (own label; distributor brand; private brand; house brand) A product sold under a distributor's own name or trademark through its own outlets. These items are either made specially for the distributor or are versions of the equivalent *manufacturer brand. Own-brand goods are promoted by the distributor rather than the manufacturer and are typically 10–20% cheaper to the distributor than an equivalent brand. Own brands are sold principally by *multiple shops.

owners' equity The beneficial interest in an organization held by its owners, i.e. the sum of its total assets less its total liabilities. The balance-sheet or *book value of the owners' equity is unlikely to be equal to its *market value. *See also* NET ASSETS; NET WORTH.

ownership Rights over property, including rights of possession, exclusive enjoyment, destruction, etc. In UK common law, land cannot be owned outright, as all land belongs to the Crown and is held in tenure by the 'owner'. However, an owner of an estate in land in fee simple is to all intents and purposes an outright owner. In general, ownership can be split between different persons. For example, a trustee has the legal ownership of trust property but the beneficiary has the equitable or beneficial ownership. If goods are stolen, the owner still has ownership but not possession. Similarly, if goods are hired or pledged to someone, the owner has ownership but no immediate right to possession.

own label *See* OWN BRAND.

own shares purchase The purchase or redemption of its own shares by a company; this is permitted subject to certain legal restrictions. For example, in the UK redeemable shares may only be redeemed if they are fully paid. If the redemption or purchase of a company's own shares would lead to a reduction of its capital, a *capital redemption reserve will need to be created. The Companies Act 2006 made it easier for private companies to reduce their capital in this way. *See also* PERMISSIBLE CAPITAL PAYMENT.

PA 1. Abbreviation for personal account, used to denote a transaction made by a professional investment adviser for his own account rather than for the firm for which he or she works. **2.** Abbreviation for *personal assistant. **3.** Abbreviation for *power of attorney. **4.** Abbreviation for particular average. *See* AVERAGE.

pa'anga (TOP) The standard monetary unit of Tonga, divided into 100 seniti.

Paasche's index *See* INDEX NUMBER.

PACE Acronym for price, assortment, convenience, entertainment. A summary of the benefits available to customers using e-commerce.

package *See* BUSINESS SOFTWARE PACKAGE.

package deal An agreement that encompasses several different parts, all of which must be accepted. A package deal may have involved either or both parties in making concessions on specific aspects of the package in order to arrive at a compromise arrangement.

packaging 1. The design of wrappers or containers for a product. **2.** The wrappers or containers themselves. **3.** An activity that combines several operations and enables the packager to deliver a finished or near-finished product to a selling organization. For example, many non-fiction books are produced by **book packagers**, who write, illustrate, typeset, and print books, which they deliver to publishers, who sell them to the public under their own imprint.

PageRank An algorithm used by the search engine Google to evaluate the importance of any individual web page. In simple terms, it does this by gauging the number of relevant and useful links between the page in question and other sites, on the assumption that this reflects the value of the page to Internet users. As PageRank determines the prominence of a page in Google's search-result listings, businesses will often take deliberate steps to secure a higher rank for their website. *See* SEARCH-ENGINE OPTIMIZATION.

paid-up policy An *endowment assurance policy in which the assured has decided to stop paying premiums before the end of the policy term. This results in a *surrender value, which instead of being returned in cash to the assured is used to purchase a single-premium *whole life policy. In this way the life assurance protection continues (for a reduced amount), while the policyholder is relieved of the need to pay further premiums. If the original policy was a *with-profits policy, the bonuses paid up to the time the premiums ceased would be included in the surrender value. If it is a unit-linked policy, capital units actually allocated would be allowed to appreciate to the end of the term.

paid-up share capital The *issued share capital of a company when this consists of *fully paid shares, payment for which has been received. *Compare* CALLED-UP SHARE CAPITAL.

paired comparisons 1. A technique used in marketing research in which consumers are presented with pairs of competing products and asked to choose the one they prefer. This technique can be used to compare, say, a number of brands of soap, giving respondents two at a time to compare. The number of times each brand is selected as a preference in a large number of such tests will reveal an order of brand preference. *Compare* MONADIC TESTING. **2.** A method of *employee evaluation in which each worker in a group is compared with each other worker on one or more performance measures. Employees are then ranked according to the number of favourable comparisons they receive.

paisa (*plural* **paise**) A monetary unit of Bangladesh, Bhutan, India, Nepal, and Pakistan, worth one hundredth of a *rupee.

pallet A wooden frame on which certain goods are stacked in warehouses and during transport. Pallets are designed to be lifted by fork-lift trucks or pallet trucks.

palmtop computer See PDA.

P & L account See PROFIT AND LOSS ACCOUNT.

Panel on Takeovers and Mergers See CITY CODE ON TAKEOVERS AND MERGERS.

paper An informal name for securities that can be bought and sold or held as an investment. It is used particularly on the *money market for *debt instruments maturing in less than 90 days. See COMMERCIAL PAPER; EURO-COMMERCIAL PAPER.

paper bid See SHARE-FOR-SHARE OFFER.

paper profit A profit shown by the books or accounts of an organization that is not a *realized profit. This is usually for one of three reasons:

- because the value of an asset has fallen below its book value;
- because the asset, although nominally showing a profit, has not actually been sold;
- because some technicality of book-keeping shows an activity to be profitable when it is not.

For example, a share that has risen in value since its purchase might show a paper profit but this would not be a real profit since the value of the share might fall again before it is sold.

paper sizes See INTERNATIONAL PAPER SIZES.

paper trail See AUDIT TRAIL.

par See PAR VALUE.

para A monetary unit of Serbia, worth one hundredth of a *dinar.

paradox of community size The observation that small groups produce more active members and stimulate individual contributions, but that large group sizes are necessary to produce enough committed members. The paradox is often cited in connection with Internet communities but has many wider applications.

parallel hedge A *hedge in which exposure to fluctuation in one foreign currency is matched by a purchase or sale of another currency, which is expected to move in sympathy with the first currency.

parallel processing A method of computing in which two or more parts of a program are executed simultaneously rather than sequentially. Strictly, parallel processing is only possible on computers with more than one arithmetic and logical unit in the central processing unit, but it is often simulated on other machines by such techniques as *time sharing.

par banking The US practice of one bank paying the full face value of a cheque drawn on another bank, without imposing a charge for encashment. Members of the *Federal Reserve System are obliged to comply with the rules of par banking.

par bond A security or financial instrument that is bought and sold at its face value, rather than at a discount or premium.

parent company (parent undertaking) See HOLDING COMPANY.

parenting The way in which the directors of the main *holding company of a large group manage their relationships with the subsidiary companies or business units. The method by which control is exercised varies, with some firms concentrating on financial control and others on the broader strategic targets. *See* STRATEGIC STYLES.

Pareto chart A type of *bar chart in which vertical bars representing the relative frequency (or cost) of a set of factors are displayed in descending order of size (i.e. with the most significant factor or cause on the left and the least so on the right). A line graph is generally superimposed to show the cumulative total of the frequencies; this will rise to 100% at the right vertical axis. The purpose is to enable an analysis of the most common causes of a problem (e.g. defects in a product) in terms of *Pareto's Rule. For example, a Pareto chart might show that some 80% of defects could be eradicated by tackling only two or three causes. The chart is one of the *seven tools of quality.

Pareto efficiency In economic theory, an alteration in the allocation of resources is said to be Pareto efficient when it leaves at least one person better off and nobody worse off. A state of **Pareto optimality** occurs when no further Pareto-efficient changes can be made. The concept was first described by the Italian economist Vilfredo Pareto (1848–1923). *Compare* KALDOR–HICKS EFFICIENCY.

Pareto's Rule (80/20 rule) A rule originally applied by the economist Vilfredo Pareto (1848–1923) to income distribution, i.e. 80% of a nation's income is earned by 20% of the population. It can be widely extended as a rule of thumb; for example: 80% of value is locked up in 20% of inventory; 80% of car breakdowns can be fixed by 20% of the spare parts range; 80% of a company's profits will come from 20% of its product range; and 80% of system failures will be caused by 20% of possible causes. The rule can be used as a guide to managers: in deciding how to spend limited funds, priority should be given to the most significant 20% of problems. Once they are eliminated the 80/20 rule will again apply to the remainder. *See* PARETO CHART. *See also* LONG TAIL.

pari passu (Latin: with equal step) Ranking equally. When a new issue of shares is said to rank *pari passu* with existing shares, the new shares carry the same dividend rights and winding-up rights as the existing shares. A *pari passu* loan is one in which the borrower agrees that this new loan will rank equally with other existing debts.

Paris Bourse From January 1991, the only stock exchange in France, incorporating the six provincial stock exchanges in Bordeaux, Lille, Lyons, Marseilles, Nancy, and Nantes. The merger recognized the dominance of the Paris Bourse, which accounted for 95% of all trading in French securities. The **CAC** (Cotation Assistée en Continue) electronic trading system was introduced in 1988 and the **NSC** (Nouveau Système de Cotation) in 1995. The **CAC-40** is the benchmark index. From the late 1990s the Paris Bourse led the way in the creation of the pan-European exchange *Euronext NV, of which it is now a division (**Euronext Paris**).

Paris Club *See* GROUP OF TEN.

parity 1. An equality between prices of commodities, currencies, or securities on separate markets. **2.** A fixed exchange rate. **3.** Another term for *par value.

parking 1. Putting company shares that one owns in the name of someone else or of nominees in order to hide their real ownership. This is often illegal. *See also* WAREHOUSING. **2.** Holding assets in a short-term riskless form pending an investment decision.

Parkinson's laws The propositions made by the British writer Cyril Northcote Parkinson (1909–93) in his book *Parkinson's Law*. Facetious but often confirmed in practice, they include such aphorisms as: work expands to fill the time available in which to do it; expenditure rises to meet income; and subordinates multiply at a fixed rate that is independent of the amount of work produced. They were devised with large organizations in mind and it is to such organizations that they principally apply—unless managers take steps to ensure that they do not. *See also* DILBERT PRINCIPLE; PETER PRINCIPLE.

p

par of exchange The theoretical *rate of exchange between two currencies in which there is equilibrium between the supply and demand for each currency. The par value lies between the market buying and selling rates. *See also* MINT PAR OF EXCHANGE.

partial loss *See* AVERAGE.

participated loan (participation financing) A large loan, exceeding the lending limit of an individual bank, that is shared among a group of lenders.

participating interest An interest held by one organization in the shares of another organization, provided these shares are held on a long-term basis for the purpose of exercising some measure of control or influence over the organization's activities. The UK Companies Act lays down that a holding of 20% or more of the shares of an organization constitutes a participating interest, unless contrary indications are given. Options to buy shares are normally treated as an interest in these shares. *See also* CONTROLLING INTEREST; MINORITY INTEREST.

participating preference share *See* PREFERENCE SHARE.

participation financing *See* PARTICIPATED LOAN.

participative decision making The inclusion of employees (or their representatives) in the process of management decision making. This can range from a fairly limited form of consultation to a situation in which workers take responsibility for major decisions. *See* INDUSTRIAL DEMOCRACY.

participator Any person having an interest in the capital or income of a company, e.g. a shareholder, loan creditor, or any person entitled to participate in the *distributions of the company.

particular average (PA) *See* AVERAGE.

partly paid share A share the full *par value of which has not been paid by the shareholder. Formerly, partly paid shares were issued by some banks and insurance companies to inspire confidence, in the knowledge that they could always call on their shareholders for further funds if necessary. Shareholders, however, did not like the liability of being called upon to pay out further sums for their shares and the practice largely died out. It has been revived for large new share issues, especially in *privatizations, in which shareholders pay an initial sum for their shares and subsequently pay one or more *calls on specified dates. *Compare* FULLY PAID SHARE. *See also* CALLED-UP SHARE CAPITAL; PAID-UP SHARE CAPITAL.

partnership An association of two or more people (**partners**) formed for the purpose of carrying on a business. Partnerships are governed by the Partnership Act 1890. Unlike an incorporated *company, a partnership does not have a legal personality of its own and therefore, as a general rule, partners are liable for the debts of the firm. **General partners** are fully liable for these debts, **limited partners** only to the extent of their investment. A **limited partnership** is one consisting of both general and limited partners and is governed by the Limited Partnership Act 1907. The *Limited Liability Partnership Act 2000 now enables some categories of business partnership to claim limited liability in a similar fashion to that enjoyed by *limited companies. A **partnership-at-will** is one for which no fixed term has been agreed. Any partner may end the partnership at any time provided that notice of the intention to do so is given to all the other partners. **Nominal partners** allow their names to be used for the benefit of the partnership, usually for a reward but not for a share of the profits. They are not legal partners. Partnerships are usually governed by a *partnership agreement.

partnership accounts The accounts kept by a *partnership. They include an *appropriation account in which the profit is shared between the partners in accordance with the *partnership agreement. This may be in the form of salaries, interest on capital, and a share of the profit in the appropriate *profit-sharing ratio. Each partner also has a *capital account and a *current account. The former is used to account for capital contributions, *goodwill, and revaluations; the latter for all other transactions, such as appropriations of profit and *drawings.

partnership agreement (articles of partnership) An agreement made between the partners of a *partnership. In the absence of either an express or an implied agreement the provisions of the Partnership Act 1890 apply. These provisions are also applicable if an agreement is silent on a particular point. The provisions are:

- partners share equally in the profits or losses of the partnership;
- partners are not entitled to receive salaries;
- partners are not entitled to interest on their capital;
- partners may receive interest at 5% per annum on any advances over and above their agreed capital;
- a new partner may not be introduced unless all the existing partners consent;
- a retiring partner is entitled to receive interest at 5% per annum on his or her share of the partnership assets retained in the partnership after his or her retirement;
- on dissolution of the partnership the assets of the firm must be used first to repay outside creditors, secondly to repay partners' advances, and thirdly to repay partners' capital. Any residue on dissolution should be distributed to the partners in the *profit-sharing ratio.

See also LIMITED LIABILITY PARTNERSHIP.

partnership-at-will *See* PARTNERSHIP.

par value (face value; nominal value) The *nominal price of a share or other security. If the market value of a security exceeds the nominal price it is said to be **above par**; if it falls below the nominal price it is **below par**. Gilt-edged securities are always repaid **at par** (usually £100), i.e. at the par value.

passing a name The disclosure by a firm of brokers of the name of the principal for whom they are acting. In some commodity trades, if brokers disclose the names of their buyers to the sellers, they do not guarantee the buyers' solvency, although they may do so in some circumstances. However, if brokers do not pass their principals' names, it is usual for them to guarantee their solvency. Thus, to remain anonymous, a buyer may have to pay an additional brokerage.

passing off Conducting a business in a manner that misleads the public into thinking that one's goods or services are those of another business. The commonest form of passing off is marketing goods with a design, packaging, or trade name that is very similar to that of someone else's goods. It is not necessary to prove an intention to deceive; innocent passing off is actionable.

passing the book Transferring the management of a financial *position from one office of a business to another in a different time zone to take advantage of *24-hour trading.

passive management A style of *portfolio management that involves holding assets over the long term and, in many cases, tracking a market index. *Compare* ACTIVE MANAGEMENT.

past-due loan A banking loan on which the interest is more than 90 days overdue. After this grace period has elapsed, the borrower becomes liable for late charges.

pataca (MOP) The standard monetary unit of Macao, divided into 100 avos.

patent The grant of an exclusive right to exploit an invention. In the UK patents are granted by the Crown through the *Intellectual Property Office (IPO). An applicant for a patent (usually the inventor or the inventor's employer) must show that the invention is new, is not obvious, and is capable of industrial application. An expert known as a *patent attorney often prepares the application, which must describe the invention in considerable detail. The IPO publishes these details if it grants a patent. A patent remains valid for 20 years from the date of application (the **priority date**) provided that the person to whom it has been granted (the **patentee**) continues to pay the appropriate fees. During this time, the patentee may assign the patent or grant licences to use it. Such transactions are registered in a public register at the IPO. If anyone infringes the patentee's monopoly, the patentee may sue for an *injunction and *damages or an account of profits. However, a patent from the Patent Office gives exclusive rights in the UK only: the inventor must obtain a patent from the European Patent Office in Munich and patents in other foreign countries to protect the invention elsewhere. For patents internationally the Patent Cooperation Treaty procedure can be used. A patent is a form of *intellectual property and as such is an *intangible asset.

patent attorney (patent agent) A member of the Chartered Institute of Patent Attorneys (CIPA), who gives advice on obtaining *patents and prepares patent applications.

paternity rights See MATERNITY RIGHTS.

pathfinder prospectus An outline *prospectus concerning the flotation of a new company in the UK; it includes enough details to test the market reaction to the new company but not its main financial details or the price of its shares. Pathfinder prospectuses are known in the USA as **red herrings**.

path-goal leadership model A theory of leadership suggesting that a leader needs to influence followers' perceptions of work goals, self-development goals, and paths to goal attainment. A leader will be successful to the extent that he or she creates an expectancy that effort will lead to accomplishment and that accomplishment will produce valued rewards. The *leadership style best suited to achieve this will depend on the characteristics of followers and the nature of the work setting. The model is a

development of the *valence-instrumentality-expectancy theory of motivation.

patronage rewards Cash or other rewards for the regular use of a certain company's products or services.

pawnbroker A person who lends money against the security of valuable goods used as collateral. Borrowers can reclaim their goods by repaying the loan and interest within a stated period. However, if the borrower defaults the pawnbroker is free to sell the goods. The operation of pawnbrokers is governed by the Consumer Credit Act 1974.

payable to bearer Describing a *bill of exchange in which neither the payee nor endorsee are named. A holder, by adding his name, can make the bill *payable to order.

payable to order Describing a *bill of exchange in which the payee is named and on which there are no restrictions or endorsements; it can therefore be paid to the endorsee.

pay-as-you-earn See PAYE.

pay-as-you-go pension system (unfunded pension system) A system in which state retirement benefits are financed by contributions levied from current workers, as opposed to a funded system in which contributions are invested to pay for future benefits. The British *National Insurance system is a pay-as-you-go system.

payback period method A method of *capital budgeting in which the time required before the projected cash inflows for a project equal the investment expenditure is calculated; this time is compared to a required payback period to determine whether or not the project should be considered for approval. If the projected cash inflows are constant annual sums, after an initial capital investment the following formula may be used:

$$payback(years) = initial\ capital\ investment/annual\ cash\ inflow.$$

Otherwise, the annual cash inflows are accumulated and the year determined when the cumulative inflows equal the investment expenditure. The method is sometimes seen as a measure of the risk involved in the project.

The two major weaknesses of the payback method are:

- the *time value of money is not considered;
- the cash flows after the investment is recovered are not considered.

However, payback is a relatively simple technique for managers to use and for this reason it remains popular. Often managers use payback and *discounted cash flow techniques at the same time, even though they are very different methods of capital budgeting (*see* DISCOUNTED PAYBACK METHOD).

PAYE Pay-as-you-earn. The UK scheme for collecting income tax and *National Insurance contributions, under which the onus is placed on employers to collect the tax from their employees as payments are made to them. There is an elaborate system of administration to ensure that broadly the correct amount of tax is deducted week by week or month by month and that the employer remits the tax collected to HM Revenue and Customs very quickly. The amount of tax due is calculated using *income tax codes and tax tables supplied to employers by the Revenue (now usually in the form of computer software). Although technically called pay-as-you-earn, the system would be better called 'pay-as-you-get-paid'.

((⊕)) SEE WEB LINKS

- An introduction to PAYE for employers from the HMRC website

payee A person or organization to be paid. In the case of a cheque payment, the payee is the person or organization to whom the cheque is made payable.

payer A person or organization who makes a payment.

paying agent A bank or other organization that contracts under a **paying agency agreement** to pay the interest and capital sums due on a *bearer security.

paying banker The bank on which a *bill of exchange (including a cheque) has been drawn and which is responsible for paying it if it is correctly drawn and correctly endorsed (if necessary).

paying-in book A book of slips used to pay cash, cheques, etc., into a bank account. The counterfoil of the slip is stamped by the bank if the money is paid in over the counter.

payment by results A system of payment in which an employee's pay is directly linked to his performance. The majority are *premium bonus schemes. *See also* PIECE RATE; LUMP SUM.

payment for honour *See* ACCEPTANCE SUPRA PROTEST.

payment in advance (prepayment) Payment for goods or services before they have been received. In company accounts, this often refers to rates or rents paid for periods that carry over into the next accounting period.

payment in due course The payment of a *bill of exchange when it matures (becomes due).

payment in kind A payment that is not made in cash but in goods or services. It is often in the form of a discount or an allowance, e.g. cheap fares for British Airways employees, staff prices for food at supermarkets, etc. Now regarded as a bonus or *fringe benefit, payment in kind in the 19th century was widespread; the Truck Acts 1831 were passed to discourage employers who insisted on paying their employees in goods instead of cash (as often the cash value of goods bought in bulk by the employer was much less than their value to the employee).

payment on account 1. A payment made for goods or services before the goods or services are finally billed. *See also*

p

DEPOSIT. **2.** A payment towards meeting a liability that is not the full amount of the liability. The sum paid will be credited to the account of the payer in the books of the payee as a part-payment of the ultimate liability.

payment supra protest *See* ACCEPTANCE SUPRA PROTEST.

payment terms The agreed way in which a buyer pays the seller for goods. The commonest are cash with order or cash on delivery; prompt cash (i.e. within 14 days of delivery); cash in 30, 60, or 90 days from date of invoice; *letter of credit; *cash against documents; *documents against acceptance; or *acceptance credit.

payoff The value of a portfolio or a single financial obligation at a particular date or at the expiry of an instrument. The value is sometimes calculated in absolute terms and sometimes in terms of the gain made over a given time period.

PayPal A secure online system that enables account holders to pay for goods or services and arrange money transfers over the Internet. PayPal, which operates in 26 currencies worldwide, became a wholly owned subsidiary of *eBay in 2002.

payroll tax A tax based on the total of an organization's payroll. The main function of such a tax would be to discourage high wages or over-employment. The current employers' Class 1 *National Insurance contributions constitute such a tax.

PBGC Abbreviation for *Pension Benefit Guaranty Corporation.

PC Abbreviation for *personal computer.

PCP Abbreviation for *permissible capital payment.

PDA (palmtop computer) Abbreviation for personal digital assistant; a small handheld device that allows the user to store and retrieve information, such as addresses, telephone numbers, dates, etc. It can usually transfer data to or from a personal computer and access the Internet via

*Bluetooth. Since the early 2000s dedicated PDAs have been rendered more or less obsolete by the advent of the *smartphone.

PDCA Abbreviation for Plan, Do, Check, Act: a four-stage cycle widely used in *feedback control. The stages are: (1) define goals and the processes required to achieve them; (2) put these into practice; (3) review the results by comparing output with objectives; (4) seek improvements by modifying the plan, the implementation, and the review process as necessary. The cycle is to be repeated indefinitely in pursuit of *continuous improvement.

PDE Abbreviation for *prepared data entry.

PDF Abbreviation for portable document format. *See* ACROBAT.

PDR (P/D ratio) Abbreviations for *price–dividend ratio.

peaceful picketing *See* PICKETING.

peak time The period of television airtime, usually the middle part of the evening, for which the highest advertising rate is charged as during this period the highest number of people are viewing.

peering arrangement A formal or informal agreement made between independent networking companies governing the way in which Internet traffic moves between their networks.

peer-to-peer lending (P2P lending; social lending) The growing practice in which those with spare funds lend money to small businesses or private borrowers via a dedicated website, thus avoiding the intermediation of a bank. This usually brings a higher return but carries a higher risk of default. Peer-to-peer lending sites were formerly unregulated but came under the remit of the new *Financial Conduct Authority in April 2014. *See also* CROWDFUNDING.

pegging 1. (pegging the exchange) The fixing of the value of a country's currency on foreign exchange markets. *See* CRAWLING PEG; FIXED EXCHANGE RATE.

2. The fixing of wages or prices at existing levels by government order to prevent them rising during a period of *inflation.

penalty An arbitrary prearranged sum that becomes payable if one party breaches a contract or undertaking. It is usually expressly stated in a **penalty clause** of the contract. Unlike liquidated *damages, a penalty will be disregarded by the courts and treated as being void. Liquidated damages will generally be treated as a penalty if the amount payable is extravagant and unconscionable compared with the maximum loss that could result from the breach. However, use of the words 'penalty' or 'liquidated damages' is inconclusive as the legal position depends on the interpretation by the courts of the clause in which they appear.

penetration *See* MARKET PENETRATION.

penni (*plural* **penniä**) A former monetary unit of Finland, worth one hundredth of a *markka (until 2002).

penny 1. A monetary unit of the UK, worth one hundredth of a *pound.   **2.** A former monetary unit of the Republic of Ireland, worth one hundredth of a *punt (until 2002).

penny shares Securities with a very low market price (although they may not be as low as one penny) traded on a stock exchange. They are popular with small investors, who can acquire a significant holding in a company for a very low cost. Moreover, a rise of a few pence in a low-priced share can represent a high percentage profit. However, they are usually shares in companies that have fallen on hard times and may, indeed, be close to bankruptcy. The investor in this type of share is hoping for a rapid recovery or a takeover.

pension A specified sum paid regularly to a person who has reached a certain age or retired from employment. It is normally paid from the date of reaching the specified age or the retirement date until death.

In the UK, contributory **retirement pensions** are usually paid by the state from the normal retirement age (until 2010 65 for men and 60 for women, now gradually adjusting to 65 for both in 2018 and 67 for both in 2028) irrespective of whether or not the pensioners have retired from full-time employment. A widow who was bereaved before 9 April 2001 may also receive a state pension based on her husband's contributions.

From 1978 state pensions were augmented by the *State Earnings-Related Pension Scheme (SERPS); this has now been replaced by a non-earnings-related scheme, the *State Second Pension.

The private sector of the insurance industry also provides a wide variety of *occupational pension schemes, *personal pension schemes, and *stakeholder pension schemes, as well as *annuities and *endowment assurances. Financial analysts predict a major pensions crisis in the mid-21st century, since demographic trends will produce an ever-growing number of people beyond retirement age drawing on insufficient state and personal provision. *See* PAY-AS-YOU-GO PENSION SYSTEM.

(⊕) SEE WEB LINKS
• Information about state pensions from the Gov.uk website

pensionable earnings The part of an employee's salary that is used to calculate the final pension entitlement. Unless otherwise stated, overtime, commission, and bonuses are normally excluded.

Pension Benefit Guaranty Corporation (PBGC) A US federal agency that insures *defined-benefit pension schemes of companies. It was established under the Employee Retirement Income Security Act 1974 (ERISA).

pensioneer trustee A person authorized to oversee the management of a *pension fund in accordance with the provisions of the Pension Trust Deed.

pension funds State and private pension contributions invested to give as high a return as possible to provide the funds from which pensions are paid. In the UK, pension funds managed by individual organizations work closely with insurance companies and investment trusts, being together the *institutional investors that have a dominant influence on many securities traded on the London Stock Exchange. An enormous amount of money is accumulated by these pension funds, which grows by weekly and monthly contributions; real estate and works of art are often purchased for investment by pension funds in addition to stock-exchange securities.

Pensions Regulator The UK regulatory body responsible for protecting the benefits of those in work-based pension schemes; this includes all occupational schemes and any other schemes in which payments are made through the employer.

PEP Abbreviation for personal equity plan.

peppercorn rent A nominal rent. In theory one peppercorn (or some other nominal sum) is payable as a rent to indicate that a property is leasehold and not *freehold, the peppercorn representing the *consideration. In practice it amounts to a rent-free lease.

P/E ratio Abbreviation for *price–earnings ratio.

per capita income The average income of a group, obtained by dividing the group's total income by its number of members. The **national per capita income** is the ratio of the national income to the population.

percent of sales method A method of setting a promotional budget in which the amount budgeted is a set percentage of the sales revenue, often a standard percentage for a given industry. Car companies are known to use a fixed percentage for promotion, based upon the final price of the car.

perceptual mapping The use of mathematical psychology to understand the structure of a market. Consumer images of different brands of a product are plotted on a graph or map; the closer two brands are on the map, the closer they are as

competitors. Perceptual mapping is also used in the development of a new product; the closer a new product appears on a map to an ideal product, the more likely the new product is to succeed. It can be useful in determining competitors' positions and what opportunities there are in unoccupied positions.

per contra Denoting a book-keeping entry of a particular amount on the opposite side of an *account. It is often used when two entries, a debit and a credit, are on opposite sides of the same page, as, for example, a transfer from cash to bank or vice versa, both recorded in the same cash book.

per diem (Latin: per day) Denoting a fee charged by a professional person who is paid a specified fee for each day that he or she is employed.

perfect competition A market in which no buyer or seller has the power to influence prices, which result solely from an equilibrium of supply and demand. For such a market to exist there would have to be a multiplicity of small buyers and sellers, no *barriers to entry, and a state of *perfect information about prices; moreover, the goods offered by the various sellers would have to be undifferentiated to prevent the development of *monopolistic competition. The idea of pure competition is mainly useful as a tool for analysing the ways in which real-world markets diverge from such a model. Probably, no such market has ever truly existed: the nearest approximations would be certain markets for agricultural products and some types of competitive auction (including online auctions).

perfect information In economic theory, a hypothetical state in which each participant in a market has complete up-to-date information about products and prices and can therefore make perfectly rational choices. Perfect information is a precondition of *perfect competition. *See also* ASYMMETRIC INFORMATION; BOUNDED RATIONALITY.

perfecting the sight *See* BILL OF SIGHT.

performance appraisal A formal review of the performance of an employee. The results of the appraisal may be used in deciding an employee's pay or other rewards, career prospects, or training requirements. It usually involves an interview between the employee and his or her immediate manager, although in some cases there may be an element of self-appraisal.

In most organizations, appraisal consists of assessing the employee's ability (or otherwise) to meet expected standards and his or her general demeanour as a member of the workforce. *See also* EMPLOYEE EVALUATION.

performance measurement The process of (a) developing indicators to assess progress towards certain predefined goals and (b) reviewing performance against these measures. Performance measures can be applied to the whole organization or to particular departments, branches, or individuals. They are often divided into:

- **strategic indicators**—related to successful and effective performance over the lifetime of an organization;
- **operational indicators**—related to the success and profitability of products and services; product mixes and portfolios; and productivity and output;
- **specific indicators**—including organization income or profit per member of staff, per customer, per offering, per outlet, per square foot; returns on investment; speed of response; product durability and longevity of usage; volume and quality targets;
- **behavioural indicators**—related to staff management aspects; prevailing attitudes and values; the extent of strikes, disputes, absenteeism, labour turnover, and accidents; harmony/discord, cooperation/conflict; the general aura of well-being;
- **confidence indicators**—reflecting the relationship between the organization and its environment, its backers, its stakeholders, its customers, and its communities;
- **ethical indicators**—reflecting the standards of behaviour and performance that an organization sets for itself and its acceptance in both markets and communities.

A distinction is also made between **financial measures**, such as *return on capital employed, *residual income, and *Economic Value Added, and **non-financial measures**, such as delivery time or customer retention. Management accountants will be particularly interested in identifying how the use of different financial and non-financial measures influences the behaviour of managers. For example, using return on capital employed as a measure will probably encourage managers to reduce investment; this may improve short-term performance figures but will damage the long-term performance of the company. Another problem may arise if managers improve delivery times to meet targets but significantly increase costs in the process. These two examples emphasize the importance of understanding the behavioural aspects of management accounting. Another issue is how to link non-financial and financial measures. The *balanced scorecard is a recent development that connects non-financial and financial performance measures to a company's overall strategy. *See also* GOODHART'S LAW.

performance standard In *standard costing, the standard level of performance to be achieved during a period. For example, a standard performance for direct labour of two standard hours to complete a task would be combined with the *rate per standard hour for labour to create the *standard direct labour cost for the task.

peril *See* RISK. *See also* EXCEPTED PERIL.

period bill (term bill) A *bill of exchange payable on a specific date rather than on demand.

period of grace *See* DAYS OF GRACE.

perks An informal word for **perquisites**, the benefits arising as a result of employment, in addition to regular renumeration.

Perks are privileges that are expected mainly by senior employees (e.g. a company car, private health insurance, gym membership). *See* BENEFITS IN KIND; SHAREHOLDERS' PERKS.

permanent diminution in value A fall in the value of an asset that is unlikely to be reversed. The *fixed asset must be shown in the *balance sheet at the reduced amount, which will be the estimated *recoverable amount. A provision has to be made through the *profit and loss account; if this is subsequently found to be no longer required, it should be written back to the profit and loss account.

permanent establishment A fixed place of business that a taxpayer of one country has in another country, thus rendering the taxpayer liable to that second country's taxation. It will include a place of management, branch, office, factory or workshop, and long-term construction projects but it may exclude some sales offices and storage depots. The concept is important in *double-taxation treaties.

permanent health insurance (PHI) A form of health insurance that provides an income (maximum 75% of salary) up to normal retirement age (or pension age) to replace an income lost by prolonged illness or disability in which the insured is unable to perform any part of his or her normal duties. Premiums are related to age and occupation and normally are fixed; benefits, which are not paid for the first 4–13 weeks of disability, are tax free for one year and thereafter are taxed. *Compare* SICKNESS AND ACCIDENT INSURANCE.

permanent interest bearing share (PIBS) A non-redeemable security, usually issued by a building society, that pays interest at a rate fixed at issue. This is often 10–13.5%, giving investors a high yield for perpetuity. However, these shares carry the risks associated with fixed-interest securities, being the last to be paid out should an issuing building society go into liquidation. Moreover, the second-hand market for PIBS is small (approximately £800 million),

making it difficult to find a buyer at any particular price.

per mille (per mill; per mil) (Latin: per thousand) Denoting that the premium on an insurance policy is the stated figure per £1,000 of insured value. Per mille is also used to mean 0.1% in relation to interest rates.

permissible capital payment (PCP) A payment made out of *capital when a company is redeeming or purchasing its own *shares and has used all available distributable profits as well as the proceeds of any new issue of shares. *See* OWN SHARES PURCHASE.

permission to deal Permission by the *London Stock Exchange to deal in the shares of a newly floated company. It must be sought three days after the issue of a *prospectus.

perpetual annuity (perpetuity) The receipt or payment of a constant annual amount in perpetuity. Although the word annuity refers to an annual sum, in practice the constant sum may be for periods of less than a year. The *present value of an annuity is obtained from the formula:

$$P = (a \times 100)/i,$$

where P is the present value, a is the annual sum, and i is the interest rate.

perpetual debenture (perpetual bond) **1.** A bond or *debenture that can never be redeemed, i.e. the issuer has neither the right nor the obligation to repay the *principal. Usually *interest is paid at a constant rate, or at a fixed margin over a benchmark rate. *See* IRREDEEMABLE SECURITIES. **2.** A bond or debenture that cannot be redeemed on demand.

perpetual FRN A *floating-rate note that is never redeemed. *See also* FLIP-FLOP FRN.

perpetual inventory A method of continuous *stock control in which an account is kept for each item of stock; one side of the account records the deliveries of that type of stock and the other side records the issues from the stock. Thus, the balance of the account at any time provides a record of either the number of items in stock or their values, or both. This method is used in large organizations in which it is important to control the amount of capital tied up in the running of the business. It also provides a means of checking pilferage. Less sophisticated organizations rely on annual *stocktaking to discover how much stock they have.

perpetual succession The continued existence of a *corporation until it is legally dissolved. A corporation, being a separate legal person, is unaffected by the death or other departure of any member but continues in existence no matter how many changes in membership occur. *See* ARTIFICIAL PERSON.

per proc (per pro; p.p.) Abbreviations for *per procurationem* (Latin: by procuration): denoting an act by an agent, not acting on his own authority but on that of his principal. The abbreviation is often used when signing letters on behalf of a firm or someone else, if formally authorized to do so. The firm or person giving the authority accepts responsibility for documents so signed.

perquisites *See* PERKS.

persistent misdeclaration penalty A penalty used in the collection of *value added tax. It applies when there has been a material inaccuracy in a VAT return, being the lower of £500,000 and 10% of the total true amount of VAT due for the quarter. The trader must also have received a *surcharge liability notice resulting from a previous error within the 15 months prior to the current VAT period. In these circumstances a penalty for repeated errors of 15% of the VAT lost will be charged.

personal accident and sickness insurance *See* SICKNESS AND ACCIDENT INSURANCE.

personal account 1. An *account in a *ledger that bears the name of an individual or of an organization; it records the state of indebtedness of the named person to the

organization keeping the account or vice versa. Personal accounts are normally kept in the sales (or total debtors) ledger and the purchases (or total creditors) ledger. **2.** *See* PA.

personal allowance The allowance to which every individual resident in the UK is entitled in calculating their *taxable income for *income tax. Under current rules, the allowance depends on the age of the taxpayer. For 2015–16 the personal allowance is £10,600 for those born on or after 6 April 1948 and £10,660 for those born before that date. The additional age-related allowance was frozen in 2013 and is due to disappear in 2016. *See also* INCOME TAX ALLOWANCES.

personal assistant (PA) A person who is appointed to help a manager or director and who has wider responsibilities than a secretary.

personal communication channels Channels through which two or more people communicate directly with each other, including face to face, person to audience, or by telephone, fax, Internet, or mail.

personal community An Internet *community of users organized around a small network of individuals. The members of a personal community usually know each other.

personal computer (PC) A microcomputer suitable for a single user, with a localized hard storage disk and a *microprocessor. Although microcomputers have limited abilities compared with the larger *mainframes, they are sufficiently powerful to meet the needs of most small businesses; their uses include producing accounts and payrolls, invoicing, word processing, and compiling mailing lists. More powerful systems can be obtained by linking several small computers by a *local area network. *See also* LAPTOP COMPUTER; TABLET COMPUTER.

personal financial planning Financial planning for individuals, which involves analysing their current financial position, predicting their short-term and long-term needs, and recommending a financial strategy. This may involve advice on pensions, the provision of independent school fees, mortgages, life assurance, and investments.

personal identification number (PIN) A number memorized by the holder of a *cash card, *credit card, or *multifunctional card and used in *automated teller machines and *electronic funds transfer at point of sale to identify the card owner. The number is given to the cardholder in secret and is memorized so that if the card is stolen it cannot be used. The number is unique to the cardholder. *See* PHANTOM WITHDRAWALS.

personal influence The effect of statements made by one person on another person's attitude or decision to purchase.

personality tests *See* PSYCHOLOGICAL TESTS. *See also* INTEREST FACTORS.

personalization Creating a specialized form of a product tailored for an individual customer.

personal ledger A *ledger containing *personal accounts, for example the debtors' ledger and the creditors' ledger.

personal loan A loan to a private person by a bank or building society for domestic purposes, buying a car, etc. There is usually no security required and consequently a high rate of interest is charged. Repayment is usually by monthly instalments over a fixed period. This is a more expensive way of borrowing from a bank than by means of an *overdraft.

personal pension scheme An arrangement in which an individual contributes part of his or her salary to a pension provider, such as an insurance company or a bank. The pension provider invests the funds so that at retirement a lump sum is available to the pensioner. This is generally used to purchase an *annuity to provide regular pension payments, although from April 2014 this is no longer a legal requirement. In the UK it was formerly possible to

contract out of the Second State Pension through a personal pension scheme; this option was removed in 2012. The administration of pensions is scrutinized by the *Financial Ombudsman Service, which is empowered to deal with complaints relating to personal pension schemes. *See also* STAKEHOLDER PENSION SCHEME.

personal property (personalty) Any property other than *real property (realty). This distinction is especially used in distinguishing property for *inheritance tax. Personal property includes money, shares, chattels, etc.

personal representative A person whose duty is to gather in the assets of the estate of a deceased person, to pay his liabilities, and to distribute the residue. Personal representatives of a person dying testate are known as *executors; those of a person dying intestate are known as his *administrators.

personal selling Person-to-person interaction between a buyer and a seller in which the seller's purpose is to persuade the buyer of the merits of the product, to convince the buyer of his or her need for it, and to develop with the buyer an ongoing customer relationship.

personalty *See* PERSONAL PROPERTY.

person–job fit The extent to which an individual's skills, interests, and personal characteristics are consistent with the requirements and rewards of their work.

personnel management *See* HUMAN-RESOURCE MANAGEMENT.

personnel selection The process of choosing the most suitable applicant for a vacancy within an organization. Normally, a *job description is written, stating the purpose of the job and the tasks, duties, and responsibilities it entails. This enables a *personnel specification to be created, listing the qualifications, experience, and personal attributes that will be required in the successful candidate (*see* KSAOs). A search for the right person then begins, using advertisements in newspapers, trade papers, or employment agencies; if the vacancy is sufficiently senior a head hunter may be employed. Initial selection is then made by inviting letters of application (or using application forms) supported by a *curriculum vitae and listing the applicants that most closely match the job specification. Screening interviews may then be held, which may include practical tests so that a short list of final candidates can be drawn up. Second interviews are sometimes required and, when appropriate, *psychological tests are used. The number of interviews and the extent of testing will depend on the organization and the level of the position within it. *See* ASSESSMENT CENTRE; SELECTION INTERVIEW.

personnel specification A document used in the recruitment process for a job that lists the skills, experience, and other qualities needed in order to perform it successfully. The specification may include general personality traits as well as more objective criteria, such as qualifications. *See also* KSAOs.

person–organization fit The extent to which an individual's values, interests, and behaviour are consistent with the culture of an organization as a whole, rather than with a specific role or task.

persuasive advertising Advertising used to build selective demand for a brand by persuading consumers that it offers the best quality for their money.

PERT Acronym for programme evaluation and review technique. *See* NETWORK MODELLING.

pervasive computing *See* UBIQUITOUS COMPUTING.

peseta Formerly, the standard monetary unit of Spain and one of the two standard monetary units of Andorra (*see also* FRANC), divided into 100 céntimos. It was replaced by the *euro in 2002.

pesewa A monetary unit of Ghana, worth one hundredth of a *cedi.

peso 1. The standard monetary unit of Argentina (ARS), Chile (CLP), Colombia (COP), Cuba (CUP), the Dominican Republic (DOP), Mexico (MXN), and the Philippines (PHP); it is divided into 100 centavos. **2.** (UYU) The standard monetary unit of Uruguay, divided into 100 centésimos.

PESTLE analysis Analysis of the external influences on a firm: the acronym stands for *p*olitical, *e*conomic, *s*ocial, *t*echnological, *l*egal, and *e*nvironmental, i.e. issues that could significantly affect the strategic development of a firm. The former acronym, **PEST**, has been expanded to include the legal and environmental aspects.

PET Abbreviation for *potentially exempt transfer.

Peter principle The observation, first formulated by the educationalist Laurence J. Peter, that in a hierarchy every employee tends to rise to his or her level of incompetence. In other words, employees are successively promoted until they reach a level where they are inadequate to the demands of the job. *See also* DILBERT PRINCIPLE; PARKINSON'S LAWS.

petrodollars Reserves of US dollars deposited with banks as a result of the steep rises in the price of oil in the 1970s. The export revenues of the oil-exporting nations increased rapidly in this period, leading to large current-account surpluses, which had an important impact on the world's financial system.

petroleum revenue tax (PRT) A tax on the profits from sales of oil and gas extracted in the UK or on the continental shelf. This tax was the principal means enabling the UK government to obtain a share in the profits made from oil in the North Sea. It has been abolished for oilfields getting development consent on or after 16 March 1993. The current rate of tax is 35%. Profits from oil extraction are also subject to a supplementary corporation tax charge of 20%.

petty cash The amount of cash that an organization keeps in notes or coins on its premises to pay small items of expense. This is to be distinguished from cash, which normally refers to amounts held at banks. Petty-cash transactions are normally recorded in a **petty-cash book**, the balance of which should agree with the amounts of petty cash held at any given time.

petty patent *See* UTILITY MODEL.

Pfennig (*plural* **Pfennige**) A former monetary unit of Germany, worth one hundredth of a *Deutschmark (until 2002).

PFI Abbreviation for *private finance initiative. *See* PUBLIC–PRIVATE PARTNERSHIP.

phantom withdrawals The removal of funds from bank accounts through *automated teller machines (ATMs) by unauthorized means and without the knowledge or consent of the account holder. Until recently most banks maintained that such withdrawals were possible only where account holders had divulged their *personal identification numbers (PINs) to a third party. However, there is now firm evidence of ATM fraud perpetrated by technological means, including the use of 'skimming' devices to copy the details of inserted cards and miniature cameras to record PINs.

PHI 1. Abbreviation for *permanent health insurance. **2.** Abbreviation for *private health insurance.

phishing A type of fraud in which victims are tricked into disclosing bank-account or credit-card details, passwords, or other sensitive information by bogus e-mails or text messages, usually purporting to be from a bank or other trustworthy source.

physical capital Items such as *plant and machinery, buildings, and land that can be used to produce goods and services. It is compared to financial capital, i.e. money, and *human capital.

physical delivery The settlement of an *option or *futures contract by the delivery of the *underlying rather than an equivalent cash settlement.

physical distribution The tasks involved in planning, implementing, and controlling the flow of materials and final goods from their points of origin to their final destinations to meet the requirements of customers at a profit. Warehousing, transportation, and other firms that enable a company to stock and move goods are known as **physical distribution firms**.

physical distribution management *See* SUPPLY-CHAIN MANAGEMENT.

physical price The price of a commodity that is available for delivery. In most forward contracts (*see* FORWARD DEALING) and *futures contracts the goods are never actually delivered because sales and purchases are set off against each other.

physicals *See* ACTUALS.

PI *See* PROFITABILITY INDEX.

piastre 1. A monetary unit of Egypt, Lebanon, South Sudan, Sudan, and Syria, worth one hundredth of a *pound. **2.** A monetary unit of Jordan, worth one hundredth of a dinar.

PIBS Abbreviation for *permanent interest bearing share.

PIC Abbreviation for *product innovation charter.

picketing A form of *industrial action in which employees gather outside a workplace in which there is a trade dispute, usually a strike. The pickets so gathered often form a **picket line**, past which they attempt to discourage other workers, delivery lorries, and customers' collection lorries from passing. The purpose is to reinforce the effects of the strike and to encourage the maximum number of employees to join it. The right to **peaceful picketing** at one's own place of work is recognized in the Trade Union and Labour Relations (Consolidation) Act 1992. It is not lawful if it has not first been authorized by a ballot of the union involved and if the reason for the action is because the employer involved is employing a non-union employee. **Secondary picketing**, i.e. picketing other people's place of work is a civil offence under the Act. In particular so-called **flying pickets**, who join a picket line although they are neither employees of the organization being picketed nor union representatives of employees, have no immunity from civil action.

pictogram A diagram providing quantitative information, using stylized drawings of people or things, in which the number of such individual drawings represents the number of people or things involved.

piece rate A payment scheme in which an employee is paid a specific price for each unit made. The rate is therefore directly related to output and not to time (*compare* TIME RATE). This method is often combined with a basic salary and takes the form of a productivity bonus, in which individual effort is rewarded. In modern factories, many tasks have been mechanized, making this method of payment less common, although it is simple to operate and popular with employees. Piece rate, to be attractive to workers, depends on speed of production, therefore the standard of quality and safety may suffer if adequate precautions are not taken. *See also* PAYMENT BY RESULTS; PREMIUM BONUS.

pie chart A diagram providing a visual representation of the proportions into which something is divided. It consists of a circle divided in sectors, the area of each sector representing the proportion of a specified component.

piggyback service A distribution service in which loaded truck trailers, or other sealed containers, are carried by rail to destinations from which they can be taken by truck to their final destination. Similar services are **fishyback service**, involving transport of containers by water, and **birdyback service**, involving transport of containers by air.

PII Abbreviation for *professional indemnity insurance.

pilot production The small-scale production of a new product in a **pilot plant**. The object is to check and, if necessary, improve the production method. The product itself is often used in a marketing exercise to monitor its reception by the market and, in some cases, to improve it.

pilot study A small-scale *marketing research study conducted as a trial so that any problems can be eliminated before a full study is undertaken. For example, a pilot study might show that changes are needed in a questionnaire because questions are ambiguous, miss the point, etc.

PIMS (Profit Impact of Market Strategies) An extensive database giving details of the performance of some 4,000 businesses in Europe and North America. The details include sales, market share, investment, research and development budget, etc. PIMS examines the relationship between expenditure, market performance, and profitability and has provided explanations for nearly 80% of the variations in profitability among the businesses in the database.

PIN Abbreviation for *personal identification number.

PINC Abbreviation for *property income certificate.

Pink Book *See* UK BALANCE OF PAYMENTS.

pink form (preferential form) An *application form in a flotation that is printed on pink paper and usually distributed to employees of the company to give them preference in the allocation of shares. Up to 10% of a share issue can be set aside under London Stock Exchange rules for applications from employees or from shareholders in a parent company that is floating a subsidiary.

pip *See* TICK.

pipeline inventory *See* INVENTORY.

piracy 1. An illegal act of violence, detention, robbery, or revenge committed on a ship or aircraft. It excludes acts committed for political purposes and during a war. In marine insurance it extends to include any form of plundering at sea. **2.** Infringement of copyright. The usual remedy is for the copyright holder to obtain an injunction to end the infringement. This may not be possible in a foreign country and many British and American books are pirated in foreign countries by copying them photographically and printing them cheaply.

pit (trading pit) An area of a stock market, financial futures and options exchange, or commodity exchange in which a particular stock, financial future, or commodity is traded, especially one in which dealings take place by *open outcry. Authorized dealers in these markets are called **pit traders**. In recent years the practice of pit trading has been largely replaced by that of screen trading. *See also* CALLOVER; FLOOR.

placing The selling of shares in a company to a selected group of individuals or institutions. Placings can be used either as a means of *flotation or to raise additional capital for a listed company (*see also* PRE-EMPTION RIGHTS; RIGHTS ISSUE). Placings are usually the cheapest way of raising capital and they also allow the directors of a company to influence the selection of shareholders. Placings of private companies (**private placings**) are often carried out without the intermediary of a stockbroker. A **public placing** is the placing of a public company. In the USA a placing is called a **placement**. *Compare* INTRODUCTION; OFFER FOR SALE.

plain vanilla Describing a financial instrument in its simplest form (e.g. a straightforward *option with no exotic features). With the advent of *structured finance, more traditional debt instruments are now sometimes described as **vanilla finance**.

planned economy *See* COMMAND ECONOMY.

planned location of industry Government intervention in the location of new industries in an area or country. As old industries in a region, such as shipbuilding, gradually decrease, new industries are required to take their place to avoid high unemployment and skilled workers moving away. Many governments provide assistance to those wishing to set up new industries in these areas.

planned obsolescence *See* OBSOLESCENCE.

planning One of the functions of *management accounting in which plans for the future activities and operations of an organization are incorporated into its *budgets, etc. *See also* BUSINESS PLAN.

planning blight Difficulty in selling or developing a site, building, etc., because it is affected by a government or local-authority development plan. Planning blight may be ended by a compulsory purchase by the government or local authority, but it may continue indefinitely if the government plans fail to mature or if the site itself is not required by the development but is rendered unsaleable or less valuable by its proximity to a development.

planning fallacy The demonstrated tendency for people to underestimate the length of time it will take them to complete a task. Various explanations have been offered, including *optimism bias, failure to allow for extraneous factors such as sickness etc., and the wish to make a good impression when submitting plans for approval. One counterintuitive finding of studies in this area is that the more detailed and specific the plan, the *more* likely it is to be seriously over-optimistic. This is perhaps because detailed planning (i) encourages people to suppose that everything will go according to plan; and (ii) narrows their focus so they fail to consider factors outside the plan (e.g. defaults by suppliers, accidents, unexpected events of all kinds). The best antidote to planning fallacy is to research how long comparable projects have taken in the past (which can be accurately known), rather than making assumptions about the future (which cannot). *See also* HOFSTADTER'S LAW; STRATEGIC MISREPRESENTATION.

planning permission Permission that must be obtained from a local authority in the UK before building on or developing a site or before changing the use of an existing site or building, in accordance with the Town and Country Planning Act 1990.

plant and machinery The equipment required to operate a business. *Capital allowances are available for plant and machinery although neither is defined in the tax legislation. The working definition often used is that given in the taxation case *Yarmouth* v *France* (1887). This defines plant and machinery as 'whatever apparatus is used by a businessman for carrying on his business – not his stock in trade which he buys or makes for resale: but all goods and chattels, fixed or moveable, live or dead, which he keeps for permanent employment in the business'. Subsequent cases have been largely concerned with the distinction between plant actively used in a business, and so qualifying for capital allowances, and expenditure on items that relate to the setting up of the business, which do not so qualify. Items ruled to be plant and machinery range from a barrister's law books to sculptures and other decorative items intended to create ambience. Although buildings and parts of buildings do not generally qualify as plant, there are various specified exceptions (e.g. safety and security features in certain types of premises).

plastic money A colloquial name for a *credit card, *debit card, or *multifunctional card. It is often shortened to **plastic**.

playing the yield curve An investment strategy designed to take advantage of differences in yield for different terms, for example by funding short term and investing longer term on a normal *yield curve.

plc Abbreviation for *public limited company. This (or its Welsh equivalent *c.c.c.) must appear in the name of a public limited company. *Compare* LTD.

pledge An article given by a borrower (**pledgor**) to a lender (**pledgee**) as a security for a debt. It remains in the ownership of the pledgor although it is in the possession of the pledgee until the debt is repaid. *See also* PAWNBROKER.

Plimsoll line *See* LOAD LINE.

ploughed-back profits *See* RETAINED EARNINGS.

PLUS Markets A stock exchange in London for shares in smaller companies: it developed from the Ofex trading facility in 2005–06 and by 2007 had become a serious rival to the London Stock Exchange's *Alternative Investment Market. It became a UK *Recognized Investment Exchange in 2007. However, trading losses in the years after 2008 led to its sale to the *inter-dealer broker ICAP in 2012.

pluvial insurance (pluvius insurance) An insurance policy covering loss of income or profits caused by rain or other weather conditions. The main demand comes from the organizers of outdoor summer events, who could suffer financially if rain caused the event to be curtailed or abandoned. For events in which any profits would be uncertain, e.g. a summer fete, the policy specifies that claims are to be based on the number of millimetres of rain that fall in an agreed period at an agreed weather station near to the site of the event. If the amount of lost revenue can be easily calculated from ticket sales at an event, such as a cricket test match or tennis match, a policy paying for lost profit can be arranged.

PM Abbreviation for *preventative maintenance.

PMTS Abbreviation for *predetermined motion-time standards.

point method An analytical method of *job evaluation in which jobs are scored on a number of different features (e.g. skills, effort, level of responsibility, working conditions, etc.). The scores are then summed and used to create a graded pay structure. The method, which is very widely used, is essentially a refinement of the *factor-comparison method. *See also* CLASSIFICATION METHOD; HAY METHOD;

JOB-COMPONENT METHOD; RANKING METHOD.

point-of-purchase promotion (POP promotion) A promotional display or demonstration that takes place at the point of sale.

point of sale (POS) The place at which a consumer makes a purchase, usually a retail shop. It may, however, also be a doorstep (in door-to-door selling), a market stall, or a mail-order house.

poisha A monetary unit of Bangladesh, worth one hundredth of a *taka.

poison pill A tactic in which a company discourages unwanted *takeover bids by ensuring that a successful bid will trigger some event that substantially reduces the value of the company. Examples of such tactics include the sale of some prized asset to a friendly company or bank or the issue of securities with a conversion option enabling the bidder's shares to be bought at a reduced price if the bid is successful. *See also* PORCUPINE PROVISIONS; STAGGERED DIRECTORSHIPS.

polarization The distinction enforced by the *Financial Services Act 1986 between intermediaries who give advice on investments and act as a representative of one company (a tied agent) and those who are fully independent and able to advise on the full range of products offered by different companies (*see* INDEPENDENT FINANCIAL ADVISER). This polarization was intended to end confusion amongst consumers and to remove any doubts about the impartiality of advice provided by independent intermediaries. However, owing to the costs associated with maintaining a fully independent status, the majority of high-street banks and building societies became tied to one particular company, prompting concerns over the limited consumer choice available at the retail level. For this reason, new regulations introduced in late 2004 enabled advisers to be 'multi-tied', i.e. to advise on products from a limited range of companies (a change sometimes referred to as **depolarization**).

policy *See* INSURANCE POLICY.

policy proof of interest (PPI) An insurance policy (usually *marine insurance) in which the insurers agree that they will not insist on the usual requirement that the insured must prove an *insurable interest existed in the subject matter before a claim is paid. The possession of the policy is all that is required. These policies are a matter of trust between insurer and insured as they are not legally enforceable. They are issued for convenience in cases in which an insurable interest exists but is extremely difficult to prove or in which an insurable interest might come into existence later in the voyage.

political and charitable contributions Donations for political or charitable purposes made by an organization. Under the Companies Act a disclosure of such a donation has to be made by companies that are not *wholly owned subsidiaries of another British company and which have on their own or with their subsidiaries given in the financial year in aggregate more than £200. Charitable purposes is taken to mean purposes that are exclusively charitable. A donation for political purposes is taken to mean the giving of money either directly or indirectly to a political party of the UK or any part of it, or to a person who is carrying on activities likely to affect support for a political party. The total amounts given for both political and charitable purposes must be separately disclosed. If the payments are for political purposes, where applicable, the following information must be provided: (a) the name of each person to whom money exceeding £200 in amount has been given for those purposes and the amount given; and (b) if more than £200 has been given as a donation or subscription to a political party, the identity of the party and the amount given must be disclosed.

political credit risk (sovereign risk) The *credit risk arising from the fact that a foreign government may decide not to honour its financial obligations or other business commitments. *Compare* TRANSFER CREDIT RISK. *See also* COUNTRY RISK.

poll tax A tax that is the same for each individual, i.e. a lump sum per head (from Middle English *polle*: head). The main benefit claimed for such taxes is that they do not distort choices, being an equal levy from everyone's resources whatever their circumstances; however, poll taxes are often criticized as being regressive in that they do not take account of *ability to pay. The **community charge**, an alternative to domestic rates, was a poll tax introduced in 1990 (1989 in Scotland) and replaced by council tax in 1993.

pollution The disposal into the environment of substances that cannot be made harmless by normal biological processes. As part of a wider and increasing concern for environmental issues, the costs of industrialization are being assessed in terms of discharges into the air and water, the disposal and long-term effects of wastes, recycling, energy efficiency, land use and degradation, and the depletion of raw materials. Legislation has been enacted, increasingly, to limit levels of pollution and in 1996 an Environmental Agency was established in the UK to coordinate the previously separate activities of various agencies. Most other advanced industrial countries have introduced legislation and similar agencies. International targets have been agreed to eliminate the use of CFCs in aerosols and as a refrigerant (because they deplete the ozone layer). The adoption of the 'Polluter Pays Principle' (the fining of major companies for pollution incidents) and increasing awareness of green consumerism has meant that many leading companies have now issued environmental policy statements and some publish annual *environmental audits. Under the UK's Pollution Prevention and Control Regulations (2000) excessive noise and vibrations are formally classed as pollutants. *See also* ENVIRONMENTAL COSTS; HAZARDOUS WASTE; WASTE DISPOSAL.

pollution permits Permits issued by a government that allow the owner to pollute the environment legally. These permits may be bought and sold; firms that improve their environmental efficiency would reduce their need for permits and be in a position to sell them to less environmentally efficient rivals. In the USA, as part of the Clean Air Act, trading in these permits has cut sulphur dioxide emissions faster and more cheaply than expected. This system of **emissions trading** appears to have two main advantages over traditional environmental regulations. First, it gives firms a financial incentive to reduce emissions for less than it would cost to buy permits, and secondly, by leaving it to companies to decide how and when to reduce emissions, it reduces not only the cost of compliance but also the bureaucracy required to enforce environmental regulations. The European Union introduced a multinational emissions trading scheme in 2005.

POP promotion Abbreviation for *point-of-purchase promotion.

population (universe) In marketing research, any complete group of entities sharing a common set of characteristics. For example, a population could be all the companies in the car-supplying industries or all the consumers in the South West of England. A population is the group from which a *sample is taken. **Population specification error** is the error that results from an incorrect definition of the population from which the sample is chosen. For example, a population of consumers defined as buyers of Brand X may contain some non-buyers in the sample.

population hypothesis In marketing research, an empirically testable proposition made by a researcher about some characteristic of a *population of interest. Typical hypotheses could be that for a particular population one method of advertising (e.g. TV) is more effective than another (e.g. the Internet) or that one brand of cereal is more popular in a selected area of the country than in other areas. In order to affirm or reject the hypothesis, a *sample is selected from the population, data are collected and evaluated, and the *sampling error is identified.

population pyramid A diagram that illustrates the distribution of a population by age. The youngest and most numerous age group forms a rectangle at the base of the pyramid; the oldest and least numerous is a small rectangle at its apex.

porcupine provisions (shark repellents) Provisions made by a company to deter *takeover bids. They include *poison pills and *staggered directorships.

portal A web site that seeks to act as an attractive user-friendly access point to the Internet. Portals typically provide services (e-mail, social networking), content (news, listings of events, etc.), *directories of useful sites, and a *search engine to search the rest of the Web.

Porter's Five Forces A framework for analysing the balance of power within a particular industry and hence its overall profitability. The frame identifies five forces in the *microenvironment that drive competition and threaten a firm's ability to make profits: (1) rivalry between existing competitors (depending on e.g. their number, size, and relative market shares); (2) the threat of new entrants (i.e. the extent to which there are significant *barriers to entry); (3) the threat of substitutes (i.e. products in another industry that the consumer may see as alternatives); (4) the strength of buyer power; and (5) the strength of supplier power. Forces (2), (3), (4), and (5) all feed back into force (1) by driving up competitive rivalry. The five-forces model is probably the most widely used tool in *industry structure analysis and is also a popular starting point in *strategic management. It was developed by Michael E. Porter of Harvard Business School in the late 1970s.

portfolio 1. The set of holdings in securities owned by an investor or institution. In building up an investment portfolio an institution will have its own investment analysts, while an individual may make use of the services of a *merchant bank that offers **portfolio management**. The choice of portfolio will depend on the mix of income and capital growth its owner expects, some investments providing good income prospects while others provide good prospects for capital growth. **2.** A list of the loans made by an organization. Banks, for example, attempt to balance their portfolio of loans to limit the risks.

portfolio analysis 1. An analysis enabling management to identify and evaluate the various business units that make up a diversified company. Various techniques are used, the best known being the *Boston matrix. **2.** An analysis of the assets in an investment *portfolio.

portfolio insurance (portfolio protection) The use of a *financial futures and *options market to protect the value of a portfolio of investments. For example, a fund manager may expect the general level of prices to fall on the stock exchange. The manager could protect the portfolio by selling the appropriate number of *index futures, which could then be bought back at a profit if the market falls. Alternately, the manager could establish the value of the portfolio at current prices by buying put options, which would provide the opportunity to benefit if there was a rise in the general level of prices.

portfolio theory A theoretical approach to investment choices based on the assumption that for any given expected return, rational investors will seek to minimize their risk and that for any given level of risk they will seek to maximize their return. On this basis a set of efficient *portfolios can be calculated from which the investor will choose the one most appropriate for their risk profile. The practical conclusions of the theory are that investors should diversify widely and hold a mixture of *long and *short positions to minimize *systematic risk. Portfolio theory was influential in the 1960s and 1970s but many of its assumptions have since been questioned by *behavioural finance. *See* *also* MARKOWITZ MODEL; PORTFOLIO INSURANCE.

port mark The markings on the packages of goods destined for export, giving the name of the overseas port to which they are to be shipped or sent by air freight.

POS Abbreviation for *point of sale.

position The extent to which an investor, dealer, or speculator has made a commitment in the market by buying or selling securities, currencies, commodities, or any financial obligation. *See* LONG POSITION; OPEN POSITION; SHORT POSITION.

position audit A systematic assessment of the current situation of an organization. This normally involves drawing up a report (either internally or through external consultants) of the strengths and weaknesses of the organization and the opportunities or threats that it faces (*see* SWOT). The position audit is a vital tool in designing the future strategies of a large organization.

positioning A marketing strategy that will position a company's products and services against those of its competitors in the minds of consumers. To achieve positioning success it is suggested that there are four basic competitive strategies that a company can follow. The three winning strategies are:

- **cost leadership**—the company tries to achieve lowest costs of production and distribution;
- **differentiation**—making use of specific *marketing mixes (*see* DIFFERENTIATED MARKETING);
- **focus**—paying attention to a few market segments.

The fourth strategy is a losing strategy in which a company pursues a middle-of-the-road path. Companies that try to be good at everything are rarely particularly good at anything.

position limit 1. A limit placed by a financial exchange on the *exposure that any single transactor may undertake. **2.** An internal risk-management limit imposed on *positions to be held by traders, desks, etc. within an organization. *See also* INTRADAY LIMIT; LIMIT.

position trading In finance, the holding of an *open position for a long period of time with an eye to achieving long-term profits from calculated risks.

possession Actual physical control of goods or land. Possession has a wide variety of meanings in English law, depending on the nature of the property and the circumstances. For example, a person may still have possession of goods that have been lost or mislaid, provided that they are not abandoned and that no-one else has physical possession of them. It is sometimes used in the sense of a right to possession, e.g. the right of a person who has pledged goods to get them back. Possession may be divorced from *ownership; for example, a thief has legal possession of stolen goods but not ownership. Possession usually requires intention to possess—a person cannot possess something without knowing that he or she does so.

postal account A savings account with a bank or a building society that can only be operated by letter or (sometimes) by *automated teller machine (i.e. not over the counter or by telephone or over the Internet). Postal accounts usually pay a higher rate of interest than those that can be operated in person because of their cost structure.

post-balance-sheet events *See* ADJUSTING EVENTS; NON-ADJUSTING EVENTS.

post-completion audit A comparison of the actual cash flows resulting from an investment project with the forecast cash flows. A post-completion audit should identify bad investments made in the past and encourage managers to use more realistic forecasts for future investment projects.

post-date To insert a date on a document that is later than the date on which it is signed, thus making it effective only from the later date. A **post-dated** (or **forward-dated**)

cheque cannot be negotiated before the date written on it, irrespective of when it was signed. *Compare* ANTE-DATE.

post-entry duty *See* OVER-ENTRY CERTIFICATE.

poster A placard or bill exhibited in a public place as an advertisement. Although there are over 200,000 legal poster sites in the UK, poster advertising accounts for less than 10% of the total advertising expenditure. Illegal attachment of posters or bills to empty shop windows, company hoardings, etc., is called **flyposting**. Flyposting is often undertaken at night by a small number of companies, all of whom jealously guard their regular territories. Flyposting is particularly popular with record companies, underground magazines, and some film companies.

post hoc segmentation The process of segmenting a market or markets empirically. *See* MARKET SEGMENTATION.

postpurchase behaviour The stage in *consumer buying behaviour in which the consumer takes further action after purchase, based on his or her satisfaction or dissatisfaction.

post-testing Testing that takes place after an advertisement has appeared to determine whether or not it has met the objectives set for it by the company that paid for it.

potential entrant An organization that is poised to enter a market and would do so if there was a small price rise or a reduction in *barriers to entry.

potentially exempt transfer (PET) A lifetime gift made by an individual that is neither an *exempt transfer for *inheritance tax purposes nor liable to an immediate charge (*see* CHARGEABLE TRANSFER). No charge occurs if the donor survives seven years after the date of the gift. If death occurs within seven years of the gift, the total lifetime gifts in the seven years preceding death are reviewed. The gifts are taken in chronological order with the first £325,000 (2009–15) worth of gifts being covered by the nil-rate band. Gifts in excess of this sum are charged at a flat rate of 40% with graduated relief for gifts made between three and seven years before death.

potential market The consumers who profess some level of interest in a particular product or service.

pound 1. (GBP) The standard monetary unit of the UK, divided into 100 pence. It dates back to the 8th century AD when Offa, King of Mercia, coined 240 pennyweights of silver from 1 pound of silver. When *sterling was decimalized in 1971 it was divided into 100 newly defined pence. The pound is also the currency unit of the Falkland Islands, Gibraltar, the Channel Islands, and the Isle of Man. *See also* PUNT. **2.** The standard monetary unit of Egypt (EGP), Lebanon (LBP), South Sudan (SSP), Sudan (SDG), and Syria (SYP), divided into 100 piastres. **3.** Formerly, the standard monetary unit of Cyprus, divided into 100 cents. Cyprus adopted the euro in 2008.

pound cost averaging A method of accumulating capital by investing a fixed sum of money in a particular share every month (or other period). When prices fall the fixed sum will buy correspondingly more shares and when prices rise fewer shares are bought. The result is that the average purchase price over a period is lower than the arithmetic average of the market prices at each purchase date (because more shares are bought at lower prices and fewer at higher prices).

power of attorney (PA) A formal document giving one person the right to act for another. A power to execute a *deed must itself be given by a deed. An attorney may not delegate these powers unless specifically authorized to do so.

power styles The characteristic ways in which different managers attempt to influence the behaviour of employees and others, overcome resistance, and achieve their goals. Power styles can be characterized as either competitive or collective.

- **Impression management** is a competitive power style in which information is controlled and manipulated in order to influence peoples' attitudes to events, policies, or personalities. This reliance on presentation and 'spin' may at times amount to actual deceit.
- **Consensus** and **charismatic power styles** are forms of the collective use of power. The consensus power style involves *participative decision making and joint problem solving, whereas the charismatic style makes use of the manager's personality to inspire the members of an organization to work together for a common purpose (*see* CHARISMATIC LEADER; TRANSFORMATIONAL LEADERSHIP).
- A **transactional power style** involves the use of negotiation and *contingent reinforcement (rewards and penalties) to influence others; it can be either competitive or collective, depending on the decision maker. Cooperation is needed for any transaction to take place: if that transaction involves the use and allocation of scarce resources it could become very competitive. *See* TRANSACTIONAL LEADERSHIP.

See also LEADERSHIP STYLE; SOURCES OF POWER.

power to manage The power to direct the affairs of a company, particularly as this is distributed between the *general meeting of members and the board of directors. The distribution of power is usually made clear in the company's constitution; for example, the model *articles of association contained in schedule 1-3 of the Companies (Model Articles) Regulations 2008 provide that there is a wide power of management vested with the board of directors.

power to sue The authority by which a company can institute legal proceedings. Where there is a wrong done to the company, the company is the proper person to act against the wrongdoer. However, the organ of the company that is empowered to take such action will depend on the company's constitution. Under the model *articles of association contained in schedules

1-3 of the Companies (Model Articles) Regulations 2008, the power is vested with the board of directors, which may, as a matter of management, decide not to sue. However, under the same model articles, the *general meeting can intervene by passing a *special resolution. Alternatively, the general meeting can use a residual power to commence proceedings where the board is unable to act, or can act as the decision-making body where the directors are themselves the wrongdoers.

p.p. Abbreviation for *per procurationem.* *See* PER PROC.

PPI 1. Abbreviation for *policy proof of interest. **2.** Abbreviation for *producer price index.

PPP 1. Abbreviation for *purchasing power parity. **2.** Abbreviation for *public–private partnership.

PR Abbreviation for *public relations.

PRA Abbreviation for *Prudential Regulation Authority.

preacquisition profit The *retained earnings of one company before it is taken over by another company. Preacquisition profits should not be distributed to the shareholders of the acquiring company by way of dividend, as such profits do not constitute income to the parent company but are a partial repayment of its capital outlay on the acquisition of the shares.

preapproach A step in the industrial selling process in which a salesperson learns as much as possible about a prospective customer before making a sales call.

preautomation analysis An analysis that should precede the replacement of a manual system by automation. Research suggests that large-scale investments in automation frequently fail to provide the expected benefits, because they are not used as an opportunity to eliminate unnecessary elements of the process. *See* BUSINESS PROCESS RE-ENGINEERING; VALUE-ADDED MANUFACTURING.

precept A command by HM Revenue and Customs to a taxpayer to make certain relevant documents available, usually by a specified date.

precious metals The metals silver, gold, and platinum. *Compare* BASE METALS.

predatory pricing strategy 1. The pricing of goods or services at such a low level that other firms cannot compete and are forced to leave the market. While it has long been accepted that some firms resort to predatory pricing on occasions, the application of *game theory to *strategic behaviour has shown that predatory pricing is unlikely to occur very often as it is at least as painful for the predator as for the victim. This encourages most potential predators to look for a more cooperative plan. *See also* KAMIKAZE PRICING, PRICE WAR. **2.** An illegal pricing strategy in which a product is offered at a low price to eliminate competition and the price is subsequently raised after the competition has been eliminated.

predetermined motion-time standards (PMTS) A *work measurement technique using libraries of pre-established times for basic human motions, to construct standard times for jobs or processes.

predetermined overhead rate An overhead *absorption rate computed in advance of operations. In practice, most absorption rates are computed from budgeted figures and are therefore predetermined overhead rates, which usually cover one year.

pre-employment health questionnaires Under the Equality Act 2010 it is generally unlawful for an employer to ask questions about disability or health before making a job offer. The rule, which applies to all enquiries by or on behalf of an employer (e.g. by a recruitment agency), is intended to prevent disability or health issues being used to reject applicants at an early stage in the recruitment process. It would be unlawful, therefore, to ask applicants to list on an application form how many days' sick leave they have taken in the last year. The rule covers questions to third parties, such as a former employer, as well as to applicants.

It is, however, permissible to make a job offer that is conditional on the applicant passing a medical examination or answering health-related questions. The employer may also ask whether an applicant will be able to carry out an intrinsic part of the job, such as handling heavy goods. In such cases, the employer is under a duty to make *reasonable adjustments and this must be considered in dealing with the answer given by the applicant.

pre-emption First refusal: the right of a person to be the first to be asked if he or she wishes to enter into an agreement at a specified price; for example, the right to be offered a house at a price acceptable to the vendor before it is put on the open market.

pre-emption rights The principle, established in UK company law, that existing shareholders should be offered a proportion of certain classes of newly issued securities before they are offered to anyone else and upon terms that are at least as favourable. To satisfy this principle a company must write to every shareholder (*see* RIGHTS ISSUE), which may be an expensive and lengthy procedure. Newer methods of issuing shares, such as *vendor placings or *bought deals, are much cheaper and easier to effect, although they violate pre-emption rights. An issue of shares with no pre-emption rights can only be made if the shareholders have agreed to this in a *special resolution. In the USA pre-emption rights have now been largely abandoned but controversy over the principle is still widespread in the UK.

pre-empt spot An advertising spot for a particular period of airtime on television, bought in advance at a discount for use only if another advertiser does not offer to take up that time at the full rate.

preference dividend A *dividend payable to the holders of *preference shares. Preference dividends not paid in previous periods will only be due to the holders of *cumulative preference shares.

preference share A share in a company yielding a fixed rate of interest rather than a variable dividend. A preference share is an intermediate form of security between an *ordinary share and a *debenture. Preference shares usually confer some degree of ownership of the company; in the event of liquidation, they are paid off after *loan capital but before *ordinary share capital.

    Participating preference shares carry additional rights to dividends, such as a further share in the profits of the company, after the ordinary shareholders have received a stated percentage. *See also* PREFERRED ORDINARY SHARE.

preference share capital *Share capital consisting of *preference shares. In the UK, preference share capital was formerly considered *non-equity share capital; however, such shares are now classified as *liabilities rather than *shareholders' equity.

preferential creditor A creditor whose debt will be met in preference to those of other creditors and who thus has the best chance of being paid in full on the bankruptcy of an individual or the winding-up of a company. Preferential creditors, who are usually paid in full after *secured liabilities and before ordinary creditors, include the trustees of occupational pension schemes, and employees in respect of any remuneration outstanding. The status of the Crown (i.e. HM Revenue and Customs) as a preferential creditor was abolished from 2003.

preferential debt A debt that will be repaid in preference to other debts. *See* PREFERENTIAL CREDITOR.

preferential duty A specially low import duty imposed on goods from a country that has a trade agreement of a certain kind with the importing country. For example, in the days of the British Empire, imports from member countries were granted Imperial Preference on imported materials, which later became Commonwealth Preference.

preferential form *See* PINK FORM.

preferential payment A payment made to a *preferential creditor.

preferred ordinary share A share issued by some companies that ranks between a *preference share and an *ordinary share in the payment of dividends.

preferred position A desirable position for an advertisement in a publication, for which a premium is charged.

preferred stock The US name for a *preference share.

prefinancing An arrangement in which a buyer (often an importer) finances the activities of a supplier by making an advance payment against delivery. This is sometimes used as a *fair trade policy, in which Western importers pay farmers in the developing world for their crops some months in advance of harvest.

preliminary announcement An early announcement of their profit or loss for the year that *listed companies are required to make under *London Stock Exchange Regulations. The minimum information is a summarized *profit and loss account, although there has been a trend for companies to provide other information, such as *balance sheets. Companies must lodge their preliminary announcement with the Stock Exchange, but there is no requirement to send the information to shareholders. A number of companies publish some of the information in national newspapers and provide *investment analysts and journalists with substantial information, which receives considerable comment in the press.

preliminary expenses Expenses involved in the formation of a company. They include the cost of producing a *prospectus, issuing shares, and advertising the flotation.

pre-market Denoting any trading that takes place before the official opening of a market.

premium 1. The consideration payable for a contract of *insurance or life assurance. **2.** An amount in excess of the nominal value of a share, bond, or other security. **3.** An amount in excess of the issue price of a share or other security. When dealings open for a new issue of shares, for instance, it may be said that the market price will be at a premium over the issue price (*see* STAG). **4.** The price paid by a buyer of an *option contract to the seller for the right to exercise the option. In general, the premium asked for an option consists of two components, its *intrinsic value and its *time value. **5.** The difference between the spot price for a commodity or currency and the forward price. **6.** A bonus given to bank customers as an inducement to open an account.

premium bonds UK government securities first issued in 1956 and now administered by *National Savings and Investments, an agency of HM Treasury. No regular income or capital gain is offered but bonds enter monthly draws for a range of tax-free prizes, winners being drawn by ERNIE (electronic random number indicating equipment). Bonds are in £1 denominations with a minimum purchase of £100 and a maximum holding of £30,000. Bonds are repaid at their face value at any time.

premium bonus A *payment by results method of paying workers, in which a standard time is set for the production of each unit and bonuses are paid related to the actual time taken. Depending on the needs of the organization, this scheme can be varied to achieve a balance between quality and speed of production; it also provides an incentive for employees. The standards were formerly set by experienced staff but more scientific attempts at classifying work units have resulted in the introduction of systematic *work-study techniques. These schemes can lead to friction between employee and employer as standard times are a permanent source of conflict. *See also* PIECE RATE.

premium currency Of two currencies, the one whose exchange rate is higher in the forward market.

premium income The total income of an insurance company from insurance policy *premiums.

premium offer A special offer of a domestic product advertised on the package of some other product. The purchaser sends a set number of package tops or labels with a small cash payment to an address given and receives the domestic product by post. Premium offers are handled by **premium houses**, who provide all the services required to distribute the products.

pre-packaged bankruptcy Bankruptcy proceedings that incorporate in advance an already agreed reorganization plan.

prepared data entry (PDE) In marketing research, a method of rapid data collection in which the respondent interacts directly with a computer instead of through the medium of an interviewer. A major advantage is the elimination of *interviewer error.

prepayment 1. The settlement of a debt before it is due, for example by the early repayment of a mortgage. **2.** *See* PAYMENT IN ADVANCE.

prepayment risk The *risk associated with early payments of obligations. A prime example is the risk that a borrower will repay a fixed-rate mortgage early at a time when interest rates are falling, leaving the lender with a lower interest income than anticipated. To offset this risk, lenders sometimes impose a **prepayment penalty** on loans.

prescriptive strategy A management approach in which business objectives are clearly defined in advance and a detailed plan for attaining them is set out and adhered to. The chief advantage of such a strategy is that targets can be identified and progress measured. The disadvantage is the risk of inflexibility. A prescriptive strategy can be contrasted with an *emergent strategy, which is more responsive to unexpected events or changed circumstances. *See also* DELIBERATE STRATEGY.

presentation 1. A verbal report, often supported by explanatory and illustrative material, in which something, such as a balance sheet, new product, etc., is presented to an audience. **2.** A step in the industrial selling process in which a salesperson explains a product to the buyer, giving a detailed description of the way in which the product will make or save money for the buyer.

present value (discounted value) The result arrived at in a *discounted cash flow calculation by multiplying a projected annual cash flow figure by a *discount factor derived from a *hurdle rate of interest and a time period.

present-value factor See DISCOUNT FACTOR.

president 1. The chief executive of a US company, equivalent to the chairman of the board of a UK company. **2.** A title sometimes given to a past chairman or managing director of a UK company, usually for an honorary position that carries little responsibility for running the company.

press conference A meeting called by an organization to announce a newsworthy event to the press. The public relations or press departments of a large organization will often prepare a **press kit**, consisting of press releases and supporting material, to provide the press with accurate information.

prestige price A high price charged for a product to convey an impression of high quality. The underlying assumption is that if a product has a low price it must be inferior to competitive products that are being sold at higher prices.

pre-tax profit The profit of a company before deduction of corporation tax.

pretesting 1. Conducting limited trials of a questionnaire, or other study document, to determine its suitability for a planned marketing research project. **2.** In the context of advertising, marketing research on the effectiveness of an advertisement; it begins at the earliest stage of development and continues until the advertisement is ready for use.

preventative maintenance (PM) An approach to the maintenance of plant, which is central to *just-in-time techniques; it emphasizes frequent proactive inspection and repair in order to reduce downtime and to extend its working life.

prevention costs See COST OF QUALITY. See also ENVIRONMENTAL COSTS.

price The amount of money charged for a product or service, or the value that a consumer exchanges for the benefits of having or using a product or service.

price-bundling strategy A pricing strategy in which the price of a set of products is lower than the total of the individual prices of the components. For example, a car with a set of optional extras may be priced in this way. See BUNDLING.

price competition Competition based on the price at which a product or service is offered. It is especially important in the marketing of products that are not distinctive, such as raw materials. Because *price wars reduce profits, sellers prefer other forms of competition, based on quality, packaging, advertising, etc.

price control Restrictions by a government on the prices of consumer goods, usually imposed on a short-term basis as a measure to control inflation. See also PRICES AND INCOME POLICY.

price discrimination The sale of the same product at different prices to different buyers. Usually practised by monopolists, it requires that a market can be subdivided to exploit different sets of consumers and that these divisions can be sustained. Pure price discrimination rarely exists, since sellers usually differentiate the product slightly (as in first-class rail travel and different types of theatre seat). See also REVENUE MANAGEMENT.

price–dividend ratio (PDR; P/D ratio) The current market price of a company share divided by the dividend per share for the previous year. It is a measure of the investment value of the share.

price–earnings ratio (P/E ratio) The current market price of a company share divided by the *earnings per share (eps) of the company. The P/E ratio usually refers to the annual eps and is expressed as a number (e.g. 5 or 10), often called the **multiple** of the company. Loosely, it can be thought of as the number of years it would take the company to earn an amount equal to its market value. High multiples, usually associated with low *yields, indicate that the company is growing rapidly, while a low multiple is associated with dull no-growth stocks. The P/E ratio is one of the main indicators used by fundamental analysts to decide whether the shares in a company are expensive or cheap, relative to the market.

price index See CONSUMER PRICE INDEX; PRODUCER PRICE INDEX; RETAIL PRICE INDEX.

price leadership The setting of the price of a product by a dominant firm in an industry in the knowledge that competitors will follow this lead in order to avoid the high cost of a *price war. This practice is often found in *oligopolies and has the effect of a *cartel. As the price leader is as anxious as the other members of the industry to achieve a stable market, it is in their interest to set the price at a sensible level; a price leader who fails to do so will soon be replaced as leader by another member of the group. *Compare* PRICE RING.

price level The average level of prices of goods and services in an economy, usually calculated as a figure on a price index. See CONSUMER PRICE INDEX; PRODUCER PRICE INDEX; RETAIL PRICE INDEX.

price-lining strategy A pricing strategy in which a seller prices individual products in a product line in accordance with certain price points that are believed to be attractive to buyers.

price method The US term for *piece rate.

price packs Products sold at a reduced price that is marked by the producer directly on the label or package of the product.

price ring A group of firms in the same industry that have agreed amongst themselves to fix a minimum retail price for their competing products, thus forming a *cartel. Price rings are illegal in many countries unless they can be shown to be in the public interest. See CONSUMER PROTECTION; PRICE LEADERSHIP.

prices and income policy A government policy to curb *inflation by directly imposing wage restraint (*see* WAGE FREEZE) and *price controls.

price-sensitive information Information (usually unpublished) about a company that is likely to cause its share prices to move. See INSIDER DEALING.

price stabilization A pricing policy aimed at avoiding widely fluctuating prices. The marketer with this objective sets prices to match competitors' prices or to maintain existing price differentials.

price support A government policy of providing support for certain basic, usually agricultural, products to stop the price falling below an agreed level. Support prices can be administered in various ways: the government can purchase and stockpile surplus produce to support the price or it can pay producers a cash payment as a *subsidy to raise the price they obtain through normal market channels. See also COMMON AGRICULTURAL POLICY.

price theory A theory that, at the micro-economic level, defines the role of prices in consumer demand and the supply of goods by firms. At a broader level, it explains the role of prices in markets as a whole. At the macroeconomic level it treats wages and interest rates as the prices of particular goods, thus implying that governments must take market forces into account when formulating such policies as incomes policy and monetary policy.

price war Competition between two or more firms in the same industry that are seeking to increase their shares of the market by cutting the prices of their products. Although this can give short-term advantages in some circumstances to one participant, in the longer run it is a situation from which no one profits. To avoid the perils of selling products at a loss in order to outdo the competition, in most industries prices are not allowed by competitors to fall below a certain level, competition being restricted to other methods, such as advertising, improving the packaging, etc.

pricing The setting of selling prices for the products and services supplied by an organization. In many cases selling prices will be based on market prices but in other circumstances pricing will be based on costs, using information provided by the *management accounting system.

prima facie (Latin: *prima facies* first appearance) At first appearances. **Prima facie evidence** is evidence that appears to be conclusive on first appearances but is not necessarily conclusive.

primage 1. A percentage added to a freight charge to cover the cost of loading or unloading a ship. **2.** An extra charge for handling goods with special care when they are being loaded or unloaded from a ship, aircraft, etc.

primary demand *See* GENERIC DEMAND.

primary-demand advertising Advertising aimed at stimulating *generic demand.

primary domain name *See* DOMAIN NAME.

primary earnings per share *See* FULLY DILUTED EARNINGS PER SHARE.

primary market The market into which a *new issue of securities is launched. *Compare* SECONDARY MARKET.

primary production *See* PRODUCTION.

prime cost *See* DIRECT COSTS.

prime rate The rate of interest at which US banks lend money to first-class borrowers. It is similar in operation to the *base rate in the UK. Competitive markets have forced many banks, both in the USA and the UK, to offer business customers credit at below prime rates. The main difference between US and UK practice is that the US prime rate is approximately equal to the dollar three-month *London Inter Bank Offered Rate (LIBOR) plus 1%, whereas the UK base rate is approximately equivalent to the sterling three-month LIBOR.

prime time The time of the day when radio and TV audiences are expected to be at a peak and therefore advertising rates are highest.

PRINCE Acronym for *projects in controlled environments. A method of project management, used by government *information technology departments, that provides a shell within which to control a project throughout its life cycle. To the extent that this enables standardized procedures to be used, it allows managers to concentrate on content rather than process. It also permits a more structured and comparative evaluation of a process to be made.

principal 1. The sum on which interest is paid. **2.** A person who has given express or implied authority for another person to act as an *agent on his or her behalf. *See* AGENCY RELATIONSHIP.

principles of motion economy (characteristics of easy movement) Guidelines that focus on efficient and effective use of the human body, arrangements of the workplace, and design of tools and equipment. *See also* ERGONOMICS; WORK STUDY.

priority date *See* PATENT.

priority percentage (prior charge) The proportion of any profit that must be paid to holders of fixed-interest capital (*preference shares and loan stock; *see* DEBENTURE) before arriving at the sums to be distributed to holders of *ordinary shares. These percentages help to assess the security of the income of ordinary shareholders and are related to the *gearing of the company's capital.

priority sequencing *See* SEQUENCING.

prior-period adjustments Adjustments applicable to prior *accounting periods arising from changes in *accounting policies or from the correction of material errors. They do not include normal recurring adjustments or corrections of accounting estimates made in prior periods. If prior-period adjustments fall within these definitions, the *financial statements for the current period should not be distorted, but comparative information for the prior periods should be restated with a note explaining the nature of the error or change in policy. Detailed guidance is given in Section 10 of the Financial Reporting Standard Applicable in the UK and Republic of Ireland. The relevant *International Accounting Standard is IAS 8, Accounting Policies, Changes in Accounting Estimates and Errors.

privacy statement A statement provided to a customer that makes clear what type of information is collected about him or her and how it is used.

private bank 1. A *commercial bank owned by one person or a partnership (*compare* JOINT-STOCK BANK). Popular in 19th-century Britain, they have been superseded by joint-stock banks. They still exist in the USA. **2.** A bank that is not a member of a *clearing house and therefore has to use a clearing bank as an agent. **3.** A bank that is not owned by the state.

private brand *See* OWN BRAND.

private carrier *See* CARRIER.

private enterprise (free enterprise) An economic system in which citizens are allowed to own capital and property and to run their own businesses with a minimum of state interference. The free-enterprise system encourages *entrepreneurs and the making of profits by private individuals and firms. *See* FREE MARKET.

private equity firm An investment firm that seeks to make high returns by (i) obtaining a controlling interest in a target company (if this is a public company it is then taken private); (ii) subjecting it to radical financial and organizational restructuring over several years with the aim of maximizing profits; and (iii) selling the revitalized company or floating it on the stock exchange. Most private equity investment is funded by debt; acquisitions generally take the form of a highly leveraged *management buy-in (or *management buy-out; *see* BIMBO). Critics of the private equity industry, which saw spectacular growth in the early 2000s, have accused it of an *asset-stripping mentality; there have also been concerns about unfair tax advantages (*see* SHAREHOLDER DEBT; TAPER RELIEF) and exemptions from disclosure.

private finance initiative (PFI) *See* PUBLIC–PRIVATE PARTNERSHIP.

private health insurance (PHI) A form of insurance that covers all the normal costs associated with private medical treatment. PHI enables those who wish to do so to choose their own consultants, choose when and where they are hospitalized, and to have private rooms (with private telephones) in hospitals. Because these facilities are often important for managers and executives, businesses often offer PHI to senior employees as a fringe benefit. Many companies offer group schemes at discounted premiums.

private ledger A *ledger containing confidential accounts. A *control account may be used to link it to the general ledger.

private limited company Any *limited company that is not a *public limited company. Such a company is not permitted to offer its shares for sale to the public and it is free from the rules that apply to public limited companies.

private placing *See* PLACING.

private sector The part of an economy that is not under government control. In a *mixed economy most commercial and industrial firms are in the private sector, run by *private enterprise. *Compare* PUBLIC SECTOR.

private-sector liquidity *See* MONEY SUPPLY.

private treaty Any contract made by personal arrangement between the buyer and seller or their agents, i.e. not by public *auction.

privatization (denationalization) The process of selling a publicly owned company or asset (*see* NATIONALIZATION) to the private sector. Privatization may be pursued for political as well as economic reasons. The economic justification for privatization is that a company will be more efficient under private ownership, although most economists would argue that privatization will only achieve this if it is accompanied by increased competition. Politically, privatization in the form of share offers to the general public is seen as a means of widening the share-owning public and thus increasing the commitment of working people to the capitalist system.

PRO Abbreviation for public relations officer. *See* PUBLIC RELATIONS.

proactive response A management strategy in which a company seeks to preempt criticisms of its social or environmental practices by devising policies to deal with such problems before they arise. This anticipatory strategy is the most engaged of responsive strategies (*compare* ACCOMMODATING RESPONSE; DEFENSIVE RESPONSE; OBSTRUCTIVE RESPONSE).

probability The likelihood that an event or a particular result will occur. It can be represented on a scale by a number between 0 (zero probability of the event happening, i.e. it is certain not to) and 1 (certainty that it will occur). It is treated mathematically on this basis in statistics.

probability sampling (random sampling) A sampling procedure in which each element of a *population has a known chance of being selected for the *sample.

Apart from simple random sampling, this includes certain forms of *stratified sampling and *systematic sampling. The process depends upon reliable, up-to-date lists of the population being available; without such lists a probability sample cannot be chosen. *Compare* NON-PROBABILITY SAMPLING.

probate A certificate issued by the Family Division of the High Court, on the application of *executors appointed by a will, to the effect that the will is valid and that the executors are authorized to administer the deceased's estate. When there is no apparent doubt about the will's validity, probate is granted in **common form** on the executors filing an *affidavit. Probate granted in common form can be revoked by the court at any time on the application of an interested party who proves that the will is invalid. When the will is disputed, probate in **solemn form** is granted, but only if the court decides that the will is valid after hearing the evidence on the disputed issues in a **probate action**.

probate price The price of shares or other securities used for *inheritance-tax purposes on the death of the owner. The price is taken as either one quarter of the interval between the upper and lower quotations of the day on which the owner died added to the lower figure or as half way between the highest and lowest recorded bargains of the day, whichever is the lower.

probate value A valuation of all the assets included in the estate of a deceased person at the time of his or her death, taking account of any restrictions on the use of the assets. A probate value is agreed with HM Revenue and Customs for the purposes of calculating *inheritance tax.

problem child *See* BOSTON MATRIX.

problem definition The first stage in *marketing research. It consists of a clear definition of the problem to be solved and the precise objectives of the research.

problem recognition The first stage in the business buying process (*see* BUSINESS BUYER BEHAVIOUR) in which someone in a company recognizes a problem or need that can be met by acquiring a good or a service.

process 1. A specific, structured, and managed set of work activities, with known inputs, designed to produce a specified output, e.g. product development, order management, and performance monitoring. **2.** A particular configuration of the workplace, with a related set of operational capabilities and restrictions. *See* PROCESS CHOICE.

process choice The selection of the type of process to be used to provide a product or service. Options range from a one-off project approach (e.g. custom-made furniture by a craftsperson), through *batch production, to *continuous processing that produces large volumes over long periods, e.g. a cement kiln. The process decision usually commits an organization to significant capital expenditure. Each option involves a different combination of workforce skills and job-design issues, planning and control problems, inventory, and scheduling criteria. The option chosen must therefore fit with the method used by the organization to win orders. For example, a decision to compete in a large-volume low-cost market suggests the need for a mass-production line-flow process.

process costing A costing system sometimes applied to production carried out by a series of chemical or operational stages or processes. Its characteristics are that costs are accumulated for the whole production process and that average unit costs of production are computed at each stage (*see* AVERAGE COST). Special rules are applied in process costing to the valuation of *work in progress, *normal losses, and abnormal losses. In process costing it is usual to distinguish between the *main product of the process, *by-products, and joint products. *Compare* CONTINUOUS-OPERATION COSTING.

process innovation *See* BUSINESS PROCESS RE-ENGINEERING.

process layout (process-oriented layout) A factory, office, or other workplace layout in which work stations and transforming resources are grouped together. The resources to be transformed move from process to process and each product or service may follow a completely unique route, according to its needs. Typical process layouts include small engineering workshops that produce medium to high volumes of similar items. *See also* BATCH PRODUCTION; PROCESS CHOICE. *Compare* PRODUCT LAYOUT.

procuration *See* PER PROC.

produce *See* COMMODITY.

produce broker *See* COMMODITY BROKER.

producer price index (PPI) A measure of the rate of *inflation among goods purchased and manufactured by UK industry (replacing the former **wholesale price index**). It measures the movements in prices of about 10,000 goods relative to the same base year. *Compare* CONSUMER PRICE INDEX; RETAIL PRICE INDEX.

product 1. Anything that can be offered to a market for attention, acquisition, use, or consumption that might satisfy a need. It includes physical objects and services. **2.** Any item, sub-assembly or *cost unit manufactured or sold by an organization.

product adaptation The adaptation of a standard product to meet local conditions or needs, especially in foreign markets.

product assortment *See* PRODUCT MIX.

product category A subset of a *product class (e.g. cars) containing products of a certain type, e.g. sports cars.

product-category extension A new item or new line of items in a *product category new to the company offering it.

product class A broad group of products that perform similar functions or provide similar benefits but differ in the way in which they do so; for example, all cars made for personal use form a product class.

product concept The idea that consumers will favour products that offer the best quality, performance, and features and that an organization marketing products should therefore devote its energy to making continuous improvements.

product costs The costs of production when charged to the *cost units and expressed as costs of individual products. Product costs may include both *direct costs and *indirect costs (overhead); many different costing methods, such as *absorption costing, *activity-based costing, and *process costing, are used in computing product costs.

product design The process of designing the function and style of a product to ensure that it is both effective and attractive, as well as easy, safe, and inexpensive to use and service. It must also be simple and economical to produce and distribute.

product development A strategy for company growth that relies on offering modified or new products to market segments currently being served. *See* PRODUCT–MARKET STRATEGY. *See also* NEW PRODUCT DEVELOPMENT.

product differentiation The creation of a distinction between products that fulfil the same purpose but are made by different producers and therefore compete with each other. The distinction may be real (i.e. one product is better than others) or largely illusory. Producers in a competitive market use packaging, advertising, etc., to enhance the idea that significant differences exist where none in fact do. *See also* MONOPOLISTIC COMPETITION.

product diversification The strategy of marketing new products to a new set of customers. *See* PRODUCT–MARKET STRATEGY.

product elimination The process used to withdraw a product from a market in an orderly fashion so that it does not disrupt

the sale of other products marketed by the same organization.

product enhancement The introduction of a new and improved version of an existing product, in order to extend the *product life cycle by keeping it in the growth stage.

product-guarantee insurance An insurance policy covering financial loss as a consequence of a fault occurring in a company's product. A product-guarantee claim would be made, for example, to pay for the cost of recalling and repairing cars that are found to have a defective component. This type of policy would not pay compensation to customers or members of the public injured as a result of the defect. Such claims would be met by a *products-liability insurance.

product idea An idea for a possible product that the company can see itself offering to the market. If the idea is pursued, the product enters its *development stage.

product innovation charter (PIC) A statement formalizing a company's new-product strategy and giving management's rationale behind the search for innovation opportunities, the product, market, and technology upon which to focus, as well as the goals and objectives to be achieved. The charter indicates the priority managers should place on developing the search for new products, changing existing ones, and imitating competitors' products.

production The *cost units manufactured by an organization. Production may be measured in units, *direct labour hours, *machine hours, or *direct labour cost.

production cost (total cost of production) The total of all the costs incurred in producing a product or *cost unit. In a *manufacturing account the production cost is represented by the total of the *direct costs and the *manufacturing overhead. *See* COST OF GOODS MANUFACTURED.

production cost centre An area of an organization, such as a function, department, section, individual, or any group of these, in which production is carried out. *See also* COST CENTRE.

production cost variance In *standard costing, the *variance arising when the standard cost of the actual production is compared with the actual cost incurred. If the standard cost is higher than the actual cost a favourable variance arises, while if the actual cost exceeds the standard cost an adverse variance occurs. The production cost variance is usually analysed into the direct materials variances, the direct labour variances, and the fixed and variable overhead variances, each of which can be further analysed within such parameters as expenditure and efficiency. *See* ANALYSIS OF VARIANCE.

production department A section of an organization in which production is carried out.

production order (manufacturing requisition) A form issued to the production department of an organization specifying the production to be carried out by the department. A production order gives, inter alia, a description of the operations to be carried out, the quantities to be produced, the time allowed, and the completion times.

production overhead *See* MANUFACTURING OVERHEAD.

production planning The administrative operations ensuring that the material, labour, and other resources necessary to carry out production are available when and where they are required, and in the necessary quantities.

production profit *See* PROFIT ON MANUFACTURE.

production-unit method (units of production method of depreciation) A method of computing the *depreciation charge for a period on a piece of machinery in which the depreciation charge is based on the number of production units manufactured by the machine. When the machinery to be depreciated is purchased

an estimate is made of the total number of units of production that will be made by the machine over its lifetime. A rate per production unit is then computed and applied to the production over the life of the machinery. The formula per production unit is as follows:

original cost − estimated residual value/
    estimated number of production units.

Unlike the *straight-line method of depreciation, which treats depreciation as a *fixed cost, the production-unit method treats it as a *variable cost.

productivity A measure of the output of an organization or economy per unit of input (labour, raw materials, capital, etc.). *See also* UNIT LABOUR COSTS.

productivity agreement An agreement between an employer and a union in which an increase in wages is given for a measured increase in *productivity. To arrive at such an agreement, **productivity bargaining** is needed to reach a compromise between the increase in wages demanded by the unions and the increase in productivity demanded by the employers.

product layout (product-oriented layout) A factory, office, or other workplace layout in which the position of all the work stations, machines, etc., is optimized to suit the product (e.g. a car assembly line). The resources to be transformed flow along a line of transforming resources in a logical sequence, which is controlled by the requirements of the product. *Compare* PROCESS LAYOUT.

product liability The liability of manufacturers and other persons for defective products. Under the Consumer Protection Act 1987, passed to conform to the requirements of EU law, the producer of a defective product that causes death or personal injury or damage to property is strictly liable for the damage. A claim may only be made for damage to property if the property was for private use or consumption and the value of the damage caused exceeds £275. The persons liable for a defective product are the producer (i.e. the manufacturer, including producers of component parts and raw materials), any persons who hold themselves out to be producers by putting their names or trademarks on the product, a person who imports the product into the EU, and a supplier who fails, when reasonably requested to do so by the person injured, to identify the producer or importer of the product.

The purchaser of a defective product may sue the seller for *breach of contract in failing to supply a product that conforms to the contract. Under the same Act suppliers of consumer goods must ensure that the goods comply with the general safety requirement. Otherwise they commit a criminal offence. Regulations establishing a new product-safety regime, based on the EU's General Product Safety Directive, came into force in the UK in late 2005. *See also* CONSUMER PROTECTION.

product-liability insurance An insurance policy that pays any compensation the insured is legally liable to pay to customers who are killed, injured, or have property damaged as a result of a defect in a product that they have manufactured or supplied.

Costs incurred as a consequence of the defect that are not legal *damages would not be covered by a policy of this kind. *Product-guarantee insurance is intended to cover these costs.

product life cycle The course of a product's sales and profitability over its lifetime. The model describes five stages, each of which represents a different opportunity for the marketer. A new product starts in the **development stage**, during which the original idea is transformed into a prototype and its marketing strategy is worked out. This is followed by the **introduction stage**, characterized by low sales: buyers are unsure about the product and it is not stocked by all distributors. In this stage the product is adapted as customers provide feedback. Sales can be increased by introductory price offers and advertising support. If purchasers are satisfied with the product, its reputation will spread and it will enter the **growth stage**: the product will become more widely available and sales will increase. Competitors' versions will then appear and eventually the **maturity stage** will be reached, in which supply and demand are matched and sales

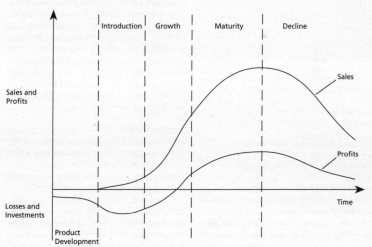

Product life cycle. Sales and profits rise during the growth and maturity stages but subsequently decline.

stabilize. The maturity stage is the longest period, characterized by intense competition. In this stage there will be an operational emphasis on reducing the costs of production in order to maximize returns, but eventually a better way of satisfying consumers' needs will almost certainly be provided by another new product and the **decline stage** will be entered. The important skill in this stage is to know when to leave the market. The duration of each stage is unique to each product. In practice, many new products will not survive beyond the introduction stage. The concept of product life cycle underpins the strategic management concept of product portfolios.

product line A group of products that are closely related because they function in a similar manner, are sold to the same customer groups, are marketed through the same types of outlets, or fall within particular price ranges. *See also* FAMILY BRAND.

product-line filling Increasing the product line by adding more items within the existing range of products. *Compare* PRODUCT-LINE STRETCHING.

product-line pricing Setting the price steps between various products in a *product line, based on differences in costs of manufacture between the products, competitors' prices, and how customers evaluate the different features in the product line.

product-line stretching Increasing the product line by lengthening it beyond its current range. *Compare* PRODUCT-LINE FILLING.

product manager *See* BRAND MANAGER.

product–market strategy (Ansoff matrix) A *marketing planning model. Companies can sell either existing or new products; and they can sell them either in markets familiar to them (existing markets) or in new markets. The resulting two-by-two matrix gives four alternative strategies for increasing sales. One is to concentrate on selling more existing products into existing markets (**market penetration**), by

Products	Old/Existing Markets	New Markets
old products	market penetration	market development
new products	product development	product diversification

Product–market strategy.

such means as price reductions and increased advertising. This is regarded as a low-risk low-gain strategy offering few prospects of sustained growth in the longer term. Alternatively, an organization can modify or improve its existing products and sell these to current customers (**product development**); for example, a lawn-mower manufacturer might install a more powerful motor in its products. The third option is to sell existing products to a new market (**market development**)—for example, to export the current range of lawn mowers to America. These two strategies are medium-risk with good prospects for growth in the medium term. The highest-risk strategy is to develop new products for new markets (**product diversification**)—for example, for the lawn-mower manufacturer to develop printing machinery for the publishing industry. Despite the higher risk, this is considered the best strategy for long-term growth. *See also* DEFENDER STRATEGY; PROSPECTOR STRATEGY.

product mix (product assortment) All the *product lines and items that a particular seller offers for sale.

product obsolescence A condition that occurs when an existing product becomes out of date as a result of the introduction of a new or improved product or changes in taste or fashion. *See* OBSOLESCENCE.

product orientation The attitude of a company that believes the product comes first and persuading customers to buy it follows. **Market orientation** typifies the attitude of a company that will only produce what it believes it can sell.

product portfolio A collection of products marketed by one company. An analysis of a product portfolio focuses on the interrelationships of products within a *product mix. The performance of the mix of products is emphasized rather than the performance of individual products.

product position The way a product is seen by consumers in terms of its important attributes, i.e. the place the product occupies in consumers' minds, relative to competing products. *See* PERCEPTUAL MAPPING; POSITIONING.

product prototype tests Tests conducted to obtain the reactions of target customers to working versions of new products in their *development stage to assess marketability. *See* NEW PRODUCT DEVELOPMENT.

product quality The ability of a product to perform its advertised functions, in the mind of the consumer. A product's quality includes its durability, reliability, precision, ease of operation, and its ability to be repaired if it goes wrong. Some of these quality attributes can be measured objectively, while others can only be assessed in terms of consumers' perceptions. It is important that companies should achieve consistency of quality. *See* TOTAL QUALITY MANAGEMENT.

product salesforce structure The structure of a company's salesforce in which salespeople specialize in selling only a portion of the company's *product lines.

product-sustaining-level activities *See* ACTIVITY.

professional indemnity insurance (PII) A form of third-party insurance that covers a professional person, such as a solicitor, surveyor, or accountant, against paying compensation in the event of being sued for *negligence. This can include giving defective advice, if the person professes to be an expert in a given field. There have been a number of very high awards made to plaintiffs (especially in the USA where PII is known as **malpractice insurance**) and

this has greatly increased the cost of obtaining cover. One solution is for firms, of accountants for example, to form *limited liability partnerships rather than traditional partnerships.

professional service technology The type of processing technology used in service industries, which are typified by high customer contact and professional service providers (e.g. legal advice, medical general practice). The service providers are constrained by the practices of their professions as much as by the needs of their organizations; the relationship between the client and the professional is central to the service. *Compare* MASS SERVICE TECHNOLOGY.

professional valuation An assessment of the value of an asset (share, property, stock, etc.) in the balance sheet or prospectus of a company, by a person professionally qualified to give such a valuation. The professional qualification necessary will depend on the asset; for example, a qualified surveyor may be needed to value property, whereas unlisted shares might best be valued by a qualified accountant.

profit 1. (margin; profit margin) For a single transaction or set of transactions, the excess of sales revenue over the costs of providing the goods or services sold. *See* GROSS PROFIT; NET PROFIT. **2.** For a period of trading, the surplus of net assets at the end of a period over the net assets at the start of that period, adjusted where relevant for amounts of capital injected or withdrawn by the proprietors. As profit is notoriously hard to define, it is not always possible to derive one single figure of profit for an organization from an accepted set of data.

profitability The capacity or potential of a project or an organization to make a *profit. Measures of profitability include *return on capital employed and the ratio of net profit to sales.

profitability index (PI) A method used in *discounted cash flow for ranking a range of projects under consideration, in which *standard cash flow patterns are projected. It is based on the ratio:

> total present values of cash inflows/
> initial investment,

the value of which is compared for each project.

The projects with a PI of less than 1 are not expected to earn the required *rate of return and are rejected. The projects with a PI in excess of 1 are ranked according to the magnitude of the PI.

profitability ratios Financial metrics that are used to measure a company's ability to generate *profit relative to other key variables, such as sales, assets, or equity. Different measures of profitability may be used, including *gross profit, *EBITDA, *EBIT, and *net profit. The ratio is applied to a particular period of trading. Some commonly employed profitability ratios include *net profit percentage, *gross profit percentage, and *return on capital employed, in which an agreed measure of profit is expressed as a proportion of total investment. *See* RATIO ANALYSIS.

profitable customer A person, household, or company providing long-term revenues that exceed, by an acceptable amount, the company's costs of attracting, selling, and servicing that customer. *See* CUSTOMER PROFITABILITY ANALYSIS.

profit and loss account (P & L account) 1. An *account in the books of an organization showing the profits (or losses) made on its business activities with the deduction of the appropriate expenses. **2. (income statement)** A statement of the profit (or loss) of an organization over a financial period. It is one of the statutory accounts that, for most limited companies, has to be filed annually with the UK Registrar of Companies (*see* ANNUAL ACCOUNTS). The profit and loss account explains what has happened since the previous *balance sheet; the users of financial statements require information on the progress and future prospects of the company. Under the Financial Reporting Standard Applicable in the UK and Republic of Ireland the P & L (or income

statement) may appear as a separate item within the *statement of total recognized gains and losses (comprehensive income statement) or as an integral part of that statement.

The P & L account typically consists of three parts. The first is a trading account, showing the total sales income less the costs of production, etc., and any changes in the value of stock or work in progress from the last accounting period. This gives the *gross profit (or loss). The second part gives any other income and lists administrative and other costs to arrive at a *net profit (or loss). From this net profit before taxation the appropriate corporation tax is deducted to give the net profit after taxation. In the third part, the net profit after tax is appropriated to dividends or to reserves (retained profit). The UK Companies Act gives a choice of four formats, one of which must be used to file a profit and loss account for a registered company.

profit centre A section or area of an organization to which revenue can be traced, together with the appropriate costs, so that profits can be ascribed to that area. Profit centres may be divisions, subsidiaries, or departments.

profiteer A person who makes excessive profits by charging inflated prices for a commodity that is in short supply, especially during a war or national disaster.

profit forecast A forecast by the directors of a public company of the profits to be expected in a stated period. If a new flotation is involved, the profit forecast must be reported on by the reporting accountants and the sponsor to the share issue. An existing company is not required to make a profit forecast with its *accounts, but if it does it must be reported on by the company's auditors.

profit margin *See* PROFIT. *See also* MARGIN.

profit on manufacture (production profit) The margin obtained when manufactured items or finished goods are transferred from the factory at a price in excess of the cost of production. The technique is used in organizations wishing to submit the production departments to market prices and therefore credit production according to some formula; for example, at a price per unit. The system may also create a **loss on manufacture**. *See also* MANUFACTURING ACCOUNT; MANUFACTURING PROFIT/LOSS.

profit-pool concept The identification of a constellation of minor purchases surrounding a major purchase, and the identification of the money value and profitability of each of these related sales.

profit-related pay (PRP) 1. The situation in which the pay of employees is related to the profit made by the employer. The purpose is to increase motivation, commitment, and effort by the workforce by ensuring that all staff have a positive stake in the commercial success of the company. For such a scheme to be a success it must be believed in, valued, and understood by all concerned. Staff must clearly understand that a bonus payment will be forthcoming if the organization has a good year but will not be if the organization does not make profits. Above all, profit-related pay should never be used as a means of cutting wage and salary bills. Its general effect is to put up wage and salary bills and this legitimately raises the expectations of the individuals concerned.

Profit-related rewards are usually offered in one of two ways. The simplest of these is to allocate an amount from the surplus generated by the organization and to share this out among employees. For maximum equality, this will be as a percentage increase in all employees' salaries. The other approach is to offer shares in the organization; the employees will thus become investors in their own future. In the UK, the Bell-Hanson Report (1989), researching 113 publicly quoted companies, found that profit-sharing companies out-performed others by an average of 27% on returns on capital, earnings per share, and profit and sales growth. *See also* GAIN SHARING; PROFIT-SHARING SCHEME. **2.** A former UK scheme enabling employees to be paid part of their salary tax-free; it was

phased out in 2000–01. Payments to employees under a registered scheme could be tax-free up to the maximum for the year.

profits available for distribution *See* DISTRIBUTABLE PROFITS.

profit-sharing ratio (PSR) The ratio in which the profits or losses of a business are shared. For a partnership, the profit-sharing ratios will be set out in the *partnership agreement. This will show the amount, usually given as a percentage of the total profits, attributable to each partner. In some agreements there is a first charge on profits, which is an allocation of the first slice of the profits for the year. The remainder will then be split in the profit-sharing ratios as specified in the agreement. The profit-sharing ratios can also apply to the capital of the partnership, but this does not always follow. The partnership agreement can specify a different capital-sharing ratio. If no specific agreement has been made, profits and losses will be shared equally in accordance with the Partnership Act 1890.

profit-sharing scheme A scheme by which employees share in the profits of a business, usually through some type of share ownership. *See* EMPLOYEE SHARE OWNERSHIP PLAN; EMPLOYEE SHARE OWNERSHIP TRUST; SAVINGS RELATED SHARE OPTION SCHEME; SHARE OPTION. *See also* GAIN SHARING; PROFIT-RELATED PAY.

profits tax Any tax on the profits of a company. *Corporation tax in the UK is a form of profits tax.

profit variance In *standard costing, the variance consisting of the difference between the *standard operating profit budgeted to be made on the items sold and the actual profits made. The analysis of the profit variance into its constituent sales, direct labour, direct material, and overhead variances provides the management of the organization with information regarding the source of the gains and losses compared to the predetermined standard. *See* ANALYSIS OF VARIANCE.

profit–volume chart (PV chart) A graph showing the profits and losses to be made at each level of activity. The profit/loss line is usually plotted as a linear function, and the graph shows the total fixed cost level as the loss at zero activity, the *breakeven point activity level, and the profits or losses at each level of production or sales.

profit warning An announcement by a company that its future profits will be significantly lower than previously announced or forecast.

proforma financial statements *Financial statements for a period prepared before the end of the period, which therefore contain estimates.

proforma invoice A *sales invoice sent in certain circumstances to a buyer, usually before some of the invoice details are known. For example, in commodity trading a proforma invoice may be sent to the buyer at the time of shipment, based on a notional weight, although the contract specifies that the buyer will only pay for the weight ascertained on landing the goods at the port of destination. When the missing facts are known, in this case the landed weight, a *final invoice is sent.

programme evaluation and review technique (PERT) *See* NETWORK MODELLING.

program trading Trading on financial markets using computer programs that trigger automatic trades once certain limits are reached. Program trading was introduced in the late 1980s and has been partly blamed for the market crash in October 1987. Although the New York Stock Exchange imposed limits on program trading, it now accounts for some 30% of trades on NYSE. Advances in technology have seen the development of program trading into the more sophisticated use of computer algorithms in *high-frequency trading.

progress chaser A person who is responsible for following the progress of work being done in a factory or office and for seeing that it is completed on time.

progressive tax A tax in which the rate of tax increases with increases in the *tax base. In the UK, the most obvious such tax is *income tax but progressive rates are also applied to *National Insurance contributions, *inheritance tax, and to a limited extent *corporation tax. Such taxes are generally justified on the *ability-to-pay principle. *Compare* FLAT TAX; REGRESSIVE TAX.

progress payment An instalment of a total payment made to a contractor, when a specified stage of the operation has been completed.

project A set of activities intended to produce a specific output, which has a definite beginning and end. The activities are interrelated and must be brought together in a particular order, based on precedence relationships between the different activities. Examples of projects include the building of the Channel Tunnel and the design of a computer system for an ambulance service. Projects are usually based on bringing together teams of

Profit–volume chart.

specialists within relatively temporary management structures. Project management techniques are increasingly being used to manage such tasks as the introduction of *total quality management within organizations.

project financing (limited recourse financing) An arrangement in which the money or loans put up for a particular project (often a major property development) are secured on that project and its foreseen earnings rather than forming part of the general borrowing of the company concerned. In case of default, the lender has no recourse to the other assets of the company.

projective techniques Methods of exploring respondents' deepest feelings in marketing research, by asking them to project these feelings into an unstructured situation. This technique, which has been borrowed from clinical psychology, encourages respondents to reveal their unconscious feelings and *attitudes, without realizing that they are doing so. Projective techniques used include: word association tests, sentence completion tests, story completion tests, and cartoons with blank balloons to fill in.

project management software Software designed to facilitate and integrate key tasks in the management of a large project. These typically include scheduling, *network modelling, budget control, and administrative support; the system may also include a collaborative *decision support system. A good system will be integrated and dynamic, so that the total knock-on effect of any departures from the original plan can be assessed in key areas (e.g. budgeting, scheduling) as the project evolves.

project progress reporting The monitoring and reporting of progress on projects, in particular time and cost variations. The successful use of project planning tools, such as critical-path analysis and PERT (*see* NETWORK MODELLING), is dependent on a regular comparison between planned and actual performance

and the consequent updating of the data used in the models. Modern *project management software can calculate the impact of individual variations and the synergistic effects of multiple variations and are able to update all forms of output. Typical outputs include: actual costs of work completed, budgeted costs of work completed, and budgeted costs of work scheduled.

promissory note A document that is a *negotiable instrument and contains a promise to pay a certain sum of money to a named person, to that person's order, or to the bearer at a specified time in the future. It must be unconditional, signed by the maker, and delivered to the payee or bearer. They are widely used in the USA but are not in common use in the UK. A promissory note cannot be reissued, unless the promise is made by a banker and is payable to the bearer, i.e. unless it is a banknote.

promoter A person involved in setting up and funding a new company, including preparing its *articles of association and *memorandum of association, registering the company, finding directors, and raising subscriptions. The promoter is in a position of trust with regard to the new company and may not make an undisclosed profit or benefit at its expense. A promoter may be personally liable for the fulfilment of a contract entered into by, or on behalf of, the new company before it has been formed.

promotion *See* SALES PROMOTION.

promotional allowance A payment or price reduction to reward dealers for participating in advertising programmes and sales-support programmes.

promotional mix An organization's total promotional effort, including personal selling, advertising, publicity, public relations, and *sales promotion. The promotional mix attempts to attain *integrated marketing communications.

promotional pricing Temporarily setting the price of products below the list price, and sometimes even below cost, to increase sales in the short term.

prompt cash Payment terms for goods or services in which payment is due within a few days (usually not more than 14) of delivery of the goods or the rendering of the service.

prompt day (prompt date) 1. The day (date) on which payment is due for the purchase of goods. In some commodity spot markets it is the day payment is due and delivery of the goods may be effected. **2.** The date on which a contract on a commodity exchange matures.

proper accounting records *Accounting records that are sufficient to show and explain an organization's transactions. For a company, the Companies Act requires that these records should be able to disclose with reasonable accuracy, at any time, the financial position of the company and enable the directors to ensure that the *balance sheet and *profit and loss account comply with the statutory regulations. In particular, the accounting records shall contain entries of all money received and spent and a record of the *assets and *liabilities of the company. If goods are being bought and sold, stock records must also be sufficient. In forming an *audit opinion an auditor performing a *statutory audit under the Companies Act will consider whether proper accounting records have been kept and proper returns adequate for audit have been received from branches not visited. Furthermore, the auditor will consider whether the accounts are in agreement with the accounting records and returns. *See also* STATUTORY BOOKS.

property Something capable of being owned (*see* PERSONAL PROPERTY; REAL PROPERTY). It may be tangible, such as a building or work of art, or intangible, such as a right of way or an *intellectual property, such as a copyright.

property bond A bond issued by a life-assurance company, the premiums for which are invested in a fund that owns property.

property income certificate (PINC) A certificate giving the bearer a share in the value of a particular property and a share of the income from it. PINCs can be bought and sold.

property insurance Insurance covering loss, damage, or destruction of any form of item from personal computers to industrial plant and machinery. Property-insurance policies are a form of *indemnity in which the insurer undertakes to make good the loss suffered by the insured. The policy may state the specific compensation payable in the event of loss or damage; if it does not, the policy will normally pay the intrinsic value of the insured object, taking into account any appreciation or depreciation on the original cost. Such policies usually have a maximum sum for which the insurers are liable.

property register *See* LAND REGISTRATION.

property tax A tax based on the value of property owned by a taxpayer. In the UK, council tax or *business rates are charged on the value of a property, as defined by a series of value bands, which depend on the region of the UK in which the property is situated.

proportional tax *See* FLAT TAX.

proportional treaty (quota share reinsurance treaty) A *reinsurance agreement in which the risks are transferred in direct proportion to the premiums paid over.

proportionate stratified sampling A *probability sampling method in which different strata in a *population are identified and the number of elements drawn from each stratum is proportionate to the relative number of elements in each stratum. For example, if the population consisted of 55% females and 45% males, then a sample would be drawn in the same proportions. *Compare* DISPROPORTIONATE

STRATIFIED SAMPLING. *See* STRATIFIED SAMPLING.

proposal solicitation The stage in the business buying process (*see* BUSINESS BUYER BEHAVIOUR) in which the buyer invites qualified suppliers to submit proposals.

proposed dividend A *dividend that has been recommended by the directors of a company but not yet paid.

proprietary company *See* PTY.

proprietary network A network of *automated teller machines (ATMs) available for use only by the customers of a specific bank or financial institution or some other limited group. Proprietary networks have been supplanted by ATM networks that allow the customers of a bank to use free of charge the withdrawal facilities of several other banks with which it has entered a reciprocal agreement.

proprietary standard A software protocol owned and controlled by a specific company. Microsoft Windows is an example of a proprietary standard.

proprietorship register *See* LAND REGISTRATION.

pro rata (Latin: in proportion) Denoting a method of dividing something between a number of participants in proportion to some factor. For example, some of the profits of a company are shared, pro rata, among the shareholders, i.e. in proportion to the number of shares each shareholder owns.

prospect fee *See* CLICKTHROUGH FEE.

prospecting In sales, the process of identifying likely customers by searching lists of previous customers, lists of trade associations, government publications, and a variety of other sources.

prospector strategy A competitive strategy that emphasizes product innovation and the search for new market opportunities. Such an approach requires creativity and organizational flexibility; it is

most likely to succeed in an area characterized by fast-developing technology. *Compare* DEFENDER STRATEGY.

prospect theory A theory, developed by the economists Daniel Kahneman and Amos Tversky, that seeks to explain how individuals make decisions when faced with uncertainty. It is central to the growing area of research known as *behavioural finance, which posits that psychology plays a major part in financial decision making. In essence, prospect theory has three components, which concern the role played by decision frames, mistakes in relation to evaluating probabilities, and a *risk preference structure. To help them make a decision individuals use a framework, which has a strong influence on the decision made. Individuals believe that improbable events are more likely to occur than they are in practice, and conversely that probable events are less likely to occur than they are in practice. Typically, they define outcomes in terms of gains and losses, with the latter having a more important impact on their welfare than the former. *See also* UTILITY THEORY.

prospectus A document that gives details about a new issue of shares and invites the public to buy shares or debentures in the company. A copy must be filed with the Registrar of Companies. The prospectus of a *listed company must comply with Stock Exchange regulations; that of an unlisted company must conform to the provisions of the Financial Services and Markets Act 2000. In either case, it will describe the aims, capital structure, and any past history of the venture, and may contain future *profit forecasts. There are heavy penalties for knowingly making false statements in a prospectus. *See* OFFER BY PROSPECTUS.

protean career A career that involves frequent changes of organization, work setting, and job content, as opposed to one that involves commitment to a single organization or line of work. Such a career will be shaped by the individual's own needs, goals, and values rather than by organizational structures or received ideas of professional development. Success will depend on adaptability, self-motivation, and a willingness to learn new skills. It has been argued that the increasing trend towards protean career patterns has radically altered the nature of *psychological contracts between organizations and their employees.

protective duty A tariff imposed on an import to protect domestic manufacturers from foreign competition.

protest A certificate signed by a *notary public at the request of the holder of a *bill of exchange that has been refused payment or acceptance. It is a legal requirement after *noting the bill (*see also* ACCEPTANCE SUPRA PROTEST). The same procedure can also be used for a *promissory note that has been dishonoured.

protocol The rules governing the communications between different computers or computer peripherals. The protocol is a formal statement of how data is to be set out when messages are exchanged, the order and priority of various messages, and so on.

prototype A preproduction model developed to evaluate the feasibility of new ideas, materials, technology, and design techniques as part of *new product development. In addition to the technological evaluation, consumer clinics may be used to establish the opinion of potential customers on the acceptability of the product.

provider-based revenue Fees paid to a website owner by other businesses to gain access to the website's visitors. Examples include advertising fees and *clickthrough fees.

provision An amount set aside out of profits in the accounts of an organization for a known liability (even though the specific amount might not be known) or for the diminution in value of an asset. Common examples include *provisions for bad debts, for *depreciation, and for *accruals. According to the UK Companies Act notes must be given to explain every material

provision in the accounts of a limited company. Because of abuses in the use of provision, current accounting rules define a provision quite narrowly as a definite liability arising from a past event that is nevertheless of uncertain timing or amount; this would not include e.g. a provision for depreciation. Detailed guidance can be found in Section 21 of the Financial Reporting Standard Applicable in the UK and Republic of Ireland. The relevant *International Accounting Standard is IAS 37, Provisions, Contingent Liabilities and Contingent Assets.

provisional liquidator A person appointed by a court after the presentation of a winding-up petition on a company (*see* COMPULSORY LIQUIDATION). The provisional liquidator, whose powers are limited, has to protect the interests of all the parties involved until the winding-up order is made. The *official receiver is normally appointed to this post. *See also* LIQUIDATOR.

provision for bad debts An amount calculated to cover the debts during an *accounting period that are not expected to be paid. A **general provision**, e.g. 2% of debtors, is not allowed as a deduction for tax purposes. A **specific provision**, in which specific debts are identified, is allowed if there is documentary evidence to indicate that these debts are unlikely to be paid. A **provision for doubtful debts** (or **allowance for doubtful accounts**) is treated in the same way for tax purposes.

provision for depreciation *See* DEPRECIATION.

proximate cause The dominant and effective cause of an event or chain of events that results in a claim on an insurance policy. The loss must be caused directly, or as a result of a chain of events initiated, by an insured peril. For example, a policy covering storm damage would also pay for items in a freezer that deteriorate because of a power cut caused by the storm, which is the proximate cause of the loss of the frozen food.

proximo *See* INSTANT.

proxy A person who acts in the place of a member of a company at a company meeting at which one or more votes are taken. The proxy need not be a member of the company but it is quite common for directors to offer themselves as proxies for shareholders who cannot attend a meeting. Notices calling meetings must state that a member may appoint a proxy and the appointment of a proxy is usually done on a form provided by the company with the notice of the meeting; it must be returned to the company not less than 48 hours before the meeting. A **two-way proxy form** is printed so that the member can state whether the proxy should vote for or against a particular resolution. A **special proxy** is empowered to act at one specified meeting; a **general proxy** is authorized to vote at any meeting.

PRP Abbreviation for *profit-related pay.

PRT Abbreviation for *petroleum revenue tax.

prudence concept The *accounting concept that insists on a realistic view of business activity and stresses that anticipated revenues and profits have no place in a *profit and loss account until they have been realized in the form of cash or other assets for which the ultimate cash value can be assessed with reasonable certainty. However, provision should be made for all known expenses and losses whether the amount of these is known with certainty or is a best estimate in the context of the information available.

The prudence concept was identified as a fundamental accounting concept in *Statement of Standard Accounting Practice (SSAP) 2, Disclosure of Accounting Policies, the UK Companies Acts, and the EU's *Fourth Company Law Directive; it is also emphasized in the Financial Reporting Standard Applicable in the UK and Republic of Ireland. However, current thinking recognizes the prudence concept as a desirable rather than a fundamental quality of financial information.

Prudential Regulation Authority (PRA) A new body established in April 2013 as the UK's prudential regulator for banks, building societies, credit unions, insurers, and major investment firms. Under the Financial Services Act 2012 it is one of two successor bodies to the *Financial Services Authority (FSA), the other being the *Financial Conduct Authority. The stated objective of the PRA is to play a more active role in promoting the safety and soundness of institutions than the FSA and to create a more resilient financial system. It is part of the Bank of England.

prudent insurer A theoretical insurer who needs to know all the *material facts before entering into a contract of insurance. The insured must not conceal any information that a prudent insurer would need to know in assessing a risk.

prudent-man rule (prudent-person rule) A US criterion for managing investments, especially in relation to pensions, that is designed to avoid reckless speculation. It requires that a *fiduciary behave as a notional prudent man or woman would when making an investment.

PSBR Abbreviation for Public Sector Borrowing Requirement. *See* PUBLIC SECTOR NET CASH REQUIREMENT.

PSNCR Abbreviation for *Public Sector Net Cash Requirement.

PSR Abbreviation for *profit-sharing ratio.

psychographic segmentation Dividing a market into different groups, based on social class, lifestyle, and personality characteristics. *See also* GEODEMOGRAPHIC SEGMENTATION; MARKET SEGMENTATION.

psychological contract The psychological nature of a contract between an organization and its staff. This encompasses the implications and expectations that arise as a result of the relationship. Psychological contracts can take various forms:

- A **coercive contract** is one in which the relationship between an organization and its staff, or between an organization and its customers, is based on coercion. An example of this occurs if sections of the community are forced into using a monopoly or near-monopoly for an essential commodity or service (electricity, telecommunication, or fuel). It can occur with institutions, such as schools and colleges, where the students attend because they are required to do so by society.

- In an **alienative contract** the relationship between staff and the employing organization is negative. This traditionally applied to large sophisticated organizations, especially to staff working on production lines and in administrative hierarchies, in which they have very little control over the quality and output of work.

- A **remunerative contract** is one in which the relationship between staff and the employing organization is clearly drawn up in terms of money paid in return for the time spent at work. It is normally used when there is a low level of mutual identity between the staff and the organization.

- A **calculative contract** is one in which the staff have a low commitment to the goals of the employing organization and a high commitment to earnings and satisfaction. It is a key feature of the wage–work bargain for production and administrative staff. For those with professional and technical expertise, the calculative relationship is based on the ability to practise, the need to find an outlet for these skills, and individual drives to serve and become expert.

- In a **normative contract** the individual is highly committed to the objectives of the employing organization. This is usually found in religious organizations, political parties, and trade unions, and also occurs with some business organizations if the wage–work bargain is sound and the organization accepts a range of obligations and responsibilities to ensure that it is maintained.

See also ORGANIZATIONAL COMMITMENT; PROTEAN CAREER.

psychological pricing An approach to pricing that reflects the psychological impact of prices and not simply the economics of the situation. There is evidence that in some instances consumers can associate higher prices with better quality. *See* PRESTIGE PRICE.

psychological tests (personality tests) Tests designed to assess the personalities and abilities of individuals to determine their suitability for a particular job and to make best use of their talents. With the increasing use of computers to analyse information, the tests used in *personnel selection have become increasingly complex; choosing the wrong person for a senior job can be costly and have far-reaching effects in a competitive market. *See also* ASSESSMENT CENTRE; INTEREST FACTORS.

Pty Abbreviation for proprietary company, the name given to a *private limited company in Australia and the Republic of South Africa. The abbreviation Pty is used after the name of the company as Ltd is used in the UK. It is also used in the USA for an insurance company owned by outside shareholders.

public company A company whose shares are available to the public through a stock exchange. *See* PUBLIC LIMITED COMPANY.

public corporation A state-owned organization set up either to provide a national service (such as the British Broadcasting Corporation) or to run a nationalized industry. The chairman and members of the board of a public corporation are usually appointed by the appropriate government minister. The public corporation attempts to reconcile public accountability for the use of public finance, freedom of commercial operation on a day-to-day basis, and maximum benefits for the community.

public debts The debts of the *public sector of the economy, including the national debt.

public deposits The balances to the credit of government departments held at the Bank of England.

public issue (public offering) An *offer for sale in which the public are invited, through advertisements in the national press, to apply for a new issue of shares or other securities at a price fixed by the company. *Compare* ISSUE BY TENDER. *See also* INITIAL PUBLIC OFFERING.

publicity The technique of attracting the attention of the public to a product, organization, or event by the mass media. Publicity involves a third party, such as a newspaper editor or TV presenter, who determines whether the message is sufficiently newsworthy to publish and what the nature of the message should be.

public-liability insurance An insurance policy that pays compensation to a member of the public and court costs in the event of the policyholder being successfully sued for causing death, injury, or damage to property by failing to take reasonable care in his or her actions or those of any employees. A business whose work brings it into contact with the public must have a public-liability policy. *Compare* PRODUCT-LIABILITY INSURANCE. *See also* EMPLOYERS' LIABILITY INSURANCE; PROFESSIONAL INDEMNITY INSURANCE.

public limited company (plc) A company registered under the Companies Act as a public company. Its name must end with the initials 'plc' (or its Welsh equivalent, c.c.c.). It must have a share capital of at least £50,000 or the euro equivalent, of which at least 25% must be paid up. The company's constitutional documents must comply with the format given in the Companies (Model Articles) Regulation 2008. It may offer shares and securities to the public. The regulation of such companies is stricter than that of private companies. Most public companies are converted from private companies, under the re-registration procedure in the Companies Act.

public offering *See* PUBLIC ISSUE. *See also* INITIAL PUBLIC OFFERING.

public policy The interests of the community. If a *contract is (on common-law principles) contrary to public policy, this will normally make it an *illegal contract. In a few cases, however, such a contract is void but not illegal, and is treated slightly more leniently (for example, by *severance). Contracts that are illegal because they contravene public policy include any contract to commit a crime or a tort or to defraud the revenue, any contract that prejudices national safety or the administration of justice, and any immoral contract. Contracts that are merely void include contracts in *restraint of trade.

public–private partnership (PPP) In the UK, any of various schemes devised to bring private-sector investment and expertise into the provision of public services. Examples include the **private-finance initiative** (**PFI**) hospital-building programme in the National Health Service, the sale of local authority housing stock to housing associations, and the failed plan to modernize and refurbish the London Underground. Advocates of the policy claim that it will result in better services and lower costs; sceptics argue that the real attraction to government is the fact that PPPs enable upfront borrowing costs to be passed to the private sector, thus improving the Treasury balance sheet.

public relations (PR) Influencing the public so that they regard an individual, firm, charity, etc., in a favourable light in comparison to their competitors. In business a good corporate image is an important asset. Some media personalities, large companies, and national charities employ their own **public relations officers (PROs)** to deal with the media, provide information in the form of handouts, and to represent their principals at *press conferences, etc. Others use **public relations agencies** to fulfil these functions. PR does not involve paid advertising, which is a quite separate activity. While an advertising agent will plan an advertising campaign, charging a percentage of the money spent, PR agencies, for a flat fee (plus expenses), will seek to promote their principals by persuading newspapers to feature them in articles, by obtaining publicity for their products, by arranging for TV and radio personalities to interview them, and by lobbying. PR agencies also handle unfavourable reports and rumours.

public sector That part of the economy that involves the activities of the government and local authorities. This includes education, the health and social services, the police, local public services, etc., as well as state-owned industries and *public corporations. *Compare* PRIVATE SECTOR.

Public Sector Net Cash Requirement (PSNCR) The amount by which UK government expenditure exceeds its income (i.e. the **public sector deficit**); this must be financed by borrowing (e.g. by selling gilt-edged securities). As an indicator of government fiscal policy the PSNCR has acquired increased status since the late 1970s. By that time many economists had come to believe that a high PSNCR is not only inflationary but also has the effect of raising interest rates, reducing private investment, and 'crowding out' private expenditure. Concern about the high level of the PSNCR again became acute in the wake of the financial crash of 2008, leading the Conservative-led government to embark on a controversial austerity programme from 2010. The PSNCR was formally known as the **Public Sector Borrowing Requirement (PSBR)**.

public trustee A state official in charge of the Public Trust Office, a trust corporation set up for certain statutory purposes. Being a *corporation sole, the office exists irrespective of the person performing it. He or she may act as *administrator of small estates, as *trustee for English trusts where required, and as *receiver when directed to do so by a court. Another duty is to hold funds of registered *Friendly Societies and trade unions.

public warehouse *See* WAREHOUSE.

published accounts Accounts of organizations published according to UK law. The most common are the accounts of *limited companies, which must be provided for their shareholders and filed with the Registrar of Companies at Companies House, Cardiff. Companies often include additional documents for shareholders that are not required by company law. *See* ANNUAL ACCOUNTS; ANNUAL RETURN.

puffery The practice of exaggerating a product's good points in advertising or other promotional media. Flamboyant claims of this kind that are not likely to be taken literally by consumers are considered part of the normal rhetoric of advertising: as such, they are not prohibited by the Fair Trading Act.

puisne mortgage A legal *mortgage of unregistered land that is not protected by the deposit of title deeds. It should instead be protected by registration.

pul (*plural* **puli**) A monetary unit of Afghanistan worth one hundredth of an *afghani.

pula (BWP) The standard monetary unit of Botswana, divided into 100 thebe.

pull manufacturing systems Systems, such as *just in time, in which production only takes place when there is a demand from the next stage in the process or from the customer.

pull strategy A strategy that requires high spending on advertising and consumer promotion to build up consumer demand for a product. If the strategy is successful, consumers will ask their retailers for the product, the retailers will ask the wholesalers, and the wholesalers will ask the producers. Thus, the product will be pulled through the *distribution channel. *Compare* PUSH STRATEGY.

pulsing The scheduling of advertisements in short bursts, over a certain period.

pumping The colloquial name for the injection of money into the US banking system by the *Federal Reserve Bank to force down interest rates.

punt The Irish pound: formerly the standard monetary unit of the Republic of Ireland, divided into 100 pence. It was replaced by the *euro in 2002.

punter A speculator on a financial market, especially one who hopes to make quick profits.

purchase day book (bought day book; purchases journal) The *book of prime entry in which invoice amounts for purchases are entered.

purchase decision *See* CONSUMER BUYING BEHAVIOUR.

purchased goodwill *Goodwill acquired when a business is purchased as opposed to that which has been internally generated.

purchased life annuity An *annuity in which a single premium purchases an income to be paid from a specified future date for the rest of the policyholder's life.

purchase fund A fund used to purchase bonds that have fallen below *par value.

purchase intent scales Scales used in marketing research to measure a respondent's intention to buy or not buy a product. They are most often used when a company is testing a new product and is attempting to gauge the potential sales of the product.

purchase ledger (creditors' ledger) The *ledger in which the personal accounts of an organization's suppliers are recorded. The total of the balances in this ledger represents the organization's *trade creditors.

purchase ledger control account An account in the *nominal ledger to which the totals of the entries in the *purchase day book are posted at regular intervals. With this procedure the balance on the purchase ledger control account should, at any time, equal the aggregate of the balances on all the individual accounts in the ledger. The balance also represents the total of *trade creditors.

purchase method In the USA, a method of accounting for business combinations in which cash and other assets are distributed or liabilities incurred. The purchase method is used if the criteria are not met for the pooling-of-interests method. With the purchase method, the acquirer records the net assets acquired at the fair value on the market. Any excess of the purchase price over fair market value is recorded as *goodwill. The net income of the acquired company is recognized from the date of acquisition.

purchases budget A budget set for the purchasing function of an organization under a system of *budgetary control, which plans the volumes and cost of the purchases to be made in a budget period. It will usually provide an analysis of the budgets by material and by *accounting period.

purchasing and supply management *See* SUPPLY-CHAIN MANAGEMENT.

purchasing officer An employee of a manufacturer, who is responsible for purchasing the raw materials used in the manufacturing process. If these include raw materials that fluctuate in price, the purchasing officer has to show that the average purchase price for the year is not excessive. The purchasing officer is also responsible for maintaining adequate stocks to tide the company over any break in the continuity of supply, without tying up excessive amounts of capital.

purchasing power The ability to purchase goods and services. In times of inflation a loss of purchasing power occurs when *monetary assets are held because of the decline in the purchasing power of the currency. If a company has monetary liabilities, a purchasing power gain will arise because the absolute sum of the loans will be repaid with currency with less purchasing power.

purchasing power parity (PPP) The theory that, after adjusting for the exchange rate, the cost of a good should be the same in all countries. In other words, the rate of exchange between two currencies should be such that each currency has exactly the same purchasing power in its own economy. This is never actually the case, although over the long term exchange rates do appear to adjust to differences in national inflation. This latter proposition is referred to as the **relative purchasing power parity theory**. *See also* BIG MAC INDEX.

pure competition *See* PERFECT COMPETITION.

pure endowment assurance An assurance policy that promises to pay an agreed amount if the policyholder is alive on a specified future date. If the policyholder dies before the specified date no payment is made and the premium payments cease. The use of the word 'assurance' for this type of contract is questionable as there is no element of life-assurance cover.

pure monopoly A market in which there is a single seller. It may be a government *monopoly, a private regulated monopoly, or a private non-regulated monopoly.

pure play A company that is dedicated to a single narrowly defined activity, as opposed to one that has diverse interests. Investing in a pure play is therefore much the same as investing in the commodity or product that the company deals in.

pure risk *See* RISK.

push manufacturing systems Systems, such as *material requirements planning (MRP), in which production is driven by a schedule derived from anticipated demand.

push money A cash inducement given to a retailer by a manufacturer or wholesaler to be used to reward sales personnel who are particularly successful in selling specified products.

push programming *See* WEBCASTING.

push strategy A strategy that makes use of a company's salesforce and trade promotion activities to create consumer demand for a product. The producer promotes the product to wholesalers, the wholesalers promote it to retailers, and the retailers promote it to consumers. Thus, the product will be pushed through the *distribution channel. *Compare* PULL STRATEGY.

put-of-more option *See* OPTION TO DOUBLE.

put option *See* OPTION.

puttable bonds Bonds issued with a provision that the holder is entitled to redeem the bond before the final maturity date. *Compare* CALLABLE BONDS.

put through Two deals made simultaneously by a *market maker on the London Stock Exchange, in which a large quantity of shares is sold by one client and bought by another, the market maker taking a very small turn.

PV chart *See* PROFIT–VOLUME CHART.

pya A monetary unit of Burma, worth one hundredth of a *kyat.

pyramiding The snowballing effect that derives from a *holding company acquiring a number of subsidiary companies.

pyramid selling A method of selling to the public using a hierarchy of part-time workers. Usually a central instigator (at the apex of the pyramid) sells a franchise to regional organizers for a certain product, together with an agreed quantity of the goods. These organizers recruit district distributors, who each take some of the stock and, in turn, recruit door-to-door salesmen, who take smaller proportions of the stock, which they attempt to sell. In some cases the last stage consists of people who sell the goods to their friends. As the central instigator can sell more goods by this means than are likely to be bought at the base of the pyramid, and someone on the way down is liable to be caught with unsaleable stock, the system is illegal in the UK.

QCA Abbreviation for *Quoted Companies Alliance.

QE Abbreviation for QUANTITATIVE EASING.

QFD Abbreviation for *quality function deployment.

qindar (*plural* **qindarka**) A monetary unit of Albania, worth one hundredth of a *lek.

QLF Abbreviation for *quality loss function.

Q ratio (Tobin's Q) A ratio devised by the US economic analyst James Tobin to measure the impact of *intangible assets on business value. It is the ratio of the market value of a business to the *replacement cost of its assets.

qualified acceptance An *acceptance of a *bill of exchange that varies the effect of the bill as drawn. If the holder refuses to take a qualified acceptance, the drawer and any endorsers must be notified or they will no longer be liable. If the holder takes a qualified acceptance, all previous signatories who did not assent from liability are released.

qualified audit report An *auditors' report in which some qualification of the *financial statements is required because (a) the auditor feels there is a limitation on the scope of the audit examination or (b) the auditor disagrees with the treatment or disclosure of a matter in the financial statements but judges, that this is not sufficiently material for an *adverse opinion to be issued.

qualified available market The consumers who have the interest, income,

access, and qualifications to buy a particular product or service.

qualifying The process of evaluating a prospective business customer's potential interest in buying a product. Key questions are whether the customer needs the product, can pay for it, and has the authority to make, or at least contribute to, a decision to purchase it.

qualifying distribution Any dividend paid by a company or other distribution from company assets to shareholders that carries a *tax credit (i.e. the shareholder is given allowance for the tax paid at source). Formerly (until 1999), this meant a distribution from a company that resulted in *advance corporation tax being paid.

qualifying loss A trading loss arising in a current accounting period as a result of computing the profits and losses of an organization in accordance with accepted *corporation-tax principles. *See* LOSS RELIEFS.

qualitative forecasting techniques Techniques used to forecast future trends, e.g. the demand for a product, when there is little meaningful data to use as the basis of statistical techniques, or when it is considered necessary to triangulate the results of statistically based projections. Typical techniques include making use of salesforce estimates, juries of expert opinion (*see* DELPHI TECHNIQUE), and surveys of user expectations. *Compare* QUANTITATIVE FORECASTING TECHNIQUES.

qualitative marketing research *Marketing research techniques that use small *samples of respondents to gain an impression of their beliefs, motivations, perceptions, and opinions. Such unstructured methods of data collection as *depth interviews and *group discussions are used to explore topics in considerable detail. Qualitative marketing research is frequently used to test an advertisement's effectiveness or to explore new products. *See also* CONCEPT TEST. In general, it is used to show why people buy a particular product, whereas *quantitative marketing research reveals how many people buy it.

quality The totality of the features and characteristics of a product or service that bear on its ability to satisfy stated or implied needs.

quality assurance The design and implementation of systematic activities aimed at preventing quality problems; British Standard 5750 provides a classic example. The approach lies somewhere between the process performance orientation of *quality control and the overall approach of *total quality management.

quality circles A technique that brings together members of a workforce to solve problems and to put forward ideas for improving a process or product. It aims to develop employee participation and process ownership at the same time as exploiting employees' creativity and expertise. Participation is voluntary, employees are paid for participating in such groups, and training is given in analytical and problem-solving techniques. Success is frequently related to whether or not senior management appears to take the recommendations of the groups seriously.

quality control The activities and techniques used to achieve and maintain a high standard of quality in a transformation process. They may include systematic inspection of inputs and outputs, or a sample of inputs and outputs at various stages in their transformation to ensure that acceptable tolerances are not being exceeded. They may also involve a statistical analysis of the data produced by this sampling (particularly in *line production); in this case, in traditional organizations, management has to balance the costs

incurred against the customer's goodwill (*see* COST OF QUALITY). Quality control is also concerned with finding, and eliminating, the causes of quality problems. *See also* SEVEN TOOLS OF QUALITY; SIX SIGMA; STATISTICAL PROCESS CONTROL; TOTAL QUALITY MANAGEMENT.

quality cues Indicators or signs that help users gauge the quality of a website or Internet service.

quality function deployment (QFD) A technique for ensuring that a new product or service meets the customer requirement that gave rise to the original concept. *See* VALUE ENGINEERING.

quality loss function (QLF) A measure of the effectiveness of *quality control techniques, which reflects the economic losses incurred by the customer as a result of:

• maintenance and failure costs;
• damage to the environment;
• the costs of operating a product.

QLF was developed by Genichi Taguchi; it differs from other quality approaches that accept *random variation within limits. QLF recognizes that any deviation from the designed specification involves extra cost for the consumer.

quango Acronym for *qu*asi-*auto*nomous *g*overnment *o*rganization. Such bodies, some members of which are likely to be civil servants and some not, are appointed by a minister to perform some public function at the public expense. Examples are the *Advisory Conciliation and Arbitration Service and the *Health and Safety Executive. While not actually government agencies, they are not independent and are usually answerable to a government minister.

quantitative easing (QE) A form of *monetary policy that is sometimes used to stimulate the economy when interest rates have already been reduced close to zero; it is regarded as a policy of last resort when there is a serious risk of *deflation. Essentially, the central bank creates new money electronically by expanding its balance sheet and uses this to buy government bonds from financial institutions. The aim is to boost the amount of money in circulation and to increase the willingness of banks to lend. QE, which was introduced in the UK from March 2009, is regarded as a high-risk strategy because of the risk of hyperinflation. Economists disagree as to how far it differs from the older and discredited policy of simply printing extra money.

quantitative forecasting techniques Techniques used to forecast future trends, e.g. the demand for a product, based on manipulation of historical data. *See* CAUSAL QUANTITATIVE MODELS; NAIVE QUANTITATIVE METHODS. *Compare* QUALITATIVE FORECASTING TECHNIQUES.

quantitative marketing research *Marketing research techniques that use large *samples of respondents to quantify behaviour and reactions to marketing activities. Typically, a structured questionnaire is used to obtain data that quantifies the numbers and proportions of respondents falling into each predetermined category; for example, a study might show how many people per thousand of the population buy a particular product. *Compare* QUALITATIVE MARKETING RESEARCH.

quantitative trading (quant trading) Any financial trading strategy based on trends or patterns identified by analysing large quantities of complex data on such variables as price and volume. Quantitative trading is used mainly by large financial institutions. In particular, the predictive models established by *data mining are used to formulate the computer algorithms used in high-volume *high-frequency trading. The mathematicians employed to analyse data and produce models are known informally as **quants**.

quantity discount *See* DISCOUNT.

quantum meruit (Latin: as much as has been earned) **1.** Denoting a payment for goods or services supplied in partial fulfilment of a contract, after the contract has been breached. **2.** Denoting a payment for

goods or services supplied and accepted, although no price has been agreed between buyer and seller.

quarter days Four days traditionally taken as the beginning or end of the four quarters of the year, often for purposes of charging rent. In England, Wales, and Northern Ireland they are Lady Day (25 March), Midsummer Day (24 June), Michaelmas (29 September), and Christmas Day (25 December). In Scotland they are Candlemas (2 February), Whitsuntide (15 May), Lammas (1 August), and Martinmas (11 November).

quarterly report In the USA, a financial report issued by a company every three months. The usual contents are an *income statement, *balance sheet, *statement of changes in financial position, and a narrative overview of business operations.

quarter up The means of arriving at the *probate price of a share or other security.

quasi-contract A legally binding obligation that one party has to another, as determined by a court, although no formal *contract exists between them. A *letter of intent may constitute a quasi-contract.

quasi-loan An arrangement in which a creditor agrees to meet some of the financial obligations of a borrower, on condition that the borrower reimburses the creditor.

quasi-manufacturing technology The type of process technology used in service industries in which there is high capital investment and relatively low customer contact, e.g. postal services. These industries involve a limited range of standardized services with a high level of reliability.

quasi money *See* NEAR MONEY.

quasi-subsidiary A company, trust, partnership, or other arrangement that does not fulfil the definition of a *subsidiary undertaking but is directly or indirectly controlled by the reporting entity and gives rise to benefits for that entity that are in substance no different from those that would arise if it was a subsidiary. If a reporting entity has a quasi-subsidiary, the substance of the transactions entered into by the quasi-subsidiary should be reported in *consolidated financial statements.

Queen's Awards for Enterprise

Awards to British industry instituted by royal warrant in 1976 to replace the Queen's Award to Industry, which was instituted in 1965. The **Queen's Award for International Trade** is given for a sustained increase in overseas earnings to an outstanding level for the products or services concerned and for the size of the applicants' organizations. The **Queen's Award for Innovation** is given for outstanding or continuous innovation in the production, development, or distribution of goods or the performance of services. There are also two more recent categories: the **Queen's Award for Sustainable Development** and the **Queen's Award for Enterprise Promotion** (which is awarded to an individual, rather than a company). The awards are announced on the Queen's actual birthday (21 April). Awards are held for five years and entitle the holders to fly a special flag and display on their packages, stationery, etc., the emblem of the award.

(⊕) SEE WEB LINKS

• Guide to the Queen's Awards for Enterprise from the Gov.uk website

query expansion The ability of a *search engine to retrieve documents that contain related items and synonyms of search terms in addition to documents containing the search terms themselves.

question mark See BOSTON MATRIX.

questionnaire A structured set of questions designed to generate the information required for a specific purpose, especially in *marketing research. The preparation of the questionnaire requires considerable expertise. The questionnaire can make use of *multiple-choice questions, with a series of formal questions designed to produce limited responses; alternatively it can use more *open-ended questions, giving

respondents an opportunity to air their views. The latter type of questions are often used with small samples to provide the basis of questionnaires for larger samples.

quetzal (*plural* **quetzales**) (GTQ) The standard monetary unit of Guatemala, divided into 100 centavos.

queuing theory An approach to simulating the way that work arrives in a system (e.g. the rate at which components queue to be processed by a machine) or customers require service, enabling the most effective process for handling these inputs to be designed and evaluated.

quick assets See LIQUID ASSETS.

quick-succession relief Relief available when the same property is assessed for *inheritance-tax purposes in the estates of two separate individuals, the second of whom dies within 5 years of the first. For example, B inherits property from A, which was subject to inheritance tax on A's death of £X. If B dies within one year of the date of the gift, the inheritance tax, £X, that was paid on A's estate will be allowed in full against the inheritance-tax liability on B's estate. If B dies within 1–2 years after the date of A's death the relief is 80% of £X, within 2–3 years relief is 60% of £X, within 3–4 years relief is 40% of £X, and within 4–5 years relief is 20% of £X. The relief is deducted from the whole estate, not simply a particular part of it.

quid pro quo (Latin: something for something) Something given as compensation for something received. *Contracts require a quid pro quo; without a *consideration they would become unilateral agreements.

quorum The smallest number of persons required to attend a meeting in order that its proceedings may be regarded as valid. For a company, the quorum for a meeting is laid down in the *articles of association.

quota 1. A limit on the import or export of a particular product imposed by a government. Import quotas may be imposed for protectionist reasons (i.e. to shield domestic manufacturers from foreign competition); export quotas may be imposed in countries that depend on the export of a particular raw material, as a means of stabilizing prices. Quotas are usually controlled by the issue of licences. **2.** Any proportional share of a whole allocated to a particular person, organization, or country.

quota sampling A method of *non-probability sampling in which the target population is divided into strata (subgroups) and a quota is set for the number of respondents to be selected from each stratum. According to the requirements of the survey, the strata could be determined by age, gender, social class, ownership of a particular product, etc. The interviewer chooses which persons to interview and allocates them to a quota until each quota is filled. This form of sampling tends to be the most frequently used form in *marketing research. *See also* STRATIFIED SAMPLING.

quotation 1. The representation of a security on a recognized *stock exchange (*see* LISTED COMPANY). A quotation allows the shares of a company to be traded on the stock exchange and enables the company to raise new capital if it needs to do so (*see* FLOTATION; LISTING REQUIREMENTS; RIGHTS ISSUE). **2.** An indication of the price at which a seller might be willing to offer goods for sale. A quotation does not,

however, have the status of a firm *offer. **3.** A bid and offer price indicated by a dealer in financial obligations.

Quoted Companies Alliance (QCA) A pressure group formed in 1992 (as the City Group for Smaller Companies) to represent the interests of smaller companies on the London Stock Exchange. It was instrumental in setting up the *Alternative Investment Market in 1995.

 SEE WEB LINKS
• Website of the QCA

quoted company *See* LISTED COMPANY.

quoted price The last price at which a security or commodity was traded. On the London Stock Exchange, quoted prices are given daily in the *Official List. Quoted prices of commodities are given by the relevant markets and recorded in the financial press.

quote driven Denoting a financial market in which prices are determined by the quotations made by *market makers or dealers. The London *Stock Exchange Automated Quotations System and the US *NASDAQ system use quote-driven arrangements. *Compare* ORDER DRIVEN.

qursh A monetary unit of Saudi Arabia, worth one twentieth of a *riyal.

q

race discrimination *See* DISCRIMINA-TION.

rack rent *See* RENT.

Radio Joint Audience Research (RAJAR) A UK organization that measures radio audiences and provides information on their listening habits. Its research is based on *quota sampling of listeners aged 15 or over living within a station's designated area. Participants record details of their radio listening in 15-minute periods in specially designed seven-day diaries. Other data about where and how they listen (e.g. over the Internet) is also collected. RAJAR is jointly owned by the BBC and the trade body representing commercial radio.

RAFT Abbreviation for *revolving acceptance facility by tender.

raider An organization or person that attempts to exploit a company with undervalued assets by making a hostile *takeover bid.

rally A rise in prices in a financial market, after a fall. This is usually brought about by a change of market sentiment. However, if the change has occurred because there are more buyers than sellers, it is known as a **technical rally**. For example, unfavourable sentiment might cause a market to fall, in turn causing sellers to withdraw at the lower prices. The market will then be sensitive to the presence of very few buyers, who, if they show their hand, may bring about a technical rally.

ramping The practice of trying to boost the image of a security and the company behind it by buying the securities in the market with the object of raising demand; if the price rises, the ramper may be able to make a quick profit by selling.

Ramsey principle In UK tax law, the principle that the court is entitled to look at a transaction or series of connected transactions as a whole in order to decide the taxpayer's liability to tax. It is named after the ruling in the case *Commissioners of Inland Revenue v W T Ramsey Ltd*, in which the House of Lords ruled against a company that had used certain self-cancelling transactions to create a non-taxable gain and a tax-relievable loss. The Ramsey principle can be seen as a limitation on the *Westminster doctrine. *See also* GENERAL ANTI-ABUSE RULE.

rand (ZAR) The standard monetary unit of South Africa, divided into 100 cents.

random-digit dialling A method of identifying the households to be contacted for a telephone interview. Either all the digits of the telephone number are randomly generated, or numbers are randomly selected from a directory and the last one or two digits are replaced by random numbers.

random number generator A computer program that produces numbers by a quasi-random process. It is often used to provide an input to financial *simulation models, notably those using a *Monte Carlo simulation.

random sampling *See* PROBABILITY SAMPLING.

random variations Unplanned and uncontrollable variations from a planned level of performance. They may arise from external influences (e.g. abnormal weather conditions) or they may be inherent in some element of the process (e.g. slight variations in the raw materials delivered). From a quality control point of view, it is important to distinguish between a random variation and one that means that the process is going out of control. *See* STATISTICAL PROCESS CONTROL.

random-walk theory The theory that prices on a financial market move, for whatever reason, without any memory of past movements and that the movements therefore follow no pattern. This theory is used to dispute the predictions of *chartists, who do rely on past patterns of movements to predict present and future prices.

range branding strategy A broad strategy in which a firm develops separate product range names for different families of product.

ranking method 1. A simple method of *job evaluation in which jobs are ranked according to an informal assessment of their overall importance to the organization. This method is quick and inexpensive but becomes difficult to sustain as organizations get larger and more complex. *Compare* CLASSIFICATION METHOD; FACTOR-COMPARISON METHOD; JOB-COMPONENT METHOD; POINT METHOD. **2.** A method of *employee evaluation in which a group of employees are ranked on the basis of relevant performance criteria.

rank-order scale A technique used in marketing research in which a respondent is asked to rank various products or brands in terms of *attitude, belief, perception, or some performance criterion. The respondent ranks the products or brands in order of the best, most important, etc.

RAROC Abbreviation for *risk-adjusted return on capital.

rate anticipation swap An *interest-rate swap in which the swap is related to predicted interest-rate changes. *See also* SWAP.

rate card A list of prices charged for advertising space, TV or radio time, etc. *See also* OFF-CARD RATE.

rate of exchange (exchange rate) The price of one currency in terms of another. It is usually expressed in terms of how many units of the home country's currency are needed to buy one unit of the foreign currency. However, in some cases, notably in the UK, it is expressed as the number of units of foreign currency that one unit of the home currency will buy. Two rates are usually given, the buying and selling rate; the difference is the profit or commission charged by the organization carrying out the exchange.

rate of interest *See* INTEREST RATE.

rate of return The annual amount of income from an investment, expressed as a percentage of the original investment. This rate is very important in assessing the relative merits of different investments. It is therefore important to note whether a quoted rate is before or after tax, since with most investments, the after-tax rate of return is most relevant. Also, because some rates are payable more frequently than annually, it may be important, in order to make true comparisons, to consider the *annual percentage rate (APR), which most investment institutions are required to state by law. *See also* RISK-FREE RATE.

rate of turnover (turnover ratio) The frequency, expressed in annual terms, with which some part of the assets of an organization is turned over (i.e. replaced by others of the same class). In order to calculate how frequently stock is turned over, the total sales revenue (or if a more accurate estimate is needed the *cost of sales) is divided by the average value of the stock. This provides a reasonable measure in terms of *current assets. Some accountants also divide the sales figure by the value of the *fixed assets to arrive at turnover of fixed assets. This is hardly realistic, although it does express the relationship of sales to the fixed assets of the organization, which in some organizations could be significant. *See also* CAPITAL TURNOVER; LABOUR TURNOVER RATE.

rate per direct labour hour A basis used in *absorption costing for absorbing the *manufacturing overhead into the *cost units produced. The formula is:

> budgeted manufacturing overhead/ budgeted direct labour hours.

A different approach to *cost allocation is used in *activity-based costing.

rate per machine hour A basis used in *absorption costing for absorbing the *manufacturing overhead into the *cost units produced. The formula is:

> budgeted manufacturing overhead/ budgeted machine hours.

This rate may not be very useful for managers if overheads do not increase or decrease as machine hours increase or decrease. *Activity-based costing systems can provide a more accurate *cause-and-effect allocation of costs.

rate per standard hour A basis used in *absorption costing for absorbing the *manufacturing overhead into the *cost units produced. The formula is:

> budgeted manufacturing overhead/ budgeted standard hours.

A different basis of *cost allocation is used in *activity-based costing systems.

rate per unit A basis used in *absorption costing for absorbing the *manufacturing overhead into the *cost units produced. The formula is:

> budgeted manufacturing overhead/ budgeted units.

A different basis of *cost allocation is used in *activity-based costing systems.

rates *See* BUSINESS RATES.

rating A *work measurement technique for adjusting data from a series of time studies against a common level of performance, corresponding to *standard performance.

rating agency An organization that monitors the credit backing of institutions and of bond issues and other forms of public borrowings. It may also give a rating of the risks involved in holding specific stocks. The three best known are Standard & Poor's, Moody's, and Fitch, all of which have been in existence for over 100 years. *See also* CREDIT RATING.

ratio analysis The use of *accounting ratios to evaluate a company's operating performance and financial stability. Such ratios as *return on capital employed and *gross profit percentage can be used to assess profitability. The *liquid ratio can be used to examine solvency and *gearing ratios to examine the financial structure of the company. In conducting an analysis comparisons will be made with other companies and with industry averages over a period of time. The analysis of ratios can indicate how well a company is run, the risks of financial insolvency, and the financial returns provided. *See also* FINANCIAL-STATEMENT ANALYSIS.

ratio covenant A form of *covenant in a loan agreement that includes conditions relating to such ratios as the *gearing ratio and *interest cover. Breaching such a covenant could indicate significant deterioration in the company's business or a major change in its nature; this will usually empower the lender to request repayment of any of the loan then outstanding, and the loan then becomes null and void.

rational appeal An appeal in an advertisement to the audience's self-interest. The advertisement shows that the product will produce the claimed benefits by, for example, appeals of product quality, economy, value, or performance.

rational choice theory A class of theory which posits that individual actors within a given set of constraints, such as a market, make rational decisions between possible courses of action with the aim of maximizing the utility of the outcome. Most conventional economics is based on this assumption and the rational choice model has also been influential in sociology and political science. More recently, critics of rational choice theory have sought to analyse why actors do not always make the decisions the theory would predict; some notable work of this kind has been done in the field of *behavioural finance. *See also* PROSPECT THEORY; UTILITY THEORY.

rational expectations The macroeconomic theory, developed since the 1960s by John F. Muth and others, that economic transactors make unbiased forecasts on the basis of all the information available. This means that although forecasts may be right or wrong, agents do not make systematic forecasting errors. Such an assumption is central to the *efficient markets hypothesis. More recently, the theory of rational expectations has been challenged by *behavioural finance. *Compare* ADAPTIVE EXPECTATIONS.

rationalization A reorganization of a firm, group, or industry to increase its efficiency and profitability. This may include closing some manufacturing units and expanding others (horizontal *integration), merging different stages of the production process (vertical integration), merging support units, closing units that are duplicating effort of others, etc. A firm may also rationalize its product range to reflect changes in demand, concentrating its sales and marketing effort on its best sellers. *See also* DOWNSIZING; RIGHTSIZING.

raw materials *Direct materials used in a production process, which are at a low level of completion compared to the final product or *cost unit. Examples include steel plate, wood, and chemicals.

RBV Abbreviation for *resource-based view.

RCH Abbreviation for *Recognized Clearing House.

reach The proportion of a total market that an advertiser hopes to reach at least once within a given period in an advertising campaign.

reaction A reversal in a market trend as a result of overselling on a falling market (when some buyers are attracted by the low prices) or overbuying on a rising market (when some buyers are willing to take profits).

reader service card *See* BINGO CARD.

real (BRL) The standard monetary unit of Brazil, divided into 100 centavos.

real account A *ledger account for some types of property (e.g. land and buildings, plant, investments, stock) as distinct from a *nominal account, which would be for revenue or expense items (e.g. sales, motor expenses, discount received, etc.). This distinction is now largely obsolete and both sets of accounts are maintained in the same ledger, usually referred to as the *nominal ledger.

real estate The US name for *real property.

real interest rate The actual interest rate less the current rate of inflation. For example, if a bank is paying 3% interest and the rate of inflation is 2%, the real growth of a deposit held for a year in the bank is 1%—this is the real rate of interest. Real interest rates are used to calculate more accurate pre-tax returns on investment, i.e. by discounting inflation.

real investment Investment in capital equipment, such as a factory, plant and machinery, etc., or valuable social assets, such as a school, a dam, etc., rather than in such paper assets as securities, debentures, etc.

realizable account An account drawn up on the dissolution of a *partnership. The account is debited with the assets of the partnership and any expenses on realization; it is credited with the proceeds of any sales made. The difference between the total debits and credits is either a *profit or loss on realization and must be shared between the partners in the *profit-sharing ratio.

realizable asset *See* LIQUID ASSETS.

realization account An *account used to record the disposal of an asset or assets and to determine the profit or loss on the disposal. The principle of realization accounts are that they are debited with the book value of the asset and credited with the sale price of the asset. Any balance therefore represents the profit or loss on disposal.

realized profit/loss A profit or loss that has arisen from a completed transaction (usually the sale of goods or services or other assets). In accounting terms, a profit is normally regarded as having been realized when an asset has been legally disposed of and not when the cash is received, since if an asset is sold on credit the asset being disposed of is exchanged for another asset, a debtor. The debt may or may not prove good but that is regarded as a separate transaction. *Compare* PAPER PROFIT.

realized yield The total return obtained on a security, including that from the investment of any interest paid.

real option An *option that arises naturally in the course of business activities rather than one purchased on a financial market. A common example of a real option is early investment in a technology, which will enable a firm to exploit the new technology should it prove successful.

real property (realty) Any property consisting of land or buildings as distinct from *personal property (personalty).

real terms A representation of the value of a good or service in terms of money, taking into account fluctuations in the *price level.

real terms accounting A system of accounting in which the effects of changing prices are measured by their effect on a company's financial capital (i.e. *shareholders' equity) to see if its value is maintained in real terms. Assets are measured at *current cost. Profit is defined as any surplus remaining after the shareholders' funds (determined by reference to the current cost of *net assets) have been

maintained in real terms. The unit of measurement may be either the nominal pound or the unit of constant purchasing power.

real-time control *See* CONCURRENT CONTROL.

real-time marketing The ability of customized goods and services to update themselves continuously and track changing customer needs, often without input from corporate personnel or conscious input from the customer.

real-time pricing Pricing that is updated continuously to reflect current conditions.

real-time processing The processing of data by a computer as soon as it is input so that the results can be output almost immediately.

realtor The US name for an estate agent or land agent.

realty *See* REAL PROPERTY.

real value A monetary value expressed in *real terms.

reasonable adjustments Under the Equality Act 2010 the employer or potential employer of a disabled person is under a duty to make 'reasonable adjustments'. Three requirements apply where a disabled person would otherwise be placed at a substantial disadvantage compared with people who are not disabled. The first involves making adjustments to any provision, criterion, or practice imposed by the employer that creates such a disadvantage (e.g. where rules on sickness absence have a disproportionate impact on a disabled employee). The second involves making changes to physical barriers in the workplace (e.g. providing a wheelchair ramp). The third involves providing an auxiliary aid or auxiliary service (e.g. special computer software). A failure to comply with any of these requirements is discrimination against a disabled person. The duty is subject to a test of reasonableness. This is judged objectively (rather than from the point of view of the employer) and will take account of such factors as practicality and cost.

rebalancing 1. In finance, the adjustment of a *hedge in order to improve its effectiveness as circumstances change. **2.** The adjustment of an investment portfolio over time to better reflect its underlying strategy. For example, a market-tracking hedge will require changes over time in order to reflect the differing importance of particular securities.

rebate 1. A discount offered on the price of a good or service, often one that is paid back to the payer, e.g. a tax rebate is a refund to the taxpayer. **2.** A discount allowed on a *bill of exchange that is paid before it matures.

recall test A test used in marketing research to ascertain how much consumers can remember about an advertisement. **Spontaneous tests** reveal which advertisements a respondent can remember without guidance or assistance. **Prompted** (*or* **aided**) **tests** indicate which advertisements respondents can remember from a series they have seen in a campaign.

recapitalization In the USA, the process of changing the balance of *debt and *equity financing of a company without changing the total amount of *capital. Recapitalization is often required as part of reorganization of a company under bankruptcy legislation.

receipt A document acknowledging that a specified payment has been made. For payments made by cheque, the cheque itself functions as the receipt. *See also* DOCK RECEIPT; MATE'S RECEIPT.

receivables Sums of money due to a business from persons or businesses to whom it has supplied goods or services in the normal course of trade.

received bill A *bill of lading that has been stamped "Goods received for shipment". This does not imply that they have been loaded but that they have been received for loading (*compare* SHIPPED BILL).

receiver A person exercising any form of *receivership. In *bankruptcy, the *official receiver becomes receiver and manager of the bankrupt's estate. Where there is a floating *charge over the whole of a company's property, which was created before 16 September 2003, and a crystallizing event has occurred, an *administrative receiver may be appointed to manage the whole of the company's business. The administrative receiver will have wide powers to carry on the business of the company, take possession of its property, commence *liquidation, etc. A receiver appointed in respect of a *fixed charge can deal with the property covered by the charge only, and has no power to manage the company's business.

receivership The situation in which a lender holds a mortgage or charge over a company's property and, in consequence of a default by the company, a receiver is appointed to realize the assets charged in order to repay the debt.

receiving inspection Quality inspections carried out on inputs as they are received into a transformation system. The alternative is a contract with the suppliers that commits them to a guaranteed level of quality, thus transferring the cost of quality control to the supplier. *See also* ACCEPTANCE SAMPLING.

recession A slowdown or fall in economic growth rate. A recession is defined by the US National Bureau of Economic Research as a decline in *gross domestic product in two successive quarters. A severe recession is called a *depression. Recession is associated with falling levels of *investment, rising unemployment, and (sometimes) falling prices. *See also* BUSINESS CYCLE.

reciprocal costs Costs apportioned from a *service cost centre to a *production cost centre that carries out work for the original service cost centre. Consequently, a proportion of the production cost centre costs should also be reapportioned to the service cost centre. Cost apportionment can be calculated either by the use of simultaneous equations or by a continuous apportionment method, until all the costs are charged to the production cost centre.

reciprocal exchange rate *See* DIRECT QUOTE.

recognition tests The *post-testing procedure used in advertising to investigate the ability of respondents to recognize advertisements to which they were previously exposed in an interview.

Recognized Clearing House (RCH) in the UK, a body authorized to act as a *clearing house under the Financial Services and Markets Act 2000. There are currently five: LCH.Clearnet (*see* LONDON CLEARING HOUSE), *Euroclear, ICE Clear Europe (*see* ICE FUTURES EUROPE), CME Clearing Europe, and European Central Counterparty (Euro CCP).

Recognized Investment Exchange (RIE) In the UK, a body authorized under the Financial Services and Markets Act 2000 to sell financial instruments. There are currently five RIEs: the *London Stock Exchange, Euronext.liffe (*see* LIFFE), ICE Futures Europe (formerly the *International Petroleum Exchange), the *London Metal Exchange, and ICAP Securities and Derivatives Exchange.

Recognized Professional Body (RPB) *See* DESIGNATED PROFESSIONAL BODY.

Recognized Supervisory Body In the UK, a body recognized as supervising and maintaining the conduct and technical standards of auditors performing *statutory audits. Currently the *Institute of Chartered Accountants in England and Wales, the Institute of Chartered Accountants of Scotland, and the Institute of Chartered Accountants in Ireland are recognized, together with the *Association of Chartered Certified Accountants; in effect, the Association of Authorized Public Accountants is also recognized.

recommended retail price (RRP) The price that a manufacturer recommends as the retail price for his product. Under the Competition Act 1998 the manufacturer has no legal power to enforce this recommendation. The RRP is also called the **manufacturers' recommended price (MRP)**. *See also* RESALE PRICE MAINTENANCE.

reconciliation *See* ACCOUNT RECONCILIATION; BANK RECONCILIATION STATEMENT.

reconciliation of movements in shareholders' funds (statement of changes in equity; statement of movements in shareholders' funds) A *financial statement bringing together the performance of an organization in a financial period, as shown in the *statement of total recognized gains and losses, with all other changes in *shareholders' equity in the period, including capital contributed by or repaid to shareholders. Under the Financial Reporting Standard Applicable in the UK and Republic of Ireland, companies are required to publish such a statement as part of the *annual accounts.

recontracting The renegotiation of contracts between a company in *financial distress and its creditors.

recorded delivery A postal service offered by the UK Post Office that provides a record of posting and delivery of inland letters for an extra fee; advice of delivery is also offered for a further fee. *Compare* SPECIAL DELIVERY.

recourse The right of redress should the terms of a contract not be fulfilled. *See* WITHOUT RECOURSE.

recourse agreement An agreement between a hire-purchase company and a retailer, in which the retailer undertakes to repossess the goods if the buyer fails to pay his regular instalments.

recoverable amount The value of an *asset treated as the greater of its *net realizable value and its *net present value. The value of an asset to a business can be regarded as the lower of the recoverable amount and the current *replacement cost.

recovery *See* TURNAROUND.

recovery stock A share that has fallen in price but is believed to have the potential of climbing back to its original level.

rectification of register 1. An alteration to any of the land registers (*see* LAND REGISTRATION), where it is thought necessary by the registrar or the court. Examples include a mistake that has been made as to the ownership of land or an entry obtained by fraud. Anyone suffering loss because of rectification or anyone who has suffered loss as a result of a refusal to rectify a mistake in the register may be entitled to state compensation. **2.** An alteration of the *register of members of a company by the court if any members have been omitted, a person's name has been wrongly entered, or delay has occurred in removing the name of a former member. The court may award damages as well as rectifying the register.

redeemable gilts *See* GILT-EDGED SECURITY.

redeemable shares *Shares (either *ordinary shares or *preference shares) that the issuing company has the right to redeem, under terms specified on issue. Redemption may be funded from *distributable profits or from a fresh issue of shares.

redeemable trust certificate *See* UNIT TRUST.

redemption The repayment of *shares, *stocks, *debentures, or *bonds. The amount payable on redemption is usually specified on issue. The **redemption date**, or dates, may or may not be specified on issue. *See also* GILT-EDGED SECURITY; MATURITY DATE.

redemption yield *See* GROSS REDEMPTION YIELD; YIELD.

rediscounting The discounting of a *bill of exchange or *promissory note that has already been discounted by someone else, usually by a *discount house. A *central bank, acting as *lender of last resort, may be said to be rediscounting securities submitted to it by brokers in the money

market, as the securities will have already been discounted in the market. In some cases the US *Federal Reserve Bank will rediscount a financial instrument that has already been discounted by a local bank.

red-tape syndrome *See* BUREAUPATHOLOGY.

reducing-balance method *See* DIMINISHING-BALANCE METHOD.

reduction of capital A reduction of a company's share *capital in accordance with the Companies Act 2006. The Act states that a private company can reduce its share capital provided that: (i) it passes a *special resolution to do so; (ii) the resolution is supported by a solvency statement; and (iii) the reduction is not restricted or prohibited by the company's articles. Alternatively, a private or public company can, subject to any restriction or prohibition in the articles, reduce its share capital on the passing of a special resolution confirmed by the court. A reduction of capital can also occur where there is a permitted redemption or repurchase of a private company's own shares out of capital.

redundancy 1. The loss of a job by an employee because the job has ceased to exist or because there is no longer work available. It involves *dismissal by the employer, with or without notice, for any reason other than a breach of the contract of employment by the employee, provided that no reasonable alternative employment has been offered by the same employer. In the UK, if the employee has been continuously employed in the business for at least two years, a **redundancy payment** must be made by the employer according to the Employment Rights Act 1996, the amount of which will depend on the employee's age, length of service, and rate of pay. **2.** *See* COMPENSATION FOR LOSS OF OFFICE.

re-exports Goods that have been imported and are then exported without having undergone any material change while in the exporting country. Countries with a major re-export or *entrepôt trade distinguish re-exports from domestic exports in their balance of payments accounts. Any import duty paid on goods imported for re-export can be reclaimed (*see* DRAWBACK).

referee 1. A person who will, if asked, give an applicant for a job a **reference**. The referee should be given a brief job description of the job the applicant is trying to secure. **2.** A person appointed by two arbitrators, who cannot agree on the award to be made in a dispute to be settled by *arbitration. The procedure for appointing a referee in these circumstances is usually laid down in the terms of arbitration. **3.** A person or organization named on some *bills of exchange as a **referee** (*or* **reference**) in case of need. If the bill is dishonoured its holder may take it to the referee for payment.

reference *See* BANKER'S REFERENCE; REFEREE.

reference bank A bank nominated under the terms of a loan agreement to provide the marker rates for the purposes of fixing interest charges on a variable-rate loan.

reference groups *See* CONSUMER GROUPS.

reference prices Prices that buyers carry in their minds and refer to when they look at a given product.

reference rate 1. An interest rate relative to which a bank prices its products, sometimes referred to as its *base rate. **2.** An interest rate relative to which financial markets price their products, for example the *London Inter Bank Offered Rate (LIBOR) or *Euro Inter Bank Offered Rate (EURIBOR). **3.** A foreign-exchange rate that a country wishes to maintain.

referring site The website from which a user reached the site currently being visited. *See also* CLICKTHROUGH; DESTINATION SITE.

refer to drawer Words written on a cheque that is being dishonoured by a bank, usually because the account of the person who drew it has insufficient funds to cover it and the manager of the bank is unwilling to allow the account to be overdrawn or further overdrawn. Other reasons for referring to the drawer are that the drawer has been made bankrupt, that there is a *third-party debt order against the drawer, that the drawer has stopped it, or that something in the cheque itself is incorrect (e.g. it is wrongly dated, words and figures don't agree, etc.). The words 'please re-present' may often be added, indicating that the bank may honour the cheque at a second attempt.

refinance bill *See* THIRD-COUNTRY ACCEPTANCE.

refinance credit A credit facility enabling a foreign buyer to obtain credit for a purchase when the exporter does not wish to provide it. The buyer opens a credit at a branch or agent of his bank in the exporting country, the exporter being paid by sight draft on the buyer's credit. The bank in the exporting country accepts a *bill of exchange drawn on the buyer, which is discounted and the proceeds sent to the bank issuing the credit. The buyer only has to pay when the bill on the bank in the exporting country matures.

refinancing The process of repaying some or all of the loan capital of a firm by obtaining fresh loans, usually at a lower rate of interest.

reflation A policy aimed at expanding the level of output of the economy by government stimulus, either fiscal or monetary policy. This could involve increasing the money supply and government expenditure on investment, public works, subsidies, etc., or reducing taxation and interest rates.

refugee capital *Hot money belonging to a foreign government, company, or individual that is invested in the country offering the highest interest rate, usually on a short-term basis.

regenerative method A procedure applied at regular intervals to the data that forms the basis of *material requirements planning (MRP). All the data is reprocessed to provide a new MRP.

registered auditor An *auditor eligible to carry out *statutory audits in any member state of the European Union, in accordance with the Eighth Company Law Directive. This was brought into UK law by the Companies Act 1989, which gave the *Recognized Supervisory Bodies power to approve such auditors. Registers of individuals and firms eligible to act as registered auditors are kept.

registered capital *See* AUTHORIZED SHARE CAPITAL.

registered company A *company incorporated in England and Wales or Scotland by registration with the *Registrar of Companies. It may be a *limited company or an *unlimited company, a private company or a public company.

registered land Land the title to which has been registered under the Land Registration Acts of 1925 and 2002. Over 90% of land in England and Wales is now registered. *See* LAND REGISTRATION; RECTIFICATION OF REGISTER.

registered name The name in which a UK company is registered. The name, without which a company cannot be incorporated, will be stated in the company's constitutional documents. Some names are prohibited by law and will not be registered; these include names already registered and names that in the opinion of the Secretary of State are offensive. The name may be changed by special resolution of the company and the Secretary of State may order a company to change a misleading name. The name must be displayed at each place of business, on stationery and e-mails, and on bills of exchange, etc., or the company and its officers will be liable to a fine.

registered office The official address of a UK company, to which all

correspondence can be sent. Statutory registers are kept at the registered office, the address of which must be disclosed on stationery, e-mails, company websites, and the company's annual return. Any change must be notified to the *Registrar of Companies within 14 days.

registered stock *See* INSCRIBED STOCK.

registered trader A *taxable person who has complied with the *registration for value added tax regulations.

register of charges 1. The register maintained by the Registrar of Companies on which certain *charges must be registered by companies. A charge is created when a company gives a creditor the right to recover a debt from specific assets. The types of charge that must be registered in this way, and the details that must be given, are set out in the Companies Act. Failure to register the charge within 21 days of its creation renders it void, so that it cannot be enforced against a liquidator or creditor of the company. The underlying debt remains valid, however, but ranks only as an unsecured debt. **2.** A list of charges that a company must maintain at its registered address or principal place of business. Failure to do so may render the directors and company officers liable to a fine. This register must be available for inspection by other persons during normal business hours.

register of companies *See* COMPANY; COMPANIES HOUSE; REGISTRAR OF COMPANIES.

register of debenture-holders A list of the holders of *debentures in a UK company. There is no legal requirement for such a register to be kept but if one exists it must be kept at the company's registered office or at a place notified to the *Registrar of Companies. It must be available for inspection, to debenture-holders and shareholders free of charge and to the public for a small fee.

register of directors and secretaries A register listing the directors and the secretary of a UK company, which must be kept at its *registered office. It must state the full names of the directors and the company secretary, an address for each, the nationality of directors, particulars of other directorships held, the occupation of directors, and in the case of a public company, their dates of birth. If the function of director or secretary is performed by another company, the name and registered office of that company must be given. The register must be available for inspection by members of the company free of charge and it may be inspected by the public for a small fee. Under the Companies Act 2006 directors may include a service address, rather than their residential address, in the register that is seen by the public.

register of directors' interests A statutory register in which a company must detail the interests of its *directors in the shares and debentures of the company. The register must be available for inspection during the *annual general meeting of the company.

register of interests in shares A statutory register required to be maintained by *public companies. Interests in shares disclosed to the company by those persons knowingly interested in 3% or more of any class of the voting share capital must be disclosed in the register. Investments held by a spouse, children under 18 years, and corporate bodies over which the person has control are added to the person's own interests.

register of members (share register) A list of the *members of a company, which all UK companies must keep at their *registered office or some other address notified to the *Registrar of Companies. It contains the names and addresses of the members, the dates on which they were registered as members, and the dates on which any ceased to be members. If the company has a share capital, the register must state the number and class of the shares held by each member and the amount paid for the shares. Entry in the register constitutes evidence of ownership.

Thus, a shareholder who loses a share certificate can obtain a replacement from the company provided proof of identity is supplied. However, as legal rather than beneficial ownership is registered, it is not always possible to discover from the register who controls the shares. Under the Companies Act 2006 the register must be open to inspection by members free of charge and by others on payment of a fee; in both cases the person seeking information must apply to the company in writing, explaining the reason for the request. A company that wishes to decline such a request must apply to the court.

registrar The appointed agent of a company whose task is to keep a register of share and stock holders of that company. The functions of a registrar are often performed by a subsidiary company of a bank.

Registrar of Companies An official charged with the duty of registering all the companies in the UK. There is one registrar for England and Wales and one for Scotland. The registrar is responsible for carrying out a wide variety of administrative duties connected with registered companies, including maintaining the **register of companies** and the *register of charges, issuing certificates of incorporation, and receiving annual returns.

registration 1. The process in which an individual subscribes to a website or requests further information from it by filling in contact details and his or her needs using an electronic form. **2.** The process of reserving a unique web address that can be used to refer to a company website. *See also* DOMAIN NAME; UNIFORM RESOURCE LOCATOR.

registration fee A small fee charged by a company whose shares are quoted on a stock exchange when it is requested to register the name of a new owner of shares.

registration for value added tax An obligation on a person making taxable supplies to register for *value added tax if at the end of any month the amount of taxable supplies in the period of 12 months ending in that month exceeds the **registration threshold** of £82,000 (2015–16).

registration statement In the USA, a lengthy document that has to be lodged with the *Securities and Exchange Commission. It contains all the information relevant to a new *securities issue that will enable an investor to make an informed decision whether or not to purchase the security.

regression analysis A statistical technique that attempts to measure the extent to which one variable is related to two or more other variables, often with the aim of predicting future values of the dependent variable. It is used extensively in financial economics and marketing theory. *See* CAUSAL QUANTITATIVE MODELS.

regressive tax A tax in which the rate of tax decreases as income increases. Indirect taxes fall into this category. Regressive taxes are said to fall more heavily on the poor than on the rich; for example, the poor spend a higher proportion of their incomes on VAT than the rich. *Compare* PROGRESSIVE TAX. *See also* FLAT TAX.

regulated company *See* COMPANY.

reinstatement of the sum insured The payment of an additional premium to return the sum insured to its full level, after a claim has reduced it. Insurance policies are, in effect, a promise to pay money if a particular event occurs. If a claim is paid, the insurance is reduced by the claim amount (or if a total loss is paid, the policy is exhausted). If the policyholder wishes to return the cover to its full value, a premium representing the amount of cover used by the claim must be paid. In the case of a total loss the whole premium must be paid again.

reinsurance The passing of all or part of an insurance risk that has been covered by an insurer to another insurer in return for a premium. The contract between the parties is usually known as a **reinsurance treaty**. The policyholder is usually not aware that reinsurance has been arranged, as no

mention is made of it on the policy. Reinsurance is a similar process to the bookmaker's practice of laying off bets with other bookmakers when too much money is placed on a particular horse. Very often an insurer will only accept a risk with a high payout if a total loss occurs (e.g. for a jumbo jet) in the sure knowledge that the potential loss can be reduced by reinsurance. *See also* FACULTATIVE REINSURANCE.

reintermediation 1. *See* DISINTERMEDIATION. **2.** The creation of a new *intermediary between customers and suppliers to provide such services as supplier search and product evaluation.

reinvestment rate The interest rate at which an investor is able to reinvest income earned on an existing investment.

relatedness needs *See* ERG THEORY.

related party An individual, partnership, or company that has the ability to control, or exercise significant influence over, another organization.

related-party transaction A transfer of resources or obligations between *related parties, regardless of whether a price is charged.

relationship banking The establishment of a long-term relationship between a bank and its customers. The main advantage is that it enables the bank to develop in-depth knowledge of a customer's business, which improves its ability to make informed decisions regarding loans to the customer. The customer expects to benefit by increased support during difficult times. *See also* BILATERAL BANK FACILITY; SYNDICATED BANK FACILITY.

relationship capital *See* INTELLECTUAL CAPITAL.

relationship marketing (relationship management) Marketing activities aimed at building long-term relationships with parties (especially customers) that contribute to a company's success. The goal is to ensure long-term value to customers, producing enduring customer satisfaction.

relationship-motivated (person-oriented) Describing a *leadership style that is concerned with maintaining positive relationships within the group, removing causes of friction, and lifting morale. A relationship-motivated leader will demonstrate trust of subordinates, respect for their ideas, and consideration for their feelings. *Compare* TASK-MOTIVATED. *See* CONTINGENCY THEORIES OF LEADERSHIP; LEAST PREFERRED CO-WORKER SCALE.

relationship roles A set of coherent, socioemotional roles that are often adopted by the different members of a group in order to sustain good working relationships within the group. Some commonly identified roles of this kind include the **encourager**, who provides praise and reassurance; the **harmonizer**, who mediates between those with opposing views; the **gatekeeper**, who maintains the channels of communication and makes sure that everyone's view is heard; and the **comedian**, who uses humour to relieve stress and lift morale. *Compare* TASK ROLES.

relaunch To reintroduce an existing product or brand into the market after changes have been made to it.

relevance 1. The accounting principle that the financial information provided by a company should be capable of influencing the decisions of users of that information. To be relevant, information must either have predictive value or act as confirmation or correction of earlier expectations. The concept is defined in the Financial Reporting Standard Applicable in the UK and Republic of Ireland. It is also recognized in the International Accounting Standards Board's Conceptual Framework. **2.** The principle in decision making that the impact of a particular decision on the performance of an organization can only be determined by identifying those elements of cost or revenue that are relevant to the decisions made. *See* RELEVANT COST.

relevant cost An expected future cost that varies with alternative courses of action. Decision making involves choosing between such alternatives, and to make the best choice a manager needs to identify the future cash flows for each decision. Costs that have already been incurred as a result of past decisions (*sunk costs) are not relevant for decision making. Likewise, a future cost that will not be changed by a decision is irrelevant to that decision. *See* DIFFERENTIAL ANALYSIS.

An understanding of relevant costs is particularly important for the following types of decision:

- special selling-price decisions;
- product-mix decisions when capacity constraints exist;
- decisions on replacement of equipment;
- outsourcing (make or buy) decisions;
- decisions on whether to drop a product or close a department.

relevant property trust From March 2006, any trust that is not an *interest-in-possession trust, an age *18–25 trust, or a trust established for a bereaved minor is a relevant property trust for *inheritance tax purposes. A relevant property trust is taxed (i) on creation, (ii) whenever there is a distribution to a beneficiary, and (iii) on each tenth anniversary of the settlement. *See also* DISCRETIONARY TRUST.

relevant transfer A situation that may arise when a business or part of a business changes ownership and staff transfer to the new owner. If the change of ownership falls within the scope of the Transfer of Undertakings Protection of Employment Regulations 2006 (**TUPE**), there is an automatic transfer of an employee's contract of employment. TUPE was first introduced in 1981, as a response to the EC's Acquired Rights Directive, the main objective of which was to safeguard employees' rights in the event of a change of employer. The situations in which a relevant transfer governed by TUPE occurs are numerous, and have been made more so in the latest regulations. The simplest situation is where one company acquires another and staff transfer. More complex situations include contracting out services, the transfer of contracts and franchises, and the transfer of leases. TUPE operates in each of these situations if staff have followed the transfer or have lost employment as a consequence.

releveraging Increasing the level of debt in the *capital structure of a business. *See* GEARING.

reliability The accounting principle that the financial information provided by a company should have the characteristics of faithful representation, neutrality, and freedom from material error. The concept is defined in the Financial Reporting Standard Applicable in the UK and Republic of Ireland. It is also recognized in the International Accounting Standards Board's Conceptual Framework.

relocation The removal of an office, factory, or other place of work from one place to another, often as a result of a merger, takeover, etc. Sometimes employees are offered a **relocation allowance**, as an incentive for them to remain with the organization.

reminder advertising Advertising in which the purpose is to remind consumers about a product and to keep them thinking about it.

remitting bank *See* COLLECTING BANK.

remoteness of damage Loss or injury that has resulted from unforeseen or unusual circumstances. In the law of *negligence, a person is presumed to intend the natural consequences of his acts. A person who is negligent will be liable for all the direct and immediate consequences of the negligence. If, however, the consequences of the acts could not be reasonably foreseen or anticipated, the resulting damage is said to be too remote. Similarly, in the law of contract, damage resulting from breach of contract will be deemed too remote unless it arises directly from the breach complained of. No *damages will be awarded for damage the courts deem to be too remote.

remuneration 1. A sum of money paid for a service given. For auditors' remuneration, *see* AUDIT FEE. **2.** A salary.

remuneration committee In UK public companies, a committee of *non-executive directors who decide the pay of executive directors. Many such bodies were set up as a result of the *Greenbury Report of 1995. Under the *Corporate Governance Code they are now recommended for all public listed companies. *See also* AUDIT COMMITTEE.

remunerative contract *See* PSYCHOLOGICAL CONTRACT.

rendu *See* FRANCO.

renewal notice An invitation from an insurer to continue an insurance policy that is about to expire by paying the **renewal premium**. The renewal premium is shown on the notice; it may differ from the previous premium, either because insurance rates have changed or because the insured value has changed. Many insurers increase the insured value of certain objects automatically, in line with inflation.

renminbi The official currency of the People's Republic of China (excluding Hong Kong and Macau); the standard monetary unit is the *yuan.

renounceable documents Documents that provide evidence of ownership, for a limited period, of unregistered shares. An allotment letter (*see* ALLOTMENT) sent to shareholders when a new issue is floated is an example. Ownership of the shares can be passed to someone else by *renunciation at this stage.

rent A payment for the use of land, usually under a *lease. The most usual kinds are *ground rent and **rack rent**. Rack rent is paid when no capital payment (premium) has been made for the lease and the rent therefore represents the full value of the land and buildings. The amount of rent may be regulated by statute in certain cases. *See also* PEPPERCORN RENT.

rentes Non-redeemable government bonds issued by several European governments, notably France. The interest, which is paid annually, for ever, is called **rente**.

rentier A person who lives on income from *rentes or on receiving rent from land. The meaning is sometimes extended to include anyone who lives on the income derived from his assets rather than a wage or salary.

renting back See LEASEBACK.

renunciation 1. The surrender to someone else of rights to shares in a rights issue. The person to whom the shares are allotted by allotment letter (see ALLOTMENT) fills in the **renunciation form** (usually attached) in favour of the person to whom the rights are to be renounced. **2.** The disposal of a unit-trust holding by completing the renunciation form on the reverse of the certificate and sending it to the trust managers.

reorder level The number of units of a particular item of stock to which the balance can fall before an order for replenishment is placed. A **reorder-level system** is a stock-control system based on the principle that orders for the replenishment of items of stock are only placed when the balance of stock for a particular item falls to a predetermined level. The **reorder quantity** is the quantity ordered to replenish stock when the stock level falls to the reorder level.

reorder point The point at which stock should be reordered. It is usually based on an optimum balance of the costs of holding stock, the costs of running out of stock, the costs of ordering stock, and the time required for the stock to arrive.

reorganization 1. In the US, the process of restructuring a company that is in financial difficulties. Protection against creditors can be sought under *chapter 11 of the Bankruptcy Reform Act 1978 while such a reorganization back to profitability is being undertaken. If creditors cannot agree on a plan, the company's assets are liquidated and the proceeds distributed by the Bankruptcy Court. **2.** The restructuring of a larger organization without the formation of a new company.

repackaged security A *new issue that uses an existing security as its backing.

repairing lease See LEASE.

repatriation The return of capital from a foreign investment to investment in the country from which it originally came.

replacement cost The cost of replacing an asset, either in its present physical form or as the cost of obtaining equivalent services. If the latter is lower in amount than the former, the conclusion is that the assets currently used by the company are not those it would choose to acquire in the market place. Replacement cost may be used to value tangible *fixed assets and in some circumstances such *current assets as stock.

replacement cycle The period over which a product or *fixed asset will need to be replaced owing to *obsolescence.

repo 1. Short for *repurchase agreement. **2.** Short for *repossession.

reporting accountant 1. An accountant or firm of accountants who report on the financial information provided in a *prospectus. They may or may not be the company's own auditors. It is usual for reporting accountants to have had previous experience of new issues and the preparation of prospectuses. **2.** See AUDIT EXEMPTION.

reporting entity See ACCOUNTING ENTITY.

reporting partner The partner in a firm of auditors who forms an *audit opinion on the *financial statements of a client company and signs and dates the *auditors' report after the financial statements have been formally approved by the directors of the company.

reporting period See ACCOUNTING PERIOD.

report of the auditor(s) See AUDITORS' REPORT.

report of the directors *See* DIRECTORS' REPORT.

repositioning Changing a product's design, formulation, packaging, price, brand image, or brand name to reposition it in the minds of the customer and in relation to its competitors. *See* PERCEPTUAL MAPPING; POSITIONING.

repossession 1. The taking back of something purchased, for nonpayment of the instalments due under a *hire-purchase agreement. **2.** The situation in which a mortgagee (lender) takes vacant possession of the property occupied by a mortgagor (borrower), usually because the latter has defaulted on payments due. *See* MORTGAGE LAW.

representation and warranty A clause in a loan agreement in which the borrower gives a contractual undertaking confirming certain fundamental facts. These will include the borrower's power to borrow and to give guarantees, as well as confirmation that it is not involved in any major litigation.

representations 1. Information given by a person wishing to arrange insurance about the nature of the risk that is to be covered. If it contains a *material fact it must be true to the best knowledge and belief of the person wishing to be insured. *See* UTMOST GOOD FAITH. **2.** Information given by one party in furtherance of a deal.

repudiation 1. The refusal of one party to pay a debt or honour a contract. It often refers to the refusal by the government of a country to settle a national debt incurred by a previous government. **2.** *See* BREACH OF CONTRACT.

repurchase 1. The purchase from an investor of a unit-trust holding by the trust managers. **2.** (**repurchase agreement**; **repo**) An agreement (in full a **sale and repurchase agreement**) in which one party sells a financial asset to another on terms that provide for the seller to buy it back later at an agreed price. The seller is paid in full and makes the agreement to raise ready money without losing the holding. The buyer negotiates a suitable repurchase price to enable a profit to be earned equivalent to interest on the money involved. Repurchase agreements originated in arrangements between the US *Federal Reserve Bank and the *money market, but are now widely used by large companies in the USA and also in Europe. Repos may have a term of only a few days— or even overnight. *See also* RETAIL REPO.

repurchase of own debt The buying back by a company of its own *debt at an amount different from the amount of the liability shown in the *balance sheet.

repurchase transaction A form of discounting in which a corporation raises funds from a bank by selling negotiable paper to it with an undertaking to buy the paper when it matures (*see* NEGOTIABLE INSTRUMENT).

reputational capital The value of an organization's good name and standing. *See also* INTELLECTUAL CAPITAL.

reputed owner A person who acts as the owner of certain goods, with the consent of the true owner. If that person becomes bankrupt, the goods are divided among the creditors and the true owner may be estopped (*see* ESTOPPEL) from claiming them.

request for proposal (RFP) In tendering, a written statement in which a business or other organization invites bids from prospective suppliers by setting out specific requirements for the good or service that it intends to purchase as well as any financial, technical, or time constraints that apply.

A good RFP indicates the exact information that the purchaser requires from suppliers in order to compare their bids objectively.

requisition A form that requires the recipient department or organization to carry out a specified procedure. Examples are purchase requisition, materials requisition, and manufacturing requisition (*see* PRODUCTION ORDER).

requisitioning The taking possession of property by a government, usually during a national emergency, with or without the consent of the owner. When the emergency has ended, the property may be **derequisitioned**, i.e. returned to its owner. A requisition differs from a *compulsory purchase in that ownership does not pass in a requisition as it does in a compulsory purchase.

resale price maintenance (RPM) Formerly, an agreement between a manufacturer, wholesaler, and retailer not to sell a specified product below a fixed price, usually one given by the manufacturer. The purpose was to ensure that all parties were allowed to make a reasonable profit without cut-throat competition. Such an agreement, however, is not in the public interest as it stifles competition; RPM contracts are now generally prohibited under UK and EU law. *See* RECOMMENDED RETAIL PRICE.

rescission The right of a party to a contract to have it set aside and to be restored to the position he or she was in before the contract was made. This is an equitable remedy, available at the discretion of the court. The usual grounds for rescission are mistake, misrepresentation, undue influence, and unconscionable bargains (i.e. those in which the terms are very unfair). No rescission will be allowed where the party seeking it has taken a benefit under the contract (affirmation), or where it is not possible to restore the parties to their former position (restitutio in integrum), or where third parties have already acquired rights under the contract.

research and development costs The costs to a company of its research and development. Section 18 of the Financial Reporting Standard Applicable in the UK and Republic of Ireland, distinguishes between research and development.

- **Research** is original investigation undertaken to gain new scientific or technical knowledge and understanding, whether or not this knowledge has any specific applications.

- **Development** is the use of scientific or technical knowledge to produce new or substantially improved materials, devices, products, processes, systems, or services prior to the commencement of commercial production.

Costs of pure and applied research should be treated as an expense in the year in which they were incurred. In the case of development expenditure, if there is reasonable expectation that the product or process involved is likely to create economic benefits, then the company has the option of capitalizing the development costs, thereby creating an *intangible asset to be shown on the *balance sheet. In all other circumstances development expenditure must be written off to the profit and loss account as soon as it is incurred.

research brief A document that defines the objectives of a *marketing research study before the research is undertaken.

reservation of title A sale of goods in which the seller retains title to the goods sold, or any products made from them, or the resulting sale proceeds, until the buyer pays for the goods. *See also* ROMALPA CLAUSE.

reserve Part of the *capital of a company, other than the share capital, largely arising from retained profit or from the issue of share capital at more than its nominal value. Reserves are distinguished from *provisions in that for the latter there is a known diminution in value of an asset or a known liability, whereas reserves are surpluses not yet distributed and, in some cases (e.g. *share premium account or *capital redemption reserve), not distributable. The directors of a company may choose to earmark part of these funds for a special purpose (e.g. a reserve for obsolescence of plant). However, reserves should not be seen as specific sums of money put aside for special purposes as they are represented by the general net assets of the company. Reserves are subdivided into *retained earnings (revenue reserves), which are available to be distributed to the shareholders by way of dividends, and *undistributable reserves, which for various reasons are not distributable as dividends, although they may be converted into permanent share capital by way of a bonus issue.

reserve assets 1. Money held by a bank that is not required or committed to outstanding loans, and is therefore available to cover shortfalls. In the USA banks must place reserve assets with the *Federal Reserve System. **2.** Gold and foreign currency held by a central bank for intervention in foreign-exchange markets.

Reserve Bank *See* FEDERAL RESERVE BANK.

reserve capital (uncalled capital) When the *issued share capital of a company consists of *partly paid shares, that part of the share capital that has not been requested from subscribers but is held in reserve until it is required (often only if the company is wound up). *Compare* CALLED-UP SHARE CAPITAL; PAID-UP SHARE CAPITAL.

reserve currency A foreign currency that is held by a government because it has confidence in its stability and intends to use it to settle international debts. The US dollar and the pound sterling fulfilled this role for many years but the Japanese yen and the euro are now also widely used.

reserve price The lowest price a seller is willing to accept for an article offered for sale by public *auction. If the reserve price is not reached by the bidding, the auctioneer is instructed to withdraw the article from sale.

reserve tranche The 25% of its quota to which a member of the *International Monetary Fund has unconditional access, for which it pays no charges, and for which there is no obligation to repay the funds. The reserve tranche corresponds to the 25% of quota that was paid not in the member's domestic currency but in *Special Drawing Rights (SDRs) or currencies of other IMF members. It counts as part of the member's foreign reserves. As before 1978 it was paid in gold, it was known as the

gold tranche. Like all IMF facilities it is available only to avert balance of payments problems, although for the reserve tranche the IMF has no power either to challenge the member's assessment of need or to impose a corrective policy. Further funds are available through credit tranches but these are subject to certain conditions (*see* CONDITIONALITY).

resident A person living or based in the UK to whom one of the following applies for a given tax year:

- the person is present in the UK for 183 days or more during that year;
- the person pays substantial visits to the UK, averaging 90 days or more for four or more consecutive years;
- the person has accommodation available for use in the UK and one visit is made during the year. This does not apply if the taxpayer is working abroad full-time nor to individuals who come to the UK for a temporary purpose only.

A UK resident or **resident company** is subject to UK tax on income or capital gains arising anywhere in the world (unless this is disapplied by a *double taxation agreement). From 15 March 1988 companies incorporated in the UK are regarded as resident in the UK for corporation-tax purposes, irrespective of where the management and control of the company is exercised. HM Revenue and Customs has an International Manual that provides more details. *Compare* DOMICILE.

residual income (residual return) The net income that a *subsidiary undertaking or division of an organization generates after being charged a percentage return for the book value of the net assets or resources deemed to be under its control. The headquarters or holding company of the organization will require the subsidiary or division to maximize its profits after the charge for the use of those assets. This approach is very similar to the *Economic Value Added technique. Residual income is often compared with *return on capital employed when measuring the performance of divisions.

residual risk *See* SYSTEMATIC RISK.

residual unemployment The number of people in an economy that remain unemployed, even when there is full employment. They consist largely of people whose physical or mental disabilities are such that they are virtually unemployable; they therefore do not usually feature in unemployment statistics.

resistance level In technical analysis, a level of prices for a security or commodity that is repeatedly reached but not exceeded. Any move beyond this ceiling (*see* BREAKOUT) is regarded as signalling a significant shift to higher prices. *Compare* SUPPORT LEVEL. *See also* DOUBLE TOP.

resistance to change Antagonism towards change among the employees in an organization. The reasons for resistance include a misunderstanding of the goal of the change, having a low tolerance for change (particularly through fear), and perceiving that something of value will be lost. In general, people will only change if they feel it will be in their interests to do so. *See also* CHANGE AGENT; CHANGE MANAGEMENT.

resolution A binding decision made by the members of a company. If a motion is put before the members of a company at a general meeting and the required majority vote in favour of it, the motion is passed and becomes a resolution. A resolution may also be passed by unanimous informal consent of the members.

UK company law recognizes several different types of resolution, each of which has different requirements in terms of the required voting majority. The type of resolution required to make a particular decision may be prescribed by the Companies Act or by the company's articles. For example, an *ordinary resolution is required to remove a director and a *special resolution is required to change the company's articles of association. *See also* WRITTEN RESOLUTION.

resource-based view (RBV) A model holding that a company's business strategy should be determined principally by its internal resources—assets, capabilities, processes, and *intellectual capital—rather than by external factors, such as market opportunity. The RBV holds that a company can create sustained *competitive advantage where its resources satisfy the so-called **VRIN** criteria: i.e. where its resources are *v*aluable, *r*are, *i*mperfectly imitable, and *n*on-substitutable. More recently, the RBV has been extended by the *dynamic capabilities approach. *See also* CORE COMPETENCY.

respondentia bond *See* HYPOTHECATION.

response bias An error that results from the tendency of people to answer a marketing research question falsely, either through deliberate misrepresentation or unconscious falsification.

restitution The legal principle that a person who has been unjustly enriched at the expense of another should make restitution, e.g. by returning property or money. This principle is not yet fully developed in English law but has a predominant place in the laws of Scotland and the USA.

restraint of trade A term in a contract that restricts a person's right to carry on his or her trade or profession. An example, in a contract covering the sale of a business, would be a clause that attempts to restrict the seller's freedom to set up in competition to the buyer. Such clauses are illegal, unless they can be shown not to be contrary to the public interest.

restricted stock (restricted securities) Shares in a company, usually held by selected employees, that are not owned outright by the holder until a stated condition is fulfilled. This may be a time limit (i.e. the employee must remain with the company for a specified number of years) or an individual or collective performance target. Restricted stock has become a popular alternative to *share option schemes. *See also* SHARE INCENTIVE SCHEME.

restricted surplus *See* UNDISTRIBUTABLE RESERVES.

restrictive covenant 1. A clause in a contract that restricts the freedom of one of the parties in some way. Employment contracts, for example, sometimes include a clause in which an employee agrees not to compete with the employer for a specified period after leaving the employment. Such clauses may not be enforceable in law. *See* RESTRAINT OF TRADE; RESTRICTIVE TRADE PRACTICES. **2.** A clause in a contract affecting the use of land. *See* COVENANT.

restrictive endorsement An endorsement on a *bill of exchange that restricts the freedom of the endorsee to negotiate it.

restrictive trade practices Agreements between traders that are not considered to be in the public interest. Under the Competition Act 1998 any agreement between two or more suppliers of goods or services restricting prices, conditions of sale, quantities offered, processes, areas and persons to be supplied, etc., must be entered in a public register and, where appropriate, investigated by the *Office of Fair Trading. Such agreements are presumed to be contrary to the public interest unless the parties are able to prove to the court that the agreement is beneficial.

retailer A *distributor that sells goods or services to consumers (*compare* WHOLESALER). There are, broadly, three categories of retailer: *multiple shops, *co-operative retailers, and *independent retailers.

retailer co-operative organization *See* CO-OPERATIVE.

retailing accordion The manner in which the width of a retailer's product assortment or operation changes over its lifetime: there tends to be a general specific general cycle, although some retailing businesses evolve over a specific general specific cycle.

Retail Price Index (RPI) An index of the prices of goods and services in retail shops purchased by average households, expressed in percentage terms relative to a base year, which is taken as 100. For example, if 1987 is taken as the base year for the UK (i.e. average prices in January 1987 = 100), then in 1946 the RPI stood at 7.4, and in May 2015 at 258.5. The RPI is published by the Office for National Statistics on a monthly basis and includes the prices of some 650 goods and services in 11 groups. The prices of the goods are checked every month and individual items and groups are weighted to reflect their relative importance. Weightings are regularly updated by the Family Expenditure Survey. Although the RPI is still widely used and quoted, it is no longer the main official measure of the rate of *inflation (*see* CONSUMER PRICE INDEX).

(⊕) **SEE WEB LINKS**
• UK RPI data

retail repo A *repurchase agreement involving a loan to a bank rather than to a company or an individual.

retail tender An application to buy a substantial number of shares in a privatization offer. The application is made through a **retail tender broker**. Usually the investor either decides on the price to bid for the shares (which may or may not be successful) or bids on a 'strike price only' basis, in which case shares will be allocated to the investor at the price paid by like institutions. Generally a retail tender will not attract the special incentives available to purchasers using a *share shop. Retail tender brokers are often also share shops.

retained earnings (retained profits; ploughed-back profits; retentions) The *net profit available for *distribution, less any distributions made, i.e. the amount kept within the company. Retained earnings are recorded in the profit and loss reserve.

retentions *See* RETAINED EARNINGS.

retiring a bill The act of withdrawing a *bill of exchange from circulation when it has been paid on or before its due date.

return The income from an investment, frequently expressed as a percentage of its cost. *See also* RETURN ON CAPITAL EMPLOYED.

returned cheque A *cheque on which payment has been refused and which has been returned to the bank on which it was drawn. If the reason is lack of funds, the bank will mark it *refer to drawer; if the bank wishes to give the customer an opportunity to pay in sufficient funds to cover it, they will also mark it 'please represent'. The collecting bank will then present it for payment again, after letting his customer know that the cheque has been dishonoured.

return on assets An *accounting ratio expressing the amount of *profit for an *accounting period as a percentage of the *assets of a company.

return on capital employed (ROCE) An *accounting ratio expressing the *profit of an organization for an *accounting period as a percentage of the capital employed. It is one of the most frequently used ratios for assessing the performance of organizations. In making the calculation, however, there are a number of differing definitions of the terms used. Profit is usually taken as profit before interest and tax, while capital employed refers to fixed assets plus *current assets minus *current liabilities. Sometimes the expression **return on investment (ROI)** is used, in which case even greater care must be used in understanding the calculation of the separate items. Management may consider that profit before interest and tax, expressed as a percentage of total assets, is a useful measure of performance. Shareholders, however, may be more interested in taking profit after interest and comparing this to total assets less all liabilities. The ratio can be further analysed by calculating profit margins and *capital turnover ratios.

For managers, ROCE highlights the benefits that can obtain by reducing investments in current or fixed assets. However, it is important to emphasize that relying on a single *performance measure is not desirable and managers should use ROCE in conjunction with other measures. For example, ROCE is often compared to *residual income.

return on equity (ROE) The net income of an organization expressed as a percentage of its equity capital.

return on investment (ROI) *See* RETURN ON CAPITAL EMPLOYED.

returns inwards (sales returns) Goods returned to an organization by customers, usually because they are unsatisfactory.

returns outwards Goods returned by an organization to its suppliers, usually because they are unsatisfactory.

Reuters A worldwide agency dealing in news, financial information, and trading services. It was founded in 1851 as a subscription information service for newspapers. It now provides a wide range of financial prices and dealing services.

revalorization of currency The replacement of one currency unit by another. A government often takes this step if a nation's currency has been devalued frequently or by a large amount. The practice is usually associated with high rates of inflation. *Compare* REVALUATION OF CURRENCY.

revaluation account In a *partnership to which a new partner is admitted or if an existing partner dies or retires, assets and liabilities must be revalued to their current market value. The differences between historical values and the revaluations are debited or credited to the revaluation account. The balance on the revaluation account will represent a profit or loss on revaluation, which must be shared between the partners in the *profit-sharing ratio.

revaluation method A method of determining the *depreciation charge on a *fixed asset against profits for an accounting period. The asset to be depreciated is revalued each year; the fall in the value is the amount of depreciation to be written off the asset and charged against the profit and loss account for the period. It is often used for such depreciating assets as loose tools or a mine from which materials are extracted.

revaluation of assets A revaluation of the assets of a company, either because they have increased in value since they were acquired or because *inflation has made the balance-sheet values unrealistic. The Companies Act makes it obligatory for the directors of a company to state in the directors' report if they believe the value of land differs materially from the value in the balance sheet. The Act also lays down the procedures to adopt when fixed assets are revalued. The difference between the net book value of a company's assets before and after revaluation is shown in a revaluation reserve account or, more commonly in the USA, an **appraisal-surplus account** (if the value of the assets has increased).

revaluation of currency An increase in the value of a currency in terms of gold or other currencies. It is usually made by a government that has a persistent balance of payments surplus. It has the effect of making imports cheaper but exports become dearer and therefore less competitive in a country; revaluation is therefore unpopular with governments. *Compare* DEVALUATION; REVALORIZATION OF CURRENCY.

revenue 1. Any form of income. **2.** Cost and income items that are either charged or credited to the *profit and loss account for an accounting period.

revenue account 1. An *account recording the income from trading operations or the expenses incurred in these operations. **2.** A budgeted amount that can be spent for day-to-day operational expenses, especially in public-sector budgeting. *Compare* CAPITAL ACCOUNT.

Revenue and Customs, HM The UK government department responsible for the care, management, and collection of direct and indirect taxes, *National Insurance contributions, and customs and excise duties within the UK. Its other responsibilities include the payment of *tax credits and child benefit. It is governed by a small board known as the Commissioners of Revenue and Customs, but the day-to-day administration is carried out by civil servants. Inspectors of Taxes are responsible for assessing taxes, which are collected by Collectors of Taxes (*see also* SELF-ASSESSMENT). A taxpayer can appeal against an inspector's assessment. HM Revenue and Customs was formed from a merger of the Board of Inland Revenue and the Board of Customs and Excise in April 2005. A Revenue and Customs Prosecution Office, responsible for the prosecution of all revenue and customs cases, was established at the same time.

(((( ))) SEE WEB LINKS
- HMRC area of the Gov.uk website provides details of all UK tax rates, codes, and allowances and facilities for making returns online

revenue bonds Loans in which the *principal and *interest are payable from the earnings of the project financed by the loan. They are sometimes issued in the USA by municipalities, to finance such projects as toll bridges.

revenue evaporation A sudden fall in income from the sale of a product or service, particularly when this is owing to fundamental change in the nature of a market, e.g. as a result of technological innovation. Recent examples of this have occurred in the telecommunications and media industries, where revenue from voice calls and print has declined owing to the advent of Internet-based alternatives.

revenue expenditure Expenditure written off to the *profit and loss account in the *accounting period in which it is made. Such expenditure is deemed to have been incurred by the revenue generated within that financial period.

revenue management (yield management) The use of sophisticated computer programs to analyse consumer behaviour, forecast demand, and adjust pricing in order to maximize revenues. Revenue management is mainly applicable to industries in which resources are fixed and perishable, such as the travel and hospitality industries. A seat on an aeroplane, for example, must be filled by the time of take-off or contribute nil revenue; companies therefore need to know the optimum moment at which to maximize the yield from a flight by offering unfilled seats at a discount. At the same time, the company will want to encourage early rather than late booking as the general rule and may devise price incentives accordingly. Revenue management attempts to optimize overall yield through a complex process of *market segmentation, *price discrimination (e.g. charging a different price for an airline ticket depending on when, where, and by whom it is bought), and differentiating the product (e.g. charging more or less for a ticket depending on what travel restrictions apply).

revenue reserve A reserve that is not a *capital reserve, i.e. a reserve that is distributable.

revenue support grant (RSG) In the UK, central government funding of local authorities to supplement income from local taxes. The grant helps local authorities to maintain services and taxes at levels comparable to other authorities. It was formerly known as the **rate support grant**.

reverse engineering Taking a finished product and analysing it to find out how it is made or how it works. In the case of a mechanical device, this usually involves disassembling it. In the case of software, it involves decompiling in order to reproduce the original source code. Reverse engineering is most often undertaken with the aim of designing a similar product in a way that does not infringe intellectual property rights. Alternatively, a patent or copyright holder may use it to check a competitor's product for any such infringement. In the EU reverse engineering of computer software is illegal where the purpose is to design a competing product.

reverse takeover 1. The buying of a larger company by a smaller company. **2.** The purchasing of a public company by a private company. This may be the cheapest way that a private company can obtain a listing on a stock exchange, as it avoids the expenses of a *flotation and it may be that the assets of the public company can be purchased at a discount. In the UK many such reverse takeovers are transacted on the *Alternative Investment Market.

reverse yield gap The situation in which the yield on long-term fixed-interest securities is greater than the dividend yield on equities (*see* YIELD GAP). In the UK, such a situation prevailed from the late 1950s until the late 2000s.

reversible lay days *See* LAY DAYS.

reversionary annuity *See* CONTINGENT ANNUITY.

reversionary bonus A sum added to the amount payable on death or maturity of a *with-profits policy. The bonus is added if the life-assurance company has a surplus or has a profit on the investment of its life funds. Once a reversionary bonus has been made it cannot be withdrawn if the policy runs to maturity or to the death of the insured. However, if the policy is cashed, the bonus is usually reduced by an amount that depends on the length of time the policy has to run.

revocable letter of credit *See* LETTER OF CREDIT.

revolving acceptance facility by tender (RAFT) An underwritten facility from a bank to place sterling *acceptance credits through the medium of a tender panel of eligible banks.

revolving bank facility (standby revolving credit) A loan from a bank or group of banks to a company in which the company has flexibility with regard to the timing and the number of *drawdowns and repayments; any loan repaid can be reborrowed subject to fulfilment of the conditions of the *committed facility. The facility can be a *bilateral bank facility or a *syndicated bank facility.

revolving credit A bank credit that is negotiated for a specified period; it allows for *drawdown and repayment within that period. Repaid amounts can be redrawn up to the agreed limit of the credit. At the end of the loan period there is a *bullet repayment of the principal and any outstanding interest; alternatively, a repayment schedule is negotiated for the outstanding principal and interest. In the USA a revolving credit is called an **open-end credit**. *See also* CONVERTIBLE REVOLVING CREDIT.

revolving underwriting facility (RUF) *See* NOTE ISSUANCE FACILITY.

RFM analysis Abbreviation for recency, frequency, monetary analysis: a marketing tool used to analyse customer behaviour in terms of how recently they have made a purchase, how frequently they have done so, and how much money they have spent. It is widely used to select customers for *direct marketing promotions, as applying RFM has been found to be more cost-effective than a blanket approach. It can also be used to identify customers who made regular purchases in the past but have for some reason ceased to do so.

RFP Abbreviation for *request for proposal.

rial 1. (IRR) The standard monetary unit of Iran. **2.** (OMR) The standard monetary unit of Oman, divided into 1,000 baizas.

rich pictures A pictorial technique used in *soft systems methodology enabling individuals and groups to compare their views of the key entities, structures, processes, relationships, and issues involved in a problem situation.

RIE Abbreviation for *Recognized Investment Exchange.

riel (KHR) The standard monetary unit of Cambodia, divided into 100 sen.

rigging a market An attempt to make a profit on a market, usually a security or commodity market, by overriding the

normal market forces. This often involves taking a *long position or a *short position in the market that is sufficiently substantial to influence price levels, and then supporting or depressing the market by further purchases or sales.

right of resale The right that the seller in a contract of sale has to resell the goods if the buyer does not pay the price as agreed. If the goods are perishable or the seller tells the buyer that the goods will be resold and the buyer still does not pay within a reasonable time, the seller may resell them and recover from the first buyer damages for any loss.

rights issue A method by which listed companies on a stock exchange raise new capital, in exchange for new shares. The name arises from the principle of *pre-emption rights, according to which existing shareholders must be offered the new shares in proportion to their holding of old shares (a **rights offer**). For example in a 1 for 4 rights issue, shareholders would be asked to buy one new share for every four they already hold. As rights are usually issued at a discount to the market price of existing shares, those not wishing to take up their rights can sell them in the market. *Compare* BOUGHT DEAL; VENDOR PLACING; SCRIP ISSUE.

rightsizing The restructuring and *rationalization of an organization to improve effectiveness and cut costs, without involving a full *downsizing operation, which can often be overdone. Rightsizing could include increasing the size of an organization to meet increased demand, but it is more often used as a euphemism for moderate and controlled downsizing.

rights letter A document sent to an existing shareholder of a company offering him shares in a *rights issue on advantageous terms. If the recipient does not wish to take advantage of the offer himself he can sell the letter and the attendant rights on the stock exchange (*see* RENUNCIATION).

ring 1. A number of manufacturers, dealers, or traders who agree among themselves to control the price or conditions of sale of a product for their own benefit. Such agreements are illegal in most countries, unless they can be shown to be in the public interest. *See* RESTRICTIVE TRADE PRACTICES. **2.** An association of dealers in an auction sale, especially a sale of antiques or paintings, who agree not to bid against each other but to allow one of their number to buy an article being auctioned at an artificially low price, on the understanding that it will be auctioned again, exclusively to members of the ring. The difference between the purchase price and the final price paid is shared among the members of the ring. This is an illegal practice.

Ringelmann effect The finding that the output of groups increases as they grow larger but that the gain in productivity becomes less for each new member added. The effect is named after Max Ringelmann (1861–1931), a French agricultural engineer who studied the output of men, animals, and machines in various combinations. It can be explained by the lower levels of efficiency and motivation characteristic of large groups. *See* COLLECTIVE EFFORT MODEL; SOCIAL LOAFING; SUCKER EFFECT.

ring-fence 1. To allow one part of a company or group to go into receivership or bankruptcy without affecting the viability of the rest of the company or group. **2.** To assign a sum of money to a particular purpose so that it does not become part of the general resources of an organization. **3.** To separate one part of a business from another for regulatory reasons. This is sometimes enforced when e.g. a public utility is acquired by a parent company with wider business interests. In the wake of the 2008 financial crisis a similar model has often been proposed for banks that engage in both everyday retail banking and more speculative activities.

ringgit (MYR) The Malaysian dollar: the standard monetary unit of Malaysia, divided into 100 sen.

ring trading *See* CALLOVER.

riot and civil commotion A risk not usually covered in householders' insurance policies or commercial policies, unless a special clause has been added to cover loss or damage due to riot or civil commotion.

rising bottoms A pattern in which the price lows within market fluctuations display a steady upward trend over time. In *chartist analysis such a pattern is seen as a sign of a *bull market. *Compare* ASCENDING TOPS.

risk 1. (**speculative risk**) A possibility of financial loss (whether in absolute terms or relative to expectations) that is inseparable from the opportunity for financial gain. Some of the major categories are *market risk, *credit risk, *liquidity risk, and *operational risk. Market risk arises from changes in prices in financial markets. Credit risk relates to non-payment of obligations or credit impairment. Liquidity risk is that of running out of cash or problems with asset enhancement. Operational risk is a catch-all category that covers a firm's internal systems and processes, as well as external events. *See also* COUNTERPARTY RISK; EXCHANGE-RATE EXPOSURE; INTEREST-RATE RISK; SPECIFIC RISK; SYSTEMATIC RISK. **2.** (**peril; pure risk**) The possibility of suffering some form of loss or damage where there is no corresponding opportunity for gain. Risks of this kind – e.g. fire, theft, or accident – are the proper domain of insurance cover. *See* INSURABLE RISK.

risk-adjusted discount rate In *capital budgeting and portfolio management, the *discount rate used in calculations of *present value; it will reflect the level of risk embodied in the cash flows being considered.

risk-adjusted return on capital (RAROC) A measure of the performance of units within a bank or financial organization, be they managerial units, products, distributional units, or such treasury-based units as trading desks. It was developed by Bankers' Trust and the Bank of America in the 1980s. In its most common form RAROC allocates *capital at risk to a unit and divides that into the return obtained from the unit. The capital is allocated in terms of a *value-at-risk methodology. A refinement of this system is known as **RAROC 2020**.

risk analysis The measurement and analysis of *risk associated with a business, project, or decision. It involves the identification of risk, the classification of risks in regard to their impact and likelihood, and a consideration of how they might best be managed. *See* RISK MANAGEMENT.

risk-averse Describing a *risk preference in which a decision maker's attraction to an investment or other economic choice rises with higher average returns and falls with greater *standard deviations of returns. *Compare* RISK-NEUTRAL; RISK-SEEKING. *See also* PORTFOLIO THEORY; UTILITY THEORY.

risk capital (venture capital) Capital invested in a project in which there is a substantial element of risk, especially money invested in a new venture or an expanding business. It is also used in buy-outs by *private equity firms and employee or *management buy-outs (*see* BIMBO). Risk capital is normally invested in the equity of the company in the hope of a high return; it is not a loan (but *see* SHAREHOLDER DEBT).

risk-free rate The *rate of return on an investment that has no risk. The return on US and UK Treasury bills is often regarded as a very close approximation to this rate. The risk-free rate is an important concept in the *capital asset pricing model.

risk management A process that aims to help organizations understand, evaluate, and take action on all their risks. A private-sector organization will need to identify and evaluate the trade-off between risk and expected return and to choose the course of action that will help it to maximize its value. Risk management is also relevant to the public sector. Common forms of risk management include taking out insurance against possible losses and the use of *derivatives to *hedge against changes in interest rates, exchange rates, or other economic variables. A bank will always try

to manage the risks involved in lending by adjusting the level of charges and interest rates to compensate for a percentage of losses.

risk matrix A method of *risk analysis customized for businesses from a basic framework developed by the US military in the identification of *operational risk. It is in essence a brainstorming technique. When applied to a business, the two dimensions of the matrix relate to those assets at risk in the business and how these assets are at risk. When considering what is at risk, the assets of the business are defined as widely as possible, including both *tangible assets and such *intangible assets as reputation and branding.

risk-neutral Describing a *risk preference in which the decision maker is influenced only by the average return on an investment or other choice and not by the *standard deviation of returns. *Compare* RISK-AVERSE; RISK-SEEKING.

risk preference The attitude of an investor or decision maker to risks. *See* RISK-AVERSE; RISK-NEUTRAL; RISK-SEEKING.

risk premium (market-risk premium) **1.** The difference between the expected *rate of return on an investment and the *risk-free rate of return over the same period. If there is any risk element at all, the rate of return should be higher than if no risk were involved. *See* CAPITAL ASSET PRICING MODEL. **2.** An addition to the normal price of a transaction to reflect any extra risk involved.

risk-seeking Describing a *risk preference in which the decision maker's attraction to an investment or other economic choice rises with higher average returns and a higher *standard deviation of returns. *Compare* RISK-AVERSE; RISK-NEUTRAL.

risky effect *See* CHOICE-SHIFT EFFECTS.

riyal 1. (SAR) The standard monetary unit of Saudi Arabia, divided into 20 qurush and 100 halala. **2.** (QAR) The standard monetary unit of Qatar, divided into 100 dirhams. **3.** (YER) The standard monetary unit of Yemen, divided into 100 fils.

road haulage The transport of goods by road vehicles. With the advent of the European Union, the network of motorways throughout Europe, *roll-on roll-off ferries, and the Channel Tunnel, much freight is now carried throughout Europe by road vehicles.

Robinson–Patman Act 1936 A US federal law intended to halt discriminatory pricing policies by specifying certain limited conditions under which a seller is permitted to charge different prices to different buyers.

robot A machine, usually controlled by computer, that is capable of performing routine and repetitive tasks without human intervention.

ROCE Abbreviation for *return on capital employed.

ROE Abbreviation for *return on equity.

ROI Abbreviation for return on investment. *See* RETURN ON CAPITAL EMPLOYED.

rolled-up coupon A certificate of interest (*see* COUPON) on a bond or other security, in which the interest is ploughed back to increase the capital value of the original bond, rather than being drawn as cash.

rolling budget A budget that is regularly updated by adding a further budget period, such as a month or a quarter, while at the same time dropping out the earliest month or quarter as appropriate.

rolling launch The process of gradually introducing a new product into the market.

rolling position A financial *position that is maintained, although the instruments comprising the position are changed over time.

roll-on roll-off ferry (RORO) A ferry that loads motor vehicles by allowing them to drive on and drive off. Such ferries are widely used for transporting road haulage vehicles across the English Channel.

roll-over CD A *certificate of deposit in which the maturity is divided into short periods to make it easier to sell on the secondary market. They are sometimes known as **roly-poly CDs**.

roll-over credit A medium- or long-term bank loan in which the rate of interest varies with short-term money-market rates (such as LIBOR) because the bank has raised the loan by short-term money-market or *interbank market borrowing.

roll-over relief A relief that permits a charge to *capital gains tax to be deferred when the proceeds from the disposal of an asset are reinvested in a new asset. Any gain arising from the disposal of the new asset will be correspondingly increased (unless the gain is once more 'rolled over'). Both the old and new asset must be business assets, but they do not have to belong to the same category. For example, the proceeds on disposal of land (the old asset) could be rolled over into the acquisition of plant and machinery (the new asset). The disposal of the old asset and the acquisition of the new asset must take place within specified time limits. Detailed regulations are available from HM Revenue and Customs.

roll-up funds An offshore investment fund using securities with *rolled-up coupons designed to avoid *income tax. However, these funds are now assessed for income tax as if the coupons were paid in cash.

roly-poly CD *See* ROLL-OVER CD.

Romalpa clause (title retention clause) A clause included in a contract of sale in which the seller retains the title of the goods sold until they have been paid for. This is of importance to accountants as it may affect the ownership of *stocks; it is essential to determine whether the commercial substance of a transaction rests ownership of an *asset in the purchaser, irrespective of any legal agreement. This clause derives its name from the case of *Aluminium Industrie Vasseen BV v Romalpa Aluminium Ltd* (1976), which was concerned with the practice of selling goods subject to *reservation of title.

RORO Abbreviation for roll-on roll-off. *See* ROLL-ON ROLL-OFF FERRY.

rotation of directors Under the *articles of association of most UK companies, the obligatory retirement of one third of the directors each year (normally at the *annual general meeting), so that each director retires by rotation every three years. Retiring directors may be re-elected.

rouble The standard monetary unit of Russia (RUB) and Belarus (BYR), divided into 100 kopeks.

round lot A round number of shares or a round amount of stock for which market makers will sometimes offer better prices than for **odd lots**.

round tripping 1. Any of various practices in which a company, A, sells an asset to a buyer, B (who is often in another jurisdiction) and then purchases an equivalent asset from B at essentially the same price. The self-cancelling nature of the transaction is usually disguised by passing the assets through a chain of intermediaries. The object may be *money laundering, *tax evasion, or a desire to inflate the company's trading figures. **2.** A transaction in which a company borrows money from one source and lends it at profit to another by taking advantage of a short-term rise in interest rates or a regulatory anomaly. For example, a company may use its bank overdraft facility to deposit funds in the money market at rates that exceed the cost of the overdraft. This practice is frowned upon by banks because they may be having to use the money market themselves to fund their customers' overdrafts.

route sheet A document showing the succession of processes through which a product passes. Computer-based scheduling systems make it possible to track individual components and products in situations that would be too complex with manual systems.

Royal Institution of Chartered Surveyors (RICS) An institution, founded in 1868 and given a Royal Charter in 1881, that aims to provide education and training for surveyors and to define and control their professional conduct. Qualification as a Chartered Surveyor can be achieved by passing the Institution's own examinations or through recognized academic or professional experience in the field. A Chartered member of RICS can use the initials MRICS after his or her name; after further experience he or she may apply for a Fellowship (FRICS). The Institution also has members who qualify by a more vocational route and use the initials TechRICS or AssocRICS.

((●)) SEE WEB LINKS

• RICS website: includes a digest of economic news and analysis and authoritative surveys of the UK's residential and commercial property markets

Royal Mint The organization in the UK that has had the sole right to manufacture English coins since the 16th century. Controlled by the Chancellor of the Exchequer, it was formerly situated in the City of London but moved to Llantrisant in Wales in 1968. It also makes banknotes, UK medals, and increasing quantities of foreign coins (now about 65% of the Mint's total output).

royalty A payment made for the right to use the property of another person for gain. This is usually an *intellectual property, such as a copyright (e.g. in a book) or a patent (e.g. in an invention). A royalty may also be paid to a landowner, who has granted mineral rights to someone else, on sales of minerals extracted from the land. A royalty is regarded as a *wasting asset as copyrights, patents, and mines have limited lives.

RPB Abbreviation for Recognized Professional Body. *See* DESIGNATED PROFESSIONAL BODY.

RPI Abbreviation for *Retail Price Index.

RPM Abbreviation for *resale price maintenance.

RRP Abbreviation for *recommended retail price.

RSG Abbreviation for *revenue support grant.

RUF Abbreviation for revolving underwriting facility. *See* NOTE ISSUANCE FACILITY.

rufiyaa (MVR) The standard monetary unit of the Maldives, divided into 100 laari.

rule-based system A computer program that makes decisions or solves problems by applying a set of 'if–then' rules. There are numerous applications: for example a program can be used to determine the kinds of special offers, promotions, and information that should be provided for visitors to a company's website. An *expert system is a sophisticated form of rule-based system.

rummage A search of a ship or aircraft by customs officers looking for contraband, illegal drugs, etc.

running-account credit A personal credit agreement that enables a person to receive loans from time to time from a bank or other lender provided that a specified credit limit is not exceeded. Interest is charged on the amount loaned during any period.

running broker A bill broker who does not himself discount *bills of exchange but acts between bill owners and discount houses or banks, on a commission basis.

running costs The expenditure incurred in order to carry out the operations of a fixed asset. Examples are power, maintenance, and consumable materials for a machine or fuel, oil, tyres, and servicing for motor vehicles.

running days Consecutive days including Saturdays, Sundays, and Bank Holidays. In chartering a vessel the period of the charter is given in running days, rather than working days.

running-down clause A clause in a *hull insurance policy covering a ship-owner against liability for compensation as a result of a collision with another vessel.

running yield *See* YIELD.

run of paper Denoting an advertisement in a paper, magazine, etc., in which the publisher decides where the advertisement shall be placed. This is offered at a lower rate than an advertisement set in a specified position in the publication.

run-out time The time that will elapse before an item in stock runs out. The concept is essential for scheduling the reordering of a range of goods. The run-out time for a product i is defined as:

$$r_i = l_i/d_i,$$

where r_i is run-out time in weeks, l_i is units in stock, and d_i is demand in units per week.

The accompanying table gives a number of examples.

run to settlement Denoting a *futures contract in a commodity that has run to its

PRODUCT	CURRENT STOCK (UNITS)	DEMAND RATE (UNITS/WEEK)	RUN-OUT TIME (WEEKS)
A	1000	200	5
B	500	150	3.3
C	2000	500	4
D	600	300	2

Run-out time. The run-out times of four products as calculated from current stock levels and demand rates.

settlement day without being set off by a corresponding sales or purchase contract so that delivery of the physical goods must be made or taken.

rupee 1. The standard monetary unit of India (INR), Pakistan (PKR), and Nepal (NPR), divided into 100 paisa. **2.** The standard monetary unit of Sri Lanka (LKR), Mauritius (MUR), and the Seychelles (SCR), divided into 100 cents.

rupiah (IDR) The standard monetary unit of Indonesia, divided into 100 sen.

S

SA 1. Abbreviation for *société anonyme*. It appears after the name of a French, Belgian, or Luxembourg company, being equivalent to the British abbreviation plc (i.e. denoting a public limited company). **2.** Abbreviation for *sociedad anónima*. It appears after the name of a Spanish public company. **3.** Abbreviation for *sociedade anónima*. It appears after the name of a Portuguese public company. *Compare* SARL.

SAB Abbreviation for *standard application blank.

safe custody A service offered by most UK commercial banks, in which the bank holds valuable items belonging to its customers in its strong room. These items are usually documents, such as deeds and bearer bonds, but they may also include items of value. The bank is a bailee for these items and its liability will depend on whether or not it has charged the customer for the service and the terms of the customer's own insurance (in the case of items of value). In a **safe deposit** the customer hires a small lockable box from the bank or safe-deposit company, to which access is provided during normal banking hours.

sagacity segmentation A form of *market segmentation developed to improve the discriminating power of demographic classifications. It combines life-cycle, income, and socio-economic information. The underlying idea is that as people pass through the various stages of their lives they have different aspirations and patterns of behaviour, which are reflected in their consumption of goods and services.

saitori Members of the Tokyo Stock Exchange who act as intermediaries between brokers. They cannot deal on their own account or for non-members of the exchange; they may only be allowed to deal in a limited number of stocks.

salaried partner A partner in a *partnership who by agreement draws a regular salary.

salary A regular payment, usually monthly, made by an employer, under a contract of employment, to an employee.

sale and leaseback A transaction in which the owner of an *asset sells it and immediately purchases back from the buyer the right to use the asset under a *lease. The lease may be a *finance lease or an *operating lease.

sale and repurchase agreement *See* REPURCHASE.

sale as seen A sale made on the basis that the buyer has inspected the goods and is buying them as a result of this inspection and not on any guarantee of quality or condition by the seller. The seller does not guarantee or imply that the goods are suitable for any particular purpose. *Compare* SALE BY DESCRIPTION; SALE BY SAMPLE.

sale by description A sale made on the basis that the quality of the goods sold will correspond to the description given of them in the contract of sale. *Compare* SALE AS SEEN; SALE BY SAMPLE.

sale by instalments *See* HIRE PURCHASE.

sale by sample A sale made on the basis of *sample, i.e. that the quality and condition of the bulk of the goods will be at least as good as that of the selling sample. In contracts in which goods are sold by sample, the contract may stipulate how and by whom the bulk should be sampled and what tests should be used to compare it to the selling sample. The contract will also usually lay down the procedure to be adopted if the bulk sample is not as good as the selling sample. *Compare* SALE AS SEEN; SALE BY DESCRIPTION.

sale by tender *See* ISSUE BY TENDER.

sale or return Terms of trade in which the seller agrees to take back from the buyer any unsold goods, usually in a specified period. Some retail shops buy certain of their goods on sale or return.

sales account An *account used to record cash and credit sales transactions resulting from the sale of goods or services.

sales analysis A detailed study of an organization's sales records, including a detailed breakdown of all sales information, to reveal patterns that can be used to evaluate the effectiveness of the marketing efforts.

sales day book (sales journal; sold day book) The *book of prime entry in which an organization records the invoices issued to its customers for goods or services supplied in the course of its trade. Postings are made from this book to the personal accounts of the customers, while the totals of the invoices are posted to the sales account in the *nominal ledger.

salesforce automation system (SFA system) A computer application used to coordinate and analyse various types of information relevant to salespeople and salesforce managers. It will include a detailed *customer database, product information, activity records, and an order management system. Most SFA systems can now be used via smartphones. *See also* CUSTOMER RELATIONSHIP MANAGEMENT SYSTEM.

salesforce management The planning, organization, direction, recruitment, training, and motivation of the salesforce within

a planned marketing strategy. It includes setting *sales objectives and evaluating the results obtained by the salesforce. In very large markets, such as the USA, there might be a hierarchy of sales managers and district managers, reporting to regional managers, who in turn report to a national sales manager.

salesforce promotion A sales promotion designed to motivate the salesforce and make its selling efforts more effective. The promotion may include bonuses, contests, prizes, or sales rallies.

sales forecast An estimate of future sales volumes and revenue. It is usually based on past trends and takes into account current and future directions, such as government regulations, economic forecasts, and industry conditions.

sales function The section of an organization responsible for selling its products and services. *See* FUNCTION.

sales invoice A document sent by the seller of goods or services to the buyer, detailing the amounts due, discounts available, payment dates, and such administrative details as the account numbers and credit limits.

sales ledger (debtors' ledger) The *ledger that records the personal accounts of an organization's customers. The total of the balances in this ledger represents the organization's trade debtors.

sales mix The relative proportions of individual products that make up the total units sold.

sales objectives The specific objectives that an organization's sales effort will attempt to meet. Sales objectives should be precise and quantifiable; they should include a time frame and should be attainable in terms of the organization's resources.

sales orientation A strategy that concentrates on selling existing products, whether or not they meet consumer needs, often by means of aggressive sales techniques and advertising. It is regarded as a strategy with a limited long-term future.

sales presentation *See* PRESENTATION.

sales promotion An activity designed to boost the sales of a product or service. It may include an advertising campaign, increased PR activity, a free-sample campaign, offering free gifts, arranging demonstrations or exhibitions, setting up competitions with attractive prizes, temporary price reductions, door-to-door calling, telephone selling, mail shots, e-mail marketing, etc.

sales quota A target set by *salesforce management for a specific area or *sales representative. Since the earnings of sales representatives are often directly related to the sales achieved, the setting of realistic quotas is imperative.

sales representative A person who sells the goods and services of an organization, either as an employee of that organization or as part of a contractual salesforce. Additional responsibilities might include generating new sales leads (*see* COLD CALLING), publicizing changes in products or prices, gathering information about competitors' activity, and *merchandising products. Sales representatives often receive a commission on what they sell.

sales response function The relationship between the likely sales of a particular product during a specified period and the level of marketing support it receives. The more advertising, sales promotion, or public-relations support for a product, the higher the sales are likely to be.

sales returns 1. *See* RETURNS INWARDS. **2.** A report on sales made in a period.

sales tax (expenditure tax; outlay tax) A tax based on the selling price of goods. Such taxes are not now generally favoured, since they have a cascade effect, i.e. if goods are sold on from one trader to another the amount of sales tax borne by the ultimate buyer becomes too great.

*Value added tax was largely designed to meet this objection.

sales territory The unit of organization of a salesforce within a company. Each *sales representative is usually assigned a geographical area, market segment, or product group in which to develop sales, and accordingly accepts the credit for the success (or otherwise) of the product within that area.

sales trend The long-term, underlying pattern of sales growth or decline for a product or service resulting from basic changes in population, capital formation, or technology.

salvage 1. Goods, property, etc., saved from a shipwreck or from a fire. If a cargo is treated as a total loss for insurance purposes, there still may be salvageable items that have a **salvage value**; these may be sold by the insurers or allowed for in the settlement of their claim. **2.** A reward paid to persons who help to save a ship, goods, etc., voluntarily and at some danger to themselves. **Salvage money** cannot be paid to anyone responsible for the care of the ship. The reward is paid by the owners of the ship or the cargo and the **salvors** have a lien on the property rescued for the salvage money.

salvage value (scrap value) The *net realizable value of an asset at the end of its useful life, when it is no longer suitable for its original use. Fixed assets, stock, or waste arising from a production process can all have a salvage value.

sample 1. A small quantity of a commodity, etc., selected to represent the bulk of a quantity of goods. *See* SALE BY SAMPLE. **2.** A small quantity of a product, given to potential buyers to enable them to test its suitability for their purposes. **3.** A group of items or individuals selected from a *population to represent the characteristics of the population as a whole. Samples are often used in *marketing research because it is not feasible to interview every member of a particular market; however, conclusions about a market drawn from a sample always contain a *sampling error and must be used with caution. The larger the sample, in general, the more accurate will be the conclusions drawn from it. In *quota sampling the composition of the sample reflects the known structure of the market. Thus, if it is known that 60% of purchasers of household DIY products are men, any sample would reflect this. An alternative sampling procedure is random or *probability sampling, which ensures that everyone in a particular market has an equal probability of being selected. Although more rigorous than quota sampling, it is also more expensive and difficult to implement. *See also* CLUSTER SAMPLING; JUDGMENTAL SAMPLING; STRATIFIED SAMPLING; SYSTEMATIC SAMPLING.

Sampling is also important in auditing, as it is not usually feasible to inspect all the available documentation.

sampling error Any difference between the true parameters of a *population and a conclusion about these parameters based on a *sample of the population. Sampling errors are of two kinds. The first, which is inevitable, arises from the laws of statistics and probability, which enable a **margin of error** to be calculated. The second, which is preventable, arises from inadequate or unrepresentative sampling techniques (*see* SELECTION ERROR). *Compare* NON-SAMPLING ERRORS.

samurai bond A *bond issued in Japan by a foreign institution. Unlike a *shogun bond, it is denominated in yen. *See also* SHIBOSAI BOND.

SAN Abbreviation for storage area network. In computing, a subnetwork of disk storage devices that replaces the local hard disks in network *servers. SANs provide very fast data access, but are expensive and hence found mostly on large networks. *Compare* NAS.

sanctions *See* ECONOMIC SANCTIONS.

sandbag A stalling tactic used by an unwilling target company in a *takeover bid. The management of the target company agrees to have talks with the unwelcome bidder, which it protracts for as long as possible in the hope that a *white knight will appear and make a more acceptable bid.

S&L Abbreviation for *savings and loan association.

S&P 500 Abbreviation for *Standard and Poor's 500 Stock Index.

sandwich course A course of study in the UK for a diploma or degree in which periods of academic study in an institution of higher education are sandwiched between periods of supervised work experience in a factory or industrial organization. The course usually lasts for four years, with six-monthly periods in both college and industry.

sans recours *See* WITHOUT RECOURSE.

santim A former monetary unit of Latvia, worth one hundredth of a *lats.

São Paulo Stock Exchange The most important of the stock exchanges in Brazil, the **Bolsa de Valores de São Paulo** or **Bovespa**; together with the older Rio de Janeiro market it accounts for over 90% of Brazilian equity trading. In 2008 it merged with the Brazilian Mercantile and Futures Exchange (BM&F) and was renamed BM&F Bovespa; the merged exchange is the largest in Latin America

Sarbanes–Oxley Act 2002 (Sarbox; Sox) Wide-ranging US legislation aiming to establish and enforce new standards in corporate governance, financial reporting, and auditing. The Act was passed in response to several high-profile corporate scandals, most notoriously the Enron scandal of 2001.

Sarl. 1. Abbreviation for *società a responsabilità*. It appears after the name of an Italian company, being equivalent to the British abbreviation Ltd (i.e. denoting a private limited liability company). **2.** Abbreviation for *société à responsibilité limitée*. It appears after the name of a French private limited company. *Compare* SA.

SAS Abbreviation for *Statement of Auditing Standards.

satang A monetary unit of Thailand, worth one hundredth of a *baht.

satisficing behaviour Behaviour by a company or an individual that is aimed at achieving satisfactory returns rather than optimum profit or growth. Given the limitations on any individual's knowledge of the total market situation, this is often a more rational approach than an abstract commitment to maximizing returns. *See* BOUNDED RATIONALITY. *See also* BEHAVIOURAL FINANCE.

save-as-you-earn (SAYE) A method of making regular savings (not necessarily linked to earnings), which carries certain tax privileges. This method has been used to encourage tax-free savings in building societies or *National Savings and also to encourage employees to acquire shares in their own organizations (*see* SAVINGS RELATED SHARE OPTION SCHEME).

savings Money set aside by individuals, either for some special purpose or to provide an income at some time in the future (often after retirement). Money saved can be placed in a *savings account with a bank or building society or an *Individual Savings Account (ISA), invested in *National Savings, or used to purchase *securities. Savings are also used to buy *pensions, *annuities, and *endowment assurance.

savings account A bank or building-society account designed for the investment of personal savings. The rates tend to be higher than old-fashioned *deposit accounts and interest-bearing *current accounts. Some accounts offer instant access to funds, while others require that notice be given, typically 30, 60, or 90 days.

savings and loan association (S&L) The US equivalent of a UK *building society. It usually offers loans with a fixed rate of interest and has greater investment flexibility than a UK building society.

savings bank A bank that specializes in setting up *savings accounts for relatively small deposits. In the UK the *National Savings Bank and *building societies perform this function. In the USA, *savings and loan associations do so.

savings certificate *See* NATIONAL SAVINGS.

savings related share option scheme (Sharesave) An approved *share option scheme established by an employer for the benefit of executives or other employees. HM Customs and Revenue has detailed rules regarding the income tax and capital gains tax chargeable to individuals benefiting from such a scheme. *See also* EMPLOYEE SHARE OWNERSHIP PLAN; EMPLOYEE SHARE OWNERSHIP TRUST; SAVE-AS-YOU-EARN; SHARE INCENTIVE SCHEME.

SAYE Abbreviation for *save-as-you-earn.

SBU Abbreviation for *strategic business unit.

SCA Abbreviation for sustainable *competitive advantage.

scalability 1. The potential for a business to replicate its activities on a wider scale, thereby increasing its customer base, without disproportionate increase in cost or diminution in quality. In retail businesses the term generally refers to the ability to add sales channels or outlets. **2.** In computer systems, the ability of a network to handle a larger number of users.

scale effect *See* ECONOMIES OF SCALE.

scalpers Traders in financial obligations who deal very frequently for small gains and may only hold a position for a few minutes.

scatter diagram A graph on which observations are plotted on the y-axis for events on the x-axis. For example, the wages incurred (y-axis) for each level of activity (x-axis) would produce a scatter graph from which a relationship can be established between the two variables, as an aid to predicting *cost behaviour.

scenario analysis A process in which the various possible developments in an industry are examined, together with a company's ability to respond flexibly and creatively. Expert opinion is used to formulate a qualitative view of the future; this will usually identify major trends and analyse long-term environmental influences but will not involve use of historical data in an attempt to 'predict' future events. By examining a range of possible scenarios managers should be able to assess the strategic options available and evaluate existing assumptions and practices. *See also* DELPHI TECHNIQUE; STRATEGIC CHOICE.

Schatzwechsel A German government Treasury bill, usually repayable in three months.

schedule 1. A plan of activities that uses the resources made available by *aggregate planning and allocates them to individual jobs, activities, or customers over a particular period. A schedule shows what has to be done, when, by whom, and with what resources. If the output of the system is being made to order, the schedule provides detailed timings for each order. If the output is being made to stock, it provides detailed timings for products. **2.** The part of legislation that is placed at the end of a UK Act of Parliament and contains subsidiary matter to the main sections of the act. **3.** In the UK, one of several schedules formerly used to classify various sources of income for *income-tax purposes and in some cases still applicable for *corporation tax. The schedules retained for corporation tax purposes are: Schedule A, rents from property in the UK; Schedule D, Case I, profits from trade; Case II, profits from professions or vocations; Case III, interest not otherwise taxed; Case IV, income from securities outside the UK; Case V, income from possessions outside the UK; Case VI, other annual profits and gains. **4.** Working papers submitted with tax returns or tax computations.

scheme of arrangement 1. An agreement between a company and its members or creditors to restructure the business in some way; the procedure is mainly used

when the company is in financial difficulties or to effect a *takeover. It must be approved by a majority in number (holding 75% in value) of those creditors or members at separate meetings, and sanctioned by the court. All creditors or members involved in the scheme are bound by it, although the court can make special provision for those who dissent. Agreements with company creditors can often be more conveniently concluded by a *voluntary arrangement. **2.** An agreement between a debtor and his or her creditors to arrange the debtor's affairs to satisfy the creditors. The debtor usually agrees to such an arrangement in order to avoid *bankruptcy. If the arrangement is agreed when no bankruptcy order has been made, it may take the form of either an ordinary private contract or a *deed of arrangement. An arrangement agreed after a bankruptcy order has been made is governed by the statutory provisions relating to bankruptcy (*see* VOLUNTARY ARRANGEMENT).

Schilling Formerly, the standard monetary unit of Austria, divided into 100 Groschen. It was replaced by the *euro in 2002.

Schumpeterian growth (endogenous growth) Economic growth that is driven by *innovation and governed by a process of *creative destruction, as described by the Austrian economist Joseph Schumpeter (1883–1950). The late 1980s and 1990s saw a major revival of interest in Schumpeter's ideas among economists, business people, and policy makers.

science park An industrial estate on or near a university or research centre, in which high-technology firms are located so as to encourage the transfer of technical knowledge and research results between the academic institution and the commercial user.

scientific management (Taylorism) One of the classic approaches to management theory, which emphasizes the rationality of organizational systems and holds that operational efficiency can be optimized by applying the appropriate scientific management principles. Developed by Frederick Taylor in the late 19th and early 20th centuries, the theory forms the basis for the techniques now known as *work study. The key principles were:

- Managers should take full responsibility for the planning of work and should use scientific methods to specify precisely how the job should be done to achieve the maximum efficiency;
- Managers should select the most appropriate person for the job, train them to do the job efficiently, and monitor their performance to ensure conformity to the specification.

Scientific management is credited with increasing productivity enormously, but only at the cost of *deskilling many areas of work. The boring, repetitive, and alienating nature of the jobs created using scientific management methods causes demotivation in staff and can lead to an extreme emphasis on pay rates as the primary form of motivation. *See also* ADMINISTRATIVE MANAGEMENT; CLASSICAL SCHOOL OF MANAGEMENT.

scope economies (economies of scope) The increases in efficiency and sales that can result from producing, distributing, and marketing a range of products, as opposed to a single product or type of product. *Bancassurance is often seen as an example of scope economies.

scorched earth policy An extreme form of *poison pill in which a company that believes it is to be the target of a *takeover bid makes its balance sheet or profitability less attractive than it really is by a reversible manoeuvre, such as borrowing money at an exorbitant rate of interest.

scorekeeping One of the functions of *management accounting in which the performance of the managers and operators is monitored and reported in accounting statements to the appropriate levels of management.

SCOUT Acronym for Shared Currency Option Under Tender: a currency *option especially designed for companies who are tendering for the same overseas job in a

foreign currency. To save each of them having to *hedge the currency risk separately, SCOUT enables them to share the cost of a single option.

SCP model *See* STRUCTURE–CONDUCT–PERFORMANCE MODEL.

scrambled merchandising The selling of certain products in a retail outlet that is not traditionally associated with these products. Many retailers have extended their product width and depth in this way. For example, most supermarkets now sell books and CDs and many offer financial services.

scrap 1. What is left of an asset at the end of its useful life, which may have a *salvage value. **2.** The waste arising from a production process, which may also have a salvage value.

scrap value *See* SALVAGE VALUE.

screening stage The stage in *new product development that involves an analysis of new ideas to determine their appropriateness in relation to an organization's goals and objectives.

screen trading *See* AUTOMATED SCREEN TRADING.

scrip The certificates that demonstrate ownership of *stocks, *shares, and *bonds (capital raised by sub*scrip*tion), especially the certificates relating to a *scrip issue.

scrip issue (bonus issue; capitalization issue; free issue) The issue of new share certificates to existing shareholders to reflect the accumulation of profits in the reserves of a company's balance sheet. The shareholders do not pay for the new shares and appear to be no better off. However, in a 1 for 3 scrip issue, say, the shareholders receive 1 new share for every 3 old shares they own. This automatically reduces the price of the shares by 25%, catering to the preference of shareholders to hold cheaper shares rather than expensive ones; it also encourages them to hope that the price will gradually climb to its former value, which will, of course, make them 25% better off. In the USA this is known as a **stock split**.

script A section of programming code used in web pages to add functionality. The script may run on the *web server (server-side script). Commonly, scripts written in Javascript are included in the HTML (*see* HYPERTEXT) of the web page and are interpreted by the *web browser when the page is opened (client-side script).

SDDE Abbreviation for *simultaneous direct data entry.

SDK Abbreviation for software development kit. A collection of the software tools, code libraries, documentation, etc., necessary to develop a specific type of computer software, commonly provided as a single installable package.

SDLT Abbreviation for *stamp duty land tax.

SDR Abbreviation for *Special Drawing Rights.

SDRT Abbreviation for *stamp duty reserve tax.

SEAQ *See* STOCK EXCHANGE AUTOMATED QUOTATIONS SYSTEM.

search engine A service provided on the Internet that enables the user to search for items of interest. Some, such as the widely used Google, Yahoo, and Bing, are free and attempt to capture information from the whole range of material available on the net. Others are subscription-based but in return provide access to specialist publications, full-text retrieval capabilities, or other added-value services.

search-engine optimization (SEO) Designing a website in such a way that its pages achieve the highest possible rank in the listings of Internet search engines, thereby generating greater traffic to the site. This generally involves using keywords and tags that are known to rank highly with search-engine algorithms as well as increasing the internal and external links on the site. SEO methods are often divided into so-called **white hat** techniques, which make use of legitimate and overt means, and **black hat** tactics, which rely on hidden coding. *See* PAGERANK.

search order A court injunction ordering the defendant to allow the plaintiff to enter named premises to search for and take copies of specified articles and documents. These orders are obtained by the plaintiff 'ex parte' (without the other party being present in court) to allow evidence to be preserved in cases in which there are grounds to think it will be destroyed. It is especially useful in 'pirating' cases. The order is not a search warrant, so entry cannot be forced, but the defendant will be in contempt of court if entry is refused. A solicitor must serve the order. It was formerly called an **Anton Piller order**, after an order made in the High Court in 1976 against Anton Piller KG.

seasonality The seasonal variability of certain economic or financial factors, for example unemployment or commodity prices. In statistical analyses of time-series data, findings may need to be adjusted for seasonal variation (e.g. a spike in sales around Christmas).

seasonal rate A rate of charging that varies according to the time of the year. This is quite common in *advertising, for example the *Radio Times* charges a higher page rate for its Christmas issue than for any other issue. **Seasonal discounts** are also common, especially in advertising, when sellers wish to encourage business in a slack period.

seasonal unemployment *Unemployment that occurs as a result of the seasonal nature of some jobs. The building trade, for example, employs more people in the summer months than the winter months. Much of the seaside holiday trade is seasonal and a considerable amount of agricultural work is seasonal. It is for this reason that UK unemployment figures are usually **seasonally adjusted**, i.e. adjusted to flatten the peaks and troughs of unemployment in certain seasons.

S

SEC Abbreviation for *Securities and Exchange Commission.

secondary bank 1. A name sometimes given to *finance houses. **2.** Any organization that offers some banking services, such as making loans, offering secondary mortgages, etc., but that does not offer the usual commercial bank services of cheque accounts, etc.

secondary data Marketing research information available to researchers that they have not gathered themselves. Examples include data provided by a government department or extracted from company records.

secondary domain name See DOMAIN NAME.

secondary market (after market) A market in which existing securities are traded, as opposed to a *primary market, in which securities are sold for the first time. In most cases a *stock exchange largely fulfils the role of a secondary market, with the flotation of *new issues representing only a small proportion of its total business. However, it is the existence of a flourishing secondary market, providing liquidity and the spreading of risks, that creates the conditions for a healthy primary market.

secondary picketing See PICKETING.

secondary production See PRODUCTION.

Second Banking Directive The most important of the EU directives on banking regulation, introduced in 1989 (see BANKING DIRECTIVES). It regulates the licensing and operation of banks based in one member state and operating in other EU countries. The directive also set *capital adequacy requirements for banks in member states.

second-hand goods scheme An arrangement in which the *value added tax due on second-hand goods sold is calculated on the trader's margin, rather than the total selling price of the goods. This applies regularly with sales of second-hand cars. In order to qualify, the trader must retain detailed records of car purchases and sales, which must be available for inspection at a VAT control visit.

second mortgage A *mortgage taken out on a property that is already mortgaged. Second and subsequent mortgages can often be used to raise money from a *finance house (but not a commercial bank or building society) if the value of the property has increased considerably since the first mortgage was taken out. See MORTGAGE LAW.

second of exchange See BILLS IN A SET.

second-tier market A market for investors to buy and sell shares in new and developing companies. Companies have access to new sources of finance and do not have to follow the complex rules that the main market requires. The *Alternative Investment Market of the *London Stock Exchange is an example of a second-tier market.

secret reserve See HIDDEN RESERVE.

secular Denoting a long-term trend or development, in contrast to seasonal or cyclical phenomena.

secured creditor A creditor who holds a fixed or floating *charge over the assets of a debtor.

secured debenture A *debenture secured by a *charge over the property of a company, such as mortgage debentures (secured on land belonging to the company). Usually a trust deed sets out the powers of the debenture holders to enforce their security in the event of the company defaulting in payment of the principal or the interest. It is usual to appoint a *receiver to realize the security.

secured liability A debt against which the borrower has provided sufficient assets as security to safeguard the lender in case of non-repayment.

secure sockets layer (SSL) See TRANSPORT LAYER SECURITY.

Securities and Exchange Commission (SEC) A US government agency established in 1934 to protect investors by regulating behaviour in the securities markets. Each year the SEC brings between 400 and 500 civil enforcement actions against individuals and companies that break the securities laws. The SEC is also responsible for monitoring and controlling corporate financial reporting and auditing practices.

(((●))) SEE WEB LINKS
• Website of the SEC

Securities Industry and Financial Markets Association (SIFMA) A US trade association for the finance industry. It was formed in 2006 from a merger of the Securities Industry Association (SIA) and the Bond Market Association.

securitization (asset securitization) The process of turning assets into *securities. Generally this involves an arrangement in which one party (the originator) sells a portfolio of assets, such as house mortgages or bank loans, to a *special purpose vehicle (the issuer), who finances the purchase by packaging the cash flows from these assets as tradable financial instruments (securities), which are sold to investors. The arrangement may be a form of *off-balance-sheet finance and now falls under the regulations of *International Accounting Standard 39, Financial Instruments: Recognition and Measurement. The prevalence of complex derivative products based on the securitization of *subprime mortgages is widely seen as a key factor in the global financial crisis of 2007–08. *See also* STRUCTURED FINANCE.

security 1. An asset or assets to which a lender can have recourse if the borrower defaults on the loan repayments. In the case of loans by banks and other money-lenders the security is sometimes referred to as *collateral. **2.** A financial asset, including shares, government stocks, debentures, bonds, unit trusts, and rights to money lent or deposited. It does not, however, include insurance policies. *See also* BEARER SECURITY; DATED SECURITY; FIXED-

INTEREST SECURITY; GILT-EDGED SECURITY; LISTED SECURITY; MARKETABLE SECURITY. **3.** In computing, measures used to prevent or protect against (a) access to information by unauthorized users or (b) unauthorized destruction or alteration of that information. Most security policies involve the use of both administrative controls (e.g. passwords) and dedicated software (e.g. firewalls and anti-virus programs). *See also* CYBERLIABILITIES. **4.** Precautions taken in e-commerce to ensure that the following attributes are safeguarded:

• **Authentication**. Are parties to a transaction who they claim to be? This is achieved by using *digital signatures.
• **Privacy and confidentiality**. Is transaction data protected? The consumer may want an anonymous purchase. Are all non-essential traces of a transaction removed from the public network and have all intermediary records been eliminated?
• **Integrity**. Are the messages sent complete? Checks are needed to ensure that messages have not been corrupted.
• **Non-repudiability**. Could the sender deny sending the message? It is essential measures are in place to protect against repudiation.
• **Availability**. How can threats to the continuity and performance of the system be eliminated?

seed capital The small amount of initial capital required to fund the research and development necessary before a new company is set up. The seed capital should enable a persuasive and accurate *business plan to be drawn up.

segmental reporting 1. The disclosure in the *annual accounts and report of certain results of major business, and geographic segments of a diversified group of companies. The argument for segmental reporting is that the disclosure of profitability, risk, and growth prospects for individual segments of a business will be of use to investors. Under *International Financial Reporting Standard 8, Operating Segments, listed companies should disclose, for both *business segments and geographic segments, total assets and liabilities, profit or loss before tax, and revenue and investment information. Entities should also disclose how segments are defined and how transactions between segments are measured. **2.** The approach in *management accounting in which the financial and quantitative performance of each definitive part of an organization is reported to the management both of the business segment and of the organization as a whole.

SEHK Abbreviation for Stock Exchange of Hong Kong. *See* HONG KONG STOCK EXCHANGE.

seigniorage The profits accruing to the issuer of legal tender, mainly as a result of the difference between the material costs of producing currency and its face value. The term is frequently used in reference to the US Treasury's earnings from producing coins and notes; as the producer of the world's major reserve currency and black market currency, the USA can obtain considerable gains from printing money.

selection error The type of *sampling error that results from following an incomplete or improper selection process in sampling (*see* SAMPLE). Often, respondents who are not relevant to the study are used in surveys. For example, ownership of a car may be a prerequisite for an interview, but a respondent may be selected who merely has the use of a car, rather than owning one.

selection interview (job interview) An interview with a candidate for a job in which a manager or personnel worker attempts to form a judgment of the applicant's suitability for the position in question. As basic biographical information about the candidate will already have been obtained (*see* BIODATA), the main purpose of the interview is usually to get an idea of his or her personality, demeanour, motivation, and interpersonal skills. The interview may be highly structured, with a large number of set questions, or virtually unstructured, to provide the candidate with more opportunity to reveal his or her

qualities. The interviewer will also use the occasion to provide more information about the job, the company, and its activities.

selective demand Demand for a specific brand of a product or service.

selective distribution The use of more than one but less than all of the intermediaries willing to carry a company's products.

selective retention The tendency of people to retain only part of the information to which they are exposed; usually they retain the information that supports their own attitudes or beliefs. The concept is important in the psychology of advertising.

self-actualization The drive people have to realize their potential and to find fulfilment. Self-actualization encompasses the human need for challenge, responsibility, creativity, and variety at work, enabling employees to take pride in their achievements, as well as in their technical or professional expertise. An integral part of the concept is for their worth to be recognized and valued by those with, and for, whom they work. *See also* MASLOW'S MOTIVATIONAL HIERARCHY; MOTIVATION.

self-administered questionnaire (self-complete questionnaire) A marketing research questionnaire filled out by a respondent with no interviewer involvement.

self-assessment A system that enables taxpayers to assess their own *income tax and *capital gains tax liabilities for the year. Major changes to the UK system occurred in the year 1996–97, since when a self-assessment section has been contained in the *tax return, in addition to the part requiring details of *taxable income, *chargeable gains, and claims for *personal allowances. At present the self-assessment is voluntary; if the taxpayer prefers to let HM Revenue and Customs calculate his or her liability, then the tax return must be submitted by September 30 following the end of the year of assessment, rather than the usual January 31. The introduction of self-assessment was accompanied by the Revenue being granted extensive audit powers to enquire into any tax return.

(⊕) SEE WEB LINKS
• Guide to self-assessment from HMRC

self-assessment for companies A scheme for the self-assessment of tax by companies. In the UK, self-assessment of *corporation tax was introduced for all companies with an accounting period ending after 1 July 1999. Tax returns must be completed and filed within 12 months of the end of the accounting period. Smaller companies must pay their tax liability within nine months of the end of the accounting period; large companies must make payments on account in advance of this date.

self-complete questionnaire See SELF-ADMINISTERED QUESTIONNAIRE.

self-employed taxpayers Persons who are not employees and who trade on their own account. They are taxed on the profits of their trades rather than by *PAYE and their *National Insurance contributions differ from those of employees.

self-financing Denoting a company that is able to finance its capital expenditure from undistributed profits rather than by borrowing.

self-liquidating 1. Denoting an asset that earns back its original cost out of income over a fixed period. **2.** Denoting a loan in which the money is used to finance a project that will provide sufficient yield to repay the loan and its interest and leave a profit. **3.** Denoting a *sales-promotion offer that pays for itself. For example, if a seller of tea bags offers a free tea mug in exchange for a specified number of vouchers, each taken from a box of tea bags, the seller expects the extra number of tea-bag boxes sold during the promotion to pay for the costs of buying and despatching the mugs.

self-service A method of retailing goods in which the customer serves himself and pays at a cash point before leaving. Widely used in food supermarkets, petrol stations, and cafés, self-service greatly reduces labour costs but offers increased opportunities for shoplifters.

self supply The *value added tax charge on a commercial building, which is used for an exempt purpose, on the grant of an interest in the building. *Output tax is charged on the land and the building costs. *Input tax is allowed on the building costs. The self supply is due to be assessed and paid within three months of the initial occupation.

self-tender A *tender offer in which a company approaches its shareholders in order to buy back some or all of its shares. There are two circumstances in which this operation can be of use. One is in the case of a hostile bid: the directors may wish to buy back shares in their company in order to reduce the chances of the bidder being able to buy a controlling interest in the company. The other circumstance is that the board may wish to show increased earnings per share; if they are unable to increase their profits it may be appropriate for them to reduce the number of shares in the company.

sellers' market A market in which the demand exceeds the supply, so that sellers can increase prices. At some point, however, buyers will cease to follow the price rises and the sellers will be forced to drop prices in order to make sales, i.e. the supply will have exceeded the demand. See BUYERS' MARKET.

sellers over A market in commodities, securities, etc., in which buyers have been satisfied but some sellers remain. This is clearly a weak market, with a tendency for prices to fall. Compare BUYERS OVER.

selling agent See AGENT.

selling concept The idea that consumers will not buy enough of an organization's products unless the organization undertakes a large-scale selling and promotion effort.

selling out The selling of securities, commodities, etc., by a broker because the original buyer is unable to pay for them. This invariably happens after a fall in market price (the buyer would take them up and sell them at a profit if the market had risen). The broker sells them at the best price available and the original buyer is responsible for any difference between the price realized and the original selling price, plus the costs of selling out. *Compare* BUYING IN.

selling overhead (selling costs) The expenses incurred by an organization in carrying out its selling activities. These would include salaries of sales personnel, advertising costs, sales commissions, etc.

selling process The steps that a sales-person may follow when selling. These include *prospecting and *qualifying potential customers, a *preapproach, approach, *presentation and demonstration, handling objections, closing, and *follow-up.

selling short *See* SHORT SELLING.

semantic differential A method of evaluating the image of a product or company by asking respondents to rate the item on a scale between a pair of words representing bipolar opposites, e.g. good and bad, modern and old-fashioned. The mean of the responses is then calculated.

semi-fixed cost (stepped cost) An item of expenditure that increases in total as activity rises but in a stepped, rather than a linear, function (*see* LINEAR COST FUNCTION). For example, the costs of one supervisor may be required for a particular range of activity, although above this level the cost of an additional supervisor would be incurred.

semisolus An advertisement that appears on a page in a publication containing another advertisement but is not placed adjacent to it. *Compare* SOLUS POSITION.

semi-variable cost An item of expenditure that contains both a *fixed-cost element and a *variable-cost element. Consequently, when activity is zero, the fixed cost will still continue to be incurred. For example, in the UK the cost of gas is made up of a standing charge plus a cost per unit consumed; therefore while the consumption of gas varies with production the fixed standing charge will still be incurred when production is zero.

sen 1. A monetary unit of Cambodia, worth one hundredth of a *riel. **2. (cent)** A monetary unit of Malaysia, worth one hundredth of a *ringgit. **3.** A monetary unit of Indonesia, worth one hundredth of a *rupiah. **4.** A former monetary unit of Japan (still used as a unit of account), worth one hundredth of a *yen.

sene A monetary unit of Samoa, worth one hundredth of a *tala.

senior capital Capital in the form of secured loans to a company (*see* SECURED CREDITOR; SECURED LIABILITY). In the event of a liquidation, the senior capital is repaid before the *shareholders' equity.

seniti A monetary unit of Tonga, worth one hundredth of a *pa'anga.

sense-of-mission marketing A principle of marketing holding that a company should define its mission in broad social terms, rather than narrow product terms.

sensitive market A market in commodities, securities, etc., that is sensitive to outside influences because it is basically unstable. For example, a poor crop in a commodity market may make it sensitive, with buyers anxious to cover their requirements but unwilling to show their hand and risk forcing prices up. News of a hurricane in the growing area, say, could cause a sharp price rise in such a sensitive market.

sensitivity analysis A method of analysing the sensitivity of a decision to a change in one or more of the assumptions used in making it. For instance, a company might analyse how its future performance might be affected by changing its level of advertising or by lowering the price of a product, to enable it to estimate the likely impact on sales and profitability. Similarly, in considering an investment decision, it could investigate the impact of changing assumptions regarding the life of an asset, the cost of borrowing, and the end value of the asset. Apart from suggesting a range of possible outcomes, a sensitivity analysis will indicate the degree of risk associated with a decision or course of action.

sent (*plural* **senti**) A former monetary unit of Estonia, worth one hundredth of a *kroon.

SEO Abbreviation for *search-engine optimization.

separable assets and liabilities *See* IDENTIFIABLE ASSETS AND LIABILITIES.

separate-entity concept *See* ACCOUNTING ENTITY.

separation point (split-off point) In *process costing, the point at which the *by-products or the joint products separate and are subsequently processed independently of each other.

sequencing (priority sequencing) Establishing an exact order for jobs, taking into account job interference and queuing times. Priority sequencing specifies the order in which waiting jobs are to be processed. It requires the adoption of a rule to decide the basis upon which priorities are to be allocated. *See* DISPATCHING RULES.

sequential product development An approach to *new product development in which one department of a company completes its stage of the process before passing the new product to the next department. *Compare* SIMULTANEOUS PRODUCT DEVELOPMENT.

sequestration The confiscation of the property of a person or organization who has not complied with a court order. This is a very drastic remedy, and will be ordered in serious cases only. It is most commonly used against companies, trade unions, and in matrimonial cases.

Serious Fraud Office (SFO) A body established in 1987 to be responsible for investigating and prosecuting serious or complex frauds in England, Wales, and Northern Ireland. The Attorney General appoints and superintends its director. Serious and complex fraud cases can go straight to the Crown Court without committal for trial. That court can hold preparatory hearings to clarify issues for the jury and settle points of law.

SERPS Abbreviation for State Earnings-Related Pension Scheme. *See* STATE SECOND PENSION.

served market *See* TARGET MARKETING.

server (file server) A computer that makes services available to users on a wider network.

service Any activity or benefit that one party can offer to another that is intangible and does not result in the transfer of ownership of any physical object.

Economic activity has traditionally been divided into extractive, constructive, manufacturing, and service sectors. With the decline of heavy engineering and the rise of the knowledge-based economy, the **service industries** make up an ever-increasing proportion of the national income in nearly all developed countries.

Essentially, services can be classified into three categories:

- **Services to trade** include banking, insurance, transport, etc.;
- **Professional services** encompass the advice and skill of accountants, lawyers, doctors, architects, business consultants, etc.;
- **Consumer services** include those given by caterers, cleaners, mechanics, plumbers, etc.;

Service providers need to define exactly what service they are providing, who they are competing with, and where their markets are. For example, does the Channel Tunnel provide a fast link to Paris for business people in competition with the

S

airlines, or a holiday route to France in competition with the ferries?

Crucially, they also need to be aware of those characteristics of services that make their management different from the production of goods. These can be summarized as:

- **Intangibility**—the exact nature of a service is often difficult to define; the product cannot be handled and ownership of an object is not transferred. The service is experiential rather than concrete and thus quality is difficult to define and measure.
- **Customer participation**—normally the customer is directly involved in the delivery of the service; e.g. hospital treatment cannot be given if the patient is absent.
- **Simultaneity**—production and consumption of a service are usually simultaneous and therefore not storable.
- **Perishability**—because a service is perishable, stocks cannot be built up; e.g. a seat on the 9 a.m. London to Glasgow train is gone forever as soon as the train departs.
- **Heterogeneity**—because the interaction between the customer and the provider is a unique experience, the same service can be perceived differently by different customers and by the same customer on different occasions. Other customers can affect the experience of a service, e.g. a quiet weekend at a small hotel can be ruined if two rival football teams are also staying in the hotel.
- **Indivisibility of operations and marketing**—frequently the same people do the selling and the delivery of the service. This has implications for training and the efficiency of the operation. Process design needs to ensure a smooth flow from one stage to the next.
- **Geographical dispersion**—most services need to be reasonably near to the customer. However, use of telecommunications and *information technology increasingly allows major service organizations to centralize large parts of their process, while retaining an interface with the customer; e.g. the use of national (or

international) *call centres and the provision by banks of *automated teller machines and *home banking facilities.

service contract (service agreement)
A contract between an employer and a director or other very senior employee. Service contracts must be kept at the registered office of a company and be open to inspection by members of the company. The Companies Act 2006 prohibits service contracts that give an employee guaranteed employment for more than five years, without the company having an opportunity to break the employment as and when it needs to. This measure prevents directors with long service agreements from suing companies for loss of office in the event of a takeover or reorganization. The 2006 Act also broadened the definition of a service contract to include a *contract for services as well as a contract of employment. *See also* COMPENSATION FOR LOSS OF OFFICE; GOLDEN PARACHUTE.

service cost centre (indirect cost centre; service department; support cost centre) In *cost accounting, a *cost centre that is necessary to carry out the production process but incidental to it as it does not handle the *cost unit. Examples of service cost centres are stores, canteens, and boiler houses.

service industry *See* SERVICE.

service level A comparison between what a customer expects from a service and the actual service received.

service package A collection of facilities, goods, and services put together. These can be tangible, e.g. the decor and fittings of a hotel, or intangible, e.g. the feeling of confidence imparted by an efficient hospital.

servicing a loan Paying the interest on a loan.

servqual The provision of high-quality products together with a high quality of customer service. It can be identified by a number of factors:

Servqual.

- **tangibles**, i.e. physical evidence of the service;
- **reliability**, i.e. consistency of performance and dependability;
- **responsiveness**, i.e. a readiness on the part of employees to provide a prompt service;
- **assurance**, i.e. competence, credibility, and access to those employees providing the service;
- **empathy**, i.e. understanding the customers' needs as well as communicating with them considerately and respectfully.

Servqual provides an important *differentiated marketing strategy. It has been repeatedly shown that providing consumers with a high level of service, combined with high-quality products, affects consumer satisfaction, which is reflected in their buying behaviour. Companies providing outstanding servqual undoubtedly achieve greater sales and profits. While servqual is difficult to quantify, many companies are anxious to know how consumers assess it, especially in terms of comparing their expectations with actual performance. If consumers' expectations do not match the actual level of service provided, a 'gap' is created. If the gap is negative it can be the cause of serious consumer dissatisfaction. On the other hand, a 'positive gap' implies that consumers' expectations are exceeded by the servqual provided, which should be the objective of every company. "We exceed your expectations" is a slogan often used in advertising. Similarly, management's perception of the consumers' expectations, rather than the consumers' actual expectations, can create a further gap.

set-off An agreement between the parties involved to set off one debt against another or one loss against a gain. A banker is empowered to set off a credit balance on one account against a debit balance on another if the accounts are in the same name and in the same currency. It is usual, in these circumstances, for the bank to issue a **letter of set-off**, which the customer countersigns to indicate agreement. A letter of set-off is also needed if the accounts are not in the same name, e.g. differently named companies in the same group.

SETS Abbreviation for *Stock Exchange Trading System.

settlement 1. The payment of an outstanding account, invoice, charge, etc. **2.** A disposition of land, or other property, made by deed or will under which a *trust is set up by the settlor. The settlement names the beneficiaries and the terms under which they are to acquire property. **3.** The document in which such a disposition is made. **4.** The voluntary conclusion of civil litigation or an industrial dispute, as a result of agreement between the parties.

settlement agreement A legally binding agreement under which parties can agree to end an employment relationship on specified terms, usually including a payment by the employer to the employee. The validity of such agreements is governed by the Employment Rights Act 1996. They must be in writing and the employee must have received independent advice from an appropriate person (e.g. a lawyer or trade union official). The effect of the agreement is that the employee waives his right to make a claim to the *employment tribunal on the matters covered in the agreement. An employer who improperly pressures an employee into entering a settlement agreement should be aware that this can amount to *constructive dismissal. Guidance is provided in a statutory ACAS Code of Practice.

settlement day The day on which trades are cleared by the delivery of the securities or foreign exchange.

settlement price The price at which an *index futures or option contract is settled on the *LIFFE (now Euronext.liffe). Officially known as the **Exchange Delivery Settlement Price** (EDSP), the settlement price is calculated on the last day of the delivery month and forms the basis for the cash settlement.

settlement risk The *risk that a transaction will not be settled as expected (i.e. that an agreed delivery or payment will not be made). It is sometimes referred to as **Herstatt risk** after a bank of that name, which failed to honour its foreign exchange transactions in 1974. *See also* COUNTERPARTY RISK.

settlor A person declaring or creating a *settlement or *trust. For tax purposes any person providing money or property for a settlement will be regarded as the settlor.

set-up reduction (SUR) An approach to operations management that seeks to reduce the *set-up time of a process by better process or product design, by using parallel rather than sequential operations, or by undertaking at least some of the set-up while the process is running, e.g.

refuelling nuclear power stations online. *See also* JUST IN TIME.

set-up time 1. The time taken to prepare a machine, process, or operation to carry out production. It may involve such operations as tool setting, calibration, and the initialization of the production process. **2.** The time that elapses between the production of the last acceptable piece in one batch and the first acceptable piece in the next batch. This unproductive time is a cost that should be minimized. *See* SET-UP REDUCTION.

seven-day money Money that has been invested in the *money market for a term of seven days. Special interest rates are quoted for seven-day money.

seven tools of quality A *quality-control schema in which seven types of diagram or chart are used to diagnose problems in any given system and to facilitate their resolution. It was developed by the Japanese management professor Kaoru Ishikawa as part of his philosophy of *total quality management. It is claimed that the use of these simple, easily interpreted charts will allow quality control to be standardized throughout a business. The diagrams are: check sheets to collect real-time data; *control charts; *flow charts; *histograms or *bar charts; *Pareto charts; *scatter diagrams; and Ishikawa's own *cause–effect diagram, which can be used to narrow down the possible causes of a problem.

severance The separation of the good parts of a contract from the bad; it applies to contracts that are not illegal but are void by statute or common law. Courts will, if possible, save contracts from complete invalidity by severance of the parts that are void.

severance payment *See* COMPENSATION FOR LOSS OF OFFICE; REDUNDANCY.

sex discrimination *See* DISCRIMINATION.

sexual harassment *See* HARASSMENT.

SFAS Abbreviation for *Statement of Financial Accounting Standards.

SFO Abbreviation for *Serious Fraud Office.

shadow director A person in accordance with whose instructions the directors of a company are accustomed to act although that person has not been appointed as a director. Certain provisions of the Companies Act that relate to directors, including *wrongful trading and the regulation of loans to directors, also extend to shadow directors.

shamrock organization A type of organizational structure described by the British human-resources expert Charles Handy, who predicts that it will become predominant in the near future. The shamrock organization consists of four 'leaves': the professional core; the contractual fringe; a flexible labour force; and customers, who are regarded as part of the organization. Of these groups only the professional core will enjoy anything like traditional permanent employment.

sham transaction A transaction in which the parties intend to create one set of rights and obligations but perform acts or enter into documents that they intend should give parties (often HM Revenue and Customs) the appearance of creating different rights and obligations. Tax benefits arising from sham transactions may be denied by the courts.

Shanghai Stock Exchange (SSE) The main stock market of the People's Republic of China. Its roots go back to the late 19th century but it was established in its present form in 1990. It is now the sixth largest stock exchange in the world by market capitalization. The main indicator is the SSE Composite Index.

share One of a number of titles of ownership in a company. Most companies are limited by shares, enabling investors to limit their liability if the company fails to the amount paid for (or owing on) the shares. A share is a *chose in action,

conferring on its owner a legal right to the part of the company's profits (usually by payment of a *dividend) and to any voting rights attaching to that share (*see* VOTING SHARES; A SHARES). Companies are obliged to keep a public record of the rights attaching to each class of share. The common classes of shares are: *ordinary shares, which have no guaranteed amount of dividend but carry voting rights; and *preference shares, which receive dividends (and/ or repayment of capital on winding-up) before ordinary shares, but which have no voting rights. Shares in public companies may be bought and sold in an open market, such as a stock exchange. Shares in a private company are generally subject to restrictions on sale, such as that they must be offered to existing shareholders first or that the directors' approval must be sought before they are sold elsewhere. *See also* CUMULATIVE PREFERENCE SHARE; DEFERRED ORDINARY SHARE; FOUNDERS' SHARES; FULLY PAID SHARE; PARTLY PAID SHARE; PREFERRED ORDINARY SHARE; REDEEMABLE SHARES; SHARES OUTSTANDING; SUBSCRIPTION SHARES; TERM SHARES.

share account 1. In the UK, a building society deposit account with no fixed investment period that confers a share of ownership in the society. It entitles the holder to vote at shareholders' meetings and to an allocation of free shares if the society is demutualized. **2.** In the USA, an account with a credit union (a non-profit making co-operative institution) that pays dividends rather than interest.

share capital That part of the *capital of a company received from its owners (i.e. its members or shareholders) in return for *shares. Every company must commence with some share capital (a minimum of two shares). *See* AUTHORIZED SHARE CAPITAL; CALLED-UP SHARE CAPITAL; ISSUED SHARE CAPITAL; PAID-UP SHARE CAPITAL; RESERVE CAPITAL.

share certificate A document that provides evidence of ownership of shares in a company. It states the number and class of shares owned by the shareholder and the serial number of the shares. It is stamped by the common seal of the company and usually signed by at least one director and the company secretary. It is not a negotiable instrument. *See* BEARER SECURITY.

shared-cost effect The consequence that a market in which one person chooses the product and another person pays for it will be less price sensitive than a market in which the same person both chooses and pays.

share exchange A service offered by most unit-trust managements and life assurance companies, in which the trust or company takes over a client's shareholding and invests the proceeds in unit-trust funds, etc., of the client's choice. The client is thereby saved the trouble and expense of disposing of his shares and if the shares are absorbed into the trust's or company's own portfolio he may receive a better price than he would on the market (i.e. he may receive the offer price rather than the bid price).

share-for-share offer (paper bid) A *takeover bid in which the directors of one company offer shares in that company as the payment for acquiring the shares in the target company. If the offer is accepted the shareholders of both companies will become the owners of the newly formed combination.

shareholder An owner of shares in a limited company or limited partnership. A shareholder is a member of the company. In the USA, the more usual word is **stockholder**.

shareholder debt A risk-bearing equity that is treated as debt for tax purposes (i.e. interest paid is tax deductible). Shareholder debt is a feature of the highly leveraged funding arrangements associated with *private equity firms.

shareholders' equity (shareholders' funds) **1.** The *share capital and *reserves of a company. **2.** The market value of a company's equity shares.

shareholders' perks Benefits offered by a company to its shareholders as a reward

for their loyalty. The benefits are given in addition to dividends and are tax-free.

shareholder value An approach to business that places the maximization of the value of shares to those who hold them above other business objectives. Normally, shareholder value can be increased in three ways: dividend payments, appreciation in the value of the shares, and cash repayments. However, this focus has been widened by companies buying back shares to increase earnings and the demerging of parts of a group in order to unlock the value of individual components by means of a separate flotation. Shareholder value can also be influenced by maximising *economic value, either by undertaking positive *present-value decisions or by running the business in such a way as to create a surplus above the market costs of funding. The shareholder-value objective has sometimes been criticized as being too narrow and contrary to the longer-term interests of other *stakeholder groups.

shareholder value analysis (SVA) A method for valuing the entire *equity in a company. SVA assumes that the value of a business is the *net present value of its future cash flows, discounted at the appropriate *cost of capital. Once the value of a business has been calculated in this way, the next stage is to calculate shareholder value using the equation:

shareholder value = value of business−
    debt.

This method was first developed by Alfred Rappaport in the 1980s. The key difference between traditional financial accounting and SVA is that the latter recognizes the *time value of money. The traditional *balance sheet and *profit and loss account report on the past performance of a company is not helpful when measuring the change in value of the company. *See also* VALUE DRIVER.

Share Incentive Plan (SIP) A plan set up by a British company, and approved by HM Revenue and Customs, under which a trustee acquires and holds shares for the benefit of employees. There are significant tax advantages as long as various conditions are met, the chief being that the SIP must be open to all employees and executive directors. *See also* EMPLOYEE SHARE OWNERSHIP TRUST.

share incentive scheme Any scheme in which employees who achieve personal or group performance targets are rewarded with shares in the company. There are many different types of scheme. *See also* EMPLOYEE SHARE OWNERSHIP PLAN; EMPLOYEE SHARE OWNERSHIP TRUST; ENTERPRISE MANAGEMENT INCENTIVES; RESTRICTED STOCK; SAVINGS RELATED SHARE OPTION SCHEME; SHARE OPTION.

share index (stock market index) An index formed by selecting a number of prominent shares traded on a *stock exchange and comparing the value of these shares with their value on a stated date in the *base year. The daily value of the index may be weighted according to the prices of the shares traded or (more commonly) by the market capitalization of the company. *See* DOW JONES INDUSTRIAL AVERAGE; FTSE INDEXES; HANG SENG INDEX; NIKKEI STOCK AVERAGE.

share issued at a discount A share issued at a price (the *issue price) below its *par value. The discount is the difference between the par value and the issue price. It is illegal to issue shares at a discount in the UK.

share of wallet The share of a customer's business that is obtained by a particular company.

share option 1. A benefit sometimes offered to employees, especially new employees, in which they are given an option to buy shares in the company for which they work at a favourable fixed price or at a stated discount to the market price. The difference between the value of the share acquired (or its sale proceeds) and the amount paid to exercise the option is usually subject to income tax. *See* ENTERPRISE MANAGEMENT INCENTIVES; SAVINGS RELATED SHARE OPTION SCHEME. **2.** *See* OPTION.

share premium The amount payable for shares in a company and issued by the company itself in excess of their nominal value (*see* NOMINAL PRICE). Share premiums received by a company must be credited to a *share premium account.

share premium account The account to which any *share premium must be credited. The balance on the share premium account may be used for specified purposes:

• the issue of *bonus shares;
• the writing-off of preliminary expenses;
• the writing-off of underwriting commissions;
• the provision of a premium to be paid on the redemption of *debentures;
• the provision of a premium to be paid on the redemption or purchase of *share capital, subject to certain limits.

The share premium account may not be used to write off *goodwill on consolidation. Relief from the creation of a share premium account is available in specified circumstances (*see* MERGER RELIEF).

share register *See* REGISTER OF MEMBERS.

ShareSave *See* SAVINGS RELATED SHARE OPTION SCHEME.

share shop A stockbroker, bank, building society, or other financial intermediary appointed by the government to promote and handle applications for shares in a *privatization issue. The purpose of these share shops is to enable those members of the public who do not usually buy shares to purchase publicly offered shares without difficulty. Share shops act on behalf of members of the public but members of the public pay no commission. Commission is paid to the share shops by the government on successful share applications. Share shops exist only for the duration of the public share offer. *See also* RETAIL TENDER.

shares outstanding (outstanding shares) The issued *share capital of a company less any shares that have been repurchased by the company. It includes shares not available to the general public, such as those held by officers of the company or reserved as part of an employee *share incentive scheme.

share splitting The division of the share capital of a company into smaller units. The effect of a share split is the same as a *scrip issue although the technicalities differ. Share splits are usually carried out when the existing shares reach such a high price that trading in them becomes difficult.

share transfer (stock transfer) A change in the ownership of a share or stock. Formerly, a **stock transfer form** had to be executed by the seller of registered securities to legalize such a transaction on the London Stock Exchange. The whole process can now be carried out instantaneously in electronic form, using the *CREST system.

share warehousing *See* WAREHOUSING.

share warrant A certificate giving the holder the right to purchase a security at a particular price at a particular date or dates in the future.

shark repellents *See* PORCUPINE PROVISIONS.

shark watcher A business consultant who specializes in helping companies to identify raiders and to provide early warning of share *warehousing and other manoeuvres used as preliminaries to takeovers.

sharpbender A firm that has been underperforming its rivals in an industry, but suddenly improves and maintains its performance at above the average. Sharpbending may be caused by a new management team, significant new product success, or other major changes in its *business strategy. *See* TURNAROUND.

SHEEP Acronym for sky-high earnings expectations possibly: applied to investments that appear to offer an unusually high return but that may prove very unreliable.

shell company 1. A non-trading company, with or without a stock-exchange listing, used as a vehicle for various company manoeuvres or kept dormant for future use in some other capacity. **2.** A company that has ceased to trade and is sold to new owners for a small fee to minimize the cost and trouble of setting up a new company. Some business brokers register such companies with the sole object of selling them to people setting up new businesses. The name and objects of such a company can be changed for a small charge. **3.** A name-plate company set up in a tax haven.

Shenzhen Stock Exchange A stock exchange in the Shenzhen special economic zone of China. Of the three Chinese exchanges, it is the only one on the mainland (the others being in Hong Kong and Shanghai). It was founded in 1990 and lists some 1500 companies, many of them state owned.

sheqel The standard monetary unit of Israel, divided into 100 agorot.

shibosai bond A *samurai bond sold direct by a company to investors, without using a stockbroker.

shilling The standard monetary unit of Kenya (KES), Somalia (SOS), Tanzania (TZS), and Uganda (UGX), divided into 100 cents.

Shingo's Seven Wastes The seven ways that wastage can occur in industrial processes, as enumerated by Shigeo Shingo, an engineer at Toyota and a noted authority on *just-in-time techniques. They are:
- waste of overproduction—make only what is needed now;
- waste of waiting;
- waste of transportation;
- waste of processing—does this product or part need to be made?;
- waste of stocks;
- waste of motion—first improve, then mechanize or automate;
- waste of making defective products—accept no defects and make no defects.

See also LEAN PRODUCTION.

shipbroker A broker who specializes in arranging charters, cargo space, and sometimes passenger bookings, in return for a brokerage on the business obtained.

shipowner's lien The *lien a shipowner has on cargo being carried, if the freight charges are not paid.

shipped bill A *bill of lading confirming that specified goods have been loaded onto a specified ship.

shipper 1. An organization that exports goods, which it usually owns, to a foreign country by sea or by air. **2.** In some trades, the importer who sells on to merchants or users, especially one that buys FOB port of shipment and pays the freight cost.

shipping and forwarding agent An organization that specializes in the handling of goods sent by sea, air, rail, or road, especially if the goods are being exported or imported. They advise on the best method of transport, book freight, cover insurance, and arrange custom clearance at both ends, if necessary. They usually do all the required paperwork and documentation. They also arrange inland transport in the exporting or importing country, arranging factory-to-factory transport, if it is required.

shipping bill A form used by HM Revenue and Customs before goods can be exported from the UK. It is also required when removing goods from a bonded warehouse before *drawback can be claimed.

shipping conference An association of shipowners whose liners ply the same routes. They combine to fix freight rates, passenger rates, and terms of contracts. Not all liners belong to conferences; those that do are called **conference line ships**.

shipping documents The documents that an exporter of goods delivers to a bank in the exporting country in order to obtain payment for the goods. The bank sends them to its branch or agents in the importing country, who only release them to the importer against payment. Once the

importer has these documents, the goods can be claimed at the port of destination. The documents usually consist of a commercial invoice, *bill of lading, insurance policy or certificate, weight note, quality certificate, and, if required, a certificate of origin, consular invoice, and export licence.

shipping ton *See* TON.

ship's certificate of registry A document that the master of a ship must always carry. It records the ship's country of registration, home port, owner's name, registered tonnage, permitted number of passengers, master's name, etc.

ship's papers The documents that the master of a ship must always have available for inspection if required. They include the *ship's certificate of registry, bill of health, log book, the ship's articles (muster roll), the charterparty if the ship is on charter (*see* CHARTERING), cargo *manifest and bills of lading, and passenger manifest if it is carrying passengers.

ship's report A report that the master of a ship must make to the port authorities on arrival at a port. It lists details of the ship, crew, passengers, and cargo.

shirkah *See* ISLAMIC FINANCE.

shogun bond A bond sold on the Japanese market by a foreign institution and denominated in a foreign currency. *Compare* SAMURAI BOND.

shopping on demand The new situation in which the Internet enables customers to shop at any time, day or night, without being curtailed by time or place.

shopping product A consumer product that a customer, in the process of selection and purchase, characteristically compares with others, taking into account its suitability, quality, price, and style.

shop steward An employee of a firm, who works in a factory or office and is the representative of a trade union. The shop steward is responsible for negotiating with the employers on behalf of the other members of the same union in the factory or office.

short bill A *bill of exchange that is payable at sight, on demand, or within ten days.

short covering The purchasing of goods that have been sold short (*see* SHORT POSITION) so that the *open position is closed. The dealer in commodities, securities, or foreign exchanges, hopes to cover the shorts at below the price at which they were sold in order to make a profit. Dealers cover their shorts when they expect the market to turn.

short-dated gilt *See* GILT-EDGED SECURITY.

short delivery A delivery of goods that has fewer items than invoiced or a smaller total weight than invoiced. This may be due to accidental loss, which could give rise to an insurance claim, or it may be due to some normal process, such as drying out during shipment, in which case the weight on arrival will be used in a *final invoice. It may also be an attempt by the seller to make an extra profit, in which case the buyer would be well advised to make a claim for short delivery.

short hedging *See* HEDGE.

short interest In marine insurance, the difference between the insured value of goods and their market value, when the insured value exceeds the market value. In these circumstances any excess premium paid can be reclaimed.

short lease A lease that has less than 50 years to run, as defined by the Companies Act. *Compare* LONG LEASE.

short position A position held by a dealer in securities, commodities, currencies, etc., in which sales exceed holdings because the dealer expects prices to fall, enabling the shorts to be covered at a profit. *Compare* LONG POSITION.

shorts 1. *See* GILT-EDGED SECURITY.
2. Securities, commodities, currencies, etc.,

of which a dealer is short, i.e. has a *short position.

short selling Selling commodities, securities, currencies, etc. that one does not currently own. A short seller expects prices to fall so that a profit can be made by buying in the assets at a lower price than that received from the sale. Normally, the short seller will borrow the asset in the interim to ensure that delivery can be made at the agreed date: when he or she omits to do so, the practice is known as **naked short selling**. Since 2008 many regulatory authorities, including the US *Securities and Exchange Commission, have placed restrictions on short selling (and especially naked short selling).

short-term capital Capital raised for a short period to cover an exceptional demand for funds over a short period. A bank loan, rather than a debenture, is an example of short-term capital.

short-term instrument A *negotiable instrument that matures in three months or less.

short-termism Any policy that aims to maximize current profits rather than long-term development and wealth. For example, cutting back on research and development reduces immediate costs but may lead to products becoming obsolescent in the future. A company may well experience problems of this kind if managers' salaries or bonuses are linked too closely to short-term results. Similarly, institutional and individual shareholders often overreact to a company's short-term results and policies, causing the company to lose the longer-term focus that is ultimately in the interests of all *stakeholders.

short ton *See* TON.

show stopper A legal action in which the target firm in an unwelcome *takeover bid seeks a permanent injunction to prevent the bidder from persisting in its attempt, on the grounds that the bid is legally defective in some way.

shrinkage The goods that disappear from a retail outlet without being registered as sales. This includes goods that are broken, damaged, stolen, or—in the case of foodstuffs—past their sell-by date and therefore thrown away or given away.

SHRM Abbreviation for *strategic human-resource management.

shut-down cost The costs to be incurred in closing down some part of an organization's activities.

SIC Abbreviation for *Standard Industrial Classification.

sickness and accident insurance A form of health insurance in which the benefits are paid for a fixed time after the onset of an illness or accident that prevents the insured from working. Premiums can increase each year and renewal can be refused if a claim has been made. *Compare* PERMANENT HEALTH INSURANCE.

side deal A private deal between two people, usually for the personal benefit of one of them, as a subsidiary to a transaction between the officials of a company, government, etc. For example, the chairman of a public company may agree to encourage the board to welcome a takeover bid, provided that a personal profit can be made in some side deal with the bidder. Side deals are rigorously investigated by the Panel on Takeovers and Mergers (*see* CITY CODE ON TAKEOVERS AND MERGERS).

SIFIs Acronym for systemically important financial institutions; those institutions, such as large banks, whose failure would jeopardize an entire financial system, whether national or international. SIFIs that are perceived as having a global importance are known as **G-SIFIs**. Following the global financial crisis of 2007–08, the UK Financial Stability Board sought to list and regulate the key attributes of such institutions. *See also* TOO BIG TO FAIL.

SIFMA Abbreviation for *Securities Industry and Financial Markets Association.

sight bill *See* AT SIGHT.

sight deposit Money deposited in a bank account that can be withdrawn without notice, e.g. money withdrawn by cheque from a current account. In the USA it is known as a *demand deposit.

sight draft Any *bill of exchange that is payable on sight, i.e. on presentation, irrespective of when it was drawn.

signalling hypothesis The idea that many actions taken by economic agents are motivated chiefly by the wish to send a positive 'signal' to other agents, rather than by their ostensible purpose. This can be a means of overcoming the problem of *asymmetric information between transactors. For example, a business may choose to spend an ostentatious amount of money on advertising a new product—not because this is the most cost-effective form of publicity, but because a large outlay by the company signals its faith in the product to investors, distributors, and other stakeholders. Similarly, a generous dividend policy can be a means by which management signals its positive view of the firm's position and future prospects to the financial markets. In this case, such signalling is a means of overcoming the mismatch between the information available to managers and that available to shareholders. *See also* AGENCY RELATIONSHIP.

simple interest *See* INTEREST.

simplified financial statements Simplified versions of the *annual accounts and report intended for readers who do not possess sophisticated financial knowledge. The financial information may be made easier to understand by using simple terminology, showing the information in the forms of graphs and diagrams, providing fuller explanations, and reducing the amount of information. One form of simplified financial statement is the *employee report, which is intended for employees and not covered by legislation; another form is the *summary financial statement intended for shareholders and subject to legislation. *See also* UNDERSTANDABILITY.

simulated test market (Hall test) A laboratory-based marketing research technique for forecasting product sales; it is based upon pretest interviews, forced advertising exposures, simulated store shopping, product trials, and follow-up interviews to measure the repurchase rate.

simulation Recreating or modelling a hypothetical situation in order to consider its likely outcomes and to develop problem-solving strategies. In **computer simulation** all the available data is fed into a computer, which enables a range of possible strategies to be compared. Uncertainty may be modelled by the use of random numbers, as in a *Monte Carlo simulation, or worst cases by the use of *stress testing. In **laboratory simulation** situations are realistically recreated in order to assess possible results or responses. Simulation is widely used in *risk analysis, financial modelling, and marketing.

simultaneous development *See* CONCURRENT ENGINEERING.

simultaneous direct data entry (SDDE) A method used in *computer-assisted telephone interviewing in which questions are displayed on a monitor and the responses (pre-coded) are keyed by the interviewer directly into the computer. It is a relatively fast method of data collection.

simultaneous engineering *See* CONCURRENT ENGINEERING.

simultaneous product development An approach to *new product development in which various departments in a company work closely together so that there is some overlap in the development stages in order to save time and increase effectiveness. *Compare* SEQUENTIAL PRODUCT DEVELOPMENT.

sine die (Latin: without a day) Denoting an adjournment of an action, arbitration, etc., indefinitely.

single-capacity system *See* DUAL-CAPACITY SYSTEM.

single column centimetre A unit used in selling advertising space in printed publications.

single-life pension A pension or *annuity that is paid for the lifetime of the beneficiary only, rather than for the lifetime of a surviving spouse. *Compare* JOINT-LIFE AND LAST-SURVIVOR ANNUITIES.

Single Market The concept of a single integrated market that underlies trading in the European Union, as codified in the **Single European Act** 1986, which was introduced in 1987 with a target date of 31 December 1992 for completion. The Single Market came into force on 1 January 1993 with between 90% and 95% of the necessary legislation enacted by all member countries. In practice, however, some of its terms have taken considerably longer to implement. The measures covered by the legislation include:

- the elimination of frontier controls (the full measures have been repeatedly delayed);
- the acceptance throughout the market of professional qualifications;
- the acceptance of national standards for product harmonization;
- open tendering for public supply contracts;
- the free movement of capital between states;
- a reduction of state aid for certain industries;
- the harmonization of VAT and excise duties throughout the market.

single-premium assurance A life-assurance policy in which the insured pays only one capital sum rather than regular premiums. *See also* INVESTMENT BOND.

single-product strategy A strategy that involves a company offering only one product or one product version with very few options. Few companies or organizations find themselves using this strategy because the risks are too high (if the single product fails).

single property ownership trust (SPOT) A single property trust; shares in the trust entitle their holder to a direct share of the property's income and capital. A form of *securitization, a share in a SPOT is similar to a *property income certificate (PINC).

single-source data systems Electronic monitoring systems that link consumers' exposure to television advertising and promotion (measured using television meters) with what they buy in stores (measured using store checkout scanners).

single-tax system A system of taxation in which there would be only one major tax, usually a *comprehensive income tax, instead of several taxes, such as income tax, capital gains tax, and National Insurance, as in the UK. Arguments in favour of such taxes are that they should be less avoidable and should simplify administration. On the other hand the present variety of taxes is designed for a variety of purposes and flexibility may be lost in a single-tax system. *See also* FLAT TAX.

sinking fund A fund set up to replace a *wasting asset at the end of its useful life. Usually a regular annual sum is set aside to enable the fund, taking into account interest at the expected rate, to replace the exhausted asset at a specified date. Some have argued that amounts set aside for *depreciation of an asset should be equal to the annual amounts needed to be placed in a notional sinking fund.

SIP Abbreviation for *Share Incentive Plan.

sister-ship clause A clause used in marine insurance policies, enabling the insurer to make a claim as a result of a collision between two ships both owned by the same insurer. Without this clause, the insurer may have no claim as it is not possible to sue oneself.

sit-down strike A strike in which workers come to their place of work, but refuse

to either work or to go home. In a **work-in**, the workers refuse to leave the place of work and continue working, usually in spite of management instructions not to do so.

site availability An indication of the ease with which a user can be connected to a website. In theory this figure should be 100%, but for technical reasons, such as failures in the server hardware or upgrades to software, users cannot always access the site and the figure can fall below 90%.

site stickiness An indication of how long a visitor stays on a website. *Log file analysers can be used to assess average visit times.

situational analysis The process of analysing the past and future situations facing an organization in order to identify problems and opportunities. *See* SWOT.

situational leadership theory A *contingency theory of leadership holding that *leadership style should be varied according to the maturity of followers, which encompasses such factors as experience in the job and willingness to take responsibility. Where maturity is low, leaders should be *task-motivated and directive; as maturity increases, leaders should be increasingly *relationship-motivated and supportive.

SI units Système International d'Unités: an international metric system of units used in science and increasingly for commercial purposes. It is based on the seven basic units: metre, kilogram, second, ampere, kelvin, candela, and mole. Derived units with special names include the hertz (frequency), joule (energy), volt (potential), and watt (power). They are used with a standard set of multiples and sub-multiples, including hecto- ($\times$ 100), kilo- ($\times$ 1000), centi- ($\times$ 1/100), and milli- ($\times$ 1/1000).

six-month money Money invested on the *money market for a period of six months. If it is withdrawn before the six months have elapsed there may be a heavy penalty, although if the market has moved in favour of the recipient of the funds, this penalty may be negligible.

Six Sigma A *quality-control system first developed at the US telecoms company Motorola in 1986 and later adopted by many large industrial businesses, including General Electric. The process systematizes production with the objective of reducing flaws to 3.4 defects per million. It involves five key stages, often summarized in the acronym **DMAIC** (pronounced 'duh-may-ick'): (i) *d*efine goals; (ii) *m*easure the current process; (iii) *a*nalyse data; (iv) *i*mprove the process; and (v) *c*ontrol future production so that faults are eradicated before they can occur.

SIX Swiss Exchange The main stock exchange in Switzerland, based in Zurich. It was created as **SWX Swiss Exchange** in 1995, when the exchanges in Zurich, Geneva, and Basle adopted a single fully automated system for trading, clearing, and settlement (the Berne exchange remains independent). The price level is given daily by the **Swiss Market Index** (**SMI**). In 2001–02 it acquired the London-based electronic exchange virt-x, which became known as **SWX Europe** until all trading was moved to the Zurich exchange in 2009. SWX became SIX in 2008, when it merged with the SIS and Telekurs groups.

skip-day The two-day period allowed before payment has to be made for a security purchased on the US *money market.

SL Abbreviation for *specification limits.

slack time (float) The difference between the amount of time an activity takes and the amount of time allocated to it in *network modelling. Activities that constitute the critical path in a project are those for which there is no slack time. Activities not on the critical path have an earliest and a latest possible start and finish time. The difference between the two is the slack time.

sleeping partner A person who has capital in a *partnership but takes no part in its commercial activities. He or she has all the legal benefits and obligations of ownership and shares in the profits of the partnership in accordance with the provisions laid down in the partnership agreement.

sliding peg *See* CRAWLING PEG.

slump *See* DEPRESSION.

slush fund A fund that is used by an individual, political organization, or company for illegal purposes. For example, a company may have a slush fund for bribing potential customers.

small company Under UK company law, a private company that satisfies at least two of the following criteria for the current and preceding financial year:

- its *net worth does not exceed £3.26 million;
- its *turnover does not exceed £6.5 million;
- the average number of employees does not exceed 50.

A company that is in its first financial year may still qualify as a small company if it falls within these limits. Alternatively, if the company has qualified in the two preceding financial years, it may qualify.

Certain small companies may prepare accounts for their members under the special provisions of the Companies Act. In addition, they may prepare and deliver *abbreviated accounts to the Registrar of Companies.

Many small companies can also claim total exemption from *statutory audit.

However, if a company is a member of a *group containing a public company, a banking or insurance company, or an authorized person under the Financial Services Act 1986, it is not eligible for the exemptions for small companies. *See also* MICRO-ENTITY; SME.

(⊕) SEE WEB LINKS
- Further details on filing and audit exemptions

Small Firms Loan Guarantee (SFLG) *See* ENTERPRISE FINANCE GUARANTEE.

small group A *group that meets two out of three of the following criteria for the current and preceding year, or the two preceding financial years:

- its *net worth should not exceed £3.26 million net or £3.9 million gross;
- its *turnover should not exceed £6.5 million net or £7.8 million gross;
- the average number of employees should not exceed 50.

If a group is in its first financial year, it may still qualify if it falls within these limits.

Under the Companies Act, a parent company is not required to prepare *group accounts for a financial year in which the group headed by that parent qualifies as a small group. A small group may file *abbreviated accounts instead of full accounts with the *Registrar of Companies.

A group containing a public company, a banking or insurance company, or an authorized person under the Financial Services Act 1986 is ineligible for the exemptions for small groups. *Compare* MEDIUM-SIZED GROUP.

small print Printed matter on a document, such as a life-assurance policy or hire-purchase agreement, in which the seller sets out the conditions of the sale and the mutual liabilities of buyer and seller. The use of a very small type size and unintelligible jargon is often intended to obscure the buyer's legal rights and safeguards. This unfair practice has largely been remedied by the various Acts that provide *consumer protection. *See also* COOLING-OFF PERIOD.

smart ad An advertisement targeted to specific users of a product or service, based on their observable characteristics and behaviour. The scope for targeted promotions of this kind has increased greatly with the rise of *Internet advertising.

smart card A plastic card that contains a microprocessor that stores and updates information, typically used in performing financial transactions. Unlike an ordinary *debit card or *cash card, a smart card memorizes all transactions in which the card is used. Other uses include storing a person's medical records.

smart money Money invested by experienced and successful people, especially those with inside information about a particular project or investment opportunity.

smart offer A dynamic presentation of an offer to an individual on a website, based on that visitor's history.

smartphone A mobile phone with computing features over and above the ability to make and take calls, and send or receive text messages. The extra features generally include data storage, *Bluetooth, GPS, location-aware applications, and touch-screen user interfaces. Many current smartphones are essentially compact personal computers.

SME Abbreviation for small or medium-sized enterprise. Although the term is very widely used, there is no standard definition of an SME based on e.g. net worth, turnover, profits, or number of employees. In the UK the terms *small company and *medium-sized company are officially defined for accounting purposes, but different criteria are employed for corporation tax and to determine eligibility for various tax allowances and government schemes. Banks and insurance companies also have their own definitions. The EU is currently attempting to harmonize the definition of an SME across member states.

Smith Report *See* HIGGS REPORT.

smokestack industries An informal name for traditional manufacturing industries, especially heavy engineering, as opposed to modern industries, such as electronics.

SMP Abbreviation for statutory maternity pay. *See* MATERNITY RIGHTS.

smurfing Slang for the practice of dividing a large transaction into numerous much smaller transactions, usually for the purpose of *laundering money. Because the individual payments are below the threshold at which financial institutions are required to report them, the attention of regulatory and law-enforcement agencies can often be avoided in this way. Owing to the threat of international terrorism, however, banks have become increasingly alert to any suspicious pattern of activity. The name alludes to the small identical-looking cartoon characters, the Smurfs. A more formal term is **structuring a deposit**.

snowball sampling In *marketing research, a sampling technique in which the selection of additional respondents is based on referrals from the initial respondents. Thus, the interviewer might ask the respondents if they know someone else who owned brand X. Clearly, the danger is that interviews are conducted with similar persons.

social accounting issues Issues that concern the impact of an entity on society, both within the organization and externally. Social accounting issues may include charitable donations of equipment and time, education initiatives (such as sponsorships and research funding), product safety, community involvement, employment of disadvantaged groups, and the provision of sports equipment or sponsorship. Environmental issues that are often also included under this heading include energy conservation and control of pollution. *See* SOCIAL RESPONSIBILITY REPORTING.

social audit An *audit of the non-financial impact of an organization on society. For example, an *environmental audit is one kind of social audit. Other aspects may be of interest to other stakeholder groups, such as customers, employees, and the wider community. The object is to enable a firm to assess its performance in relation to society. *See also* SOCIAL RESPONSIBILITY REPORTING.

Social Chapter The section of the founding treaty of the *European Union that reflects the agreement of member states with respect to social policy. The objectives of the Social Chapter are to promote employment, improve living and working conditions, establish dialogue between management and workers by means of works councils, implement proper social protection, and develop human resources with a view to lasting high employment. After much resistance, the British government finally agreed to the incorporation of these social aims and objectives into the main body of the treaty in 1997. This has led to a number of changes to UK law, including the implementation of unpaid parental leave and new rights for part-time workers (who are now entitled to be treated no less favourably than comparable full-time workers in their contractual terms and conditions).

social classes A system for classifying the population according to social status. According to the classification issued by the UK *Office for National Statistics, there are seven classes for those in work and an eighth class for those on benefit:

- 1A—Large employers and higher managers: includes senior administrators, senior police and service officers, etc.;
- 1B—Senior professional people: includes lawyers, doctors, headteachers, airline pilots, etc.;
- 2—Other managerial and professional occupations: includes journalists, technicians, nurses, actors, NCOs, etc.;
- 3—Intermediate occupations: includes most clerical, sales, and service jobs, and professional sportspeople;
- 4—Small employers and the nonprofessional self-employed: includes plumbers, electricians, small farmers;
- 5—Skilled workers: includes train drivers, craftspeople, foremen, etc.;
- 6—Semi-routine occupations: includes caretakers, gardeners, assembly-line workers, etc.;
- 7—Routine occupations: includes cleaners, road workers, farm labourers, etc.;
- 8—The long-term unemployed and chronically sick.

social cost The cost of a product that is not paid by its producer but is paid by society in general. An example would be the environmental cost involved in a production process that involves the discharge of pollutants into the environment (e.g. into the sea or the atmosphere). *See also* EXTERNALITY.

social entrepreneurship A form of entrepreneurship in which a company or organization is established to further a defined social goal rather than to pursue maximum profit. Typically, a social entrepreneur recognizes a need not currently met by for-profit business, government, or charity and aims to fill this gap through his or her own initiative, rather than by campaigning against existing business practices or public policy.

social lending *See* PEER-TO-PEER LENDING.

social loafing The general tendency for people to expend less effort on a task when working as part of a group than when working individually. There have been various attempts to explain this phenomenon. *See* COLLECTIVE EFFORT MODEL; RINGELMANN EFFECT; SUCKER EFFECT.

socially responsible investment *See* ETHICAL INVESTMENT.

social marketing *See* NONPROFIT MARKETING.

social media Applications that enable users to interact with one another over the Internet by posting or linking to text, pictures, and videos (*see* USER-GENERATED CONTENT). Social media platforms became very popular in the 2000s and now have billions of users worldwide. In a simple case, an individual maintains a *blog, an online journal that can be freely accessed and commented on. Other applications are more sophisticated and specialized. *Facebook, founded in 2004 and the leading site for informal social networking, allows users to specify which content is visible to all users and which is visible only to a specified set of 'friends'; *Twitter, founded in 2006, involves the posting of short messages ('tweets') that are received by all users who have chosen to 'follow' the sender. The application encourages users

to make new contacts, thereby building up their networks. *Linked-In, founded in 2003, is the premier tool for business and professional networking.

The number of people using social media and the speed and ease with which information can be exchanged make these sites an increasingly vital channel for business communication. Because they enable companies to interact directly with customers, they have become an important vehicle for public relations, marketing, and marketing research, as well as advertising (*see* VIRAL MARKETING). The fact that social media are now increasingly accessed from mobile devices means that business messaging can be both time- and location-sensitive. Maintaining a lively blog and a presence on Facebook and Twitter is now considered essential by many companies, who may employ staff specifically to manage their social-media operations.

social overhead capital *See* INFRASTRUCTURE.

social responsibility reporting (corporate social reporting) The reporting of *social accounting issues by a business. These may be discussed in the *annual accounts and report or form the basis of a separate report. Social responsibility costs are the costs to the business of e.g. equipment donated, sponsorship given, or charitable donations. The monetary quantification of social benefits is much harder to measure and necessarily subjective. Owing to the concerns of consumers, investors, and other stakeholders, companies are increasingly obliged to be environmentally and socially conscious. *See also* GREEN REPORTING; SOCIAL AUDIT; TRIPLE BOTTOM-LINE ACCOUNTING.

social security A government system for paying allowances to the sick and the unemployed, as well as maternity benefits and retirement pensions. Other low-income members of society are also eligible, such as the disabled and single-parent families. In the UK this is now the responsibility of the Department for Work and Pensions; the *National Insurance scheme that funds the social security payments is administered by HM Revenue and Customs.

sociedad anónima *See* SA.

sociedade anónima *See* SA.

società a responsabilità limitata *See* SARL.

societal marketing concept 1. A form of marketing that takes into consideration the long-term welfare of society. For many years the individual needs of consumers dominated the practice of marketing. For example, two cars might be compared in terms of their acceleration. It is now recognized, however, that both cars may have jeopardized the long-term welfare of society as a result of the pollution they cause. Adapting both cars to run on lead-free petrol is an example of the way in which societal marketing concepts are being used. **2.** Marketing techniques applied to a social cause, such as an anti-pollution campaign or an anti-smoking campaign.

società per azioni *See* SPA.

societas Europea A business entity created by the merger of two or more companies resident in different member states of the European Union.

société anonyme *See* SA.

société à responsabilité limitée *See* SARL.

sociogram A diagrammatical representation of patterns of interpersonal relationships amongst group members (likes or dislikes, communication links, etc.). Usually, each member is represented by a letter or symbol and the various links are shown by arrows. The use of sociograms to analyse intergroup relationships is known as **sociometry**.

socio-technical system A system involving the interaction of *hard systems and human beings, in ways that either cannot be separated or are thought to be inappropriate to separate.

soft benefits Such benefits as improved quality and customer satisfaction that are hard to measure but have indirect benefits to the firm.

soft commodities (softs) Commodities, other than metals. They include cocoa, coffee, grains, potatoes, and sugar.

soft currency A currency that is not freely convertible and for which there is only a *thin market. *Compare* HARD CURRENCY.

soft landing The situation in which an economy slows down but does not go into a recession. The term was first used in astronautics journals of the late 1950s to describe a safe moon landing.

soft loan A special type of government loan in which the terms and conditions of repayment are more generous (or softer) than they would be under normal finance circumstances. For example, the interest rate might be less and the repayment term might be for a longer period.

soft sell The use of unobtrusive methods of selling as opposed to those employed in a *hard sell. Implication, rather than forceful statement and relentless repetition, form the basis of a soft sell.

soft systems methodology (SSM) A method for intervening in problem situations that have a human or social component, as opposed to being purely technological. The method suggests that systems capable of producing desired outputs frequently fail because the participants in these systems have differing views of the world, based on differing values and standards. It involves the widest possible research into the nature of the problem, the production of root definitions and conceptual models, the identification of feasible and desirable changes, and, finally, recommendations for action.

software The programs used with a computer, together with their documentation, as opposed to the physical parts of the computer system (*hardware).

A distinction is made between systems software, or those programs that control the functioning of the computer itself, and *applications software, such as accounting or *audit software, which is designed to serve a particular specialized function. *See* BUSINESS SOFTWARE PACKAGE.

software development kit *See* SDK.

sogo shosha The Japanese name for a large overseas trading company with a wide spread of commercial and industrial activities. The leading *sogo shosha* include Mitsubishi and Toyota.

sol *See* NEW SOL.

sold day book *See* SALES DAY BOOK.

sold note *See* CONTRACT NOTE.

sole agency An agreement between an agent and a principal that gives the agent exclusive rights to sell a product or service in a particular territory for a specified period.

sole proprietor An individual who runs an unincorporated business on his or her own. Generally, a sole proprietor of a business is known as a **sole trader** and a sole proprietor of a professional practice, such as an accountant or solicitor, as a **sole practitioner**.

solicitor's letter A letter written by a solicitor, usually threatening to take a matter to court.

solo (sola) A single *bill of exchange of which no other copies are in circulation.

solus position An isolated position for a poster or press advertisement, so that it is separated from any competitive announcement. *Compare* SEMISOLUS.

solus site A retail outlet, such as a petrol station, that carries the products of only one company.

solvency 1. The financial state of a person or company that is able to pay all debts as they fall due. **2.** The amount by which the assets of a bank exceed its liabilities.

solvency ratio 1. Any of various *accounting ratios used to measure a company's longer-term solvency. One of the most widely used is: *net assets / (*long-term liabilities + *short-term liabilities), expressed as a percentage; sometimes net after-tax profit is substituted for net assets. *See also* LIQUID RATIO. **2.** A ratio used by the UK regulatory authorities to evaluate the stability of insurance companies; it is the ratio of the company's net assets to its non-life premium income. **3.** *See* CAPITAL ADEQUACY RATIO.

som (*plural* **somy**) **(KGS)** The standard monetary unit of Kyrgyzstan, divided into 100 tiyin.

somoni (TJS) The standard monetary unit of Tajikistan, divided into 100 diram.

SONIA Acronym for Sterling Overnight Index Average, a *reference rate computed as a weighted average of sterling overnight funding rates in the interbank market. *Compare* EONIA; EURONIA. *See* OVERNIGHT RATE.

sort code In the UK, a sequence of numbers that serves to identify the branch holding a bank account.

source and application of funds (source and disposition of funds) A statement showing how an organization has raised and used its funds for a specified period. Sources of funds are typically trading profits, issues of shares or loan stock, sales of fixed assets, and borrowings. Applications are typically trading losses, purchases of fixed assets, dividends paid, and repayment of borrowings. In UK accountancy practice, it has been replaced by the *cash-flow projection.

source document The first document to record a transaction.

sources of power The six major areas that can be used to build a power base by a person or unit working in a large organization:

- **Political network**—support is built up by communication with peers, subordinates, and those not in direct authority. This method is dependent on the person's communication channels within an organization.

- **Perception of dependence**—support comes from the belief that the person controls scarce resources and has the power to allocate them.
- **Work unit power**—power deriving from a department's ability to deal with uncertainty, the uniqueness of its functions, changes in its external environment, etc.
- **Work activities**—power arising by exploiting the visible and necessary differences within the organization.
- **Charisma**—a person who is continuously successful, especially one who takes high risks, often comes to be highly regarded by others, who become inspired by his or her ideas and committed to implement them (*see* CHARISMATIC LEADER; TRANSFORMATIONAL LEADERSHIP). This in turn strengthens the person's knowledge, reputation, and credibility.

See also POWER STYLES.

sovereign debt Debt issued by a national government in the form of bonds in a *reserve currency. The level of risk in the bond is reflected in the rate of interest payable on it. Traditionally, sovereign debt had been considered low-risk, as governments were believed to have a variety of means to ensure they did not default on their obligations. However, since the 1990s there have been several **sovereign debt crises**, in which high ratios of debt to GDP have resulted in a perceived risk of default on sovereign bonds. Following the financial crisis of 2008–09, sovereign debt in some eurozone countries, notably Greece and Cyprus, reached levels that required international intervention to avoid the risk of default (*see* EUROPEAN STABILITY MECHANISM).

sovereign risk *See* POLITICAL CREDIT RISK.

sovereign wealth fund (SWF) An investment fund that is owned by a sovereign nation and managed by a central bank, state pension fund, or official investment company. Most such funds originated in

foreign-exchange reserves built up from the sale of commodity exports (notably oil). The growing size and influence of SWFs attracted much comment in the late 2000s, when sovereign funds acquired major stakes in many Western banks and financial institutions. Most of the world's largest SWFs belong to developing nations (e.g., Abu Dhabi, Singapore, Saudi Arabia, Kuwait) but important funds are also held by Norway, Russia, and Australia.

Sox Abbreviation for the *Sarbanes–Oxley Act 2002.

SpA Abbreviation for *società per azioni*. It appears after the name of a public limited company in Italy, being equivalent to the British abbreviation plc. *Compare* SARL.

spamming Sending unsolicited and unwanted e-mails in bulk for advertising purposes. The proliferation of such material, which now accounts for some 85% of all e-mails sent, has become a serious nuisance to business users. Software that identifies spam and separates it from genuine e-mail messages has therefore become essential.

SPC Abbreviation for *statistical process control.

special clearing The clearing of a cheque through the UK banking system in less than the normal three days, for a small additional charge. A cheque for which a special clearing has been arranged can usually be passed through the system in one day.

Special Commissioners A body of civil servants who are specialized tax lawyers appointed to hear appeals against assessments to income tax, corporation tax, capital gains tax, and inheritance tax. Hearings are informal and appellants may present their own case or be represented. *See also* GENERAL COMMISSIONERS.

special crossing A crossing on a *cheque in which the name of a bank is written between the crossing lines. A cheque so crossed can only be paid into the named bank.

special delivery A postal service offered by the UK Post Office for urgent, valuable, or important items. Next-day delivery is guaranteed and the progress of the parcel can be tracked online or via a mobile phone. The recipient's signature on delivery can also be viewed electronically. *Compare* RECORDED DELIVERY.

special deposits Deposits that the UK government may instruct the clearing banks to make at the Bank of England, as a means of restricting credit in the economy. The less money the clearing banks have at their disposal, the less they are able to lend to businesses. A similar system has been used by the Federal Reserve System in the USA.

special dividend (extra dividend) A single irregular *dividend payment. It is usually made after an especially profitable year but is sometimes associated with the restructuring of companies.

Special Drawing Rights (SDRs) The standard unit of account used by the *International Monetary Fund (IMF). In 1970 members of the IMF were allocated SDRs in proportion to the quotas of currency that they had subscribed to the fund on its formation. There have since been further allocations. SDRs can be used to settle international trade balances and to repay debts to the IMF itself. On the instructions of the IMF a member country must supply its own currency to another member, in exchange for SDRs, unless it already holds more than three times its original allocation. The value of SDRs was originally expressed in terms of gold, but since 1974 it has been valued in terms of its members' currencies. SDRs provide a credit facility for IMF members in addition to their existing credit facilities (hence the name); unlike these existing facilities they do not have to be repaid, thus forming a permanent addition to members' reserves and functioning as an international reserve currency.

specialized industry An industry in which there are many opportunities for a firm to create a competitive advantage that

gives a high pay-off. *Compare* STALEMATE INDUSTRY.

special manager A person appointed by the court in the liquidation of a company or bankruptcy of an individual to assist the *liquidator or *official receiver to manage the business of the company or individual. The special manager's powers are decided by the court.

special notice *See* RESOLUTION.

special purpose vehicle (SPV) A legal entity established for the sake of a single transaction, for example in the *credit enhancement of a securitization.

special resolution A *resolution of the members of a company that must be approved by at least 75% of the members to be valid. Members must have been given at least 14 days' notice of the meeting at which the resolution is proposed and the notice of the meeting must give details of the special resolution. Matters requiring a special resolution include any emendation to the *articles of association of a company. *Compare* ORDINARY RESOLUTION. *See also* WRITTEN RESOLUTION.

specialty goods Consumer goods with unique characteristics or a strong brand identification for which a significant number of buyers is willing to make a special purchase effort. For example, if a store is out of stock of this brand, the consumer will go to another store to find it; if it is not available there, they will wait until new supplies become available.

specialty store A retail store that carries a narrow *product line with a wide assortment within that line. Specialty stores include specialist record shops, PC retail outlets, etc.

specie Money in the form of coins, rather than bank notes or bullion.

specification limits (SL) The limits of acceptable variation in the characteristics of a component or product. Outside those limits the item is not fit for use. *See* STATISTICAL PROCESS CONTROL.

specific bank guarantee An uncondi- tional guarantee from the *Export Credits Guarantee Department to a UK bank enabling that bank to finance an exporter's medium-term credit to an export customer without recourse; the arrangement is known as **supplier credit** in contrast to the buyer credit under which the bank finances the overseas buyer to pay the exporter on cash terms.

specific charge *See* CHARGE; FIXED CHARGE.

specific indicators *See* PERFORMANCE MEASUREMENT.

specific performance An equitable legal remedy requiring the parties to carry out the contract they have entered into. This will be granted by a court only if damages are an inadequate remedy and if it is possible to perform the contract. It is the usual remedy in cases in which there is a breach of contract for the sale of land.

specific risk (non-systematic risk) The *risk associated with each of the individual assets in a *portfolio, as opposed to the *systematic risk associated with the market as a whole. It can be eliminated by *diver- sification. *Portfolio theory holds that investors should maintain a diversified portfolio in order to maximize the utility of their investments. Because specific risk can be eliminated in this way, there is no requirement for a *risk premium for taking specific risks. This is an important under- lying principle of the *capital asset pricing model and *arbitrage pricing theory. Spe- cific risk is measured by the *alpha coefficient.

speculation The purchase or sale of something for the sole purpose of making a capital gain. For professional speculators the security, commodity, and foreign exchange markets are natural venues as they cater for speculation as well as invest- ment and trading. Indeed, speculators help to make a viable market and thus smooth out price fluctuations. This is particularly true of commodity futures and option markets.

speculative risk *See* RISK. *See also* INSURABLE RISK.

spend management A systematic attempt to optimize a company's spending by achieving best value for money in every area of its expenditure. This is to be distin- guished from simple cost cutting, which often achieves only short-term benefits. Spend management begins with an ana- lysis of current spending behaviour and develops a strategic approach integrating such areas as sourcing, procurement, con- tract management, supply-chain logistics, and a company's invoicing and payment processes. Specialized software is now available.

spidering *See* WEB CRAWLER.

spin-off 1. A commercially valuable product or process that emerges as an unexpected benefit from a research project in another field. For example, the non-stick saucepan coating Teflon (trademark) came from the US space programme. **2.** A type of corporate restructuring in which a parent company divests itself of a wholly-owned subsidiary by distributing shares in the lat- ter to its own shareholders, usually on a pro rata basis. The subsidiary thus becomes an independent company. Spin-offs are usu- ally carried out with the aim of increasing shareholder value and making both com- panies more focused, particularly where the subsidiary underperformed as part of the whole. It is nearly always more tax effi- cient for a company to spin off a subsidiary in this way than to sell it. *Compare* CARVE- OUT; SPLIT-OFF.

splash page A preliminary page that precedes the normal *home page of a website. Site users can either wait to be redirected to the home page or can follow a link to do so. Splash pages are now less commonly used than formerly as they slow down the process by which customers find the information they need.

split *See* SHARE SPLITTING.

split-capital investment trust (split- level trust; split trust) An *investment trust with a limited life in which the equity capital is divided into various classes of income shares and capital shares. Holders of income shares receive all or most of the income earned plus a predetermined capital value on liquidation. Holders of capital shares receive little or no income but are entitled to all of the assets remaining after repayment of the income shares.

split-off A type of corporate restructuring in which a parent company divests itself of a wholly-owned subsidiary by giving its members the chance to exchange their shares for shares in the subsidiary, which thereby becomes an independent undertaking. In contrast to a *spin-off, where shares are distributed automatically, the parent makes a *tender to its shareholders, who can choose whether or not to acquire shares in the new company. A *premium is often used to encourage the exchange. *See also* CARVE-OUT.

spoilage *See* WASTE.

sponsor 1. The financial institution, usually a merchant bank or investment bank, that handles the *flotation of a company. It will supervise the preparation of the *prospectus and make sure that the company is aware of the benefits and obligations of being a public company. **2.** The lender in a *project financing agreement.

sporadic problem A short-term non-random problem that may cause a process to deviate from its control limits. *See* STATISTICAL PROCESS CONTROL.

SPOT Abbreviation for *single property ownership trust.

spot goods Commodities that are available for immediate delivery, as opposed to futures (*see* FUTURES CONTRACT) in which deliveries are arranged for named months in the future. The price of spot goods, the **spot price**, is usually higher than the forward price, unless there is a glut of that particular commodity but an expected shortage in the future.

spot market A market that deals in commodities or *foreign exchange for immediate delivery. Immediate delivery in foreign currencies usually means within two business days. For commodities it usually means within seven days. *Compare* FORWARD DEALING; FUTURES CONTRACT.

spot month The month during which goods bought on a futures contract will become available for delivery.

spot price *See* SPOT GOODS.

spread 1. The difference between the buying and selling price made by a *market maker on the stock exchange. **2.** The diversity of the investments in a *portfolio. The greater the spread of a portfolio the less volatile it will be. **3.** The simultaneous purchase and sale of commodity futures (*see* FUTURES CONTRACT) in the hope that movement in their relative prices will enable a profit to be made. This may include a purchase and sale of the same commodity for the same delivery, but on different commodity exchanges (*see* STRADDLE), or a purchase and sale of the same commodity for different deliveries.

spreadsheet A computer application used for tabular calculations. A spreadsheet display consists of a large number of cells arranged in rows and columns. Generally, columns are labelled by a letter, or combination of letters, and rows are labelled by numbers. Each cell in the array has a unique identification: A1, A2, etc., B1, B2, etc. The user can enter text, numbers, or formulas into individual cells. The formulas can be used to perform calculations on values in other cells. For example, A1*100/B1 takes the value in cell A1 and expresses it as a percentage of the value in cell B1. A formula of the type sum (A1:A20) adds all the values in the cells from A1 to A20. Values and formulas can be copied from a single cell to a block of cells. In this way it is possible to set up complex calculations for accounting or financial modelling purposes. Spreadsheet programs generally have a facility for producing graphs and charts automatically from the data. Widely used spreadsheets include Excel and Lotus 1-2-3.

S

SPV Abbreviation for *special purpose vehicle.

spyware Software that sends unauthorized details of a computer's data or of its use (for example, a log of all keystrokes) to a third party, usually over the Internet. Spyware is often concealed in downloaded web pages and installs itself surreptitiously, either by exploiting security weaknesses or by tricking the user into giving consent, and is difficult to remove. It is a type of *malware.

Square Mile *See* CITY.

squeeze 1. Controls imposed by a government to restrict inflation. An income (pay) squeeze limits increases in wage and salaries, a *credit squeeze limits the amounts that banks and other moneylenders can lend, a dividend (profits) squeeze restricts increases in dividends. **2.** Any action on a market that forces buyers to come into the market and prices to rise. In a bear squeeze (*see* BEAR) dealers holding a *short position are forced to cover in order to deliver. It may be restricted to a particular commodity or security or a particular delivery month may be squeezed, pushing its price up against the rest of the market.

SSAP Abbreviation for *Statement of Standard Accounting Practice.

SSE Abbreviation for *Shanghai Stock Exchange.

SSM Abbreviation for *soft systems methodology.

SSP 1. Abbreviation for *statutory sick pay. **2.** Abbreviation for *State Second Pension.

staff management *See* LINE AND STAFF MANAGEMENT.

stag A person who applies for shares in a *new issue in the hope that the price when trading begins will be higher than the *issue price. Often measures will be taken by the issuers to prevent excessive stagging; it is usually illegal for would-be investors to attempt to obtain large numbers of shares by making multiple applications. Issuers will often scale down share applications to prevent such quick-profit taking, e.g. by ballot.

stagflation A combination of slow economic growth with rising prices. The UK and the USA experienced stagflation for the first time in the 1970s.

staggered directorships A measure used as a defence against unwanted *takeover bids. If the company concerned resolves that the terms of office served by its directors are to be staggered and that no director can be removed from office without due cause, a bidder cannot gain control of the board for some years, even if he has a controlling interest of the shares. *See* POISON PILL.

STAGS Acronym for Sterling Transferable Accruing Government Securities. These European sterling bonds are backed by a holding of Treasury stock. They are *deep-discount bonds paying no interest.

stakeholder pension scheme In the UK, a type of low-cost pension available since April 2001. Stakeholder pensions are bought from authorized financial institutions, such as insurance companies, banks, and building societies. The pension providers can only charge a maximum of 1% of the value of the pension fund each year to manage the fund, plus costs. Any extra services and any extra charges not provided for by law, such as advice on choosing a pension or life assurance cover, must be optional. All stakeholder schemes will accept contributions of as little as £20, payable weekly, monthly, or at less regular intervals. The scheme must be run by trustees or by an authorized stakeholder manager.

Employers with five or more employees were formerly required to make a stakeholder pension scheme available to their staff; from 2017 this will be replaced by automatic enrolment of most employees into workplace pension schemes, most of which will be stakeholder schemes in form.

SEE WEB LINKS
- Guide to stakeholder pensions from the Pensions Regulator

stakeholders All those with interests in an organization; for example, as *shareholders, employees, suppliers, customers, or members of the wider community (who could be affected by environmental consequences of an organization's activities). **Stakeholder theory** is an approach to business that attempts to incorporate the interests of all stakeholders in a business, as opposed to the view that a firm is responsible only to its owners (*see* SHAREHOLDER VALUE). It thus attempts to adopt an inclusive rather than a narrow approach to business responsibility.

stale bull A dealer or speculator who has a *long position in something, usually a commodity, which is showing a *paper profit but which the dealer cannot realize as there are no buyers at the higher levels. Being fully committed financially and therefore unable to increase the bull position, the dealer may be unable to trade.

stale cheque A cheque that, in the UK, has not been presented for payment within six months of being written. The bank will not honour it, returning it marked 'out of date'.

stalemate industry An industry in which there are few opportunities to create competitive advantages against existing products. *Compare* SPECIALIZED INDUSTRY.

stamp duty A tax collected by stamping the legal documents giving effect to certain transactions: the rate of duty is ½% of the consideration given, the charge being rounded up to the nearest £5. Since 1 December 2003 stamp duty proper has been charged solely on traditional stampable documents relating to shares and securities (including bearer instruments). A transfer of shares and securities that is made without a stampable document (i.e. electronically) is charged to *stamp duty reserve tax. A transfer of land is now charged to *stamp duty land tax.

stamp duty land tax (SDLT) A tax charged on the consideration given for the sale of land in the UK. Until 4 December 2014 the tax charge was a percentage of the total purchase price of the property, with a higher percentage being charged on the more expensive properties. It is now calculated on a banded basis similar to income tax, with a charge of 0.3% on that part of the sale price that falls between £100,000 and £150,000, 0.8% on that between £150,000 and £200,000, 1.3% between £200,000 and £250,000, and so on, up to a maximum of 10.3% for £5 million and above.

stamp duty reserve tax (SDRT) A tax levied on the transaction when a shareholding is transferred without a document, or when the document is kept outside the UK. The majority of transactions on UK exchanges are now electronic and 'paperless'. Like *stamp duty, stamp duty reserve tax is charged on the consideration given, not on the market value of the shareholding.

Standard and Poor's 500 (S&P) A US *credit rating agency and financial services company based in New York. S&P rates the bonds issued by companies, public corporations, and sovereign states on a scale from AAA downwards to D: a rating of BBB or above denotes 'investment grade', lower ratings 'speculative grade'. The company also publishes a series of stock-market indexes, the widest being the **S&P 500**.

SEE WEB LINKS
- Website of Standard and Poor's

standard application blank (SAB) A standardized application form used to obtain *biodata on the candidates for a job. This enables objective scoring of the candidates according to the information supplied. In a **weighted application blank (WAB)** different weightings are applied to the various categories of data according to their importance as predictors of success in the job.

standard cash flow pattern In a *discounted cash flow calculation, the situation in which the projected cash flows are made up of an initial cash outflow followed by subsequent cash inflows over the life of the project, there being no net cash outflows in subsequent years. Such patterns are rare in practice.

standard cost In *standard costing systems, a predetermined unit cost of a product or service. It is important to emphasize that standard cost is a unit cost concept.

standard cost allowance Under a *standard costing system, the level of expenditure allowed to be incurred for *variable costs, taking into account the actual levels of activity achieved. For example, the standard cost allowance for *direct materials is obtained from the actual number of units produced multiplied by the *standard direct materials cost per unit.

standard costing A system of cost ascertainment and control in which predetermined *standard costs and income for products and operations are set and periodically compared with actual costs incurred and income generated in order to establish any *variances. Standard costing systems are very expensive to develop and maintain; they were also designed for traditional manufacturing systems in which direct labour and direct materials are the most important costs. Recent years have seen a decline in the use of such systems as companies become less labour intensive.

standard deviation A measure of the dispersion of statistical data. For a series of n values x_1, x_2, x_n, it is given by the formula

$$\sqrt{[(1/n)\sum(x_i - x)]}$$

where x is the average of the n values. The standard deviation of the returns from an investment can be used as a measure of the risk associated with that investment.

standard direct labour cost In *standard costing, a standard cost derived from the *standard time allowed for the performance of an operation and the *standard direct labour rate for the operators specified for that operation.

standard direct labour rate A predetermined rate of pay for *direct labour operators used for establishing *standard direct labour costs in a *standard costing system; it provides a basis for comparison with the actual direct labour rates paid.

standard direct materials cost In *standard costing, a standard cost derived from the standard quantity of materials allowed for the production of a product and the *standard direct materials price for the materials specified for that product.

standard direct materials price In *standard costing, a predetermined price for *direct materials used for establishing *standard direct materials costs in order to provide a basis for comparison with the actual direct material prices paid.

standard fixed overhead cost In *standard costing, a standard cost derived from the standard time allowed for the performance of an operation or the production of a product and the standard fixed overhead *absorption rate per unit of time for that operation or product.

standard hour A measure of production (not time) that represents the amount of work, number of units produced, etc., that can be achieved within an hour under normal conditions. It is used to calculate the *efficiency ratio and a range of *variances that measure the more or less efficient use of *direct labour or production time.

Standard Industrial Classification (SIC) A system developed by the UK and US governments for classifying various industries in order to produce official industrial statistical information. The basis of the classification is an industry's supply characteristic. The British classification now follows the principles of the UN's International Standard Industrial Classification.

standardization strategy See GLOBALIZATION STRATEGY.

standardized marketing mix A marketing strategy adopted by multinational companies for using basically the same products, advertising, distribution channels, and other elements of the *marketing mix in all the company's international markets. *See* GLOBALIZATION STRATEGY.

standard marginal costing In a *marginal costing system, a system of cost ascertainment and control in which predetermined standards for marginal costs and income generated for products and operations are set and periodically compared with actual marginal costs incurred and income generated in order to establish any *variances.

standard materials usage In *standard costing, a predetermined quantity of materials to be used in the manufacture of a product; this is compared with actual usage of *direct materials to calculate any *variance.

standard mix 1. The predetermined proportions in which a mixture of different materials are intended to be used in a manufacturing process. It is set as a standard for the purposes of calculating any *variances arising from differences in the proportions or quantity of direct materials used. **2.** The budgeted total volume of sales of an organization expressed in predetermined proportions of its range of related products. It is set as a standard for the purposes of calculating any variances arising from differences in the actual *sales mix or volume of sales achieved.

standard operating cost The total of all the *standard cost allowances for the actual level of activity achieved by an organization.

standard operating profit The *budgeted revenue from an operation less the *standard operating cost.

standard overhead cost A standard cost for the fixed and/or variable overhead of an operation derived from the standard time allowed for the performance of the operation or the production of a product and the standard overhead *absorption rate per unit of time for that operation or product.

standard performance (standard operator performance) A concept used in *work measurement to achieve comparability between a range of observations, for determining standard overhead costs, and as the basis for the calculation of some performance-related bonus schemes. Standard performance is defined as the rate of output that a qualified worker achieves as an average over the working day, shift, or hour provided that the worker adheres to the specified work method and is well motivated. This performance is denoted as 100 on the standard rating and performance scales.

standard production cost The *production costs of products and operations calculated from predetermined levels of performance and cost in order to provide a yardstick against which actual production costs can be compared for the purposes of cost ascertainment and control.

standard purchase price A predetermined price set for each commodity of *direct material for a specified period. These prices are compared with the actual prices paid during the period in order to establish *direct materials price variances in a system of *standard costing.

standard rate 1. The rate of *value added tax applied to all items sold by *taxable persons that are not specified as either *exempt supplies, *zero-rated goods and services, or taxable at a special rate. The rate for 2015–16 is 20%. **2.** The marginal rate of tax for most taxpayers. *See* BASIC RATE OF INCOME TAX.

standard rate of pay A predetermined rate of pay set for each classification of labour for a period. These rates are compared with the actual rates paid during the period in order to establish *direct labour rate of pay *variances in a system of *standard costing.

standard selling price A predetermined selling price set for each product sold for a specified period. In *standard costing, these prices are compared with the actual prices obtained during the period in order to establish any *variance.

standard time The time allowed to carry out a production task in a *standard costing system. It may be expressed as the standard time allowed or alternatively, when expressed in *standard hours, as the output achieved.

standard variable overhead cost A standard cost derived from the standard time allowed for the performance of an operation or the production of a product and the standard variable overhead *absorption rate per unit of time for that operation or product.

standby agreement An agreement between the *International Monetary Fund and a member state, enabling the member to arrange for immediate drawing rights in addition to its normal drawing rights in such cases of emergency as a temporary balance of payments crisis.

standby credit A *letter of credit that guarantees a loan or other form of credit facility. The bank that issues it promises to refund the amount borrowed if the borrower defaults on repayment. It calls for a certificate of default by the applicant. In a *note issuance facility a standby credit is a third-party guarantee to honour an issue to an investor who may have a low credit rating. *See also* REVOLVING BANK FACILITY.

standing order An instruction by a customer to a bank (**banker's order**) or building society to pay a specified amount of money on a specified date or dates to a specified payee. Standing orders are widely used for such regular payments as insurance premiums, subscriptions, etc. *See also* CREDIT TRANSFER.

standstill agreement 1. An agreement between two countries in which a debt owed by one to the other is held in abeyance until a specified date in the future. **2.** An agreement between an unwelcome bidder for a company and the company, in which the bidder agrees to buy no more of the company's shares for a specified

period. **3.** An arrangement between banks who have loans to a company in trouble, in which they each agree to maintain their existing credit facilities and not to force the company into receivership by acting alone.

star *See* BOSTON MATRIX.

start-up A new business or other project, especially one seeking finance.

start-up costs The initial expenditure incurred in the setting up of an operation or project. The start-up costs may include the capital investment costs plus the initial revenue expenditure prior to the start of operations.

state banks Commercial banks in the USA that were established by state charter rather than federal charter (*compare* NATIONAL BANKS). The rules governing their trading are controlled by state laws and there are therefore differences in practices from state to state. State banks are not compelled to join the *Federal Reserve System, although national banks are. State banks are regulated by state banking departments and by the Federal Deposit Insurance Corporation (FDIC). Even if they choose not to join the Federal Reserve System, they must abide by its rules, particularly on consumer credit protection.

State Earnings-Related Pension Scheme (SERPS) *See* STATE SECOND PENSION.

statement of account A document recording the transactions of an organization with its customer for a specified period and normally showing the indebtedness of one to the other. Many firms issue statements to their customers every month to draw attention to any unpaid invoices.

statement of affairs A statement showing the assets and liabilities of a person who is bankrupt or of a company in liquidation.

Statement of Auditing Standards (SAS) Any of a series of statements issued by the Auditing Practices Board (APB) on basic principles and essential procedures in auditing. Auditors were required to comply with an SAS, except where otherwise stated in the SAS concerned, in the conduct of any audit of *financial statements for periods commencing before 15 December 2004. For periods commencing on or after that date, *International Standards on Auditing (UK and Ireland) are to be applied.

statement of cash flows The usual *International Financial Reporting Standard term for a *cash-flow statement.

statement of changes in equity (SOCE) The usual *International Financial Reporting Standard term for the *reconciliation of movements in shareholders' funds.

statement of changes in financial position The US equivalent of the UK *cash flow statement.

statement of comprehensive income The usual *International Financial

Reporting Standard term for the *statement of total recognized gains and losses.

Statement of Financial Accounting Standards (SFAS) In the USA, any of the statements detailing the *financial accounting and reporting requirements of the Financial Accounting Standards Board. These accounting standards are *generally accepted accounting principles and should be followed by accountants responsible for the preparation of *financial statements.

statement of financial position The usual *International Financial Reporting Standard term for a *balance sheet.

statement of movements in shareholders' funds *See* RECONCILIATION OF MOVEMENTS IN SHAREHOLDERS' FUNDS.

Statement of Standard Accounting Practice (SSAP) Any of a series of accounting standards issued by the Accounting Standards Committee between

---

STATEMENTS OF STANDARD ACCOUNTING PRACTICE

1. Accounting for the Results of Associated Companies
2. Disclosure of Accounting Policies
3. Earnings per Share
4. The Accounting Treatment of Government Grants
5. Accounting for Value Added Tax
6. Extraordinary Items and Prior Year Adjustments
7. Accounting for the Changes in the Purchasing Power of Money (provisional)
8. The Treatment of Taxation under the Imputation System
9. Stocks and Work in Progress
10. Statement of Sources and Application of Funds
11. Accounting for Deferred Taxation
12. Accounting for Depreciation
13. Accounting for Research and Development
14. Group Accounts
15. Current Cost Accounting
16. Accounting for Post Balance Sheet Events
17. Accounting for Contingencies
18. Accounting for Investment Properties
19. Foreign Currency Translation
20. Accounting for Leases and Hire Purchase Contracts
21. Accounting for Goodwill
22. Accounting for Acquisitions and Mergers
23. Accounting for Pension Costs
24. Segmental Reporting

1971 and 1990. Many were subsequently replaced by the later *Financial Reporting Standard and all have now been superseded by the Financial Reporting Standard Applicable in the UK and Republic of Ireland.

statement of terms of employment

A statement in writing that an employer must give to certain employees under the terms of the Employment Rights Act 1996, which aims to comply with the EU Proof of Employment Relationship Directive. Not later than two months after the beginning of employment, an employer must give to every employee a written statement setting out the following information:

- the names of employer and employee;
- the date employment began;
- the date when the employee's continuous employment began;
- the scale or rate of remuneration or method of calculating remuneration;
- the intervals at which remuneration is paid;
- the hours of work;
- the holiday entitlement (which must be sufficiently specific to allow the employee's holiday entitlement to be precisely calculated);
- the procedure to be adopted in the event of incapacity for work as a result of sickness or injury (including sick pay provisions, if any);
- pensions and pension schemes;
- the length of notice the employee is obliged to give and entitled to receive to terminate the contract;
- the title of the job the employee is employed to do or, as an alternative to the job title, a brief description of the work;
- if the employment is not intended to be permanent, the period for which it is expected to continue or, if it is for a fixed term, the date it is intended to end;
- either the place of work or, if the employee is required to work at various places, an indication that this is the case;
- any collective bargaining agreements that directly affect the terms and conditions of employment.

Where there are no particulars to be given (for example, if there is no pension scheme), this must be indicated.

If the employee is required to work outside the UK for more than one month there is a requirement for additional information to be given relating to the length of the period of this employment, the currency in which remuneration is to be paid in that period, details of additional remuneration or benefits connected with working outside the UK, and the repatriation arrangements.

The statement must also include a note giving certain details of the employer's disciplinary and grievance procedures and stating whether or not a pensions contracting-out certificate is in force. The note of disciplinary and grievance procedures must cover any disciplinary rules and dismissal procedures that apply to the employee.

Some of these particulars may be provided by way of reference to documents other than the written statement, provided the employee has reasonable opportunities to read these documents in the course of his employment.

If any amendment is made to any of these terms after the statement has been (or should have been) issued, the employer must give the employee a written statement setting out the details of the change not later than one month after the change has been made.

Failure to comply with any of these requirements gives the employee the right to complain to an *employment tribunal at any time during the currency of the employment, or within three months of the employment coming to an end.

The written statement, although providing evidence of the terms of employment, is not itself the *contract of employment.

statement of total recognized gains and losses (statement of comprehensive income)

A *financial statement showing the extent to which *shareholders' equity has increased or decreased from all the various gains and losses recognized in the period. It includes profits and losses for the period, together with all other movements on *reserves reflecting recognized gains and losses attributable to shareholders. Such a statement has been a required item in the annual accounts of UK companies since 1993.

state ownership *See* NATIONALIZATION; PUBLIC SECTOR.

State Second Pension (SSP; S2P) A scheme run by the UK government to provide a *pension in addition to the basic state retirement pension. It was introduced in April 2002 to replace the existing **State Earnings Related Pension Scheme (SERPS)**. Contributions are made through National Insurance payments. It was formerly possible to contract out of SSP by subscribing to an occupational pension scheme or a personal pension scheme; from 2012, however, it is only possible to contract out through a defined-benefit scheme operated by an employer.

static risk *See* INSURABLE RISK.

Stationery Office (TSO) The privatized body that took over most of the functions of **Her Majesty's Stationery Office** (HMSO) in 1996. TSO publishes and sells government publications, such as White Papers, Acts of Parliament, and official statistical information, etc., both online and through selected bookshops.

(((⊕))) SEE WEB LINKS
• TSO's online bookshop

statistical demand analysis A set of statistical procedures used to discover the most important real factors affecting sales and their relative influence; the most commonly analysed factors are prices, income, population, and promotion.

statistical process control (SPC) A technique for checking whether or not a product or service is conforming to its design specification, by means of sampling during production or delivery. Small variations in the output of a process are inevitable. For example, when cutting a machine part slight changes in material hardness, operating temperature, etc., will cause dimensions to vary very slightly.

Using statistical techniques, SPC defines the limits of these variations that can be accepted. Provided sampled outputs stay within this range the process is in control. *See* CONTROL CHART.

statistics 1. The branch of mathematics concerned with the collection, analysis, organization, and presentation of information in numerical form. It is based on the assumption that if a group is sufficiently large, it will, unlike an individual, behave in a regular and reproducible manner. For groups that are not large enough for this assumption to be true, a measure of the likelihood of an event happening is its *probability. Much of statistics is concerned with calculating and interpreting probabilities. *See also* DISTRIBUTION; STANDARD DEVIATION. **2.** The numbers by which information is expressed. *See also* OFFICE FOR NATIONAL STATISTICS.

status enquiry *See* BANKER'S REFERENCE.

statute-barred debt A debt that has not been collected within the period allowed by law. *See* LIMITATION OF ACTIONS.

statutory accounts Accounts required by law, as by the Companies Act. *See also* STATUTORY BOOKS.

statutory audit An *audit of a company as required by the Companies Act, subject to *small company exemptions. The auditors are required to report to the company's members on all accounts of the company, copies of which are laid before the company in general meeting. Companies with a *turnover of not more than £6.5 million and a *balance sheet total of not more than £3.26 million may be exempt from the statutory audit. The government has increased the audit threshold significantly in recent years to reduce costs for small companies.

Statutory Audit Directive An EU directive (2006) designed to enhance public confidence in the auditing profession within the EU, chiefly by increasing accountability. Together with the *Company Reporting Directive, the Statutory

Audit Directive is often seen as providing a European equivalent to the US *Sarbanes–Oxley Act (Sox); as such, the two directives are often referred to jointly as **Eurosox**.

statutory books The *books of account that the Companies Act requires a company to keep. They must show and explain the company's transactions, disclose with reasonable accuracy the company's financial position at any time, and enable the directors to ensure that any accounts prepared therefrom comply with the provisions of the act. They must also include entries from day to day of all money received and paid out together with a record of all assets and liabilities and statements of stockholding (where appropriate). *See also* PROPER ACCOUNTING RECORDS.

statutory company *See* COMPANY.

statutory maternity pay (SMP) *See* MATERNITY RIGHTS.

statutory sick pay (SSP) A compulsory scheme operated by an employer. Payments are made to an employee for up to 28 weeks of absence as a result of sickness. There are two rates of statutory sick pay, the applicable level being determined by the employee's earnings. The two qualifying conditions for SSP are:

• there must be a period of incapacity for work;
• there must be one or more qualifying days.

The first three days do not count and so it is only on the fourth consecutive day that an entitlement to SSP begins.

stealth tax (hidden tax) A tax, the incidence of which may be hidden from the person who is suffering it. An example could be a tax levied on goods at the wholesale level, which increases the retail price in such a way that the final customer cannot detect either that it has happened or the amount of the extra cost. The term is also applied to various mechanisms by which the government can increase the tax paid by individuals without raising tax rates, notably the abolition or restriction of tax allowances and the adjustment of thresholds.

stepped costs *See* SEMI-VARIABLE COST.

stepped preference share A *preference share that earns a predetermined income, which rises steadily by a set amount each year to the winding-up date; there is also a predetermined capital growth.

stereotyping Making assumptions about individuals (which may or may not be correct) on the basis of the groups to which they belong or are held to belong. Such assumptions may be based on age, class, gender, ethnic origin, nationality, religion, or sexuality. Unfortunately, human beings are liable to have selective prejudices towards their fellows, seeing only what they want to see and ignoring factors that do not fit in with their preconceived beliefs. They also tend to assume that all members of a group have the same, or similar, characteristics. Thus:

• all graduates are clever
• all unemployed people are lazy

are two of the stereotypes that have to be resisted in carrying out job selection interviews. *See also* HORNS AND HALO EFFECT.

sterling The UK *pound, as distinguished from the pounds of other countries. The name derives from the small star *steorra* (Old English) that appeared on early Norman pennies.

Sterling Overnight Index Average *See* SONIA.

Sterling Transferable Accruing Government Securities *See* STAGS.

Stewardship Code A code of best practice for institutional investors, such as pension funds, insurance companies, and *investment trusts, first issued in 2010. It provides guidelines on how such vehicles should engage with their investee companies, notably in the exercise of voting rights. The Code operates on the same 'comply or explain' basis as the UK *Corporate Governance Code.

(((●))) SEE WEB LINKS
• Full text of the UK Stewardship Code (2012)

stickiness A tendency for certain economic variables, notably prices and wages, to 'stick' at or near their existing levels despite changes in supply and demand. For example, companies tend not to cut the wages of existing employees, even where market forces might seem to demand this; wages (like prices) are therefore said to be 'sticky downward'. Various factors have been cited to explain such stickiness: these include the limited information available to transactors, the role of long-term fixed-price or fixed-wage contracts, the hidden costs of repricing (*see* MENU COSTS), and consumer resistance to sudden or frequent change.

stock 1. In the UK, a fixed-interest security (*see* GILT-EDGED SECURITY) issued by the government, local authority, or a company in fixed units, often of £100 each. They usually have a *redemption date on which the *par value of the unit price is repaid in full. They are dealt in on stock exchanges at prices that fluctuate, but depend on such factors as their *yield and the time they have to run before redemption. *See also* TAP STOCK. **2.** The US name for an *ordinary share. **3.** The stock-in-trade of an organization. *See* INVENTORY. **4.** Any collection of assets, e.g. the stock of plant and machinery owned by a company.

stock appreciation/depreciation The amount by which the value of the *inventory of an organization has increased or decreased over any given period. This may be owing to inflation, in which case the increase in value will be recorded in the accounts as a profit, although it is not a real profit as when the goods are sold they will need to be replaced at an inflated price. Stock-in-trade may also appreciate or depreciate genuinely as a result of market fluctuations, especially of raw materials.

stockbroker An agent who buys and sells securities on a stock exchange on behalf of clients and receives remuneration for this service in the form of a commission. Before October 1986 (*see* BIG BANG), stockbrokers on the *London Stock Exchange were not permitted to act as principals

(*stockjobbers) and worked for a fixed commission laid down by the Stock Exchange. Since October 1986, however, many London stockbrokers have taken advantage of the new rules, which allow them to buy and sell as principals, in which capacity they are now known as *market makers. This change has been accompanied by the formal abolition of fixed commissions, enabling stockbrokers to vary their commission in competition with each other. Stockbrokers have traditionally offered investment advice, especially for their institutional investors.

stock control (inventory control) Regulation of the *inventory (stock-in-trade) of a company so that all components or items are available without delay but without tying up unnecessarily large sums of money. Stock control is a discipline well suited to computerization. Many large manufacturers, retailers, etc., have a computerized stock-control system with automatic reordering when the stock of an item reaches a predetermined low level. In retail supermarkets, for example, the act of registering a sale at the check-out reduces the quantity of that item on the computer-held stock record; new deliveries are entered as they arrive. Thus, the stock at any instant can be read from the computer. A periodic check of the actual stock reveals the extent of pilfering. *See also* PERPETUAL INVENTORY.

stock cover The time for which a company's stock of raw materials would last, without replenishment at the current rate of sale or use.

stock depreciation *See* STOCK APPRECIATION/DEPRECIATION.

stock exchange (stock market) A market in which *securities are bought and sold, prices being controlled by supply and demand. Stock markets have developed hand in hand with *capitalism since the 17th century, constantly growing in importance and complexity. The basic function of a stock exchange is to enable public companies, governments, and local authorities to raise *capital by selling securities to investors. The secondary market function of a stock exchange is to enable these investors to sell their securities to others, providing liquidity and reducing the risks attached to investment. Most countries now have stock exchanges. The major international stock exchanges are based in New York, London, Tokyo, Hong Kong, and Shanghai.

Stock Exchange Automated Quotations System (SEAQ) A computerized system used on the *London Stock Exchange to record the prices quoted by *market makers. The shares in the FTSE 250 Index are now traded in the Stock Exchange Trading System (SETS) rather than via SEAQ; this means that SEAQ is now mainly used to record prices on the *Alternative Investment Market.

Stock Exchange Trading System (SETS) The London Stock Exchange order-driven electronic trading system that came into operation in 1997. It has increasingly replaced the previous quote-driven system (*see* STOCK EXCHANGE AUTOMATED QUOTATIONS SYSTEM). Buyers and sellers enter their orders, which are matched automatically. The price of the transaction is then automatically recorded on a trading report and passes into the settlement system. SETS covers the 250 shares of the FTSE 250 index and other *blue chip securities.

stockholder The usual US name for a *shareholder.

stock-in-trade 1. *See* INVENTORY. *See also* STOCK APPRECIATION/DEPRECIATION; STOCK CONTROL; STOCK TURNOVER. **2.** The goods or services that an organization normally offers for sale.

stockjobber (jobber) A wholesale dealer on the *London Stock Exchange prior to the *Big Bang (October 1986). Stockjobbers were only permitted to deal with the general public through the intermediary of a *stockbroker. This single capacity system was replaced by the *dual-capacity system of *market makers after the Big Bang.

stockless production system A production system that does not permit stocks to be held in the process. *See* JUST IN TIME.

stock market 1. *See* STOCK EXCHANGE. **2.** A market in which livestock are bought and sold.

stock market index *See* SHARE INDEX.

stock of money *See* MONEY SUPPLY.

stock option 1. *See* SHARE OPTION. **2.** *See* OPTION.

stock-out costs The extra costs incurred when stocks are not available to meet demand. These extra costs result from lost sales, overtime spent trying to make up the deficiency, and penalty clauses.

stockpile 1. An unusually large stock of a raw material held by an organization in anticipation of a shortage, transport strike, planned production increase, etc. **2.** A large stock of strategic materials, food, etc., built up by a government in anticipation of a war, a break in trading relations with a supplier nation, etc.

stock policy An insurance policy covering the goods stocked and sold by a commercial company for specified risks or for all risks (*see* ALL-RISKS POLICY). Policies of this kind are usually based on the price paid for the stock, not the price at which it might be sold, i.e. the insurance does not cover loss of profit or mark-up on the stock.

stock split *See* SCRIP ISSUE.

stocktaking The process of counting and evaluating inventory (stock-in-trade), usually at an organization's year end in order to value the total stock for preparation of the accounts. In more sophisticated organizations, in which permanent stock records are maintained, stock is counted on a random basis throughout the year to compare quantities counted with the quantities that appear in the, usually, computerized records.

stock turnover The number of times in a year that the *stock-in-trade of an organization is deemed to have been sold. This is best found by dividing the total cost of the goods sold in a year by an average value of the stock-in-trade (*see* RATE OF TURNOVER). The faster the stock is turned over, the more opportunities there are to make profits on it and therefore the lower the margins that are required; for example a supermarket, in which the stock is turned over frequently, makes lower margins than a jeweller's shop, in which high-priced goods are sold infrequently.

stock valuation *See* INVENTORY VALUATION.

Stock Watch The unit of the New York Stock Exchange that monitors share dealing to identify irregular or illegal behaviour.

stock watering 1. Any of various practices in which a company inflates the value of its assets or exaggerates its profits as a pretext for issuing an unjustified amount of shares. Fraudulent practices of this kind were particularly associated with the US railway boom of the late 19th century. **2.** A derogatory term for the *dilution of equity in a company.

stop-loss order An order placed with a broker in a security or commodity market to close an *open position at a specified price in order to limit a loss. It may be used in a volatile market, especially by a speculator, if the market looks as if it might move strongly against his position.

stop notice A court procedure available to protect those who have an interest in shares but have not been registered as company members. The notice prevents the company from registering a transfer of the shares or paying a dividend upon them without informing the server of the notice. It was formerly known as **notice in lieu of distringas**.

stop order An order placed with a broker in a security or commodity market to buy if prices rise to a specified level or sell if they fall to another specified level.

stoppage *in transitu* A remedy available to an unpaid seller of goods when the buyer has become insolvent and the goods are still in course of transit. If the seller gives notice of stoppage to the carrier or other bailee of the goods, the seller is entitled to have them redelivered and may then retain possession of them until the price is paid. If the right is not exercised, the goods will fall into the insolvent buyer's estate and go towards satisfying the creditors.

storage area network *See* SAN.

store card A plastic card issued by a store or retail chain that entitles the holder to purchase goods or services up to a prescribed limit from that store or outlets in the chain. Customers receive monthly statements from the retailer, or a finance company appointed by the retailer; they may settle the bill in full without interest, or make a specified minimum payment and pay interest on the outstanding balance. *See also* CHARGE CARD.

store image The image formed by a consumer of a particular store. It is affected by the personnel, the range of merchandise, the external and internal appearance of the store, the level of prices, and the standard of service provided.

storyboard A sequence of sketches and cartoons to show the main elements in a television or cinema advertisement.

stotin A former monetary unit of Slovenia worth one hundredth of a *tolar.

stotinka (*plural* **stotinki**) A monetary unit of Bulgaria, worth one hundredth of a *lev.

stowage plan A plan of a ship showing where all the cargo on a particular voyage was stowed.

straddle A strategy used by dealers in *options or *futures contracts. In the option market it involves simultaneously purchasing put and call options; it is most profitable when the price of the underlying security is very volatile. *Compare* BUTTERFLY. In commodity and currency futures a straddle may involve buying and selling options or both buying and selling

S

the same commodity or currency for delivery in the future, often on different markets. Undoing half the straddle is known as *breaking a leg.

straight *See* EUROBOND.

straight bond A *bond issued in the *primary market that carries no equity or other incentive to attract the investor; its only reward is an annual or biannual interest coupon together with a promise to repay the capital at par on the redemption date.

straight-line method A method of calculating the amount by which a *fixed asset is to be depreciated in an accounting period, in which the *depreciation to be charged against income is based on the original cost or valuation, less the asset's estimated *net residual value, divided by its estimated life in years. This has the effect of a constant annual depreciation charge against profits year by year. In some circumstances the net residual value is ignored.

straight product extension Marketing a product in a foreign market without any change to the product sold in the home market.

straight rebuy *Business buyer behaviour characterized by automatic and regular repurchasing of familiar products from regular suppliers.

stranding The running aground of a ship as a consequence of an unusual event. For the purposes of *marine insurance, stranding does not include running aground and being refloated; it might involve being driven onto rocks when taking avoiding action, or a similar event.

strap A triple *option on a share or commodity market, consisting of one put option and two call options at the same price and for the same period. *Compare* STRIP.

strapline A slogan often used in conjunction with a brand's name in advertising and other promotions.

strategic alliance (alliance; strategic partnership) An agreement between two or more firms to engage in an activity on a shared basis. The outside activities of each partner are not affected by the alliance, which is designed to build on the expertise of each member and the way in which they complement each other. Strategic alliances are generally less formal and far-ranging than *joint ventures and may often be designed to last for a limited time. *See also* CONSORTIUM.

strategic asset A source of *competitive advantage derived from factors outside a firm rather than from its own competence. Such sources could include proximity to raw materials or aspects of government policy. *See also* ABSOLUTE COST ADVANTAGE.

strategic behaviour The behaviour of firms or individuals that is aimed at influencing the structure of a *market. In traditional economics, such situations as *monopoly or *oligopoly were seen as the outcome of technological conditions and the state of demand. More recently, it has been observed that a particular firm or individual can influence its competitors in the market in various ways, for example by threatening a *price war if other firms attempt to enter the market. *See* INDUSTRIAL ORGANIZATION ECONOMICS. *See also* GAME THEORY; MARKETING WARFARE STRATEGY; PREDATORY PRICING STRATEGY.

strategic business unit (SBU) An autonomous division of a large company that is responsible for planning the marketing of a particular range of products.

strategic choice The alternative strategic plans available to an organization. The degree of choice in formulating a firm's *business strategy is likely to be determined by its resources and by such external factors as competition and environmental issues. Managerial competence, in terms of a firm's ability to manage a new area of activity or an acquisition, will also influence the choice and, therefore, a firm's future strategic development. *See*

DIVERSIFICATION; EXTERNAL GROWTH; INTERNAL GROWTH.

strategic decision making The process in which senior management makes long-term policy decisions that set the general direction and objectives of a company. It involves looking at the challenges and opportunities an industry faces over time and evaluating the most appropriate course of action for the company as a whole. *See* BUSINESS STRATEGY; STRATEGIC MANAGEMENT.

strategic drift The limitations placed on *strategic choice by assumptions made in the past and the application of previously tried remedies. It may restrict a firm from making the radical strategies required to deal with a changing environment.

strategic financial management An approach to management that applies financial techniques to strategic decision making. *See also* STRATEGIC MANAGEMENT ACCOUNTING.

strategic fit The extent to which *diversification into another field fits with the future scope of a firm. To evaluate whether or not the proposed action would fit strategically with a firm's plans requires the strategic logic to be examined in detail and the extent to which integration could be achieved to be evaluated.

strategic gap analysis A method of examining a business strategy and establishing whether or not it will meet a desired objective. If a failure to achieve this objective is predicted, there is a performance gap between the hoped-for and expected states. This gap can be closed by means of a modified strategy, which will need to be formulated.

strategic group A sub-group of firms within a market or industry that occupy a similar position in terms of e.g. product range, geographic coverage, pricing policy, and distribution channels. These companies have adopted similar business strategies, face similar challenges and opportunities, and must be considered

direct competitors. Strategic group analysis will show which companies are the closest competitors, and can also be used to identify potential gaps or opportunities in a market sector. *See also* MOBILITY BARRIERS.

strategic human-resource management (SHRM) A systematic attempt to integrate the use of human resources with the wider long-term business strategy of an organization. *See* HUMAN-RESOURCE MANAGEMENT; STRATEGIC MANAGEMENT.

strategic indicators *See* PERFORMANCE MEASUREMENT.

strategic intent A clearly understood statement of the direction in which a firm intends to develop. It should be both understood and interpreted by each employee in relation to their work and is a crucial element in the strategic management of a firm. *See also* MISSION STATEMENT.

strategic investment appraisal An appraisal of an investment decision based on wider grounds than that provided by a purely financial appraisal. It is also necessary to evaluate possible long-term strategic benefits and any intangible factors that may be relevant to the decision, particularly if advanced manufacturing technology is concerned.

strategic management An approach to management that formulates overall long-term objectives for the company, develops policies to achieve these objectives, and takes concrete steps to implement policy across all the functions of the organization. The process begins with a *position audit that analyses the strengths and weaknesses of the company and the opportunities and threats of the market (*see* INDUSTRY STRUCTURE ANALYSIS; SWOT). This should lead to a statement of *strategic intent and a *strategic plan. Implementation of the plan will require the allocation of sufficient resources (financial, human, technical), the establishment of appropriate structures, and constant monitoring of results. Finally, mechanisms must be set in place that allow

S

for the reassessment of individual policies and the overall strategy itself as circumstances evolve. *See also* BUSINESS STRATEGY.

strategic management accounting A *management accounting system organized so that it is capable of providing the information needed for long-term strategic decision making, as opposed to the more traditional approach of providing short-term costs. Strategic management accounting, for example, provides information that will assist in the pricing strategy for new products and decisions relating to the expansion of capacity.

strategic misrepresentation In planning and budgeting, the tendency for those presenting projects for approval knowingly to understate costs and overstate benefits. This is a matter of deliberate policy and thus distinct from *optimism bias, *planning fallacy, or simple miscalculation. Those who adopt such a policy would probably justify it as an expected part of the negotiation 'game' and argue that many worthwhile projects would never get approval if the true costs were revealed at the start.

strategic plan A plan describing how a firm will adapt to take advantage of opportunities in its constantly changing environment, in order to maintain a *strategic fit between the firm's goals and capabilities and these market opportunities.

strategic styles The ways in which large diversified businesses control their subsidiary companies. Broadly, three strategies have been defined:

- **strategic planning**, in which the central organization develops a detailed overall masterplan with specified targets for the subsidiaries;
- **financial control**, in which the central organization acts as banker to the subsidiaries, setting tight financial targets and regularly monitoring performance;
- **strategic control**, in which the central organization sets an overall strategy, but agrees a *business plan with each

subsidiary and monitors each one against the agreed plan.

See also PARENTING.

stratified sampling A sampling procedure in which a population is divided into two or more mutually exclusive and collectively exhaustive strata and a fixed proportion of the total sample is drawn from each stratum. *See* DISPROPORTIONATE STRATIFIED SAMPLING; PROPORTIONATE STRATIFIED SAMPLING; QUOTA SAMPLING.

street-name stocks The US name for nominee stocks (*see* NOMINEE SHAREHOLDING).

stress reduction A decrease in the number of situations that cause a person stressful experiences. Personal strategies that achieve this end include avoiding situations that cause distress and planning ahead. Organizational strategies include training programmes and job redesign. Individuals can also increase their ability to endure stress, without experiencing dysfunctional results; this stress resilience is helped by exercise, diet, and weight control.

stress testing A method of *risk analysis in which *simulations are used to estimate the impact of worst-case situations. It is commonly used by regulators, rating agencies, and financial institutions, which base their simulations on both historical and hypothetical crises.

strike An organized refusal on the part of a group of employees to work, in an attempt to force their employers to concede to their demands for higher pay, shorter hours, better working conditions, etc. An **official strike** is one that takes place on the instructions of a trade union, whereas an **unofficial strike** is one that takes place without union backing. A **wildcat strike** is called at short notice in contravention of an agreement not to strike and it does not have union backing. A **sympathetic strike** is one in which one union calls its members out on strike to support another union, although it is not in dispute with its own employers. A **token strike** is a short withdrawal of labour, e.g. for an hour or two or even for one day, to threaten employers of more serious action to come if the employees' demands are not met. In a **general strike** most of the trade unions in a country call out their members, virtually bringing the country to a standstill.

Under UK law, a trade union cannot call its members out on strike unless a majority has voted for the action in a secret ballot.

strike price (striking price) 1. *See* EXERCISE PRICE. **2.** The price fixed by the sellers of a security after receiving bids from would-be buyers in an *issue by tender. Usually, those who bid below the strike price receive nothing, while those who bid at or above it receive some proportion of the amount they have bid for.

string diagrams A technique employed in *work study that uses string wrapped around points on a scale layout diagram to calculate movement. Computerized methods are replacing manual methods, but the generic name is still used.

strip A triple *option on a share or commodity market, consisting of one call option and two put options at the same price and for the same period. *Compare* STRAP.

stripped bond 1. A bond in which payments are sold as a set of 300 coupon bonds. **2.** A bond or stock that has been subjected to *dividend stripping.

structural capital *See* INTELLECTUAL CAPITAL.

structure–conduct–performance model (SCP model) A commonly used paradigm in *industrial organization economics. It states that the *structure* or form of a particular market (i.e. the level of *concentration and presence or absence of *barriers to entry) will determine the *conduct* (i.e. *strategic behaviour) of buyers and sellers and the overall *performance* (i.e. social efficiency) of that market. As the number of significant players within a market increases, the ability of firms to

influence prices declines and the efficiency of the market is enhanced.

structured finance The creation of complex debt instruments by *securitization or the addition of *derivatives to existing instruments. Structured finance typically involves the pooling of assets, the tranching of liabilities (*see* TRANCHE), and the creation of *special purpose vehicles to limit risk. The prevalence of structured finance products based on *subprime mortgages is generally seen as a key factor precipitating the financial crisis of 2007–08.

structured interview An interview used in *marketing research in which the interviewer asks the questions exactly as they appear on the questionnaire, adding and explaining nothing to the respondent. The questions can only be answered 'yes', 'no', or 'don't know'. Although this type of marketing research produces easily tabulated data quickly, it places a heavy burden on the designer of the questionnaire to ensure that the data is not misleading.

Structured questionnaires and (less rigidly) structured interviews are also sometimes used in *personnel selection.

structured investment vehicle (SIV) An *arbitrage fund that raises finance by selling asset-backed *commercial paper (CP) and *medium-term notes and invests predominantly in *asset-backed securities (ABSs). The SIV makes its profit from the difference between the short-term rate paid to the holders of CP and the longer-term rate earned on the ABSs. By late 2008 all known SIVs had failed as a result of the global financial crisis.

structuring a deposit *See* SMURFING.

sub-agent A person or firm that is employed to buy or sell goods as an *agent of an agent. A firm may hold the agency for certain goods in a particular country, for example, and employ sub-agents to represent it in outlying districts of that country.

subjective goodwill The *goodwill of an enterprise calculated by deducting its net tangible assets from the *net present value of its estimated future *cash flows.

sub-lease *See* HEAD LEASE.

suboptimization A situation that arises when the individual components of a system fail to work together to achieve maximum *synergy. This can result from:

- the failure of one or more elements to produce their own outputs to a sufficient standard;
- poor communication of objectives at a strategic level, so that there is no shared understanding of those objectives;
- poor communication across component boundaries, either through ineffective use of the available tools or through deliberate control and manipulation of information;
- the development of subcultures that do not share the overall objectives of the organization.

Most organizations recognize that individual members have a range of personal needs that may not be entirely compatible with the organization's aims. Desired outputs are necessarily a compromise between personal needs and the ideals of an organization. *See also* GOAL DIVERGENCE.

subordinated debt A debt that can only be claimed by an unsecured creditor, in the event of a liquidation, after the claims of *secured creditors have been met. In **subordinated unsecured loan stocks** loans are issued by such institutions as banks, in which the rights of the holders of the stock are subordinate to the interests of the depositors. Debts involving *junk bonds are always subordinated to debts to banks, irrespective of whether or not they are secured.

subpoena (Latin: under penalty) An order made by a court instructing a person to appear in court on a specified date to give evidence, or to produce specified documents. The party calling for the witness must pay all reasonable expenses. Failure to comply with a subpoena is *contempt of court.

subprime lending The provision of loans (especially home loans) to borrowers with a poor credit rating. Because such loans are considered high risk, the costs of borrowing are also higher. Reckless subprime lending by US financial institutions, compounded by the *securitization of these loans in high-risk off-balance-sheet instruments, precipitated a financial and banking crisis in 2007–08.

subrogation The principle that, having paid a claim, an insurer has the right to take over any other methods the policyholder may have for obtaining compensation for the same event. For example, if a neighbour is responsible for breaking a person's window and an insurance claim is paid for the repair, the insurers may, if they wish, take over the policyholder's legal right to claim the cost of repair from the neighbour.

subscribed share capital *See* ISSUED SHARE CAPITAL.

subscriber A person who signs the *memorandum of association of a new company and who joins with other members in paying for a specified quantity of shares in the company, signing the *articles of association, and appointing the first directors.

subscription shares 1. Shares in a building society that are paid for by instalments; they often pay the highest interest rates. **2.** The shares bought by the initial *subscribers to a company.

subsidiary undertaking (group undertaking) An undertaking that is controlled by another undertaking (the parent or *holding company). The extent of the control needed to define a subsidiary is given in the Companies Act. The financial statements of a subsidiary undertaking are normally included in the *consolidated financial statements of the group. *See also* QUASI-SUBSIDIARY; WHOLLY OWNED SUBSIDIARY.

subsidy A payment by a government to producers of certain goods to enable them to sell the goods to the public at a low price, to compete with foreign competition, to avoid making redundancies and creating unemployment, etc. In general, subsidies distort international trade and are unpopular but they are sometimes used by governments to help to establish a new industry in a country. *See also* COMMON AGRICULTURAL POLICY.

subsistence crop A crop grown by a farmer for consumption by himself and his family, rather than for sale. *Compare* CASH CROP.

substance over form An important concept in accounting, according to which transactions and other events are accounted for by their commercial reality rather than their legal form. *Off-balance-sheet finance and *creative accounting depend on accounting according to the legal form, often established in complex agreements.

substantiality The extent to which a market segment is sufficiently large or profitable to provide a worthwhile attempt to service it.

substantive motion *See* MOTION.

substitute awareness effect An effect that depends on the relation between a customer's price sensitivity and his or her awareness of the existence of alternatives. The substitute awareness effect usually lowers a customer's willingness to pay high prices.

substitute cheque *See* CHEQUE TRUNCATION.

succession planning In *human-resource management, the process of identifying potential successors to key positions in the organization and providing training, *mentoring, and other opportunities to prepare them for these roles. Ideally, this should involve longer-term planning as well as the grooming of immediate replacements and should not be confined to the most senior positions in the company. Some common pitfalls associated with succession planning are: (a) the tendency to look for 'clones' of existing

leaders, thereby neglecting talented individuals of a different gender, background, or personality type; (b) the tendency to 'fast-track' those seen as potential leaders by moving them up the hierarchy before they have had a chance to broaden their experience; and (c) the failure to realize that the future needs of the organization may be quite different from those of the past. The problem of succession planning can be particularly acute in small privately owned businesses that have depended on one or two very gifted individuals.

sucker effect The finding that some individuals will reduce their individual effort when working on a group task because they fear becoming, or being seen as, a 'sucker', i.e. someone who contributes more to the group than others but receives the same reward. *See also* COLLECTIVE EFFORT MODEL; RINGELMANN EFFECT; SOCIAL LOAFING.

sue and labour clause A clause in a *marine insurance policy extending the insurance to cover costs incurred by the policyholder in preventing a loss from occurring or minimizing one that could not be avoided. Without this clause the policy would only cover damage that had actually occurred.

sugging (survey under the guise of research) The unethical practice of deliberate deception by telemarketers masquerading as market researchers. Respondents are often invited to take part in a survey as a lead-in to a sales presentation or as an attempt to get information that could be used for sales leads or mailing lists. *Compare* FRUGGING.

sum (*plural* **sumy**) (UZS) The standard monetary unit of Uzbekistan, divided into 100 tyin.

sum insured The maximum amount the insurers will pay in the event of a claim.

summarizer *See* TASK ROLES.

summary financial statement An abbreviated form of the *annual accounts and report that, providing certain conditions are met, may be sent by *listed companies to their shareholders instead of the full report. *See also* ABBREVIATED ACCOUNTS; SIMPLIFIED FINANCIAL STATEMENTS.

sum-of-the-digits method A method of calculating the amount by which a *fixed asset is depreciated in an accounting period. The estimated life is expressed in years, and the digits for each year of its life are totalled. The proportion of the asset's cost or valuation less residual value to be written off as depreciation in a particular year is determined by the number of years remaining before the asset's removal from commission, expressed as a proportion of the sum of the years; the greatest amount is therefore written off in the early years of the asset's life. For example, for an asset with an estimated life of 5 years, the sum of the digits is $5 + 4 + 3 + 2 + 1 = 15$. Thus 5/15 is written off in the first year, 4/15 in year 2, 3/15 in year 3, and so on. In some circumstances the *net residual value is ignored.

sundry expenses Costs incurred as small items of expenditure, which do not lend themselves to easy classification under any other heading. Sometimes they refer to a specific area, such as sundry office expenses or sundry production costs.

sunk capital The amount of an organization's funds that has been spent and is therefore no longer available to the organization, frequently because it has been spent on either unrealizable or valueless assets.

sunk costs **1.** (**sunk capital**) Expenditure, usually on capital items, that once having been incurred can be included in a company's books of account as an asset, although this value cannot be recovered. **2.** In *management accounting, expenditure that has already been incurred and that cannot be recovered. Such costs are not relevant to any subsequent spending decisions. An example of a sunk cost is the original cost of a machine when the decision is whether or not to replace this machine. *Compare* RELEVANT COST.

superannuation *See* OCCUPATIONAL PENSION SCHEME.

supermajority provisions Provisions in the byelaws of a company that call for more than a simple majority of its members when voting on certain *motions, such as the approval of a merger or whether or not to agree to a takeover. In these circumstances the provisions may call for a supermajority of between 70% and 80% of the votes cast.

supermarket A large self-service store that carries a wide variety of food, household products, and other goods, which it sells in high volumes at relatively low prices. *See also* HYPERMARKET.

superstore A store usually about twice the size of a regular *supermarket, which is often found on the edge of a town. It carries a large assortment of food and nonfood items and offers such services as dry cleaning, a pharmacy, lunch counters, car care, etc.

supervisory board A board of *non-executive directors who appoint and oversee the members of the executive board of a company. This arrangement is common in Continental Europe. *See* TWO-TIER BOARD.

supplementary costs *See* OVERHEAD.

supplier A firm or individual that provides the resources needed by a company and its competitors to produce goods and services.

supplier credit *See* SPECIFIC BANK GUARANTEE.

supplier search The stage of the business buying process (*see* BUSINESS BUYER BEHAVIOUR) in which the buyer tries to find the best vendors.

supplier selection The stage of the business buying process (*see* BUSINESS BUYER BEHAVIOUR) in which the buyer reviews proposals from suitable vendors and selects a supplier or suppliers.

supply and demand *See* MARKET FORCES.

supply chain The series of linked stages in a supply network along which a particular set of goods or services flows; it usually consists of: suppliers, vendors of the suppliers, producers, distribution partners, and customers. *See* SUPPLY-CHAIN MANAGEMENT.

supply-chain management The management of the links between an organization and its suppliers and customers to achieve strategic advantage. Many specialist companies now offer to manage the whole of the supply chain, on behalf of manufacturers. Supply-chain management covers:

- **Materials management**—the management of the flow of materials through an organization's supply chain, including first-tier suppliers, inventory management, operations planning and control, and distribution to first-tier customers.
- **Logistics**—the management of materials and information flows from an organization to its customers. (Sometimes 'logistics' is also used as a synonym for 'supply-chain management'.)
- **Physical distribution management**—the management of the process that connects the producer and the first-tier customers, including storage and transport.
- **Purchasing and supply management**—the management of an organization's interface with suppliers, ensuring that the right quantity is bought at the right time, at the right price, to the right quality specification, and from the right sources.
- **Information flow management**—the management of the flow of information between an organization and both its suppliers and its customers. For every unit of material flow in one direction through the supply chain, there should be at least one corresponding information flow in the opposite direction. Many of the more recent improvements in materials management have come from the use of computers and information technology in the flow of information.

supply-chain support A network of vendors, dealers, and distribution partners linked online so that queries in one category can lead to related information in another.

supply risk 1. The inherent risk in *project financing that the raw materials necessary for the operation of the plant to be constructed may become unavailable.

Supply chain management.

Compare COMPLETION RISK; TECHNOLOGICAL RISK. **2.** More generally, the risk of disruption of inputs into a firm.

support level In technical analysis, a floor level of prices for a security or commodity at which the price tends to stop falling and begin to rebound. A fall below this level is regarded as marking a significant shift to lower prices. *Compare* RESISTANCE LEVEL. *See also* DOUBLE BOTTOM.

supra protest *See* ACCEPTANCE SUPRA PROTEST.

SUR Abbreviation for *set-up reduction.

surcharge liability notice A notice issued when a trader is late with a *value added tax return or with the payment of the tax. The surcharge period is specified on the notice and it will run to the anniversary of the end of the period in which the default occurred. Any default during the surcharge period will result in a further notice extending the period to the anniversary of the end of the VAT period in which the second default occurred.

surety 1. A guarantor for the actions of someone. **2.** A sum of money held as a *guarantee or as evidence of good faith.

surfer Someone who dips into the information and other services available on the Internet with no clear objective in mind, often following the links from one site to another out of simple curiosity.

surrender value The sum of money given by an insurance company to the insured on a life policy that is cancelled before it has run its full term. The amount is calculated approximately by deducting from the total value of the premiums paid any costs, administration expenses, and a charge for the life-assurance cover up to the cancellation date. There is little or no surrender value to a life policy in its early years. Not all life policies acquire a surrender value; for example, term assurance policies have no surrender value.

survey research Any form of *marketing research in which data is gathered systematically from a sample of people by means of a questionnaire. Surveys are usually conducted by means of face-to-face interviews, telephone interviews, or mailed questionnaires.

sushi bond A bond issued by a Japanese-registered company in a currency other than yen but targeted primarily at the Japanese institutional investor market.

suspense account A temporary account in the books of an organization to record balances to correct mistakes or balances that have not yet been finalized (e.g. because a particular deal has not been concluded).

sustainable competitive advantage *See* COMPETITIVE ADVANTAGE.

SVA Abbreviation for *shareholder value analysis.

swap A means by which a borrower can exchange the type of funds most easily raised for the type of funds required, usually through the intermediary of a bank. For example, a UK company may find it easy to raise a sterling loan when they really want to borrow euros; a German company may have exactly the opposite problem. A swap will enable them to exchange the currency they possess for the currency they need. This is called a *currency swap. The other common type of swap is an *interest-rate swap, in which borrowers exchange fixed-for floating-interest rates. The essence of a swap is that the parties exchange the net cash flows of different types of borrowing instruments on an *over-the-counter market. *See also* BASIS SWAP; CROSS-CURRENCY INTEREST-RATE SWAP.

swap line A line of credit between two central banks in different countries, when securities of equal value are exchanged but the borrowing bank repays on a forward contract.

swaption An *option to enter into a *swap contract.

sweep facility A service provided by a bank which automatically transfers funds above a certain level from a current account to a higher-interest earning account. The process can work in reverse when funds in the current account fall below a certain level. The purpose is to provide the customer with the greatest amount of interest, with the minimum personal intervention.

SWF Abbreviation for *sovereign wealth fund.

swingline bank facility (swingline loan) A facility that enables a borrower to avail itself of funds at very short notice, usually on a same-day basis, often to cover shortfalls in other credit arrangements. It may form part of a multi-option facility.

switching 1. Using the cash from the sale of one investment to purchase another. This may, or may not, involve a liability for capital gains tax, depending on the circumstances. **2.** Closing an *open position in a commodity market and opening a similar position in the same commodity but for a different delivery period. For example, a trader may switch a holding of sugar for October delivery FOB to an equal quantity of sugar for March delivery FOB for the next year. **3.** A country's intervention in the international currency market to stop an outflow of its currency. **4.** Exporting and importing through a third nation, where the currency paying for the goods can be easily exchanged into one acceptable to the seller.

switching cost A means of building a *competitive advantage into a product or service by involving buyers in an extra cost if they switch to an alternative supplier. It may form part of the physical characteristics of the product, which make it incompatible with the equipment of alternative suppliers (such as a different computer operating system), or the switching cost may result from the disruption of the quality of service formed by a long-established and close working relationship.

SWOT Acronym for strengths, weaknesses, opportunities, and threats. When planning to market of a new product a company needs to embark on a SWOT analysis to assess its strengths and weaknesses (internally) and the opportunities and threats facing it (externally). Internal strengths could be a good distribution system and adequate cash flow. Weaknesses might be identified as an already extended product line or poor servicing facilities. Opportunities could be consumer demand for a particular product or the vulnerability of a competitor, while threats might be forthcoming government legislation or diversification by a competitor. A SWOT analysis can also provide the framework for an organization's managerial *position audit (*see* STRATEGIC MANAGEMENT).

SWX Swiss Exchange *See* SIX SWISS EXCHANGE.

symbol retailer (voluntary retailer) A voluntary group of independent retailers formed to buy in large quantities from *wholesalers at lower prices than they could achieve independently. Originally a defensive move by independents to counter the increasing dominance and expansion of the multiple stores, supermarkets, hypermarkets, etc., these groups can also provide each other with such services as promotional support and management advice. The members of a group often use a common name or symbol to identify themselves.

sympathetic strike *See* STRIKE.

syndicate 1. A group of bankers, insurers, contractors, etc., who join together to work on a large project. Notable activities undertaken by such a group may include syndicated loans and underwriting (*see also* SYNDICATED BANK FACILITY.) **2.** A number of *Lloyd's underwriters who accept insurance risks as a group; each syndicate is run by a syndicate manager or agent. The **names** in the syndicate accept an agreed share of each risk in return for the same proportion of the premium. The names do not take part in organizing the underwriting business but treat their involvement with the syndicate as an investment. Since the reorganization of Lloyd's in the 1990s, limited companies have been allowed to become names. Although a syndicate underwrites as a group, each member is financially responsible for only his or her own share.

syndicated bank facility (syndicated loan) A very large loan made to one borrower by a group of banks headed by one *lead manager, which usually takes only a small percentage of the loan itself, syndicating the rest to other banks and financial institutions. The loans are usually made on a small margin. The borrower can reserve the right to know the names of all the members of the syndicate. If the borrower states which banks are to be included, it is known as a **club deal**. A syndicated bank facility is usually a *revolving bank facility. There is only one loan agreement.

syndicated research A large-scale marketing research project undertaken by market-research companies and subsequently offered for sale to interested parties. It is not therefore undertaken on behalf of a client.

syndicated selling See AFFILIATE MODEL.

synergy The added value created by joining two separate firms, enabling a greater return to be achieved than by their individual contributions as separate entities; i.e. the overall return is greater than the sum of its parts. The synergy is usually anticipated and analysed during merger or takeover activities; for example, one firm's strength in marketing would be complementary to the other firm's versatility in new product development. Although synergy is often optimistically sought, it can be hard to achieve in practice owing to resistance to change, particularly after a contested takeover. The corporate culture that each participant may have built up over many years of separate existence may prove too inflexible to enable a productive merger to be achieved without friction. The condition that arises when, far from adding value, a merger produces an outcome that is less than the sum of the parts is known as **anergy**. See also SUBOPTIMIZATION.

synthetic standard times A *work measurement technique that produces standard times for new tasks (see STANDARD PERFORMANCE) by assembling data from previous time studies of component parts of the task.

system An assembly of components or elements connected together in an organized way to produce outputs; the components of the assembly are affected by being in the system and the behaviour of the system is changed if any component leaves it.

systematic risk (residual risk) The element of *risk in a *portfolio of investments that cannot be reduced by *diversification, because it is common to all securities of the same general class. The compensation that an investor requires for undertaking such risks forms the basis for the *risk premium calculation of the *capital asset pricing model and *arbitrage pricing theory. Systematic risk is measured by the *beta coefficient. Compare SPECIFIC RISK.

systematic sampling A sampling procedure in which every kth element is selected from the frame, after a random start somewhere within the first k elements, where k = the sampling interval. For example, an alphabetical list of first-year students might be obtained from a college and every fifth student selected for the sample.

system capacity See CAPACITY.

systemic risk The *risk of a failure in a whole system, such as the *clearing-house system in commodity markets. The notion that certain banks or financial institutions are effectively *too big to fail is based on the idea that the collapse of such a bank would involve a systemic risk to the financial system as a whole. See SIFIs.

systems analysis The examination or analysis of the objectives and problems of a system for the purpose of developing and improving the system by the use of computers. Systems analysis entails producing a precise statement of what is to be accomplished, determining the methods of achieving the objectives that are most cost-effective, and preparing a feasibility study. If the study is accepted by the customer, the **systems analysts** will advise on the hardware and software needed, provide programmers with the details they need to write the programs, produce documentation describing the system, plan staff training on it, and monitor the system once it is installed.

systems dynamics A computer-based system, developed at the Massachusetts Institute of Technology, for modelling the behaviour of transient systems. It attempts to unravel the synergistic effects (*see* SYNERGY) of numerous individual changes being made at various points in a system; it also allows 'what if' questions to be asked.

systems selling The selling of a total system rather than an individual product. For example, some computer manufacturers sell VDUs, keyboards, printers, and the necessary software for their computers, while other companies might only supply the software for these computers.

systems software Computer programs that control the functioning of the computer itself, rather than directly meeting the user's computing needs (*compare* APPLICATIONS SOFTWARE). Examples are *operating systems and utility programs, which perform such tasks as copying *files, checking the integrity of magnetic disks, etc. These programs are usually supplied with the computer and may even be built into it (*see* FIRMWARE).

systems thinking Any way of thinking that attempts to understand how interactions between elements of a complex system can influence the functioning of the system as a whole and vice versa. Problem solving within such a context will involve a detailed analysis of the relationship between the parts and the whole rather than a simple focus on the part or parts in question. The systems-thinking approach can be applied to virtually any system, whether this is a computer network, a business, or a complex society. It has therefore proved influential in disciplines ranging from organizational design to town planning and ecology.

system utilization *See* UTILIZATION.

S

tablet computer (tablet) A portable personal computer that is operated using a touchscreen interface rather than a mouse and keyboard. Tablets generally provide an on-screen keyboard for typing, although some hybrid models also have a physical keyboard. A typical tablet is about half the size of a laptop computer but larger than a *smartphone. The first successful tablet was Apple's iPad, launched in 2010; it remains the market leader.

tachistoscope A projection device used in studies of visual perception and memory. In advertising and marketing research it is used to measure the extent to which the features of an advertisement or brand are registered by consumers. The tachistoscope shows a package or advertisement for a very brief period (which can be varied), enabling researchers to test the effectiveness of the design, colour, lay-out, or name. Tachistoscope tests are often undertaken before the product or advertisement is released. Various methods of achieving the same effect on a computer screen have been explored but the projection method is still generally preferred.

tactical asset allocation An attempt to increase *portfolio returns in the short term by altering the asset composition of the portfolio. The academic literature is sceptical as to whether this will result in higher returns for any reason other than chance.

Taffler's Z score *See* Z SCORE.

Taguchi methods Methods of testing the design of a new product or service in the most extreme circumstances likely to occur. In theory, all possible design variables and combinations are investigated to achieve the optimum combination. In reality, this would be impossible; therefore a range of statistical techniques are used to determine the best combinations, leading to the lowest cost and the highest degree of uniformity. The methods were devised by Genichi Taguchi.

taka (BDT) The standard monetary unit of Bangladesh, divided into 100 oisha.

takeover bid (offer to purchase) An offer made to the shareholders of a company by an individual or organization to buy their shares at a specified price in order to gain control of that company. In a welcome takeover bid the directors of the company will advise shareholders to accept the terms of the bid. This is usually known as a *merger. If the bid is unwelcome, or the terms are unacceptable, the board will advise against acceptance (*see* HOSTILE BID). In the ensuing **takeover battle**, the bidder may improve the terms offered and will then usually write to shareholders outlining the advantages that will follow from the successful takeover. In the meantime bids from other sources may be made (*see* GREY KNIGHT; WHITE KNIGHT) or the original bidder may withdraw as a result of measures taken by the board of the *target company (*see* POISON PILL; PORCUPINE PROVISIONS). In an **unconditional bid**, the bidder will pay the offered price irrespective of the number of shares acquired, while the bidder of a **conditional bid** will only pay the price offered if sufficient shares are acquired to provide a controlling interest. Takeovers in the UK are subject to the rules and disciplines of the *City Code on Takeovers and Mergers, which now incorporates articles of the EU's Takeover Directive (2005).

Takeover Panel *See* CITY CODE ON TAKEOVERS AND MERGERS.

taker The buyer of a traded *option. *Compare* WRITER.

tala (WST) The standard monetary unit of Samoa, divided into 100 sene.

tally clerk (tallyman) A worker at a port or airport, who checks that the goods unloaded from a ship or aircraft tally with the documents covering them and the ship's or aircraft's manifest.

talon A printed form attached to a *bearer bond that enables the holder to apply for a new sheet of *coupons when the existing coupons have been used up.

tambala A monetary unit of Malawi, worth one hundredth of a *kwacha.

tangible assets Literally, *assets that can be touched, i.e. physical objects such as land, buildings, or machinery. However, tangible assets may also include leases and company shares. They are therefore best defined as the *fixed assets of an organization excluding such *intangible assets as goodwill, patents, and trademarks, which are even more intangible than leases and shares.

tanker A ship designed to carry liquids in bulk in large storage tanks. Most carry oil but some carry wine, sugar products, and liquefied gases.

Tannenbaum–Schmidt continuum (leadership continuum theory) A model of leadership that sees *leadership style as a continuum varying from leader-centred (autocratic) to subordinate-centred (democratic). The type of leadership that is practical and desirable in any given situation will depend on three types of force: forces in the leader (e.g. self-confidence, personal philosophy); forces in the followers (e.g. experience, willingness to take responsibility); and forces in the situation (e.g. the complexity of the problem, time pressures). *See also* CONTINGENCY THEORIES OF LEADERSHIP.

tape Any reporting system for the latest stock-market information, primarily prices. The earliest such system was known as **tickertape**, from the noise made by telegraphic printing machines. 'Tape' systems are all now computerized.

taper relief Formerly, a relief applied in computing the *capital gains tax (CGT) charge on a capital gain. The maximum reduction available was 40% for a non-business asset and 75% for a business asset. Taper relief was introduced in 1998 and abolished from April 2008, largely because of disquiet at the extent to which *private equity firms were using it to avoid paying tax on their profits. It was replaced by *entrepreneurs' relief.

tap issue The issue of UK government securities or bills to selected market makers, usually to influence the price of gilts. The government can control their volume and price, like turning a tap on or off.

tap stock A gilt-edged security from an issue that has not been fully subscribed and is released onto the market slowly when its market price reaches predetermined levels. **Short taps** are short-dated stocks and **long taps** are long-dated taps.

TAR Abbreviation for throughput accounting ratio. *See* THROUGHPUT ACCOUNTING.

tare *See* GROSS WEIGHT.

target company A company that is subject to a *takeover bid.

target costing A method of costing products or services to reflect the price that customers are willing to pay. Target costing has four stages:
(1) Identify the **target price** that customers will pay for the product. This involves market research to identify competitors' products and prices.
(2) Identify the **target cost** by deducting a target profit margin from the target price. The target profit margin will vary from company to company. Sony is an example of a company that would

require a high profit margin to cover the investment in new technology.

(3) Forecast the **actual cost** of the product.

(4) If the forecast actual cost is greater than the target cost, the company will have to identify ways of lowering the forecast actual cost. Product designers may have to change the design so that it is cheaper to manufacture. Manufacturing engineers may also look into ways of making the production processes more efficient. If the company cannot bring actual costs down to the target cost, then the product should not be manufactured.

This approach to pricing is very different from *cost-plus pricing.

Target Group Index (TGI) An annual marketing research report compiled from the returned questionnaires of a random sample of thousands of respondents on their use of hundreds of products and thousands of brands. The questionnaires, which are completed with no interviewer present, also collect information on respondents' demographics, attitudes and values, leisure activities, and exposure to the media. TGI was originated in the UK in 1969 but is now operated in over 60 countries.

target marketing The selection of one or more segments of an available market as a target for marketing a product or service. This is known as the **target market** or **served market**. Since it has become almost impossible to market products that will satisfy everyone, target marketing enables companies to aim the products at specific groups of consumers.

target population A *population of interest in *marketing research. It is from this population that the *samples to be researched are drawn.

tariff 1. Any list of charges for goods or services. **2.** A tax or customs duty payable on imports or exports, or a list detailing such duties. HM Revenue and Customs issues tariffs stating which goods attract duty and what the rate of duty is. **3.** A list of charges in which the charging rate changes after a fixed amount has been purchased or in which a flat fee is imposed in addition to a quantity-related charge, as in two-part tariffs for gas or telephone services.

tariff office An insurance company that bases its premiums on a tariff arranged with other insurance companies. A **non-tariff office** is free to quote its own premiums.

task identity *See* CORE JOB CHARACTERISTICS.

task-motivated (task-oriented) Describing a *leadership style that is concerned with setting goals, structuring tasks, and measuring performance. A task-motivated leader will focus on such activities as planning, scheduling, defining roles and responsibilities, and providing performance-related feedback. *Compare* RELATIONSHIP-MOTIVATED. *See* CONTINGENCY THEORIES OF LEADERSHIP; LEAST PREFERRED CO-WORKER SCALE.

task roles A set of coherent roles that are often adopted by the different members of a group in order to solve problems, make decisions, and meet targets. Some commonly identified roles of this kind include the **initiator**, who defines goals, recognizes problems, and initiates procedures; the **opinion giver**, who provides ideas and information; the **opinion seeker**, who elicits the ideas or expertise of others; and the **summarizer**, who clarifies and sums up the ideas of the group. *Compare* RELATIONSHIP ROLES.

task significance *See* CORE JOB CHARACTERISTICS.

taxable income Income liable to taxation. It is calculated by deducting *income tax allowances and any tax deductible expenses from the taxpayer's *total income. *Compare* NON-TAXABLE INCOME.

taxable person In UK *value added tax legislation, an individual, partnership, limited company, club, association, or charity that makes regular *taxable supplies above a certain annual value. Value added tax is charged on taxable supplies made by taxable persons in the course or furtherance of a business.

taxable supply In UK *value added tax legislation, any supply of goods or services made in the UK other than an *exempt supply. As well as straightforward sales, taxable supplies include rentals, hirings, the granting of rights, and the distribution of promotional gifts.

taxation A levy on individuals or corporate bodies by central or local government in order to finance the expenditure of that government and also as a means of implementing its fiscal policy. Payments for specific services rendered to or for the payer are not regarded as taxation. In the UK, an individual's income is taxed by means of an *income tax (see also PAYE), while corporations pay a *corporation tax. Increases in individual wealth are taxed by means of *capital gains tax and by *inheritance tax. See also DIRECT TAXATION; INDIRECT TAXATION; VALUE ADDED TAX.

taxation brackets Figures between which taxable income or wealth is taxed at a specified rate. For example, in the UK taxable income up to £31,785 attracts tax at the basic rate of 20%, whereas over £31,785 the higher rate of 40% applies. See also BRACKET INDEXATION.

tax avoidance (tax planning) Minimizing tax liabilities legally and by means of full disclosure to the tax authorities. In the UK there has generally been a clear distinction between tax avoidance and illegal *tax evasion, with the authorities legislating to forbid specific arrangements where this seems desirable (see WESTMINSTER DOCTRINE). However, the recently introduced *General Anti-Abuse Rule breaks new ground in its attempt to outlaw all tax avoidance measures that can be deemed 'artificial and abusive'.

tax base The specified domain on which a tax is levied, e.g. an individual's income for *income tax, the estate of a deceased person for *inheritance tax, the profits of a company for *corporation tax.

tax break A tax advantage for a particular activity.

tax burden The total loss of real income suffered by an individual or organization as the result of a tax. This may not be the same as the tax obligation imposed by law, because of the possibility of shifting the *incidence of taxation to others.

tax clearance See CLEARANCE.

tax code 1. See INCOME TAX CODE. **2.** The body of tax law applicable in a country, in which the tax law is codified rather than laid down by statute.

tax credit 1. The tax allowance associated with the *dividend paid by a company. The shareholder is given allowance for the tax paid at source by the tax credit, at the same rate, 10/90; i.e. a dividend of £90 received by the shareholder has an associated tax credit of £10. For those whose taxable income does not exceed £31,785 there is no further tax to pay. For those who pay the *higher rate of income tax, income from dividends is charged at a rate of 32.5%; for those who pay the additional rate, the tax is 37.5%. From April 2016 the tax credit system will be replaced by a *dividend tax. **2.** Any other allowance against a tax liability. **3.** In the UK, a social security payment such as the Working Tax Credit or Child Tax Credit that is administered by HM Revenue and Customs. Despite their titles, neither of these payments affects the amount of tax that is payable. Both these credits are due to be replaced by the new Universal Credit.

tax-deductible Denoting an amount that can be deducted from income or profits, in accordance with the tax legislation, before establishing the amount of income or profits that is subject to tax.

tax-deferred Describing a financial instrument in which tax is paid at maturity.

tax deposit certificate A certificate issued by HM Revenue and Customs to a taxpayer who has made an advance payment in anticipation of future income tax, capital-gains tax, or corporation tax. The initial payment must not be less than £500 and should be made to HMRC; payments of £100,000 or over can be made directly to the Bank of England. The certificates bear interest, which is liable to tax. The interest rate depends on whether the certificate is withdrawn for cash or surrendered to meet a tax demand. A higher rate is paid on the latter. Interest normally runs to the date of encashment but if the certificate is used to pay tax, it runs only to the due date of payment of the liability, not the actual date of payment.

tax-effective Denoting a procedure that is in accordance with the tax legislation and results in a reduction in the tax charge.

tax evasion Minimizing tax liabilities illegally, usually by not disclosing that one is liable to tax or by giving false information to the authorities. If a person donates money to a bona fide charity in order to reduce his tax burden he is practising *tax avoidance; if he informs the Revenue that he has made such donations when this is not the case, he is guilty of tax evasion. As Denis Healey once remarked, 'The difference between tax avoidance and tax evasion is the thickness of a prison wall'.

tax exile A person with a high income or considerable wealth who chooses to live in a *tax haven in order to avoid the high taxation of his or her native country.

tax-free Denoting a payment, allowance, benefit, etc., on which no tax is payable.

tax harmonization The process of increasing the compatibility of various taxation systems by limiting the variations between them. The main areas of difference in taxation are the *tax base and the rates of tax applicable. There is often strong resistance to tax harmonization between independent states as, by setting limits within which the tax rates can be set, the authority of individual governments is eroded.

tax haven A country or area that has a low rate of tax and therefore offers advantages to retired wealthy individuals or to

companies that can arrange their affairs so that their tax liability falls at least partly in the low-tax haven. In the case of individuals, the cost of the tax saving is usually residence in the tax haven for a majority of the year (*see* TAX EXILE). For multinational companies, an office in the tax haven, with some real or contrived business passing through it, is required. Luxembourg, Monaco, Liechtenstein, the Bahamas, Bermuda, and the Cayman Islands are examples of tax havens. *See also* OFFSHORE FINANCIAL CENTRES.

tax holiday A period during which a company, in certain countries, is excused from paying corporation tax or profits tax (or pays them on only part of its profits) as an export incentive or an incentive to start up a new industry.

tax invoice A detailed *value added tax invoice that must be provided by a *taxable person to another taxable person when the *taxable supply is made for over £250. The tax invoice must show:

- the supplier's name, address, and VAT registration number;
- the tax point and invoice number;
- the name and address of the customer;
- a description of the transaction and the goods supplied;
- the amount of VAT and the amount excluding VAT.

A less detailed invoice is required for a supply of less than £250.

tax loss A loss made by an organization in one period, that can be carried forward to another period to reduce the tax payable by that organization in the subsequent period. *See* LOSS RELIEFS.

tax month Under the UK taxation system, the month running from the 6th day of one month to the 5th day of the following month. This ensures that there are 12 complete tax months in the *fiscal year.

tax planning *See* TAX AVOIDANCE.

tax point Under the *value added tax rules, the date on which goods are removed or made available to a customer, or the date on which services to a customer are completed. The tax point determines the tax period for which the *output tax must be accounted for to HM Revenue and Customs.

tax rebate A repayment of tax paid. A repayment claim must be made and approved by an *Inspector of Taxes and the refund due to the taxpayer will be made by the Collector of Taxes following the Inspector's instructions.

tax relief A deduction from a taxable amount, usually given by statute. In the UK, income-tax reliefs are given in respect of income from tax-exempt sources (e.g. ISAs), as well as tax-deductible expenses, personal allowances, tax credits, and *gift aid. *See* INCOME TAX ALLOWANCES.

The reliefs against *capital gains tax include an annual exemption, exemption from the proceeds of the sale of an only or a principal private residence, and *entrepreneurs' relief.

For *inheritance tax there is an annual relief as well as relief in respect of gifts between spouses and gifts to political parties and charities; agricultural and business reliefs are also available.

tax return A form upon which a taxpayer makes an annual statement of income and personal circumstances, enabling claims to be made for personal allowances. In the UK an income tax return also requires details of *capital gains in the year. The onus is on the taxpayer to provide HM Revenue and Customs with the appropriate information even if the taxpayer receives no tax return. Categories of tax payer who can expect to receive a tax return include the self-employed, company directors, people with a high investment income, and those acting as trustees or personal representatives. Since 1996–97 income tax returns have included a section for *self-assessment, in which the tax payer calculates his or her own liability for income tax. Separate returns are required for *inheritance tax purposes and in respect of VAT and excise duties. It is possible to complete and send back a tax return over the Internet.

(()) SEE WEB LINKS
• Information on making an online tax return from the Gov.uk website

tax schedules *See* SCHEDULE.

tax shelter (tax shield) Any financial arrangement made to lower a person's or a company's tax liabilities.

tax tables Tables issued by HM Revenue and Customs to employers to assist them in calculating the tax due from their employees under the pay-as-you-earn system (*see* PAYE). The tables are provided for either weekly or monthly payments. In practice, employers now calculate salaries, wages, and tax deductions by computer, using a program into which the tax tables are incorporated.

tax treaty An agreement between two countries, identifying the treatment of income, profits, or gains that are subject to tax in both countries. The amount of *double taxation relief will be specified in the treaty.

tax year *See* FISCAL YEAR.

Taylorism *See* SCIENTIFIC MANAGEMENT.

TBL Abbreviation for *triple bottom-line accounting.

team-building exercises Various interventions designed to increase the extent to which a work group functions as a team; that is, as a cohesive, united, emotionally bonded group in which individual inputs (skills, effort, personal characteristics) are combined to maximum effect in pursuit of the common goal. Such exercises usually involve an element of group problem solving, which may or may not be related to the usual professional activities of the group. *See* BUSINESS GAMES; OUTDOOR TRAINING PROGRAMME.

team selling The use of teams of people drawn from a number of departments in a company to service large and complex accounts. The team may include personnel from sales, marketing, production, finance, and technical support departments; it may also be headed by a member of the upper management.

technical analysis *See* INVESTMENT ANALYST.

technical rally *See* RALLY.

technical reserves The assets held by an insurance company against future claims or losses.

technological change An increase in the level of output resulting from automation and computerized methods of production. Apart from increasing output, technological change can affect the ratio of capital to labour used in a factory. If it involves reducing the labour force it can lead to **technological unemployment** in an area or industry.

technological risk 1. The *risk to a business from changing technology. **2.** The inherent risk in *project financing schemes that the newly constructed plant etc. will not operate to specification. *Compare* COMPLETION RISK; SUPPLY RISK.

technology transfer The transfer of technological knowledge to a third party, which often occurs when a patent holder grants a licence to another firm to use a technology, process, or product. In many instances this transfer takes place between countries, when a firm establishes an overseas subsidiary or grants a licence to a local producer. It is therefore a means by which countries gain new technology or update their existing technological base, enabling them to build up their industrial infrastructure. *See* MULTINATIONAL ENTERPRISE.

telecommuting *See* TELEWORKING.

teleconferencing Any telecommunications facility enabling users in two or more locations to participate in a live exchange of information or views. It may involve the transmission of voice only (*audioconferencing), voice and pictures (*videoconferencing), or the written word only. The main business advantage is that teleconferencing reduces the time and money spent in travelling to meetings; it also permits meetings to be scheduled at very short notice.

telegraphic transfer (TT) A method of transmitting money overseas by means of an electronic transfer between banks. The transfer is usually made in the currency of the payee and may be credited to his account at a specified bank or paid in cash to the payee on application and identification.

telemarketing *See* TELEPHONE SELLING.

telephone banking A *home banking facility enabling customers to use banking services by means of a telephone link.

telephone focus groups *Focus groups that are conducted by means of *audioconferencing or *videoconferencing.

telephone research A marketing research technique in which **telephone interviews** are conducted. It is cheaper than personal interviewing and, perhaps because it avoids face-to-face confrontations, seems to be more popular with respondents.

telephone selling (telemarketing) A method of *direct marketing in which the telephone is used to contact potential customers in order to reduce the time spent in making personal visits. Certain products, such as double glazing and central heating, are frequently marketed using this technique. Orders may be taken over the phone, or arrangements are made for sales representatives to visit interested clients. *See also* COLD CALLING.

teletext An information service in which pages of text are transmitted to the home or office for display on a television set. The information is given under various headings, with a *menu call-up system. With the growth in Internet access and the switch to digital television in the 2000s, many leading broadcasters no longer transmit teletext. *See also* VIEWDATA.

television home shopping A cable or digital television shopping service in which consumers see a product on their home TV screens and are able to place orders by telephone. *See also* HOME SHOPPING CHANNELS.

television rating (TVR) The measurement of the popularity of a television programme based on survey research. Equipment attached to sets in selected homes records which channel the set is tuned to, while *diary panels are used to determine how many people are watching the set. In this way ratings can be calculated for each programme and expressed as a percentage of the total households that can receive TV. Survey research is undertaken in the UK by the Broadcasters Audience Research Board (*BARB).

teleworking (telecommuting) A work arrangement in which employees work at remote locations, usually at home, using computers and telecommunications links to carry out their responsibilities and communicating with others as necessary.

Telex A method of communicating written messages over the international telephone network, using a Telex (teleprinter) machine. Although *e-mail has replaced Telex in virtually all business applications, it is still used by shipping, news services, and the military.

teller The US name for a bank or building society cashier, i.e. someone who accepts deposits and pays out cash over the counter to customers.

temporal method In accounting, a method of converting a foreign currency involved in a transaction; the local currency is translated at the exchange rate in operation on the date on which the transaction occurred. If rates do not fluctuate significantly, an average for the period may be used as an approximation. Any exchange gain or loss on translation is taken to the *profit and loss account. This contrasts with the closing rate or net-investment method of translation, which uses the exchange rate ruling at the balance-sheet date for translation and takes exchange differences to *reserves. Traditionally, UK accounting

practice allowed either method to be adopted. This area is now governed by the detailed regulations in Section 30 of the Financial Reporting Standard Applicable in the UK and Republic of Ireland. In general, items should be recorded using the temporal method except for (i) foreign currency monetary items and (ii) items measured at fair value. The relevant *International Accounting Standard is IAS 21.

temporary assurance *See* TERM ASSURANCE.

temporary employee An *employee who is employed for a specified period or for a specific task. Under the Fixed-term Employees (Prevention of Less Favourable Treatment) Regulations 2002, they are entitled to be treated no less favourably than permanent employees if they are doing the same or similar work. It is open to the employer to justify less favourable treatment if good reason can be shown. Under new regulations implemented in 2010 temporary *workers who are not employees are likewise entitled to equal treatment if they have worked for a company for 12 consecutive weeks or longer. *See also* AGENCY WORKER; CONTINGENT WORKER.

tenancy agreement An agreement to let land. *See* LEASE.

tenancy in common Two or more persons having an interest in the same piece of land. Each person can bequeath his or her interest by will, although the land itself has not been physically divided. Trustees must hold the legal estate and the tenancy in common exists in equity. *See also* JOINT TENANTS.

tender 1. A written offer to purchase something at a stated price. **2.** A means of auctioning an item of value to the highest bidder. Tenders are used in many circumstances, e.g. for allocating valuable construction contracts, for selling shares on a stock market (*see* OFFER FOR SALE; ISSUE BY TENDER), or for the sale of government securities (*see* GILT-EDGED SECURITY).

tender offer 1. An offer by one company to buy the shares of another from the shareholders at a stated price (usually at a premium above the market price). It is normally made as part of a *takeover bid. *See also* SELF-TENDER; TWO-TIER TENDER OFFER. **2.** *See* ISSUE BY TENDER.

tender panel A group of banks who are asked to subscribe as a syndicate for the issue of *euronote facilities.

tenesi A monetary unit of Turkmenistan, worth one hundredth of a *manat.

tenge (KZT) The standard monetary unit of Kazakhstan, divided into 100 tiyn.

tenor The time period elapsing between the issue of a security (such as a *bill of exchange) and its maturity.

Ten Windows Formerly, ten institutions in the People's Republic of China that were authorized to borrow abroad.

terabyte A billion kilobytes, i.e. a million megabytes, a thousand gigabytes, or a trillion bytes.

term 1. The period of time before a security expires or is redeemed. **2.** *See* TERM ASSURANCE. **3.** A clause in a contract that refers to a particular obligation between the contracting parties.

term assurance (temporary assurance) A life-assurance policy that operates for a specified period of time. No benefit is paid if the insured person dies outside the period. This form of insurance is often used to cover the period of a loan, mortgage, etc. If the insured person dies before the loan has been repaid, it is settled by the insurance company. *See also* DECREASING TERM ASSURANCE.

term bill *See* PERIOD BILL.

terminable annuity *See* CERTAIN ANNUITY.

terminal A computer input and output device. It commonly consists of a keyboard and display screen, connected to the computer. Terminals that are distant from the computer and connected to it by a communications link are called remote terminals. Terminals with some computing power, often incorporating a *microprocessor, are called *intelligent terminals. Specialized terminals have been developed for use in banking and retailing.

terminal bonus An additional amount of money added to payments made on the maturity of an insurance policy or on the death of an insured person, because the investments of the insurer have produced a profit or surplus. Bonuses of this kind are paid at the discretion of the life office and usually take the form of a percentage of the sum assured.

terminal date The date on which a *futures contract expires.

terminal-loss relief Relief for a loss made by a company, partnership, or sole trader during the last 12 months of trading. The business or profession must be permanently discontinued. For partnerships and sole traders, the loss of the last 12 months can be set against the profits of the three years prior to the final tax year, taking the most recent year first. For companies, the trading loss arising in the accounting period in which the trade ceases may be carried back and offset against the profits of the three years ending immediately before the commencement of the final period of trading. *See* LOSS RELIEFS.

terminal market A commodity market in a trading centre, such as London or New York, rather than a market in a producing centre, such as Calcutta or Singapore. The trade in terminal markets is predominantly in *futures, but *spot goods may also be bought and sold.

terminal value (TV) The value of an investment at the end of an investment period taking into account a specified rate of interest over the period. The formula is the same as that for compound *interest, i.e.

$$TV = P(1 + r)^t,$$

where *TV* is the final amount at the end of period, *P* is the principal amount invested, *r* is the interest rate, and *t* is the time in years for which the investment takes place.

term loan A loan from a bank to a company. The term of the loan is fixed and it is drawn down (*see* DRAWDOWN) immediately or within a short period of signing the loan agreement as set out in the *amortization schedule.

term shares Shares that cannot be sold for a given period (term). They are usually shares in a building society that cannot be cashed on demand and consequently carry a higher rate of interest.

terms of trade A measure of the trading prospects of a country expressed as an index of export prices divided by an index of import prices. A country's terms of trade improve if this ratio rises, because it can purchase more imports for a particular volume of exports.

term structure of interest rates A set of discount rates for each year to maturity, applied to fixed-rate securities such as government bonds. The term structure of interest rates is related to the *yield curve, but differs from this in that it gives a discount rate appropriate for individual years to maturity, rather than the discount rate for all years on a bond to maturity.

terotechnology The branch of technology that involves the use of management, financial, and engineering skills in installing, operating, and maintaining plant and machinery. *See* LIFE-CYCLE COSTING.

territorial salesforce structure A salesforce organization that assigns an exclusive geographic territory to a particular salesperson, who carries the company's full line.

territorial waters The part of the sea around a country's coastline over which it has jurisdiction according to international law. Historically, it was the sea within three nautical miles of the coast, a practical distance determined by the range of a cannon ball. Since disputes have arisen over fishing rights, off-shore oil mining, and mineral rights below the ocean, the universal three-mile

rule has been abrogated and various nations have made different claims, some, but not all, of which have been accepted internationally. Ten to fifteen nautical miles is now quite common in definitions of territorial waters. The Territorial Sea Act 1987 fixes the UK territorial waters at 12 nautical miles. The UN Convention on the Law of the Sea (1982) defines a 200-mile **exclusive economic zone**, giving a country sovereign rights over all the resources of the sea, seabed, and subsoil within this zone. To date, this Convention has been subscribed to by 148 nations, including the UK.

tertiary production *See* PRODUCTION.

testimonial advertisement An advertisement that makes use of the implied or explicit patronage of a product by a well-known person or organization.

test marketing (market testing) A procedure for launching a new product in a restricted geographical area to test consumers' reactions. If the product is unsuccessful, the company will have minimized its costs and can make the necessary changes before a wider launch. Test marketing is typically undertaken in large towns or in areas served by a particular commercial television company. Test marketing has the disadvantage that competitors learn about the new product before its full launch. *See also* NEW PRODUCT DEVELOPMENT.

tetri A monetary unit of Georgia, worth one hundredth of a *lari.

TGI Abbreviation for *Target Group Index.

thebe A monetary unit of Botswana, worth one hundredth of a *pula.

theory of constraints (TOC) An approach to the planning of production that focuses attention on the *capacity constraints or bottlenecks that occur in the process, rather than attempting to maximize loading across the whole system.
   Examples of TOC solutions include:
*   providing additional training for employees to improve working speeds;

- replacing an existing bottleneck machine with a faster one;
- changing the design of a product to reduce manufacturing time.

See also OPTIMIZED PRODUCTION TECHNOLOGY.

theory of games *See* GAME THEORY.

theory of institutional deficiencies (TIDE) A theory of social and business organization, developed by Maris Martinsons from 1997, which suggests that in countries without effective law-governed institutions, business will tend to be carried on through informal and potentially corrupt relationships rather than through rule-based markets. This can be a major obstacle to growth, and in particular it may inhibit the transition from the physical to the electronic marketplace, as buyers and sellers are reluctant to give up their direct personal connections.

theory of the firm The branch of economic theory that is concerned with the nature of the firm or company, as opposed to the nature of the market. It addresses itself to perhaps four main questions:

- Why do firms exist at all—i.e. why do markets include organized corporate bodies and not just a myriad of individual transactors?
- How and why do firms emerge, change over time, and collapse?
- What determines the boundaries of the firm with the market—i.e. which transactions are performed internally, which externally, and why?
- What factors determine the internal organization of firms?

Whereas early neoclassical answers to these questions concentrated largely on the company's role in reducing *transaction costs, subsequent approaches have incorporated insights from psychology, sociology, *game theory, and the study of *agency relationships.

Theory X and Theory Y Two conflicting theories regarding the human motivation to work, put forward by the US psychologist Douglas McGregor (1906–64), which have

relevance in *human-resource management.

Theory X is based on the premise that people are inherently lazy, dislike work, and will avoid it if they can. They prefer being directed to accepting responsibility; their only use for creativity is in getting round the rules of an organization. Because they are motivated to work only by money, they require coercion and tight control to make them function adequately.

Theory Y, on the other hand, assumes that people wish to be interested in their work and, given the right conditions, will enjoy it. Motivated by the wish to achieve, and to have their achievements recognized, most people will work to the best of their capabilities, creativity, and ingenuity. They accept responsibility and the rules of the organization they work for, imposing self-discipline on their work, given accepted targets.

The generally accepted view is that if management follow Theory Y they will achieve better operational performance. *See also* THEORY Z.

Theory Z An alternative approach to *human-resource management put forward by William Ouchi, as a way of enabling US companies to integrate aspects of the Japanese approach to human resource management (*compare* THEORY X AND THEORY Y). The theory proposes: more secure employment, better career prospects, greater employee participation in decision making, greater emphasis on the team spirit, recognition of the contributions of employees, and the development of greater mutual respect between managers and employees. The implementation of this theory requires a commitment to consultation and to training by top management.

thin capitalization An arrangement in which a company is incorporated (typically in another jurisdiction) with a small share capital and financed with a large loan from its parent company. The arrangement is often designed to give tax relief on the interest payment on the loan, whereas no relief would be available on dividends paid on shares. In the UK a special tax regime is applied in certain instances of thin capitalization, so that excessive interest paid on the loan is treated as if it were a dividend, thus denying the right to a tax deduction.

thin market A market for a security, commodity, currency, etc. in which there are currently few transactions. In such a market the *spread between bid and offer prices will be wide and any sizable transactions will have a direct effect on prices. Large investors tend to avoid a thin market because of its low liquidity. *Compare* DEEP MARKET.

third-country acceptance (refinance bill) An international trade *time draft drawn on a country other than that of the importer or exporter. *See also* BANKER'S ACCEPTANCE.

third-line forcing Forcing a buyer to take a supply of something unwanted as a condition of supplying him or her with a desired product. The practice is deprecated by the Restrictive Practices Court (*see* RESTRICTIVE TRADE PRACTICES).

third-party debt order An order made by a judge on behalf of a *judgment creditor restraining a third party (often a bank) from paying money to the judgment debtor until sanctioned to do so by the court. The order may also specify that the third party must pay a stated sum to the judgment creditor, or to the court, from the funds belonging to the judgment debtor. It was formerly called a **garnishee order**.

third-party insurance Insurance of a person's legal liabilities to others. The insurer and the policyholder are the two parties to the insurance contract, any other person to whom there is a legal obligation is therefore a third party. Some forms of third-party insurance are compulsory, e.g. motorists must have third-party cover for any loss or damage suffered by members of the public as a result of their driving and employers must cover against any results of injury to employees at work. Professional indemnity insurance is a form of third-party insurance that is optional.

third sector That part of a society or an economy that comprises non-governmental, voluntary, and *nonprofit organizations. This is known as the third sector to distinguish it from both the profit-making or private sector and the governmental or public sector.

360° feedback A system that provides employees with all-round performance *feedback from colleagues, manager(s), customers, and others. Crucially, it also compares the individual's self-perception with performance ratings supplied by others.

threshold agreement An agreement between an employer and employees (or their union) that pay will increase by a specified amount if the rate of inflation exceeds a specified figure in a specified period. Threshold agreements are seen by some as providing an inflationary pressure of their own but others claim that they reduce inflation by making it unnecessary for unions to press for excessive settlements to protect their members against inflation.

threshold effect The point at which advertising begins to show signs of increasing sales. As advertising is expensive, the threshold effect is important because it sets the minimum level for an advertising budget.

threshold price *See* COMMON AGRICULTURAL POLICY.

throughput accounting An approach to short-term decision making in manufacturing in which all *conversion costs are treated as though they were fixed and products are ranked if a particular *constraint or scarce resource exists. Decisions are made using the **throughput accounting ratio (TAR)** as follows:

return per factory hour/cost per factory hour,

where return per factory hour =

(sales price − material cost)/hours on scarce resource;

and cost per factory hour =

> total factory cost/total available hours of constraint.

More recently, throughput accounting has been applied in more general areas of *management accounting.

tick The smallest possible price movement on a financial market; this is usually a single *basis point (0.01%). In foreign-exchange trading, the term **pip** is often preferred.

TIDE Abbreviation for *theory of institutional deficiencies.

tied adviser *See* INDEPENDENT FINANCIAL ADVISER; POLARIZATION.

tied loan A loan made by one nation to another on condition that the money loaned is spent buying goods or services in the lending nation. It thus helps the lending nation, by providing employment, as well as the borrowing nation.

tied outlet A retail outlet that is obliged to sell only the products of one producer (and possibly other noncompeting products). The outlet is usually owned by the producer; in other cases the outlet agrees to become tied in return for financial concessions.

tie-in A collaboration between two or more organizations, working as partners in a promotional effort.

tiger markets A colloquial name for four economies in the Pacific Basin that experienced rapid export-led growth from the 1960s to the 1980s: namely, Hong Kong, South Korea, Singapore, and Taiwan. *Compare* DRAGON MARKETS.

tight money *See* DEAR MONEY.

TIGR Abbreviation for Treasury Investors Growth Receipt. These *zero-coupon bonds are linked to US Treasury bonds. They are denominated in dollars and are usually referred to as **Tigers**.

time and motion study A method of finding the best way of performing a complex task by breaking the task into small steps and measuring the time taken to perform each step. This enables standards of performance to be set. These standards can then be used to plan and control production, estimate prices and delivery times, and devise incentive schemes. Time and motion studies are associated with the school of *scientific management.

time bargain A contract in which securities have to be delivered at some date in the future.

time card (clock card) A card on which is recorded the time spent by an employee at the place of work or the time spent on a particular job. The card is usually marked by mechanical or electronic means by recording the starting and ending times, enabling the elapsed time to be calculated.

time charter The hire of a ship or aircraft for a specified period of time rather than for a specified number of voyages (*compare* VOYAGE CHARTER).

time deposit A deposit of money in an interest-bearing account for a specified period. In the USA, a time deposit requires at least 30 days' notice of withdrawal.

time draft A *bill of exchange drawn on and accepted by a US bank. *See also* BANKER'S ACCEPTANCE.

time fence A period during which a *master production schedule (MPS) must not be changed, to enable the *material requirements planning to stabilize. Once the system is stable, the MPS can change.

time inconsistency In *utility theory, the idea that an individual's economic preferences may vary over time, sometimes in ways that do not accord with simple views of his or her rational self-interest. For example, if on 1 January 2015 a person was asked to choose between receiving £10,000 on 1 January 2030 or £11,000 on 1 July 2030, it seems certain that he would opt for the larger sum. However, if the same person was offered the same choice on 31 December 2029 the prospect of receiving an immediate £10,000 might be too attractive to resist. Time inconsistency is of major interest in the field of *behavioural finance. At the macroeconomic level, it has been used to explain *inflationary bias and to argue for a rules-based approach to *monetary policy.

time pacing The practice of producing, or introducing, new products according to a given schedule.

time rate A rate of pay expressed as a sum of money paid to an individual for the time worked, rather than for a specified output (*compare* PIECE RATE).

time-series analysis A marketing research technique for forecasting sales, in which past sales are broken down into trends, cycles, seasons, and erratic components; these components are then recombined to produce a sales forecast. *See also* NAIVE QUANTITATIVE METHODS.

time sharing A method of operating a computer in which several programs apparently run at the same time. Although the computer actually divides its time between the programs, it is fast enough to allow each program to operate at an acceptable speed. Most *multitasking and multiuser systems are time sharing systems.

time sheet A form on which is recorded the employee time or machine time spent on each activity during a period. It is used for costing jobs, operations, or activities.

time to market (TTM) The time taken to bring a new product or service from the initial concept stage to its introduction to the market. Shortening TTM can often deliver a substantial competitive advantage. *See* CONCURRENT ENGINEERING.

time value The market value of an *option over and above its *intrinsic value. The time value represents the value of the possibility that a movement in the price of the underlying will make the option worth exercising, even if it is not currently *in the money. This value declines exponentially as the expiry date approaches. At expiry the value of an option, if any, consists solely of its intrinsic value.

time value of money The concept, used as the basis for *discounted cash flow calculations, that cash received earlier is worth more than a similar sum received later, because the sum received earlier can be invested to earn interest in the intervening period. For the same reasons, cash paid out later is worth less than a similar sum paid at an earlier date.

tipping point The point at which a new idea, behaviour, or product suddenly breaks out from being a minority or elite interest and becomes a mass trend. The term originated in epidemiology but was widely popularized by Malcolm Gladwell's 2000 book *The Tipping Point*, which analysed why some trends achieve exponential growth while others fail to do so.

title deed A document proving the ownership of land. The document must go back at least 15 years to give a good root of title. If the land is registered, the *land certificate now takes the place of the title deed. *See* ABSTRACT OF TITLE.

tiyn A monetary unit of Kazakhstan, worth one hundredth of a *tenge.

TLF Abbreviation for *transferable loan facility.

TLS Abbreviation for *transport layer security.

Tobin's Q *See* Q RATIO.

Tobin tax A proposed low-level tax on foreign-exchange dealings. It has been suggested that such a tax could have the effect of restraining destabilizing currency speculation while also raising large sums that could be used to aid developing nations. The tax was first proposed by the US economist James Tobin (1918–2002). In the wake of the global financial crisis of 2008 there has been considerable interest in the idea of implementing a wider Tobin tax in the form of a general **Financial Transactions Tax (FTT)** or **Financial Activities Tax (FAT)**.

TOC Abbreviation for *theory of constraints.

toea A monetary unit of Papua New Guinea, worth one hundredth of a *kina.

toehold An initial stake in a company obtained as a prelude to an acquisition attempt.

token strike *See* STRIKE.

tokkin A special investment fund on the Japanese stock markets owned by companies using their cash surpluses to generate extra income, although their main business is not in the financial markets.

Tokyo Stock Exchange (TSE) The principal stock exchange of Japan, which is currently the third largest in the world by market capitalization. There are three sections. The first lists some 1,700 of the largest issues in the market. Around 70% of first-section companies are also listed in the markets in Osaka and Nagoya. The second section has around 500 stocks, with less stringent listing requirements, while the third section is for new high-growth companies (currently about 160). The TSE also has an *over-the-counter market in shares registered with the Japanese Securities Dealers Association. Electronic trading for all transactions was introduced in 2000. TSE members are either regulars, who deal in securities as principals, or agents (saitori), who can only act as intermediaries between regular members. The main market indicator is the *Nikkei Stock Average of 225 Japanese industrial companies.

(⊕) SEE WEB LINKS

• English-language version of the TSE website

tolar Formerly, the standard monetary unit of Slovenia, divided into 100 stotin. Slovenia adopted the euro in 2007.

tombstone An advertisement in the financial press giving brief deals of the amount and maturity of a recently completed bank facility. The names of the *lead managers are prominently displayed, as well as the co-managers and the managers. It is customary for the borrower to pay although he or she receives little benefit from the advertisement.

ton The formerly widely used **long ton** of 2240 pounds has now been replaced by the **metric ton** or **tonne** of 1,000 kilograms for all purposes of trade and commerce. In the USA the **short ton** of 2000 lb is still in use (consisting of 20 short hundredweights of 100 lb each). The **shipping ton** is a measure of cargo-carrying capacity and consists of 100 cubic feet of space (*see* TONNAGE).

tone The sentiment of a market. If a stock exchange or commodity market has a firm or strong tone, prices are tending upwards, whereas if the tone is weak, nervous, unsettled, etc., prices are tending to fall.

tonnage A measure of the volume or cargo-carrying capacity of a ship. The **gross register tonnage (GRT)** is the volume of a ship below the upper deck measured in shipping *tons of 100 cubic feet. The **net register tonnage (NRT)** is the GRT less the space occupied by engines, fuel, stores, and accommodation for crew and passengers. Harbour and port dues are usually based on the NRT and dry dock dues are usually based on the GRT. In the UK it is now mandatory to measure tonnage in either GRT or NRT, rather than in any of the various alternative ways sometimes used formerly.

tonnage tax A means of calculating the charge to *corporation tax of a shipowning company. Since 2000 a company may elect to pay corporation tax on the basis of the net register tonnage of its shipping, rather than on the basis of the profit or loss made.

tonne *See* TON.

tontine *See* LAST-SURVIVOR POLICY.

too big to fail The notion that certain banks or other financial institutions will always be supported in a crisis, because their failure would have an unacceptable effect on the stability of the national or international financial system. If such an institution should get into trouble, it is argued, the central bank would be compelled to bail it out; awareness of this fact creates a significant *moral hazard by making such a bank more willing to take risks. The counterargument is that even if it received aid, there might still be serious consequences for the managers and shareholders of the bank. In any case, the theory only applies to the largest financial institutions, and then not inevitably. Notoriously, in 2007 the US investment bank Lehman Brothers was allowed to fail after sustaining major losses on the *sub-prime mortgage market, with systemic effects in both the USA and abroad. By contrast, the Federal Reserve Bank provided a $30 billion loan to prevent the collapse of Bear Sterns in 2008. In the UK the Bank of England and HM Treasury provided over £25 billion of emergency support to the mortgage bank Northern Rock in 2007–08; the government also bought an 82% stake in the Royal Bank of Scotland to prevent its collapse. *See* SIFIs.

top-box score A high score in a scale used in marketing research to estimate purchase intentions. When companies are assessing the intention of potential customers to buy a product or service, they often use a 3-, 4-, 5-, 6-, or 7-point scale representing 'very unlikely to buy' (or some similar statement) to 'very likely to buy'. It is argued that companies should only use those percentages in the highest category ('very likely to buy') to estimate purchase intention.

top-down design An approach to product design based on general principles or deductive reasoning, rather than on empirical research or user feedback. *Compare* BOTTOM-UP DESIGN.

top-hat scheme A pension plan for a senior executive of a company. *See* EXECU-TIVE PENSION PLAN.

top slicing A method of assessing the taxable gain on a *life-assurance policy. The proceeds of the policy plus all capital withdrawals, less the premiums paid, are divided by the number of years for which the policy has been in force. This amount is added to any other income for the year in which the chargeable event occurred; if this places the taxpayer in a higher tax band, the whole gain is charged at the appropriate

marginal rate, i.e. the tax rate in that band less the basic rate of tax. If the sum does not exceed the basic rate tax, no further tax is due.

top up To increase the benefits due under an existing insurance scheme, especially to increase the provision for a pension when a salary increase enables the insured to pay increased premiums.

Toronto Stock Exchange (TSX) The main exchange for Canadian shares. Trading has been entirely electronic since April 1997, when the physical trading floor was closed. The main market indicators are the TSX 60 index and the wider TSX Composite index.

tort A civil wrong other than one relating to a contract. The law of tort is concerned with providing *damages for personal injury and damage to property resulting from negligence. It is also concerned with protecting against defamation of character and preserving personal freedom, enjoyment of property, and commercial interests. A person who commits a tort is called a **tortfeasor**.

total absorption costing *See* ABSORPTION COSTING.

total income The income of a taxpayer from all sources, before any *income-tax allowances are deducted. This is often referred to as **statutory total income** and comprises income from some sources calculated on the basis of the income of the current *fiscal year and income from other sources calculated on the basis of the *accounting period ending in the current fiscal year. This artificial concept is used to calculate a person's income tax for a given year. *See* BASIS OF ASSESSMENT.

total market demand The total volume of a product or service that would be bought by a defined consumer group in a defined geographic area in a defined period in a defined marketing environment under a defined level and mix of industry marketing effort.

total productive management (TPM)
An approach to management that
empowers the employees operating a piece
of equipment to take responsibility for a
wide range of routine maintenance tasks,
traditionally carried out by a separate
engineering function, and to develop a
proactive approach to the prevention of
failure. Integral to *total quality management, TPM is an essential part of *just-in-
time techniques. The overall objective is to
optimize the effectiveness of plant by
eliminating downtime, less-than-max-
imum speed of throughput, and process-
generated defects.

total profits Profits chargeable to *corporation tax (PCTCT), including profits
from trading, property, investment income,
overseas income, and chargeable gains,
less charges.

total quality management (TQM) An
approach to management that seeks to
integrate all the elements of an organization in order to meet the needs and
expectations of its customers. A number of
people have pioneered this approach,
including W. Edwards Deming, Armand
V. Feigenbaum, Kaoru Ishikawa, Joseph
M. Juran, and Genichi Taguchi. Some
details of their various methods are in
conflict, but all share a commitment to ensuring that all the parts of an organization
and all the individuals within the organization understand and contribute to the
desired outputs. The implementation of
TQM involves:

- a systematic and long-term commitment,
  in particular by senior management;
- a commitment to getting things right the
  first time;
- a commitment to *continuous improvement;
- an understanding of both internal and
  external customer–supplier relationships;
- an understanding of the total costs
  involved in the purchase of products and
  services, e.g. cheap inputs of low quality
  can cause serious faults in processes
  and products;

- a commitment to aligning systems to
  organizational needs, which may involve
  a radical redesign of work processes;
- appropriate management and training
  techniques to improve communications
  between sections and between staff and
  management;
- improved workplace training and a
  degree of employee *empowerment;
- meaningful measures of performance to
  enable workers to understand what they
  are contributing and how they can
  improve.

TQM as a philosophy should be able to
incorporate other programmes of management change. However, many organizations fail to exploit its full potential by
abandoning it too soon, either through lack
of commitment or because it costs too
much.

total return The total income plus the
capital growth obtained from an
investment.

total standard cost In *standard costing, the *total standard production cost
plus the *standard cost allowance for the
non-production overhead.

total standard production cost In
*standard costing, the total of *standard
direct materials cost, *standard direct
labour cost, the *standard fixed overhead
cost, and the *standard variable overhead
cost.

total standard profit The difference
between the sales at *standard selling
prices and the *standard overhead cost of
these sales.

TPM Abbreviation for *total productive
management.

TQM Abbreviation for *total quality
management.

tracker fund See INDEX TRACKING.

tracking stock A stock whose value
depends on the performance of a specific
unit or division of a company, rather than
that of the company as a whole, and which

is traded separately from the *ordinary shares of the company.

trade 1. The activity of selling goods or services in order to make a profit. Profits from trade are taxed under *income tax or *corporation tax on income, rather than under *capital gains tax or corporation tax on capital gains. The concept of trade is difficult to define for taxation purposes (*see* BADGES OF TRADE). **2.** To buy or sell in a market.

trade advertising Advertising that is aimed at members of the distribution channel of a product or service rather than at the consumer. It is sometimes advantageous to draw the attention of the trade to a product either in addition to *consumer advertising or instead of it (usually because it is much cheaper). For example, book publishers rarely go to the great expense of consumer advertising (say, on TV) but usually advertise a new book in the trade journals seen by booksellers, so that the staff in bookshops are kept advised of forthcoming productions.

trade agreement A commercial treaty between two (**bilateral trade agreement**) or more (**multilateral trade agreement**) nations.

trade association An association of companies in the same trade, formed to represent them in negotiations with governments, unions, other trade associations, etc., and to keep members informed of new developments affecting the trade. Trade associations also frequently draw up contracts for their members to use and provide arbitration procedures to settle disputes between members.

trade barrier Any action by a government that restricts free trading between organizations within that country and the world outside. Tariffs, quotas, embargoes, sanctions, and restrictive regulations all present barriers to free trade.

trade bill A *bill of exchange used to pay for goods. They are usually either held until they mature, as they do not command a

favourable discount rate compared to bank bills, or they are discounted by banks.

trade bloc A group of nations united by trade agreements between themselves; for example, the European Union.

trade credit Credit given by one company to another; it usually results when a supplier of goods or services allows the customer a period (e.g. 14 days, 90 days) before expecting an invoice to be settled.

trade creditor One who is owed money by an organization for having provided goods or services to that organization.

trade cycle *See* BUSINESS CYCLE.

trade description Any direct or indirect indication of certain characteristics of goods or of any part of them, such as their quantity, size, fitness for their purpose, time or place of origin, method of manufacture or processing, and price. Under the Trade Descriptions Act 1968, it is a criminal offence to apply a false trade description to goods or to supply or offer any goods to which a false description is applied.

trade discount (trade terms) A reduction on the recommended retail price of a product or service that is offered to distributors because they buy regularly in bulk. The difference between the retail price and the discounted price provides the retailer with his overheads and profit. The amount of the trade discount will often depend on the size of an order. Thus, a supermarket chain buying goods in very large quantities expects a higher trade discount than a corner shop buying in small quantities. It is also usual for members of the same trade to offer each other trade terms as a matter of course.

trade dispute (industrial dispute) A dispute between an employer and employees (or their trade union), usually about wages or conditions of working. Under the Trade Union and Labour Relations (Consolidation) Act 1992, a person cannot be sued in *tort for an act that is committed in furtherance of a trade dispute on the grounds that it induces or threatens any breach of interference with the performance of a contract. Generally, such immunity extends only to the acts of employees against their own employer. Secondary industrial action (*see* PICKETING) may be unlawful when it is directed against an employer who is neither a party to the dispute nor the customer or supplier of the employer in dispute. Moreover, there is no immunity in respect of action taken to enforce a *closed shop.

The 1992 Act gives similar immunity to trade unions for their acts committed in contemplation or furtherance of a trade dispute provided the act concerned is authorized by a majority vote in favour of the action in a secret ballot of the union's members. A trade union member can obtain a court order preventing industrial action being taken if it has not been authorized by a ballot.

When a trade union's immunity does not apply and it is ordered to pay damages (other than for causing personal injury or for breach of duty concerning the ownership, control, or use of property, or for *products liability under the Consumer Protection Act 1987), the amount awarded may not exceed specified limits. These limits depend on the number of members in the union.

traded option *See* OPTION. *See also* EXCHANGE-TRADED OPTION.

trade gap The difference between the value of a nation's imports and the value of its exports. *See also* BALANCE OF PAYMENTS.

trade investment Shares in or loans made to another company with a view to facilitating trade with the other company.

trademark A distinctive symbol that identifies particular products of a trader to the general public. The symbol may consist of a device, words, or a combination of these. A trader may register a trademark at the Register of Trade Marks, which is at the *Intellectual Property Office. This authorizes the trader to enjoy the exclusive right to the trademark in connection with the products for which it was registered. Any manufacturer, dealer, importer, or retailer

may register a trademark. Registration is initially for ten years and is then renewable. The right to remain on the register may be lost if the trademark is not used or is misused. The owner of a trademark may assign it or, subject to the Registrar's approval, allow others to use it. If anyone uses a registered trademark without the owner's permission, or uses a mark that is likely to be confused with a registered trademark, the owner can sue for an *injunction and *damages or an *account of profits.

A trademark is a form of *intellectual property and as such is an *intangible asset. Since 1996 it has been possible to obtain Community Trade Marks for the whole of the EU.

trade price The price paid for goods to a wholesaler or manufacturer by a retailer. It is usually the recommended retail price less the *trade discount.

trade promotion A sales promotion designed to gain reseller support and to improve reseller selling efforts. These include discounts, allowances, free goods, cooperative advertising, and push money, as well as conventions and trade shows. *See also* TRADE ADVERTISING.

trade reference A reference concerning the creditworthiness of a trader given by another member of the same trade, usually to a supplier. If a firm wishes to purchase goods on credit from a supplier, the supplier will usually ask for a trade reference from another member of the same trade, in addition to a *banker's reference.

trade secret Knowledge of some process or product belonging to a business, disclosure of which would harm the business's interests. In the UK, the courts will generally grant injunctions to prohibit any threatened disclosure of trade secrets by employees, former employees, and others to whom the secrets have been disclosed in confidence. *See also* INDUSTRIAL ESPIONAGE.

trade show A meeting or convention of members of a particular industry, at which business-to-business contacts are routinely made.

Trades Union Congress (TUC) The central UK organization to which most *trade unions belong. It represents the trade union movement in negotiations with the government and such bodies as the *Confederation of British Industry. It also acts as an arbitrator in disputes between member unions.

 SEE WEB LINKS
• Website of the TUC

trade terms *See* TRADE DISCOUNT.

trade union An organization whose principal purposes include the regulation of relations between employees and employers or employers' associations. A **house** (*or* **company**) **union** is an association of employees all belonging to the same company, which will probably have no connection with the trade union movement. An **industrial** (*or* **general**) **union** has members who work in the same industry; it is usually very large. A **craft union** is a small union of skilled workers. Unions' affairs are now regulated by the Trade Union and Labour Relations (Consolidation) Act 1992. This provides that secret ballots must be held for election of unions' executive committees and before any industrial action backed by the union is taken. The Act gives a right to trade union members not to be unjustifiably disciplined by their union (for example for failing to take industrial action). A member can apply to an *employment tribunal for a declaration that he or she has been unjustifiably disciplined.

trading account The part of a *profit and loss account in which the *cost of sales is compared with the money raised by their sale in order to arrive at the *gross profit.

trading estate (industrial estate) An area of land that has been granted planning permission for the development of factories, warehouses, offices, retail outlets, etc. Originating in the late 19th century (e.g. at Trafford Park, Manchester in 1896), they

offer land away from residential areas that is well served by transport and services; they also enable premises to be acquired at low rentals. *See also* SCIENCE PARK.

trading floor *See* FLOOR.

trading halt 1. The cessation of trading on a financial market when price movements reach the permitted *limit. **2.** The halting of trading in a particular security, usually as a result of a major news development or destabilizing rumour.

trading pit *See* PIT.

trading post The base on the trading *floor from which a specialist on a US stock exchange operates.

trading profit The *profit of an organization before deductions for such items as interest, directors' fees, auditors' remuneration, etc.

trading stock *See* STOCK-IN-TRADE.

traditional costing system Any of the systematic costing methods that prevailed before the rise of *activity-based costing in the 1990s. Because they rely on an essentially *arbitrary allocation of *indirect costs, such systems do not give managers accurate product cost information, which means that accurate calculation of product profitability is not possible. The overhead rate in a traditional costing system would typically be calculated using direct labour hours, machine hours, or units. This could lead to accurate product costs when direct costs were high and indirect costs were low, as was usually the case 50 years ago; however, modern organizations typically have low direct costs and higher indirect costs.

The strengths of traditional costing systems are:
• simplicity—the calculation of overhead rates is relatively straightforward;
• they are widely understood in the business;
• they are not expensive to operate;
• until the late 1980s they were seen as fairly accurate;

- they are still being used after many decades.

The weaknesses of traditional costing systems are:

- their reliance on arbitrary rather than *cause-and-effect allocation of overheads;
- their inability to give accurate product costs in multiproduct companies;
- their failure to analyse non-manufacturing costs.

traditional option See OPTION.

trait theories of leadership See LEADERSHIP THEORIES.

tramp ship A cargo-carrying ship that does not have a planned itinerary but carries its cargo to any ports for which its charterers can find cargo. Tramps are available for *voyage charter or *time charter (the latter is now more common) and many are tankers.

tranche (French: slice) **1.** A part or instalment of a large sum of money. In the International Monetary Fund the first 25% of a loan is known as the **reserve** (formerly **gold**) **tranche**. In **tranche funding**, successive sums of money become available on a prearranged basis to a new company, often linked to the progress of the company and its ability to reach the targets set in its *business plan. **2.** In a *securitization, any of several classes of debt instrument created from the same pool of assets but having different risk–return profiles to attract different classes of investor. The junior tranches bear a higher level of *credit risk than the senior tranches and consequently pay a higher coupon. See STRUCTURED FINANCE.

tranche CD A *certificate of deposit that has one maturity date but is sold by the issuing bank in portions (*tranches) to other investors.

transactional database A computerized database of the purchases made by a particular customer. See CUSTOMER DATABASE.

transactional leadership A *leadership style based on the setting of clear goals and objectives for followers and the use of rewards and punishments to encourage compliance. Compare TRANSFORMATIONAL LEADERSHIP. See also CONTINGENT REINFORCEMENT; POWER STYLES.

transaction costs In economics, the costs incurred in making a bargain, over and above the benefit exchanged. They typically include research costs, bargaining costs, and enforcement costs; there will also be agency costs if an agent is used (see AGENCY RELATIONSHIP). A simple example of a transaction cost is the commission paid to a broker when buying or selling securities.

transfer 1. The movement of money from one bank account to another. **2.** The movement of funds through the banking system's *clearing house. **3.** A large movement of dollars in the USA through the *fedwire system. **4.** The conveyance of property ownership by the transfer of deeds. **5.** See SHARE TRANSFER.

transferable Denoting a deed or other document the ownership of which can be transferred freely, e.g. a *negotiable instrument.

transferable loan facility (TLF) A bank loan facility that can be traded between lenders, in order to reduce the credit risk of the bank that provided the loan. It is a form of *securitization but can have an adverse effect on *relationship banking.

transfer credit risk The *credit risk that arises, especially on long-term contracts, as a result of a foreign debtor's inability to obtain foreign currency from the central bank at the appropriate time. This may occur even when the debtor is able and willing to pay. Compare POLITICAL CREDIT RISK. See also COUNTRY RISK.

transferee A person to whom an asset is transferred.

transfer of value The reduction in the value of a person's estate by a gratuitous transfer. Unless specifically exempted, such transfers are subject to *inheritance tax if made in a given period before the date of the donor's death. *See also* CHARGEABLE TRANSFER; EXEMPT TRANSFERS; POTENTIALLY EXEMPT TRANSFER.

transferor A person who transfers an asset to another (the transferee).

transfer payment (transfer income) A payment made or income received in which no goods or services are being paid for. Pensions, unemployment benefits, subsidies to farmers, etc., are transfer payments; they are excluded in calculating *gross national product.

transfer prices The prices at which goods and services are bought and sold between divisions or subsidiaries within a group of companies.

The transfer price is a cost to the receiving division and revenue to the supplying division: therefore the transfer price will affect the profitability of each division. In a complex organization there may be several buying and selling divisions in a group. Transfer prices can also apply between *cost centres.

Managers need to consider a complex range of issues when setting a transfer price. This is because transfer pricing can be used for several quite different purposes:

- to provide information that motivates managers to make good economic decisions;
- to provide information for evaluating the managerial and economic performance of divisions;
- to maintain divisional autonomy;
- to move profits between divisions, which may involve moving profits from one country to another to minimize tax on profits. (In the UK the scope for doing this has been greatly reduced by legislation passed in 2002 and 2010).

As a result, those setting transfer prices may find that they face a conflict of objectives. For example, senior managers of a group may want to maximize profitability even though this will means reducing the autonomy of divisional managers. This may

result in short-term increases in profitability but at the expense of the motivation of divisional managers in the long run.

There are six main transfer-pricing methods: *see* COST-PLUS TRANSFER PRICES; DUAL-RATE TRANSFER PRICES; FULL-COST TRANSFER PRICES; MARGINAL-COST TRANSFER PRICES; MARKET-BASED TRANSFER PRICES; NEGOTIATED TRANSFER PRICES.

transformational leadership A *leadership style that involves generating a vision for the organization and inspiring followers to meet the challenges that it sets. Transformational leadership depends on the leader's ability to appeal to the higher values and motives of followers and to inspire a feeling of loyalty and trust. Successful leadership of this kind usually has four components:

- individualized consideration—each team member is recognized and respected for their individual contribution;
- intellectual stimulation—the free exchange of ideas and opinions is encouraged;
- inspirational motivation—an optimistic but clear and attainable vision is set by the leader;
- charisma—the leader is seen to take responsibility, make personal sacrifices, show determination in the face of setbacks, and share any glory.

Compare TRANSACTIONAL LEADERSHIP.

transformation system A system that takes inputs and converts them into desired outputs. *See* OPERATIONS; TRANSFORMED RESOURCES; TRANSFORMING RESOURCES.

transformed resources Resources input into a *transformation system that are changed or acted upon by the system to produce the desired outputs. Examples include steel rod converted into bolts, survey data converted into market-research forecasts, and passengers transported from A to B. *Compare* TRANSFORMING RESOURCES.

transforming resources Resources input into a *transformation system that act upon, or facilitate action upon, *transformed resources to produce the desired outputs. Examples include machine tools, trained market researchers, and railway stations.

transhipment The shipment of goods from one port to another with a change of ship at an intermediate port. Tranship-ments are usually made because there is no direct service between the ports of ship-ment and destination, or because it is necessary for some political reason, e.g. wishing to conceal the port of shipment from the buyers, whose government may have embargoed goods from the country of that port.

transire A two-part document in which the cargo loaded onto a coaster is detailed. It is supplied by the Customs at the port of shipment; one part has to be handed to the Customs at the port of destination to prove that the cargo comes from a home port rather than an overseas port.

transparency 1. An essential condition of a free market in securities, in which trans-action prices and volumes of trade are vis-ible for all to see. **2.** The quality of a financial product that makes clear to the purchaser what the *front-end load and other charges will be.

transparent customization Changes in a product suggested by observed user behaviour rather than a user request.

transport layer security (TLS) A com-monly used *encryption technique for scrambling data, such as credit card num-bers, as they are passed across the Internet from a *web browser to a *web server. TLS was developed as a successor to the **secure sockets layer (SSL)** protocol.

travel insurance An insurance policy covering a variety of risks for the duration of a business trip or holiday. Although pol-icies vary, an average policy covers the policyholder's baggage and personal effects for all risks (*see* ALL-RISKS POLICY); com-pensation for delays while travelling to or from the destination; refund of deposits lost if the trip has to be cancelled for any of a number of specific causes; theft or loss of money, traveller's cheques, or credit cards; payment of medical expenses or costs of flying home in the event of illness or injury; and payment of legal compensation for injuring other people or damaging their property because of negligence.

traveller's cheque A cheque issued by a bank, building society, travel agency, credit-card company, etc., to enable a traveller to obtain cash in a foreign cur-rency when abroad. They may be cashed at banks, exchange bureaus, restaurants, hotels, some shops, etc., abroad on proof of identity. The traveller has to sign the cheque twice, once in the presence of the issuer and again in the presence of the paying bank, agent, etc. Most traveller's cheques are covered against loss.

treasure Under the Treasure Act 1996, any item with no known owner that is at least 300 years old and contains over 5% precious metal (except single coins). All such treasure belongs to the Crown, which will reward the finder.

treasurer 1. A person who is responsible for looking after the money and other assets of an organization. This may include overseeing the provision of the organiza-tion's finances as well as some stewardship over the way in which the money is spent. **2.** In more recent times, the man-ager responsible for an organization's rela-tionship with financial markets.

Treasury The UK government department responsible for the country's financial pol-icies and management of the economy. The First Lord of the Treasury is the Prime Minister, but the Treasury is run by the Chancellor of the Exchequer.

(((●))) SEE WEB LINKS

• HM Treasury area of the Gov.uk website: includes latest economic indicators and forecasts for the UK economy

Treasury bill A *bill of exchange issued by the Bank of England on the authority of the UK government that is repayable in three months. They bear no interest, the yield being the difference between the purchase price and the redemption value. The US Treasury also issues Treasury bills.

Treasury bill rate The rate of interest obtainable by buying a *Treasury bill at a discount and selling it at its redemption value.

Treasury bill tender A weekly sale of Treasury bills to UK *discount houses by the Bank of England. The cost of the bills is set by the **Treasury bill tender rate**.

Treasury bond A bond issued by the US Treasury.

Treasury Investment Growth Receipts *See* TIGR.

treasury stock A US term for shares that have been repurchased by the issuing company, thereby reducing the number of its shares on the open market. *See* BUY-BACK.

Treasury stocks *See* GILT-EDGED SECURITY.

treaty 1. Any formal agreement in writing between nations. A **commercial treaty** relates to trade between the signatories. **2.** A transaction in which a sale is negotiated between the parties involved (**by private treaty**) rather than by auction. **3.** An agreement, usually in reinsurance, in which a reinsurer agrees automatically to accept risks from an insurer, either when a certain sum insured is exceeded or on the basis of a percentage of every risk accepted. With such a treaty an insurer has the confidence and capacity to accept larger risks than would otherwise be possible, as the necessary reinsurance is already arranged.

Treaty of Rome The 1957 treaty that set up the *European Economic Community (EEC), now the *European Union.

Treynor's alpha *See* ALPHA COEFFICIENT.

trial balance A listing of the balances on all the accounts of an organization, with debit balances in one column and credit balances in the other. If the rules of *double-entry book-keeping have been accurately applied, the totals of each column should be the same. If they are not the same, checks must be carried out to find the discrepancy. The figures in the trial balance after some adjustments, e.g. for closing stocks, prepayments and accruals, depreciation, are used to prepare the final accounts (profit and loss account and balance sheet). *See also* EXTENDED TRIAL BALANCE.

trial sampling The distribution as free samples of newly marketed products to consumers to enhance familiarity with the product. If a favourable impression is made by the free sample, consumers are encouraged to place a trial order.

Trinity House A UK corporation granted its first charter in 1514. It is responsible for lighthouses, aids to navigation maintained by local harbours, and dealing with wrecks that present a hazard to navigation in England and Wales and the Channel Islands. A separate authority, the **Northern Lighthouse Board**, is responsible for these matters in Scotland and the Isle of Man.

triple bottom-line accounting (TBL) A method of measuring a company's social and environmental impact in addition to its economic value. Triple bottom-line accounting seeks to appraise not only (i) the conventional 'bottom line' of economic profit and loss, but also (ii) a company's 'people account', a measure of *corporate social responsibility, and (iii) its 'planet account', a gauge of its environmental impact. The concept was introduced by John Elkington in 1994.

triple witching hour The third Friday of each March, June, September, and December, when stock-index options, futures, and individual stock options all expire at the same time. This makes for very volatile trading conditions.

true and fair view Auditors of the published accounts of companies are required to form an opinion as to whether the accounts they audit show a 'true and fair view' of the organization's affairs. This is an important concept in the UK and may be used as an override to depart from legal requirements. Despite its importance there is no legal definition of the expression. The meaning of 'true and fair view' develops over time as accounting standards are issued and new accounting issues are debated. The US and *International Accounting Standards equivalent of the concept is *fair presentation.

trunking Delivering goods by road over long distances, usually by means of a service that has local distribution depots, from which collections and deliveries are made.

trust 1. An arrangement enabling property to be held by a person or persons (the *trustees) for the benefit of some other person or persons (the beneficiaries). The trustee is the legal owner of the property but the beneficiary has an equitable interest in it. A trust may be intentionally created or it may be imposed by law (e.g. if a trustee gives away trust property, the recipient will hold that property as constructive trustee for the beneficiary). Trusts are commonly used to provide for families and in commercial situations (e.g. pensions trusts). *See also* DISCRETIONARY TRUST; 18–25 TRUST; INTEREST-IN-POSSESSION TRUST; RELEVANT PROPERTY TRUST. **2.** In the USA, a form of monopoly in which the owners of merging corporations gave their stock to a board of trustees, who were empowered to act on their behalf. Such monopolies were largely outlawed by the antitrust laws.

trust bank A Japanese bank that both lends and accepts savings; it also carries out trust activities, usually involving property or pension funds.

trust deed The document creating and setting out the terms of a *trust. It will usually contain the names of the trustees, the identity of the beneficiaries, and the nature of the trust property, as well as the powers and duties of the trustees. Trusts of land must be declared in writing; trusts of other property need not be although there is often a trust deed to avoid uncertainty.

trustee A person who holds the legal title to property but who is not its beneficial

owner. Usually there are two or more trustees of a *trust and for some trusts of land this is necessary. The trustee may not profit from the position but must act for the benefit of the beneficiary, who may be regarded as the real owner of the property. Either an individual or a company may act as trustee. It is usual to provide for the remuneration of trustees in the trust deed, otherwise there is no right to payment. Trustees may be personally liable to beneficiaries for loss of trust property.

trust fund A fund consisting of the assets belonging to a *trust, including money and property, that is held by the *trustees for the beneficiaries.

trust letter A document that assigns goods to a bank as security against a loan and enables the borrower to regain title of the goods in order to sell them to pay off the loan.

trust receipt A document given by a bank holding a borrower's goods as security against a loan (*see* TRUST LETTER), when the borrower takes possession of these goods in order to sell them to pay off the loan.

Truth in Lending Act US consumer protection legislation, dating from 1969, that requires lenders to state how they calculated interest on loans and other charges and to express them as an *annual percentage rate. The Act also allows the borrower a 'cooling off' period, authorizing withdrawal from a financial agreement on a mortgage, within three days of signing a consumer credit agreement.

TSE Abbreviation for *Tokyo Stock Exchange.

TSX Abbreviation for *Toronto Stock Exchange.

TT Abbreviation for *telegraphic transfer.

TTM Abbreviation for *time to market.

TUC Abbreviation for *Trades Union Congress.

tugrik (MNT) The standard monetary unit of Mongolia, divided into 100 möngös.

TUPE See RELEVANT TRANSFER.

turnaround (recovery) A strategy designed to reverse the decline in profitability of a firm or subsidiary, enabling it to achieve a viable and sustainable future. Firms in crisis require drastic action to effect a turnaround, which may involve managerial changes, redundancies (*see* DOWNSIZING), or closure to avoid receivership. See SHARPBENDER.

Turnbull Report A report (1999) providing directors of UK listed companies with guidance on *risk management and *internal controls and their obligations with regard to both under the *Corporate Governance Code. It was prepared by a working party of the Institute of Chartered Accountants in England and Wales and endorsed by the London Stock Exchange. Revised guidelines were issued in 2005 and 2014.

turnkey system 1. The planning and execution of a major capital project, in which one company has responsibility for its overall management, so that the client only has to 'turn the key' in order to start the operation. **2.** A computer system that is ready to start work as soon as it is installed. All the necessary programs and equipment are supplied with the system.

turnover 1. The total sales figure of an organization for a stated period. Turnover is defined in the Companies Acts as the total revenue of an organization derived from the provision of goods and services, less trade discounts, VAT, and any other taxes based on this revenue. **2.** More generally, the rate at which some asset is sold and replaced by one of the same class. See CAPITAL TURNOVER; LABOUR TURNOVER RATE; STOCK TURNOVER. See also RATE OF TURNOVER. **3.** The total value of the transactions on a market or stock exchange in a specified period.

turnover ratio See RATE OF TURNOVER.

turnover tax A tax on the sales made by a business, i.e. on its turnover. See SALES TAX.

turn-round rate The total cost of a transaction on a commodity market, including the broker's commission and the fee charged by the *clearing house.

Turquoise An electronic pan-European trading platform established by a consortium of nine leading investment banks in 2008. Turquoise was originally limited to equities trading but subsequently expanded into futures and options. The London Stock Exchange acquired a controlling interest in 2009 and in 2011 Turquoise was merged with the LSE's derivatives platform EDX London.

TV 1. Abbreviation for television. **2.** Abbreviation for *terminal value.

TVR Abbreviation for *television rating.

24-hour trading Round-the-clock dealings in securities, bonds, and currency. In practice, it is not normally carried out from any one office of a securities house; instead, the dealers in one time zone pass on their *position to associates in another time zone. Thus, a London office may pass its position to its New York office, which is passed, in turn, to Tokyo, and back to London. Twenty-four-hour trading has been encouraged by the rise in cross-border share trading.

Twitter A *social-media platform, first launched in 2006, that enables users to post and read short messages over the Internet. Messages, known as **tweets**, may be up to 140 characters in length and are received by all users who have chosen to 'follow' the sender. As those who receive messages may opt to 'retweet' them to their followers, and so on, a popular tweet may quickly reach a very large readership. Twitter now has over 270 million active users (2014) and is widely used by businesses for marketing and publicity.

two-factor theory of motivation
See HYGIENE FACTORS; MOTIVATION.

two-handed process chart A technique used in *work study to identify the individual movements of both hands. *See* ERGONOMICS.

two-tier board A method of running a large organization in which, in addition to a board of management, there is a *supervisory board. It is claimed that this practice, which is common in Continental Europe, provides an effective method of *corporate governance. In the UK, the normal practice is for a single board to consist of both executive and *non-executive directors.

two-tier tender offer In a *takeover bid, a *tender offer to purchase in which shareholders are offered a high initial offer for sufficient shares to give the bidder a controlling interest in the company, followed by an offer to acquire the remaining shares at a lower price. Bidders use this technique in order to provide an incentive to shareholders to accept the initial offer quickly. Such offers are usually for a combination of cash and shares in the bidder's own company. They are illegal in some countries, notably the UK. *See also* BOOTSTRAP.

tyiyn A monetary unit of Kyrgyzstan, worth one hundredth of a *som.

uberrima fides See UTMOST GOOD FAITH.

ubiquitous computing (ambient computing; pervasive computing) A model for the development of computing in the early 21st century. It envisages a movement away from 'computers' as distinct specialized devices; rather, many objects used in everyday life will contain embedded computing devices that can interact in useful ways with each other and with their environment. Such a model becomes possible as the size of computing devices decreases and wireless networking makes the ad-hoc self-configuring networks necessary for ubiquitous computing viable. Ubiquitous computing is currently a subject of both academic and commercial research.

UBR Abbreviation for Uniform Business Rate. See BUSINESS RATES.

UCITS Acronym for Undertakings for Collective Investment in Transferable Securities: *unit trusts or *investment trusts that are permitted to operate throughout the EU on the basis of their admission by the domestic regulator in one member state. A set of rules making this possible was adopted in 1985 and widened in 2001 and 2009.

UGC Abbreviation for *user-generated content.

UK Balance of Payments An annual publication of the *Office for National Statistics. It is often known as the **Pink Book** and is now available online as well as in printed form. See BALANCE OF PAYMENTS.

UK Export Finance See EXPORT CREDITS GUARANTEE DEPARTMENT.

UK National Accounts An annual publication of the *Office for National Statistics. It is often known as the **Blue Book** and is now available online as well as in printed form. It provides figures for the *gross domestic product and separate accounts of production, income, and expenditure.

UK Payments Administration (UKPA) A body established in 2009 as successor to the **Association for Payment Clearing Services (APACS)**, the organization set up by UK banks in 1985 to manage payment clearing and overseas money transmission. UKPA provides services and facilities to four main operating companies: **Bacs** (formerly Bankers' Automated Clearing System), which is responsible for automated interbank clearing and settlement services in the UK, including direct debits and credits; **Cheque and Credit Clearing Co. Ltd**, which operates a bulk clearing system for cheques and other paper instruments; **CHAPS Co**, which provides high-value same-day electronic funds transfer in sterling and euros; and **Faster Payments**, a new service that enables customers to make express payments by phone or online. UKPA also works closely with the UK Cards Association, the body representing the card payments industry, and LINK, the network of UK cash machines. See also VOCALINK.

(())) SEE WEB LINKS
• Website of the UK Payments Administration

ullage 1. The amount by which the full capacity of a barrel or similar container exceeds the volume of the contents, as a result of evaporation or leakage. **2.** As defined by HM Revenue and Customs, the actual contents of a barrel or similar container at the time of importation into the UK. The difference between this volume and the full capacity is called the **vacuity**.

ULS Abbreviation for *unsecured loan stock.

ultimate holding company (ultimate parent company) A *company that is the *holding company of a group in which some of the subsidiary companies are themselves *immediate holding companies of their own groups.

ultimo *See* INSTANT.

ultra vires (Latin: beyond the powers) Denoting an act of an official or corporation for which there is no authority. The powers of officials exercising administrative duties and of corporations are limited by the instrument from which their powers are derived. If they act outside these powers, their action may be challenged in the courts. Until recently, a company's powers were limited by the *objects clause in its *memorandum of association; if it entered into an agreement outside these objects, the agreement could be challenged. The Companies Act 2006 removes the requirement for a company to restrict its objects in this way (unless it is a charitable company).

umbrella fund An *offshore fund consisting of a *fund of funds that invests in other offshore funds.

umpire *See* ARBITRATION.

unabsorbed cost The part of the overhead costs of a production process that is not covered by its revenue when the output falls below a specified level. Overheads are sometimes added to the *direct costs of a process and divided by the output to give a *unit cost. The output for this calculation is often set at such a level that the whole of the overheads are absorbed by the unit cost. If, in fact, the output falls below this level, the whole of the overheads will not be absorbed, the deficit being the unabsorbed cost.

unamortized cost 1. The *historical cost of a *fixed asset less the total *depreciation shown against that asset up to a specified date. **2.** The value given to a fixed asset in the accounts of an organization after *revaluation of assets less the total depreciation shown against that asset since it was revalued.

unappropriated profit The part of an organization's *profit that is neither allocated to a specific purpose nor paid out in *dividends. *See* APPROPRIATION.

unbundling 1. The separation of a business into its constituent parts, generally by selling off certain subsidiaries or business lines. **2.** The selling off of separate parts of a security, for example its *coupon.

uncalled capital *See* RESERVE CAPITAL.

uncertificated units A small number of units purchased for an investor in a *unit trust by reinvestment of dividends. If the number of units is too small to warrant the issue of a certificate they are held on account for the investor and added to the total when the holding is sold.

uncleared effects Financial documents lodged with a bank for collection, still held by the bank pending the completion of the collection.

uncommitted facility An agreement between a bank and a company in which the bank agrees in principle to make funding available to the company but is under no obligation to provide a specified amount of funding; if a loan is made it will be for only a short period. Examples of an uncommitted facility include a *money-market line or an *overdraft. *Compare* COMMITTED FACILITY.

unconditional bid *See* TAKEOVER BID.

unconfirmed letter of credit *See* LETTER OF CREDIT.

unconscionable bargain *See* CATCHING BARGAIN.

unconsolidated subsidiary An undertaking that, although it is a *subsidiary undertaking of a group, is not included in the *consolidated financial statements of the group.

uncontrollable costs (non-controllable costs) Items of expenditure appearing on a manager's *management accounting statement that cannot be controlled or influenced by that level of management. Costs regarded as uncontrollable by one level of management may, however, be controllable at a higher level. There is always potential for disagreement over what is or is not an uncontrollable cost. Correctly identifying such costs is important for *performance measurement. *Compare* CONTROLLABLE COSTS. *See also* CONTROLLABILITY CONCEPT.

uncontrollable turnover *See* LABOUR TURNOVER RATE.

uncoupling inventory *See* INVENTORY.

UNCTAD Abbreviation for *United Nations Conference on Trade and Development.

undated security A *fixed-interest security that has no *redemption date. *See* CONSOLS.

underabsorbed overhead (underapplied overhead) In *absorption costing, the circumstance in which the absorbed overhead is less than the overhead costs incurred for a period. This adverse *variance represents a reduction of the budgeted profits of the organization.

undercapitalization The state of a company that does not have sufficient *capital or *reserves for the size of its operations. For example, this may be due to the company growing too quickly. Although such a company may be making profits it may be unable to convert these profits sufficiently quickly into cash to pay its debts. *Compare* OVERCAPITALIZATION.

underlying The asset, measure, or obligation on which a *derivative, such as an option or futures contract, is based.

underpositioning A *positioning error involving a failure to position a company, its product, or brand correctly.

understandability The accounting principle that the financial information provided by a company should be such that its significance is capable of being perceived by a person with a reasonable knowledge of business and accounting and a willingness to study it with reasonable diligence. The information should not leave out anything material, but should not be so comprehensive that the main points of significance are obscured.

The concept is defined in the Financial Reporting Standard Applicable in the UK and Republic of Ireland. It is also recognized in the International Accounting Standards Board's Conceptual Framework.

undersubscription *See* OVERSUBSCRIPTION.

underwriter 1. A person who examines a risk, decides whether or not it can be insured, and, if it can, works out the premium to be charged, usually on the basis of the frequency of past claims for similar risks. Underwriters are either employed by insurance companies or are members of *Lloyd's. The name arises from the early days of marine insurance, when a merchant would, as a sideline, *write* his name *under* the amount and details of the risk he had agreed to cover, on a slip of paper. 2. The firm that issues an insurance policy, thereby accepting liability for specified losses. 3. A financial institution, usually a *merchant bank, that guarantees to buy a proportion of any unsold shares, bonds, etc. when a new issue is offered to the public. Underwriters usually work for a commission, and a number may combine together to buy all the unsold shares, provided that the minimum subscription stated in the prospectus has been sold to the public. 4. Any person or enterprise that accepts financial responsibility for a transaction or project.

undifferentiated marketing The marketing of a product aimed at the widest possible market. An early example was the

u

Model T Ford, which was mass-produced, aimed at a very wide market, and only available in black. Ford now produce a wide range of models, with different engine capacities, colours, and prices aimed at attracting a wide variety of tastes and requirements. *Compare* DIFFERENTIATED MARKETING.

undischarged bankrupt A person whose *bankruptcy has not been discharged. Such persons may not obtain credit (above £500) without first informing the creditor that they are undischarged bankrupts, become directors of companies, or trade under another name. Undischarged bankrupts may not hold office as a JP, MP, mayor, or councillor.

undisclosed factoring A form of *factoring in which the seller of goods does not wish to disclose the use made of a factor. In these circumstances, the factor buys the goods that have been sold (rather than the debt their sale incurred) and, as an *undisclosed principal, appoints the original seller to act as agent to recover the debt. The factor assumes responsibility in the case of non-payment so that from the point of view of the seller, the factor offers the same service as in normal factoring.

undisclosed principal A person who buys or sells through an agent or broker and remains anonymous. The agent or broker must disclose when dealing on behalf of an undisclosed principal; failure to do so may result in the agent being treated in law as the principal and in some circumstances the contract may be made void.

undistributable reserves (capital reserves) *Reserves that may not be distributed according to the Companies Act. They include *share capital, *share premium account, *capital redemption reserve, certain *unrealized profits, or any other reserve that the company may not distribute according to some other Act or its own constitutional documents. In the USA such reserves are known as **restricted surplus**. *Compare* DISTRIBUTABLE PROFITS.

undistributed profit Profit earned by an organization but not distributed to its shareholders by way of *dividends. Such sums are available for later distribution but are frequently used by companies to finance their activities. *See* RETAINED EARNINGS.

undiversifiable risk *See* SYSTEMATIC RISK.

undue influence Unfair pressure exerted on a person to sign a contract that is not a true expression of that person's aims or requirements at the time, but is to the advantage of another party (either a party to the contract or a third party). Such a contract may be set aside by a court.

unearned income Income not derived from trades, professions or vocations, or from the emoluments of office. In the UK it was formerly taxed more heavily than earned income, through the imposition of an investment-income surcharge. Earned and unearned income are now taxed at essentially the same rates, with some minor differences in the treatment of income from savings and company dividends.

unemployment An inability to find work although it is actively sought. Theoretically the unemployed are those members of the active labour force who are out of work, although in most cases statistics are based on the number of people claiming jobseeker's allowance. Unemployment has been a persistent problem in industrial economies during *recession over the last 200 years. *See also* FRICTIONAL UNEMPLOYMENT; HIDDEN UNEMPLOYMENT; RESIDUAL UNEMPLOYMENT; SEASONAL UNEMPLOYMENT.

unexpired cost The balance of an item of expenditure, recorded in the books of account of an organization, that has not been written off to the profit and loss account. For example, the *net book value of an asset represents the unexpired cost of that asset.

unfair contract terms In consumer contracts, certain terms relating to the exclusion or restriction of a manufacturer's liability that, under the Unfair Contract Terms Act 1977 and Unfair Terms in Consumer Contracts Regulations 1999, are either ineffective or effective only so far as is reasonable.

unfair dismissal Any *dismissal of an employee that the employer cannot show to be fair. Under the Employment Rights Act 1996 employees have the right not to be unfairly dismissed, provided they have served the required period of continuous employment (52 weeks for full-time employment). Dismissal for membership or non-membership of a trade union is always regarded as unfair dismissal, whatever the employee's length of service. Employees who consider that they have been unfairly dismissed can apply within three months after the effective date of termination of their employment contract to an *employment tribunal for reinstatement, re-engagement, or compensation. The tribunal will make an award unless the employer shows that the principal reason for the dismissal was the employee's incapability, lack of qualifications, or conduct; redundancy; the fact that it would be illegal to continue employing the person; or some other substantial reason. The employer must also show that he acted reasonably in dismissing the employee. *Compare* WRONGFUL DISMISSAL.

unfair prejudice Conduct in the running of a company's affairs that may entitle members to a remedy under the Companies Act. In small companies, the unfairness may consist of a failure by some members to honour a common understanding reached when the company was formed, e.g. that a member be allowed to assist in the management and be paid accordingly. The usual remedy sought is for the purchase of the member's shares at a fair price. *See also* MINORITY PROTECTION.

unfair trading *See* CONSUMER PROTECTION.

unfavourable balance A *balance of trade or *balance of payments deficit.

unfunded pension system *See* PAY-AS-YOU-GO PENSION SYSTEM.

Unicode In computing, a coding standard in which one or more bytes are used to represent each character. Unicode allows unique definition of symbols, foreign alphabets, Chinese ideographs, etc. To date over 110,000 have been defined.

UNIDO Abbreviation for *United Nations Industrial Development Organization.

Unified Patent Court *See* EUROPEAN PATENT COURT.

Uniform Business Rate (UBR) *See* BUSINESS RATES.

uniform delivered pricing A geographic pricing strategy in which a company charges the same price, including freight charges, to all its customers, regardless of their location.

uniform load scheduling (level scheduling) An approach to scheduling work that aims to produce small quantities of each product each day, throughout the day. *just-in-time techniques are designed to work on the basis of level scheduling.

uniform resource locator (universal resource locator; URL) An address for a specific resource on the Internet. The URL always starts with the protocol for data transfer (http for web pages and ftp for file transfer protocol). A web page has a URL of the form

    http://www.domain-name.extension/filename.html

See also DOMAIN NAME.

unilateral contract A *contract in which one party (the promisor) undertakes to do or refrain from doing something if the other party (the promisee) does or refrains from doing something, but the promisee does not undertake to do or refrain from doing that thing. An example of a unilateral contract is one in which the promisor offers a reward for the giving of information. *Compare* BILATERAL CONTRACT.

unilateral relief Relief against *double taxation given by the UK authorities for tax paid in another country with which the UK has no double-taxation agreement.

uninsurable risk *See* INSURABLE RISK.

unique selling proposition (USP) A product benefit that can be regarded as unique and therefore can be used in advertising to differentiate it from the competition. The concept is not now as popular as it was as not every product can have a USP.

unique value effect Features and benefits of a product that make it unique in its field, thereby lowering the price sensitivity of potential customers. The unique value effect raises consumers' willingness to pay higher prices.

unissued share capital The difference between the *authorized share capital of a company and the *issued share capital.

unit banking A system of banking in which a bank must be a single enterprise without branches. This was once common practice in the USA, but regulators have turned against this form of bank, following the collapse of the Continental Illinois Bank in 1984.

unit cost Expenditure incurred by an organization expressed as a rate per unit of production or sales. It may be difficult to make valid comparisons of unit costs between organizations. The main problem is the *arbitrary allocation of *fixed overhead costs.

United Nations Conference on Trade and Development (UNCTAD) A permanent organization set up by the UN in 1964 to encourage international trade, particularly to help developing countries to finance their exports. Under its auspices the **UN Common Fund for Commodities (CFC)** was established in 1989 to provide finance for international commodity organizations to enable *buffer stocks to be maintained and to carry out research into the development of *commodity markets.

United Nations Industrial Development Organization (UNIDO) An international organization that became a specialized agency of the UN in 1986, having developed from the Centre for Industrial Development, set up in 1961. With headquarters in Vienna, its aim is to promote the industrialization of developing countries by providing planning policies and technical advice and assistance. UNIDO suffered a major crisis in the mid 1990s, when the USA, Canada, and Australia withdrew from the organization. It has since reformed its structures and processes.

unitization The process of changing an *investment trust into a *unit trust.

unit labour costs The total expenditure on labour per unit of output. A comparison between changes in *productivity and unit labour costs in different countries enables economists to make predictions about changes in their *competitiveness. For example, if unit labour costs and productivity both rise by the same amount in the UK, UK producers do not have to change the prices of their goods; if, however, Japanese unit labour costs rise by less than productivity, Japanese prices could fall, making them increasingly competitive.

unit-level activities *See* ACTIVITY.

unit-linked policy A *life-assurance policy in which the benefits depend on the performance of a portfolio of shares. Each premium paid by the insured person is split: one part is used to provide life-assurance cover, while the balance (after the deduction of costs, expenses, etc.) is used to buy units in a *unit trust. In this way a small investor can benefit from investment in a *managed fund without making a large financial commitment. As they are linked to the value of shares, unit-linked policies can go up or down in value. Policyholders can surrender the policy at any time and the *surrender value is the selling price of the units purchased by the date of cancellation (less expenses). Recent decades have also seen a widespread increase in **unit-linked savings plans**, both with and without life-assurance cover.

unit of account 1. A function of *money enabling its users to calculate the value of their transactions and to keep accounts. **2.** The standard unit of currency of a country. **3.** An artificial currency used only for accounting purposes.

unit price The price paid per unit of item purchased or charged per unit of product sold.

unit pricing The practice of showing the price of a single unit of a product in order that shoppers can compare the price against the cost of a multipack. A single bag of crisps in a supermarket might cost 30p. A larger bag containing six single bags could be offered at £1.50, i.e. a unit price of 25p each. The shopper can therefore see at a glance that the larger purchase is the more economical.

unit profit (*or* **loss**) The profit (or loss) attributable to one unit of production. *See* UNIT COST.

unit standard operating profit The *standard operating profit, expressed as a rate per unit of production or sales.

unit standard production cost The *standard production cost, expressed as a rate per unit of production or sales.

unit trust 1. In the UK, an investment fund shared by a large number of different investors. A unit trust is an 'open-ended fund', which means that the fund gets bigger as more people invest and smaller as people withdraw their money. A fund manager is responsible for the fund and makes the investment decisions. The fund is divided into segments called 'units'. Investors take a stake in the fund by buying these units, the price of which will vary as the value of the investments the trust has invested in increase or decrease. The *Financial Conduct Authority authorizes firms that sell unit trusts, most of which belong to the *Investment Management Association (IMA). Investors should always look carefully at the charges associated with unit trusts. Basic-rate tax is deducted from the dividends paid by unit trusts and

capital gains on the sale of a holding are subject to capital gains tax. In the USA unit trusts are called **mutual funds**. **2.** A trust scheme (also called a **unit investment trust**) in the USA in which investors purchase **redeemable trust certificates**. The money so raised is used by the trustees to buy such securities as bonds, which are usually held until they mature. Usually both the number of certificates issued and the investments held remain unchanged during the life of the scheme, but the certificates can be sold back to the trustees at any time.

univariate statistics *See* DESCRIPTIVE STATISTICS.

universal banking Banking that involves not only services related to loans and savings (retail or commercial banking) but also trading on financial markets and making investments in companies. Universal banking has traditionally been most common in Germany, Switzerland, and the Netherlands. The *Glass–Steagall Act 1933 prohibited universal banking in the USA, but the restrictions placed on it were effectively removed in 1999. In the UK it was largely avoided until the late 1990s, after which there was rapid expansion in the trading activities of leading banks. In the wake of the financial crisis of 2007–08 there have been growing calls for a renewed separation between retail and *investment banking.

universal product code (**UPC**) The form of *bar code found on most products for sale in retail outlets in the UK, North America, and Australia.

universe *See* POPULATION.

UNIX A computer operating system that originated in Bell Laboratories in 1969. Originally used mainly by universities, it proved significant in the development of the Internet and is now widely used in workstations, mobile devices, and mid-range systems.

unlimited company A *company whose *shareholders do not benefit from limited liability (*compare* LIMITED COMPANY). Such companies are exempt from filing accounts with the *Registrar of Companies.

unlimited liability A liability to pay all the debts incurred by a business. For a *sole proprietor or general partner (*see* PARTNERSHIP), liability is not limited to the amount he or she has agreed to invest. All debts of the business must not only be paid out of the assets of the business but also, if necessary, out of personal assets.

unliquidated damages *See* DAMAGES.

unlisted securities (unquoted securities) Securities (usually *equities) in companies that are not on an official stock-exchange list. They are therefore not required to satisfy the standards set for listing (*see* LISTED SECURITY). Unlisted securities are usually issued in relatively small companies and their shares usually carry a high degree of risk. In London, unlisted securities are traded on the *Alternative Investment Market. Other exchanges have similar markets.

unofficial strike *See* STRIKE.

unorganization An approach to *organizational design that aims to maximize a company's flexibility by dismantling most of its formal structures and processes. In practice this will usually mean *delayering of management, *outsourcing of projects, and the encouragement of *teleworking by employees. *See also* ADHOCRACY; SHAMROCK ORGANIZATION; VIRTUAL ORGANIZATION.

unpaid cheque A cheque that has been sent to the payee's bank and then through the clearing process only to be returned to the payee because value cannot be transferred. If the reason is lack of funds the bank will mark the cheque 'refer to drawer'.

unquoted securities *See* UNLISTED SECURITIES.

unrealized profit/loss A profit or loss that results from holding *assets rather than using them; it is therefore a profit or loss that has not been realized in cash.

unsecured creditor A person who is owed money by an organization but who has not arranged that in the event of non-payment specific assets would be available as a fund out of which he or she could be paid in priority to other creditors. *Compare* SECURED CREDITOR.

unsecured debt A debt that is not covered by any kind of collateral.

unsecured loan stock (ULS; unsecured debenture) A loan stock or *debenture in which no specific assets have been set aside as a fund out of which the debenture holders could be paid in priority to other creditors in the event of non-payment. *Compare* SECURED DEBENTURE.

unsocial hours Working hours, other than normal office or factory hours, that prevent an employee from enjoying family life and the usual social activities. Shift workers and workers who have to work unsocial hours are often paid at higher rates than 9–5 workers.

unsubscribe To *opt out from an e-mail newsletter, mailing list, online discussion group, etc.

unvalued policy An insurance policy for property that has a sum insured shown for each item although the insurers do not acknowledge that this figure is its actual value. As a result, if a claim is made the insured must provide proof of the value of the item lost, damaged, or stolen before a payment will be made. The policy may have a maximum specified payment. *Compare* VALUED POLICY.

UPC Abbreviation for universal product code. *See* BAR CODE.

upload To transfer a copy of a file from a local computer to a remote server. It is usually achieved using *FTP.

up-selling A sales technique in which the customer is encouraged to buy something in addition to his or her intended purchase or to consider a more expensive alternative. For example, customers who buy expensive consumer goods are usually encouraged to take out an extended warranty. *See also* CROSS-SELLING.

upstream Denoting a loan from a subsidiary company to its parent, for example a loan from a subsidiary of a bank to its holding company to enable the holding company to pay its dividends.

URL Abbreviation for *uniform resource locator, i.e. an address on the Internet.

URL placement 1. The relative position of a website address in the pages of results generated by keying relevant words into a leading search engine. Various strategies can be used to achieve a higher placement and thereby increase traffic to the site: *see* SEARCH-ENGINE OPTIMIZATION **2.** Displaying the web address of a company in those settings (e.g. advertisements, company literature, other related websites) that are most likely to generate traffic.

usance 1. The time allowed for the payment of short-term foreign *bills of exchange. It varies from country to country but is often 60 days. **2.** Formerly, the rate of interest on a loan.

US Customary units The units of measurement in use in the USA. They are based on *Imperial units but the US gallon is equal to 0.8327 Imperial gallons and the hundredweight is taken as 100 lb, making the *ton 2,000 lb (instead of the Imperial 2,240 lb). The USA has fallen behind Europe in converting to metric units, but intends to complete the process.

useful economic life (useful life) The period for which the present owner of an *asset will derive economic benefits from its use. In standard accounting practice, a fixed asset is depreciated over its useful economic life.

USENET (user's network) A very large network of online newsgroups, run very informally to discuss particular topics, such as a sport, hobby, or business area. USENET predates the *Internet: some Internet hosts do not subscribe to USENET and some USENET hosts are not on the Internet.

user *See* CONSUMER BUYING BEHAVIOUR. *See also* DECISION-MAKING UNIT.

user-friendly Denoting a computer system that is intended to be easy to use by people who are not computer specialists.

user-generated content (UGC) Media content that is produced by users of that medium rather than by media professionals. Although traditional media have often included some UGC (e.g. the letters page of a newspaper), the term is mainly associated with modern electronic media and embraces such phenomena as *blogs, *wikis, *social media, and digital video (*YouTube).

USP Abbreviation for *unique selling proposition.

usury An excessively high rate of interest. In Christian countries the term was formerly used to condemn all forms of lending on interest, a prohibition that has been maintained by Islam. *See* ISLAMIC FINANCE.

utility model (petty patent) A type of short-term *patent that is available in many EU and other jurisdictions but not the UK. A utility model is usually much easier to obtain than a full patent and gives the holder an exclusive right to exploit an invention for a limited period of time (generally 7 to 10 years).

utility theory A class of theory concerned with the behaviours, strategies, and mental processes adopted by individuals faced with making a risky choice or decision. Utility is usually taken as the subjective value to the individual of a particular outcome or attribute. The main applications of utility theory in business and finance are in relation to consumer and investment choices. Different structures of utility and *risk preference are considered in *portfolio theory. *See also* BEHAVIOURAL FINANCE; CONJOINT ANALYSIS; PROSPECT THEORY; RATIONAL CHOICE THEORY; TIME INCONSISTENCY.

u

utilization (system utilization) The ratio of the actual output of an *operating system to its designed capacity. For example, if the designed capacity of a plant is 4,000 units per week and the output is 3,000 units per week, the utilization is 75%. However, it is important to remember that 75% represents the utilization of the most restricted part of the operating system, i.e. the bottleneck. If other parts of the plant are capable of more than 4,000 units per week their utilization will be lower.

utmost good faith (*uberrima fides*)
The fundamental principle of insurance practice, requiring that a person wishing to take out an insurance cover must provide all the information the insurer needs so as to calculate the correct premium for the risk involved. Nothing must be withheld from the insurers, even if they do not actually ask for the information on an application form. The principle is essential because an insurer usually has no knowledge of the facts involved in the risk they are being asked to cover; the only source of information is the person requiring the insurance. If an insured person is found to have withheld information or given false information, the insurer can treat the policy as void and the courts will support a refusal to pay claims. *See* ASYMMETRIC INFORMATION.

u

vacuity *See* ULLAGE.

valence-instrumentality-expectancy theory (VIE theory) A theory of *motivation stating that the level of effort individuals will exert in any task can be computed from three variables: expectancy, or the belief that action or effort will lead to a successful outcome; instrumentality, or the belief that success will bring rewards; and valence, or the desirability of the rewards on offer. The theory, which was proposed by Victor H. Vroom in 1964, inspired the *path-goal leadership model.

valium holiday (valium picnic) A colloquial name for a non-trading day on a stock exchange or other commercial market; or a day on which trading is slow.

valorization The raising or stabilization of the value of a commodity or currency by artificial means, usually by a government. For example, if a government wishes to increase the price of a commodity that it exports it may attempt to decrease the supply of that commodity by encouraging producers to produce less, by stockpiling the commodity itself, or, in extreme cases, by destroying part of the production.

VALS *See* LIFESTYLE.

valuation risk The *risk that arises from problems of valuation. For example, it can be difficult to value a business during the acquisition process or to put an accurate value on an option on the *over-the-counter market.

value added (added value) The value added to goods or services by a step in the chain of original purchase, manufacture or other enhancement, and retail. *See* VALUE-ADDED STATEMENT; VALUE CHAIN. *See also* ECONOMIC VALUE ADDED.

value-added manufacturing A method of optimizing the efficiency of a process by eliminating any element that does not add value to the product or service.

value-added statement (added-value statement) A *financial statement showing how much wealth (value added) has been created by the collective effort of capital, employees, and others and how it has been allocated for an *accounting period. Value added is normally calculated by deducting materials and bought-in services from *turnover. The value added is then allocated to employees in the form of wages, to shareholders and lenders in the form of dividends and interest, and to the government in the form of taxes, with a proportion being retained in the company for reinvestment.

value added tax (VAT) A charge on *taxable supplies of goods and services made in the UK by a *taxable person in the course or furtherance of a business. Where appropriate, each trader adds VAT to sales and must account to HM Revenue and Customs for the *output tax. The *input tax paid on purchases can be deducted from the output tax due. VAT, indirect taxation that falls on the final customer, was introduced in 1973 when the UK joined the European Economic Community. Unless they are *zero-rated goods and services, *exempt supplies, or taxed at a special rate, all goods and services in the UK now bear VAT at a rate of 20%.

((●)) SEE WEB LINKS

• VAT information from the Gov.uk website

value analysis An examination of every feature of a product to ensure that its cost is no greater than is necessary to carry out its functions. Value analysis can be applied to a new product idea at the design stage and also to existing products. *See also* VALUE ENGINEERING.

value-at-risk (VAR) A measure of risk developed at the former US bank J. P. Morgan Chase in the 1990s, now most frequently applied to measuring *market risk and *credit risk. It is the level of losses over a particular period that will only be exceeded in a small percentage of cases. A cut-off value for gains and losses is established that excludes a certain proportion of worst-case results (e.g. the bottom 1% of outcomes); the value-at-risk is then measured relative to that cut-off value. VAR was initially designed to measure the overnight risk in certain highly diversified *portfolios. It has since developed into a finance industry standard and has been incorporated into the regulatory requirements applying to financial institutions. Recently there have been claims that VAR methodology may have contributed to the global financial crisis of 2007–08 by creating false confidence and encouraging excessive risk-taking.

value-based pricing Setting the price for a product or service on the basis of the buyer's perception of its value, rather than its cost.

value chain The chain of activities by which a good or service is produced, distributed, and marketed. Each step of the chain (which may consist of the activities of one company or of several) creates different amounts of value for the consumer. There are five value-creating activities:

- inbound distribution
- operations
- outbound distribution
- marketing
- after-sales service;
  and four supporting activities:
- buying

- research and development
- human resource management
- infrastructure of the firm.

For management, the main application of the value-chain concept is that a company should examine its costs and performance at each stage, and decide, among other things, whether it is best to carry out a particular stage in house or externally. The value chain can provide the basis for a strategic analysis in terms of the search for *competitive advantage.

value date 1. The date on which specified funds (e.g. a remittance sent through the bank clearing cycle) become available for use. **2.** The date on which a transaction actually takes place. **3.** The date on which foreign exchange is due to be delivered.

valued policy An insurance policy in which the value of the subject matter is agreed when the cover starts. As a result, the amount to be paid in the event of a total-loss claim is already decided and does not need to be negotiated.

value driver Any variable that significantly affects the value of an organization. In his development of *shareholder value analysis, Alfred Rappaport identified seven key drivers of value:

- sales growth rate
- operating profit margin
- tax rate
- fixed capital investment
- working capital investment
- planning period
- cost of capital.

Of these, the first five can be used to forecast the future cash flows of a business, whereas the remaining two can be used to calculate the *present value of these cash flows.

In practice, different companies will have different value drivers. For example, Sony is a company that produces high-quality products for which customers are prepared to pay a relatively high price. Maintaining a high operating profit margin is therefore more important for Sony than sales growth. For another company, however, sales growth may well be the more important factor.

value engineering Designing a product to eliminate any costs that do not contribute to the value of the product, i.e. the performance (or some other attribute) that leads the customer to purchase the product in preference to other similar products.

value for money audit An audit of a government department, charity, or other non-profit-making organization to assess whether or not it is functioning efficiently and giving value for the money it spends.

value investment An investment strategy guided by a view of the real underlying value of a company and its long-term potential for growth, as opposed to one that tries to make short-term gains from market fluctuations.

value marketing A principle of enlightened marketing holding that a company should put most of its resources into value-building marketing investments.

value migration The inevitable flow of profit and shareholder value away from companies with outmoded business models and towards those better equipped to meet consumers' changing priorities. Typically, a company will go through a sequence of three phases: (i) value flows into the company as its business model proves better adapted to meeting consumer demand than those of its competitors; (ii) value stabilizes as a competitive equilibrium is reached; and (iii) value starts to flow out of the company as new forms of competition emerge.

value positioning A range of *positioning alternatives based on the value and price a product offers.

value received Words that appear on a *bill of exchange to indicate that the bill is a means of paying for goods or services to the value of the bill. However, these words need not appear on a UK bill as everyone who has signed a UK bill is deemed to have been a party to it for value.

value statement A statement of a company's central principles, which are meant to inform all its activities and goals. Such a statement is usually directed both internally, to the company's managers and other employees, and externally, to its customers, suppliers, and investors. Value statements may include commitments to ethical practices or social engagement. *See also* MISSION STATEMENT.

value to the business (deprival value) In *current cost accounting, the value of an *asset taken as the lower of the *replacement cost and the *recoverable amount. The latter is the greater of the *net realizable value and *net present value. It is claimed that generally an asset should never be worth more to a business than its replacement cost, because if the business were deprived of the asset it would replace it. If an asset is not worth replacing it would be sold (net realizable value), unless the net present value were higher.

value transferred The amount by which a donor's estate is diminished by making a *transfer of value. The term is used in the computation of *inheritance tax.

vanilla finance *See* PLAIN VANILLA.

VAR Abbreviation for *value-at-risk.

variable A characteristic of a product or service that can be measured on a continuously variable scale, e.g. length, weight, time, price. *Compare* ATTRIBUTE.

variable cost An item of expenditure that, in total, varies directly with the level of activity achieved. For example, *direct materials cost will tend to double if output doubles, a characteristic being that it is incurred as a constant rate per unit. In practice, there are few examples of true variable costs or true *fixed costs, most costs being *semi-variable costs.

variable costing *See* MARGINAL COSTING.

variable cost ratio The ratio of *variable cost to sales revenue, expressed as a percentage.

v

variable life assurance A *unit-linked policy in which the policyholder can vary the amount of life assurance cover provided.

variable output plan See CHASE DEMAND STRATEGY.

variable overhead cost The elements of an organization's indirect costs for a product that vary in total in proportion to changes in the levels of production or sales. Examples can include power, commission earned by sales personnel, and consumable materials.

variable production overhead The elements of an organization's indirect manufacturing costs that vary in total in proportion to changes in the level of production or sales. Examples can include factory power and depreciation of machinery using the *production-unit method.

variable-rate mortgage A *mortgage in which the rate of interest is varied from time to time by the mortgagee (lender) according to market conditions.

variable-rate note (VRN) A *bond, usually with a fixed maturity, in which the interest coupon is adjusted at regular intervals to reflect the prevailing market rate (usually a margin over the *London Inter Bank Offered Rate). A VRN differs from a *floating-rate note in that the margin is not fixed and will be adjusted to take into account market conditions at each coupon setting date.

variable-rate security A *security in which the interest rate varies with market rates. *Floating-rate notes, *eurobonds, and 90-day *certificates of deposit are examples of variable-rate securities.

variance 1. In *standard costing and *budgetary control, the difference between the standard or budgeted levels of cost or income for an activity and the actual costs incurred or income achieved. If the actual performance is better than standard then a **favourable variance** results, while if actual performance is worse than standard there is an **adverse variance**. Adverse

variances may be subjected to detailed analysis in order to pinpoint their precise causes. See ANALYSIS OF VARIANCE. **2.** In statistics, a measure of the dispersion (spread) of a distribution of outcomes. It is the square of the *standard deviation.

variation margins The gains or losses on open contracts in future markets, calculated on the basis of the closing price at the end of each day. They are credited by the *clearing house to its members' accounts and by its members to their customers' accounts.

variety-seeking buying behaviour *Consumer buying behaviour in situations characterized by low consumer involvement, but significant perceived brand differences.

VAT Abbreviation for *value added tax.

vatu (VUV) The standard monetary unit of Vanuatu.

VCT Abbreviation for *venture capital trust.

Veblen good A good for which the demand increases as its price increases. This is contrary to conventional economic theory, which posits that a rise in price leads to a fall in demand. Veblen goods are those products that confer on the purchaser a high perceived status in line with the high price paid; typically these are luxury goods, such as designer clothes or sports cars. They are named after the economist Thorstein Veblen. *Compare* GIFFEN GOOD.

velocity of circulation The average number of times that a unit of money is used in a specified period, approximately equal to the total amount of money spent in that period divided by the total amount of money in circulation. The **income velocity of circulation** is the number of times that a particular unit of currency forms part of a person's income in a specified period. It is given by the ratio of the gross national product to the amount of money in circulation. The **transactions velocity of circulation** is the number of times that a particular unit of currency is spent in a money transaction in a specified period, i.e. the ratio of the total amount of money spent in sales of goods or services to the amount of money in circulation.

vendor A person who sells goods or services.

vendor placing A type of *placing used as a means of acquiring another company or business. For example, if company X wishes to buy a business from company Y, it issues company X shares to company Y as payment with the prearranged agreement that these shares are then placed with investors in exchange for cash. Vendor placings have been popular with companies in recent years as a cheaper alternative to a *rights issue. *See also* BOUGHT DEAL.

venture capital *See* RISK CAPITAL.

venture capital trust (VCT) An *investment trust that provides *risk capital for smaller unlisted trading companies. The trust managers accept sums of money from investors who wish to share in the profits of the trust. This form of investment is relatively high risk but has certain tax advantages in the UK, in that any profits are free of *capital gains tax and income is untaxed. They have the additional advantages that up to £200,000 can be invested in any year; and 30% of any investment in a VCT can be claimed back from previously paid tax, provided the VCT is held for five years. By investing a taxable gain in a VCT that is held for three years, the payment of the capital gains tax is deferred until the VCT investment is sold (and the annual exemptions from capital gains tax can be carried forward).

vertical integration *See* INTEGRATION.

vertical job enlargement *See* JOB ENLARGEMENT.

vertical marketing system (VMS) A *distribution channel structure in which producers, wholesalers, and retailers act as a unified system. One channel member owns the others, has contracts with them, or has so much power that they all have to cooperate. *See* ADMINISTERED VMS; CONTRACTUAL VMS; CORPORATE VMS.

vertical mobility *See* MOBILITY OF LABOUR.

vertical spread A strategy used with *options, consisting of buying a long call option and a short call option with the same exercise date.

vested benefit A benefit owing to a member of a pension scheme, whether or not the member is employed by the organizers of the scheme.

vested interest 1. In law, an interest in property that is certain to come about rather than one dependent upon some event that may not happen. For example, a gift to 'A for life and then to B' means that A's interest is **vested in possession**, because A has the property now. B's gift is also vested (but not in possession) because A will certainly die sometime and then B (or B's estate if B is dead) will inherit the property. A gift to C 'if C reaches the age of 30' is not vested, because C may die before reaching that age. An interest that is not vested is known as a **contingent interest**. **2.** An involvement in the outcome of some business, scheme, transaction, etc., usually in anticipation of a personal gain.

vestibule training A form of training in which new employees learn the job in a setting that approximates as closely as is practicable to the actual working environment. An example is the training of airline pilots in a simulated cockpit. This type of training is generally used when the use of actual equipment by untrained employees would be too risky or when the actual work setting would be unconducive to learning (e.g. because of noise levels).

Vickers Report *See* INDEPENDENT COMMISSION ON BANKING.

videoconferencing A *teleconferencing facility enabling groups of people at various locations to see and speak to each other, making it possible to hold meetings, seminars, etc., without travel. Desk-top

PC-based systems are now readily available, as are systems that can be used with mobile devices. *See also* VoIP.

videotex An information system in which information from a distant computer is displayed on a television screen. There are two types: in *viewdata the information is sent to the video display using telephone lines or cables; in *teletext, the information is broadcast as a part of the normal signal from a television station.

VIE theory Abbreviation for *valence-instrumentality-expectancy theory.

viewdata A *videotex system in which information from a distant computer is sent along telephone wires to a television set or VDU. Viewdata has been largely superseded by the Internet but is still widely used in the travel industry for booking flights and hotels.

view to resale Grounds on which a *subsidiary undertaking may be excluded from the *consolidated financial statements of a group, i.e. because the group's interest in the subsidiary is held exclusively with a view to subsequent resale. The subsidiary undertaking should not previously have been consolidated in group accounts prepared by the *holding company. Where a subsidiary undertaking is excluded on these grounds, it should be recorded in the consolidated financial statements as a *current asset at either (i) cost less impairment or (ii) fair value. Detailed rules are set out in Section 27 of the Financial Reporting Standard Applicable in the UK and Republic of Ireland.

vigilance A person's ability to perform a task at a constant level of efficiency and effectiveness over a period.

vigilance decrement A decline in a person's ability to perform a task at a constant level of efficiency and effectiveness as that person becomes tired or less able to respond due to psychological factors.

vigilante bondholders (bond vigilantes) Investors who react to government policies they believe likely to cause

inflation, such as expansion of the money supply and high budget deficits, by selling government bonds and thereby pushing up bond yields. The term was widely used in the USA in the 1990s and revived after the crisis of 2008.

vigilantibus non dormientibus jura subveniunt (Latin: the law will not help those who sleep on their rights). *See* LACHES.

vineyard organization A model of organizational structure in which the company's mission is pictured as a vine and the various units of employees as 'clusters' of grapes. The major clusters will include a team of core management, a series of largely autonomous business units, staff units providing back-up services, and a range of project teams assembled for specific short-term purposes.

viral marketing 1. A marketing strategy in which various unconventional techniques are used to generate word-of-mouth excitement about a product. Conventional media outlets may be deliberately avoided in order to create an air of mystery or exclusivity. **2.** More specifically, a form of *direct marketing in which a company encourages Internet users to forward its material in e-mails, usually by including jokes, games, or other entertaining features. The aim is that publicity for the company will spread in the manner of a computer virus.

virement In some systems of *budgetary control, an agreed practice in which funds may be transferred from one part of the budget to another during a financial year. So, for example, a projected surplus under one budget head may be used to make up for a deficit under another.

virtual auction An auction conducted completely online, with no physical location. Virtual auctions are conducted on the Internet by such auction houses as *Ebay.

virtualization A process by which a company develops some of the characteristics of a *virtual organization.

virtual mall (electronic mall) A website that brings together different electronic retailers at a single online location.

virtual organization An organization that uses information and communications technology to enable it to operate without clearly defined physical boundaries. It usually provides customized services by outsourcing production and other functions to third parties.

virtual reality (VR) A computer modelling system capable of creating three-dimensional simulated environments that give the user the experience of being inside, and interacting with, the environment being modelled. Used as part of *computer-aided design systems, VR enables customers to view new products without the expense of creating prototypes. Building layouts, for example, can be optimized by allowing customers to 'walk through' the VR model. Most systems allow them to move elements of the design, with any modifications (e.g. repositioned doors) being translated into new drawings and blueprints. VR can also be used to train staff without exposing them to hazardous conditions.

virtual trade show An online site that shows new products, technologies, and services to current or potential buyers.

virtual value activities The strategies that firms use to make website information more valuable.

virtuous cycle A cycle of growth that produces positive returns. Each success in the loop promotes another success in another part of the loop.

visible control A technique used in *total quality management to make defects visible to employees so that resources can be focused on removing the source of the problem. For example, flashing lights, called *andon*, can be linked to electronic sensors that detect a failure to complete all stages of a process.

visibles Earnings from exports and payments for imports of goods, as opposed to services (such as banking and insurance). The *balance of trade is made up of visibles and is sometimes called the **visible balance**.

vision statement *See* MISSION STATEMENT.

visit duration The length of time a user spends on a website during a visit, or the number of pages viewed during a visit.

visual load profile A graph that compares workloads with available capacity against time (see diagram).

vital statistics Statistics relating to a nation's or region's population, including its birth rate, death rate, marriage rate, etc.

vitamin model A model that compares the effect of certain factors on *job satisfaction to the effect of vitamins on the body. Nine 'vitamins' are identified, and the employee will require a minimum level of each if he or she is to remain satisfied. Of these nine, three (money, security, and social position) can be taken in very large amounts with no ill effects. However, an excess of the other six factors (externally set goals, clarity, variety, control, use of skills, and contact with others) can be problematic.

VMS Abbreviation for *vertical marketing system.

VocaLink The company that owns and operates the UK's national bank payments infrastructure. VocaLink works closely with both Bacs, the automated payments scheme used by British banks, and LINK, the nationwide network of cash machines. *See* UK PAYMENTS ADMINISTRATION.

vocational training Training in a trade or occupation. In the UK, the Business and Technology Education Council (**BTEC**) was set up in 1983 to develop a national system of vocational training. BTEC certificates and diplomas are now awarded by Edexcel, a privatized body. National Vocational Qualifications (**NVQs**) recognize ability in a particular trade or occupation.

Visual load profile.

voice broking Carrying out a financial trade by telephoning a broker, rather than using an electronic trading system. Voice broking is most common for large-volume trades or those involving complex instruments.

VoIP Abbreviation for Voice over Internet Protocol. The use of a packet-switched network, in particular the Internet, to carry spoken communications. This has been a major growth area in recent years, with several companies offering services that not only allow conversations between their members but also connect to the global telephone network. Indeed, many traditional telephone providers now use VoIP internally. Implementing conversations in real time imposes special constraints because they are particularly sensitive to any delay or lost data.

volatile Denoting a market, commodity, share, bond, etc., that may be expected to fluctuate greatly and frequently in value.

volume 1. The space occupied by something. **2.** A measure of the amount of

trade that has taken place, usually in a specified period. On the *London Stock Exchange, for example, the number of shares traded in a day is called the volume, and the value of these shares is called the **turnover**. In commodity markets, the daily volume is usually the number of lots traded in a day.

voluntary arrangement 1. (company voluntary arrangement; CVA) A procedure provided for by the Insolvency Act 1986, in which a company may come to an arrangement with its creditors to pay off its debts and to manage its affairs so that it resolves its financial difficulties. This arrangement may be proposed by the directors, an *administrator, or a *liquidator, and must be approved by meetings of both the company and its creditors. Once approved, the arrangement becomes binding on all the parties, and a qualified insolvency practitioner is appointed to supervise it. The aim is to assist the company to solve its financial problems without the need for a winding-up (*see* LIQUIDATION). **2. (individual voluntary**

arrangement; IVA) A similar agreement between a debtor and his or her creditors under the Insolvency Act 1986. It takes the form of either a *scheme of arrangement or a *composition and can be made either before or after a bankruptcy order is made. The terms of the arrangement must be agreed at a meeting between the debtor and his or her creditors and an insolvency practitioner appointed. If no agreement is reached, or the debtor subsequently fails to comply with the terms of an IVA, bankruptcy proceedings may be initiated or resumed. *See* BANKRUPTCY LAW.

voluntary liquidation (voluntary winding-up) *See* CREDITORS' VOLUNTARY LIQUIDATION; MEMBERS' VOLUNTARY LIQUIDATION.

voluntary registration Registration for *value added tax by a *taxable person whose taxable turnover does not exceed the registration threshold.

voluntary retailer *See* SYMBOL RETAILER.

volunteer A person who, in relation to any transaction, has not given valuable *consideration.

vostro account A bank account held by a foreign bank with a UK bank, usually in sterling. *Compare* NOSTRO ACCOUNT.

voting shares Shares in a company that entitle their owner to vote at the annual general meeting and any extraordinary meetings of the company. Shares that carry **voting rights** are usually *ordinary shares, rather than *A shares or *debentures. The company's articles of association will state which shares carry voting rights.

voucher A receipt for money or any document that supports an entry in a book of account.

voyage charter A charter of a ship or of cargo space for a fixed number of voyages rather than for a fixed period (*compare* TIME CHARTER). The shipowner usually warrants that the ship will arrive at an agreed port on an agreed day, will be in seaworthy condition, and will be properly equipped. The charterer agrees to load and unload in the agreed number of *lay days.

VR Abbreviation for *virtual reality.

VRIN *See* RESOURCE-BASED VIEW.

VRN Abbreviation for *variable-rate note.

Vroom–Yetton–Jago model A *contingency theory of leadership holding that leaders should vary the extent to which they allow followers to participate in decision making according to certain key factors in the situation. These include the nature of the task, the extent to which followers can be expected to disagree over the best solution, and the extent to which followers will accept decisions they personally disagree with. A *decision tree is used to assess these factors and to decide which of a range of *leadership styles is most appropriate.

vulture fund An investment fund that buys the distressed debts of sovereign states or companies. The creditor fund then seeks to profit by suing or otherwise pressuring the debtor country or company for repayment of the debt. The operation of such funds in highly indebted developing countries has been controversial.

v

WA Abbreviation for with average. *See* AVERAGE.

WAB Abbreviation for weighted application blank. *See* STANDARD APPLICATION BLANK.

WACC Abbreviation for *weighted average cost of capital.

wafer seal A modern form of seal used on such documents as *deeds. It is usually a small red disc stuck onto the document to represent the seal.

wage differential The difference in earnings between workers with similar skills in different industries or between workers with different skills in the same industry. There may also be differentials between urban and non-urban wages or between regions (wages in the UK are highest in the Southeast, where the cost of living is highest). The Equality Act 2010 (as previously the Equal Pay Act 1970) makes it illegal for a differential to exist between the pay of men and women doing like work in the same employment.

wage freeze An attempt by a government to counter inflation by fixing wages at their existing level for a specified period. For various reasons, including the use of overtime and bonuses to defeat the measure, this is no longer considered an effective policy. **Wage restraint** is a less rigidly applied attempt to control prices by obtaining union agreement to make only modest and essential claims for wage increases.

wagering contract *See* GAMING CONTRACT.

wages The remuneration paid to hourly paid employees for the work done, usually based on the number of hours spent at the place of work.

waiter An attendant at *Lloyd's (and formerly at the *London Stock Exchange) who carries messages and papers etc. The name goes back to the 17th-century London coffee houses from which these institutions grew, in which the waiters also performed these functions.

waiting time The period during which the operators of a machine or the machinery itself are idle or waiting for work, material, or repairs. *See also* IDLE TIME.

waiver The setting aside or non-enforcement of a right. This may be done deliberately or it may happen by the operation of law. For example, if a tenant is in breach of a covenant in a lease and the landlord demands rent in spite of knowing of the breach, the landlord may be held to have waived the right to terminate the lease.

walk-through test An *audit test that takes a few transactions from the records of a business and follows them through every stage of the accounting system. For example, a walk-through test of a purchases system would follow through from the material requisition to settlement of the supplier's invoice.

Wall Street 1. The *New York Stock Exchange, which stands on Wall Street in New York. **2.** The financial institutions, collectively, of New York, including the stock exchange, banks, money markets, commodity markets, etc.

WAP Abbreviation for *wireless application protocol.

warehouse Any building in which goods are stored; a **public warehouse** is one at or near a port in which goods are stored after being unloaded from a ship or before being loaded onto a ship (*see also* BONDED WAREHOUSE). When goods are taken into a public warehouse a warehouse *warrant is issued, which must be produced before the goods can be removed.

warehouse club (wholesale club; membership warehouse) A cut-price retailer that sells a limited selection of brand-name grocery items, appliances, clothing, and other goods at substantial discounts to members, who pay an annual membership fee.

warehouse keeper The person in charge of a warehouse. A *bonded warehouse also has a **warehouse officer**, employed by HM Customs and Excise, to inspect goods entering and leaving the warehouse.

warehousing 1. The storage of goods in a warehouse. **2.** Building up a holding of shares in a company prior to making a *takeover bid, by buying small lots of the shares and 'warehousing' them in the name of nominees. The purpose is for the bidder to remain anonymous and to avoid having to make the statutory declaration of interest. This practice is contrary to the *City Code on Takeovers and Mergers.

war loan A government stock issued during wartime; it has no redemption date, pays only 3½% interest, and stands at less than half its face value.

warrant 1. (**share warrant**) A security that offers the owner the right to subscribe for the *ordinary shares of a company at a fixed date, usually at a fixed price. Warrants are themselves bought and sold on *stock exchanges and are equivalent to stock options. Subscription prices usually exceed the market price, as the purchase of a warrant is a gamble that a company will prosper. They have proved increasingly

popular in recent years as a company can issue them without including them in the balance sheet. **2.** A document that serves as proof that goods have been deposited in a public *warehouse. The document identifies specific goods and can be transferred by endorsement. Warrants are frequently used as security against a bank loan. Warehouse warrants for warehouses attached to a *wharf are known as **dock warrants** or **wharfinger's warrants**.

warranty 1. A statement made clearly in a contract (**express warranty**) or, if not stated clearly, understood between the parties to the contract (*see* IMPLIED WARRANTY). An unfulfilled warranty does not invalidate the contract (as it would in the case of an unfulfilled *condition) but could lead to the payment of damages. *See also* FLOATING WARRANTY. **2.** A condition in an insurance policy that confirms that something will or will not be done or that a certain situation exists or does not exist. If a warranty is breached, the insurer is entitled to refuse to pay claims, even if they are unconnected with the breach. For example, if a policy insuring the contents of a house has a warranty that certain locks are to be used on the doors and windows and these are found not to have been used, the insurers could decline to settle a claim for a burst pipe. In practice, however, this does not happen as insurers have agreed that they will only refuse to pay claims if the breach of warranty has affected the circumstances of the claim. **3.** A manufacturer's written promise to repair or replace a faulty product, usually free of charge, during a specified period subsequent to the date of purchase. This is often called a **guarantee**.

wash sale A US name for the sale and purchase by a single investor, or a group in collusion, of a block of securities, either simultaneously or in a short space of time, to establish a loss or a gain; it may also be used to create the impression that the security in question is trading actively. It is similar to the practice known in the UK as *bed and breakfast.

w

waste 1. (spoilage) The amount of material lost as part of a production process. Acceptable levels of waste, known as a *normal loss, are part of the cost of production and as such are allowed for in the product costs. **2.** Any process or activity that does not add value. *See* SHINGO'S SEVEN WASTES.

waste disposal Under the Control of Pollution Act 1974 household, commercial, and industrial waste may be disposed of only in licensed sites. Local authorities are generally required to collect household refuse free of charge but there is a charge for the collection of waste from business premises. Businesses now have a duty of care in respect of waste removed from their property by builders, scrap-metal merchants, etc. If the contractors are not registered with the Environment Agency as authorized carriers of waste, the business may be liable for a fine. Waste has traditionally been buried in landfill sites but recent European and UK legislation has placed strict controls on the amount and type of material sent to landfill. Stringent controls on emissions from the incineration of waste were introduced by the Waste Incineration Directive (WID), which applies from December 2005. There are special regulations dealing with the treatment, carriage, and disposal of *hazardous waste. *See* POLLUTION.

wasting asset An *asset that has a finite life; for example, a lease may lose value throughout its life and become valueless when it terminates. It is also applied to such assets as plant and machinery, which wear out during their life and therefore lose value.

watered stock *See* STOCK WATERING.

waybill 1. *See* CONSIGNMENT NOTE.
2. *See* AIR WAYBILL.

WDA Abbreviation for *writing-down allowance.

WDV Abbreviation for *written-down value.

wealth management The practice of offering *high net-worth individuals investment management, financial advice, and estate and tax-planning services as a unified professional service. In recent years this part of the financial sector has grown rapidly with the increasing number of wealthy individuals around the world.

Wealth Management Association (WMA) A representative body for private-client investment managers and stockbrokers, formed as the **Association of Private Client Investment Managers and Stockbrokers (APCIMS)** in 1990. It aims to improve the environment and expand the market in which private investors' business is transacted. The association represents 95% of eligible firms with a network of over 550 offices throughout the UK and Ireland. It publishes a directory of private-client stockbrokers, with details of members and the services they provide. The association, which adopted its current name in 2013, is run by an elected committee with a small permanent secretariat based in London, assisted by specialist practitioner committees.

((🌐)) **SEE WEB LINKS**
• WMA website

wealth tax A tax used in some European countries, not including the UK, consisting of an annual levy on wealth. In practice, the implementation of a wealth tax requires a clear identification of the assets to be charged and an unassailable valuation of these assets.

wear and tear A diminution in the value to an organization of a fixed asset due to the use and damage that it inevitably sustains throughout its working life. It is one of the causes of *depreciation.

weather insurance *See* PLUVIAL INSURANCE.

weather working days *Working days on which the weather permits work to be carried out. This often refers to the days allowed in a charter for loading or unloading a ship. *See* LAY DAYS.

web address *See* UNIFORM RESOURCE LOCATOR.

web browser A software application, such as Microsoft Internet Explorer or Google Chrome, that provides an easy method of accessing, viewing, and interacting with information stored as HTML web documents on different *web servers.

webcasting 1. The transmission of audio or video content over the Internet using streaming technology. **2.** (**push programming**) In marketing, a process in which an online marketer sends advertisements or information over the Internet, directly to the desktops of target customers. Companies can also sign on with a webcasting service provider, who will automatically download customized information to the personal computers of subscribers to their service.

web crawler (web spider) A computer application that systematically and continuously traverses the *World Wide Web for some purpose, typically the indexing of websites by assigning keywords and phrases. Web *search engines, for example, use web crawlers to refresh their data by periodically revisiting registered websites and following hyperlinks to new pages. Performing such traversals is called **spidering**.

web feed A web document that contains a summary of and link to another document. Web feeds are often used to notify subscribers to a service of updated content.

web log *See* BLOG.

webmaster A person responsible for ensuring the quality of a website. This means achieving suitable availability, speed, working links between pages, and connections to company databases. In small companies the webmaster may also be responsible for graphic design and *content development.

web server A store of web pages that can be accessed by a *web browser. Web servers may also contain databases of customer or product information, which can be queried and retrieved using a web browser.

website *Content accessible on the *World Wide Web created by a particular organization or individual. The location and identity of a website is indicated by its web address (*see* UNIFORM RESOURCE LOCATOR). It may be stored on a single server in a single location, or on a cluster of servers.

website brand impact The benefits to a particular brand that result from a website visit.

website reach The fraction of the total number of web users that visit a specified website during a specified time interval.

web spider *See* WEB CRAWLER.

weighted aggregate indices *See* INDEX NUMBER.

weighted application blank (WAB) *See* STANDARD APPLICATION BLANK.

weighted average (weighted mean) An arithmetic average that takes into account the importance of the items making up the average. For example, if a person buys a commodity on three occasions, 100 tonnes at £70 per tonne, 300 tonnes at £80 per tonne, and 50 tonnes at £95 per tonne, the purchases total 450 tonnes; the simple average price would be $(70+80+95)/3 = £81.7$. The weighted average, taking into account the amount purchased on each occasion, would be $[(100 \times 70)+(300 \times 80)+(50 \times 95)]/450 = £79.4$ per tonne.

In calculating the value of a *share index, the share prices are usually weighted in some way, most often by the market capitalization of the company. An **unweighted average** is an average calculated on the basis of price only.

weighted average cost of capital (WACC) A method for calculating the average cost of a company's different sources of finance. The WACC is calculated on the assumption that the company will maintain the same *debt–equity ratio.

Managers should only use the WACC as an appropriate *discount rate for a project when the project has about the same level of risk as the company. The most difficult part of the calculation is the estimate for the cost of equity.

In theory, a company can lower its weighted average cost of capital by increasing the proportion of debt. However, this could become a problem for shareholders, who may feel that higher levels of debt will increase the risk of their investment. *See also* COST OF CAPITAL.

weighted ballot A *ballot held if a new issue of shares has been oversubscribed, in which the allocation of shares is based on the number of shares applied for and biased towards either the smaller investor or the larger investor.

weightless 1. Denoting a business that has very few *tangible assets, especially one involved in Internet trading. **2.** Denoting that part of the economy that is based on ideas and information rather than trade in physical goods.

weight note A document produced by a seller of goods in which the *gross weights of the packages are listed. It also gives the marks and numbers of the packages and an indication of the average tare.

weight or measurement *See* FREIGHT.

Westminster doctrine In UK tax law, the principle that a person is entitled to make any lawful arrangement that he or she sees fit in order to reduce liability to tax. It is named after the ruling in the case *Commissioners of Inland Revenue v the Duke of Westminster* (1936), in which the House of Lords upheld the Duke's right to pay his gardener through a covenant scheme, thus reducing his liability to surtax. *Compare* RAMSEY PRINCIPLE. *See also* GENERAL ANTI-ABUSE RULE.

wharf The quay at which ships dock in a port, together with the adjacent warehouses in which goods are stored before loading or after unloading. The

wharfinger is the firm or individual responsible for running the wharf.

wharfage The charge made by a wharfinger for the use of a wharf for loading or unloading cargo onto or from a ship.

wharfinger's receipt *See* DOCK RECEIPT.

wharfinger's warrant *See* WARRANT.

wheel of retailing concept A retailing concept assuming that new-style retailers usually begin as low-margin, low-price, and low-status operations but later evolve into higher-priced higher-service operations, eventually resembling the conventional retailers they attempted to replace.

whipsawing 1. A procedure in which individual employees or groups of employees are made to compete with one another on a task, usually with the aim of increasing productivity. Employers have sometimes used whipsawing as a means of undermining trade unions. **2.** A bargaining tactic employed by trade unions in which there is an attempt to spread wage and other concessions from one employer to another using 'coercive comparisons'.

whisper stock Shares in a company that is rumoured to be the target of a takeover. Such stocks may rise rapidly in anticipation of a deal, even though the information cannot be shown to be reliable.

whistle-blower An employee who reveals evidence of wrongdoing or malpractice within a business or other organization. In the UK the practice is now officially termed 'making a disclosure in the public interest'. The disclosure may be made to an authorized person within the company, to an authorized body outside the company, or in some cases to the media. Employees in many jurisdictions have legal protection against dismissal resulting from whistle-blowing where the company's behaviour endangers others, damages the environment, or breaks the law.

white-collar worker Any non-manual office worker, including clerical, administrative, managerial, and professional personnel. *Compare* BLUE-COLLAR WORKER.

white goods A class of consumer durables that includes washing machines, dishwashers, refrigerators, tumble-dryers, deep-freezers, and cookers; they are so named because they are usually finished in white enamel paint, although browns and other colours are now being used to make them fit less starkly into modern kitchens. *Compare* BROWN GOODS.

white knight A person or firm that makes a welcome *takeover bid for a company on improved terms to replace an unacceptable and unwelcome bid from a *black knight. If a company is the target for a takeover bid from a source of which it does not approve or on terms that it does not find attractive, it will often seek a white knight, whom it sees as a more suitable owner for the company, in the hope that a more attractive bid will be made. *Compare* GREY KNIGHT.

whole life policy (whole of life policy) A *life-assurance policy that pays a specified amount on the death of the life assured. Benefits are not made for any other reason and the cover continues until the death of the life assured, provided the premiums continue to be paid, either for life or until a specified date. They may be *with-profits policies or *unit-linked policies.

wholesale banking Interbank lending as well as lending to or by other large financial institutions, pension funds, and government agencies. *See* INTERBANK MARKET; MONEY MARKET. In the USA, wholesale banking also refers to the provision of banking services to large corporate businesses at special rates.

wholesale club *See* WAREHOUSE CLUB.

wholesale deposit A large deposit obtained by a bank, financial institution, or large corporate business.

wholesale market *See* MONEY MARKET.

Wholesale Market Brokers' Association (WMBA) The trade association for UK brokers in the *money market. The WMBA provides the *SONIA and *EURONIA indexes for overnight lending in the sterling and euro markets respectively.

(⊕) SEE WEB LINKS
• Website of the WMBA

wholesale price index *See* PRODUCER PRICE INDEX.

wholesaler A *distributor that sells goods in large quantities, usually to other distributors. Typically, a wholesaler buys and stores large quantities of several producers' goods and breaks into the bulk deliveries to supply *retailers with smaller amounts assembled and sorted to order.

wholesaler-sponsored voluntary chain A *vertical marketing system initiated by a *wholesaler, in which a group of independent retailers participate in a relationship linked to the wholesaler supplier.

wholly owned subsidiary A *subsidiary undertaking that is owned 100% by a holding company (i.e. there is no *minority interest).

WiFi A wireless technology that enables a computer or mobile device to link to a network or access the Internet using radio waves in the 2.4 GHz band. WiFi has a range of up to 100m but this is very dependent on the location.

wiki A *website whose content can be changed and extended by users via their web browsers. Wikis provide a useful way of rapidly assembling and disseminating 'collective wisdom' ('wiki wiki' is Hawaiian for 'fast' or 'quick'). They have become popular on many levels, ranging from small private wikis through internal departmental or corporate wikis to such websites as **Wikipedia**, the Internet encyclopedia. Their major drawback is the possibility of inappropriate or malicious changes. All wikis maintain lists of recent changes to and often a complete history of each web page, to aid the 'user community' in discovering and reversing unwanted changes. However, such self-policing has been found inadequate for highly exposed websites with their large but unknown user base. *See* USER-GENERATED CONTENT.

wildcat strike *See* STRIKE.

windbill *See* ACCOMMODATION BILL.

windfall gains and losses Gains and losses arising from actual or prospective receipts that differ from those originally predicted or from changes in the *net present value of the receipts as a result of differences in discount rates.

winding-up *See* LIQUIDATION.

winding-up order An order given by a British court, under the Insolvency Act 1986, compelling a company to be wound up.

windmill *See* ACCOMMODATION BILL.

window 1. An opportunity to borrow or invest that may be only temporary and should therefore be taken while it is available. **2.** A period during the day during which interbank transfers and clearance may be enacted.

window dressing Any practice that attempts to make a situation look better than it really is. It has been used extensively by accountants to improve the look of balance sheets. For example, banks used to call in their short-term loans and delay making payments at the end of their financial years, in order to show spuriously high cash balances. Another example is when a company borrows cash from an associated undertaking to disguise a short-term liquidity problem. These practices fall within the remit of the *Financial Reporting Council. *See* CREATIVE ACCOUNTING; OFF-BALANCE-SHEET.

Windows *Trademark* A *graphical user interface developed by Microsoft for *microprocessors. It is the most widely used operating system on personal computers. There have been a number of versions, including versions for mobile

devices. It was originally based on *MS-DOS.

WIP Abbreviation for *work in progress.

wireless access point *See* ACCESS POINT.

wireless application protocol (WAP) A standard that enables mobile phones to access text from websites.

with average (WA) *See* AVERAGE.

withholding tax Tax deducted at source from *dividends or other income paid to non-residents of a country. If there is a *double-taxation agreement between the country in which the income is paid and the country in which the recipient is resident, the tax can be reclaimed.

without prejudice Words used as a heading to a document or letter to indicate that what follows cannot be used in any way to harm an existing right or claim, cannot be taken as the signatory's last word, cannot bind the signatory in any way, and cannot be used as evidence in a court of law. For example, a solicitor may use these words when making an offer in a letter to settle a claim, implying that the client may decide to withdraw the offer. It may also be used to indicate that although agreement may be reached on the terms set out in the document on this occasion, the signatory is not bound to settle similar disputes on the same terms.

without-profits policy A life-assurance or pension policy that does not share in the profits of the life-assurance office that issued it. *Compare* WITH-PROFITS POLICY.

without recourse (sans recours) Words that appear on a *bill of exchange to indicate that the holder has no recourse to the person from whom it was bought, if it is not paid. It may be written on the face of the bill or as an endorsement. If these words do not appear on the bill, the holder does have recourse to the drawer or endorser if the bill is dishonoured at maturity.

w

with-profits bond An investment bond that has a cash-in value to some extent protected by the payment and accrual of bonuses.

with-profits policy A life-assurance policy that has additional amounts added to the sum assured, or paid separately as cash bonuses, as a result of a surplus or profit made on the investment of the fund or funds of the life-assurance office. *Compare* UNIT-LINKED POLICY.

WMA Abbreviation for *Wealth Management Association.

WMBA Abbreviation for *Wholesale Market Brokers' Association.

won The standard monetary unit of North Korea (KPW) and South Korea (KRW), divided into 100 chon.

word association A technique used in *marketing research in which a series of words is presented to a respondent, who is asked to respond to each one with the first word that comes to mind. The researcher seeks to interpret the results.

word-of-mouth advertising (word-of-mouth influence) The process in which the purchaser of a product or service tells friends, family, neighbours, and associates about its virtues, especially when this happens in advance of media advertising. *See* VIRAL MARKETING.

word processor (WP) A computerized text-processing system consisting of a computer unit with a keyboard, display screen, printer, and hard disk. Modern word processors enable text to be justified and correctly hyphenated, a variety of fonts and typefaces to be used, tables and footnotes to be automatically generated, and graphics to be incorporated. Most word processors are now capable of producing documents that are equivalent in quality to a printed book.

work breakdown structure A preliminary stage in producing a project network model (*see* NETWORK MODELLING) in which the work to be done is broken down into broad categories, the resources required are identified, and details of the deliverables expected at each stage are listed.

work centre A machine, set of machines, or a work station that performs a transformation or provides a service as part of a job. A product may pass through several such work centres in the course of manufacture.

worker Under UK employment law 'worker' is a wider category than *employee, as it encompasses those who work regularly for another party but have not been given a *contract of employment. This means that they are free to accept or decline work as they choose and the other party has no obligation to provide work. At the same time, such a worker is to be distinguished from a genuinely self-employed person because he or she is economically dependent on the employer, who cannot be considered a client or customer of the worker. Some employment legislation extends to all workers (e.g. the *minimum wage) while some covers only employees (e.g. *unfair dismissal). *See also* AGENCY WORKER; TEMPORARY EMPLOYEE.

workers' participation *See* INDUSTRIAL DEMOCRACY.

work-in *See* SIT-DOWN STRIKE.

working capital The part of the capital of a company that is employed in its day-to-day trading operations. It consists of *current assets (mainly trading stock, debtors, and cash) less *current liabilities (mainly trade creditors). In the normal trade cycle—the supply of goods by suppliers, the sale of stock to debtors, payments of debts in cash, and the use of cash to pay suppliers—the working capital is the aggregate of the net assets involved, sometimes called the **working assets**. The management of working assets is very important to a company. Holding sufficient levels of finished goods to meet customer requirements is important, but managers must also be aware of the cost of holding these goods.

w

working days In commerce, the days of the week excluding Sunday and, in some cases, Saturday (depending on the custom of the trade). Public holidays (*see* BANK HOLIDAYS) are also excluded from working days. In shipping and some other trades it is usual to distinguish *weather working days. *See also* LAY DAYS.

working director *See* EXECUTIVE DIRECTOR.

working hours The EU **Working Time Directive** of 1993 required all member states to limit the working week of employees to 48 hours, except where employees have agreed otherwise. The provisions of this directive were enacted by the British government in the Working Time Regulations (1998). Key elements of the Regulations require a maximum working week of 48 hours, daily rest breaks, weekly rest periods, and annual paid leave of 24 days for those working a five-day week (rising to 28 days from April 2009). They are enforced by the Health and Safety Executive.

work in progress (WIP) Materials, parts, and unfinished products within an *operating system, in which they represent locked-up capital. *Just-in-time techniques aim to minimize WIP, while more traditional systems see WIP as necessary to provide a head of work. WIP is normally valued at the lower of cost or *net realizable value, using either the *first-in-first-out cost, the *last-in-first-out cost, or the *average cost method of valuation. In the USA, **work in process** is the more common term.

workload approach An approach to setting the size of a salesforce in which a company groups accounts into classes of different sizes in order to determine how many salespeople are needed to call on the members of each class the desired number of times.

work measurement The application of techniques to establish the time required for a qualified worker to carry out a specified task at a defined level of performance. *See* WORK STUDY.

workplace pension *See* OCCUPATIONAL PENSION SCHEME; STAKEHOLDER PENSION SCHEME.

work-sample tests In *personnel selection, an assessment procedure that requires candidates to carry out tasks sampled from the job(s) in question. For example, an applicant may be required to use actual or simulated equipment or to make a decision based on complex financial data. An **in-basket test** is a work-sample test in which the candidate is presented with a typical manager's in-basket full of memos, letters, etc. and is asked to prioritize and deal with these items.

work sampling *See* ACTIVITY SAMPLING.

workstation *See* LOCAL AREA NETWORK.

work study A systematic examination of human work processes, designed to identify the ways in which the efficiency and effectiveness of these processes can be improved. It usually consists of a *method study to compare existing methods with proposed methods and *work measurement to establish the time required by a qualified worker to do the job to a specified standard. Traditionally, work study techniques have been associated with the school of *scientific management and applied by specialists known as *industrial engineers (or more colloquially as time-and-motion experts), working in *management services departments. The introduction of such approaches as *total quality management has enabled managers and staff to take responsibility for the design and management of their own systems. Recent techniques, such as *business process re-engineering, share many of the same objectives as work study but exploit *information technology, which was not available to earlier industrial engineers.

work-to-rule A form of *industrial action in which employees pay a slavish obedience to employers' regulations in order to dislocate working procedures, without resorting to a *strike. A work-to-rule usually involves an *overtime ban.

World Bank The name by which the *International Bank for Reconstruction and Development, combined with its affiliates, the *International Development Association and the *International Finance Corporation, is known.

World Economic Forum A not-for-profit organization that holds an annual meeting of business leaders, politicians, academics, and opinion formers, usually in Davos, Switzerland. It also holds several regional meetings each year. The Forum, which first met in 1971, has its headquarters in Geneva; there are also offices in New York and Beijing.

(⊕) SEE WEB LINKS
• Website of the World Economic Forum

World Trade Organization (WTO) An international trade organization formed under the *General Agreement on Tariffs and Trade (GATT) to replace GATT and implement measures agreed at the Uruguay round in 1994. The WTO's aims are to continue the work of GATT in agreeing international trading rules and furthering the liberalization of international trade. The WTO has wider and more permanent powers than GATT and extends its jurisdiction into such aspects of trading as *intellectual property rights. WTO rules are very important in international trade contracts. The highest authority of the WTO is the Ministerial Conference, held approximately every two years. There are currently (2015) 161 members of the WTO.

(⊕) SEE WEB LINKS
• Website of the WTO: includes a comprehensive statistics database

World Wide Web (WWW; Web) *See* INTERNET.

WP Abbreviation for *word processor.

wrap fund (wrap; wrap account) A *portfolio consisting of investments in a wide range of *unit trusts, *open-end trusts, and similar vehicles; the balance of the portfolio can be tailored to the requirements of the purchaser. Wraps are generally sold through intermediaries such as financial advisers, so that the investor deals directly with a single fund manager and pays a single annual fee.

write To cover an insurance risk, accepting liability, under an insurance contract as an *underwriter.

write off 1. To reduce the value of an asset to zero in a balance sheet. An expired lease, obsolete machinery, or an unfortunate investment would be written off. **2.** To reduce to zero a debt that cannot be collected (*see* BAD DEBT). Such a loss will be shown in the *profit and loss account of an organization.

writer The seller of a traded option. *Compare* TAKER.

writing-down allowance (WDA) A *capital allowance available to a UK trader. Any additions to *plant and machinery are added to the *written-down value of assets acquired in previous years and the writing-down allowance is calculated as 18% of the total. For certain long-life assets it is calculated at 8% in the same way. *See also* ANNUAL INVESTMENT ALLOWANCE.

writ of execution An order issued by a court to enforce a judgment; it is addressed to a court officer instructing that officer to carry out an act, such as collecting money or seizing property. A **writ of delivery** is a writ of execution directing the High Court Enforcement Officer to seize goods and deliver them to the plaintiff or to obtain their value in money, according to an agreed assessment. If the writ does not offer the defendant the option to retain the goods by paying the assessed value, the writ is a **writ of specific delivery**.

written-down value (WDV) The value of an asset for tax purposes after taking account of its reduction in value below the initial cost, as a result of its use in the trade. An asset acquired for a trade is eligible for *capital allowances. A *writing-down

		£
YEAR 1	Cost	1000
	WDA 25%	(250)
	WDV	750
YEAR 2	WDA 25%	(187)
	WDV	563

Written-down value.

allowance of 25% is available in the year of purchase, which is deducted from the initial cost to establish the written-down value. In the following year the written-down value is subject to the 25% writing-down allowance, which is deducted to arrive at the written-down value at the end of the second year. The table shows the WDA and WDV for an asset acquired for £1000. The written-down value of the asset, for tax purposes, at the end of year 2 is £563.

written resolution Under the Companies Act 2006, a *resolution signed by a majority of company members and treated as effective even though it is not passed at a properly convened company meeting. A *special resolution requires the support of 75% of members to become effective. Private companies can, in most circumstances, pass resolutions in this way; other companies may have power to do so under their constitutional documents. Under previous legislation, a written resolution required the signature of all members.

written statement of terms of employment See STATEMENT OF TERMS OF EMPLOYMENT.

wrongful dismissal The termination of an employee's contract of employment in a manner that is not in accordance with that contract. Thus when an employee is dismissed without the correct notice entitlement (in circumstances that do not justify summary dismissal) or when the employer prematurely terminates the employee's fixed-term contract, the employee is entitled to claim *damages in the courts for wrongful dismissal. The court's jurisdiction concerns only the parties' contractual rights and not their statutory rights under the employment protection legislation (*compare* UNFAIR DISMISSAL). The Employment Protection (Consolidation) Act 1978 empowers the Secretary of State for Employment to give industrial tribunals jurisdiction to hear claims of wrongful dismissal.

wrongful trading Trading during a period in which a company had no reasonable prospect of avoiding insolvent *liquidation. The liquidator of a company may petition the court for an order instructing a director of a company that has gone into insolvent liquidation to make a contribution to the company's assets. The court may order any contribution to be made that it thinks proper if the director knew, or ought to have known, of the company's situation. A director would be judged liable if a reasonably diligent person carrying out the same function in the company would have realized the situation: no intention to defraud need be shown. *Compare* FRAUDULENT TRADING.

WTO Abbreviation for *World Trade Organization.

WWW Abbreviation for World Wide Web. *See* INTERNET.

w

XBRL Abbreviation for *Extensible Business Reporting Language.

xd Abbreviation for ex-dividend (*see* EX-).

xerography A dry electrostatic process for making photocopies and printing computer output with a *laser printer. In a **plain-paper photocopier** an electrostatic image is formed on a selenium-coated plate or cylinder. This is dusted with a resinous toner, which sticks selectively to the charged areas, the image so formed being transferred to a sheet of paper, on which it is fixed by heating.

xu A monetary unit of Vietnam, worth one hundredth of a *dồng.

Yankee bond A *bond issued in the USA by a foreign borrower.

yearling bond A UK local authority bond that is redeemable one year after issue.

year of assessment *See* FISCAL YEAR.

Yellow Book The colloquial name for *Admission of Securities to Listing*, a book issued by the *Financial Conduct Authority that sets out the regulations for admission to the *Official List of the London Stock Exchange and the obligations of companies with *listed securities. *See* LISTING REQUIREMENTS.

Yellow Pages *See* CLASSIFIED DIRECTORIES.

yen (IPY) The standard monetary unit of Japan, formerly divided into 100 *sen.

yield 1. The income from an investment expressed in various ways. The **nominal yield** of a fixed-interest security is the interest it pays, expressed as a percentage of its *par value. For example, a £100 stock quoted as paying 8% interest will yield £8 per annum for every £100 of stock held. However, the **current yield** (also called **running yield**, **earnings yield**, or **flat yield**) will depend on the market price of the stock. If the 8% £100 stock mentioned above was standing at a market price of £90, the current yield would be $100/90 \times 8 = 8.9\%$. As interest rates rise, so the market value of fixed-interest stocks (not close to redemption) fall in order that they should give a competitive current yield. The capital gain (or loss) on redemption of a stock, which is normally redeemable at £100, can also be taken into account. This is called the **yield to redemption** (or the

redemption yield). The redemption yield consists approximately of the current yield plus the capital gain (or loss) divided by the number of years to redemption. Thus, if the above stock had 9 years to run to redemption, its redemption yield would be about $8.9 + 10/9 = 10\%$. The yields of the various stocks on offer are usually listed in commercial papers as both current yields and redemption yields, based on the current market price. However, for an investor who actually owns stock, the yield will be calculated not on the market price but the price the investor paid for it. The annual yield on a fixed-interest stock can be stated exactly once it has been purchased. This is not the case with *equities, however, where neither the dividend yield (*see* DIVIDEND) nor the capital gain (or loss) can be forecast, reflecting the greater degree of risk attaching to investments in equities. Yields on fixed-interest securities and equities are normally quoted gross, i.e. before deduction of tax. **2.** The income obtained from a tax.

yield curve A curve on a graph in which the *yield on deposits or fixed-interest securities is plotted against the length of time they have to run to maturity. The yield curve usually slopes upwards, indicating that investors expect to receive a premium for holding securities that have a long time to run. However, a downward-sloping or negative yield curve may occur when the market anticipates falling interest rates or deflation. A flat or 'humped' yield curve is usually taken as a sign of market uncertainty.

yield gap The difference between the average annual dividend yield on equities and the average annual yield on long-dated fixed-income bonds. Before the 1960s yields obtained from UK equities usually exceeded the yields provided by long-dated UK gilts, reflecting the greater degree of risk involved in an investment in equities. In the 1960s, however, rising equity prices led to falling dividend yields causing a *reverse yield gap. This was regarded as acceptable, as equities were seen to provide a better hedge against inflation than fixed-interest securities (i.e. their greater risk element was compensated by the possibility of higher capital gains). The yield from UK equities once more overtook that from bonds in the 2000s.

yield management *See* REVENUE MANAGEMENT.

yield to maturity *See* GROSS REDEMP-TION YIELD.

yield to redemption *See* YIELD.

YouTube A website dedicated to sharing video files uploaded by its users. Established in 2005, by 2012 it was receiving more than four billion views per day. It is now a subsidiary of Google. *See* USER-GENERATED CONTENT.

yuan (CNY) The standard monetary unit of China, divided into 10 jiao or 100 fen.

yuppie Slang for a successful and ambitious young person, especially one from the world of business or finance. The word, which is now somewhat dated, was formed from *y*oung *u*pwardly-mobile *p*rofessional.

zaibatsu A Japanese conglomerate. It differs from a *keiretsu in having a bank as its dominant member.

ZBB Abbreviation for *zero-base budget.

Zebra A discounted *zero-coupon bond, in which the accrued income is taxed annually rather than on redemption.

zero-base budget (ZBB) A *cash-flow budget in which the manager responsible for its preparation is required to prepare and justify the budgeted expenditure from a zero base, i.e. assuming that initially there is no commitment to spend on any activity.

zero-coupon bond A type of *bond that offers no interest payments. In effect, the interest is paid at maturity in the redemption value of the bond. Investors sometimes prefer zero-coupon bonds as they may confer more favourable tax treatment. A zero-coupon bond is the ultimate deep-discount bond (*see* DEEPLY DISCOUNTED SECURITY). *See also* TIGR; ZEBRA.

zero defects A component of *total quality management aimed at changing workers' attitudes to quality by stressing the goal of error-free performance. In practice, error-free performance is neither economically nor practically realizable. Experience suggests that, while short-term improvements may be achieved by these programmes, performance usually returns to previous levels quite quickly. *See* ABSOLUTE PERFORMANCE STANDARD.

zero-hours contract A *contract of employment in which an employee is not guaranteed any fixed working hours; the employer is not obliged to offer a minimum amount of work and the employee is paid only for the time he or she actually works. Such contracts were formerly associated with industries in which labour is required at short notice, such as catering, but have now spread to many other areas. Concerns have been raised about the uncertainty of income and lack of employment rights provided to workers by such contracts, particularly those that allow employers to offer shifts entirely at their discretion but oblige employees to take whatever work is offered.

zero-rated goods and services Goods and services that are taxable for *value added tax purposes but are currently subject to a tax rate of zero. These differ from *exempt supplies in that the VAT attributable is allowable for *input tax credit. Zero-rated supplies include:

- most food items,
- sewerage and water services for non-industrial users,
- periodicals and books,
- certain charitable supplies,
- new domestic buildings,
- transport fares for vehicles designed to carry not less than 10 passengers,
- banknotes,
- drugs and medicines,
- clothing and footwear for children,
- fuel for air ambulances and lifeboats,
- all exports.

ZIP A format for storing compressed versions of one or more files within a single archive file (a **ZIP file**). It is now used on many systems and is a de facto standard.

zip code The US name for a postcode. It consists of a five- or nine-digit code, the first five digits indicating the state and postal zone or post office, the last four digits the rural route, building, or other delivery location.

zloty (PLN) The standard monetary unit of Poland, divided into 100 groszy.

Zone of Possible Agreement (ZOPA)

In a negotiation or business discussion, that area in which the parties may eventually find common ground to resolve their differences and conclude a deal. Such a zone can only exist if there is an area of overlap between the bottom lines of the parties.

zone pricing A pricing strategy in which a company delineates two or more geographic zones. All the customers within a zone pay the same price for a product; the more distant the zone from the company's headquarters or warehouse, the higher the price.

Z score A multivariate formula, devised by Edward I. Altman in 1968, that attempts to measure the susceptibility of a business to failure. It is computed by applying *beta coefficients to a number of selected ratios taken from an organization's final accounts using the technique of multiple discriminant analysis. A UK-based version was introduced by Richard J. Taffler in 1983.

Z

Appendix: Checklist for a Business Plan

The business

The following information about the nature and objectives of the business should be given:

Personal details For the founder, proprietor, partners, or directors state each person's name, address, age, and profession if it is relevant to the business. Some details of their background and experience should also be given.

Structure of the business State whether the business is or will be set up as a sole trader, a partnership, or a limited company.

Business activities Describe the product or service the business will offer for sale and to what extent (if at all) it will manufacture the product.

Commencement date State the date on which trading will start (for a new business) and why this date has been selected.

Objectives State what the business is expected to achieve in general terms of sales and profitability, referring to a more detailed analysis later in the plan.

History A new business will probably have no history; however, something should be said of how it came into being. A restructured business or a business seeking new capital will have a history and this should be given here, paying special attention to any mergers or takeovers.

Personnel

State the number of employees (other than directors, partners, etc.). For all senior personnel give names, ages, qualifications, position, and salary. If no staff are currently employed but some will be required, state the numbers you propose to recruit and their salaries as accurately as possible. An overall plan of staff requirements, together with any further recruitment or redundancies, should be given. If this requires considerable detail it should be given in an appendix.

The product(s) or service(s) in relation to the market

Product or service details Provide details of all products and their proposed sale prices. Explain your pricing policy, taking into account the price and quality of competing products or services.

Market details State the nature of the market; whether it is growing, declining, static, or seasonal. Give brief details of any market testing undertaken and profiles of intended customers. If substantial orders, or letters stating an intent to place substantial orders, have been received, attach copies. State if any market research has been undertaken.

The competition Give the names of major competitors, their pricing policy, strengths, weaknesses, etc. Explain how the company's products or services will be better than those of competitors, and any other ideas you have about overcoming competition.

Proposed marketing methods Give details of how you propose to market your products or services and the cost of doing so. Include in your budgeted expenditure a figure for advertising. If advertising and PR are important to your sales plan, give details in an appendix.

Suppliers Give details of your principal suppliers as well as alternative sources of supply. Give a brief account of the advantages in using the chosen supplier. If you have any letters from suppliers that could be of interest, attach copies.

Premises

Property type State whether offices and any manufacturing or storage units will be leased or bought. If the premises are to be leased, state the length of the lease, whether there is an option to renew, the present rent, and the frequency of rent reviews. Mention should also be made of who bears responsibility for internal and external repairs. If you own the premises, state the purchase price and when they were bought. If a valuer's report has been obtained, enclose a copy. If the property is freehold, state its *written-down value. In both leasehold and freehold property state the amounts payable in rates.

Specifications State the overall size of the premises and how they are (or will be) subdivided, e.g. production space, storage space, retailing space, office space. If appropriate, supply a plan.

Equipment required

If the business manufactures or is intended to manufacture its product(s), it may be useful to give a brief outline here of the process involved.

Manufacturing equipment Give details of equipment already owned, including the purchase price, *depreciation, and current value. Also give financial details of any manufacturing equipment currently hired, leased, or borrowed. Add a note about the cost of servicing equipment.

General trading equipment Give details of any equipment owned for trading purposes, e.g. computers, cash tills, company vans or cars, including the depreciation, present value, and purchase price. Mention any such items leased or borrowed, stating the rent paid and terms of leasing.

Equipment on hire purchase Give details of any equipment currently being bought on hire purchase, together with the date and terms of the contract.

Equipment required Give details of all equipment you intend to buy, either to begin trading or to increase existing production. State the prices, leasing arrangements, and source of funds.

Sales forecasts

The business plan should state how sales are to be achieved, with details of any

distribution network. Discounts and agency fees should be stated, and a breakdown of the sale price in the form of a pie chart is often useful. Provide a detailed forecast of sales either on a monthly basis, if this is feasible, or on a quarterly or annual basis. The sales forecasts should be projected as far into the future as possible (certainly three years but longer if a sensible forecast can be made). These figures will form the basis of the all-important *cash-flow projections.

Financial summary

Source of funds For an existing business the *capital structure should be given. This may consist of shares, loan stock, and debt. The long-term debt may consist of *debentures, while the short-term debt may be in the form of bank loans. For a new business, the intended capital structure should be outlined together with a list of shareholders, stock and debenture holders, etc. For a business seeking new capital, state your requirements precisely and explain what form of security you can offer.

Cash-flow projection This is probably the most important part of the business plan. If the plan is to be credible, it is essential that the cash-flow projection should not contain any estimates that cannot be substantiated as fair and likely. For a convincing business plan the cash-flow projection might cover the first three years in detail and the next two years in less detail. If an outline projection for ten years can be provided the picture becomes increasingly credible.

Projection of profits Give an estimate of the profit over at least three years. This should be realistic, even if it shows that the venture is unlikely to be profitable in its initial year (or two).

For a restructured business or a business seeking new capital the supporting documents should also include copies of the *balance sheets and *profit and loss accounts for at least the past three years.

Oxford Quick Reference

A Dictionary of Psychology
Andrew M. Colman

Over 9,000 authoritative entries make up the most wide-ranging dictionary of psychology available.

'impressive ... certainly to be recommended'
Times Higher Education Supplement

'probably the best single-volume dictionary of its kind.'
Library Journal

A Dictionary of Economics
John Black, Nigar Hashimzade, and Gareth Myles

Fully up-to-date and jargon-free coverage of economics. Over 3,400 terms on all aspects of economic theory and practice.

'strongly recommended as a handy work of reference.'
Times Higher Education Supplement

A Dictionary of Law

An ideal source of legal terminology for systems based on English law. Over 4,200 clear and concise entries.

'The entries are clearly drafted and succinctly written ... Precision for the professional is combined with a layman's enlightenment.'
Times Literary Supplement

A Dictionary of Education
Susan Wallace

In over 1,250 clear and concise entries, this authoritative dictionary covers all aspects of education, including organizations, qualifications, key figures, major legislation, theory, and curriculum and assessment terminology.

Oxford Quick Reference

A Dictionary of Sociology
John Scott

The most wide-ranging and authoritative dictionary of its kind.

'Readers and especially beginning readers of sociology can scarcely do better ... there is no better single volume compilation for an up-to-date, readable, and authoritative source of definitions, summaries and references in contemporary Sociology.'

A. H. Halsey, *Emeritus Professor, Nuffield College, University of Oxford*

The Concise Oxford Dictionary of Politics
Iain McLean and Alistair McMillan

The bestselling A–Z of politics with over 1,700 detailed entries.

'A first class work of reference ... probably the most complete as well as the best work of its type available ... Every politics student should have one'

Political Studies Association

A Dictionary of Environment and Conservation
Chris Park and Michael Allaby

An essential guide to all aspects of the environment and conservation containing over 8,500 entries.

'from *aa* to *zygote*, choices are sound and definitions are unspun'

New Scientist

Oxford Quick Reference

The Concise Oxford Dictionary of Quotations
SIXTH EDITION
Edited by Susan Ratcliffe

Based on the highly acclaimed seventh edition of *The Oxford Dictionary of Quotations*, this dictionary provides extensive coverage of literary and historical quotations, and contains completely up-to-date material. A fascinating read and an essential reference tool.

Oxford Dictionary of Quotations by Subject
Edited by Susan Ratcliffe

The ideal place to discover what's been said about what, the dictionary presents quotations on nearly 600 areas of special interest and concern in today's world.

The Oxford Dictionary of Humorous Quotations
Edited by Ned Sherrin

From the sharply witty to the downright hilarious, this sparkling collection will appeal to all senses of humour.

The Oxford Dictionary of Political Quotations
Edited by Antony Jay

This lively and illuminating dictionary from the writer of 'Yes Minister' presents a vintage crop of over 4,000 political quotations. Ranging from the pivotal and momentous to the rhetorical, the sincere, the bemused, the tongue-in-cheek, and the downright rude, examples include memorable words from the old hands as well as from contemporary politicians.

'funny, striking, thought-provoking and incisive ... will appeal to those browsing through it at least as much as to those who wish to use it as a work of reference'
Observer

Oxford Quick Reference

The Oxford Dictionary of Art & Artists
Ian Chilvers

Based on the highly praised *Oxford Dictionary of Art*, over 2,500 up-to-date entries on painting, sculpture, and the graphic arts.

'the best and most inclusive single volume available, immensely useful and very well written'

Marina Vaizey, *Sunday Times*

The Concise Oxford Dictionary of Art Terms
Michael Clarke

Written by the Director of the National Gallery of Scotland, over 1,800 entries cover periods, styles, materials, techniques, and foreign terms.

A Dictionary of Architecture and Landscape Architecture
James Stevens Curl

Over 5,000 entries and 250 illustrations cover all periods of Western architectural history.

'splendid ... you can't have a more concise, entertaining, and informative guide to the words of architecture.'

Architectural Review

'excellent, and amazing value for money ... by far the best thing of its kind.'

Professor David Walker

Oxford Quick Reference

The Concise Oxford Companion to English Literature
Dinah Birch and Katy Hooper

Based on the best-selling *Oxford Companion to English Literature*, this is
an indispensable guide to all aspects of English literature.

Review of the parent volume:
'the foremost work of reference in its field'

Literary Review

A Dictionary of Shakespeare
Stanley Wells

Compiled by one of the best-known international authorities on the
playwright's works, this dictionary offers up-to-date information on all
aspects of Shakespeare, both in his own time and in later ages.

The Oxford Dictionary of Literary Terms
Chris Baldick

A best-selling dictionary, covering all aspects of literature, this is an
essential reference work for students of literature in any language.

A Dictionary of Critical Theory
Ian Buchanan

The invaluable multidisciplinary guide to theory, covering movements,
theories, and events.

'an excellent gateway into critical theory'

Literature and Theology

Oxford Quick Reference

The Kings and Queens of Britain
John Cannon and Anne Hargreaves

A detailed, fully-illustrated history ranging from mythical and pre-conquest rulers to the present House of Windsor, featuring regional maps and genealogies.

A Dictionary of World History

Over 4,000 entries on everything from prehistory to recent changes in world affairs. An excellent overview of world history.

A Dictionary of British History
Edited by John Cannon

An invaluable source of information covering the history of Britain over the past two millennia. Over 3,000 entries written by more than 100 specialist contributors.

Review of the parent volume
'the range is impressive ... truly (almost) all of human life is here'

Kenneth Morgan, *Observer*

The Oxford Companion to Irish History
Edited by S. J. Connolly

A wide-ranging and authoritative guide to all aspects of Ireland's past from prehistoric times to the present day.

'packed with small nuggets of knowledge'   *Daily Telegraph*

The Oxford Companion to Scottish History
Edited by Michael Lynch

The definitive guide to twenty centuries of life in Scotland.
'exemplary and wonderfully readable'

Financial Times

OXFORD

Oxford Quick Reference

A Dictionary of Marketing
Charles Doyle

Covers traditional marketing techniques and theories alongside the latest concepts in over 2,000 clear and authoritative entries.

'Flick to any page [for] a lecture's worth of well thought through information'

Dan Germain, Head of Creative, innocent ltd

A Dictionary of Media and Communication
Daniel Chandler and Rod Munday

Provides over 2,200 authoritative entries on terms used in media and communication, from concepts and theories to technical terms, across subject areas that include advertising, digital culture, journalism, new media, radio studies, and telecommunications.

'a wonderful volume that is much more than a simple dictionary'
Professor Joshua Meyrowitz, University of New Hampshire

A Dictionary of Film Studies
Annette Kuhn and Guy Westwell

Features terms covering all aspects of film studies in 500 detailed entries, from theory and history to technical terms and practices.

A Dictionary of Journalism
Tony Harcup

Covers terminology relating to the practice, business, and technology of journalism, as well as its concepts and theories, organizations and institutions, publications, and key events.

Oxford Quick Reference

Concise Medical Dictionary

Over 12,000 clear entries covering all the major medical and surgical specialities make this one of our best-selling dictionaries.

'"No home should be without one" certainly applies to this splendid medical dictionary'

Journal of the Institute of Health Education

'An extraordinary bargain' *New Scientist*

A Dictionary of Nursing

Comprehensive coverage of the ever-expanding vocabulary of the nursing professions. Features over 10,000 entries written by medical and nursing specialists.

A Dictionary of Dentistry
Robert Ireland

Over 4,000 succinct and authoritative entries define all the important terms used in dentistry today. This is the ideal reference for all members of the dental team.

A Dictionary of Forensic Science
Suzanne Bell

In over 1,300 entries, this new dictionary covers the key concepts within Forensic Science and is a must-have for students and practitioners of forensic science.